ISBN 978-1-334-24346-2
PIBN 10549096

Forgotten Books is a registered trademark of FB &c Ltd.
Copyright © 2018 FB &c Ltd.
FB &c Ltd, Dalton House, 60 Windsor Avenue, London, SW19 2RR.
Company number 08720141. Registered in England and Wales.

For support please visit www.forgottenbooks.com

1 MONTH OF
FREE
READING

at

www.ForgottenBooks.com

By purchasing this book you are eligible for one month membership to ForgottenBooks.com, giving you unlimited access to our entire collection of over 1,000,000 titles via our web site and mobile apps.

To claim your free month visit:

www.forgottenbooks.com/free549096

English
Français
Deutsche
Italiano
Español
Português

www.forgottenbooks.com

Mythology Photography **Fiction**
Fishing Christianity **Art** Cooking
Essays Buddhism Freemasonry
Medicine **Biology** Music **Ancient**
Egypt Evolution Carpentry Physics
Dance Geology **Mathematics** Fitness
Shakespeare **Folklore** Yoga Marketing
Confidence Immortality Biographies
Poetry **Psychology** Witchcraft
Electronics Chemistry History **Law**
Accounting **Philosophy** Anthropology
Alchemy Drama Quantum Mechanics
Atheism Sexual Health **Ancient History**
Entrepreneurship Languages Sport
Paleontology Needlework Islam
Metaphysics Investment Archaeology
Parenting Statistics Criminology
Motivational

WORLD HEADQUARTERS BUILDING—Marchant Calculators, Inc.

RICHMOND CONSTRUCTION COMPANY, General Contractors

JANUARY 1958

"Can't get this dad-burned sliver o' wood to burn," rumbled Paul Bunyan to Babe, the Blue Ox. A mountain top trembled and fell, damming up a river. "Babe, what the cuss do you suppose them Baxter folks done to this here piece o' plywood? She's dry—but she JEST DON'T BURN!"

BAXCO
FIRE-
RETARDANT
PLYWOOD
(*Pressure treated with Protexol*)

Sorry, Paul, old timer—but even you couldn't get that wood to burn! It's BAXCO's new fire-resistant plywood, pressure treated with Protexol fire retardants and kiln dried after treatment. These are the most effective and widely approved fire retardants. Protexol-Pyresote affords termite and decay protection as well to the treated plywood. Protexol meets all important fire hazard and flame-spread classifications. BAXCO will quote promptly—send your inquiry today.

RECOMMENDED USES: *Partitions ... Core Stock—Panels and doors ... Interior trim and finish ... Barns, stables and stalls ... Railroad car flooring ... Ship and Yacht interiors ... Cabinet work.*

©J. H. Baxter & Co. 1955

J. H. BAXTER & CO. *120 Montgomery Street, San Francisco 4, California*

Quality <u>can</u> be measured . . .

Quality in a roof scuttle can be measured
in many ways . . . by its ease of operation—the
safety it affords the user—the virtually
indefinite trouble free service it gives the
building owner. Bilco scuttles offer your clients
"floating" cover action, one hand operation
and the finest of materials and workmanship—at
a price of little more if any, than ordinary access doors.
For lasting satisfaction specify Bilco—the measure
of roof scuttle quality for more than 20 years.
A size for every requirement—see our catalog in Sweets.

Only the Best is stamped

California Representatives

—— *ARCHITECT & ENGINEER is indexed regularly by ENGINEERING INDEX, INC.; and ART INDEX* ——

Contents for

JANUARY

THE OLDEST PROFESSIONAL MONTHLY BUSINESS MAGAZINE OF THE ELEVEN WESTERN STATE

ARCHITECT AND ENGINEER (Established 1905) is published on the 15th of the month by The Architect an
Engineer, Inc., 68 Post St., San Francisco 4; Telephone EXbrook 2-7182. President, K. P. Kierulff; Vice
President and Manager, L. B. Penhorwood; Treasurer, E. N. Kierulff. — Los Angeles Office: Wentworth F
Green, 438 So. Western Ave., Telephone DUnkirk 7-6135 — Portland, Oregon, Office: R. V. Vaughn, 711
Canyon Lane. — Entered as second class matter, November 2, 1905, at the Post Office in San Francisco
California, under the Act of March 3, 1879. Subscriptions United States and Pan America, $3.00 a year
$5.00 two years; foreign countries $5.00 a year; single copy, 50c.

EDITORIAL NOTES .

YOU PAY THE BILL

The Federal budget just presented to the Congress by President Eisenhower forecasts a $400-million deficit for fiscal 1958 but a $500-million surplus for fiscal 1959. Increased expenditures for national defense and a slackening of economic activity account for the prospective deficit in 1958.

The probable impact of the proposed budget on the nation's economy is hard to evaluate. There are so many imponderables. In addition to the size of the budget itself, what happens will depend on time lags in the spending program, the speed of various reactions of the private economy to government fiscal operations, the non-budgetary cash flows between the government and the public, how the budget affects private expectations and many other factors.

The budget appears to be predicated on a high-employment economy and reflects the President's State of the Union Message when he said, "There are solid grounds for believing that economic growth will be resumed without extended interruption." If recession continues, increased spending on military orders during the first half of 1958 and planned outlays for 1959 will help to buoy up flagging private demand. Even the prospect of such increases may have favorable effect on business expectations.

But, there's little prospect for a tax reduction as Percival Brundage, Director of the Budget points out: "It is a balanced budget which requires the continuation of present tax rates for another year." The proposed budget for Washington, Oregon and California, totaling some $9,573.7-million must still come from the taxpayer—and that's YOU.

* * *

The American Society of Civil Engineers, oldest national organization of engineers in the US, has passed the 40,000 mark in membership:—William H. Wisely, exec-Secty, New York.

* * *

GET YOUR DOLLAR'S WORTH

With construction costs at an all time high, school districts across the country are striving to get the fullest value for every dollar spent on new building.

Starting this past summer, one of the hottest debates raging in education today still centers around comparative building costs and whether schools are actually doing all they can to keep costs in line. There are two extreme views in approaching the problem: one group asks "must our schools be palaces?" and the other asks "must our schools be shacks?"

Aside from apparent differences in what constitutes necessities for our modern-day schools, one of the basic points of contention between the two opposing thoughts is determining a fair basis of cost comparison

among different schools. Cost per square foot, cost per pupil and cost per classroom can be distorted to either raise or lower the construction cost figure to any desired level.

A new basis for measuring the relative construction costs of schools of various kinds and sizes in various parts of the country has been propounded by Nickolaus L. Engelhardt, Jr., New York educational consultant. In a long list of influences which determine costs, Engelhardt includes: Educational Specifications, Nature of Site, Design—function and efficiency, Design—architectural character, Labor and materials, Type and quality of Construction; financial expense, Geographica; location, Time of Bidding, Market Conditions generally, Value of the Construction dollar.

In setting up construction programs, school boards will find the cost problem answered if they will "give a real clue to value received by minimizing the effect on the comparison of all those factors which are not really controllable."

Probably the best practical answer to school construction costs is to make sure those in charge of design and construction are well qualified to do a good job.

* * *

The US Bureau of the Census has just reported the number of non-farm households in the nation, was 44,325,000 as compared to 43,136,000 a year ago—a gain of almost 1,190,000 households in the past year:—Geo. S. Goodyear, president National Association of Home Builders.

* * *

FEDERAL-STATE RELATIONS IMPROVE

Progress continues in the efforts of the Joint Federal-State Action Committee to improve relationships between the national government and state and local governments through the return of functions and revenue sources. The third meeting of this group held recently in Washington, D. C. developed several significant specific actions:

It was agreed that the states would undertake financial responsibility for planning grants for urban renewal and extended state programs of technical assistance.

It was agreed that support would be given to amendments to the Atomic Energy Act of 1954, recognizing state responsibility for the health and safety aspects of the peaceful uses of atomic energy and for training state employees.

Action was deferred on the school lunch and school milk programs pending further study.

The governors affirmed state and local responsibility for school construction and proposed further federal tax relinquishment in order that states might meet their needs.

No action was taken on old-age assistance pending further study.

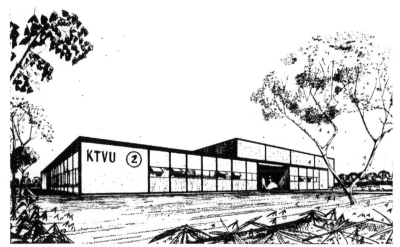

KTVU-CHANNEL 2

STUDIO BUILDING

OAKLAND, CALIFORNIA

A studio building for KTVU-Channel 2, the Bay area's newest television station, scheduled for construction on the Oakland waterfront at Jack London Square, is nearing completion.

The proposed one-story building, designed by Welton Becket, F.A.I.A. and Associates, San Francisco, architects and engineers, will be unique because of its new approach to acoustical problems. It will house two television studios, office space and a storage area for props.

The studio area will have "tilt-up" concrete walls, which are poured flat and then raised into place by

crane, while the frame office wing will be built on the modular system, a type of construction featuring a series of complete sections of equal size which insure flexibility in future planning. The exterior of the building will express the modular principle with colored duraply panels set between batten-covered posts. Dudley Deane & Associates are electrical and mechanical engineers for the project.

Channel 2 will go on the air March 1, according to William D. Pabst, San Francisco-Oakland Television, Inc., owners of the new facilities, and will be available to television viewers within a radius of approximately 100 miles.

NEWS and COMMENT ON ART

M. H. deYOUNG MEMORIAL MUSEUM

The M. H. deYoung Memorial Museum, Golden Gate Park, San Francisco, under the direction of Walter Heil, is offering a number of special exhibits and events for January including the following:

EXHIBITIONS: Paintings by Dorr Bothwell; Watercolors by Sister Mary Luke; Paintings by Cameron Booth; Swiss Peasant Art, comprising a group of Paintings and Handicraft circulated by the Smithsonian Institution; Paintings in Gouache by Elizabeth Duquette, and Contemporary Danish Design in Textiles and Furniture.

EVENTS: An illustrated lecture "The Enjoyment of Painting" by Theodore Rousseau, Curator of Painting at the Metropolitan Museum of Art, New York City, is scheduled for Monday, February 3rd at 3 p.m., sponsored by the deYoung Museum Society.

Classes in Art Enjoyment for adults, conducted by Charles Lindstrom, include Exercises in Oil Painting, Part II; Seminars in the History of Art Thursday mornings at 10:30, are informal illustrated lectures and discussions; and for the children are classes in Picture Making, Art and Nature and the Art Club, conducted by Miriam Lindstrom. All classes are free of charge.

The Museum is open daily—free parking area provided.

PORTLAND ART MUSEUM

A special exhibition is currently being shown at the Portland (Oregon) Art Museum entitled "The Artist in Architecture", and includes the showing of a motion picture "Architecture in Mexico" and Gallery Tour; a Forum on "Integration of Art in Architecture Today" featuring Walter Church, AIA, Architect, Thos. K. Welch, General Contractor, Richard J. Turner, Chairman of the Portland Art Commission, and Manuel Izquierdo, Sculptor.

Other highlights include film showings 'From Doric to Gothic" and Gallery Tour, and "Architecture West" and Gallery Tour. Two slide lectures will be featured: "Art in Architecture" by Lewis P. Crutcher, AIA Architect, and "Contemporary Church Art in Architecture" by the Reverend John M. Domin.

ANCIENT ART IN MODERN FORM PLACED ON EXHIBIT

Twenty colorful jewel-like mosaics, made from various domestic and imported tiles, semi-precious stones, beads, glasses, jewelry and shells imbedded in colorful cement were placed on exhibit at the National Housing Center in Washington, D. C. this month. The mosaics are the products of adult education students at the Immaculate Heart College of Los Angeles, and were created under the direction of Sister Magdalen Mary, I. H. M., Chairman of Art at the College.

The mosaics will be on exhibition at the Housing Center through February.

Both religious and secular subjects form the designs of the mosaics, which range in size from 12" x 16" to one that stands 77" high. The making of mosaics is a centuries-old art, but today it is enjoying a spectacular revival and in Southern California particularly, architects are commissioning local artists to design and execute mosaic murals for public and commercial buildings, as indoor and outdoor decoration.

Most of the mosaic makers exhibiting are non-professionals and include housewives, scientists, school teachers, laboratory technician, engineer, secretary and nurse. After the present showing at the Housing Center this collection will be shown in museums and art centers throughout the nation.

CITY OF PARIS

The Rotunda Gallery of the City of Paris, San Francisco, under the direction of André Laherrere, is offering an Exhibition of Paintings by Nat Levy and Fred Fredden Goldberg for January.

The Exhibit comprises a group of twenty paintings by Nat Levy and a group of twenty-six paintings by Fred Fredden Goldberg.

SAN FRANCISCO MUSEUM OF ART

The San Francisco Museum of Art, War Memorial Building, Civic Center, under the direction of Dr. Grace L. McCann Morley, announces the following special exhibitions and events for this month

EXHIBITIONS: "Contemporary Ceramics" featuring the work of Beatrice Wood of Southern California, and J. B. Blunk, Ruby O'Burke, Antonio Prieto, and Margurite Wildenhain of the San Francisco Bay Area. "The Blue Four", honoring the work of Feininger, Jawlensky, Kandinsky and Klee; "The World of Edward Weston"; "Collection of Modern Art", the collection of Mr. and Mrs. Harry Lewis Winston and selected loans from Bay Region collections; "Paintings by Young Africans of South Rhodesia", a collection done at the Chirodzo Art Center, and "Arts From Morocco".

SPECIAL EVENTS: Lecture tours of the Museum, based on current exhibitions, are conducted each Sunday afternoon at 3 o'clock; discussions in art each

Wednesday evening at 9 o'clock. General Museum activities include Studio-Art for the Layman, a course by Prof. Henry Schaefer-Simmern, Director of the Institute of Art Education, designed to awaken and develop inherent artistic potentialities of the layman. Children's Saturday morning Art Classes, 10 to 11 for children 6 to 14 years, who may work in charcoal, paint, collage, and papier mache.

The Museum is open daily.

KATE NEAL KINLEY
MEMORIAL FELLOWSHIP

The Board of Trustees of the University of Illinois have again authorized the announcement of the twenty-seventh annual consideration of candidates for the Kate Neal Kinley Memorial Fellowship, which was established in 1931 by late President-Emeritus David Kinley in memory of his wife and in recognition of her influence in promoting the Fine Arts and similar interests upon the Campus.

The Fellowship yields the sum of one thousand five hundred dollars which is to be used by the recipient toward defraying the expense of advanced study of the Fine Arts in America or abroad. It is open to graduates of the College of Fine Arts and Applied Arts of the University of Illinois and to graduates of similar institutions of equal educational standing whose principal or major studies have been in one of Music, Art, and Architecture—Design or history. Applicants should not exceed twenty-four years of age on June 1, 1958, but Veterans may deduct amount of time spent in service.

Applications should reach the Committee not later than May 15, 1958 and should be addressed to Dean Allen S. Weller, College of Fine and Applied Arts, Room 110, Architecture Bldg, University of Illinois, Urbana.

OAKLAND ART MUSEUM

The Oakland Art Museum, 1000 Fallon Street, under the direction of Paul Mills, Curator, announces the award winners of the Museum's California Painters' Annual Exhibition.

The exhibition, a competitive show open to artists residing in California, attracted nearly six hundred entries from all parts of the state. Jurors for the exhibition were Richard Diebenkorn, faculty member of Mills College and the California College of Arts and Crafts; Peter Blos, well known portrait artist and painter of Southwest scenes; and Wilfrid Zogbaum, New York abstractionist and visiting professor at the University of California Art Department. Each juror selected just over 25 paintings for inclusion in the show. The individual choices are shown in separate galleries. Each also selected five works for Honorable Mention. From the resultant list of fifteen, the mu-

seum in turn selected paintings to receive the one thousand dollars in Women's Board purchase Awards and the Adele Hyde Morrison Medals. A tradition in the museum for many years, the medals have not, however, carried the Morrison name before this year. In naming them after her, the museum honors the benefactress who provided the award money for the competitive shows for several decades.

Principal winner in the exhibition is Fred Martin, "Guest of Honor" one-man show during 1958 and a Women's Board Purchase award. Martin, in addition to being an active painter whose work has been shown in Paris galleries as well as frequently in the United States, is Registrar on the museum staff and Chairman of the Artists Council of the San Francisco Art Association. He is an Oakland resident; Juror Diebenkorn selected his work for Honorable Mention.

The Silver Morrison Medal went to Maurice Lapp, whose work was selected by Peter Bios, was formerly an art instructor in the Oakland schools and now teaches in Santa Rosa. Philip Wofford, studying at the University of California Art Department, won the Bronze Morrison Medal. His work was selected by Wilfrid Zogbaum.

Women's Board Purchase Awards went to William H. Brown and Mary Navratil, San Francisco, and Sylvia Vince, Oakland, from Richard Diebenkorn's selection. Glenn Wessels of Berkeley, whose work was selected by Peter Blos, also received a purchase award. From Wilfrid Zogbaum's selection, Manuel Neri of San Francisco and Carol Haerer of Berkeley received purchase awards.

A purchase award from the Art League of the East Bay went to William Brown of Davis for a painting selected by the museum.

Additional Honorable Mentions went to Blanch Brody, June Felter, Sue McCauley, George Miyasaki, St. John Moran, Robert Qualters and Joseph Smith.

CALIFORNIA PALACE OF THE
LEGION OF HONOR

The California Palace of the Legion of Honor, Lincoln Park, San Francisco, under the direction of Thomas Carr Howe, Jr., has arranged a number of special exhibition and events for January including the following:

SPECIAL EXHIBITIONS: Watercolors and Gouaches by Jason Schoener; Paintings by A. Sheldon Pennoyer, a Memorial exhibition; Paintings by Roger Bolomey; Indonesian Paintings; Color Photographs by Margaret Morse; Paintings by Cecil Everley, and Paintings by Robert Sterling.

ACHENBACH FOUNDATION for Graphic Arts: At the Museum is being shown "The Story of Christ"

(See Page 32)

NEWLY DESIGNED EXTERIOR . . . Innes Shoes, Downtown Los Angeles.

SHOE STORE – Modernized

Los Angeles, California

TRADITIONAL WARMTH felt in friendly
entrance of new appearance

DESIGNERS: Burke, Kober & Nicolais, Los Angeles
Harold J. Nicolais, A.I.A.

COST OF THE MODERNIZATION PROGRAM:
$500,000

The new Innes Shoe Company's store combines contemporary design with a variety of interesting new materials, many of which are enjoying their Los Angeles debut.

The exterior is faced with white Travertine marble, dominated by large expanse of show windows set between massive columns of textured Italian fulget. A heavily patterned marble floor leads from the sidewalk to the interior.

Street floor feature, is a men's shoe section. Masculine atmosphere is developed through use of large expanse of finished wood; in this case roughly textured African Jeweltree, semi-polished. Display backgrounds are of untanned calf, lighting fixtures of polished brass, shaped like oriental hats. They are bright enough and low enough to provide light for package wrapping, yet they give a soft effect because of the textured plastic lenses which diffuse the light. Focal point is the back wall, faced with textured all white Italian fulget marble which provides a background for the unique figures from a 17th century Samuri print, executed in wire and perforated metal.

New customer convenience added by the installation of an escalator to the second level. Separate shoe shops are grouped around the escalator well.

The Innes Downtown is carpeted and air-conditioned throughout and is setting a new standard of customer convenience and comfort.

ABOVE: Good use of escalator well as focal point for important merchandise displays at second store level.

BELOW: Existing structural units are used. Heavy column serves as hub around which shoe salon exists.

NEW PLANT NEARING COMPLETION

NEW WORLD HEADQUARTERS BUILDING

MARCHANT CALCULATORS, Inc.

OAKLAND, CALIFORNIA

ARCHITECT: Albert P. Roller, A.I.A.

STRUCTURAL ENGINEER: H. J. Brunnier

MECHANICAL ENGINEERS: Dudley Deane & Associates

ELECTRICAL ENGINEERS: Lyle E. Patton

GENERAL CONTRACTORS: Dinwiddie Construction Co.

The initial move into the "new world headquarters" executive offices and main factory of the Marchant Calculators, was successfully completed recently when the company's assembly division commenced operation in a newly constructed factory section of the building.

The new Marchant plant, full occupancy of which must await completion of construction in mid-1958, is a one block wide building on an industrial site in the Oakland metropolitan area bounded by San Pablo avenue, 67th street in Oakland, Folger avenue in Berkeley, and a Southern Pacific railway right of way on the west. To complicate exact location further the rear corner of the building is in the City of Emeryville, thus making the facilities a new, enlarged enterprise for Oakland, Berkeley and Emeryville.

Initial occupancy of the building was unusual in that the second floor of the factory section became the first scene of operations in Marchant's new home. The move was required because the assembly division plant was on part of the building site.

The old structure was removed to permit extension of the new building to its full depth.

Marchant's assembly division is now in only a portion of its permanent quarters on the second floor of the factory section. The plant, stretching approxi-

mately 800 feet east to west and a full block north and south, remains to be completed to the full extent of the factory section.

Upon completion there will be approximately one-third more floor space for the assembly division. The parts production division will occupy corresponding space on the first floor.

Administrative and engineering divisions, on San Pablo avenue is 250 feet wide and 120 feet long and will occupy a four-story section. The total floor space of the new Marchant plant will be 507,000 square feet, a size well over twice the total area of the firm's present facilities in Oakland.

Design

The new building phases of the firm's expansion program, and which is now under construction in progressive stages of completion for occupancy and use, will house Marchant Calculators, Inc., "international headquarters and main production plant." This will, when completed, consolidate under one roof their widely scattered home office and factory operations which include Administrative Activities, Production of equipment and parts, Assembly and the Na-

(See Page 13)

SITE . . . as it appeared prior to start of new construction, partially used as parking area. Berkeley hills in background.

WORLD HEADQUARTERS . . .

In every way possible the new building is designed to provide ideal working conditions:
Plenty of light and fresh air—42,000 square feet of window space which is equipped to admit light but not heat or cold.

Modern first aid rooms—Cafeteria and dining rooms, and rest room facilities.

Pictured here are two views of construction in progress: LOWER, shows pouring of concrete for walls, and UPPER view shows some of window glass in place and building nearing completion.

(From Page 11)

...onal Sales, National Service, and Engineering di-
...sion.

The structure is 351 feet wide by 770 feet long,
...ontaining an administration portion of four floors,
...nd a factory area, two floors in height with provisions
...or a future third floor. A full basement extends under
...he entire building. Reinforced concrete was used
...hroughout and more than 35,000 cubic yards of
...oncrete and 2800 tons of reinforcing steel were used
...n construction. The factory areas are designed with a
flat slab, and drop-head column to obtain a maximum
unobstructed working height. All windows in the
administration area are continuous aluminum case-

VIEW AT RIGHT: Construction in factory section where heavy machinery will be installed—heat ducts in ceiling, and piping installed.

STOPPING POINT of phase one of the construction program. After Plant II has been removed, building will continue westward.

ments. Continuous strip steel sash was used in the factory. Door frames throughout the structure are either channel iron or hollow metal type frames. Exterior doors are hollow metal type frames, the interior fire doors in the factory area are weldwood. In the administration section hollow metal frames with either birch, oak or walnut are used.

New Radiant Heating

All windows are glazed with glare reducing glass to minimize strain in manufacturing and assembly of small parts. The administration offices are air conditioned, utilizing radiant ceilings, which consist of half inch steel pipes one foot on the center to which are snapped aluminum acoustical panels. Centrally heated and chilled water is circulated through these pipes to create the desired temperature. This leaves the floor space completely unencumbered by radiators and air conditioning units. This system of overhead heating and cooling is relatively new to the West Coast, but is rapidly gaining recognition as an improved method of comfort conditioning.

All factory areas will be heated and mechanically

(See Page 17)

MOVED IN and running on all schedules is this portion of the manufacturing and assembly department—note ideal lighting.

**FOUNDATION
IS STARTED**

Wall forms and column forms begin
to take shape . . . about 5% of some
35,000 cubic yards of concrete required to the entire building will be
used for these walls and columns.

BELOW: First floor of new building as seen from roof of adjacent building, showing supports for a plywood base serving as the first "layer" of the lower floor of the Factory section . . . reinforcing steel is placed on top of the plywood then a layer of concrete is poured
. . . concrete columns will extend upward as supports for the second floor.

WORLD HEADQUARTERS . . .

POURING CONCRETE

Excavation of ground for basement has been completed and forms set in place to start pouring of concrete . . . steel reinforcing bars have been laid in "criss cross" pattern to strengthen foundation.

As concrete is poured into forms from concrete truck on ground level workmen "agitate" mix as it settles in place.

BELOW: Is an overall view of the construction site . . . foreground shows supports from basement that hold forms for construction of the ground level floors . . . in the background may be seen supports in use for constructing the second floor; reinforcing bars extending upward through flooring is where main support columns will be constructed.

**EXCAVATION
FOR HUGE
BASEMENT**

Work is being completed
on column footings, tem-
porary shoring in place
and preparations being
made to install forms
for concrete.

(From Page 14)

ventilated. All working areas throughout the building
are lighted by continuous fluorescent fixtures with recessed incandescent units used in the cafeteria and
specialized locations.

Cafeteria-Dining Rooms

The employees' dining room will be approximately
71'-0" wide by 125'-0" long. Lively colors have been
used to decorate this room to produce a pleasant
atmosphere for dining. The exterior walls are in pale

WORLD HEADQUARTERS . . .

**CLOSE-UP VIEW
OF CEILING**
Newly designed radiant heating, cooling and
acoustical ceiling is feature of building . . . is
ideal lighting as well.

yellow with a blue-green color selected for most of the interior walls. A bright coral is used adjacent to the serving area, bringing out the lustre of the polished stainless steel cafeteria counters which will be used. Wallpaper in harmonizing colors cover one of the walls.

The officers' dining room is decorated in tones of brown, blue and copper. A recessed panel of wallpaper was used on one end of this room. Light fixtures are copper with suspended globes of white glass.

An exterior terrace is seen through a glass wall on the east side of the employees' dining room. This area will be planted with shrubs and a full size tree in brick planting boxes which are raised to provide seating space in the sun.

Two large stainless steel cafeteria serving counters designed for fast, easy service, and including hot food units, automatic plate lowerators, refrigerated salad and dessert sections and self-help coffee units will be

(See Page 20)

. . . MARCHANT CALCULATORS, Inc.

CEILING DETAIL

Multi-purpose functional ceiling (see completed picture on opposite page) details of installing new method radiant heating, radiant cooling coils. Workmen weld supports in place and install piping.

UP IT GOES . . .

Three electrical sub-stations in the basement will supply power for the entire building, with each of the units costing more than $185,000.

On the front of the building, facing San Pablo Avenue, a pylon section will be erected to a height of approximately five stories.

The primary construction of this project will provide newest facilities for assembly operations and plant factory, subsequent construction will represent new and improved general offices, including sales and service and executive.

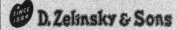

WORLD HEADQUARTERS . . .

**EXCAVATION
COMPLETED**

First phase of new construction following completion of basement excavation is installation of wall forms for concrete sidewalls of basement and first floor.

(From Page 18)

available in the employees' dining area. Additionally, space has been provided for a third quick serve counter to be used as necessary. Automatic, electrically heated dishwashing facilities are a part of the scullery, assuring clean, sterilized table ware. Electric ranges and ovens take care of the heavy duty cooking, in addition to stainless steel steam jacketed kettles and steam pressure cookers. All of this equipment will be under a stainless steel patented ventilator, which, in addition to making for a cool kitchen, removes all odors and grease. Adequate refrigeration is, of course, provided in the kitchen.

General Features

The facade facing San Pablo Avenue is dominated by a pylon faced with brick, supported by concrete columns over the main entrance to the building. To the left of the foyer is located the museum which will house Marchant's interesting collection of historical items pertaining to calculating. This collection is displayed in free-standing glass cases and recessed shadow

MARCHANT CALCULATORS, Inc.

ing onto a paved and landscaped terrace partially covered by a porch. The executive offices and Board Room Suite are on the third floor. These rooms will be finished in walnut paneling. Wood and glass screens will be done in the same material.

The foremost problem in design was to provide a building with a maximum of flexibility for manufacturing as well as administration in a densely populated urban area.

READY-MIX concrete trucks supply more than 35,000 cubic yards of concrete.

boxes. The museum room as well as the adjacent sales area can be viewed from the street through floor to ceiling glass walls. A cafeteria, which offers complete food preparation and serving for the entire organization, is located on the second floor of the administration building. One wall of the cafeteria is glass, open-

BANCO

HIPOTECARIO

DE EL SALVADOR

San Salvador

Central America

ARCHITECT: Raymond R. Shaw, A.I.A.

The Directors of Banco Hipotecario de El Salvador have authorized Architect Raymond R. Shaw A.I.A. and William D. Coffey, Consulting Structural Engineer of Los Angeles to design and supervise the construction of the bank's new $2,000,000.00 Head-Office building. The building is to be erected in San Salvador, the Capital of the Republic of El Salvador, and its largest city.

Several parcels of property, totaling 39,090 square feet, have been purchased in the central business district; and the building to be erected thereon will have a usable floor area of 150,000 square feet. A full basement covering the entire property is included. The number of stories will vary with use and location. The front section of building, back to a depth of 140 feet, with a width of 165 feet, will be three stories. The rear section, 52 feet by 165 feet, will be five stories in height. The remaining section will be two stories, designed to add three stories at some future date.

Construction of the building is to be steel frame with steel floor decking and concrete slabs. Perimeter walls are to be reinforced concrete. On the two principal street frontages, Black Diamond Granite is to be used to a height of 16 feet above the sidewalk. Flanking the main entrance and extending into the outer and inner banking room lobbies, rose-colored Carnelian Granite is to be used on the vertical surfaces.

The exterior has been designed in a Modern Greek style. Interiors will be Contemporary Modern. The principal banking room is located on the second floor

and access thereto will be furnished by four modern elevators, also by two escalators operating between the ground floor and the second floor. The fourth floor in the rear of the building contains a large Assembly Room with a seating capacity of 400 persons. Eight vaults are provided, three of which will be Security Vaults equipped with the most modern types of doors and other vault equipment. A Night Depository is included for after-hour deposits. On the ground floor, two motor-windows, off the rear parking driveway, are available to customers. There are two automobile parking levels. The basement, or subterranean, parking will accommodate 58 automobiles; and the ground floor space will accommodate 21 automobiles.

The entire building is to be air-conditioned. A large cistern will be installed under the basement with sufficient capacity to assure a minimum three-day water supply at all times. This is in addition to the regular storage tank on the roof. A stand-by electric generating plant is being installed to furnish electrical energy to bookkeeping machines and illuminating equipment in the event of power failure. A Short Wave Telephone System will make it possible for the bank to maintain communications with its branch banks, under all circumstances. Air-conditioning, Electrical and Hydraulic Engineering services are to be furnished by Herbert L. Wollman, M.E., a well known California Engineer.

Structural drawings are scheduled to be completed and ready for Steel quotations about the middle of December.

SEAOSC AND ASCE HOLD
JOINT MEETING ON QUAKE

The Structural Engineers Association of Southern California and the American Society of Civil Engineers held a joint meeting January 8 to listen to the report of seven structural engineers from the Los Angeles and San Francisco areas concerning their observations of the Mexico City earthquake last year. Two of the speakers, John M. Sardis and G. W. Housner, were on their vacations in Mexico City at the time of the disaster.

Approximately 400 SEAOSC and ASCE members attended the meeting, making it the largest gathering of engineers ever held in the history of these local associations.

Joseph Sheffet, 1958 SEAOSC president acted as host for the evening.

John M. Sardis, San Francisco consulting engineer opened the discussion. Sardis was asleep on the eighth floor in the Reforma Hotel in Mexico City when the earthquake struck at about 2:40 a.m. He reported that the quake sounded like thunder with the building cracking and groaning, and the building swayed considerably. The amplitude of the first wave of the earthquake did not feel as large as the amplitude of the second wave which was about two or three minutes later. At daylight Sardis was able to assay the damage to the hotel which appeared to be mainly plaster cracking.

However, Sardis observed the Hilton Hotel was not as fortunate as the Reforma Hotel since many of the unreinforced filler walls had fractured and collapsed. If this earthquake had happened during the daytime many more casualties would have occurred because of the debris falling from the buildings. Many of the buildings that collapsed were inadequate for their vertical loads and thus little additional resistance was available for the earthquake loads.

John Sardis' conclusions were as follows: the seismic design coefficient is not as important as properly designed and executed details; unreinforced masonry is unsatisfactory in an earthquake area; the structural frame of a building should be of a high strength ductile material that can take overstress, and a definition of failure for a structure is needed—does failure occur when people refuse to re-enter a building because of excessive movements? Does failure occur when the filler walls are fractured or collapsed?

Foundation Conditions

Professor Martin Duke of U.C.L.A. spoke principally about foundation conditions as related to the Mexico City earthquake, and the effects of the quake in other areas of Mexico other than Mexico City. Duke flew to Mexico shortly after the earthquake occurred observing the effects. The city of Acapulco is situated 50 miles from the epicenter of the quake but suffered small damage. However, Mexico City,

which was 170 miles from the epicenter, had considerable damage. The reason for this appears to be due to the foundation conditions. The city of Acapulco is founded upon granite while the portion of Mexico City that was severely damaged was founded upon an old lake bed which is composed of unconsolidated clays and silts.

Professor Duke noted that the magnitude of this earthquake was 7.5 which is about the same as the Kern County quake in 1952. The intensity of the earthquake by the Mercalli Scale in the damaged portion of Mexico City was about seven plus and in the remainder of the city about four or less.

Murray Erick, consulting engineer in Los Angeles, spent four weeks in Mexico studying the Hilton Hotels in Acapulco and Mexico City. He noted that this earthquake acted quite differently than the earthquakes of California acquaintance, and he felt that this was mainly due to geological differences.

Erick classified the buildings in Mexico City and their types of failures into four broad classifications: **Type one:** Low, heavy, rigid structures. These buildings were usually very old and of very poor construction and often had high reinforced parapets. With few exceptions there were no failures of this type of structure or even cracks in the parapets. **Type two:** Low concrete or steel framed buildings of less than six stories. The damage to this type of structure was far more than expected for the intensity of earthquake that was experienced. Many failures occurred. **Type three:** Intermediate height concrete or steel framed buildings, six to ten stories in height. These buildings fared somewhat better than the frame buildings of lower height. **Type four:** Ten stories and higher concrete or steel framed buildings. There were a good many cases of trouble in these buildings with the reinforced concrete badly damaged. Many of these buildings should be condemned.

Filler Walls

Erick also noted that the structural steel frames of most buildings had only a small amount of structural damage, but that the adjacent filler walls of masonry had failed as also the plaster partitions and glass walls. There were only a few difficulties with some of the connections of some steel frames. Erick felt that the filler walls contained by the concrete or steel frames may have at first contributed to the initial failure, but may also have prevented the final failure of the entire structure.

Some of the items that Erick believed contributed to the failures in Mexico City are: substandard qualities of materials and workmanship; many irregular buildings producing excessive torsional forces; insufficient separation between structures permitting considerable pounding between buildings; unreinforced masonry walls not tied into the structure; poor structural design, and bad foundation conditions.

Vincent R. Bush, engineer for the Pacific Fire Rat-

(See Page 25)

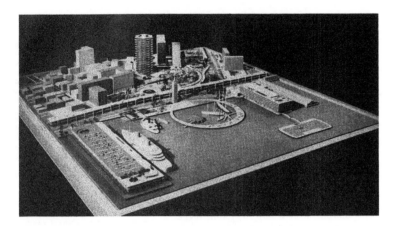

SAN FRANCISCO'S

GOLDEN GATEWAY - FERRY PARK

REHABILITATION OF FERRY BUILDING—WHOLESALE PRODUCE AREA

ARCHITECT: Mario J. Ciampi

A plan to develop the area around the Ferry Building at the foot of Market Street into a park has been announced by the San Francisco City Planning Commission. Architect Mario J. Ciampi prepared the plan as consultant to the Department of City Planning. The park development would tie in with previously announced plans for the Golden Gateway redevelopment project, in which multi-story office buildings, apartments and parking garages would replace the city's present wholesale produce market area.

Carried out, the plan would vitalize an area that should be one of the city's most important focal points, an area which, in the days of ferry boat commuting, was the most important gateway to the city. At present, signs of life in the area are reflected in new construction activities such as the building of the Embarcadero freeway, the establishment of the World Trade Center in the north wing of the Ferry Building, new office construction along lower Market Street, and Matson Lines' desire to build a new passenger terminal south of the Ferry Building.

The double decker freeway being built directly in front of the Ferry Building creates esthetic problems which the Ciampi plan proposes to handle with landscaping and with the ultimate removal of both wings of the Ferry Building, permitting a vista under the freeway to the bay and leaving the tower freestanding as the well-known landmark of the city.

The area will become a terminal for all kinds of transportation. Ramps will lead off the freeway into the Golden Gateway project with its public and private garages with capacity for 4000 cars. The California cable car will terminate in the park at the present foot of Market Street; Municipal Railway buses will terminate in the ground floor of a new building on Mission Street and the Embarcadero. Pedestrians will receive their due; the landscaped plaza on the land side of the park will be a pleasant and festive place for strolling, sunning and eating lunches, and an underpass with moving sidewalks will take them under the freeway and Embarcadero surface traffic to the water side of the park. There, within a circular pier, historic ships, refurbished, will be on display, and a pavilion will house other historic exhibits. The terminal for large

passenger ships on the pier south of the Ferry tower would serve the liners docking at San Francisco, and would have on its roof automobile parking and a restaurant overlooking the bay. A ferry slip and facilities for excursion boats would be provided next to the circular pier. The World Trade Center would be relocated to a new building on the pier north of the Ferry tower. A heliport would be built on the bay off of this pier.

A major office building of outstanding design is proposed in the plan, next to the plaza on the north side of Market Street, as a part of the Golden Gateway redevelopment project.

The park landscaping will continue along the freeway ramps into the heart of the Golden Gateway project, which envisions generously spaced office building towers on terraces two stories high in the area south of the ramps, and high-rise apartments north of the ramps. Public parking garages would be built in the tier of blocks between the ramps, and between the office development and the apartments. Some new and some existing light industrial uses would also be a part of the redevelopment project.

The architectural firm of Skidmore, Owings and Merrill prepared the Golden Gateway plans with a gift of money from a group of public-spirited San Franciscans known as the Zellerbach-Blyth committee. The city will apply for federal aid for carrying out the redevelopment project.

Funds to develop the Ferry park will be sought from various sources, the State Park Commission, Board of State Harbor Commissioners, and other public and private groups.

QUAKE MEETING
(From Page 23)
ing Bureau, presented many interesting slides showing the various failures of structures in Mexico City. Bush's conclusions were that foundation conditions were the primary cause of the failures in Mexico City. He believed that the unconsolidated silts and clays caused magnification of the earthquake shocks.

Not too severe
Gilbert E. Morris, Superintendent of Building for the City of Los Angeles, noted that after reviewing the effects of this earthquake he came to the conclusion that the Los Angeles building standards are not too severe but are very sound. He felt that it is unwise to build up a metropolitan area without the regulation of some governmental building agency. Morris commented on one particular building which was essentially an inverted pendulum without any damping. This building suffered considerable damage to the columns, and he felt that this type of structure should be designed for a much greater factor than the usual 12 or 13 per cent. Morris requested that SEAOSC recommend to the Department of Building and Safety a factor cognizant of this type of structure.

How sound was the new Los Angeles Code Pro-

visions for unlimited height buildings was a major concern for R. W. Binder during his observations of the Mexico earthquake. He felt that there was substantiation on a broad basis of our present engineering knowledge regarding seismic design. Also he felt that if sound design is combined with appropriate materials and good construction a satisfactory structure will result.

Binder also commented that stiff and heavy elements without any strength and not tied into the structure provided damping only at the start of the earthquake and then merely acted as dead weight and were hazardous to the structure. Poor construction, lack of overall design, large torsional forces due to lack of symmetry, and foundation failures all contributed to the poor record in Mexico City. The greatest damage occurred in that part of Mexico City which has had the most settlement of the underlying unconsolidated silts and clays. Binder also noted some diaphragm failures which he thought were due to poor construction.

Same as Tehachapi
Dr. G. W. Housner, Professor of California Institute of Technology, was on vacation in Mexico City at the time of the quake and thus had a good opportunity to further his knowledge in his special field. He noted that the magnitude of the 1952 Tehachapi earthquake was about the same as this 1957 Mexico City earthquake. Also the ground displacements during the 1952 quake in North Hollywood are about the same as occurred in Mexico City; but here the similarity ends as the North Hollywood location was 65 miles from the epicenter while Mexico City was about 200 miles away!

He noted that the reason for so many structural failures in Mexico City due to an earthquake that would cause only minor damage here was that Mexican engineers designed their buildings for lesser earthquakes.

WENDELL R. SPACKMAN, AIA ELECTED CHAIRMAN BICB
Wendell R. Spackman, AIA, architect and partner in the San Francisco architectural firm of Corlett & Spackman, has been elected chairman of the Building Industry Conference Board of San Francisco, succeeding K. E. Parker, general contractor.

Elected to serve with Spackman during the ensuing year as vice-chairman was Dudley Deane, Consulting Engineer, and William E. Hague of the Associated General Contractors will continue to serve as Honorary Secretary.

Wendell R. Spackman, AIA BICB Chairman

25

American Institute of Architects

WASHINGTON STATE CHAPTER

Lewis Crutcher, Skidmore, Owings and Merrill's Portland office featured the January meeting in the New Washington Hotel, Seattle, with a discussion on "Old World Architecture—and Current efforts in American Urban Design." Slides were used to underscore the similarities and disparities in the European and American approaches to city planning. New members: Edwin Butler, Anchorage, Alaska, Corporate Member; John Graham, Associate; Calvin L. Wilson, Junior Associate; Ronald D. Lockwood, William Charles Thacker, and Milton D. Hunt, Student Associate members.

PASADENA CHAPTER

1958 Officers of the Chapter, the Women's Architectural League and the Associates were installed at the January meeting by William Glenn Balch, President of the California Council of Architects AIA. Dean Arthur Gallion, U.S.C. entertained with a description and showing of slides of his extensive trip around the world.

NORTHERN CALIFORNIA CHAPTER

"A Management Analyst Looks at the Business Problems of the Architectural Profession" was the subject of the January meeting, held in the Press and Union League Club, San Francisco, with John Paul Jones, president of John Paul Jones Associates, Inc., the speaker. New members include Theodore T.

Boutmy, and David Coleman; and Wilfred W. Davies, Junior Associate.

SAN FRANCISCO ARCHITECTURAL CLUB ELECTS 1958 OFFICERS

Camiel Van De Wegbe, has been elected president of the San Francisco Architectural Club for 1958.

Other new officers chosen to serve with Camiel Van De Wegbe are: O. Huchenlooper, vice-president; James O. Brummett, secretary; and J. W. Tasker, treasurer.

The Architectural Club meets at 507 Howard Street, and included in its activities are spring classes in architecture for students, and "refresher" courses for taking the State architectural examination.

SOUTHERN CALIFORNIA CHAPTER

William C. Eldridge, partner in the firm of Booz Allen and Hamilton, Management Consultants in nine cities throughout the nation, was the guest speaker at a recent meeting discussing the subject "Developing a Clientele."

The January meeting, held in the Venetian Room of the Ambassador Hotel, was the annual installation banquet with new officers of the chapter and WAL being installed. Chapter officers were installed by Philip Will, Jr., Second Vice-President of the American Institute of Architects, while WAL officers were installed by Floyd Rible, Regional Director, California-Nevada-Hawaii District.

CALIFORNIA COUNCIL OF ARCHITECTS

President William Glenn Balch, AIA, Los Angeles, announces that the Council's 1957 13th annual convention will be held in Monterey on October 15-19, with the Mark Thomas Inn serving as official convention headquarters and the business and technical sessions to be held at the Monterey County Fairgrounds.

Loy Chamberlain, AIA, Oakland, was named Chairman of the convention and will be assisted by William Gillis, Elisabeth Kendall Thompson, Worley K. Wong and Walter Stromquist.

OREGON CHAPTER

Harry Berry of the Douglas Fir Plywood Association was the principal speaker at the January meeting giving a talk and showing a film and slides on the manufacture of plywood and advanced engineering design of stressed skin and other structural techniques.

First award of the Artists Equity, Oregon Chapter, at the opening of the "Artist in Architecture" Show at the Portland Art Museum was presented to Walter Gordon, AIA, for "outstanding contribution toward the use of painting and sculpture in architecture."

WELDON L. RICHARDS HEADS CENTRAL CALIFORNIA CHAPTER OF THE AGC

Weldon L. Richards, partner in the Pacific Company, Berkeley, has been elected president of the Central California Chapter, Associated General Contractors for 1958, succeeding Franklin Erickson.

Others elected to serve with Richards were: Curtis E. Smith, Jr., Vice-President, vice president Dinwiddie Construction Company; Bruce McKenzie was retained as secretary, and Franklin Erickson automatically becomes treasurer.

Richards has been active in the contracting business for the past nine years; is a graduate civil engineer, a member of the Structural Engineers Association of Northern California, an associate member of the American Society of Civil Engineers and has been prominent in civic affairs in Berkeley and the East Bay.

WITH THE ENGINEERS

STRUCTURAL ENGINEERS ASSOCIATION OF SOUTHERN CALIFORNIA

Joseph Sheffet was elected President of the Structural Engineers Association of Southern California at the recent annual meeting. Harald Omsted was elected Vice-President, and Marvin J. Kudroff, Secretary-Treasurer. Named as members of the Board of Directors were: Robert M. Wilder, and Norman B. Green.

Recent new members include: Leonard Melberg, Robert O. Greenawalt, MEMBERS. Associate Members Charles L. Nichols, Alan D. Roberts, James E.

Amrhein, Philip H. Benton, J. A. Krabbe, Paul B. Maurer, A. John Rosier and Earl L. Watson. Robert L. Phelps, Martin H. Powell and John E. Richter, Affiliate Members. Calvin S. Burns and Brittain Poteet, III, Junior Members. Lewis M. Nerenbaum, Student.

STRUCTURAL ENGINEERS ASSOCIATION OF CALIFORNIA

Henry J. Degenkolb, member of the firm of John J. Gould and H. J. Degenkolb, Structural Engineers, San Francisco, was elected president of the Structural Engineers Association of California at the recent annual meeting in Coronado. Named to serve with him during the ensuing year as officer of the Association was Charles D. De Maria, Secretary.

William E. Dreusike has been appointed general convention chairman for the 1958 convention.

Henry J. Degenkolb
President SEAOC

Degenkolb has been very active in the engineering profession for a number of years and has served as president of the SEAONC, numerous committees and is also active in many civic activities.

FEMINEERS

The Femineers January meeting was held on the 15th at the San Francisco Women's Athletic Club, with the following being elected to serve as new officers during the ensuing year:

Mrs. Burr H. Randolph, President; Mrs. J. Albert Paquette, Vice-President; Mrs. James Smith, Recording Secretary; Mrs. Herman Yank, Treasurer; Mrs. Donald H. Moyer, Corresponding Secretary; Mrs. Cedric H. Anderson and Mrs. Fred Nicholson, Directors.

STRUCTURAL ENGINEERS ASSOCIATION OF NORTHERN CALIFORNIA

The February 3rd meeting will be a joint meeting with the AIA in the Fairmont Hotel, San Francisco, with the program devoted to a discussion of reinforced concrete thin shells, a kind of structure that presents theoretical, asthetic and construction problems not encountered before in the field of concrete. Some interesting results of shell design will be illustrated by means of slides. Speakers will include Mario G. Salvadori, Professor of Civil Engineering, Columbia University.

New Members: Kjartan O. Armann, CE; H. Wayne Taul, CSE; Etienne D. Rolin, CE; James W. Pereira, CE. Junior Member Robert P. Clark, and Affiliate Members Samuel D. Burks, and Richard C. Clark.

AMERICAN SOCIETY FOR TESTING MATERIALS SOUTHERN CALIFORNIA

Alvin J. Herzig, President, Climax Molybdenum Company of Michigan, and Richard T. Kropf, ASTM President, Vice-President and Director of Research, Belding Heminway Company, Inc., were the principal speakers at the January meeting of the Los Angeles Chapter in the Rodger Young Auditorium.

Herzig spoke on "Molybdenum Metal and Its Promising Alloys," and Kropf discussed "The Road to the Future."

AMERICAN SOCIETY OF CIVIL ENGINEERS—San Francisco

For the first time in its more than 52 years of existence the Section now has a permanent office in charge of a paid secretary to handle the rapidly expanding affairs of the engineers. Offices have been opened in Room 302, Atlas Bldg., 604 Mission St., San Francisco and are in charge of Mrs. Ola H. Dewell.

It is anticipated that the establishment of this per-

manent office will materially aid the elected secretary and treasurer in the performance of many of their time-consuming duties.

SOCIETY OF AMERICAN MILITARY ENGINEERS—San Francisco Post

Major General Frank A. Heilman, Army, RET, Director of Advanced Research, Division of Hiller Helicopters, was the principal speaker at the January meeting in the Officer's Club, Presidio of San Francisco, speaking on the subject "Some New Concepts of Vertical Take-Off Aircraft with Military Significance."

Use of slide and movies emphasized the new developments in this particular field of aircraft development.

AMERICAN SOCIETY OF CIVIL ENGINEERS—Los Angeles

Prof. Everett D. Howe, Chairman, Department of Mechanical Engineering, University of California, Berkeley, will be the principal speaker at the February 12th meeting to be held in the Rodger Young Auditorium, Los Angeles.

He will speak on the subject "Desalting of Sea Water," and is very familiar with the latest developments in sea-water conversion research. His discussion will be illustrated by slides.

STRUCTURAL ENGINEERS ASSOCIATION OF NORTHERN CALIFORNIA

J. Albert Paquette, San Francisco, has been elected President of the Structural Engineers Association of Northern California for 1958.

Named to serve with him were: Charles DeMaria, Vice-President; Arthur R. Weatherbe, Secretary; Samuel H. Clark, Assistant Secretary; William K. Cloud, Treasurer, and Henry J. Degenkolb, Harold S. Kellam, Marvin A. Larson, John M. Sardis and Richard J. Woodward, Directors.

The above photo shows the new metal shop in the Sunnyvale, California high school building. Constructed with plexiglas windows which has made progress in the past few years toward acceptance by the architects, engineering profession and the construction industry. This economical window has been used the last few years in the construction of many buildings across the nation.

Architectural advantages for uses of these windows are many. It is transparent as fine optical glass and available in a wide range of transparent and translucent colors. Time proven ability to withstand exposure to weather. Reduces breakage, is lighter weight than glass, and has six to seventeen times greater resistance to impact in thickness of $\frac{1}{8}''$ to $\frac{1}{4}''$.

(See Page 32)

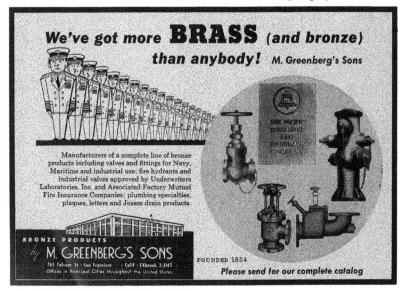

CLARK A. DUNN CHOSEN PRESIDENT NATIONAL SOCIETY PROF. ENGINEERS

Clark A. Dunn, administrative head of the School of General Engineering at Oklahoma State University, has been nominated for the office of president of the National Society of Professional Engineers. He is also executive director of the office of engineering research at the university, and is currently serving a second term as vice president of the Southwestern Region of the National Society.

Dunn will assume his office for the administrative year which begins in July.

HARRY FABRIS IS APPOINTED SALES MANAGER

U. A. "Harry" Fabris has been appointed sales manager of both M. Greenberg's Sons and Josam Pacific Company, according to an announcement by Stuart N. Greenberg, president.

Fabris has been associated with both M. Greenberg's Sons and its subsidiary the Josam Pacific Company for the past 16 years, starting as Sales Engineer and in the past 8 years has served as Assistant Sales Manager.

MacDONALD, YOUNG AND NELSON, CONTRACTORS MOVING TO OAKLAND

MacDonald, Young and Nelson, Inc., San Francisco general contracting firm, have announced they will move their headquarters from San Francisco to Oakland on February 15th. The announcement was made by Graeme K. MacDonald, president of the firm.

In announcing the move, MacDonald declared that the new location for the firm will provide ample room for future expansion and will provide for more complete integration of warehousing and equipment storage facilities.

The new offices and plant will be located at 8907 Railroad Avenue in East Oakland on a 5-1/2 acre site owned by MacDonald, Young and Nelson, where a new administrative building is now being constructed and which was designed by the architectural firm of Wurster, Bernardi & Emmons, San Francisco.

CALAVERAS CEMENT INAUGURATES AUTOMATIC SYSTEM

A completely automatic system of kiln operation has been "on stream" for the past three months at the Calaveras Cement Company plant in San Andreas, California, according to Grant W. Metzger, plant manager.

The company's steps toward perfecting a sensitive complex of instruments to regulate its 360 foot long revolving fifth kiln have been closely watched in the cement industry, which regards the control system as a major move toward automation in the manufacture of cement.

The new system was designed jointly by Lewis A. Parsons, Calaveras consulting engineer, and Mel C. Sutton, Calaveras chief chemist, with the technical assistance of Nels Swanson, and provides a method of measuring the temperature of the mix in the calcining zone of the kiln, approximately 110 feet from the start of the burning zone. Temperature in this area averages 1400 degrees F.

The new system of precision control

makes possible a uniformity of production not previously attainable.

AISE SCHEDULE ANNUAL MEETING

The fifth annual western meeting of the Association of Iron and Steel Engineers will be held February 24-26 at the Statler Hotel in Los Angeles.

Technical sessions to be held the first two days of the meeting will offer papers by leading steel mill authorities on topics of particular interest to western steel producers, and will include such topics as automatic numerical data logging and processing, static control for blast furnaces, a modern forging press and its control, immersion thermocouple practice, electrical equipment for a modern sheet temper mill.

Individuals associated with the iron, steel and allied industries, whether or not they are members of the AISE, are invited to attend the meetings.

ENCINA HALL STANFORD RENOVATION

Encina Hall on Stanford University campus, Palo Alto, will be completely renovated during the summer vacation period at a cost of $1,350,000, according to an announcement by the Stanford University Board of Trustees.

The project will be completed by September and the opening of the fall term.

SUNNYVALE SCHOOL
(From Page 30)

Translucent white sheets diffuse light evenly in all directions. Heated to pliable state, can be formed to intricate shapes and curves. It is easily sawed, machined, drilled and cemented.

Architects for the Sunnyvale High School are Masten, Hurd and Abrams and the general contractors O. E. Anderson and Carl Swenson.

PHOTO CREDITS: Albert W. Roller, Architect, Cover; Welton Becket, FAIA and Associates, Architects and Engineers, page 5; Julius Shulman Photos, pages 8, 9; George W. Reed & Co., page 10; Marchant Calculating Company, pages 11, 12, 13, 15, 16; Industrial Lighting Company, page 14; Cramer Acoustics, pages 18, 19; Pacific Cement & Aggregates, pages 20, 21; Raymond R. Shaw, AIA Architect, page 22; and Mario J. Ciampi, Architect, page 24.

ART COMMENT
(From Page 7)

in Prints by Albert Duerer and his Contemporaries, and Modern Prints in Color. On Loan Exhibition at the San Francisco Public Library is being shown a group of Photographs of California by Hugo P. Rudinger.

SPECIAL EVENTS: Organ Recital each Sunday and Saturday afternoon at 3 o'clock. Educational Activities include the Spring series of art classes for children and adults.

The Museum is open daily.

SISTER MARY LUKE PAINTINGS SHOWN AT deYOUNG MUSEUM

Sister Mary Luke, Head of the Art Department of the College of the Holy Names in Oakland, who has won wide recognition for her paintings on architectural themes, is exhibiting a selection of watercolors—primarily impressions of southern California missions—at the M. H. deYoung Memorial Museum January 1 through January 26.

The exhibition includes impressions of the southern-most eight of the 21 California missions: San Diego de Acala, San Luis Rey, San Juan Capistrano, San Gabriel, Nuestra Senora la Reina de los Angeles, San Fernando, Santa Barbara and Santa Ines.

On occasion of a recent exhibition of this series at the Santa Barbara Museum it was written: "Sister Mary Luke has her roots buried deep in California's soil, descending as she does from an old line of Spanish caballeros. With such an ancestry she brings to her subject, California Missions, an innate appreciation and a sparkling enthusiasm which shines forth in her paintings. Her creative work—though the product of a long period of observation, reading, and study—has been fused in an artistic synthesis styled expressionism, for it is the 'Spirit of the Mission' rather than the pictorial representation which emerges."

BOOK REVIEWS
PAMPHLETS AND CATALOGUES

ECONOMICS OF ATOMIC ENERGY. By Mary Goldring, B.A. Philosophical Library, Inc., 15 E. 40th St., New York 16, N.Y. Price $6.00.

This is another book in the "Atoms for Peace Series" and deals with the fact that nuclear power has become economic, and electricity will be produced at a cost equivalent to that from ordinary coal and oil-fired power stations within the next three or four years.

The author discusses critically the growth of Britain's nuclear power from the viewpoint of one who is well informed, yet outside and therefore free from the trammels imposed by either membership of the U. K. Atomic Energy Authority or the companies. The book endeavors to outline clearly and authoritatively the major trends of a subject which is inevitably, because of its youth and rapid growth, subjected to more rapid shifts of opinion and fact than practically any other sphere of economics.

ESTIMATING GENERAL CONSTRUCTION COSTS, Second Edition. By Louis Dallavia. F. W. Dodge Corp., 119 W. 40th St., New York 18, N.Y. Price $8.50.

This is an estimating handbook that cannot become out of date; it provides an accurate, foolproof method of estimating all direct production costs in Earthwork, Reinforced Concrete Work, Structural Steel Work, Masonry and Carpentry. The author tells how to estimate jobs involving any operation by a system determining your productivity percentage and applying it against only three tables to find your shift cost, output range, and unit cost. Once the unit costs for each operation are found, simple arithmetic will provide the total cost to you on any general construction job. The author has spent all of his professional career as a construction estimator and field engineer.

STRENGTH OF MATERIALS. By Prof. F. R. Shanley. McGraw-Hill Book Co., 330 W. 42nd St., New York 36, N.Y. Price $8.50.

The book is designed to be used as a first text in college courses in engineering and science, and because of this the order of presentation has been given careful attention by the author, Professor of Engineering at the University of California, Los Angeles. The text does not emphasize any particular field of structures, such as aeronautical or civil, but instead contains material which forms the basis for all types of structural analysis and design. Examples and problems include practical cases from fields of civil, aeronautical, and mechanical engineering, and the scope of the book has been expanded considerably beyond the usual limits for a text of this type. Illustrative examples, numerous problems with answers to most of them, and key questions for each chapter complete the text.

NEW CATALOGUES AVAILABLE

Architects, Engineers, Contractors, Planning Commission members—the catalogues, folders, new building products material, etc., described below may be obtained by directing your request to the name and address given in each item.

Heavy-duty shoring for bridges, etc. Illustrated brochure containing many details of heavy duty shoring for bridges, overpass and heavy slab work, including cost comparison with lumber and steel; drawings of applications to actual construction. Free copy write DEPT-A&E, Laurence Myers Scaffolding Co., 61 Bluxome St., San Francisco 7.

Modern stone age is here. "The Modern Stone Age is Here," a colorful brochure pictorially reviews the use of stone through the ages from the time of the cave man, the Egyptian, Grecian, Roman, Byzantine, Medieval, Renaissance Periods, the present time and portrays a panorama of the City of the Future; also depicts every type of quarried stone in natural colors. Free copy write DEPT-A&E, Building Stone Institute, 420 Lexington Ave., New York 17, N.Y.

Structural and slab perimeter insulations. New catalog (A.I.A. File No. 37-C-1) describes entire line of structural and slab perimeter insulation of spun mineral wool products for home and industry; technical descriptions and specifications for full thick blankets, semi-thick blankets, builders

batts, blowing wool and Perimsul; describes physical and thermal properties of all materials as well as appropriate facings; size data, density, conductivity, conductance and thermal resistance; installation instructions and methods of application. Free copy write DEPT·A&E, Building Materials Division, Baldwin-Hill Co., 500 Breunig Ave., Trenton 2, N.J.

Ceramic veneer in shopping centers. Four-page folder (AIA File No. 9a) describes the use of ceramic veneer in shopping -centers; printed in 2-color, illustrates with examples of ceramic veneer installations in shopping centers; information on Screen Decorative Ceramic Veneer which provides permanent, personalized design; also data on CV panelwall construction. Copy free write DEPT·A&E, Architectural Products Division, Gladding McBean & Co., 2901 Los Feliz Blvd., Los Angeles 39.

Fire warning systems. Completely revised and comprehensive catalog covering all types of fire warning systems available to architects, engineers and contractors concerned with planning, designing, installing, and maintaining fire alarm systems; every type of property, schools, hospitals, office buildings, public and private institutions, and industrial installations. Write DEPT·A&E, The Autocall Company, 57 Tucker Avenue, Shelby, Ohio.

Radar-Eye. New colored brochure describes operation and uses of "Radar-Eye" in commercial, industrial, and residential uses; a new electric motion device that uses the same principle used by planes and ships and by the military to alert our country to air attack; intruders cannot crawl over it, slide under it, cut through it or in any way tamper with either the unit or wiring system without setting off alarm. For complete details write Sullivan Sales, Radar-Eye Corpn., 1605 Solano Ave., Berkeley 7, California.

Acousti-Booths for Better Hearing. New bruchure, in color and profusely illustrated, gives design, and installation details of telephone booth design to absorb extraneous noises; proved by years of service in all types of public and industrial locations. Free copy write DEPT·A&E, Cramer Acoustics, Burgenn-Manning Co., 560-9th St., San Francisco.

3-Way functional ceiling. Descriptive brochure in color (AIA File No. 17-A) gives detailed data on a completely self-contained suspended ceiling that offers radiant panel heating, radiant panel cooling, and acoustic control; installation details, charts, specifications, and photographs of installations. Free copy write DEPT·A&E, Cramer Acoustics, Burgenn-Manning Co., 560-9th St., San Francisco.

Design in color. Illustrated catalog shows complete line of stools and tables plus electric hand and hair dryers for all washrooms, for free copy write DEPT·A&E, The Chicago Hardware Foundry Co., North Chicago, Ill.

Ceramic veneer, descriptive booklet. Ceramic Veneer, the modern, high fired glazed facing material, is pictured and described in a new 8-page, four color booklet (AIA File No. 9a), issued by Architectural Division of Gladding, McBean & Co., describes adhesion, anchored, mold pressed, CV Panelwall, screen, decorative and sculptured types of the building product; booklet offers a ready guide to construction details, installation and specifications. Copies available, write DEPT·A&E, Gladding, McBean & Co., Seattle, Spokane, Portland, Phoenix, San Francisco, or 2901 Los Feliz Blvd., Los Angeles 39, California.

ESTIMATOR'S GUIDE

BUILDING AND CONSTRUCTION MATERIALS

PRICES GIVEN ARE FIGURING PRICES AND ARE MADE UP FROM AVERAGE QUOTATIONS FURNISHED BY
LeROY CONSTRUCTION SERVICES. 4% SALES TAX ON ALL MATERIALS BUT NOT LABOR.

All prices and wages quoted are for San Francisco and the Bay District. There may be slight fluctuation of prices in the interior and southern part of the state. Freight cartage and labor travel time must be added in figuring country work.

BONDS—Performance or Performance plus Labor and Material Bond(s), $10 per $1000 on contract price. Labor & Material Bond(s) only, $5.00 per $1000 on contract price.

BRICKWORK—MASONRY—

BUILDING BRICK—estimated cost per sq. ft.
WALL	BRICK	AVERAGE
8"	Jumbo	$2.30
8"	Norman	2.40
10"	Standard	2.40
12"	Jumbo	2.55
14"	Standard	2.60

FACE BRICK—estimated cost per sq. ft.
WALL	BRICK	AVERAGE
8"	Jumbo	$2.55
8"	Brick Block	2.30
10"	Standard	2.90
10"	Norman	2.80
14"	Norman	3.05

Common Brick—Per 1 M laid—$175.00 up (according to class of work).
Face Brick—Per 1 M laid—$265.00 and up (according to class of work).
Brick Steps—$2.75 per lin. ft. & up.

BRICK VENEER

BUILDING BRICK—estimated cost per sq. ft.
WALL	BRICK	AVERAGE
3"	Jumbo	$1.15
3"	Norman	1.25
4"	Standard	1.40

FACE BRICK—estimated cost per sq. ft.
WALL	BRICK	AVERAGE
3"	Jumbo	$1.35
4"	Standard	1.60
4"	Norman	1.50
4"	Roman	1.80

Common Brick Veneer on Frame Bldgs.—Approx. $1.75 and up—(according to class of work).
Face Brick Veneer on Frame Bldgs.—Approx. $2.25 and up (according to class of work).
"Bricketts" (Brick Veneer) per M, f.o.b. Niles, $50.00.

Glazed Structural Units—Walls Erected—
Clear Glazed—
2 x 6 12 Furring	$1.95 per sq. ft.
4 x 6 x 12 Partition	2.25 per sq. ft.

4 x 6 x 12 Double Faced
Partition	2.50 per sq. ft.

For colored glaze add........ .30 per sq. ft.
Mantel Fire Brick $150.00 per M—F.O.B. Pittsburgh.
Fire Brick—2½"x9x4½—$110.00.
Cartage—Approx. $10.00 per M.
Paving—$75.00.

Building Tile—
8x5½x12-inches, per M	$159.40
6x5½x12-inches, per M	124.00
4x5½x12-inches, per M	96.90

Hollow Tile—
12x12x3-inches, per M	156.85
12x12x4-inches, per M	177.10
12x12x6-inches, per M	235.30
F.O.B. Plant	

BUILDING PAPER and FELTS—
1 ply per 1000 ft. roll	$5.30
2 ply per 1000 ft. roll	7.80
3 ply per 1000 ft. roll	9.70
Brownskin, Standard 500 ft. roll	6.85
Sisalkraft, reinforced, 500 ft. roll	8.50

Sheathing Papers—
Asphalt sheathing, 15-lb. roll	$2.70
30-lb. roll	3.70
Dampcourse, 216-ft. roll	2.95
Blue Plasterboard, 60-lb. roll	5.10

Felt Papers—
Deadening felt, ¾-lb., 50-ft. roll	$4.30
Deadening felt, 1-lb.	5.05
Asphalt roofing, 15-lbs.	2.70
Asphalt roofing, 30-lbs.	3.70

Roofing Papers—
Standard Grade, 108-ft. roll, Light	$2.50
Smooth Surface, Medium	2.90
Heavy	3.40
M. S. Extra Heavy	3.95

CONCRETE AGGREGATES—
The following prices net to Contractors unless otherwise shown. Carload lots only.

	Bunker per ton	Del'd per ton
Gravel, all sizes	$3.10	$3.90
Top Sand	3.30	4.10
Concrete Mix	3.20	4.00
Crushed Rock, ½" to ¾"	3.30	4.10
Crushed Rock, ¾" to 1½"	3.30	4.10
Roofing Gravel	3.25	4.15

Sand—
Lapis (Nos. 2 & 4)	4.05	4.85
Olympia (Nos. 1 & 2)	3.35	3.95

Cement—
Common (all brands, paper sacks).
Per Sack, small quantity (paper)	$1.35
Carload lots, in bulk, per bbl.	4.14

Cash discount on carload lots, 10c a bbl., 10th Prox., less than carload lots, $5.20 per bbl. f.o.b. warehouse or $5.60 delivered.
Cash discount on L.C.L. 2%
Trinity White	1 to 100 sacks, $4.00
Medusa White	sack, warehouse or delivered.

CONCRETE READY-MIX—
Delivered in 5-yd. loads; 6 sk.
in bulk $14.80
Curing Compound, clear, drums,
per gal. .... .90

CONCRETE BLOCKS—
	Haydite	Basalt
4x8x16-inches, each	$ .22½	$ .22½
6x8x16-inches, each	.28½	.28½
8x8x16-inches, each	.33	.33
12x8x16-inches, each	.49	.49½
12x8x24-inches, each	.70	.70

Aggregates—Haydite or Basalite Plant
¾-inch to ¾-inch, per cu. yd.	$6.00	$7.50
¾-inch to ¾-inch, per cu. yd.	6.00	7.50
No. 6 to 0-inch, per cu. yd.	6.00	7.50

DAMPPROOFING and Waterproofing—
Two-coat work, $9.00 per square and up.
Membrane waterproofing—4 layers of saturated felt, $13.00 per square and up.
Hot coating work, $5.50 per square & up.
Medusa Waterproofing, $3.50 per lb. San Francisco Warehouse.
Tricosal concrete waterproofing, 60c a cubic yd. and up.
Anhi Hydro, 50 gal., $2.20.

ELECTRIC WIRING—$20 to $25 per outlet for conduit work (including switches) $18-20. Knob and tube average $7.00 to 9.00 per outlet.

ELEVATORS—
Prices vary according to capacity, speed and type. Consult elevator companies. Average cost of installing a slow speed automatic passenger elevator in small four story apartment building, including entrance doors, about $9,500.00.

EXCAVATION—
Sand, $1.25, clay or shale, $2.00 per yard. Trucks, $35 to $55 per day.
Above figures are an average without water. Steam shovel work in large quantities, less; hard material, such as rock, will run considerably more.

FIRE ESCAPES—
Ten-foot galvanized iron balcony, with stairs, $275 installed on new buildings; $325 on old buildings.

FLOORS—
Asphalt Tile, ⅛ in. gauge 25c to 35c per sq. ft.
Composition Floors, such as Magnesite, 50c-$1.25 per sq. ft.
Linoleum, standard gauge, $3.75 sq. yd. & up laid.
Mastipave—$1.90 per sq. yd.
Battleship Linoleum—$6.00 sq. yd. & up laid.
Terazzo Floors—$2.50 per sq. ft.
Terazzo Steps—$3.75 per lin. ft.
Mastic Wear Coat—according to type—45c per sq. ft. and up.

Hardwood Flooring—
Oak Flooring—T & G—Unfin.—
	1¼x2¼	1½x2	¾x2	¾x2
Clear Qtd., White	$405	$405	$	
Clear Qtd., Red	405	380		
Select Qtd., Red or White	355	340		
Clear Pln., Red or White	355	340	335	315
Select Pln., Red or White	340	330	325	300
#1 Common, red or White	315	310	305	780
#2 Common, Red or White	305			

Prefinished Oak Flooring—
	Prime	Standard
½ x 2½	$369.00	$359.00
½ x 2½	380.00	370.00
½ x 3¼	390.00	381.00
½ x 3¼	375.00	355.00
½ x 3¾	395.00	375.00
½ x 2¼ & 3¼ Ranch Plank		415.00

Unfinished Maple Flooring—
	Prime
⅞ x 2¼ First Grade	$390.00
⅞ x 2¼ 2nd Grade	365.00
⅞ x 2¼ 2nd & Btr. Grade	375.00
⅞ x 2¼ 3rd Grade	240.00
x 3¼ 3rd & Btr., Jtd. EM	380.00
x 3½ 2nd & Btr., Jtd. EM	390.00
33/32 x 2¼ First Grade	400.00
33/32 x 2¼ 2nd Grade	360.00
33/32 x 2¼ 3rd Grade	320.00
Floor Layer Wage $2.83 per hr.	

GLASS—
Single Strength Window Glass	$ .30 per ☐ ft.
Single Strength Window Glass	$ .30 per ☐ ft.
Double Strength Window Glass	.60 per ☐ ft.
Plate Glass, ¼ polished to 75	1.80 per ☐ ft.
75 to 100	2.10 per ☐ ft.
¼ in. Polished Wire Plate Glass	2.70 per ☐ ft.
¼ in. Rgh. Wire Glass	.80 per ☐ ft.
⅛ in. Obscure Glass	.55 per ☐ ft.
⅞ in. Obscure Glass	.70 per ☐ ft.
⅛ in. Heat Absorbing Obscure	.54 per ☐ ft.
¼ in. Heat Absorbing Wire	.72 per ☐ ft.
⅛ in. Ribbed	.55 per ☐ ft.
⅞ in. Ribbed	.75 per ☐ ft.
⅛ in. Rough	.55 per ☐ ft.
⅞ in. Rough	.75 per ☐ ft.

Glazing of above additional $.15 to .30 per ☐ ft.
Glass Blocks, set in place. 3.50 per ☐ ft.

HEATING—Installed
Furnaces—Gas Fired
Floor Furnace, 25,000 BTU
25,000 BTU	$42.00- 80.00
35,000 BTU	47.00- 87.00
45,000 BTU	55.00- 95.00
Automatic Control, Add	39.00- 45.00

Dual Wall Furnaces, 25,000 BTU
25,000 BTU	72.00-134.00
35,000 BTU	149.00
45,000 BTU	161.00
With Automatic Control, Add	45.00-161.00
Unit Heaters, 50,000 BTU	215.00
Gravity Furnace, 65,000 BTU	210.00
Forced Air Furnace, 75,000 BTU	342.00

Water Heaters—5-year guarantee
With Thermostat Control,
20 gal. capacity	96.00
30 gal. capacity	112.00
40 gal. capacity	135.00

INSULATION AND WALLBOARD—
Rockwool Insulation—
Full thick 3" $66.00
(2") Less than 1,000 ☐ ft................ 64.00
(2") Over 1,000 ☐ ft........................ 59.00
Cotton Insulation—Full-thickness
(1") ....$41.60 per M sq. ft.
Sisalation Aluminum Insulation—Aluminum
coated on both sides ....$23.50 per M sq. ft.
Tileboard—4'x6' panel ....$9.00 per panel
Wallboard—½" thickness ....$55.00 per M sq. ft.
Finished Plank ....69.00 per M sq. ft.
Ceiling Tileboard ....69.00 per M sq. ft.

IRON—Cost of ornamental iron, cast iron, etc., depends on designs.

LUMBER—Ex Lumber Yards
S4S Construction Grade
O.P. or D.F., per M. f.b.m.............$105.00
Flooring—

	Per M Delvd
V.G.-D.F., B & Btr. 1 x 4 T & G Flooring...$215.00	
"C" and better—all...........	205.00
"D" and better—all...........	135.00
Rwd. Rustic—"A" grade, medium dry......	185.00
8 to 24 ft.	

Plywood, per M sq. ft.
¼-inch, 4.0x8.0-S1S $110.00
½-inch, 4.0x8.0-S1S 190.00
¾-inch, per M sq. ft.................................... 240.00
Plyform 220.00

Shingles (Rwd. not available)—
Red Cedar No. 1—$12.25 per square; No. 2,
$10.25; No. 3, $6.25.
Average cost to lay shingles, $7.50 per square.
Cedar Shakes—½" to ¾" x 24/26 in handsplit
tapered or split resawn, per square......$16.00
¾" to 1¼" x 24/26 in split resawn,
per square 18.00
Average cost to lay shakes, $12.50 per square.
Pressure Treated Lumber—
Salt Treated ....Add $45 per M to above
Creosoted,
8-lb. treatment ....Add $52 per M to above

MARBLE—(See Dealers)

METAL LATH EXPANDED—
Standard Diamond. 3.40, Copper
Bearing, LCL, per 100 sq. yds.......$45.50
Standard Ribbed, ditto.....................$49.50

MILLWORK—Standard.
D. F. $200 per 1000, R. W. Rustic air dried
$225 per 1000 (delivered).
Complete door unit, $21-$32.
Screen doors, $10 to $15 each.
Patent screen windows, $1.75 a sq. ft.
Cases for kitchen and pantries seven ft.
high, per lineal ft., upper $10 to $15;
lower $12 to $18.
Dining room cases, $20.00 per lineal foot.
Rough and finish about $2.00 per sq. ft.
Labor—Rough carpentry, warehouse heavy
framing (average), $115 per M.
For smaller work average, $125 to $135 per
1000.

PAINTING—
Two-coat work ....per yard $ .90
Three-coat work ....per yard 1.35
Cold water painting............per yard .45
Whitewashing ....per yard .25

Linseed Oil, Strictly Pure	Wholesale	
(Basis 7½ lbs. per gal.)	Raw	Boiled
Light Iron drums....................per gal.	$2.28	$2.34
5-gallon cans ....per gal.	2.40	2.46
1-gallon cans ....each	2.52	2.58
Quart cans ....each	.71	.72
Pint cans ....each	.38	.39
½-pint cans ....each	.24	.24

Turpentine	Pure Gum
(Basis, 7.2 lbs. per gal.)	Spirits
Light iron drums..........................	per gal. $1 65
5-gallon cans	per gal. 1.76
1-gallon cans	each 1.88
Quart cans	each .54
Pint cans	each .31
½-pint cans	each .20

**Pioneer White Lead in Oil Heavy Paste and
All-Purpose (Soft-Paste)**

	List Price		Price to Painters	
Net Weight	Per 100	Pr. per	per 100	Pr. per
Packages	lbs.	pkg.	lbs.	pkg.
100-lb. kegs	$28.35	$29.35	$27.50	$27.50
50-lb. kegs	30.05	15.03	28.15	14.08
25-lb. kegs	30.35	7.50	28.45	7.12
5-lb. cans*	33.35	1.34	31.25	1.25
1-lb. cans*	36.00	.36	33.75	.34

500 lbs. (one delivery) ¾c -per pound less than
above.
*Heavy Paste only.

**Pioneer Dry White Lead—Litharge—Dry Red Lead
Red Lead in Oil**

Price to Painters—Price Per 100 Pounds			
	100	50	25
	lbs.	lbs.	lbs.
Dry White Lead........................	$26.30	$....	$....
Litharge..................................	25.95	26.60	26.90
Dry Red Lead	27.20	27.85	28.15
Red Lead in Oil	30.65	31.30	31.60

Pound cans, $.37 per lb.

PATENT CHIMNEYS—Average
6-inch ....$2.75 lineal foot
8-inch .... 3.25 lineal foot
10-inch .... 4.10 lineal foot
12-inch .... 5.20 lineal foot
Installation ....75c to $1.50 lineal foot

PLASTER—
Neat wall, per ton delivered in S. F. in
paper bags, $27.00.

PLASTERING (Interior)—

	Yard
3 Coats, metal lath and plaster....................	$3.75
Keene cement on metal lath.........................	4.25
Ceilings with ¾ hot roll channels metal lath	
(lathed only)	3.75
Ceilings with ¾ hot roll channels metal lath	
plastered	5.60
Single partition ¾ channels and metal lath	
1 side (lath only)	3.75
Single partition ¾ channels and metal lath	
2 inches thick plastered........................	8.75
4-inch double partition ¾ channels and	
metal lath 2 sides (lath only)................	6.25
4-inch double partition ¾ channels and	
metal lath 2 sides plastered..................	10.25

PLASTERING (Exterior)—

	Yard
2 coats cement finish, brick or concrete	
wall	$2.25
3 coats cement finish, No. 18 gauge wire	
mesh	3.00

Lime—$4.25 per bbl. at yard.
Processed Lime- $4.95 per bbl. at yard.
Rock or Grip Lath—⅜"—35c per sq. yd.
Composition Stucco—$4.50 sq. yd. (applied).
Lime Putty—$3.75 per bbl.

PLUMBING—
From $250.00 - $300.00 per fixture up,
according to grade, quality and runs.

ROOFING—
"Standard" tar and gravel, 4 ply....$15.00
per sq. for 30 sqs. or over.
Less than 30 sqs. $18.00 up per sq.
Tile $40.00 to $50.00 per square.
No. 1 Redwood Shingles in place.
4½ in. exposure. per square.........$18.25
5/2 No. 1 Cedar Shingles, 5 in. ex-
posure, per square.............................. 16.50
5/8 x 16"—No. 1 Little Giant Cedar
Shingles, 5" exposure, per square.. 18.25
4/2 No. 1-24" Royal Cedar Shingles
7½" exposure, per square.............. 23.00
Re-coat with Gravel $5.50 up per sq.

Compo Shingles, $17 to $25 per sq. laid
½ to ¾ x 25" Resawn Cedar Shakes,
10" Exposure ....$24.00 to $30.00
¾ to 1¼ x 25" Resawn Cedar Shakes,
10" Exposure ....$28.00 to $35.00
1 x 25" Resawn Cedar Shakes,
10" Exposure ....$20.00 to $22.00
Above prices are for shakes in place.

SEWER PIPE—
Vitrified, per foot: L.C.L. F.O.B. Ware-
house, San Francisco.
Standard, 4-in. ....$ .28
Standard, 6-in. .... .51
Standard, 8-in. .... .74
Standard, 12-in. 1.61
Standard, 24-in. 6.42
Clay Drain Pipe, per 1,000 L.F.
L.C.L., F.O.B. Warehouse, San Francisco:
Standard, 6-in. per M..................$240.00
Standard, 8-in. per M.................. 400.00

SHEET METAL—
Windows—Metal, $2.50 a sq. ft.
Fire doors (average), including hardware
$2.80 per sq. ft., size 12'x12'. $3.75 per
sq. ft., size 3'x6'.

SKYLIGHTS—(not glazed)
Galvanized iron, per sq. ft..................$1.50
Vented hip skylights, per sq. ft......... 2.50
Aluminum, puttyless,
(unglazed), per sq. ft......................... 1.25
(installed and glazed), per sq. ft... 1.85

STEEL—STRUCTURAL—10 to 50 Tons
$325 & up per ton erected, when out of
mill.
$350 per ton erected, when out of stock.

STEEL REINFORCING—
$185.00 & up per ton, in place.
¼-in. Rd. (Less than 1 ton) per 100 lbs.......$8.90
⅜-in. Rd. (Less than 1 ton) per 100 lbs........ 7.80
½-in. Rd. (Less than 1 ton) per 100 lbs........ 7.50
⅝-in. Rd. (Less than 1 ton) per 100 lbs........ 7.25
¾-in. & ⅞-in. Rd. (Less than 1 ton)............. 7.15
1 in. & up (Less than 1 ton)........................ 7.10
1 ton to 5 tons, deduct 25c.

STORE FRONTS—
Individual estimates recommended. See
ESTIMATORS DIRECTORY for Architec-
tural Veneer (3), and Mosaic Tile (35).

TILE—
Ceramic Tile Floors—Commercial $1.45 to $1.70
per square foot.
Cove Base—$1.20 per lineal foot.
Quarry Tile Floors—6x6 with 6" base @ $1.35
per sq. ft.
Tile Wainscots and Floors—Residential, 4¼x4¼
@ $1.75 to $2.00.
Tile Wainscots—Commercial Jobs 4¼x4¼ Tile
$1.60 to $1.85 per sq. ft.
Asphalt Tile Floor ⅛".. ⅜"...$ .25 - $ .35 sq. ft.
Light shades slightly higher.
Cork Tile—$.60-$.70 per sq. ft.
Mosaic Floors—See dealers.
Linoleum tile, per ☐ ft............................$ .65
Rubber tile, per ☐ ft............................$ .55 to $ .75

Furring Tile	
Scored	F.O.B. S. F.
12 x 12, each.................................	$ .17

Kraftile: Per square foot	
Patio Tile—Niles Red	
12 x 12 x ⅞-inch, plain........................	$ .40
6 x 12 x ⅞-inch, plain..........................	.43
6 x 6 x ⅞-inch, plain............................	.46

Building Tile—	
8x5½x12-inches, per M........................	$139.50
6x5½x12-inches, per M........................	105.00
4x5½x12-inches, per M........................	84.00

Hollow Tile—	
12x12x2-inches, per M........................	$146.75
12x12x3-inches, per M........................	156.85
12x12x4-inches, per M........................	177.10
12x12x6-inches, per M........................	235.30

F.O.B. Plant

VENETIAN BLINDS—
45c per square foot and up. Installation
extra.

WINDOWS—STEEL—INDUSTRIAL—
Cost depends on design and quality required.

ESTIMATOR'S DIRECTORY
Building and Construction Materials

ACOUSTICAL ENGINEERS
L. D. REEDER CO.
San Francisco: 1255 Sansome St., DO 2-5050
Sacramento: 3026 V St., GL 7-3505

AIR CONDITIONING
E. C. BRAUN CO.
Berkeley: 2115 Fourth St., TH 5-2356
GILMORE AIR CONDITIONING SERVICE
San Francisco: 1617 Harrison St., UN 1-2000
KAEMPER & BARRETT
San Francisco: 233 Industrial St., JU 6-6200
LINFORD AIR & REFRIGERATION CO.
Oakland: 174-12th St., TW 3-6521
MALM METAL PRODUCTS
Santa Rosa: 724-2nd St., SR 454
JAMES A. NELSON CO.
San Francisco: 1375 Howard St., HE 1-0140

ALUMINUM BLDG. PRODUCTS
MICHEL & PFEFFER IRON WORKS (Wrought Iron)
So. San Francisco: 212 Shaw Road, PLaza 5-8983
REYNOLDS METALS CO.
San Francisco: 3201 Third St., MI 7-2990
SOULE STEEL CO.
San Francisco: 1750 Army St., VA 4-4141
UNIVERSAL WINDOW CO.
Berkeley: 950 Parker St., TH 1-1600

ARCHITECTURAL PORCELAIN ENAMEL
CALIFORNIA METAL ENAMELING CO.
Los Angeles: 6904 E. Slauson, RA 3-6351
San Francisco: Continental Bldg. Products Co.,
    178 Fremont St.
Portland: Portland Wire & Iron Works,
    4644 S.E. Seventeenth Ave.
Seattle: Foster-Bray Co., 2412 1st Ave. So.
Spokane: Bernhard Schafer, Inc., West 34. 2nd Ave.
Salt Lake City: S. A. Roberts & Co., 109 W. 2nd So.
Dallas: Offenhauser Co., 2201 Telephone Rd.
El Paso: Architectural Products Co.,
    506 E. Yandell Blvd.
Phoenix: Haskell-Thomas Co., 3808 No. Central
San Diego: Maloney Specialties, Inc., 823 W. Laurel St.
Boise: Intermountain Glass Co., 1417 Main St.

ARCHITECTURAL & AERIAL PHOTOGRAPHS
FRED ENGLISH
Belmont, Calif.: 1310 Old County Road, LY 1-0385

ARCHITECTURAL VENEER
Ceramic Veneer
GLADDING, McBEAN & CO.
San Francisco: Harrison at 9th St., UN 1-7400
Los Angeles: 2901 Los Feliz Blvd., OL 2121
Portland: 110 S.E. Main St., EA 6179
Seattle 99: 945 Elliott Ave., West, GA 0330
Spokane: 1102 N. Monroe St., BR 3259
KRAFTILE COMPANY
Niles, Calif., Niles 3611

Porcelain Veneer
PORCELAIN ENAMEL PUBLICITY BUREAU
Oakland 12: Room 601, Franklin Building
Pasadena 8: P. O. Box 186, East Pasadena Station

Granite Veneer
VERMONT MARBLE COMPANY
San Francisco 24: 6000 3rd St., VA 6-5024
Los Angeles: 3522 Council St., DU 2-6339

Marble Veneer
VERMONT MARBLE COMPANY
San Francisco 24: 6000 3rd St., VA 6-5024
Los Angeles: 3522 Council St., DU 2-6339

BANKS - FINANCING
CROCKER-ANGLO NATIONAL BANK
San Francisco: 13 Offices

BLINDS
PARAMOUNT VENETIAN BLIND CO.
San Francisco: 5929 Mission St., JU 5-2436

BRASS PRODUCTS
GREENBERG'S, M. SONS
San Francisco 7: 765 Folsom, EX 2-3143
Los Angeles 23: 1258 S. Boyle, AN 3-7108
Seattle 4: 1016 First Ave. So., MA 5140
Phoenix: 3009 N. 19th Ave., Apt. 92, PH 2-7663
Portland 4: 510 Builders Exch. Bldg., AT 6443

BRICKWORK
Face Brick
GLADDING McBEAN & CO.
San Francisco: Harrison at 9th, UN 1-7400
KRAFTILE CO.
Niles, Calif., Niles 3611
UNITED MATERIALS & RICHMOND BRICK CO.
Point Richmond, BE 4-5032

BRONZE PRODUCTS
GREENBERG'S M. SONS
San Francisco: 765 Folsom St., EX 2-3143
MICHEL & PFEFFER IRON WORKS
So. San Francisco: 212 Shaw Road, PLaza 5-8983
C. E. TOLAND & SON
Oakland: 2635 Peralta St., GL 1-2580

BUILDING HARDWARE
E. M. HUNDLEY HARDWARE CO.
San Francisco: 662 Mission St., YU 2-3322

BUILDING PAPERS & FELTS
PACIFIC CEMENT & AGGREGATES INC.
San Francisco: 400 Alabama St., KL 2-1616

CABINETS & FIXTURES
CENTRAL MILL & CABINET CO.
San Francisco: 1595 Fairfax Ave., VA 4-7316
THE FINK & SCHINDLER CO.
San Francisco: 552 Brannan St., EX 2-1513
MULLEN MFG. CO.
San Francisco: 64 Rausch St., UN 1-5815
PARAMOUNT BUILT IN FIXTURE CO.
Oakland: 962 Stanford Ave., OL 3-9911
ROYAL SHOWCASE CO.
San Francisco: 770 McAllister St., JO 7-0311

CEMENT
CALAVERAS CEMENT CO.
San Francisco: 315 Montgomery St.
DO 2-4224, Enterprise 1-2315
PACIFIC CEMENT & AGGREGATES INC.
San Francisco: 400 Alabama St., KL 2-1616

CONCRETE AGGREGATES
Ready Mixed Concrete
CENTRAL CONCRETE SUPPLY CO.
San Jose: 610 McKendrie St.
PACIFIC CEMENT & AGGREGATES INC.
San Francisco: 400 Alabama St., KL 2-1616
Sacramento: 16th and A Sts., GI 3-6586
San Jose: 790 Stockton Ave., CY 2-5620
Oakland: 2400 Peralta St., GL 1-0177
Stockton: 820 So. California St., ST 8-8643
READYMIX CONCRETE CO.
Santa Rosa: 50 W. Cottage Ave.
RHODES-JAMIESON LTD.
Oakland: 333-23rd Ave., KE 3-5275
SANTA ROSA BLDG. MATERIALS CO.
Santa Rosa: Roberts Ave.

CONCRETE ACCESSORIES
Screed Materials
C. & H. SPECIALTIES CO.
Berkeley: 909 Camelia St., LA 4-5358

CONCRETE BLOCKS
BASALT ROCK CO.
Napa, Calif.

CONCRETE COLORS—HARDENERS
CONRAD SOVIG CO.
875 Bryant St., HE 1-1345

CONSTRUCTION SERVICES
LE ROY CONSTRUCTION SERVICES
San Francisco, 143 Third St., SU 1-8914

DECKS—ROOF
UNITED STATES GYPSUM CO.
2322 W. 3rd St., Los Angeles 54, Calif.
300 W. Adams St., Chicago 6, Ill.

DOORS
THE BILCO COMPANY
New Haven, Conn.
Oakland: Geo. B. Schultz, 190 MacArthur Blvd.
Sacramento: Harry B. Ogle & Assoc., 1331 T St.
Fresno: Healey & Popovich, 1703 Fulton St.
Reseda: Daniel Dunner, 6200 Alonzo Ave.

Cold Storage Doors
BIRKENWALD
Portland: 310 N.W. 5th Ave.

Electric Doors
ROLY-DOOR SALES CO.
San Francisco, 5976 Mission St., PL 5-5089

Folding Doors
WALTER D. BATES & ASSOCIATES
San Francisco, 693 Mission St., GA 1-6971

Hardwood Doors
BELLWOOD CO. OF CALIF.
Orange, Calif., 533 W. Collins Ave.

Hollywood Doors
WEST COAST SCREEN CO.
Los Angeles: 1127 E. 63rd St., AD 1-1108
T. M. COBB CO.
Los Angeles & San Diego

W. P. FULLER CO.
Seattle, Tacoma, Portland
HOGAN LUMBER CO.
Oakland: 700 - 6th Ave.

HOUSTON SASH & DOOR
Houston, Texas

SOUTHWESTERN SASH & DOOR
Phoenix, Tucson, Arizona
El Paso, Texas

WESTERN PINE SUPPLY CO.
Emeryville: 5760 Shellmound St.
GEO. C. VAUGHAN & SONS
San Antonio & Houston, Texas

Screen Doors
WEST COAST SCREEN DOOR CO.

DRAFTING ROOM EQUIPMENT
GENERAL FIREPROOFING CO.
Oakland: 332-19th St., GL 2-4280
Los Angeles: 1200 South Hope St., RI 7-7501
San Francisco: 1025 Howard St., HE 1-7070

DRINKING FOUNTAINS
HAWS DRINKING FAUCET CO.
Berkeley: 1435 Fourth St., LA 5-3341

ELECTRICAL CONTRACTORS
COOPMAN ELECTRIC CO.
San Francisco: 85 - 14th St., MA 1-4438
ETS-HOKIN & GALVAN
San Francisco: 551 Mission St., EX 2-0432

ELECTRICAL CONTRACTORS (cont'd)

LEMOGE ELECTRIC CO.
San Francisco: 212 Clara St., DO 2-6010
LYNCH ELECTRIC CO.
San Francisco: 937 McAllister St., WI 5158
PACIFIC ELECTRIC & MECHANICAL CO.
San Francisco: Gough & Fell Sts., HE 1-5904

ELECTRIC HEATERS

WESIX ELECTRIC HEATER CO.
San Francisco: 390 First St., GA 1-2211

FIRE ESCAPES

MICHEL & PFEFFER IRON WORKS
South San Francisco: 212 Shaw Road, PLaza 5-8983

FIRE PROTECTION EQUIPMENT

FIRE PROTECTION PRODUCTS CO.
San Francisco: 1101-16th St., UN 1-2420
ETS-HOKIN & GALVAN
San Francisco: 551 Mission St., EX 2-0432
BARNARD ENGINEERING CO.
San Francisco: 35 Elmira St., JU 5-4642

FLOORS

Floor Tile

GLADDING McBEAN & CO.
San Francisco: Harrison at 9th St., UN 1-744
Los Angeles: 2901 Las Feliz Bldg., OL 2121
KRAFTILE CO.
Niles, Calif., Niles 3611

Resilient Floors

PETERSON-COBBY CO.
San Francisco: 218 Clara St, EX-2-8714
TURNER RESILIENT FLOORS CO.
San Francisco: 2280 Shafter Ave., AT 2-7720

FLOOR DRAINS

JOSAM PACIFIC COMPANY
San Francisco: 765 Folsom St., EX 2-3142

GAS VENTS

WM. WALLACE CO.
Belmont, Calif.

GENERAL CONTRACTORS

O. E. ANDERSON
San Jose: 1075 No. 10th St., CY 3-9844
BARRETT CONSTRUCTION CO.
San Francisco: 1800 Evans Ave., MI 7-9700
JOSEPH BETTANCOURT
South San Francisco: 125 So. Linden St., PL 5-9185
DINWIDDIE CONSTRUCTION CO.
San Francisco: Crocker Bldg., YU 6-2718
D. L. FAULL CONSTRUCTION CO.
Santa Rosa: 1236 Cleveland Ave.
HAAS & HAYNIE
San Francisco: 275 Pine St., DO 2-0678
HENDERSON CONSTRUCTION CO.
San Francisco: 33 Ritch St., GA 1-0856
JACKS & IRVINE
San Francisco: 620 Market St., YU 6-0511
G. P. W. JENSEN & SONS
San Francisco: 320 Market St., GA 1-2444
RALPH LARSEN & SON
San Francisco: 64 So. Park, YU 2-5682
LINDGREN & SWINERTON
San Francisco: 200 Bush St., GA 1-2980
MacDONALD, YOUNG & NELSON
San Francisco: 351 California St., YU 2-4700
MATTOCK CONSTRUCTION CO.
San Francisco: 220 Clara St., GA 1-5516
OLSEN CONSTRUCTION CO.
Santa Rosa: 125 Brookwood Ave., SR 2030
BEN ORTSKY
Cotati: Cypress Ave., Pet. 5-4383
PARKER, STEFFANS & PEARCE
San Mateo: 135 So. Park, EX 2-6639

RAPP, CHRISTENSEN & FOSTER
Santa Rosa: 705 Bennett Ave.
STOLTE, INC.
Oakland: 8451 San Leandro Ave., LO 2-4611
SWINERTON & WALBERG
San Francisco: 200 Bush St., GA 1-2980

FURNITURE—INSTITUTIONAL

GENERAL FIREPROOFING CO.
San Francisco: 1025 Howard St., HE 1-7070
Oakland: 332-19th St., GL 2-4280
Los Angeles: 1200 South Hope St., RI 7-7501

HEATING & VENTILATING

ATLAS HEATING & VENT. CO.
San Francisco: 557-4th St., DO 2-0377
E. C. BRAUN CO.
Berkeley: 2115 Fourth St., TH 5-2356
C. W. HALL
Santa Rosa: 1665 Sebastopol Rd., SR 6354
S. T. JOHNSON CO.
Oakland: 940 Arlington Ave., OL 2-6000
LOUIS V. KELLER
San Francisco: 289 Tehama St., JU 6-6252
L. J. KRUSE CO.
Oakland: 6247 College Ave., OL 2-8332
MALM METAL PRODUCTS
Santa Rosa: 724-2nd St., SR 454
JAS. A. NELSON CO.
San Francisco: 1375 Howard St., HE 1-0140
SCOTT COMPANY
Oakland: 1919 Market St., GL 1-1937
WESIX ELECTRIC HEATER CO.
San Francisco: 390 First St., GA 1-2211
Los Angeles: 530 W. 7th St., MI 8096

INSULATION WALL BOARD

PACIFIC CEMENT & AGGREGATES, INC.
San Francisco: 400 Alabama St., KL 2-1616

INTERCEPTING DEVICES

JOSAM PACIFIC CO.
San Francisco: 765 Folsom St., EX 2-3142

IRON—ORNAMENTAL

MICHEL & PFEFFER IRON WKS.
So. San Francisco. 212 Shaw Rd., PL 5-8983

LATHING & PLASTERING

ANGELO J. DANERI
San Francisco: 1433 Fairfax Ave., AT 8-1582
K-LATH CORP.
Alhambra: 909 So. Fremont St., Alhambra
A. E. KNOWLES CORP.
San Francisco: 3330 San Bruno Ave., JU 7-2091
G. H. & C. MARTINELLI
San Francisco: 174 Shotwell St., UN 3-6112
FREDERICK MEISWINKEL
San Francisco: 2155 Turk St., JO 7-7587
RHODES-JAMIESON LTD.
Oakland: 933-23rd Ave., KE 3-5225
PATRICK J. RUANE
San Francisco: 44 San Jose Ave., MI 7-6414

LIGHTING FIXTURES

SMOOT-HOLMAN COMPANY
Inglewood, Calif., OR 8-1217
San Francisco: 55 Mississippi St., MA 1-8474

LUMBER

CHRISTENSEN LUMBER CO.
San Francisco: Quint & Evans Ave., VA 4-5832
ART HOGAN LUMBER CO.
1701 Galvez Ave., ATwater 2-1157
MEAD CLARK LUMBER CO.
Santa Rosa: 3rd & Railroad
ROLANDO LUMBER CO.
San Francisco: 5th & Berry Sts., SU 1-6901
STERLING LUMBER CO.
Santa Rosa: 1129 College Ave., S. R. 82

MARBLE

JOS. MUSTO SONS-KEENAN CO.
San Francisco: 555 No. Point St., GR 4-6365
VERMONT MARBLE CO.
San Francisco: 6000-3rd St., VA 6-5024

MASONRY

BASALT ROCK CO.
Napa, Calif.
San Francisco: 260 Kearney St., GA 1-3758
WM. A. RAINEY & SON
San Francisco: 323 Clementina St., SU 1-0072
GEO. W. REED CO.
San Francisco: 1390 So. Van Ness Ave., AT 2-1226

METAL EXTERIOR WALLS

THE KAWNEER CO.
Berkeley: 930 Dwight Way, TH 5-8710

METAL FRAMING

UNISTRUT OF NORTHERN CALIFORNIA
Berkeley: 2547-9th St, TH. 1-3031
                                    Enterprise 1-2204

METAL GRATING

KLEMP METAL GRATING CORP.
Chicago, Ill.: 6601 So. Melvina St.

METAL LATH—EXPANDED

PACIFIC CEMENT & AGGREGATES, INC.
San Francisco: 400 Alabama St., KL 2-1616

METAL PARTITIONS

THE E. F. HAUSERMAN CO.
San Francisco: 485 Brannan St., YU 2-5477

METAL PRODUCTS

FORDERER CORNICE WORKS
San Francisco: 269 Potrero Ave., HE 1-4100

MILLWORK

CENTRAL MILL & CABINET CO.
San Francisco: 1595 Fairfax Ave., VA 4-7316
THE FINK & SCHINDLER CO.
San Francisco: 552 Brannan St., EX 2-1513
MULLEN MFG. CO.
San Francisco: 64 Rausch St., UN 1-5815
PACIFIC MFG. CO.
San Francisco: 16 Beale St., GA 1-7755
Santa Clara: 2610 The Alameda, S. C. 607
Los Angeles: 6820 McKinley Ave., TH 4156
SOUTH CITY LUMBER & SUPPLY CO.
So. San Francisco: Railroad & Spruce, PL 5-7085

OFFICE EQUIPMENT

GENERAL FIREPROOFING CO.
Los Angeles: 1200 South Hope St., RI 7-7501
San Francisco: 1025 Howard St., HE 1-7070
Oakland: 332-19th St., GL 2-4280

OIL BURNERS

S. T. JOHNSON CO.
Oakland: 940 Arlington Ave., GL 2-6000
San Francisco: 585 Potrero Ave., MA 1-2757
Philadelphia, Pa.: 401 North Broad St.

ORNAMENTAL IRON

MICHEL & PFEFFER IRON WORKS
So. San Francisco: 212 Shaw Rd., PL 5-8983

PAINTING

R. P. PAOLI & CO.
San Francisco: 2530 Lombard St., WE 1-1632
SINCLAIR PAINT CO.
San Francisco: 2112-15th St., HE 1-2196
D. ZELINSKY & SONS
San Francisco: 165 Groove St., MA 1-7400

PHOTOGRAPHS

Construction Progress

FRED ENGLISH
Belmont, Calif.: 1310 Old County Road, LY 1-0385

PLASTER

PACIFIC CEMENT & AGGREGATE INC.
San Francisco: 400 Alabama St., KL 2-1616

PLASTIC PRODUCTS

PLASTIC SALES & SERVICE
San Francisco: 409 Bryant St., DO 2-6433
WEST COAST INDUSTRIES
San Francisco: 3150-18th St., MA 1-5657

18

PLUMBING
BROADWAY PLUMBING CO.
San Francisco: 1790 Yosemite Ave., MI 8-4250
E. C. BRAUN CO.
Berkeley: 2115 Fourth St., TH 5-2356
C. W. HALL
Santa Rosa: 1665 Sebastopol Rd., SR 6354
HAWS DRINKING FAUCET CO.
Berkeley: 1435 Fourth St., LA 5-3341
JOSAM PACIFIC CO.
San Francisco: 765 Folsom St., EX 2-3143
LOUIS V. KELLER
San Francisco: 289 Tehama St., YU 6-6252
L. J. KRUSE CO.
Oakland: 6247 College Ave., OL 2-8332
JAS. A. NELSON CO.
San Francisco: 1375 Howard St., HE 1-0140
RODONI-BECKER CO., INC.
San Francisco: 455-10th St., MA 1-3662
SCOTT CO.
Oakland: 1919 Market St., GL 1-1937
PLUMBING FIXTURES
BRIGGS MANUFACTURING COMPANY
Warren, Michigan
POST PULLER
HOLLAND MFG. CO.
No. Sacramento: 1202 Dixieanne
PUMPING MACHINERY
SIMONDS MACHINERY CO.
San Francisco: 816 Folsom St., DO 2-6794
ROOFING
ANCHOR ROOFING CO.
San Francisco: 1671 Galvez Ave., VA 4-8140
ALTA ROOFING CO.
San Francisco: 1400 Egbert Ave., MI 7-2173
REGAL ROOFING CO.
San Francisco: 930 Innes Ave., VA 4-3261
ROOF SCUTTLES
THE BILCO CO.
New Haven, Conn.
Oakland: Geo. B. Schultz, 190 MacArthur Blvd.
Sacramento: Harry B. Ogle & Assoc., 1331 T St.
Fresno: Healey & Popovich, 1703 Fulton St.
Reseda: Daniel Dunner, 6200 Alonzo Ave.
ROOF TRUSSES
EASYBOW ENGINEERING & RESEARCH CO.
Oakland: 13th & Wood Sts., GL 2-0805
SAFES
THE HERMANN SAFE CO.
San Francisco: 1699 Market St., UN 1-6644
SEWER PIPE
GLADDING, McBEAN & CO.
San Francisco: 9th & Harrison, UN 1-7400
Los Angeles: 2901 Los Feliz Blvd., OL 2121

SHEET METAL
MICHEL & PFEFFER IRON WORKS
So. San Francisco: 212 Shaw Rd., PL 5-8983
SOUND EQUIPMENT
STROMBERG-CARLSON CO.
San Francisco: 1805 Rollins Rd., Burlingame, OX 7-3630
Los Angeles: 5414 York Blvd., CL 7-3939
SPRINKLERS
BARNARD ENGINEERING CO.
San Francisco: 35 Elmira St., JU 5-4642
STEEL—STRUCTURAL & REINFORCING
COLUMBIA-GENEVA DIV., U. S. STEEL CORP.
San Francisco: Russ Bldg., SU 1-2500
Los Angeles: 2087 E. Slauson, LA 1171
Portland, Ore.: 2345 N.W. Nicolai, BE 7261
Seattle, Wn.: 1331-3rd Ave. Bldg., MA 1972
Salt Lake City, Utah: Walker Bank Bldg., SL 3-6733
HERRICK IRON WORKS
Oakland 18th & Campbell, GL 1-1767
INDEPENDENT IRON WORKS, INC.
Oakland: 780 Pine St., TE 2-0160
JUDSON PACIFIC MURPHY CORP.
Emeryville: 4300 Eastshore Highway, OL 3-1717
REPUBLIC STEEL CORP.
San Francisco: 116 New Montgomery St., GA 1-0977
Los Angeles: Edison Bldg.
Seattle: White-Henry Stuart Bldg.
Salt Lake City: Walker Bank Bldg.
Denver: Continental Oil Bldg.
SOULE STEEL CO.
San Francisco: 1750 Army St., VA 4-4141
STEEL FORMS
STEELFORM CONTRACTING CO.
San Francisco: 666 Harrison St., DO 2-5582
SWIMMING POOLS
SIERRA MFG. CO.
Walnut Creek, Calif.: 1719 Mt. Diablo Blvd.
SWIMMING POOL FITTINGS
JOSAM PACIFIC CO.
San Francisco: 765 Folsom St., EX 2-3143
TESTING LABORATORIES
(ENGINEERS & CHEMISTS
ABBOT A. HANKS, INC.
San Francisco: 624 Sacramento St., GA 1-1697
ROBERT W. HUNT COMPANY
San Francisco: 500 Iowa, MI 7-0224
Los Angeles: 3050 E. Slauson, JE 9131
Chicago, New York, Pittsburgh
PITTSBURGH TESTING LABORATORY
San Francisco: 651 Howard St., EX 2-1747

TILE—CLAY & WALL
GLADDING McBEAN & CO.
San Francisco: 9th & Harrison Sts., UN 1-7400
Los Angeles: 2901 Los Feliz Blvd., OL 2121
Portland: 110 S.E. Main St., EA 6179
Seattle: 945 Elliott Ave. West, GA 0330
Spokane: 1102 No. Monroe St., BR 3259
KRAFTILE CO.
Niles, Calif.: Niles 3611
San Francisco: 50 Hawthorne St., DO 2-3780
Los Angeles: 406 So. Main St., MA 7241
TILE—TERRAZZO
NATIONAL TILE & TERAZZO CO.
San Francisco: 198 Mississippi St., UN 1-0273
TIMBER—TREATED
J. H. BAXTER CO.
San Francisco: 200 Bush St., YU 2-0200
Los Angeles: 3450 Wilshire Blvd., DU 8-9591
TIMBER TRUSSES
EASYBOW ENGINEERING & RESEARCH CO.
Oakland: 13th & Wood Sts., GL 2-0805
TRUCKING
PASSETTI TRUCKING CO.
San Francisco: 264 Clementina St., GA 1-5297
UNDERPINNING & SHORING
D. J. & T. SULLIVAN
San Francisco: 1942 Folsom St., MA 1-1545
VAULT DOORS—FIRE RESISTANT
THE HERMANN SAFE CO.
San Francisco: 1699 Market St., UN 1-6644
WALL PAPER
WALLPAPERS, INC.
Oakland: 384 Grand Ave., GL 2-0451
WAREHOUSE AND STORAGE EQUIPMENT AND SHELVING
GENERAL FIREPROOFING CO.
Los Angeles: 1200 South Hope St., RI 7-7501
San Francisco: 1025 Howard St., HE 1-7070
Oakland: 332-19th St., GL 2-4280
WATERPROOFING MATERIALS
CONRAD SOVIG CO.
San Francisco: 875 Bryant St., HE 1-1345
WATERSTOPS (P.V.C.)
TECON PRODUCTS, LTD.
Vancouver, B.C.: 681 E. Hastings St.
Seattle: 304 So. Alaskan Way
WINDOW SHADES
SHADES, INC.
San Francisco: 80 Tehama St., DO 2-7092

CLASSIFIED ADVERTISING

RATE: 20c PER WORD . . . CASH WITH ORDER   MINIMUM $5.00

CONSTRUCTION INDUSTRY WAGE RATES

Table 1 has been prepared by the State of California, Department of Industrial Relations, Division of Labor Statistics and Research. The rates are the union hourly wage rates established by collective bargaining as of January 2, 1958, as reported by reliable sources.

TABLE 1—UNION HOURLY WAGE RATES, CONSTRUCTION INDUSTRY, CALIFORNIA

Following are the hourly rates of compensation established by collective bargaining, reported as of January 2, 1958 or later

CRAFT	San Francisco	Alameda	Contra Costa	Fresno	Sacramento	San Joaquin	Santa Clara	Solano	Los Angeles	San Bernardino	San Diego	Santa Barbara	Kern
ASBESTOS WORKER	$3.55	$3.55	$3.55	$3.55	$3.55	$3.55	$3.55	$3.55	$3.55	$3.55	$3.55	$3.55	$3.55
BOILERMAKER	3.675	3.675	3.675	3.675	3.675	3.675	3.675	3.675	3.675	3.675	3.675	3.675	3.675
BRICKLAYER	3.95	3.75	3.75	3.75	3.80	3.75	3.875	3.95	3.80	3.90	3.75		3.85
BRICKLAYER HODCARRIER		3.10	3.10	2.90	3.10	2.90	3.00	3.10	2.75	2.75	2.75		2.75
CARPENTER	3.175	3.175	3.225	3.225	3.225	3.225	3.225	3.225	3.225	3.225	3.225	3.225	3.225
CEMENT MASON	3.22	3.22	3.22	3.22	3.22	3.22	3.22	3.22	3.15	3.15	3.25	3.15	3.15
ELECTRICIAN	3.936A	3.936A	3.936A		3.94A	3.50	4.03A	3.666A	3.90A	3.90A	3.90	3.85A	3.70
GLAZIER	3.09	3.09	3.09	3.135	3.065	3.055	3.09	3.09	3.105	3.105	3.03	3.105	3.135
IRON WORKER													
ORNAMENTAL	3.625	3.625	3.625	3.625	3.625	3.625	3.625	3.625	3.625	3.625	3.625	3.625	3.625
REINFORCING	3.375	3.375	3.375	3.375	3.375	3.375	3.375	3.375	3.375	3.375	3.375	3.375	3.375
STRUCTURAL	3.625	3.625	3.625	3.625	3.625	3.625	3.625	3.625	3.625	3.625	3.625	3.625	3.625
LABORER, GENERAL OR CONSTRUCTION	2.505	2.505	2.505	2.505	2.505	2.505	2.505	2.505	2.50	2.50	2.48	2.50	2.50
LATHER	3.4375	3.84	3.84	3.45	3.60B	3.40C	3.60D	3.50E	3.9375		3.725	3.625F	
OPERATING ENGINEER													
Concrete mixer (up to 1 yard)	2.89	2.89	2.89	2.89	2.89	2.89	2.89	2.89					
Concrete mixer operator—Skip Type									2.96	2.96	2.96	2.96	2.96
Elevator Hoist Operator									3.19	3.19	3.19	3.19	3.19
Material Hoist (1 drum)	3.19	3.19	3.19	3.19	3.19	3.19	3.19	3.19					
Tractor Operator	3.33	3.33	3.33	3.33	3.33	3.33	3.33	3.33	3.47	3.47	3.47	3.47	3.47
PAINTER													
Brush	3.20	3.20	3.20	3.13	3.325	3.175	3.20	3.20	3.26B	3.25	3.19	3.13H	3.10
Spray	3.20	3.20	3.20	3.38	3.575	3.325	3.20	3.20	3.51G	3.50	3.74	3.38H	3.35
PILEDRIVERMAN	3.305	3.305	3.305	3.305	3.305	3.305	3.305	3.305	3.355	3.355		3.355	3.355
PLASTERER	3.69	3.545	3.545	3.35	3.60B	3.55C	3.58	3.50	3.9375	3.725			
PLASTERER HODCARRIER	3.25	3.42	3.42	3.10	3.10	3.00C	3.20	3.15	3.6875	3.5625	3.475	3.50	3.6875
PLUMBER	3.67		3.935I	3.80J	3.70	3.80J	3.60	3.675	3.70	3.70	3.70	3.70	3.375
ROOFER	3.35	3.35	3.35	3.20	3.25	3.35	3.35	3.10K	3.20L	3.25	3.10	3.30	3.775
SHEET METAL WORKER	3.45	3.45	3.45	3.425	3.45	3.465	3.45	3.325	3.50	3.50	3.45	3.55	3.10
STEAMFITTER	3.67	3.96	3.96	3.80J	3.70	3.80J	3.60	3.675	3.70	3.70	3.70	3.70	3.775
TRUCK DRIVER— Dump Trucks under 4 yards	2.55	2.55	2.55	2.55	2.55	2.55	2.55	2.55	2.63	2.63	2.63	2.63	2.63
TILE SETTER	3.275	3.275	3.275	3.375	3.28	3.30	3.275	3.275	3.36	3.40	3.375	3.36	

A Includes 4% vacation allowance.
B Includes 5c hour for industry promotion and 5c hour for vacation fund.
C ½% withheld for industry promotion.
D 1½% withheld for industry promotion.
E Includes 5c hour for industry promotion and 5c hour for vacation fund. Hourly rate for part of county adjacent to Sacramento County is $3.60.
F Northern part of County: $3.75.

G Pomona Area: Brush $3.25; Spray $3.50.
H Southern half of County: Brush $3.20; Spray $3.28.
I Includes 30c hour for vacation pay.
J Includes 15c hour which local union may elect to use for vacation purposes.
K Includes 10c hour for vacation fund.
L Includes 10c hour savings fund wage.

ATTENTION: The above tabulation has been prepared by the State of California, Department of Industrial Relations, Division of Labor Statistics and Research, and represents data reported by building trades councils, union locals, contractor organizations, and other reliable sources. The above rates do not include any payments to funds for health and welfare, pensions, vacations, industry promotion, apprentice training, etc., except as shown in the footnotes.

CONSTRUCTION INDUSTRY WAGE RATES — TABLE 2

Employer Contributions to Health and Welfare, Pension, Vacation and Other Funds
California Union Contracts, Construction Industry

(Revised March, 1957)

CRAFT	San Francisco	Fresno	Sacramento	San Joaquin	Santa Clara	Los Angeles	San Bernardino	San Diego
ASBESTOS WORKER	.10 W / .11 hr. V	.10 W / .11 hr. V	.10 W / .11 hr. V	.10 W / .11 hr. V	.10 W / .11 hr. V	.10 W	.10 W	.10 W
BRICKLAYER	.15 W / .14 P / .05 hr. V		.15 W		.15 W			
BRICKLAYER HODCARRIER	.10 W / .10 P / .10 V	.10 W	.10 W	.10 W	.10 W	.075 W	.075 W	.075 W
CARPENTER	.10 W / .10 hr. V	.10 W	.10 W	.10 W	.10 W	.10 W	.10 W	.10 W
CEMENT MASON	.10 W	.10 W	.10 W	.10 W	.10 W	.10 W	.10 W	.10 W
ELECTRICAL WORKER	.10 W / 1% P / 4% V	.10 W / 1% P / 4% V	.075 W / 1% P	.075 W / 1% P / 4% V	1% P	1% P	1% P	.10 W / 1% P
GLAZIER	.075 W / .085 V	.075 W / 40 hr. V	.075 W / .05 V	.075 W / .05 V	.075 W / .085 V	.075 W / 40 hr. V	.075 W / 40 hr. V	.075 W / 40 hr. V
IRONWORKER: REINFORCING / STRUCTURAL	.10 W / .10 W	.10 W / .10 W	.10 W / .10 W	.10 W / .10 W	.10 W / .10 W	.10 W / .10 W	.10 W / .10 W	.10 W / .10 W
LABORER, GENERAL	.10 W	.10 W	.10 W	.10 W	.10 W	.075 W	.075 W	.075 W
LATHER	.60 day W / .70 day V		.10 W	.10 W	.075 W / .05 V	.90 day W	.70 day W	.10 W
OPERATING ENGINEER TRACTOR OPERATOR (MIN.) / POWER SHOVEL OP. (MIN.)	.10 W / .10 W	.10 W / .10 W	.10 W / .10 W	.10 W / .10 W	.10 W / .10 W	.10 W / .10 W	.10 W / .10 W	.10 W / .10 W
PAINTER, BRUSH	.095 W	.08 W	.075 W	.10 W	.095 W / .07 V	.085 W	.08 W	.09 W
PLASTERER	.10 W / .10 V	.10 W	.10 W	.10 W	.10 W / .15 V		.10 W	.90 day W	.10 W
PLUMBER	.10 W / .10 V	.15 W / .10 P	.10 W / .10 P / .125 V	.10 W	.10 W / .10 P / .125 V	.10 W	.90 day W	.10 W
ROOFER	.10 W / .10 V	.10 W	.10 W / .10 V	.10 W	.075 W / .10 V	.085 W	.10 W	.075 W
SHEET METAL WORKER	.075 W / 4% V	.075 W / 7 day V	.075 W / .10 V	.075 W / .12 V	.075 W / 4% V	.085 W / .10 V	.085 W / .10 V	.085 W / 5 day V
TILE SETTER	.075 W / .09 V				.075 W / .09 V	.025 W / .06 V		

ATTENTION: The above tabulation has been prepared and compiled from the available data reported by building trades councils, union locals, contractor organizations and other reliable sources. The table was prepared from incomplete data; where no employer contributions are specified, it does not necessarily mean that none are required by the union contract.

The type of supplement is indicated by the following symbols: W—Health and Welfare; P—Pensions; V—Vacations; A—Apprentice training fund; Adm—Administration fund; JIB—Joint Industry Board; Prom—Promotion fund.

CONSTRUCTION CONTRACTS AWARDED AND MISCELLANEOUS PERSONNEL DATA

GREENHOUSE & HEADHOUSE, University of California at Davis, Yolo county. University of California, Berkeley, owner. Some steel and glass in the greenhouse construction; precast concrete and steel frame construction of the Headhouse —$167,000. ARCHITECT: Donald Mackey, 1444 Webster St., Oakland. GENERAL CONTRACTOR: Robert E. Griffin, 5356 Rosalind Ave., El Cerrito.

SCHOOL ADD'N, Placerville, El Dorado county. Gold Oak Unified School District, Placerville, owner. 1 Story concrete block wall with wood laminated beams—$159,-150. ARCHITECT: Kaestner & Kaestner, 115 Eye St., Modesto. GENERAL CONTRACTOR: George W. Reed Co., 920 9th St., Sacramento.

CONCRETE BLEACHERS, Funston Playground, San Francisco. City and County of San Francisco, owner. Construction of concrete grandstands at the baseball diamonds in the Funston Playground — $169,650. ARCHITECT: Charles W. Griffiths, City Architect, City Hall, San Francisco. GENERAL CONTRACTOR: Morris Daley, 1145 California Drive, Burlingame.

APARTMENT, San Rafael, Marin county. Jack Gowland, owner. 2 Story, 17 unit apartment building; 20x40 ft. swimming pool, each unit to have carport; 2nd story with deck patio—$150,000. DESIGNER: Philip Hussey, 509 4th St., San Rafael. GENERAL CONTRACTOR: Filippo Const. Co., 32 Woodland Ave., San Rafael.

SR. HIGH SCHOOL ADD'N, Antioch, Contra Costa county. Antioch-Live Oak Unified School District, Antioch, owner. Construction includes addition of 10 classrooms to the present building—$163,793. ARCHITECT: John Lyon Reid & Partners, 1019 Market St., San Francisco. GENERAL CONTRACTOR: Pagni Const. Co., 84 Bishop Rd., Crockett.

ELECTRONIC MFG. PLANT, Sunnyvale, Santa Clara county. Holbrook Merrill Co., San Francisco, owner. 1 Story manufacturing plant and office building, approximately 40,000 sq. ft. area, tilt-up concrete construction; 3000 sq. ft. in office area—$153,500. STRUCTURAL ENGINEER: Simpson & Stratta, 325 5th St., San Francisco. GENERAL CONTRACTOR: Leonard Semas Const., 2885 Homestead Road, Santa Clara.

MEDICAL BLDG., Monterey. Paloma Land Co., Monterey, owner. 1 Story wood frame construction, aluminum framed windows, approximately 8,000 sq. ft. of area —$119,633. ARCHITECT: William D. Concolino, 588 Huston St., Monterey. GENERAL CONTRACTOR: Henry Jewell & Associates, 620 Lake St., Seaside.

GARDEN CENTER, McKinley Park, Sacramento, owner. Wood frame construction,

stone and wood siding, tar and gravel roofing, considerable glass; Exhibit building for exhibitions and meetings—$112,250. ARCHITECT: Raymond Franceschi, 2015 J St., Sacramento. GENERAL CONTRACTOR: J. K. Beals & R. M. Poore, 4205 57th St., Sacramento.

SOCIAL HALL, Methodist Church, San Jose, Santa Clara county. Calvary Methodist Church, San Jose, owner. 1 Story frame and stucco construction to provide facilities for a Social Hall and Educational Building—$209,700. ARCHITECT: Higgins & Root, 220 Meridian Rd., San Jose. GENERAL CONTRACTOR: Aiken Const. Co., 333 Phelan Ave., San Jose.

ELEMENTARY SCHOOL, Floyd, Kerman, Fresno county. Kerman-Floyd Union School District, Kerman, owner. Concrete and slab foundation, asphalt tile floor, plaster exterior, plywood interior, gravel roof; to provide facilities for administration unit, 6-classrooms, music room, covered passageway, site development, and toilet facilities—$199,750. ARCHITECT: Horn & Mortland, 2016 Merced St., Fresno. GENERAL CONTRACTOR: R. G. Fisher Co., P. O. Box 4081 Fresno.

CHURCH, Stockton, San Joaquin county. Lincoln Presbyterian Church, Stockton, owner. Timber construction, concrete block, 5,000 sq. ft. area. ARCHITECT: Donald Powers Smith, 133 Kearny St., San Francisco. GENERAL CONTRACTOR: C. S. Plumb Co., P. O. Box 247, Stockton.

U. S. NAVAL SUPPORT (Industrial), Sunnyvale, Santa Clara county. Lockheed Aircraft Corpn., Missile System Division, Sunnyvale, owner. Tilt-up concrete construction approximately 150,000 sq. ft. area for classified industry—$2,650,000. GENERAL CONTRACTOR: Carl N. Swenson, 1095 Stockton Ave., San Jose.

ELEMENTARY SCHOOL, Crestmoor, San Bruno, San Mateo county. 1-story

wood frame, built-up roofing, concrete slab floors, asphalt tile covering to provide facilities for administration, 16-classrooms, 2-kindergartens, multi-use room, connecting corridors, toilet rooms, site development, driveways, paths, playgrounds—$478,493. ARCHITECT: Ernest Kump & Associates, 450 Ramona St., Palo Alto. GENERAL CONTRACTOR: Harvis Const. Co., 946 El Camino Real, South San Francisco.

DAIRY BARN, Oakdale, Stanislaus county. J. L. Sawyer, Oakdale, owner. Construction of a dairy barn and site facilities—$104,881. ARCHITECT: Clowdsley & Whipple, 142 N. California St., Stockton. GENERAL CONTRACTOR: Don P. Clark, P. P. Box 1767 Stockton.

PARISH HALL, Culver City, Los Angeles county. Grace Lutheran Church, Culver City, owner. Two story parish hall and educational building; reinforced masonry construction, concrete slab, wood subfloor, asphalt tile, acoustic tile, heating and ventilating and toilet facilities. ARCHITECT: Orr, Strange & Inslee, 3142 Wilshire Blvd., Los Angeles. GENERAL CONTRACTOR: Petersen Construction Co., 4205 S. Sepulveda Blvd., Culver City.

ELEMENTARY SCHOOL, Addition, McSwain, Merced county. Merced School District, Merced, owner. Frame and stucco construction addition to the McSwain Elementary School—$62,835. ARCHITECT: Horn & Mortland, 2016 Merced St., Fresno. GENERAL CONTRACTOR: Cullen & Cullen, 1311 W. 21st, Merced.

CHURCH CHAPEL, La Mirada, Los Angeles county. Prince of Peace Lutheran Church, La Mirada, owner. Frame and stucco church chapel building, approximately 3000 sq. ft. area; asphalt shingle roofing, asphalt tile floors, concrete slab, acoustical tile ceiling, interior plaster, electrical and plumbing—$34,795. ARCHITECT: Culver Heaton, 228 N. El Molino, Pasadena. GENERAL CONTRACTOR: Voge, Inc., 7601 Crenshaw Blvd., Los Angeles.

FIRE DRILL TOWER, San Rafael, Marin county. City of San Rafael, owner. One story wood frame tower, pent house, chemically treated siding—$17,890. ARCHITECT: Eugene E. Crawford, 920 5th St., San Rafael. GENERAL CONTRACTOR: Don Presco, 55 Broadview Drive, San Rafael.

EDUCATIONAL UNIT, Community Presbyterian Church, West Covina, Los Angeles county. First Presbyterian Church of West Covina, owner. One story, 7-classroom concrete block educational unit building of irregular shape 104x68 ft.; composition roof, wood roof sheathing, concrete slab, asphalt tile, aluminum siding and fixed sash, forced air heating, toilet facilities with some terrazzo work. ARCHITECTS: Orr, Strange & Inslee, 3142 Wilshire Blvd., Los Angeles. GENERAL CONTRACTOR: Searles Constn. Co., 739 Werden Way, Covina.

DEPARTMENT STORE, Del Amo Center, Torrance, Los Angeles county. Broadway Hale Stores, Los Angeles, owner. Department store development, reinforced concrete construction, 3-stories, penthouse and basement, metal sash and trim, resilient flooring, heating and ventilating, ceramic tile, acoustical, fire sprinklers and related work including site de-

velopment. ARCHITECT: Welton Becket & Associates, 5657 Wilshire Blvd., Los Angeles. GENERAL CONTRACTOR: Louis C. Dunn Inc., 3101 Wilshire Blvd., Los Angeles.

OIL KING SCHOOL, Coalinga, Fresno county. Oil King School District, Coalinga, owner. Project comprises construction of a complete new school plant at a cost of $237,050. ARCHITECT: Benjamin Lippold, 1272 Wishon St., Fresno. GENERAL CONTRACTOR: Hemco Const. Co., P. O. Box 152, Avenal.

AUTO AGENCY, Merced, Merced county. John Roth Chevrolet Agency, Merced, owner. Construction included service facilities and new car showroom, administration offices, toilet facilities — $140,000. ARCHITECT: Walter Wagner & Partners, Thornington Bldg., Merced. GENERAL CONTRACTOR: Kul-Ber Const. Co., 1305 W. 10th St, Merced.

MEMORIAL ADD'N, Oroville, Butte county. Butte County Pioneer Assn., Oroville, owner. Wood frame and hollow masonry construction of addition to present building—$22,757. ARCHITECT Thomas A. Hayes, 1442 Lincoln St., Oroville. GENERAL CONTRACTOR: Fisci Bros., 5515 Clard Rd., Paradise.

SCHOOL BLDG., High School Monterey, Monterey county. Monterey Union High School District, Monterey, owner. Facilities will include a girls' gymnasium platform, corrective exercise rooms, administration, storage lockers, showers, transformer vault; structural steel frame for assembly hall, wood frame and stucco for remaining facilities, built-up roofing, ceramic tile, lockers and showers, maple flooring in gym—$284,120. ARCHITECT: Wallace Holm & Associates, 321 Webster St., Monterey. GENERAL CONTRACTOR: Tombleson & Huck Inc., P. O. Box 1388, Salinas.

INTERMEDIATE SCHOOL, Santa Clara, Santa Clara county. Jefferson School District, Santa Clara, owner. Wood frame and structural steel construction to provide facilities for administration, classrooms, shops, multi-purpose and toilet facilities— each building separate—$780,143. ARCHITECT: Kress & Goudie, 363 Park Ave., San Jose. GENERAL CONTRACTOR: Leonard Semas Const. Co., 2885 Homestead Road, Santa Clara.

ELEMENTARY SCHOOL, South Shores, San Pedro, Los Angeles county. Los Angeles Board of Education, owner. The project includes 10-classrooms, 2-kindergartens—$433,000. ARCHITECT: James R. Friend, Kress Bldg., Long Beach. GENERAL CONTRACTOR: C. V. Holder Co., 18011 S. La Salle St., Gardena.

NEWSPAPER PLANT, San Luis Obispo, San Luis Obispo county. John P. Scripps, San Luis Obispo, owner. One story reinforced concrete slab, tilt-up, steel decks to provide for offices and publishing plant. ARCHITECT: Kenneth H. Hess, 620 E. Main St., Ventura. SUPERVISING ARCHITECT: John R. Ross. 1149 Marsh St., San Luis Obispo. GENERAL CONTRACTOR: Maino Const. Co., 2238 Broad St., San Luis Obispo.

HOSPITAL ALTERATION, Oroville, Butte county. Butte County Board of Supervisors, Oroville, owner. Work com-

prises remodeling of the heating system in various wards, alterations to the scullery area, remodel nurses call system and install night lights — $90,372. ARCHITECT (DESIGNER): L. L. Ward, 336 Broadway, Chico. GENERAL CONTRACTOR: Modern Bldg. Co., P. O. Box 635, Chico.

CHURCH ADD'N, Carlsbad, San Diego county. Carlsbad Union Church, Carlsbad, owner. Project includes site work and additions to the present building of 9200 sq. ft.; frame and stucco, built-up roofing, metal windows, resilient floor covering, slab floor, laminated plastic counter tops, plumbing, heating, toilets—$76,344. ARCHITECT: Walter C. See, 4460 Park Blvd., San Diego. GENERAL CONTRACTOR: R. L. Watson Constn. Co., 2601 State St., Carlsbad.

AIRCRAFT HANGAR, Municipal Airport Sacramento, City of Sacramento, owner. Work includes furnishing and erecting a prefabricated metal hangar at the Sacramento Municipal Airport—$22,157. GENERAL CONTRACTOR: Pascoe Steel Co., 1301 E. Lexington, Pomona.

STORE REMODEL, Marysville, Yuba county. Bradley's, Marysville, owner. Present store building is 1 and 2 story, new construction will add additional floor to 1 story portion, also extensive remodeling throughout the entire building —$47,865. ARCHITECT: Robert S. Oliver, 916 F. St., Marysville. GENERAL CONTRACTOR: C. A. Otto, P. O. Box 1385 Marysville.

STUDENT UNION-DORMITORY, Menlo School & College, Atherton, San Mateo county. Menlo School & College, Atherton, owner. Student union building includes recreation facilities, snack bar, book store; cement block construction 2-story Dormitory and Faculty building concrete and concrete blocks; both buildings have concrete floors, asbestos shingle roofing on wood sheathing—$435,848. ARCHITECT: J. S. Gould, 407 Sansome St., San Francisco. GENERAL CONTRACTOR: B. & R. Const. Co., 110 Market St., San Francisco.

OFFICE, Oakland, Alameda county. Federal Credit Union, Oakland, owner. Two story office building; light steel frame construction, wood and concrete retaining wall forming 2-sides of building, some asphalt paving and site development. ARCHITECT: Hansen & Winkler, 251 Post St., San Francisco. GENERAL CONTRACTOR: Jack Burns, 1612 Everett St., El Cerrito.

ELEMENTARY SCHOOL, Raymond Temple School, Buena Park, Los Angeles county. Centralia School District, Buena Park, owner. New Raymond Temple elementary school includes: 16-classrooms, 2-kindergartens, multipurpose building, administration building and related facilities; 1-story, frame and stucco construction—$411,268. ARCHITECT: Frick & Frick, 340 N. Altadena Dr., Pasadena. GENERAL CONTRACTOR: Smith-Campbell Co., 6510 E. Cherry Ave., Long Beach.

OFFICE BLDG., Huntington Park, Los Angeles county. Ideal Roller & Mfg. Co., Huntington Park, owner. One story concrete block and stone veneer office building; 40x50 ft., composition roofing, metal jalousies and aluminum sliding sash, sliding glass doors, concrete slab floor with

asphalt tile and cork covering, forced air heating and air conditioning, restrooms, plumbing, electrical work, blacktop paving in parking area, landscaping. ENGINEER: B. C. Adams, 12692 SW Singing Wood Dr., Santa Ana, and R. S. Jones, 9721 Orangewood Ave., Garden Grove. GENERAL CONTRACTOR: Besco Constructors, 4316 E. Gage Ave., Bell.

FOOD MARKET, Orinda, Contra Costa county. Hagstrom Food Stores, Oakland, owner. One story, steel frame and concrete, built-up roofing—$185,876. ARCHITECT: Jack Buchter, AIA & Associates, 3729 Mt. Diablo Blvd., Lafayette. GENERAL CONTRACTOR: Harry K. Jensen, 1025 44th Ave., Oakland.

TV-STATION, Oakland, Alameda county. Port of Oakland, Oakland, owner. New TV Studio, offices for Channel No. 2, to be built in Jack London Square, Oakland; building to have 13,900 sq. ft. area: Studio space 9200 sq. ft., special designed acoustical treatment for walls and ceilings, lighting grids, other features—$214,980. ARCHITECT: Welton Becket & Associates, 153 Maiden Lane, San Francisco. GENERAL CONTRACTOR: Able Builders, 15363 E. 14th St., Oakland.

RECTORY, St. Brigid's, San Francisco. Archbishop of San Francisco, owner. Wood frame construction, shingle tile roof, brick veneer—$127,500. ARCHITECT: Wilton Smith, 2143 Lombard St., San Francisco. GENERAL CONTRACTOR: John A. Rademann, 4828 Geary Blvd., San Francisco.

HORSE BARNS, Fairgrounds, Pleasanton, Alameda county. County of Alameda, Oakland, owner. New barns to replace present wooden facilities; 5-concrete barns, each to contain 38 stalls and 8 tack rooms—$245,156. ARCHITECT: Hale & Jacobsohn, 241 Vallejo St., Mission San Jose. GENERAL CONTRACTOR: C. A. Gossett & Sons, 10048 Madison Ave., Castro Valley.

HOSPITAL, Sequoia, Redwood City, San Mateo county. Sequoia Hospital District, Redwood City, owner. Additions and alterations to present facilities: new administration unit, central supply unit, new emergency area, 3 operating rooms new bedroom area for 140 beds, new hydro-

therapy with pool and appurtenances, laboratory, work shop, radiographic unit, shop, kitchen, storage and locker rooms—$2,927,400. ARCHITECT: Stone, Mulloy, Marraccini & Patterson, 536 Mission St., San Francisco. STRUCTURAL ENGINEER: Washington & Mitchell, 204 Sansome St., San Francisco. MECHANICAL & ELECTRICAL ENGINEERS: Buonacorsi & Murray, 350 Mission St., San Francisco. GENERAL CONTRACTOR: Barrett Const. Co., 1800 Evans Ave., San Francisco.

FIRE HOUSE, Santa Clara, Santa Clara county. City of Santa Clara, owner. Frame and stucco construction, concrete slab floor, asbestos shingle—$30,530. ARCHITECT: L. F. Richards, 1033 Jackson St., San Francisco. GENERAL CONTRACTOR: Sundahl Const. Co., 840 Circle Drive, Santa Clara.

IN THE NEWS

LOCKHEED AIRCRAFT ANNOUNCE YEAR-LONG ENGINEER STUDY

The Lockheed Missile Systems Division of the Lockheed Aircraft Company, Palo Alto, and Holmes & Narver, Inc., Los Angeles engineering and construction firm, have started a year-long study of the effects of earthquake on nuclear power reactors, according to an announcement by the U.S. Atomic Commission.

Holmes & Narver will carry prime responsibility for structural and seismic analyses, while Lockheed will study design problems of nuclear reactors themselves.

Dr. George W. Housner, president of the Earthquake Engineering Research Institute and professor of civil engineering and applied mechanics at California Institute of Technology, is acting as consultant to Holmes & Narver on Seismology.

The study is expected to evaluate earthquake hazards to major types of stationary reactors and to develop criteria for inclusion in design requirements to minimize or eliminate such hazards. Results of the study will be published in an AEC handbook for the guidance of industrial firms interested in the design and construction of large reactors.

ST. JOHN LUTHERAN CHURCH PLANNED FOR MONTEBELLO

Architect O. J. Bruer, 120 N. Montebello Blvd, Montebello, has completed plans and specifications for construction of a 1 and 2-story, with basement, frame and stucco and stone veneer church in Montebello for the St John's Lutheran Church.

The new building will contain 13,200 sq. ft. of area, asbestos shingle and built-up composition roofing, steel sash, stained leaded glass, Flemish cathedral and plate glass windows, concrete and wood floors with carpet and vinyl asbestos covering, forced air heating, restrooms, plumbing and electrical work.

BOSTON ARCHITECT AWARDED HIGHEST ART GOLD MEDAL

Henry R. Shepley of Boston, ranking American architect and designer of the New York Hospital-Cornell Medical Center, has been chosen to receive the Gold Medal for Architecture of the National Institute of Arts and Letters for 1958, it has been announced by Malcolm Cowley, president of the Institute. He will receive the honor at the Joint Annual Ceremonial of the National Institute and the American Academy of Arts and letters in May.

The Gold Medal of the Institute is conferred annually in each of two categories of literature and the arts, ten categories being designated over a five year period. Among previous recipients of The Gold Medal for Architecture are Frank Lloyd Wright, Frederick Law Olmsted and William Adams Delano.

STRUCTURAL COMPONENT PLANT ANNOUNCED NEAR PORTLAND, OREGON

A new industrial plant is being constructed in Beaverton, eight miles west of Portland, Oregon, for Structural Laminates, Inc., manufacturers of Struc-

tural Panels for construction of roofs, floors and walls, particularly adapted for roof decks for school classrooms, and industrial and commercial buildings.

Principals in the new plant are C. D. Johnson, Jr., and Chas. R. Wilson, Sales Manager.

NEW McQUAY CONDENSER HAS 50 TON CAPACITY

A new air cooled condenser which has a capacity of up to 50-tons in a single unit is this "AB" model AIRCON; belt driven, remote, and is designed for waterless refrigeration and air conditioning; single fan and motor assembly.

For commercial and industrial application such as air conditioning and refrigerating super-markets, shopping centers, office buildings or large industrial plants. AIRCON coils are constructed of copper tubes with exclusive McQuay Ripple Aluminum Fins. For complete data inquire McQuay, Inc., Minneapolis, Minn.

BANK AMERICA BUILDS IN SHOPPING CENTER

The Utah Construction Company, 100 Bush Street, San Francisco, is starting construction of a new bank building in the South Shore Shopping Center, near Alameda, for the Bank of America.

The new facilities will provide a complete banking service and related activities and will cost $220,000.

GEORGE B. QUAMBY RETIRES FROM FENESTRA INC.

George B. Quamby, associated with the Fenestra organization for some 38 years, and head of the San Francisco office since 1943, was retired the first of this month, according to an announcement by R. E. Sechler, assistant Western regional manager.

TENTH ANNUAL INDUSTRIAL ENGINEERING INSTITUTE SCHEDULED FOR U.C.

The University of California's Tenth Annual Industrial Engineering Institute will be conducted on the Berkeley Campus, February 7-8, and will include discussions on "Industrial Engineering in the Small Company"; "Applying Mathematical Techniques to Industrial Engineering Problems"; "Use of Digital Techniques in Industrial Control Systems"; "Automatic Manufacturing and its Implication to the Small Businessman"; "The Impact of Numerically Controlled Machine Tools,"

and "Practical Implications of Human Relations Research."

The purpose of the program is to present to industrial engineers and managers the latest developments in research and practice.

NEW SCHOOL
PLANNED FOR
CARMICHAEL

Architect Gordon Stafford, 1024 "J" Street, Sacramento, is completing plans for construction of a new elementary school in the city of Carmichael, near Sacramento, to be know as the Jonas Salk Elementary School.

The construction of light steel frame and combination of grouted brick and precast slab will provide facilities for administration offices, 15-classrooms, kitchen, multipurpose classrooms for mentally retarded children and rest rooms. Estimated cost is $500,000.

KAISER STEEL NAMES
JAMES A. MAGGETTI
TO NAPA PLANT

James A. Maggetti has been named assistant plant manager of Kaiser Steel Corporation's Napa, California plant, according to an announcement by Ernest L. Ilsley, vice president and general manager of the company's Fabricating Division plants at Napa and Fontana, California.

He will be responsible for sales, production, and certain administration functions relating to operation of the plant, and will continue as manager of the Napa plant's planning and estimating department.

Maggetti is a native of Napa and a graduate of the University of California, business administration and engineering.

WATSONVILLE
TO BUILD
AIRPORT BUILDING

Architect Robert R. Jones, Ocean Avenue at Mission Street in Carmel, has been commissioned by the City of Watsonville, to design a terminal building to be built at the Watsonville municipal airport.

Preliminary plans have been completed.

SCHOLARSHIP FOR
SAN FRANCISCO
BAY AREA STUDENT

The Bay Area's top ranking high school science student will be chosen to receive a $500 college scholarship as a highlight of this year's observance of National Engineers' Week, which will be observed nationally February 16-22.

The Bay Area Engineers' Week committee, sponsors of the scholarship awards, will also select two runners-up to receive $300 each toward their college education.

To be eligible for the awards, students must be in their senior year, graduating in February or June. The scholarship awards program, as well as other Engineers' Week activities, is being sponsored and supported by Bay area business and industry in cooperation with the professional engineering society chapters.

RADAR CENTER
DEVELOPMENT
NEAR RENO

Plans are being completed for construction of a radar center at the Stead Air Force Base, near Reno, Nevada, at an estimated cost of $5,000,000.

The center will be a part of the Defense network of Nevada, and will serve as a portion of the overall National Defense System.

Actual construction and equipment installation will begin about March 1st according to present plans.

"STELLAR" WIDE SPAN
MIRROR AND
COSMETIC CABINET

The new "Stellar" series of 32 inch high Jensteel units are now available in 18″, 36″, 42″ and 48″ widths.

These smart wide-span plate mirrored medicine and cosmetic cabinets come with full capacity stain-proof tops and baked enamel interiors. The rich, luxurious waffle glass doors silently glide on plastic runners inside a polished stainless steel picture frame matching the frame enclosing the copper backed plate mirror. Special "easy-hang" mounting bracket

makes installation almost instantaneous. Full data from Jensen Industries, 159 S. Anderson St., Los Angeles, California.

C. D. RAMSDEN
NAMED PRESIDENT
PACIFIC COAST

C. D. Ramsden has been named president and general manager of the Pacific Coast Engineering Company of Alameda, California, according to an announcement by the Board of Directors of the firm.

Ramsden joined the company in 1946 as Chief Engineer and served in that position until 1956 when he was appointed Vice-President and General Manager. He has directed equipment design and fabri-

LIBRARY TO
BE BUILT
IN CONCORD

Architect Donald Powers Smith, 133 Kearny St, San Francisco, has completed working drawings for construction of a new Library building in Concord for the City of Concord.

The Library is to be built in the City's new Civic Center; will be "T" shaped with the main unit for storage and reading facilities; a wing for meeting rooms and a wing for children's books and activities. Construction will be of concrete and wood frame at an estimated cost of $200,000.

MYRON A. KENDALL
AWARDED COVETED
A.S.M.E. "AWARD"

Myron A. "Mike" Kendall, 75, dean of conveyor engineers, and Board Chairman of the Stephens-Adamson Mfg. Co., has been awarded the American Society of Mechanical Engineers' "Fellow Award."

Competition for the award is extremely keen as the science of engineering covers such a broad scope of activity. Each candidate nominated by the committee is carefully screened by a regional committee and then by the national body of the A.S.M.E. The screening process not only encompasses the candidate's engineering activity but his contributions to his com-

cation for Columbia River Hydroelectric projects, St. Lawrence River Hydroelectric projects, atomic projects of the Atomic Energy Commission and the world's largest oil barges and most powerful dredges.

munity and mankind in general.

Kendall has spent 50 years in engineering achievement in the conveyor industry and has been prominently identified with community projects.

NEW HOWE CO.
PORTABLE
VEHICLE SCALE

The Howe Scale Company, Rutland, Vermont, a subsidiary of Safety Industries, Inc., announces a portable vehicle scale that requires no pit, and is available in capacities to 70 tons and lengths of 60 feet.

Additional scale sections may be joined for greater length and capacity, requiring only 9 standard bolts, and can be re-located as the job requires.

These portable vehicle scales incorporate Howe's unique Parallel Link Load Suspension assembly in their platform construction, designed to absorb loading shocks and to reduce wear on the scale pivots. They are recommended for road contractors, quarrymen, gravel and other rock product producers, farmers and many other similar users in industry. Complete data from the manufacturer, Howe Scale Co., Rutland, Vermont.

FRANK LLOYD WRIGHT
NATIONAL CONCRETE
MASONRY SPEAKER

Frank Lloyd Wright, dean of American architects, will be a featured speaker at the 1958 convention of the National Concrete Masonry Association, February 17-20, in Chicago.

Upwards of 1500 persons are expected to attend the four-day conference, according to Walter W. Underwood, executive director. Theme of the session will be "Looking Ahead," and other speakers will include: Dr. A. Allan Bates, vice president for research and development, Portland Cement Association; Edith B. Evans, editor, Living for Young Homemakers magazine; Alfred M. Baltzer, director,

small business and associations program, National Safety Council; and William Avery, editor, Concrete Products magazine.

UC EXTENSION
CLASSES MOVE
LARGER SPACE

The University of California Extension lecture series on Space Technology, being held in San Francisco, were moved from the Morrison Planetarium to the Scottish Rite Auditorium to accommodate the large attendance.

Lectures are being given by L. M. K. Boelter, Dean of the College of Engineering at UCLA, and H. Guyford Stever, Associate Dean of Engineering and professor of Aeronautical Engineering at the Massachusetts Institute of Technology.

The series of weekly programs will continue through May 14th.

ARCHITECT
GIVEN
COMMISSION

Architect Andrew P. Anderson, 5335 College Avenue, Oakland, has been commissioned by the Oakland Unified School District to prepare plans and specifications for the construction of a new Auditorium at the Lockwood Elementary School in Oakland.

AUTOMOBILE
LICENSE
BUILDING

The Arizona State Highway Commission, Phoenix, has announced plans are underway for construction of a Drivers' License Building in Phoenix.

RUBY ANNOUNCES
UNBREAKABLE
LIGHT FIXTURE

Especially designed to be unbreakable, even when submitted to rough usage, the new Ruby "Security" fluorescent light fixture has many uses in schools, colleges, commercial and industrial installations. Fixture fits flush against ceiling or wall and can be opened for re-lamping only with a special tool.

Completely dust proof and bug proof. So watertight can be cleaned with hose at full pressure as the sturdy plexiglas lens can withstand almost any attack without breaking; ideal for shower rooms, toilet facilities, swimming pool areas, dining halls, infirmaries, and kitchens. Available in units to carry two, three or four fluorescent lamps, and in addition an 8-watt "night lamp" which can be operated independently to provide a night safety lamp. Finished in white baked enamel. Complete data available, Ruby Lighting Corp., 802 W. Whittier Blvd., Whittier, Calif.

MODERN NEW
MOTEL RISES
IN STOCKTON

Architect Jack Chernoff, 3060 11th Avenue, Los Angeles, is completing plans for construction of a new 54-unit motel in Stockton for owner Ben Rishwin.

The new motel will include 54 units with 12 kitchens, landscaped courts, offices, paved parking area, swimming pool. The buildings will be in a "U" shape, of contemporary design, considerable glass, brick and masonite construction. Estimated cost of the project is $500,000.

BANK SERVICE
BUILDING FOR
BANK OF AMERICA

Architects Wurster, Bernardi & Emmons, 202 Green St., San Francisco, are completing plans for construction of a new bank service building in San Francisco for the Bank of America. Construction will allow for future expansion of the facilities.

Estimated cost is $5,000,000.

INDUSTRIAL
PLANT SITE
IS BOUGHT

Ernest and Jack Ingold, Russ Building, San Francisco, announce the purchase of a 12 acre site in the Ingold Industrial Center on Rollins Road in Burlingame, which will be developed as a planned industrial unit.

The anticipated expenditure for development is $3,000,000.

AMADOR COUNTY
HOSPITAL HAS
NEW ADDITION

Architects Fingardo & Kern, 2910 Telegraph Avenue, Oakland, are preparing preliminary plans for construction of a

A bullet for Charlemagne

THE thickset Caco general got slowly to his feet. Behind him, in the darkness, stood an ug backdrop of a hundred Haitian outlaws. At his feet, a woma stirred a small fire.

Confronting him, the tattered youg man in blackface disguise saw the fire gleam on his whte silk shirt and pearl handled pistol and knew this was t? murderous chieftain, Charlemagne Masena Peralte. The man he'd come for, through a jungle and a 1200-manencampment, past six hostile outposts, risking detection ad certain death.

Charlemagne squinted across thefire. "Who is it?" he challenged in Creole.

There was no alternative; Marine sergeant Herman Hanneken dropped his disguise, drew anautomatic, and fired.

The night exploded into gunflame nost of it from Hanneken's second-in-command, Marine Crporal Button, and his handful of disguised Haitian gendanes. But the shot that killed Charlemagne was the one whic would finally end Caco terror and bring peace to Haiti.

Sergeant Hanneken is retired now—as Brigadier General Hanneken, USMC, with a Silver Star for Guadalcanal, a Legion of Merit for Peleliu, a Bronze Star for Cape Gloucester, a Gold Star, and a Navy Cross. And, for his incredible expedition against Charlemagne, November 1, 1919, the Medal of Honor.

The Herman Hannekens are a rare breed, it is true. Yet in all Americans there is much of the courage and character which they possess in such unusual abundance. Richer than gold, greater, even, than our material resources, it is the *living* wealth behind one of the world's soundest investments— United States Savings Bonds. It backs our country's guarantee: safety of principal up to any amount, and an assured rate of return. For real security, buy Bonds regularly, through your bank or the Payroll Savings Plan, and hold onto them!

Now Savings Bonds are better than ever! Every Series E Bond purchased since February 1, 1957, pays 3¼% interest when held to maturity. It earns higher interest in the early years than ever before, and matures in only 8 years and 11 months. Hold your *old* E Bonds, too. They earn more as they get older.

PART OF EVERY AMERICAN'S SAVINGS BELONGS IN U.S. SAVINGS BONDS

The U.S. Government does not pay for his advertisement. It is donated by this publication in cooperation with the Advertising uncil and the Magazine Publishers of America.

40-bed concrete and frame construction addition to the Amador County Hospital in Jackson.

The additional facilities will also provide a storage area, nursing home, small laundry, recreation area and four psychiatric rooms.

ST. JAMES CHURCH AND RECTORY FOR REDONDO BEACH

Architects Comeau & Brooks, 16611 Ventura Blvd., Encino, are completing plans for construction of a masonry church and rectory at St. James Parish, Redondo Beach, for the Roman Catholic Archbishop of Los Angeles.

Construction will be concrete slab, tile roof, cathedral glass, forced air heating, plumbing, paving and landscaping. Seating capacity will be 1000 persons.

SCATENA YORK CO. BUILDS NEW NC WAREHOUSE

Gale Santocono, designer, has completed plans and specifications for construction of a new 12,000 sq. ft. combination warehouse and office to be built in San Francisco for the Scatena York Company, exclusive Northern California distributors of York air conditioning, McCray refrigerated display cases and other supermarket equipment.

The modern steel frame structure will provide 3,000 sq. ft. of office and working area for 30 employees as well as display room, and according to J. A. Scatena and C. J. Scatena, brother partners, steadily increasing sales and an expanding business make the move to larger facilities imperative.

PORCELAIN ENAMEL TERM DEFINITION UPHELD BY COURT

A firm definition of the term "porcelain enamel" was established by the U. S. Court of Appeals for the Third Circuit in its review of a previous decision by the Federal Trade Commission.

The action of the court affirmed the Commission in its decision against Arrow Metal Products Corpn., et al, and successfully culminates more than two years work through the FTC, by the Porcelain Enamel Institute, its legal counsel and legal committee, to prohibit the company from using the word "porcenamel" to describe the organic paint finish on their products.

The Federal Trade Commission had originally issued a cease and desist order stating that the phrase was misleading to a substantial portion of the public. In its opinion, the Appeals Court held that the findings of the Commission were adequately supported and its order affirmed.

A bullet for Charlemagne

THE thickset Caco general got slowly to his feet. Behind him, in the darkness, stood an ugly backdrop of a hundred Haitian outlaws. At his feet, a woman stirred a small fire.

Confronting him, the tattered young man in blackface disguise saw the fire gleam on his white silk shirt and pearl handled pistol and knew this was the murderous chieftain, Charlemagne Masena Peralte. The man he'd come for, through a jungle and a 1200-man encampment, past six hostile outposts, risking detection and certain death.

Charlemagne squinted across the fire. "Who is it?" he challenged in Creole.

There was no alternative; Marine Sergeant Herman Hanneken dropped his disguise, drew an automatic, and fired.

The night exploded into gunflame, most of it from Hanneken's second-in-command, Marine Corporal Button, and his handful of disguised Haitian gendarmes. But the shot that killed Charlemagne was the one which would finally end Caco terror and bring peace to Haiti.

Sergeant Hanneken is retired now—as Brigadier General Hanneken, USMC, with a Silver Star for Guadalcanal, a Legion of Merit for Peleliu, a Bronze Star for Cape Gloucester, a Gold Star, and a Navy Cross. And, for his incredible expedition against Charlemagne, November 1, 1919, the Medal of Honor.

The Herman Hannekens are a rare breed, it is true. Yet in all Americans there is much of the courage and character which they possess in such unusual abundance. Richer than gold, greater, even, than our material resources, it is the *living* wealth behind one of the world's soundest investments— United States Savings Bonds. It backs our country's guarantee: safety of principal up to any amount, and an assured rate of return. For real security, buy Bonds regularly, through your bank or the Payroll Savings Plan, and hold onto them!

Now Savings Bonds are better than ever! Every Series E Bond purchased since February 1, 1957, pays 3¼% interest when held to maturity. It earns higher interest in the early years than ever before, and matures in only 8 years and 11 months. Hold your *old* E Bonds, too. They earn more as they get older.

As General Contractors and Builders, we share pride with

MARCHANT'S WORLD HEADQUARTERS
NEW BUILDING

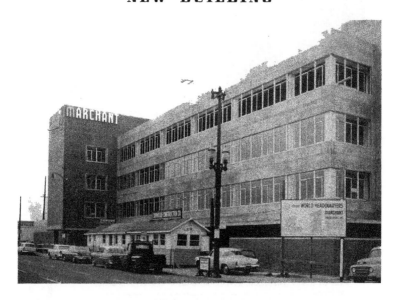

The construction and design of the Marchant's World Headquarters building offered important challenges to all who were concerned with making it a reality. To have played a part in finding able men to face these challenges . . . to have worked with such able associates to make this idea of a magnificent building a reality . . . has been a great privilege!

ALBERT F. ROLLER, A.I.A., *Architect*

   H. J. BRUNNIER, *Structural Engineer*

      DUDLEY DEANE & ASSOCIATES, INC., *Mechanical Engineers*

        LYLE E. PATTON, *Electrical Engineer*

DINWIDDIE CONSTRUCTION CO.

210 Crocker Building   San Francisco 4, Calif.   YUkon 6-2718

RCHITECT
NGINEER

MODERN KITCHENS

As General Contractors and Builders, we share pride with

MARCHANT'S WORLD HEADQUARTERS NEW BUILDING

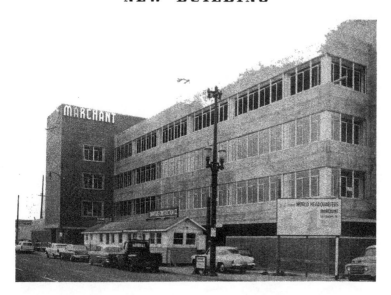

The construction and design of the Marchant's World Headquarters building offered important challenges to all who were concerned with making it a reality. To have played a part in finding able men to face these challenges . . . to have worked with such able associates to make this idea of a magnificent building a reality . . . has been a great privilege!

ALBERT F. ROLLER, A.I.A., *Architect*

H. J. BRUNNIER, *Structural Engineer*

DUDLEY DEANE & ASSOCIATES, INC., *Mechanical Engineers*

LYLE E. PATTON, *Electrical Engineer*

DINWIDDIE CONSTRUCTION CO.

210 Crocker Building   San Francisco 4, Calif.   YUkon 6-2718

RCHITECT

NGINEER

MODERN KITCHENS

——ARCHITECT & ENGINEER is indexed regularly by ENGINEERING INDEX, INC.; and ART INDEX——

Contents for

FEBRUARY

THE OLDEST PROFESSIONAL MONTHLY BUSINESS MAGAZINE OF THE ELEVEN WESTERN STATES

ARCHITECT AND ENGINEER (Established 1905) is published on the 15th of the month by The Architect and
Engineer, Inc., 68 Post St., San Francisco 4; Telephone EXbrook 2-7182. President, K. P. Kierulff; Vice-
President and Manager, L. B. Penhorwood; Treasurer, E. N. Kierulff. — Los Angeles Office: Wentworth F.
Green, 439 So. Western Ave., Telephone DUnkirk 7-8135 — Portland, Oregon, Office: R. V. Vaughn, 7117
Canyon Lane. — Entered as second class matter, November 2, 1905, at the Post Office in San Francisco,
California, under the Act of March 3, 1879. Subscriptions United States and Pan America, $3.00 a year;
$5.00 two years; foreign countries $5.00 a year; single copy, 50c.

. EDITORIAL NOTES .

SPUTNIKS AND SPENDING

Investigations into the status of American scientific development, particularly as it concerns weapons advancement and the military situation, continue. From the maze of reactions which have occurred since the Soviet satellite went into space, several encouraging facts are becoming evident.

The approach to appraising and solving such problems as may exist is taking a constructive course under the leadership of the President and other high governmental officials, as responsible officials seem to be well on the road to meeting the state of urgency which faces the nation carefully, analytically and constructively.

There is a recognition that economic strength as well as military strength is important in the international competition in which this nation is engaged with Russia. Federal spending and tax considerations are being given careful review, recognizing that a victory in the military field must be based upon a strong economic health.

And of particular importance to economy advocates is a growing recognition in many quarters that current happenings have made the need for constructive economy and governmental reform more imperative than ever. More flexibility in administering research and development funds, greater control over them by the Defense Department, and a lessening of the means by which the Pentagon can engage in wasteful rivalries are in the immediate offing.

* * *

"We shall need a minimum of 3,000 additional engineers between now and 1961 to keep abreast of the growing lighting field":—Marshall N. Waterman, president Illumination Engineering Society.

* * *

WHAT RECESSION?

We have been trying for a long time to "educate" executives in advertising agencies handling important advertising schedules of many dealers, distributors, and manufacturers of products that are consumed in the construction industry, that there is a "market" opportunity on the West Coast for sale of building products never before equalled.

Of course, quite naturally, we have tried to point out to these individuals charged with the responsibility of producing a maximum of value for every advertising dollar expended, that ARCHITECT & ENGINEER magazine readers throughout the West represented the "key" buyers of construction products, and therefore, advertising scheduled in ARCHITECT & ENGINEER magazine was the "best" investment that could be made for present and even future business.

Our contention has been based upon the fact that all types of construction in the eleven western states, dollar for dollar, is far above the national average, and that while economic adjustments might occur in certain areas of the nation, the dollar spent for construction, per capita, in the West would remain far above the national average for some time to come.

Having beaten the tom-toms on this subject among prospective advertisers, and even manufacturers, from Los Angeles to Seattle, and from San Francisco to Denver, frankly without too much success, we have almost come to the conclusion that the old proverb, "A prophet is without honor in his own town" certainly holds true.

With the "slight recession" reported nationally during the past few months, and particularly since the turn of the new year, and with a number of building material manufacturers "retrenching" because of the 'uncertainty" of business, what do the records for construction on the West Coast show?

The San Francisco Bay Area alone reports $66,000,-000 construction permits for December, up sharply from previous months and compared with $40,000,000 in December a year ago.

New dwelling units authorized dropped seasonally to 2,321 units, some 700 above the November figure of a year ago, and Max D. Kossoris, director of the western region of the Department of Labor's Bureau of Labor Statistics, recently reported that the total construction authorized for 1957 in the Bay Area amounted to $648,000,000, only 1 per cent short of the record total reached in 1956. Housing construction came close to the 1956 level with 31,100 units being issued as against 32,200 in 1956.

These official figures do not lead us to believe that construction projects, and prospects for a continuance of a substantial volume of building for some time to come, are falling apart at the seams. Nor are we sympathetic to those who think a "retrenchment" is the answer to construction industry problems which in many instances do not apply to the West Coast.

Ever optimistic and inclined to look at the problem objectively, we feel there is a tremendous opportunity for the sale of building materials and products throughout the entire West today, tomorrow and day after tomorrow. Who will make these sales, and beat what obviously in many instances is a "propaganda recession"? Well! we have given the answer many, many times, but we will repeat it again for any late comers—the fellow who goes out after business enthusiastically and with energy, . . . and don't forget, the sales effort backed by a consistent advertising schedule in ARCHITECT & ENGINEER magazine, will have an edge over the other fellow.

GENERAL
VIEW OF
MEXICO
CITY

OBSERVATIONS

ON THE MEXICO CITY EARTHQUAKE
OF JULY 28, 1957

By

JOHN J. GOULD

John J. Gould &
H. J. Degenkolb,
Consulting Engineers

The 1957 earthquake that caused spectacular damage in Mexico City had its epicenter about 218 miles to the south. In other cities like Taxco, located about half-way between, I saw no evidence of any damage. The dominant period of the shock was estimated to be about 1½-2 seconds with a maximum double amplitude of about 3". The period of destruction lasted about 16 seconds.

The maximum intensity measured by the modified Mercalli Scale seemed to be about 7' with great variations of intensity being observed in the city. Its general effects appeared similar to those of the after shocks of the Tehachapi Earthquake of 1951.

Mexico City has a population of about four and one-half million, and an area of 85 square miles. When the Spanish arrived in 1520, the area consisted of a number of islands surrounded by a huge lake which was subsequently filled in with lava and ashes through the volcanic eruptions. A heavily saturated soil is found near the surface extending down to substantial layers of clay, sand and gravel about 100' below the ground. Most important buildings are supported on concrete or wood piles driven into these layers, the wood piles being in short lengths spliced with steel dowels. Some footings were provided with permanent jacks to permit adjustment for relative subsidence.

(See Page 23)

NOTE: This paper was presented to members of the San Francisco Post of the Military Engineers and the Structural Engineers Association of Northern California on November 14, 1957, and the Reno, Nevada Section of the American Society of Civil Engineers on November 20, 1957. The Editor.

NEWS and COMMENT ON ART

SAN FRANCISCO MUSEUM OF ART

The San Francisco Museum of Art, War Memorial Building, Civic Center, under the direction of Dr. Grace L. McCann Morley, will feature the following special exhibition and museum activities during February: .

EXHIBITIONS: Highlights of the Spring Rental Gallery; Retrospective, Piet Mondrian; Contemporary Ceramics, Beatrice Wood of Southern California and Ruby O'Burke, Antonia Prieto and Margurite Wildenhain of the Bay Area; The World of Edward Weston; The Blue Four—Feininger, Jawlensky, Kandinsky and Klee; and Collecting Modern Art featuring the collection of Mr. and Mrs. Harry Lewis Winnston and selected loans from Bay Region collections;

SPECIAL EVENTS: Include Concert and Programs; Lecture Tours, each Sunday at 3 o'clock; and Museum activities including Adventures in Drawing; Studio-Art for the Layman, and Children's Saturday morning Art Classes.

The Museum is open daily.

M. H. deYOUNG MEMORIAL MUSEUM

The M. H. deYoung Memorial Museum, Golden Gate Park, San Francisco, under the direction of Walter Heil, has announced the following special exhibits and activities for this month:

EXHIBITIONS: Paintings by Frank H. Myers, a memorial exhibition; Chinese Paintings by Huang Chun-Pi; Paintings by Cameron Booth, and Watercolors by Sister Mary Luke.

SPECIAL EVENTS: Classes in Art Enjoyment for adults includes Exercises in Oil Painting, Part II, and Seminars in History of Art. For the children there are classes in Picture Making each Saturday morning, Art and Nature, Wednesday 3:30 to 4:30, and the Art Club for students 12-18 years old each Thursday 3:30 to 4:30 p.m.

The Museum is open daily, auto parking provided.

OAKLAND ART MUSEUM

The Oakland Art Museum, 1000 Fallon Street, under the direction of Paul Mills, Curator, is presenting one of the greatest collections of old master paintings to be seen in the Bay Region in the Hammer Collection, lent by the Hammer Galleries of New York.

Immortals whose works are included are Rubens, represented by two paintings; Frank Hals, whose laughing peasant boy is a popular favorite; Rembrandt, Tintoretto, Fra Filippo Lippi and many others to make up a collection of forty paintings. Exhibited under auspices of the Los Angeles Art Commission before coming to Oakland, the collection has also been shown at the Virginia Museum of Art.

Several special events planned for this month will include Dr. Alfred Neumeyer, director of the Mills Art Gallery; Dr. Walter Horn, Chairman of the University of California Art Department; and guided tours through the museum, in charge of Marjory Young, formerly of the Toledo Museum of Art.

CALIFORNIA PALACE OF THE LEGION OF HONOR

The California Palace of the Legion of Honor, Lincoln Park, San Francisco, under the direction of Thomas Carr Howe, is presenting the following special exhibits and activities during February:

EXHIBITS: Postera U. S. A. representing an exhibition of 69 American posters illuminating the American scene from 1832 through World War I, presented in cooperation with American Heritage, the Detroit Historical Society, Levi Berman, and the American Federation of Arts; Pre-Marshall Plan Germany, pictures by Boris Von Clodt; Watercolors and Gouaches by Jason Schoener; Painting by Roger Bolomey; Indonesian Paintings, and Paintings by A. Sheldon Pennoyer, A Memorial Exhibition.

The ACHENBACH FOUNDATION for Graphic Arts: Modern Prints in Color; and an exhibition of early prints and drawings of California from the collection of Robert B. Honeyman.

SPECIAL EVENTS: Organ Recital every Saturday and Sunday at 3:00 p.m. Educational activities—the Spring Session of art classes for children and juniors will begin on Saturday, March 15th.

The Museum is open daily, 10:00 a.m. to 5:00 p.m.

EXHIBITION OF STUDENT WORK RUDOLF SCHAEFFER SCHOOL

The East-West Arts Gallery of the Rudolph Schaeffer School of Design, 350 Union Street, San Francisco, will be the setting of the "Mid-term Interior Design

and Color Exhibition of Student Work," this month.

Representing the work of 134 students, the exhibition will include models of interiors, presentation drawings, fabric and wall-paper designs, color studies and three dimensional design ideas.

Highlight of the exhibition will be a coordinated class project, "A San Francisco Penthouse", utilizing scale models executed by the students of Peter Rocchia, Interior Color and Design instructor, and Furniture Design instructor Paul Palmer.

The Rudolph Schaeffer School of Design, a non-profit institution under the sponsorship of the Rudolph Schaeffer Foundation, in now in its thirty-first year. It offers to the professional and non professional student a complete color and design program.

**DR. GRACE L. McCANN MORLEY
WILL RETIRE AS DIRECTOR**

Dr. Grace L. McCann Morley and the Trustees of the San Francisco Museum of Art announced early this month, Dr. Morley's resignation as Director of the Museum, effective December 31, 1960. This date coincides with the 25th anniversary of Dr. Morley's service to the Museum as its Director.

Dr. Morley helped organize the Museum in 1935 and has served as its Director during its entire existance. Under her guidance, the Museum has achieved international recognition as one of the outstanding institutions in its field, and has played an important and prominent part in the Artistic life of San Francisco.

M. H. DE YOUNG MEMORIAL MUSEUM

Golden Gate Park   San Francisco

Mother and Child

by FRANCOIS BOUCHER

French. 1703-1770

Gift of Brooke Postley

FEBRUARY, 1958

SOLID MASS OF ROCK SITE OF

MODERN HOME

Oakland, California

Architect: B. D. Thorne

Consulting Engineer: Carl Replogle

"If you can't move it, use it!"

That's what Architect David Thorne exclaimed the first time he viewed the 50 by 100-foot lot his client, Jazz Pianist Dave Brubeck, had purchased in the Oakland hills.

With a matured $1,000 war bond his father had given him and $100 from his own savings, Brubeck had purchased what amounted to one huge rock. This piece of real estate was anything but level. A rocky snag poked out toward the rear 42 feet higher than the front elevation. It was well wooded with tall spruce and eucalyptus, and from the rock crest the Bay Area unfolded in a magnificent panorama.

But this crest completely obscured the view from the remaining three-quarters of the lot. Burbeck wanted this view from every point in the house. He also wanted what he called "an isolation booth" where he could do his writing without disturbance of any sort. On this rather steep hillside, Brubeck's wife, Iola, wanted safe playing areas for their four children. She also wanted to be able to divide the house to accommodate both jam sessions and the needs of the nursery.

Architect Thorne met every one of these requirements with striking results. His solution was to literally "lift" 3,000 square feet of house on five fingers of steel. He used the rock mass as a solid anchor from which to cantilever these steel fingers in two directions. Architect Thorne calls this design a house of structural necessities. In almost every case, he took what was a lot limitation to begin with, and by simply using steel, surmounted the problem. He was also able to preserve the natural beauty of the lot, leaving very large and very tall trees intact. The structure has the appearance of growing from a solid rock, yet its spectacular cantilever gives one the impression of soaring eloquence.

Thorne's five fingers of steel are composed of three 16-inch wide flange sections, supporting the living, dining room, and kitchen wing of the house, including the upper deck area in one direction and two heavier 18-inch wide flange sections supporting the bedroom wing. At one end, each of the five steel sections is anchored to footings, each of which is seated on the solid rock mass of the lot.

Each footing is tied in laterally on the downhill portion of the lot with a 16 by 16-inch reinforced concrete grade beam which ties in with the forward shear wall of reinforced concrete block, seated on the rock mass. In some cases the beams and footings were keyed into the rock mass with a jackhammer. The steel members from which the house was to be floated thus formed the top portion of a continuous rigid frame, imbedded in solid rock. In the bedroom wing, Thorne

was able to achieve a spectacular cantilever of over 16 feet. The 16-inch wide flange sections provided a cantilever of over 8 feet for the entire dining and living room side of the house, a distance of 40 feet. Where the front 18-inch wide flange section cornered on the 16-inch wide flange section like the index finger and thumb, the two pieces were welded together providing greater rigidity.

In the shop, an 8-foot module was set up on each steel section by welding angle brackets to which 6 by 14-inch wooden floor joists could be bolted once the steel was erected. The consulting engineer was Carl Replogle of Oakland.

In the filed, the fabricator was hampered by having to leave trees intact and the steep terrain. But one simplification aided greatly. Instead of landing the heavy steel directly on anchor bolts, the foundations were equipped with an anchor plate which had been welded to reinforcing rods, seated and grouted into the concrete piers. The wide flange beams were then fastened to the anchor plate by welding.

Floating the house on this hand of steel, here's what Thorne was able to accomplish:

View—Glass in virtually every area of the entire house covers 360 degrees. Mrs. Brubeck can watch her children playing on the lot from the kitchen located in the center. An ingenious mirror arrangement by her dressing table in the master bedroom takes in the porch play area. At night, Dave Brubeck composes jazz in the living room, studio area. A hole, which thoughtful neighbors trimmed through a pair of pine trees, frames the Golden Gate Bridge far in the distance. The lights of Berkeley, Oakland, and San Francisco sparkle like a carpet of diamonds.

Play area—Inside and off the bedroom area in the center of the house is a 16 by 9-foot play area which can be expanded on rainy days by moving a wall partition between it and the living room. Combined with the hallway, this offers children 80-feet of running space. An upper deck is enclosed by a fence and gate with a reverse latch, and opens off the dining room through sliding glass doors for additional play area. Like a giant trampolin is the 22 by 24-foot deck area provided by the carport roof. In this, Architect Thorne utilized steel again. The forward part of the deck is supported by an 18-inch wide flange section which provides a 16-foot cantilever at the extreme corner of the deck and gives a bouncy feel to the deck flooring.

Practicality—The bedroom wing is divided into four small bedrooms for the children with a large master bedroom at the end of the hall. This portion of the house soars out spectacularly on a 16-foot cantilever.

The childrens' bedrooms are separated by movable closet units, and the entire area can be made into one large dormitory if need arises. Each of the childrens' bedroom doors has glass to sill height. Not only is the view unhampered in two directions, but Mrs. Brubeck can take quick inventory of the offspring at night-time.

A small service yard opens off the utility room to provide outdoor play area for the children. A "training sink" at the entrance to the utilities room was installed so that they could wash up before entering the house.

Privacy—In spite of all the glassed areas, the design provides for privacy. The master bedroom, while having floor to ceiling glass in the front part of the house, is cantilevered out into space some 20 feet off the ground, high enough to give complete privacy to the occupants. Nothing can beat the privacy of Dave Brubeck's isolation "booth" located under the bedroom wing. In the space between the concrete block shear wall and the rear foundation supporting the cantilever, Thorne designed a completely sound proof room, the ceiling of which is better than 4-feet below the floor of the house.

"I use the 'booth' if I really want to get away," Brubeck says. Located as it is on the concrete footing —a pad nearly three feet thick—not even vibrations can get through. While he does a lot of composing right in the middle of play activities with the children, Brubeck admits, "there comes a time when it's great to get away from distractions of any kind. Inner peace

of mind is by far the most important atmosphere for writing."

As for features—by using steel to carry the structural load of the house, Architect Thorne was able to capitalize on many innovations: the cantilevered bedroom wing soaring out into space; the same for the music room area; the contrast of openness, yet complete privacy for living areas. And even in contrast to "the out in space" feeling, Thorne brings one back to solid terra firma with emphasis. In the living room, he uses the rocky snag, allowing it to come up out of the floor of the house and form the centerpiece for an attractive indoor planter.

In the garage or carport area, Thorne again takes advantage of the tremendous leverage of the rock mass, using it as a counterbalance by which he anchors the steel 18-inch wide flange beam by means of 4-foot foundation bolts imbedded through a concrete slab. As a finishing touch, Thorne garnished the top of the beam with a huge bolder.

Satisfaction in a house is hard to come by. Yet in the case of the Brubeck residence, after three years of living and with their family increased to five, the Brubecks are extremely happy. Instead of moving to a larger house, they have again commissioned the architect to add on a utility and play area, and extend the living room. Brubeck now owns the crest of the entire hill which the house overlooks, and is planning outdoor play areas—a pool and guest house.

"The way I look at it," says Artist-Composer Brubeck, "this house expresses much of my wife's and my own personality. To us, it's a house that is full of common sense. To someone else perhaps their reaction might be, 'I would never live in a house like this.' I feel that if inspiration can come from good surroundings then it will come from here. This is a house full of windows. It's completely open and honest. You have almost every form of nature surrounding it. In fact, I feel sometimes we're living in a tree house."

One of his rare pleasures Dave says is to lie in bed in the morning to watch and listen to the birds in the branches of the tall pines, one of which was so close to the master bedroom that it was necessary to cut back the eaves to accommodate it. "My favorite character," Brubeck says, "is some old owl that's always hanging around looking wise."

PLAY AREA

Canvas covered deck doubles as roof of car port; front is supported by an 18-inch wide flange steel beam cantilevered from a rock mass at side of lot.

Composer Brubeck on front steps leading to upper deck of house holds son Daniel. Christopher, Michael, Darius and Mrs. Brubeck.

WATERFALLS combine with warmth of natural red cedar paneling and old brick to create friendly entrance lobby.

NEWLY DESIGNED PILUSO'S

and attention-getting design ideas.

The main dining room, serving 375 guests, is 72 feet, 10 inches by 90 feet, 8 inches and surrounds a 20 by 40 foot swimming pool. This unique dining area, which includes a cedar cocktail bar and lounge, is post free and supported by three glu-lam fir beams. These man-made beams, nine by forty-two inches in size, have a graceful, upsweeping curve and camber and were designed especially for this job. The beams are so large and so attractive they immediately catch the attention of guests.

The three main beams are placed on 22-foot, six-inch spacing and the roof slope is 2:12. One end of the beams rests on tapered glu-lam columns which are 19 feet, 7¾ inches high, and the other rests on concrete pilasters.

The theatre restaurant was constructed at a cost of $7.80 a square foot, with John LaPorte doing the general contracting. One reason given by Designer Eska for the extremely low cost is the use of post and beam bent type modular design with the main glu-lam beams

supporting the entire roof section.

The beams overhang on either side of the building, one seven-foot, four-inch overhang sheltering a long lanai high above the ground on the low side which will serve as an outdoor cocktail area during the warm summer months. The other overhang is six feet, six inches and shelters a walkway which serves the 200-car, paved lot.

Other economies were realized by using heavy glu-lam supporting members for the floors. These beams are 9 by 19⅜ inches and are spaced twelve feet, six inches on center.

The restaurant is remarkable for its variety of services and entertainment. From the time the guest enters the warm, friendly lobby until he is ready to leave, he is constantly seeing something different.

Bathing beauties are featured twice nightly in an attractive water ballet seen from the main dining room. In the Marine Lounge on a lower level, guests may sip cocktails while viewing the ballet underwater through a 10 x 10 foot plate glass window. A floating

SWIMMING POOL is center attraction in main dining room; sweeping beam forming striking and dramatic roof supports.

THEATRE RESTAURANT . . .

dance floor powered by cable and electric motor, covers the pool between water shows at night. It operates on steel rails.

The lobby entrance is designed in western red cedar and old brick with a stone waterfall adding charm and enchantment. Well designed glu-lam fir beams and exposed tongue-and-groove cedar form the ceiling of the lobby. The cedar cocktail bar on the main floor near the lobby features cedar panels and backbar and laminated plastic decorative panels behind the bar which appear as outside windows. An egg crate fir ceiling of 2x8's on two-foot modules makes the bar more friendly by lowering the ceiling.

A garden room is also designed in cedar and stone for 140 guests who may view a velvet green, nine-hole pitch and putt golf course through a full wall of glass. A small bar serves this room and a girl swimming in a fish bowl offers added attraction for guests. A 500-capacity banquet room on the Marine Lounge level is often converted on weekends to public use to help handle the crowds.

Heavy glu-lam beams have been left exposed on the lower level to continue the country club theme of informality.

The dance floor has a maple parquet surface which is three feet below the level of the main dining room. A bandstand faces one end of the pool and contains a diving board hydraulically operated. The electric organ also may be raised and lowered hydraulically.

The firm, headed by Ernest Piluso, long-time Eugene restaurateur, already has invested $250,000 in this theatre restaurant and on tap for spring and summer construction is another $100,000 worth of added attractions, including the pitch and putt golf course,

MARINE LOUNGE on lower level is designed for complete relaxation. Plate glass window on left looks into underwater pool where mermaids perform nightly. Leather overstuffed TV furniture adds glamor.

now nearly completed, and outdoor barbecue area with six barbecue pits to be located in an old apple orchard with privacy for small parties a feature of this area. Barbecue customers will be catered by the kitchen on the adjoining lower floor.

A small stream flows along the golf course and will be equipped with a lighted waterwheel.

Exterior siding is rough-sawn western red cedar installed vertically and stained a dark brown. The same material went into the forty-foot tall, lighted pylon which marks the restaurant for motorists passing by on Highway 99 entering Portland from the south. Piluso's is about fifteen minutes' drive from downtown Portland and reached by main arterials. It is set away from the highway about 150 feet and is located on the old Piluso homestead.

All equipment, broilers, ranges and barbecue, in the two kitchens is gas-fired and heat from the building and pool is also supplied from gas-fired furnaces. Furniture in each room has been carefully designed. White leather overstuffed TV chairs are a feature of the Marine Lounge. White leather predominates in the furniture in both the main dining room and cedar cocktail bar lounge, with white bleached wood used with the leather in the lounge and wrought iron in the dining room. The Garden Room features special garden furniture.

The low lines in the main dining room, made possible by the sturdy, cambered beams on a low pitch, combined with the warmth of naturally finished cedar accounts to a considerable degree for the atmosphere of western friendliness.

GARDEN ROOM offers facilities for 140 guests and is a favorite for private parties. Full wall of glass on left overlooks nine hole pitch and putt golf course. Small bar and a girl in a fish bowl are added attractions. Bandstand can be seen at middle right.

THEATRE RESTAURANT . . .

Most supper clubs appear drab and lifeless in daylight, but not Piluso's. There is plenty of light from a half wall of glass along one entire side of the main dining room which overlooks the barbecue area and pitch and putt course. The full wall of glass in the Garden Room lights up the west end of the main dining room where the two connect, separated only by the bandstand and sheltering walls. Indirect light comes from clerestory lights located in a special recess area in the ceiling between two of the main beams.

The walls throughout are of western red cedar which has been finished with a sealer of clear plastic brushed on, adding to the richness of the setting in both daytime and evening. Indirect lights above the cedar paneling adds a definite charm and brings out many of the highlights of this autumn-toned wood. An acoustical plaster covers the entire ceiling excepting for the exposed beams.

When Designer Arnold Eska started out to translate owner Ernest Piluso's wishes into workable form, the basic idea back of the plan was to create one of the great ballroom palladiums of the 1920's, but with contemporary ideas for entertaining, and for food and drink service.

It had to be large, but it must be warm and friendly, Eska determined. He felt his best opportunity to get spaciousness and warmth could be achieved with a low, snug roof section relatively close to the dining floor, yet high enough to avoid a feeling of crowding. He decided on using glu-lam beams because they would combine beauty and sweeping lines with the strength necessary to carry the 90 foot roof span.

Eska calls the design "northwest contemporary" and this seems to be an excellent designation since it features native woods to an extraordinary degree in the most contemporary form.

CORNER OF BANQUET ROOM in basement has adjoining kitchen. Heavy timber beams help create post-free area for complete enjoyment of some 500 diners.

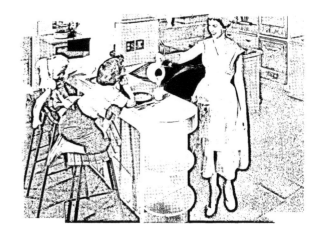

FAMILY KITCHEN

Example of the open area home of Pacific Northwest.

The Sam Rubinstein home, by Tom Balshizer, Architect.

WESTERN ARCHITECTS DEVELOP

MODERN KITCHENS

. . . an Amazing World

By ARTHUR W. PRIAULX

Since World War II, appliance and material manufacturers have been wooing the American public with the wonder kitchens of the future, equipped with every conceivable type of gadget. Some even serve up hot coffee or cold coke from conventional taps. These were dream kitchens with custom-made conveniences to tempt the most reactionary old grandmother still sold on functional kitchens "without all that falderal."

Architects and women's clubs in many a city helped spread the word with conducted kitchen tours. Every woman with an older home overnight became kitchen conscious. Today much of the remodeling is in the kitchen and be it said for the manufacturers of those fabulous appliances, they have come through handsomely, making available all of the newest devices and

conveniences in a wide range of colors, sizes and price ranges.

But, to the architects here in the west who have done so much to develop the beautiful, functional, casual contemporary home design, must go credit for developing as well the kitchen of the future, today. All of the kitchen talk of the past decade and more since the end of the last world war seems to have come to fruition in the past couple of years. All at once, the kitchen supreme seems to have burst into full bloom. A look at some of the most carefully designed homes along the Pacific Coast will convince even the most casual observer that kitchens with amazing versatility and beauty are no longer the exception but have become one of the key features of the modern home.

THEATRE RESTAURANT . . .

Most supper clubs appear drab and lifeless in daylight, but not Piluso's. There is plenty of light from a half wall of glass along one entire side of the main dining room which overlooks the barbecue area and pitch and putt course. The full wall of glass in the Garden Room lights up the west end of the main dining room where the two connect, separated only by the bandstand and sheltering walls. Indirect light comes from clerestory lights located in a special recess area in the ceiling between two of the main beams.

The walls throughout are of western red cedar which has been finished with a sealer of clear plastic brushed on, adding to the richness of the setting in both daytime and evening. Indirect lights above the cedar paneling adds a definite charm and brings out many of the highlights of this autumn-toned wood. An acoustical plaster covers the entire ceiling excepting for the exposed beams.

When Designer Arnold Eska started out to translate wner Ernest Piluso's wishes into workable form, the asic idea back of the plan was to create one of the reat ballroom palladiums of the 1920's, but with con mporary ideas for entertaining, and for food and drir service.

I iad to be large, but it must be warm and friendly, Esk determined. He felt his best opportunity to get spa ousness and warmth could be achieved with a lov snug roof section relatively close to the dining floc yet high enough to avoid a feeling of crowding. He lecided on using glu-lam beams because they wo d combine beauty and sweeping lines with the streigth necessary to carry the 90 foot roof span.

Ika calls the design "northwest contemporary" and thi seems to be an excellent designation since it fea res native woods to an extraordinary degree in the nost contemporary form.

CORNER OF BANQUET ROOM in basement has adjoining kitchen. Heavy timber beams help create post-free area for complete enjoyment of some 500 diners.

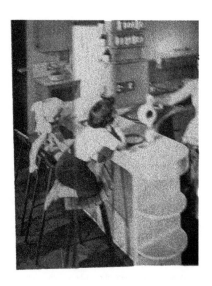

FAMILY KITCHEN

Example of the open area home of Pacific Northwest.

The Sam Rubinstein home, by Tom Bakhizer. Architect.

WESTERN ARCHITECTS DEVELOP

MODERN KITCH

. . . an Amazing World

By ARHUR W. PRIAULX

Since World War II, appliance and material manufacturers have been wooing the American public with the wonder kitchens of the future, equipped with every conceivable type of gadget. Some even serve up hot coffee or cold coke from conventional taps. These were dream kitchens with custom-made conveniences to tempt the most reactionary old grandmother still sold on functional kitchens "without all that falderal."

Architects and women's clubs in many cities have spread the word with conducted kitchen tours. Every woman with an older home overnight became kitchen conscious. Today much of the remodeling is in the kitchen and be it said for the manufacturers of fabulous appliances, they have come through handsomely, making available all of the newest ideas

conveniences in a wide price ranges

But, to

done so

usual

devel

MODERN KITCHENS . . .

Even the lower cost dwelling units have kitchens in the dream category and this goes for apartments as well.

Kitchens Are Roomier

Kitchens are roomier, because they have become the heart of the home, the food center as well as the ordinary living center. They have become the outdoor food preparing and serving headquarters, and are equally attractive for parties as well. Lovely to look at, the modern kitchen is a dream of functionalism.

The key to these kitchens is space use, integration of appliances with custom-built storage units, utilization of the walls and handy-to-reach areas for storage, and care in planning workable units for placement of pots, pans and utensils. And, the next most important step is to plan the kitchen work areas: grouping such areas as the cooking, food preparation and baking units to cut down on steps and expedite mealtime chores.

Color has come into the kitchens with a rush, breathtaking, beautiful and practical. Here the housewife has an opportunity to give vent to her own personality, her own pet color schemes when worked out in cooperation with her architect. Appliances can be had in a wide variety of colors and hues from the tawny copper finishes and silver tones, which fit so well with the natural wood texture and colorings of

the wooden cabinets, to pastels and brighter colors.

More and more west coast architects are calling on western softwoods, like the incomparable west coast hemlock and the golden Douglas fir, as the background for their kitchens. The soft, neutral shades of these woods are not only easy to incorporate in any color scheme, but the wide flexibility of these woods make them ideal for custom-made cabinets, builtins and storage units. When the architect and the housewife have agreed, finally, upon the exact location of every major appliance, the problem then resolves itself down to building interconnecting storage and work areas which tie the appliances together into a smooth, streamlined unit and still provide all of the other functions required in a kitchen. The easy-to-work softwoods can be cut, fitted and shaped into any desirable unit. Since both fir and hemlock are very durable, withstand scratches, wear and tear, and have intricate beauty as well, they are among the most popular materials in the kitchen of today.

More Utility Use

It is said there have been two revolutions in our lifetime in kitchen design. First the dingy kitchen we knew in 1915 and before gave way a decade and a half ago to the gleaming, snow-white hospital purity job dominated by white-faced appliances. Both kitch-

**OPENNESS
of
MODERN KITCHEN**

Shows architect's handling of interconnection between cooking and dining areas, in the R. H. Parker home.

Designed by
Richard Marlitt,
Architect.

ens were a virtual prison for the housewife during meal preparations. She was shut off from the family, and since the kitchens were uninviting in appearance and cold with sterile white facades of stoves and refrigerators, the family generally stayed away unless put to work.

The biggest feature of the modern kitchen is the release of the housewife from this prison. A majority of the modern trends make the kitchen an integrated part of the home, joined up after the fashion of the old New England kitchen-living room or keeping room plan with the rest of the living area. While it is true that not all new homes are designed in the open area trend, it is true that most kitchens today integrate, with scarcely any division, into the dining area, and the two are so spacious and attractive the family just naturally seems to gravitate there at meal preparation time, at snack time, and many families almost live in this part of the home, especially if the designer has been thoughtful enough to provide a place for the television set.

Still other homes are being designed so the kitchen joins with the living room, and many a home places the family room next to the kitchen. There are many

COMPACTNESS is keynote of this kitchen in home of Milton Foland, designed by Richard Sundeleaf—note stacked utensil storage and stairstep spice shelves as outstanding examples of compact planning.

LIGHT, airy and friendly kitchen in the Robert Dwyer home designed by Richard Sundeleaf, Architect.

COTTAGE TYPE HOME of Leslie Coons in open area theme shows how smoothly kitchen can be incorporated with the adjoining dining and family living areas.

ways to separate the kitchen area from these other rooms. Serving bars, hanging cabinets, low divider walls, decorative screens, and even folding walls which can shut off the kitchen from living or family rooms when not in use, all are effectively used.

Unusual Kitchens

Architect Tom Balshizer designed a rather unusual kitchen in the Sam Rubenstein home in Eugene (see page 15), which joins not only to the dining area but to the family room as well. Using Douglas fir effectively for cabinets to set forth the wall ovens and surface cooking units in their metal finishes, his kitchen is smart, well arranged and highly functional. A serving bar which also serves as a snack bar at odd times, separates dining and kitchen areas. A half wall on which has been built a brick barbecue grill which is accessible from either the kitchen or family room sets up the line of demarcation between these living spaces. The Douglas fir is vertical grained and has been finished in natural colors.

An example of the kitchen-dining area separation is seen to good advantage in the Richard Parker home in Portland, designed by Architect Richard Marlitt

(see cover and page 16). Here a work unit, containing surface cooking unit and tiled work top with storage cabinets accessible from both the kitchen and dining areas, serves as a definite divider. A suspended cabinet above with vision area below makes a partial wall but does not shut off the kitchen. This suspended cabinet contains the fan over the range unit, condiment and utensil storage on the kitchen side and china storage on the dining side. Made of soft-toned west coast hemlock to match the walls and cabinets in both rooms, it also enhances the smart appearance of the metal faced wall ovens and surface range units. The china cabinet is open storage shelving with the background of the cupboards painted a soft pastel blue to feature the special china pieces on display.

Kitchens can be spacious without losing that compactness which means stepsaving during a long day. In the Robert Dwyer home in Portland, Architect Richard Sundeleaf has designed a kitchen which has all the attributes of a tiny, campact pullman kitchen, yet is large, airy and inviting (see page 17). A peninsula type island of storage drawers and cabinets, reached from both sides, serves to enclose the actual kitchen area and separate it from the breakfast dining

area. In order not to create a separation above the level of the surface top of the peninsula, Sundeleaf has erected plate glass shelves supported by attractively carved posts. These shelves are used for choice bits of china, bric-a-brac and tiny vases, in a most effective manner. By using wrought iron hinges and drawer pulls, the blonde hemlock cabinets and builtins create a pleasing Colonial atmosphere in this kitchen which at the same time has every possible modern convenience.

In the Milton A. Foland home in Portland, Architect Richard Sundeleaf demonstrates what can be done to bring about the greatest compactness in a kitchen without sacrifice of adequate storage space (see page 17). Made of blonde-finished west coast hemlock, this kitchen features some interesting storage ideas. Cooking utensils are stored on sliding shelves which pull out, permitting easy access to those at the back of the shelf. Spice cabinet has been built with a series of tiny raised shelves without the usual hunting. Again a triumph for careful planning and space utilization.

One of the many features which makes the modern kitchen so desirable and so workable is to plan for the adjoining utility room to be equally as attractive,

OUTDOOR BROOM CLOSET featured in this home, adjacent to kitchen, takes cleaning odors outside.

L-SHAPED SUSPENDED CABINET and storage peninsula separate kitchen and breakfast room in the Eugene, Oregon, home.

19

MODERN KITCHENS . . .

handy and open to light and air. Most of the utility rooms today either join directly with the kitchen, some being divided by only a low cabinet space, or they are separated only by a door. Most of these rooms are designed to match the kitchen. As in the Norman Richards home of Cottage Grove, Oregon (see page 21), designed also by Architect Tom Balshizer, where the smooth lines of vertical grain Douglas fir were used effectively in the utility room as in the kitchen. This room does not have the usual cluttered appearance of the laundry. All appliances have been enclosed in Douglas fir cabinets which are closed when not in use. A ·formica-covered table top fits snugly over washer and dryer, and when closed down provides welcome added work space. Other cabinets in the room match this and contain soiled clothes and washing materials. The utility room is as attractive as any other room in this lovely, modern home.

The James Luckey home in Eugene (see page 21), designed by Louis F. Bronson, III, features a utility room with a slightly different plan. Washer and dryer are not enclosed, but facing these units is a very attractive full wall of cabinets built of flat-grained fir to match the walls, and the center feature of this wall cabinet is a formica-covered work table which drops down when needed and becomes a large matching cabinet door when folded back. The table also serves as an accounting desk, with pigeonholes installed in the back wall. Washing materials are stored in drawers and cabinets in this storage wall. This utility room joins kitchen and garage and because it is handy to the garage it provides storage for some of the play and game equipment of the family as well as fishing and hunting gear.

An interesting variation of the kitchen-living room theme was developed in the Leslie Coons home in Portland (see page 18). This is a completely open area home, with dining area immediately adjoining the kitchen without any divider. The living room is around a corner from the kitchen, and the western red cedar paneling of the kitchen has been carried as well in the living room, effectively tying the home together

UTILITY ROOM is part of the kitchen in the Barney McPhillips home designed by Whittier and Fritsch, divided only by counter high bar.

UTILITY ROOM which is easy to keep neat as architect has provided simplicity in functional use as kitchen with utilities being covered with table top when not in use.

into one unit, so much so that the kitchen, although visible from both living and dining areas does not appear as a kitchen. This is probably due to the use of cedar paneling and cabinets which have been finished to bring out the rich reds and brown of the cedar. A cedar wood box beside the fireplace serves to add to the tie-up between the three different adjoining use areas of this home.

To utilize a corner hall between kitchen and dining room in the Milton Foland home mentioned above, Architect Richard Sundeleaf has made use of this narrow passageway to create a compact pantry, which doubles as a pass cupboard and a bar. Linen and silver storage is provided in interestingly designed cabinets below the bar top, and two tiny cabinets on either side of a window allow for storage of glassware and bottled goods. Builtins in the pantry as in the kitchen were designed in hemlock and finished in a light, neutral tone.

In the Barney McPhillips home at McMinnville, Oregon (see page 20), Architect George Whittier of Whittier and Fritsch made use of an extra large kitchen to combine utility room and kitchen in one

area. A serving bar reaching part way out in the kitchen containing storage drawers and shelves on the kitchen side, is the only divider. Washer and dryer are along one wall, flanked by adequate working surface for ironing, folding, and a tiny sink provides water for sprinkling. A storage unit above with matched cabinet doors provides all the storage room needed for washing supplies. These units and utility area walls were built of vertical grained Douglas fir to match the walls and builtins found in the remainder of the kitchen.

Not every home is designed so that floor and cleaning equipment can be kept outside. But Architect John Stafford arranged the Henry Hall home in Eugene (see page 19 top), so that this equipment, always a nuisance to store, could be out of the way in its own closet which opens onto the back porch and is reached handily through a door from the kitchen. Smells of solvents, waxes and cleaning fluids are thus kept outdoors, yet handy to the housewife. This closet is compact and has floor room for polisher, mops and mop bucket and brooms. Canvas pouches hung on the

MODERN KITCHENS . . .

door contain brushes, and small items which are so easy to lose.

Architects have commented freely that the grain of fine wood, like Douglas fir and hemlock, have as much as any other single thing given distinction and charm to many a kitchen where these woods have been used intelligently and judiciously to carry out a well-thought-out plan. With the present wax and plastic finishes, these woods can be made to reflect a flattering light, and the deep patina of fir and hemlock adds softness and beauty. Yet, they are easy to maintain.

The modern kitchen is called upon to meet two requirements and these two basic elements are uppermost in the minds of architects bent on creating kitchens more expressive than the common run found in many indifferently planned homes. They must first be as comprehensive as possible in their functional assets, and secondly, they must manifest a definite mark of aesthetic thought.

More Than Kitchens

It has taken designers a long time to learn that kitchens are not merely a string of appliances assembled with surgical detachment and determination, but rather that they should be highly personable rooms where the housewife not only must spend many hours, but where she will enjoy spending those hours. They must reflect the owner's whims, needs, tastes and personality.

The architect who would please his client—and that means the women of the family—faces a real challenge when working out kitchen details, but at the same time, he probably has in this room the widest possible latitude for his skill and imagination. He can make the room simple or elaborate, full of time-saving devices or skimp, colorful as a sunset or hospital white. But, whatever he does with these rooms, he would have one thing always uppermost in his mind; the kitchen has to work, has to be foolproof and functional. Beyond that the housewife asks only that the room meet her own concept of a kitchen, and Heaven only knows what that is.

GENERAL UTILITY areas of a home can be attractive, as well as convenient . . . portion of wall drops down to make work area table top — Dutch door to carport provides fresh air.

MEXICO CITY EARTHQUAKE

(From Page 3)

LOTTERY BUILDING, at right on mat foundation, is 18 stories high, steel frame and concrete walls, suffered no damage.

Reforma No. 1, at left, built before 1941, was damaged considerably.

Most buildings up to three or four stories high are built on spread footings or mats using a soil pressure of about 2-300#/$\square'$. Settlements of many feet occurred on some of the older structures.

My first reaction in Mexico City was that the effects of this quake were much less severe, but also quite different from those observed in Long Beach and Tehachapi. The highly ornamented stone structures, the towers and churches built since the Sixteenth Century, showed little if any damage. Likewise, most low, rigid type masonry and brick buildings built since the Spanish settlement appear to be in excellent condition. This leads me to believe that this city, for the past three or four centuries, has suffered shocks of comparative moderate intensity only. Many masonry buildings resembling the French Hospital in San Francisco or the old City Hall in San Jose, had no apparent damage. Mr. Jose E. Fernandez, a prominent structural engineer of Mexico City, was kind enough to make available the following summary of damage:

"A study of 320 buildings, out of a total of 1500 damaged, shows that 305 buildings were damaged in the lower section of the city. The damage was classified as follows: Dangerous 9%, Major Damage 16%, Slight Damage 55%. The classification by Structure was: Damaged buildings with steel structure 7%, Damaged Buildings with Concrete structures 36%, Damaged Modern and Old Buildings with Load Bearing brick walls 33%. In some cases there was evidence that resonance occurred, they were simple structures, frames and long columns."

To evaluate the effects of this earthquake, and its relation to our California practice, attention should be called to various aspects of building construction in Mexico. Since the previous severe shocks in 1941, buildings were required to be designed for a horizontal force equal to 2½% of gravity, but these requirements were generally not enforced. Often buildings are designed for architectural appearance and layout only; competitive bids are then taken which include the structural design. In these cases the designing engineers are employees of the contractor, with limited authority and with little if any opportunity to supervise the work. Wages in the construction industry are very low by our standards; concrete is carried in buckets from the mixers to the site by laborers, resulting in more contruction joints than good practice allows.

Some buildings have 4" thick exterior curtain walls consisting of extremely soft brick combined with poor mortar and poor workmanship. This brick can readily be crushed by hand. It was noted that large panels were pushed out or fractured by the more flexible structural frame. The solution to this problem could, I believe, be one of the key objectives of the Mexican building industry. Many modern buildings are enclosed entirely with glass; occasionally they are built with a structural steel frame, but more often with reinforced concrete. Column spacings are quite often small, and partitions are mostly built of clay tile, plastered direct, without mesh.

In Mexico City, about half a dozen structures totally

collapsed, but considerable evidence exists that collapse or severe damage should be attributed to overstress due to the vertical loads and vertical load moments. As a whole, a large portion of the damage was in flexible structures where the natural period of vibration seemed to be in close proximity to the dominant period of the earthquake. In addition, some Mexican engineers believe that destructive effects were greater where the weaker ground prevailed. The vast majority, probably 99% of the structures, seemed to be totally unharmed, most likely the result of peculiar long period action of the quake rather than sound construction.

Latin American Building

A 43-story high structure. Tower about 70' square at the typical floor.

This building represents the most radical departure from usually accepted methods of earthquake design and construction. The frame is built of structural steel and concrete floors.

The building was designed by Adolfo Zeevaert and Professor Newmark by means of a dynamic analysis rather than by static design. Computed horizontal shears in the design resulted in assumptions that are 20% greater at the base and roughly twice as large at the top as compared to the San Francisco Building Code. The building is about 456 feet high plus a 138 foot high tower.

The maximum horizontal shears computed from three modes of vibrations were used in computing overturning moments which resulted in an increase of about 25% of the piles.

Devices were set up in the building to measure deflection at three floors during an earthquake of about

¼" on a typical floor—total top deflection about 12".

The partitions and fireproofing were completely separated from the steel frame. A clearance of ½" was provided between each 4½ x 6' glass panel.

The piles were driven into solid ground about 110' below the curb.

I visited the two sub-basements — several typical floors and the top of the building. I saw no damage of any kind. No glass damage occurred.

Based on measured deflection it was computed that this earthquake stressed the structure to about its designed capacity.

This structure represents a real step forward in its many phases towards a logical solution of the modern skyscraper where full advantage can be taken of the flexibility of a steel frame with small or no property damage.

Lottery Building

This building is 18-stories high—built with a steel frame, and concrete walls. Building was designed for 9% G earthquake loading according to the designer.

The designing Engineer Cuevas told me that no damage of any kind was observed although the structure was built on a mat foundation without any piles. The Engineer first loaded the ground with steel ingots equal to the weight of the building compressing the sills by several feet. To compensate for future unequal subsidence a number of water tanks were installed permitting adjustment which so far have proven to be successful.

In view of the constant moving of the water table in Mexico City, Engineer Cuevas believes that the mat type of foundation possesses many advantages over pile foundation.

The Reforma #1 was badly damaged in 1941 and the July shocks. A Mexican Engineer advised me that the large extent of damage from this earthquake was the result of poor details of previous reconstruction of 1941. He stated that haunches gunited to the columns and gunite walls acted as battering effect during the recent shock.

Reforma #51

This 25-story steel frame is also one of the finest earthquake resistant buildings in Mexico City, designed by Mexican Engineers. I was told that the frame was provided with lateral force coefficient of 5%. The building is supported on piles and is only one bay wide. Partitions were of typical construction, i.e., not separated from the frame.

I walked from the top floor down to the first floor; I saw no damage.

The American Embassy Building—22-story building. Was reported badly damaged with considerable damage on the 15th and 16th floors.

Banco Nationale

The Banco Nationale, widely publicized, was damaged heavily. In Mexico I was told that the collapse was:

1. Caused by a concrete column failure located in the interior pulling steel columns on the outside down.
2. The floor was of grid (waffle) type concrete joists, the shear connection between the floor and the steel frame being very poor failed.
3. Its failure was due to the fact that the slender (steel) columns couldn't take the horizontal thrust without excessive deflection.

It appears that engineers in Mexico enjoy as many differences of opinion as we do.

Conclusion

Mexico City is very beautiful and has many modern structures that are a tribute to the highest skill of their architects and engineers.

Additional information is needed from local professional groups to evaluate further details of these events. It appears, however, that a few pertinent facts stand out as being worthy of our attention at this time.

20-STORY Reforma No. 69 building on left settled four inches and suffered slight exterior damage. Center is 25-story Reforma No. 51, steel frame structure, no damage observed. American Embassy, at right, suffered considerable 15th and 16th floor damage.

1. **Overturning:** Study and pictures indicate that many structures are quite slender, and are resting on soft soil. I found no evidence that any had a tendency to overturn, because the rapid change in the ground motions seem to allow no time for a structure to turn over. While a few buildings showed unequal settlements, some Mexican engineers attributed this to poor details of pile splices and not to overturning effects. On a recent project an architect engaged a seismologist to advise on earthquake loadings. Because of the general lack of masonry walls and masonry partitions, the seismologist suggested a lateral force coefficient over four times as large as that required by the San Francisco Code. Overturning factors were six times as large and would have required a foundation mat 27' thick to provide enough dead weight to prevent column uplift. This illustrates the extreme wide gulf of opinion between engineers and scientists on this basic question.

2. **Foundation Design:** Foundation conditions in Mexico are considered very poor by Mexican engineers. I saw little evidence that serious structural damage developed from settlements attributed to this quake. It seems to me that soil conditions in Mexico City are no worse than in many of the filled-in areas of the Bay Region.

3. **Dampening Effects:** There was considerable evidence that cracking of partitions and exterior walls created a dampening effect, benefiting the safety of many structures.

4. **Flexible Structures:** In these cases, the use of

(See Page 30)

THE OLD and NEW. Structures directly opposite the Reforma Hotel. No damage was observed in either building.

13-STORY concrete structure near Reforma Hotel—note slenderness of building. No damage observed.

collapsed, but considerable evidence exists that collapse or severe damage should be attributed to overstress due to the vertical loads and vertical load moments. As a whole, a large portion of the damage was in flexible structures where the natural period of vibration seemed to be in close proximity to the dominant period of the earthquake. In addition, some Mexican engineers believe that destructive effects were greater where the weaker ground prevailed. The vast majority, probably 99% of the structures, seemed to be totally unharmed, most likely the result of peculiar long period action of the quake rather than sound construction.

Latin American Building

A 43-story high structure. Tower about 70' square at the typical floor.

This building represents the most radical departure from usually accepted methods of earthquake design and construction. The frame is built of structural steel and concrete floors.

The building was designed by Adolfo Zeevaert and Professor Newmark by means of a dynamic analysis rather than by static design. Computed horizontal shears in the design resulted in assumptions that are 20% greater at the base and roughly twice as large at the top as compared to the San Francisco Building Code. The building is about 456 feet high plus a 138 foot high tower.

The maximum horizontal shears computed from three modes of vibrations were used in computing overturning moments which resulted in an increase of about 25% of the piles.

Devices were set up in the building to measure deflection at three floors during an earthquake of about

$\frac{1}{4}$" a typical floor—total top deflection about 12".

The partitions and fireproofing were completely separated from the steel frame. A clearance of $\frac{1}{2}$" was provided between each $4\frac{1}{2}$ x 6' glass panel.

The piles were driven into solid ground about 110' below the curb.

I sited the two sub-basements — several typical floors and the top of the building. I saw no damage of any nd. No glass damage occurred.

Based on measured deflection it was computed that this earthquake stressed the structure to about its design capacity.

This structure represents a real step forward in its many phases towards a logical solution of the modern skyscraper where full advantage can be taken of the flexibility of a steel frame with small or no property damage.

Lottery Building

This building is 18-stories high—built with a steel frame and concrete walls. Building was designed for 9% earthquake loading according to the designer.

The designing Engineer Cuevas told me that no damage of any kind was observed although the structure was built on a mat foundation without any piles. The Engineer first loaded the ground with steel ingots equal to the weight of the building compressing the soil by several feet. To compensate for future unequal subsidence a number of water tanks were installed permitting adjustment which so far have proven to be successful.

In view of the constant moving of the water table in Mexico City, Engineer Cuevas believes that the mat type of foundation possesses many advantages over pile foundation.

The Reforma #1 was badly damaged in 1941 and the July shocks. A Mexican Engineer avised me that the large extent of damage from this erthquake was the result of poor details of previous reonstruction of 1941. He stated that haunches gunited > the columns and gunite walls acted as battering efect during the recent shock.

Reforma #51

This 25-story steel frame is also on of the finest earthquake resistant buildings in Meco City, designed by Mexican Engineers. I wastold that the frame was provided with lateral force coefficient of 5%. The building is supported on pils and is only one bay wide. Partitions were of typica construction, i.e., not separated from the frame.

I walked from the top floor down to he first floor; I saw no damage.

The American Embassy Building—'-story building. Was reported badly damaged wit considerable damage on the 15th and 16th floors.

Banco Nationale

The Banco Nationale, widely publicied, was damaged heavily. In Mexico I was told tha the collapse was:

1. Caused by a concrete column faire located in the interior pulling steel columns n the outside down.
2. The floor was of grid (waffle) ype concrete joists, the shear connection betwee the floor and the steel frame being very poor faed.
3. Its failure was due to the fact tha the slender (steel) columns couldn't take te horizontal thrust without excessive deflection

It appears that engineers in Mexico ejoy as many differences of opinion as we do.

Conclusion

Mexico City is very beautiful and has 1any modern structures that are a tribute to the highe skill of their architects and engineers.

Additional information is needed frm local pro-

20-STORY Reforma No. 69 building on left settled four inches and suffered slight exterior damage. Center is 25-story Reforma No. 51, steel frame structure, no damage observed. American Embassy, at right, suffered considerable 15th and 16th floor damage.

fessional groups to evaluate further details of these events. It appears, however, that a few pertinent facts stand out as being worthy of our attention at this time.

1. **Overturning:** Study and pictures indicate that many structures are quite slender, and are resting on soft soil. I found no evidence that any had a tendency to overturn, because the rapid change in the ground motions seem to allow no time for a structure to turn over. While a few buildings showed unequal settlements, some Mexican engineers attributed this to poor details of pile splices and not to overturning effects. On a recent project an architect engaged a seismologist to advise on earthquake loadings. Because of the general lack of masonry walls and masonry partitions, the seismologist suggested a lateral force coefficient over four times as large as that required by the San Francisco Code. Overturning factors were six times as large and would have required a foundation mat ?' thick to provide enough dead weight to prevent column uplift. This illustrates the extreme wide gulf of opinion between engineers and scientists on this hot question.

2. **Foundation Design:** Foundation conditions in Mexico are considered very poor by Mexican engineers. I saw little evidence that serious damage developed from settlements of the earthquake. It seems to soil con. City are no worse of the Bay Region.

American Institute of Architects

Leon Chatelain, Jr., President

John N. Richards, 1st Vice President
Philip Will, Jr., 2nd Vice President

Edward L. Wilson, Secretary
Raymond S. Kastendieck, Treasurer

Edmund R. Purves, Executive Secretary

National Headquarters—1735 New York Avenue, N. W., Washington, D. C.

REGIONAL DIRECTORS — **Northwest District**, Donald J. Stewart, Portland, Oregon; **Western Mountain District**, Bradley P. Kidder, Santa Fe, New Mexico; **California-Nevada-Hawaii District**, Ulysses Floyd Rible, Los Angeles, Calif.

Arizona Chapters:

CENTRAL ARIZONA: James W. Elmore, President; Martin Ray Young, Jr., Vice-President; Robert T. Cox, Secretary; David Sholder, Treasurer; Ex. Com. Elmore, Cox, Fred Weaver, Richard E. Drover & Ralph Haver. Office of Secy. 1902 E. Camelback Rd., Phoenix.

SOUTHERN ARIZONA: Fred Jobusch, President; Santry C. Fuller, Vice-President; Edward H. Nelson, Secretary; Gerald I. Cain, Treasurer; and Jobusch, Nelson, E. D. Herreras, Ellsworth Ellwood, and Emerson C. Scholer, Exec. Comm. Office of Secy. 234 E. 6th St., Tucson.

Coast Valleys Chapter:

William L. Higgins (San Jose), President; Paul J. Huston (Palo Alto), Vice-President; William H. Daseking (Menlo Park), Treasurer; Edward N. Chamberlain (San Jose), Secretary. Office of Secy., 390 Park Ave., San Jose.

Central Valley of California:

Edward H. de Wolf (Stockton), President; Whitson Cox (Sacramento), Vice-President; Joe Jozens (Sacramento), Secretary; Albert M. Dreyfuss (Sacramento), Treasurer. Directors: Doyt Early (Sacramento), Jack Whipple (Stockton). Office of Secty., 914 11th St., Sacramento.

Colorado Chapter:

Casper F. Hegner, President; C. Gordon Sweet, Vice President; Norton Polivnick, Secretary; Richard Williams, Treasurer. Directors: James M. Hunter, Robert K. Fuller, Edward L. Bunts. Office of Secy., 1225 Bannock St., Denver, Colorado.

East Bay Chapter:

Hachiro Yuasa (Oakland), President; George T. Kern (Oakland), Vice-President; William M. Gillis (San Francisco), Secretary; J. A. Zerkle (Berkeley), Treasurer. Directors H. B. Clausen. F. A. Lockwood, John Oyarzo, G. M. McCue. Marjorie Montgomery, Ex. Secy. Office of Secy., Mezzanine, Hotel Claremont, Berkeley 5.

Idaho Chapter:

Anton E. Dropping, Boise, President; Charles W. Johnston, Payette, Vice-President; Glenn E. Cline, Boise, Sec.-Treas. Executive Committee, Chester L. Shawver and Nat J. Adams, Boise. Office of Sec., 624 Idaho Bldg., Boise.

Monterey Bay Chapter:

Thomas S. Elston, Jr., President (Carmel); Robert Stanton, Vice-President (Carmel); George F. Rhoda, Secretary (Monterey); Walter Burde, Treasurer. Office of Secty., 2281 Prescott St., Monterey.

Montana Chapter:

William J. Hess, President (Great Falls); John E. Toohey, Vice-President (Billings); H. C. Cheever, Sec.-Tress. (Bozeman). Directors: Oscar J. Ballas, Wm. J. Hess, John E. Toohey. Office of Secy., Bozeman, Montana.

Nevada Chapter:

RENO: Lawrence A. Gulling, President; William E. Cowell, Vice-President; Albert W. Alegre, Secretary; Ralph A. Casazza, Treasurer. Graham Erskine, Raymond M. Hellman, George L. F. O'Brien, Directors. Office of the Secy., 500 Plumas St., Reno.

PASADENA CHAPTER AIA

February's meeting was a visit to the Stuart Company's new pharmaceutical plant in Pasadena, where Edward D. Stone, architect of the building, described construction on a tour of the property. Stone is also the architect of the Museum of Modern Art in New York City, the United States Embassy in New Delhi, India, and the American Pavilion for the Brussels World's Fair.

Recent new members include: John J. Harman, Jr., 625 E. Comstock Ave., Glendora.

COAST VALLEYS CHAPTER AIA

Architect Ernest J. Kump was the featured speaker at a recent meeting in Los Altos, taking as his subject "Space Module Schools".

Announcement has been made of the appointment of an Executive Secretary. Mrs. Katherine Jenks, 18921 Loree Ave., Cupertino, will serve in this capacity.

WASHINGTON STATE CHAPTER AIA

Architect Paul Thiry's picture slide tour of South America featured the February meeting held in the Sorrento Hotel in Seattle. John Detlie made a brief report on the activities of the national committee of which he is a member, the Architectural Museum

Committee. The Seminar and Education Committee sponsored a "Public Design" Seminar on February 20, including discussion of public structures, freeways, tunnels, bridges.

ARCHITECT A. H. ALBERTSON HONORED:

Marking the 50th anniversary of the founding of his architectural practice in Seattle, friends and associates of A. H. Albertson, FAIA, gathered at his home recently. Among those present were: William J. Bain, Lincoln Bouillon, Edward Graef, J. Lister Holmes, Arthur Loveless, Earnest Osgood, John Stevenson and Frank Stanton.

SAN FRANCISCO ARCHITECTURAL CLUB

Discussion of San Francisco's latest fire laws and building code featured the February meeting held in the Club, 507 Howard Street. First "Field Trip" of the new year was to the new Westmoor High School in Daly City with architect of the project Mario Ciampi conducting a tour of the project. Junior AIA members participated in the tour.

PRODUCERS COUNCIL SEMINAR

Technological developments in curtain wall panel construction will be the subject of a building industry

seminar in San Francisco Monday, March 17. At an all-day session in the Sheraton-Palace Hotel in San Francisco, local architects, structural engineers, contractors and other interested people will have an opportunity to learn of the latest developments in this field resulting from the extensive research programs currently being conducted by many building products' manufacturers.

The program is being sponsored by the Producers' Council, Inc.—the national organization of building products manufacturers and associations—in conjunction with its San Francisco chapter.

In explaining the purpose of the meeting, Chapter President John O'Connor of H. H. Robertson Company stated, "Curtain wall panel construction, which is a comparatively recent development, refers to the enclosing of a structure with various types of panels

which are fastened to the structural frame, but do not support the weight of the building. Top research and product development experts from several firms will speak on important aspects of this subject."

He added, "The seminar will also be highlighted by an exhibition of products utilized in this type of building."

Permanent speakers who will represent various phases of the construction industry where curtain walls would be used, will present specialized discussions in the particular subjects where they are qualified to talk. The all-day meeting will have such qualified speakers who will cover subjects such as: design and fabrication, erection, types of sealants, joints and flashings, aluminum, masonry, steel, glass, types of panels, specification studies, auxiliary construction,

(See Page 30)

WITH THE ENGINEERS

SOCIETY OF AMERICAN MILITARY ENGINEERS—SAN FRANCISCO POST

Captain James Douglas, CEC, USN, was the principal speaker at the February meeting held in the Officers Club, Presidio of San Francisco, taking as his subject "Operation Deep-Freeze." Captain Douglas gave many interesting comments on his activities as Director, Seebee Division, Bureau Of Yards and Docks, in the Armed Forces support of the International Geophysical Year expedition to the South Pole. He was associated with the planning and administrative phases of Operation Deep Freeze from its incep-

tion to the actual landing and all support construction including runway and dock facilities. Many of the activities were illustrated by slides.

Annual Dinner Dance, honoring retiring president C. R. Graff and officers, has been scheduled for March 21 in the Officers Club, Presidio of San Francisco.

STRUCTURAL ENGINEERS ASSOCIATION OF SOUTHERN CALIFORNIA

A panel discussion on the subject "Where Are We Going in Engineering Education," featured the February meeting held in the Rodger Young Auditorium, Los Angeles, with panel members comprising: R. E. Vivian, Dean, School of Engineering, University of Southern California, who discussed the phase "Professional vs. Technical Level Trends in Engineering Education from the Technical Subject Standpoint"; Daniel E. Whelan, Jr., Dean of Engineering, Loyola University discussed "The Distribution of Humanities and Social Studies Courses in the College Curriculum; Charles F. Horne, vice president and division manager of Convair, Pomona, who discussed "Salaries and Qualifications in Developing College Faculties"; and Murray Erick, Consulting Structural Engineer, who discussed "Practicing Structural Engineers Requirements for New Engineering Graduates."

Recent new members include: George W. Coleman, Bernard K. Kent, John D. Lemons, Robert D. Lichti, and Philip H. Skarin, Members; Samuel J. Colyer, Affiliate; Richard L. Hegle, Associate, and Chang J. Park, Student.

AMERICAN SOCIETY OF CIVIL ENGINEERS SAN FRANCISCO SECTION

Francis N. Hveem, Materials and Research Engineer with the State of California, Division of Highways, was the principal speaker at the February meeting, discussing the various aspects of the project sponsored by the American Association of State Highway Officials to construct a highway test track in the State of Illinois with funds contributed by 47 states, three territories, the Bureau of Public Roads, Automobile manufacturers and other interested agencies. Some

$23,000,000 is being spent on the project, to determine 1) Engineering facts concerning design of highways and bridges, 2) Information for betterment of existing pavements; 3) Arrive at an engineering basis for legislation for design loading; 4) Provide information to highway equipment manufacturers, and 5) Provide information concerning cost of highways.

STRUCTURAL ENGINEERS ASSOCIATION OF NORTHERN CALIFORNIA

Mario G. Salvadori, Professor of Civil Engineering, Columbia University, was the speaker at a joint meeting of SEANC, AIA and ASCE members in the Fairmont Hotel, taking as his subject: "Thin Shell Structure." Numerous slides were used to illustrate his remarks on unusual structures designed by the speaker which resemble giant sea shells. By using a series of curved surfaces formed of reinforced concrete his structures achieve the characteristics of strength and rigidity found in such natural shapes as sea shells, egg shells, and even soap bubbles.

J. Albert Paquette, Structural Engineer of San Francisco, was elected President of the SEANC to serve

J. ALBERT PAQUETTE
President SEANC

for the ensuing year. He is a graduate from the University of Toronto School of Applied Science with a degree of BASC.

From 1926 to 1930 he was associated with Smith Hinchman and G r y l l s, Architects and Engineers of Detroit. From 1930 to 1931 he was with Sydney E. Junkins Co., of Vancouver, B.C. He joined the late F. W. Kellberg in San Francisco in 1932 and became a partner in what is now known as Kellberg, Paquette & Maurer.

Paquette was licensed as a Structural Engineer in California in 1934. He is active in the San Francisco Section of the American Society of Civil Engineers, and his wife, Lois is presently serving as Vice President of the Femineers, an organization of wives of members of the American Society of Civil Engineers and the Structural Engineers Association of Northern California. He has two children, a boy in College, and a daughter attending high school.

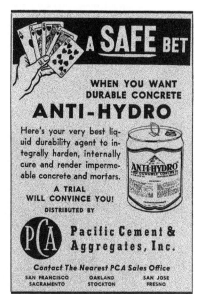

MEXICO CITY EARTHQUAKE

(From Page 25)

structural steel as a moment resisting frame appears advisable. The high resistance of steel in shear, tension and its ductility in case of large movements should minimize major failures. The design for vertical loads should account for secondary stresses and provide for the effects of deflection. The Latino-American Building furnishes an excellent example of how flexible structures can be built with adequate safety and a minimum of property damage.

5. **Property Damage:** Proportionately, damage in certain modern tall structures was high. The cost of repairs, loss of revenue and loss of confidence by the public in the stability of the building represent a major financial problem. It appears to me that our local practice to build rigid walls with a flexible frame has much merit. The wall elements are adequate to resist moderately strong quakes and provide long range property protection. A. moment resisting frame acts after cracking of the walls but furnishes added ultimate resistance to severe shocks.

6. **New Type Buildings:** The use of all glass exterior walls and metal partitions for taller buildings raises many new problems. This type represents a radical departure from the older practice that has successfully survived shocks. The progressive cracking-up of plaster and wall elements furnished a welcome relief to our many factors of ignorance. For new types, more consideration should be given to deflections and the dynamic characteristics of the structural system. A prominent Mexican engineer, Mr. Jose A. Cuevas, suggested a research program sponsored by the United Nations which should include seismic loadings of the modern skyscraper.

7. **Basic Earthquake Loadings:** Honesty of design and construction are still fundamental factors in earth-quake resistant design. Based on my observations in Mexico City, Long Beach, Tehachapi, and studies of other California earthquakes, it seems that the present San Francisco Building Code is amply conservative. Its provisions for the design of low rigid buildings appear sufficient to protect life and to prevent large property damage. The Code's recognition of the merit of flexibility to achieve safety with economy represents progress in seismic design.

The Mexican authorities have now adopted a new code governing the earthquake design of buildings. This code sets up lateral force requirements in some cases 2-3 times as severe as our San Francisco Code. I feel confident that these provisions, unnecessarily conservative, will give way to more considerate judgment as the hysteria of the July events no longer prevails.

ACKNOWLEDGEMENT: Mr. Fred Merritt; Mr. John E. Kearny; Mr. Jose A. Cuevas; Mr. Jose E. Fernandez; Dr. Emilio Rosenblueth; Mr. Federico De Palacio; Mr. Candella.

PRODUCERS' COUNCIL SEMINAR

(From Page 26)

and other points.

Several nationally known authorities on these subjects will be among those who will present the topics.

The sessions will start around 9 a.m. and continue throughout the day.

This is one in a series of such seminars to be conducted by the Producers' Council in the major marketing areas of the nation. Nationally known firms will be participating in the discussions and the exhibits.

The Producers' Council was organized 36 years ago as a manufacturers' committee of the American Institute of Architects. Since its incorporation in 1929, it has maintained an affiliation with the A.I.A.

SAN DIEGO CHAPTER AIA INSTALLS NEW OFFICERS

The San Diego Chapter AIA and Women's Architectural League recently conducted a "annual meeting" and dinner with many prominent architects and guests attending. It also served as an "installation," with officers of both organizations taking office.

OFFICER INSTALLATION—San Diego Chapter AIA (l. to r.): Sim Bruce Richards, Past President; Glenn Balch, President, California Council AIA, and Raymond Lee Eggers, new Chapter President.

CALIFORNIA STATE POLYTECHNIC COLLEGE ARCHITECTURAL EXHIBIT

The California State Polytechnic College, San Luis Obispo, will present its 26th annual Poly Royal on April 25-26, planned and produced entirely by students at the "learn-by-doing" campus.

Among featured department displays will be an exhibit featuring the work of the architectural students at the college. Campus tours, rodeo, carnival, dances and a variety of entertainment will be offered visitors during the two-day event.

ERLE T. PLUMMER NAMED GENERAL SALES MANAGER OF UNION ASBESTOS

Erle T. Plummer has been named general sales manager of the Union Asbestos & Rubber Company's Fibrous Products Division, according to an announcement by Edwin E. Hokin, president.

Plummer, a native of Alameda, California, began his business career with the Wells Fargo Bank in San Francisco in 1939. He joined UNARCO in 1950 as a sales representative for the Fibrous Products Division in the San Francisco office and later served in a similar capacity in the company's Houston, Texas, office. He will now make his headquarters in Chicago.

J. J. DURKIN IS NAMED SEATTLE DISTRICT MANAGER

J. J. Durkin has been named Seattle district manager for the "Automatic" Sprinkler Corpn. of America, according to an announcement by W. E. O'Neill, sales manager.

Durkin has been a Contracting Engineer for the firm in New York City since joining the firm in 1946. He is an associate member of the National Fire Protection Association.

WILLARD WOODROW WINS GAS INDUSTRY AWARD

Willard Woodrow of Bellflower, California, has been awarded the 1957 Gas Industry Builder Award in recognition of outstanding contributions to the home building industry.

The award, first of its kind to be made by the billion-dollar gas industry, was presented to Woodrow by C. S. Stackpole, managing director of the American Gas Association during the National Association of Home Builders' Convention in Chicago the latter part of January.

The award is based on builders' advanced methods of production, use of new materials and equipment, and modern merchandising techniques. As president of the Aldon Construction Company, Woodrow, has built his company's reputation on giving the public quality homes at moderate prices. His company has built and sold more than 26,000 homes in Southern California and Arizona.

SCHOOL DESIGN FORUM HELD BY TACOMA LUMBERMEN

A state educational official, local educator and architect discussed "school design" at a meeting held in the Winthrop Hotel, Spokane this month, sponsored by the Tacoma Lumbermen's Club.

Corydon Wagner, Jr., club president, declared the meeting was "to take an objective look at the commonsense use of wood in creative school design," and to "seriously consider modern uses of wood in school design" as a factor in meeting Tacoma's need for additional school facilities.

Speakers at the Forum included: Lloyd J. Andrews, State Superintendent of Public Instruction; Robert B. Price, AIA, Architect, and James Hopkins, Assistant Superintendent of Tacoma schools.

GORDON F. THRUELSEN GENERAL SALES MANAGER LOS ANGELES FARR CO.

Gordon F. Thruelsen has been appointed general sales manager of the Farr Company, Los Angeles, manufacturers of air filtration equipment, according to a recent announcement.

He was formerly general manager of Dust Control, Inc., a Farr Company subsidiary and their Southern California sales and certified filter service representative. He will be in charge of all marketing operations for the commercial-industrial, railroad and electronic sales divisions, which formerly was under the direction of President R. S. Farr.

ARCHITECT CONTINI SPEAKER

Edgardo Contini, partner in the Architectural firm of Victor Gruen Associates, Beverly Hills, was a guest speaker at the Annual Meeting of the American Institute of Planners, California Chapter, held in the Riverside Hotel, Riverside, the first part of this month.

Contini spoke before the group on the subject "The Downtown Area," and discussed the new concepts of urban development and the approaches his organization has made to solve the problem in the central business district.

Here is the
DISTINGUISHED APPEARANCE
that only
HAWS
can give

Model 77—Semi-recessed

HAWS Model 77 is a brilliant departure from stereotyped drinking facilities...ready to match the imagination and dignity of your project, superbly styled, precision-engineered. Model 77 is a semi-recessed wall fountain—in durable vitreous china, available in striking colors, with automatic volume and pressure controls. And the same design is available in stainless steel (Model 73); or in remarkably tough, lightweight fiberglass (Model 69, in choice of colors at no extra cost).

WRITE FOR DETAILS
Ask for HAWS complete new catalog, too!

For nearly 50 years, HAWS has provided finer drinking facilities to match forward-looking architectural design. Here's a design in vitreous china, stainless steel and fiberglass worthy of your attention.

HAWS DRINKING FAUCET COMPANY
1441 FOURTH STREET (Since 1909) BERKELEY 10, CALIFORNIA

SAN FRANCISCO ARCHITECTURAL CLUB AGAIN OFFERS SEMINAR

The San Francisco Architectural Club is offering an architectural seminar, or review course, for those who plan to take the examination of the California State Board of Architectural Examiners this year.

The seminar will consist of twenty-three lectures given by well qualified men of the architectural and engineering profession and will cover all the divisions of the examination. With a few exceptions, the seminar lectures will be given only once a week, thus affording an opportunity to read reference material between class meetings. Each lecture will last approximately two hours, and the first will be given on Monday, February 3rd.

Instructors for this year's Spring Seminar include: Clyde E. Bentley, Consulting Engineer, San Francisco; Leo E. Dwyer, Mechanical Engineer with Clyde E. Bentley, Lecturer, Extension Division, U. of C.; Don Ralston, Electrical Engineer, San Francisco; Donald Powers Smith, AIA, Architect, San Francisco; Clement A. Mullins, AIA, Architect, Bureau of Architecture, City of San Francisco; Howard Moise, Architect, Berkeley; Gordon Dean, Civil and Structural Engineer, San Francisco; and Clyde F. Trudell, Architect, San Francisco.

MODERN PRODUCTS

The demands of today's architecture have brought about radical changes in the design and construction of doors for horizontal access. Shown here is a modern out-of-sight roof design that continues a stair tower right up to roof level with a normal rise and run of steps and without need of the old fashioned Pent House type of construction. The roof scuttle has a clear opening of 2'6" x 8'0", and can be obtained from the manufacturer in any special size to suit any architectural requirements.

Manufactured by the Bilco Company, manufactur-

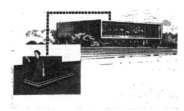

NEW BILCO PRODUCT

ers and designers of a complete line of "Spring-balanced" doors that will meet the need for access through any horizontal surface, whether it be a roof, a ceiling, a floor or a sidewalk. The firm has pioneered the application of built-in springs for effortless operation and the use of new materials for life-long, trouble-free service.

RELIGIOUS BUILDINGS FOR TODAY. By John Knox Shear, AIA. F. W. Dodge Corp., 119 W. 40th St., New York 18, N.Y.

Here is a stimulating collection of recently completed religious building projects from many areas of the world, selected and edited by John Knox Shear, AIA, Editor-in-Chief of Architectural Record. Each case study includes interior and exterior photographs, with detailed floor plans; many structural diagrams are also shown, exemplifying a great variety of faiths, sites, budgets, program requirements, structural methods, and attitudes. The choice of projects was highly selective. The book is a valuable addition to the library of clergymen of all faiths, architects, religious building committees, and for anyone interested in learning more of both the practical and the esthetic significance of this most important segment of the world's architectural culture.

SOLAR RADIATION IN AIR CONDITIONING. By Ivor S. Groundwater, A.M.I. Mech. E., John De Graff, Inc., 31 E. 10th St., New York 3, N.Y. Price $5.00.

Written primarily for the consulting engineer, architect, and air-conditioning engineer, this book is useful in that it deals factually with the most difficult problem in air conditioning— solar radiation. The first part deals with the source of solar design data, and of building absorption coefficients. Next, ways of reducing the flow of solar heat into roofs are discussed, and finally the various ways are tabulated to show their advantages and disadvantages from several points of view. Methods of calculation favored by successful commercial enterprise in the East are surveyed and answers tabulated for ease of comparison.

BASIC SOILS ENGINEERING. By B. K. Hough, Prof. Civil Engineering, Cornell University. The Ronald Press Co., 15 E. 26th St., New York 10, N.Y. Price $8.00.

It is generally agreed that the analytical approach to investigation of the engineering behavior of soil was first brought to the attention of many engineers in this country by the work of Dr. Karl Terzaghi, which began to gain recognition in the mid-twenties. Initiation of courses of instruction in the subject in engineering courses did not become general until after World War II. In this book, information on fundamental properties of soil has been assembled, not only from engineering sources, but from agronomy and the soil sciences and is presented in engineering terms. Throughout the text, numerous illustrative examples are given as an aid to explanation of the subject material, and at the end of each chapter an unusual number of questions and problems has been provided for use as assignments in courses of instruction.

NEW CATALOGUES AVAILABLE

Architects. Engineers. Contractors, Planning Commission members—the catalogues. folders, new building products material. etc.. described below may be obtained by directing your request to the name and address given in each item.

Sidewall panels for industrial sound control. Newly published brochure (AIA FILE No. 37-B-1) describes Tectum sidewall panels; numerous illustrations, drawings, design data. Specifications, and complete description of product and its uses. Free copy write DEPT-A&E, Cramer Acoustics, 560-9th St., San Francisco.

"Beyond the water mains." New, 28-page, illustrated booklet outlines history of man's search for water and his development of mechanical means of delivering it for domestic uses; sketches the story of water from Genesis through current times; of particular interest to engineers, contractors, educational leaders, engineering schools, distributors of water systems, and architects. For free copy write DEPT-A&E, Franklin Electric Co., Inc., 350 E. Spring St., Bluffton, Indiana.

Lighting, miniature troffers. New brochure highlighting "Miniature" troffers which are just 5" wide and 4" deep; also 8" and 12"-wide troffers, which are 6" in depth; accommodate two lamps despite their extremely narrow width, and require less headroom due to their extra shallow depth; 24",

36" and 48" lengths with choice of six frame finishes and 5 light diffusers; 8" and 12" troffers available in 24" and 48" lengths, variety of diffusers and frame finishes. Free copy, write Dept-A&E, Alkco Mfg. Co., 4242 Lincoln Ave., Chicago 18, Ill.

Construction data handbook. New pocket size Construction Data Handbook just published by A. C. Horn Co., Inc., subsidiary of Sun Chemical Corp., is available to engineers, contractors, purchasing agents, and architects. Completely revised, contains 160 pages with detailed information on almost 100 Horn construction and maintenance specialities; over 30 construction tables, guides and time saving charts; indexes streamlined for quick reference and easy use; each product concisely described. Free copy write DEPT-A&E, A. C. Horn Co., Inc., 10th St. & 44th Ave., Long Island City, N. Y.

Latex emulsion and oil paint guide. Two-color, 12-page "paintcyclopedia" features comprehensive specification chart for all interior surfaces; also includes section on specifying paint for metal surfaces and machinery; 2 pages devoted to general painting specifications and surface preparation; brief description of 74 products. Free copy write DEPT-A&E, Paint Selector, Luminall Paints, Chicago 9, Ill.

Public address and high fidelity loudspeakers. New 12-page, illustrated catalog describes public address and high fidelity loudspeakers for use in mining, construction and architectural fields; full product descriptions, specifications and application information as well as prices, also list and description of accessories. Free copy write DEPT-A&E, University Loudspeakers Inc., 80 S. Kensico Ave., White Plains, N. Y.

Handrail systems. Two-color brochure (AIA FILE 14-D-4) describes and illustrates new handrail system that makes possible sharp reductions in railing installation costs; eliminates need for detail design, templates, prefabrication or welding and permits a finished job on site, without waste or scrap; Complete details write DEPT-A&E, Universal Railing Co., 275 Klamath, Denver 23, Colorado.

Heavy duty shoring. New booklet describes heavy duty shoring for bridges, overpasses, and heavy slab work; numerous detail drawings and descriptions of design applications. Free copy write DEPT-A&E, Laurence Myers Scaffolding Co., 61 Bluxome St., San Francisco.

Where to buy. More than 200 mills in Oregon, Washington and northern California producing Douglas Fir, West Coast hemlock, Western Red Cedar and Sitka spruce lumber are listed in the 1958 edition of "Where-To-Buy"; the 40-page book included WCLA member mills and detailed information on lumber fabricating and treating plants in the Douglas fir region; lists key personnel, capacity and facilities of each member and product. Free copy, write DEP-A&E, West Coast Lumbermen's Association, 1410 S. W. Morrison St., Portland 5, Oregon.

Doors for special services. New two-color catalog, describes in detail, with design, specifications, and photographs, various types and installations of a wide variety of doors for all purposes; Roof scuttles, and ceiling access doors; interior/exterior doors for sidewalk; basement doors. For free copy write DEPT-A&E, The Bilco Company, New Haven 5, Conn.

ESTIMATOR'S GUIDE

BUILDING AND CONSTRUCTION MATERIALS

PRICES GIVEN ARE FIGURING PRICES AND ARE MADE UP FROM AVERAGE QUOTATIONS FURNISHED BY
LeROY CONSTRUCTION SERVICES. 4% SALES TAX ON ALL MATERIALS BUT NOT LABOR.

All prices and wages quoted are for San Francisco and the Bay District. There may be slight fluctuation of prices in the interior and southern part of the state. Freight cartage and labor travel time must be added in figuring country work.

BONDS—Performance or Performance plus Labor and Material Bond(s), $10 per $1000 on contract price. Labor & Material Bond(s) only, $5.00 per $1000 on contract price.

BRICKWORK—MASONRY—

BUILDING BRICK—estimated cost per sq. ft.

WALL	BRICK	AVERAGE
8"	Jumbo	$2.30
8"	Norman	2.40
10"	Standard	2.40
12"	Jumbo	2.55
14"	Standard	2.60

FACE BRICK—estimated cost per sq. ft.

WALL	BRICK	AVERAGE
8"	Jumbo	$2.55
8"	Brick Block	2.30
10"	Standard	2.60
10"	Norman	2.80
14"	Norman	3.05

Common Brick—Per 1 M laid—$175.00 up (according to class of work).
Face Brick—Per 1 M laid—$265.00 and up (according to class of work).
Brick Steps—$2.75 per lin. ft. & up.

BRICK VENEER

BUILDING BRICK—estimated cost per sq. ft.

WALL	BRICK	AVERAGE
3"	Jumbo	$1.15
3"	Norman	.25
4"	Standard	.40

FACE BRICK—estimated cost per sq. ft.

WALL	BRICK	AVERAGE
3"	Jumbo	$1.35
4"	Standard	1.60
4"	Norman	1.50
4"	Roman	1.80

Common Brick Veneer on Frame Bldgs.—Approx. $1.75 and up—(according to class of work).
Face Brick Veneer on Frame Bldgs—Approx. $2.25 and up (according to class of work).
"Bricketts" (Brick Veneer) per M, f.o.b. Niles, $50.00.

Glazed Structural Units—Walls Erected—
Clear Glazed—

2 x 6 12 Furring	$1.95 per sq. ft.
4 x 6 x 12 Partition	2.25 per sq. ft.
4 x 6 x 12 Double Faced Partition	2.50 per sq. ft.
For colored glaze add	.30 per sq. ft.

Mantel Fire Brick $150.00 per M—F.O.B. Pittsburgh.
Fire Brick—2½"x9x4½—$110.00.
Cartage—Approx. $10.00 per M.
Paving—$75.00.

Building Tile—

8x5½x12-inches, per M		$159.40
6x5½x12-inches, per M		124.00
4x5½x12-inches, per M		96.90

Hollow Tile—

12x12x3-inches, per M		156.85
12x12x4-inches, per M		177.10
12x12x6-inches, per M		235.30

F.O.B. Plant

BUILDING PAPER & FELTS—

1 ply per 1000 ft. roll	$5.30
2 ply per 1000 ft. roll	7.80
3 ply per 1000 ft. roll	9.70
Brownskin, Standard 500 ft. roll	6.85
Sisalkraft, reinforced, 500 ft. roll	8.50

Sheathing Papers—

Asphalt sheathing, 15-lb. roll	$2.70
30-lb. roll	3.70
Dampcourse, 216-ft. roll	2.95
Blue Plasterboard, 60-lb. roll	5.10

Felt Papers—

Deadening felt, ¾-lb., 50-ft. roll	$4.30
Deadening felt, 1-lb.	5.05
Asphalt roofing, 15-lbs.	2.70
Asphalt roofing, 30-lbs.	3.70

Roofing Papers—

Standard Grade, 108-ft. roll, Light	$2.50
Smooth Surface, Medium	2.90
Heavy	3.40
M. S. Extra Heavy	3.95

CONCRETE AGGREGATES—

The following prices net to Contractors unless otherwise shown. Carload lots only.

	Bunker per ton	Del'd per ton
Gravel, all sizes	$3.10	$3.90
Top Sand	3.30	4.10
Concrete Mix	3.20	4.00
Crushed Rock, ¼" to ¾"	3.30	4.10
Crushed Rock, ¾" to 1½"	3.30	4.10
Roofing Gravel	3.25	4.15

Sand—

Lapis (Nos. 2 & 4)	4.05	4.95
Olympia (Nos. 1 & 2)	3.35	3.95

Cement—
Common (all brands, paper sacks),
Per Sack, small quantity (paper) $1.35
Carload lots, in bulk, per bbl............ 4.14
Cash discount on carload lots, 10c a bbl., 10th Prox., less than carload lots, $5.20 per bbl. f.o.b. warehouse or $5.60 delivered.

Cash discount on L.C.L. 2%

Trinity White	1 to 100 sacks, $4.00
Medusa White	sack, warehouse or delivered.

CONCRETE READY-MIX—

Delivered in 5-yd. loads; 6 sk.
in bulk $14.80
Curing Compound, clear, drums,
per gal. .... .90

CONCRETE BLOCKS—

	Haydite	Basalt
4x8x16-inches, each	$ .22½	$ .22½
6x8x16-inches, each	.28½	.28½
8x8x16-inches, each	.33	.33
12x8x16-inches, each	.49	.49½
12x8x24-inches, each	.46	.70

Aggregates—Haydite or Basalite Plant

¾-inch to ⅜-inch, per cu. yd.	$6.00	$7.50
⅜-inch to ⅜-inch, per cu. yd.	6.00	7.50
No. 6 to 0-inch, per cu. yd.	6.00	7.50

DAMPPROOFING and Waterproofing—

Two-coat work; $9.00 per square and up.
Membrane waterproofing—4 layers of saturated felt, $13.00 per square and up.
Hot coating work, $5.50 per square and up.
Medusa Waterproofing, $3.50 per lb. San Francisco Warehouse.
Tricosal concrete waterproofing, 60c a cubic yd. and up.
Anhi Hydro, 50 gal., $2.20.

ELECTRIC WIRING—$20 to $25 per outlet for conduit work (including switches) $18-20. Knob and tube average $7.00 to 9.00 per outlet.

ELEVATORS—

Prices vary according to capacity, speed and type. Consult elevator companies. Average cost of installing a slow speed automatic passenger elevator in small four story apartment building, including entrance doors, about $9,500.00.

EXCAVATION—

Sand, $1.25, clay or shale, $2.00 per yard.
Trucks, $35 to $55 per day.
Above figures are an average without water. Steam shovel work in large quantities, less; hard material, such as rock, will run considerably more.

FIRE ESCAPES—

Ten-foot galvanized iron balcony, with stairs, $275 installed on new buildings; $325 on old buildings.

FLOORS—

Asphalt Tile, ⅛ in. gauge 25c to 35c per sq. ft.
Composition Floors, such as Magnesite, 50c-$1.25 per sq. ft.
Linoleum, standard gauge, $3.75 sq. yd. & up laid.
Mastipave—$1.90 per sq. yd.
Battleship Linoleum—$6.00 sq. yd. & up laid.
Terazzo Floors—$2.50 per sq. ft.
Terazzo Steps—$3.75 per lin. ft.
Mastic Wear Coat—according to type—45c per sq. ft. and up.

Hardwood Flooring—
Oak Flooring—T & G—Unfin.—

	⅜⅜x2¼	½x2	⅜x2	⅜x2
Clear Qtd., White	$425	$405	$	$
Clear Qtd., Red	405	380		
Select Qtd., Red or White	355	340		
Clear Pln., Red or White	355	340	335	315
Select Pln., Red or White	340	330	325	300
#1 Common, red or White	315	310	305	280
#2 Common, Red or White	305			

Prefinished Oak Flooring—

		Prime	Standard
½ x 2		$369.00	$359.00
x 2½		380.00	370.00
x 2¼		390.00	380.00
x 2¼		390.00	355.00
x 2¼		395.00	375.00
x 2¼ & ¾ Ranch Plank			415.00

Unfinished Maple Flooring—

			Prime	Standard
⅜⅜ x 2¼ First Grade			$390.00	
⅜⅜ x 2¼ 2nd & Btr. Grade			365.00	
⅜⅜ x 2¼ 3rd Grade			375.00	
⅜⅜ x 2¼ 2nd Grade			240.00	
⅜ x 3¼ 3rd & Btr. Jtd. EM			380.00	
⅜ x 3½ 2nd & Btr. Jtd. EM			390.00	
33/32 x 2¼ First Grade			400.00	
33/32 x 2¼ 2nd Grade			360.00	
33/32 x 2¼ 3rd Grade			320.00	

Floor Layer Wage $2.83 per hr.

GLASS—

Single Strength Window Glass	$ .30 per ☐ ft.
Single Strength Window Glass	$ .30 per ☐ ft.
Double Strength Window Glass	.60 per ☐ ft.
Plate Glass, ¼ polished to 75	1.80 per ☐ ft.
75 to 100	2.10 per ☐ ft.
¼ in. Polished Wire Plate Glass	2.70 per ☐ ft.
¼ in. Rgh. Wire Glass	.80 per ☐ ft.
⅛ in. Obscure Glass	.55 per ☐ ft.
⅞ in. Obscure Glass	.70 per ☐ ft.
⅛ in. Heat Absorbing Obscure	.54 per ☐ ft.
⅛ in. Heat Absorbing Wire	.72 per ☐ ft.
⅛ in. Ribbed	.55 per ☐ ft.
⅛ in. Ribbed	.75 per ☐ ft.
⅛ in. Rough	.55 per ☐ ft.
⅛ in. Rough	.75 per ☐ ft.
Glazing of above additional $.15 to .30 per ☐ ft.
Glass Blocks, set in place	3.50 per ☐ ft.

HEATING—Installed

Furnaces—Gas Fired

Floor Furnace, 25,000 BTU	$42.00-80.00
35,000 BTU	47.00-87.00
45,000 BTU	55.00-95.00
Automatic Control, Add	39.00-45.00
Dual Wall Furnaces, 25,000 BTU	72.00-134.00
35,000 BTU	149.00
45,000 BTU	161.00
With Automatic Control, Add	45.00-161.00
Unit Heaters, 50,000 BTU	215.00
Gravity Furnace, 65,000 BTU	210.00
Forced Air Furnace, 75,000 BTU	342.00

Water Heaters—5-year guarantee
With Thermostat Control,

20 gal. capacity	96.00
30 gal. capacity	112.00
40 gal. capacity	135.00

INSULATION AND WALLBOARD—

Rockwool Insulation—
Full thick 3" $66.00
(2") Less than 1,000 □ ft. 64.00
(2") Over 1,000 □ ft. 59.00
Cotton Insulation—Full-thickness (1") .... $41.60 per M sq. ft.
Sisalation Aluminum Insulation—Aluminum coated on both sides .... $23.50 per M sq. ft.
Tileboard—4'x6' panel .... $9.00 per panel
Wallboard—½" thickness .... $55.00 per M sq. ft.
Finished Plank .... 69.00 per M sq. ft.
Ceiling Tileboard .... 69.00 per M sq. ft.

IRON—Cost of ornamentai iron, cast iron, etc., depends on designs.

LUMBER—Ex Lumber Yards

S4S Construction Grade
O.P. or D.F., per M. f.b.m. $105.00

Flooring—

Per M Delvd

V.G.-D.F. B & Btr. 1 x 4 T & G Flooring $215.00
"C" and better—all 205.00
"D" and better—all 135.00
Rwd. Rustic—"A" grade, medium dry 8 to 24 ft. 185.00

Plywood, per M sq. ft.
¼-inch, 4.0x8.0-S1S $110.00
½-inch, 4.0x8.0-S1S 190.00
¾-inch, per M sq. ft. 240.00
Plysform 220.00

Shingles (Rwd. not available)—
Red Cedar No. 1—$12.25 per square; No. 2, $10.25; No. 3, $6.25.
Average cost to lay shingles, $7.50 per square.
Cedar Shakes—½" to ¾" x 24/26 in handsplit tapered or split resawn, per square $16.00
¾" to 1¼" x 24/26 in split resawn, per square 18.00
Average cost to lay shakes, $12.50 per square.

Pressure Treated Lumber—
Salt Treated .... Add $45 per M to above
Creosoted, 8-lb. treatment .... Add $52 per M to above

MARBLE—(See Dealers)

METAL LATH EXPANDED—

Standard Diamond. 3.40, Copper Bearing, LCL, per 100 sq. yds. $45.50
Standard Ribbed, ditto $49.50

MILLWORK—Standard.

D. F. $200 per 1000, R. W. Rustic air dried $225 per 1000 (delivered).

Complete door unit, $21-$32.

Screen doors, $10 to $15 each.

Patent screen windows, $1.75 a sq. ft.

Cases for kitchen and pantries seven ft. high, per lineal ft., upper $10 to $15; lower $12 to $18.

Dining room cases, $20.00 per lineal foot. Rough and finish about $2.00 per sq. ft.

Labor—Rough carpentry, warehouse heavy framing (average), $115 per M.

For smaller work average, $125 to $135 per 1000.

PAINTING—

Two-coat work .... per yard $ .90
Three-coat work .... per yard 1.35
Cold water painting .... per yard .45
Whitewashing .... per yard .25

Linseed Oil, Strictly Pure (Basis 7¾ lbs. per gal.)		Wholesale Raw	Boiled
Light iron drums	per gal.	$2.28	$2.34
5-gallon cans	per gal.	2.40	2.46
1-gallon cans	each	2.52	2.58
Quart cans	each	.71	.72
Pint cans	each	.38	.39
½-pint cans	each	.24	.24

Turpentine (Basis, 7.2 lbs. per gal.)		Pure Gum Spirits
Light iron drums	per gal.	$1.65
5-gallon cans	per gal.	1.76
1-gallon cans	each	1.88
Quart cans	each	.54
Pint cans	each	.31
½-pint cans	each	.20

Pioneer White Lead in Oil Heavy Paste and All-Purpose (Soft-Paste)

Net Weight Packages	List Price Per 100 lbs.	List Price Pr. per pkg.	Price to Painters per 100 lbs.	Price to Painters Pr. per pkg.
100-lb. kegs	$28.35	$29.35	$27.50	$27.50
50-lb. kegs	30.05	15.03	28.15	14.08
25-lb. kegs	30.35	7.50	28.45	7.12
5-lb. cans*	33.35	1.34	31.25	1.25
1-lb. cans*	36.00	.36	33.75	.34

500 lbs. (one delivery) ¾c per pound less than above.
*Heavy Paste only.

Pioneer Dry White Lead—Litharge—Dry Red Lead Red Lead in Oil

Price to Painters—Price Per 100 Pounds

	100 lbs.	50 lbs.	25 lbs.
Dry White Lead	$26.30	$.... ...	$.... ...
Litharge	25.95	26.60	26.90
Dry Red Lead	27.20	27.85	28.15
Red Lead in Oil	30.65	31.30	31.60

Pound cans, $.37 per lb.

PATENT CHIMNEYS—Average

6-inch .... $2.75 lineal foot
8-inch .... 3.25 lineal foot
10-inch .... 4.10 lineal foot
12-inch .... 5.20 lineal foot
Installation .... 75c to $1.50 lineal foot

PLASTER—

Neat wall, per ton delivered in S. F. in paper bags, $27.00.

PLASTERING (Interior)—

Yard
3 Coats, metal lath and plaster $3.75
Keene cement on metal lath 4.25
Ceilings with ¾ hot roll channels metal lath (lathed only) 3.75
Ceilings with ¾ hot roll channels metal lath plastered 5.60
Single partition ¾ channels and metal lath 1 side (lath only) 3.75
Single partition ¾ channels and metal lath 2 inches thick plastered 8.75
4-inch double partition ¾ channels and metal lath 2 sides (lath only) 6.25
4-inch double partition ¾ channels and metal lath 2 sides plastered 10.25

PLASTERING (Exterior)—

Yard
2 coats cement finish, brick or concrete wall $2.25
3 coats cement finish, No. 18 gauge wire mesh 3.00
Lime—$4.25 per bbl. at yard.
Processed Lime—$4.95 per bbl. at yard.
Rock or Grip Lath—⅜"—35c per sq. yd.
Composition Stucco—$4.50 sq. yd. (applied).
Lime Putty—$3.75 per bbl.

PLUMBING—

From $250.00 - $300.00 per fixture up, according to grade, quality and runs.

ROOFING—

"Standard" tar and gravel, 4 ply .... $15.00 per sq. for 30 sqs. or over.
Less than 30 sqs. $18.00 up per sq.
Tile $40.00 to $50.00 per square.
No. 1 Redwood Shingles in place. 4½ in. exposure, per square $18.25
5/2 No. 1 Cedar Shingles, 5 in. exposure, per square 16.50
5/8 x 16"—No. 1 Little Giant Cedar Shingles, 5" exposure, per square.. 18.25
4/2 No. 1-24" Royal Cedar Shingles 7½" exposure, per square 23.00
Re-coat with Gravel $5.50 up per sq.

ESTIMATOR'S DIRECTORY
Building and Construction Materials

ACOUSTICAL ENGINEERS
L. D. REEDER CO.
San Francisco: 1255 Sansome St., DO 2-5050
Sacramento: 3026 V St., GL 7-3505

AIR CONDITIONING
E. C. BRAUN CO.
Berkeley: 2115 Fourth St., TH 5-2356
GILMORE AIR CONDITIONING SERVICE
San Francisco: 1617 Harrison St., UN 1-2000
KAEMPER & BARRETT
San Francisco: 233 Industrial St., JU 6-6200
LINFORD AIR & REFRIGERATION CO.
Oakland: 174-12th St., TW 3-6521
MALM METAL PRODUCTS
Santa Rosa: 724-2nd St., SR 454
JAMES A. NELSON CO.
San Francisco: 1375 Howard St., HE 1-0140

ALUMINUM BLDG. PRODUCTS
MICHEL & PFEFFER IRON WORKS (Wrought Iron)
So. San Francisco: 212 Shaw Road, PLaza 5-8983
REYNOLDS METALS CO.
San Francisco: 3201 Third St., MI 7-2990
SOULE STEEL CO.
San Francisco: 1750 Army St., VA 4-4141
UNIVERSAL WINDOW CO.
Berkeley: 950 Parker St., TH 1-1600

ARCHITECTURAL PORCELAIN ENAMEL
CALIFORNIA METAL ENAMELING CO.
Los Angeles: 6904 E. Slauson, RA 3-6351
San Francisco: Continental Bldg. Products Co.,
178 Fremont St.
Portland: Portland Wire & Iron Works,
4644 S.E. Seventeenth Ave.
Seattle: Foster-Bray Co., 2412 1st Ave. So.
Spokane: Bernhard Schafer, Inc., West 34, 2nd Ave.
Salt Lake City: S. A. Roberts & Co., 109 W. 2nd So.
Dallas: Offenhauser Co., 2201 Telephone Rd.
El Paso: Architectural Products Co.,
506 E. Yandell Blvd.
Phoenix: Haskell-Thomas Co., 3808 No. Central
San Diego: Maloney Specialties, Inc., 823 W. Laurel St.
Boise: Intermountain Glass Co., 1417 Main St.

ARCHITECTURAL & AERIAL PHOTOGRAPHS
FRED ENGLISH
Belmont, Calif.: 1310 Old County Road, LY 1-0385

ARCHITECTURAL VENEER
Ceramic Veneer
GLADDING, McBEAN & CO.
San Francisco: Harrison at 9th St., UN 1-7400
Los Angeles: 2901 Los Feliz Blvd., OL 2121
Portland: 110 S.E. Main St., EA 6179
Seattle 99: 945 Elliott Ave., West, GA 0330
Spokane: 1102 N. Monroe St., BR 3259
KRAFTILE COMPANY
Niles, Calif.: Niles 3611

Porcelain Veneer
PORCELAIN ENAMEL PUBLICITY BUREAU
Oakland 12: Room 601, Franklin Building
Pasadena 8: P. O. Box 186, East Pasadena Station

Granite Veneer
VERMONT MARBLE COMPANY
San Francisco 24: 6000 3rd St., VA 6-5024
Los Angeles: 3522 Council St., DU 2-6339

Marble Veneer
VERMONT MARBLE COMPANY
San Francisco 24: 6000 3rd St., VA 6-5024
Los Angeles: 3522 Council St., DU 2-6339

BANKS - FINANCING
CROCKER-ANGLO NATIONAL BANK
San Francisco: 13 Offices

BLINDS
PARAMOUNT VENETIAN BLIND CO.
San Francisco: 5929 Mission St., JU 5-2436

BRASS PRODUCTS
GREENBERG'S, M. SONS
San Francisco 7: 765 Folsom, EX 2-3143
Los Angeles 23: 1258 S. Boyle, AN 3-7108
Seattle 4:1016 First Ave. So., MA 5140
Phoenix: 3009 N. 19th Ave., Apt. 92, PH 2-7663
Portland 4: 510 Builders Exch. Bldg., AT 6443

BRICKWORK
Face Brick
GLADDING McBEAN & CO.
San Francisco: Harrison at 9th, UN 1-7400
KRAFTILE CO.
Niles, Calif., Niles 3611
UNITED MATERIALS & RICHMOND BRICK CO.
Point Richmond, BE 4-5032

BRONZE PRODUCTS
GREENBERG'S M. SONS
San Francisco: 765 Folsom St., EX 2-3143
MICHEL & PFEFFER IRON WORKS
So. San Francisco: 212 Shaw Road, PLaza 5-8983
C. E. TOLAND & SON
Oakland: 2635 Peralta St., GL 1-2580

BUILDING HARDWARE
E. M. HUNDLEY HARDWARE CO.
San Francisco: 662 Mission St., YU 2-3322

BUILDING PAPERS & FELTS
PACIFIC CEMENT & AGGREGATES INC.
San Francisco: 400 Alabama St., KL 2-1616

CABINETS & FIXTURES
CENTRAL MILL & CABINET CO.
San Francisco: 1595 Fairfax Ave., VA 4-7316
THE FINK & SCHINDLER CO.
San Francisco: 552 Brannan St., EX 2-1513
MULLEN MFG. CO.
San Francisco: 64 Rausch St., UN 1-5815
PARAMOUNT BUILT IN FIXTURE CO.
Oakland: 962 Stanford Ave., OL 3-9911
ROYAL SHOWCASE CO.
San Francisco: 770 McAllister St., JO 7-0311

CEMENT
CALAVERAS CEMENT CO.
San Francisco: 315 Montgomery St.
DO 4-2224, Enterprise 1-2315
PACIFIC CEMENT & AGGREGATES INC.
San Francisco: 400 Alabama St., KL 2-1616

CONCRETE AGGREGATES
Ready Mixed Concrete
CENTRAL CONCRETE SUPPLY CO.
San Jose: 610 McKendrie St.
PACIFIC CEMENT & AGGREGATES INC.
San Francisco: 400 Alabama St., KL 2-1616
Sacramento: 16th and A Sts., GI 3-6586
San Jose: 790 Stockton Ave., CY 2-5620
Oakland: 2400 Peralta St., GL 1-0177
Stockton: 820 So. California St., ST 8-8643
READYMIX CONCRETE CO.
Santa Rosa: 50 W. Cottage Ave.
RHODES-JAMIESON LTD.
Oakland: 333-23rd Ave., KE 3-5225
SANTA ROSA BLDG. MATERIALS CO.
Santa Rosa: Roberts Ave.

CONCRETE ACCESSORIES
Screed Materials
C. & H. SPECIALTIES CO.
Berkeley: 909 Camelia St., LA 4-5358

CONCRETE BLOCKS
BASALT ROCK CO.
Napa, Calif.

CONCRETE COLORS—HARDENERS
CONRAD SOVIG CO.
875 Bryant St., HE 1-1345

CONSTRUCTION SERVICES
LE ROY CONSTRUCTION SERVICES
San Francisco, 143 Third St., SU 1-8914

DECKS—ROOF
UNITED STATES GYPSUM CO.
2322 W. 3rd St., Los Angeles 54, Calif.
300 W. Adams St., Chicago 6, Ill.

DOORS
THE BILCO COMPANY
New Haven, Conn.
Oakland: Geo. B. Schultz, 190 MacArthur Blvd.
Sacramento: Harry B. Ogle & Assoc., 1331 T St.
Fresno: Healey & Popovich, 1703 Fulton St.
Reseda: Daniel Dunner, 6200 Alonzo Ave.

Cold Storage Doors
BIRKENWALD
Portland: 310 N.W. 5th Ave.

Electric Doors
ROLY-DOOR SALES CO.
San Francisco, 5976 Mission St., PL 5-5089

Folding Doors
WALTER D. BATES & ASSOCIATES
San Francisco, 693 Mission St., GA 1-6971

Hardwood Doors
BELLWOOD CO. OF CALIF.
Orange, Calif., 533 W. Collins Ave.

Hollywood Doors
WEST COAST SCREEN CO.
Los Angeles: 1127 E. 63rd St., AD 1-1108
T. M. COBB CO.
Los Angeles & San Diego
W. P. FULLER CO.
Seattle, Tacoma, Portland
HOGAN LUMBER CO.
Oakland: 700 - 6th Ave.
HOUSTON SASH & DOOR
Houston, Texas
SOUTHWESTERN SASH & DOOR
Phoenix, Tucson, Arizona
El Paso, Texas
WESTERN PINE SUPPLY CO.
Emeryville: 5760 Shellmound St.
GEO. C. VAUGHAN & SONS
San Antonio & Houston, Texas

Screen Doors
WEST COAST SCREEN DOOR CO.

DRAFTING ROOM EQUIPMENT
GENERAL FIREPROOFING CO.
Oakland: 332-19th St., GL 2-4280
Los Angeles: 1200 South Hope St., RI 7-7501
San Francisco: 1025 Howard St., HE 1-7070

DRINKING FOUNTAINS
HAWS DRINKING FAUCET CO.
Berkeley: 1435 Fourth St., LA 5-3341

ELECTRICAL CONTRACTORS
COOPMAN ELECTRIC CO.
San Francisco: 85 - 14th St., MA 1-4438
ETS-HOKIN & GALVAN
San Francisco: 551 Mission St., EX 2-0432

ELECTRICAL CONTRACTORS (cont'd)

LEMOGE ELECTRIC CO.
San Francisco: 212 Clara St., DO 2-6010
LYNCH ELECTRIC CO.
San Francisco: 937 McAllister St., WI 5158
PACIFIC ELECTRIC & MECHANICAL CO.
San Francisco: Gough & Fell Sts., HE 1-5904

ELECTRIC HEATERS

WESIX ELECTRIC HEATER CO.
San Francisco: 390 First St., GA 1-2211

FIRE ESCAPES

MICHEL & PFEFFER IRON WORKS
South San Francisco: 212 Shaw Road, PLaza 5-8983

FIRE PROTECTION EQUIPMENT

FIRE PROTECTION PRODUCTS CO.
San Francisco: 1101-16th St., UN 1-2420
ETS-HOKIN & GALVAN
San Francisco: 551 Mission St., EX 2-0432
BARNARD ENGINEERING CO.
San Francisco: 35 Elmira St., JU 5-4642

FLOORS

Floor Tile

GLADDING McBEAN & CO.
San Francisco: Harrison at 9th St., UN 1-744
Los Angeles: 2901 Las Feliz Bldg., OL 2121
KRAFTILE CO.
Niles, Calif., Niles 3611

Resilient Floors

PETERSON-COBBY CO.
San Francisco: 218 Clara St., EX 2-8714
TURNER RESILIENT FLOORS CO.
San Francisco: 2280 Shafter Ave., AT 2-7720

FLOOR DRAINS

JOSAM PACIFIC COMPANY
San Francisco: 765 Folsom St., EX 2-3142

GAS VENTS

WM. WALLACE CO.
Belmont, Calif.

GENERAL CONTRACTORS

O. E. ANDERSON
San Jose: 1075 No. 10th St., CY 3-8844
BARRETT CONSTRUCTION CO.
San Francisco: 1800 Evans Ave., MI 7-9700
JOSEPH BETTANCOURT
South San Francisco: 125 So. Linden St., PL 5-9185
DINWIDDIE CONSTRUCTION CO.
San Francisco: Crocker Bldg., YU 6-2718
D. L. FAULL CONSTRUCTION CO.
Santa Rosa: 1236 Cleveland Ave.
HAAS & HAYNIE
San Francisco: 275 Pine St., DO 2-0678
HENDERSON CONSTRUCTION CO.
San Francisco: 33 Ritch St., GA 1-0856
JACKS & IRVINE
San Francisco: 620 Market St., YU 6-0511
G. P. W. JENSEN & SONS
San Francisco: 320 Market St., GA 1-2444
RALPH LARSEN & SON
San Francisco: 64 So. Park, YU 2-5682
LINDGREN & SWINERTON
San Francisco: 200 Bush St., GA 1-2980
MacDONALD, YOUNG & NELSON
San Francisco: 351 California St., YU 2-4700
MATTOCK CONSTRUCTION CO.
San Francisco: 220 Clara St., GA 1-5516
OLSEN CONSTRUCTION CO.
Santa Rosa: 125 Brookwood Ave., SR 2030
BEN ORTSKY
Cotati: Cypress Ave., Pet. 5-4383
PARKER, STEFFANS & PEARCE
San Mateo: 135 So. Park, EX 2-6639

RAPP, CHRISTENSEN & FOSTER
Santa Rosa: 705 Bennett Ave.
STOLTE, INC.
Oakland: 8451 San Leandro Ave., LO 2-4611
SWINERTON & WALBERG
San Francisco: 200 Bush St., GA 1-2980

FURNITURE—INSTITUTIONAL

GENERAL FIREPROOFING CO.
San Francisco: 1025 Howard St., HE 1-7070
Oakland: 332-19th St., GL 2-4280
Los Angeles: 1200 South Hope St., RJ 7-7501

HEATING & VENTILATING

ATLAS HEATING & VENT. CO.
San Francisco: 557-4th St., DO 2-0377
E. C. BRAUN CO.
Berkeley: 2115 Fourth St., TH 5-2356
C. W. HALL
Santa Rosa: 1665 Sebastopol Rd., SR 6354
S. T. JOHNSON CO.
Oakland: 940 Arlington Ave., OL 2-6000
LOUIS V. KELLER
San Francisco: 289 Tehama St., JU 6-6252
L. J. KRUSE CO.
Oakland: 6247 College Ave., OL 2-8332
MALM METAL PRODUCTS
Santa Rosa: 724-2nd St., SR 454
JAS. A. NELSON CO.
San Francisco: 1375 Howard St., HE 1-0140
SCOTT COMPANY
Oakland: 1919 Market St., GL 1-1937
WESIX ELECTRIC HEATER CO.
San Francisco: 390 First St., GA 1-2211
Los Angeles: 530 W. 7th St., MI 8096

INSULATION WALL BOARD

PACIFIC CEMENT & AGGREGATES, INC.
San Francisco: 400 Alabama St., KL 2-1616

INTERCEPTING DEVICES

JOSAM PACIFIC CO.
San Francisco: 765 Folsom St., EX 2-3142

IRON—ORNAMENTAL

MICHEL & PFEFFER IRON WKS.
So. San Francisco, 212 Shaw Rd., PL 5-8983

LATHING & PLASTERING

ANGELO J. DANERI
San Francisco: 1433 Fairfax Ave., AT 8-1582
K-LATH CORP.
Alhambra: 909 So. Fremont St., Alhambra
A. E. KNOWLES CORP.
San Francisco: 3330 San Bruno Ave., JU 7-2091
G. H. & C. MARTINELLI
San Francisco: 174 Shotwell St., UN 3-6112
FREDERICK MEISWINKEL
San Francisco: 2155 Turk St., JO 7-7587
RHODES-JAMIESON LTD.
Oakland: 333-23rd Ave., KE 3-5225
PATRICK J. RUANE
San Francisco: 44 San Jose Ave., MI 7-6414

LIGHTING FIXTURES

SMOOT-HOLMAN COMPANY
Inglewood, Calif., OR 8-1217
San Francisco: 55 Mississippi St., MA 1-8474

LUMBER

CHRISTENSEN LUMBER CO.
San Francisco: Quint & Evans Ave., VA 4-5832
ART HOGAN LUMBER CO.
1701 Galvez Ave., ATwater 2-1157
MEAD CLARK LUMBER CO.
Santa Rosa: 3rd & Railroad
ROLANDO LUMBER CO.
San Francisco: 5th & Berry Sts., SU 1-6901
STERLING LUMBER CO.
Santa Rosa: 1129 College Ave., S. R. 82

MARBLE

JOS. MUSTO SONS-KEENAN CO.
San Francisco: 555 No. Point St., GR 4-6365
VERMONT MARBLE CO.
San Francisco: 6000-3rd St., VA 6-5024

MASONRY

BASALT ROCK CO.
Napa, Calif.
San Francisco: 260 Kearney St., GA 1-3758
WM. A. RAINEY & SON
San Francisco: 323 Clementina St., SU 1-0072
GEO. W. REED CO.
San Francisco: 1390 So. Van Ness Ave., AT 2-1226

METAL EXTERIOR WALLS

THE KAWNEER CO.
Berkeley: 930 Dwight Way, TH 5-8710

METAL FRAMING

UNISTRUT OF NORTHERN CALIFORNIA
Berkeley: 2547-9th St., TH 1-3031
Enterprise 1-2204

METAL GRATING

KLEMP METAL GRATING CORP.
Chicago, Ill.: 6601 So. Melvina St.

METAL LATH—EXPANDED

PACIFIC CEMENT & AGGREGATES, INC.
San Francisco: 400 Alabama St., KL 2-1616

METAL PARTITIONS

THE E. F. HAUSERMAN CO.
San Francisco: 485 Brannan St., YU 2-5477

METAL PRODUCTS

FORDERER CORNICE WORKS
San Francisco: 269 Potrero Ave., HE 1-4100

MILLWORK

CENTRAL MILL & CABINET CO.
San Francisco: 1595 Fairfax Ave., VA 4-7316
THE FINK & SCHINDLER CO.
San Francisco: 552 Brannan St., EX 2-1513
MULLEN MFG. CO.
San Francisco: 64 Rausch St., UN 1-5815
PACIFIC MFG. CO.
San Francisco: 16 Beale St., GA 1-7755
Santa Clara: 2610 The Alameda, S. C. 607
Los Angeles: 6820 McKinley Ave., TH 4156
SOUTH CITY LUMBER & SUPPLY CO.
So. San Francisco: Railroad & Spruce, PL 5-7085

OFFICE EQUIPMENT

GENERAL FIREPROOFING CO.
Los Angeles: 1200 South Hope St., RI 7-7501
San Francisco: 1025 Howard St., HE 1-7070
Oakland: 332-19th St., GL 2-4280

OIL BURNERS

S. T. JOHNSON CO.
Oakland: 940 Arlington Ave., GL 2-6000
San Francisco: 585 Potrero Ave., MA 1-2757
Philadelphia, Pa.: 401 North Broad St.

ORNAMENTAL IRON

MICHEL & PFEFFER IRON WORKS
So. San Francisco: 212 Shaw Rd., PL 5-8983

PAINTING

R. P. PAOLI & CO.
San Francisco: 2530 Lombard St., WE 1-1632
SINCLAIR PAINT CO.
San Francisco: 2112-15th St., HE 1-2196
D. ZELINSKY & SONS
San Francisco: 165 Groove St., MA 1-7400

PHOTOGRAPHS

Construction Progress
FRED ENGLISH
Belmont, Calif.: 1310 Old County Road, LY 1-0385

PLASTER

PACIFIC CEMENT & AGGREGATE INC.
San Francisco: 400 Alabama St., KL 2-1616

PLASTIC PRODUCTS

PLASTIC SALES & SERVICE
San Francisco: 409 Bryant St., DO 2-6433
WEST COAST INDUSTRIES
San Francisco: 3150-18th St., MA 1-5657

CLASSIFIED ADVERTISING

CONSTRUCTION INDUSTRY WAGE RATES

Table 1 has been prepared by the State of California, Department of Industrial Relations, Division of Labor Statistics and Research. The rates are the union hourly wage rates established by collective bargaining as of January 2, 1958, as reported by reliable sources.

TABLE 1—UNION HOURLY WAGE RATES, CONSTRUCTION INDUSTRY, CALIFORNIA

Following are the hourly rates of compensation established by collective bargaining, reported as of January 2, 1958 or later

CRAFT	San Francisco	Alameda	Contra Costa	Fresno	Sacramento	San Joaquin	Santa Clara	Solano	Los Angeles	San Bernardino	San Diego	Santa Barbara	Kern
ASBESTOS WORKER	$3.55	$3.55	$3.55	$3.55	$3.55	$3.55	$3.55	$3.55	$3.55	$3.55	$3.55	$3.55	$3.55
BOILERMAKER	3.675	3.675	3.675	3.675	3.675	3.675	3.675	3.675	3.675	3.675	3.675	3.675	3.675
BRICKLAYER	3.95	3.75	3.75	3.75	3.80	3.75	3.875	3.95	3.80	3.90	3.75		3.86
BRICKLAYER HODCARRIER		3.10	3.10	2.90	3.10	2.90	3.00	3.10	2.75	2.75	2.75		2.75
CARPENTER	3.175	3.175	3.225	3.225	3.225	3.225	3.225	3.225	3.225	3.225	3.225	3.225	3.225
CEMENT MASON	3.22	3.22	3.22	3.22	3.22	3.22	3.22	3.22	3.15	3.15	3.25	3.15	3.15
ELECTRICIAN	3.936ᴀ	3.936ᴀ	3.936ᴀ		3.94ᴀ	3.50	4.03ᴀ	3.666ᴀ	3.90ᴀ	3.90ᴀ	3.90	3.85ᴀ	3.70
GLAZIER	3.09	3.09	3.09	3.135	3.055	3.055	3.09	3.09	3.105	3.105	3.03	3.105	3.135
IRON WORKER													
ORNAMENTAL	3.625	3.625	3.625	3.625	3.625	3.625	3.625	3.625	3.625	3.625	3.625	3.625	3.625
REINFORCING	3.375	3.375	3.375	3.375	3.375	3.375	3.375	3.375	3.375	3.375	3.375	3.375	3.375
STRUCTURAL	3.625	3.625	3.625	3.625	3.625	3.625	3.625	3.625	3.625	3.625	3.625	3.625	3.625
LABORER, GENERAL OR CONSTRUCTION	2.505	2.505	2.505	2.505	2.505	2.505	2.505	2.505	2.50	2.50	2.48	2.50	2.50
LATHER	3.4375	3.84	3.84	3.45	3.60ʙ	3.40ᴄ	3.60ᴅ	3.50ᴇ	3.9375		3.725	3.625ꜰ	
OPERATING ENGINEER													
Concrete mixer (up to 1 yard)	2.89	2.89	2.89	2.89	2.89	2.89	2.89	2.89					
Concrete mixer operator—Skip Type									2.96	2.96	2.96	2.96	2.96
Elevator Hoist Operator									3.19	3.19	3.19	3.19	3.19
Material Hoist (1 drum)	3.19	3.19	3.19	3.19	3.19	3.19	3.19	3.19					
Tractor Operator	3.33	3.33	3.33	3.33	3.33	3.33	3.33	3.33	3.47	3.47	3.47	3.47	3.47
PAINTER													
Brush	3.20	3.20	3.20	3.13	3.325	3.175	3.20	3.20	3.26ɢ	3.25	3.19	3.13ʜ	3.10
Spray	3.20	3.20	3.20	3.38	3.575	3.325	3.20	3.20	3.51ɢ	3.50	3.74	3.38ʜ	3.35
PILEDRIVERMAN	3.305	3.305	3.305	3.305	3.305	3.305	3.305	3.305	3.355	3.355		3.355	3.355
PLASTERER	3.69	3.545	3.545	3.35	3.60ʙ	3.55ᴄ	3.58	3.50	3.9375	3.9375	3.75		
PLASTERER HODCARRIER	3.25	3.42	3.42	3.10	3.10	3.00ᴄ	3.20	3.15	3.6875	3.5625	3.475	3.50	3.6875
PLUMBER	3.67		3.935ı	3.80ᴊ	3.70	3.80ᴊ	3.60	3.675	3.70	3.70	3.70	3.70	3.375
ROOFER	3.35	3.35	3.35	3.20	3.25	3.35	3.35	3.10ᴋ	3.20ʟ	3.25	3.10	3.30	3.775
SHEET METAL WORKER	3.45	3.45	3.45	3.425	3.45	3.465	3.45	3.325	3.50	3.50	3.45	3.55	3.10
STEAMFITTER	3.67	3.94	3.94	3.80ᴊ	3.70	3.80ᴊ	3.60	3.675	3.70	3.70	3.70	3.70	3.775
TRUCK DRIVER— Dump Trucks under 4 yards	2.55	2.55	2.55	2.55	2.55	2.55	2.55	2.55	2.63	2.63	2.63	2.63	2.63
TILE SETTER	3.275	3.275	3.275	3.375	3.28	3.30	3.275	3.275	3.36	3.60	3.375	3.36	

ᴀ Includes 4% vacation allowance.
ʙ Includes 5c hour for industry promotion and 5c hour for vacation fund.
ᴄ ½% withheld for industry promotion.
ᴅ 1½c withheld for industry promotion.
ᴇ Includes 5c hour for industry promotion and 5c hour for vacation fund. Hourly rate for part of county adjacent to Sacramento County is $3.60.
ꜰ Northern part of County: $3.75.

ɢ Pomona Area: Brush $3.25; Spray $3.50.
ʜ Southern half of County: Brush $3.28; Spray $3.28.
ı Includes 30c hour for vacation pay.
ᴊ Includes 15c hour which local union may elect to use for vacation purposes.
ᴋ Includes 10c hour for vacation fund.
ʟ Includes 10c hour savings fund wage.

ATTENTION: The above tabulation has been prepared by the State of California, Department of Industrial Relations, Division of Labor Statistics and Research, and represents data reported by building trades councils, union locals, contractor organizations, and other reliable sources. The above rates do not include any payments to funds for health and welfare, pensions, vacations, industry promotion, apprentice training, etc., except as shown in the footnotes.

CONSTRUCTION INDUSTRY WAGE RATES — TABLE 2

Employer Contributions to Health and Welfare, Pension, Vacation and Other Funds
California Union Contracts, Construction Industry

(Revised March, 1957)

CRAFT	San Francisco	Fresno	Sacramento	San Joaquin	Santa Clara	Los Angeles	San Bernardino	San Diego
ASBESTOS WORKER	.10 W / .11 hr. V	.10 W / .11 hr. V	.10 W / .11 hr. V	.10 W / .11 hr. V	.10 W / .11 hr. V	.10 W	.10 W	.10 W
BRICKLAYER	.15 W / .14 P / .05 hr. V		.15 W / .10 P		.15 W			
BRICKLAYER HODCARRIER	.10 W / .10 P / .10 V	.10 W	.10 W	.10 W	.10 W	.075 W	.075 W	.075 W
CARPENTER	.10 W / .10 hr. V	.10 W	.10 W	.10 W	.10 W	.10 W	.10 W	.10 W
CEMENT MASON	.10 W	.10 W	.10 W	.10 W	.10 W	.10 W	.10 W	.10 W
ELECTRICAL WORKER	.10 W / 1% P / 4% V	.10 W / 1% P / 4% V	.075 W / 1% P	.075 W / 1% P / 4% V	1% P	1% P	1% P	.10 W / 1% P
GLAZIER	.075 W / .085 V	.075 W / 40 hr. V	.075 W / .05 V	.075 W / .05 V	.075 W / .085 V	.075 W / 40 hr. V	.075 W / 40 hr. V	.075 W / 40 hr. V
IRONWORKER: REINFORCING	.10 W	.10 W	.10 W	.10 W	.10 W	.10 W	.10 W	.10 W
STRUCTURAL	.10 W	.10 W	.10 W	.10 W	.10 W	.10 W	.10 W	.10 W
LABORER, GENERAL	.10 W	.10 W	.10 W	.10 W	.10 W	.075 W	.075 W	.075 W
LATHER	.60 day W / .70 day V		.10 W	.10 W	.075 W / .05 V	.90 day W	.70 day W	.10 W
OPERATING ENGINEER								
TRACTOR OPERATOR (MIN.)	.10 W	.10 W	.10 W	.10 W	.10 W	.10 W	.10 W	.10 W
POWER SHOVEL OP. (MIN.)	.10 W	.10 W	.10 W	.10 W	.10 W	.10 W	.10 W	.10 W
PAINTER, BRUSH	.095 W	.08 W	.075 W	.10 W	.095 W / .07 V	.085 W	.08 W	.09 W
PLASTERER	.10 W / .10 V	.10 W	.10 W	.10 W	.10 W / .15 V	.10 W	.90 day W	.10 W
PLUMBER	.10 W / .10 V	.15 W / .10 P	.10 W / .10 P / .125 V	.10 W	.10 W / .10 P / .125 V	.10 W	.90 day W	.10 W
ROOFER	.10 W / .10 V	.10 W	.10 W / .10 V	.10 W	.075 W / .075 V	.085 W	.10 W	.075 W
SHEET METAL WORKER	.075 W / 4% V	.075 W / 7 day V	.075 W / .10 V	.075 W / .12 V	.075 W / 4% V	.085 W / .10 V	.085 W / .10 V	.085 W / 5 day V
TILE SETTER	.075 W / .09 V				.075 W / .09 V	.025 W / .06 V		

ATTENTION: The above tabulation has been prepared and compiled from the available data reported by building trades councils, union locals, contractor organizations and other reliable sources. The table was prepared from incomplete data; where no employer contributions are specified, it does not necessarily mean that none are required by the union contract.

The type of supplement is indicated by the following symbols: W—Health and Welfare; P—Pensions; V—Vacations; A—Apprentice training fund; Adm—Administration fund; JIB—Joint Industry Board; Prom—Promotion fund.

CONSTRUCTION CONTRACTS AWARDED AND MISCELLANEOUS PERSONNEL DATA

HIGH SCHOOL ADD'N, McClymonds, Oakland, Alameda county. Oakland Unified School Dist., owner. Project includes a new shop building providing facilities for auto, cabinet, wood and metal machine shops—$223,550. ARCHITECT: Anderson, Yde & Anderson, Bank of America Bldg., Oakland. GENERAL CONTRACTOR: Gaspard Const. Co., 6629 Beck St., Oakland.

MEMORIAL HOSPITAL, New Wing, Redding, Shasta county. Memorial Hospital Association, Redding, owner. One story, basement, approximately 20,000 sq. ft. area, reinforced concrete and masonry block construction, built-up roofing, concrete floors—$353,367. ARCHITECT: Smart & Clabaugh, 1001 Yuba St., Redding. GENERAL CONTRACTOR: L. Singleton Co., P. O. Box 271, Eureka.

COLLEGE LIBRARY, State College, Sacramento, Sacramento county. State of California, Sacramento, owner. Three story addition, with penthouse, to the college library at the Sacramento State College—$525,985. ARCHITECT: Anson Boyd, California State Architect, Sacramento. GENERAL CONTRACTOR: Campbell Const. Co., P. O. Box 390, Sacramento.

TELEPHONE BLD. ADD'N., San Bernardino. Pacific Tel. & Tel., Los Angeles, owner. Part 2, 3 and 4 story building addition, steel frame, reinforced concrete, masonry, built-up roofing, slab floors, metal sash, plastering, floor covering, ceramic tile work, heating, ventilating and air conditioning, electrical work, rest rooms; 29,360 sq. ft. area. ARCHITECT: Woodford & Bernard, 410 N. La Brea Ave., Los Angeles. GENERAL CONTRACTOR: Robinson and Wilson, 179 4th St., San Bernardino.

OFFICE & EQUIPMENT BLDG., Los Gatos, Santa Clara County. Western Calif. Telephone Company, San Francisco, owner. 1-story reinforced concrete construction—$273,231. ARCHITECT: Clarence O. Pererson, 116 New Montgomery St., San Francisco. GENERAL CONTRACTOR: Moroney Const. Co., 1408 Chapin Ave., Burlingame.

AUTO CLUB OFFICE, Huntington Park, Los Angeles County. Automobile Club of Southern California, Los Angeles, owner. Wood siding, frame and stucco, cement tile veneeer office building in Huntington Park; composition gravel roof, plate glass, store fronts, laminated wood beams, steel framing, acoustical tile, terrazzo, concrete slab, asphalt tile flooring, air conditioning, metal toilet partitions, interior plaster, landscaping; 5400 sq. ft. of area. ARCHITECT: Larsen Associates (H. L. Kahn & E. Farrell, architects); ENGINEER: B. L. Larsen, 6255 Van Nuys Blvd., Van Nuys. GENERAL CONTRACTOR: Saffell &

McAdams, 860 W. Foothill Blvd., Monrovia.

NEW WAREHOUSE, South San Francisco, San Mateo County. Sterling Furniture Company, San Francisco, owner. 1-story warehouse building providing employees lunch room, recreational features including outside sports facilities, 211,000 sq. ft. floor area—$750,000. CONSULTING ENGINEERS: Cline, Zerkle & Agee, 1810 6th St., Berkeley. GENERAL CONTRACTORS: Utah Const. Co.

DESERT MUSEUM, Palm Springs, Riverside County. Palm Springs Desert Museum, owner. 1-story with provisions for second floor at later date, concrete block and adobe brick construction—$80,875. ARCHITECT: Frey and Chambers, 879 N. Palm Canyon Drive, Palm Springs. GENERAL CONTRACTOR: Robinson & Wilson, 179 4th St., San Bernardino.

FIRE STATION, Danville, Contra Costa County. Danville Fire District, owner. Wood frame, concrete slab, wood siding and masonry exterior walls, radiant heating; 2500 sq. ft. area—$37,666. ARCHITECT: Schachtman & Velikonia, 333 Maryland St., Vallejo. GENERAL CONTRACTOR: Franz Muller, P.O. Box 1061, Walnut Creek.

BIOLOGY-GEOLOGY BLDG., Pomona College campus, Pomona, Los Angeles County. Pomona College, Pomona, owner. Reinforced steel and concrete, 3 floors, 40,000 sq. ft. floor area, includes 150-seat auditorium, library, classrooms, offices, and laboratory for work in general physics, atomic and radiation physics, electricity, electronics, and engineering—$1,300,000.

ARCHITECT: Smith, Powell & Morgridge, 208 W. 8th St., Los Angeles.

LIBRARY, Mountain View, Santa Clara County. City of Mt. View, owner. 1-story, rigid steel frame with wood, some brick veneer, masonry curtain wall, 8,500 sq. ft. area—$119,997. ARCHITECT: Paul J. Huston, 744 Cowper St., Palo Alto. GENERAL CONTRACTOR: Wells P. Goodenough Const. Co., P. O. Box 120, Palo Alto.

BUILDERS EXCHANGE BLDG., San Carlos, San Mateo County. Peninsula Builders Exchange, Belmont, owner. 1-story wood frame and stucco construction, 6000 sq. ft. of area—$55,492. GENERAL CONTRACTOR: Carl Sjoberg & Co., 334 Hudson St., Redwood City.

CHURCH SCHOOL, Sunnyvale, Santa Clara County. First Methodist Church, Sunnyvale, owner. Wood frame construction to provide kindergarten facilities at church—$21,561. ARCHITECT: Edwin Wadsworth, 130 Summerhill Lane, Woodside. GENERAL CONTRACTOR: Delano H. Large, 851 Southhampton Dr., Palo Alto.

BOWLING ALLEY, Canoga Park, Los Angeles County. Canoga Park Bowling Center, owner. Concrete construction, composition roof, plaster, acoustical tile and hardwood panel work, tile, concrete, vinyl tile and rubber tile floors, plywood partitions, glass sliding, metal and wood slab doors, metal sash, sound insulation, plate glass, pipe columns and brick fireplace: 34,000 sq. ft. of area—$325,000. ENGINEERS: Adams, Morgan, Latham, Kripp & Wright, Engineers, 3601 Long

Beach Blvd., Los Angeles. GENERAL CONTRACTORS: Jim Ray, 11959 E. Slauson Ave., Whittier.

GLASS FIBER MFG. PLANT, Corona, Riverside County. L.O.F. Glass Fibers Co., Toledo, Ohio, owner. Glass fiber manufacturing plant, 105,000 sq. ft. of space (5000 sq. ft. in offices); landscaped California type building of concrete, tilt-up construction—$1,000,000. ARCHITECT: Stiles and Robert Clements, 210 W. 7th St., Los Angeles. GENERAL CONTRACTOR: Jackson Bros., Los Angeles.

JR. HIGH SCHOOL, Bret Harte, Oakland. Oakland Unified School District, owner. 2-story reinforced concrete construction; facilities for Administration unit, library, music, auditorium, cafeteria, shops, arts and crafts, and toilets—$909,825. ARCHITECT: Ponsford & Price, 524 20th St., Oakland. GENERAL CONTRACTOR: Herbert E. Ellis, P. O. Box 146 Station-A, Berkeley.

OFFICE BLDG., San Francisco. California State Automobile Association, San Francisco, owner. 9-floor and basement, structural steel frame, basement and roof areas for auto parking, external aluminum curtain walls, concrete and ceramic tile, fireproofing — $1,199,200 ARCHITECT: Albert F. Roller, 1 Montgomery St., San Francisco. STRUCTURAL ENGINEER: H. J. Brunnier, Sharon Bldg., San Francisco. CONSULTING ENGINEER: Dudley Deane & Associates, 182 2nd St., San Francisco and Lyle E. Patton, 604 Mission St., San Francisco. GENERAL CONTRACTOR: Rothchild-Faffin & Weirick, 274 Brannan St., San Francisco.

ELEMENTARY SCHOOL, Ridgewood, Cutten, Humboldt County. Cutten School District, owner. 1-story wood frame, interior dry wall, exterior wood, built-up roofing, concrete floors—$122,685. ARCHITECT: Gerald Matson, 537 G St., Eureka. GENERAL CONTRACTOR: Ole Antonsen, 4255 Broadway, Eureka.

SCHOOL ADD'N, North Brae, San Bruno, San Mateo County. San Bruno Park School District, owner. 1-story wood frame construction, built-up roofing, concrete slab floor and asphalt tile floors; to provide facilities for administration unit, 2 classrooms—$100,217. ARCHITECT: Ernest Kump & Associates, 450 Ramona St., Palo Alto. GENERAL CONTRACTOR: Hub-Pacific Bldrs., 3637 Haven Ave., Redwood City.

OFFICE IMPROVEMENTS, Department of Finance, Sacramento, California. State of California, Sacramento, owner. Work comprises installing new entrance with glazed aluminum doors, new concrete stairs and interior alterations to mezzanine floor consisting of alterations to partitions, installing wood stud and gypsum board partitions and movable partitions, gypsum and acoustical tile ceilings, ceramic tile and linoleum floors, millwork, painting, toilet fixtures, plumbing, electrical—$28,240. ARCHITECT: Anson Boyd, California State Architect, Sacramento. GENERAL CONTRACTOR: Bingham Const. Co., 6329 Elvas Ave., Sacramento.

THEATER ALTERATIONS, Hollywood, Los Angeles County. Grauman's Chinese Theater, Hollywood, owner. Work comprises widening of proscenium arch, flooring, electrical, painting, plastering, seating changes—$139,930. ENGINEER:

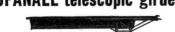

William D. Coffey, 649 S. Olive St., Los Angeles. GENERAL CONTRACTOR: Contracting Engineers, 2310 W. Vernon Ave., Los Angeles.

LIBRARY BLDG., Jr. College, Visalia. Sequoia Jr. College District, Visalia, owner. Construction of a new library building on the Sequoia Jr. College campus—$251,500. ARCHITECT: Robert C. Kaestner, 210 N. Encina Ave., Visalia. GENERAL CONTRACTOR: Lewis C. Nelson & Sons, 2915 McCall St., Selma.

BAPTIST SEMINARY, Golden Gate Theological, Strawberry Point, Marin County. Golden Gate Baptist Theological Seminary, Berkeley, owner. Work of Phase No. 2, consists of dormitory and individual housing for students, wood frame construction—$1,332,745. ARCHITECT: John Carl Warnecke, 111 New Montgomery St., San Francisco. GENERAL CONTRACTOR: Williams & Burrows, 500 Harbor Blvd., Belmont.

AUTO SHOW ROOM, San Rafael, Marin County. Wood frame, and concrete block construction, wood exterior, concrete slab floors, tar and gravel roof, concrete foundations, dry wall and wood panel interior — $31,428. DESIGNER: Edward Hageman & Associates, 255 W. End Ave., San Rafael. GENERAL CONTRACTOR: Custom Builders, 47 Louise St., San Rafael.

MEDICAL BLDG., Monte Vista, San Bernardino County. Dr. A. E. Gillotte, Monte Vista, owner. 1-story frame, stucco and brick veneer medical building; 7800 sq. ft. of area, rock roofing, aluminum louvers and fixed plate glass windows, asphalt tile floors, interior plaster, air conditioning, laminated plastic counters, plumbing, electrical, asphalt paving. ENGINEER: L. L. Penn, 278 E. Palmer St., Costa Mesa, and John G. Snyder, 8074 Archibald Ave., Cucamonga. GENERAL CONTRACTOR: Larson Const. Co., 718 E. Yale St., Ontario.

OFFICE BLDG., Turlock, Stanislaus County. Turlock Irrigation District, Turlock, owner. Structural steel frame and concrete, dry wall interior, composition roofing, stone veneer, porcelain enamel panels, air conditioning—$608,941. ARCHITECT: Donald L. Hardison, 160 Broadway, Richmond. GENERAL CONTRACTOR: Delphia-Shadle Co., P.O. Box 607, Patterson.

ELEMENTARY SCHOOL, Whipple, Decoto, Alameda County. Decoto School District, owner. 1-story frame and stucco construction, concrete slab floors—$269,300. ARCHITECT: John Hudspeth, 339 15th St., Oakland. GENERAL CONTRACTOR: E. H. Moore & Sons, 693 Mission St., San Francisco.

MOTEL ADD'N, Richelieu, San Francisco. Richelieu Hotel Co., San Francisco, owner. Work consists of additions to presently existing buildings — $117,900. ARCHITECT: Bruce E. Heiser, 251 Post St., San Francisco. GENERAL CONTRACTOR: Clovis Const. Co., 521 Brannan St., San Francisco.

COURTHOUSE ALTERATIONS, San Rafael, Marin County. County of Marin, San Rafael, owner. Work consists of alterations to the basement annex building of the present building. ARCHITECT: Schubart & Friedman, 52 Vallejo St., San Francisco. GENERAL CONTRACTOR:

Larkins Const. Co., 60 Upland Rd., Kentfield.

AUTOMOBILE AGENCY, West Los Angeles. Walker-Buerge Ford Agency, owner. 1 and part 2-story, reinforced brick, lift-slab, 20,000 sq. ft. floor area, plumbing, electrical, plate glass, aluminum sliding windows, aluminum framed entrance doors, asphalt paving. ENGINEER: C. F. Knowlton, and Wilbur and Evans, 246 26th St., Santa Monica. GENERAL CONTRACTOR: Herbert Goldsworthy, 409 Santa Monica Blvd., Santa Monica.

ELEMENTARY SCHOOL ADD'N, Corning, Tehama County. Corning Unified School District, owner. 1-story frame construction will provide facilities for 5-class-rooms — $72,926. ARCHITECT: Lawrence G. Thompson, 125 W 3rd St., Chico. GENERAL CONTRACTOR: Lamon Const. Co., 881 Market St., Yuba City.

CHURCH & RECTORY, Sacred Heart Parish, Covina, Los Angeles County. Roman Catholic Archbishop of Los Angeles, owner. Work includes a reinforced concrete and masonry church and a 2-story frame and stucco rectory; 15,300 sq. ft. in area, Rectory 5000 sq. ft.; composition roofing, steel sash, cathedral glass, asphalt tile, permanent seating, forced-air-heating, ceramic tile—$334,999. ARCHITECT: Verge & Clatworthy, 4342 Eagle Rock Blvd., Los Angeles. GENERAL CONTRACTOR: Theisen Co., 358 Del Monte St., Pasadena.

SCHOOL ADD'N, James Marshall, West Sacramento. Washington Unified School District, West Sacramento, owner. 1-story wood frame and steel joists, built up roofing, some grouted brick work; 40,000 sq. ft. area—$720,144. ARCHITECT: Barovetto & Thomas, 718 Alhambra Blvd., Sacramento. GENERAL CONTRACTOR: United Const. Co., 3839 Riverside Blvd., Sacramento.

BANK BLDG., Rancho Cordova, Sacramento County. Bank of America, San Francisco, owner. 1-story, mezzanine, concrete slab floors, shingle roof, concrete block construction — $91,000. ARCHITECT: Continental Service, Architectural Division, Flood Bldg., San Francisco. GENERAL CONTRACTOR: Affiliated Engineers & Contractors, 2228 Sutterville Rd., Sacramento.

MEMORIAL HOSPITAL ADD'N, Redding, Shasta County. Memorial Hospital Ass'n, Redding, owner. 1-story, plus basement; approximately 20,000 sq. ft. area; reinforced concrete and masonry block construction, built-up roofing, concrete floors. ARCHITECT: Smart & Clabaugh, 1001 Yuba St., Redding. GENERAL CONTRACTOR: L. Singleton Co., P.O. Box 271, Eureka.

ELEMENTARY SCHOOL, Jefferson, Cloverdale, Sonoma County. Cloverdale Union School District, owner. 1-story, wood frame, plaster exterior, concrete slab floors, composition roofing; facilities for Administration unit, 8-classrooms, kindergarten and toilets—$235,160. ARCHITECT: Clarence Felciano, 4010 Montecito Ave., Santa Rosa. GENERAL CONTRACTOR: R. R. Todd, 915 Beaver St., Santa Rosa.

IN THE NEWS

AIA GIVEN FUNDS FOR STUDY OF NEGLECTED AREAS

The American Institute of Architects has been granted funds by the National Science Foundation to conduct a conference to identify neglected areas of basic research in architecture, and plans for the workshop-conference are being made for next fall in Washington, D.C.

Approximately 30 authorities from all parts of the U.S. will be invited to participate in the conference, scheduled for three days, "to determine the relationships of the physical, biological and social sciences in the problems of optimum created environ-

ment for human activities."

Members of the conference board include Dr. Robert King Merton, Columbia University sociologist; Dr. Albert H. Hastorf, Dartmouth College psychologist; Dr. C. P. Yaglou, Harvard University School of Public Health; Prof. Myle Holley, MIT Structural Engineer; and Walter E. Campbell, AIA, Boston architect and chairman of the AIA Research Committee.

LARGE SHOPPING CENTER STARTS NEAR SAN JOSE

Architect John S. Bolles, San Francisco, has announced the start of site work on a $10,000,000 shopping center project to be built near San Jose in Santa Clara County.

The project will comprise some 44 acres with the shopping center buildings containing 70 air-conditioned stores, occupying 500,000 sq. ft. of area. Paved parking will provide facilities for 4000 cars.

WALTER VILLARREAL FORMS MANUFACTURERS REPRESENTATIVE AGENCY

Walter Villarreal recently announced the formation of the W. J. Villarreal Company with offices at 2525 El Camino Real, Redwood City, to act as manufacturers representative for gas-heating and gas-ventilating equipment.

Villarreal has been in the sheet metal and heating field since 1932, during which time he has worked with many architects and engineers on venting system layouts. He was formerly district manager for William Wallace Company in Northern California and Nevada.

The new company will operate in California, Nevada and Hawaii.

PROMINENT ARCHITECTS OPEN NEW OFFICES IN STANFORD CENTER

Albert Sigal, Jr., and Milton F. Johnson have formed a partnership for the practice of Architecture and have opened new offices in the Stanford Professional Center, Palo Alto.

The new firm will direct its efforts without specialization to the best needs of client and community in terms of use-space, economy and design.

Both members of the firm are graduates of Stanford University.

STANLEY M. SMITH JOINS PALO ALTO OFFICE OF KUMP

Stanley M. Smith, AIA, has joined the Palo Alto office of the architectural firm of Ernest J. Kump and Associates.

Smith, a graduate of the University of California, has spent the past six years

working as an architect and planning consultant for the Arabian-American Oil Company and the Aramco Overseas Company in Rome, The Hague, and Saudi Arabia.

US PLYWOOD OPENS OREGON OFFICES

United States Plywood Corporation has announced the opening of a new distribution center in Eugene, Oregon, the 110th branch office of the firm in the United States.

The Eugene branch is located at 410 Garfield Street, across from the company's Associated Division Mill.

Eugene McDonald, formerly resident salesman in Eugene, will be in charge of the office.

EQUIPMENT FIRM OPENS FACILITIES IN OAKLAND

M. L. Regensburger, vice president and general manager of Laurence Myers & Company, Inc., contractors' equipment distributors, San Francisco, has announced the opening of new facilities at 801 73rd Avenue in Oakland.

The new Oakland facility will house the company's office and warehouse, repair, service and maintenance activities and will also serve in the capacity of scaffold sales, rentals and erection.

PONDEROSA PINE DOORS REVISED STANDARD

A recommended revision of Commercial Standard SC120-53, Ponderosa Pine Doors, which is designed to aid architects, builders and other users of these doors, as well as manufacturers and distributors, has been presented to the industry for consideration by the Commodity Standards Division, office of Technical Services, U.S. Department of Commerce.

The revision was recommended by the National Woodwork Manufacturers Association and approved by the Standing Committee for Commercial Standards. Chief purpose of this trade standard is to establish uniform specifications, design, and size of doors as well as methods of grading and labeling those doors that comply. It also serves as the basis for fair competition.

C. J. HOLZMUELLER ADDS ENGINEERING DIVISION SERVICE

C. J. Holzmueller, oldest theatrical supply house in the West, and for more than 50 years a source of equipment and services in connection with all types of theatrical presentations and lighting effects, has added a Theatre Engineering Division with consulting services in all phases of theatre and auditorium stage lighting, rigging, drapery and associated requirements.

James Jewell, Yale University graduate, will head the new division. He has had considerable experience as a technician and lighting designer.

LOS ANGELES FIRM WINS NATIONAL ARCHITECTURAL AWARDS

The architectural firm of Palmer and Krisel, AIA, Los Angeles, has been awarded four top honors from three separate national organizations, according to a recent announcement.

The National Association of Home builders, for the third successive year, presented two of their six Design Merit Awards to Palmer and Krisel, one for a Palm Springs residence designed for the George Alexander Co., and the other for a subdivision house in El Paso. At the same time the magazine Living for Young

44

Homemakers announced that the architects' "Living-Conditioned Home" designed for Sanford D. Adler in Northridge had won first prize in nation-wide competition, and the American Builder presented the firm with a Merit Award for the same house.

The firm of Palmer and Krisel have designed more than 20,000 homes in the last six years, most of them for merchant builders in Southern California.

KENNETH E. HILL APPOINTED FACTORY SALES ENGINEER

Kenneth E. Hill has been appointed Factory Sales Engineer in the Southern California area for the Payne Company of La Puente, according to an announcement by Owen McComas, National Sales Manager of the company.

Hill will serve the San Fernando Valley and West Los Angeles area with engineering and sales aid to dealers in the gas appliance and new construction field.

MEDICAL CENTER STORES AND APARTMENT

Architect A. Reid Street of Beverly Hills, has completed working drawings for construction of a 1- and part 2-story frame, plaster and brick veneer medical building to include 8200 sq. ft. of area and will be of concrete slab construction.

STRUCTURAL WORK STARTS ON NEW ZELLERBACH BUILDING

Structural steel work has begun on the construction site of the 20-story Crown Zellerbach headquarters building in San Francisco, with a giant derrick installing 18 massive steel legs which will serve as a support for the building.

These base columns will be erected in three sections and will extend a total of 67 feet from the sub-basement floor up to the second floor level. They weigh approximately 2500 pounds per foot and are the heaviest structural steel members ever used in building construction west of the Mississippi river.

Over 8000 tons of structural steel will be used in the building, which will be bolted and welded to eliminate the noise of riveting.

When completed the building will rise 320 feet above street level.

HIGH SCHOOL STADIUM FOR BAKERSFIELD

Architect Ernest L. McCoy of Bakersfield is completing plans for construction of a stadium at the South Hill High School in Bakersfield, for the Kern County Union High School and College District.

The reinforced concrete stadium will seat 3000 persons.

BLUE CROSS TO BUILD SEATTLE OFFICE BUILDING

John Maloney, AIA, Architect of Seattle, has completed plans for a modern, efficient office building to be constructed in Seattle, by the Washington Blue Cross Plan, according to C. J. Kretchmer, executive director of the prepaid hospital service organization.

The new structure will provide more efficient work space than present quarters and has been designed to reduce operating

costs and give better service to Blue Cross members.

A fireproof building of stilt-type construction, will have the appearance of two stories, and will contain some 36,455 sq. ft. of floor space. Parking space will be provided for about 50 cars.

FRUIN-COLNON CONTRACTING
COMPANY SAN FRANCISCO
ANNOUNCES AWARDS PROGRAM

On occasion of the 85th Anniversary of the Fruin-Colnon Contracting Company, Engineers and Constructors, with offices in San Francisco, St. Louis and Indianapolis, a national Awards Program has been announced by John P. Soult, President.

The awards are to stimulate consideration of the needs of urban and metro-

politan communities and to recognize significant contributions towards the improvement and development of urban and metropolitan areas. The program is to be co-sponsored by the National Municipal League. Any individual or group which publishes a report, book or monograph, conducts a research project, or completes an action program which makes a significant contribution in line with the purposes of the awards is eligible.

WASHINGTON STATE
CHAPTER PRODUCERS
COUNCIL TABLE-TOP

The Producers Council, Inc., Washington State Chapter, held a "Table Top" exhibition recently in the Washington Athletic Club, Seattle, Washington.

The latest in building materials available and usable in the Northwest were shown, with more than 37 members exhibiting their products.

ARCHITECT GETS
COMMISSION FOR
HIGH SCHOOL

Architect William H. Harrison of Los Angeles, has been commissioned by the Whittier High School District, Whittier, to prepare plans for construction of a new high school in Whittier.

The project will include classrooms, administration unit, cafeteria and gymnasium.

BANK OF AMERICA
TO BUILD NEW SAN
FRANCISCO OFFICE

The Bank of America has announced plans for construction of a new 8-story building, with provision for extension to a 13-story building, on Market Street in San Francisco.

The new building will be located be-

tween 11th street and South Van Ness, and will contain 550,000 sq. ft. of office space for 1000 employees in 15 of the bank's service departments. Off-street auto parking will be provided on the ground floor level.

HIGH SCHOOL
PLANNED
FOR OROVILLE

The Oroville Union High School District has acquired a new site for construction of a $1,500,000 new high school building, which will provide facilities for an administration unit, 16-classrooms, cafeteria, shop building, arts and crafts, home economics, gymnasium with lockers and showers, and toilets.

Architect Lawrence G. Thomsen, 325 W. 3rd Street, Chico, is preparing plans and specifications.

COLFAX WILL
BUILD NEW
HIGH SCHOOL

Architect Lawrence G. Thomson, 325 W. 3rd St., Chico, is preparing plans for construction of a new high school in Colfax for the Placer Union High School District.

The project represents a complete new high school building with facilities for an administration unit, classrooms, multi-purpose unit, kitchen, cafeteria, shops, library, gymnasium and locker rooms. Estimated cost of the work is $700,000.

JOHN S. BARRY
PROMOTED BY
GLADDING, McBEAN

John S. Barry, formerly staff assistant to the Manager of Marketing Solar Aircraft Company in San Diego, has been appointed Market Research Analyst of Gladding, McBean & Company, according to an announcement by C. W. Planje, firm president.

The position is a new one and will comprise directing market research activities for all divisions of the Company, under the direction of vice president H. K. Swenerton.

CALIFORNIA STATE
ARCHITECT ANNOUNCES
EXTENSIVE SCHEDULE

California State Architect Anson Boyd, recently announced that the Division of Architecture expects to begin construction on over $170,000,000 of State building projects during 1958. This more than doubles the division's 1957 construction program and is the result of several very large projects being initiated during the year. The program is divided into over

$70,000,000 for Northern California, and $99,000,000 for Southern California.

Included in the work is a large program of college residence hall construction authorized by the Legislature in 1957. The program will require over 3,900,000 man days of labor by the construction trades, and $63,000,000 of manufactured materials.

AIRTEMP NAMES NEW WEST COAST DIVISION MANAGER

Joseph S. Topp has been named Manager of the Airtemp Construction West Coast Zone headquarters in Los Angeles, a position created by the establishment of six new zone offices throughout the country.

Topp was formerly manager of the Contract and Order Administration at the firm's Dayton, Ohio, plant.

DONALD BRADSHAW IS NAMED MANAGER SAN FRANCISCO OFFICE

Donald Bradshaw, formerly manager of the Phoenix, Arizona branch of the Fiberglas Engineering & Supply Division of Owens-Corning Fiberglas Corpn., has been appointed manager of the division's San Francisco branch, according to an announcement by W. E. Munsey, Santa Clara, gneral manager of the Fiberglas Engineering & Supply Division.

Bradshaw, born and educated in England, joined Owens-Corning in 1951 in the General Engineering Department of the company's Santa Clara plant, transferred to the company's sales office in San Francisco in December 1952, and two

years later was named Phoenix manager of the firm. He is a member of the American Society of Refrigeration Engineers, and is a registered professional mechanical engineer, State of California.

ALBERT E. JOHANN APPOINTED BY WEBER SHOWCASE

Albert E. Johann has been appointed Director of Industrial Relations for the Weber Showcase & Fixture Company, Inc., Los Angeles, according to an announcement by Alexander Black, Executive Vice President of the firm.

Johann's entire background has been in the industrial relations field. His most recent position being with the Meredith Publishing Company of Des Moines, Iowa, where he served as Director of Industrial Relations and Personnel.

ARCHITECTS DESIGN NEWLY DEDICATED COVINA SCHOOL

Dedication of the Badillo Elementary School in the Charter Oak School District, second in a program of twelve elementry schools in the Covina, California district, was observed this month, with Frank W. Kittinger, District Superintendent, in charge of ceremonies.

Planned, designed and engineered by Daniel, Mann, Johnson & Mendenhall, Los Angeles, architects and engineers, the plant's facilities include 16-classrooms, a double kindergarten, administration building, a multi-use with a complete kitchen and a teachers' dining room, and attendant facilities, and will provide for 680 students.

Careful design and a good choice of materials enabled the buildings to be completed at an average cost of $11.97 per sq. ft., which is considerably less than the figure set for State Aid allowance.

EDSEL CURRY IS NAMED WEBERWALL SALES DIRECTOR

Edsel Curry, youthful civic leader and former USC athlete, has been named sales director of Weber Showcase & Fixture's Weberwall Division for the 11 western states, Oklahoma and Texas, according to an announcement by Alexander Black, executive vice president and co-ordinator for the company's Laboratory Equipment Division, Los Angeles.

Curry, in his new position, will be responsible for sales in every section of the country in which Weber movable walls and partitions are marketed.

DONALD H. McLAUGHLIN GIVEN HIGHEST AWARD OF AMERICAN INSTITUTE

Donald H. McLaughlin of San Francisco, president of the Homestake Mining Company, together with Dr. Champion H. Mathewson, Professor Emeritus of Metallurgy and Metallography at Yale University since 1950 and former President of AIME; and Fred Searls, Jr., of New York, Chairman of the Board of Newmont Mining Corpn., was elected to Honorary Membership in the American Institute of Mining, Metallurgical, and Petroleum Engineers.

This is the highest distinction conferred

by AIME, and presentations will be made at the annual meeting of AIME in New York City on February 19.

McLaughlin and Searls, Jr., are native Californians, and both are graduates of the University of California.

OTIS D. GOUTY JOINS ASCE HEADQUARTERS

Otis D. Gouty of Kansas City, Mo., has joined the headquarters staff of the American Society of Civil Engineers in New York City as assistant to the secretary. His duties will be primarily concerned with the student chapters and local sections of ASCE.

Gouty, graduate of the University of Kansas with a degree in civil engineering, formerly served as engineer with the Central States Pipe Lines Division of the Socony Mobil Oil Company at Wichita, Kansas.

ROBERT G. HILL IS HONORED BY ADVERTISERS

Robert G. Hill, advertising manager for Columbia-Geneva Steel Division of United States Steel, San Francisco, has been named "Industrial Advertising's Manager-of-the-Year" for 1957, the first West Coast adman selected for the award in the 21 years of the competition.

He was chosen for the honor by "Industrial Marketing," national publication covering the industrial advertising and selling field. The award is given annually to an industrial advertising man who produces or who oversees the production of outstanding advertisements for his company during the year. Many of the advertisements appeared in ARCHITECT & ENGINEER magazine during the past year.

BUYS LARGE ACREAGE CALAVERAS CEMENT BUYS LARGE ACERAGE IN REDDING AREA

Caliveras Cement Company, San Francisco, has exercised four options to purchase acreage and mining claims totaling approximately 550 acres in the Redding area of the Sacramento Valley.

The land was acquired for its limestone deposits, and is being bought by the company as part of a long range program of adding to reserves. Calaveras completed an extensive test drilling program on the properties several months ago.

The firm also has options on several other properties in the area as potential sites for a new cement plant.

THE UNLADYLIKE BEHAVIOR
OF MARIA MITCHELL

In a quiet house in Lynn, Massachusetts, in 1889, an old woman lay waiting for death. "Well," she said in amused wonder, "if this is dying, there is nothing very unpleasant about it." And the book closed for one of the most remarkable of the many remarkable women America has produced.

Her story began on a night very long ago when, as a Quaker girl in Nantucket, Maria Mitchell discovered a comet—and got a gold medal worth 20 ducats from the Danish King.

Overnight she became a celebrity. But many people, wedded to the popular notion of woman as a "household ornament," regarded Maria as an unwelcome phenomenon and her discovery as only an accident.

That was because they didn't know Maria Mitchell. At 12 she could regulate a ship's chronometer; at 17 she understood Bowditch's "Practical Navigator" and was studying science in self-taught French, German and Latin. In time she would become the first woman member of the American Academy of Arts and Sciences, the first woman astronomy professor—in Matthew Vassar's Female College—and a member forever of New York University's Hall of Fame.

Moreover, all her adult life she was to work with growing success in the crusade to make American women free.

No one these days would question the rewards of Maria Mitchell's crusade. Women today enrich every level of public life. And, in family life, they guard financial security two times out of three. One reason, probably, why their families have more than $40,000,000,000 saved—in guaranteed-safe United States Savings Bonds.

Women know there is no *safer* way to save. Trust them. Through Payroll Savings or at your bank, start *your* Bond program, too. Today.

Now Savings Bonds are better than ever! Every Series E Bond purchased since February 1, 1957, pays 3¼% interest when held to maturity. It earns higher interest in the early years than ever before, and matures in only 8 years and 11 months. Hold your *old* E Bonds, too. They earn more as they get older.

As General Contractors and Builders, we share pride with

MARCHANT'S WORLD HEADQUARTERS
NEW BUILDING

The construction and design of the Marchant's World Headquarters building offered important challenges to all who were concerned with making it a reality. To have played a part in finding able men to face these challenges . . . to have worked with such able associates to make this idea of a magnificent building a reality . . . has been a great privilege!

ALBERT F. ROLLER, A.I.A., *Architect*

    H. J. BRUNNIER, *Structural Engineer*

        DUDLEY DEANE & ASSOCIATES, INC., *Mechanical Engineers*

           LYLE E. PATTON, *Electrical Engineer*

DINWIDDIE CONSTRUCTION CO.

210 Crocker Building   San Francisco 4, Calif.   YUkon 6-2718

S. DAVID UNDERWOOD, Architect

H 1958

San Jose City Hall — now under construction

Architect: Donald F. Haines A.I.A.   Contractor: Carl N. Swenson Co. Inc.

Michel & Pfeffer Iron Works, Inc.

212 Shaw Road
South San Francisco, California
Plaza 5-8983

ARISTON
Metal Products
SINCE 1912

WILDER

TING EDITORS:

W. LITTLE, Dean,
Architecture, Univer-
egon, Eugene, Oregon

g
i R. MOCINE, City
Engineer, Oakland,

*uing and
:enters*
EMERY COX, Sales
& Business Develop-
lyst, Berkeley, Califor-

slopment
DRACHMAN, Sub-
nd Realty Developer,
Arizona

ming
). McCONNEL, Stan-
ool Planning Dept.,
a, California

Planning
NES, Architect,
aho

chitecture
FIELD, Architect,
:les, California

. BLUME, Consulting
:ctural Engineer, San
, California

4 A. ULLNER,

NES
dvertising

★

VER PICTURE

:K

SAVINGS &
)CIATION
Y.

dler's Diamond Anniver-
s extensive variety of in-
abinet work, being done
in with West Coast con-

for details.
Phil Fein & Associates
Photographers

CTS' REPORTS—
By

ENGINEER

——ARCHITECT & ENGINEER *is indexed regularly by* ENGINEERING INDEX, INC.; *and* ART INDEX——

Contents for

MARCH

THE OLDEST PROFESSIONAL MONTHLY BUSINESS MAGAZINE OF THE ELEVEN WESTERN STATES

ARCHITECT AND ENGINEER (Established 1905) is published on the 15th of the month by The Architect and
Engineer, Inc., 68 Post St., San Francisco 4; Telephone EXbrook 2-7182. President, K. P. Kierulff; Vice-

. EDITORIAL NOTES .

DEVELOPING ENGINEERING

American engineering colleges—already carrying on nearly one-half of the government-sponsored basic research in engineering now underway in the nation—have appealed for expanded national support for fundamental research and promised in return to assume even greater responsibilities for the success of such a program.

In a comprehensive summary of the status and needs of research in engineering colleges, The American Society for Engineering Education, points out:

That engineering research valued at $100 million a year is now in progress on college campuses.

Another $10 million could be accommodated immediately with the present educational staff.

The progress of engineering in future years in the Nation requires a greatly expanded program of basic research today in all technical fields.

Increased support of research in educational institutions is vital for the professional development of the faculties, for new knowledge which will result, and for the qualified students it will help to train.

Budget uncertainties of late 1957 damaged the "good relationships and the spirit of mutual confidence" which had been built up between the Defense Department and educational institutions. Many cuts remain unrestored, and some new programs are still uncertain.

Summing up the report Dr. Frederick C. Lindvall, President of The American Society for Engineering Education, and Chairman of the Division of Engineering at the California Institute of Technology, declared, "Research is an integral part of modern engineering education as well as the foundation upon which new technology is built."

Electric power Utilities, privately owned, are paying taxes at the rate of $1.7-billion a year . . . that supplies a lot of government services.

* * *

COMPLACENCY

Too often we take for granted the private ownership of our basic national industries.

It is, therefore, worth noting the excellent progress being made in the synthetic rubber industry which was recently denationalized, following its birth as an economic wartime activity.

Little more than two years ago, the synthetic rubber producing facilities were disposed of at prices considered to be beneficial to taxpayers.

The record since then makes it fortunate for a private enterprise system that this denationalization took place. As late as 1941, synthetic production accounted for less than 1% of total rubber production. In 1954, before denationalization, synthetic's share was 52%. In 1956, synthetic production has risen to 61% of the market and in 1957, to 64%. Projected into 1960, synthetic production is expected to account for more than 70% of the total.

Clearly, had denationalization not taken place, we would have had a subtle, long-run process of nationalization of the total productive facilities of the rubber industry. It is most fortunate, therefore, that the eleventh hour attempt on the floor of Congress to defeat denationalization was beaten back. This industry is now able to grow and progress is rightfully service to American consumers.

* * *

It's a good idea to give preference to American made items in the plumbing brass line — says the Plumbing-Heating-Cooling Information Bureau.

• • •

ARCHITECTURE IS BIG BUSINESS

A carefully prepared report from the California State Board of Architectural Examiners, and delivered to the California Council, American Institute of Architects, at their last annual meeting, discloses some rather interesting information about the architectural profession in California.

According to this official governmental report, there are now some 2791 architects registered in the State of California and licensed to practice architecture.

This figure represents a total of 11.6 per cent of all the architects registered to practice architecture in the United States, and as the population of California is approximately 7.6 per cent of that of the entire 48 states, the numbrer of architects licensed to practice in California is some 66 per cent greater, per state, than the national average.

Obviously such an abundance of architects in California means just one thing! California is a keystone construction center in the nation and work being done, and on the boards of California architects, represents a tremendous potential of building material products and services consumption. Yes, indeed! Architecture is BIG business in California.

* * *

FEDERAL ENGINEERING CIVIL SERVICE

The American Society of Civil Engineers has announced support of measures designed to remove "inequities" in the Federal Classification Act, particularly as related to the grades and salary schedules of the professional and scientific employees in federal civil service.

At the same time, the Society recommended interim salary adjustments for professional engineers in the Uniformed Services that will be comparable to those recommended for Civil Service engineers.

VALLEY HIGH SCHOOL

Woodland Hills,
California

Balch,
Bryan,
Perkins,
Hutchason,
Architects

A combination of aluminum, glass and porcelain panel curtain walls, is featured in the plans just completed for the new $5,000,000 William Howard Taft High School at east Woodland Hills, California.

Located on a 28-acre site in the San Fernando Valley, the new school was designed for the Los Angeles City Board of Education by Architects Balch-Bryan-Perkins-Hutchason.

It will have 244,000 sq. ft., and will provide facilities for 2500 students in permanent structures. Future expansion under the master plan calls for the school to accommodate a total of 3200 students.

The school will have three two-story classroom buildings, plus boys and girls gymnasium and multipurpose unit, with a large covered lunch shelter and music rooms. Other buildings will be for industrial arts, agriculture, utilities, driver education, library and administration.

Two-story classroom buildings, with concrete floors and roofs, were included in the plans to accommodate all required facilities on the only practical school site in the vicinity.

Plans for the new school were authorized last summer by the City Board of Education as a part of a special crash program. Under the program $180,000 is being spent for plans and specifications from current tax funds, rather than waiting until the school district voted the needed bond issue.

This procedure will advance the start of construction on the new school by one year, with completion expected late in 1960.

Interiors will have fluorescent lighting, asphalt tile flooring, acoustical tile ceilings and plaster walls. Classrooms will be equipped with audio-visual darkening blinds.

The multi-purpose building will have a platform-type stage and will seat an audience of about 650. Larger gatherings will be cared for in an outdoor assembly area, with stage. This area will be placed between two of the larger classroom buildings.

Folding bleachers for basketball spectators will seat 1250 persons in the gymnasium. It will have a hardwood spring-type playing floor.

Other athletic facilities will include a football field, with bleachers to seat 3000 persons, four tennis courts, baseball diamond and general athletic areas. Two large paved car parking sections and adequate landscaping are included.

NEWS and COMMENT ON ART

M. H. deYOUNG
MEMORIAL MUSEUM

The M. H. deYoung Memorial Museum, Golden Gate Park, San Francisco, under the direction of Walter Heil, is presenting the following special exhibitions and events during the month of March:

EXHIBITIONS: Paintings, by Jose Juan Capuletti; Kimona Stencils, by famous artists of the 18th and 19th Centuries. An exhibition from the collection of John Huston of San Francisco, courtesy of the Japan Air Lines.

SPECIAL EVENTS: Seminars in the History of Art are held each Thursday morning at 10:30. These are informal illustrated lectures and discussions with the theme of the current series being "Contemporary Sculpture." Classes in Art Enjoyment for adults include exercises in Oil Painting, Part II, which is a continuation course of 10 weekly experiments intended to develop self-command in seeing and painting. The course is given Saturday morning at 10:30; Saturday afternoon at 1:30; Wednesday morning at 10:30 and Wednesday afternoon at 1:30. Art Classes for Children include Picture Making, ages 4-8, Saturday morning from 10:15 to 11:30; Art and Nature, ages 9-11, Wednesday afternoon 3:30 to 4:30, and the Art Club, for students 12-18, each Thursday afternon 3:30 to 4:30.

Free automobile parking is provided. The Museum is open daily.

OAKLAND ART MUSEUM

The Oakland Art Museum, 1000 Fallon Street, under the direction of Paul Mills, Curator, is offering a number of outstanding exhibits and events during March, including:

EXHIBITIONS: California Design IV, comprising furniture, accessories, textiles, ceramics and other well designed objects for the home, all designed by Southern California designers for production. A juried show organized by the Pasadena Art Museum. FURNITURE, by Sam Maloof, who has received international recognition for his hand crafted furniture. SHELL FORMS of Felix Candela, a photographic exhibition of the new frontiers in architectural structure being explored by this Mexican architect, organized by the University of Southern California and the Southern California Chapter of the AIA. KEITH GALLERY, treasures from St. Mary's, a selection from the outstanding paintings assembled by Brother Cornelius of the St. Mary's College Keith Gallery.

SPECIAL EVENTS: Wednesday nights at the Museum, programs begin at 8:30 p.m., and include

showing of slides, discussions on art, and other phases of activities closely identified with art. Classes in "Looking At Art", each Tuesday evening at 8 o'clock, and Leader Training Classes, craft instruction designed to help Girl Scout and Campfire leaders provide interesting and different projects for their troops. Tuesdays and Thursdays 10 a.m.

The Museum is open daily.

CALIFORNIA PALACE OF THE
LEGION OF HONOR

The California Palace of the Legion of Honor, Lincoln Park, San Francisco, under the direction of Thomas Carr Howe, Jr., is offering the following special exhibits and events for this month:

EXHIBITS: CALIFORNIA COLLECTS: North and South. An exhibition sponsored by the patrons of Art and Music of the California Palace of the Legion of Honor and the Art Council of the University of California, Los Angeles. "YALLAH", an exhibition of photographs by Peter W. Haeberlin, done for the book by Paul Bowles. PAINTINGS, by Cosmy. POSTERS U.S.A., an exhibition of 69 American posters illuminating the American scene from 1832 through World War I, presented in cooperation with American Heritage, the Detroit Historical Society, Levi Berman, and the American Federation of Arts. PRE-MARSHALL PLAN GERMANY, Pictures by Boris Von Clodt.

The Achenbach Foundation for Graphic Arts. Early Prints and Drawings of California from the collection of Robert B. Honeyman. The Iconography of Anthony Van Dyck.

SPECIAL EVENTS: Organ Program each Saturday and Sunday at 3 p.m. Educational activities include two art classes for children ages 6-11, Saturday mornings at 10 o'clock; Drawing and Painting from Observation and Imagination, a class for juniors ages 12-17 will be held Saturday afternoon at 2 o'clock. All classes are free of charge and materials are furnished.

The Museum is open daily, admission free.

CALIFORNIA SCHOOL OF
FINE ARTS

The California School of Fine Arts, 800 Chestnut Street, San Francisco, is presenting a special group of exhibits during this month, including the following:

The 77th Annual Exhibition of the San Francisco Art Association, a juried showing with awarding of prizes; and a Special Exhibition of European, American and Bay Area Art, from the private collection of John Bolles, Architect.

SAN FRANCISCO MUSEUM OF ART

The San Francisco Museum of Art, War Memorial Building, Civic Center, under the direction of Dr. Grace L. McCann Morley, will feature the following special exhibits and events during this month:

EXHIBITIONS: Adventure in Glass originates in Sweden and is devoted to the famous Orrefors Glassbruk; includes interesting displays of technical processes involved in making glass and emphasizes the various physical and decorative properties of the material. The exhibit is touring the United States under auspices of the American Federation of Arts. CONTEMPORARY PRINTS FROM ITALY, second of a series of international print exchanges, organized and directed in Europe by Matila Simon and in this country by Prof. Gordon W. Gilkey, Head of the Art Department, Oregon State College. Exhibit includes lithographs, etchings, dryprints and woodcuts. ADALINE KENT MEMORIAL EXHIBITION, presented in honor of an artist long beloved in the Bay Area, includes drawings and paintings, sculpture, and emphasizes especially work of the last seven or eight years. SPRING RENTAL GALLERY. CONTEMPORARY JAPANESE AND WESTERN PAINTING: Shokuku and selected works. COLLECTING MODERN ART, the collection of Mr. and Mrs. Harry Lewis Weston, and selected from Bay Area collections. RETROSPECTIVE, Piet Mondrian.

SPECIAL EVENTS: Art Travel Series, Tuesday evenings at 8:30; Fashion Group Career Course, Thursday evenings at 7:30; Lecture Tours, Sundays at 3:30; Wednesday evening programs include round table art discussions and museum activities; Adventures in Drawing and Painting, Friday evenings at 7:30, include the Sketch Club, Painting Class. Studio: Art for the Layman on Tuesday mornings at 10:00; Children's Saturday Morning Art Classes, ages 10-11 and 6-14.

The Museum is open daily.

SAN FRANCISCO ART ASSOCIATION

One of the most interesting private collections of contemporary art on the West Coast belongs to John Bolles, internationally famous Bay Area architect. Selections from this collection will be shown to the public for the first time in the San Francisco Art Association Gallery, 800 Chestnut street, San Francisco. Approximately twenty-five paintings, the work of American and European artists chosen by a committee of the San Francisco Art Association Artists' Council, will be shown.

John Bolles' interest in art springs from his early study of the ancient architecture of Persia, Egypt, Yucatan and other countries during the early 20's and 30's when he was turning his skills as an engineer and architect to the field of archaeology.

OAKLAND ART MUSEUM EXHIBITIONS NOW TOURING UNITED STATES MUSEUMS

New project for 1958 at the Oakland Art Museum is sending exhibitions to other museums throughout the country. Seven different exhibitions have been scheduled or are being scheduled for showings, according to Curator Paul Mills. "Through this program, the whole nation is learning to think of Oakland not as an industrial but as a cultural center," Mills states.

"Contemporary Bay Area Figurative Painting," the first exhibition in the country covering the new application of abstract painting techniques to subject matter, was shown in the Oakland museum in September. A larger, travelling version of the show, which features the work of David Park, Elmer Bischoff, Richard Diebenkorn and other painters, most of them residents of the East Bay, was prepared by the museum. During December, the exhibition was presented by the Los Angeles County Museum and this current month is on show at the Dayton Art Institute. The third distinguished American museum which will present the show is the Colorado Springs Fine Arts Center.

First of the museum exhibitions to tour was the Bay Printmakers Society First Annual, which was shown in galleries in every corner of the country for two years. The society, headed by local printmaker Robert Strohmeier, and the museum have just sent off the Third Annual for another two-year tour. 'The Painted Flower," the collection of floral paintings belonging to Mr. and Mrs. Herbert Mortimer Stoll, Jr., is receiving enthusiastic response. Mrs. Stoll is General Chairman of the Oakland Museums Association's Women's Board. The exhibition was first shown at the Vancouver, Canada, Art Museum, and has bookings scheduled in Seattle, Salt Lake City, Tacoma, Portland, Memphis, Reno, Long Beach, Spokane and other cities.

"New Museums, U.S.A." is an exhibition of photographs and drawings of new museum buildings built or planned in recent years. The material was assembled with the help of the museums association and presented in brief form at the California Spring Garden Show last year. Bookings are scheduled in several cities, and the exhibition, now a larger, more finished production than during its first showing here, will be presented again in Oakland during the year.

OUR PROBLEM OF IGNORANCE

By LEON CHATELAIN, JR.

President, The American
Institute of Architects

Several decades ago, any address by an architect to a major convention of genaral contractors would have been considered surprising, if not downright odd. The architect, in those days, frequently doubled as a builder. At the same time, the general contractor dabbled in design and operated on the theory that he could get along just fine without an architect to bother him. During this period of rapid growth in America, we both made many mistakes and they are still cluttered around us in the form of buildings. That's the awful thing about a bad building. You can't burn it easily, as you would a poor piece of music or a bad book, and you can't turn it to the wall, as you can with a bad painting. Like Everest, the building just stands there and outlives all our apologies. Needless to say, there has been a vast improvement in design and building over the past half century. One major reason for that improvement is the effective teamwork which exists today between the architect and the general contractor. The American Institute of Architects will not have a member who builds or who, in any way, profits from the use or sale of materials. As a professional man, the architect must serve only one person—the client. He relies on the skill and experience of the contractor for the translation of design into structure. The contractor relies upon the architect for design. Today, we are partners, well-equipped to help each other, and—more important—to serve the public. It is a very good thing that we enjoy this harmony, trust and mutual faith because we bear a tremendous responsibility, you and I.

Future of Architecture

We represent the biggest industry in the United States—the construction industry. It is going to grow bigger, and even today, it is changing before our very

NOTE: Herewith is a talk by Leon Chatelain, Jr., Washington, D. C., president of The American Institute of Architects, given before the 39th annual convention of the Associated General Contractors of America, Inc., in Dallas, Texas, on February 11, 1958, in which several phases of architect, builder, public relationships are discussed. Editor.

eyes. In these changes, we—you and I—are going to have to accept many new ideas and learn many new things. We may also find that our responsibility does not end with building alone. In fact, I believe that this is here now.

For one thing, our client has changed. It is very seldom today that we design a building for one person. This is the age of the corporate client—the collective client, if you will. The criteria for an office building are decided by a committee appointed by and responsible to a board of directors. A church project is supervised by a building committee. A school—when the job is planned properly—is dependent upon the entire community for the conceptual process which guides the design. There is no segment of the public to which we can point and say—it has no connection with architecture and building. The Girl Scout leader and housewife of today are among the people who will decide upon a new civic center, a church, a school, or even a bank tomorrow. They will participate in planning a new kind of architecture—building in the mass.

If the client is seldom an individual today, the building may not be an individual tomorrow. Architecture is no longer a single house, a church, a school. It is a plaza, a community redevelopment, a vast clearance of worn-out buildings and congested land. We are finding that we must adjust our minds and imagination to new ideas—tearing down and re-building to fit rapidly-changing needs — re-building on a scale which, a few years ago, seemed more fancy than fact.

We also will find, in the near future, a demand for the new types of buildings. The suburb, as a word and idea, is disappearing as metropolitan belts overlap. Middle-aged people are moving back to the nerve centers of the population areas. This has given rise to new architectural thinking about a new type of city house, designed and built to provide utility, economy, and privacy in the busy life of the metropolis.

Development of West

In the not-to-distant future, we may find ourselves

designing and building new types of reinforced structures for blast protection—at the very least we will have to provide shelters against nuclear fall-out. A more pleasant thought is that the conjunction of nuclear energy with automation and new developments in water purification promise almost certainly that we will soon break the chains that now hold us to the transportation lines. This is an exciting thought. When man first emerged from the cave and began to do business with his neighbor, his commerce grew up along the footpaths. Later, business expanded along the waterways, and, still later, acquired new room by stringing itself along the railroad lines. Man has always needed facilities at hand to renew his source of power. Today, we face real change.

According to the Atomic Energy Commission, there were one hundred and two nuclear reactors being operated by industry in the United States as of last October. If you count all kinds of reactors—civilian and military—those used for research and training as well as power—an estimated two hundred and forty reactors are either operating, being built, or in the planned stage. If you still have any doubt that we are in what we might call the practical nuclear age, consider this: In Washington, D. C., a private school for technical training is inaugurating a home-study correspondence course for high school graduates in the operation and maintenance of nuclear reactors. This is a serious, practical project, which has the blessing of the government.

Water Resources

Now we are told that, within the next ten years, it almost certainly will be commercially feasible to pipe sea water into the great southwestern desert and turn it into fresh water. This could make the frontier-era migration to the western United States look like a Sunday outing by a bird-watchers' club. At the same time, progress is being made with the reclamation of used water—so that a given quantity of water may be used over and over again for a variety of purposes. Entire industrial communities—powered by nuclear packages and supplied by inexhaustible supplies of water—will spring up and transform that great western desert which for thousands of miles today looks like the face of the moon without benefit of telescope. This is the future—in our country—on earth, and one could wish that outer space were not so near, because we have so much to do here.

However, some doubts about our future are being raised today because we seemed to have lagged behind Russia in some areas. To overcome this lag, there's a good deal of talk going on about how to catch up. Some of this talk involves us—the architect and the builder—and we had better pay heed. We had better pay heed because there's confusion and misunder-

standing about public education. A good deal of this confusion involves school buildings—what they are, what they're worth, and what they should cost. The confusion comes from ignorance, and this is a sad commentary on American life. The average parent and home owner is affected more by the condition of his schools than nearly anything else in his community life. His schools cost him money and affect the welfare of his children—they hit him in the pocketbook and in the family. Yet, by and large, the public knows next to nothing about its schools. The ignorance is not confined to the proverbial John Smith of Everytown, U.S.A. It has been disseminated recently by a number of prominent non-educational writers, thus compounding the confusion, and, even worse, encouraging school boards to embark upon unwise and wasteful ventures.

School Building

In the matter of public education, basically, we are dealing with two kinds of things—those we know, and those we do not know.

The architects and general contractors do know about the planning and building of schools, and the fact that many people do not know is our own fault. It is this story which we must tell, not for our own aggrandizement but because, without public understanding and public support, the building of enough good schools that combine quality with economy, will not be possible. There are many opinions about school design and construction, and also a number of facts. Here are some of the facts:

The cost of school buildings has doubled in the past twenty years, due to advances in the price of land, materials, labor, and other expenses. Yet during this same period in which school-building costs doubled, the costs of buildings generally has tripled. In the difference between the two figures lies a real tribute to the dedication and ingenuity of the nation's educators, contractors, and architects. The fact is that the school-building is still the best bargain, dollar-for-dollar, on the building market today.

Yet some people claim that schools are over-priced and represent a heavy tax burden upon the home-owner. Are they a tax burden? The simple fact is that if schools were built for nothing at all, it would make very little difference on the average tax bill. Let's say that Mr. John Smith receives an annual property tax bill of two hundred dollars. The chances are his bill will show about half, or one hundred dollars of that amount, will be spent for education. But of that one hundred dollars, only about ten per cent, or ten dollars, will be spent on his municipal school-building program. In other words, Mr. Smith's share of his community's school-building costs will cost about the same amount that he would spend in one evening by hiring a baby-sitter and taking his wife to dinner and a

movie.

If school building increased at the same pace for fifteen years, Mr. Smith would pay about as much for his new school buildings during that time as he spends on one modest television set. This does not seem unreasonable.

The substantial expense of school buildings is the interest paid on financing and the annual cost of maintenance and repair. For this reason, we have this seeming paradox—only the wealthy community can afford a cheap school. We reject the argument that school buildings should be monuments. We feel that we won this argument many years ago. We can save money by avoiding the trappings and ornaments of the past—the fake columns, the parapet roofs, and the gingerbread. Forcing schools into a certain "look" adds nothing to education, creates community eye-sores, and wastes imagination and money. Contemporary design is simply the freedom to solve a problem without boxing a building into an artificial style.

School Costs

Recently, several writers have stated that schools are being designed as palaces, and that they're costing too much; that this is so because educators, architects, and contractors want it that way. This is sheer nonsense. In each of these diatribes, the writers have pointed to two or three specific schools as examples which prove their statements. The alleged high cost of one of the schools was cited over and over again. However, no one mentioned that the community in which the school is located has an average annual family income of twenty-one thousand dollars. Who are we, or anyone else, to say that the citizens of this rich suburb wasted their money by buying a truly first-class school?

On what should they have spent their money? Has anyone criticized them for buying new cars, new clothes, and new television sets? Since when is a school less important than incidental, personal luxuries? It seems to me there is a serious question of human values at issue here.

Money can be saved on schools. Of course it can. But it is rare when very much of it can be saved on the job site. The real savings to the community accrue through long-range planning of school buildings. A ten-year advance program is not unrealistic. Community studies on population trends, projected located of industry, residential building plans, and zoning development can be made at great future savings to the community. Planning targets can be adjusted from year to year. Architects are given time to make thoughtful design studies. Contractors may bid more accurately. Jobs are not dumped together on saturated building markets which deprive the school board of bidding competition. School boards are not stampeded into rash

decisions and cut-rate schemes. Communities are not persuaded to accept temporary 'package" buildings, fabricated without professional advice and without the needs of the individual site and educational program in mind. It may seem a new though to some, but the fact is that it would be hard to find two municipal school systems in our entire nation which teach the same thing in exactly the same way. This is basic to American education. As the architect and contractor know, seemingly minor changes in teaching methods and material can make substantial differences in the school building. Take a science classroom, for example. Will the students be taught mainly at their desks, or while standing at the chalkboards? The answer to just this one question will affect the amount of wall space needed, the size of the wall boards, the amount of storage required, the type and size of seating equipment, and the intensity and location of lighting.

School Planning

When you add to these questions of curriculum and method the peculiar needs of the local soil, the climate, the degree of natural light available, and the availability of materials and labor, you begin to realize why educational facilities cannot be mass-produced on a stock basis.

Besides long-range planning and design tailored to specific community needs, permanence of building is essential to economy. Consider the cost of replacing temporary buildings; not just the construction, but the financing. The difference between a two per cent and three per cent interest rate can be twenty per cent of the cost of the entire building. Today's school should be built of first-class materials and it should be built to last for forty years. This is not incompatible with flexibility. The good school is situated on enough ground to allow for expansion. It is designed so that additional units can easily be added without tearing down existing walls and laying new utility lines. It is designed, as we like to say, for ultimate use.

These are some of the things that we know about education, and it is our job, yours and mine, to tell this story through our organizations and individually, to the people we meet and do business with. There are many other things that we do not know, but which are of interest to all of us.

I hope I have not given the impression that we know all there is to know about designing for education. One considerable area of uncertainty concerns the psychological effects of architecture upon man. There is considerable hope, I am happy to report to you today, that we will shortly begin to find out many new things about this subject. The National Science Foundation has granted a sum of money for us to hold a conference —which will include psychologists and sociologists—to define needed areas of basis research in architecture. These definitions have not yet been made but I believe

it can be predicted fairly that some of them will have to do with finding the answers to questions about human scale and the psychological effects of color. We know, for example, that lower ceilings cut down the cubic footage of a room, and, all things being equal, help reduce the building cost of the unit. However, what effect does this have on the students in a schoolroom? We really do not know. This may seem a rather obscure question. But is **not** when you consider that the design of one building can give the occupant a sense of freedom and space while another—containing the same square footage—seems to cramp and constrict. We know this much by observation. We also know that we must find out the **why** to these questions before we can do as much as we should to design a building which materially **encourages** the learning process.

Scientific Development

Let us examine another part of the educational problem. There is an avalanche of effort today to provide more and better scientists through public education. As architects—the people who plan human environment and whose work must be tailored to the function of the structure in question—we are greatly interested in this subject. Frankly, I had intended to come before you today with recommendations of a specific nature on what we should try to do about improvement of public education. However, the things which we do not know and cannot find out are so vital to a clear understanding of our educational condition that a clear-cut recommendation is ill advised.

The United States Department of Health, Education, and Welfare has proposed a far-ranging scholarship award program to worthy high school students throughout the nation. When we heard this, we immediately thought of the logical connection between the awarding of scholarships—mostly for science students — and the need for physical facilities in the schools. It doesn't make sense to have one without the other. We've been told by Secretary Folsom that we're in trouble because only one out of three high school students get a year of chemistry, and only one out of **four** takes physics. It seemed to me that someone should speak out about the obvious need for new and better classroom facilities for science. It did, until my staff looked into the subject a little further. The available facts were, to say the least, confusing.

According to the Department of Health, Education, and Welfare, **ninety-two per cent** of the senior high schools in the country were offering chemistry and physics in 1956. **But,** at the same time, only **thirty-six per cent** of the senior high school students were taking chemistry and only **twenty-six per cent** were taking physics. The figures seem to show clearly that the facilities are there, the courses **are** available—the students just aren't taking them.

There is another disturbing factor here. The figures themselves don't tell us what **kind** of facilities our schools have; what **sort** of programs are being offered. Are they good programs? We couldn't find out. Several educational organizations have told us within the past few days that they're just now planning to find out. The National Science Teachers Association tells us that we don't even know how many science classrooms in the country have gas, electrical outlets, and running water. In this proud nation of push-buttons, new car styles, color television, and the chemise, this is lamentable ignorance. There is another element which is much harder to measure. This is the imagination and interest of the teacher. The best laboratory in the country won't produce a good science program if the teacher is inadequate. However, it can be argued that an imaginative teacher can conduct a good science program **without** elaborate classroom facilities. Physics can be taught with a book, a buzzer, a dry cell, and a few brain cells. A running stream near a schoolhouse can be used for water-flow experiments and chemical analysis. Another question we must ask concerns the number of science students we want. Is it a bad thing that one out of three high school pupils takes chemistry? Isn't that enough? Will mass scholarships and more facilities produce Einsteins? Would more music schools produce Beethovens? You can **encourage** geniuses, but can you **mass-produce** them? It is relatively easy to raise many serious questions concerning all of the crash programs which have been outlined to us.

Teaching Methods

Obviously, we need a thorough understanding of our assets and needs before we can draw enough solid conclusions to put us on the proper path. This is of more than passing interest to architects and contractors, because the improvement of teaching methods and curricula will inevitably lead to improvement in the physical facilities of schools. One leads irresistably to another.

From what we now know, I offer several personal observations. They are not original or new, yet I think they are valid. We **do** know that we need more school buildings so that classes do not become too large for effective teaching. We **do** know that we should pay our teachers more—much more—in order to get and hold the best possible people for the important job of teaching.

I believe we also face a fundamental problem of reassuring our thinking about education. We cannot turn back the clock and say that everything will be much better if we just re-concentrate on the three R's. There are no longer sharply divergent schools of progressive and conservative education. Experimentation is always necessary to progress. In many American cities today, school boards are experimenting with teaching by

(Continued on Page 32)

PROCESS BUILDING . . . Roy A. Lippincott, Architect

HEAVY CONCRETE SLAB CONSTRUCTION

RESEARCH CENTER

SHELL DEVELOPMENT COMPANY

Emeryville, California

TOP VIEW:

Shows architectural rendering of the new Process Building as it will appear when completed.

LOWER VIEW:

Mobile crane equipment starts to raise one of the 34-ton sections into place.

Some of the heaviest, cast concrete slabs ever raised in light construction on the West Coast, were recently hoisted into place at the Shell Development Company's new Research Center being built in Emeryville, California.

The slabs, each weighing 34 tons, were the first walls raised for Shell's new 10,000 square foot process laboratory, and a check with R. A. Lippcott, Los Angeles architect who designed the building, and M. S. McDuffie, project engineer in charge representing Swinnerton-Walberg Company, general contractors, showed that no heavier tilt-up slabs have ever been raised in the area.

Of the thirty-four panels being used, some will be as much as 11 inches thick.

The three story, $500,000 building, is scheduled for completion about June 1st, and will be used by the physical chemistry, oil reaction process, chemical separation, and chemical reaction process departments.

Portions of its interior will be open from ground to roof to allow indoor construction of 35-foot models of distillation columns and absorption towers which in full scale will rise more than 100 feet.

In this lab, Shell will be able to develop processes for manufacture of new products to the point where they can be scaled up more quickly to commercial production.

Tests in the new process development lab will give engineers many of the answers before they go into pilot plant development.

ABOVE—one of the thirty-four panels being raised into final construction position.

BELOW—two of the huge concrete slab panels have been raised into wall position.

UNIVERSITY CITY . . . Largest Health Center *Photos by Hamilton Wright*

VENEZUELAN CAPITAL

ARCHITECTURE

POLYCLINIC HOSPITAL, in foreground of above picture, dominates all of University City at Caracas by its strategic location on the campus. . . . Its activities are closely integrated with those of the University's schools of medicine, pathological anatomy, experimental medicine, and tropical medicine.

Together with the schools of nursing, hygiene, dentistry, and pharmacy, it comprises the largest health center in all of South America in one of the most complete of all educational centers in the western hemisphere. . . . Costing $33,000,000 the hospital contains 1,515 beds for patients, of which 400 are reserved for the care of the student body of 5,000. The entire sixth floor is devoted exclusively to surgical and operating

Thriving City of

CARACAS

An oil fed boom has transformed the South American City of Caracas in Venezuela, from a sleepy Spanish village of some three-hundred thousand persons in 1941, to a throbbing metropolis of over one million population today. A tidal wave of people descending upon this mountain capital of Venezuela has brought about a complete transformation of the face of the city.

The dramatic results seen in the recent helicopter views shown on these four pages, are startling. With no place to go but "up," huge 15-story apartment buildings rise on hillsides levelled by bulldozers to replace squatters' shacks. Whole blocks of sprawling ancient buildings have given way to skyscraper office buildings and modern super-highways.

Architecture knows no single master, and whether school, office building or express highway, each contains daring new features in design and construction. The City Planning Commission works overtime to keep abreast of all of the architectural influences.

By 1960, when Caracas will play host to 79 nations for its International World's Fair, today's skyscrapers will be overshadowed by the amazing "Helicoid" or spiral in space building now taking shape. This unusual structure will be 25 stories high on one side, only 10 stories tall on the other, and its site has been cut out of the side of a mountain. A 58-storey building for which foundations are already completed is also planned for inaugural by 1960 in this South American city's vast "face lifting" program.

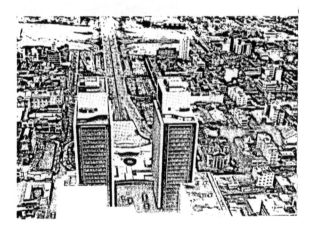

LOOKING DOWN

On the core of modern Caracas, the business and commercial center are reminiscent of New York's Rockefeller Center . . . nine blocks of the old city were demolished to make room for this development which can house 30,000 office workers.

Main arterial traffic moves underneath the two 30-story buildings which have two underground parking lots for 1,600 cars . . . modern shops, restaurants and a bus terminal.

BELOW is shown architectural model of the "Helicoid" business center . . . which will
house business offices, showrooms and shops, and also a permanent exhibition hall and
complete TV station, all reached by a spiral ramp connecting with the main arterial
approach shown at lower right . . . the site is located at one end of the Avenida Fuerzas
Armadas, principal North-South highway route bisecting the city. Dr. Jorge Romero
Gutierrez is the architect and designer.

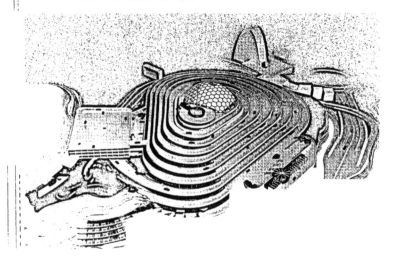

**ALL OF CITY'S MODERN HIGHWAYS
LEAD TO THE "BEISBOL" STADIUM**

A dramatic helicopter view looking down on the spacious stadium that is part of University City. It can seat 30,000 persons comfortably, without a single column to mar their vision. It's "home" for the Venezuela Winter League teams that sent Chico Overhead highway link is the Avenida Roosevelt, important connection from Caracas

Overhead highway link is the Avenida Roosevelt, important connection from Caracas to the Pan American highway. Below it is the "Autopista del Este," extension of the express route that connects Caracas with its international airport at LaGuaira now only 30 minutes drive from the capital.

VIEW ... Looking toward the West.

EXCITING DESIGN OF NEW

CITY HALL

SAN JOSE, CALIFORNIA

Donald F. Haines, A.I.A., Architect
Gould & Degenkolb, Structural Engineers,
Carl N. Swenson Co., Inc., General Contractor

DETAIL

Of the Northeast eleva-
tion showing liberal use
of glass for natural day
lighting.

Unusual in design, to say the least, is the new City Hall being completed in San Jose, California. It is built along the arc of a giant circular curve and combines architectural beauty with practicality, resulting in a contemporary styling in which form has truly followed function.

All weather comfort of every area of the building is assured by radiant heating and cooling systems equipped with flexible automatic controls.

Structurally the building is based on a 3 foot thick concrete mat foundation which has been used in preference to the frequently used spread footings because of the possibility of differential settlement of the clay types of soil on which the structure stands. However, in spite of numerous special construction features the cost of construction has been held to the nominal figure of $18.60 per square foot of floor space.

The architect's problem in designing the building was to come up with a style which would be impressive, yet not massive or gaudy, and so he decided on the curved form, which tends to catch the eye and to lead it along the structure. An added effect of movement is given the viewer by this form, and the result is a prominent building along a graceful arc.

CURVED ARC design gives eye-catching prominence. Council wing at left and upper tier utility housing break the usual monotony of a single form.

NORTHWEST elevation shows liberal use of decorative brick and stone, while general impression favorably accepts sweeping curve of large arc design.

The building is a four-story, reinforced concrete structure with an additional two-story wing which includes the dining hall and city council chambers. A two-way reinforced, 10-inch thick, concrete slab floor, with drop panels at supporting points, sets on three rows of columns. One advantage of this type of floor is that its freeing the undersides permits location of an elaborate air conditioning network of ducts and piping. The floor is cantilevered a distance of 11 feet beyond the interior row of columns to make a public corridor along the interior curved side.

The rows of columns are 22½ feet apart, with 20 foot intervals along the interior curve and 25 feet along the exterior curve. The two rows of columns along the curves with greater radii are 18 x 18 in. reinforced with No. 6 or 7 bars. To provide longitudinal rigidity against seismic loads, the inner curve row of columns was designed to a 18 x 48 in. size, the larger dimension extending parallel to the curve. Lateral shearwalls—four spaced evenly along the building—act to give rigidity in the other direction.

A structural steel roof frame tops the council chamber. A collular steel deck covers the frame to act as a diaphragm in resisting earthquake forces.

Soil and foundation studies made by Woodward-Clyde & Associates of Oakland, Calif., indicated the strong possibility of differential settlement in a clay-type soil if conventional spread footings were used. As a consequence a solidmat foundation was decided on to assure even settlement. That the decision was correct has been proved by the 2 in. of even settlement which has occurred already.

The foundation mat was designed as a flat 3 ft slab with 2 way reinforcing steel at both top and bottom. No. 8 to No. 11 sized reinforcing rods went into this slab. The pour took 29 hours using three transit batch plants and 15 cu yd trucks for the haul. The mat was

poured in one pour with a total of 3,400 cu yd of concrete. Peak rate for the pour was 170 cu yd per hour.

A total of 75 tons of structural steel was used in the building. Some 1,000 tons of reinforcing rods were used in conjunction with the 10,000 cu yd of structural concrete poured. A 6 sack mix with $1\frac{1}{2}$ in. aggregate was used for the foundation and shear walls; a $6\frac{1}{2}$ sack mix with $\frac{3}{4}$ in. aggregate was used for the floor slab. Both were designed for a 28 day strength of 3,250 psi.

A radiant comfort conditioning system is being installed throughout the building. This system has the advantage over conventional air conditioning in its rapid response and maximum flexibility in dividing areas to meet tenant requirements. A pneumatic type automatic control system with independent thermostats to control each zone as dictated both by interior and exterior loads is used.

Ducted air is forced through the ceiling plenum to assure circulation up to 4 air changes per hour in working spaces. But the air itself is not the governing temperature regulator, since this occurs by means of the $\frac{1}{2}$ in. piping network in contact with perforated aluminum acoustical panels—through radiation.

A centrifugal type 250 hp chilling unit and a 50 hp reciprocating chilling unit with a total capacity of 300 tons of refrigeration handle the cooling needs. Two gas-fired hot water boilers give heat to the system as necessary.

The building is enclosed on its curved sides with porcelain enamel panels and glass, mounted on steel

BUILDING'S principal entrance . . . attractive and inviting.

MAIN STAIRWAY . . . showing unique design and spaciousness.

mullions extending from ground to roof. A heat-resistant glass is being used on the sunny side with all windows being the inoperable type.

Since the corridor along the inner curve faces south, it tends to insulate the adjoining office spaces, in addition to assuring soft lighting of the working spaces.

Because San Jose is a rapidly growing city, providing for flexibility in use of office spaces proved an important consideration. This was done by using metal-baked enamel partitions to panel much of the interior.

ATTRACTIVE FOYER of San Jose's new City Hall.

In this way office spaces can be changed easily to meet the need for increased work areas. Another way of insuring such flexibility was to provide an underfloor duct system embedded in all floors which will give power, telephone, and intercommunication service as needed directly at each desk.

The total cost of the city hall is $2.5 million with the greater part being financed through a local bond issue of $1,950,000.

C. N. Swenson of San Jose was awarded the contract with his basic bid of $2,218,000. Construction began in July, 1956, with completion scheduled for early in 1958.

TODAY'S MODERN MANUFACTURING PLANT

DIAMOND ANNIVERSARY

FINK AND SCHINDLER CO.

PIONEERS IN FINE WOOD CRAFTSMANSHIP

San Francisco, California

Seventy-five years ago, Conrad Fink and Adam C. Schindler were listed in the San Francisco Directory of 1882 as cabinet makers, with shops in their respective residences. Each was an artist at his trade, who had served an exacting apprenticeship in Europe, and whose high standard of craftsmanship was a matter of intense pride.

The architect and decor of the period created a particular demand for the type of service offered by these two men, especially among the fast growing business and financial houses where their painstaking pre-

YESTERDAY . . . 1882 to 1906, plant was located on site now occupied by the Western Furniture Mart on Market Street at Ninth.

cision in the construction of fixtures was most appreciated.

Bq 1883, Conrad Fink and Adam Schindler had decided that it would be more profitable to work together than in competition, and the following year found them making and selling "Artistic Furniture" together up at Ninth and Market, where San Francisco's Western Merchandise Mart now towers. The two partners were also purveyors, according to the current advertising, of "Upholstery and Draperies, Bank, Office and Saloon Fittings, Parquetry Floors, Wood Mantels and Interiors."

Three quarters of a century and three generations later, Fink and Schindler is now the oldest company of its kind continuously in business in the West. Located, after a number of outgrowings, at 552-560 Brannan street, it is still building wood interiors, cabinets and specialized fixtures, as well as custom-made furniture, for Western stores, banks and offices—and saloons, too.

That beautiful and precise workmanship with which Conrad Fink and Adam Schindler met the exacting demands of early San Francisco's large corporations and institutions continues under the watchful supervision of President Charles F. Stauffacher, Sr., a nephew of Adam Schindler. Mr. Stauffacher has had on-the-job training since 1899, when he started to work at 16 as bookkeeper, for his uncle.

The current head of the firm will employ none but dedicated craftsmen in wood; men who enjoy their skills and know their materials intimately; who consider every piece that is turned and joined as an indi-

Joseph Magnin's beautiful new "Valley Fair" store in San Jose, California.

Shown below is a portion of the elaborate Fink & Schindler Co.'s installation in Shreve & Company's San Francisco store.

vidual work of art. That he succeeds in upholding the old standards is attested to by the continuing demand for Fink & Schindler made cabinets and fixtures.

Fink & Schindler has progressed as San Francisco has progressed, growing with the booms, weathering the depressions, rising from the earthquake and fire to work with busy architects, contractors and businessmen to help build a bigger and better city. The firm's list of store clients alone reads like a Who's Who of the merchandising field.

Some outstanding recent jobs may be observed in

St. Ambrose Church, Berkeley, showing hand carved oak lectern.

Aleck Wilson, Architect

the functional cases and handsome wood interiors of Shreve & Company and of Blum's in San Francisco; of the Joseph Magnin stores at Las Vegas and Valley Fair, The Emporium in Santa Clara, and Hastings' at Stanford Village.

Other examples of Fink & Schindler craftsmanship include the laboratory cabinets and work areas in the Physics Building and the Virus Laboratories at the University of California, the interior woodwork, individual wordrobes, nurses' charting desks and laboratory equipment at the Mount Eden Hospital, and the interior woodwork of over two hundred Bank of America branches built during the past 38 years—most

with every modern improvement in finishing equipment, now occupy 42,000 square feet at the Brannan street location, where the firm has been expanding since 1933.

Though keeping in step with the demands of modern architectural progress, there is no "planned obsoles-

(See Page 32)

of it as beautiful as the day it was completed.

To handle the increased production volume flowing through its plant, The Fink & Schindler Company recently expanded its own facilities by an additional 14,000 square feet of floor space. The new offices and display area, the doubled-in-size fabricating department, and the completely new finishing department

American Institute of Architects

Leon Chatelain, Jr., President

John N. Richards, 1st Vice President
Philip Will, Jr., 2nd Vice President

Edward L. Wilson, Secretary
Raymond S. Kastendieck, Treasurer

Edmund R. Purves, Executive Secretary

National Headquarters—1735 New York Avenue, N. W., Washington, D. C.

REGIONAL DIRECTORS — **Northwest District,** Donald J. Stewart, Portland, Oregon; **Western Mountain District,** Bradley P. Kidder, Santa Fe, New Mexico; **California-Nevada-Hawaii District,** Ulysses Floyd Rible, Los Angeles, Calif.

Arizona Chapters:

CENTRAL ARIZONA: David Sholder, President; A. John Brenner, Vice-President; Jimmie R. Nunn, Secretary; Kemper Goodwin, Treasurer; James W. Elmore, Director; Ralph Haver, Director; Martin Ray Young, Jr., Director. Office of Secy., P.O. Box 904, Phoenix.

SOUTHERN ARIZONA: Santry Clay Fuller, President; Edward H. Nelson, Vice-President; David S. Swanson, Secretary; Robert J. Ambrose, Treasurer; D. Burr DuBois, Director; Eleazar D. Herreras, Director; Emerson C. Scholer, Director. Office of Secy., 2343 South Tucson Avenue, Tucson.

Coast Valleys Chapter

William L. Higgins (San Jose), President; Paul J. Huston (Palo Alto), Vice-President; William H. Daseking (Menlo Park), Treasurer; Edward N. Chamberlain (San Jose), Secretary. Office of Secy., 390 Park Ave., San Jose.

Central Valley of California:

Edward H. de Wolf (Stockton), President; Whitson Cox (Sacramento), Vice-President; Joe Jozens (Sacramento), Secretary; Albert M. Dreyfuss (Sacramento), Treasurer. Directors: Doyt Early (Sacramento), Jack Whipple (Stockton). Office of Secty., 914 11th St., Sacramento.

Colorado Chapter:

Casper P. Hegner, President; C. Gordon Sweet, Vice President; Norton Polivnick, Secretary; Richard Williams, Treasurer. Directors: James M. Hunter, Robert K. Fuller, Edward L. Bunts. Office of Secy., 1225 Bannock St., Denver, Colorado.

East Bay Chapter:

Hachiro Yuasa (Oakland), President; George T. Kern (Oakland), Vice-President; William M. Gillis (San Francisco), Secretary; J. A. Zerkle (Berkeley), Treasurer. Directors H. B. Clausen, F. A. Lockwood, John Oyarzo, G. M. McCue. Marjorie Montgomery, Ex. Secy. Office of Secy., Mezzanine, Hotel Claremont, Berkeley 5.

Idaho Chapter:

Anton E. Dropping, Boise, President; Charles W. Johnston, Payette, Vice-President; Glenn E. Cline, Boise, Sec.-Treas. Executive Committee, Chester L. Shawver and Nat J. Adams, Boise. Office of Sec., 624 Idaho Bldg., Boise.

Monterey Bay Chapter:

Thomas S. Elston, Jr., President (Carmel); Robert Stanton, Vice-President (Carmel); George F. Rhoda, Secretary (Monterey); Walter Burde, Treasurer. Office of Secty., 2281 Prescott St., Monterey.

Montana Chapter:

William J. Hess, President (Great Falls); John E. Toohey, Vice-President (Billings); H. C. Cheever, Sec.-Treas. (Bozeman). Directors: Oscar J. Ballas, Wm. J. Hess, John E. Toohey. Office of Secy., Bozeman, Montana.

Nevada Chapter:

RENO: Lawrence A. Gulling, President; William E. Cowell, Vice-President; Albert W. Alegre, Secretary; Ralph A. Casazza, Treasurer. Graham Erskine, Raymond M. Hellman, George L. F. O'Brien, Directors. Office of the Secy., 500 Plumas St., Reno.

PASADENA CHAPTER

The March meeting, held in the Eaton's Restaurant, Arcadia, was the annual joint meeting of the AIA and Producers Council. Door prizes and unusual features highlighted the meeting.

Recent new members include: Ray Chermak, Fred P. Dinger, William L. Duquette and Harland H. Perersen, Corporate Members; Rudolph J. Landa, Associate Member.

SAN DIEGO CHAPTER

Committee Chairmen appointed to serve during the 1958 year include Robert desLauriers, Membership; Herbert P. Fifield, Practice of Architecture; Stanley J. French, Construction Industry; William Lumpkins, Public Relations; C. J. Paderewski, Education and Registration; Walter Rein, Public Information; Sim B. Richards, Allied Arts, and Frank L. Hope, Civic Design.

WASHINGTON STATE CHAPTER

"Sculpture as Architecture" was the theme of the March meeting held in The Sorrento Hotel, Seattle, with William Atkin, Editor, Art and Architectural Books, Reinhold Publishing Corp. of New York, the principal speaker. Being responsible for the publication of more than 75 books on architecture, city

planning, and various aspects of art, houses and gardens, gave the speaker a wealth of material upon which to base his remarks.

New members: Arnold C. Amundsen, Jr., Anthony Callison, Barden G. Erickson, Clark B. Goldsworthy, Dean E. Hardy, Francis M. Johnson, Gunnar R. Lie, Robert E. Messer, Robert J. Pope, James A. Van Drimmelen, F. Wayne White, and James E. Zervas, Junior Associates; Sigurdur Geirsson, Student Associate.

CALIFORNIA COUNCIL AIA

Directors gave approval of a plan for reapportionment of director members from AIA Chapters, based upon total membership, at the last Board meeting held in Berkeley. The plan gives each Chapter one voting director plus one additional voting director for each 50 members. The four Chapters with less than 50 members will also have one non-voting director on the Board.

The Board also unanimously passed a resolution again petitioning the Institute to make California a Region in itself, removing it from Nevada and Hawaii. California accounts for more than 93 percent of the AIA members in the present Region which embraces California, Nevada and Hawaii.

COLLEGE OF ENVIRONMENTAL DESIGN FOR UNIVERSITY OF CALIFORNIA

Dean William W. Wurster, FAIA, of the University of California College of Architecture, outlined a plan to establish a new "College of Environmental Design," at a recent meeting of the California Council AIA of architects in Berkeley.

The new college would include departments of architecture, city and regional planning, and landscape architecture. Creation of the new college would not affect the architectural curriculum degree now being given at the college. Aside from internal administrative advantages, the principal benefit of the enlarged program would be a closer relationship and understanding between students of the three professions involved.

EAST BAY CHAPTER AIA

Publicity and the Architect was the subject of a panel discussion at the March meeting held at Spenger's.

Appearing on the panel were Miss Nes Young, Home Editor of the San Francisco Chronicle; Kenneth MacDonald, Pacific Coast Editor of Institutions; and Richard Moore, Pacific Affairs Director for TV station KQED, San Francisco. A. P. Anderson, past president of the Chapter, served as moderator.

PASADENA CHAPTER

The March meeting, held in the Eaton's Restaurant, Arcadia, was the annual joint meeting of the AIA and Producers Council. Door prizes and unusual features highlighted the meeting.

Recent new members include: Ray Chermak, Fred P. Dinger, William L. Duquette and Harland H. Pereren, Corporate Members; Rudolph J. Landa, Associate Member.

SAN DIEGO CHAPTER

Committee Chairmen appointed to serve during the 1958 year include Robert desLauriers, Membership; Herbert P. Fifield, Practice of Architecture; Stanley J. French, Construction Industry; William Lumpkins, Public Relations; C. J. Paderewski, Education and Registration; Walter Rein, Public Information; Sim B. Richards, Allied Arts, and Frank L. Hope, Civic Design.

WASHINGTON STATE CHAPTER

"Sculpture as Architecture" was the theme of the March meeting held in The Sorrento Hotel, Seattle, with William Atkin, Editor, Art and Architectural Books, Reinhold Publishing Corp. of New York, the principal speaker. Being responsible for the publication of more than 77 books on architecture, city planning, and various aspects of art, houses and gardens, gave the speaker a wealth of material upon which to base his remarks.

New members: Arnold C. Amundsen, Jr., Anthony Callson, Barden G. Erickson, Clark B. Goldsworthy, Dee E. Hardy, Francis M. Johnson, Gunnar R. Lie, Ralph E. Messer, Robert J. Pope, James A. Van Drimelen, F. Wayne White, and James E. Zervas, Junior Associates; Sigurdur Geirsson, Student Associate.

CALIFORNIA COUNCIL AIA

Directors gave approval of a plan for reapportionment of director members from AIA Chapters, based upon total membership, at the last Board meeting held in Berkeley. The plan gives each Chapter one voting director plus one additional voting director for each 50 members. The four Chapters with less than 50 members will also have one non-voting director on the Board.

The Board also unanimously passed a resolution again petitioning the Institute to make California a Region in itself, removing it from Nevada and Hawaii. California accounts for more than 93 percent of the AIA members in the present Region which embraces California, Nevada and Hawaii.

LAS VEGAS: Walter F. Zick, President; Aloysius McDonald, Vice-President; Edward B. Hendricks, Sec.-Treas.; Directors: Walter F. Zick, Edward Hendricks, Charles E. Cox. Office of Secty., 106 S. Main St., Las Vegas.

Nevada State Board of Architects:
L. A. Ferris, Chairman; Aloysius McDonald, Sec.-Treas., Members: Russell Mills (Reno), Edward S. Parsons (Reno), R. Stadelman (Las Vegas). Office 1420 S. 5th St., Las Vegas.

Northern California Chapter:
William Corlett, President; Donald Powers Smith, Vice-President; George T. Rockrise, Secretary; Richard S. Banwell, Treasurer; Directors: W. Clement Ambrose, John Kruse, Bernard J. Sabaroff, Corwin Booth. Exec. Secty., May B. Hershman, Office, 47 Kearny St., San Francisco.

Orange County Chapter:
John A. Nordbak, President (Downey); Willard T. — Vice-President (Costa Mesa); Don M. Williamson, Secretary (Laguna Beach); Gordon P. Powers, Treasurer (Long Beach). Office of Secty., 361 Park Ave., Laguna Beach.

Oregon Chapter:
John K. Dukehart, President; Keith R. Maguire, Vice-President; Robert Douglas, Secretary; Harry K. Stevens, Treasurer; Directors: Daniel McGoodwin, Earl F. Newberry, Patient F. Robert W. Fritsch, Donald W. Edmundson. Office of Secty., S.W. 18th Ave., Portland 1.

Pasadena Chapter:
H. Douglas Byles, President; Edward D. Davis, Vice-President; Ward W. Deems, Secretary; Robert F. Gordon, Treasurer; Directors: Mal Gianni, Lee B. Kline, Keith P. Marston, George Neptune. Office of the Secty., 170 E. California St., Pasadena.

San Diego Chapter:
Raymond Lee Eggers, President; William F. Wilmurt, Vice-President; Lloyd P. A. Ruocco, Secretary; Delmar S. Mitchell, Treasurer; Directors: John C. Deardorf, Richard George Wheeler, Sim Bruce Richards. Office of the Secty., 3003 4th Ave., San Diego 3.

San Joaquin Chapter:
Allen Y. Lew, President (Fresno); William G. Hyberg, Vice-President (Fresno); Paul H. Harris, Secretary; Edwin S. Darden, Treasurer (Fresno). Office of Pres., 408 Fulton St., Fresno.

Santa Barbara Chapter:
Darwin E. Fisher, President (Ventura); Wallace W. Arendt, Vice-President (Santa Barbara); Donald H. Miller, Secretary; Donald A. Kimball, Treasurer (Santa Barbara). Office of Treas., 1045 Via Tranquila, Santa Barbara.

Southern California Chapter:
Cornelius M. Deasy, President; Robert Field, Jr., Vice-President; Stewart D. Kerr, Treasurer; Edward H. Fickett, Secretary; Directors: Stewart S. Granger, Burnett C. Turner, George V. Russell, Paul R. Hunter. Exec. Secty., Miss Eva E. Miller, 3757 Wilshire Blvd., Los Angeles 5.

Southwest Washington Chapter:
Charles T. Pearson, President (Tacoma); Robert T. Olson, 1st Vice-President (Olympia); Donald Burr, 2nd Vice-President; Alan Liddle (Tacoma); Percy G. Ball, Secretary (Tacoma); Silas Woehn and Gordon N. Johnston, Trustees—Gilbert M. Woehn and Gordon N. Johnston (Tacoma). Office of Sec., 2715 Center St., Tacoma, Washington.

Utah Chapter:
W. J. Monroe, Jr., President, 433 Atlas Bldg., Salt Lake City; M. E. Harris, Jr., Secretary, 703 Newhouse Bldg., Salt Lake City.

Washington State Chapter:
James J. Chiarelli (Seattle), President; Robert H. Dietz (Seattle), 1st Vice-President; Walter H. Rothe (Yakima), 2nd Vice-President; Talbot Wegg (Seattle), Secretary; Albert O. Bumgardner (Seattle), Treasurer; Directors: Arnold O. Gangnes, Harrison J. Overturf, Lloyd J. Lovegren, and John L. Wright. Miss Gwen Myer, Executive Secretary, 409 Central Bldg., Seattle 4.

Spokane Chapter:
Wm. C. James, President; Carl H. Johnson, Vice-President; Keith T. BoYington, Secretary; Ralph J. Bishop, Treasurer; Lawrence G. Evanoff, Carroll Martell, Kenneth W. Brooks, Directors. Office of the Secty., 615 Realty Bldg., Spokane, Washington.

Hawaii Chapter:
Robert M. Law, President; Harry W. Seckel, Vice-President; Richard Dennis, Secretary. Directors: Edwin Bauer, George J. Wimberly. Office of Secty., P.O. Box 3288, Honolulu, Hawaii.

CALIFORNIA COUNCIL, THE A.I.A.
L. F. Richards, Santa Clara, President; Lee B. Kline, Los Angeles, Vice-President; Edward H. Fickett, Los Angeles, Secretary; Allen Y. Lew, Fresno, Treasurer. Miss Mary E. White, Office Secretary. 703 Market Street, San Francisco 3.

CALIFORNIA STATE BD. ARCHITECTURAL EXAMINERS:
C. J. Paderewski (San Diego), President; Malcolm D. Reynolds (Oakland), Secretary; Kenneth S. Wing (Long Beach); Wendell R. Spackman (San Francisco); and Paul O. Davis (Los Angeles). Exec. Secty., Richard A. Patrick, Room 312, 145 So. Spring St., Los Angeles; San Francisco Office, Room 300, 507 Polk St.

ALLIED ARCHITECTURAL ORGANIZATIONS

San Francisco Architectural Club:
C. Van De Weghe, President; O. Hickenlooper, Vice-President; James O. Brummett, Secretary; J. W. Tasker, Treasurer. Directors: Morris Barnett, Art Swisher, Stan Howatt, Frank Barsotti, Franco Capone. Office of Secty., 507 Howard St., San Francisco 5.

Producers' Council—Southern California Chapter:
Clay T. Snider, President, Minneapolis-Honeywell Regulator Co., L.A.; E. J. Lawson, Vice-President, Aluminum Company of America, L.A.; E. Phil Filsinger, Secretary, Gladding, McBean & Co., L.A.; William G. Aspy, Treasurer, H. H. Robertson Co., L.A.; Henry E. North, Jr., National Director, Arcadia Metal Products, L.A.; Office of the Secty., 2901 Los Feliz Blvd.

Producers' Council—Northern California Chapter:
John J. O'Connor, President, H. H. Robertson Co.; Stanley L. Basterash, Vice-President, Western Asbestos Co.; Howard W. DeWeese, Treasurer, Pomona Tile Mfg. Co.; Robert W. Harrington, Secretary, Clay Brick & Tile Ass'n. Office of Sec'y, 55 New Montgomery St., San Francisco 5.

Producers' Council—San Diego Chapter:
Eugene E. Bean, President, Fenestra Inc.; James J. Hayes, Vice-President, Westinghouse Electric Co.; E. K. Shelby, Secretary, The Celotex Corp. (El Cajon); Joseph C. Langley, Treasurer, Republic Steel Corp'n., Truscon Steel Div. (Lemon Grove). Office of Secty., 1832 Wedgemere Rd., El Cajon.

Construction Specifications Institute—Los Angeles:
R. R. Coghlan, Jr., President; George Lamb, Vice-President; E. Phil Filsinger, Secretary; Harry L. Miller, Treasurer; Directors: Harold Keller, Jack Whiteside, Walter Hagedohm, Raymond Whalley, Charles Field Wetherbee, Martin A. Hegsted. Advisory Member, D. Stewart Kerr. Office of Secty., 2901 Los Feliz Blvd., L.A.

Construction Specifications Institute—San Francisco:
Henry C. Collins, President; Leonard M. Tivel, Vice-President; Leonard P. Grover, Treasurer; Marvin E. Hirchert, Secretary. Office of Secty., 585 Whitewood Drive, San Rafael.

COLLEGE OF ENVIRONMENTAL DESIGN FOR UNIVERSITY OF CALIFORNIA

Dean William W. Wurster, FAIA, of the University of California College of Architecture, outlined a plan to establish a new "College of Environmental Design," at a recent meeting of the California Council AIA of architects in Berkeley.

The new college would include departments of architecture, city and regional planning, and landscape architecture. Creation of the new college would not affect the architectural curriculum degree now being given at the college. Aside from internal administrative advantages, the principal benefit of the enlarged program would be a closer relationship and understanding between students of the various professions involved.

EAST BAY CHAPTER AIA

Publicity and the Architect was the subject of a panel discussion at the March meeting. Spen...

WITH THE ENGINEERS

STRUCTURAL ENGINEERS ASSOCIATION OF NORTHERN CALIFORNIA

The new Crown Zellerbach Corporation Headquarters Office Building in San Francisco was the topic of discussion at the March meeting, held in the Engineers Club, with speakers including Herbert L. Lyell, Andrew P. Stevens, Charles D. DeMaria, and Stanley E. Teixeira. This building has received considerable publicity since construction was started last year.

The Board of Directors has endorsed the principles embodied in the Jenkins-Keogh bill now pending in Congress, which would allow self-employed persons to set aside a portion of their income, up to a maximum of 10 per cent, for investment in a private retirement fund under the same status as is now accorded retirement funds for employed persons or for those who are doing business as a corporation.

Recent new members include: Pecos H. Calahan, Howard D. Eberhart, Leslie A. Irvin, and Walter T. Norris—Members; Richard E. Biggs and Ronald D. Blotter—Junior Members.

STRUCTURAL ENGINEERS ASSOCIATION OF SOUTHERN CALIFORNIA

"Design of Composite Concrete and Steel Structures—An Example of Practical Utilization of Research Studies," was the subject of the March meeting held in the Rodger Young Auditorium with Dr. Ivan M. Viest, Consulting Engineer, the principal speaker. Dr. Viest was formerly research professor, Department of Theoretical and Applied Mechanics at the University of Illinois, and also was associated for several years with the A. A. S. H. O. Research Program.

New members include: George O. Dyer, Glenn C. Gordon, and Robert E. Tobin, Associate; Robert H. Hanson, Student, and C. Y. Jernigan, Affiliate.

SOCIETY OF AMERICAN MILITARY ENGINEERS ELECT OFFICERS

The Society of American Military Engineers, national organization with general offices in Washington,

D. C., and local chapters throughout the United States, recently elected the following officers to serve during the ensuing year:

Maj. Gen. Emerson C. Itschner, Chief of Engineers, U.S. Army, President; Vice Adm. William O. Hiltabidle, U.S. Navy, ret., Vice-President. Regional vice-presidents included Col. John H. Carruth, San Antoio, Southwestern Region, and Brig. Gen. Dwight F. Johns, San Francisco, Western Region.

The 38th annual meeting of the Society will be held in Washington, D. C. May 20 and 21. The tentative program includes an inspection of the nuclear reactor now furnishing electric power at Fort Belvoir, Virginia.

SOUTHERN CALIFORNIA ENGINEERS HEAR EDUCATIONAL DISCUSSION

The Structural Engineers of Southern California heard a panel discussion recently on "Where Are We Going in Engineering Education?" The panel consisted of Robert E. Vivian, Dean, School of Engineering, University of Southern California, Daniel E. Wilhelm, Jr., Dean, College of Engineering, Loyola University, Murray Erick, Murray Erick Associates, consulting structural engineers, and Charles F. Horne, vice president and division manager of Convair. John B. Howe, partner, Maurseth & Howe, foundation engineers, was moderator.

Dean Vivian's subject was Professional Versus Technical Level Trends in Engineering Education from the Technical Subject Standpoint. Dean Vivian commented on the problems confronting faculties in preparing curricula to satisfy the expanding needs of science in industry, pointing out that there is an ever increasing demand for graduate training in the universities. Of a total of two thousand students enrolled in the School of Engineering at U.S.C., seven hundred are graduate students. Cost of providing graduate courses is considerably higher than for undergraduate courses on account of the need for more highly qualified instructors and more elaborate equipment. Dean Vivian predicted that college enrollment in engineer-

ing courses will need to be doubled within the next 10 to 15 years if America is to stay in the race for scientific supremacy, and that the cost of engineering education will need to be increased—not doubled, but trebled.

Dean Vivian suggested that the Ackerman Report on Engineering Education, sponsored by ASCE, should be required reading.

An increase in the length of college engineering undergraduate courses from four to five years was not considered to be essential at the present time, though this should be one of the aims in the development of curricula. It was pointed out that an engineering student is required to complete 140 units during his four years, none of which is earned in so-called "snap" courses.

It is pointed out that civil engineering is closer to the public health and welfare than any other branch of engineering; however, on account of poor promotion, it is considered to be the least promising of any of the branches of engineering. Even many of the members of the ASCE are found to be unenthusiastic about the economic aspects of the profession. Since World War II, enrollment in civil engineering courses has increased only 20% while mechanical has increased 50% and electrical 100%. Another interesting observation is that 80% of all graduates in civil engineering find employment in governmental agencies, while 80% of graduates in other fields of engineering go to private industry.

Dean Daniel E. Whelan, Jr. spoke on the subject of Distribution of Humanities and Social Studies Courses in the College Curriculum. He asserted that as a profession engineers suffer from an inferiority complex stemming from inability in self-expression. The student of engineering should concentrate on engineering fundamentals and at the same time try to broaden his outlook on society by understanding

moral and philosophical problems. College engineering courses have not been static in their development. Dean Whelan pointed out that there has been a definite trend away from more practical vocational type courses.

Engineering courses have not at any time been completely devoid of cultural education; however, the Grinter report on Engineering Education sug-

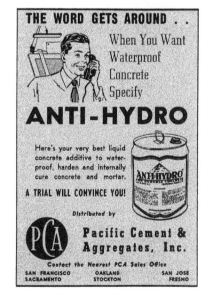

gests that courses should consist of about 20% human-
ities. The Hammond report of 1945 on General Education in Engineering pointed up the fields in which
an engineer should strive to become proficient so that
he may be in a position to be called upon for community leadership. He should be equipped with the
necessary knowledge to place himself in a position
where he may "control the products of his own
genius."

Charles F. Horne spoke on the Salaries and Qualifications in Developing College Faculties. He stated
that the increased demand for scientific education
calls for both an increase in the number of teachers
and an increase in the quality of teachers. Since our
political system does not allow us to direct all students of greater-than-average intelligence into scientific pursuits as in the case of Russia, we must endeavor to compete on a quality rather than quantity
basis.

Mr. M. J. Skinner, partner, Murray Erick Associates, presented the views of Mr. Erick who had been
unexpectedly called to Mexico City on business.

CALIFORNIA COUNCIL OF ARCHITECTS ELECTS L. F. RICHARDS PRESIDENT

The California Council of Architects, AIA, at the
annual meeting of the Board of Directors in Berkeley
the first of the month, elected L. F. Richards of Santa

L. F. RICHARDS
President, CCA

Clara president of the
CCA for the ensuing
year. Richards served as
vice president of the
Council last year and has
held the offices of secretary, treasurer, and president of the Coast Val-
leys Chapter of the AIA.

Officers named to serve
with Richards during the
year include: Lee B.
Kline of Los Angeles,
Vice-President; Edward
H. Fickett of Los Ange-

les, Secretary; Allen Y. Lew of Fresno, treasurer, and
Corwin Booth of San Francisco, member-at-large of
the CCA Administrative Committee.

The Board of Directors also approved a plan for
reapportionment of Chapter delegates, and reaffirmed
its proposal that California be made an Institute Region in itself. At present California is a part of the
California-Nevada-Hawaii Region, and the reapportionment plan, if approved, would increase the Northern California Chapter delegates from 4 to 7, and
increase the Southern California Chapter delegates
from 4 to 11.

GENERAL CONTRACTOR MOVES OFFICES TO NEW LOCATION

The general offices of John A. Rademann Company, general contractors, has been moved to 307 12th Avenue, San Francisco, according to a recent announcement by the contracting firm.

ARCHITECT SPEAKS AT ART CLUB

Victor Gruen, Los Angeles architect and planner, and head of the architectural firm of Victor Gruen Associates, was a guest speaker at the Kingsley Art Club in the E. B. Crocker Art Gallery, Sacramento, recently.

Gruen spoke on the subject of "The Architect and Urban Cultures."

McGEE APPOINTED REPRESENTATIVE FOR WASHINGTON

Al McGee has been appointed representative in the State of Washington for the West Coast Lumbermen's Association, according to an announcement by Hal V. Simpson, executive vice president of the association.

McGee will make his headquarters in Seattle. He is a former editor of employee publications for Weyerhaeuser Timber Company in Tacoma, and has worked in sawmills, plywood plants and logging operations.

AMERICAN WOOD PRESERVERS MEET IN LOS ANGELES

The American Wood-Preservers' Association will hold its 54th Annual Meeting in Los Angeles, Hotel Statler, April 14-16, with a full three days devoted to technical discussions and panel's by specialists in the wood treating industry.

A. Dale Chapman, general convention chairman, announces a number of special events have been arranged for members and guests. It is the first time the convention has been held in California, since 1921, and according to W. W. Barger, president, a large number of members from all sections of the nation will attend.

ELKS LODGE TO BUILD IN PITTSBURG

Architects Cantin & Cantin of 5652 College Ave., Oakland, have completed plans for construction of a single story Elks lodge building in the City of Pittsburg, Contra Costa county.

The new building will be of wood frame with stucco exterior construction.

KRAFTILE CO. OBSERVES A SAFETY RECORD

Completion of four years of operation by the Kraftile Company of Niles, California, without a single lost-time accident was observed recently by the firm when they "treated" employees at the mid-morning "break" with soft drinks on the house.

L. R. Alt, vice-president in charge of production, and C. W. Kraft, president, spoke briefly to the employees, thanking each for their part in observing "safety" at all times and particularly during the extremely adverse conditions at the time

of the flood in December 1955.

Kraft noted that a good safety record is an indication of high morale. "I have never known a plant that was not run in a clean, efficient manner where the men were discouraged and disgruntled to have a good safety record!"

ARCHITECT SELECTED SAN JOSE

The architectural firm of Stone, Mulloy, Marraccini & Patterson of 536 Mission street, San Francisco, has been commissioned by the State of California, Division of Architecture, to design an addition to the San Jose State College in San Jose and to draft plans and specifications for con-

struction of a new Health Center on the campus.

It is estimated the college additions will cost $1,816,000, while the cost of the health center will be $1,176,000.

PIERSON MOVES TO OFFICES IN SAN FRANCISCO

Aaron A. Pierson, vice president of Fruin-Colnon Contracting Company, has been placed in charge of the firm's Western Division, with offices in Burlingame, California.

He was formerly District Manager of the Indiana Division of the company in Indianapolis.

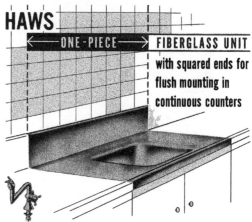

Diamond Anniversary

FINK & SCHINDLER CO.

(From Page 25)

cence" incorporated in Fink & Schindler built fixtures. The old style craftsmanship goes on, now under the additional supervision of young Charles F. Stauffacher, Jr., third generation member of the company, who has already proved his outstanding ability to carry on in

INTERIOR . . . Bank of America, Polk-Van Ness Branch in San Francisco.

the tradition in which he has been steeped—with an additional solid background in architecture. He received his Master's degree in this subject at the University of California, and worked for four years with Ambrose & Spencer, well known San Francisco architects, before joining with his father in the family business as vice president in 1951.

Under the eagle eyes of these two perfectionists, each job that goes through the shop is given thorough individual attention, down to the most minute phase. Each order is detailed in full scale drawings, submitted for client approval before the fixtures are fabricated, finished and installed by the same type of skilled work-

men who have kept the Fink & Schindler reputation for precision bright for seventy-five years.

" And that's the way it's going to go on, both Stauffachers agree.

OUR PROBLEM OF IGNORANCE

(From Page 9)

means of closed-circuit television systems. This can hardly be called a frill or a waste of money.

I do think, however, that we need to place a good deal more emphasis on scholastic excellence, on competition among students within the schoolroom. I also firmly believe that we all have a big job to do outside the schoolroom. We blame youth for lack of interest in science and explain it on the ground that our youth considers scientists to be 'egg-heads" and therefore social oddities. Yet in the face of this statement, youthful experimentation in rocketry has become so widespread that there is serious concern over the likelihood of personal injuries. This does not sound as though youth lacks interest in science. Our priceless and unique characteristic of youth is its perpetual curiosity. We, as adults, have the power to direct that curiosity into worthy channels. There seems to be evidence that we have failed to do this; instead, we have forfeited these opportunities through preoccupation with amusing and coddling ourselves with material comforts and needless luxuries.

Scholastic Excellence

Perhaps it is we who really need re-education. Certainly we need re-education which will make us want to put our spare dollars into better schools rather than into more personal gadgets. It is for us to set the examples, else youth, as it always has, will reflect our attitudes and lose sight of those things in life which are worthy of its time.

I am not at all sure that the education our children are getting today is any worse than it was twenty years ago. However, I am sure that today's children need far more and better education than has been necessary in the past. As architects and contractors, it is our joint responsibility to build schools which, unlike the prison-like, pompous buildings of yesterday, serve to encourage learning. If such buildings can be combined with imaginative teaching that stimulates student curiosity in the physical sciences—and the arts—it is entirely possible that our young people may come to consider the acquisition of knowledge as something which is not only socially desirable, but pleasurable. If this is done, we as a nation will have nothing to fear from anybody —not even ourselves.

PHOTO CREDITS: Phil Fein & Associates, Cover, Pages 22 (top), 23, 24, 25; Balch, Bryan, Perkins, Hutchason, Architects, Page 3; Shell Development Co., Pages 10, 11; Hamilton Wright, Pages 12, 13, 14, 15; Gordon Bartels, Pages 16, 17, 18, 19, 20, 21; Miss Cecil Davis, Page 30.

SPECIFICATIONS AND COSTS — Data Book for Civil Engineers, Vol. II. By Elwyn E. Seelye. John Wiley & Sons, Inc., 440 4th Ave., New York 16, N.Y. Price $20.00.

This book, comprising as it does contract documents, specifications, and cost data, together with excursions into such subjects as evaluation, depreciation and obsolescence, glossary, mechanical and electrical power costs, has been particularly popular with engineers in the progressive and administrative echelons. In this edition the author has tried not only to widen the cost data coverage and bring it up to date, but also to enrich the book with such items as Special Foundation Specifications; Warnings related to specification writing; Riprap specifications, and suggested form of agreement between engineer and client. A valuable addition to any engineer's, architect's and contractor's library.

APPLIED STRENGTH OF MATERIALS. By Prof. Alfred Jensen. McGraw-Hill Book Co., 330 W. 42nd St., New York, N.Y. Price $5.75.

The purpose of this book by Alfred Jensen, Professor of Architectural Engineering, University of Washington, is to acquaint the student, as well as architects, engineers and contractors, with the strength and other properties of common engineering materials, and to teach how to design various types of structural members and connection usually found in machines and buildings. The book features the development of all design formulas without the use of calculus; a large number of solved illustrative problems are included; illustrations are profuse, and the many helpful tables are noteworthy.

COMPOSITION AND PROPERTIES OF CONCRETE. By George Earl Troxell and Harmer E. Davis. McGraw-Hill Book Co., 330 W. 42nd St., New York 36, N.Y. 434 pages. Price $7.75.

This book by George Earl Troxell, Professor of Civil Engineering, University of California; and Harmer E. Davis, Professor of Civil Engineering, University of California; with Chapters on Proportioning of Concrete Mixtures and Strength of Concrete by J. W Kelly, includes information on the control of concrete making and concrete construction; the materials of concrete; and the desirable and undesirable characteristics of concrete. The book is divided into two parts: Part I covers the characteristics of cement, aggregates, admixtures, and water used in concrete mixes, the proportioning of these materials, and the batching, mixing, placing and curing of the concrete to produce a finished product of suitable and predictable quality and economy. Part II comprises instructions for laboratory tests, selected to illustrate the most important facts and principles connected with the use of cement, aggregate and concrete. Numerous examples are given in many cases, and a list of questions is included at the end of each chapter.

NEW CATALOGUES AVAILABLE

Architects, Engineers, Contractors, Planning Commission members—the catalogues, folders, new building products material, etc., described below may be obtained by directing your request to the name and address given in each item.

Doorware that radiates charm. New 4-color catalog illustrates wide variety of combinations in distinctive new designs in doorware knobs and escutcheons executed in combinations of wood, ceramics, and metals; these new knobs and escutcheons can be combined in a great number of motifs suitable for most contemporary trends in architecture and interior design. Free copy write DEPT-A&E, Russel & Erwin, New Britain, Conn.

Non-combustible acoustical materials. New 4-page, 2-color bulletin describes and pictures two non-combustible acoustical materials; manufactured of spun mineral wool for insulating home and industry; gives complete characteristics and specifications; sound absorption coefficients, light reflectance values and flame resistance ratings; styles and methods of installation discussed and shown by photographs. Free copy write DEPT-A&E, Acoustical Products Div., Baldwin-Hill Co., 500 Breunig Ave., Trenton 2, N. J.

Testing laboratories. New descriptive folder (AIA FILE No. 35-E-4) outlines scope and activities of the Association of Cali-

fornia Testing and Inspection Laboratories, including Code of Ethics; described origin and object, and operation of Association. Free copy write DEPT·A&E, Abbot A. Hanks, Inc., 624 Sacramento St., San Francisco, or any Association member.

Western Pine Association Directory. Lists more than 350 lumber manufacturing plants and their sales offices; facilities and products of Western Pine mills in the 12-state region are tabulated in this 20-page publication; Shows species each mill manufacturers; staple products made; dry kiln facilities and plant brand products. Free copy write DEPT·A&E, Western Pine Association, Yeon Bldg., Portland 4, Oregon.

Unit plan for greater educational flexibility and economy. A new brochure entitled "The Unit Plan for Greater Educational Flexibility and Economy" has been produced by Warren H. Ashley, architect; outlines briefly the primary advantages of the Unit Plan in increasing educational efficiency of the structure, reducing congestion, creating a more stimulating environment, and reducing building and expansion cost. Free copy write DEPT·A&E, Warren H. Ashley, Architect, 740 N. Main St., West Hartford, Conn.

Classrooms for easy listening. New concept in classroom acoustical design is explained in this 16-page booklet entitled "Classrooms for Easy Listening"; use of sound reflective ceilings, with limited application of acoustical treatment is covered in easy-to-read language; explanatory drawings; also illustrated importance of voice reinforcement and the control of reverbration time in good student-teacher hearing. Free copy write DEPT·A&E, The Flexicore Co., Inc., 1932 E. Monument Ave., Dayton 2, Ohio.

Metal letters. New catalog (AIA FILE No. 15-R-1) of metal letters for both interior and exterior use; metal letter styles are illustrated, available in heights 2" to 24" in aluminum, bronz, stainless steel, as well as plastic-face and baked enamel sign letters; on location photo's shown, factories, churches, schools, stores and other non-residential buildings; explains methods for specifying and ordering special-design lettering and procedure for mounting letters on masonry and other materials. Copies free, Write DEPT·A&E, Spanjer Brothers, 1160 N. Howe St., Chicago 10.

Architectural color chart. New architectural color chart card and brochure showing color-flected and solid colored, textured paints; graphically displays 20 multicolored spray chips as well as 10 new solid colored finishes; complete information about multi-colored paints for use by architects and decorators. Copies available write DEPT·A&E, Plextone Corpn. of America, 2141 McCarter Highway, Newark, N.J.

Aluminum shade screen. New brochure (AIA FILE No. 35-P-1) gives complete information on Kaiser aluminum shade screen, its function, advantages, installation recommendations and availabilities; has chart giving estimates of air conditioning economies brought about by the use of shade screens over windows; also includes drawings showing basic screening applications and typical installation details. Free write DEPT·A&E, Kaiser Aluminum & Chemical Sales Inc., 919 N. Michigan Ave., Chicago 11.

Salt treated wood. New brochure on proven, effective, low-cost wood preservative, "Boliden Salt" from Sweden; illustrated shows numerous applications and uses; descriptive matter on tests. Free copy write DEPT·A&E, McCormick & Baxter Creosoting Co., Portland, San Francisco, Glendale.

ESTIMATOR'S GUIDE

BUILDING AND CONSTRUCTION MATERIALS

PRICES GIVEN ARE FIGURING PRICES AND ARE MADE UP FROM AVERAGE QUOTATIONS FURNISHED BY LeROY CONSTRUCTION SERVICES. 4% SALES TAX ON ALL MATERIALS BUT NOT LABOR. ITEMS IN ITALIC INCLUDE LABOR AND SALES TAX.

BONDS—Performance or Performance plus Labor and Material Bond(s), $10 per $1000 on contract price. Labor and Material Bond(s) only, $5.00 per $1000 on contract price.

BRICKWORK & MASONRY

COMMON BRICKWORK, Reinforced:		
8" walls	SF	2.95
12" walls	SF	4.15
SELECT COMMON, Reinforced:		
8" walls	SF	3.05
12" walls	SF	4.30
CONCRETE BLOCK, Reinforced:		
6" walls	SF	1.40
8" walls	SF	1.55
12" walls	SF	1.90
BRICK VENEER:		
4" Select Common	SF	1.65
4" Roman	SF	2.50
4" Norman	SF	2.40
4" Aggrelite	SF	2.40

BRICKWORK & MASONRY

All Prices—F.O.B. Plant.

COMMON BRICK		
Common 2½ x 3¾ x 8¼	M	45.00
Select 2½ x 3¾ x 8¼	M	52.00
Clinker 2½ x 3¾ x 8¼	M	48.00
Jumbo 3½ x 3 x 11½	M	90.00
FACE BRICK		
Standard	M	59.80 - 83.20
Jumbo	M	114.40 - 130.00
Roman	M	88.40 - 109.20
Norman	M	101.40 - 124.80
Brik Blox (6")	M	202.80
Brik Blox (8")	M	239.20
Braile Veneer	M	26.00
BUILDING TILE		
8 x 5½ x 12 inches	M	165.78
6 x 5½ x 12 inches	M	128.96
HOLLOW TILE		
12 x 12 x 3 inches	M	163.12
12 x 12 x 4 inches	M	184.18
12 x 12 x 6 inches	M	244.71
MANTEL FIRE BRICK		
2½ x 9½ x 4½ inches	M	140.40
GLAZED STRUCTURAL UNITS		
2 x 6 x 12 Furring	SF	.90
4 x 6 x 12 Furring	SF	1.20
6 x 6 x 12 Furring	SF	1.50
4 x 6 x 12 Partition	SF	1.60
Add for color	SF	.20
CONCRETE BLOCKS		
4 x 8 x 16 inches	EA	.22
6 x 8 x 16 inches	EA	.265
8 x 8 x 16 inches	EA	.30
12 x 8 x 16 inches	EA	.435
Colored Add	EA	.02
AGGREGATE—Haydite or Basalite		
All sizes in bulk	CY	6.24

BUILDING PAPERS & FELTS

1 ply per 1000 ft. roll	3.95
2 ply per 1000 ft. roll	6.03
3 ply per 1000 ft. roll	8.22
Sisalkraft, reinf. 500 ft. roll	7.54
SHEATHING PAPERS:	
Asphalt sheathing, 15-lb. roll	2.50
Asphalt sheathing, 30-lb. roll	3.50
Dampcourse, 216-ft. roll	3.05
FELT PAPERS:	
Deadening felt, ¾-lb. 50 ft. roll	4.10
Deadening felt, 1-lb. 50 ft. roll	4.78
Asphalt roofing, 15-lbs.	2.50
Asphalt roofing, 30-lbs.	3.50
ROOFING PAPERS:	
Standard Grade, Smooth Surface	
108-ft. roll, Light	2.35
Medium	2.75
Heavy	3.22
Extra Heavy	3.75

CHIMNEYS, PATENT

F.O.B. Warehouse

6"	LF	1.45
8"	LF	2.05
10"	LF	2.85
12"	LF	3.45

Rates for 10 - 50 Lin. Ft.

CONCRETE AGGREGATES

	Bunker Per Ton	Del'd Per Ton
Gravel, All Sizes	3.38	4.16
Top Sand	3.59	4.37
Concrete Mix	3.48	4.26
Crushed Rock		
¼" to ¾"	3.43	4.26
¾" to 1½"	3.43	4.26
Roofing Gravel	3.54	4.42
SAND		
Lapis (Nos. 2 & 4)	4.47	5.30
Olympia (Nos. 1 & 2)	3.75	4.32

CEMENT		
Common All Brands (Paper Sacks)		
Small Quantities	Per Sack	1.40
Large Quantities	Per Bbl.	4.00
Trinity White & Mendusa White	Per Sack	4.16
CONCRETE READY-MIX		
6 sack in 5 yd. loads	Per Yd.	15.40
CURING COMPOUND, Clear		
5 gal. drums	Per Gal.	1.46

CARPENTRY & MILLWORK

Hardware not included

FRAMING:		
Floors	BM	.20 - .25
Walls	BM	.25 - .30
Ceilings	BM	.18 - .22
Roofs	BM	.22 - .27
Furring & Blocking	BM	.30 - .50
SHEATHING:		
1 x 8 straight	BM	.20 - .25
1 x 8 diagonal	BM	.23 - .28
5/16" Plyscore	SF	.16 - .20
⅜" Plywood	SF	.25 - .30
SIDING:		
1 x 8 Bevel	BM	.35 - .40
1 x 4 V-Rustic	BM	.40 - .45
EXTERIOR TRIM:		
Fascia and Molds	BM	.40 - .50
Bolted Framing—Add 50%		
ENTRANCE DOORS & FRAMES:		
Singles		*60.00 & Up*
Doubles		*100.00 & Up*
INTERIOR DOORS & FRAMES:		
Singles		*35.00 & Up*
Pocket Sliding		*45.00 & Up*
Closet Sliding (Pr.)		*50.00 & Up*
WINDOWS:		
D/H Sash & Frames	SF	*1.75 & Up*
Casement Sash & Frames	SF	*1.90 & Up*
SHELVING:		
1 x 12 S4S	BM	.30 - .50
¾" Plywood	SF	.40 - .60
STAIRS:		
Oak steps D.F. Risers		
Under 36" wide	Riser	12.00
Under 60" wide	Riser	17.00
Newel posts and rail extra		
WOOD CASES & CABINETS:		
D.F. Wall Hung	LF	13.00 - 18.00
D.F. Counters	LF	15.00 - 20.00

DAMPPROOFING & WATERPROOFING

MEMBRANE:		
1 layer 50 lb. felt	SQ.	9.00
4 layers Dampcourse	SQ.	13.00
Hot coat walls	SQ.	6.00
Tricosal added to concrete	CY	1.00
Anti-Hydro added to concrete	CY	1.50

ELECTRIC WIRING

Per Outlet:

Knob & Tube	EA	9.00
Armor	EA	16.00
Conduit	EA	20.00
110 V Circuit	EA	25.00
220 V Circuit	EA	95.00

ELEVATORS & ESCALATORS

Prices vary according to capacity, speed and type. Consult Elevator Companies.

Slow speed apartment house elevator including doors and trim, about $5000.00 per floor.

EXCAVATION

MACHINE WORK in common ground:		
Large Basements	CY	.75 - 1.00
Small Pits	CY	1.25 - 1.75
Trenches	CY	1.50 - 2.25
HAND WORK in common ground:		
Large pits and trenches	CY	4.50 - 5.50
Small pits and trimming	CY	5.00 - 6.50

Hard Clay & Shale 2 times above rates.
Rock and large boulders 4-6 times above rates.
Shoring, bracing and disposal of water not included.

FLOORS

⅛" Asp. tile, dark colors	SF	.25 - .30
⅛" Asp. tile, light colors	SF	.30 - .35
⅛" Rubber tile	SF	.60 - .70
.080 Vinyl Asbestos Tile	SF	.40 - .45
.080 Vinyl Tile	SF	.85 - .95
Lino, Standard Gauge	SY	3.75 - 4.25
Lino, Battleship	SY	5.25 - 5.75
4" Rubber Base, Black	LF	.35 - .40
Rubber Stair Nosing	LF	1.00 - 1.75

Above rates based on quantities of 1000 - 5000 SF per job.

HARDWOOD FLOORS

Select Oak, filled, sanded, stained and varnished:		
5/16" x 2¼" strip	SF	.45 - .50
5/16" Random Plank	SF	.50 - .55
25/32" x 2¼" T&G	SF	.70 - .80
Maple, 2nd Grade and Better, filled, sanded, stained and varnished:		
25/32" x 2¼" T&G	SF	.80 - .95
Wax Finish, add	SF	.10

HARDWOOD FLOORING

Oak 5/16" x 2" Strip—		
Clear	M	229.00
Select	M	218.00
#1 Common	M	203.00
Oak 5/16" Random Plank—		
Select & Btr.	M	286.00
#1 Common	M	244.00
Oak 25/32" x 2¼" T&G—		
Select	M	260.00
#1 Common	M	203.00
Maple 25/32" x 2¼" T&G—		
#1 Grade	M	317.00
#2 Grade	M	281.00
#3 Grade	M	208.00
Nails—1" Floor Brads	KEG	17.20

GLASS & GLAZING

S.S.B. Clear	SF	.48
D.S.B. Clear	SF	.78
Crystal	SF	.92
¼" Plate	SF	2.17
⅛" Obscure	SF	.68
⅛" Heat Absorbing	SF	1.12
¼" Tempered Plate	SF	4.38
½" Tempered Plate	SF	7.84
¼" Wire Plate, Clear	SF	3.65
¼" Wire Plate, Rough	SF	1.08

GLASS—CUT TO SIZE

F.O.B. Warehouse

S.S.B. Clear, Av. 6 SF	SF	.34
D.S.B. Clear, Av. 10 SF	SF	.56
Crystal, Av. 35 SF	SF	.66
¼" Polished Plate, Av. 100 SF	SF	1.55
⅛" Obscure, Av. 10 SF	SF	.49
⅛" Ribbed, Av. 10 SF	SF	.49
⅛" Rough, Av. 10 SF	SF	.49
¼" Wire Plate, Clear, Av. 40 SF	SF	2.61
¼" Wire Plate, Rough, Av. 40 SF	SF	.77
⅛" Heat Absorbing, Av. 10 SF	SF	.80
¼" Tempered Plate, Av. 50 SF	SF	3.13
½" Tempered Plate, Av. 50 SF	SF	5.60

Glazing—Approx. 40-50% of Glass
Glass Blocks—Check with Dealer

HEATING

FURNACES—Gas Fired—Av. Job:	
FLOOR FURNACE:	
25,000 BTU	*100.00 - 125.00*
35,000 BTU	*107.00 - 135.00*
45,000 BTU	*115.00 - 150.00*
AUTOMATIC CONTROL:	
Add	*25.00 - 35.00*

HEATING—Cont'd

DUAL WALL FURNACE:		
25,000 BTU		*110.00 - 125.00*
35,000 BTU		*125.00 - 145.00*
50,000 BTU		*150.00 - 180.00*
AUTOMATIC CONTROL:		
Add		*25.00 - 35.00*
GRAVITY FURNACE:		
75,000 BTU		*375.00 - 450.00*
85,000 BTU		*425.00 - 525.00*
95,000 BTU		*475.00 - 600.00*
FORCED AIR FURNACE:		
Add		*75.00 - 125.00*
AUTOMATIC CONTROL:		
Add		*15.00 - 25.00*
HEAT REGISTERS:		
Outlet		*7.50 - 15.00*

INSULATION & WALLBOARD

F.O.B. Warehouse

ROCKWOOL Insulation—		
2" Semi-thick	Per M SF	63.02
3⅝" Full Thick	Per M SF	80.50
COTTON Insulation		
1" Full Thick	Per M SF	43.26
SOFTBOARDS—Wood Fiber—		
½" thick	Per M SF	88.00
1½" thick	Per M SF	275.00
2" thick	Per M SF	385.00
ALUMINUM Insulation—		
80# Kraft paper with alum. foil		
1 side only	Per M SF	18.30
2 sides	Per M SF	31.00
GYPSUM Wallboard—		
⅜" thick	Per M SF	49.50
½" thick	Per M SF	54.50
⅝" thick	Per M SF	83.00
⅜" Gyplap	Per M SF	85.00
HARDBOARDS—Wood Fiber—		
⅛" thick, Sheathing	Per M SF	78.75
3/16" thick, Sheathing	Per M SF	90.48
¼" thick, Sheathing	Per M SF	109.20
⅛" thick, Tempered	Per M SF	98.80
3/16" thick, Tempered	Per M SF	140.40
¼" thick, Tempered	Per M SF	194.48
CEMENT Asbestos Board—		
⅛" C.A.B. Flat Sheets	Per M SF	156.00
3/16" C.A.B. Flat Sheets	Per M SF	218.40
¼" C.A.B. Flat Sheets	Per M SF	280.80

LATH & PLASTER

Diamond 3.40 copper bearing	SY	.50
Ribbed 3.40 copper bearing	SY	.55
⅜" rock lath	SY	.37
2" Standard Channel	LF	.085
1½" Standard Channel	LF	.065
¾" Standard Channel	LF	.045
3¼" steel studs	LF	.09
4" steel studs	LF	.105
Stud shoes	EA	.025
Hardwall, Browning	Sack	1.46
Hardwall, Finish	Sack	1.72
Stucco	Sack	2.50

LATH & PLASTERWORK

CHANNEL FURRING:		
Suspended Ceilings	*SY*	*2.20 - 2.50*
Walls	*SY*	*2.30 - 2.60*
METAL STUD PARTITIONS:		
3¼" Studs	*SY*	*1.70 - 2.00*
4" Studs	*SY*	*1.95 - 2.25*
Over 10'0 high, add	*SY*	*.20 - .30*
3.40 METAL LATH AND PLASTER:		
Ceilings	*SY*	*3.60 - 4.00*
Walls	*SY*	*3.75 - 4.15*
KEENE'S CEMENT FINISH:		
Add	*SY*	*.40 - .60*
ROCK LATH & PLASTER:		
Ceilings	*SY*	*2.50 - 2.80*
Walls	*SY*	*2.60 - 2.90*
WIRE MESH AND ⅞" STUCCO:		
Walls	*SY*	*3.60 - 4.10*
STUCCO ON CONCRETE:		
Walls	*SY*	*2.30 - 2.80*
METAL ACCESSORIES	*LF*	*.20 - .50*

LINOLEUM

Lino. Standard Gauge	SY	2.65 - 2.85
Lino. Battleship	SY	3.90 - 4.10
⅛" Asp. tile, Dark	SF	.10 - .11
⅛" Asp. tile, Light	SF	.14 - .16
⅛" Rubber Tile	SF	.40 - .44
.080 Vinyl Asb. tile	SF	.18 - .19
.080 Vinyl tile	SF	.59 - .61
⅛" Vinyl tile	SF	.78 - .82
4" Base, Dark	LF	.15 - .16
4" Base, Light	LF	.24 - .26
Rubber Nosing	LF	.60 - 1.30
Lino Paste	GAL	.75 - .90

Above rates based on quantities of 1000-5000 SF per job.

LUMBER

DOUGLAS FIR:	M.B.M.
#1 2x4—2x10	88.00 - 92.00
#2 2x4—2x10	85.00 - 90.00
#3 2x4—2x10	68.00 - 74.00
#4 2x4—2x10	64.00 - 72.00
Clear, Air Dried	180.00 - 210.00
Clear, Kiln Dried	210.00 - 240.00
REDWOOD:	
Foundation Grade	120.00 - 130.00
Construction Heart	110.00 - 120.00
A Grade	180.00 - 210.00
Clear Heart	190.00 - 220.00
D.F. PLYWOOD	M.S.F.
¼" AB	95.00 - 105.00
¼" AD	90.00 - 95.00
¼" Ext. Waterproof	115.00 - 125.00
⅜" AB	130.00 - 145.00
⅜" AD	115.00 - 125.00
⅜" CD	70.00 - 85.00
½" AB	170.00 - 185.00
½" AD	110.00 - 115.00
½" CD	....
⅝" AB	185.00 - 200.00
⅝" AD	165.00 - 180.00
⅝" CD	115.00 - 125.00
¾" AB	210.00 - 230.00
¾" AD	195.00 - 210.00
¾" CD	125.00 - 140.00
⅝" Plyform	160.00 - 170.00
SHINGLES:	Square
Cedar #1	14.00 - 15.50
Cedar #2	11.50 - 12.50
SHAKES:	
CEDAR	
½ to ¾" Butt	17.50 - 18.50
¾ to 1¼" Butt	18.50 - 19.50
REDWOOD	
¾ to 1¼" Butt	21.00 - 24.00

MILLWORK

All Prices F.O.B. Mill

D.F. CLEAR, AIR DRIED:		
S4S	MBM	220.00 - 250.00
D.F. CLEAR, KILN DRIED:		
S4S	MBM	225.00 - 275.00
DOOR FRAMES & TRIM:		
Residential Entrance		17.00 & up
Interior Room Entrance		7.50 & up
DOORS:		
1⅜" D.F. Slab, Hollow Core		8.00 & up
1¾" D.F. Slab, Solid Core		19.00 & up
1⅜" Birch Slab, Hollow Core		10.00 & up
1¾" Birch Slab, Solid Core		22.00 & up
WINDOW FRAMES:		
D/H Singles	SF	.80
Casement Singles	SF	.90
WOOD SASH:		
D/H in pairs (1 lite)	SF	.45
Casement (1 lite)	SF	.50
WOOD CABINETS:		
¾" D.F. Ply with ¼" ply backs		
Wall Hung	LF	10.00 - 15.00
Counter	LF	12.00 - 17.00

BIRCH OR MAPLE—Add 25%

PAINTING

EXTERIOR:		
Stucco Wash 1 ct.	*SY*	*.30*
Stucco Wash 2 cts	*SY*	*.55*
Lead and Oil 2 cts	*SY*	*.90*
Lead and Oil 3 cts	*SY*	*1.30*
INTERIOR:		
Primer Sealer	*SY*	*.40*
Wall Paint, 1 ct.	*SY*	*.50*
Wall Paint, 2 cts	*SY*	*.95*
Enamel, 1 ct.	*SY*	*.60*
Enamel, 2 cts	*SY*	*1.10*
Doors and Trim	*EA*	*10.00*
Sash and Trim	*EA*	*12.00*
Base and Molds	*LF*	*.12*

Old Work—Add 15-30%

PLUMBING

Lavatories	*EA*	*100.00 - 150.00*
Toilets	*EA*	*200.00 - 300.00*
Bath Tubs	*EA*	*250.00 - 350.00*
Stall Shower	*EA*	*80.00 - 150.00*
Sinks	*EA*	*125.00 - 175.00*
Laundry Trays	*EA*	*80.00 - 130.00*
Water Heaters	*EA*	*100.00 - 300.00*

Prices based on average residential and commercial work. Special fixtures and excessive piping not included.

PAINT

All Prices F.O.B. Warehouse

Thinners—5-100 gals.	GAL	.45
Turpentine—5-100 gals.	GAL.	1.35
Linseed Oil, Raw	GAL	2.00
Linseed Oil, Boiled	GAL	1.95
Primer-Sealer	GAL	2.95
Enamel	GAL	5.00
Enamel Undercoat	GAL	3.25
White Lead in Oil	LB.	.26
Red Lead in Oil	LB.	.29
Litharge	LB.	.24

ROOFING

STANDARD TAR & GRAVEL	Per Square
4 ply	*14.00 - 18.00*
5 ply	*17.00 - 20.00*
White Gravel Finish—Add	*2.00 - 4.00*
Asph. Compo. Shingles	*16.00 - 20.00*
Cedar Shingles	*20.00 - 24.00*
Cedar Shakes	*26.00 - 30.00*
Redwood Shakes	*28.00 - 34.00*
Clay Tiles	*40.00 - 50.00*

SEWER PIPE

VITRIFIED:		
Standard 4 in.	LF	.31
Standard 6 in.	LF	.56
Standard 8 in.	LF	.81
Standard 12 in.	LF	1.76
Standard 24 in.	LF	6.95
CLAY DRAIN PIPE:		
Standard 6 in.	LF	.34
Standard 8 in.	LF	.59

Rate for 100 Lin. Ft. F.O.B. Warehouse

STEEL

REINFORCING BARS:		
¼" rounds	LB	.122
⅜" rounds	LB	.111
½" rounds	LB	.107
⅝" rounds	LB	.104
¾" rounds	LB	.102
⅞" rounds	LB	.102
1" rounds	LB	.102
REINFORCING MESH (1050 SF Rolls)		
6x6 X 10x10	SF	.035
6x6 x 6x6	SF	.067
16 GA. TYING WIRE	LB	.130

Rates 100-1000 Lbs. F.O.B. Warehouse

STRUCTURAL STEEL

$325.00 and up per ton erected when out of mill.
$350.00 and up per ton erected when out of stock.

SHEET METAL

ROOF FLASHINGS:		
18 ga. Galv. Steel	*SF*	*.60 - 1.00*
22 ga. Galv. Steel	*SF*	*.50 - .90*
26 ga. Galv. Steel	*SF*	*.40 - .80*
18 ga. Aluminum	*SF*	*1.00 - 1.50*
22 ga. Aluminum	*SF*	*.80 - 1.30*
26 ga. Aluminum	*SF*	*.60 - 1.10*
24 oz. Copper	*SF*	*1.90 - 2.40*
20 oz. Copper	*SF*	*1.70 - 2.20*
16 oz. Copper	*SF*	*1.50 - 2.00*
26 ga. Galv. Steel		
4" o.g. gutter	*LF*	*.90 - 1.30*
Mitres and Drops	*EA*	*2.00 - 4.00*
22 ga. Galv. Louvres	*SF*	*2.50 - 3.50*
20 oz. Copper Louvres	*SF*	*3.00 - 4.50*

TILE WORK

CERAMIC TILE, Stock colors:		
Floors	*SF*	*1.95 - 2.45*
Walls	*SF*	*2.05 - 2.55*
Coved Base	*LF*	*1.05 - 1.45*
QUARRY TILE:		
6" x 6" x ½" Floors	*SF*	*1.60 - 2.00*
9" x 9" x ¾" Floors	*SF*	*1.75 - 2.15*
Treads and risers	*LF*	*3.00 - 4.50*
Coved Base	*LF*	*.90 - 1.30*

Mosaic Tile — Rates vary with design and colors. Each job should be priced from Manufacturer.

TERRAZZO & MARBLE

Terrazzo Floors	*SF*	*2.00 - 2.50*
Cond. Terr. Floors	*SF*	*2.20 - 2.75*
Precast treads and risers	*LF*	*3.50 - 4.50*
Precast landing slabs	*SF*	*3.00 - 4.00*

TILE

CERAMIC:

F.O.B. Warehouse

4¼" X 4¼" glazed	SF	.69
4¼" X 4¼" hard glazed	SF	.72
Random unglazed	SF	.73
6" X 2" cap	EA	.17
6" coved base	EA	.22
¼" round bead	LF	.18
QUARRY:		
6 x 6 x ½" Red	SF	.49
6 x 6 x ¾" Red	SF	.52
9 x 9 x ¾" Red	SF	.60
6 x 6" coved base	EA	.21
White Cement Grout	Per 100 Lbs.	6.25

VENETIAN BLINDS

Residential	SF	.40 & Up
Commercial	SF	.45 & Up

WINDOWS

STEEL SASH:		
Under 10 SF	SF	2.50 & Up
Under 15 SF	SF	2.00 & Up
Under 20 SF	SF	1.50 & Up
Under 30 SF	SF	1.00 & Up
ALUMINUM SASH:		
Under 10 SF	SF	2.75 & Up
Under 15 SF	SF	2.25 & Up
Under 20 SF	SF	1.75 & Up
Under 30 SF	SF	1.25 & Up

Above rates are for standard sections and stock sizes F.O.B. Warehouse

QUICK REFERENCE
ESTIMATOR'S DIRECTORY
Building and Construction Materials

ACOUSTICAL ENGINEERS
L. D. REEDER CO.
San Francisco: 1255 Sansome St., DO 2-5050
Sacramento: 3026 V St., GL 7-3505

AIR CONDITIONING
E. C. BRAUN CO.
Berkeley: 2115 Fourth St., TH 5-2356
GILMORE AIR CONDITIONING SERVICE
San Francisco: 1617 Harrison St., UN 1-2000
KAEMPER & BARRETT
San Francisco: 233 Industrial St., JU 6-6200
LINFORD AIR & REFRIGERATION CO.
Oakland: 174-12th St., TW 3-6521
MALM METAL PRODUCTS
Santa Rosa: 724-2nd St., SR 454
JAMES A. NELSON CO.
San Francisco: 1375 Howard St., HE 1-0140

ALUMINUM BLDG. PRODUCTS
MICHEL & PFEFFER IRON WORKS (Wrought Iron)
So. San Francisco: 212 Shaw Road, PLaza 5-8983
REYNOLDS METALS CO.
San Francisco: 3201 Third St., MI 7-2990
SOULE STEEL CO.
San Francisco: 1750 Army St., VA 4-4141
UNIVERSAL WINDOW CO.
Berkeley: 950 Parker St., TH 1-1600

ARCHITECTURAL PORCELAIN ENAMEL
CALIFORNIA METAL ENAMELING CO.
Los Angeles: 6904 E. Slauson, RA 3-6351
San Francisco: Continental Bldg. Products Co.,
178 Fremont St.
Portland: Portland Wire & Iron Works,
4644 S.E. Seventeenth Ave.
Seattle: Foster-Bray Co., 2412 1st Ave. So.
Spokane: Bernhard Schafer, Inc., West 34, 2nd Ave.
Salt Lake City: S. A. Roberts & Co., 109 W. 2nd So.
Dallas: Offenhauser Co., 2201 Telephone Rd.
El Paso: Architectural Products Co.,
506 E. Yandell Blvd.
Phoenix: Haskell-Thomas Co., 3808 No. Central
San Diego: Maloney Specialties, Inc., 823 W. Laurel St.
Boise: Intermountain Glass Co., 1417 Main St.

ARCHITECTURAL & AERIAL PHOTOGRAPHS
FRED ENGLISH
Belmont, Calif.: 1310 Old County Road, LY 1-0385

ARCHITECTURAL VENEER
Ceramic Veneer
GLADDING, McBEAN & CO.
San Francisco: Harrison at 9th St., UN 1-7400
Los Angeles: 2901 Los Feliz Blvd., OL 2121
Portland: 110 S.E. Main St., EA 6179
Seattle 99: 945 Elliott Ave., West, GA 0330
Spokane: 1102 N. Monroe St., BR 3259
KRAFTILE COMPANY
Niles, Calif., Niles 3611

Porcelain Veneer
PORCELAIN ENAMEL PUBLICITY BUREAU
Oakland 12: Room 601, Franklin Building
Pasadena 8: P. O. Box 186, East Pasadena Station

Granite Veneer
VERMONT MARBLE COMPANY
San Francisco 24: 6000 3rd St., VA 6-5024
Los Angeles: 3522 Council St., DU 2-6339

Marble Veneer
VERMONT MARBLE COMPANY
San Francisco 24: 6000 3rd St., VA 6-5024
Los Angeles: 3522 Council St., DU 2-6339

BANKS - FINANCING
CROCKER-ANGLO NATIONAL BANK
San Francisco: 13 Offices

BLINDS
PARAMOUNT VENETIAN BLIND CO.
San Francisco: 5929 Mission St., JU 5-2436

BRASS PRODUCTS
GREENBERG'S, M. SONS
San Francisco 7: 765 Folsom, EX 2-3143
Los Angeles 23: 1258 S. Boyle, AN 3-7108
Seattle 4:1016 First Ave. So., MA 5140
Phoenix: 3009 N. 19th Ave., Apt. 92, PH 2-7663
Portland 4: 510 Builders Exch. Bldg., AT 6443

BRICKWORK
Face Brick
GLADDING McBEAN & CO.
San Francisco: Harrison at 9th, UN 1-7400
KRAFTILE CO.
Niles, Calif., Niles 3611
UNITED MATERIALS & RICHMOND BRICK CO.
Point Richmond, BE 4-5032

BRONZE PRODUCTS
GREENBERG'S M. SONS
San Francisco: 765 Folsom St., EX 2-3143
MICHEL & PFEFFER IRON WORKS
So. San Francisco: 212 Shaw Road, PLaza 5-8983
C. E. TOLAND & SON
Oakland: 2635 Peralta St., GL 1-2580

BUILDING HARDWARE
E. M. HUNDLEY HARDWARE CO.
San Francisco: 662 Mission St., YU 2-3322

BUILDING PAPERS & FELTS
PACIFIC CEMENT & AGGREGATES INC.
San Francisco: 400 Alabama St., KL 2-1616

CABINETS & FIXTURES
CENTRAL MILL & CABINET CO.
San Francisco: 1595 Fairfax Ave., VA 4-7316
THE FINK & SCHINDLER CO.
San Francisco: 552 Brannan St., EX 2-1513
MULLEN MFG. CO.
San Francisco: 64 Rausch St., UN 1-5815
PARAMOUNT BUILT IN FIXTURE CO.
Oakland: 962 Stanford Ave., OL 3-9911
ROYAL SHOWCASE CO.
San Francisco: 770 McAllister St., JO 7-0311

CEMENT
CALAVERAS CEMENT CO.
San Francisco: 315 Montgomery St.
DO 2-4224, Enterprise 1-2315
PACIFIC CEMENT & AGGREGATES INC.
San Francisco: 400 Alabama St., KL 2-1616

CONCRETE AGGREGATES
Ready Mixed Concrete
CENTRAL CONCRETE SUPPLY CO.
San Jose: 610 McKendrie St.
PACIFIC CEMENT & AGGREGATES INC.
San Francisco: 400 Alabama St., KL 2-1616
Sacramento: 16th and A Sts., GI 3-6586
San Jose: 790 Stockton Ave., CY 2-5620
Oakland: 2400 Peralta St., GL 1-0177
Stockton: 820 So. California St., ST 8-8643
READYMIX CONCRETE CO.
Santa Rosa: 50 W. Collage Ave.
RHODES-JAMIESON LTD.
Oakland: 333-23rd Ave., KE 3-5225
SANTA ROSA BLDG. MATERIALS CO.
Santa Rosa: Roberts Ave.

CONCRETE ACCESSORIES
Screed Materials
C. & H. SPECIALTIES CO.
Berkeley: 909 Camelia St., LA 4-5358

CONCRETE BLOCKS
BASALT ROCK CO.
Napa, Calif.

CONCRETE COLORS—HARDENERS
CONRAD SOVIG CO.
875 Bryant St., HE 1-1345

CONSTRUCTION SERVICES
LE ROY CONSTRUCTION SERVICES
San Francisco, 143 Third St., SU 1-8914

DECKS—ROOF
UNITED STATES GYPSUM CO.
2322 W. 3rd St., Los Angeles 54, Calif.
300 W. Adams St., Chicago 6, Ill.

DOORS
THE BILCO COMPANY
New Haven, Conn.
Oakland: Geo. B. Schultz, 190 MacArthur Blvd.
Sacramento: Harry B. Ogle & Assoc., 1331 T St.
Fresno: Healey & Popovich, 1703 Fulton St.
Reseda: Daniel Dunner, 6200 Alonzo Ave.

Cold Storage Doors
BIRKENWALD
Portland: 310 N.W. 5th Ave.

Electric Doors
ROLY-DOOR SALES CO.
San Francisco, 5976 Mission St., PL 5-5089

Folding Doors
WALTER D. BATES & ASSOCIATES
San Francisco, 693 Mission St., GA 1-6971

Hardwood Doors
BELLWOOD CO. OF CALIF.
Orange, Calif., 533 W. Collins Ave.

Hollywood Doors
WEST COAST SCREEN CO.
Los Angeles: 1127 E. 63rd St., AD 1-1108
T. M. COBB CO.
Los Angeles & San Diego
W. P. FULLER CO.
Seattle, Tacoma, Portland
HOGAN LUMBER CO.
Oakland: 700 - 6th Ave.
HOUSTON SASH & DOOR
Houston, Texas
SOUTHWESTERN SASH & DOOR
Phoenix, Tucson, Arizona
El Paso, Texas
WESTERN PINE SUPPLY CO.
Emeryville: 5760 Shellmound St.
GEO. C. VAUGHAN & SONS
San Antonio & Houston, Texas

Screen Doors
WEST COAST SCREEN DOOR CO.

DRAFTING ROOM EQUIPMENT
GENERAL FIREPROOFING CO.
Oakland: 332-19th St., GL 2-4280
Los Angeles: 1200 South Hope St., RI 7-7501
San Francisco: 1025 Howard St., HE 1-7070

DRINKING FOUNTAINS
HAWS DRINKING FAUCET CO.
Berkeley: 1435 Fourth St., LA 5-3341

ELECTRICAL CONTRACTORS
COOPMAN ELECTRIC CO.
San Francisco: 85 - 14th St., MA 1-4438
ETS-HOKIN & GALVAN
San Francisco: 551 Mission St., EX 2-0432

ELECTRICAL CONTRACTORS (cont'd)

LEMOGE ELECTRIC CO.
San Francisco: 212 Clara St., DO 2-6010
LYNCH ELECTRIC CO.
San Francisco: 937 McAllister St., WI 5158
PACIFIC ELECTRIC & MECHANICAL CO.
San Francisco: Gough & Fell Sts., HE 1-5904

ELECTRIC HEATERS

WESIX ELECTRIC HEATER CO.
San Francisco: 390 First St., GA 1-2211

FIRE ESCAPES

MICHEL & PFEFFER IRON WORKS
South San Francisco: 212 Shaw Road, PLaza 5-8983

FIRE PROTECTION EQUIPMENT

FIRE PROTECTION PRODUCTS CO.
San Francisco: 1101-16th St., UN 1-2420
ETS-HOKIN & GALVAN
San Francisco: 551 Mission St., EX 2-0432
BARNARD ENGINEERING CO.
San Francisco: 35 Elmira St., JU 5-4642

FLOORS

Floor Tile

GLADDING McBEAN & CO.
San Francisco: Harrison at 9th St., UN 1-744
Los Angeles: 2901 Las Feliz Bldg., OL 2121
KRAFTILE CO.
Niles, Calif., Niles 3611

Resilient Floors

PETERSON-COBBY CO.
San Francisco: 218 Clara St., EX 2-8714
TURNER RESILIENT FLOORS CO.
San Francisco: 2280 Shafter Ave., AT 2-7720

FLOOR DRAINS

JOSAM PACIFIC COMPANY
San Francisco: 765 Folsom St., EX 2-3142

GAS VENTS

WM. WALLACE CO.
Belmont, Calif.

GENERAL CONTRACTORS

O. E. ANDERSON
San Jose: 1075 No. 10th St., CY 3-8844
BARRETT CONSTRUCTION CO.
San Francisco: 1800 Evans Ave., MI 7-9700
JOSEPH BETTANCOURT
South San Francisco: 125 So. Linden St., PL 5-9185
DINWIDDIE CONSTRUCTION CO.
San Francisco: Crocker Bldg., YU 6-2718
D. L. FAULL CONSTRUCTION CO.
Santa Rosa: 1236 Cleveland Ave.
HAAS & HAYNIE
San Francisco: 275 Pine St., DO 2-0678
HENDERSON CONSTRUCTION CO.
San Francisco: 33 Ritch St., GA 1-0856
JACKS & IRVINE
San Francisco: 620 Market St., YU 6-0511
G. P. W. JENSEN & SONS
San Francisco: 320 Market St., GA 1-2444
RALPH LARSEN & SON
San Francisco: 64 So. Park, YU 2-5682
LINDGREN & SWINERTON
San Francisco: 200 Bush St., GA 1-2980
MacDONALD, YOUNG & NELSON
San Francisco: 351 California St., YU 2-4700
MATTOCK CONSTRUCTION CO.
San Francisco: 220 Clara St., GA 1-5516
OLSEN CONSTRUCTION CO.
Santa Rosa: 125 Brookwood Ave., SR 2030
BEN ORTSKY
Cotati: Cypress Ave., Pet. 5-4383
PARKER, STEFFANS & PEARCE
San Mateo: 135 So. Park, EX 2-6639

RAPP, CHRISTENSEN & FOSTER
Santa Rosa: 705 Bennett Ave.
STOLTE, INC.
Oakland: 8451 San Leandro Ave., LO 2-4611
SWINERTON & WALBERG
San Francisco: 200 Bush St., GA 1-2980

FURNITURE—INSTITUTIONAL

GENERAL FIREPROOFING CO.
San Francisco: 1025 Howard St., HE 1-7070
Oakland: 332-19th St., GL 2-4280
Los Angeles: 1200 South Hope St., RI 7-7501

HEATING & VENTILATING

ATLAS HEATING & VENT. CO.
San Francisco: 557-4th St., DO 2-0377
E. C. BRAUN CO.
Berkeley: 2115 Fourth St., TH 5-2356
C. W. HALL
Santa Rosa: 1665 Sebastopol Rd., SR 6354
S. T. JOHNSON CO.
Oakland: 940 Arlington Ave., OL 2-6000
LOUIS V. KELLER
San Francisco: 289 Tehama St., JU 6-6252
L. J. KRUSE CO.
Oakland: 6247 College Ave., OL 2-8332
MALM METAL PRODUCTS
Santa Rosa: 724-2nd St., SR 454
JAS. A. NELSON CO.
San Francisco: 1375 Howard St., HE 1-0140
SCOTT COMPANY
Oakland: 1919 Market St., GL 1-1937
WESIX ELECTRIC HEATER CO.
San Francisco: 390 First St., GA 1-2211
Los Angeles: 530 W. 7th St., MI 8096

INSULATION WALL BOARD

PACIFIC CEMENT & AGGREGATES, INC.
San Francisco: 400 Alabama St., KL 2-1616

INTERCEPTING DEVICES

JOSAM PACIFIC CO.
San Francisco: 765 Folsom St., EX 2-3142

IRON—ORNAMENTAL

MICHEL & PFEFFER IRON WKS.
So. San Francisco: 212 Shaw Rd., PL 5-8983

LATHING & PLASTERING

ANGELO J. DANERI
San Francisco: 1433 Fairfax Ave., AT 8-1582
K-LATH CORP.
Alhambra: 909 So. Fremont St., Alhambra
A. E. KNOWLES CORP.
San Francisco: 3320 San Bruno Ave., JU 7-2091
G. H. & C. MARTINELLI
San Francisco: 174 Shotwell St., UN 3-6112
FREDERICK MEISWINKEL
San Francisco: 2155 Turk St., JO 7-7587
RHODES-JAMIESON LTD.
Oakland: 333-23rd Ave., KE 3-5225
PATRICK J. RUANE
San Francisco: 44 San Jose Ave., MI 7-6414

LIGHTING FIXTURES

SMOOT-HOLMAN COMPANY
Inglewood, Calif., OR 8-1217
San Francisco: 55 Mississippi St., MA 1-8474

LUMBER

CHRISTENSEN LUMBER CO.
San Francisco: Quint & Evans Ave., VA 4-5832
ART HOGAN LUMBER CO.
1701 Galvez Ave., ATwater 2-1157
MEAD CLARK LUMBER CO.
Santa Rosa: 3rd & Railroad
ROLANDO LUMBER CO.
San Francisco: 5th & Berry Sts., SU 1-6901
STERLING LUMBER CO.
Santa Rosa: 1129 College Ave., S. R. 82

MARBLE

JOS. MUSTO SONS-KEENAN CO.
San Francisco: 555 No. Point St., GR 4-6365
VERMONT MARBLE CO.
San Francisco: 6000-3rd St., VA 6-5024

MASONRY

BASALT ROCK CO.
Napa, Calif.
San Francisco: 260 Kearney St., GA 1-3758
WM. A. RAINEY & SON
San Francisco: 323 Clementina St., SU 1-0072
GEO. W. REED CO.
San Francisco: 1390 So. Van Ness Ave., AT 2-1226

METAL EXTERIOR WALLS

THE KAWNEER CO.
Berkeley: 930 Dwight Way, TH 5-8710

METAL FRAMING

UNISTRUT OF NORTHERN CALIFORNIA
Berkeley: 2547-9th St., TH 1-3031
Enterprise 1-2204

METAL GRATING

KLEMP METAL GRATING CORP.
Chicago, Ill.: 6601 So. Melvina St.

METAL LATH—EXPANDED

PACIFIC CEMENT & AGGREGATES, INC.
San Francisco: 400 Alabama St., KL 2-1616

METAL PARTITIONS

THE E. F. HAUSERMAN CO.
San Francisco: 485 Brannan St., YU 2-5477

METAL PRODUCTS

FORDERER CORNICE WORKS
San Francisco: 269 Potrero Ave., HE 1-4100

MILLWORK

CENTRAL MILL & CABINET CO.
San Francisco: 1595 Fairfax Ave., VA 4-7316
THE FINK & SCHINDLER CO.
San Francisco: 552 Brannan St., EX 2-1513
MULLEN MFG. CO.
San Francisco: 64 Rausch St., UN 1-5815
PACIFIC MFG. CO.
San Francisco: 16 Beale St., GA 1-7755
Santa Clara: 2610 The Alameda, S. C. 607
Los Angeles: 6820 McKinley Ave., TH 4156
SOUTH CITY LUMBER & SUPPLY CO.
So. San Francisco: Railroad & Spruce, PL 5-7085

OFFICE EQUIPMENT

GENERAL FIREPROOFING CO.
Los Angeles: 1200 South Hope St., RI 7-7501
San Francisco: 1025 Howard St., HE 1-7070
Oakland: 332-19th St., GL 2-4280

OIL BURNERS

S. T. JOHNSON CO.
Oakland: 940 Arlington Ave., GL 2-6000
San Francisco: 585 Potrero Ave., MA 1-2757
Philadelphia, Pa.: 401 North Broad St.

ORNAMENTAL IRON

MICHEL & PFEFFER IRON WORKS
So. San Francisco: 212 Shaw Rd., PL 5-8983

PAINTING

R. P. PAOLI & CO.
San Francisco: 2530 Lombard St., WE 1-1632
SINCLAIR PAINT CO.
San Francisco: 2112-15th St., HE 1-2196
D. ZELINSKY & SONS
San Francisco: 165 Groove St., MA 1-7400

PHOTOGRAPHS

Construction Progress
FRED ENGLISH
Belmont, Calif.: 1310 Old County Road, LY 1-0385

PLASTER

PACIFIC CEMENT & AGGREGATE INC.
San Francisco: 400 Alabama St., KL 2-1616

PLASTIC PRODUCTS

PLASTIC SALES & SERVICE
San Francisco: 409 Bryant St., DO 2-6433
WEST COAST INDUSTRIES
San Francisco: 3150-18th St., MA 1-5657

PLUMBING
BROADWAY PLUMBING CO.
San Francisco: 1790 Yosemite Ave., MI 8-4250
E. C. BRAUN CO.
Berkeley: 2115 Fourth St., TH 5-2356
C. W. HALL
Santa Rosa: 1665 Sebastopol Rd., SR 6354
HAWS DRINKING FAUCET CO.
Berkeley: 1435 Fourth St., LA 5-3341
JOSAM PACIFIC CO.
San Francisco: 765 Folsom St., EX 2-3143
LOUIS V. KELLER
San Francisco: 289 Tehama St., YU 6-6252
L. J. KRUSE CO.
Oakland: 6247 College Ave., OL 2-8332
JAS. A. NELSON CO.
San Francisco: 1375 Howard St., HE 1-0140
RODONI-BECKER CO., INC.
San Francisco: 455-10th St., MA 1-3662
SCOTT CO.
Oakland: 1919 Market St., GL 1-1937

POST PULLER
HOLLAND MFG. CO.
No. Sacramento: 1202 Dixieanne

PUMPING MACHINERY
SIMONDS MACHINERY CO.
San Francisco: 816 Folsom St., DO 2-6794

ROOFING
ANCHOR ROOFING CO.
San Francisco: 1671 Galvez Ave., VA 4-8140
ALTA ROOFING CO.
San Francisco: 1400 Egbert Ave., MI 7-2173
REGAL ROOFING CO.
San Francisco: 930 Innes Ave., VA 4-3261

ROOF SCUTTLES
THE BILCO CO.
New Haven, Conn.
Oakland: Geo. B. Schultz, 190 MacArthur Blvd.
Sacramento: Harry B. Ogle & Assoc., 1331 T St.
Fresno: Healey & Rapovich, 1703 Fulton St.
Reseda: Daniel Dunner, 6200 Alonzo Ave.

ROOF TRUSSES
EASYBOW ENGINEERING & RESEARCH CO.
Oakland: 13th & Wood Sts., GL 2-0805

SAFES
THE HERMANN SAFE CO.
San Francisco: 1699 Market St., UN 1-6644

SEWER PIPE
GLADDING, McBEAN & CO.
San Francisco: 9th & Harrison, UN 1-7400
Los Angeles: 2901 Los Feliz Blvd., OL 2121

SHEET METAL
MICHEL & PFEFFER IRON WORKS
So. San Francisco: 212 Shaw Rd., PL 5-8983

SOUND EQUIPMENT
STROMBERG-CARLSON CO.
San Francisco: 1805 Rollins Rd., Burlingame, OX 7-3630
Los Angeles: 5414 York Blvd., CL 7-3939

SPRINKLERS
BARNARD ENGINEERING CO.
San Francisco: 35 Elmira St., JU 5-4642

STEEL—STRUCTURAL & REINFORCING
COLUMBIA-GENEVA DIV., U. S. STEEL CORP.
San Francisco: Russ Bldg., SU 1-2500
Los Angeles: 2087 E. Slauson, LA 1171
Portland, Ore.: 2345 N.W. Nicolai, BE 7261
Seattle, Wn.: 1331-3rd Ave. Bldg., MA 1972
Salt Lake City, Utah: Walker Bank Bldg., SL 3-6733
HERRICK IRON WORKS
Oakland 18th & Campbell, GL 1-1767
INDEPENDENT IRON WORKS, INC.
Oakland: 780 Pine St., TE 2-0160
JUDSON PACIFIC MURPHY CORP.
Emeryville: 4300 Eastshore Highway, OL 3-1717
REPUBLIC STEEL CORP.
San Francisco: 116 New Montgomery St., GA 1-0977
Los Angeles: Edison Bldg.
Seattle: White-Henry Stuart Bldg.
Salt Lake City: Walker Bank Bldg.
Denver: Continental Oil Bldg.
SOULE STEEL CO.
San Francisco: 1750 Army St., VA 4-4141

STEEL FORMS
STEELFORM CONTRACTING CO.
San Francisco: 666 Harrison St., DO 2-5582

SWIMMING POOLS
SIERRA MFG. CO.
Walnut Creek, Calif.: 1719 Mt. Diablo Blvd.

SWIMMING POOL FITTINGS
JOSAM PACIFIC CO.
San Francisco: 765 Folsom St., EX 2-3143

TESTING LABORATORIES (ENGINEERS & CHEMISTS
ABBOT A. HANKS, INC.
San Francisco: 624 Sacramento St., GA 1-1697
ROBERT W. HUNT COMPANY
San Francisco: 500 Iowa, MI 7-0224
Los Angeles: 3050 E. Slauson, JE 9131
Chicago, New York, Pittsburgh
PITTSBURGH TESTING LABORATORY
San Francisco: 651 Howard St., EX 2-1747

TILE—CLAY & WALL
GLADDING, McBEAN & CO.
San Francisco: 9th & Harrison Sts., UN 1-7400
Los Angeles: 2901 Los Feliz Blvd., OL 2121
Portland: 110 S.E. Main St., EA 6179
Seattle: 945 Elliott Ave. West, GA 0330
Spokane: 1102 No. Monroe St., BR 3259
KRAFTILE CO.
Niles, Calif.: Niles 3611
San Francisco: 50 Hawthorne St., DO 2-3780
Los Angeles: 406 So. Main St., MA 7241

TILE—TERRAZZO
NATIONAL TILE & TERAZZO CO.
San Francisco: 198 Mississippi St., UN 1-0273

TIMBER—TREATED
J. H. BAXTER CO.
San Francisco: 200 Bush St., YU 2-0200
Los Angeles: 3450 Wilshire Blvd., DU 8-9591

TIMBER TRUSSES
EASYBOW ENGINEERING & RESEARCH CO.
Oakland: 13th & Wood Sts., GL 2-0805

TRUCKING
PASSETTI TRUCKING CO.
San Francisco: 264 Clementina St., GA 1-5297

UNDERPINNING & SHORING
D. J. & T. SULLIVAN
San Francisco: 1942 Folsom St., MA 1-1545

WALL PAPER
WALLPAPERS, INC.
Oakland: 384 Grand Ave., GL 2-0451

WAREHOUSE AND STORAGE EQUIPMENT AND SHELVING
GENERAL FIREPROOFING CO.
Los Angeles: 1200 South Hope St., RI 7-7501
San Francisco: 1025 Howard St., HE 1-7070
Oakland: 332-19th St., GL 2-4280

WATERPROOFING MATERIALS
CONRAD SOVIG CO.
San Francisco: 875 Bryant St., HE 1-1345

WATERSTOPS (P.V.C.)
TECON PRODUCTS, LTD.
Vancouver, B.C.: 681 E. Hastings St.
Seattle: 304 So. Alaskan Way

WINDOW SHADES
SHADES, INC.
San Francisco: 80 Tehama St., DO 2-7092

CONSTRUCTION INDUSTRY WAGE RATES

Table 1 has been prepared by the State of California, Department of Industrial Relations, Division of Labor Statistics and Research. The rates are the union hourly wage rates established by collective bargaining as of January 2, 1958, as reported by reliable sources.

TABLE 1—UNION HOURLY WAGE RATES, CONSTRUCTION INDUSTRY, CALIFORNIA

Following are the hourly rates of compensation established by collective bargaining, reported as of January 2, 1958 or later

CRAFT	San Francisco	Alameda	Contra Costa	Fresno	Sacramento	San Joaquin	Santa Clara	Solano	Los Angeles	San Bernardino	San Diego	Santa Barbara	Kern
ASBESTOS WORKBR	$3.70	$3.70	$3.70	$3.70	$3.70	$3.70	$3.70	$3.70	$3.70	$3.70	$3.70	$3.70	$3.70
BOILERMAKER	3.675	3.675	3.675	3.675	3.675	3.675	3.675	3.675	3.675	3.675	3.675	3.675	3.675
BRICKLAYER	3.95	3.75	3.75	3.75	3.80	3.75	3.875	3.95	3.80	3.90	3.75		3.85
BRICKLAYER HODCARRIER	3.15	3.15	3.15	3.15	2.90	2.90	3.00	3.10	2.75	2.75	2.75		2.75
CARPENTER	3.175	3.175	3.225	3.225	3.225	3.225	3.225	3.225	3.225	3.225	3.225	3.225	3.225
CEMENT MASON	3.22	3.22	3.22	3.22	3.22	3.22	3.22	3.22	3.15	3.15	3.25	3.15	3.15
ELECTRICIAN	3.936A	3.936A	3.936A		3.94A	3.50	4.03A	3.666A	3.90A	3.90A	3.90	3.85A	3.70
GLAZIER	3.09	3.09	3.09	3.135	3.055	3.055	3.09	3.09	3.105	3.105	3.03	3.105	3.135
IRON WORKER, ORNAMENTAL	3.625	3.625	3.625	3.625	3.625	3.625	3.625	3.625	3.625	3.625	3.625	3.625	3.625
REINFORCING	3.375	3.375	3.375	3.375	3.375	3.375	3.375	3.375	3.375	3.375	3.375	3.375	3.375
STRUCTURAL	3.625	3.625	3.625	3.625	3.625	3.625	3.625	3.625	3.625	3.625	3.625	3.625	3.625
LABORER, GENERAL OR CONSTRUCTION	2.505	2.505	2.505	2.505	2.505	2.505	2.505	2.505	2.50	2.50	2.48	2.50	2.50
LATHER	3.4375	3.84	3.84	3.45	3.60B	3.40C	3.60D	3.50E	3.9375		3.725	3.625F	
OPERATING ENGINEER Concrete mixer (up to 1 yard)	2.89	2.89	2.89	2.89	2.89	2.89	2.89	2.89					
Concrete mixer operator—Skip Type									2.96	2.96	2.96	2.96	2.96
Elevator Hoist Operator									3.19	3.19	3.19	3.19	3.19
Material Hoist (1 drum)	3.19	3.19	3.19	3.19	3.19	3.19	3.19	3.19					
Tractor Operator	3.33	3.33	3.33	3.33	3.33	3.33	3.33	3.33	3.47	3.47	3.47	3.47	3.47
PAINTER Brush	3.20	3.20	3.20	3.13	3.325	3.175	3.20	3.20	3.26G	3.25	3.19	3.13H	3.10
Spray	3.20	3.20	3.20	3.38	3.575	3.325	3.20	3.20	3.51G	3.50	3.74	3.38H	3.35
PILEDRIVERMAN	3.305	3.305	3.305	3.305	3.305	3.305	3.305	3.305	3.355	3.355		3.355	3.355
PLASTERER	3.69	3.545	3.545	3.35	3.60B	3.55C	3.58	3.50	3.9375	3.9375	3.725		
PLASTERER HODCARRIER	3.25	3.42	3.42	3.10	3.10	3.00C	3.20	3.15	3.6875	3.5625	3.475	3.50	3.6875
PLUMBER	3.67		3.935I	3.80J	3.70	3.80J	3.60	3.675	3.70	3.70	3.70	3.70	3.375
ROOFER	3.35	3.35	3.35	3.20	3.25	3.35	3.35	3.10K	3.20L	3.25	3.10	3.30	3.775
SHEET METAL WORKER	3.45	3.45	3.45	3.425	3.45	3.465	3.45	3.325	3.50	3.50	3.45	3.55	3.10
STEAMFITTER	3.67	3.96	3.96	3.80J	3.70	3.80J	3.60	3.675	3.70	3.70	3.70	3.70	3.775
TRUCK DRIVER— Dump Trucks under 4 yards	2.55	2.55	2.55	2.55	2.55	2.55	2.55	2.55	2.63	2.63	2.63	2.63	2.63
TILE SETTER	3.275	3.275	3.275	3.375	3.28	3.30	3.275	3.275	3.36	3.36	3.60	3.375	3.36

A Includes 4% vacation allowance.
B Includes 5c hour for industry promotion and 5c hour for vacation fund.
C ½% withheld for industry promotion.
D 1½c withheld for industry promotion.
E Includes 5c hour for industry promotion and 5c hour for vacation fund.
    Hourly rate for part of county adjacent to Sacramento County is $3.60.
F Northern part of County: $3.75.

G Pomona Area: Brush $3.25; Spray $3.50.
H Southern half of County: Brush $3.28; Spray $3.28.
I Includes 30c hour for vacation pay.
J Includes 15c hour which local union may elect to use for vacation purposes.
K Includes 10c hour for vacation fund.
L Includes 10c hour savings fund wage.

ATTENTION: The above tabulation has been prepared by the State of California, Department of Industrial Relations, Division of Labor Statistics and Research, and represents data reported by building trades councils, union locals, contractor organizations, and other reliable sources. The above rates do not include any payments to funds for health and welfare, pensions, vacations, industry promotion, apprentice training, etc., except as shown in the footnotes.

CONSTRUCTION INDUSTRY WAGE RATES — TABLE 2

Employer Contributions to Health and Welfare, Pension, Vacation and Other Funds
California Union Contracts, Construction Industry

(Revised March, 1957)

CRAFT	San Francisco	Fresno	Sacramento	San Joaquin	Santa Clara	Los Angeles	San Bernardino	San Diego
ASBESTOS WORKER	.10 W .11 hr. V	.10 W .11 hr. V	.10 W .11 hr. V	.10 W .11 hr. V	.10 W .11 hr. V	.10 W	.10 W	.10 W
BRICKLAYER	.15 W .14 P .05 hr. V		.15 W		.15 W			
BRICKLAYER HODCARRIER	.10 W .10 P .10 V	.10 W	.10 W	.10 W	.10 W	.075 W	.075 W	.075 W
CARPENTER	.10 W .10 hr. V	.10 W	.10 W	.10 W	.10 W	.10 W	.10 W	.10 W
CEMENT MASON	.10 W	.10 W	.10 W	.10 W	.10 W	.10 W	.10 W	.10 W
ELECTRICAL WORKER	.10 W 1% P 4% V	.10 W 1% P 4% V	.075 W 1% P	.075 W 1% P 4% V	1% P	1% P	1% P	.10 W 1% P
GLAZIER	.075 W .085 V	.075 W 40 hr. V	.075 W .06 V	.075 W .05 V	.075 W .085 V	.075 W 40 hr. V	.075 W 40 hr. V	.075 W 40 hr. V
IRONWORKER: REINFORCING	.10 W	.10 W	.10 W	.10 W	.10 W	.10 W	.10 W	.10 W
STRUCTURAL	.10 W	.10 W	.10 W	.10 W	.10 W	.10 W	.10 W	.10 W
LABORER, GENERAL	.10 W	.10 W	.10 W	.10 W	.10 W	.075 W	.075 W	.075 W
LATHER	.60 day W .70 day V		.10 W	.10 W	.075 W .05 V	.90 day W	.70 day W	.10 W
OPERATING ENGINEER TRACTOR OPERATOR (MIN.)	.10 W	.10 W	.10 W	.10 W	.10 W	.10 W	.10 W	.10 W
POWER SHOVEL OP. (MIN.)	.10 W	.10 W	.10 W	.10 W	.10 W	.10 W	.10 W	.10 W
PAINTER, BRUSH	.095 W	.08 W	.075 W	.10 W	.095 W .07 V	.085 W	.08 W	.09 W
PLASTERER	.10 W .10 V	.10 W	.10 W	.10 W	.10 W .15 V	.10 W	.90 day W	.10 W
PLUMBER	.10 W .10 V	.15 W .10 P	.10 W .10 P .125 V	.10 W	.10 W .10 P .125 V	.10 W	.90 day W	.10 W
ROOFER	.10 W .10 V	.10 W	.10 W .10 V	.10 W	.075 W .10 V	.085 W	.10 W	.075 W
SHEET METAL WORKER	.075 W 4% V	.075 W 7 day V	.075 W .10 V	.075 W .12 V	.075 W 4% V	.085 W .10 V	.085 W .10 V	.085 W 5 day V
TILE SETTER	.075 W .09 V				.075 W .09 V	.075 W .025 W .06 V		

ATTENTION: The above tabulation has been prepared and compiled from the available data reported by building trades councils, union locals, contractor organizations and other reliable sources. The table was prepared from incomplete data; where no employer contributions are specified, it does not necessarily mean that none are required by the union contract.

The type of supplement is indicated by the following symbols: W—Health and Welfare; P—Pensions; V—Vacations; A—Apprentice training fund; Adm—Administration fund; JIB—Joint Industry Board; Prom—Promotion fund.

CONSTRUCTION CONTRACTS AWARDED AND MISCELLANEOUS PERSONNEL DATA

NEW JUNIPER SCHOOL, Palmdale, Los Angeles County. New Juniper School for elementary and intermediate students in Palmdale; 21-classrooms, 2 kindergartens, music room, shop and home making buildings, and multi-use unit; 52,000 sq. ft. in area; reinforced concrete and precast concrete panels, composition roofing, concrete slabs, glare reducing glass, radiant flooring heating, steel sash, covered walkways, metal decking, terrazzo—$734,057. ARCHITECT: Balch, Bryan, Perkins & Hutchason, 2933 Rowena Ave., Los Angeles. GENERAL CONTRACTOR: Larsen-Ratto Const. Co., 1901 Hedges Ave., Fresno.

GYMNASIUM, High School, Kelseyville, Lake County. Kelseyville Union High School District, owner. Structural steel frame, wood, concrete slab, glue laminated arches—$157,328. ARCHITECT: Bruce

E. Heiser, 251 Post St., San Francisco. GENERAL CONTRACTOR: C. H. Smythe, P.O. Box 207 Lakeport.

NEW ELEMENTARY SCHOOL, Bidwell, Antioch, Contra Costa County. Antioch School District, owner. 1-story slab on concrete, light weight steel frame, wood joists, some curtain wall, exterior wood and ceramic tile; facilities for 16-classroom, multi-purpose unit, library, kitchen, toilets—$687,118. ARCHITECT: John Lyon Reid & Partners, 1019 Market St., San Francisco. GENERAL CONTRACTOR: Pagni Const. Co., 84 Bishop Rd., Crockett.

KEZAR STADIUM, San Francisco. City of San Francisco, owner. Improvements and reconstruction of Kezar Stadium — $82,800. ARCHITECT: Chas. W. Griffiths, City Architect, City Hall, San Fran-

cisco. GENERAL CONTRACTOR: Martinelli Const. Co., 1580 Folsom St., San Francisco.

EXHIBIT BLDG., Junior, Ukiah, Mendocino County. 12th District Agricultural Association, Ukiah, owner. Construction of a 40x80 rigid steel frame exhibit building to be used for junior activities and the District Fair Grounds in Ukiah — $28,566. GENERAL CONTRACTOR: Leake & White Co., 772, Robinson Rd., Sebastopol.

LUCKY MARKET, South Shore Center, Alameda. South Shore Shopping Center, Inc., San Francisco, owner. 1-story reinforced concrete construction with all facilities for modern super market—$236,-283. GENERAL CONTRACTOR: Utah Const. Co., 100 Bush St., San Francisco.

ELEMENTARY SCHOOL, Rheem, Moraga, Contra Costa County. Moraga School District, owner. 1-story, wood frame, built-up roofing; facilities for administration unit, 8-classrooms, kitchen, multi-purpose, kitchen, toilets—$197,000. ARCHITECT: Jack Buchter, 3729 Mt. Diablo Blvd.,

Lafayette. GENERAL CONTRACTOR: Edward Eoff Co., 1439 Nevin Ave., Richmond.

SANCTUARY, Palo Alto, Santa Clara county. College A v e n u e Methodist Church, Palo Alto, owner. New 1-story building of concrete and laminated wood arches, 45x100 ft., facilities for 350 persons and choir of 400—$88,500. ARCHITECT: Carlton A. Steiner, 2941 Telegraph Ave., Berkeley. GENERAL CONTRACTOR: Aro & Okerman, P.O. Box 433, Palo Alto.

SCHOOL AND RESIDENCE, St. Bernards Parish, Tracy, San Joaquin county. Archbishop of San Francisco, San Francisco, owner. 1-story, part tilt-up and part wood frame construction, some masonry, concrete slab and asphalt tile floor, plaster wall interior, built-up roofing—$194,240. ARCHITECT: George J. Steuer, 705 Maud Ave., San Leandro. GENERAL CONTRACTOR: Anthony Morsilli, 8060 Crescent Ave., Hayward.

ELEMENTARY SCHOOL, John Fremont, additions, Antioch, Contra Costa county. Antioch-Live Oak Unified School District, Antioch, owner. Wood frame construction of additions to present building, to provide facilities for 2-kindergartens, library, storage, covered corridors —$96,712. ARCHITECT: John Lyon Reid & Partners, 1019 Market St., San Francisco. GENERAL CONTRACTOR: Vezey Const. Co., 3760 Ardley Ave., Oakland.

OLYMPIC WINTER GAMES, Squaw Valley, Placer county. California Olympic Games Committee, San Francisco, owner. Project comprises Phase 2 and consists of 3 buildings, Unit J—athlete's center, Unit K—Press Bldg., and Unit L—Recreation Center—$649,500. ARCHITECTS: Corlett & Spackman, and Kitchen & Hunt, San Francisco. STRUCTURAL ENGINEER: H. J. Brunnier and John M. Sardis, San Francisco. CONSULTING ENGINEERS: Punnet, Parz & Hutchinson, San Francisco. LANDSCAPE ARCHITECTS: Eckbo,

K-Lath 2" solid partitions save space, time, money.

K-LATH
galvanized
paper-backed · flat

K-Lath Corporation, Dept. 9
909 S. Fremont,
Alhambra, California
Please send me more information about K-Lath □. Name and address of nearest K-Lath dealer □.

Name_____
Street_____
City_____ State_____

Royston & Williams, San Francisco. MECHANICAL & ELECTRICAL ENGINEERS: Vandament & Darmsted, San Francisco. GENERAL CONTRACTOR: Diversified Builders, P.O. Box 390, Montebello.

SCHOOL ADD'N, Jefferson and Monroe Schools, Hanford, Kings county. Hanford School District owner. Wood and frame construction to provide facilities for 4-classrooms in wing, teachers workroom—$88,200. ARCHITECT: Alexander & Dorman, Architects and Engineers, 128 E. 8th St., Hanford. GENERAL CONTRACTOR: R. G. Fisher Co., P.O. Box 4081, Fresno.

ELEMENTARY SCHOOL, Cotati, Sonoma county. Cotati School District, owner. Frame and stucco construction, composition roof, concrete floors; facilities for administration unit, 6-classrooms, kindergarten, toilets—$102,500. ARCHITECT: C. A. Caulkins, Jr., Rosenberg Bldg., Santa Rosa. GENERAL CONTRACTOR: David C. Walker, P.O. Box 191, Cloverdale.

MOTEL, Moro Bay, San Luis Obispo county. Golden Tee Motel Co., Moro Bay, owner. 2 Story motel unit with lodge, wood, stone and glass construction, heavy crushed stone roof; facilities for banquet room for 200 persons, dining room for 100 persons, cocktail lounge and coffee shop; site is near golf course—$476,833. ARCHITECT: John R. Ross, 1149 Market St., San Luis Obispo. GENERAL CONTRACTOR: Nichols & Peterson, P.O. Box 476, Atascadero.

EXHIBIT BLDG., Hanford, Kings county. 24th-A District Agricultural Association, Hanford, owner. Metal, prefabricated, exhibit building, 70x110 ft., concrete block walls, complete with kitchen and toilets—$45,000. GENERAL CONTRACTOR: Lou Richardson, 123 Colonial Dr., Hanford.

PHONE BLDG., Corcoran, Kings county. Pacific Tel. & Tel., San Francisco, owner. Project consists of alterations and additions to present telephone exchange building—$23,800. ARCHITECT: Alastair Simpson, 64 N. Fulton St., Fresno. GENERAL CONTRACTOR: Robert Jolly, 4564 E. Tyler St., Fresno.

LIBRARY ADD'N, Dixon, Solano county. Dixon Unified School District, owner. 1 Story additions to present Carnegie library building; 2000 sq. ft. area; concrete slab on grade, concrete block walls, glued laminated wood beams and columns, 2x4 laminated roof decking, built-up roofing, asphalt tile floors—$34,997. ARCHITECT: Corlett & Spackman, 347 Clay St., San Francisco. GENERAL CONTRACTOR: Jay Bailey Const. Co., P.O. Box 148, Woodland.

CHURCH, Lor Lady of Guadalupe, Sacramento, owner. Concrete construction, poured in place and some tilt-up panels—$170,170. ARCHITECT: Harry J. Devine, 1012 J St., Sacramento. GENERAL CONTRACTOR: Continental Const. Co., P.O. Box 2551 Sacramento.

ELEMENTARY SCHOOL, new Marina Vista, Marina, Monterey county. Marina School District, owner. Concrete block construction, wood frame partitions, built-up roof, almost entirely glass skylights; facilities for Administration unit, 6 classrooms, kindergarten, toilets—$177,200; ARCHITECT: Wallace Holm & Associates, 321 Webster St., Monterey. GENERAL CONTRACTOR: Ekelin & Small, 273 E. Alisal, Salinas.

FIRE STATION, San Bruno, San Mateo county. City of San Bruno, owner. Project comprises central fire station for 5 engines, drill tower, living quarters, dormitory and toilet facilities—$111,674. ARCHITECT: William Rowe, 251 Post St., San Francisco. GENERAL CONTRACTOR: Peterson Const. Co., 715 El Camino Real, San Bruno.

ELEMENTARY SCHOOL, McDowell, Petaluma, Sonoma county. Petaluma City School District, owner. New wood frame elementary school building, tar and gravel roof, wood siding, plywood interior, asphalt tile floor; complete facilities for administration unit, 6 classrooms, toilets—$144,000. ARCHITECT: Stanton, Keeble & Rhoda, P.O. Box 2177 Carmel. GENERAL CONTRACTOR: Postmeier Const., 920 I St., Petaluma.

DORMITORY, Mudd College, Claremont, Los Angeles county. Harvey Mudd College, Claremont, owner. Construction of a new dormitory building will include: composition roof, concrete floor, asphalt tile floor covering, painting, plastering, plumbing, electrical, heating, ventilating, sheet metal structural and miscellaneous metal. ARCHITECT: Heitschmidt & Thompson, 2010 Wilshire Blvd., Los Angeles. GENERAL CONTRACTOR: Escherich Bros. Inc., 645 S. Ave. 21, Los Angeles.

NEW HOSPITAL, Quincy, Plaumas county. Plumas Hospital District, owner. 1 Story reinforced brick masonry construction with metal roof deck, metal lath and plaster, aluminum window walls, Type 1 building, 13,500 sq. ft. of area—$403,000. ARCHITECT: Cox & Liske, 926 J St., Sacramento. GENERAL CONTRACTOR: Bishop-Mattei Const., Pier 7, San Francisco.

PRINTING PLANT, Bellflower, Los Angeles county. B. J. Abraham, Bellflower, owner. Frame and stucco construction, composition roof, tapered steel girders, plaster interior, aluminum sash, slab floors, toilets, asphalt paving; 3850 sq. ft. of area—$24,000. DESIGNER: E. A. Brakensiek. GENERAL CONTRACTOR: Bert Pinckney, 405 Via Chico, Palos Verdes Estates.

COLLEGE OF NOTRE DAME, Additions, Belmont, San Mateo county. Sisters of Notre Dame, owner. Wood frame construction of a 3-story dormitory addition to existing buildings; expansion of cafeteria and kitchen—$379,998. ARCHITECT: Vincent G. Raney, 233 Post St., San Francisco. GENERAL CONTRACTOR: Leon M. Wheatley, 149 N. Gordon Way, Los Altos.

Y.M.C.A. BLDG., Westchester, Los Angeles Young Men's Christian Association, owner. 2 Story reinforced brick building with all facilities, 175x155 ft.—$317,000. ARCHITECT: Smith, Powell & Morgridge, 208 W. 8th St., Los Angeles. GENERAL CONTRACTOR: Kemp Bros., 8750 Mettler St., Los Angeles.

ELKS LODGE, Fresno. Fresno Elks Club, owner. Construction of new Elks Club

building to include offices, club rooms, and all facilities—$299,139. ARCHITECT: Swartz & Hyberg, 627 Rowell Bldg., Fresno. GENERAL CONTRACTOR: Midstate Const. Co., 505 Bank of America Bldg., Fresno.

ELEMENTARY SCHOOL, Piute School, Lancaster, Los Angeles county. Project will include administrative unit, multi-use rooms, 2 kindergartens, library and home economics units, music, arts, and shop units—$662,939. ARCHITECT: H. L. Gogerty, 3123 W. 8th St., Los Angeles. GENERAL CONTRACTOR: Vinnell Co., Inc., 1145 Westminster Ave., Alhambra.

HIGH SCHOOL ADD'N, Hughson, Stanislaus county. Hughson Union High School District, owner. Work consists of two buildings: 1 Story each, reinforced concrete tilt-up walls, wood laminated beams, concrete and tile floors, composition roof; to provide facilities for multi-use unit, cafeteria, music room, and 2 class-rooms — $320,527. ARCHITECT: Kaestner & Kaestner, 1115 Eye St., Modesto. GENERAL CONTRACTOR: Harris Const. Co., 264 Palm Ave., Fresno.

MEDICAL BLDG., Downey, Los Angeles county. David-Julius Inc., Downey, owner. 2 Story masonry and wood frame, medical building; composition roof, concrete slab, asphalt tile, interior plaster, acoustical work, heating and ventilating, metal sash — $150,000. ARCHITECT: Kazumi Adachi, 3305 Wilshire Blvd., Los Angeles. GENERAL CONTRACTOR: Integrated Constructors & Engineers, Inc., 7668 Telegraph Rd., Los Angeles.

FIRE STATION, Fig Garden, Fresno. Fig Garden Fire Department, owner. Work will consist of alerations and additions to the present fire house building, including the addition of two apartments—$35,208. ARCHITECT: Alastair Simpson, 64 N. Fulton St., Fresno. GENERAL CONTRACTOR: George Noricks, 2706 N. Cedar St., Fresno.

BANK BLDG., Willits, Mendocino county. Bank of America, San Francisco, owner. 1 Story building for complete banking facilities, including lobby, vault; 20,000 sq. ft. of space in the site—$101,880. ARCHITECT: Continental Service Co., San Francisco. GENERAL CONTRACTOR: Frank M. Crane, 4 Banker Blvd., Ukiah.

STUDENT RESIDENCE, UC Medical Center, San Francisco. University of California, Board of Regents, Berkeley, owner. Project will include construction of combined structure representing Unit No. 3—$281,000. GENERAL CONTRACTOR: Midstate Const. Co., 347 Clay St., San Francisco.

HIGH SCHOOL ADD'N, Yuba City, Sutter county. Yuba City Union High School District, owner. Light steel frame construction with combination of grouted brick and pre-cast concrete slab; facilities for cafeteria and multi-purpose rooms—$359,359. ARCHITECT: Gordon Stafford, 1024½ J St., Sacramento. GENERAL CONTRACTOR: Chapek, Dorville-Gallino & Kohler, P.O. Box 875 Grass Valley.

OFFICE & WAREHOUSE, Menlo Park, San Mateo county. Parke, Davis Co., Detroit, Michigan, owner. 1 Story, addition to warehouse approximately 6,000 sq. ft. of area; Eastern type construction for all of company's operations in Northern California, western Nevada; most sections of building prefabricated, including poured concrete roof, roof framing work, precast concrete arches and steel ties, white marble chip waterproofing, glass exterior walls, landscaping — $500,000. ARCHITECT: Minoru Yamasaki, Detroit, Michigan. GENERAL CONTRACTOR: Williams & Burrows, 500 Harbor Blvd., Belmont.

MOTEL, Upland, San Bernardino county. Walter C. Muller, Arcadia, owner. 2 Story frame and stucco 62-unit motel, comprising 3 buildings; 35,000 sq. ft. total area, composition roof, metal sash, concrete slab and wood floors, forced air heating, tile stall showers, tile top pullmans and drainboards, paved parking area, swimming pool 28x58, utility buildings. ARCHITECT: Thornton Ladd & Associates, 160 W. Holly St., Pasadena. GENERAL CONTRACTOR: Walter C. Muller, 161 Colorado Pl., Arcadia.

ELEMENTARY SCHOOL, Santa Fe, Oakland, Alameda county. Oakland Unified School District, owner. Work consists of additions to existing buildings to provide facilities for: Administration unit, 21 classrooms, multi-purpose unit without kitchen, library, 2 kindergartens, 2 special classrooms, and toilet facilities—$628,566. ARCHITECT: Bruno & Cerruti, 1440 Broadway, Oakland. GENERAL CONTRACTOR: Gaspard Const. Co., 6629 Beck St., Oakland.

DENTAL OFFICE, Sherman Oaks, Los Angeles county. Wayne B. Ford, Sherman Oaks, owner. Frame and stucco building, composition roof, concrete slab, carpeting, asphalt tile flooring, interior plaster, wood paneling, acoustical tile, plate glass, plumbing and electrical, asphaltic concrete paving. ARCHITECT: Alex J. Arany, 14611 Ventura Blvd., Sherman Oaks. GENERAL CONTRACTOR: Gilbert Oberman, 2928 Roscomare Rd., Los Angeles.

RESIDENCE HALLS, Units 2 and 3, University of California, Berkeley, Alameda county. University of California, Board of Regents, Berkeley, owner. Work comprises 2 residence halls, each unit consisting of a central two-level dining hall, kitchen and services building of 36,680 sq. ft. in area; surrounded by four similar 9-story residence hall buildings of 38,900 sq. ft. each—$7,733,000. ARCHITECT: Wernecke & Warnecke, 111 New Montgomery St., San Francisco; MECHANICAL ENGINEER: Dudley Deane & Associates, 182 2nd St., San Francisco. STRUCTURAL ENGINEERS: Isadore Thompson, 133 Kearney St., San Francisco. GENERAL CONTRACTOR: Dinwiddie Const. Co., 210 Crocker Bldg., San Francisco.

OFFICE BLDG., Long Beach, Los Angeles county. Sully-Miller Contracting Co., owner. Frame stucco and masonry building —$106,081. ARCHITECT: Hugh Gibbs, 441 E. 1st St., Long Beach. GENERAL CONTRACTOR: Patrick Prizio, 2427 Oakmont, Santa Ana.

IN THE NEWS

DEAN SIDNEY W. LITTLE OREGON ARCHITECT TO RESIGN SCHOOL POST

Sidney W. Little, Dean of the School of Architecture and Allied Arts at the University of Oregon, has announced his resignation from this administrative position and return to academic status as Professor of Architecture, effective July first of this year. He has been in this administrative post for the past twelve years, and came to Oregon from the Alabama Polytechnic Institute, where he served as Associate Professor of Architecture.

Dean Little will leave early in July on a six-month sabbatical leave for travel in

Europe and the United States, returning to the University of Oregon in January, 1959.

PORTLAND FIRM OF ARCHITECTS CHANGE NAME

The architectural firm of Sundeleaf, Hagestad & Peace of Portland, Oregon, recently announced the changing of the firm's name to Sundeleaf and Hagestad, A.I.A. Their address is Portland Trust Bldg., 319 S. W. Washington Street, Portland 4.

Richard Sundeleaf, AIA, and Wallace P. Hagestad, AIA, comprise the members of the firm.

BEAVER AWARD IS GIVEN TO LeTOURNEAU

Robert G. LeTourneau, Longview, Texas, manufacturer of earthmoving equipment, was presented with a "Beaver Award" in Los Angeles at the 3rd Annual Awards Dinner of The Beavers, in recognition of the contribution of his firm to the equipment and services to the heavy construction industry.

Close to 1000 leaders in the heavy construction industry witnessed the presentation in Los Angeles, which was made by George H. Atkinson, Beaver president, who said: "There is hardly any phase of this vast industry that has not been benefited and advanced through the products of Mr. LeTourneau's inventive genius."

MULTI-MILLION DOLLAR MOTEL IS ANNOUNCED

The Flamingo Hotels, Inc., operators of nineteen motels and hotels stretching across the country from Chicago to California, have acquired a site near San Leandro on Alameda county's Eastshore Freeway, and have announced the immediate construction of a 500-unit Motel.

The first phase of the 2-story Motor Motel will provide for 160 units and will be set in a developed 38-acre area. Construction in Phase 1 will include a large swimming pool, offices and medical center and neighborhood shopping center.

RADICAL DEPARTURE IN GYMNASIUM DESIGN OBSERVED

A radical new departure in gymnasium design, planned to provide an aesthetically attractive as well as athletically functional environment, was introduced in Pasadena this month with the opening of the

newest unit of the Flintridge Preparatory School's long range building program.

Designed by Thornton Ladd and Associates, the gymnasium is a concrete block structure of grey-green, with the building outlined by white sheet metal gutters and downspouts which form an arresting decorative pattern that is further dramatized by recessed plaster panels and projecting panels at the two main entrances. Inside, the white concrete block walls and off-white exposed ceiling are accentuated by laminated beams and vertical pilasters painted ebony. Two full length skylights provide natural lighting during the day. Floor is of maple hardwood.

NEW INTERIOR LOCK ANNOUNCED BY SCHLAGE

A new interior lock has been announced by Schlage, following five years of design, engineering, and development, for use in residences.

It is specifically engineered for today's streamlined building methods and is fast to install. The new lock embodies the following features: Surface mounted face plates and strike plate; pre-set mounting screws; anti-rattle, adjustable strike tongue; ingenious snap-in knob assembly; snap-on rose; and panic-proof push button. Is available in Tulip or Plymouth design knobs in brass, bronze and aluminum. Manufactured by Schlage Lock Co., San Francisco.

DONNER LAKE LODGE PLANS IMPROVEMENTS

Elvin Riley, Architect of Design Associates, 2090 Willow Pass Road, Concord, is completing preliminary plans for the construction of extensive additions to the Donner Lake Lodge at Donner Lake in Place county.

The work will consist of additiontl facilities to provide for a Coffee Shop, Gift Shop, additions to the dining area, and possible addition of 60 rental units.

FRED W. HELDENFELS, JR. INSTALLED AS PRESIDENT OF ASSOCIATED GEN. CONT.

Fred W. Heldenfels, Jr., of the firm of Heldenfels Brothers of Corpus Christi, Texas, was recently installed as 1958 presi-

dent of The Associated General Contractors of America. He served the organization last year as vice-president, and has served as preseident of the Texas Highway Branch of the AGC for two years, and as chairman of the Texas AGC Executive Council which includes 15 Texas AGC chapters.

Named to serve as vice president was James W. Cawdrey, partner in the firm of Cawdrey & Vemo of Seattle, Washington. He served as president of the Seattle AGC chapter in 1949, and was chairman of the Building Division of the national association in 1955.

CLARK COUNTY
COURT HOUSE
AT LAS VEGAS

The Board of Commissioners of Clark county, Nevada, have announced plans for construction of a new Clark County Court House to be built in Las Vegas at an estimated cost of $3,550,000.

The new facilities, being designed by Welton Becket & Associates, Architects of Los Angeles, and Zick & Sharp, Architects of Las Vegas, will include a part 3 and part 4 story building with reinforced concrete and steel construction; refrigerated air conditioning, metal sash, marble work, ornamental iron work, sprinkler system fire protection, ceramic tile and all utilities.

ELFSTROM TO HEAD
ADVERTISING FOR
UTILITY, MISSION

John K. Elfstrom has been appointed advertising manager of Utility Appliance Corp. and Mission Appliance Corp., according to an announcement by P. L.

Chabre, vice president of the firm in charge of marketing and sales.

Elfstrom joined the firm in 1949 as layout artist and later became advertising manager of Utility only. A native of Chicago he received his art training at the Chicago Art Institute, the Evanston Academy of Fine Arts and the Los Angeles Art Center. He was an Armed Forces camouflage instructor during World War II.

AMAZING NEW
NIGHT WRITER
BALL POINT PEN

Known as "Infra," new modern design ball point pen, eliminates fumbling in the dark with flashlight and pen, as both are combined in this "Night Writer."

Includes a regular superior quality ball-point pen with long life cartridge; ball

point pen with built-in light, and point may be removed and used as small flashlight. Complete data from Silver Bells Limited, P.O. Box 982, Carmel, California.

DES-MARK CORPORATION
NOW IN PRODUCTION OF
"METAL CURTAIN WALL"

The Des-Mark Corporation, with general offices at 165 O'Farrell Street, San Francisco, has engineered, designed and is now in production of "Metal Curtain Wall," an entirely new concept of controlling light, particularly for the modern glass curtain wall buildings.

In accordance with architect's specifications, slat widths can be had in a range of from 3" to 6", and in lengths from 5' to 15'. The outside of slats is painted white and the interior any color the architect selects.

"Curtain Wall" is well named because its multiple lengths will form a continuous curtain the full length of the wall, giving complete protection from the sun, while the panels will give a maximum of light and visibility. It is adaptable to ceiling and floor installation. Slats may be removed without the use of tools or equipment, may be cleaned and hung from the same level.

SOLAR HOUSE
BEING BUILT
IN PHOENIX

The Phoenix, Arizona, Association of Home Builders are building a solar heated and cooled house from the designs which recently won a contest sponsored by the Association for Applied Solar Energy.

The design calls for the trapping of solar

rays by a series of mobile louvers, electronically controlled to move with the sun and adjust with the seasons, so that heating and cooling can be accomplished by the same system.

When completed, it is estimated the house will cost about $25,000, and will be put on display to the public this spring, according to John I. Yellot, executive director of the Association for Applied Solar Energy.

**TWA BUILDS NEW
FACILITIES AT THE
LOS ANGELES AIRPORT**

Construction of a new maintenance hangar and administration building for Trans-World Airlines, Inc., is well under

way at the Los Angeles International Airport at an estimated cost of $5,000,000.

Designed by Holmes & Narver, Inc., Los Angeles engineering and construction firm, the new building is being built on a 50-acre site, 35 acres of which are involved in the present development.

The huge hangar, of double cantilever construction, will accommodate six airliners, three to a side. The 490-foot long building will be all open floor area with the exception of a two-story building which divides the hangar for its entire length. Hangar roofs extend outward from this center building to house instrument repair shops, offices, medical unit, training quarters and crew lounges. Total area of hangar, office building and garage is 250,000 sq. ft. Paved parking areas and access roads will total some 1,220,000 sq. ft.

**KENT VICKERY NAMED
CALAVERAS CEMENT
REPRESENTATIVE**

Kent Vickery has been appointed sales representative for Calaveras Cement Company in Stanislaus, Merced, and Mariposa counties according to a recent announcement by William G. Jeffrey, sales manager of the cement firm.

Vickery will have his headquarters in the Modesto Builders Exchange, and will reside in Modesto with his wife and two children. He succeeds James White in the tri-county area. White having been advanced to assistant sales manager and transferred to the San Francisco office.

**KAWNEER INTRODUCES
A NEW PORCELAIN
ENAMEL PRODUCT**

Color Wall is a new porcelain enamel

panel for facing building exteriors with a coat of economical and permanent color. This latest addition to wall systems and store front materials is a laminated panel with the fadeproof porcelain on steel bonded to tempered hardboard and backed with a metal moisture barrier.

In addition to this heavy-duty exterior panel, the Color Wall program includes a lighter panel designed for interior partitions and walls. Since the panels are complimentary with ¼" glass, double face Color Wall can also be used in place of glass or in combination with it in fixed glazing systems to achieve numerous window wall and spandrel effects.

Color Wall panels are available in ten semi-gloss colors—Blue, Teal, Turquoise, Black, Pepper Green, Ash Gray, White, Jasmine Yellow, Deep Red and Sunset Red —and a stippled surface of pastel blue and mint green. In addition, other colors will be available on special order. Panel sizes include 2'x8', 2'x10', 3'x8' and 3'x10'. Smaller sizes are easily obtained by cutting Color Wall panels to the required size at the job site.

Color Wall facing applications are easily obtained by the use of mastic and aluminum trim mouldings. When applying it in a Kawneer glazing system the panels are held firmly in place by dry vinyl glazing or the use of glass stops.

**LESTER A. JACOBSON
ELECTED PRESIDENT
TIMBER CONSTRUCTION**

Lester A. Jacobson of Berkeley, has been elected president of the American Institute of Timber Construction, a nationwide organization with executive headquarters in Washington, D.C., at the 6th annual meeting of the structural timber fabricating industry recently held in Chandler, Arizona.

Jacobson, a native of Orland, California, is a graduate engineer and presi-

dent of Associated Wood Products, Inc., and engineered timber construction firm of Berkeley. He succeeds Val Gardner of Springfield, Oregon, as head of the timber fabricators.

Other officers chosen included: J. P. Weyerhauser, St. Paul, Minn., vice-president; A. W. Talbot, Bellingham, Washington, member of the Board; and Ward Mayer, Portland, Oregon, a Director.

NEW SORORITY HOUSE FOR BERKELEY

Architects Ratcliff & Ratcliff of Berkeley, have completed plans for construction of a three-story Sorority House in Berkeley for Alpha Epsilon Phi Sorority.

The new building will be a 3-story, with basement, concrete and wood construction and will cost an estimated $325,000.

ADVERTISING AGENCY IN NEW OFFICES

The Pacific Advertising Staff, advertising specialists serving a number of firms in the construction and building materials industry, has moved into new offices, according to an announcement by Carl W. Sickler, executive.

The new offices and production facilities will be located at 3770 Piedmont Avenue, Oakland 11.

MORMON CHAPEL BEING BUILT IN SAN LUIS OBISPO

The architectural firm of Clark-Montgomery & Associates, Nolan L. Montgomery, Architect of Reseda, is completing plans for construction of a 19,000 sq. ft. area Mormon Chapel in San Luis Obispo

for the Church of Jesus Christ of Latter Day Saints.

The building will be of steel frame, concrete block and stucco construction, composition roofing, steel beams, metal sash, frame steeple, concrete slab floors with carpeting and vinyl flooring, and asphaltic concrete paving.

REINFORCED EPOXY PIPE AVAILABLE

Corrosion - resistant reinforced plastic pipe, 1/4th the weight of steel, is now available in 2 to 12-inch diameters to meet piping, tubing and ducting needs in the building field. Manufactured by a patented process employing interwoven fiber glass filaments, impregnated with epoxy resins and heat cured.

The new pipe comes in rigid 20 ft. lengths with ends plain, bell-and-spigot or flanged. Other lengths, as well as up to 40″ available on special order. Pipe is nontoxic, nonflammable and collapse-resistant, does not cold flow or sag in use; smooth, friction-free interior surface resists scale. Two standard series, one with nominal working pressure of 250 psi, and another rated at 500 psi. Both have a 10-to-1 safety factor. Complete data on Bondstrand from manufacturer Amercoat Corpn., 4809 Firestone Blvd., South Gate, California.

ENGINEER DESIGNS BOAT FACTORY AT LA MESA

Robert E. Scherrer, Structural Engineer of Santa Ana, is preparing drawings for construction of a boat factory in Costa Mesa for Hubert Longtin.

The manufacutring facilities will be housed in a 1-story structure of concrete block construction containing 3000 sq. ft. of area. Estimated cost of the work is $10,000.

BEVERAGE COMPANY TO BUILD BOTTLING PLANT IN OAKLAND

The Par-T-Pak Beverage Company announces leasing of a site from the Port of Oakland, Board of Commissioners, on Hegenberger Road north of San Leandro, where they will build a 41,000 sq. ft. area bottling plant.

The proposed plant will cost an estimated $400,000 and will provide for production and storage, shops, and offices.

ARCHITECT GWATHMEY BECOMES ASSOCIATE OF MASTEN AND HURD

Cabell Gwathmey, registerde architect in the State of California, has joined the firm of Masten and Hurd, Architects, 526

Powell Street, San Francisco, as a principal.

Gwathmey recently retired as Director of the Department of Licenses and Inspections of the District of Columbia. Prior to heading the department responsible for enforcing the zoning, building and housing laws of the national capital, Gathmey served for more than twenty years with the Corps of Engineers in the design and construction of military projects and civil works in the United States and overseas.

**NEW DI CARLO
PEN POINT SET
CHANGEABLE**

Artists and draftsmen will have a wide array of pen points at their immediate command in this new Di Carlo set of interchangeable nibs molded of Tenite butyrate plastic. The treated nibs, each of which holds a steel point, screw readily into the Di Carlo pen holder.

This means that a point can be changed in two seconds or less, with no jamming, tugging, or soiling of fingers.

The nibs are made in a whole array of bright butyrate colors. Points, firmly anchored in the plastic, are aligned with the center of the nib and, never loosen or become wobbly. For complete information write to the Di Carlo Pen Company, 3 Station Road, Madison, New Jersey.

**NEW PLANT
SITE ACQUIRED
IN SALINAS**

The Nestle Chocolate Company has acquired a large factory site in the Bruce Church Industrial area in Salinas, Monterey county, and announces it will soon start construction on a $5,000,000 new plant and factory.

Walter Baker, Engineer, is making test well borings and will determine actual location of plant and spur railroad track.

---

48   ARCHITECT AND ENGINEER

She Helped a Burglar make his Getaway

Her home was in a part of the city where anything could happen

WAKING ONE MIDNIGHT, she surprised a burglar in her room. As he leapt for the window, she stopped him. "You'll be hurt. Go down by the stairs and let yourself out."

Calm, kind, and acutely intelligent, she had long ago learned to stay human in emergencies—by living where emergencies were routine, in the heart of one of Chicago's poorest immigrant neighborhoods.

Here she had settled down to her life work—helping people. No sociologist or social worker, she left it for others to make this a science. To her, it was an art. An art she practiced so beautifully that, eventually, while she was loved around Halsted Street, she was admired around the world.

When, in 1935, Jane Addams of Hull House died, her little grandniece, seeing hundreds of children among the mourners, asked, "Are we all Aunt Jane's children?"

In a sense, we all are. For the work Jane Addams did and the lessons she taught still help us all. And they prove magnificently the fact that America's greatest wealth lies in Americans.

It is the character and abilities of her people that make this country strong. And it is these selfsame people who make our nation's Savings Bonds one of the world's finest investments. For in U. S. Savings Bonds your principal is guaranteed safe to any amount—and your interest guaranteed sure—by the government that represents the united strength of 168 million Americans. So for your family's security, buy Savings Bonds. Buy them at your bank or through the Payroll Savings Plan at work. And hold on to them.

PART OF EVERY AMERICAN'S SAVINGS BELONGS IN U.S. SAVINGS BONDS

A Sectorial Structure of Striking Splendor

San Jose City Hall
San Jose, California

Donald Francis Haines, A. I. A.
Architect

Main Vestibule and
Circular Staircase

CARL N. SWENSON CO., INC.
General Contractors

Since 1923

1095 STOCKTON AVE., SAN JOSE

TELEPHONE CYPRESS 4-3232

A Sectorial Structure of Striking Splendor

San Jose City Hall
San Jose, California

Donald Francis Haines, A. I. A.
Architect

Main Vestibule and
Circular Staircase

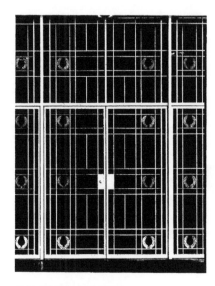

ONE OF TEN ALUMINUM
AND BRONZE FOYER GATES
INSTALLED IN THE TEMPLE

ORNAMENTAL
AND
MISCELLANEOUS
METAL WORK
IN THE
CALIFORNIA MASONIC
MEMORIAL TEMPLE
SAN FRANCISCO

ALBERT F. ROLLER, A.I.A. Architect
MacDONALD, YOUNG &
NELSON, INC., Contractors

Michel & Pfeffer Iron Works, Inc.
212 Shaw Road
South San Francisco, California
PLaza 5-8983

Since 1912 Fabricators of Architectural Metal • Metal Windows and Doors • Steel Buildings

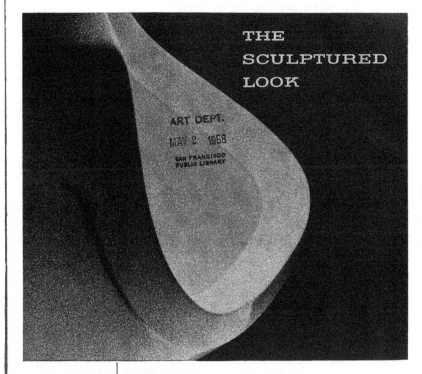

THE
SCULPTURED
LOOK

B3461—MILTON: 24" x 20" vitreous
china lavatory with back, 8" centers.

B4911—LAWTON: Vitreous china
wall hung washout urinal; extended shields.

B4012—MERCURY: Vitreous china
drinking fountain with glass filler.

B6782—SULTAN: Vitreous china
syphon jet, wall hung bowl.

Briggs combines a new design in commercial plumbing fixtures with more than 70 years of vitreous china experience!

Briggs now brings the simplicity of sculptured form to commercial plumbing ware—in a complete new line designed by Harley Earl, Inc. These vitreous china fixtures are built to quality standards set by more than 70 years of continuous experience in manufacturing fine vitreous china. Available in any of Briggs six compatible colors or white. Complete specifications on request.

A COMPLETE LINE OF PLUMBING FIXTURES FOR RESIDENTIAL, COMMERCIAL AND INDUSTRIAL USE

BRIGGS

B E A U T Y W A R E

ncture...

Vol. 213   No. I

EDWIN H. WILDER
Editor

CONTRIBUTING EDITORS:

Education
SIDNEY W. LITTLE, Dean,
School of Architecture, University of Oregon, Eugene, Oregon

City Planning
CORWIN R. MOCINE, City
Planning Engineer, Oakland,
California

*Urban Planning and
Shopping Centers*
FRANK EMERY COX, Sales
Research & Business Development Analyst, Berkeley, California

Realty Development
ROY P. DRACHMAN, Subdivider and Realty Developer,
Tucson, Arizona

School Planning
DR. J. D. McCONNEL, Stanford School Planning Dept.,
Palo Alto, California

Residential Planning
JEDD JONES, Architect,
Boise, Idaho

General Architecture
ROBERT FIELD, Architect,
Los Angeles, California

Engineering
JOHN A. BLUME, Consulting
and Structural Engineer, San
Francisco, California

Advertising
WILLIAM A. ULLNER,
Manager
FRED JONES
Special Advertising

★

COVER PICTURE

CALIFORNIA
MASONIC MEMORIAL
TEMPLE
San Francisco

Albert F. Roller, A.I.A.,
Architect
MacDonald, Young & Nelson,
General Contractors.

View of the new California Masonic
Memorial Temple as seen from California Street. For complete details see
page 12.

Photo by
Gabriel Moulin Studio

Nelson, Inc.

Telephone: LOckhaven 9-4433

AND ENGINEER

ARCHITECTS' REPORTS—
Published Daily
Archie MacCorkindale, Manager
Telephone DOuglas 2-8311

ARCHITECT
AND
ENGINEER

——ARCHITECT & ENGINEER is indexed regularly by ENGINEERING INDEX, INC. and ART INDEX——

Contents for

APRIL

THE OLDEST PROFESSIONAL MONTHLY BUSINESS MAGAZINE OF THE ELEVEN WESTERN STATE

ARCHITECT AND ENGINEER (Established 1905) is published on the 15th of the month by The Architect and
Engineer, Inc., 68 Post St., San Francisco 4; Telephone EXbrook 2-7182. President, K. P. Kierulff; Vice
President and Manager, L. B. Penhorwood; Treasurer, E. N. Kierulff. — Los Angeles Office: Wentworth
Green, 439 So. Western Ave., Telephone DUnkirk 7-8135 — Portland, Oregon, Office: R. V. Vaughn, 717
Canyon Lane. — Entered as second class matter, November 2, 1905, at the Post Office in San Francisco,
California, under the Act of March 3, 1879. Subscriptions United States and Pan America, $3.00 a year;
$5.00 two years; foreign countries $5.00 a year; single copy, 50c.

. EDITORIAL NOTES .

SPRING CLEAN-UP

For many years the National Board of Fire Underwriters has encouraged the Spring Clean-up movement emphasizing the need to repair and thoroughly clean homes and places of business.

Cooperative efforts to give communities a thorough cleaning at least once a year were first undertaken many years ago.

The first campaigns were day long and devoted to ridding homes and yard of rubbish and waste that had accumulated during the winter months and which represented fuel for accidental fires. Later campaigns were spread over a period of a week or even longer.

In recent years the movement has spread so rapidly that practically every city has a Spring Clean-up campaign, some repeating the effort in the fall, during Fire Prevention Week.

These campaigns do much to foster community spirit. Streets are cleaned, homes are beautifully repaired, and accumulated waste and rubbish disposed of.

* * *

Do not attempt to adjust or repair your house heating boiler yourself and particularly do not tinker with the controls—says the Plumbing-Heating-Cooling Information Bureau.

* * *

GIVE IT A TRY

Recently concluded hearings by the House Ways and Means Committee indicated that most of some 300 persons testifying before the group recommended tax reductions in some form or another.

Whether the 300 individuals were from the business, worker, educational, professional, or agricultural level a uniformity of desire existed and should be given very careful consideration by members of Congress, and all other governing bodies having to do with the assessment and collection of taxes.

Every individual producer of income is faced with the problem of meeting tax requirements—sales taxes, city taxes, county taxes, state taxes, luxury taxes, special taxes on real property, use taxes, and state and federal income taxes, to name a few.

Quite naturally therefore, any consideration of tax reduction should contain a correction to obvious inequities in our present tax structure and should remove numerous existing barriers to greater productivity and investment for all income groups, as it is no secret that the existing tax rate structure is so unreasonably high that it operates to discourage full exercise of individual initiative, effort and productivity.

We have tried the "full tax" treatment, now let's try reducing taxes to a realistic basis of personal income.

HOME BUILDING

If our economy were such that someone could push a button and start building 200,000 new homes, let's take a look and see just what it would represent.

Records and statistics indicate that about 3,000 different items go into every new home. The 200,000 new houses would consume 3.8-million gallons of paint, 200-million square feet of asphalt roofing shingles, 1.9-billion board feet of lumber, 280-million square feet of wall and ceiling insulation, 1-billion square feet of gypsum wallboard and lath.

Add 60-million square feet of asphalt, rubber or vinyl tile and linoleum, 230-million board feet of finish flooring, 208-million square feet of softwood plywood, 940-million bricks, a half-million tons of steel, 22-million square feet of ceramic tile, 250,000 sets of bathroom fixtures, 200,000 heating units, plus thousands of washers, ranges, water heaters, clothes dryers, dishwashers and refrigerators.

It's estimated that a new home generates the sale of about $1,500 of furnishings and equipment just in the first year of occupancy. And, of course more homes mean more schools, churches, stores, and utilities.

Boost housing activity back to the 1955 level, and it should exceed that figure considerably on the West Coast, and you can just double each of the above statistics.

* * *

The government's own Voluntary Home Mortgage Credit Program, set up to search out money for hard-to-finance housing, says it has more money than it has takers.

* * *

WHO OWNS BIG BUSINESS?

Contrary to popular notion the larger companies usually are owned by the smaller stockholders.

Small firms, on the other hand, principally are owned by the larger stockholders.

That is why proposals now before Congress for a graduated income tax on corporations are basically unsound and unfair, for as everyone knows, the tax would actually fall on the individual—either the consumer or the stockholder or both. And they are not necessarily big simply because the corporation is big.

There is no justification for reducing the dividend of the small stockholder or increasing the price to the small consumer simply because one is the owner and the other a customer of a large company.

The tax proposals are described as "an aid to small business." But once the principle of increasing corporate tax rates as corporate income goes up, is accepted, the rates can always be steepened toward the bottom, as happened with the individual income tax rates.

This would put a crushing burden on YOU.

California Masonic Memorial Temple

ALBERT F. ROLLER, *Architect*
DUDLEY DEANE & ASSOCIATES, MECHANICAL ENGINEERS

PLUMBING
HEATING
AIR CONDITIONING
by

JAMES A. NELSON CO.

1375 HOWARD ST., SAN FRANCISCO

TELEPHONE: HEMLOCK 1-0140

NEWS and COMMENT ON ART

CALIFORNIA PALACE OF THE LEGION OF HONOR

The California Palace of the Legion of Honor, Lincoln Park, San Francisco, under the direction of Thomas Carr Howe, Jr., is offering the following schedule of special exhibits and museum activities during this month:

EXHIBITS: California Collects—North and South, an exhibition sponsored by the Patrons of Art and Music of the California Palace of the Legion of Honor and the Art Council of the University of California at Los Angeles; Pre-Marshall Plan Germany — Pictures, by Boris Klodt; Watercolors by William Wintle; Offhand Blown Glass by John Burton; and Studies or Pre-Columbian Objects from Mexico—Photographs by Lee Boltin.

The Achenbach Foundation for Graphic Arts Features The Iconography of Anthony Van Dyck, and the Society of California Etchers Annual Exhibition.

SPECIAL ACTIVITIES: Organ Program each Saturday and Sunday at 3:00 p.m. featuring Ludwig Altman and Richard Purvis. Educational activities include art classes for children ages 6-11 on Saturday afternoons at 2:00 p.m.

The Museum is open daily.

ARCHITECTURAL GALLERY BUILDING CENTER LOS ANGELES

A special exhibition is being shown in the Architectural Gallery of the Building Center, 7933 West Third Street, Los Angeles, featuring the works of two prominent Southern California architectural and engineering firms.

The first exhibit, April 1-15, features the work of Austin, Field and Fry, Architects and Engineers, and the second special exhibit April 16-30, features work of Thornton Ladd & Associates, Architects.

M. H. deYOUNG MEMORIAL MUSEUM·

The M. H. deYoung Memorial Museum, Golden Gate Park, San Francisco, under the direction of Walter Heil, is showing the following special exhibitions and Museum events for the month of April:

EXHIBITS: Painting by Tomioka Tessai (1836-1924), and exhibition of works selected from the collection of Kiyoshi Kojin Temple, Takarazuka, Japan, and originated by the Metropolitan Museum of Art, New York City, in cooperation with the Reverend Bishop Kojo Sakamoto of Kyoshi Kojin, and the Kokusai Bunka Shinkokai of Tokyo. The exhibit is being circulated by the Smithsonian Institution Traveling Exhibition Service; Association of San Francisco Potters 1958 Biennial Exhibition.

SPECIAL EVENTS: Seminars in the History of Art, Thursday morning at 10:30; Classes in Art Enjoyment for adults each Saturday morning 10:30, Saturday afternoon at 1:30, and Wednesday morning and Wednesday afternoon; Art Classes for Children include Picture Making, Satuday mornings; Art and Nature, Wednesday afternoon, and the Art Club for students each Thursday afternoon 3:30 to 4:30.

The Museum is open daily, free auto parking.

POTTERS AT deYOUNG MEMORIAL MUSEUM

The San Francisco Potters Association annual exhibition "Pottery '58" will be shown this month at the M. H. deYoung Memorial Museum, Golden Gate Park, San Francisco.

Judges for this year's exhibition include Ralph Du Casse, painter and teacher at the California School of Fine Arts; Betty Feves, ceramic sculptor, Pendleton, Oregon; Charles Feingarten, Feingarten Galleries in San Francisco; Miriam Lindstrom, curator at the deYoung Museum; and Gordon Woods, sculptor and director of the California School of Fine Arts.

The exhibition is a cross section of the most recently produced pottery on the Pacific Coast.

GEORGE D. CULLER IS APPOINTED ASSISTANT DIRECTOR OF THE SAN FRANCISCO MUSEUM OF ART

W. W. Crocker, Chairman, and E. Morris Cox, president of the board of trustees of the San Francisco Museum of Art, recently announced the appointment of George D. Culler to the post of Associate Director of the Museum.

Culler will assume his new duties this summer and comes to San Francisco from the Art Institute of Chicago, where he has been Director of Museum education. Prior to 1955, he was Director of the Akron Art Institute of Akron, Ohio, before that time was on the staff of the Cleveland Museum of Art.

A graduate of the Cleveland Institute of Art, Culler received his Bachelor's degree from the School of Education, Western Reserve University. His Master's degree in aesthetics and art history was also awarded by Western Reserve University in 1939. Married, Culler is the father of two chilldren.

CALIFORNIA CREATIVE ART ON PACIFIC COAST TOUR

A broad cross section of creative art now being done in California received public acclaim at the

recent Fourth Annual California Design Exhibit at the Pasadena Art Museum, and is now on tour of Pacific Coast states.

Hundreds of articles are featured in the exhibit including such materials as chinaware, pottery, ceramic tile, furniture, carpeting, draperies, kitchen appliances, electronic equipment and numerous others. Work done on both an individual basis and a commercial scale is included, being selected by Clifford Nelson, architectural designer and director of the exhibit.

The exhibit, conducted with the assistance of a grant from the Los Angeles County Board of Supervisors, was shown at the Pasadena Art Museum early in the year, and is scheduled to be shown in the Oakland Municipal Art Museum, Department of Art at Oregon State College at Corvallis, October, and Long Beach Museum of Art in November. Other showings are planned.

DOG PORTRAITURE WILL FEATURE deYOUNG MUSEUM EXHIBIT BY REUBEN BLAKE

Drawings by Reuben Lloyd Blake, San Francisco artist specializing in dog portraiture, will be displayed at the M. H. de Young Memorial Museum this month and through May 11.

A dog owner and fancier himself, Blake has made a careful study of dog anatomy, growth of hair and expression. With few textbooks or instructions available in rendering this subject, he has developed his own style and interprets his work as "Fine Point Technique" striving to capture with complete fidelity every characteristic and individual personality of the animal as does the portraitist of human life.

Blake has presented one-man shows in the Press and Union League Club of San Francisco and at the

(See page 32)

M. H. DE YOUNG MEMORIAL MUSEUM

Golden Gate Park   San Francisco

**"PORTRAIT OF
A FRIEND OF TITIAN"
By TITIAN**

A Venetian Painter

**Born in 1477 and
Died in 1576**

**From the
Samuel H. Kress Collection**

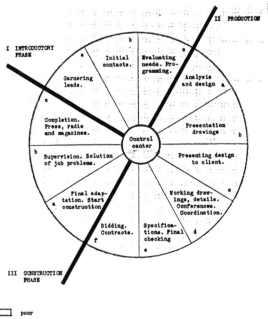

II PRODUCTION

I INTRODUCTORY PHASE

b
a Initial contacts.
Evaluating needs. Programming. c

Garnering leads.
Analysis and design a

c
Presentation drawings b

Completion. Press, radio and magazines.
Control center

b Supervision. Solution of job problems.
Presenting design to client.

Final adaptation. Start construction a
Working drawings, details. Conferences. Coordination. c

Bidding. Contracts. f
Specifications. Final checking d

e

III CONSTRUCTION PHASE

▭ poor
▤ mediocre
▥ good
■ outstanding

▯ Capacity for teamwork

ARCHITECT'S MIRROR

By **SEWALL SMITH**

Architect

Do you agree it might be helpful to analyze the nature of the contribution within your firm which you and the members of your architectural team can make? Whether you are a lone architect, just starting your practice, or a staff member of a firm, the big purpose of this little article is to show you how you can graphically SEE in chart form the assets and liabilities which you possess. If you are the owner of an established architectural firm, you can compile a composite office chart from the individual charts showing the assets and liabilities of your entire staff and the all-important pattern of their correlation. Of course what is said here would apply just as well to an engineering or construction firm engaged in the planning of buildings, or to an A-E firm. When this has been done, another essential ingredient should also be assessed . . . . the capacity for teamwork which you and the others possess, for upon this faculty depends the smooth and successful operation of the business as a whole.

The first broad segments of our chart obviously are (I) Introductory Phase; (II) Production of Documents, and (III) Construction Phase. You can think of these as major segments of a continuing circle; for

surely each construction job (III) should lead again to further projects (I). Each of these major segments is composed of small segments and in any of the latter a man may be poor, mediocre, good or outstanding. Your own best abilities—or those of your associates and employees—may be scattered through all three phases, or they may be concentrated in one major segment. Knowing them in a general way is not enough; recognition of the precise nature of your own assets and liabilities, as well as those of your co-workers, is mandatory today.

The segments as I see them—see if you agree with me—are then as follows, shown also in chart form to bring out graphically the circle idea:

I. Introductory Phase*:
  a) Garnering leads from all sources.
  b) Initial contacts with prospect or committee. Presenting your firm's qualifications for handling the work. Reaching agreement.
  c) Evaluating essential needs, after further conferences with client, committee or board. Programming.

II. Production:
  a) Analysis and design.
  b) Presentation drawings.
  c) Presenting design to client.
  d) Working drawings, details, incidental design. Conferences with client or committee and with material and equipment dealers. Coordination.
  e) Specifications. Final checking.
  f) Bidding. Contracts.

III. Construction Phase:
  a) Final adaptations, if any, resulting from bids. Commencement of construction.
  b) Supervision. Solution of job problems. Helping to expedite work to the completion date.
  c) Completion. Recognition of job's merit channelled to newspapers, radio, trade journals, perhaps television and magazines. (Earlier opportunities for illustrated news releases occur at acceptance of design, IIc; and at commencement of construction, IIIa.)

---

*This might well be called—let's face it!—the Procurement Phase, for most offices. There are some firms where work comes in automatically, of course. In these cases, and in the case of civil service work, our chart would merely start at Ib and at Ic, respectively.

In normal good practice, IIIc leads of course to Phase I, again.

To get a graphic picture of your individual chart, shade in lightly the small segments in which you are mediocre, double crosshatch those where you are good, and pochet solidly the areas of your outstanding contributions. The white segments left will stand out as areas where you may want to develop meager abilities, or if you'd prefer, think of these as areas where you'll need to supplement your abilities with those of others. That will require teamwork, no matter what

"level" you are on; more on that later. If you are an employee you may find assets that your employer does not know you have and will be glad to use.

If you are an employer, now, with all the charts which you and your men have made, you are in a position to make a composite or office chart of your firm's abilities. You'll quickly see precisely where partners' or co-workers' abilities nicely complement your own and each others. You'll know exactly where weak spots are and what abilities need to be supplemented or where there may be overlapping. You may be surprised at the total results and discover attributes you never suspected in some of the men you've been working with for years.

Some years ago when major projects were not so common or so complex, it was perhaps possible for one man to embrace within himself all the qualifications on our chart . . . at a "good" level for most segments and maybe outstanding for one or two. Today, the needed qualifications transcend those of any one person. Your first rate architect can no longer get by as a single principal. The day of the prima donna architect is past. On larger work the client is a committee or group. The architect today deals with groups of widely varying abilities: the make-up of his own organization, his associate engineers and other collaborators. With the complexity of today's projects, it is a day of teamwork and intelligent collaboration if ever there was one.

It's encouraging to note that even if his co-workers may have only "good" abilities for the most part, rather than "outstanding," if a spirit of teamwork pervades the organization, the resulting work can be surprisingly impressive. But there lies" the catch!" Each member of the team must recognize his limitations to the point of being ready for real collaboration with his fellow workers. Not showing in the chart or wheel— but permeating it—is the vital lubricant: capacity for teamwork. The need for this capacity is paramount for the employer himself, who has his place at the hub of the wheel in the Control Center, but is also vitally needed by every man under him. So score yourself and your fellow workers in this essential capacity!

In view of the increasing need for intelligent and effective group work, courses in basic applied or business psychology will undoubtedly become part of the required curricula in schools of architecture. Refresher and evening courses could supply the need now. The laws and psychological conditions governing effective group work must become familiar to all. Perhaps a quotation from one excellent source, Laird's "Practical Business Psychology," might be pertinent here:

"Praise, in short, makes people work harder and feel more cooperative. This neglect of encouraging praise is often deliberate. The horse-trading type of boss believes a praised worker will want a raise, and that faultfinding keeps the worker trying harder. This psychology is completely wrong. The bosses of an

(See page 32)

NEVADA'S NEWEST

CLARK COUNTY COURTHOUSE

LAS VEGAS, NEVADA

ARCHITECTS: WELTON BECKET & ASSOCIATES,

Architects and Engineers

ZICK & SHARP, Architects

Associated Architects

GENERAL CONTRACTORS: DIVERSIFIED BUILDERS

Two Los Angeles firms will team to create the $4 million courthouse for Clark County, Nevada, due for immediate construction in downtown Las Vegas.

General contract has been awarded to Diversified Builders of Los Angeles, whose actual bid of $3,433,052 was more than $50,000 under Clark County's budget. Bids do not include furnishings and other equipment.

Welton Becket and Associates, Los Angeles architects and engineers, designed the new courthouse in association with Zick and Sharp, Las Vegas architects.

The building has been planned to meet requirements of Las Vegas in 1978. Welton Becket's survey department studied official files and other records to

project needs of law enforcement, population, and court loads for 20 years hence.

The tiny, 42-year-old original Clark County courthouse building will be demolished to make way for the new structure. Its site will become the landscaped court of the building.

Main unit of the new, 135,000-square-foot courthouse will rise four stories from the front entrance. A long three-story wing will cut through the main unit, while a two-level parking garage will complete the "U"-shaped structure.

Plans also call for remodeling the existing 11,000-square-foot extension to the original courthouse, completed in 1950. When this building has been finished

to harmonize with the new building the Clark County Courthouse will cover the entire city block, and will be some 14 times larger than the little courthouse that served county needs in 1916.

The main surface of the new building will give an appearance of being finished entirely of glass. Exterior walls of the first floor are full windows. Upper floors will appear as strips of windows alternating with strips of glass over insulating panels of white styrofoam that will give a deep, glistening effect. The end panel of the main unit will be a three-story panel of molded architectural concrete floating on one-story high square columns.

Areas of the building that are exposed to the sun will be protected with a special window glass that sandwiches tiny aluminum-louvred screens within its panes.

The building, entirely air conditioned, will feature a floating lobby staircase that leads directly to the area most often approached by taxpayers—the county assessor's office. Three high-speed elevators will also service the upper floors. The building includes a freight elevator, a prisoner elevator, and a jail kitchen elevator. Other features are an 80-person auditorium, a jail chapel, a barber shop, and a jail hospital.

First level of the building will be devoted to court activities. It will include five full courtrooms with private jury roms, judge's chambers, and toilets. A separate judges' corridor connects all courtrooms with private entrances. Also in this area are two non-contest courts, four jury dormitories capable of handling two complete juries, and two jury lounges.

District courts, the county clerk, the law library, a marriage license bureau with a 24-hour entrance, and other general offices are on the first level.

County prisoners will arrive at the first level at a security parking area and be taken by special elevator to booking and jail areas on the second and third floors. Jail facilities, including dining room and kitchen are located on the second floor of the wing. County Commissioners' quarters and hearing room are on this level in the main four-story unit, together with other county administrative offices. Existing judges' chambers in the 1950 building's second floor will be remodeled to become the court of the justice of the peace.

The third floor, top level of the wing, includes more jail facilities and the prisoner booking desk with a special closed circuit television system which allows observation of jail corridors at all times. This television circuit is also monitored by the sheriff's offices on the third floor of the main unit. Near the sheriff's offices are the district attorney and the detective bureau.

Located on the fourth floor will be the building and planning departments, the county engineer, treasurer and tax collector, auditor, and county recorder.

A basement is also included in the building. Engineers' testing laboratories, a photo laboratory, multilith department, microfilm room and vault, mainte-

nance and receiving areas, and mechanical and boiler rooms will be located on this level.

Parking for more than 200 cars will be provided on the two-level parking structure.

An amazing amount of flexibility has been designed into the courthouse floor plan by Becket and Zick and Sharp architects. To allow for a 20-year program, unassigned areas have been located between departments for department expansions. Inside walls on each floor can be moved on any multiple of six and a half feet to provide complete office facilities in that area—lighting, air conditioning, telephone, and electrical outlets.

Basic construction of the new courthouse will be reinforced concrete. Its curtainwall facade will have horizontal sliding sash windows to allow easy cleaning. The design provides for an addition of two more floors to the administrative unit and one floor to the jail wing.

VIBRATIONS
IN STRUCTURES

STRUCTURAL ENGINEERS ASSOCIATION OF SOUTHERN CALIFORNIA REPORT

Can the structure take it! Tall stacks, buildings in earthquakes, supports for turbines and reciprocating machinery are some examples of structures subjected to vibrating loads. The structural engineer must provide for the effect of vibration in his design.

Three authorities on vibrating loads gave their views on this subject to the members at the meeting of the Structural Engineers Association held in the Rodger Young Auditorium, Los Angeles, early this month. Walter L. Dickey of Wailes Precast Concrete Corp. presented material on vibration of stacks due to wind. Ray Clough of the University of California at Berkeley gave a general theoretical treatment of vibrations and their effect on supports. William W. Moore of Dames & Moore, San Francisco, spoke on foundation design to carry vibrating loads.

Mr. Dickey told how the engineer must design his stack to be high enough to avoid having the discharge gases contaminate the ground surface. What is called the downwind plume must meet certain specified limits as to proximity to the ground. The higher the stack the lower becomes the ground level contamination. The diameter of the stack must be suitable to power requirements. The larger the diameter, the lower the power consumption. On the other hand, stack costs go up with diameter and height. After weighing all these factors, the designer selects the size of satck.

Mr. Dickey stated that there are two ways a stack vibrates. It may bend back and forth as a cantilever beam. Or a breathing action may result causing the

(See page 30)

NEVADA'S NEWEST

CLARK COUNTY COURTHO⌐

LAS VEGAS, NVADA

ARCHITECTS: WELTON BECCET & ASSOCIATES,

Architects an Engineers

ZICK & SHA¹P, Architects

Associated A·hitects

GENERAL CONTRACTORS: ⅡVERSIFIED BUILDERS

Two Los Angeles firms will team to create the $4 million courthouse for Clark County, Nevada, due for immediate construction in downtown Las Vegas.

General contract has been awarded to Diversified Builders of Los Angeles, whose actual bid of $3,433-052 was more than $50,000 under Clark County's budget. Bids do not include furnishings and other equipment.

Welton Becket and Associates, Los Angeles architects and engineers, designed the new courthouse in association with Zick and Sharp, Las Vegas architects.

The building has been planned to meet requirements of Las Vegas in 1978. Welton Becket's survey department studied official files and other records to

rʲject needs of law enforcem c⌐rt loads for 20 years hence.

The tiny, 42-year-old origi ʰuse building will be den t⌐ new structure. Its site cᴜrt of the building.

Main unit of the new ʰuse will rise four sto ⌐ long three-story win uit, while a two-level ⌐ te "U"-shaped structur

Plans also call for ren ﹐uare-foot extension to t ⌐ted in 1950. When thi

to harmonize with the new building the first
Courthouse will cover the entire co... st... and will
be some 14 times larger than the little courthouse
that served county needs in 1910

The main surface of the new building will... appearance of being brushed aluminum... a glass curtain walls of the first floor the full windows... floors will appear as strips of windows alternating with strips of glass over insulating panels of white... ... will give a deep, glistening effect. The... ... the main unit will be a three-story... building architectural concrete floating in massive high square columns.

Areas of the building that are exposed to the sun will be protected with a special window glass... sandwiches may aluminum-louvered screens without window panes.

The building, entirely air conditioned, will feature a floating lobby staircase that leads directly to this area most often approached by taxpayers—the county assessor's office. Three high-speed elevators will service the upper floors. The building includes freight elevator, a prisoner elevator, and a jail elevator. Other features are an 90-person audit a jail chapel, a barber shop, and a jail hospital.

First level of the building will be devoted to activities. It will include five full courtrooms private jury rooms, judge's chambers, and... separate judges' corridor connects all courtrooms private entrances. Also in this area are... test courts, four jury dormitories capable of... two complete juries, and two jury lounges.

District courts, the county clerk, the... marriage license bureau with a 24-hour... other general offices are on the first level.

County prisoners will arrive at the lower level security parking area and be taken by special... to booking and jail areas on the second and... floors. Jail facilities, including dining rooms... are located on the second floor in the... Commissioners' quarters and hearing rooms... level in the main, four-story unit... other county administrative offices... chambers in the 1950 building... remodeled to become the court of the... peace.

The third floor, top level of the main... jail facilities and the... special closed circuit... observation of jail corridors... circuit is also monitored... third floor of the main... are the district attorney...

Located on the fourth... planning department... and tax collector, ...

A basement is... neers' testing laboratory... lth department...

' COURTHOU...

... & ASSOCIATES

... and Engineers

... Architects

... ...

... SIFIED BUILDERS

VIBRA...
IN ST...

STRUCTURE...
OF SOU...

Corne...
ies in...
copper...
mporary...
Street is th...
two massi...
ymbolic of...
n's Temple,...
and weighs m...

Entrance Foyer

marble which en...
gnified simplicity,...
historical window,...
impressive features...
window depicts Maso...

CALE
MASON

...tures the main facade of...

WHITE MARBLE ENTRANCE

Photos, Gabriel Moulin Studios

CALIFORNIA
MASONIC MEMORIAL TEMPLE

SAN FRANCISCO

ARCHITECT: ALBERT F. ROLLER, A.I.A.

GENERAL CONTRACTOR: MacDONALD, YOUNG & NELSON

Completion of the new six-million dollar, white marble California Masonic Memorial Temple, located on San Francisco's Nob Hill at the southwest corner of California and Taylor Streets, will be formaly dedicated in September of this year when the next annual Grand Lodge session is to be held.

Like Rome, this beautiful structure was not "built in a day". Ten or twelve years ago it became evident that as a result of California Masonry's continuing

growth, the facilities of the Masonic Temple at 25 Van Ness Avenue, were rapidly becoming inadequate for the needs of the annual Grand Lodge communications.

In 1947 it was recommended that a suitable site for the erection of a new Temple be acquired, and following a thorough study by a special committee, a recommendation was made that the Nob Hill property at California and Taylor Streets be acquired and that

a new and modern Grand Lodge home and headquarters be built there.

It was not until 1953 that the recommendations
were approved and the Memorial Temple Board of
Trustees appointed to carry out the numerous details
of site clearance, planning and design, and construction program.

Temple Site

Location of the Temple is on an area adjacent to
hotels, shops and theatres. The famed California Street
cable cars pass the door, and it is convenient to public
transportation, taxicab or private automobile. The
building occupies some 200 feet on California Street,
200 feet on Taylor Street and there is a rear entrance
of 25 feet on Pine Street.

The building itself is in the form of a memorial,
dedicated to those California and Hawaiian Masons
who gave their lives in their country's service, and will
serve as headquarters building for the California
Masonic Grand Lodge, and the Masonic Homes of
California. Its white marble facing commands immediate attention in the Nob Hill surroundings. Pure white
marble is also used in the terraces, entrance porch,
foyer and two major sides of the Temple's exterior.

One of the features of the main facade, fronting on
California Street, is the symbolic memorial sculpture
with a vertical theme depicting four branches of our
country's armed services with a horizontal abstraction
of the eternal, honoring California and Hawaiian

Masonic war dead, and suitably inscribed with a dedi-
catory message. It is executed in white Italian marble,
gold Masonic and ceramic bands representing land,
sea, and air.

Terrace and Entrance Porch

Rising by a short flight of steps from California
Street, the Memorial Temple's north frontage is occupied by the terrace and entrance porch. The terrace,
accessible both from the street and from the auditorium, features five growing olive trees, emblematic
of peace. At night the terrace and trees are illuminated
by soft electric lighting.

In the northeast wall is the Cornerstone, laid with
impressive Masonic ceremonies in September 1956,
and within the stone is a copper casket containing
historic Masonic and contemporary documents.

Fronting on California Street is the colonnaded entrance porch flanked by two massive white marble
pillars. The pillars are symbolic of the pillars in the
porch of King Solomon's Temple, and each pillar is
twenty-three feet high and weighs more than fourteen
tons.

Entrance Foyer

Finished in white marble which emphasizes its striking beauty and dignified simplicity, the foyer is dominated by a huge historical window, one of the most
outstanding and impressive features of the Temple.
The picture window depicts Masonry's coming to

CLOSE-UP VIEW of symbolic memorial sculpture that features the main facade of the
building fronting on California Street.

MASONIC TEMPLE . . .

MEMORIAL FOYER

Dominated by a large end-mosaic window glowing in natural colors and depicting the history of Masonry in California.

California, and its subsequent part in our State's growth and development.

The central window is topped by a representation of the All-Seeing Eye, and seven important Masonic symbols. Beneath them is the large central figure representing today's Master Mason. Around this central figure are depictions of tools and facilities with which modern Masons work, and illustrative of California's economy.

To the right and left of the central figure are representations of the wayfarer and seafarer—important in Masonic and California history. The first wayfarer is seen holding a fruit, representing the farmer, rancher, and agriculture. The second holds a musket and powder horn, representative of trapper, hunter, land trader, and overland scout. The third holds the miner's pick, symbolizing the gold mines and miners of the gold rush era, in which Masonry had a prominent part.

In the seafaring group to the right of the central figure, the first figure, holding a compass, symbolizes the early arriving sea captains and seamen. The next

figure is shown holding a rolled charter, symbolic of the arrival of the first lodge charters by sea. The final figure is the fisherman.

Below the lower frieze of symbols, at the base of the window are various strata of the earth composed of the actual gravels and soils of the 58 counties of California and the islands of Hawaii, symbolizing the antiquity of the Masonic fraternity.

Below the historical window, panels of clear plate glass looking beyond a balcony provide a panoramic view of much of the San Francisco Bay area to the east, south, and west.

Opening from the foyer to the right of the main entrance is a reception room and visitors' lounge, This comfortably furnished room will provide a convenient meeting place for Masons and their families, especially those visiting San Francisco from outside communities.

. To the left of the main entrance, on the Temple's north wall, are listed the date for its formal dedication (September, 1958); the names of the Memorial Temple Board of Trustees; the architect for the building;

DETAIL VIEW of Auditorium. Note center area of ceiling, which represents an enlarged vent and is made of many small sheet metal cylinders.

and the names of the Past Grand Masters since 1947. It has been during the eleven years since 1947 that the Memorial Temple was proposed, planned, and built.

In preparation is the Open Book, to be placed in the foyer. It will contain the names of all donors to the Memorial Temple Building Fund.

Memorial Auditorium

The main entrance to the auditorium is from the foyer, turning left from the California Street portal.

Opening the way into the carpeted concourse and auditorium are aluminum and bronze grille gates, whose decorative theme is featured by bronze wreaths of victory.

Above the gates is an inscription suitably expressing the principal Memorial Theme of the entire building.

INTERIOR VIEW of Memorial Auditorium, which has a seating capacity of 2,800 persons—main floor and balcony.

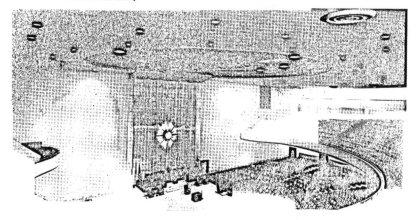

FOYER

Looking towards the Auditorium, showing some detail of the aluminum and bronze grill work; also, a memorial tablet overhead of entrance.

The auditorium will seat 2000 on the main floor and 1200 in the balcony. All seating is in modern upholstered opera chairs designed for bodily comfort. All seats have an unobstructed view of the stage.

The auditorium's acoustics have been carefully planned to achieve perfection in oratory and in music, and include the best modern features in high fidelity sound reproduction.

The electronic organ, one of the largest of its type on the West Coast, was designed and built expressly for the Memorial Temple. Traditional tones, typical of the finest pipe organ, are produced by an electronic process. Electric circuits and amplifiers permit transmission of organ or recorded music into many portions of the building.

The background of the platform, or stage, is a wall of Roman Travertine marble, surrounded by a gold leaf panel, and surmounted by a gold-leafed canopy. Central ornament of the wall is a gold sunburst. In its center is a transparent letter "G" which can be illumi-

MAIN RAMP of the Garage on California Street extends down several floors and has a capacity of 500 cars.

nated as desired, the light shining through from the back.

The two hardwood pillars in the auditorium, like those on the main entrance porch, represent the pillars on the porch of King Solomon's Temple. They were lovingly and carefully made from especially selected woods, by Master Masonic craftsmen.

All auditorium lighting is of special plan and design to provide the most modern effects.

Central Facilities

Another of the Memorial Temple's major features is

the multi-purpose room, 17,000 square feet in area, on the ground floor with direct access by a short flight of steps from California Street, or from within the building. This room is planned for exhibits or displays, or will provide dining capacity for 1200 diners served from an adjoining fully-equipped kitchen.

Adjoining and below the multi-purpose room, and also back of the auditorium on the first floor, are a series of air-conditioned committee rooms and offices. Several are accessible directly from the California Street ground-floor entrance. Six offices and four large, or eight small, committee rooms are available for con-

ventions and group meetings. The large committee rooms will seat 80 to 100. They can be divided by roll-back wall curtains, and when so arranged will provide eight rooms, each with a seating capacity of 40 to 50.

Also adjoining the multi-purpose room, and with direct access from California Street by an easy-slope ramp, is the public garage, private operated, with 500-car parking capacity.

Automatic electric elevators serve all floors of the building, from the garage to the top floor.

Mezzanine Floor, Auditorium Balcony, and Museum

This floor gives access to the auditorium balcony. Here too is space for a Masonic Museum, in which will

be maintained an exhibit of historic Masonic articles.

From the balcony an additional view can be obtained of the endomosaic window.

Third Floor

The third, and top, floor is occupied by the administrative offices of the California Masonic Grand Lodge and the Masonic Homes of California; the Grand Master, Grand Secretary; and the staff.

Here too will be the Bronze Plaque listing the "Merit Roll" lodges, who are designated as "BUILDERS OF THE TEMPLE."

Opening from the third floor is an open-air loggia from which is visible still another sweeping panoramic view of the San Francisco Bay region.

**PROJECT
COMPLETED**

*Kawneer
Photo*

TWENTY-FIVE FIRST STREET, San Francisco

MODERNIZING
A BASICALLY GOOD BUILDING

By **WILLIAM B. McCORMICK, A.I.A.**

JOS. L. BARNES, General Contractor

a modern building a number of years ago to meet the specific needs at that time of a large, easily accessible, merchandise storage building which could be combined to some degree and serve as also having industrial purpose possibilities.

Area Changes

The general area of the city in which the building is located had changed considerably in type of business activity during the past few years so that at the present time the owners felt it was desirable from an economic standpoint that the structure be remodeled and used as a modern office building, rather than continue to serve as a light industrial and warehouse type building as was originally planned and provided for. After giving the matter considerable consideration, the owner decided definitely that the structure could better serve the area and as income property as an office building with an office clientele and that in conformity with the trends of the area it was advisable to immediately alter the building in its entire basic utility concept and make the changes necessary which would permit the future use of the building as desirable office space.

Located between Market and Mission Streets on First Street in downtown San Francisco, the site is in close proximity to the East Bay Transit Terminal which serves as the San Francisco terminal for East Bay public transportation service crossing the Oakland-San Francisco Bay Bridge. This, plus the fact that the area also serves as the downtown San Francisco "Loop" area for street car and bus transportation service, makes it an ideal location for an office building, where personnel working in offices depend upon public transportation to and from work.

Old Building

The building to be altered was a six-story and basement structure of reinforced concrete design utilizing flat slab floors throughout. It had one small passenger elevator serving the six floors and one small freight elevator, both of which were located on opposite sides of the building near the center. The ground floor had served pretty generally as a warehouse area with ample facilities for loading and unloading trucks.

At the time it was decided to proceed with plans to remodel the building, it was being occupied by only two tenants. One of these tenants occupied all of the fifth and sixth floors, while the other tenant occupied the remaining four floors and the basement, so there was not too much consideration necessary to the factor of disturbing tenants by remodeling. The basic building arrangement was not too satisfactory in itself at any time prior to remodeling because of the limited freight and passenger elevator service.

Recognizing the need for a complete adjustment of the premises, if anything was to be done at all, preliminary sketches of the proposed work, together with estimates of the construction costs, were made by the architect and general contractor respectively, and with this detailed information available it was possible for the real estate firm of Coldwell, Banker & Company to look around the city for a firm seeking expansion of office facilities and found the Bechtel Corporation, Contractors and Engineers, were in need of additional offices. Arrangements were completed and the Bechtel Corporation leased the first four floors, as well as the basement, of the remodeled building. The two upper floors remained occupied by the tenant in the building prior to the remodeling and there was no major alteration to these floors except, of course, the provisions necessary for the installation of modern elevators in supplemental shafts which would better serve the entire structure.

Because of the sturdy floor construction used in the original erection of the building, it was found most economical to install the new elevators in the middle of bays, and two new automatic elevators were in-

stalled in the remodeling process. One was placed in the location of the old passenger elevator shaft and the other one was placed in the adjacent bay. While this treatment separated the two elevators a little more distance than is usual, they are not too far apart for good usability of the tenants of the building and the public. Placement of the elevators as was done also represented a great deal less complication structurally.

New Facilities

In providing the two new elevator facilities, it was decided to build a new elevator penthouse and in this newly constructed area to provide for possible future elevator expansion when tenant requirements might necessitate the providing of additional service to the upper fifth and sixth floors.

To meet the varying weather conditions of San Francisco's cool summers, overcast-foggy days, and rainy season, the remodeled building is adequately ventilated and heated by a modern tempered air conditioning system. The main boiler and hot water heater for this newly installed system is conveniently located in a planned portion of the new penthouse construction. Location of this equipment in the penthouse eliminates the necessity of placing the equipment in an area which can otherwise be used by occupants of the building. The large ventilating fans, which are a part of the air conditioning and heating unit, were

DETAIL OF ENTRANCE

DETAIL OF
FOYER

showing unique and very attractive mosaic wall of modernistic design.

Also, interesting light fixtures by Mary Henry.

also placed on the roof of the building and designed with the supply and exhaust ducts running into a rear court. In this way no space was taken out of the building area for mechanical equipment.

Conversion of the lighting facilities from typical warehouse installation to a modern office building presented no particular problem. The first four floors have been provided with a modern lighting of 100 foot-candle intensity, which is adequate for lighting in an office area. The building's new spacious lobby has also been provided with modern lighting, fifty foot candle intensity being used in the receptionist desk and public waiting areas.

In planning the re-arrangement of the first floor, it was decided to design the area to serve as a reception space with a desk and inter-office communication system for the tenant and at the same time serve as a public lobby where anyone could wait comfortably for appointments with tenants or their personnel. The large wall on the left side as you enter the lobby is a very striking exposed light tan Roman brick wall, while on the opposite side the wall is attractively finished in oak boards. The elevator shaft walls are com-

FIRST FLOOR LOBBY: Receptionist area has exposed brick wall combined with wood paneling for beauty, indirect overhead lighting, and asphaltic tile floor.

pletely covered with a new plastic wall covering of a somewhat pumpkin color, and the entire lobby area is lighted from the ceiling by fluorescent tubes which are shielded by an overall $\frac{1}{2}$" x $\frac{1}{2}$" metal grid. The floor of the lobby has been done in an attractive terrazzo.

The spacious foyer of the building, as completed, has two quite unusual and distinctive features for an office building, both of which have been designed by Mrs. Mary Henry of Los Altos. The first unusual feature is a ten by sixteen foot glass tile mosaic, and the other feature of special note is a unique lighting fixture of panels complementing the large colored mosaic.

Construction

Construction wise, the interior facade above the first floor level is faced with an aluminum frame curtain wall with porcelain enameled iron panels and windows of plate glass. The porcelain panels are a strong blue-green and are a striking contrast to adjacent buildings and structures in the area.

The first story columns are sheathed in attractive Deer Island granite, a warm mottled grey with suggestions of pink in it, which also offer a striking contrast to the blue porcelain enamel panels of the building itself and surrounding structures.

The office area of the building was planned by the tenant to meet the particular needs of a large organi-

24

CONFERENCE ROOM: Second floor incorporates today's modern trend to include furniture as well as building materials and design.

zation engaged in the construction and engineering business with activities on a world-wide basis, and the work was executed by the general contractor under the supervision of the Architect.

Another phase of construction was the installation of new under-floor ducts for both extensive telephone and electrical outlets. These were provided in the existing floor by filling over the old concrete floors with a light fill of lightweight concrete and thereby imbedding the new ducts.

The new concrete floors of the building were then covered with a vinyl asbestos tile throughout, except for several executive offices, conference rooms, and the library where individual carpeting was used to meet the tenants desire. Ceilings of all the offices and conference rooms are acoustical tile to better serve in the modern environment of noise control.

It is conservatively estimated that the alterations to this older downtown building enhanced its value considerably, so that it will now hold its own with the projected growth of the entire area and can be considered as one of the more desirable office space areas for many years to come. The results of this remodeling project is conclusive proof that it is economically desirable to modernize a basically good building in a metropolitan city to meet current trends and conditions in business activities.

FIRST FLOOR LOBBY: Rece onist area has exposed br bined with wood paneling f beauty, indirect overhea asphaltic tile floor.

pletely ered with a ne
a somew t pumpkin colo
is lighte rom the ceilin
are shiel d by an over
floor of he lobby h
terrazzo

The ecious foye
has two nite unus
office bu ling, bot
Mrs. Ma Henry
ture is ien by
other fe ure of
ture of nels

Conside
first flo
tain wa
dows o
blue-gre
buildin

The
Deer
gesti
tras
ing its

The
tenan

CONFERENCE ROOM: Second floor incorporates today's modern trend to include furniture as well as building materials and design.

zation engaged in the construction and engineering business with activities on a worldwide basis, and all work was executed by the general contractor under the supervision of the Architect.

Another phase of construction was the installation of new under-floor ducts for both telephone and electrical outlets. These were provided in the existing floor by filling over the old or with a light fill of lightweight concrete imbedding the new ducts.

The new concrete floors of the building were covered with a vinyl asbestos tile except for several executive offices and the library where individual carpeting was used as the tenants desired. Ceilings of the conference rooms are acoustically treated to meet the modern environment of the building.

American Institute of Architects

Leon Chatelain, Jr., President

John N. Richards, 1st Vice President
Philip Will, Jr., 2nd Vice President
Edmund R. Purves, Executive Secretary

Edward L. Wilson, Secretary
Raymond S. Kastendieck, Treasurer

National Headquarters—1735 New York Avenue, N.W., Washington, D.C.

REGIONAL DIRECTORS—Northwest District, Donald J. Stewart, Portland, Oregon: Western Mountain District, Bradley P. Kidder, Santa Fe, New Mexico; California-Nevada-Hawaii District, Ulysses Floyd Rible, Los Angeles, California

ARIZONA CHAPTERS:
CENTRAL ARIZONA: David Sholder, President; A. John Brenner, Vice-President; Jimmie R. Nunn, Secretary; Kemper Goodwin, Treasurer; James W. Elmore, Director; Ralph Haver, Director; Martin Ray Young, Jr., Director. Office of Secy., P.O. Box 904, Phoenix.

SOUTHERN ARIZONA: Santry Clay Fuller, President; Edward H. Nelson, Vice-President; David S. Swanson, Secretary; Robert J. Ambrose, Treasurer; D. Burr DuBois, Director; Eleazar D. Herreras, Director; Emerson C. Scholer, Director. Office of Secy., 2343 South Tucson Avenue, Tucson.

COAST VALLEYS CHAPTER:
William L. Higgins (San Jose), President; Paul J. Huston (Palo Alto), Vice-President; William H. Daseking (Menlo Park), Treasurer; Edward N. Chamberlain (San Jose), Secretary. Office of Secy., 390 Park Ave., San Jose.

CENTRAL VALLEY OF CALIFORNIA:
Joseph J. Jozens, President (Sacramento); Armsby Tod Hart, Vice-President (Sacramento); Albert M. Dreyfuss, Secretary (Sacramento); Whitson W. Cox, Treasurer. Office of Secy., 2127 "J" St., Sacramento.

COLORADO CHAPTER:
Casper F. Hegner, President; C Gordon Sweet, Vice President; Norton Polivnick, Secretary; Richard Williams, Treasurer. Directors: James M. Hunter, Robert K. Fuller, Edward L. Bunts. Office of Secy., 1225 Bannock St., Denver, Colorado.

EAST BAY CHAPTER:
Hachiro Yuasa (Oakland), President; George T. Kern (Oakland), Vice-President; William M. Gillis (San Francisco), Secretary; J. A. Zerkle (Berkeley), Treasurer. Directors: H. B. Clausen, F. A. Lockwood. John Oyarzo, G. M. McCue. Marjorie Montgomery, Exec. Secy. Office of Secy., Mezzanine, Hotel Claremont, Berkeley 5.

IDAHO CHAPTER:
Anton E. Dropping, Boise, President; Charles W. Johnston, Payette, Vice-President; Glenn E. Cline, Boise, Sec.-Treas. Executive Committee; Chester L. Shawver and Nat J. Adams, Boise. Office of Secy., 624 Idaho Bldg., Boise.

MONTEREY BAY CHAPTER:
Robert Stanton, President (Carmel); Walter Burde, Vice-President; William L. Cranston, Secretary; George Kuska, Treasurer. Office of Secy., P.O. Box 1846, Carmel.

MONTANA CHAPTER:
William J. Hess, President (Great Falls); John E. Toohey, Vice-President (Billings); H. C. Cheever, Secy.-Treas. (Bozeman). Directors: James J. Ballas, Wm. J. Hess. John E. Toohey. Office of Secy., Bozeman. Montana.

NEVADA CHAPTER:
RENO: Lawrence A. Gulling, President; William E. Cowell, Vice-President; Albert W. Alegre, Secretary; Ralph A. Casazza, Treasurer. Graham Erskine, Raymond W. Hellman, George L. F. O'Brien, Directors. Office of the Secy., 500 Plumas St., Reno.

LAS VEGAS: Walter F. Zick, President; Aloysius McDonald, Vice-President; Edward B. Hendricks, Secy.-Treas. Directors: Walter F. Zick, Edward Hendricks, Charles E. Cox. Office of Secy., 106 S. Main St., Las Vegas.

NEVADA STATE BOARD OF ARCHITECTS:
L. A. Ferris, Chairman; Aloysius McDonald, Secy.-Treas. Members: Russell Mills (Reno), Edward S. Parsons (Reno), Richard R. Stadelman (Las Vegas). Office: 1420 S. 5th St., Las Vegas.

NORTHERN CALIFORNIA CHAPTER:
William Corlett, President; Donald Powers Smith, Vice-President; George T. Rockrise, Secretary; Richard S. Banwell, Treasurer. Directors; W. Clement Ambrose, John Kruse, Bernard J. Sabaroff, Corwin Booth. Exec. Secy., May B. Hipshman. Chapter Office, 47 Kearny St., San Francisco.

ORANGE COUNTY CHAPTER:
William T. Jordan, President (Costa Mesa); Donald M. Williamson. Vice-President (Laguna Beach); J. Herbert Brownell, Secretary; Rumont W. Hougan, Treasurer. Office of Secy., 1950 W. Coast Highway, Newport Beach.

OREGON CHAPTER:
John K. Dukehart, President; Keith R. Maguire. Vice-President; Robert Douglas, Secretary; Harry K. Stevens, Treasurer. Directors: Daniel McGoodwin, Earl P. Newberry, Everett B. Franks, Robert W. Fritsch, Donald W. Edmundson. Office of Secy., 2041 S.W. 58th Ave., Portland 1.

(See opposite page)

SAN DIEGO CHAPTER

The Annual Theater party at the Old Globe was held this month, sponsored by the WAL, with members of the Producers Council participating. "Desk Set" turned out to be a comedy enjoyed by all attending.

Favorable comments are still being heard about the A.I.A. exhibit at the recent Home Show, an exhibition due to the efforts of Sim Bruce Richards, Jim Bernard, Naomi Parfel and many other A.I.A. and W.A.L. members.

NORTHERN CALIFORNIA CHAPTER

Robert Denny, national AIA Public Relations Council , was the principal speaker at the April meeting, discussing the Institute's national public relations program and at the same time he exhibited two semi-animated films of the AIA, "A School for Johnny" and "What's a House".

Leonard Tivol, chairman of the Codes Committee, has informed Sherman Duckel, Director of Public Works for the City and County of San Francisco, that unless further review is made of the final draft of the proposed new Housing Code for San Francisco, "the Chapter must in good conscience oppose the Code as written."

New members: Ernest E. Lee of Hansen & Winkler, Corporate Member. Louis E. Gelwicks and William M. Lee, Junior Associates.

CALIFORNIA COUNCIL AIA

Loy Chamberlain, Oakland, chairman of the 1958 Convention Advisory Committee, reported recently that the program for the CCAIA 13th Annual Convention, October 15-19 at Monterey, was beginning to take form. The Convention will start Wednesday the 15th, with registration and the first event of the professional program in the afternoon. Thursday will be a short day, leaving the late afternoon free, and Friday will be a full schedule of professional activities, and as in the past, Saturday will be given over to Producers' Council events and tours.

This year's program will be primarily concerned with the creative approach to architecture with speeches and seminars dealing with such things as the evolution of a creative idea; creative methods with new materials; the creative approach to structures; analyses

of specific buildings by their architects, and a general design analysis by an outstanding architect speaker.

SANTA CLARA & SANTA CRUZ COUNTIES CHAPTER

Members of the two counties were treated to a guided tour through the new Santa Clara County Jail, which was designed by architect Frank Treseder, as a feature of a recent meeting. Through the cooperation of Howard Campen, County Executive, and the Sheriff's department, dinner was served at the jail.

Member Jerry Erickson of Higgins & Root, Design Committee, is compiling a list of Architectural Model Makers, Mural Makers and other related artists.

EAST BAY CHAPTER

Presentation of prizes to winner-student in the High School Competition sponsored by the East Bay WAL, in cooperation with the AIA Awards Committee, and a discussion of "Curtain Wall Panel Construction" arranged by Harry Bruno and moderated by J. H. Anderson, featured the April meeting held in the Bow and Bell, Jack London Square, Oakland.

The first public hearing on the new preliminary General Plan for Oakland was held in the Oakland City Hall early this month.

The Chapter co-sponsored a program on architec-

(See page 30)

WALLS OF CLEANLINESS--
KRAFTILE GLAZED STRUCTURAL UNITS
Easy To Clean — Low Maintenance — Wear Forever

1 FOR Shower Rooms, Dressing Rooms, Wash Rooms — in schools, factories, institutions. Not affected by steam, chemicals, stains or odors.

2 FOR Surgeries, Laboratories, First Aid Rooms, Veterinary Hospitals. Fire resistant, vermin proof. Won't chip, crack or fade.

3 FOR Food Processing Plants, Kitchens, Lunchrooms, Dairies — or wherever low cost maintenance, high sanitation standards and permanent, economical construction are indicated. Never needs patching or painting.

Complete wall and finish combined. Modular 6" x 12" face size for easy, low-cost installation by masons alone. Wall thicknesses, 2", 4" and 6". Kraftile quality control assures uniformity in color, size, shape and structural strength. Available in clear and 12 lifelong ceramic color glazes.

Ask for free Fact Sheets, specifications, Graphic Standards Manual.

KRAFTILE COMPANY
NILES, CALIFORNIA

MADE IN THE WEST...FOR WESTERN CONSTRUCTION

27

STRUCTURAL ENGINEERS ASSOCIATION NORTHERN CALIFORNIA

A panel type discussion on the experiences of the California State Division of Architecture in various types of concrete construction featured the April meeting held in the Engineer's Club, San Francisco.

The panel members included: C. M. Herd, State Division of Architecture, Sacramento; A. H. Brownfield, State Division of Architecture, Sacramento; A. H. Stubbs, Western Concrete Structures, Inc., Los Angeles; M. J. Heller, Continental Construction Company, Sacramento, and Charles Peterson, State Division of Architecture, Sacramento.

The panel covered the comparative costs, and problems of design and construction of conventional and prestressed poured-in-place slabs, as well as lift slabs.

* *

Members of the San Francisco Engineers Speakers Club gave some 75 addresses to local service groups during the recent Engineers Week.

FEMINEERS

The Femineers, wives of members of the Structural Engineers Association, observed their annual costume Dinner Dance this month. The event, featuring the theme of "The Roaring Twenties" was held in The Village, San Francisco.

STRUCTURAL ENGINEERS ASSOCIATION OF OREGON

The Structural Engineers Association of Oregon, Charles H. Woodworth of Portland, President, sponsored a panel discussion at the Second Structural Engineer's Conference held recently at the University of Washington at Seattle, on the subject "Highway Structures."

Moderator of the conference was A. M. James of James and Honey, Consulting Engineers, and speakers included: G. S. Paxson, Assistant Highway Engineer, Oregon State Highway Department; David M. Goodall, Assistant Regional Bridge Engineer, Bureau of

Public Roads; and Charles E. Andrew, Principal Consulting Engineer, Washington Toll Bridge Authority.

John Skilling of Worthington and Skilling, Seattle, highlighted a recent meeting devoted to the subject of thin shell construction.

Scheduled for a fall meeting is a lecture by Professor Guido Oberti, Professor of Structures, Milan, Italy, on the subject "The I S M E S of Bergama, Italy," a Modern institute for research on structures of models.

STRUCTURAL ENGINEERS ASSOCIATION SOUTHERN CALIFORNIA

"Vibrations in Structures" was the subject of discussion at the April meeting with a four part discussion including "Support of Elements of Vibrating Decks," "Vibration of Stacks Due to Wind," "Support of Vibrating Units on Beams," and "Vibrating Foundation Masses on Resilient Soil."

Speakers included Walter L. Dickey, Structural Engineer, Wailes Precast Concrete Corp.; Ray Clough, Civil Engineering Dept., University of California at Berkeley, and William W. Moore, Dames and Moore, San Francisco.

* *

Some 842 persons attended the Engineers' Week Banquet, held in the Biltmore Bowl recently.

* *

Recent new members include: Herbert J. McLeod, Victor R. Preston, and Julius A. Sonne, Associate Members.

AMERICAN SOCIETY OF HEATING AND AIR CONDITIONING ENGINEERS

The semi-annual meeting of the American Society of Heating and Air-Conditioning Engineers will be held June 23-25 in Minneapolis, Minnesota. In as much as the 54th Annual Meeting of the American Society of Refrigerating Engineers will take place at the same time, the two Societies plan on holding several joint sessions and special events.

James S. Locke is the General Chairman of the

ASHAE Minnesota Chapter Committee on Arrangements. Honorary Chairmen are John E. Haines and F. B. Rowley, both past presidents of ASHAE. Assisting are G. M. Kendrick and J. F. Siegel.

NATIONAL SOCIETY OF PROFESSIONAL ENGINEERS

Highlight of the Annual Meeting of the National Society of Professional Engineers, to be held June 11-14, in St. Louis Missouri, will be the presentation of the 1958 NSPE Award to Nathan W. Dougherty, dean emeritus of engineering at the University of Tennessee.

Dean Dougherty was chosen for the Award "In recognition of his outstanding leadership in his profession as evidenced by his devotion to the advancement of engineering education, his sympathetic encouragement of students of engineering, his zealous promotion of the ideals and principals of his profession, and his humanitarian interest in his fellow men."

The eighth individual to receive the Award since it was first made in 1949, Dean Dougherty served as a member of the faculty of the College of Engineering for forty years before his retirement in 1956.

Others having received the Award are: Herbert Hoover, 1949; David B. Steinman, 1952; Charles F. Kettering, 1953; Harry A. Winne, 1954; A. A. Potter, 1955; Donald A. Quarles, 1956, and Granville M. Read, 1957.

AMERICAN SOCIETY OF CIVIL ENGINEERS SAN FRANCISCO SECTION

Dr. Samuel Benesch, Superintendent of the Research Group at the Jet Propulsion Laboratory, a branch of the California Institute of Technology, was the principal speaker at a meeting of the Section held this month in the Engineers Club, San Francisco.

Dr. Benesch took as his subject: "After Satellites—What?" and presented a color movie "X-80 Days", which described the activity which followed the order to proceed as quickly as possible, following the launching of Russia's Sputnik.

Another point discussed by Dr. Benesch was the role of the Civil Engineer in this era of satellites and rockets, particularly in the field of design of airframes and launching towers.

LEWIS A. PARSONS, Consulting Engineer for Calaveras Cement Company, was honored recently at a company luncheon in San Francisco in recognition of his formal retirement after twenty-one years on the Calaveras staff. He was presented with a gold wrist watch by Wm. Wallace Mein, Jr., Calaveras President.

CONSTRUCTION SPECIFICATIONS INSTITUTE LOS ANGELES CHAPTER

"Quality Control of Structural Steel in Buildings" was the subject of a meeting this month in the Rodger Young Auditorium, with discussions considering the subject from the standpoint of Practice in Office, Shop, Laboratory and Field.

Speakers included George E. Brandow, Consulting Structural Engineer; A. L. Collin, Chief Development Engineer, Kaiser Steel Fabricators, and E. F. MacDonald of the Smith-Emery Company.

SOCIETY OF AMERICAN MILITARY ENGINEERS SAN FRANCISCO POST

Orien L. Hogan, Rocketdyne Division, North American Aviation Corp., was the principal speaker at the April meeting, discussing the subject: "Road To The Stars." Mr. Hogan augmented his remarks by showing a prize-winning film covering the latest developments in the rocket and missile field.

A.I.A. ACTIVITIES
(From page 27)
ture at the Oakland Art Museum, with an exhibit of shell forms by Felix Candela, a film on Mexican architecture, and a talk by Stephen Jacob, architect and faculty member of the University of California at Berkeley.

New Member: Roy F. Johnson, Junior Associate.

SOUTHERN CALIFORNIA CHAPTER

Ira J. Bach, Chicago, First Commissioner of Planning for Chicago, and a city planner and architect by training and profession, was the principal speaker at the April meeting held in the Biltmore Hotel, Los Angeles. He participated in the planning of war housing in Utah, Colorado and Wyoming, served as Director of the Tri-County Regional Planning Commission in Denver, and was later appointed executive director of the Chicago Land Clearance Commission
(See page 32)

VIBRATIONS IN STRUCTURES
(From page 11)
shell to fluctuate, forming ovals on horizontal sections. Movement of some stacks during a typhoon on Okinawa were described as being as spectacular as the vibration failure of the Tacoma Narrows Bridge. A steady wind is an essential factor in causing vibration. What is known as the Von Karman Vortex Trail, where small vortices or eddies drop away around the stack, cause it to vibrate at right angles to the wind.

Prevention of excessive stack vibration entails the study of many features. The diameter should not be too small. Damping characteristics of material should be known. For example, concrete has 30 times the damping characteristics of steel. Beam supports may be too flexible. Foundation conditions must be suitable. Studies of models may prove useful.

After the stack is built it may be tested by pulling sidewise with cables and releasing instantly. The resulting movement is measured with instruments.

Mr. Clough stated that the problem of vibration control involves three factors: Psychological, cost and theory. You can seldom achieve a perfect solution. You must satisfy somebody that vibration is okay. People will report a vibration to be to 1/16 of an inch when the actual magnitude may be only 1/1000 of an inch. The client may feel a vibration excessive, but when confronted with the cost of improvements, decide the vibration quite acceptable!

On the theoretical side, it is desirable to minimize the transmissibility of the vibration. This is best managed by keeping the ratio of the frequency of the vibrating machine to the frequency of the support system greater than the square root of 2. Above this value transmission of vibrations reduces. Also various methods of damping may be employed, such as use of dash pots or other friction devices attached to the machine. Since a machine in start up must pass through the natural frequency of the supporting stucture, damping in this range is of particular merit.

When there is more than one degree of freedom to a vibrating body, it is important to line up the center of gravity of the body with the resultant of the resisting forces.

Mr. Moore stressed the importance of proper soil investigations in the design of foundations for supporting vibrating machinery. Just to classify a soil is not enough. A designer should know the characteristics of the particular material since the properties of clays, sands, silts, etc., may have considerable variation. Effects of overturning, sub-surface layers, and elastic properties must be weighed. Even then you may be in for trouble. But design the best you can, then be prepared to fix your structure if it still vibrates too much.

Mainly the problem of foundation design is to determine the mass of soil which will vibrate the concrete footing and to evaluate a spring constant for this soil system. Try to determine what will be the inertia forces and distortion of the system.

Mr. Moore stated that seismic exploration methods are directly related to soil mass under dynamic loading.

He demonstrated how the spring constant of soils may be arrived at by evaluating the shear modulus of the various soils, assuming a stress distribution along sides of the soil mass, and computing the resulting deflection of the system. Considerably more research on this method is desirable.

The meeting wound up with a short but lively question period.

DOUGLAS McHENRY ELECTED PRESIDENT AMERICAN CONCRETE INSTITUTE 1958

Douglas McHenry, Director of Development, Research and Development Division, Portland Cement Association, was elected president of the American Concrete Institute at the Institute's 54th annual convention in Chicago, succeeding Walter Price, Director of Engineering Laboratories, U. S. Bureau of Reclamation.

McHenry has served the past two years as vice president of the Institute, has served on the Board of Direction, and numerous committees.

OPENS ENGINEERING OFFICE

New offices for Albert A. Erkel & Associates, consulting structural engineers, have been opened at 3515 Cahuenga Blvd., Los Angeles, according to a recent announcement.

The firm is presently engaged in engineering work on a number of major construction projects under way in Los Angeles and Orange counties.

Erkel is an engineering graduate of the California Institute of Technology and completed post graduate work at the University of Southern California.

HOWARD H. DeWEESE NEW EASTERN SALES DIRECTOR FOR POMONA

Howard H. DeWeese has been named eastern sales director of Pomona Tile Manufacturing Company, according to a recent announcement by Richard Scherbacher, sales director.

DeWeese has been with Pomona Tile since 1954 as a sales representative in the firm's San Francisco branch. He will make his headquarters in the company's Kansas City district offices, and will be in charge of expanding the eastern markets.

ARCHITECT NAMED TO ADVISORY BOARD ARIZONA COLLEGE

C. M. Deasy, Los Angeles architect, has been appointed to the advisory board of the department of architecture at Arizona State College, Tempe, Arizona, according to an announcement by Grady Gammage, college president.

Deasy's function will be to advise the department, which is new to Arizona State, on curriculum development. A graduate of USC, Deasy is also immediate past president of the Southern California Chapter AIA.

ARCHITECT WRIGHT RE-NAMED CHAIRMAN CONFERENCE GROUP

Architect Henry L. Wright, FAIA, of Los Angeles, has been re-elected chairman of the Architects and Engineers Conference Committee of California. He is a representative of the California Council AIA, on the Conference Committee which includes Wesley T. Hayes, San Francisco, re-elected vice-president, and representing the Structural Engineers Association of California.

Other member organizations are the Consulting Engineers Association of California and the California Council of Civil Engineers and Land Surveyors.

The Conference Committee was formed by the four organizations in 1956 to provide a means for exchanging information and planning cooperative action at the State level in fields of mutual interest to the architectural and engineering professions.

ENGINEERS GROUP HOLD INSTALLATION

New officers of the Civil Engineers and Land Surveyors Association of California were installed at a banquet in the Beverly Wilshire Hotel, Beverly Hills, recently.

Glenn I. Voorheis of Van Nuys was installed as president; F. William Pafford, vice-president; and C. S. Northrop of Arcadia, secretary - treasurer. Directors included: A. M. Fickes and Don D. Hillyard of Santa Ana, Harold A. Barnett of Pasadena, E. F. Koenig of Los Angeles and Leslie V. Olson, immediate past president of Downey, and A. Richard Drown of Buena Park. The association is affiliated with the California Council of Civil Engineers and Land Surveyors.

TENNIS CLUB FACILITIES EXPANDED

The architectural firm of Rickey & Brooks, 2015 J. Street, Sacramento, has completed drawings for construction of additional facilities at the South Hills Raquet Club in Sacramento.

The project includes a new clubhouse, dressing, shower and locker rooms, tennis courts, volley ball court, putting green, Olympic-size "L" shaped swimming pool, and off-street parking.

A.I.A. ACTIVITIES

(From page 30)

where he supervised the organization and progress of ten redevelopment projects involving more than 500 acres and costing an estimated $50,000,000.

OREGON CHAPTER

Richard Turner, Chairman of the Portland Art Commission was a recent speaker at a regular meeting, taking as his subject "Portland's Cultural Inferiority Complex". He also discussed the mural at the airport.

Recent new members: Frank Shell, Corporate Member. 1st Lt. P. J. Penn and 1st Lt. A. M. Staehli. Portland Air Base, Jr. Associate Members.

SAN FRANCISCO ARCHITECTURAL CLUB

Rear Admiral A. G. Cook, USN Ret. was the principal speaker at the April business meeting, taking as his subject some revealing points of the nation's defense, and showing motion pictures.

A tour of the American President Line's passenger ship is scheduled for June 7th, you must register at Club headquarters, 507 Howard Street. O. Hickenlooper is in charge.

Recent new members include Louis Gelwicks, with Rex Allen, and Gerald Johnson, Architectural Draftsman of Redwood City.

DON WEAVER, AIA, Architect, has been appointed a member of the Ukiah, California, Planning Commission.

ARCHITECT'S MIRROR

(From page 9)

eastern company were instructed to talk with each of the nearly 800 skilled workers and give each one praise for some little thing. The management had expected this to bring a rash of requests for salary increases. In anticipation of such requests, a review board had been set up to handle them. But there was not a single request for a raise! Yet production increased; absenteeism and tardiness declined."

Tested instructions in how to increase efficiency, in ability to concentrate, making memory more efficient, ways to plan and organize work for more efficiency are needed by architects as well as by other businessmen.

The architect employer needs to study and absorb the nature and basis and strategies of leadership . . . the motivations needed to build morale and the will to work. He should know the rules leading to group cooperation and group spirit, if he is to meet the challenge of today.

PHOTO CREDITS: Gabriel Moulin Studio, Cover, Pages 12, 13, 14, 15, 16, 17, 19; M. H. deYoung Memorial Museum, Page 7; Sewall Smith, Page 8; Welton Becket & Associates, Page 10; Kawneer Company, Page 20; Loren Smith, Pages 22, 23, 24, 25.

NEWS AND COMMENT ON ART

(From page 7)

Shell Oil Company, and is an honorary Life member and on the Advisory Board of the Society of Western Artists.

SAN FRANCISCO MUSEUM OF ART

The San Francisco Museum of Art, War Memorial Building, Civic Center, under the direction of Dr. Grace L. McCann Morley, is presenting the following exhibitions and events for April:

EXHIBITIONS: The 77th Annual Painting and Sculpture Exhibition of the San Francisco Art Association; Abstract Photography, an American Federation of Arts Exhibition; the Adaline Kent Memorial Exhibition, Contemporary Prints from Italy, and Adventure in Glass.

SPECIAL EVENTS: Lecture tours of the Museum each Sunday at 3:00 o'clock, featuring the current exhibitions; Round-table discussions on various phases of Art each Wednesday evening at 8:30; and the special activities include Adventures in Drawing and Painting—the Sketch Club, and the Painting Class, Friday evenings at 7:30; Children's Saturday Morning Art Classes from 10:00 to 11:00 o'clock.

The Museum is open daily.

PAINTINGS OF NOTED JAPANESE ARTIST AT DeYOUNG MUSEUM

A special exhibition of 53 hanging scrolls and painted screens by the revered Japanese artist Tomioka Tessai is being shown at the M. H. DeYoung Memorial Museum, San Francisco, this month.

The exhibition was organized by the Society of International Cultural Relations and the National Museum of Modern Art in Tokyo and is being circulated among leading museums of this country by the Smithsonian Institution Traveling Exhibition Service.

The selection of works spans the development from Tessai's early works in the style of Yamoto-e painting and his more robust works in the manner of Otsu-e and Ukiyo-e, to the final culmination in the luxuriance of the art of his late period.

BOOK REVIEWS
PAMPHLETS AND CATALOGUES

TECHNIQUES OF PLANT MAINTENANCE & EN-
ENGINEERING—1957. Proceedings of Technical Sessions, Eighth National Plant Maintenance and Engineering Show. Plant Maintenance Show, Inc., 341 Madison
Ave., New York 17, N.Y. 273 pages. Price $10.00.
The latest in the annual series of reports on the changing
patterns of maintenance and engineering; includes 29 papers
presented by discussion leaders, and has 890 specific problems presented in the form of questions and answers; contains
46 charts, diagrams, tables and other illustrations. Although
most papers have application to all industry, a number are
devoted to specific industries and include the maintenance of
metal working plants, chemical plants, steel mills, metal fabricating plants, foundries, paper mill and paper product plants,
petroleum refineries, food processing plants, rubber mills and
rubber product plants, and textile mills.

ATOMIC ENERGY FACTS. U. S. Atomic Energy Commission. U. S. Government Printing Office, Washington 25,
D. C. 216 pages. Price $2.00.
This up to date compilation of facts in the atomic energy
field is a handbook on nuclear operations in the United States
for industrial management and others active or interested in
atomic energy. The text is entirely devoted to peaceful uses
of atomic energy, organization and technical services of the
Commission, conditions under which qualified individuals and
organizations may gain access to classified information, special
materials and services available from the Commission, and how
to obtain patents and licenses. The volume contains eight
appendices covering: basic principles of controlled thermo-
nuclear program, categories of restricted data available to
access permit holders, depository libraries of U. S. Atomic
Energy Commission, a bibliography, power reactor data tables,
data for representative research reactors, gamma irradiation
facilities, and a catalog of materials standards.

MODERN SCHOOL SHOP PLANNING. Prakken Publications, 330 Thompson St., Ann Arbor, Michigan. 184
pages. Price $3.85.
Carefully compiled to be of the utmost practical help in the
planning of modern facilities for school shops, this revised and
enlarged edition features the addition of extensive check lists
of standards for evaluating shop plans and facilities which will
enable architects, engineers and contractors who design shop
facilities for schools to check their work against the judgments
of experts in various areas such as ventilation, fenestration,
space requirements, visual comfort, and other details. It also
carries inclusive recommendations for handling storage of
tools, projects, and equipment.

METALLURGICAL PROGRESS — 3. A Third Series of
Critical Reviews. Philosophical Library Inc., 15 E. 40th
St., New York 16. 88 pages. Price $6.00.
Following the success of earlier series, the publication of
surveys of the present state of knowledge on various industrial
subjects is here continued with reviews by a number of leading specialists in four further branches of the iron and steel
industry, i.e., refractories, non-destructive testing, coke, and
foundry technology. Each of these new reviews comprises a
compilation and analysis of published information which would
represent many months of research for the student in these
fields.

NEW CATALOGUES AVAILABLE

*Architects, Engineers, Contractors, Planning Commission
members—the catalogues, folders, new building products
material, etc., described below may be obtained by directing
your request to the name and address given in each item.*

Aluminum radiant-acoustical ceilings. New 4-page brochure
(AIA File No. 30-C-44) on aluminum radiant-acoustical
ceilings; fully explains newly developed Airtex ceiling that
can be used in conjunction with standard acoustical tiles for
radiant heating, cooling and noise reduction; complete description of components and schematic illustration of installation included. Free copy write DEPT-A&E, Airtex Corpn.,
2900 N. Western Ave., Chicago 18.
How good is your electrical wiring. A handy calculator
that architects can use to determine home electrical require-

ments; designed to provide an easy method to calculate "housepower"; 2-color folder consists of a check list by means of which total, room by room, wattage required for a home's electrical service can be determined. Copy available write DEPT-A&E, Federal Pacific Electric Co., 50 Paris St., Newark, N.J.

Mercury vapor floodlights. New 18-page bulletin, 2-color, contains latest information on operating characteristics and economics, and color characteristics of all currently available mercury lamps; thoroughly informative section on how to select ballasts with illustrations of the typical ballast types and mountings; various sizes are explained; excellent short-cut method for estimating floodlighting requirements with sample layout diagrams and selection tables. Free copy write DEPT-A&E, Pyle-National Co., 1334 N. Kostner Ave., Chicago 51.

Effective sewage disposal. 40-Page primer on sewage pumping and treatment is available to architects and engineers, builders, and others interested in community facilities entitled "The Home Builders Guide to Effective Sewage Disposal"; covers comprehensive variety of situations encountered by builders in the collection, disposition and treatment of sewage; non-technical case history presentation spells out the ABC's of sewage handling for single homes as well as developments up to 1500 homes. Copy free write DEPT-A&E, Yeomans Bro's Co., 1999 N. Ruby St., Melrose Park, Ill.

Overhead doors. New 16-page catalog (AIA File No. 16-D) presents line of residential, commercial, and industrial overhead doors; gives full information on new Weather-King flush overhead door sections, combining high-insulation-value sandwich construction with guaranteed weather proof facing; electric operators, cam-action closing hardware, radio controls, and special controls also fully described and extensively illustrated; specifications, instructions, detailed drawings. Free copy write DEPT-A&E, Barber-Colman Co., Rockford, Ill.

Pressure treated forest products. Illustrated brochure (AIA FILE No. 19-A-3) describes pressure-treatment of wood that assures dependable protection against wood borers and decay fungi; numerous photographs of typical uses, and other details. Free copy, write DEPT-A&E, McCormick & Baxter Creosoting Co., 485 California St., San Francisco; or P.O. Box 3344, Portland, Oregon.

Stone laboratory equipment. Booklet describes standard material for the permanent equipment of laboratories in industrial, educational and research institutions; many illustrations of installations; drawings and specifications. Free copy write DEPT-A&E, Stiehle & Co., 605 Addison St., Berkeley, Calif.

Flush valves. 20-Page catalog describes complete line of Haws-Kramer Flush Valves, Division of Haws Drinking Faucet Co.; features their Nyla-Phragm flush valves along with their Piston type flush valves; rough-in drawings for 40 combination installations; operational and repair parts drawings, stop valves, vacuum breakers, flush valve variations, comparison charts and complete listing of representatives. Free copy write DEPT-A&E, Haws-Kramer Flush Valves, 819 Bryant St., San Francisco 3, Calif.

Facebrick. New 6-page folder (AIA FILE No. 9a) describes varied line of distinctive facebrick manufactured by the Pacific Northwest Division of Gladding, McBean & Co., 945 Elliott Ave., West, Seattle 99, Wash.

ESTIMATOR'S GUIDE

BUILDING AND CONSTRUCTION MATERIALS

PRICES GIVEN ARE FIGURING PRICES AND ARE MADE UP FROM AVERAGE QUOTATIONS FURNISHED BY LeROY CONSTRUCTION SERVICES. 4% SALES TAX ON ALL MATERIALS BUT NOT LABOR. ITEMS IN ITALIC INCLUDE LABOR AND SALES TAX.

BONDS—Performance or Performance plus Labor and Material Bond(s), $10 per $1000 on contract price. Labor and Material Bond(s) only, $5.00 per $1000 on contract price.

BRICKWORK & MASONRY

COMMON BRICKWORK, Reinforced:
8" walls ... SF 2.95
12" walls ... SF 4.15
SELECT COMMON, Reinforced:
8" walls ... SF 3.05
12" walls ... SF 4.30
CONCRETE BLOCK, Reinforced:
6" walls ... SF 1.40
8" walls ... SF 1.55
12" walls ... SF 1.90
BRICK VENEER:
4" Select Common ... SF 1.65
4" Roman ... SF 2.50
4" Norman ... SF 2.40
4" Aggrelite ... SF 2.40

BRICKWORK & MASONRY

All Prices—F.O.B. Plant.
COMMON BRICK
Common 2½ x 3¾ x 8¼ ... M 45.00
Select 2½ x 3¾ x 8¼ ... M 52.00
Clinker 2½ x 3¾ x 8¼ ... M 48.00
Jumbo 3½ x 3 x 11½ ... M 90.00
FACE BRICK
Standard ... M 59.80 - 83.20
Jumbo ... M 114.40 - 130.00
Roman ... M 88.40 - 109.20
Norman ... M 101.40 - 124.80
Brik Blox (6") ... M 202.80
(8") ... M 239.20
Braile Veneer ... M 26.00
BUILDING TILE
8 x 5½ x 12 inches ... M 165.78
6 x 5½ x 12 inches ... M 128.96
HOLLOW TILE
12 x 12 x 3 inches ... M 163.12
12 x 12 x 4 inches ... M 184.18
12 x 12 x 6 inches ... M 244.71
MANTEL FIRE BRICK
2½ x 9½ x 4½ inches ... M 140.40
GLAZED STRUCTURAL UNITS
2 x 6 x 12 Furring ... SF .90
4 x 6 x 12 Furring ... SF 1.20
6 x 6 x 12 Furring ... SF 1.50
4 x 6 x 12 Partition ... SF 1.60
Add for color ... SF .20
CONCRETE BLOCKS
4 x 8 x 16 inches ... EA .22
6 x 8 x 16 inches ... EA .265
8 x 8 x 16 inches ... EA .30
12 x 8 x 16 inches ... EA .435
Colored Add ... EA .02
AGGREGATE—Haydite or Basalite
All sizes in bulk ... CY 6.24

BUILDING PAPERS & FELTS

1 ply per 1000 ft. roll ... 3.95
2 ply per 1000 ft. roll ... 6.03
3 ply per 1000 ft. roll ... 8.22
Sisalkraft, reinf. 500 ft. roll ... 7.54
SHEATHING PAPERS:
Asphalt sheathing, 15-lb. roll ... 2.50
30-lb. roll ... 3.50
Dampcourse, 216-ft. roll ... 3.05
FELT PAPERS:
Deadening felt, ¾-lb. 50 ft. roll ... 4.10
1-lb. 50 ft. roll ... 4.78
Asphalt roofing, 15-lbs. ... 2.50
30-lbs. ... 3.50
ROOFING PAPERS:
Standard Grade, Smooth Surface
108-ft. roll, Light ... 2.35
Medium ... 2.75
Heavy ... 3.22
Extra Heavy ... 3.75

CHIMNEYS, PATENT

F.O.B. Warehouse
6" ... LF 1.45
8" ... LF 2.05
10" ... LF 2.85
12" ... LF 3.45
Rates for 10 - 50 Lin. Ft.

CONCRETE AGGREGATES

	Bunker Per Ton	Del'd Per Ton
Gravel, All Sizes	3.38	4.16
Top Sand	3.59	4.37
Concrete Mix	3.48	4.26
Crushed Rock		
¼" to ¾"	3.43	4.26
¾" to 1½"	3.43	4.26
Roofing Gravel	3.54	4.42
SAND		
Lapis (Nos. 2 & 4)	4.47	5.30
Olympia (Nos. 1 & 2)	3.75	4.32

CEMENT
Common All Brands (Paper Sacks)
Small Quantities ... Per Sack 1.40
Large Quantities ... Per Bbl. 4.00
Trinity White & Mendusa White ... Per Sack 4.16
CONCRETE READY-MIX
6 sack in 5 yd. loads ... Per Yd. 15.40
CURING COMPOUND, Clear
5 gal. drums ... Per Gal. 1.46

CARPENTRY & MILLWORK

Hardware not included
FRAMING:
Floors ... BM .20 - .25
Walls ... BM .25 - .30
Ceilings ... BM .18 - .22
Roofs ... BM .22 - .27
Furring & Blocking ... BM .30 - .50
SHEATHING:
1 x 8 straight ... BM .20 - .25
1 x 8 diagonal ... BM .23 - .28
5/16" Plyscore ... SF .16 - .20
⅜" Plywood ... SF .25 - .30
SIDING:
1 x 8 Bevel ... BM .35 - .40
1 x 4 V-Rustic ... BM .40 - .45
EXTERIOR TRIM:
Fascia and Molds ... BM .40 - .50
Bolted Framing—Add 50%
ENTRANCE DOORS & FRAMES:
Singles ... 60.00 & Up
Doubles ... 100.00 & Up
INTERIOR DOORS & FRAMES:
Singles ... 35.00 & Up
Pocket Sliding ... 45.00 & Up
Closet Sliding (Pr.) ... 50.00 & Up
WINDOWS:
D/H Sash & Frames ... SF 1.75 & Up
Casement Sash & Frames ... SF 1.90 & Up
SHELVING:
1 x 12 S4S ... BM .30 - .50
¾" Plywood ... SF .40 - .60
STAIRS:
Oak steps D.F. Risers
Under 36" wide ... Riser 12.00
Under 60" wide ... Riser 17.00
Newel posts and rail extra
WOOD CASES & CABINETS:
D.F. Wall Hung ... LF 13.00 - 18.00
D.F. Counters ... LF 15.00 - 20.00

DAMPPROOFING & WATERPROOFING

MEMBRANE:
1 layer 50 lb. felt ... SQ. 9.00
4 layers Dampcourse ... SQ. 13.00
Hot coat walls ... SQ. 6.00
Tricosal added to concrete ... CY 1.00
Anti-Hydro added to concrete ... CY 1.50

ELECTRIC WIRING

Per Outlet:
Knob & Tube ... EA 9.00
Armor ... EA 16.00
Conduit ... EA 20.00
110 V Circuit ... EA 25.00
220 V Circuit ... EA 95.00

ELEVATORS & ESCALATORS

Prices vary according to capacity, speed and type. Consult Elevator Companies.

Slow speed apartment house elevator including doors and trim, about $5000.00 per floor.

EXCAVATION

MACHINE WORK in common ground:
Large Basements ... CY .75 - 1.00
Small Pits ... CY 1.25 - 1.75
Trenches ... CY 1.50 - 2.25
HAND WORK in common ground:
Large pits and trenches ... CY 4.50 - 5.50
Small pits and trimming ... CY 5.00 - 6.50
Hard Clay & Shale 2 times above rates.
Rock and large boulders 4-6 times above rates.
Shoring, bracing and disposal of water not included.

FLOORS

⅛" Asp. tile, dark colors ... SF .25 - .30
⅛" Asp. tile, light colors ... SF .30 - .35
⅛" Rubber tile ... SF .60 - .70
.080 Vinyl Asbestos Tile ... SF .40 - .45
.080 Vinyl Tile ... SF .85 - .95
Lino, Standard Gauge ... SY 3.75 - 4.25
Lino, Battleship ... SY 5.25 - 5.75
4" Rubber Base, Black ... LF .35 - .40
Rubber Stair Nosing ... LF 1.00 - 1.75
Above rates based on quantities of 1000 - 5000 SF per job.

HARDWOOD FLOORS

Select Oak, filled, sanded, stained and varnished:
5/16" x 2¼" strip ... SF .45 - .50
5/16" Random Plank ... SF .50 - .55
25/32" x 2¼" T&G ... SF .70 - .80
Maple, 2nd Grade and Better, filled, sanded, stained and varnished:
25/32" x 2¼" T&G ... SF .80 - .95
Wax Finish, add ... SF .10

HARDWOOD FLOORING

Oak 5/16" x 2" Strip—
Clear ... M 229.00
Select ... M 218.00
#1 Common ... M 203.00
Oak 5/16" Random Plank—
Select & Btr. ... M 286.00
#1 Common ... M 244.00
Oak 25/32" x 2¼" T&G—
Select ... M 260.00
#1 Common ... M 203.00
Maple 25/32" x 2¼" T&G—
#1 Grade ... M 317.00
#2 Grade ... M 281.00
#3 Grade ... M 208.00
Nails—1" Floor Brads ... KEG 17.20

GLASS & GLAZING

S.S.B. Clear ... SF .48
D.S.B. Clear ... SF .78
Crystal ... SF .92
¼" Plate ... SF 2.17
⅛" Obscure ... SF .68
⅛" Heat Absorbing ... SF 1.12
¼" Tempered Plate ... SF 4.38
½" Tempered Plate ... SF 7.84
¼" Wire Plate, Clear ... SF 3.65
¼" Wire Plate, Rough ... SF 1.08

GLASS—CUT TO SIZE

F.O.B. Warehouse
S.S.B. Clear, Av. 6 SF ... SF .34
D.S.B. Clear, Av. 10 SF ... SF .56
Crystal, Av. 35 SF ... SF .66
¼" Polished Plate, Av. 100 SF ... SF 1.55
⅛" Obscure, Av. 10 SF ... SF .49
⅛" Ribbed, Av. 10 SF ... SF .49
⅛" Rough, Av. 10 SF ... SF .49
¼" Wire Plate, Clear, Av. 40 SF ... SF 2.61
¼" Wire Plate, Rough, Av. 40 SF ... SF .77
⅛" Heat Absorbing, Av. 10 SF ... SF .80
¼" Tempered Plate, Av. 50 SF ... SF 3.13
½" Tempered Plate, Av. 50 SF ... SF 5.60
Glazing—Approx. 40-50% of Glass
Glass Blocks—Check with Dealer

HEATING

FURNACES—Gas Fired—Av. Job:
FLOOR FURNACE:
25,000 BTU ... 100.00 - 125.00
35,000 BTU ... 107.00 - 135.00
45,000 BTU ... 115.00 - 150.00
AUTOMATIC CONTROL:
Add ... 25.00 - 35.00

HEATING—Cont'd

DUAL WALL FURNACE:	
25,000 BTU	*110.00 - 125.00*
35,000 BTU	*125.00 - 145.00*
50,000 BTU	*150.00 - 180.00*
AUTOMATIC CONTROL:	
Add	*25.00 - 35.00*
GRAVITY FURNACE:	
75,000 BTU	*375.00 - 450.00*
85,000 BTU	*425.00 - 525.00*
95,000 BTU	*475.00 - 600.00*
FORCED AIR FURNACE:	
Add	*75.00 - 125.00*
AUTOMATIC CONTROL:	
Add	*15.00 - 25.00*
HEAT REGISTERS:	
Outlet	*7.50 - 15.00*

INSULATION & WALLBOARD

F.O.B. Warehouse

ROCKWOOL Insulation—		
2" Semi-thick	Per M SF	63.02
3⅝" Full Thick	Per M SF	80.50
COTTON Insulation		
1" Full Thick	Per M SF	43.26
SOFTBOARDS—Wood Fiber—		
½" thick	Per M SF	88.00
1½" thick	Per M SF	275.00
2" thick	Per M SF	385.00
ALUMINUM Insulation—		
80# Kraft paper with alum. foil		
1 side only	Per M SF	18.30
2 sides	Per M SF	31.00
GYPSUM Wallboard—		
⅜" thick	Per M SF	49.50
½" thick	Per M SF	54.50
⅝" thick	Per M SF	83.00
⅝" Gyplap	Per M SF	85.00
HARDBOARDS—Wood Fiber—		
⅛" thick, Sheathing	Per M SF	78.75
3/16" thick, Sheathing	Per M SF	90.48
¼" thick, Sheathing	Per M SF	109.20
⅛" thick, Tempered	Per M SF	98.80
3/16" thick, Tempered	Per M SF	140.40
¼" thick, Tempered	Per M SF	194.48
CEMENT Asbestos Board—		
⅛" C.A.B. Flat Sheets	Per M SF	156.00
3/16" C.A.B. Flat Sheets	Per M SF	218.40
¼" C.A.B. Flat Sheets	Per M SF	280.80

LATH & PLASTER

Diamond 3.40 copper bearing	SY	.50
Ribbed 3.40 copper bearing	SY	.55
⅜" rock lath	SY	.37
2" Standard Channel	LF	.085
1½" Standard Channel	LF	.065
¾" Standard Channel	LF	.045
3¼" steel studs	LF	.09
4" steel studs	LF	.105
Stud shoes	EA	.025
Hardwall, Browning	Sack	1.46
Hardwall, Finish	Sack	1.72
Stucco	Sack	2.50

LATH & PLASTERWORK

CHANNEL FURRING:		
Suspended Ceilings	*SY*	*2.20 - 2.50*
Walls	*SY*	*2.30 - 2.60*
METAL STUD PARTITIONS:		
3¼" Studs	*SY*	*1.70 - 2.00*
4" Studs	*SY*	*1.95 - 2.25*
Over 10'0 high, add	*SY*	*.20 - .30*
3.40 METAL LATH AND PLASTER:		
Ceilings	*SY*	*3.60 - 4.00*
Walls	*SY*	*3.75 - 4.15*
KEENE'S CEMENT FINISH:		
Add	*SY*	*.40 - .60*
ROCK LATH & PLASTER:		
Ceilings	*SY*	*2.50 - 2.80*
Walls	*SY*	*2.60 - 2.90*
WIRE MESH AND ⅞" STUCCO:		
Walls	*SY*	*3.60 - 4.10*
STUCCO ON CONCRETE:		
Walls	*SY*	*2.30 - 2.80*
METAL ACCESSORIES	*LF*	*.20 - .50*

LINOLEUM

Lino. Standard Gauge	SY	2.65 - 2.85
Lino. Battleship	SY	3.90 - 4.10
⅛" Asp. tile, Dark	SF	.10 - .11
⅛" Asp. tile, Light	SF	.14 - .16
⅛" Rubber Tile	SF	.40 - .44
.080 Vinyl Asb. tile	SF	.18 - .19
.080 Vinyl tile	SF	.59 - .61
⅛" Vinyl tile	SF	.78 - .82
4" Base, Dark	LF	.15 - .16
4" Base, Light	LF	.24 - .26
Rubber Nosing	LF	.60 - 1.30
Lino Paste	GAL	.75 - .90

Above rates based on quantities of 1000-5000 SF per job.

LUMBER

DOUGLAS FIR:	M.B.M.
#1 2x4—2x10	88.00 - 92.00
#2 2x4—2x10	85.00 - 90.00
#3 2x4—2x10	68.00 - 74.00
#4 2x4—2x10	64.00 - 72.00
Clear, Air Dried	180.00 - 210.00
Clear, Kiln Dried	210.00 - 240.00
REDWOOD:	
Foundation Grade	120.00 - 130.00
Construction Heart	110.00 - 120.00
A Grade	180.00 - 210.00
Clear Heart	190.00 - 220.00
D.F. PLYWOOD	M.S.F.
¼" AB	95.00 - 105.00
¼" AD	90.00 - 95.00
¼" Ext. Waterproof	115.00 - 125.00
⅝" AB	130.00 - 145.00
5/16" AD	115.00 - 125.00
⅜" CD	70.00 - 85.00
½" AB	170.00 - 185.00
½" AD	110.00 - 115.00
½" CD	....
⅝" AB	185.00 - 200.00
⅝" AD	165.00 - 180.00
⅝" CD	115.00 - 125.00
¾" AB	210.00 - 230.00
¾" AD	195.00 - 210.00
¾" CD	125.00 - 140.00
⅝" Plyform	160.00 - 170.00
SHINGLES:	Square
Cedar #1	14.00 - 15.50
Cedar #2	11.50 - 12.50
SHAKES:	
CEDAR	
½ to ¾" Butt	17.50 - 18.50
¾ to 1¼" Butt	18.50 - 19.50
REDWOOD	
¾ to 1¼" Butt	21.00 - 24.00

MILLWORK

All Prices F.O.B. Mill

D.F. CLEAR, AIR DRIED:		
S4S	MBM	220.00 - 250.00
D.F. CLEAR, KILN DRIED:		
S4S	MBM	225.00 - 275.00
DOOR FRAMES & TRIM:		
Residential Entrance		17.00 & up
Interior Room Entrance		7.50 & up
DOORS:		
1⅜" D.F. Slab, Hollow Core		8.00 & up
1¾" D.F. Slab, Solid Core		19.00 & up
1⅜" Birch Slab, Hollow Core		10.00 & up
1¾" Birch Slab, Solid Core		22.00 & up
WINDOW FRAMES:		
D/H Singles	SF	.80
Casement Singles	SF	.90
WOOD SASH:		
D/H in pairs (1 lite)	SF	.45
Casement (1 lite)	SF	.50
WOOD CABINETS:		
¾" D.F. Ply with ¼" ply backs		
Wall Hung	LF	10.00 - 15.00
Counter	LF	12.00 - 17.00

BIRCH OR MAPLE—Add 25%

PAINTING

EXTERIOR:		
Stucco Wash 1 ct	*SY*	*.30*
Stucco Wash 2 cts	*SY*	*.35*
Lead and Oil 2 cts	*SY*	*.90*
Lead and Oil 3 cts	*SY*	*1.30*
INTERIOR:		
Primer Sealer	*SY*	*.40*
Wall Paint, 1 ct	*SY*	*.50*
Wall Paint, 2 cts	*SY*	*.95*
Enamel, 1 ct	*SY*	*.60*
Enamel, 2 cts	*SY*	*1.10*
Doors and Trim	*EA*	*10.00*
Sash and Trim	*EA*	*12.00*
Base and Molds	*LF*	*.12*

Old Work—Add 15-30%

PLUMBING

Lavatories	*EA*	*100.00 - 150.00*
Toilets	*EA*	*200.00 - 300.00*
Bath Tubs	*EA*	*250.00 - 350.00*
Stall Shower	*EA*	*80.00 - 150.00*
Sinks	*EA*	*125.00 - 175.00*
Laundry Trays	*EA*	*80.00 - 130.00*
Water Heaters	*EA*	*100.00 - 300.00*

Prices based on average residential and commercial work. Special fixtures and excessive piping not included.

PAINT

All Prices F.O.B. Warehouse

Thinners—5-100 gals.	GAL	.45
Turpentine—5-100 gals.	GAL.	1.35
Linseed Oil, Raw	GAL	2.00
Linseed Oil, Boiled	GAL	1.95
Primer-Sealer	GAL	2.95
Enamel	GAL	5.00
Enamel Undercoat	GAL	3.25
White Lead in Oil	LB.	.26
Red Lead in Oil	LB.	.29
Litharge	LB.	.24

ROOFING

STANDARD TAR & GRAVEL	Per Square
4 ply	*14.00 - 18.00*
5 ply	*17.00 - 20.00*
White Gravel Finish—Add	*2.00 - 4.00*
Asph. Compo. Shingles	*16.00 - 20.00*
Cedar Shingles	*20.00 - 24.00*
Cedar Shakes	*26.00 - 30.00*
Redwood Shakes	*28.00 - 34.00*
Clay Tiles	*40.00 - 50.00*

SEWER PIPE

VITRIFIED:		
Standard 4 in.	LF	.31
Standard 6 in.	LF	.56
Standard 8 in.	LF	.81
Standard 12 in.	LF	1.76
Standard 24 in.	LF	6.95
CLAY DRAIN PIPE:		
Standard 6 in.	LF	.34
Standard 8 in.	LF	.59

Rate for 100 Lin. Ft. F.O.B. Warehouse

STEEL

REINFORCING BARS:		
¼" rounds	LB	.122
⅜" rounds	LB	.111
½" rounds	LB	.107
⅝" rounds	LB	.104
¾" rounds	LB	.102
⅞" rounds	LB	.102
1" rounds	LB	.102
REINFORCING MESH (1050 SF Rolls)		
6x6 x 10x10	SF	.035
6x6 x 6x6	SF	.067
16 GA. TYING WIRE	LB	.130

Rates 100-1000 Lbs. F.O.B. Warehouse

STRUCTURAL STEEL

$325.00 and up per ton erected when out of mill.
$350.00 and up per ton erected when out of stock.

SHEET METAL

ROOF FLASHINGS:		
18 ga. Galv. Steel	*SF*	*.60 - 1.00*
22 ga. Galv. Steel	*SF*	*.50 - .90*
26 ga. Galv. Steel	*SF*	*.40 - .80*
18 ga. Aluminum	*SF*	*1.00 - 1.50*
22 ga. Aluminum	*SF*	*.80 - 1.30*
26 ga. Aluminum	*SF*	*.60 - 1.10*
24 oz. Copper	*SF*	*1.90 - 2.40*
20 oz. Copper	*SF*	*1.70 - 2.20*
16 oz. Copper	*SF*	*1.50 - 2.00*
26 ga. Galv. Steel		
4" o.g. gutter	*LF*	*.90 - 1.30*
Mitres and Drops	*EA*	*2.00 - 4.00*
22 ga. Galv. Louvres	*SF*	*2.50 - 3.50*
20 oz. Copper Louvres	*SF*	*3.00 - 4.50*

TILE WORK

CERAMIC TILE, Stock colors:		
Floors	*SF*	*1.95 - 2.45*
Walls	*SF*	*2.05 - 2.55*
Coved Base	*LF*	*1.05 - 1.45*
QUARRY TILE:		
6" x 6" x ½" Floors	*SF*	*1.60 - 2.00*
9" x 9" x ¾" Floors	*SF*	*1.75 - 2.15*
Treads and risers	*LF*	*3.00 - 4.50*
Coved Base	*LF*	*.90 - 1.30*

Mosaic Tile — Rates vary with design and colors. Each job should be priced from Manufacturer.

TERRAZZO & MARBLE

Terrazzo Floors	*SF*	*2.00 - 2.50*
Cond. Terr. Floors	*SF*	*2.20 - 2.75*
Precast treads and risers	*LF*	*3.50 - 4.50*
Precast landing slabs	*SF*	*3.00 - 4.00*

TILE

CERAMIC:

F.O.B. Warehouse

4¼" x 4¼" glazed	SF	.69
4¼" x 4¼" hard glazed	SF	.72
Random unglazed	SF	.73
6" x 2" cap	EA	.17
6" coved base	EA	.22
¼" round bead	LF	.18
QUARRY:		
6 x 6 x ½" Red	SF	.49
6 x 6 x ¾" Red	SF	.52
9 x 9 x ¾" Red	SF	.60
6 x 6" coved base	EA	.21
White Cement Grout	Per 100 Lbs.	6.25

VENETIAN BLINDS

Residential	SF	.40 & Up
Commercial	SF	.45 & Up

WINDOWS

STEEL SASH:		
Under 10 SF	SF	2.5 &
Under 15 SF	SF	2.0 &
Under 20 SF	SF	1.50 & Up
Under 30 SF	SF	1.00 & Up
ALUMINUM SASH:		
Under 10 SF	SF	2.75 &
Under 15 SF	SF	2.25 &
Under 20 SF	SF	1.75 &
Under 30 SF	SF	1.25 & Up

Above rates are for standard sections and stock sizes Up
F.O.B. Warehouse

ESTIMATOR'S DIRECTORY
Building and Construction Materials

ACOUSTICAL ENGINEERS
L. D. REEDER CO.
San Francisco: 1255 Sansome St., DO 2-5050
Sacramento: 3026 V St., GL 7-3505

AIR CONDITIONING
E. C. BRAUN CO.
Berkeley: 2115 Fourth St., TH 5-2356
GILMORE AIR CONDITIONING SERVICE
San Francisco: 1617 Harrison St., UN 1-2000
KAEMPER & BARRETT
San Francisco: 233 Industrial St., JU 6-6200
LINFORD AIR & REFRIGERATION CO.
Oakland: 174-12th St., TW 3-6521
MALM METAL PRODUCTS
Santa Rosa: 724-2nd St., SR 454
JAMES A. NELSON CO.
San Francisco: 1375 Howard St., HE 1-0140

ALUMINUM BLDG. PRODUCTS
MICHEL & PFEFFER IRON WORKS (Wrought Iron)
So. San Francisco: 212 Shaw Road, PLaza 5-8983
REYNOLDS METALS CO.
San Francisco: 3201 Third St., MI 7-2990
SOULE STEEL CO.
San Francisco: 1750 Army St., VA 4-4141
UNIVERSAL WINDOW CO.
Berkeley: 950 Parker St., TH 1-1600

ARCHITECTURAL PORCELAIN ENAMEL
CALIFORNIA METAL ENAMELING CO.
Los Angeles: 6904 E. Slauson, RA 3-6351
San Francisco: Continental Bldg. Products Co.,
178 Fremont St.
Portland: Portland Wire & Iron Works,
4644 S.E. Seventeenth Ave.
Seattle: Foster-Bray Co., 2412 1st Ave. So.
Spokane: Bernhard Schafer, Inc., West 34, 2nd Ave.
Salt Lake City: S. A. Roberts & Co., 109 W. 2nd So.
Dallas: Offenhauser Co., 2201 Telephone Rd.
El Paso: Architectural Products Co.,
506 E. Yandell Blvd.
Phoenix: Haskell-Thomas Co., 3808 No. Central
San Diego: Maloney Specialties, Inc., 823 W. Laurel St.
Boise: Intermountain Glass Co., 1417 Main St.

ARCHITECTURAL & AERIAL PHOTOGRAPHS
FRED ENGLISH
Belmont, Calif.: 1310 Old County Road, LY 1-0385

ARCHITECTURAL VENEER
Ceramic Veneer
GLADDING, McBEAN & CO.
San Francisco: Harrison at 9th St., UN 1-7400
Los Angeles: 2901 Los Feliz Blvd., OL 2121
Portland: 110 S.E. Main St., EA 6179
Seattle 99: 945 Elliott Ave., West, GA 0330
Spokane: 1102 N. Monroe St., BR 3259
KRAFTILE COMPANY
Niles, Calif., Niles 3611

Porcelain Veneer
PORCELAIN ENAMEL PUBLICITY BUREAU
Oakland 12: Room 601, Franklin Building
Pasadena 8: P. O. Box 186, East Pasadena Station

Granite Veneer
VERMONT MARBLE COMPANY
San Francisco 24: 6000 3rd St., VA 6-5024
Los Angeles: 3522 Council St., DU 2-6339

Marble Veneer
VERMONT MARBLE COMPANY
San Francisco 24: 6000 3rd St., VA 6-5024
Los Angeles: 3522 Council St., DU 2-6339

BANKS - FINANCING
CROCKER-ANGLO NATIONAL BANK
San Francisco: 13 Offices

BLINDS
PARAMOUNT VENETIAN BLIND CO.
San Francisco: 5929 Mission St., JU 5-2436

BRASS PRODUCTS
GREENBERG'S, M. SONS
San Francisco 7: 765 Folsom, EX 2-3143
Los Angeles 23: 1258 S. Boyle, AN 3-7108
Seattle 4:1016 First Ave. So., MA 5140
Phoenix: 3009 N. 19th Ave., Apt. 92, PH 2-7663
Portland 4: 510 Builders Exch. Bldg., AT 6443

BRICKWORK
Face Brick
GLADDING McBEAN & CO.
San Francisco: Harrison at 9th, UN 1-7400
KRAFTILE CO.
Niles, Calif., Niles 3611
UNITED MATERIALS & RICHMOND BRICK CO.
Point Richmond, BE 4-5032

BRONZE PRODUCTS
GREENBERG'S M. SONS
San Francisco: 765 Folsom St., EX 2-3143
MICHEL & PFEFFER IRON WORKS
So. San Francisco: 212 Shaw Road, PLaza 5-8983
C. E. TOLAND & SON
Oakland: 2635 Peralta St., GL 1-2580

BUILDING HARDWARE
E. M. HUNDLEY HARDWARE CO.
San Francisco: 662 Mission St., YU 2-3322

BUILDING PAPERS & FELTS
PACIFIC CEMENT & AGGREGATES INC.
San Francisco: 400 Alabama St., KL 2-1616

CABINETS & FIXTURES
CENTRAL MILL & CABINET CO.
San Francisco: 1595 Fairfax Ave., VA 4-7316
THE FINK & SCHINDLER CO.
San Francisco: 552 Brannan St., EX 2-1513
JONES KRAFT SHOP,
San Francisco: 1314 Ocean Avenue., JU 7-1545
MULLEN MFG. CO.
San Francisco: 64 Rausch St., UN 1-5815
PARAMOUNT BUILT IN FIXTURE CO.
Oakland: 962 Stanford Ave., OL 3-9911
ROYAL SHOWCASE CO.
San Francisco: 770 McAllister St., JO 7-0311

CEMENT
CALAVERAS CEMENT CO.
San Francisco: 315 Montgomery St.
DO 2-4224, Enterprise 1-2315
PACIFIC CEMENT & AGGREGATES INC.
San Francisco: 400 Alabama St., KL 2-1616

CONCRETE AGGREGATES
Ready Mixed Concrete
CENTRAL CONCRETE SUPPLY CO.
San Jose: 610 McKendrie St.
PACIFIC CEMENT & AGGREGATES INC.
San Francisco: 400 Alabama St., KL 2-1616
Sacramento: 16th and A Sts., GI 3-6586
San Jose: 790 Stockton Ave., CY 2-5620
Oakland: 2400 Peralta St., GL 1-0177
Stockton: 820 So. California St., ST 8-8643
READYMIX CONCRETE CO.
Santa Rosa: 50 W. Cottage Ave.
RHODES-JAMIESON LTD.
Oakland: 333-23rd Ave., KE 3-5225
SANTA ROSA BLDG. MATERIALS CO.
Santa Rosa: Roberts Ave.

CONCRETE ACCESSORIES
Screed Materials
C. & H. SPECIALTIES CO.
Berkeley: 909 Camelia St., LA 4-5358

CONCRETE BLOCKS
BASALT ROCK CO.
Napa, Calif.

CONCRETE COLORS—HARDENERS
CONRAD SOVIG CO.
875 Bryant St., HE 1-1345

CONSTRUCTION SERVICES
LE ROY CONSTRUCTION SERVICES
San Francisco, 143 Third St., SU 1 8914

DECKS—ROOF
UNITED STATES GYPSUM CO.
2322 W. 3rd St., Los Angeles 54, Calif.
300 W. Adams St., Chicago 6, Ill.

DOORS
THE BILCO COMPANY
New Haven, Conn.
Oakland: Geo. B. Schultz, 190 MacArthur Blvd.
Sacramento: Harry B. Ogle & Assoc., 1331 T St.
Fresno: Healey & Popovich, 1703 Fulton St.
Reseda: Daniel Dunner, 6200 Alonzo Ave.

Cold Storage Doors
BIRKENWALD
Portland: 310 N.W. 5th Ave.

Electric Doors
ROLY-DOOR SALES CO.
San Francisco, 5976 Mission St., PL 5-5089

Folding Doors
WALTER D. BATES & ASSOCIATES
San Francisco, 693 Mission St., GA 1-6971

Hardwood Doors
BELLWOOD CO. OF CALIF.
Orange, Calif., 533 W. Collins Ave.

Hollywood Doors
WEST COAST SCREEN CO.
Los Angeles: 1127 E. 63rd St., AD 1-1108
T. M. COBB CO.
Los Angeles & San Diego
W. P. FULLER CO.
Seattle, Tacoma, Portland
HOGAN LUMBER CO.
Oakland: 700 - 6th Ave.
HOUSTON SASH & DOOR
Houston, Texas
SOUTHWESTERN SASH & DOOR
Phoenix, Tucson, Arizona
El Paso, Texas
WESTERN PINE SUPPLY CO.
Emeryville: 5760 Shellmound St.
GEO. C. VAUGHAN & SONS
San Antonio & Houston, Texas

Screen Doors
WEST COAST SCREEN DOOR CO.

DRAFTING ROOM EQUIPMENT
GENERAL FIREPROOFING CO.
Oakland: 332-19th St., GL 2-4280
Los Angeles: 1200 South Hope St., RI 7-7501
San Francisco: 1025 Howard St., HE 1-7070

DRINKING FOUNTAINS
HAWS DRINKING FAUCET CO.,
Berkeley: 1435 Fourth St., LA 5-3341

ELECTRICAL CONTRACTORS
COOPMAN ELECTRIC CO.
San Francisco: 85 - 14th St., MA 1-4438
ETS-HOKIN & GALVAN
San Francisco: 551 Mission St., EX 2-0432

ELECTRICAL CONTRACTORS (cont'd)
LEMOGE ELECTRIC CO.
San Francisco: 212 Clara St., DO 2-6010
LYNCH ELECTRIC CO.
San Francisco: 937 McAllister St., WI 5158
PACIFIC ELECTRIC & MECHANICAL CO.
San Francisco: Gough & Fell Sts., HE 1-5904

ELECTRIC HEATERS
WESIX ELECTRIC HEATER CO.
San Francisco: 390 First St., GA 1-2211

FIRE ESCAPES
MICHEL & PFEFFER IRON WORKS
South San Francisco: 212 Shaw Road, PLaza 5-8983

FIRE PROTECTION EQUIPMENT
FIRE PROTECTION PRODUCTS CO.
San Francisco: 1101-16th St., UN 1-2420
ETS-HOKIN & GALVAN
San Francisco: 551 Mission St., EX 2-0432
BARNARD ENGINEERING CO.
San Francisco: 35 Elmira St., JU 5-4642

FLOORS
Floor Tile
GLADDING McBEAN & CO.
San Francisco: Harrison at 9th St., UN 1-744
Los Angeles: 2901 Las Feliz Bldg., OL 2121
KRAFTILE CO.
Niles, Calif., Niles 3611

Resilient Floors
PETERSON-COBBY CO.
San Francisco: 218 Clara St., EX 2-8714
TURNER RESILIENT FLOORS CO.
San Francisco: 2280 Shafter Ave., AT 2-7720

FLOOR DRAINS
JOSAM PACIFIC COMPANY
San Francisco: 765 Folsom St., EX 2-3142

GAS VENTS
WM. WALLACE CO.
Belmont, Calif.

GENERAL CONTRACTORS
O. E. ANDERSON
San Jose: 1075 No. 10th St., CY 3-8844
BARRETT CONSTRUCTION CO.
San Francisco: 1800 Evans Ave., MI 7-9700
JOSEPH BETTANCOURT
South San Francisco: 125 So. Linden St., PL 5-9185
DINWIDDIE CONSTRUCTION CO.
San Francisco: Crocker Bldg., YU 6-2718
D. L. FAULL CONSTRUCTION CO.
Santa Rosa: 1236 Cleveland Ave.
HAAS & HAYNIE
San Francisco: 275 Pine St., DO 2-0678
HENDERSON CONSTRUCTION CO.
San Francisco: 33 Ritch St., GA 1-0856
JACKS & IRVINE
San Francisco: 620 Market St., YU 6-0511
G. P. W. JENSEN & SONS
San Francisco: 320 Market St., GA 1-2444
RALPH LARSEN & SON
San Francisco: 64 So. Park, YU 2-5682
LINDGREN & SWINERTON
San Francisco: 200 Bush St., GA 1-2980
MacDONALD, YOUNG & NELSON
San Francisco: 351 California St., YU 2-4700
MATTOCK CONSTRUCTION CO.
San Francisco: 220 Clara St., GA 1-5516
OLSEN CONSTRUCTION CO.
Santa Rosa: 125 Brookwood Ave., SR 2030
BEN ORTSKY
Cotati: Cypress Ave., Pet. 5-4383
PARKER, STEFFANS & PEARCE
San Mateo: 135 So. Park, EX 2-6639

RAPP, CHRISTENSEN & FOSTER
Santa Rosa: 705 Bennett Ave.
STOLTE, INC.
Oakland: 8451 San Leandro Ave., LO 2-4611
SWINERTON & WALBERG
San Francisco: 200 Bush St., GA 1-2980

FURNITURE—INSTITUTIONAL
GENERAL FIREPROOFING CO.
San Francisco: 1025 Howard St., HE 1-7070
Oakland: 332-19th St., GL 2-4280
Los Angeles: 1200 South Hope St., RI 7-7501

HEATING & VENTILATING
ATLAS HEATING & VENT. CO.
San Francisco: 557-4th St., DO 2-0377
E. C. BRAUN CO.
Berkeley: 2115 Fourth St., TH 5-2356
C. W. HALL
Santa Rosa: 1665 Sebastopol Rd., SR 6354
S. T. JOHNSON CO.
Oakland: 940 Arlington Ave., OL 2-6000
LOUIS V. KELLER
San Francisco: 289 Tehama St., JU 6-6252
L. J. KRUSE CO.
Oakland: 6247 College Ave., OL 2-8332
MALM METAL PRODUCTS
Santa Rosa: 724-2nd St., SR 454
JAS. A. NELSON CO.
San Francisco: 1375 Howard St., HE 1-0140
SCOTT COMPANY
Oakland: 1919 Market St., GL 1-1937
WESIX ELECTRIC HEATER CO.
San Francisco: 390 First St., GA 1-2211
Los Angeles: 530 W. 7th St., MI 8096

INSULATION WALL BOARD
PACIFIC CEMENT & AGGREGATES, INC.
San Francisco: 400 Alabama St., KL 2-1616

INTERCEPTING DEVICES
JOSAM PACIFIC CO.
San Francisco: 765 Folsom St., EX 2-3142

IRON—ORNAMENTAL
MICHEL & PFEFFER IRON WKS.
So. San Francisco, 212 Shaw Rd., PL 5-8983

LATHING & PLASTERING
ANGELO J. DANERI
San Francisco: 1433 Fairfax Ave., AT 8-1582
K-LATH CORP.
Alhambra: 909 So. Fremont St., Alhambra
A. E. KNOWLES CORP.
San Francisco: 3330 San Bruno Ave., JU 7-2091
G. H. & C. MARTINELLI
San Francisco: 174 Shotwell St., UN 3-6112
FREDERICK MEISWINKEL
San Francisco: 2155 Turk St., JO 7-7587
RHODES-JAMIESON LTD.
Oakland: 333-23rd Ave., KE 3-5225
PATRICK J. RUANE
San Francisco: 44 San Jose Ave., MI 7-6414

LIGHTING FIXTURES
SMOOT-HOLMAN COMPANY
Inglewood, Calif., OR 8-1217
San Francisco: 55 Mississippi St., MA 1-8474

LUMBER
CHRISTENSEN LUMBER CO.
San Francisco: Quint & Evans Ave., VA 4-5832
ART HOGAN LUMBER CO.
1701 Galvez Ave., ATwater 2-1157
MEAD CLARK LUMBER CO.
Santa Rosa: 3rd & Railroad
ROLANDO LUMBER CO.
San Francisco: 5th & Berry Sts., SU 1-6901
STERLING LUMBER CO.
Santa Rosa: 1129 College Ave., S. R. 82

MARBLE
JOS. MUSTO SONS-KEENAN CO.
San Francisco: 555 No. Point St., GR 4-6365
VERMONT MARBLE CO.
San Francisco: 6000-3rd St., VA 6-5024

MASONRY
BASALT ROCK CO.
Napa, Calif.
San Francisco: 260 Kearney St., GA 1-3758
WM. A. RAINEY & SON
San Francisco: 323 Clementina St., SU 1-0072
GEO. W. REED CO.
San Francisco: 1390 So. Van Ness Ave., AT 2-1226

METAL EXTERIOR WALLS
THE KAWNEER CO.
Berkeley: 930 Dwight Way, TH 5-8710

METAL FRAMING
UNISTRUT OF NORTHERN CALIFORNIA
Berkeley: 2547-9th St., TH 1-3031
Enterprise 1-2204

METAL GRATING
KLEMP METAL GRATING CORP.
Chicago, Ill.: 6601 So. Melvina St.

METAL LATH—EXPANDED
PACIFIC CEMENT & AGGREGATES, INC.
San Francisco: 400 Alabama St., KL 2-1616

METAL PARTITIONS
THE E. F. HAUSERMAN CO.
San Francisco: 485 Brannan St., YU 2-5477

METAL PRODUCTS
FORDERER CORNICE WORKS
San Francisco: 269 Potrero Ave., HE 1-4100

MILLWORK
CENTRAL MILL & CABINET CO.
San Francisco: 1595 Fairfax Ave., VA 4-7316
THE FINK & SCHINDLER CO.
San Francisco: 552 Brannan St., EX 2-1513
MULLEN MFG. CO.
San Francisco: 64 Rausch St., UN 1-5815
PACIFIC MFG. CO.
San Francisco: 16 Beale St., GA 1-7755
Santa Clara: 2610 The Alameda, S. C. 607
Los Angeles: 6820 McKinley Ave., TH 4156
SOUTH CITY LUMBER & SUPPLY CO.
So. San Francisco: Railroad & Spruce, PL 5-7085

OFFICE EQUIPMENT
GENERAL FIREPROOFING CO.
Los Angeles: 1200 South Hope St., RI 7-7501
San Francisco: 1025 Howard St., HE 1-7070
Oakland: 332-19th St., GL 2-4280

OIL BURNERS
S. T. JOHNSON CO.
Oakland: 940 Arlington Ave., GL 2-6000
San Francisco: 585 Potrero Ave., MA 1-2757
Philadelphia, Pa.: 401 North Broad St.

ORNAMENTAL IRON
MICHEL & PFEFFER IRON WORKS
So. San Francisco: 212 Shaw Rd., PL 5-8983

PAINTING
R. P. PAOLI & CO.
San Francisco: 2530 Lombard St., WE 1-1632
SINCLAIR PAINT CO.
San Francisco: 2112-15th St., HE 1-2196
D. ZELINSKY & SONS
San Francisco: 165 Groove St., MA 1-7400

PHOTOGRAPHS
Construction Progress
FRED ENGLISH
Belmont, Calif.: 1310 Old County Road, LY 1-0385

PLASTER
PACIFIC CEMENT & AGGREGATE INC.
San Francisco: 400 Alabama St., KL 2-1616

PLASTIC PRODUCTS
PLASTIC SALES & SERVICE
San Francisco: 409 Bryant St., DO 2-6433
WEST COAST INDUSTRIES
San Francisco: 3150-18th St., MA 1-5657

PLUMBING
BROADWAY PLUMBING CO.
San Francisco: 1790 Yosemite Ave., MI 8-4250
E. C. BRAUN CO.
Berkeley: 2115 Fourth St., TH 5-2356
C. W. HALL
Santa Rosa: 1665 Sebastopol Rd., SR 6354
HAWS DRINKING FAUCET CO.
Berkeley: 1435 Fourth St., LA 5-3341
JOSAM PACIFIC CO.
San Francisco: 765 Folsom St., EX 2-3143
LOUIS V. KELLER
San Francisco: 289 Tehama St., YU 6-6252
L. J. KRUSE CO.
Oakland: 6247 College Ave., OL 2-8332
JAS. A. NELSON CO.
San Francisco: 1375 Howard St., HE 1-0140
RODONI-BECKER CO., INC.
San Francisco: 455-10th St., MA 1-3662
SCOTT CO.
Oakland: 1919 Market St., GL 1-1937

POST PULLER
HOLLAND MFG. CO.
No. Sacramento: 1202 Dixieanne

PUMPING MACHINERY
SIMONDS MACHINERY CO.
San Francisco: 816 Folsom St., DO 2-6794

ROOFING
ANCHOR ROOFING CO.
San Francisco: 1671 Galvez Ave., VA 4-8140
ALTA ROOFING CO.
San Francisco: 1400 Egbert Ave., MI 7-2173
REGAL ROOFING CO.
San Francisco: 930 Innes Ave., VA 4-3261

ROOF SCUTTLES
THE BILCO CO.
New Haven, Conn.
Oakland: Geo. B. Schultz, 190 MacArthur Blvd.
Sacramento: Harry B. Ogle & Assoc., 1331 T St.
Fresno: Healey & Rapovich, 1703 Fulton St.
Reseda: Daniel Dunner, 6200 Alonzo Ave.

ROOF TRUSSES
EASYBOW ENGINEERING & RESEARCH CO.
Oakland: 13th & Wood Sts., GL 2-0805

SAFES
THE HERMANN SAFE CO.
San Francisco: 1699 Market St., UN 1-6644

SEWER PIPE
GLADDING, McBEAN & CO.
San Francisco: 9th & Harrison, UN 1-7400
Los Angeles: 2901 Los Feliz Blvd., OL 2121

SHEET METAL
MICHEL & PFEFFER IRON WORKS
So. San Francisco: 212 Shaw Rd., PL 5-8983

SOUND EQUIPMENT
STROMBERG-CARLSON CO.
San Francisco: 1805 Rollins Rd., Burlingame, OX 7-3630
Los Angeles: 5414 York Blvd., CL 7-3939

SPRINKLERS
BARNARD ENGINEERING CO.
San Francisco: 35 Elmira St., JU 5-4642

STEEL—STRUCTURAL & REINFORCING
COLUMBIA-GENEVA DIV., U. S. STEEL CORP.
San Francisco: Russ Bldg., SU 1-2500
Los Angeles: 2087 E. Slauson, LA 1171
Portland, Ore.: 2345 N.W. Nicolai, BE 7261
Seattle, Wn.: 1331-3rd Ave. Bldg., MA 1972
Salt Lake City, Utah: Walker Bank Bldg., SL 3-6733
HERRICK IRON WORKS
Oakland 18th & Campbell, GL 1-1767
INDEPENDENT IRON WORKS, INC.
Oakland: 780 Pine St., TE 2-0160
JUDSON PACIFIC MURPHY CORP.
Emeryville: 4300 Eastshore Highway, OL 3-1717
REPUBLIC STEEL CORP.
San Francisco: 116 New Montgomery St., GA 1-0977
Los Angeles: Edison Bldg.
Seattle: White-Henry Stuart Bldg.
Salt Lake City: Walker Bank Bldg.
Denver: Continental Oil Bldg.
SOULE STEEL CO.
San Francisco: 1750 Army St., VA 4-4141

STEEL FORMS
STEELFORM CONTRACTING CO.
San Francisco: 666 Harrison St., DO 2-5582

SWIMMING POOLS
SIERRA MFG. CO.
Walnut Creek, Calif.: 1719 Mt. Diablo Blvd.

SWIMMING POOL FITTINGS
JOSAM PACIFIC CO.
San Francisco: 765 Folsom St., EX 2-3143

TESTING LABORATORIES (ENGINEERS & CHEMISTS)
ABBOT A. HANKS, INC.
San Francisco: 624 Sacramento St., GA 1-1697
ROBERT W. HUNT COMPANY
San Francisco: 500 Iowa, MI 7-0224
Los Angeles: 3050 E. Slauson, JE 9131
Chicago, New York, Pittsburgh
PITTSBURGH TESTING LABORATORY
San Francisco: 651 Howard St., EX 2-1747

TILE—CLAY & WALL
GLADDING McBEAN & CO.
San Francisco: 9th & Harrison Sts., UN 1-7400
Los Angeles: 2901 Los Feliz Blvd., OL 2121
Portland: 110 S.E. Main St., EA 6179
Seattle: 945 Elliott Ave. West, GA 0330
Spokane: 1102 No. Monroe St., BR 3259
KRAFTILE CO.
Niles, Calif.: Niles 3611
San Francisco: 50 Hawthorne St., DO 2-3780
Los Angeles: 406 So. Main St., MA 7241

TILE—TERRAZZO
NATIONAL TILE & TERRAZZO CO.
San Francisco: 198 Mississippi St., UN 1-0273

TIMBER—TREATED
J. H. BAXTER CO.
San Francisco: 200 Bush St., YU 2-0200
Los Angeles: 3450 Wilshire Blvd., DU 8-9591

TIMBER TRUSSES
EASYBOW ENGINEERING & RESEARCH CO.
Oakland: 13th & Wood Sts., GL 2-0805

TRUCKING
PASSETTI TRUCKING CO.
San Francisco: 264 Clementina St., GA 1-5297

UNDERPINNING & SHORING
D. J. & T. SULLIVAN
San Francisco: 1942 Folsom St., MA 1-1545

WALL PAPER
WALLPAPERS, INC.
Oakland: 384 Grand Ave., GL 2-0451

WAREHOUSE AND STORAGE EQUIPMENT AND SHELVING
GENERAL FIREPROOFING CO.
Los Angeles: 1200 South Hope St., RI 7-7501
San Francisco: 1025 Howard St., HE 1-7070
Oakland: 332-19th St., GL 2-4280

WATERPROOFING MATERIALS
CONRAD SOVIG CO.
San Francisco: 875 Bryant St., HE 1-1345

WATERSTOPS (P.V.C.)
TECON PRODUCTS, LTD.
Vancouver, B.C.: 681 E. Hastings St.
Seattle: 304 So. Alaskan Way

WINDOW SHADES
SHADES, INC.
San Francisco: 80 Tehama St., DO 2-7092

CONSTRUCTION INDUSTRY WAGE RATES

Table 1 has been prepared by the State of California, Department of Industrial Relations, Division of Labor Statistics and Research. The rates are the union hourly wage rates established by collective bargaining as of January 2, 1958, as reported by reliable sources.

TABLE 1—UNION HOURLY WAGE RATES, CONSTRUCTION INDUSTRY, CALIFORNIA

Following are the hourly rates of compensation established by collective bargaining, reported as of January 2, 1958 or later

CRAFT	San Francisco	Alameda	Contra Costa	Fresno	Sacramento	San Joaquin	Santa Clara	Solano	Los Angeles	San Bernardino	San Diego	Santa Barbara	Kern
ASBESTOS WORKER	$3.70	$3.70	$3.70	$3.70	$3.70	$3.70	$3.70	$3.70	$3.70	$3.70	$3.70	$3.70	$3.70
BOILERMAKER	3.675	3.675	3.675	3.675	3.675	3.675	3.675	3.675	3.675	3.675	3.675	3.675	3.675
BRICKLAYER	3.95	3.75	3.75	3.75	3.80	3.75	3.875	3.95	3.80	3.90	3.75		3.85
BRICKLAYER HODCARRIER	3.15	3.15	3.15	2.90	3.10	2.90	3.00	3.10	2.75	2.75	2.75		2.75
CARPENTER	3.175	3.175	3.225	3.225	3.225	3.225	3.225	3.225	3.225	3.225	3.225	3.225	3.225
CEMENT MASON	3.22	3.22	3.22	3.22	3.22	3.22	3.22	3.22	3.15	3.15	3.25	3.15	3.15
ELECTRICIAN	3.936A	3.936A	3.936A		3.94A	3.50	4.03A	3.666A	3.90A	3.90A	3.90	3.85A	3.70
GLAZIER	3.09	3.09	3.09	3.135	3.055	3.055	3.09	3.09	3.105	3.105	3.03	3.105	3.135
IRON WORKER													
ORNAMENTAL	3.625	3.625	3.625	3.625	3.625	3.625	3.625	3.625	3.625	3.625	3.625	3.625	3.625
REINFORCING	3.375	3.375	3.375	3.375	3.375	3.375	3.375	3.375	3.375	3.375	3.375	3.375	3.375
STRUCTURAL	3.625	3.625	3.625	3.625	3.625	3.625	3.625	3.625	3.625	3.625	3.625	3.625	3.625
LABORER, GENERAL OR CONSTRUCTION	2.505	2.505	2.505	2.505	2.505	2.505	2.505	2.505	2.50	2.50	2.48	2.50	2.50
LATHER	3.4375	3.84	3.84	3.45	3.60B	3.40C	3.60D	3.50E	3.9375		3.725	3.625F	
OPERATING ENGINEER													
Concrete mixer (up to 1 yard)	2.89	2.89	2.89	2.89	2.89	2.89	2.89	2.89					
Concrete mixer operator—Skip Type									2.96	2.96	2.96	2.96	2.96
Elevator Hoist Operator									3.19	3.19	3.19	3.19	3.19
Material Hoist (1 drum)	3.19	3.19	3.19	3.19	3.19	3.19	3.19	3.19					
Tractor Operator	3.33	3.33	3.33	3.33	3.33	3.33	3.33	3.33	3.47	3.47	3.47	3.47	3.47
PAINTER													
Brush	3.20	3.20	3.20	3.13	3.325	3.175	3.20	3.20	3.26a	3.25	3.19	3.13H	3.10
Spray	3.20	3.20	3.20	3.38	3.575	3.325	3.20	3.20	3.51a	3.50	3.74	3.38H	3.35
PILEDRIVERMAN	3.305	3.305	3.305	3.305	3.305	3.305	3.305	3.305	3.355	3.355		3.395	3.355
PLASTERER	3.69	3.545	3.545	3.35	3.60B	3.55C	3.58	3.50	3.9375	3.9375	3.725		
PLASTERER HODCARRIER	3.25	3.42	3.42	3.10	3.10	3.00C	3.20	3.15	3.6875	3.5625	3.475	3.50	3.6875
PLUMBER	3.67		3.935I	3.80J	3.70	3.80J	3.60	3.675	3.70	3.70	3.70	3.70	3.375
ROOFER	3.35	3.35	3.35	3.20	3.25	3.35	3.35	3.10K	3.20L	3.25	3.10	3.30	3.775
SHEET METAL WORKER	3.45	3.45	3.45	3.425	3.45	3.465	3.46	3.325	3.50	3.50	3.45	3.55	3.10
STEAMFITTER	3.67	3.96	3.96	3.80J	3.70	3.80J	3.60	3.675	3.70	3.70	3.70	3.70	3.775
TRUCK DRIVER—													
Dump Trucks under 4 yards	2.55	2.55	2.55	2.55	2.55	2.55	2.55	2.55	2.63	2.63	2.63	2.63	2.63
TILE SETTER	3.275	3.275	3.275	3.375	3.28	3.30	3.275	3.275	3.36	3.60	3.375	3.36	

A Includes 4% vacation allowance.
B Includes 5c hour for industry promotion and 5c hour for vacation fund.
C ½% withheld for industry promotion.
D 1½c withheld for industry promotion.
E Includes 5c hour for industry promotion and 5c hour for vacation fund. Hourly rate for part of county adjacent to Sacramento County is $3.60.
F Northern part of County: $3.75.

a Pomona Area: Brush $3.25; Spray $3.50.
H Southern half of County: Brush $3.28; Spray $3.28.
I Includes 30c hour for vacation pay.
J Includes 15c hour which local union may elect to use for vacation purposes.
K Includes 10c hour for vacation fund.
L Includes 10c hour savings fund wage.

ATTENTION: The above tabulation has been prepared by the State of California, Department of Industrial Relations, Division of Labor Statistics and Research, and represents data reported by building trades councils, union locals, contractor organizations, and other reliable sources. The above rates do not include any payments to funds for health and welfare, pensions, vacations, industry promotion, apprentice training, etc., except as shown in the footnotes.

CONSTRUCTION INDUSTRY WAGE RATES — TABLE 2

Employer Contributions to Health and Welfare, Pension, Vacation and Other Funds
California Union Contracts, Construction Industry

(Revised March, 1957)

CRAFT	San Francisco	Fresno	Sacramento	San Joaquin	Santa Clara	Los Angeles	San Bernardino	San Diego
ASBESTOS WORKER	.10 W .11 hr. V	.10 W .11 hr. V	.10 W .11 hr. V	.10 W .11 hr. V	.10 W .11 hr. V	.10 W	.10 W	.10 W
BRICKLAYER	.15 W .14 P .05 hr. V		.15 W		.15 W			
			.10 P					
BRICKLAYER HODCARRIER	.10 W .10 P .10 V	.10 W	.10 W	.10 W	.10 W	.075 W	.075 W	.075 W
CARPENTER	.10 W .10 hr. V	.10 W	.10 W	.10 W	.10 W	.10 W	.10 W	.10 W
CEMENT MASON	.10 W	.10 W	.10 W	.10 W	.10 W	.10 W	.10 W	.10 W
ELECTRICAL WORKER	.10 W 1% P 4% V	.10 W 1% P 4% V	.075 W 1% P	.075 W 1% P 4% V	1% P	1% P	1% P	.10 W 1% P
GLAZIER	.075 W .085 V	.075 W 40 hr. V	.075 W .05 V	.075 W .05 V	.075 W .085 V	.075 W 40 hr. V	.075 W 40 hr. V	.075 W 40 hr. V
IRONWORKER: REINFORCING	.10 W	.10 W	.10 W	.10 W	.10 W	.10 W	.10 W	.10 W
STRUCTURAL	.10 W	.10 W	.10 W	.10 W	.10 W	.10 W	.10 W	.10 W
LABORER, GENERAL	.10 W	.10 W	.10 W	.10 W	.10 W	.075 W	.075 W	.075 W
LATHER	.60 day W .70 day V		.10 W	.10 W	.075 W .05 V	.90 day W	.70 day W	.10 W
OPERATING ENGINEER								
TRACTOR OPERATOR (MIN.)	.10 W	.10 W	.10 W	.10 W	.10 W	.10 W	.10 W	.10 W
POWER SHOVEL OP. (MIN.)	.10 W	.10 W	.10 W	.10 W	.10 W	.10 W	.10 W	.10 W
PAINTER, BRUSH	.095 W	.08 W	.075 W	.10 W	.095 W .07 V	.085 W	.10 W	.09 W
PLASTERER	.10 W .10 V	.10 W	.10 W	.10 W	.10 W .15 V	.10 W	.90 day W	.10 W
PLUMBER	.10 W .10 V	.15 W .10 P	.10 W .10 P .125 V	.10 W	.10 W .10 P .125 V	.10 W	.90 day W	.10 W
ROOFER	.10 W .10 V	.10 W	.10 W .10 V	.10 W	.075 W .10 V	.085 W	.10 W	.075 W
SHEET METAL WORKER	.075 W 4% V	.075 W 7 day V	.075 W .10 V	.075 W .12 V	.075 W 4% V	.085 W .10 V	.085 W .10 V	.085 W 5 day V
TILE SETTER	.075 W .09 V				.075 W .09 V	.025 W .06 V		

ATTENTION: The above tabulation has been prepared and compiled from the available data reported by building trades councils, union locals, contractor organizations and other reliable sources. The table was prepared from incomplete data; where no employer contributions are specified, it does not necessarily mean that none are required by the union contract.

The type of supplement is indicated by the following symbols: W—Health and Welfare; P—Pensions; V—Vacations; A—Apprentice training fund; Adm—Administration fund; JIB—Joint Industry Board; Prom—Promotion fund.

CONSTRUCTION CONTRACTS AWARDED AND MISCELLANEOUS PERSONNEL DATA

STORY BLDG., Rednodo Beach, Los Angeles county. Ward-Richards Inc., Redondo Beach, owner. Frame and stucco and stone veneer store building, 3880 sq. ft. area; composition roof, concrete slab, drywall interior, plumbing, electrical, fixed glass, asphalt paving. ARCHITECT: Smith & Gray, Architects and Engineers, 1820 S. Elena Ave., Redondo Beach. GENERAL CONTRACTOR: Joe Czarske, 515 Camino del Campo, Redondo Beach.

RECREATIONAL FACILITIES, Washington Park, Pomona, Los Angeles county. Pomona City Council, owner. Project will involve lighted basketball courts, picnic shelter, tot lot, revamping of blacktop and protected fencing at ball diamond, remodel and add to administration center, automatic sprinkler system, asphalt concrete paving—$31,493. ARCHITECTS: Associated Architects Amos Randall and Don Yinger, 341 W. Orange Grove Ave., Pomona. GENERAL CONTRACTOR: Claremont Contractors, 911 E. Foothill Blvd., Claremont.

MEMORIAL CHAPEL, Los Angeles, Hillside Memorial Park, owner. Built-up roof, concrete slab floor, perimeter heating and cooling, plumbing and electrical work, acoustical plaster ceilings, laminated arches, aluminum front material, compacted fill and millwork: 4000 sq. ft. area. ARCHITECT: Robert Kliegman, 8858 Melrose Ave., Los Angeles. GENERAL CONTRACTOR: Chotiner & Gumbiner, Inc., 5316 Venice Blvd., Los Angeles 19.

INDUSTRIAL LAUNDRY, South San Francisco, San Mateo county. Acme Towel Supply Co., San Francisco, owner. 1-Story pre-cast concrete construction, timber roof; 15,000 sq. ft. area—$82,972. ARCHITECT: Cline, Zerkle & Agee, 1810 6th St., Berkeley. GENERAL CONTRACTOR: A. S. Holmes & Son, Inc., 9300 G St. Oakland.

CAFE BLDG., Los Angeles. Junior Realty Company, Los Angeles, owner. 2-story frame and stucco addition to present Cafe building, composition roofing, interior drywall, acoustical plaster ceilings, terrazzo cement and linoleum floors, slab and glass and metal doors, metal sash partitions, pipe columns, wood stairs and metal railings, 36 x 55 ft. — $12,000. ARCHITECT: Kenneth T. Thompson, 9278 Santa Monica, Beverly Hills. GENERAL CONTRACTOR: Aetna Construction Co., 1308 Shatto St., Los Angeles.

HOSPITAL ADD'N, Burlingame, San Mateo County Peninsula Hospital, owner. Project comprises extensions on ground and 1st floor, and the addition of a 5th, 6th, 7th, and 8th floors to existing 4-story building — $2,906,190. ARCHITECT:

Stone, Mulloy, Marraccini & Patterson, 536 Mission St., San Francisco. STRUCTURAL ENGINEER: Smith & Moorehead, 709 Mission St., San Francisco. MECHANICAL & ELECTRICAL ENGINEERS: Buonaccorsi & Murray, 350 Mission St., San Francisco. GENERAL CONTRACTOR: Williams & Burrows, 500 Harbor Blvd, Belmont.

ATHLETIC FIELD, Flood lights, High School, Needles, San Bernardino county. Needles Union High School District, owner. Work consists of installation of floodlighting equipment at High School athletic field — $38,937. STRUCTURAL ENGINEER: H. C. Whittlesey, 525 N. Normandie Ave., Los Angeles. ELECTRICAL ENGINEER: W. E. Nance, 229 Michigan St., Redlands. GENERAL CONTRACTOR: R. D. Feil, 2839 June St., San Bernardino.

APARTMENT, Lafayette, Contra Costa county. 45-unit apartment building, wood frame and stucco construction, built-up roof. ARCHITECT: James Lucas, 61 Moraga Highway, Orinda. GENERAL CONTRACTOR: Don Lawrie, 3680 Mt. Diablo Blvd., Lafayette.

LIFE SCIENCE BLDG, State College, Tempe, Arizona. Regents of the University and State College of Arizona, Tempe, owner. Life Science building on the Arizona State College campus, 3-stories containing 88,694 sq. ft. of area; structural steel and masonry construction—$943,000. ARCHITECT: Kemper Goodwin, 115 E. 5th St, Tempe, Arizona. GENERAL CONTRACTOR: T G K Construction Co, 2750 W. McDowell Rd, Phoenix, Ariz.

ADMINISTRATION HEADQUARTERS, Oakland, Alameda county. Children's Home Society of Northern California, Oakland, owner. 1-story concrete block front, batten and tile roof; 12,200 sq. ft. area—$181,899. ARCHITECT: Warnecke & Warnecke, Financial Center Bldg, Oakland. GENERAL CONTRACTOR: Marvin E. Collins, 635 San Diego St, El Cerrito.

GOLF CLUB HOUSE, Camarillo, Ventura county. Las Posas Country Club, owner. Contains 17,000 sq. ft.; frame construction, stone and siding exterior, built-up roof, slab and wood floors, floor covering, metal sash, metal sliding doors, toilets, plaster and wood paneling, acoustical work, dining room, kitchen, toilet, electrical, heating and ventilating—$200,000. ARCHITECT: Fish & Wilde, 20 S.

Ash St, Ventura. GENERAL CONTRACTOR: Walter Scholtz Const. Co, 2788 E. Main St, Ventura.

SANITARIUM, Spottswood, Los Gatos, Santa Clara county. Spottswood Sanitarium-Resthome, Inc., Los Gatos, owner. Work consists of construction of 2-bedwards, dayroom, offices and waiting rooms, nurses lounge and isolation room — $106,984. ARCHITECT: Higgins & Root, 220 Meridian Rd, San Jose. GENERAL CONTRACTOR: Hilding Hernstedt, 12975 Blossom Rd, San Jose.

KAISER CENTER, office bldg, Oakland, Alameda county. Henry J. Kaiser Co, Oakland, owner. 25-story office building will contain 850,000 sq. ft. area; reinforced concrete construction, structural steel, aluminum and glass ceilings, elevators, escalators, air conditioning, acoustical and related work—$3,831,000. ARCHITECT: Welton Becket & Associates, 153 Maiden Lane, San Francisco. GENERAL CONTRACTOR: Robert E. McKee, Inc., 4700 San Fernando Rd., West Los Angeles.

DEPARTMENT STORE, Fresno, Pacific Mutual Life Ins. Co., Fresno, owner. 2-Story reinforced concrete construction. 110,000 sq. ft. area; exterior of ceramic tile facing with wood trim, color-lighted interior, heating and air conditioning, off-street parking for 1000 automobiles—$1,750,000. ARCHITECT: Walter Wagner & Partners, Architects and Engineers, 1830 Van Ness, Fresno.

COUNTY HOSPITAL, San Luis Obispo. County of San Luis Obispo owner. Work consists of an addition to the existing structures; Type 1 construction, 3-story addition and three 1-story buildings; rehabilitation of existing hospital buildings, kitchen equipment, laboratory equipment, elevator, air conditioning, fire alarm system, intercom system and some site work—$1,155,700. ARCHITECT: John R. Ross, 1149 Marsh St, San Luis Obispo. GENERAL CONTRACTOR: Maino Const. Co., 2238 S. Broad St., San Luis Obispo.

2-WAREHOUSE BLDGS, North Hollywood, Los Angeles county. Blue Star Mines, Ltd., North Hollywood, owner. Reinforced brick warehouse and offices; 10,00 and 60,000 sq. ft. in area, glued tied arches, composition roofing, concrete slab, plumbing, electrical, sheet metal, some asphalt paving. ENGINEER: David T. Witherly, 7233 Beverly Blvd. Los Angeles. GENERAL CONTRACTOR: Carpenter & Smallwood, 3838 W. Santa Barbara Ave., Los Angeles.

ELKS LODGE, remodel, Eureka, Humboldt county. Eureka Elks Club, owner. Work includes remodel of 1st and 2nd floors; ground floor remodeled into dining and recreation area—$168,492. ARCHITECT: Gerald D. Matson, 537 G. St., Eureka. GENERAL CONTRACTOR: Beacom Const. Co, P.O. Box 297, Fortuna.

CHAPEL & Educational Wing, Travis Air Force Base, Solano county. U. S. Army Engineer Post, Sacramento, owner. Project comprises construction of a new wing to the existing building to serve as a Chapel and for educational activities—$72,099. GENERAL CONTRACTOR: Vaca Const. Co., 147 Brown St., Vacaville.

STORE & OFFICE, Studio City, Los Angeles county. Gladys L. Carr, North Hollywood, owner. 2-story concrete block store and office building; 4500 sq. ft. area,

built-up composition roof, metal sash, concrete slab floor, interior plaster, acoustical ceiling, plate glass, toilets, store doors—$30,000. ENGINEERS: Campbell & Farrell, 4155 Bellaire Ave, Studio City. GENERAL CONTRACTOR: M. Lococo, 711 W. Palm, El Segundo.

ELEMENTARY SCHOOL, Los Ranchos, San Luis Obispo Uuion School District, owner. Wood frame construction to provide facilities for administration unit, 3-classrooms, teachers lounge, caretakers room, toilets, and some site work—896. ARCHITECT: Falk & Booth, 16 Beale St, San Francisco. GENERAL CONTRACTOR: Eugene Jackson, 660 Caudill St, San Luis Obispo.

RESTAURANT, South Gate, Los Angeles county. Al Lee, South Gate, owner. 1-story, frame and stucco restaurant building; 30 x 50 ft. in area. Composition roof, plate glass windows, concrete slab floor partially covered with asphalt tile, fluorescent lighting, restrooms, asphalt concrete paving. ENGINEER: Jules A. Juge, Jr., 3831 W. 187th St., Torrance. GENERAL CONTRACTOR: Olin Homes, Inc., 817 W. Foothill Blvd., Claremont.

TELEPHONE BLDG, Additions, Costa Mesa, Orange County. Pacific Tel & Tel, Los Angeles, owner. 2-story and basement addition to telephone building in Costa Mesa; reinforced concrete and masonry, built-up roofing, slab and asphalt tile floors, steel sash, air conditioning, heating, electrical, plumbing, ceramic tile, plastering and acoustic tile. ARCHITECT: Woodford & Bernard, 410 S. La Brea Ave, Los Angeles. GENERAL CONTRACTOR: Walter C. Markel, 915 Riviera Dr, Santa Ana.

PROFESSIONAL BLDG, Burbank, Los Angeles county. E. G. Chapman, Burbank, owner. Frame and stucco professional building, composition roof, concrete slab floor, vinyl and carpet floor covering, interior plaster, aluminum sash, plate glass, air conditioning, masonry veneer, ceramic tile — $45,000. DESIGNER: Zemke & Hartfelder, Don A. Hartfelder, 616 E. Glenoaks Blvd, Glendale. GENERAL CONTRACTOR: Carl M. King, 641 N. Myers St, Burbank.

CITY HALL, additions, Vallejo, Solano county. City of Vallejo, owner. Work consists of a wood frame and stucco addition to the City Hall, aluminum sash, composi-

tion roofing — $9,348. ARCHITECT: Schactman & Velikonia, 333 Maryland Ave., Vallejo. GENERAL CONTRACTOR: E. E. Clark, 737 Valle Vista, Vallejo.

CHURCH, Westchester, Los Angeles county. Westchester Methodist Church, owner. Reinforced pre-cast concrete and brick church building, composition roof, glass, glazing, finish harware, sheet metal, metal doors and windows, structural and miscellaneous metal, plastering, insulation, acoustical, floor covering, tile and marble work, plumbing, heating and ventilating, some ground improvements — $217,700. ARCHITECT: Walter R. Hagedohm, 2033 W. 7th St., Los Angeles. GENERAL CONTRACTOR: Davies-Keusder & Brown, 4915 Exposition Blvd., Los Angeles.

CAFETERIA BLDG., grade school, Gonzales, Monterey county. Gonzales Union Elementary School District, owner. 1-Story structural steel frame construction with complete cafeteria equipment and facilities—$124,600. ARCHITECT: Stanton, Keeble & Rhoda, 6th and Dolores, Carmel. GENERAL CONTRACTOR: Tombleson & Huck, 651 S. Sanborn Rd., Salinas.

MARKET, Lakewood, Los Angeles county. Iowa Pork Shops, Lakewood, owner. Tilt-up concrete market building, 22,100 sq. ft. area, tapered steel girders, composition roof, plywood roof deck, concrete slab and asphalt tile floors, suspended acoustical tile ceilings, plumbing, electrical, air conditioning, steel roll-up doors, metal doors, automatic entrance doors, insulation, mosaic tile, drywall, plastic finished panels, asphalt paving. ENGINEERS: Novikoff Engineers, 3858 W. Santa Barbara Ave., Los Angeles. GENERAL CONTRACTOR: Ernest W. Hahn Inc., 219 S. Hawthorne, Lakewood.

TACK ROOMS, Fairgrounds, Vallejo, Solano county. County of Solano, owner. Work includes construction of a complete new tack room at the Solano County Fairgrounds near Vallejo at a cost of $23,620. ARCHITECT: Bond & Dougherty, Architects and Engineers, 2118 Sacramento St., Vallejo. GENERAL CONTRACTOR: Val Nap Builders, 1402 Ohio St., Vallejo.

ELEMENTARY SCHOOL, Mohave, Kern county. Mohave Unified School District, owner. Construction of a new school to include 6-classrooms, toilets and all school building facilities—$100,700. ARCHITECT: Stuhr and Hicks, 924 Truxtun Ave., Bakersfield. GENERAL CONTRACTOR: Staiger Const. Co., P.O. Box 488, Fresno.

JR. HIGH SCHOOL, Thomas A. Edison, Fresno. Fresno Unified School District, owner. Wood frame and stucco construction, concrete floors, asbestos shingle roof; complete facilities for 15-classrooms, boy's and girl's locker rooms, toilet rooms—$619,554. ARCHITECT: Allen Lew, Fulton-Fresno Bldg., Fresno. GENERAL CONTRACTOR: R. G. Fisher Co., P.O. Box 4081, Fresno.

HOSPITAL ADD'N, Santa Ana, Orange county. Santa Ana Community Hospital, owner. Additions and alterations to present hospital building including 2-story maternity wing, Type 1, reinforced concrete, concrete roof and floor slabs, metal sash, heating and ventilating, resilient flooring,

elevator, steel decking, hollow metal doors — $498,852. ARCHITECT: Walker, Kalionzes & Klingerman, 488 S. San Vicente Blvd., Los Angeles. GENERAL CONTRACTOR: William D. Greschner Co., 1108 E. Washington, Santa Ana.

RECREATION CENTER, Hayward, Alameda county. Hayward Area Park and Recreation District, owner. Concrete block construction, 1200 sq. ft. of area — $14,526. ARCHITECT: Wahamaki & Corey, 1065 A St., Hayward. GENERAL CONTRACTOR: D. Ross McMellan Const. Co., 1737 Fairview Ave., Hayward.

PAROCHIAL SCHOOL, Holy Innocence Parish, Long Beach, Los Angeles county. Roman Catholic Archbishop of Los Angeles, owner. 8-Classroom school building, 12,000 sq. ft. area, reinforced concrete and masonry construction, interior plaster and acoustic work, electrical and plumbing. ARCHITECT: Verge & Clatworthy, 4342 Eagle Rock Blvd., Los Angeles. GENERAL CONTRACTOR: Hight Construction Co., 4344 Eagle Rock Blvd., Los Angeles.

FELLOWSHIP HALL, Palo Alto, Santa Clara county. Congregational Church, Palo Alto, owner. 1-Story, wood frame construction, redwood siding, built-up roof, some concrete block and brickwork—$72,377. ARCHITECT: White & Hermann, 75 Castle St., San Francisco. GENERAL CONTRACTOR: Wells P. Goodenough, P.O. Box 120, Palo Alto.

STORE BLDG., Reseda, Los Angeles county. Earl Cohler, Sherman Oaks, owner. Frame and stucco 7-unit store building, 72x110 ft., composition roof, evaporative coolers, tapered steel beams, forced air heating, jalousie sash, plate glass, aluminum facia, pipe columns, asphalt tile flooring, concrete slab, plater interior, acoustical plaster ceiling, toilets, concrete block fence, asphaltic concrete paving — $48,000. ARCHITECT: A. J. Arany, 14611 Ventura Blvd., Sherman Oaks. GENERAL CONTRACTOR: A. Glenn Hoiby, 16045 Royal Oak Rd., Encino.

SHASTA COLLEGE, Redding, Shasta county. Shasta Union High School and Jr. College District, Redding, owner. Work consists of constructing an auto shop building at the Shasta College campus, and a lunch shelter addition to the Central Valley High School; 1 Story tilt-up con-

crete panels on concrete foundation for the auto shop and a large concrete floored area with wood frame and roofed with entrances into existing buildings for lunch shelter; also some storage rooms at high school—$1,385,000. ARCHITECT: Satterlee & Tomich, 1521 I St., Sacramento. GENERAL CONTRACTOR: Singleton Const. Co., P.O. Box 271, Eureka.

OFFICE BLDG., North Hollywood, Los Angeles county. Richard Modiano, North Hollywood, owner. Frame and stucco office building, 75x60 ft., composition roof, air conditioning, concrete slab, asphalt tile, terrazzo flooring, interior plaster, acoustical plaster, wood paneling, toilets, asphaltic concrete paving—$70,000. ARCHITECT: Murray Siegel, 6500 Mary Ellen Ave., Van Nuys. GENERAL CONTRACTOR: Richard Modiano, 5437 Laurel Canyon, North Hollywood.

IN THE NEWS

MEDICAL-DENTAL BUILDING FOR SAN BERNARDINO

Plans are being prepared by Michael J. Murphy, 427 13th St., San Bernardino, for construction of a 2-story, fourteen-unit medical-dental building in San Bernardino for Tom Johnson.

Construction will be frame and stucco and involves a 13,370 sq. ft. floor area; built-up rock roof, plate glass and aluminum front, sliding aluminum patio doors, rock veneer, individual winter and summer air conditioning units, acoustical tile ceiling, plaster interior, vinyl floors, wood

ALBERT L. REEVES IS NAMED VICE PRESIDENT UTAH CONSTRUCTION CO.

Albert L. Reeves has been named vice-president of Utah Construction Company, according to a recent announcement by Allen D. Christensen, president and general manager of the firm.

His duties will include general administration and contract negotiations for the international engineering and contracting firm.

Reeves is a partner in the Washington, D.C. law firm of Cummings, Sellers, Reeves, Conner and Kendall and was a member of the 80th U.S. Congress as Representative of the 5th Missouri District from 1947 to 1949.

AMADOR COUNTY HOSPITAL WILL BE EXPANDED

Architects Fingado & Kern of 2910 Telegraph Avenue, Oakland, are completing drawings for construction of a 40-bed addition to the Amador County Hospital in Jackson.

Of concrete and frame construction the new facilities will also provide a storage area, small laundry unit, 4 psychiatric rooms, a recreation area and a new nursing home.

ARCHITECT SELECTED FOR SCHOOL

Architects Anderson, Hyde & Anderson, Jr., Bank of America Bldg., Oakland, have been commissioned by the Oakland Unified School District to draft plans and specifications for construction of a new Castlemont High School building.

Estimate cost of the project is $3,433,-000.

SAN DIEGO'S LARGEST APARTMENT HOUSE PROJECT STARTED

The largest apartment project ever to be built in San Diego county, a tremendous $13,000,000 development comprising 1062 family units, has been started at Point Loma.

Occupying a 58-acre area south of West Loma Blvd., Loma Palisades, as the development will be known, will consist almost entirely of two-story garden apartments with downstairs living area, two or three bedrooms upstairs, and private patios. Ten

swimming pools and children's playgrounds, as well as ten laundry areas and other community facilities, will also be provided, and the site will be landscaped with ample parking facilities for a community the size of an average American town.

The buildings have been designed by the architectural firm of Palmer and Krisel, AIA, Los Angeles, who also did the site planing and landscaping.

VETERANS MEMORIAL PETALUMA

Architect J. Clarence Felciano, 4010 Montecito, Santa Rosa, is completing plans and specifications for construction of a $500,000 Veterans Memorial Building in Petaluma for the Sonoma County board of supervisors.

The building will include an auditorium, banquet hall, two meeting halls, kitchen, showers, lockers and toilet facilities.

AUTOMATIC SPRAY HUMIDIFIER MADE AVAILABLE NOW

An automatic spray humidifier that fires all forced air heating systems has been announced by John W. Norris, president of Lennox Industries, Inc.

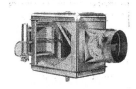

This new Lennox "Humidispray" will evaporate up to 18 gallons per day, and automatically meter proper amount of humidity according to the severity of weather. A manual control regulates flow of air through fine spray of water so exact humidity level can be determined and evenly maintained. Unevaporated droplets of water from spray are trapped by filter pad partially visible in above illustration, and drain downward into the bottom tray where a hose or tubing carries excess water away. For complete data, inquire Lennox Industries, Inc., c/o 39 S. La Salle St., Chicago 3. Theo. R. Sills & Co.

NEW COLFAX HIGH SCHOOL PLANS READY

Architect Lawrence G. Thompson, 125 W. 3rd St., Chico, has completed plans for construction of a new wood frame High School building in Colfax, for the Placer Union High School District of Colfax.

The new facilities will comprise an administration unit, classrooms, multi-use unit, kitchen, cafeteria, shops, library, gymnasium with boys and girls locker and shower rooms, and toilets. Estimated cost of the work is $700,000.

SAN DIEGO PROFESSIONAL ENGINEERS REJECT GUILD OFFER

Professional engineers and technical employees of the San Diego Gas & Electric Company voted against union representation in a recent NLRB-conducted ballot. In separate voting groups, among four professional employees, three voted against

representation by the San Diego Chapter, Engineers and Architects Association. In the technician unit the vote was 115 against and 49 for representation by the union.

The Engineers and Architects Association, with six West Coast chapters, is one of the spearheads in the formation of a new federation of engineering and technician unions, known as the Engineers and Scientists Guild.

NEW CLASSROOM BUILDING FOR U. OF NEVADA

Architects Walter Zick and Harris Sharp, 1806 S. Main Street, Las Vegas, Nevada, are preparing working drawings for construction of a 2-story classroom building at the University of Nevada campus site in Las Vegas, for the University of Nevada, Reno.

The new structure will contain 11 classrooms, library, offices, shower and locker rooms, 60x260 ft.; construction will be lift-slab type, with some structural steel, reinforced concrete slab floors, masonry filler walls, composition roof, metal sash, insulation, ceramic tile work, plastering, sheet metal, plumbing, refrigeration air conditioning, estimated cost is $425,000.

GENE WIECZOREK ELECTED PRESIDENT CONSTRUCTION INSPECTORS ASSOCIATION

Eugene Wieczorek, construction supervisor for Daniel, Mann, Johnson & Mendenhall, Architects and Engineers, Los Angeles, has been elected president of the Construction Inspectors Association of Southern California for 1958, succeeding Gene F. Girdner.

Other officers elected to serve during the ensuing year were: Charles H. Stimson, vice president; and Louis Walters, Secretary-treasurer.

The Association, founded in 1956 and now comprising members in all areas of Southern California, was formed originally to help school construction inspectors discuss their common problems. It has expanded both its purpose and scope of membership.

D. J. MORAN APPOINTED BY PABCO

D. J. Moran has been appointed manager of Sales Service for "Pabco" building materials Division of Fibreboard Paper Products Corp., according to an announcement by R. R. Galloway, vice president and general manger of the division.

Moran, will make his headquarters in San Francisco at the company's general offices.

BEN F. DINGMAN APPOINTED MANAGER OF LA OFFICES

Ben F. Dingman has been appointed West Coast Division manager of a new West Coast warehouse and factory being opened in Los Angeles by Kaiser Manufacturing, Inc., of Houston, Texas, according to a recent announcement by C. E. Kaiser, president of the firm.

The new facilities are located at 683 So. Clarence Street and occupy some 6000 sq. ft. of space.

Dingman is a 1932 graduate of Washburn University of Topeka, Kansas, and has been engaged in aircraft and construction material work since coming to California in 1933. More recently he has served as sales manager of the Pacific Tile and Porcelain Company.

NEW LIGHTING FIXTURE SERVES DUAL PURPOSE

One ceiling opening serves for both air supply and illumination with this Kno-Draft Air Diffuser and Holophane lighting fixture combination, solving any conflict that may exist between air outlets and making for cleaner, less cluttered ceilings.

The simple two-cone design of the dif-

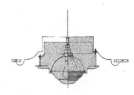

fuser and its sleeve type damper provides ample space for the Holophane light without interfering with air volume or direction. Made in 6 to 16 inch neck diameters, accommodating 100 to 500 watt bulbs. Manufactured by the Connor Engineering Corp., Danbury, Conn.

**GEORGE E. FOWLER
NAMED SALES
ENGINEER OF FIRM**

George E. Fowler and Donald C. Maginski have joined the staff of the Nudor Mfg. Company of North Hollywood, according to a recent announcement by Murrell R. Spence, president of the firm.

Fowler will serve as sales engineer, while Maginski will act as chief engineer. Both men have broad backgrounds in the engineering field.

**SANTA ANA PLANT
OF BORG-WARNER CORP.
RECEIVES AIA AWARD**

The Merit Award of The American Institute of Architects, "In recognition of

outstanding architectural achievement." was presented to BJ Electronics, Borg-Warner Corpn, for their Santa Ana plant.

John J. Kewell, AIA Architect of Los Angeles, made the presentation to John R. Harkness, vice president and general manager of Borg-Warner Corpn at recent ceremonies.

The Santa Ana facility, designed by John J. Kewell and Associates, has been named a "truly fine example of industrial architecture" by the Pasadena Chapter AIA awards committee. The 90,000 sq. ft. development is divided among three principal buildings, engineering and test laboratory, administration and manufacturing plant plus various mechanical equipment installations.

**AUTOMOBILE
SALES BUILDING
FOR MONTEREY**

Architects Wallace Holm & Associates, 321 Webster Street, Monterey, are completing plans and specifications for construction of a new automobile sales building in Monterey for the Roller Chevrolet Company.

The building will be of structural steel frame and masonry construction with concrete floors and built-up roofing. Estimated cost is $50,000.

**MARSH COMPANY
DISTRIBUTOR FOR
RUBBER FLOORING**

The Murray B. Marsh Company of Los Angeles, has been named distributor of Goodyear Tire & Rubber Company vinyl and rubber flooring products for an eight-

state Pacific Coast and Pacific Northwest area, according to a recent announcement by Robert W. Maney, vice-president of Goodyear's western division.

The Marsh Company will provide sales, service and warehousing facilities for all Goodyear flooring products in Arizona, California, Idaho, Montana, Nevada, Oregon, Utah and Washington. Branch sales and warehousing facilities are located in Fresno, Sacramento, Oakland, San Diego, Portland, Seattle, Spokane and Salt Lake City.

**RECREATION BLDG
FOR TRAILER
PARK PLANNED**

Architect Pierre Woodman, 208 S. Laurel Ave., Ontario, has completed plans for construction of a 1-story frame and stucco recreation building in Ontario as a part of the Grove Manor Trailer Park.

The building will have a shake roof, plate glass windows and louvered sash, built-up wood trusses, concrete slab floor, etched plywood walls, open beam ceilings kitchen with laminated plastic drainboard, built-in range and oven, service bar, brick fireplace, and combination dining and recreation room.

**OFFICERS QUARTERS
MATHER AIR FORCE
BASE READIED**

Concept drawings for a multi-story officers quarters building to be constructed at Mather Air Force Base, Sacramento, have been approved by Col. A. E. McCollam, Chief of the U. S. Army Corps of Engineers office in Sacramento.

Designed and engineered by Daniel, Mann, Johnson & Mendenhall, Architects and Engineers of Los Angeles, the structure is designed to combat the rising costs of land and site development. It will be 8-stories high and accommodate 408 men. Construction will be exposed concrete with aluminum windows and louvers for sun control and will contain more than 160,000 sq. ft.; estimated cost of the project is $3,000,000.

**GENEVA NUCLEAR
REACTOR TO BE
BUILT BY NARVER**

Holmes & Narver, Inc., Los Angeles, engineering and construction company, has been selected by the Atomic Energy Commission to construct the United States nuclear reactor safety exhibit for the Second International Conference on Peaceful Uses of Atomic Energy at Geneva, Switzerland, in September.

As in the first "Atoms-for-Peace" conference, held in 1955, scientists from iron

curtain countries as well as the free world will exchange ideas and techniques for constructive and peaceful uses of the atom. The U. S. exhibit will feature as its central point of interest a working model of the SPERT-1 reactor developed at the National Testing Laboratory, Arco, Idaho, and an explanation of the exhibit will be carried in four languages—English, Spanish, French and Russian.

TWELVE STORY HOTEL PLANNED FOR LONG BEACH

Structural Engineer Francis H. Gentry, 306 Insurance Exchange Building, Long Beach, has completed preliminary plans for construction of a 12-story hotel in Long Beach for the Queen Beach Investment Corpn.

The new building will be constructed on a bluff, with 3 stories below the bluff level on the ocean side, and will contain a coffee shop, 2 public dining rooms, 2 bars, banquet rooms, swimming pool on the 4th floor. The first floor will be glass curtain wall, and each room will have a glass sliding door leading to a balcony.

Max Nessel, 3719 E. 1st Street, Long Beach, is the general contractor.

WILLIAM F. STEINER PROMOTED BY PAYNE COMPANY

William F. Steiner of San Francisco, has been appointed Assistant National Sales Manager of the Payne Company of La Puente, California, according to a recent announcement by Owen McComas, National Sales Manager of the Southern California firm.

Steiner's new duties will include overall supervision of the field sales force, ex-

cluding the Southern California area, and interpretation of national sales policy in the field. He will bring to his new position over fifteen years experience in the gas appliance and heating industry.

NEW MODEL MASONRY SAW INTRODUCED

For the first time a masonry saw is being offered with a standard cutting head that will take 14", 18" or 20" blades.

Now a masonry saw user can buy the Target "Super 20" and use it with 14" blades for cutting brick and tile. Later change to 18" for refractories or stone, or to 20" blades for block sawing. An outstanding engineering feature is the fact that shaft speed has been scientifically calculated so it is never necessary to change belts or pulleys when switching to a different diameter blade. Just choose the right diameter blade for each job and use it.

Additional feature is the "lifetime" Targaloy conveyor cart, precision molded with replaceable insert that prevents sawing through the cart; also slope front water reservoir. Manufactured by Robert G. Evans Co., 6024 Troost Ave., Kansas City 10, Mo.

SCHOOL BONDS VOTED AND STATE AID

The architectural firm of Barovetto & Thomas, 718 Alhambra Blvd., Sacramento, has completed drawings for construction of additions to the North and East Davis Elementary Schools in Davis of the Davis Joint Elementary School District, to provide administration unit, 2 classrooms for the North Davis School and 5 classrooms, storage room and toilets for the East Davis School.

Funds for the work have been made available by a School Bond issue of $600,000 and a State Aid grant of $300,000.

BETHLEHEM STEEL TO BUILD OFFICE BUILDING FOR SELF

Design details of the newly announced 15-story office building to be built for Bethlehem Pacific Coast Steel Corporation in downtown San Francisco, have been announced by H. Harrison Fuller, president of Bethlehem Pacific and Welton Becket, F.AIA, and Associates, architects.

The massive marble, glass and stainless

steel structure will be the first new building adjacent to Redevelopment Area E, 80 acres of old waterfront and produce market buildings which the city hopes to tear down and replace with new office and apartment buildings, parks, and light industrial and parking facilities. Site has been cleared and construction will start in the immediate future with completion date for the Fall of 1959.

The structure will occupy a full block on Davis Street and a half block on California Street, and will be suspended between free standing exterior steel columns. It will contain 300,000 sq. ft. of area.

Dudley Deane & Associates are the mechanical and electrical engineers; Hayes & Little and John A. Blume & Associates are the structural engineers.

SAN JOSE VOTERS APPROVE LARGE SCHOOL BOND

Voters of the San Jose School District recently approved one of the largest School Bond issues ever undertaken by the District, when they authorized issuance and sale of $11,577,000 of School Bonds.

Funds derived by the sale of bonds will be used in construction of a new Senior High School, a Junior High School, and three new Elementary Schools, together with improvements to existing schools in the District.

ROBINSON BRICK TO MARKET NEW VENEER PRODUCT

An agreement has been reached between the Robinson Brick and Tile Company of Denver and the Stylon Corp. of Milford, Mass., for marketing in the western United States and Canada of Stylon's thin ceramic veneer.

John E. Ryan, manager of Robco's Ceramic Veneer Sales Division, pointed out that the addition of this new light-weight ceramic veneer would add considerably to the building products being offered by his firm.

NEW SCREWDRIVER WITH BUILT-IN FLASHLIGHT

Precision made new product of chrome finished steel is a screwdriver with a built-in flashlight, ideal for those hidden work areas.

Gets light where you want it; complete with 4-interchangeable bits, 2 Phillip's head screwdrivers, removable chuck. Takes standard flashlight cells and is a compact flashlight unit without attachments. Complete data from Silver Bells Limited, P.O. Box 982, Carmel, California.

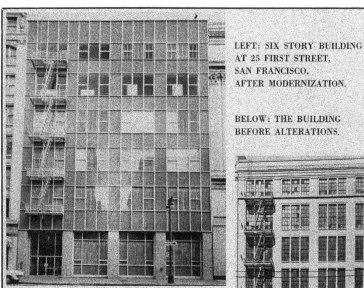

SYMPHONY IN MARBLE

VIEW OF CALIFORNIA MASONIC MEMORIAL TEMPLE
FROM HUNTINGTON PARK, SAN FRANCISCO

ARCHITECT: ALBERT F. ROLLER, A.I.A.

Vermont Eureka Danby Marble

VERMONT MARBLE COMPANY

SAN FRANCISCO   LOS ANGELES

Vol. 213   No. 2

EDWIN H. WILDER
Editor

CONTRIBUTING EDITORS:

Education
SIDNEY W. LITTLE, Dean,
School of Architecture, University of Oregon, Eugene, Oregon

City Planning
CORWIN R. MOCINE, City
Planning Engineer, Oakland,
California

*Urban Planning and
Shopping Centers*
FRANK EMERY COX, Sales
Research & Business Development Analyst, Berkeley, California

Realty Development
ROY P. DRACHMAN, Subdivider and Realty Developer,
Tucson, Arizona

School Planning
DR. J. D. McCONNEL, Stanford School Planning Dept.,
Palo Alto, California

Residential Planning
JEDD JONES, Architect,
Boise, Idaho

General Architecture
ROBERT FIELD, Architect,
Los Angeles, California

Engineering
JOHN A. BLUME, Consulting
and Structural Engineer, San
Francisco, California

Advertising
WILLIAM A. ULLNER,
Manager

FRED JONES
Special Advertising

★

COVER PICTURE

STRUCTURAL STEEL
OF NEW
CROWN ZELLERBACH BUILDING
EXTENDS 20 STORIES HIGH

The new Crown Zellerbach Building,
Market at Sansome, Pine and Battery
Streets, is San Francisco's newest Skyline addition.

Hertzka & Knowles, Skidmore, Owings
& Merrill, Architects.

H. J. Brunnier, Structural Engineer.

Haas & Haynie, General Contractors.

Bethlehem-Pacific Coast Steel, Steel
Fabricators.

ARCHITECTS' REPORTS—
Published Daily
                    Telephone DOuglas 2-8311

—ARCHITECT & ENGINEER is indexed regularly by ENGINEERING INDEX, INC.; and ART INDEX—

Contents for

MAY

THE OLDEST PROFESSIONAL MONTHLY BUSINESS MAGAZINE OF THE ELEVEN WESTERN STATES

ARCHITECT AND ENGINEER (Established 1905) is published on the 15th of the month by The Architect and
Engineer, Inc., 68 Post St., San Francisco 4; Telephone EXbrook 2-7182. President, K. P. Kierulff; Vice-
President and Manager, L. B. Penhorwood; Treasurer, E. N. Kierulff. — Los Angeles Office: Wentworth F.
Green, 439 So. Western Ave., Telephone DUnkirk 7-8135 — Portland, Oregon, Office: R. V. Vaughn, 7117
Canyon Lane. — Entered as second class matter, November 2, 1905, at the Post Office in San Francisco,
California, under the Act of March 3, 1879. Subscriptions United States and Pan America, $3.00 a year;
$5.00 two years; foreign countries $5.00 a year; single copy, 50c.

. EDITORIAL NOTES .

VALUABLE ENGINEERING LIBRARY

Just as the value of a college education can not be measured by the actual facts an individual knows, but by his ability to know where to go to find these facts when needed, so the value of an Engineering Library is not measured alone by its holdings but by the ability of its Librarian to know where to go for material to augment its collection.

An Engineering Library specializes in the subject field that is of direct interest to the company served. However, there are many times when material is required from related fields. Here is where the Engineering Librarian's knowledge of special collections in other libraries is of great assistance.

The Colorado School of Mines Library at Golden, Colorado, represents an Engineering Library which serves the school's 1000 students in the field of mineral engineering; a faculty of 140, many of whom are engaged in research problems; and its services are available to more than seventy-five permanent staff members of the Colorado School of Mines Research Foundation, all working on some phase of research in the mineral industries. Its facilities are also available to 5,275 alumni practicing their profession in all parts of the world serving industry and the engineering profession.

Virginia Lee Wilcox, Librarian, sums up the Library's activities when she says: "It is an integral part of one of the world's foremost mineral engineering schools, and we feel an obligation to foster and encourage research in fields of the School in every way possible, and at every opportunity."

* * *

A GOVERNMENT TAKE-OVER

Under a bill which has been introduced in the House of Representatives the Tennessee Valley Authority would be authorized to finance additional power facilities through the issue of revenue bonds.

Remembering the purposes for which the TVA was created, many people still think that its power operations are only a by-product of its flood control and navigation dams. Actually, TVA's power operations now constitute the major part of its activities, and more than 70% of its power is generated by burning fuel in steam plants.

This legislation would have the effect of extending TVA's power business even further. The only limitation which exists today on TVA expansion is Congressional control of the purse strings. The House bill would do away with that limitation entirely, and the Senate bill, also introduced at the present time, would all but abolish it.

There is no more reason for the Federal Government to be in the electrical power business than there is for it to be in any other business presently conducted by individual effort and financing under our system of free enterprise.

But this proposed legislation is objectionable wholly apart from the serious problem of government in competition with private enterprise.

Under its terms the TVA would be effectively removed from any congressional or executive control. As proponents of the legislation have pointed out, all decisions on how much new capacity is needed, where the capacity shall be located, when bonds will be issued and in what amounts and on what terms would be confined to the TVA board.

While current TVA physical properties are far from the Pacific Coast, population growth and industrial development in the West offers a "golden opportunity" for advocates of Government ownership of power development and using TVA as a springboard, TVA expansion could well leap right into your front yard.

NATIONAL HOME WEEK

National Home Week, the nation's biggest observation of new home ownership, will celebrate its 10th anniversary September 6-14 this year.

The nation-wide event, shared by home builders, manufacturers, suppliers and others in the home building industry, has been observed each year since 1948, and present indications are that approximately 10,000 new homes, incorporating the newest ideas in home design, will be on display throughout the country this year. They will probably be seen by upwards of 10,000,000 interested people.

Purpose of the week is to provide practical education for the public on home building, and to demonstrate the newest and best in homes in all price classes.

The week takes two forms.

In a standard national Home Week, exhibit houses are opened throughout metropolitan and city areas. In a "Parade of Homes", the exhibit houses are built side-by-side on one street where all of them can conveniently be inspected at one time.

This year's event should be particularly interesting as quite a campaign is being conducted to buy a new home, and today's new home is being built by the contractor, and builders, with the aid of architectural and design specialists to represent the finest investment a family can make in happiness and security. The finest houses in the world will be open for inspection this year . . . it is predicted.

HANDLERY MOTELS, INC.

PARKING & MOTEL BUILDING
SAN DIEGO, CALIFORNIA

PADEREWSKI, MITCHELL and DEAN, A.I.A. ARCHITECTS
and ASSOCIATES

M. H. GOLDEN CONSTRUCTION CO.
General Contractors

Bids received recently by Paderewski, Mitchell and Dean, Architects, for construction of a multi-story parking garage and motel building on Seventh Avenue, between Ash and Beech Streets, were not only extremely competitive, but unusually low for a downtown structure.

This became evident when it was announced that the total bid of the low general contractor, the M. H. Golden Construction Co., plus the low bid of Elevator Electric, Inc., for the considerable elevator work, totaled only $2,117,009.00. With a total of 282,130

(See page 30)

ABOVE: Cortez Hill Parking and Motel Building at left — moving sidewalk in center from parking into lobby of El Cortez Hotel.

BELOW: Looking west, moving sidewalk from front of Parking and Motel Building.

NEWS and COMMENT ON ART

OAKLAND ART MUSEUM

The Oakland Art Museum, 1000 Fallon Street, under the direction of Paul Mills, curator, is presenting a number of outstanding exhibitions during this month, including:

"The Painted Flower," honoring the annual California Spring Home and Garden Show, presents floral paintings by Northern California artists selected by a jury; "Ludwig Bemelmans Takes a Holiday," paintings of scenes throughout the world by this beloved artist and illustrator, an exhibit lent by the Hammer Galleries of New York; "Man's Impact on the Bay Area Landscape," a photographic commentary showing the effect of man's work on the native bay area landscape; "Recent Paintings" by John Saccaro; "Early Prints and Drawings of California," from the collection of Robert B. Honeyman, Jr.

Special events: Wednesday Nights at the Museum, program begins at 8:30 p.m., special lectures.

The William Keith Gallery, main library building, is currently exhibiting Keith Treasures from St. Mary's College and the Southwest Museum.

Museum is open daily.

SAN FRANCISCO MUSEUM OF ART

The San Francisco Museum of Art, War Memorial Building, Civic Center, under the direction of Dr. Grace L. McCann Morley, is featuring the following special exhibition and events during May:

Exhibitions: Retrospective, The Art of Albert Marquet; Enrique Climent — a group of paintings, watercolors and drawings; Gifts of the Women's Board, representing the period of 1935-1958; Architectural Photography II, an exhibition prepared by the Smithsonian Institution Traveling Exhibition; the 77th Annual Painting and Sculpture Exhibition of the San Francisco Art Association; and Abstract Photography, an American Federation of Arts Exhibition.

Special events include: Concerts and art programs, lecture tours, and special museum activities include Adventures in Drawing and Painting, each Friday evening at 7:30; the Children's Saturday Morning Art Classes; and Studio-Art for the Layman.

The Museum is open daily.

M. H. deYOUNG MEMORIAL MUSEUM

The M. H. deYoung Memorial Museum, Golden Gate Park, San Francisco, under the direction of Walter Heil, announces a number of special exhibits and events that have been scheduled for May.

Exhibits: Israel, a group of contemporary paintings and prints commemorating Israel's tenth anniversary,

by 13 contemporary artists. This is a portion of 35 works selected by the America-Israel Cultural Foundation in Israel, and being shown on the West Coast under the sponsorship of the Consulate of Israel in Los Angeles. Following its San Francisco showing this exhibit will be shown in Portland, Seattle and Denver museums.

Small Greek Bronzes and Renaissance Medals and Plaquettes, from the collection of Sigmund Morgenroth of Santa Barbara. A comprehensive exhibition of coins, medals and plaquettes.

Paintings by Afro; Sculpture by Tom Hardy; the Biennial Exhibition of the Association of San Francisco Potters, featuring pottery of 1958; and a group of drawings by Reuben Lloyd Blake.

Events: Include classes in Art Enjoyment (recessed after May 24th); classes for adults: Color Exercises, a new course of six weekly experiments in color organization and harmony; seminars in the History of Art; and classes in art for the children: Picture Making, each Saturday morning; Art and Nature, on Wednesday afternoons; and the Art Club for students 12-18 each Thursday.

The museum is open daily.

ARCHITECTURAL GALLERY LOS ANGELES

A special exhibition has been prepared by the architectural firm of Harold W. Levitt, A.I.A., architect, and Ernest W. LeDuc, associate, and has been placed on exhibition in the Architectural Galley of the Los Angeles Building Center, 7933 West Third Street.

CALIFORNIA PALACE OF THE LEGION OF HONOR

The California Palace of the Legion of Honor, Lincoln Park, San Francisco, under the direction of Thomas Carr Howe, Jr., has arranged the following group of special exhibitions and museum activities for May:

Exhibitions: Southwest Indian Arts, an exhibition of old and contemporary arts by Indian craftsmen of the Southwest, presented in cooperation with the California League for American Indians; Ink Drawings by Ivan Majdrakoff; Paintings by John Johanson; Paintings by Frederick Black; Offhand Blown Glass by John Burton; and an exhibition of watercolors by William Wintle.

The Achenbach Foundation for Graphic Arts is featuring The Society of California Etchers Annual Exhibition and the Armin Hansen Memorial Exhibition.

Special Events: Organ program each Saturday and

Sunday afternoon at 3 o'clock, featuring Richard Purvis and Ludwig Altman at the organ. Educational activities include art classes for children Saturday mornings; Drawings and Painting from Observation and Imagination, a class for junior ages 12-17, Saturday afternoons at 2 o'clock.

The museum is open daily.

AMERICAN INSTITUTE OF ARCHITECTS NAMES CALIFORNIA FELLOWS

The American Institute of Architects, national organization of the Architectural profession, has recently named five California architects to honor roll of Fellowship.

Names by the Jury of Fellows for this outstanding honor were: William Clement Ambrose, San Francisco, "for Service to the Institute"; William L. Pereira, Los Angeles, in the field of "Design"; John L. Rex, Los Angeles, in the field of ' Design'"; Malcolm D. Reynolds, Oakland, for "Service to the Institute," and George Vernon Russell, Los Angeles, in the field of "Design."

The new Fellows will receive their certificates and medals at the Annual AIA convention which is to be held in Cleveland, Ohio, in July.

USC SCHOOL OF ARCHITECTURE

The 1957 graduating class of the University of Southern California School of Architecture has presented to the school a piece of sculpture by Stephen Zakian, Los Angeles sculptor, which has been installed in the patio of Harris Hall, SC's architecture building.

Zakian was commissioned by last year's graduates to do the steel and stained glass abstraction.

SAN FRANCISCO MUSEUM OF ART

WAR MEMORIAL BUILDING CIVIC CENTER

THE HAMBURG DOCKS

1909

OIL, 25¾ x 32"

By
ALBERT MARQUET
(1875-1947)

Lent by Mme. Albert Marquet to the exhibition,

"The Art of Albert Marquet"

Marquet, an outstanding member of the Fauve group — like Matisse, who is already well known to the Bay Region public— continued to develop his individual vision and style until his death in 1947. This large exhibition, borrowed from French museums and the Marquet family and supplemented by loans from collections and museums in this country, after its showing here will go to other major museums in the United States during the following 8 months. A supplementary section of work by other artists of the Fauve group will complete the exhibition here.

ENTRANCE with theme of informality—to be landscaped.

CITY-COUNTY BUILDING

A LESSON IN ECONOMY

CRESCENT CITY, DEL NORTE COUNTY,
CALIFORNIA

By ARTHUR W. PRIAULX

At Crescent City in California's northernmost Del Norte County there has just been completed what may well be the nation's smallest city-county building.

For $409,000, Del Norte County has a courthouse which is unique in a field of public structures which lean toward being architectural monuments, for this is a delightful, rambling, single-story frame building.

It houses, in addition to all the county offices, space leased to the Crescent City government, and there is room in one of the three wings of the attractive courthouse for a separate public library.

The basic problem confronting Architect William M. Van Fleet of Eureka, Cailfornia, was to design a structure capable of housing all the combined governmental functions of a small county and city at a figure

WILLIAM M. VAN FLEET,
Architect

H. BERNARD,
General Contractor

within their financial capabilities. The citizens of Del Norte County also desired to give permanent recognition in this county courthouse to the massive and magnificent redwood forests which have their northernmost range in this county.

The design of the courthouse naturally made liberal use of the region's native woods, its redwoods and Douglas firs. The low, spreading structure, whose three wings occupy nearly all of a city block, has much of the unaffected beauty of this remote county. Exterior walls are rough-sawn boards-and-battens of redwood, and interior walls of the main rooms are of west coast hemlock flooring applied vertically. Exposed timber beams of Douglas fir provide the structural ele-

ments for the building and support the roof over corridors and offices.

The two show rooms of the building are the county supervisors' chambers, which double in brass as the city council chambers on stated occasions, and the superior courtroom. Giant glulam arches fabricated in Portland, Oregon, span the 40-foot wide rooms. These beautiful man-made curved arches set the architectural theme for the entire building.

They frame the roof and the walls and form a support for the lacing of the purlin framework of the ceiling.

The two chambers are separated by a lobby, but collapsible doors may be opened up to provide double

FLOOR PLAN demonstrates skill of space arrangement.

space for larger-than-normal public gatherings.

Two-inch Douglas fir timber decking covers the entire structure and forms the base for a built-up roof and the surface on which acoustical tile was applied. Floors are also two-inch Douglas fir tongue-and-groove material, and they have been covered with cork and asphalt tile. Two-foot square plastic diffusers are the lighting fixtures in the superior courtroom and supervisors' chambers, and conventional fluorescent fixtures are used in the smaller offices and the corridors. Hot water baseboard heating is employed throughout the building.

Two features of this remarkably simple public building stand out at once as a tribute to the planning and imagination of Architect William M. Van Fleet. One is the solution of the traffic flow into the courthouse so that patrons of various city and county offices and the library may enter directly from the street into the offices desired. The other outstanding feature is the development of a garden court theme for the building, which makes a complete break with tradition and the ordinary concept of the monumental type of public structure. The Del Norte County Courthouse looks more like an attractive, rambling apartment building which has had some fine landscape design added.

The attractive garden court adds a charming beauty spot to several offices which front on this colorful, walled garden. Trees and shrubs are planned for cul-de-sac garden courts which fill in areas between the several wings.

An idea of the ingenuity and planning of the traffic flow can be had from a study of the floor plan of the courthouse. It will be noted that separate entrances have been provided for the library, superintendent of schools, welfare, superior court, county clerk's office and the city offices, as well as the city police headquarters.

In this rainy county, a sheltered walkway from the

UNUSUAL SUPERIOR COURT ROOM—framed in inspiring upsweeping glulam arches which blend with walls of vertically applied West Coast hemlock.

SUPERVISORS' CHAMBERS double as City Council chambers. Daylight comes from skylights as well as glass wall opening onto small street-side court.

street forms the main entrance and leads into a long corridor from which open most of the county offices. From this covered walkway there is also direct access to police headquarters.

Architect Van Fleet says the building was constructed for a cost of $17.00 per square foot, which is much below what a heavier, masonry building would have cost. He gave special care to providing a fireproof building, using a gyp board sheathing ⅝ inches thick under the boards-and-battens siding, with fireproof insulating material below the windows. The Van Fleet design was ably executed by H. Barnard of Medford, Oregon, who was general contractor.

The informality of this courthouse design seems to have found ready approval and acceptance among the people of this far western county, who do not need to be impressed by imposing buildings when nature has provided them with magnificent, sky-reaching redwoods to admire.

In any appraisal of the Del Norte County Courthouse, it is readily apparent that architect and clients found a common meeting ground. Both wanted something different, something in keeping with their timbered tradition, and both were confronted with providing an adequate structure which could house all the city and county governmental functions at a cost the

taxpayers could afford.

It may well be that this break with tradition in design of what Americans have come to consider the classic style for courthouses will give the taxpayer a break. The Del Norte County pioneering offers other hard-pressed county officials something tangible to ponder.

Provisions for leasing of space to the city government may also open up new considerations for economies in public buildings. Especially will this be true where two small governmental units are not large enough to warrant excessive expenditures for individual buildings, but could pool their resources to provide an adequate and modest facility which is not burdensome on those who are required to pay for it.

A lesson to be learned from the Del Norte County Courthouse is that a permanent and attractive building with maximum functional advantages may be designed in durable woods. Unquestionably, much of the striking beauty and charm of this interesting courthouse stems from the dramatic impact of the upsweeping glulam arches in the two main chambers. The beautiful arches are in sharp contrast to the right angles and vertical lines of conventional design and stand apart from the more conventional features of the building.

HOUSING DEVELOPMENT located at edge of school playground.

AN ARCHITECT TAKES A LOOK AT

INTER-CULTURAL RELATIONS
IN COSTA RICA

By CLARENCE CULLIMORE
Fellow, American Institute of Architects

The International Cooperation Administration of the United States (ICA), working with Costa Rica's National Institute for Housing and City Planning (INVU), is doing a splendid job. Edmond H. Hoben, a graduate of the School of Architectural Engineering at the University of Michigan, and with twenty-five years of experience in architectural construction, slum-clearance and town-planning, is the chief advisor from the United States in this work in Costa Rica. He is ably assisted by Ronald C. Kephart, as housing construction advisor.

Project

Mr. Hoben, speaking of the program, makes it clear that the function of technical assistance is to stimulate cultural interchange as well as economic development, thus helping to make Costa Rica a better place in which to live, as well as strengthening resistance to subversive propaganda.

This United States agency, ICA, which Mr. Hoben represents in San Jose, the capital of Costa Rica, is helping to show the people of that small coffee and banana republic, through its governmental officials,

ROOF TERRACE of the new Hotel Oriental at San Jose, Costa Rica.

how it can best solve its problems of housing and city-planning. Assistance is rendered, largely, by making available the experience gained in other American countries with similar problems.

The program is not designed to give financial aid to Costa Rica or to any group within that country.

Program Limited

It does not engage in the actual construction of housing or in city development; but it is prepared to promote such considerations and to offer technical advice that will prove beneficial when such undertakings are in the initial planning stages.

It is through Mr. Hoben's good offices that a better understanding is promoted between the United States and Costa Rica through their respective planning commissions, their schools of architecture and engineering, and the representatives of their government.

Our country, through ICA, is primarily concerned with the gradual improvement, on a long-term basis; with reconstruction of poorly planned and poorly built communities; and with stimulating the local government to use most efficiently its manpower and materials. The rapidity with which this idea is taking hold in Costa Rica is gratifying.

Construction

Construction involving public facilities has been

RONALD C. KEPHART,

housing construction
advisor (left) showing
author Cullimore
Costa Rica's newest
structure, the
Hotel Oriental in
San Jose.

stepped up and new sewers, water systems, the widening of streets, more modern schools, and ample recreation areas have found wide popularity in San Jose. By the employment of properly trained young men the ICA has been able to prove, by results, that it is more economical to do initial planning than to ignore it.

The important thing is that the citizens for whom the planning is done see its necessity and urge their government to cooperate. Thus, education goes hand in hand with technical assistance.

With the lusty support of the man-about-town in San Jose the work of United States technicians in Costa Rica is proving of untold value.

Costa Rica's National Institute for Housing and Planning (INVU) with headquarters in San Jose is especially concerned in community planning and with

a type of construction that will withstand to-be-expected earthquake shocks.

It is hoped that this new construction will replace squalid and unsanitary hovels that for generations have restricted the enjoyment of living for the less privileged workman's family. The shot-in-the-arm to these blighted areas in this Central American republic did not just happen. It came about through the foresight of that country's governing body, in establishing in INVU a group of engineers, sanitary experts, city-planners and architects trained in Latin America and several trained in the United States.

U. S. Cooperation

Our government is cooperating under the established Costa Rican program and the results are paying off for Costa Rica.

The new housing projects are noteworthy, par-

HATILLO HOUSING PROJECT

overlooking the capital city was initiated and constructed through efforts of Costa Rica's National Institute for Housing and Planning.

ticularly because of their new concept of a floor plan arrangement. It is these contemporary floor plans that break dramatically from the traditional Costa Rican houses, that since the Conquistadores have been built around an inner court with all the rooms opening thereon.

New Style Homes

The new Coasta Rican floor plans for homes, as promoted by the INVU, are much like our own, with due emphasis on light and air, the placement of bath rooms, and with ample regard for a well-arranged,

(See page 24)

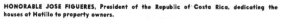

HONORABLE JOSE FIGUERES, President of the Republic of Costa Rica, dedicating the houses at Hatillo to property owners.

GENEROUS DECK AREAS take in sweeping panorama of San Francisco Bay.

STEEL BEAMS USED IN

HILLSIDE HOUSE

DR. and MRS. R. E. SCHMIDT,

BELVEDERE ISLAND, CALIFORNIA

FELIX M. WARBURG,

Designer

JOHN E. BROWN,

Civil Engineer

H. S. MEINBERGER & SON,

General Contractor

Structural steel was the key to the solution of the problems imposed by a steep and wooded building site in the newly completed Belvedere home of Dr. and Mrs. R. E. Schmidt. It permitted them to build on a steep slope without disturbing natural growth, and also proved to be less costly than other more conventional structural systems on such a slope.

The three-bedroom, two-bath house, designed by Felix M. Warburg, faces a sweeping panorama that includes San Francisco, Golden Gate Bridge, Sausalito, and Mt. Tamalpais. So completely undisturbed is the landscape, that a natural setting of pine, cypress, live oak, toyon and eucalyptus surrounds the house on four sides. The deck of the house is at a level 150 feet above the shoreline. With a 140-foot frontage on Belvedere Avenue, the house is located downhill from the street. The lot depth is some 300 feet with better than 150 feet difference in elevation.

HOUSE is "floated" on sturdy steel legs tied into a continuous footing. Building touches ground at only five places.

"The logical conclusion in planning this house was to have it touch the ground at as few points as possible," according to Warburg. As a result, except for a retaining wall on the uphill side, the house only touches the ground in five places.

Civil Engineer, John E. Brown of San Francisco, designed the structural frame.

The frame was composed of 16-inch wide flange steel sections. These were supported on five steel columns, also composed of 16-inch wide flange shapes. The column footings were tied to each other in the downhill direction with 12 by 12-inch reinforced concrete grade beams.

By using fairly heavy steel sections, the designer and engineer were able to achieve long spans, keeping their columns and footings to a minimum. Lighter steel sections tie in the frame laterally. In some places, the heavy steel sections cantilever 8 feet over the columns. Coupled with a span of 36 feet between columns, this gave a maximum use of over 40 feet per column.

The engineer estimated $1,000 to $2,000 was saved by using the steel frame instead of a conventional foundation.

"The beauty of this system is that 48 hours after you pour your concrete you can have the steel in place and welded and can be starting on your subflooring," according to Warburg. "Conventional post and beam construction would take from five days to a week in addition to which considerable scaffolding would be necessary.

"In California, particularly because of lateral prob-

FLOOR PLAN . . . upper and lower deck areas have sweeping panorama of the San Francisco shoreline.

lems involving earthquake design, steel has the desired rigidity with the simplest connections. It can have clean and economical shape. The properties of the material provide lateral ties by simple welding."

By using the steel frame, Warburg was able to eliminate the usual wood joist system and thus effect another saving. The contractor, H. S. Meinberger and Son, Kentfield, installed a laminated flooring of Douglas fir 2 x 4's and 2 x 6's. The 2 x 6's were used for a span of 16-feet and the 2 x 4's for a 12-foot span. The wood which is set on edge and nailed at frequent intervals gives great lateral strength as well as sufficient insulation to eliminate the need for a soffit in temperate climates. The wood was sanded, filled and varnished as a finished floor.

The contractors original figure for a conventional joist floor this high off the ground was $4,000 for labor and materials. The actual cost of the laminated floor was $2,500. In addition, this system eliminated the need for any scaffolding or staging as the laminations cantilevered 4-feet beyond the building line around the entire house.

The Schmidt's Belvedere home contains 1,900 square feet of floor space, plus 500 square feet of deck. Another 500 square feet is contained in the parking platform which abuts onto the street. Laminated 2 x 6's were used as decking for the parking platform.

The designer repeated the pattern of lamination in

his roof. To provide more light in certain areas, he designed skylights which were framed by leaving out pairs of laminations in 6 and 8-foot lengths. Clear plastic panels are laid over the openings, providing a light and shadow pattern in the interior. Resawn redwood boards are laid vertically in exterior and interior walls.

Another feature is the fireplace which is faced with pre-cast concrete post and lintel panels only 1½ inches thick. Lamp black is mixed in the concrete as it is cast in plywood forms in order to pick up the pattern of the wood grain. After installation, the panels are waxed to bring out the texture. The house is of wood post and beam construction with a 4-foot module and a pitched tar and gravel roof.

Warburg's philosophy is: "Be careful with nature. Every time you try to improve upon it, you're asking for trouble.

"Sooner or later we will run out of flat building sites in the west, particularly near our cities. A solution such as this may encourage economical hillside construction. The mass reduction and denuding of our natural landscape for building purposes is becoming a more and more alarming trend."

By using a steel frame, he was able to construct a tree top platform while leaving the natural landscape intact. Because only five columns were used, even the

(See page 32)

Placing steel foundation beams in concrete bases.

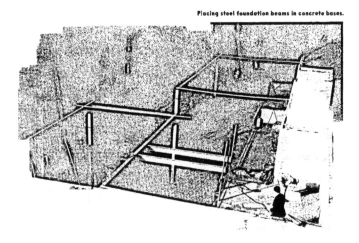

NEW
DESIGN
CONCEPT

for

CURTAIN
WALLS

By
FRANK E. COX

Western Sales Manager
Metal Wall Division
Kawneer Company

MODERN CURTAIN WALL with simple, clean lines.

Modern design for the walls of buildings, as conceived by the architectural profession, has imposed new obligations on the suppliers of materials, general contractors and the entire construction industry. This is true whether these walls be one story in height or fifty stories. This responsibility implies that there must be greater research and analysis given not only to production but to erection, installation and fulfilling the complete desires of the designer both functionally and esthetically.

The principal problems which this new design concept has brought about, are:

1. Products that will permit flexibility of design and use.

2. Integration of various kinds of materials into a "package," such as aluminum and other non-ferrous metals, glass of various kinds for both "see-through" and spandrel purposes; steel, sealants, anchors, and other components.

3. The mastering of movement that comes about as a result of thermal action, both horizontally and vertically.

4. The development of responsibility for weather tightness on the part of reliable and financially stable contractors and sub-contractors.

5. The achievement of time-saving methods to

make possible the application of the wall in less man-hours than has been the custom in the past with masonry or other conventional construction.

Importance of the Specification

To fulfill the obligation which is imposed because of these new trends, there must of necessity be a definite, specific, written description of the building and the

LIC Typical Mock-Up for testing weather-tightness and deflection of curtain walls prior to installation on buildings.

construction procedures and the component parts, that is both precise and comprehensive. This description must define the details not only in the drawings so that there is no possible chance for a misunderstanding and disappointment, but they must be delineated in the actual written manual which constitutes the specifications so that these misunderstandings cannot occur.

In the traditional phases of construction such as masonry or concrete—custom, usage and trade practices are usually dependable and reduce to some extent the need for specific and concise specification.

In curtain walls of either metal or glass, or a combination of both, with so many more variables, a more exact definition and firm specification is necessary.

In order to understand then, the character of these specifications, it would be worthwhile to discuss the many phases which should be covered. These conditions could very understandably be described as follows:

1. Scope of work of the curtain wall contractor.

2. How the design features such as mullion pro-

Right View shows the workman completing a maximum prefabrication: frames are assembled complete except for glass.

Below is view of workmen also performing a prefabrication step at manufacturing plant.

files, panel color and rigidity, and patterns must be executed.

3. The manner in which expansion and contraction of the various elements must be performed. This would include fastenings, sealants, and the many variables which become a part of this expansion and contraction family.

4. Finish.

5. Erection and installation.

6. The elimination of ripples and the achievement of vertical plumbness and horizontal precision of planes.

7. The defining of the desired "U" factor along with the determination for controlling the con-

Inside Setting: No scaffolding. Note interior back-up.

ductivity of heat and cold from one side of the wall to the other.

8. The definition of the insulations that would achieve the end result desired.

9. The defining of the backup material, how it is to be finished, and the method for other work to meet it.

For the purpose of protecting the owner, the architect, the general contractor and the sub-contractor, a firm specification to be satisfactory must accomplish the following:

1. The requirements of the curtain wall.

2. How it is to be applied.

3. The function it is to perform.

This specification then assures proper directions for execution of the work and sets the standards by which this work must be performed.

The Advantages of Rigid Specifications

Competition can be more accurately judged by such rigid outlines:

1. A definite, firm specification makes it possible to accurately judge New York Steak quality vs. New York Steak quality, not New York Steak quality vs. Hamburger.

2. The architect has a document that can insure faithful reproduction of his design.

3. It sets up a written standard and serves as a part of a contract so that the architect can

Factory prefabricated frames delivered to jobs on pallets bundled six to each pallet and hoisted to floors.

ARCHITECT AND ENGINEER

Maximum flexibility for expansion and contraction during thermal changes is made possible by split mullions. Note the studs for fastening into angle clips in upper left of frame.

enforce his intentions, his desires and his will on the various contractors and sub-contractors involved.

4. Misunderstandings and "passing the buck" by a bidder of the specification becomes difficult and well-nigh impossible.

"Base Bid" form of bidding is made possible.

1. This form of bidding has evolved out of the work of many proffessional groups such as the A.I.A., Producers Council, the B.R.I., and the Construction Specifications Institute.

2. Faithful interpretation of the architect's design is assured by designating the fabricator who most adequately served him during the preliminary and working drawing phases of the project as the most logical acceptable bidder on the base bid.

3. Competition is maintained by calling for alternate bids from several additional fabricators.

   a. Relative merits of the alternate details and costs can be best judged by the architect.

   b. Control can be kept completely under the administration of the architect.

   c. Bids from unacceptable vendors can be eliminated.

4. The general contractor is protected:

   a. With all general contract bidders quoting on the same basis, the only variable cost is the individual general contractor's markup of the fabricator's bid.

   b. "Deals" or "chiseling" become impossible.

Guarantees

The "hottest" issue currently affecting specifications is the guarantee.

Accepted guarantees set forth in the A.I.A. General Conditions Form, Article No. 20, should be sufficient.

Actual problem is one of responsibility:

1. A five-year guarantee from an unstable or financially unsound firm, or one that may be out of business next year, is no guarantee whatever.

2. Wall failure cannot be determined without first locating the source of the trouble. The source of any trouble should be anticipated during the detailing stage and corrected there and eliminated. Thus there will be no need to correct deficiencies after the job is installed. The specification firmly assures that the correct details

will be followed and the obligation of the contractor will be fulfilled.

A guarantee that would truly protect the architect and his client would have to be written by a lawyer, not a specification writer.

1. A vague guarantee is false security if the company issuing such a guarantee is financially incapable to remedy his error, or if the owner is forced to resort to litigation to enforce it.

2. Considering the large number of fabricators now engaged in producing curtain walls of metal or glass, or a combination of both, it should be obvious that quality standards, technical skills and production facilities will vary greatly.

3. A cheap curtain wall poorly done can be far more costly than a properly fabricated system that may cost more at the time of bidding, no matter what unsupported statements might be made by salesmen during the preliminary planning.

4. Elaborate guarantees are unnecessary if the curtain wall work is assigned to fabricators with a well-established record of experience, quality workmanship and technical skill.

5. There is nothing wrong, and as a matter of fact it can be considered good practice, to insist on a five-year guarantee against water leakage, but the guarantee should only be considered from financially responsible firms.

How To Achieve Good Specifications

In the preliminary design stage it would seem, from observation and experience, that good practice would dictate calling in various fabricators deemed capable of properly handling the contract in question:

1. This discussion should determine—

   a. Whether a system of standard design and profiles or a custom-designed wall should be used.

   b. The type of metal, i.e., aluminum, stainless steel, bronze, or other materials.

   c. Type of glass to be used in the "see-through" areas.

   d. Type of windows to be used, which involves operating for ventilation; operating for washing only; fixed glazing—the latter two implying an air-conditioned building; or other.

   e. Design loads, allowable deflections.

   f. Spandrel material, together with insulation determined by a specific "U" factor (what to be used); consideration of vapor seals; back-up pans; and other items used in the spandrels.

   g. Resolve any special problems such as unique materials, i.e., ceramic veneer panels or

Weather Tightness

insured by precision use of sealants under factory fabrication conditions.

others; special or unusual finishes; production and erection methods.

h. Determine a time schedule which the fabricator would be expected to follow and specify this in definite form.

2. Eliminate those fabricators that cannot meet job requirements.

During preparation of working drawings:

1. Obtain preliminary details from selected wall fabricators along with budget prices.

2. Secure special details of problem areas from wall fabricators.

3. Establish coordination of component parts within the curtain wall system and with the other trades that will be involved in the application of this system.
   a. Glass.
   b. Spandrel panels.
   c. Flashing.
   d. Sealants.
   e. Anchors and attachments to structure.

4. Establish finish standards.

5. Establish work to be included in the curtain wall section of the specification:
   a. Anchors and where they are to be fastened (in the specifications these should be defined as they relate to other trades and suppliers).
   b. Stools and convector covers.
   c. Blind boxes.
   d. Partition closures.
   e. Trim.
   f. Final cleaning.

g. Guarantees.

h. Where curtain wall contractor starts and where his complete responsibility begins.

Writing the specification for the curtain wall:

1. Have fabricators still active on project submit suggested specifications.

2. Take suggestions of fabricators, plus architect's own requirements. The specification writer can then prepare a firm specification:
   a. Set out base bid fabricator.
   b. List by name other acceptable fabricators to be bid as alternates.
   c. Scope of work should cover areas to be considered as part of curtain wall work.
   d. At points of transfer of responsibility, clearly set forth materials and services to be provided by each contractor.
   e. Set forth test requirements, design loads, deflection allowances, samples and mock-up required.
   f. Set up durometer standards for neoprene, vinyl and thiokol sealants.
   g. Allocate work to be done for curtain wall contractor by other sub-contractors.
   h. Designate responsibility for clean down after erection and glazing prior to turning over to owner, insisting on curtain wall subcontractor doing the work himself and being completely responsible for such performance.
   i. Designate responsibility for protecting curtain after installation and prior to acceptance by owner.
   j. Guarantee to owner.

Another Method

of inside setting of panels by use of the angle clips.

INTER-CULTURAL RELATIONS
(From page 13)
modern kitchen and living areas.

The Hatillo small-house development on the out-skirts of San Jose is a tribute to this progress. The first section of this project was dedicated by Church officials and auspiciously opened for occupancy by its individual purchasers by the Honorable Jose Figueres, President of the Republic of Costa Rica.

The housing units at Hatillo have been sold under long term contracts to families scrutinized as to need and character and ability to pay. Hatillo community is in the flush of its dawn, with church, school and shopping centers adjacent.

Children have adequate playgrounds and there are cultural advantages for the grown-ups.

Hatillo is only one of the many projects that the INVU has on the board. They range from experiments with interlocking blocks made of soil stabilized with cement, suitable for small inexpensive houses, to the complete town planning of the banana port of Golfito on the Costa Rican Pacific seaboard.

Self-Help Housing

A unique idea promoted under the INVU plan, and already in its intermediate stages, is one whereby a group of fifteen workers in various building trades may enter into an Aided-Self-Help contract for the con-struction of their own homes during off-hours, at night by artificial light, on holidays, and during spare hours.

For this purpose an admirable building site has been selected on an oak-studded hillside overlooking the capital city. The streets, the water-mains, sewers and utilities are in. Already thirty foundations have been poured.

There is a waiting family represented by each foun-dation, the man of which is by trade a carpenter, a cement-finisher, a bricklayer, a ditch-digger, electri-cian, plumber or some other trade that may be em-ployed in the construction of a house.

In this way the houses, which will be constructed under architectural supervision and from architectural plans, will actually be built by experts, each in his chosen field.

In this particular project the wall construction con-sists of precast concrete columns that support the forms for 3" poured concrete walls. Dowels in the columns and footings are provided so that when the walls are poured the whole wall is bonded together and to the footing.

A poured crown-beam at the top ties the walls to-gether over door and window openings, takes up unevenness of height of wall slabs and columns, and takes the load of the roof. Standardized, reusable forms are utilized.

Not a Do-It-Yourself

This is in no sense a "Do-it-yourself" project, at-tempted by a group of persons unversed in building operations.

Each house will be a professional job from its planning stage to the last nail driven and the last brush full of paint.

This Aided-Self-Help method, under which each of the workmen donates his specialty in the building trades, for himself and for others, seems a sensible plan. At least, it is working well for these Costa Ricans.

U. S. Materials

The use of machinery and materials from the United States, in demonstrations carried on by the ICA tech-nicians, frequently stimulates a market for these goods. For instance, in the technical assistance program in housing, an overhead radial-arm saw, brought in by U. S. technicians, was so well received that the INVU eagerly acquired others of the same make for their own use.

The ICA technical assistance program also provides for training Costa Rican technicians outside of their own country.

Under the housing and city planning operations men may be sent to the United States for research and study in the field of savings and loan. Engineers and community organization specialists may complete their training in the United States. Costa Rican young men are currently enrolled in architecture and city planning in several universities of this country. These contacts, of course, strengthen the bond of friendship between the two countries.

THE REAL VALUE OF ART
By ELMER GREY

Art in its manifold forms has a real spiritual value. Of course its value greatly varies in different examples. We are all instruments in the hands of a supreme Intel-ligence, a master Artist, who works through us; and some are better channels for the flow of His influence in the form of art than are others; which of course is natural for we are all created different from one an-other.

From books or from sermons we receive inspiration and are well aware of it, but from art we receive it unconsciously. A little book published in London in 1715 has, in its quaint language, this to say about the art of painting: "Because Pictures are unusually de-lightful, many, I believe, consider the art of Painting as but a pleasing superfluity; at best that it holds but a low rank with respect to its Usefulness to Mankind. If it were only one of those Sweets that the Divine Providence has bestowed on us to render the Good of our present Being superior to the Evil of it, it ought to be considered as a Bounty from Heaven and to hold a place in our esteem accordingly."

By uplifting our thought art often brings us vital aspects of truth. Its highest forms are invariably found where the highest thoughts are expressed. Henry Van Dyke has said that without the aim to cheer, console,

purify or enoble, the art of literature has "never sent an arrow close to the mark."

This would be a drab world indeed, and spiritually dead without the uplifting influence of many forms of art. Sculpture is one of these. That which largely inspired the design of the Lincoln Shrine in Redlands is a magnificent bust of Lincoln carved out of Carrara marble by the eminent sculptor George Grey Barnard, whose fame has long been international and whose masterpieces are to be found in state Capitols and national centers in many lands. It is not an ordinary portrait bust, but one which once seen is never forgotten. It seems to breathe forth the very soul of the Lincoln whom the world acknowledges as immortal. His strength, his patience and his great compassion are all there expressed.

When the Administration Building of the California Institute of Technology (now called Throop Hall) was being planned many years ago the architects felt that, since it was to be the central and in a way the most important of a large group of buildings, symbolic sculpture of the right kind over its main entrance would be most fitting. A majority of the directors of the institute considered the idea unnecessary expense and were about to turn it down, whereupon Dr. Norman Bridge, himself a director, arose and said that he felt otherwise, that he deemed it quite necessary and that he had a check in his pocket that would cover the entire expense! So the sculpture, done by a renowned sculptor, Alexander Sterling Calder, was adopted.

Most people who go through art galleries either in this country or abroad, do not go solely for pleasure. Undoubtedly some do, but Andrew Mellon would not have spent what he did in building the National Gallery of Art in Washington, D.C., if he did not know that its contents would be of inestimable value to the people of his country. As the Baltimore Sun once put it, "both the building and the art treasures it contains can be described only in superlatives!" "The largest marble edifice of its kind in the world!" ". . . eighty million dollars worth of art housed in the building at the outset!" ". . . the Mellon collection alone appraised at $50,000,000!"

That a man of Mr. Mellon's extremely practical mind should have alloted such an enormous sum of money to an institution of that nature constitutes the very strongest possible testimony that could be offered for the real value of art in the community.

CALIFORNIA COUNCIL AIA

Getting off to an early start, Loy Chamberlain, Oakland, chairman of the Convention Advisory Committee, announces the program for the 1958 Annual Convention is nearing final form, and will feature the creative approach to architecture, following preferences expressed by architects and Women's Architectural

League members in a poll of convention suggestions. Scheduled for October 15-19, the convention will be held in Monterey with business and technical sessions held at the Monterey County Fairgrounds.

To better serve the profession and schools of architecture, President L. F. Richards has appointed a special committee headed by John Lyon Reid, FAIA, San Francisco. Members of the committee include Reid, William Corlett, Malcolm D. Reynolds, Frederick L. R. Confer, William Stephen Allen Jr., George T. Rockrise, William Henry Taylor, John Rex, Stanley R. Gould, Herbert J. Powell and Maynard Lyndon.

The next meeting of the Board of Directors will be held June 5-6 in the Balboa Bay Club, Newport Beach.

EAST BAY CHAPTER AIA

The May meeting was a joint meeting with the East Bay Structural Engineers Society, and featured a number of speeches by members of the California Assembly of the State Legislature including: Samuel R. Gedded of the Fifth District; Donald Doyle of the 10th District; Carlos Bee of the 13th District, and Walter I. Dahl of the 16th District. George T. Kern served as moderator of discussions which featured "Small Business and Its Relationship to Government."

The June meeting will be the annual Honor Awards Dinner and presentation of the College of Architecture, University of California.

New members include: Russell William Barnecut, David F. Costa, Jr., and Lee Stuart Darrow, corporate members.

MAYBECK MEMORIAL TOUR
OF SAN FRANCISCO AND
BAY AREA SCHEDULED

The Northern California Chapter of the AIA and the Women's Architectural League, are sponsoring a Maybeck Memorial Tour of buildings and residences in the San Francisco, Marin County, and East Bay communities, on Sunday, May 25th, 11 a.m. to 5 p.m.

During the tour talks will be given on architect Maybeck.

NORTHERN CALIFORNIA
WAL ACTIVITIES

The regular April meeting was held in the Garden Room of the Hotel Claremont in Berkeley, with a visit of the Hotel's gardens following luncheon.

A Homes Tour is being sponsored jointly by the WAL and AIA for Sunday, May 18th. Homes on the tour are in the Oakland and Piedmont areas. Tickets are available from the AIA offices in the Claremont Hotel.

American Institute of Architects

Leon Chatelain, Jr., President

John N. Richards, 1st Vice President
Philip Will, Jr., 2nd Vice President
Edmund R. Purves, Executive Secretary

Edward L. Wilson, Secretary
Raymond S. Kastendieck, Treasurer

National Headquarters—1735 New York Avenue, N.W., Washington, D.C.

REGIONAL DIRECTORS—**Northwest District**, Donald J. Stewart, Portland, Oregon; **Western Mountain District**, Bradley P. Kidder, Santa Fe, New Mexico; **California-Nevada-Hawaii District**, Ulysses Floyd Rible, Los Angeles, California

ARIZONA CHAPTERS:
CENTRAL ARIZONA: David Sholder, President; A. John Brenner, Vice-President; Jimmie R. Nunn, Secretary; Kemper Goodwin, Treasurer; James W. Elmore, Director; Ralph Haver, Director; Martin Ray Young, Jr., Director. Office of Secy., P.O. Box 904, Phoenix.
SOUTHERN ARIZONA: Santry Clay Fuller, President; Edward H. Nelson, Vice-President; David S. Swanson, Secretary; Robert J. Ambrose, Treasurer; D. Burr DuBois, Director; Eleazar D. Herreras, Director; Emerson C. Scholer, Director. Office of Secy., 2343 South Tucson Avenue, Tucson.

COAST VALLEYS CHAPTER:
William L. Higgins (San Jose), President; Paul J. Huston (Palo Alto), Vice-President; William H. Daseking (Menlo Park), Treasurer; Edward N. Chamberlain (San Jose), Secretary. Office of Secy., 390 Park Ave., San Jose.

CENTRAL VALLER OF CALIFORNIA:
Joseph J. Jozens, President (Sacramento); Armsby Tod Hart, Vice-President (Sacramento); Albert M. Dreyfuss, Secretary (Sacramento); Whitson W. Cox, Treasurer. Office of Secy., 2127 "J" St., Sacramento.

COLORADO CHAPTER:
Casper F. Hegner, President; C. Gordon Sweet, Vice President; Norton Polivnick, Secretary; Richard Williams, Treasurer. Directors: James M. Hunter, Robert K. Fuller, Edward L. Bunts. Office of Secy., 1225 Bannock St., Denver, Colorado.

EAST BAY CHAPTER:
Hachiro Yuasa (Oakland), President; George T. Kern (Oakland), Vice-President; William M. Gillis (San Francisco), Secretary; J. A. Zerkle (Berkeley), Treasurer. Directors: H. B. Clausen, F. A. Lockwood, John Oyarzo, G. M. McCue, Marjorie Montgomery, Exec. Secy. Office of Secy., Mezzanine, Hotel Claremont, Berkeley 5.

IDAHO CHAPTER:
Anton E. Dropping, Boise, President; Charles W. Johnston, Payette, Vice-President; Glenn E. Cline, Boise, Sec.-Treas. Executive Committee: Chester L. Shawver and Nat J. Adams, Boise. Office of Secy., 624 Idaho Bldg., Boise.

MONTEREY BAY CHAPTER:
Robert Stanton, President (Carmel); Walter Burde, Vice-President; William L. Cranston, Secretary; George Kuska, Treasurer. Office of Secy., P.O. Box 1846, Carmel.

MONTANA CHAPTER:
William J. Hess, President (Great Falls); John E. Toohey, Vice-President (Billings); H. C. Cheever, Secy.-Treas. (Bozeman). Directors: Oscar J. Ballas, Wm. J. Hess, John E. Toohey. Office of Sec., Bozeman, Montana.

NEVADA CHAPTER:
RENO: Lawrence A. Gulling, President; William E. Cowell, Vice-President; Albert W. Alegre, Secretary; Ralph A. Casazza, Treasurer. Graham Erskine, Raymond W. Hellman, George L. F. O'Brien, Directors. Office of the Secy., 500 Plumas St., Reno.
LAS VEGAS: Walter F. Zick, President; Aloysius McDonald, Vice-President; Edward B. Hendricks, Secy.-Treas. Directors: Walter F. Zick, Edward Hendricks, Charles E. Cox. Office of Secy., 106 S. Main St., Las Vegas.

NEVADA STATE BOARD OF ARCHITECTS:
L. A. Ferris, Chairman; Aloysius McDonald, Secy.-Treas. Members: Russell Mills (Reno), Edward S. Parsons (Reno), Richard R. Stadelman (Las Vegas). Office: 1420 S. 5th St., Las Vegas.

NORTHERN CALIFORNIA CHAPTER:
William Corlett, President; Donald Powers Smith, Vice-President; George T. Rockrise, Secretary; Richard S. Banwell, Treasurer. Directors: W. Clement Ambrose, John Kruse, Bernard J. Sabaroff, Corwin Booth. Exec. Secy., May B. Hipshman. Chapter Office, 47 Kearny St., San Francisco.

ORANGE COUNTY CHAPTER:
William T. Jordan, President (Costa Mesa); Donald M. Williamson, Vice-President (Laguna Beach); J. Herbert Brownell, Secretary; Rumont W. Hougan, Treasurer. Office of Secy., 1950 W. Coast Highway, Newport Beach.

OREGON CHAPTER:
John K. Dukehart, President; Keith R. Maguire, Vice-President; Robert Douglas, Secretary; Harry K. Stevens, Treasurer. Directors: Daniel McGoodwin, Earl P. Newberry, Everett B. Franks, Robert W. Fritsch, Donald W. Edmundson. Office of Secy., 2041 S.W. 58th Ave., Portland 1.

PASADENA CHAPTER

Ladies' Night was observed this month with a program of "People and Places in Russia," with a camera report of Russia as seen through the eyes of Rev. Michael J. Colton, who, while attending Oxford University, was invited to tour Russia as the only American observer with a British student delegation. Mr. Colton is now assistant minister at the La Canada Presbyterian Church.

New members to the Chapter include: John Field Kelsey, Corporate; Donald R. Whited, Associate.

NORTHERN CALIFORNIA CHAPTER

The annual meeting, together with Council Night, was observed on the 14th of this month. In addition to election of officers and voting on four by-law changes, members had the opportunity of meeting with the administrative committee of the California Council AIA and hearing of plans and projects currently under way and anticipated.

Newly elected officers included Donald Powers Smith, president; Corwin Booth, vice president; Joseph Esherick, secretary; Richard Banwell, treasurer, and John Lord King, Alexander Yuill-Thornton, and Andrew T. Haas, directors.

SOUTHERN CALIFORNIA CHAPTER

The May meeting was the annual meeting of the student chapter at the University of Southern California, and was held in the Town and Gown, University of Southern California campus building.

Minoru Yamasaki, one of the country's foremost architects, was the principal speaker, taking as his subject "New Forms in Architecture." He is a principal in the firm of Yamasaki, Leinweber and Associates of Royal Oak, Mich.

SAN DIEGO CHAPTER

Dr. Roger Revelle was the principal speaker at the May meeting held in the Hotel at San Diego.

The annual spring outing of the Producers' Council was observed May 22 at the Mission Valley Country Club, with many door prizes and entertainment.

EDUCATION FOR ARCHITECTURE AND INDUSTRIAL DESIGN

The first comprehensive exhibition of all phases of student work at the University of Southern California School of Architecture entitled "Education For Architecture and Industrial Design" was opened early in May at the California Museum of Science and Industry, Exposition Park, Los Angeles. It will remain on display through June 1.

Planned to give the public an idea of the complexity of today's architectural education, the exhibition includes current examples of all major problems assigned in each of the professional courses in the school's five-year program. The exhibition, being staged by Prof. Emmet Wemple, includes drawings, blueprints and models done in design, engineering, professional practice, city planning, landscape, freehand drawing, water color, graphics, history, and senior thesis classes.

BRUNNER MEMORIAL PRIZE WINNER IS ARCHITECT

Paul Rudolph, young American architect, has been named to receive the $1,000 Brunner Memorial Prize in Architecture of the National Institute of Arts and Letters for 1958, according to an announcement by Malcolm Cowley, president of the Institute. Formal presentation of the award was made at the joint annual ceremonial of the National Institute and the American Academy of Arts and Letters on May 21.

WITH THE ENGINEERS

AMERICAN SOCIETY OF CIVIL ENGINEERS NATIONAL CONVENTION IN PORTLAND

The summer national convention of the ASCE will be held in Portland, Oregon, June 23-27, with an outstanding program of technical, educational and entertainment sessions. Excursions both technical and scenic will be offered for all members and their families.

Field trips to be offered in the area include excursions to Swift Creek Dam, lumber industry plants, City of Portland water supply headworks, Bonneville hydraulics laboratory, operated by the Corps of Engineers, express-way construction, The Dalles Dam, and a trip through scenic Columbia gorge.

Family entertainment includes a get-to-gether barbecue in the beautiful Tualatin Valley a few miles west of Portland, a dinner dance at the Hotel Multnomah, various ladies programs, and a post convention tour to Hawaii.

STRUCTURAL ENGINEERS ASSOCIATION OF SOUTHERN CALIFORNIA

"Use of Models in Structural Engineering" was the subject of a discussion at the May meeting held in the Rodger Young Auditorium, with Prof. Howard D. Eberhardt, Professor of Civil Engineering, University of California at Berkeley, the speaker. He outlined the theory and application of displacement models using both simple and complicated equipment for plane and three-dimensial structures, also models for stress analysis compared to models for structural analysis. The two basic types of models for structural analysis, loaded and displacement, and the possibilities of using loaded models. Illustrated slides assisted in the presentation.

Recent new member: James S. Colton, Associate Member.

AMERICAN SOCIETY OF CIVIL ENGINEERS SAN FRANCISCO SECTION

The Legislative Committee reports that the major issue concerning civil engineers which is before the current legislators is that of water, a problem that will probably not be resolved for quite some time to come due to the variance of opinion between Northern and Southern California areas.

It has been reported that in the three years, 1955-56-57 the Armed Forces contracted for over $10-billion of supplies, services and construction with California firms.

FEMINEERS

The Femineers celebrated their eighth birthday anniversary this month with a luncheon at the Ondine in Sausalito. A contest to identify baby pictures of prominent members was held, with Mrs. T. D. Wosser and Mrs. Earl M. Kelly in charge of the meeting.

Miss Donna Morrell gave a monologue.

STRUCTURAL ENGINEERS ASSOCIATION OF CALIFORNIA

General Convention Chairman William Dreusike, and his committee, have announced a preliminary program of technical, social and sports activities as well advanced in preparedness for the Annual Meeting of the Structural Engineers Association of California, scheduled to be held October 2-3-4 in Yosemite Valley, California.

Plans should be made now to attend.

STRUCTURAL ENGINEERS ASSOCIATION OF NORTHERN CALIFORNIA

Professors Howard D. Eberhart of the University of California and Jack R. Benjamin of Stanford University presented a program of graduate students from the two universities at the regular May meeting held in the Engineers Club, San Francisco.

Participating students included Robert Taylor, Albert Knott, Edward Wilson, Travis Smith, and Raymond Itaya from the University of California; and Frederick Willsea, Samuel M. Holmes, and Frank Hedges of Stanford University.

The meeting with the students was designed to give a report, from the people directly involved, of some of the research work that is being done in the universi-

ties in the San Francisco-Bay area on various structural engineering problems, and to give an opportunity to meet and talk with outsanding senior graduate civil engineering students.

Recent new members include: Ben C. Albritton, Nicholas F. Forell, Ernest S. Ihlen, Ottomar T. Illerich, Richard D. Karr, Stefan J. Medwadowski, Michael P. Superak, and Robert J. Toft, Members; Raj T. Desai and James W. Murray, Junior Members; and Charles A. Pratt, Affiliate Member.

ENGINEER IS ELECTED
DIRECTOR OF BANK

Francis J. Murphy, graduate of the University of Santa Clara and Chief Engineer of the Judson-Pacific Murphy Corporation, has been appointed a Director of the Central Valley National Bank of Oakland, according to a recent announcement.

Murphy is also Chairman of the Board on the Maritime Equipment and Precast Concrete Corporation; was project manager in the construction of the Richmond-San Rafael state highway bridge, and is currently project manager of the new Glen Canyon Bridge in Arizona which will cross the Colorado River.

UNIVERSITY OF WASHINGTON
CELEBRATES COLLEGE OF ARCHITECTS

A celebration commemorating the establishment of the College of Architecture and Urban Planning at the University of Washington was observed this month in Seattle. Highlights of the program included an open house in the architecture building at the University where exhibits of student and alumni work was displayed, tours of outstanding examples of architecture in' the Puget Sound region, and the annual banquet at which student prizes and scholarships were awarded.

Dr. Henry Schmitz, president of the University, addressed guests at the open house, and Welton Becket, FAIA, distinguished alumnus, was the principal banquet speaker.

The Department of Architecture was established at the UW in 1914, becoming the School of Architecture of the College of Arts and Sciences in 1935. Professor Arthur P. Herrman, FAIA, director of the School of Architecture since 1937, was appointed Dean of the College in 1957.

says NEIL O'HAIR, *President, P. E. O'Hair & Co.*
Wholesale Plumbing and Heating Supplies
Headquarters, San Francisco

"We've been using
GREENBERG bronze
products *for over 50 years*"

Don't you agree . . . half a century is a long time to test any company's product or service? Since 1854, M. Greenberg's Sons has been supplying brass and bronze products for nearly every type of industry.

Today, as the largest bronze manufacturer in the West, M. Greenberg's Sons complete line includes such items as bronze valves for Navy, maritime, and industrial use; fire hydrants and industrial valves approved by Underwriters' Laboratories, Inc., and the Associated Factory Mutual Fire Insurance Companies; plumbing specialties, plaques and letters; many other ornamental bronze products.

Please send for our complete catalog. FOUNDED 1854

BRONZE PRODUCTS
by M. GREENBERG'S SONS
765 Folsom St • San Francisco, Calif. • EXbrook 2-3143
Offices in Principal Cities throughout the United States

PARKING AND MOTEL BUILDING

(From page 3)

square feet in the proposed structure, the cost is only $7.504 per square foot. A total of nine bids was received, and there was a range of only 10% between the low and the high bid.

The multi-story project will have some unique and unusual features. The sever topography of the site has enabled the architects to provide several entrances from different levels and streets.

The building is nine stories in height, and yet from Seventh Avenue projects a maximum of only four floors above ground level. There will be six levels of self parking accommodating 500 cars, including three partial levels of offices and stores, and three floors of motel facilities (140 suites with private balconies). Also planned are a coffee shop, cocktail lounge and dining terrace. The finish will be painted concrete exterior stucco, porcelain enamel and glass.

The structure will feature three outside glass elevators, one of which will enable people on Sixth Avenue to ride vertically to a bridge at the sixth floor elevation. They can then be transported horizontally by means of a moving sidewalk from the motel building, across Seventh Avenue, to the lobby area of the El Cortez Hotel. The moving sidewalk will be constructed under a separate contract. The building will be completed in February, 1959.

The combined parking and motel building is a Type I construction consisting of a nine-story high 100' x 300' main building and a three-story and roof deck 100' x 100' West wing. (The main structure has a reinforced concrete frame from the first to the sixth floor, and a structural steel frame from the seventh floor to the roof. The West wing structure consists of a reinforced concrete frame.)

All reinforced concrete frames are made up of one-way concrete slabs supported on continuous concrete beams, which in turn are supported on spirally reinforced circular concrete columns, tied concrete columns or concrete walls. The concrete frames are designed as rigid frames for carrying vertical forces. For lateral forces the floor slabs are designed as diaphragms carrying the forces to the side concrete walls.

The soil pressure on the East wall is carried by the wall spanning between floor slabs, which in turn carry the load to the end walls and to a compression member at the center of the building, from whence the forces are transferred through a concrete wall down an 8" thick slab on grade. A system of tie beams and shear diaphragms will finally carry the forces from the soil pressure to the footings in the whole West wing area, where the neecssary friction is available. The shear wall and diaphragms were reinforced on basis of the

(See page 32)

PHOTO CREDITS: Bethlehem Pacific Coast Steel Corp., Cover and Pages 14 and 15; Paderewski, Mitchell & Dean, Architects, Page 3; William M. Van Fleet, Architect, Page 6; Commercial Studio's Photo, Page 7; Don Gabriel Solera, Pages 10, 11, 12, 13; R. L. Copeland Photos, Page 17; Loren Smith, Pages 18 (top), 19, 20 (top), 21, 22; and Hainlin Studio, Pages 18 (bottom), 20 (bottom) and 23.

ARCHITECTS NAMED TO STUDY LAND

Architects Richard J. Neutra and Robert E. Alexander of Los Angeles, have been commissioned by the Santa Ana Council to make a land-use study in relation to anticipated population increases to determine the requirements for an adequate Civic Center.

The City has begun acquisition of property for Civic Center use and construction of a new City Library soon. The new study will determine needs for the ultimate construction of the city facilities in the center.

DRAWINGS COMPLETED FOR NEW SANTA ROSA ELEMENTARY SCHOOL

The architectural firm of Kenney & Cullimore of 2 Niles Street, Bakersfield, has completed working drawings for construction of the new Santa Rosa Elementary School at Atascadero for the Atascadero School district.

Facilities will include an administration unit, 13-classrooms, toilet facilities and other features at an estimated cost of $300,000. Construction will be tilt-up concrete, structural steel decking, concrete and asphalt tile floors, air-floor heating, plywood partitions, steel sash, and ceramic tile.

ARCHITECT WRIGHT PRESENTS DRAWINGS FOR CIVIC CENTER

Architect Frank Lloyd Wright presented preliminary sketches of a proposed new Civic Center to the Board of Supervisors of Marin County and the public recently.

The new county buildings are to be constructed on a 40-acre site just north of the city of San Rafael, and at an estimated cost of $5,000,000. Preliminary sketches indicate the project will be ultra modern in design and when constructed the facilities will be one of the show places in Northern California.

PLAN FEDERAL COURTS BUILDING FOR SAN FRANCISCO

The U. S. Federal Government, Washington, D. C., has announced contemplated purchases of a building site adjacent to the Civic Center in San Francisco, to be used for construction of a new Courts Building. The contemplated project will cost approximately $13,000,000. The building would contain 400,000 sq. ft. of area.

An option plan announced would be the construction of an addition to the present Post Office building at 7th and Mission. Such a program would involve additional space of 250,000 sq. ft. of area to present facilities.

GUSTAV O. HOGLUND RECENTLY ELECTED PRESIDENT OF THE AMERICAN WELDING SOCIETY

Gustav O. Hoglund, head of the Welding Section of the Aluminum Company of America, Process Development Laboratory, has been elected President of the American Welding Society at the 39th Annual Meeting of the Society in St. Louis, Missouri, and will take office on June 1st.

Born in Milwaukee, Wisconsin, he studied aeronautical engineering at the University of Michigan graduating in 1925 with a B.C. degree. After two years with the Bureau of Aeronautics, Hoglund joined the faculty of the University of Minnesota, leaving in 1928 to join the Aluminum Company of America.

He has been very active in the work of the American Welding Society, and has made many noteworthy contributions to the welding industry.

SOUTHERN CALIFORNIA CONTRACTORS TOURING EUROPE

A delegation of 17 Southern California building trades contractors, and their wives, left Los Angeles International Airport early this month for a 30-day tour of Europe to evaluate and compare contracting methods, requirements and progress abroad, under the auspices of the Los Angeles Chamber of Commerce.

Walter J. Escherich, general contractor, was appointed an honorary vice-president of the Chamber to serve as spokesman for the group who will visit in Copenhagen, Leningrad and Moscow, Stockholm, Helsinki, Berlin, Frankfurt, Paris, Brussels and Amsterdam. The group will be meeting with contractors' associations, building commissions, the Ministry of Building Trades Society of Paris, and other architectural and engineering societies and representatives of building material associations.

GENERAL CONTRACTOR MOVES INTO NEW OFFICES

John A. Rademann Company, general contractors, have moved into new offices at 307 12th Avenue, San Francisco, according to a recent announcement by the firm.

CALIFORNIA LEGISLATURE TO TAKE LOOK AT ARCHITECTURE

Glenn E. Coolidge of Felton and Francis C. Lindsay of Loomis, members of the California State Assembly, are co-authors of a resolution passed in the closing sessions of the Legislature calling for a study of production and management activities of the California Division of Architecture.

It is hoped such a study may lead to procedures whereby the facilities of private architects can be made more readily available to the State and thereby relieve the Department of Architecture of some of the heavy load of State design work.

The resolution calls for the employment of a competent firm of management experts to conduct the study, which would also include the possibility of making the Department a separate identity under a reorganization plan, or place it under the State Department of Finance.

John L. Rex, Southern California architect of Los Angeles, has recently been advanced to Fellowship in The American Institute of Architects, national organization of the architectural profession with general offices in Washington, D.C.

Architect Rex was awarded this high honor by a jury of Fellows for his outstanding contribution in the field of Design.

He served as president of the Southern California Chapter AIA in 1952, and on the California Council of Architects in 1953. He is a principal in

**JOHN L. REX, Architect
Fellow, A.I.A.**

the firm of Honnold and Rex, and has received Southern California Chapter awards for the Liebig and Eckdale residences, the Red Cross building in Los Angeles, the Pomona Shops, and an honorable mention award from School Executive Magazine for Westchester Junior High School.

Our congratulations to Mr. John L. Rex.

HILLSIDE HOUSE
(From page 32)

ground underneath the house could be kept open. He also avoided harmful undercutting of the ground which so often results in landslides.

"The simplicity and ease of steel framing made this possible," Warburg says. 'I don't know of any other system on a steep slope where you could get a structural platform off the ground faster and disturb the landscape less."

The mechanical engineer for the Schmidt house was Daniel Yanow, San Francisco. The landscape architect was Lawrence Halpin, San Francisco.

PARKING AND MOTEL BUILDING
(From page 30)

principal stresses.

The structural steel frame starts at the 6th parking floor level with steel columns resting on concrete columns or concrete walls. At the first motel floor a change in column location takes place and the new columns are supported on heavy steel girders.

The floor system consists of a corrugated steel deck spanning between steel joists, with a structural reinforcing lightweight concrete slab on top. The roof system is a poured gypsum deck spanning between open-web steel joists.

The lateral forces in the motel portion are carried partly by a number of vertical and horizontal bracing systems in the steel frame, partly by concrete stair walls. The forces were distributed to the bracing members and the walls on the basis of their relative rigidities.

The concrete frame is monolithic and is designed for forces caused by shrinkage. The concrete slabs have been provided with initial camber and continuous top reinforcement in order to reduce sagging.

The reinforced concrete bridges are designed partly as rigid frames and stresses caused by shrinkage combined with temperature changes have been considered.

SO SORRY!

Inadvertently, the article appearing in the April, 1958, issue featuring the Remodeling of the Building at 25 First Street, San Francisco, carried a By-Line of William B. McCormick, A.I.A. The article should have identified Mr. William B. McCormick, A.I.A. as the Architect in charge of design for alterations of the building, and not the author of the article. Graham & Hayes served as Structural Engineers; Keller & Gannon, Consulting Engineers, and Jos. L. Barnes, General Contractors.

BOOK REVIEWS
PAMPHLETS AND CATALOGUES

BUILDINGS FOR INDUSTRY. An Architectural Record Book. F. W. Dodge Corp., 119 W. 40th St., New York 18, N.Y. 310 pages. Price $9.75.

Represents an outstanding selection of new industrial buildings, together with a series of informative studies on trends, and factors in present-day industrial building design. Brilliantly illustrated with over 500 photographs and 200 line illustrations. Seventy-four separate projects from all over the U. S., and several other countries, are shown. Architects, engineers, industrial executives, and everyone else interested in the buildings that house all types of industry, will find the precise text and numerous illustrations a valuable source of new ideas and practical design data.

BUILDERS' HOMES — For Better Living. By A. Quincy Jones, Frederick E. Emmons, John L. Chapman, Associate. Reinhold Publishing Corp., 430 Park Ave., New York 22, N.Y. 220 pages. Price $8.95.

Much has been written and said of the destructive consequences to the community by the indiscriminate growth of tract housing, an uninspired collection of houses, unrelated to their sites, depressing in their superficial attempts to avoid repetition, and lacking integration with the surrounding community. This book deals with the business of building; materials and method of structure; design concepts of the house; relationship of the house to the individual lot and landscaping; and community planning. Since the builder house will continue to be constructed and sold, the welfare of the community and the nation as a whole will be strongly affected by the manner in which this is done. This book is an invaluable source of information, to all interested in an improved pattern of living.

BUILDING THE NEW CHURCH. By William S. Clark. The Religious Publishing Co., Jenkintown, Pa. 68 pages. Price $????.

The book explores and explains the very practical aspects of new construction, covering the entire subject from the day the new church is conceived to the day the completed edifice is dedicated. It also contains an analysis of current American church architecture; many illustrations of contemporary church architecture and a very practical working bibliography for the minister and his building committee members.

NEW CATALOGUES AVAILABLE

Architects, Engineers, Contractors, Planning Commission members—the catalogues, folders, new building products material, etc., described below may be obtained by directing your request to the name and address given in each item.

Rubber calk and other construction sealants. New 1958 catalog contains up-to-date application and technical information on "rubber calk" and other construction sealants; complete data, application illustrations dealing with curtain wall and tilt-up construction sealing problems. Free copy write DEPT-A&E, Products Research Co., 3126 Los Feliz Blvd., Los Angeles.

Safe chimney construction. New brochure (AIA File No. 5H) gives standard recommendations for safe chimney construction; drawings and ASTM specifications; completely illustrated, describes advantages of clay flue lining in chimney construction, making them fire safe; adaptable to any fuel. Copies free write DEPT-A&E, Clay Flue Lining Institue, 161 Ash St., Akron 8, Ohio.

Ventilating and air conditioning products. New 12-page bulletin describes complete line of Herman Nelson heating, ventilating and air conditioning products; includes illustrations and descriptions of convector radiators, finned radiation, unit heaters, console heaters, propeller fans, unit blowers, industrial exhausters and centrifugal fans; charts outlining performances, capacities, dimensions, range and numerous arrangements of units. Free copy write DEPT-A&E, American Air Filter Co., Inc., 215 Central Ave., Louisville, Ky.

Designing school kitchens for all-paper service. Booklet of architectural sketches and explanatory text that shows how the use of all-paper food service can reduce construction and

equipment costs in school kitchens; includes 5 representative paper service installations contrasted with equivalent conventional facilities; savings in space needs, lower equipment costs, smaller kitchen and cafeteria staffs in kitchens designed to serve 100 to 3,500 meals daily. Free copy write Field Research Division, Paper Cup and Container Institute, 342 Madison Ave., New York 17, N. Y.

Prefabricated lumber and timbers. New booklet (AIA FILE No. 19B) features many different types and uses of prefabricated lumber and timbers; illustrated applications to commercial and industrial buildings, schools and churches; also explains light roof framing, bridges, mines, railroads, and public utilities requirements. Free copy write DEPT-A&E, Rosboro Lumber Co., Springfield, Oregon.

Commercial gas water heaters. Newly-revised commercial catalog describes complete line of Ruud Mfg. Co.'s commercial gas water heaters; 17 models, AGA Use Approved Classifications; application, construction specifications, controls, hot water deliveries, and space requirement data. Free copy write DEPT-A&E, Ruud Mfg. Co., Kalamazoo, Mich.

Sound conditioning for schools and colleges. New 12-page brochure describes advantage of well-planned acoustical ceilings for educational buildings; features 1) reduction of noise, 2) establishment of an optimum reverberation time, 3) limiting the radiation of sound from its source so that separate groups can work independently in same room; case histories, pictures, design, layout, site planning. Free copy write DEPT-A&E, Celotex Corpn, 120 S. LaSalle St., Chicago 3, Ill.

Outdoor lighting fixtures. New 4-page brochure describes outdoor lighting fixtures in multi-purpose units; featuring shatter-resistant diffuser designed to defeat vandalism; three types of light sources may be used; installation detail, light distribution curves, specifications and suggested typical uses. Write DEPT-A&E, Silvray Lighting Inc., Bound Brook, N. Y.

Suspended Metal Lath and Plaster Ceilings! Technical bulletin No.'s 12-1 and 2, feature large illustrations covering the size and spacing of all metal components for a metal lath suspended ceiling; covering the minimum size of hangers, maximum spacing of wire hangers along each main runner, the size and weights of cold-controlled main runner channels, the maximum spacing of runners and maximum spans of furring; maximum spacing of cross furring, types of cross furring, and the types of weights of metal lath; also featured is ventilation of concealed ceiling areas; channel ties and splices, and channel clearances. Write for free copy DEPT-A&E, Metal Lath Mfg's Assn., Engineers Bldg., Cleveland 14, Ohio.

Loss possibilities from fire and natural hazards. New 22-page booklet explains building loss possibilities from fire and natural hazards; discusses causes of losses and tells how to provide safeguards against them; explains factors affecting loss possibilities, i.e. type of building construction, enclosures of stairways, elevators and other floor openings, subdivision of large areas, protection against fires in adjoining property, fire resistant roof coverings and safe chimney construction; also covers automatic sprinklers, standpipes, portable extinguishers and other fire protection equipment. Free copy Write DEPT-A&E, National Board of Fire Underwriters, Engineering Dept., 85 John St., New York City 38, or 465 California St., San Francisco, Calif.

ESTIMATOR'S GUIDE

BUILDING AND CONSTRUCTION MATERIALS

PRICES GIVEN ARE FIGURING PRICES AND ARE MADE UP FROM AVERAGE QUOTATIONS FURNISHED BY LeROY CONSTRUCTION SERVICES. 4% SALES TAX ON ALL MATERIALS BUT NOT LABOR. ITEMS IN ITALIC INCLUDE LABOR AND SALES TAX.

BONDS—Performance or Performance plus Labor and Material Bond(s), $10 per $1000 on contract price. Labor and Material Bond(s) only, $5.00 per $1000 on contract price.

BRICKWORK & MASONRY

COMMON BRICKWORK, Reinforced:		
8" walls	SF	2.95
12" walls	SF	4.15
SELECT COMMON, Reinforced:		
8" walls	SF	3.05
12" walls	SF	4.30
CONCRETE BLOCK, Reinforced:		
6" walls	SF	1.40
8" walls	SF	1.55
12" walls	SF	1.90
BRICK VENEER:		
4" Select Common	SF	1.65
4" Roman	SF	2.50
4" Norman	SF	2.40
4" Aggrelite	SF	2.40

BRICKWORK & MASONRY

All Prices—F.O.B. Plant.

COMMON BRICK		
Common 2½ x 3¾ x 8¼	M	45.00
Select 2½ x 3¾ x 8¼	M	52.00
Clinker 2½ x 3¾ x 8¼	M	48.00
Jumbo 3½ x 3 x 11½	M	90.00
FACE BRICK		
Standard	M	59.80 - 83.20
Jumbo	M	114.40 - 130.00
Roman	M	88.40 - 109.20
Norman	M	101.40 - 124.80
Brik Blox (6")	M	202.80
(8")	M	239.20
Braile Veneer	M	26.00
BUILDING TILE		
8 x 5½ x 12 inches	M	165.78
6 x 5½ x 12 inches	M	128.96
HOLLOW TILE		
12 x 12 x 3 inches	M	163.12
12 x 12 x 4 inches	M	184.18
12 x 12 x 6 inches	M	244.71
MANTEL FIRE BRICK		
2½ x 9½ x 4½ inches	M	140.40
GLAZED STRUCTURAL UNITS		
2 x 6 x 12 Furring	SF	.90
4 x 6 x 12 Furring	SF	1.20
6 x 6 x 12 Furring	SF	1.50
4 x 6 x 12 Partition	SF	1.60
Add for color	SF	.20
CONCRETE BLOCKS		
4 x 8 x 16 inches	EA	.22
6 x 8 x 16 inches	EA	.265
8 x 8 x 16 inches	EA	.30
12 x 8 x 16 inches	EA	.435
Colored Add	EA	.02
AGGREGATE—Haydite or Basalite		
All sizes in bulk	CY	6.24

BUILDING PAPERS & FELTS

1 ply per 1000 ft. roll	3.95
2 ply per 1000 ft. roll	6.03
3 ply per 1000 ft. roll	8.22
Sisalkraft, reinf. 500 ft. roll	7.54
SHEATHING PAPERS:	
Asphalt sheathing, 15-lb. roll	2.50
30-lb. roll	3.50
Dampcourse, 216-ft. roll	3.05
FELT PAPERS:	
Deadening felt, ¾-lb. 50 ft. roll	4.10
1-lb. 50 ft. roll	4.78
Asphalt roofing, 15-lbs.	2.50
30-lbs.	3.50
ROOFING PAPERS:	
Standard Grade, Smooth Surface	
108-ft. roll, Light	2.35
Medium	2.75
Heavy	3.22
Extra Heavy	3.75

CHIMNEYS, PATENT

F.O.B. Warehouse

6"	LF	1.45
8"	LF	2.05
10"	LF	2.85
12"	LF	3.45

Rates for 10 - 50 Lin. Ft.

CONCRETE AGGREGATES

	Bunker Per Ton	Del'd Per Ton
Gravel, All Sizes	3.38	4.16
Top Sand	3.59	4.37
Concrete Mix	3.48	4.26
Crushed Rock		
¼" to ¾"	3.43	4.26
¾" to 1½"	3.43	4.26
Roofing Gravel	3.54	4.42
SAND		
Lapis (Nos. 2 & 4)	4.47	5.30
Olympia (Nos. 1 & 2)	3.75	4.32

CEMENT		
Common All Brands (Paper Sacks)		
Small Quantities	Per Sack	1.40
Large Quantities	Per Bbl.	4.00
Trinity White & Mendusa White	Per Sack	4.16
CONCRETE READY-MIX		
6 sack in 5 yd. loads	Per Yd.	15.40
CURING COMPOUND, Clear		
5 gal. drums	Per Gal.	1.46

CARPENTRY & MILLWORK

Hardware not included

FRAMING:		
Floors	BM	.20 - .25
Walls	BM	.25 - .30
Ceilings	BM	.18 - .22
Roofs	BM	.22 - .27
Furring & Blocking	BM	.30 - .50
SHEATHING:		
1 x 8 straight	BM	.20 - .25
1 x 8 diagonal	BM	.23 - .28
5/16" Plyscore	SF	.16 - .20
⅜" Plywood	SF	.25 - .30
SIDING:		
1 x 8 Bevel	BM	.35 - .40
1 x 4 V-Rustic	BM	.40 - .45
EXTERIOR TRIM:		
Fascia and Molds	BM	.40 - .50
Bolted Framing—Add 50%		
ENTRANCE DOORS & FRAMES:		
Singles		*60.00 & Up*
Doubles		*100.00 & Up*
INTERIOR DOORS & FRAMES:		
Singles		*35.00 & Up*
Pocket Sliding		*45.00 & Up*
Closet Sliding (Pr.)		*50.00 & Up*
WINDOWS:		
D/H Sash & Frames	SF	*1.75 & Up*
Casement Sash & Frames	SF	*1.90 & Up*
SHELVING:		
1 x 12 S4S	BM	.30 - .50
¾" Plywood	SF	.40 - .60
STAIRS:		
Oak steps D.F. Risers		
Under 36" wide	Riser	12.00
Under 60" wide	Riser	17.00
Newel posts and rail extra		
WOOD CASES & CABINETS:		
D.F. Wall Hung	LF	13.00 - 18.00
D.F. Counters	LF	15.00 - 20.00

DAMPPROOFING & WATERPROOFING

MEMBRANE:		
1 layer 50 lb. felt	SQ.	9.00
4 layers Dampcourse	SQ.	13.00
Hot coat walls	SQ.	6.00
Tricosal added to concrete	CY	1.00
Anti-Hydro added to concrete	CY	1.50

ELECTRIC WIRING

Per Outlet:

Knob & Tube	EA	9.00
Armor	EA	16.00
Conduit	EA	20.00
110 V Circuit	EA	25.00
220 V Circuit	EA	95.00

ELEVATORS & ESCALATORS

Prices vary according to capacity, speed and type. Consult Elevator Companies.

Slow speed apartment house elevator including doors and trim, about $5000.00 per floor.

EXCAVATION

MACHINE WORK in common ground:		
Large Basements	CY	.75 - 1.00
Small Pits	CY	1.25 - 1.75
Trenches	CY	1.50 - 2.25
HAND WORK in common ground:		
Large pits and trenches	CY	4.50 - 5.50
Small pits and trimming	CY	5.00 - 6.50

Hard Clay & Shale 2 times above rates.
Rock and large boulders 4-6 times above rates.
Shoring, bracing and disposal of water not included.

FLOORS

⅛" Asp. tile, dark colors	SF	.25 - .30
⅛" Asp. tile, light colors	SF	.30 - .35
⅛" Rubber tile	SF	.60 - .70
.080 Vinyl Asbestos Tile	SF	.40 - .45
.080 Vinyl Tile	SF	.85 - .95
Lino, Standard Gauge	SY	3.75 - 4.25
Lino, Battleship	SY	5.25 - 5.75
4" Rubber Base, Black	LF	.35 - .40
Rubber Stair Nosing	LF	1.00 - 1.75

Above rates based on quantities of 1000 - 5000 SF per job.

HARDWOOD FLOORS

Select Oak, filled, sanded, stained and varnished:		
5/16" x 2¼" strip	SF	.45 - .50
5/16" Random Plank	SF	.50 - .55
25/32" x 2¼" T&G	SF	.70 - .80
Maple, 2nd Grade and Better, filled, sanded, stained and varnished:		
25/32" x 2¼" T&G	SF	.80 - .95
Wax Finish, add	SF	.10

HARDWOOD FLOORING

Oak 5/16" x 2" Strip—		
Clear	M	229.00
Select	M	218.00
#1 Common	M	203.00
Oak 5/16" Random Plank—		
Select & Btr.	M	286.00
#1 Common	M	244.00
Oak 25/32" x 2¼" T&G—		
Select	M	260.00
#1 Common	M	203.00
Maple 25/32" x 2¼" T&G—		
#1 Grade	M	317.00
#2 Grade	M	281.00
#3 Grade	M	208.00
Nails—1" Floor Brads	KEG	17.20

GLASS & GLAZING

S.S.B. Clear	SF	.48
D.S.B. Clear	SF	.78
Crystal	SF	.92
¼" Plate	SF	2.17
⅛" Obscure	SF	.68
⅛" Heat Absorbing	SF	1.12
¼" Tempered Plate	SF	4.38
½" Tempered Plate	SF	7.84
¼" Wire Plate, Clear	SF	3.65
¼" Wire Plate, Rough	SF	1.08

GLASS—CUT TO SIZE

F.O.B. Warehouse

S.S.B. Clear, Av. 6 SF	SF	.34
D.S.B. Clear, Av. 10 SF	SF	.56
Crystal, Av. 35 SF	SF	.66
¼" Polished Plate, Av. 100 SF	SF	1.55
⅛" Obscure, Av. 10 SF	SF	.49
⅛" Ribbed, Av. 10 SF	SF	.49
⅛" Rough, Av. 10 SF	SF	.49
¼" Wire Plate, Clear, Av. 40 SF	SF	2.61
¼" Wire Plate, Rough, Av. 40 SF	SF	.77
⅛" Heat Absorbing, Av. 10 SF	SF	.80
¼" Tempered Plate, Av. 50 SF	SF	3.13
½" Tempered Plate, Av. 50 SF	SF	5.60

Glazing—Approx. 40-50% of Glass
Glass Blocks—Check with Dealer

HEATING

FURNACES—Gas Fired—Av. Job:	
FLOOR FURNACE:	
25,000 BTU	*100.00 - 125.00*
35,000 BTU	*107.00 - 135.00*
45,000 BTU	*115.00 - 150.00*
AUTOMATIC CONTROL:	
Add	*25.00 - 35.00*

HEATING—Cont'd

DUAL WALL FURNACE:		
25,000 BTU		*110.00 - 125.00*
35,000 BTU		*125.00 - 145.00*
50,000 BTU		*150.00 - 180.00*
AUTOMATIC CONTROL:		
Add		*25.00 - 35.00*
GRAVITY FURNACE:		
75,000 BTU		*375.00 - 450.00*
85,000 BTU		*425.00 - 525.00*
95,000 BTU		*475.00 - 600.00*
FORCED AIR FURNACE:		
Add		*75.00 - 125.00*
AUTOMATIC CONTROL:		
Add		*15.00 - 25.00*
HEAT REGISTERS:		
Outlet		*7.50 - 15.00*

INSULATION & WALLBOARD

F.O.B. Warehouse

ROCKWOOL Insulation—		
2" Semi-thick	Per M SF	63.02
3⅝" Full Thick	Per M SF	80.50
COTTON Insulation		
1" Full Thick	Per M SF	43.26
SOFTBOARDS—Wood Fiber—		
½" thick	Per M SF	88.00
1½" thick	Per M SF	275.00
2" thick	Per M SF	385.00
ALUMINUM Insulation—		
80# Kraft paper with alum. foil		
1 side only	Per M SF	18.30
2 sides	Per M SF	31.00
GYPSUM Wallboard—		
⅜" thick	Per M SF	49.50
½" thick	Per M SF	54.50
⅝" thick	Per M SF	83.00
⅜" Gyplap	Per M SF	85.00
HARDBOARDS—Wood Fiber—		
⅛" thick, Sheathing	Per M SF	78.75
3/16" thick, Sheathing	Per M SF	90.48
¼" thick, Sheathing	Per M SF	109.20
⅛" thick, Tempered	Per M SF	98.80
3/16" thick, Tempered	Per M SF	140.40
¼" thick, Tempered	Per M SF	194.48
CEMENT Asbestos Board—		
⅛" C.A.B. Flat Sheets	Per M SF	156.00
3/16" C.A.B. Flat Sheets	Per M SF	218.40
¼" C.A.B. Flat Sheets	Per M SF	280.80

LATH & PLASTER

Diamond 3.40 copper bearing	SY	.50
Ribbed 3.40 copper bearing	SY	.55
⅜" rock lath	SY	.37
2" Standard Channel	LF	.085
1½" Standard Channel	LF	.065
¾" Standard Channel	LF	.045
3¼" steel studs	LF	.09
4" steel studs	LF	.105
Stud shoes	EA	.025
Hardwall, Browning	Sack	1.46
Hardwall, Finish	Sack	1.72
Stucco	Sack	2.50

LATH & PLASTERWORK

CHANNEL FURRING:		
Suspended Ceilings	*SY*	*2.20 - 2.50*
Walls	*SY*	*2.30 - 2.60*
METAL STUD PARTITIONS:		
3¼" Studs	*SY*	*1.70 - 2.00*
4" Studs	*SY*	*1.95 - 2.25*
Over 10'0 high, add	*SY*	*.20 - .30*
3.40 METAL LATH AND PLASTER:		
Ceilings	*SY*	*3.60 - 4.00*
Walls	*SY*	*3.75 - 4.15*
KEENE'S CEMENT FINISH:		
Add	*SY*	*.40 - .60*
ROCK LATH & PLASTER:		
Ceilings	*SY*	*2.50 - 2.80*
Walls	*SY*	*2.60 - 2.90*
WIRE MESH AND ⅞" STUCCO:		
Walls	*SY*	*3.60 - 4.10*
STUCCO ON CONCRETE:		
Walls	*SY*	*2.30 - 2.80*
METAL ACCESSORIES	*LF*	*.20 - .50*

LINOLEUM

Lino. Standard Gauge	SY	2.65 - 2.85
Lino. Battleship	SY	3.90 - 4.10
⅛" Asp. tile, Dark	SF	.10 - .11
⅛" Asp. tile, Light	SF	.14 - .16
⅛" Rubber Tile	SF	.40 - .44
.080 Vinyl Asb. tile	SF	.18 - .19
.080 Vinyl tile	SF	.59 - .61
⅛" Vinyl tile	SF	.78 - .82
4" Base, Dark	LF	.15 - .16
4" Base, Light	LF	.24 - .26
Rubber Nosing	LF	.60 - 1.30
Lino Paste	GAL	.75 - .90

Above rates based on quantities of 1000-5000 SF per job.

LUMBER

DOUGLAS FIR:	M.B.M.
#1 2x4—2x10	88.00 - 92.00
#2 2x4—2x10	85.00 - 90.00
#3 2x4—2x10	68.00 - 74.00
#4 2x4—2x10	64.00 - 72.00
Clear, Air Dried	180.00 - 210.00
Clear, Kiln Dried	210.00 - 240.00
REDWOOD:	
Foundation Grade	120.00 - 130.00
Construction Heart	110.00 - 120.00
A Grade	180.00 - 210.00
Clear Heart	190.00 - 220.00
D.F. PLYWOOD	M.S.F.
¼" AB	95.00 - 105.00
¼" AD	90.00 - 95.00
¼" Ext. Waterproof	115.00 - 125.00
⅜" AB	130.00 - 145.00
⅜" AD	115.00 - 125.00
⅜" CD	70.00 - 85.00
½" AB	170.00 - 185.00
½" AD	110.00 - 115.00
½" CD	
⅝" AB	185.00 - 200.00
⅝" AD	165.00 - 180.00
⅝" CD	115.00 - 125.00
¾" AB	210.00 - 230.00
¾" AD	195.00 - 210.00
¾" CD	125.00 - 140.00
⅝" Plyform	160.00 - 170.00
SHINGLES:	Square
Cedar #1	14.00 - 15.50
Cedar #2	11.50 - 12.50
SHAKES:	
CEDAR	
½ to ¾" Butt	17.50 - 18.50
¾ to 1¼" Butt	18.50 - 19.50
REDWOOD	
¾ to 1¼" Butt	21.00 - 24.00

MILLWORK

All Prices F.O.B. Mill

D.F. CLEAR, AIR DRIED:		
S4S	MBM	220.00 - 250.00
D.F. CLEAR, KILN DRIED:		
S4S	MBM	225.00 - 275.00
DOOR FRAMES & TRIM:		
Residential Entrance		17.00 & up
Interior Room Entrance		7.50 & up
DOORS:		
1⅜" D.F. Slab, Hollow Core		8.00 & up
1¾" D.F. Slab, Solid Core		19.00 & up
1⅜" Birch Slab, Hollow Core		10.00 & up
1¾" Birch Slab, Solid Core		22.00 & up
WINDOW FRAMES:		
D/H Singles	SF	.80
Casement Singles	SF	.90
WOOD SASH:		
D/H in pairs (1 lite)	SF	.45
Casement (1 lite)	SF	.50
WOOD CABINETS:		
¾" D.F. Ply with ¼" ply backs		
Wall Hung	LF	10.00 - 15.00
Counter	LF	12.00 - 17.00

BIRCH OR MAPLE—Add 25%

PAINTING

EXTERIOR:		
Stucco Wash 1 ct.	*SY*	*.30*
Stucco Wash 2 cts.	*SY*	*.55*
Lead and Oil 2 cts.	*SY*	*.90*
Lead and Oil 3 cts.	*SY*	*1.30*
INTERIOR:		
Primer Sealer	*SY*	*.40*
Wall Paint, 1 ct.	*SY*	*.50*
Wall Paint, 2 cts.	*SY*	*.95*
Enamel, 1 ct.	*SY*	*.60*
Enamel, 2 cts.	*SY*	*1.10*
Doors and Trim	*EA*	*10.00*
Sash and Trim	*EA*	*12.00*
Base and Molds	*LF*	*.12*

Old Work—Add 15-30%

PLUMBING

Lavatories	*EA*	*100.00 - 150.00*
Toilets	*EA*	*200.00 - 300.00*
Bath Tubs	*EA*	*250.00 - 350.00*
Stall Shower	*EA*	*80.00 - 150.00*
Sinks	*EA*	*125.00 - 175.00*
Laundry Trays	*EA*	*80.00 - 130.00*
Water Heaters	*EA*	*100.00 - 300.00*

Prices based on average residential and commercial work. Special fixtures and excessive piping not included.

PAINT

All Prices F.O.B. Warehouse

Thinners—5-100 gals.	GAL	.45
Turpentine—5-100 gals.	GAL	1.35
Linseed Oil, Raw	GAL	2.00
Linseed Oil, Boiled	GAL	1.95
Primer-Sealer	GAL	2.95
Enamel	GAL	5.00
Enamel Undercoat	GAL	3.25
White Lead in Oil	LB.	.26
Red Lead in Oil	LB.	.29
Litharge	LB.	.24

ROOFING

STANDARD TAR & GRAVEL	Per Square
4 ply	*14.00 - 18.00*
5 ply	*17.00 - 20.00*
White Gravel Finish—Add	*2.00 - 4.00*
Asph. Compo. Shingles	*16.00 - 20.00*
Cedar Shingles	*20.00 - 24.00*
Cedar Shakes	*26.00 - 30.00*
Redwood Shakes	*28.00 - 34.00*
Clay Tiles	*40.00 - 50.00*

SEWER PIPE

VITRIFIED:		
Standard 4 in.	LF	.31
Standard 6 in.	LF	.56
Standard 8 in.	LF	.81
Standard 12 in.	LF	1.76
Standard 24 in.	LF	6.95
CLAY DRAIN PIPE:		
Standard 6 in.	LF	.34
Standard 8 in.	LF	.59

Rate for 100 Lin. Ft. F.O.B. Warehouse

STEEL

REINFORCING BARS:		
¼" rounds	LB	.122
⅜" rounds	LB	.111
½" rounds	LB	.107
⅝" rounds	LB	.104
¾" rounds	LB	.102
⅞" rounds	LB	.102
1" rounds	LB	.102
REINFORCING MESH (1050 SF Rolls)		
6x6 x 10x10	SF	.035
6x6 x 6x6	SF	.067
16 GA. TYING WIRE	LB	.130

Rates 100-1000 Lbs. F.O.B. Warehouse

STRUCTURAL STEEL

$325.00 and up per ton erected when out of mill.
$350.00 and up per ton erected when out of stock.

SHEET METAL

ROOF FLASHINGS:		
18 ga. Galv. Steel	*SF*	*.60 - 1.00*
22 ga. Galv. Steel	*SF*	*.50 - .90*
26 ga. Galv. Steel	*SF*	*.40 - .80*
18 ga. Aluminum	*SF*	*1.00 - 1.50*
22 ga. Aluminum	*SF*	*.80 - 1.30*
26 ga. Aluminum	*SF*	*.60 - 1.10*
24 oz. Copper	*SF*	*1.90 - 2.40*
20 oz. Copper	*SF*	*1.70 - 2.20*
16 oz. Copper	*SF*	*1.50 - 2.00*
26 ga. Galv. Steel		
4" o.g. gutter	*LF*	*.90 - 1.30*
Mitres and Drops	*EA*	*2.00 - 4.00*
22 ga. Galv. Louvres	*SF*	*2.50 - 3.50*
20 oz. Copper Louvres	*SF*	*3.00 - 4.50*

TILE WORK

CERAMIC TILE, Stock colors:		
Floors	*SF*	*1.95 - 2.45*
Walls	*SF*	*2.05 - 2.55*
Coved Base	*LF*	*1.05 - 1.45*
QUARRY TILE:		
6" x 6" x ½" Floors	*SF*	*1.60 - 2.00*
9" x 9" x ¾" Floors	*SF*	*1.75 - 2.15*
Treads and risers	*LF*	*3.00 - 4.50*
Coved Base	*LF*	*.90 - 1.30*

Mosaic Tile—Rates vary with design and colors. Each job should be priced from Manufacturer.

TERRAZZO & MARBLE

Terrazzo Floors	*SF*	*2.00 - 2.50*
Cond. Terr. Floors	*SF*	*2.20 - 2.75*
Precast treads and risers	*LF*	*3.50 - 4.50*
Precast landing slabs	*SF*	*3.00 - 4.00*

TILE

CERAMIC:

F.O.B. Warehouse

4¼" x 4¼" glazed	SF	.69
4¼" x 4¼" hard glazed	SF	.72
Random unglazed	SF	.73
6" x 2" cap	EA	.17
6" coved base	EA	.22
¼" round bead	LF	.18
QUARRY:		
6 x 6 x ½" Red	SF	.49
6 x 6 x ¾" Red	SF	.52
9 x 9 x ¾" Red	SF	.60
6 x 6" coved base	EA	.21
White Cement Grout	Per 100 Lbs.	6.25

VENETIAN BLINDS

Residential	SF	.40 & Up
Commercial	SF	.45 & Up

WINDOWS

STEEL SASH:		
Under 10 SF	SF	2.50 & Up
Under 15 SF	SF	2.00 & Up
Under 20 SF	SF	1.50 & Up
Under 30 SF	SF	1.00 & Up
ALUMINUM SASH:		
Under 10 SF	SF	2.75 & Up
Under 15 SF	SF	2.25 & Up
Under 20 SF	SF	1.75 & Up
Under 30 SF	SF	1.25 & Up

Above rates are for standard sections and stock sizes F.O.B. Warehouse

QUICK REFERENCE
ESTIMATOR'S DIRECTORY
Building and Construction Materials

ACOUSTICAL ENGINEERS
L. D. REEDER CO.
San Francisco: 1255 Sansome St., DO 2-5050
Sacramento: 3026 V St., GL 7-3505

AIR CONDITIONING
E. C. BRAUN CO.
Berkeley: 2115 Fourth St,. TH 5-2356
GILMORE AIR CONDITIONING SERVICE
San Francisco: 1617 Harrison St., UN 1-2000
KAEMPER & BARRETT
San Francisco: 233 Industrial St., JU 6-6200
LINFORD AIR & REFRIGERATION CO.
Oakland: 174-12th St., TW 3-6521
MALM METAL PRODUCTS
Santa Rosa: 724-2nd St., SR 454
JAMES A. NELSON CO.
San Francisco: 1375 Howard St., HE 1-0140

ALUMINUM BLDG. PRODUCTS
MICHEL & PFEFFER IRON WORKS (Wrought Iron)
So. San Francisco: 212 Shaw Road, PLaza 5-8983
REYNOLDS METALS CO.
San Francisco: 3201 Third St., MI 7-2990
SOULE STEEL CO.
San Francisco: 1750 Army St., VA 4-4141
UNIVERSAL WINDOW CO.
Berkeley: 950 Parker St., TH 1-1600

ARCHITECTURAL PORCELAIN ENAMEL
CALIFORNIA METAL ENAMELING CO.
Los Angeles: 6904 E. Slauson, RA 3-6351
San Francisco: Continental Bldg. Products Co.,
178 Fremont St.
Portland: Portland Wire & Iron Works,
4644 S.E. Seventeenth Ave.
Seattle: Foster-Bray Co., 2412 1st Ave. So.
Spokane: Bernhard Schafer, Inc., West 34, 2nd Ave.
Salt Lake City: S. A. Roberts & Co., 109 W. 2nd So.
Dallas: Offenhauser Co., 2201 Telephone Rd.
El Paso: Architectural Products Co.,
506 E. Yandell Blvd.
Phoenix: Haskell-Thomas Co., 3808 No. Central
San Diego: Maloney Specialties, Inc., 823 W. Laurel St.
Boise: Intermountain Glass Co., 1417 Main St.

ARCHITECTURAL & AERIAL PHOTOGRAPHS
FRED ENGLISH
Belmont, Calif.: 1310 Old County Road, LY 1-0385

ARCHITECTURAL VENEER
Ceramic Veneer
GLADDING, McBEAN & CO.
San Francisco: Harrison at 9th St., UN 1-7400
Los Angeles: 2901 Los Feliz Blvd., OL 2121
Portland: 110 S.E. Main St., EA 6179
Seattle 99: 945 Elliott Ave., West, GA 0330
Spokane: 1102 N. Monroe St., BR 3259
KRAFTILE COMPANY
Niles, Calif., Niles 3611

Porcelain Veneer
PORCELAIN ENAMEL PUBLICITY BUREAU
Oakland 12: Room 601, Franklin Building
Pasadena 8: P. O. Box 186, East Pasadena Station
Granite Veneer
VERMONT MARBLE COMPANY
San Francisco 24: 6000 3rd St., VA 6-5024
Los Angeles: 3522 Council St., DU 2-6339
Marble Veneer
VERMONT MARBLE COMPANY
San Francisco 24: 6000 3rd St., VA 6-5024
Los Angeles: 3522 Council St., DU 2-6339

BANKS - FINANCING
CROCKER-ANGLO NATIONAL BANK
San Francisco: 13 Offices

BLINDS
PARAMOUNT VENETIAN BLIND CO.
San Francisco: 5929 Mission St., JU 5-2436

BRASS PRODUCTS
GREENBERG'S, M. SONS
San Francisco 7: 765 Folsom, EX 2-3143
Los Angeles 23: 1258 S. Boyle, AN 3-7108
Seattle 4:1016 First Ave. So., MA 5140
Phoenix: 3009 N. 19th Ave., Apt. 92, PH 2-7663
Portland 4: 510 Builders Exch. Bldg., AT 6443

BRICKWORK
Face Brick
GLADDING McBEAN & CO.
San Francisco: Harrison at 9th, UN 1-7400
KRAFTILE CO.
Niles, Calif., Niles 3611
UNITED MATERIALS & RICHMOND BRICK CO.
Point Richmond, BE 4-5032

BRONZE PRODUCTS
GREENBERG'S M. SONS
San Francisco: 765 Folsom St,. EX 2-3143
MICHEL & PFEFFER IRON WORKS
So. San Francisco: 212 Shaw Road, PLaza 5-8983
C. E. TOLAND & SON
Oakland: 2635 Peralta St., GL 1-2580

BUILDING HARDWARE
E. M. HUNDLEY HARDWARE CO.
San Francisco: 662 Mission St., YU 2-3322

BUILDING PAPERS & FELTS
PACIFIC CEMENT & AGGREGATES INC.
San Francisco: 400 Alabama St., KL 2-1616

CABINETS & FIXTURES
CENTRAL MILL & CABINET CO.
San Francisco: 1595 Fairfax Ave., VA 4-7316
THE FINK & SCHINDLER CO.
San Francisco: 552 Brannan St., EX 2-1513
JONES KRAFT SHOP,
San Francisco: 1314 Ocean Avenue., JU 7-1545
MULLEN MFG. CO.
San Francisco: 64 Rausch St., UN 1-5815
PARAMOUNT BUILT IN FIXTURE CO.
Oakland: 962 Stanford Ave., OL 3-9911
ROYAL SHOWCASE CO.
San Francisco: 770 McAllister St., JO 7-0311

CEMENT
CALAVERAS CEMENT CO.
San Francisco: 315 Montgomery St.
DO 2-4224, Enterprise 1-2315
PACIFIC CEMENT & AGGREGATES INC.
San Francisco: 400 Alabama St., KL 2-1616

CONCRETE AGGREGATES
Ready Mixed Concrete
CENTRAL CONCRETE SUPPLY CO.
San Jose: 610 McKendrie St.
PACIFIC CEMENT & AGGREGATES INC.
San Francisco: 400 Alabama St., KL 2-1616
Sacramento: 16th and A Sts., GI 3-6586
San Jose: 790 Stockton Ave., CY 2-5620
Oakland: 2400 Peralta St., GL 1-0177
Stockton: 820 So. California St., ST 8-8643
READYMIX CONCRETE CO.
Santa Rosa: 50 W. Cottage Ave.
RHODES-JAMIESON LTD.
Oakland: 333-23rd Ave., KE 3-5225
SANTA ROSA BLDG. MATERIALS CO.
Santa Rosa: Roberts Ave.

CONCRETE ACCESSORIES
Screed Materials
C. & H. SPECIALTIES CO.
Berkeley: 909 Camelia St., LA 4-5358

CONCRETE BLOCKS
BASALT ROCK CO.
Napa, Calif.

CONCRETE COLORS—HARDENERS
CONRAD SOVIG CO.
875 Bryant St., HE 1-1345

CONSTRUCTION SERVICES
LE ROY CONSTRUCTION SERVICES
San Francisco, 143 Third St., SU 1 8914

DECKS—ROOF
UNITED STATES GYPSUM CO.
2322 W. 3rd St., Los Angeles 54, Calif.
300 W. Adams St., Chicago 6, Ill.

DOORS
THE BILCO COMPANY
New Haven, Conn.
Oakland: Geo. B. Schultz, 190 MacArthur Blvd.
Sacramento: Harry B. Ogle & Assoc., 1331 T St.
Fresno: Healey & Popovich, 1703 Fulton St.
Reseda: Daniel Dunner, 6200 Alonzo Ave.

Cold Storage Doors
BIRKENWALD
Portland: 310 N.W. 5th Ave.

Electric Doors
ROLY-DOOR SALES CO.
San Francisco, 5976 Mission St., PL 5-5089

Folding Doors
WALTER D. BATES & ASSOCIATES
San Francisco, 693 Mission St., GA 1-6971

Hardwood Doors
BELLWOOD CO. OF CALIF.
Orange, Calif., 533 W. Collins Ave.

Hollywood Doors
WEST COAST SCREEN CO.
Los Angeles: 1127 E. 63rd St., AD 1-1108
T. M. COBB CO.
Los Angeles & San Diego
W. P. FULLER CO.
Seattle, Tacoma, Portland
HOGAN LUMBER CO.
Oakland: 700 - 6th Ave.
HOUSTON SASH & DOOR
Houston, Texas
SOUTHWESTERN SASH & DOOR
Phoenix, Tucson, Arizona
El Paso, Texas
WESTERN PINE SUPPLY CO.
Emeryville: 5760 Shellmound St.
GEO. C. VAUGHAN & SONS
San Antonio & Houston, Texas

Screen Doors
WEST COAST SCREEN DOOR CO.
DRAFTING ROOM EQUIPMENT
GENERAL FIREPROOFING CO.
Oakland: 332-19th St., GL 2-4280
Los Angeles: 1200 South Hope St., RI 7-7501
San Francisco: 1025 Howard St., HE 1-7070

DRINKING FOUNTAINS
HAWS DRINKING FAUCET CO.
Berkeley: 1435 Fourth St., LA 5-3341

ELECTRICAL CONTRACTORS
COOPMAN ELECTRIC CO.
San Francisco: 85 - 14th St., MA 1-4438
ETS-HOKIN & GALVAN
San Francisco: 551 Mission St., EX 2-0432

ELECTRICAL CONTRACTORS (cont'd)

LEMOGE ELECTRIC CO.
San Francisco: 212 Clara St., DO 2-6010
LYNCH ELECTRIC CO.
San Francisco: 937 McAllister St., WI 5150
PACIFIC ELECTRIC & MECHANICAL CO.
San Francisco: Gough & Fell Sts., HE 1-5904

ELECTRIC HEATERS

WESIX ELECTRIC HEATER CO.
San Francisco: 390 First St., GA 1-2211

FIRE ESCAPES

MICHEL & PFEFFER IRON WORKS
South San Francisco: 212 Shaw Road, PLaza 5-8983

FIRE PROTECTION EQUIPMENT

FIRE PROTECTION PRODUCTS CO.
San Francisco: 1101-16th St., UN 1-2420
ETS-HOKIN & GALVAN
San Francisco: 551 Mission St., EX 2-0432
BARNARD ENGINEERING CO.
San Francisco: 35 Elmira St., JU 5-4642

FLOORS

Floor Tile

GLADDING McBEAN & CO.
San Francisco: Harrison at 9th St., UN 1-744
Los Angeles: 2901 Los Feliz Bldg., OL 2121
KRAFTILE CO.
Niles, Calif., Niles 3611

Resilient Floors

PETERSON-COBBY CO.
San Francisco: 218 Clara St., EX 2-8714
TURNER RESILIENT FLOORS CO.
San Francisco: 2280 Shafter Ave., AT 2-7720

FLOOR DRAINS

JOSAM PACIFIC COMPANY
San Francisco: 765 Folsom St., EX 2-3142

GAS VENTS

WM. WALLACE CO.
Belmont, Calif.

GENERAL CONTRACTORS

O. E. ANDERSON
San Jose: 1075 No. 10th St., CY 3-8844
BARRETT CONSTRUCTION CO.
San Francisco: 1900 Evans Ave., MI 7-9700
JOSEPH BETTANCOURT
South San Francisco: 125 So. Linden St., PL 5-9185
DINWIDDIE CONSTRUCTION CO.
San Francisco: Crocker Bldg., YU 6-2718
D. L. FAULL CONSTRUCTION CO.
Santa Rosa: 1236 Cleveland Ave.
HAAS & HAYNIE
San Francisco: 275 Pine St., DO 2-0678
HENDERSON CONSTRUCTION CO.
San Francisco: 33 Ritch St., GA 1-0856
JACKS & IRVINE
San Francisco: 620 Market St., YU 6-0511
G. P. W. JENSEN & SONS
San Francisco: 320 Market St., GA 1-2444
RALPH LARSEN & SON
San Francisco: 64 So. Park, YU 2-5682
LINDGREN & SWINERTON
San Francisco: 200 Bush St., GA 1-2980
MacDONALD, YOUNG & NELSON
San Francisco: 351 California St., YU 2-4700
MATTOCK CONSTRUCTION CO.
San Francisco: 220 Clara St., GA 1-5516
OLSEN CONSTRUCTION CO.
Santa Rosa: 125 Brookwood Ave., SR 2030
BEN ORTSKY
Cotati: Cypress Ave., Pet. 5-4383
PARKER, STEFFANS & PEARCE
San Mateo: 135 So. Park, EX 2-6639

RAPP, CHRISTENSEN & FOSTER
Santa Rosa: 705 Bennett Ave.
STOLTE, INC.
Oakland: 8451 San Leandro Ave., LO 2-4611
SWINERTON & WALBERG
San Francisco: 200 Bush St., GA 1-2980

FURNITURE—INSTITUTIONAL

GENERAL FIREPROOFING CO.
San Francisco: 1025 Howard St., HE 1-7070
Oakland: 332-19th St., GL 2-4280
Los Angeles: 1200 South Hope St., RI 7-7501

HEATING & VENTILATING

ATLAS HEATING & VENT. CO.
San Francisco: 557-4th St., DO 2-0377
E. C. BRAUN CO.
Berkeley: 2115 Fourth St., TH 5-2356
C. W. HALL
Santa Rosa: 1665 Sebastopol Rd., SR 6354
S. T. JOHNSON CO.
Oakland: 940 Arlington Ave., OL 2-6000
LOUIS V. KELLER
San Francisco: 289 Tehama St., JU 6-6252
L. J. KRUSE CO.
Oakland: 6247 College Ave., OL 2-8332
MALM METAL PRODUCTS
Santa Rosa: 724-2nd St., SR 454
JAS. A. NELSON CO.
San Francisco: 1375 Howard St., HE 1-0140
SCOTT COMPANY
Oakland: 1919 Market St., GL 1-1937
WESIX ELECTRIC HEATER CO.
San Francisco: 390 First St., GA 1-2211
Los Angeles: 530 W. 7th St., MI 8096

INSULATION WALL BOARD

PACIFIC CEMENT & AGGREGATES, INC.
San Francisco: 400 Alabama St., KL 2-1616

INTERCEPTING DEVICES

JOSAM PACIFIC CO.
San Francisco: 765 Folsom St., EX 2-3142

IRON—ORNAMENTAL

MICHEL & PFEFFER IRON WKS.
So. San Francisco, 212 Shaw Rd., PL 5-8983

LATHING & PLASTERING

ANGELO J. DANERI
San Francisco: 1433 Fairfax Ave., AT 8-1582
K-LATH CORP.
Alhambra: 909 So. Fremont St., Alhambra
A. E. KNOWLES CORP.
San Francisco: 3330 San Bruno Ave., JU 7-2091
G. H. & C. MARTINELLI
San Francisco: 174 Shotwell St., UN 3-6112
FREDERICK MEISWINKEL
San Francisco: 2155 Turk St., JO 7-7587
RHODES-JAMIESON LTD.
Oakland: 333-23rd Ave., KE 3-5225
PATRICK J. RUANE
San Francisco: 44 San Jose Ave., MI 7-6414

LIGHTING FIXTURES

SMOOT-HOLMAN COMPANY
Inglewood, Calif., OR 8-1217
San Francisco: 55 Mississippi St., MA 1-8474

LUMBER

CHRISTENSEN LUMBER CO.
San Francisco: Quint & Evans Ave., VA 4-5832
ART HOGAN LUMBER CO.
1701 Galvez Ave., ATwater 2-1157
MEAD CLARK LUMBER CO.
Santa Rosa: 3rd & Railroad
ROLANDO LUMBER CO.
San Francisco: 5th & Berry Sts., SU 1-6901
STERLING LUMBER CO.
Santa Rosa: 1129 College Ave., S. R. 82

MARBLE

JOS. MUSTO SONS-KEENAN CO.
San Francisco: 555 No. Point St., GR 4-6365
VERMONT MARBLE CO.
San Francisco: 6000-3rd St., VA 6-5024

MASONRY

BASALT ROCK CO.
Napa, Calif.
San Francisco: 260 Kearney St., GA 1-3758
WM. A. RAINEY & SON
San Francisco: 323 Clementina St., SU 1-0072
GEO. W. REED CO.
San Francisco: 1390 So. Van Ness Ave., AT 2-1226

METAL EXTERIOR WALLS

THE KAWNEER CO.
Berkeley: 930 Dwight Way, TH 5-8710

METAL FRAMING

UNISTRUT OF NORTHERN CALIFORNIA
Berkeley: 2547-9th St., TH 1-3031
Enterprise 1-2204

METAL GRATING

KLEMP METAL GRATING CORP.
Chicago, Ill.: 6601 So. Melvina St.

METAL LATH—EXPANDED

PACIFIC CEMENT & AGGREGATES, INC.
San Francisco: 400 Alabama St., KL 2-1616

METAL PARTITIONS

THE E. F. HAUSERMAN CO.
San Francisco: 485 Brannan St., YU 2-5477

METAL PRODUCTS

FORDERER CORNICE WORKS
San Francisco: 269 Potrero Ave., HE 1-4100

MILLWORK

CENTRAL MILL & CABINET CO.
San Francisco: 1595 Fairfax Ave., VA 4-7316
THE FINK & SCHINDLER CO.
San Francisco: 552 Brannan St., EX 2-1513
MULLEN MFG. CO.
San Francisco: 64 Rausch St., UN 1-5815
PACIFIC MFG. CO.
San Francisco: 16 Beale St., GA 1-7755
Santa Clara: 2610 The Alameda, S. C. 607
Los Angeles: 6820 McKinley Ave., TH 4156
SOUTH CITY LUMBER & SUPPLY CO.
So. San Francisco: Railroad & Spruce, PL 5-7085

OFFICE EQUIPMENT

GENERAL FIREPROOFING CO.
Los Angeles: 1200 South Hope St., RI 7-7501
San Francisco: 1025 Howard St., HE 1-7070
Oakland: 332-19th St., GL 2-4280

OIL BURNERS

S. T. JOHNSON CO.
Oakland: 940 Arlington Ave., GL 2-6000
San Francisco: 585 Potrero Ave., MA 1-2757
Philadelphia, Pa.: 401 North Broad St.

ORNAMENTAL IRON

MICHEL & PFEFFER IRON WORKS
So. San Francisco: 212 Shaw Rd., PL 5-8983

PAINTING

R. P. PAOLI & CO.
San Francisco: 2530 Lombard St., WE 1-1632
SINCLAIR PAINT CO.
San Francisco: 2112-15th St., HE 1-2196
D. ZELINSKY & SONS
San Francisco: 165 Groove St., MA 1-7400

PHOTOGRAPHS

Construction Progress
FRED ENGLISH
Belmont, Calif.: 1310 Old County Road, LY 1-0385

PLASTER

PACIFIC CEMENT & AGGREGATE INC.
San Francisco: 400 Alabama St., KL 2-1616

PLASTIC PRODUCTS

PLASTIC SALES & SERVICE
San Francisco: 409 Bryant St., DO 2-6433
WEST COAST INDUSTRIES
San Francisco: 3150-18th St., MA 1-5657

CLASSIFIED ADVERTISING

RATE: 20c PER WORD . . . CASH WITH ORDER   MINIMUM $5.00

CONSTRUCTION INDUSTRY WAGE RATES

Table 1 has been prepared by the State of California, Department of Industrial Relations, Division of Labor Statistics and Research. The rates are the union hourly wage rates established by collective bargaining as of January 2, 1958, as reported by reliable sources.

TABLE 1—UNION HOURLY WAGE RATES, CONSTRUCTION INDUSTRY, CALIFORNIA

Following are the hourly rates of compensation established by collective bargaining, reported as of January 2, 1958 or later

CRAFT	San Francisco	Alameda	Contra Costa	Fresno	Sacramento	San Joaquin	Santa Clara	Solano	Los Angeles	San Bernardino	San Diego	Santa Barbara	Kern
ASBESTOS WORKER	$3.70	$3.70	$3.70	$3.70	$3.70	$3.70	$3.70	$3.70	$3.70	$3.70	$3.70	$3.70	$3.70
BOILERMAKER	3.675	3.675	3.675	3.675	3.675	3.675	3.675	3.675	3.675	3.675	3.675	3.675	3.675
BRICKLAYER	3.95	3.75	3.75	3.75	3.80	3.75	3.875	3.95	3.80	3.90	3.75		3.86
BRICKLAYER HODCARRIER	3.15	3.15	3.15	2.90	3.10	2.90	3.00	3.10	2.75	2.75	2.75		2.75
CARPENTER	3.175	3.175	3.225	3.225	3.225	3.225	3.225	3.225	3.225	3.225	3.225	3.225	3.225
CEMENT MASON	3.22	3.22	3.22	3.22	3.22	3.22	3.22	3.22	3.15	3.15	3.25	3.15	3.15
ELECTRICIAN	3.936ᴀ	3.936ᴀ	3.936ᴀ		3.94ᴀ	3.50	4.03ᴀ	3.666ᴀ	3.90ᴀ	3.90ᴀ	3.90	3.85ᴀ	3.70
GLAZIER	3.09	3.09	3.09	3.135	3.055	3.055	3.09	3.09	3.105	3.105	3.03	3.105	3.135
IRON WORKER													
ORNAMENTAL	3.625	3.625	3.625	3.625	3.625	3.625	3.625	3.625	3.625	3.625	3.625	3.625	3.625
REINFORCING	3.375	3.375	3.375	3.375	3.375	3.375	3.375	3.375	3.375	3.375	3.375	3.375	3.375
STRUCTURAL	3.625	3.625	3.625	3.625	3.625	3.625	3.625	3.625	3.625	3.625	3.625	3.625	3.625
LABORER, GENERAL OR CONSTRUCTION	2.505	2.505	2.505	2.505	2.505	2.505	2.505	2.505	2.50	2.50	2.48	2.50	2.50
LATHER	3.4375	3.84	3.84	3.45	3.60ᴇ	3.40ᴄ	3.60ᴅ	3.50ᴇ	3.9375		3.725	3.625ꜰ	
OPERATING ENGINEER													
Concrete mixer (up to 1 yard)	2.89	2.89	2.89	2.89	2.89	2.89	2.89	2.89					
Concrete mixer operator—Skip Type									2.96	2.96	2.96	2.96	2.96
Elevator Hoist Operator									3.19	3.19	3.19	3.19	3.19
Material Hoist (1 drum)	3.19	3.19	3.19	3.19	3.19	3.19	3.19	3.19					
Tractor Operator	3.33	3.33	3.33	3.33	3.33	3.33	3.33	3.33	3.47	3.47	3.47	3.47	3.47
PAINTER													
Brush	3.20	3.20	3.20	3.13	3.325	3.175	3.20	3.20	3.26ɢ	3.25	3.19	3.13ʜ	3.10
Spray	3.20	3.20	3.20	3.38	3.575	3.325	3.20	3.20	3.51ɢ	3.50	3.74	3.38ʜ	3.35
PILEDRIVERMAN	3.305	3.305	3.305	3.305	3.305	3.305	3.305	3.305	3.355	3.355		3.355	3.355
PLASTERER	3.69	3.545	3.545	3.35	3.60ᴇ	3.55ᴄ	3.58	3.50	3.9375	3.9375	3.725		
PLASTERER HODCARRIER	3.25	3.42	3.42	3.10	3.10	3.00ᴄ	3.20	3.15	3.6875	3.5625	3.475	3.50	3.6875
PLUMBER	3.67		3.935ɪ	3.80ᴊ	3.70	3.80ᴊ	3.60	3.675	3.70	3.70	3.70	3.70	3.375
ROOFER	3.35	3.35	3.35	3.20	3.25	3.35	3.35	3.10ᴋ	3.20ʟ	3.25	3.10	3.30	3.775
SHEET METAL WORKER	3.45	3.45	3.45	3.425	3.45	3.465	3.45	3.325	3.50	3.50	3.45	3.55	3.10
STEAMFITTER	3.67	3.96	3.96	3.80ᴊ	3.70	3.80ᴊ	3.60	3.675	3.70	3.70	3.70	3.70	3.775
TRUCK DRIVER—													
Dump Trucks under 4 yards	2.55	2.55	2.55	2.55	2.55	2.55	2.55	2.55	2.63	2.63	2.63	2.63	2.63
TILE SETTER	3.275	3.275	3.275	3.375	3.28	3.30	3.275	3.275	3.36	3.60	3.375	3.36	

ᴀ Includes 4% vacation allowance.
ʙ Includes 5c hour for industry promotion and 5c hour for vacation fund.
ᴄ ¹/₂% withheld for industry promotion.
ᴅ 1¹/₂c withheld for industry promotion.
ᴇ Includes 5c hour for industry promotion and 5c hour for vacation fund. Hourly rate for part of county adjacent to Sacramento County is $3.60.
ꜰ Northern part of County: $3.75.

ɢ Pomona Area: Brush $3.25; Spray $3.50.
ʜ Southern half of County: Brush $3.28; Spray $3.28.
ɪ Includes 30c hour for vacation pay.
ᴊ Includes 15c hour which local union may elect to use for vacation purposes.
ᴋ Includes 10c hour for vacation fund.
ʟ Includes 10c hour savings fund wage.

ATTENTION: The above tabulation has been prepared by the State of California, Department of Industrial Relations, Division of Labor Statistics and Research, and represents data reported by building trades councils, union locals, contractor organizations, and other reliable sources. The above rates do not include any payments to funds for health and welfare, pensions, vacations, industry promotion, apprentice training, etc., except as shown in the footnotes.

CONSTRUCTION INDUSTRY WAGE RATES — TABLE 2

Employer Contributions to Health and Welfare, Pension, Vacation and Other Funds
California Union Contracts, Construction Industry

(Revised March, 1957)

CRAFT	San Francisco	Fresno	Sacramento	San Joaquin	Santa Clara	Los Angeles	San Bernardino	San Diego
ASBESTOS WORKER	.10 W .11 hr. V	.10 W .11 hr. V	.10 W .11 hr. V	.10 W .11 hr. V	.10 W .11 hr. V	.10 W	.10 W	.10 W
BRICKLAYER	.15 W .14 P .05 hr. V		.15 W .10 P		.15 W			
BRICKLAYER HODCARRIER	.10 W .10 P .10 V	.10 W	.10 W	.10 W	.10 W	.075 W	.075 W	.075 W
CARPENTER	.10 W .10 hr. V	.10 W	.10 W	.10 W	.10 W	.10 W	.10 W	.10 W
CEMENT MASON	.10 W	.10 W	.10 W	.10 W	.10 W	.10 W	.10 W	.10 W
ELECTRICAL WORKER	.10 W 1% P 4% V	.10 W 1% P 4% V	.075 W 1% P	.075 W 1% P 4% V	1% P	1% P	1% P	.10 W 1% P
GLAZIER	.075 W .085 V	.075 W 40 hr. V	.075 W .05 V	.075 W .05 V	.075 W .085 V	.075 W 40 hr. V	.075 W 40 hr. V	.075 W 10 hr. V
IRONWORKER: REINFORCING	.10 W	.10 W	.10 W	.10 W	.10 W	.10 W	.10 W	.10 W
STRUCTURAL	.10 W	.10 W	.10 W	.10 W	.10 W	.10 W	.10 W	.10 W
LABORER, GENERAL	.10 W	.10 W	.10 W	.10 W	.10 W	.075 W	.075 W	.075 W
LATHER	.60 day W .70 day V		.10 W	.10 W	.075 W .05 V	.90 day W	.70 day W	.10 W
OPERATING ENGINEER TRACTOR OPERATOR (MIN.)	.10 W	.10 W	.10 W	.10 W	.10 W	.10 W	.10 W	.10 W
POWER SHOVEL OP. (MIN.)	.10 W	.10 W	.10 W	.10 W	.10 W	.10 W	.10 W	.10 W
PAINTER, BRUSH	.095 W	.08 W	.075 W	.10 W	.095 W .07 V	.085 W	.08 W	.09 W
PLASTERER	.10 W .10 V	.10 W	.10 W	.10 W	.10 W .15 V	.10 W	.90 day V	.10 W
PLUMBER	.10 W .10 V	.15 W .10 P	.10 W .10 P .125 V	.10 W	.10 W .10 P .125 V	.10 W	.90 day V	.10 W
ROOFER	.10 W .10 V	.10 W	.10 W .10 V	.10 W	.075 W .10 V	.065 W	.10 W	.075 W
SHEET METAL WORKER	.075 W 4% V	.075 W 7 day V	.075 W .10 V	.075 W .12 V	.075 W 4% V	.085 W .10 V	.085 W .10 V	.085 W 5 day V
TILE SETTER	.075 W .09 V				.075 W .09 V	.075 W .025 W .06 V		

ATTENTION: The above tabulation has been prepared and compiled from the available data reported by building trades councils, union locals, contractor organizations and other reliable sources. The table was prepared from incomplete data; where no employer contributions are specified, it does not necessarily mean that none are required by the union contract.

The type of supplement is indicated by the following symbols: W—Health and Welfare; P—Pensions; V—Vacations; A—Apprentice training fund; Adm—Administration fund; JIB—Joint Industry Board; Prom—Promotion fund.

CONSTRUCTION CONTRACTS AWARDED AND MISCELLANEOUS PERSONNEL DATA

ELKS CLUB, Swimming Pool and Bath House, Palo Alto, Santa Clara county. Elks Club of Palo Alto, owner. Bath house construction of concrete block, open beam ceiling, built-up roofing, some structural steel and tile floors—$194,500. ARCHITECT: H. C. Arnfeldt, 131 University Ave., Palo Alto. GENERAL CONTRACTOR: Tropical Pools Inc., 2856 Middlefield Road, Redwood City (Swimming pool) and Wells P. Goodenough Inc., P.O. Box 120, Palo Alto (Bath house).

STORAGE BLDG., Los Angeles. Hirsch Pipe & Supply Co., Los Angeles, owner. Brick storage building 71 x 105 ft., composition roof, wood partitions, metal sash, concrete floor, wood slab and roll-up doors, plate glass, structural steel, asphalt concrete paving—$30,000. ENGINEER: David T. Witherly, 7233 Beverly Blvd., Los Angeles. GENERAL CONTRACTOR: Contracting Engineering, 2310 W. Vernon Ave., Los Angeles.

WAREHOUSE, North Hollywood, Los Angeles county. J. B. McGalliard, 131112 Saticoy St, North Hollywood, owner. Brick warehouse building, 80 x 160 ft., composition roof, tapered steel girders, rotary roof vents, concrete slab floors, toilets, overhead doors, steel sash, paving—$50,-000. CONSULTING ENGINEER: H. L. Standefer, 4344 Laurel Canyon Blvd, North Hollywood.

CONVALESCENT HOME, Concord, Contra Costa county, Valley Manor Convalescent Home, Concord, owner. Work consists of an addition to the present facilities by improving 8-bedrooms, toilets, showers, basement laundry rooms: 2,780 sq. ft. area; wood frame, composition roofing—$34,500. ARCHITECT: Hansen & Winkler, 251 Post St, San Francisco. GENERAL CONTRACTOR: James L. Petersen, 5504 Pine Hollow Rd, Concord.

OFFICE BLDG, Glendale. Los Angeles county. Smith & Mock, Glendale. owner. Frame and stucco, 50 x 100 ft., concrete slab and asphalt tile floors, refrigerated air conditioning, heating system, metal toilet partitions, stone veneer, asphalt paving. ENGINEER: Nelson Engineering Co, 1560 Victory Blvd., Los Angeles. GENERAL CONTRACTOR: John Pagliouso, 545 W. Glenoaks Blvd., Glendale.

HIGH SCHOOL ADD'N, Placer Union, Auburn, Placer county. Placer Union High School, Auburn, owner. Wood frame construction to add cafeteria facilities—$149,-950. ARCHITECT: Lawrence G. Thomson, 125 3rd St, Chico. GENERAL CONTRACTOR: Lamon Const. Co, 881 Market St, Yuba City.

SCHOOL ADD'N, Elbow Elementary, Ivanhoe, Tulare county. Ivanhoe School

District, owner. 1-Story masonry exterior, concrete floors, built-up roofing, to provide classroom facilities — $58,970. ARCHITECT: James P. Lockett, Bank of America Bldg, Visalia. GENERAL CONTRACTOR: Jack Campbell Const., 2014 E. Home St, Fresno.

HIGH SCHOOL ADD'N, Watsonville, Santa Cruz county. Watsonville Joint Union High School District, owner. Wood frame and reinforced concrete slab on grade construction, to provide facilities for 20 classrooms—$360,446. ARCHITECT: John Lyon Reid & Partners, 1019 Market St., San Francisco.

FACTORY & OFFICE, Norwalk, Los Angeles. Tilt-up concrete and stone veneer, 10,000 sq. ft. area, bow string arches, composition roofing, concrete slab and asphalt tile floors, steel sash, wood sectional overhead doors, plaster, painting, plumbing, electrical, steel pipe and H-columns, roof ventilators. ENGINEER: R. J. Twohy, 231-B, Vista del Mar, Redondo Beach. GENERAL CONTRACTOR: Tuco Inc., 1431 Hackett St., Long Beach.

PROFESSIONAL BLDG., Epley, Marysville, Yuba county. Epley Professional Bldg., Marysville, owner. Concrete block construction of 4 general offices and related facilities — $46,960. ARCHITECT: Robert S. Oliver, 916 F. St., Marysville. GENERAL CONTRACTOR: C. A. Otto, P. O. Box 1385, Marysville.

FIRST BAPTIST CHURCH, Bakersfield, Kern county. First Baptist Church of Bakersfield, owner. First stage of construction will be a 1-story frame and stucco chapel and educational unit containing 5000 sq. ft. of area; rock roof, carpet and asphalt tile floors, metal sash, forced air heating, evaporating cooling, interior plaster, movable partitions, glued laminated beams, chalk and tack boards, blacktop off-street parking, men's and women's toilet facilities—$40,000. ARCHITECT: Farrar, Hudson & Associates, 661 Hwy 99, San Bernardino.

ROCKET STORAGE BLDG., Hubbard Field, Reno, Washoe county, Nevada. U. S. Army Engineers, Sacramento, California, owner. Work includes construction of buildings, excavation, water system, piping, paving, fencing and related work—$97,278. ENGINEER: U. S. Army, Corps of Engineers, Wright Bldg., 1209 8th St., Sacramento. GENERAL CONTRACTOR: Frank Capriotti, P. O. Box 2388, Reno.

GAS SERVICE OFFICE, Pomona, Los Angeles county. Suburban Gas Service, Inc., Pomona, owner. New building will contain 10,000 sq. ft. of area; general offices, air conditioned throughout; 1-story, brick faced, 2½-acre site, illuminated sign, landscaped terraces—$200,000. ARCHITECT: Victor Gruen Associates, 435 So. Doheny Drive, Beverly Hills. GENERAL CONTRACTOR: Collins & McPherson, Pasadena.

INDUSTRIAL BLDG. ADD'N, Beverly Hills, Los Angeles county. E. L. Payne, Beverly Hills, owner. 2-Story concrete block addition to industrial building; 11,000 sq. ft. area, composition and gravel roofing, concrete slab, steel sash, elevator, plumbing, electrical, steel studs and metal lath and plaster, sheet metal. ARCHITECT: Marshall P. Wilkinson, 151 N. Fairfax Ave., Los Angeles.

GIRAFFE & PONY BARNS, San Francisco Zoological Gardens. City and County of San Francisco, owner. Construction includes bars for giraffes, also paddocks; pony barns and paddocks — $72,625. ARCHITECT: Charles W. Griffiths, City Architect, City Hall, San Francisco. GENERAL CONTRACTOR: Antone Petersen & Sons, 2758 San Bruno Ave., San Francisco.

DRUG STORE, Long's El Cerrito, Contra Costa county. Albert Lovett Co., Oakland, owner. New building to be built in the Plaza Shopping Center on San Pablo Avenue, 1-story, storage area and basement, 70 x 115 ft. — $250,000. ARCHITECT: Paul Hammarburg, 2941 Telegraph Ave., Berkeley. GENERAL CONTRACTOR: Marvin E. Collins, 635 San Diego St., El Cerrito.

U. S. MINT BUILDING CONVERSION, San Francisco. General Services Administration, owner. Work comprises alteration of the U. S. Mint building at

Market and Duboce streets; 1st floor and all space on the second floor, 3 floor, 4 floor and 5 floors; conversion of elevators to automatic and 2 freight elevators to passenger elevators; new entrance and lobby; plumbing, heating and electrical work; conversion is to office space—$512,900. ARCHITECT: Wurster, Bernardi & Emmons, 202 Green St., San Francisco. GENERAL CONTRACTOR: Wilco Const. Co., 725 2nd St., San Francisco.

FLORICULTURE & HOME ECONOMICS BLDG., Fairgrounds, Monterey. 7th District Agricultural Association, Monterey, owner. Project comprises construction of exhibit facilities and related work at county fairgrounds—$29,471. ARCHITECT: C. J. Ryland, 847 Abrego St., Monterey. GENERAL CONTRACTOR: Jake D. Huizenga, P. O. Box "L," Seaside.

ST. HELENA HIGH SCHOOL ADD'N, Napa county. St. Helena Unified School District, owner. Wood frame, prestressed concrete construction, concrete floors; facilities for a new science building—$48,363. ARCHITECT: Lillis & Smith, 912 Tennessee St., Vallejo. GENERAL CONTRACTOR: A. A. Douglas, 130 Franklin St., Napa.

COURTHOUSE, Eureka, Humboldt county. County of Humboldt, Eureka, owner. Type I construction, five story and basement with all facilities for a county courthouse — $3,332,300. ARCHITECT: Mitchell Van Bourg, Hotel Claremont, Berkeley. STRUCTURAL ENGINEER: H. J. Brunnier, Sharon Bldg., San Francisco. MECHANICAL & ELECTRICAL ENGINEER: G. L. Gendler & Associates, 1044 University Ave., Berkeley. GENERAL CONTRACTOR: Dinwiddie Const. Co., 347 Clay St., San Francisco.

OFFICE & MFG. BLDG., San Jose, Santa Clara county. Eureka Western Printing Co., San Jose, owner. Construction will be of steel frame and provide facilities for complete printing plant. ARCHITECT: John S. Bolles, Pier 5, Embarcadero, San Francisco. STRUCTURAL ENGINEER: Chin & Hensolt, 555 Sutter St., San Francisco. MECHANICAL ENGINEER: Eagleson Engineers, 615 Sansome St., San Francisco. ELECTRICAL ENGINEER: Charles H. Krieger, 580 Washington St., San Francisco. GENERAL CONTRACTOR, Carl N. Swenson, P. O. Box 558, San Jose.

KINDERGARTEN, McKinley School, Santa Barbara. Santa Barbara School District, owner. Construction of a new kindergarten building—$65,269. ARCHITECT: William B. Wade, 812 Anacapa St., Santa Barbara. GENERAL CONTRACTOR: J. W. Bailey Construction Co., P. O. Box 506, Santa Barbara.

ARMY RESERVE CENTER, Reno, Nevada. U. S. Army Engineers, Sacramento, owner. Construction of a grouted brick masonry maintenance shop building, army reserve center building, chain link fencing, flood lighting, road mix surfacing, concrete curbs and gutters, air conditioning—$226,093. ENGINEER: Corps of Engineers, 1209 8th St., Sacramento, California. GENERAL CONTRACTOR: J. C. Dillard, 1333½ Forest St., Reno, Nevada.

TRACK & FOOTBALL FIELD, Hugh School, Tustin, Orange county. Tustin Union High School District, owner. Construction of a new running track and football field, field lighting, fence, grounds lighting and asphalt paving of parking

area—$75,299. ARCHITECT: Pleger, Blurock and Hougan, 2515 E. Coast Highway, Corona del Mar. GENERAL CONTRACTOR: Hardy & Harper, 440 W. 1st St., Tustin.

RESIDENCE HALLS, Humboldt State College, Arcata, Humboldt county. State of California, Division of Architecture, Sacramento, owner. Construction consists of two 3-story reinforced concrete and concrete block residence halls, plus a certain amount of site development work—$1,167,140. ARCHITECT: Anson Boyd, California State Architect, Sacramento. GENERAL CONTRACTOR: MacDonald, Young and Nelson, 8907 Railroad Ave., Oakland.

OFFICE & FACTORY, El Monte, Los Angeles county. Microtech Corp., Pasadena, owner. 1-Story tilt-up concrete construction office and factory building in El Monte; 2300 sq. ft. in area; composition roofing, concrete floor, painting, plumbing, electrical work, heating and ventilating, air filtering and air conditioning, sheet metal, structural and miscellaneous metal. ARCHITECT: Samuel E. Lundeen & Associates, 548 S. Spring St., Los Angeles. GENERAL CONTRACTOR: H. M. Keller Co., 2311 Empire Ave., Burbank.

STEEL GRANDSTAND, Fairgrounds, Watsonville, Santa Cruz county. 14th District Agricultural Association, Watsonville, owner. Construction of a 120 x 56 ft. steel grandstand — $34,187. PLANS: E. P. Johnson, Sec.-Mgr. District Fair, Watsonville. GENERAL CONTRACTOR: O. E. Anderson, 1075 No. 10th, San Jose.

MEDICAL-DENTAL OFFICE, Richmond, Contra Costa county. 1-Story, wood frame, masonry exterior, built-up roofing, aluminum sash, concrete slab floors—$43,260. ARCHITECT: Johnson & Cometta, Oakie C. Johnson, Architect, 3516 MacDonald Ave., Richmond. GENERAL CONTRACTOR: Carl Lundberg, 2603 Mesa Vista Dr., El Cerrito.

NEW ELEMENTARY SCHOOL, Middletown, Lake county. Middletown Unified School District, owner. Work included construction of a new school building to provide facilities for administration unit, 7 classrooms, and toilet rooms—$96,422. ARCHITECT: Bruce E. Heiser, 251 Post St., San Francisco. GENERAL CONTRACTOR: Reynolds Const. Co., 55 Mt.

View Ave., Santa Rosa.

INSURANCE BLDG., John Hancock Mutual, San Francisco. John Hancock Mutual Life Insurance Co., San Francisco, owner. 12-Story office building, reinforced concrete construction throughout; exterior walls faced with polished granite, fixed plate glass windows in bronze frames. ARCHITECT: Skidmore, Owings & Merrill, 1 Montgomery St., San Francisco. GENERAL CONTRACTOR: Cahill Bros., Inc., 350 Sansome St., San Francisco.

CASA CLARA INN, Santa Clara. 1-Story approximately 2200 sq. ft. of floor area; concrete block construction—$31,425. ARCHITECT: Donnell E. Jackie and Donald G. French, Associate, 586 N. 1st St., San Jose. GENERAL CONTRACTOR: Aiken Const. Co., 333 Phelan Ave., San Jose.

IN THE NEWS

ARCHITECT WINS ALGER AWARD FOR 1958

Architect William B. Tabler, 401-15, Seventh Avenue, New York, has been selected by vote of 3000 campus leaders of more than 500 American schools and colleges to receive the 12th annual Horatio Alger Award sponsored by the Association of American Schools and Colleges.

Tabler started his designing and building career at the age of 11, worked his way through school and college and is today acclaimed one of the world's leading hotel architects.

His work includes the Statler-Hilton in Los Angeles, the Brown Palace West in Denver, the San Francisco Airport Inn, first of the Hilton's -Horizontal Hotels, and is currently designing the 1000 Hilton Hotel to be built in the heart of downtown San Francisco.

LOWELL GARRETT TO REPRESENT CALAVERAS CEMENT

Lowell Garrett has been appointed sales representative of the Calaveras Cement Company for western Nevada, southern Oregon and the Sierra Nevada counties of California, according to a recent announcement by Wm. G. Jeffrey, Calaveras Cement sales manager.

Garrett will maintain headquarters in Reno, Nevada. He was formerly sales representative for the firm in Sacramento.

UNIVERSITY OF SC DENTAL CLINIC CONSTRUCTION STARTS

Construction is now underway on a $230,000 addition to the present Dental Clinic at the University of Southern California, Los Angeles. This is the second step toward the completion of the master plan for the School of Dentistry, which calls for the later addition of a second story on the present Dental Clinic.

The 12,500 sq. ft., two-story addition, will provide facilities for three lecture rooms, administrative offices, library and record storage facilities.

PRELIMINARY PLANS FOR NEW FEDERAL BLDG

Architect Henry J. Devine, R. Franceschi, Herbert Goodpastor, and Drefuss, Rickey & Brooks, all of Sacramento, are collaborating in the preparation of preliminary plans for construction of a new Federal Office Building and Court House, to be built in Sacramento for the General Services Administration.

Estimated cost of the project is $10,000,000.

CONCRETE MIXER STANDARDS ARE NOW REVISED

The Associated General Contractors of America recently announced publication of the 23rd revision of its Concrete Mixer Standards and the 11th revision of its Contractor Pump Standards.

The Concrete Mixer Standards were first prepared by the Mixer Manufacturers Bureau, an affiliate of the AGC, in 1924, and now include specifications for construction mixers, paving mixers and plaster and mortar mixers. The Contractors Pump Standards cover specifications for diaphragm and self priming centrifugal pumps, standards which are widely used by procurement agencies and contractors, and are revised as the need occurs to meet changing industry conditions.

IMPROVED PRECISION BENCH SHAPER

An improved 7" stroke precision Bench Shaper for smooth operation at high speeds, and equipped with an automatic pressure lubricating system has just been announced by the South Bend Lathe Works, South Bend, Indiana.

A cam operated piston pump circulates lubricating oil from a large reservoir to all important bearing surfaces. Oil pressure is adjustable and can be maintained at all speeds which cushions the shock of reciprocating ram action and interrupted cuts, resulting in exceptionally smooth and quiet operation even at maximum speeds. Additional information obtainable from the manufacturer.

ALLISON AND RIBLE ARCHITECTURAL FIRM EXPANDS

George B. Allison, F.A.I.A., and Ulysses Floyd Rible, F.A.I.A., outstanding West Coast architectural firm with general offices at 3670 Wilshire Blvd., Los Angeles, has announced the admittance to partnership of Rodney T. Robinson, AIA, and Raymond Ziegler, AIA, architects.

The firm will continue under the name of Allison and Rible, Architects.

DRYWALL ASS'N DIRECTORS IN LAS VEGAS

Directors of the International Drywall Contractors Association, recently concluded a four day meeting in Las Vegas, Nevada, with members from 13 states and Canada in attendance, according to a report by Wayne W. Vaughan of Los Angeles, president of the association.

Technical discussions were led by Lloyd Yeager of Chicago, association general manager, and committee reports included developments in the fields of standards and specifications, government liaison and communications.

Officers of the association include: Wayne W. Vaughan of Los Angeles, president; Melvin L. Scott of Seattle, vice-president; M. R. McColley of San Diego, secretary; Sherwood M. Sitz of Los Angeles executive director; and Max O. Jensen,

Salt Lake City, Utah; H. A. Olson, Campbell, California; Robert A. Shepard, Phoenix, Arizona, and William J. Thompson, San Francisco, directors.

GRISWOLD RAETZE, AIA SPEAKER AT CITY COLLEGE OF SAN FRANCISCO

Griswold Raetze, AIA, architect, director of Welton Becket, FAIA, and Associates, San Francisco architects and engineers, was a recent speaker to 320 engineering students at the City College of San Francisco, taking as his subject "The Architect as Part of a Team."

The talk was part of a program designed to acquaint City College undergraduates with various phases of architecture and engineering.

HIGH SCHOOL STADIUM FOR BAKERSFIELD

Architect Ernest L. McCoy, 2811 "H" Street, Bakersfield, has completed drawings for construction of an athletic stadium at the South Side High School in Bakersfield for the Kern County High School District.

The stadium of concrete construction will seat 3000 persons.

ARCHITECT KERR APPOINTED TO GOVERNING BOARD

Architect D. Stewart Kerr, AIA, of the Los Angeles architectural firm of H. L. Gogerty Associates, has been elected a member of the governing board of the School Facilities Council, a national organization with headquarters in New York City. Membership on the governing board, which consists of 36 members from the fields of architecture, education, industry, is for three years.

The purpose of the organization is to assist education through improvement of school building design, school sites, school facilities and school equipment.

Kerr, a graduate of the University of Minnesota, has been an associate architect in the Gogerty organization for the past twelve years, and is active in the Southern California Chapter of the American Institute of Architects, Washington, D. C.

OPENS NEW PHOENIX WAREHOUSE

Gene Hartwell of Texarkana, Texas, has been named manager of a new warehouse and factory outlet opened in Phoenix recently by the Royal Tile Manufacturing Company of Fort Worth.

The new facilities will serve seven western states with a fast and efficient service.

Hartwell has had extensive tile experience having been a ceramic tile contractor in Texarkana for several years before assuming his present position.

ROY F. CARTER APPOINTED SALES ENGINEER

Roy F. Carter has been appointed sales engineer for the air conditioning division of Westinghouse Electric Corporation, according to an announcement by W. L.

Constance, Pacific Coast manager of the firm.

Carter will have his headquarters in Fresno, California, and his sales responsibilities will include Bakersfield, the San Joaquin Valley and the Northern Sacramento Valley. Carter joined Westinghouse in 1956 as heat pump specialist for the Pacific Coast Region, and is a graduate of the California State Polytechnic College.

SEATTLE FIRM
APPOINTED
REPRESENTATIVE

Coast Associates, Inc. of Seattle, Washington, have been appointed franchise

TOP QUALITY CEMENTS FOR EVERY ARCHITECTURAL USE

CALAVERAS CEMENT COMPANY
315 MONTGOMERY ST., SAN FRANCISCO 4

sales and service representative for Yale industrial lift trucks in Western Washington and Alaska, according to an announcement by Clyde R. Dean, Jr., general sales manager of Yale Materials Handling Division, Yale & Towne Mfg. Co.

The new representative firm occupies a modern 3600 sq. ft. sales and service center with considerable ground for demonstration, and convenient customer parking, in Seattle's "Industrial South End."

William G. Hathaway has been named general manager of the company and he will be assisted by Bob Wiren.

JOSEPH W. COFFY
APPOINTED MANAGER
NEW DEPARTMENT

Joseph W. Coffy has been appointed manager of a new Contractor Department recently established by the Republic Supply Company of California in Los Angeles to meet the Southern California contracting needs in highly specialized services.

The new department will offer contractors and sub-contractors special services in the fields of corrosion, temperature and hydraulic piping installations with instrumentation problems, power tool applications such as conveyors and heavy belts.

NEW CHURCH BLDG
IS PLANNED
FOR BAKERSFIELD

Farrar, Hudson & Associates, 661 Hwy 99, San Bernardino, are completing plans and specifications for construction of a new First Baptist Church in Bakersfield at an estimated cost for the first phase of construction of some $40,000.

The first phase will comprise a 1-story frame and stucco chapel and educational unit with toilet facilities; approximately 5000 sq. ft. of area; rock roof, carport and asphalt tile floors, metal sash, forced air heating, interior plaster, moveable partitions and glued laminated beams.

NEW HYDRO-HINGE
AVAILABLE FOR
INTERIOR DOORS

Door control hinges for residential doors and light special-purpose doors in business and institutional buildings including half-doors, movable partition doors and gates are now available.

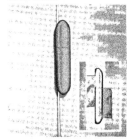

Designated type 2-H, the hinges operate to provide both closing pressure and hydraulic damping action. Fully adjustable for rate of closing and latching speed; easy to install and adjust with simple tools provided with each set; fitted to door and jamb in same manner as conventional hinges, but concealed spring and hydraulic units eliminate need for a separate closer or mechanism in floor or ceiling. Offered in contemporary finishes; bright or dull brass, bronze, chromium. For complete information write the manufacturer, Bakewell Products, 1128 Mission Street, South Pasadena, California.

LOS ANGELES FIRM
DESIGNS CONSULATE
BUILDING IN CANADA

The architectural firm of Thornton Ladd and Associates, AIA, Los Angeles, has been commissioned by the U.S. State Department, Office of Foreign Buildings, to execute plans for construction of the new U.S. Consulate in Niagara Falls, Canada.

The Canadian Consulate, latest to be sponsored by the State Department, com-

prises a pavilion-like office building and residence, linked together by a series of landscaped gardens and raised above the level of the site on an elevated "podium" of off-white pebbled concrete. The buildings themselves, rectangular in form, alternate steel columns with panels of clear and translucent glass, with both structures, including the gardens, surmounted by a single roofed portico.

NEW CASEMENT AND HOPPER-TYPE WINDOWS FOR CONCRETE WALLS

The Kewanee Mfg., Co., Kewanee, Illinois, announces the addition of Casement and Hopper Venty-type Windows to its new line of Buck Windows, windows specially designed for poured basement walls.

All units have built-in bucks, eliminating the need for steel or wood bucks, and are of welded construction. Design provides complete inside-outside trim, an important cost-saving feature when finishing basement recreation rooms, etc., full recess for screens and combinations, rapid installation. Line covers full range of types,

sizes, and wall thicknesses; shipped completely assembled, glazed or unglazed. Complete information from manufacturer.

MENLO PARK CHURCH ADDITION

Architects Arnold and Francis Constable, 95 Spencer Avenue, Sausalito, are working on drawings for construction of an adition to the Catholic Church in Menlo Park at an estimated cost of $75,000.

The new addition will be of concrete construction with a slate roof and will provide facilities for a music room, vestry, ten nun cells and book binding room.

EL CAMINO HOSPITAL PLANNED

The architectural firm of Stone, Mulloy, Marraccini & Paterson of 536 Mission St., San Francisco, are preparing plans and specifications for construction of the El Camino Hospital in Mountain View, at an estimated cost of $7,000,000.

The facilities will include all provisions for a 450 bed hospital and will be a four or five story building with basement.

MANHATTAN BEACH PLANS NEW POLICE STATION

The firm of Quigley & Clark, Engineer and Architect, 43 Cove Plaza, Palos Verdes Estates, is preparing working drawings for construction of a police station, including pistol range and jail, in Manhattan Beach for the City of Manhattan Beach.

The facilities will include 11,000 sq. ft. of floor area; composition roof, concrete slab floors, plaster work, plumbing, electrical work and asphalt paving.

SOUTHERN CALIFORNIA GETS ST. PAUL WORK ARCHITECTURAL FIRM

Victor Gruen Associates, nationwide architectural and planning firm with headquarters at 135 So. Doheny Drive, Los Angeles, has announced the completion of research and analysis studies for the revitalization of downtown St. Paul, Minnesota, a city of some 340,000 population.

The firm expects to complete schematic studies by June with completion of the overall plan in December of this year.

SUPER FOOD MARKET FOR OAKLAND

Architect Paul Hammarberg, 2941 Telegraph Ave., Berkeley, is completing plans and specifications for construction of a new Super Market at Broadway and 45th Street in Oakland, for Lynch Foods, Inc.

The new facilities will be 1-story containing 17,000 sq. ft. of area; 400 ft. of refrigerator display cases and parking area for 125 automobiles. The estimated cost of the project is $500,000.

REINFORCING FOR WATERPROOF PAPERS ANNOUNCED

More strength is being built into the edges of Sisilkraft waterproof papers, according to an announcement by R. S. Youngsberg, manager of the firm's Western Division in San Francisco.

The new innovation involves special Triple-Edge fiber reinforcing along edges of the sheet for the purpose of adding strength and resistance to tearing due to

rough handling and high winds, increasing edge tear resistance by 600 per cent.

HOSPITAL ADDITIONS SCHEDULED

The architectural firm of Fingardo & Kern, 2910 Telegraph Avenue, Oakland, is completing drawings for construction of a 40-bed addition to the Amador County Hospital in Jackson for the Amador county board of supervisors.

Of frame and concrete construction the new facilities will include a storage area, nurses home, small laundry, 4-psychiatric rooms, a recreation area and 40-beds.

PLANS ARE COMPLETED FOR CHURCH

Architect John H. Carter, 1401 21st Street, Sacramento, has completed drawings for construction of the first phase of a new church plant in Sacramento for the First Unitarian Society.

The work comprises a social hall and two Sunday School departments. Construction will be of thin shell concrete, steel arches, flat roof with light weight steel, and preliminary costs are estimated at $125,000. The complete project will cost an estimated $450,000.

NEW BANK PLANNED FOR STOCKTON

The architectural firm of Mayo & DeWolf, Exchange Bldg., Stockton, is completing plans for construction of a new bank building in Stockton for the Stockton Savings & Loan Bank.

The new building will occupy a half block site, 150 x 300 ft. with the building itself 96 x 160 feet. Construction will be 1 or 2 story with full basement; drive-in deposit area and off-street parking.

PETERSEN NAMED WESTERN REGIONAL MARKET MANAGER

Warren A. Petersen, sales manager of the Time Switch Division of the Paragon Electric Company of Two Rivers, Wisconsin, has been appointed to the position of Western Regional Marketing Manager for the firm, according to a recent announcement by Read W. Eldred, vice-president in charge of sales.

Petersen will supervise all sales in the Intermountain and West Coast areas and will operate from general offices in Los Angeles.

YOUR FUTURE IS GREAT IN A GROWING AMERICA

AMERICA ALWAYS OUTPERFORMS ITS PROMISES

We grow so fast our goals are exceeded soon after they are set!

7 BIG REASONS FOR CONFIDENCE IN AMERICA'S FUTURE

1. More People—Four million babies yearly. U. S. population has *doubled* in last 50 years! And our prosperity curve has always followed our population curve.

2. More Jobs—Though employment in some areas has fallen off, there are 15 million more jobs than in 1939—and there will be *22 million more* in 1975 than today.

3. More Income—Family income after taxes is at an all-time high of $5300—is expected to pass $7000 by 1975.

4. More Production—U.S. production *doubles* every 20 years. We will require millions more people to make, sell and distribute our products.

5. More Savings—Individual savings are at highest level ever—*$340 billion*—a record amount available for spending.

6. More Research—*$10 billion* spent each year will pay off in more jobs, better living, whole new industries.

7. More Needs—In the next few years we will need more than *$500 billion* worth of schools, highways, homes, durable equipment. Meeting these needs will create new opportunities for everyone.

 Add them up and you have the makings of another big upswing. Wise planners, builders and buyers will act now to get ready for it.

FREE! Send for this new 24-page illustrated booklet, "Your Great Future in a Growing America." Every American should know these facts. Drop a post card today to: THE ADVERTISING COUNCIL, Box 10, Midtown Station, New York 18, N. Y.

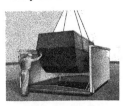

Vol. 213   No. 3

EDWIN H. WILDER
   Editor

CONTRIBUTING EDITORS:

Education
   SIDNEY W. LITTLE, Dean,
   College of Fine Arts and Department of Architecture, University
   of Arizona, Tucson, Arizona.

City Planning
   CORWIN R. MOCINE, City
   Planning Engineer, Oakland,
   California

*Urban Planning and
Shopping Centers*
   FRANK EMERY COX, Sales
   Research & Business Develop-
   ment Analyst, Berkeley, Califor-
   nia

Realty Development
   ROY P. DRACHMAN, Sub-
   divider and Realty Developer,
   Tucson, Arizona

School Planning
   DR. J. D. McCONNEL, Stan-
   ford School Planning Dept.,
   Palo Alto, California

Residential Planning
   JEDD JONES, Architect,
   Boise, Idaho

General Architecture
   ROBERT FIELD, Architect,
   Los Angeles, California

Engineering
   JOHN A. BLUME, Consulting
   and Structural Engineer, San
   Francisco, California

Advertising
   WILLIAM A. ULLNER,
   Manager

   FRED JONES
   Special Advertising

★

COVER PICTURE

Artist's Drawing
of the new home.

ASSOCIATED CONSTRUCTION
& ENGINEERING COMPANY

In South San Francisco's Airport Boulevard Industrial Park.

Completion of 10,000 sq. ft. building
coincides with firm's seventh anniversary.

See page 18 for details.

ARCHITECTS' REPORTS—
Published Daily
         Archie MacCorkindale, Manager
         Telephone DOuglas 2-8311

—ARCHITECT & ENGINEER *is indexed regularly by* ENGINEERING INDEX, INC.; *and* ART INDEX—

Contents for

JUNE

THE OLDEST PROFESSIONAL MONTHLY BUSINESS MAGAZINE OF THE ELEVEN WESTERN STATES

ARCHITECT AND ENGINEER (Established 1905) is published on the 15th of the month by The Architect and
Engineer, Inc., 68 Post St., San Francisco 4; Telephone EXbrook 2-7182. President, K. P. Kierulff; Vice-
President and Manager, L. B. Penhorwood; Treasurer, E. N. Kierulff. — Los Angeles Office: Wentworth F.
Green, 439 So. Western Ave., Telephone DUnkirk 7-8135 — Portland, Oregon, Office: R. V. Vaughn, 7117
Canyon Lane. — Entered as second class matter, November 2, 1905, at the Post Office in San Francisco,
California, under the Act of March 3, 1879. Subscriptions United States and Pan America, $3.00 a year;
$5.00 two years; foreign countries $5.00 a year; single copy, 50c.

. EDITORIAL NOTES .

WOMEN IN ARCHITECTURE

The Association of Women in Architecture will hold their national convention in Los Angeles the latter part of this month at which time architects, landscape architects, and women in closely allied professions will gather from Chapters throughout the nation, to plan and discuss problems of women presently engaged in the practice of Architecture and related fields.

According to national President Jean Driskel, three major projects will come up for consideration:

First: Reports on the first complete biographical and historical survey of American women in architecture, some of whom have achieved national and worldwide recognition in the architectural field.

Second: To aid governmental agencies and architectural firms seeking trained personnel, and to assist young graduates completing related studies in colleges throughout the United States to secure speedier placement, the Association will sponsor undergraduate Chapters in creating and maintaining an up-to-date job file list.

Third: Because of the demand for trained personnel in architecture, the Association will complete development of a student advisory program to encourage high school students who show particular aptitude and interest in the field of architecture.

In addition the Convention program includes tours of outstanding architectural examples in Southern California, including mosaics, ceramics, sculpturing, weaving, landscape architecture, land planning and engineering.

Public recognition of women in architecture is just beginning, however national gatherings of this type will speed-up the realization by many that women are taking a more independent position in architecture and related arts.

* * *

California was by far the leading state in total construction contracts for 1957 . . . ARCHITECT & ENGINEER magazine reaches this market.

*

NOW IS THE TIME

The central fact emerging from Primary Elections now being held throughout the nation is that conservatives of both parties will face their greatest battle in recent United States history in the upcoming fall general elections, when many state officials and representatives to the Congress of the United States will be chosen by the voters.

Elections this year will determine, to a great extent, whether the people will halt the steady march of power toward central government, or whether they will elect representatives in government who will demand more right to direct their own affairs through state and local governments.

How many times have you heard employees on government payrolls, payrolls which you provide through payment of taxes, declare "If you don't like the law, why don't you change it?"—This is your opportunity, and only one, to do something about it.

Give very careful consideration to the qualifications of candidates for office, make sure the man, or woman, you vote for, will represent you and your ideas, once they get into office. Make up your mind now to cast your vote this Fall, and in the meantime, determine for yourself what you want in the way of government—then select the candidate who will commit himself to your wishes.

ARCHITECT & ENGINEER MAGAZINE APPRECIATED

City of Geneva   April 11, 1958.
Museum of Art and History,
Rath Museum-Ariana Museum,
Library of Art and Archeology.

Mr. E. H. Wilder,
Architect & Engineer,
68 Post Street,
San Francisco, Calif.

Sir:

Some specimen of your review "Architect and Engineer," have been received and we have appreciated greatly the articles and the documentation of your publication. Our library being the research center of the principle school of architecture, is especially interested in your review so well documented, and principally in the new construction of your country.

We would be particularly grateful if it was possible for you to furnish us gratuitously with your review. Our students have requested several times the new brochures of "Architect and Engineer," and we would be very happy to be able to satisfy them, in making them benefit of this advantage.

Please believe, Sir, in our sincere thanks, and the gratitude of your distinguished consideration.

M. Weigle,
Librarian.

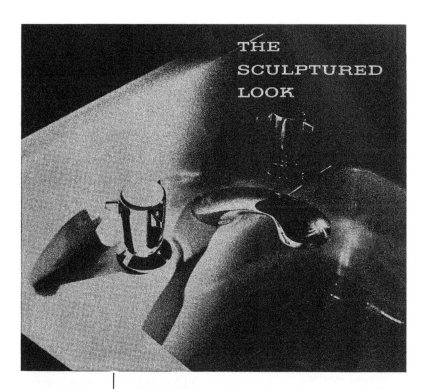

THE SCULPTURED LOOK

B-3662—DRYDEN: 24" x 20" vitreous china lavatory with 8" combination fitting.

B-6901—SPARTON: Vitreous china 18" wide stall urinal with integral flushing rim.

B-4002-H—MARS: Wall-hung exposed vitreous china drinking fountain.

B-6700—QUIETON: Vitreous china zyphon jet quiet-action floor-outlet bowl.

Briggs completely new design concept for commercial plumbing fixtures and fittings is backed by more than 70 years experience in manufacturing vitreous china.

Now, Briggs brings to its new line of commercial plumbing fixtures and fittings the contemporary look of sculptured form. Each unit and fitting, designed by Harley Earl, Inc., incorporates the same clean, simple lines—giving your plans a continuity of design. And the entire line is backed by more than 70 years experience in producing fine vitreous china of constant quality. Available in Briggs six colors or white. Complete specifications are available to you on request.

BRIGGS MANUFACTURING CO. • WARREN, MICHIGAN

A COMPLETE LINE OF PLUMBING FIXTURES FOR RESIDENTIAL, COMMERCIAL AND INDUSTRIAL USE

BRIGGS
B E A U T Y W A R E

NEWS and COMMENT ON ART

OAKLAND ART MUSEUM

The Oakland Art Museum, 1000 Fallon Street, under the direction of Paul Mills, curator, is offering a variety of exhibitions and special events during this month, including:

Exhibits: The Rietz Collection. Artifacts collected by Mr. Carl Rietz over a period of thirty years of world travel, includes Chinese and Persian ceramics, Coptic and pre-Columbian textiles and ceramics in stone, metal, wood, fiber and clay are represented.

The William Keith Gallery, main library building, is currently exhibiting Keith treasures from St. Mary's College and the Southwest Museum.

Events: The usual Wednesday evening programs will be discontinued during the summer months.

Summer Art Classes: Each year the Museum offers art activities for children from the ages of four through twelve, with additional classes in July and August.

The Museum is open daily 10 a.m. to 5 p.m.

COLLEGE OF ARCHITECTURE UNIVERSITY OF CALIFORNIA

An exhibit of student work from the College of Architecture and the Department of City and Regional Planning and Landscape Architecture will be shown in the Architecture Building of the University of California, Berkeley, this month.

M. H. de YOUNG MEMORIAL MUSEUM

The M. H. deYoung Memorial Museum, Golden Gate Park, San Francisco, under the direction of Walter Heil, is presenting the following special exhibitions and events during June:

Exhibitions: Paintings, Drawings and Etchings by Gui Ignon and the faculty, students and alumni of the Thacher School. Gui Ignon, native of France, is head of the art department of the Thacher School and director of the Thacher Museum at the Thacher College Preparatory School for Boys in Ojai, California.

Paintings by Ng Kung Fu, a group of watercolors painted in traditional Chinese style including representative tiger and bamboo paintings for which the artist is most noted.

Watercolors by Lois Langhorst, Bay area architect and painter. Recently associated with the office of Gardner Daily, Architect, Mrs. Langhorst is currently a lecturer in architectural design at the University of California, Berkeley.

The Prophets, by Aleijadinho. A group of 48 photographs illustrating stone sculptures of old testament prophets carved by the noted 18th century Brazilian sculptor, Antonio Francisco Lisboa, better known as Aleijadinho. The pictures were taken by Hans Mann, a German photographer who specializes in recording sculpture and architecture.

Paintings by Afro. One of the outstanding Italian artists in contemporary painting, who is now associated with the Mills College Fine Arts faculty conducting special classes in painting and working on a large scale mural which he has been commissioned to do for the new UNESCO building in Paris. The exhibition consists of works completed within the last three years and is assembled from museums and private collections throughout the country.

Small Greek Bronzes and Renaissance Medals and Plaquettes, from the collection of Sigmund Morgenroth of Santa Barbara.

Sculpture by Tom Hardy, showing animal forms in metal and drawings. Nationally acclaimed for his fresh approach to sculptural art, Tom Hardy is currently lecturer in Art at the University of California at Berkeley and instructor in Metal Sculpture at the California School of Fine Arts.

Special Events: All classes in Art Enjoyment have been recessed until July 9, and the art classes for children, now in recess, will be resumed early in July.

The museum is open daily.

ARCHITECTURAL GALLERY EXHIBITING ARCHITECTS

The Architectural Gallery in the Building Center, 7933 West Third Street, Los Angeles, is currently exhibiting works of the following architects:

Gerard R. Colcord, AIA; Daniel L. Dworsky, AIA; Faxon, Gruys and Sayler, Architects and Engineers; Howard W. Frank, AIA; Hudson and Hanson, AIA; Kegley, Westphall and Arbogast, AIA; Kenneth H. Neptune, AIA; Allen G. Siple, AIA; Stephen A. Stepanian, AIA; and William R. Stephenson, AIA.

A special exhibition of the work of Paul R. Williams, FAIA, will also be shown during June.

Exhibitions are open to the public.

SAN FRANCISCO MUSEUM OF ART

The San Francisco Museum of Art, War Memorial Building, Civic Center, under the direction of Dr. Grace L. McCann Morley, is presenting the following schedule of exhibitions and special events during this month:

Exhibitions: The Art of Albert Marquet, one of the major art events of the year, bringing to San Francisco the work of an important figure in the 20th century school of Paris. The Marquet Retrospective was made possible by generous loans from French

museum collections, and from the Marquet family. After its showing in San Francisco it will travel to other American museums, including the Baltimore Museum of Art, the Cincinnati Art Museum, the Munson-Proctor Williams Institute of Utica, New York, and the Seattle Art Museum.

Drawing—Memory and Discovery, by Jose Perotti, Otis Oldfield and others.

Prints, by Edvard Munch, consisting of 45 lithographs, woodcuts and etchings based on an exhibition presently recently at the Museum of Modern Art, New York, and being circulated throughout the United States under the museum's international program. The exhibit includes many prints being shown for the first time in this country, lent through the co-operation of the Norwegian government from the most extensive collection of Munch's graphic art in the world, that of the Municipal Collection in Oslo, and from the Museum of Modern Art's own Abby Aldrich Rockefeller Print Room.

Prints, by Alberto Burri, a surgeon by profession who gave up his profession when he was a prisoner of war in Texas during World War II. He turned to making collages put together from bits of cloth, sacking, canvas, old tattered clothing, which take on a direct emotional force from their materials.

Architectural Photography II, an exhibition sponsored by the American Institute of Architects in co-operation with the Architectural Photoghaphers Association, and touring the country under auspices of the Smithsonian Institution Traveling Exhibition Service. The 32 prints were selected from photographs submitted from all over the country.

Special Events: The Museum, in association with Mills College, will present the Hollywood Quartet in a series of four concerts on Friday evenings starting June 6 at 8:30 p.m. Lecture-Tours, based upon current exhibitions; Wednesday Evening Programs; and Adventures in Drawing and Painting, Children's Saturday Morning Art Classes, and the Studio Art for the Layman, the former two being recessed for the summer.

The museum is open daily.

GRETA WILLIAMS GALLERY

A comprehensive group of Paintings, Drawings and Prints by Charles Mattox, together with a special exhibition of Drawings and Watercolors by Victor Wong, are being shown this month at the Greta Williams Gallery, 2059 Union Street, San Francisco.

CALIFORNIA PALACE OF THE LEGION OF HONOR

The California Palace of the Legion of Honor, Lincoln Park, San Francisco, under the direction of Thomas Carr Howe, Jr., has announced the following special exhibits and museum events for this month:

Exhibits: Southwest Indian Arts, an exhibition of old and contemporary arts by Indian craftsmen of the Southwest, presented in cooperation with the California League for American Indians; Paintings by John Johannsen; Ink Drawings by Ivan Majdrakoff; Paintings by Frederick Black; The Fourth International Hallmark Art Award Exhibition; and Paintings by Frederic Hobbs.

The Achenbach Foundation for Graphic Arts is featuring the Armin Hansen Memorial Exhibition.

Special Events: Organ Program each Saturday and Sunday afternoon at 3 o'clock. Summer Classes for Children, a six-week summer session of art classes for children and juniors, will meet on Tuesday and Thursday mornings from 10 to 11; and classes for Juniors, age 12-17, meet each Wednesday and Friday morning from 10 to 12.

The museum is open daily.

APPOINTED TO STAFF OF deYOUNG MUSEUM

Colonel Ian Ferguson MacLeod Macalpine has been appointed secretary to the Board of Trustees of the M. H. deYoung Memorial Museum, San Francisco.

He brings to the museum a richly diversified background. Born in Scotland, he was educated by private tutor and the English public school, passing entrance to Cambridge University. In 1915 he was commissioned the youngest officer in the British Army and was promoted to Captain at age 18. He served in both world wars and following the end of World War II became a resident of the state of Wyoming and an American citizen.

DIRECTORY OF SCHOLARSHIPS

Publication of a new Directory of International Scholarships in the Arts has been announced by the Institute of International Education. The new guide catalogues awards for study abroad offered by government and private organizations throughout the world in architecture, creative writing, dance, design, music, painting and sculpture, and theater arts. Copies are available from the Institute of International Education, 1 E. 67th Street, New York 21.

NEW ART CLASSES FOR ADULTS AT deYOUNG

Free art classes for adults and children will be resumed in July at the M. H. deYoung Memorial Museum, Golden Gate Park, San Francisco, and will include a new painting workshop for adults conducted by Charles Lindstrom, education director.

Beginning July 9 students may paint independently subjects of their own choosing in the workshops at any time on two days of the week, Wednesday and Saturdays, between the hours of 10 a.m. and 5 p.m.

PRESTRESSED CONCRETE PILES OF UNPRECENDENTED LENGTH

BEING USED IN PEARL HARBOR PROJECT

By IVAN F. MENDENHALL, Partner

Daniel, Mann, Johnson & Mendenhall,

Architects and Engineers

and MORRIS ZUKERMAN, Chief

Structural Engineer, Honolulu Office,

Daniel, Mann, Johnson & Mendenhall,

Architects and Engineers

One of the best examples of progressive thinking and fine cooperation between a government agency and a private architectural and engineering firm has been displayed in the solution of the difficult design problems involved in the project of the reconstruction of berths B1, B2, and B3 at Pearl Harbor, Oahu.

In 1957 the firm of Daniel, Mann, Johnson & Mendenhall of Los Angeles was awarded this $4 million project. Preliminary discussions and conferences between the A&E and District Public Works Office of the 14th Naval District at Pearl Harbor indicated an open-minded approach to the engineering problems involved on the part of both parties to the extent that no stone was left unturned in the quest for the best solutions. This spirit of research and cooperation has prevailed throughout the design stage of this project, and the final outcome will result in a structurally sound and economical design.

The berths under consideration are situated north of Dry Dock No. 1 at Pearl Harbor. Berth B2 was built in 1915, before the other two. It consists of reinforced concrete slab 12" thick supported on precast concrete transverse beams spaced at 14'-0" o.c. These beams are supported on precast concrete columns that extend several feet below the mudline. There are three such columns in each bent and each column is supported by a poured-in-pile cap resting on a cluster of wood piles. At the present time the mudline elevation at the outboard face of the dock is about 30' below M.L.W. and 3' to 5' below M.L.W. at the inboard face.

Berth B1, south of B2 and wedged between the latter and Dry Dock No. 1, was built in 1923. It is 67' wide and 348' long. It consists of a 10" concrete slab on reinforced concrete transverse beams at 10'-0" o.c. supported partly on precast concrete piles and partly on composite piles, i.e., top portion precast concrete and bottom portion wood. Berth B3 was built in two stages in the early and late 20s, and is similar to B1 in physical characteristics. It is known as the north quay wall and pier. The total length is 704', and this berth connects with the north end of B2, so that the over-all length of all three berths is 2,063'. This berth is a quay wall for 179' of its length and is 68' wide. The northerly 525 feet is a pier 80' in width. The deck elevation is 8'-0" above M.L.W. line.

Project Requirements

The current project is the solution to a number of basic requirements to satisfy present and future needs of the shipyard.

Since the current trend in ship repair work is toward heavier type repairs, greater live load capacities and additional draft alongside berths are required for the heavier ships. Consequently, the requirements are as follows:

1. Liveload capacity—750 lbs. per sq. ft.

2. Draft to be increased from about 30' to 45'.

3. Portal crane service with maximum wheel loads of 88.3^k plus 15% impact, or an equivalent uniform load of 28^k per linear foot.

4. Adequate electrical and mechanical utilities.

Berths B1 and B3 have been designed for 750 lbs. per sq. ft. L. L. and are in good structural condition. However, since it is required to dredge the bottom to a new 45-foot draft, it was felt that this operation may undermine the piles by exposing the tops of the wood portion of the composite pile above the mudline, thus making them subject to the action of marine borers. There was also the need to provide new trackage for heavy crane loads as well as new mechanical and electrical installations below deck.

To solve all these problems it was decided to widen Berths B1 and B2 10 feet outboard from the existing face. This new construction will carry the outboard rail of the new crane track and its below-deck framing is especially designed to house electrical ducts and mechanical utilities. The portal crane rails are 28'-2-3/6" o.c. Therefore, to provide support for the inboard rail at Berth B3 it was necessary to cut a strip

of deck about 9' wide, drive new piles and pour a new concrete strip.

Berth B2 was originally designed for 400 lbs. per sq. ft. L.L. However, the structure has deteriorated in recent years to the extent that a maximum live load of only 250 lbs. per sq. ft. is now permitted. Inspection of the underside of the deck has revealed many bad crack in the slab, spalling of the concrete cover at the columns and corrosion of exposed reinforcing bars. This berth has therefore been declared inadequate and will be completely demolished and rebuilt to satisfy new loading and service conditions. However, by extending the outboard edge 10' to match the widening of B1 and B2 the new structure would have been 52' wide. It was found to be more economical to make the new structure only 38' wide and to backfill the rear portion against precast concrete sheet piling.

Bearing Piles

A considerable amount of pile driving data, compiled for the existing structures, was available to the A&E. No borings were ever made. The available data indicated that some of the piles had to be driven to great lengths in order to reach the required resistance. Come of the composite piles were 155' long. In the absence of any other information, it was assumed that the new piles will have to match in length the existing piles in the same vicinity.

This posed a serious problem. First of all, the piles will have to act as unstayed columns from the underside of the deck to some point below the mudline, where the material can be relied upon to be sufficiently solid to offer lateral stability to the pile. Secondly, there is the problem of handling such long piles.

A considerable amount of research was devoted to the study of the following possibilities:

1. Union Metal Monotube Type.
2. Precast.
3. Composite.
4. Prestressed.

From the outset, it was evident that, due to the extremely heavy crane loads, greater economy would be obtained by using high capacity piles. However, Navy criteria limited the maximum capacity of a composite pile to 30 tons, and precast or prestressed to 50 tons.

In recent years, much progress has been made in the use of prestressed piles with great success. These piles have many basic advantages.

1. The chances of cracking due to handling and shrinkage is practically eliminated.
2. A smaller section can be used, thus reducing the weight in handling.
3. Better driving characteristics are obtained, due to reduction in rebound during driving.

Furthermore, cost comparison of the various types of piles indicated that the prestressed piles, in addition to having the special advantages listed above, are also the most economical. These piles were finally adopted in the design.

In order to obtain further economy by reducing pile lengths where warranted, soils investigations will be made and test piles driven and load tested, so as to obtain more accurate data for establishing pile lengths.

Driving of the piles will be controlled by a modified E.N.R. formula taking into account the weight of the pile and further modified by field data obtained from the test piles.

In the present design, the pile lengths range from 70 to 155 feet. All the piles 140' and under are 16" octagonal, while those over 140' are 18" octagonal.

The lift points are designed for equal reactions at all points of lift, and for a bending stress of such magnitude that there will always be compression over the entire section during lifting and handling. Thus, all piles 80' and under have a two-point lift, those between 81' and 110', three points, and all those over 110', four points. The points of lift are based on a factor of the pile lengths and will be accurately figured for each length of pile used.

The piles will be pretensioned with high-tensile stress relieved seven-wire strands. Each strand is approximately 3/8" diameter. The 16" piles will have 13 strands and 18" piles 16. The initial tension in the wire is 175,000 p.s.i. placing an effective compression in the concrete of about 1,600 p.s.i. taking into account assumed losses of elastic and inelastic deformations.

The total number of piles to be used in this project is about 1,600, with an average length of 90' per pile. If all the piles are placed end to end, the total length would be over 27 miles, or about the distance from downtown Los Angeles to Pomona.

The total length of strand used, including waste, will be long enough to stretch from Los Angeles to San Francisco, and there will be enough concrete to pave a four-foot-wide sidewalk four-inches thick about 33 miles long.

CHICAGO ARCHITECT ROOT TO RECEIVE GOLD AWARD

John Wellborn Root of Chicago, architect of many of America's distinguished buildings, has been named the winner of the 1958 Gold Medal of The American Institute of Architects, and will receive the coveted award at the AIA banquet held in the course of the Institute's annual convention in Cleveland, Ohio, July 7-11.

Born 71 years ago, the son of the famous architect John Root, Sr., Root is widely known as one of the leaders in freeing American architecture from its "period" bonds. Many of the buildings he designed in the 1920s foreshadowed present-day building design.

The Gold Medal is the highest honor the Institute can bestow, and may be awarded annually in recognition of most distinguished service to the architectural profession of the Institute. Previous Gold Medal winners include Louis Skidmore in 1957; Clarence S. Stein, 1956; William M. Dudok in 1955, and Frank Lloyd Wright in 1949.

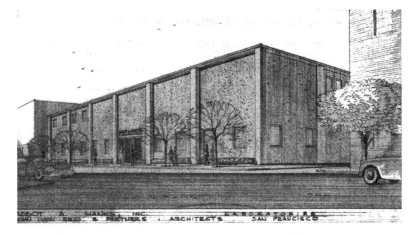

ABBOT A. HANKS LABORATORY

San Francisco, California

Ground has been broken to the new Abbot A. Hanks, Inc., laboratory at Sansome and Filbert Streets in San Francisco. John Lyon Reid and Partners are the architects and engineers, and Elvin C. Stendell, the general contractor.

The building site covers 20,000 sq. ft. of area, and ample allowance has been made for a paved parking area. It will be a two-story tilt-up reinforced concrete structure to provide complete facilities for an increasing demand for laboratory and testing services in connection with structural materials, soil mechanics, chemical, metallurgical, spectrographic and assay work.

The laboratory of Abbot A. Hanks, Inc., was established ninety-two years ago by Henry G. Hanks, who was the first California State mineralogist. It is the oldest established laboratory of its kind in the United States to maintain continuous operation during the entire period. Special consideration has been given to the requirements of its clients by providing well established technical equipment and a force of sixty trained personnel. The corporation, formed in 1924, is almost entirely owned by employees who have been with the firm for many years. Herbert D. Imrie is president of the corporation, and Theodore P. Dresser, Jr., is vice president and chief engineer.

It is expected that the new building will be ready for occupancy in November of this year.

LEFT TO RIGHT: Elvin C. Stendell, General Contractor; Theo. P. Dressler, Jr., Vice-Pres., Abbot A. Hanks, Inc.; Herbert D. Imrie, Pres. Abbot A. Hanks, Inc.; and John Lyon Reid, Architect, at ground breaking fete.

UNITED AIR LINES
JET AGE HANGAR
San Francisco, California

SKIDMORE, OWINGS and MERRILL,
Architects

DINWIDDIE CONSTRUCTION CO.
General Contractors

The largest welded plate girders ever made in the United States have been fabricated in Los Angeles and set in place for one of the nation's new Jet Age hangars which the United Air Lines is building on a site adjacent to San Francisco's International Airport in San Mateo county.

TOP VIEW shows 365 foot long steel beams in place. VIEW at right shows massive beam projecting from concrete core—one of seven welded plate girders, largest ever made in the United States.

The spectacular hangar is a double cantilever structure with a three-story concrete core for mechanical and maintenance shops, company offices, and general storerooms. Inclined trusses are employed in a special engineering technique in construction, which results in greater economy and cleaner design. The roof of the building is supported by seven plate girders, resting on pillars which enclose the core. Each girder is 365 feet long and weighs 125 tons.

One of the features of construction is the high strength bolting which made it easy to erect the seven giant 125-ton steel plate girders that form the structural ribs of the unusual roof of the building.

The girders, said to be the largest ever made in this country, measure 365 feet from tip to tip. They are fabricated from steel plate ranging from $\frac{1}{2}$ to 2 inches in thickness.

To facilitate and speed the erection of these girders, they were erected in sections. The two exterior girders on either side of the building were erected in three sctions, and the five interior girders in four sections. The most critical phase of the erection was in lifting two 120-foot sections of the exterior girders into position simultaneously and splicing them to the center of the girder. A fifty and a sixty-ton crane teamed to lift the huge pieces of steel 50 feet into the air and hold them to the center section of the girder while the three were bolted together. Each of these splices took 240 bolts, $1\frac{1}{4}$ inches in diameter.

The girders were connected together with a horizontal bracing system of inclined trusses composed of light structural steel. These were lifted in units by smaller cranes and bolted to the heavy girders. This system involved 288 individual truss units. High-strength bolts used in the job varied from $1\frac{1}{2}$-inch

diameter to ⅝-inch diameter. A total of 27,795 high strength bolts were used in the structure.

Bolting of the heavy girder splices greatly aided and speeded the erection process. The heavy sections could be kept in camber while being held by the cranes since the splice connections could be securely lined up with drift pins. As the bolts tightened, the sections came into perfect alignment.

When completed, sometime this fall, the hangar will provide 153,000 square feet of floor space for turn-around line maintenance of aircraft. This is large enough to house simultaneously two DC-7 Mainliners and four of United Air Lines forthcoming DC-8 jet planes. Aircraft will be positioned on the front and rear sides of the core.

TESTING CALIBRATIONS on high tensile bolts used to splice flanges of 365-ft. girders which cantilever 142-ft. each way.

CHARMING ENTRANCE . . . in contemporary theme.

RESIDENTIAL ENTRANCES
WITH A SMILE APPEAL

By ARTHUR W. PRIAULX

We've come a long way from the bearskin hung over the cave entrance, as one leading western architect observes, but too many architects and designers are apparently overlooking one of the finest fields of expression in the entrance and entryway and are just putting hinges on the tepee flap.

The entrance should set the pace for the rest of the home. It should give that first cheery welcome to the visitor. This same architect observes that too many architects today appear to be frustrated mystery story writers who throw in a blank slab door and dare the visitor to guess what's behind it.

Actually, the contemporary home of today, a creation largely of the inventive imagination and daring of the western architect, offers a limitless variety of styling and original thinking in the home entrance.

Informal living, epitomized in the contemporary modern home design, brings the outdoors right into the living room with large areas of glass and open walls. Styling throughout the exterior and interior of the home-of-today subtly proclaims the informality of modern family living. When the entrance section is not utilized to continue this theme, much of the charm of otherwise fine designing is lost and reduced in effectiveness.

More than ever before the modern architect has the tools and the materials to exploit fully the opportunities for design in the entrance and entryway. The texture and natural colorings of native western woods, the amazingly flexible uses of glass, the texture and native attractiveness of stone and brick put in his hands the basic materials which lend themselves to

ARCHITECT AND ENGINEER

hundreds of original designs, treatments and finishes.

The warm friendliness of these materials lend themselves readily to creating the entrance with the smile appeal—light, cheerful, pleasing and appealing. Architect George Nakashima says wood has a romantic grain which can be developed with great sympathy and feeling around the entrances to set the mode for the rest of the home, and this romantic character can be accentuated with proper blending of stone, glass and brick.

Architect Day W. Hilborn has achieved a remarkably cheerful entrance in his Ernest Christensen home at Vancouver with skillful harmonizing of western red cedar with glass (see page 12). A fir door with three large glass panels is centered in a full glass wall in the recessed entrance to the Christensen home. The entire entrance hall is lighted up, as is a tiny planetarium on either side of the door. Interesting variety is obtained by using boards-and-batten cedar siding on one exterior wall as it comes up to the entrance and rough-sawn cedar siding on the other. The mingling

of texture and line focusses attention on the entrance and creates an altogether charming and friendly entry section.

Here is an example of uniting the outdoors with the interior of the home, for shrubs are brought right up to the entrance for a unity with the plantings inside the home.

Another excellent example of the clever mingling of glass with western red cedar siding to develop a unique and pleasant entrance is the work of Architect Paul Bogen in the Tad Luckey home at Eugene (see page 17, bottom). A glass-paneled fir door forms the outer section of a glass wall at one side and above the door. A ribbed panel of glass alongside the door gives some privacy, but creates the feeling of cheerful welcome. Still more glass has been installed at the right of the entrance above eye level where an outer wall joins at right angles just to the right of the entrance section. The L-shape created points up and enhances in a cozy manner the entrance to the home.

The Oliver Willard home at Eugene utilizes still

Walls and ceiling of west coast hemlock finished with clear rex bring out natural tones to this simply designed entrance.

another device for harmonizing the contemporary theme of this home and tying together outdoors and home interior. Architect John Stafford has designed his entrance door directly beneath a modified porte cochere which has been achieved by a wide overhanging roof section. The door is solid, but surrounded by glass sections on either side. An all-cedar home, the boards-and-batten exterior siding mingles through the glass with the cedar panelled storage section which

separates the entryway from the living area. Simple lines, and soft, subtle use of wood and glass as a single entity create a remarkably informal welcome area. Part of this has been achieved by the use of brick surfacing beneath the porte cochere. Several cedar planter boxes have been placed beneath the overhang to extend the greenery and shrubbery of the outer yard more intimately into the home. The glass walls serve to lighten up the entry area inside.

Another John Stafford creation in Eugene is the Henry Hall home located halfway up a hill on the outskirts of the city. A colonial ranch-type styling depends for its effectiveness and faithfulness of theme on a combination of the rough texture of boards-and-batten cedar with contrasting use of dark and light gray stains. The entrance door is a solid, two-panel job with small windows above. The effect of friendliness comes from the light gray coloring of the solid louvers of cedar set in the angle walls which form the entrance. Light gray ceiling of the ranch-type porch and light gray trim have been used to develop a soft, warm atmosphere in this sheltered entrance area. Again, an effort has been made to achieve in-

ROOF OVERHANG in combination with focussing solid cedar screen calls attention to this charming entrance door framed in glass.

formality with low, long cedar planters along the entire
length of the cement-floored porch. Small, old-style
brass carriage lamps, one on either side of the door,
give contrasting texture to the rough cedar walls.

High atop a hill six miles west of Eugene on Green
Hill Road, the Warren Weiseth home offers ideas in
contemporary design which accentuate and highlight
the possibilities for originality in entrances. Designed
by Architects Wilmsen and Endicott, this two-level
residence demonstrates utilization of hillside site (see
page 15, bottom), adaptation of design to timbered
surroundings and skill of the architects in turning an
awkward entrance problem into an attractive and
different situation.

A brick retaining wall divides upper and lower
lawn levels, forms a natural break for the terrain as
it leads up to the story-and-a-half high entrance area.
Here again cedar siding and glass have been married
with skill and thought. The solid birch door, finished
in its natural color to contrast with the deeper tones
of cedar, marks the entrance. A glass section, full on
one side of the door and rising ten feet high above

gives height and dimension to conform to the vertical
lines of the structure and avoids that out-of-character
situation which a conventional entrance would have
created. While most of the siding is rough tongue-and-
groove installed vertically, the section around the

Story and a half entrance . . . becomes a study in glass.

RESIDENTIAL ENTRANCES . . .

entrance and continuing on to the triple garage doors adjoining is contrasting horizontal drop siding. The use of the horizontal siding to break the effect of height of the vertical siding is a fine use of line and contrasting texture and serves to pinpoint attention on the entrance area.

One real value of the well-lighted entrance door and side glass area is the welcome additional light such installations provide for the inner entryway of the home. Architect Richard Sundeleaf has done a fine job of bringing outside light into the large entry hall of the Gordon Carey home in McMinnville, Oregon (see page 13). In order to reflect this light to better advantage, Sundeleaf designed the Carey entrance hall in light-toned west coast hemlock. The natural soft tones and soft gold colorings of this wood when used on walls and ceilings in this entrance pick up the outside light and create a warm, friendly spot where the visitor first gets an inside view of this residence. A device for tying in the outdoors into the home is the extension of the stone tile of the outer porch into the entrance hall. The combination of the

natural texture of the stone and wood creates hardly a break as the visitor steps from outside into this entrance with its dramatic simple informality.

Some devices made popular by our forebears in their colonial styling are being utilized today to serve different purposes in the contemporary world. The dutch door served a purpose in the past, and has an equally useful purpose in the present. Architect Graham Smith has put it to work in the Frank Graham home at Jasper, Oregon (see page 14, top), where this family spends much of its time outside. This ranch home serves a family which has many outside interests and a yard full of pets. The lower section of the door serves to keep pets in their domain, and the upper door section of solid glass panels has a friendly appearance for frequent visitors which farm life invites. Much traffic between nearby kitchen and equally close outdoor patio can be reduced by using the upper door section as a pass-through for dishes and foodstuffs.

In many of the small, compact homes of today, where it is difficult because of space limitations to have an entrance hall, some designers and architects have

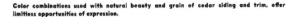

Color combinations used with natural beauty and grain of cedar siding and trim, offer limitless opportunities of expression.

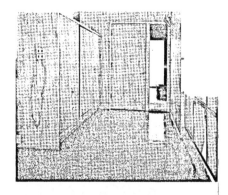

solved the problem with screening walls which serve to separate the visitor from abrupt entry into the living room and yet do not rob too much of the space. On the Orlo Bagley home at Cottage Grove (see page 15, top), a simple louvered screen of specially cut one-and-a-half by six-inch Douglas fir boards set on a slight angle to obstruct direct view from the living room, forms an attractive entrance area. The screen serves also to block out view from the living room into the hall closets on an opposite wall just beside the entrance door.

Sometimes the effect of a friendly, warm and cheerful entrance is created by the simple use of naturally textured wood with a small glass area as in the Nils Hult home at Eugene (see page 17, top). Because the family and friends almost invariably enter this home from the carport side into the keeping room, or from the more informal inner courtyard from the carport breezeway, the front entrance has been designed by Architect Clare Hamlin in a more formal tone. However, even the formality has not detracted from the suggestion of light, airy welcome. A solid flush birch door has been softened by the installation beside it of a full height matching panel of unbroken glass just half the size of the door. The visitor can see through this panel into a long hallway, a cul-de-sac which joins a solarium. The visitor can see right

through this house into the inner garden and play area, so the effect is one of intimacy and friendliness created by the simple device of clear glass and long vistas which seem to make home and outdoors one.

Many of our contemporary homes have a sweeping simplicity which is disarming once one looks inside, and again the entrance can retain this simple styling and clever use of line and form and yet be utilized as a means of suggesting to the visitor what charms and thrills await him inside.

Take the case of the Ralph P. Christensen home in

(See Page 30)

Simple lines and form in
harmony with a delicate
use of glass areas make
a lovely entrance.

Air view of Millsdale Industrial Park.

CELEBRATES SEVENTH ANNIVERSARY

ASSOCIATED CONSTRUCTION & ENGINEERING

BUILDS AND MOVES INTO NEW BUILDING

South San Francisco, California

By DICK HARRIS

Horace Greeley was once reported to have said to a group of interested citizens, "Go West Young Man—Go West," and just how far West Mr. Greeley had in mind as the land of opportunity is not too clearly defined in the records of the occasion.

However, there is little speculation in the minds of business, commercial and industrial leaders throughout the nation today, that one of the great opportunities of all time exists on the Pacific Coast where population growth is phenomenal and business opportunities already available are standing by to expand into the far east just as soon as economic conditions are settled somewhat.

Firm Organized

Realizing the existence of the tremendous opportunities available on the West Coast, and pin-pointing their initial effort in the San Francisco Bay Area, two young men, World War II veterans, decided to cast their lot together and in 1951 established the Asso-

ciated Construction and Engineering Company, with general offices at 2903 Geneva Avenue in San Francisco.

The youthful pair, both engineers, John L. Chapman and William H. Acheson, today head a growing firm specializing in industrial and commercial building construction, with completed projects and work under contract representing a wide variety of construction in many localities.

Not inclined to overlook the many opportunities for specialized construction which existed in the immediate Bay Area, the firm was quick to participate in the development and construction of one of the larger planned industrial developments on the Coast.

Area Development

When plans were completed to reclaim a portion of the tideland areas of South San Francisco and Northern San Mateo county adjacent to the rapidly developing San Francisco International Airport, and develop the area into one of the nation's newest and most modern industrial areas, the firm immediately became a part of the project through the construction of commercial and industrial buildings which were designed by numerous architects and engineers to meet the specific needs of a particular type of business activity. Thus this comparatively young organization, which began operations with a minimum staff of employees, and which has now grown to regular staff of more than 100 people, has been a definite part of and instrumental in the development of the famed Millsdale, located between Burlingame and Millbrae on the west side of the Bayshore Freeway; and the South San Francisco industrial areas. They have indeed been one of the leaders in building facilities in South San Francisco for the post-war industrial development boom which shows no sign of slackening at this time.

To keep pace with the firm's progress and growth in the construction field, it soon became evident that the original office and work facilities in San Francisco would become obsolete. Therefore, and coincidentally with the observance this year of the company's seventh anniversary, it was decided to build a new office and headquarters building in the South San Francisco Airport Boulevard Industrial Park, 127 Beacon Street.

COMPANY OFFICIALS: John L. Chapman, seated, and partner William H. Acheson of the Associated Construction and Engineering Company, this month celebrate the contracting firm's seventh birthday with the opening of new headquarters building in South San Francisco.

GARRATT-CALLAHAN COMPANY of the Millsdale Industrial Park, San Mateo county, one of the nation's leading engineering firms in the field of water treatment . . . constructed by Associate Construction and Engineering Company last year. J. FRANCIS WARD, Architect.

Build Own Building

Construction on such a building was commenced early this year, and this month the Associated Construction and Engineering Company moved into their new, considerably expanded, general headquarters building amid ceremonies marking the event.

Associated Construction and Engineering Company, according to its president, John L. Chapman, who now resides in the Hillsborough residential area and not too far from his offices, has constructed some one hundred and thirty-seven commercial and industrial buildings since the firm was organized in 1951. Operations of the company have become so diversified that it has become necessary to employ many workmen who are experts and specialists in their particular field

of endeavor. The result of an enlarged program in the construction industry has led to an increased staff and at the present time there are more than 100 men regularly employed by the company in its normal operations.

Associated Construction and Engineering Company has been keenly interested in and particularly active in the several rapidly expanding industrial areas of South San Francisco and Millsdale where the firm has been awarded numerous contracts and has built a wide variety of plants and facilities for many of the country's major commercial and industrial industries, where such organizations have moved to the West Coast or have expanded their activities to include larger areas of western America.

NEW HOME of the New Method Fur Company's headquarters building in South San Francisco, nearing completion.

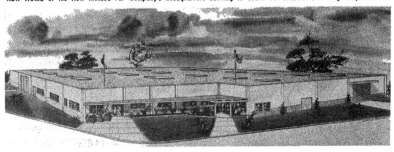

ARCHITECT AND ENGINEER

RELIANCE ELECTRIC & ENGINEERING COMPANY'S new West Coast assembly plant and distribution center . . . the 40,000 square foot plant was one of the first to be constructed in the Millsdale Industrial Park where Associated Construction and Engineering Company has been one of the most active builders. George Jennings, Engineer.

Projects Are Many

Included among activities in the South San Francisco area are plants for Spice Islands; the H. D. Lee Company, manufacturer of work clothes; Morris Manufacturing Company; the Pioneer Motor Bearing Company, Thermoid Company, the Mueller Brass Company, Coleman Company, Manhattan Shirt Company, the American Chesterfield Company, Quality Foods, Incorporated; and the J. H. Coffman and Son plant.

In the new Millsdale planned industrial area, where bay shoreline lands affected by high and low tides, and land which was between the Bayshore Freeway and the San Francisco International Airport and the higher ground east of the Southern Pacific railroad tracks, could be reclaimed by a dirt fill, a number of outstanding industrial plants have been built by the firm. In many instances the building owner utilized the opportunity of a new site to incorporate innovations in structure design and utility use so that the area as a whole represents a complete new concept in design, construction, customer parking facilities and landscaping.

Among the structures built in this area are the Frank Edwards Company building; the Reliance Electric Company plant; the Sylvania Electric Company distributing center; CIBA Drug Company, center for world-wide distribution of drug products; the Stromberg-Carlson Company general distribution facilities; John Wood Company, Harris and Strch, Jeffrey Manufacturing Company, the Garratt-Callahan Company, Burroughs-Wellcome and Company, the Biro Manufacturing Company, and the Jaeger and Branch facilities.

Recent Activities

Two recent and rather interesting projects which the firm has completed have been the attractive Marathon Paper Company's new dock-high, 100,000 square feet of floor space building in Modesto, California. This plant is a subsidiary operation of Continental Can Company, and was completed in just ninety

days after construction was started; and the 120,000-square-foot Koch Luggage factory near Corte Madera in Marin County—a building designed to harmonize and blend into the surrounding residential areas with eye appeal from the nearby Redwood Highway, and a structure which was completed in just seventy-five days following start of construction.

Associated Construction and Engineering Company's current jobs under contract are many. However, among the more interesting because of some

Sylvania Electric Company's modern West Coast headquarters has become a landmark facing Bayshore Freeway in the Millsdale Industrial Park . . . built by Associated Construction and Engineering Company. John S. Bolles, Architect.

NEW MARATHON PAPER COMPANY plant at Modesto, California. Built by Associated Construction and Engineering Company. Simpson & Stratta, Engineers.

particular phase of construction are the new million dollar Corte Madera modern shopping center in Marin county; a 50,000-square-foot addition to the Marathon Paper Company facilities in Modesto; and a new 40-lane bowling alley in San Jose which embodies all of the facilities for men and women bowlers, a cocktail lounge and snack bar, and allied factors; also a new 50,000-square-foot building is now under construction for the McKesson and Robbins drug wholesalers in the South San Francisco Industrial Park, which will serve as an expanded distribution center for the West Coast.

Associated with Mr. Chapman in the construction and engineering business is William H. Acheson, who resides with his family in Woodside. The two men, both of whom are engineers with many years of diversified experience in the building and construction industry, joined forces for formation of the firm in 1951.

World War II Veterans

Chapman, a graduate of the University of Michigan at Ann Arbor, is a World War II veteran, having seen service with the U.S. Army during the War. Following the end of hostilities and his discharge from active service, Chapman served as production manager for

the air conditioning division of the Philco Corporation, and from 1946-1950 his attentions were turned to the duties of executive vice president of the Carew Steel Company, general contractors and steel fabricators with offices and plant in York, Pennsylvania. Selling his interests in the steel business, Chapman left the east to settle in California and establish the Associated Construction and Engineering Company, an activity which has taken his full time and effort since.

One of the first major companies to establish West Coast distribution headquarters in South San Francisco was the H. D. Lee Company, one of the world's largest manufacturers of work clothing. Located in the new Airport Boulevard Industrial Park, the new plant serves all of the Western United States . . . built by Associated Construction and Engineering Company.

J.
FRANCIS
WARD,
Architect

Acheson also saw action in World War II, serving in the U.S. Navy. He is a graduate of the University of Alaska and obtained considerable experience in the building industry as a young man. Leaving Alaska he served from 1947 to 1949 as manager of the Titan Metal Products Company of Seattle. Again feeling the urge to move south, Acheson went to Oakland, California, where he formed and conducted the California Steel Buildings Company of Oakland until selling the business to become associated with Chapman in the present Associated Construction and Engineering Company.

Since its inception seven years ago, the firm, through a program of careful planning, thoroughness of work,

**FRANK
EDWARDS
COMPANY
Milsdale Park,
California**

and application to the principle of best serving their clients and associates in all construction projects, has grown into one of the leading commercial and industrial building contracting firms in Northern California.

Some evidence of the firm's success along these lines is in the fact that despite what many consider as a general downtrend in the building-construction business, Associated Construction and Engineering Company now enjoys its largest backlog of business in the company's history. Much of the firm's work is with industrial realtors on a lease-back building arrangement using leading architects and engineers of the San Francisco bay area on design and structural work.

American Institute of Architects

Leon Chatelain, Jr., President

John N. Richards, 1st Vice President
Philip Will, Jr., 2nd Vice President
Edmund R. Purves, Executive Secretary

Edward L. Wilson, Secretary
Raymond S. Kastendieck, Treasurer

National Headquarters—1735 New York Avenue, N.W., Washington, D.C.

REGIONAL DIRECTORS—**Northwest District**, Donald J. Stewart, Portland, Oregon; **Western Mountain District**, Bradley P. Kidder, Santa Fe, New Mexico; **California-Nevada-Hawaii District**, Ulysses Floyd Rible, Los Angeles, California

ARIZONA CHAPTERS:
CENTRAL ARIZONA: David Sholder, President; A. John Brenner, Vice-President; Jimmie R. Nunn, Secretary; Kemper Goodwin, Treasurer; James W. Elmore, Director; Ralph Haver, Director; Martin Ray Young, Jr., Director. Office of Secy., P.O. Box 904, Phoenix.
SOUTHERN ARIZONA: Santry Clay Fuller, President; Edward H. Nelson, Vice-President; David S. Swanson, Secretary; Robert J. Ambrose, Treasurer; D. Burr DuBois, Director; Eleazar D. Herreras, Director; Emerson C. Scholer, Director. Office of Secy., 2343 South Tucson Avenue, Tucson.

COAST VALLEYS CHAPTER:
William L. Higgins (San Jose), President; Paul J. Huston (Palo Alto), Vice-President; William H. Daseking (Menlo Park), Treasurer; Edward N. Chamberlain (San Jose), Secretary. Office of Secy., 390 Park Ave., San Jose.

CENTRAL VALLEY OF CALIFORNIA:
Joseph J. Jozens, President (Sacramento); Armsby Tod Hart, Vice-President (Sacramento); Albert M. Dreyfuss, Secretary (Sacramento); Whitson W. Cox, Treasurer. Office of Secy., 2127 "J" St., Sacramento.

COLORADO CHAPTER:
Casper F. Hegner, President; C. Gordon Sweet, Vice President; Norton Polivnick, Secretary; Richard Williams, Treasurer. Directors: James M. Hunter, Robert K. Fuller, Edward L. Bunts. Office of Secy., 1225 Bannock St., Denver, Colorado.

EAST BAY CHAPTER:
Hachiro Yuasa (Oakland), President; George T. Kern (Oakland), Vice-President; William M. Gillis (San Francisco), Secretary; J. A. Zerkle (Berkeley), Treasurer. Directors: H. B. Clausen, F. A. Lockwood, John Oyarzo, G. M. McCue, Marjorie Montgomery, Exec. Secy. Office of Secy., Mezzanine, Hotel Claremont, Berkeley 5.

IDAHO CHAPTER:
Anton S. Dropping, Boise, President; Charles W. Johnston, Payette, Vice-President; Glenn E. Cline, Boise, Sec.-Treas. Executive Committee: Chester L. Shawver and Nat J. Adams, Boise. Office of Secy., 624 Idaho Bldg., Boise.

MONTEREY BAY CHAPTER:
Robert Stanton, President (Carmel); Walter Burde, Vice-President; William L. Cranston, Secretary; George Kuska, Treasurer. Office of Secy., P.O. Box 1846, Carmel.

MONTANA CHAPTER:
William J. Hess, President (Great Falls); John E. Toohey, Vice-President (Billings); H. C. Cheever, Secy.-Treas. (Bozeman). Directors: Oscar J. Ballas, Wm. J. Hess, John E. Toohey. Office of Sec., Bozeman, Montana.

NEVADA CHAPTER:
RENO: Lawrence A. Gulling, President; William E. Cowell, Vice-President; Albert W. Alegre, Secretary; Ralph A. Casazza, Treasurer. Graham Erskine, Raymond W. Hellman, George L. F. O'Brien, Directors. Office of the Secy., 500 Plumas St., Reno.
LAS VEGAS: Walter F. Zick, President; Aloysius McDonald, Vice-President; Edward B. Hendricks, Secy.-Treas. Directors: Walter F. Zick, Edward Hendricks, Charles E. Cox. Office of Secy., 106 S. Main St., Las Vegas.

NEVADA STATE BOARD OF ARCHITECTS:
L. A. Ferris, Chairman; Aloysius McDonald, Secy.-Treas. Members: Russell Mills (Reno); Edward S. Parsons (Reno), Richard R. Stadelman (Las Vegas). Office: 1420 S. 5th St., Las Vegas.

NORTHERN CALIFORNIA CHAPTER:
William Corlett, President; Donald Powers Smith, Vice-President; George T. Rockrise, Secretary; Richard S. Banwell, Treasurer. Directors: W. Clement Ambrose, John Kruse, Bernard J. Sabaroff, Corwin Booth. Exec. Secy., May B. Hipshman. Chapter Office, 47 Kearny St., San Francisco.

ORANGE COUNTY CHAPTER:
William T. Jordan, President (Costa Mesa); Donald M. Williamson, Vice-President (Laguna Beach); J. Herbert Brownell, Secretary; Rumont W. Hougan, Treasurer. Office of Secy., 1950 W. Coast Highway, Newport Beach.

OREGON CHAPTER:
John K. Dukehart, President; Keith R. Maguire, Vice-President; Robert Douglas, Secretary; Harry K. Stevens, Treasurer. Directors: Daniel McGoodwin, Earl P. Newberry, Everett B. Franks, Robert W. Fritsch, Donald W. Edmundson. Office of Secy., 2041 S.W. 58th Ave., Portland 1.

WASHINGTON STATE CHAPTER AIA

Four fifth-year architectural students of the University of Washington were honored at a banquet at the Hotel Edmond Meany recently, at a joint meeting of the Chapter, the Architectural Alumni Association of the University, and the University's College of Architecture and Urban Planning.

Awards were made to Glenn Brewer, Richard Mayo, Alfred Westberg, Albert Nelson, Smith Nakata, Thomas Muths, Albert Nelson, Milton Hunt, William Thacker, Paul Thienes, John Morrell, Herbert Seablom, Douglas Babbit, Philip Korell and Thomas Picton. The banquet was part of a special three-day program celebrating the elevation of the University's School of Architecture to collegiate status. Dean Arthur Herrmann, F.A.I.A.; James Chiarelli, president of the Chapter, and Pro. Keith Kolb of the Alumni Association, made the presentations.

John Rohrer attended the Aspen Design Conference on "The City" this month.

NORTHERN CALIFORNIA CHAPTER AIA

Two outstanding annual events featured this month's Chapter calendar. One was the annual awards dinner at the University of California, traditionally the joint meeting of the East Bay Chapter and the Northern California Chapter; the other was the awards ceremony for students, observed this year in the courtyard of the Architecture Building, University of California at Berkeley.

On July 25, the joint AIA-WAL social evening will be held at the home of Ann and Lawrence Halprin in Kentfield, Marin county. A modern dance program and refreshments have been planned.

SANTA CLARA AND SANTA CRUZ COUNTIES AIA MEETING

The AIA's new motion pictures "What Is a House" and "A School for Johnny" were shown at a recent meeting with Allan Walter, Public Relations Committee, discussing the possibilities of local use in the interest of architecture.

A special committee has been appointed to serve with the Planning Commission of the City of Palo Alto in studying the height and set-back requirements of buildings in downtown Palo Alto. Members of the committee include Morgan Stedman, chairman;

Birge Clark and Chester Root.

The July meeting will be a joint meeting with the Monterey Chapter AIA.

New members include Ruddle Gast, junior associate member.

CALIFORNIA COUNCIL AIA

The newly expanded Board of Directors held its June meeting at the Balboa Bay Club to discuss legislation affecting the practice of architecture, including a proposed bill to license "Professional Designers." The bill was presented to the Administrative Committee by Gale Santocono, president of the California Society of Designers, and has the support of the American Institute of Building Designers. The proposed measure defines a "professional designer" as "any person who engages in the practice of creating esthetic design for objects, vehicles or structures."

A "Rule of Procedure" regarding proposals for engineering services, adopted by directors of the Consulting Engineers Association of California, was also taken under consideration.

"Creativeness in Architecture" will be the theme of the 13th Annual Convention scheduled for October 15-19 in Monterey, California.

OREGON CHAPTER AIA

"Relationship of the Professional Engineer to His Architect" was the subject of a recent panel discussion with Grant Kelly, electrical engineer; Tom Taylor, mechanical engineer; Roland Rose, structural engineer, and H. Abbott Lawrence, architect and moderator, participating.

New members include: Frederick L. Rudat, Tom Burns, Wyman K. Bear and Harold C. McNeil, corporate members. Frank A. Schumaker, Jr., architect of Oregon City, and Harry C. Newton, architect of Portland, associate members.

EAST BAY CHAPTER AIA

The June meeting consisted of participation in the annual College of Architecture Awards Dinner, University of California, Berkeley.

The Board of Directors has voted to establish a new committee to be named the Governmental Relations Committee.

New Members: Albert Anthony Perata, Junior Associate; and Henry Hill, transferred from Northern California Chapter.

SOUTHERN CALIFORNIA CHAPTER AIA

A. I. Stewart of Pasadena, member of the California State Assembly, was honored at the June meeting held in the Statler Hotel, Los Angeles. Assemblyman Stewart is retiring from the California Legislature this year and was given Chapter recognition for his many years of interest in the problems of the profession while serving as a legislator.

Principal speaker for the occasion was Major General John S. Bragdon, special assistant to the Presi-

(See Page 32)

PASADENA CHAPTER:
H. Douglas Byles, President; Edward D. Davies, Vice-President; Ward W. Deems, Secretary; Robert F. Gordon, Treasurer. Directors: Mal Gianni, Lee B. Kline, Keith B. Marston, Donald E. Neptune. Office of the Secy., 170 E. California St., Pasadena.

SAN DIEGO CHAPTER:
Raymond Lee Eggers, President; William F. Wilmurt, Vice-President; Lloyd P. A. Ruocco, Secretary; Delmar S. Mitchell, Treasurer. Directors: John C. Deardorf, Richard George Wheeler and Sam Bruce Richards. Office of the Secy., 3603 5th Ave., San Diego 3.

SAN JOAQUIN CHAPTER:
Robert C. Kaestner, President (Visalia); William G. Hyberg, Vice-President (Fresno); Lawrence B. Alexander, Secretary; Edwin S. Darden. Office of Secy., 128 E. 8th St., Hanford.

SANTA BARBARA CHAPTER:
Wallace W. Arendt, President (Santa Barbara); Darwin E. Fisher, Vice-President (Ventura); Walter Tibbetts, Secretary; Kenneth H. Hess, Treasurer. Office of Secy., 630 Para Grande Lane, Santa Barbara.

SOUTHERN CALIFORNIA CHAPTER:
George Vernon Russell, President; Maynard Lyndon, Vice-President; Ralph C. Crosby, Secretary; Thornton Abell, Treasurer. Office of Secy., 124 W. 4th St., Los Angeles.

SOUTHWEST WASHINGTON CHAPTER:
Charles T. Pearson, President (Tacoma); Robert T. Olson, 1st Vice-President (Olympia); Donald Burr, 2nd Vice-President (Tacoma); Percy G. Ball, Secretary (Tacoma); Alan Liddle, Treasurer (Tacoma); Trustees —Gilbert M. Wojahn and Gordon N. Johnston (Tacoma). Office of Secy., 2715 Center St., Tacoma.

UTAH CHAPTER:
W. J. Monroe, Jr., President, 433 Atlas Bldg., Salt Lake City; M. E. Harris, Jr., Secretary, 703 Newhouse Bldg., Salt Lake City.

WASHINGTON STATE CHAPTER:
James J. Chiarelli (Seattle), President; Robert H. Dietz (Seattle), 1st Vice-President; Walter H. Rothe (Yakima), 2nd Vice-President; Talbot Wegg (Seattle), Secretary; Albert O. Bumgardner (Seattle), Treasurer. Directors: Arnold G. Gangnes, Harrison J. Overturf, Lloyd J. Lovegren, and John L. Wright. Miss Gwen Myer, Executive Secretary, 409 Central Bldg., Seattle 4.

SPOKANE CHAPTER:
Wm. C. James, President; Carl H. Johnson, Vice-President; Keith T. Boyington, Secretary; Ralph J. Bishop, Treasurer; Lawrence G. Evanoff, Carroll Martell, Kenneth W. Brooks, Directors. Office of the Secy., 615 Realty Bldg., Spokane.

HAWAII CHAPTER:
Robert M. Law, President; Harry W. Seckel, Vice-President; Richard Dennis, Secretary. Directors: Edwin Bauer, George J. Wimberly. Office of Secy., P. O. Box 3288, Honolulu, Hawaii.

CALIFORNIA COUNCIL, THE A.I.A.:
L. F. Richards, Santa Clara, President; Lee B. Kline, Los Angeles, Vice-President; Edward H. Fickett, Los Angeles, Secretary; Allen Y. Lew, Fresno, Treasurer. Miss Mary E. White, Office Secretary, 703 Market Street, San Francisco 3.

CALIFORNIA STATE BD. ARCHITECTURAL EXAMINERS:
Malcolm D. Reynolds, President (Oakland); Kenneth Wing, Secretary (Long Beach); Wendell R. Spackman (San Francisco); Paul Davis (Santa Ana), and Frank Cronin, Executive Secy., 1020 N St., Sacramento 14.

ALLIED ARCHITECTURAL ORGANIZATIONS

SAN FRANCISCO ARCHITECTURAL CLUB:
C. Van De Weghe, President; O. Hickenlooper, Vice-President; James O. Brummett, Secretary; J. W. Tasker, Treasurer. Directors: Morris Barnett, Art Swisher, Stan Howatt, Frank Barsoti, Frances Capone. Office of Secy., 507 Howard St., San Francisco 5.

PRODUCERS' COUNCIL—SOUTHERN CALIFORNIA CHAPTER:
Clay T. Snider, President, Minneapolis-Honeywell Regulator Co., L.A.; E. J. Lawson, Vice-President, Aluminum Company of America, L.A.; E. Phil Filsinger, Secretary, Gladding, McBean & Co., L.A.; William G. Aspy, Treasurer, H. H. Robertson Co., L.A.; Henry E. North, Jr., National Director, Arcadia Metal Products, L.A.; Office of the Secy., 2901 Los Feliz Blvd.

PRODUCERS' COUNCIL—NORTHERN CALIFORNIA CHAPTER:
John J. O'Connor, President, H. H. Robertson Co.; Stanley L. Basterash, Vice-President, Western Asbestos Co.; Howard W. DeWeese, Treasurer, Pomona Tile Mfg. Co.; Robert W. Harrington, Secretary, Clay Brick & Tile Assn. Office of Secy., 55 New Montgomery St., San Francisco 5.

PRODUCERS' COUNCIL—SAN DIEGO CHAPTER:
Eugene E. Bean, President, Penestra Inc.; James I. Hayes, Vice-President, Westinghouse Electric Co.; E. R. Shelby, Secretary, The Celotex Corp. (El Cajon); Joseph C. Langley, Treasurer, Republic Steel Corp., Truscon Steel Div. (Lemon Grove). Office of Secy., 1832 Wedgemore Rd., El Cajon.

CONSTRUCTION SPECIFICATIONS INSTITUTE—LOS ANGELES:
R. R. Coghlan, Jr., President; George Lamb, Vice-President; E. Phil Filsinger, Secretary; Harry L. Miller, Treasurer; Directors: Harold Keller, Jack Whiteside, Walter Hagedohm, Raymond Whalley, Charles Field Wetherbee, Martin A. Hegsted, Advisory Member, D. Stewart Kerr. Office of Secy., 2901 Los Feliz Blvd., L.A.

CONSTRUCTION SPECIFICATIONS INSTITUTE—SAN FRANCISCO:
Henry P. Collins, President; Leonard M. Tivol, Vice-President; Leonard P. Grover, Treasurer; Marvin E. Hirchert, Secretary. Office of Secy., 585 Whitewood Drive, San Rafael.

27

WITH THE ENGINEERS

CALIFORNIA ENGINEERS STUDY PRE-STRESSED CONCRETE

The Research Committee of the Structural Engineers Association of Northern California, has formed a Sub-Committee on Prestressed Concrete headed by Theodore C. York, and members of the Prestressed Concrete Institute.

Purpose of the committee is to present standards and specifications for professional consideration of prestressed concrete to the Association's Building Code Committee in an effort to bring about their inclusion in the various Northern California building codes.

Serving with York are: F. W. Cheesebrough, Robert C. Clark, George F. Durhin, Frank D. Gaus, Don Higgins, Walter F. Koller, Prof. T. Y. Lin, Ray A. McCann, Mac Silvert, and Dr. Alexander G. Tarics.

SOCIETY OF AMERICAN MILITARY ENGINEERS—SAN FRANCISCO POST

Bernard Ellis, propulsion staff of Lockheed Aircraft Corpn., was the principal speaker at the June meeting held in the Officers' Club, Presidio of San Francisco. Taking as his subject "Rocket Flights Through Space," Ellis continued discussion of the subject which was introduced at the April meeting. He described in easy-to-understand terms the theory of operation of rocket motors and certain unique problems, physical and mechanical, which are anticipated in space travel.

Because of the strong appeal which this subject had evidenced to youngsters, it was a "Father and Son" meeting, and Ellis gave a number of tips on do's and don't's to the young rocketeers.

STRUCTURAL ENGINEERS ASSOCIATION OF NORTHERN CALIFORNIA

"Symposium on Welding" featured the June meeting held in the Engineers Club, San Francisco, with Samuel H. Clark, American Institute of Steel Construction and SEAONC member, serving as moderator.

The panel of speakers included: "Quality Control and Radiographic Inspection of Welding," John L. Beaton, Supervising Highway Engineer, State of California, Division of Highways, Sacramento; "Comparison of Welding Controls," Adolph M. Hubbard, Welding Engineer, Pittsburgh-Des Moines Steel Company, Santa Clara; "Practical Welded Design," Charles Orr, District Engineer, American Bridge Division, U.S. Steel Corpn., Los Angeles; and "New Equipment and Welding Methods," S. H. Taylor, Western Manager, The Lincoln Electric Company, Emeryville.

The advance of welding technology in the past few years has been tremendous. Structural welding has been increased, and its quality improved, and all phases of the subject, design and inspection were covered during the discussions.

The annual Golf Tournament will be held July 18th at the Olympic Club, Ocean Course, and the Annual Picnic will be held July 26th at Turtle Rock Ranch.

SAN FRANCISCO ENGINEERS SPEAKERS CLUB

The San Francisco Engineers' Speakers Club held its 19th annual banquet and speech contest early this month at Sabella's Capri Room.

Several three-minute speeches were presented, followed by the William H. Popert Trophy, a Ladies' Choice cup, Coach Popert's cash award for the best Engineers' Week speech, and the Bay Area National Engineers' Week Committee trophy.

Harry Moses, president, presided at the meeting, assisted by Don Teixeira as toastmaster.

STRUCTURAL ENGINEERS ASSOCIATION ANNUAL STATE CONVENTION

The 27th annual convention of the Structural Engineers Association of California will be held October 2-4 in Yosemite Valley, California.

General Convention Chairman William Dreusike announces many preliminary plans are under way, and it is not too early to think about making reservations.

AMERICAN SOCIETY OF CIVIL ENGINEERS—SAN FRANCISCO

Casper Weinberger, Assemblyman, 21st District, State of California, addressed the San Francisco Section meeting early this month, discussing previous attempts of the California Legislature to solve the State's critical water problem, and outlined his views on the best course of action to be taken.

FEMINEERS SF

The Femineers held their annual "poolside" party at the home of Mrs. Charles J. Lindgren in Sonoma this month. A picnic lunch was served, swimming and bridge completed the day's activities. Co-chairmen of the event were Mrs. Mark Falk and Mrs. A. V. Saph, Jr. There will be no meeting of the organization during July or August.

RESIDENTIAL ENTRANCES
(From Page 17)

Eugene as an example (see page 14, bottom). Located on a corner lot on a sloping terrain, the home spreads out along the full length of the lot and because the living areas face on an inner courtyard, the street exposure is confined largely to bedrooms with high windows. The promise of this home is concealed, so the answer was for Architect John Stafford to design an entrance which would give some warmth and appeal to the street side yet retain the flavor of simplicity which marks this home exterior. A plain but well-designed roof overhang calls attention to the entrance, set out from the flush lines of the front elevation. A solid screen of western red cedar to match the boards-and-batten siding reaches part way out from the house along the entering sidewalk as a sort of invitation to the visitor.

The entrance is simple yet inviting, with a solid wooden door of fir set in a glass section which reveals some of the charm and promise of the home to the visitor. The glass panels on either side of the door are unbroken, as is the glass section above the door and panels. Here the architect has used some of the exciting texture of cedar in combination with glass to create a most attractive and unusual opening to this home.

It is remarkable the effects that can be obtained with either plain or intricate interlacing of line, plane and substance to achieve some amazingly effective results around the entrance area of these wonderfully informal homes of today. The decorative effect of wood, glass, stone and brick are real tools in the hands of the architect who wants an opportunity for expression and the satisfaction of creating a home with real individuality and character.

Entrances can be dramatic and sensational without in any way detracting from the home. They can set the pace of casual informality, prepare the guest for an exciting experience, ready him for the beauty and wonders of the modern home where architecture reaches heights of genuine achievement; or they can let him down with a dull thud and dull his appetite for appreciation of the real charm and beauty of an otherwise lovely residence.

Most contemporary homes are good looking from all angles, both inside and outside, but the real challenge is the way the outdoor and indoor themes are linked together. The secret is the creation of that easy flow between the interior of the home and the natural surroundings of the outdoors, and the first chance to develop this mingling is right at the entrance to the home, generally the most-used portion where family members as well as all guests get their first introduction. The key feature of most homes can properly be the entrance.

BOZEMAN REGIONAL COUNCIL MEETING

Presidents of the seven AIA chapters which comprise the Northwest Region of the AIA met in Montana recently to hear reports of Don Stewart, director, on the Institute's board meeting in Scottsdale, Arizona, and other matters of regional importance including expansion of the AIA's Octagon property in Washington, D.C., membership structure, limitation of the Institute President's term to one year, Regional Judiciary Committee nominations, Regional Directorship nomination to be made at the Harrison Hot Springs Conference, and the Committee on the Profession.

ARCHITECT HOOVER
JOINS WARNECKE

Announcement has been made of the association of Albert Arthur Hoover, AIA, with the architectural firm of John Carl Warnecke, AIA, San Francisco.

Hoover attended the University of Denver, University of Michigan, and received his Bachelor of Science in Architecture from the University of Illinois in 1948. He holds certificates to practice architecture in Colorado, Connecticut, Illinois, Iowa, Massachusetts, New Jersey, New York, and holds a Junior certificate from the National Council of Architectural Registration Boards.

NATIONAL HEADQUARTERS BUILDING ASSOCIATED GENERAL CONTRACTORS

The new National Headquarters Building of The Associated General Contractors of America in Washington, D.C., was officially opened this month with dedication ceremonies at which Vice President Richard M. Nixon officiated.

Predictions of the physical facilities of the world of tomorrow were sealed in a time capsule in the building's cornerstone to be removed from the cornerstone at the turn of the 21st century and compared to the realities of that age.

Taking part in the ceremonies were: Fred W. Heldenfels, Jr., president of the AGC, Corpus Christi, Texas; Frank J. Rooney, Miami, Florida, past president and chairman of the building committee and a number of governmental officials.

Located at 20th and E Streets, N.W., in Washington, the building was designed by Leon Chatelain, Jr., of the firm of Chatelain, Gauger and Nolan, Washington, D.C.

ENGINEER SELECTED FOR CALIFORNIA AIR NATIONAL GUARD

Arthur A. Sauer, Structural Engineer, 2203 13th, Sacramento, has been selected by the Division of Architecture, Department of Public Works, State of California, to design a new Wing group building for the California Air National Guard to be built at the airport in Fresno.

SPANISH CONTRACTORS STUDY SOUTHERN CALIFORNIA

Nine Spanish contractors and engineers, recent visitors to the Los Angeles area, declared the use of mechanical equipment such as concrete buggies and automatic hoisting devices, represent one of the greatest differences in construction methods used in California and those employed in Spain.

The contractors visited the McNeil Construction Company facilities while in Southern California, their trip being under auspices of the Housing and Home Finance Agency of Washington, D.C.

ARCHITECT IS SELECTED FOR OFFICE BLDG.

Architect Grant D. Caywood, 1435 Alhambra Blvd., Sacramento, has been selected by the Division of Architecture, Department of Public Works, State of California, to draft plans and specifications for construction of a new office for the California Highway Patrol, to be built in the City of Sacramento.

The new facilities will also provide a carport.

PROFESSIONAL ENGINEERS FALL MEETING

Major issues now facing the nation's engineering profession will come under discussion at the forthcoming Fall meeting of the National Society of Professional Engineers to be held in San Francisco October 22-25.

More than 500 engineers are expected to attend the meeting, which is the first of its kind to be held on the West Coast, including more than 150 directors of the Society, representing some 46,000 members of the organization throughout the United States and its possessions.

Business sessions will be devoted to hearing committee reports on the effects of space travel on the engineering profession; effective utilization of present engineering manpower; encouraging capable high school students to consider careers in engineering; and the role of the Federal Government in engineering education.

The California Society of Professional Engineers will serve as host Society to the convention.

SAN DIEGO HEALTH CENTER BUILDING CEREMONIES

City, county, medical, civic and business leaders participated in ground breaking ceremonies in San Diego, recently when construction of a modern 5-story Health Association Building at 328 Maple Street was started.

Charles G. Polacek, Architect, has designed a modern, spacious, flexible type medical clinic with a "Pacific Modern" design theme. Each floor will be constructed to serve specific departments and on short notice can be expanded to greater capacity through the convenience of movable partitions throughout the building.

The first four floors will serve the needs of the patients and the fifth floor will be for the staff. It will consist of a penthouse council room, locker rooms, and employees' lounge.

Haas-Haynie-Frandsen, Inc., are the general contractors.

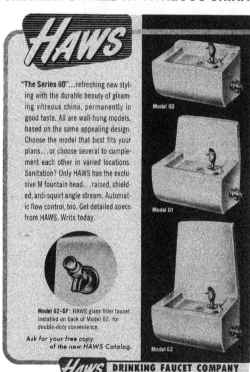

FOUR DISTINCTIVE HAWS FOUNTAINS SMARTLY STYLED IN VITREOUS CHINA

"The Series 60"...refreshing new styling with the durable beauty of gleaming vitreous china, permanently in good taste. All are wall-hung models, based on the same appealing design. Choose the model that best fits your plans...or choose several to complement each other in varied locations. Sanitation? Only HAWS has the exclusive M fountain head...raised, shielded, anti-squirt angle stream. Automatic flow control, too. Get detailed specs from HAWS. Write today.

Model 60

Model 61

Model 62-GF: HAWS glass filler faucet installed on back of Model 62, for double-duty convenience.

Ask for your free copy of the new HAWS Catalog.

Model 62

HAWS DRINKING FAUCET COMPANY

1441 FOURTH STREET (Since 1909) BERKELEY 10, CALIFORNIA

The first East Bay Chapter AIA member to be advanced to Fellowship in the American Institute of Architects is Malcolm Dames Reynolds, partner in the firm of Reynolds & Chamberlain, Architects.

Fellowship, and the election to membership in the College of Fellows, was awarded Mr. Reynolds for "his notable contribution in service to the Institute."

Active in Chapter affairs, Reynolds has served on a large number of committees, and in 1953 was president of the East Bay Chapter AIA. In 1954

MALCOLM D. REYNOLDS
Fellow

he served as president of the California Council of Architects, and is currently acting as president of the California State Board of Architectural Examiners, and is also a director of the Oakland Builders Exchange. He is a former chairman of the Urban Renewal Committee and the Construction Industries' Committee of the Oakland Chamber of Commerce.

Malcolm D. Reynolds is a member of the Reynolds family who have resided in the East Bay area for nearly 100 years. He is a graduate in architecture at the University of California, and served his first duties as an architect in the offices of E. Geoffrey Bangs, Oakland architect. Licensed to practice architecture in California in 1936, he formed a partnership with Loy Chamberlain in 1937. Today the firm owns its own building in Oakland and maintains a staff of 14 draftsmen, a full-time secretary and a part-time secretary.

During the World War II days, when building materials were difficult to obtain, the firm began designing

school buildings, an area in which they are very successful, even though their practice covers all building types at the present time.

A.I.A. ACTIVITIES
(From Page 27)

dent of the United States for the Co-ordination of Public Works Planning. He spoke on the subject: "Public Works and Prosperity."

PASADENA CHAPTER AIA

"Tomorrow's School" was the subject of a discussion at the June meeting with a panel of four experts participating: Dr. Robert E. Jenkins, superintendent of Pasadena Schools; Robert E. Kelly, associate superintendent in the Division of Secondary Education of Los Angeles City Schools; E. R. C. Billerbeck, chief architect for the Los Angeles Board of Education; and Robert E. Alexander, architect. Donald E. Neptune, chairman of the Chapter's School Committee, served as moderator.

Recent new members include: George A. Bissell, Jr., and Philip M. Davies, corporate members.

WAL CONDUCTS MAYBECK TOUR

A two-day, tri-county Memorial Tour of selected buildings designed by Bernard Ralph Maybeck was recently conducted by the Northern California Chapter AIA and the Women's Architectural League, which included twenty-two structures in Marin and San Francisco counties and Berkeley.

In addition, photographs, drawings, sketches and historical data concerning Maybeck's work was displayed in Berkeley, San Francisco and Mill Valley, and the event included a series of three lectures on Maybeck by Prof. Kenneth Cardwell of the University of California College of Architecture.

Maybeck, who died in Berkeley last November at the age of 96, is regarded as the father of Bay Area architecture and was the founder of the university's College of Architecture Department.

He designed the general plans for Mills College; he was the originator and manager of the Hearst International Competition for the plan of the University of California; he was architect of the Palace of Fine Arts in San Francisco; architect of the Associated Charities in San Francisco; advisory architect of Temple Emanuel and War Memorial Opera House in San Francisco; winner of two medals from the Eleve de Beaux-Arts, Paris, and gold medals from the St. Louis Exposition and Panama-Pacific International Exposition.

PHOTO CREDITS: Associated Construction & Engineering Co., Cover; Haas & Associates, Page 8; United Air Lines, Page 9; Bethlehem Pacific Steel, Page 10, 11; West Coast Lumbermen's Association, Page 12; Photo-Art Commercial Studios, Page 13, 14, 15, 16, 17; Gabriel Moulin, Page 18, 25; Camera Photo Service, Page 19; George Knight Photo, Page 21; Tom Vano Photo, Page 22 top; Pacific Air Industries, Page 23.

CONTRACT SPECIFICATIONS and LAW FOR ENGI-
NEERS. By Clarence W. Dunham and Robert D. Young.
McGraw-Hill Book Co., Inc., 330 W. 42nd St., New
York 36. 550 pages. Price $7.50.

A text for advanced students of architectural and civil engineering and a reference for practicing engineers and architects, contractors, and teachers. The entire treatment, including
illustrations, is fairly simple and non-legalistic. A practical
approach begins with forthright and firm statements of legal
principles and contracts, then goes into those practical situations where the student is most likely to encounter the applications of the principles. The authors Clarence W. Dunham,
CE., is associate professor of Civil Engineering at Yale University; consulting Structural Engineer for New York engineering office of Anaconda Company, and was formerly
asistant engineer, Port of New York Authority; while Robert
D. Young is an attorney for the Travelers Insurance Company
and a member of the Connecticut and New York Bar.

BRIDGES and Their Builders. By David B. Steinman and
Sara Ruth Watson. Dover Publications, Inc., 920 Broadway, New York 10. 402 pages, Illustrated. Price $1.95.

From the dawn of recorded time the construction of bridges
has reflected the progress of civilization. This book begins
with natural bridges and covers the field of primitive log
spans to the modern use of the arch, cantilever, suspension,
bascule, and vertical lift bridges. Engineers, historians, and
every person who has ever been fascinated by great spans,
will find this book an endless source of information and interest. The author, Dr. Steinman, was the 1957 recipient of
the Louis E. Levy Medal for engineering, is one of the world's
leading authorities on bridge construction.

NAVAL ARCHITECTURE OF SMALL CRAFT. By D.
Phillips-Birt, A.M.I.N.A. Philosophical Library, Inc.,
15 E. 40th Street, New York 16. 351 pages, Illustrations.
Price $15.00.

The book is concerned with naval architecture in its application to the smaller vessels—those of about 120 ft. in length
or less. In this category come the many types of working
boat, such as inshore and middle-ground fishing vessels,
patrol, pilot, and custom launches, tenders, research vessels,
and the high speed craft used for so many different purposes
today. Yachts, both sail and power, are also considered in
detail. The introductory chapter is a historical review of the
ideas that have influenced the design of ships from the
earliest times to the most modern high-speed motor boats.

NEW CATALOGUES AVAILABLE

*Architects, Engineers, Contractors, Planning Commission
members—the catalogues, folders, new building products
material, etc., described below may be obtained by directing
your request to the name and address given in each item.*

Concrete vibrators and grinders. New, larger 1958 catalog
covering line of concrete vibrators and grinders features two
new and more powerful oneman vibrators which now permits
the use of head sizes from ¾" in dia., to 1-⅞" in dia.; also
shows new form cleaner attachment and hole boring head for
the WYCO concrete grinders, as well as the WYCO "Junior"
and standard electric and gasoline vibrators. For free copy
write DEPT-A&E, Wyzenbeek & Staff, Inc., 223 N. California
Ave., Chicago 12, Ill.

Problems of excessive noise. Newly published booklet "How
To Quiet Your Home" describes effective methods for dealing
with the problem of excessive noise in the home; explains in
layman's terms what causes noise; outlines general plan for
home noise reduction, points out chief noise sources; sections
on sound conditioning materials and information where they
should be used, and exactly what they will and will not accomplish. Free copy write DEPT-A&E, Acoustical Materials
Assn., 335 E. 45th St., New York City.

Guide for housepower controls. A new guide (AIA File
No. 31-D) listing all of the newest and latest devices; over 100
pages of technical information on cabinet sizes, knockout ar-

rangements, etc., for industrial safety switches, general duty safety switches, service equipment both fusible and circuit breakers, raintight switches both service equipment and general duty, panelboards both fusible and circuit breakers and wiring troughs and fittings; many illustrations and wiring diagrams, simplified index. Free copy write Wadsworth Electric Mfg. Co., Inc., Covington, Ky.

Successful school planning. A new 28-page brochure has just been published by Warren H. Ashley, architect of 740 W. Main St., W. Hartford, Conn. designed to help school committees, educators, P.T.A. groups and civic organizations obtain the kind of school they want within budget limitations; packed with ideas that represent the best thinking that has gone into the building of more than 900 classrooms in more than 30 schools throughout New England; illustrated, describes site selection and planning; printed in two colors. Free, write DEPT-A&E, Warren H. Ashley, Architect, 740 N. Main St., West Hartford, Conn.

Insulating siding, new standard. Recent publication by the U.S. Dept. of Commerce, Standard CS216-58 entitled AS-PHALT INSULATING SIDING, culminates several years' study by the Technical Committee of the Insulating Siding Association, American Society for Testing Materials, and the FHA; provides the industry with one of the most complete sets of standards and specifications enjoyed by any building material. Copies available by writing DEPT-A&E, Insulating Siding Association, Box 103, Glenview, Ill.

Decorator colors for steel equipment. A newly issued card illustrates six new decorator colors for steel equipment; actual paint samples, gray, tan and green for steel lockers; gray and green for steel shelving and steel cabinets; additional optional decorator colors are spray green, rose amber, sage blue, warm gray, vista green and sand. These new colors will enable users to achieve more eye-appealing color schemes in offices, schools, hospitals, hotels, clubs, stores, industrial plants and warehouses where Penco products are used. Complete details write DEPT-A&E, Penco Products Division, Alan Wood Steel Co., 200 Brower Ave., Oaks, Pa.

Stadium and auditorium concreting. New 20-page folder describes case histories of concreting problems encountered and successfully solved in stadium and auditorium construction; data on 16 outstanding stadiums and auditorium projects in this country and abroad. Free copy write DEPT-A&E, The Masters Builders Co., 7016 Euclid Ave., Cleveland 3, Ohio.

Color for slab concrete. New 4-page brochure in color (AIA File No. 3-K, 3-B-1, 23-D) describes proven method for building in life-long color in concrete floors, exterior or interior surfaces—patios, swimming pools, driveways, walks, terraces, floors for stores, showrooms, offices, churches, schools and public buildings. Free copy write DEPT-A&E, The Master Builders Co., 7016 Euclid Ave., Cleveland 3, Ohio.

Surface-mounted shower fixtures. New catalog (AIA File No. 29-H-3) describes the 7600 Series, Arvin type Logan Showergon; various types for multi-station, complete ready for installation; concealed pipe, vandal proof construction, easily accessible for maintenance, exposed brass fixtures, chrome plated finish. For free copy write DEPT-A&E, The Logan Mfg. Co., P.O. Box 111, Glendale, California.

ESTIMATOR'S GUIDE

BUILDING AND CONSTRUCTION MATERIALS

PRICES GIVEN ARE FIGURING PRICES AND ARE MADE UP FROM AVERAGE QUOTATIONS FURNISHED BY LeROY CONSTRUCTION SERVICES. 4% SALES TAX ON ALL MATERIALS BUT NOT LABOR. ITEMS IN ITALIC INCLUDE LABOR AND SALES TAX.

BONDS—Performance or Performance plus Labor and Material Bond(s), $10 per $1000 on contract price. Labor and Material Bond(s) only, $5.00 per $1000 on contract price.

BRICKWORK & MASONRY

COMMON BRICKWORK, Reinforced:		
8" walls	*SF*	*2.95*
12" walls	*SF*	*4.15*
SELECT COMMON, Reinforced:		
8" walls	*SF*	*3.05*
12" walls	*SF*	*4.30*
CONCRETE BLOCK, Reinforced:		
6" walls	*SF*	*1.40*
8" walls	*SF*	*1.55*
12" walls	*SF*	*1.90*
BRICK VENEER:		
4" Select Common	*SF*	*1.65*
4" Roman	*SF*	*2.50*
4" Norman	*SF*	*2.40*
4" Aggrelite	*SF*	*2.40*

BRICKWORK & MASONRY

All Prices—F.O.B. Plant.

COMMON BRICK		
Common 2½ x 3¾ x 8¼	M	45.00
Select 2½ x 3¾ x 8¼	M	52.00
Clinker 2½ x 3¾ x 8¼	M	48.00
Jumbo 3½ x 3 x 11½	M	90.00
FACE BRICK		
Standard	M	59.80 - 83.20
Jumbo	M	114.40 - 130.00
Roman	M	88.40 - 109.20
Norman	M	101.40 - 124.80
Brik Blox (6")	M	202.80
(8")	M	239.20
Braile Veneer	M	26.00
BUILDING TILE		
8 x 5½ x 12 inches	M	165.78
6 x 5½ x 12 inches	M	128.96
HOLLOW TILE		
12 x 12 x 3 inches	M	163.12
12 x 12 x 4 inches	M	184.18
12 x 12 x 6 inches	M	244.71
MANTEL FIRE BRICK		
2½ x 9½ x 4½ inches	M	140.40
GLAZED STRUCTURAL UNITS		
2 x 6 x 12 Furring	SF	.90
4 x 6 x 12 Furring	SF	1.20
6 x 6 x 12 Furring	SF	1.50
4 x 6 x 12 Partition	SF	1.60
Add for color	SF	.20
CONCRETE BLOCKS		
4 x 8 x 16 inches	EA	.22
6 x 8 x 16 inches	EA	.265
8 x 8 x 16 inches	EA	.30
12 x 8 x 16 inches	EA	.435
Colored Add	EA	.02
AGGREGATE—Haydite or Basalite		
All sizes in bulk	CY	6.24

BUILDING PAPERS & FELTS

1 ply per 1000 ft. roll	3.95
2 ply per 1000 ft. roll	6.03
3 ply per 1000 ft. roll	8.22
Sisalkraft, reinf. 500 ft. roll	7.54
SHEATHING PAPERS:	
Asphalt sheathing, 15-lb. roll	2.50
30-lb. roll	3.50
Dampcourse, 216-ft. roll	3.05
FELT PAPERS:	
Deadening felt, ¾-lb. 50 ft. roll	4.10
1-lb. 50 ft. roll	4.78
Asphalt roofing, 15-lbs.	2.50
30-lbs.	3.50
ROOFING PAPERS:	
Standard Grade, Smooth Surface	
108-ft. roll, Light	2.35
Medium	2.75
Heavy	3.22
Extra Heavy	3.75

CHIMNEYS, PATENT

F.O.B. Warehouse

6"	LF	1.45
8"	LF	2.05
10"	LF	2.85
12"	LF	3.45

Rates for 10 - 50 Lin. Ft.

CONCRETE AGGREGATES

	Bunker Per Ton	Del'd Per Ton
Gravel, All Sizes	3.38	4.16
Top Sand	3.59	4.37
Concrete Mix	3.48	4.26
Crushed Rock		
¼" to ¾"	3.43	4.26
¾" to 1½"	3.43	4.26
Roofing Gravel	3.54	4.42
SAND		
Lapis (Nos. 2 & 4)	4.47	5.30
Olympia (Nos. 1 & 2)	3.75	4.32

CEMENT		
Common All Brands (Paper Sacks)		
Small Quantities	Per Sack	1.40
Large Quantities	Per Bbl.	4.00
Trinity White & Mendusa White	Per Sack	4.16
CONCRETE READY-MIX		
6 sack in 5 yd. loads	Per Yd.	15.40
CURING COMPOUND, Clear		
5 gal. drums	Per Gal.	1.46

CARPENTRY & MILLWORK

Hardware not included

FRAMING:		
Floors	*BM*	*.20 - .25*
Walls	*BM*	*.25 - .30*
Ceilings	*BM*	*.18 - .22*
Roofs	*BM*	*.22 - .27*
Furring & Blocking	*BM*	*.30 - .50*
SHEATHING:		
1 x 8 straight	*BM*	*.20 - .25*
1 x 8 diagonal	*BM*	*.23 - .28*
5/16" Plyscore	*SF*	*.16 - .20*
⅜" Plywood	*SF*	*.25 - .30*
SIDING:		
1 x 8 Bevel	*BM*	*.35 - .40*
1 x 4 V-Rustic	*BM*	*.40 - .45*
EXTERIOR TRIM:		
Fascia and Molds	*BM*	*.40 - .50*
Bolted Framing—Add 50%		
ENTRANCE DOORS & FRAMES:		
Singles		*60.00 & Up*
Doubles		*100.00 & Up*
INTERIOR DOORS & FRAMES:		
Singles		*35.00 & Up*
Pocket Sliding		*45.00 & Up*
Closet Sliding (Pr.)		*50.00 & Up*
WINDOWS:		
D/H Sash & Frames	*SF*	*1.75 & Up*
Casement Sash & Frames	*SF*	*1.90 & Up*
SHELVING:		
1 x 12 S4S	*BM*	*.30 - .50*
¾" Plywood	*SF*	*.40 - .60*
STAIRS:		
Oak steps D.F. Risers		
Under 36" wide	*Riser*	*12.00*
Under 60" wide	*Riser*	*17.00*
Newel posts and rail extra		
WOOD CASES & CABINETS:		
D.F. Wall Hung	*LF*	*13.00 - 18.00*
D.F. Counters	*LF*	*15.00 - 20.00*

DAMPPROOFING & WATERPROOFING

MEMBRANE:		
1 layer 50 lb. felt	*SQ.*	*9.00*
4 layers Dampcourse	*SQ.*	*13.00*
Hot coat walls	*SQ.*	*6.00*
Tricosal added to concrete	*CY*	*1.00*
Anti-Hydro added to concrete	*CY*	*1.50*

ELECTRIC WIRING

Per Outlet:		
Knob & Tube	*EA*	*9.00*
Armor	*EA*	*16.00*
Conduit	*EA*	*20.00*
110 V Circuit	*EA*	*25.00*
220 V Circuit	*EA*	*95.00*

ELEVATORS & ESCALATORS

Prices vary according to capacity, speed and type. Consult Elevator Companies.

Slow speed apartment house elevator including doors and trim, about $5000.00 per floor.

EXCAVATION

MACHINE WORK in common ground:		
Large Basements	*CY*	*.75 - 1.00*
Small Pits	*CY*	*1.25 - 1.75*
Trenches	*CY*	*1.50 - 2.25*
HAND WORK in common ground:		
Large pits and trenches	*CY*	*4.50 - 5.50*
Small pits and trimming	*CY*	*5.00 - 6.50*

Hard Clay & Shale 2 times above rates.
Rock and large boulders 4-6 times above rates.
Shoring, bracing and disposal of water not included.

FLOORS

⅛" Asp. tile, dark colors	*SF*	*.25 - .30*
⅛" Asp. tile, light colors	*SF*	*.30 - .35*
⅛" Rubber tile	*SF*	*.60 - .70*
.080 Vinyl Asbestos Tile	*SF*	*.40 - .45*
.080 Vinyl Tile	*SF*	*.85 - .95*
Lino, Standard Gauge	*SY*	*3.75 - 4.25*
Lino, Battleship	*SY*	*5.25 - 5.75*
4" Rubber Base, Black	*LF*	*.35 - .40*
Rubber Stair Nosing	*LF*	*1.00 - 1.75*

Above rates based on quantities of 1000 - 5000 SF per job.

HARDWOOD FLOORS

Select Oak, filled, sanded, stained and varnished:		
5/16" x 2¼" strip	*SF*	*.45 - .50*
5/16" Random Plank	*SF*	*.50 - .55*
25/32" x 2¼" T&G	*SF*	*.70 - .80*
Maple, 2nd Grade and Better, filled, sanded, stained and varnished:		
25/32" x 2¼" T&G	*SF*	*.80 - .95*
Wax Finish, add	*SF*	*.10*

HARDWOOD FLOORING

Oak 5/16" x 2" Strip—		
Clear	M	229.00
Select	M	218.00
#1 Common	M	203.00
Oak 5/16" Random Plank—		
Select & Btr.	M	286.00
#1 Common	M	244.00
Oak 25/32" x 2¼" T&G—		
Select	M	260.00
#1 Common	M	203.00
Maple 25/32" x 2¼" T&G—		
#1 Grade	M	317.00
#2 Grade	M	281.00
#3 Grade	M	208.00
Nails—1" Floor Brads	KEG	17.20

GLASS & GLAZING

S.S.B. Clear	*SF*	*.48*
D.S.B. Clear	*SF*	*.78*
Crystal	*SF*	*.92*
¼" Plate	*SF*	*2.17*
⅛" Obscure	*SF*	*.68*
⅛" Heat Absorbing	*SF*	*1.12*
¼" Tempered Plate	*SF*	*4.38*
½" Tempered Plate	*SF*	*7.84*
¼" Wire Plate, Clear	*SF*	*3.65*
¼" Wire Plate, Rough	*SF*	*1.08*

GLASS—CUT TO SIZE

F.O.B. Warehouse

S.S.B. Clear, Av. 6 SF	SF	.34
D.S.B. Clear, Av. 10 SF	SF	.56
Crystal, Av. 35 SF	SF	.66
¼" Polished Plate, Av. 100 SF	SF	1.55
⅛" Obscure, Av. 10 SF	SF	.49
⅛" Ribbed, Av. 10 SF	SF	.49
⅛" Rough, Av. 10 SF	SF	.49
¼" Wire Plate, Clear, Av. 40 SF	SF	2.61
¼" Wire Plate, Rough, Av. 40 SF	SF	.77
⅛" Heat Absorbing, Av. 10 SF	SF	.80
¼" Tempered Plate, Av. 50 SF	SF	3.13
½" Tempered Plate, Av. 50 SF	SF	5.60

Glazing—Approx. 40-50% of Glass
Glass Blocks—Check with Dealer

HEATING

FURNACES—Gas Fired—Av. Job:	
FLOOR FURNACE:	
25,000 BTU	*100.00 - 125.00*
35,000 BTU	*107.00 - 135.00*
45,000 BTU	*115.00 - 150.00*
AUTOMATIC CONTROL:	
Add	*25.00 - 35.00*

HEATING—Cont'd

DUAL WALL FURNACE:		
25,000 BTU		*110.00 - 125.00*
35,000 BTU		*125.00 - 145.00*
50,000 BTU		*150.00 - 180.00*
AUTOMATIC CONTROL:		
Add		*25.00 - 35.00*
GRAVITY FURNACE:		
75,000 BTU		*375.00 - 450.00*
85,000 BTU		*425.00 - 525.00*
95,000 BTU		*475.00 - 600.00*
FORCED AIR FURNACE:		
Add		*75.00 - 125.00*
AUTOMATIC CONTROL:		
Add		*15.00 - 25.00*
HEAT REGISTERS:		
Outlet		*7.50 - 15.00*

INSULATION & WALLBOARD

F.O.B. Warehouse

ROCKWOOL Insulation—		
2" Semi-thick	Per M SF	63.02
3⅝" Full Thick	Per M SF	80.50
COTTON Insulation		
1" Full Thick	Per M SF	43.26
SOFTBOARDS—Wood Fiber—		
½" thick	Per M SF	88.00
1½" thick	Per M SF	275.00
2" thick	Per M SF	385.00
ALUMINUM Insulation—		
80# Kraft paper with alum. foil		
1 side only	Per M SF	18.30
2 sides	Per M SF	31.00
GYPSUM Wallboard—		
⅜" thick	Per M SF	49.50
½" thick	Per M SF	54.50
⅝" thick	Per M SF	83.00
⅝" Gyplap	Per M SF	85.00
HARDBOARDS—Wood Fiber—		
⅛" thick, Sheathing	Per M SF	78.75
3/16" thick, Sheathing	Per M SF	90.48
¼" thick, Sheathing	Per M SF	109.20
⅛" thick, Tempered	Per M SF	98.80
3/16" thick, Tempered	Per M SF	140.40
¼" thick, Tempered	Per M SF	194.48
CEMENT Asbestos Board—		
⅛" C.A.B. Flat Sheets	Per M SF	156.00
3/16" C.A.B. Flat Sheets	Per M SF	218.40
¼" C.A.B. Flat Sheets	Per M SF	280.80

LATH & PLASTER

Diamond 3.40 copper bearing	SY	.50
Ribbed 3.40 copper bearing	SY	.55
⅜" rock lath	SY	.37
2" Standard Channel	LF	.085
1½" Standard Channel	LF	.065
¾" Standard Channel	LF	.045
3¼" steel studs	LF	.09
4" steel studs	LF	.105
Stud shoes	EA	.025
Hardwall, Browning	Sack	1.46
Hardwall, Finish	Sack	1.72
Stucco	Sack	2.50

LATH & PLASTERWORK

CHANNEL FURRING:		
Suspended Ceilings	*SY*	*2.20 - 2.50*
Walls	*SY*	*2.30 - 2.60*
METAL STUD PARTITIONS:		
3¼" Studs	*SY*	*1.70 - 2.00*
4" Studs	*SY*	*1.95 - 2.25*
Over 10'0 high, add	*SY*	*.20 - .30*
3.40 METAL LATH AND PLASTER:		
Ceilings	*SY*	*3.60 - 4.00*
Walls	*SY*	*3.75 - 4.15*
KEENE'S CEMENT FINISH:		
Add	*SY*	*.40 - .60*
ROCK LATH & PLASTER:		
Ceilings	*SY*	*2.50 - 2.80*
Walls	*SY*	*2.60 - 2.90*
WIRE MESH AND ⅛" STUCCO:		
Walls	*SY*	*3.60 - 4.10*
STUCCO ON CONCRETE:		
Walls	*SY*	*2.30 - 2.80*
METAL ACCESSORIES	*LF*	*.20 - .50*

LINOLEUM

Lino. Standard Gauge	SY	2.65 - 2.85
Lino. Battleship	SY	3.90 - 4.10
⅛" Asp. tile, Dark	SF	.10 - .11
⅛" Asp. tile, Light	SF	.14 - .16
⅛" Rubber Tile	SF	.40 - .44
.080 Vinyl Asb. tile	SF	.18 - .19
.080 Vinyl tile	SF	.59 - .61
⅛" Vinyl tile	SF	.78 - .82
4" Base, Dark	LF	.15 - .16
4" Base, Light	LF	.24 - .26
Rubber Nosing	LF	.60 - 1.30
Lino Paste	GAL	.75 - .90

Above rates based on quantities of 1000-5000 SF per job.

LUMBER

DOUGLAS FIR:	M.B.M.
#1 2x4—2x10	88.00 - 92.00
#2 2x4—2x10	85.00 - 90.00
#3 2x4—2x10	68.00 - 74.00
#4 2x4—2x10	64.00 - 72.00
Clear, Air Dried	180.00 - 210.00
Clear, Kiln Dried	210.00 - 240.00
REDWOOD:	
Foundation Grade	120.00 - 130.00
Construction Heart	110.00 - 120.00
A Grade	180.00 - 210.00
Clear Heart	190.00 - 220.00
D.F. PLYWOOD	M.S.F.
¼" AB	95.00 - 105.00
¼" AD	90.00 - 95.00
¼" Ext. Waterproof	115.00 - 125.00
⅜" AB	130.00 - 145.00
⅜" AD	115.00 - 125.00
⅜" CD	70.00 - 85.00
½" AB	170.00 - 185.00
½" AD	110.00 - 115.00
½" CD	....
⅝" AB	185.00 - 200.00
⅝" AD	165.00 - 180.00
⅝" CD	115.00 - 125.00
¾" AB	210.00 - 230.00
¾" AD	195.00 - 210.00
¾" CD	125.00 - 140.00
⅝" Plyform	160.00 - 170.00
SHINGLES:	Square
Cedar #1	14.00 - 15.50
Cedar #2	11.50 - 12.50
SHAKES:	
CEDAR	
½ to ¾" Butt	17.50 - 18.50
¾ to 1¼" Butt	18.50 - 19.50
REDWOOD	
¾ to 1¼" Butt	21.00 - 24.00

MILLWORK

All Prices F.O.B. Mill

D.F. CLEAR, AIR DRIED:		
S4S	MBM	220.00 - 250.00
D.F. CLEAR, KILN DRIED:		
S4S	MBM	225.00 - 275.00
DOOR FRAMES & TRIM:		
Residential Entrance		17.00 & up
Interior Room Entrance		7.50 & up
DOORS:		
1⅜" D.F. Slab, Hollow Core		8.00 & up
1¾" D.F. Slab, Solid Core		19.00 & up
1⅜" Birch Slab, Hollow Core		10.00 & up
1¾" Birch Slab, Solid Core		22.00 & up
WINDOW FRAMES:		
D/H Singles	SF	.80
Casement Singles	SF	.90
WOOD SASH:		
D/H in pairs (1 lite)	SF	.45
Casement (1 lite)	SF	.50
WOOD CABINETS:		
¾" D.F. Ply with ¼" ply backs		
Wall Hung	LF	10.00 - 15.00
Counter	LF	12.00 - 17.00

BIRCH OR MAPLE—Add 25%

PAINTING

EXTERIOR:		
Stucco Wash 1 ct.	*SY*	*.30*
Stucco Wash 2 cts.	*SY*	*.55*
Lead and Oil 2 cts.	*SY*	*.90*
Lead and Oil 3 cts.	*SY*	*1.30*
INTERIOR:		
Primer Sealer	*SY*	*.40*
Wall Paint, 1 ct.	*SY*	*.50*
Wall Paint, 2 cts.	*SY*	*.95*
Enamel, 1 ct.	*SY*	*.60*
Enamel, 2 cts.	*SY*	*1.10*
Doors and Trim	*EA*	*10.00*
Sash and Trim	*EA*	*12.00*
Base and Molds	*LF*	*.12*

Old Work—Add 15-30%

PLUMBING

Lavatories	*EA*	*100.00 - 150.00*
Toilets	*EA*	*200.00 - 300.00*
Bath Tubs	*EA*	*250.00 - 350.00*
Stall Shower	*EA*	*80.00 - 150.00*
Sinks	*EA*	*125.00 - 175.00*
Laundry Trays	*EA*	*80.00 - 130.00*
Water Heaters	*EA*	*100.00 - 300.00*

Prices based on average residential and commercial work. Special fixtures and excessive piping not included.

PAINT

All Prices F.O.B. Warehouse

Thinners—5-100 gals.	GAL	.45
Turpentine—5-100 gals.	GAL.	1.35
Linseed Oil, Raw	GAL	2.00
Linseed Oil, Boiled	GAL	1.95
Primer-Sealer	GAL	2.95
Enamel	GAL	5.00
Enamel Undercoat	GAL	3.25
White Lead in Oil	LB.	.26
Red Lead in Oil	LB.	.29
Litharge	LB.	.24

ROOFING

STANDARD TAR & GRAVEL	Per Square
4 ply	*14.00 - 18.00*
5 ply	*17.00 - 20.00*
White Gravel Finish—Add	*2.00 - 4.00*
Asph. Compo. Shingles	*16.00 - 20.00*
Cedar Shingles	*20.00 - 24.00*
Cedar Shakes	*26.00 - 30.00*
Redwood Shakes	*28.00 - 34.00*
Clay Tiles	*40.00 - 50.00*

SEWER PIPE

VITRIFIED:		
Standard 4 in.	LF	.31
Standard 6 in.	LF	.56
Standard 8 in.	LF	.81
Standard 12 in.	LF	1.76
Standard 24 in.	LF	6.95
CLAY DRAIN PIPE:		
Standard 6 in.	LF	.34
Standard 8 in.	LF	.59

Rate for 100 Lin. Ft. F.O.B. Warehouse

STEEL

REINFORCING BARS:		
¼" rounds	LB	.122
⅜" rounds	LB	.111
½" rounds	LB	.107
⅝" rounds	LB	.104
¾" rounds	LB	.102
⅞" rounds	LB	.102
1" rounds	LB	.102
REINFORCING MESH (1050 SF Rolls)		
6x6 x 10x10	SF	.035
6x6 x 6x6	SF	.067
16 GA. TYING WIRE	LB	.130

Rates 100-1000 Lbs. F.O.B. Warehouse

STRUCTURAL STEEL

$325.00 and up per ton erected when out of mill.
$350.00 and up per ton erected when out of stock.

SHEET METAL

ROOF FLASHINGS:		
18 ga. Galv. Steel	*SF*	*.60 - 1.00*
22 ga. Galv. Steel	*SF*	*.50 - .90*
26 ga. Galv. Steel	*SF*	*.40 - .80*
18 ga. Aluminum	*SF*	*1.00 - 1.50*
22 ga. Aluminum	*SF*	*.80 - 1.30*
26 ga. Aluminum	*SF*	*.60 - 1.10*
24 oz. Copper	*SF*	*1.90 - 2.40*
20 oz. Copper	*SF*	*1.70 - 2.20*
16 oz. Copper	*SF*	*1.50 - 2.00*
26 ga. Galv. Steel		
4" o.g. gutter	*LF*	*.90 - 1.30*
Mitres and Drops	*EA*	*2.00 - 4.00*
22 ga. Galv. Louvres	*SF*	*2.50 - 3.50*
20 oz. Copper Louvres	*SF*	*3.00 - 4.50*

TILE WORK

CERAMIC TILE, Stock colors:		
Floors	*SF*	*1.95 - 2.45*
Walls	*SF*	*2.05 - 2.55*
Coved Base	*LF*	*1.05 - 1.45*
QUARRY TILE:		
6" x 6" x ½" Floors	*SF*	*1.60 - 2.00*
9" x 9" x ¾" Floors	*SF*	*1.75 - 2.15*
Treads and risers	*LF*	*3.00 - 4.50*
Coved Base	*LF*	*.90 - 1.30*

Mosaic Tile — Rates vary with design and colors. Each job should be priced from Manufacturer.

TERRAZZO & MARBLE

Terrazzo Floors	*SF*	*2.00 - 2.50*
Cond. Terr. Floors	*SF*	*2.20 - 2.75*
Precast treads and risers	*LF*	*3.50 - 4.50*
Precast landing slabs	*SF*	*3.00 - 4.00*

TILE

CERAMIC:

F.O.B. Warehouse

4¼" x 4¼" glazed	SF	.69
4¼" x 4¼" hard glazed	SF	.72
Random unglazed	SF	.73
6" x 2" cap	EA	.17
6" coved base	EA	.22
¼" round bead	LF	.18
QUARRY:		
6 x 6 x ½" Red	SF	.49
6 x 6 x ¾" Red	SF	.52
9 x 9 x ¾" Red	SF	.60
6 x 6" coved base	EA	.21
White Cement Grout	Per 100 Lbs.	6.25

VENETIAN BLINDS

Residential	SF	.40 & Up
Commercial	SF	.45 & Up

WINDOWS

STEEL SASH:		
Under 10 SF	SF	2.50 & Up
Under 15 SF	SF	2.00 & Up
Under 20 SF	SF	1.50 & Up
Under 30 SF	SF	1.00 & Up
ALUMINUM SASH:		
Under 10 SF	SF	2.75 & Up
Under 15 SF	SF	2.25 & Up
Under 20 SF	SF	1.75 & Up
Under 30 SF	SF	1.25 & Up

Above rates are for standard sections and stock sizes F.O.B. Warehouse

ACOUSTICAL ENGINEERS
L. D. REEDER CO.
San Francisco: 1255 Sansome St., DO 2-5050
Sacramento: 3026 V St., GL 7-3505

AIR CONDITIONING
E. C. BRAUN CO.
Berkeley: 2115 Fourth St., TH 5-2356
GILMORE AIR CONDITIONING SERVICE
San Francisco: 1617 Harrison St., UN 1-2000
KAEMPER & BARRETT
San Francisco: 233 Industrial St., JU 6-6200
LINFORD AIR & REFRIGERATION CO.
Oakland: 174-12th St., TW 3-6521
MALM METAL PRODUCTS
Santa Rosa: 724-2nd St., SR 454
JAMES A. NELSON CO.
San Francisco: 1375 Howard St., HE 1-0140

ALUMINUM BLDG. PRODUCTS
MICHEL & PFEFFER IRON WORKS (Wrought Iron)
So. San Francisco: 212 Shaw Road, PLaza 5-8983
REYNOLDS METALS CO.
San Francisco: 3201 Third St., MI 7-2990
SOULE STEEL CO.
San Francisco: 1750 Army St., VA 4-4141
UNIVERSAL WINDOW CO.
Berkeley: 950 Parker St., TH 1-1600

ARCHITECTURAL PORCELAIN ENAMEL
CALIFORNIA METAL ENAMELING CO.
Los Angeles: 6904 E. Slauson, RA 3-6351
San Francisco: Continental Bldg. Products Co.,
   178 Fremont St.
Portland: Portland Wire & Iron Works,
   4644 S.E. Seventeenth Ave.
Seattle: Foster-Bray Co., 2412 1st Ave. So.
Spokane: Bernhard Schafer, Inc., West 34, 2nd Ave.
Salt Lake City: S. A. Roberts & Co., 109 W. 2nd So.
Dallas: Offenhauser Co., 2201 Telephone Rd.
El Paso: Architectural Products Co.,
   506 E. Yandell Blvd.
Phoenix: Haskell-Thomas Co., 3808 No. Central
San Diego: Maloney Specialties, Inc., 823 W. Laurel St.
Boise: Intermountain Glass Co., 1417 Main St.

ARCHITECTURAL & AERIAL PHOTOGRAPHS
FRED ENGLISH
Belmont, Calif.: 1310 Old County Road, LY 1-0385

ARCHITECTURAL VENEER
Ceramic Veneer
GLADDING, McBEAN & CO.
San Francisco: Harrison at 9th St., UN 1-7400
Los Angeles: 2901 Los Feliz Blvd., OL 2121
Portland: 110 S.E. Main St., EA 6179
Seattle 99: 945 Elliott Ave., West, GA 0330
Spokane: 1102 N. Monroe St., BR 3259
KRAFTILE COMPANY
Niles, Calif., Niles 3611

Porcelain Veneer
PORCELAIN ENAMEL PUBLICITY BUREAU
Oakland 12: Room 601, Franklin Building
Pasadena 8: P. O. Box 186, East Pasadena Station

Granite Veneer
VERMONT MARBLE COMPANY
San Francisco 24: 600Q 3rd St., VA 6-5024
Los Angeles: 3522 Council St., DU 2-6339

Marble Veneer
VERMONT MARBLE COMPANY
San Francisco 24: 6000 3rd St., VA 6-5024
Los Angeles: 3522 Council St., DU 2-6339

BANKS - FINANCING
CROCKER-ANGLO NATIONAL BANK
San Francisco: 13 Offices

BLINDS
PARAMOUNT VENETIAN BLIND CO.
San Francisco: 5929 Mission St., JU 5-2436

BRASS PRODUCTS
GREENBERG'S, M. SONS
San Francisco 7: 765 Folsom, EX 2-3143
Los Angeles 23: 1258 S. Boyle, AN 3-7108
Seattle 4:1016 First Ave. So., MA 5140
Phoenix: 3009 N. 19th Ave., Apt. 92, PH 2-7663
Portland 4: 510 Builders Exch. Bldg., AT 6443

BRICKWORK
Face Brick
GLADDING McBEAN & CO.
San Francisco: Harrison at 9th, UN 1-7400
KRAFTILE CO.
Niles, Calif., Niles 3611
UNITED MATERIALS & RICHMOND BRICK CO.
Point Richmond, BE 4-5032

BRONZE PRODUCTS
GREENBERG'S M. SONS
San Francisco: 765 Folsom St., EX 2-3143
MICHEL & PFEFFER IRON WORKS
So. San Francisco: 212 Shaw Road, PLaza 5-8983
C. E. TOLAND & SON
Oakland: 2635 Peralta St., GL 1-2590

BUILDING HARDWARE
E. M. HUNDLEY HARDWARE CO.
San Francisco: 662 Mission St., YU 2-3322

BUILDING PAPERS & FELTS
PACIFIC CEMENT & AGGREGATES INC.
San Francisco: 400 Alabama St., KL 2-1616

CABINETS & FIXTURES
CENTRAL MILL & CABINET CO.
San Francisco: 1595 Fairfax Ave., VA 4-7316
THE FINK & SCHINDLER CO.
San Francisco: 552 Brannan St., EX 2-1513
JONES KRAFT SHOP,
San Francisco: 1314 Ocean Avenue., JU 7-1545
MULLEN MFG. CO.
San Francisco: 64 Rausch St., UN 1-5815
PARAMOUNT BUILT IN FIXTURE CO.
Oakland: 962 Stanford Ave., OL 3-9911
ROYAL SHOWCASE CO.
San Francisco: 770 McAllister St., JO 7-0311

CEMENT
CALAVERAS CEMENT CO.
San Francisco: 315 Montgomery St.
DO 2-4224, Enterprise 1-2315
PACIFIC CEMENT & AGGREGATES INC.
San Francisco: 400 Alabama St., KL 2-1616

CONCRETE AGGREGATES
Ready Mixed Concrete
CENTRAL CONCRETE SUPPLY CO.
San Jose: 610 McKendrie St.
PACIFIC CEMENT & AGGREGATES INC.
San Francisco: 400 Alabama St., KL 2-1616
Sacramento: 16th and A Sts., GI 3-6586
San Jose: 790 Stockton Ave., CY 2-5620
Oakland: 2400 Peralta St., GL 1-0177
Stockton: 820 So. California St., ST 8-8643
READYMIX CONCRETE CO.
Santa Rosa: 50 W. Cottage Ave.
RHODES-JAMIESON LTD.
Oakland: 333-23rd Ave., KE 3-5225
SANTA ROSA BLDG. MATERIALS CO.
Santa Rosa: Roberts Ave.

CONCRETE ACCESSORIES
Screed Materials
C. & H. SPECIALTIES CO.
Berkeley: 909 Camelia St., LA 4-5358

CONCRETE BLOCKS
BASALT ROCK CO.
Napa, Calif.

CONCRETE COLORS—HARDENERS
CONRAD SOVIG CO.
875 Bryant St., HE 1-1345

CONSTRUCTION SERVICES
LE ROY CONSTRUCTION SERVICES
San Francisco, 143 Third St., SU 1-8914

DECKS—ROOF
UNITED STATES GYPSUM CO.
2322 W. 3rd St., Los Angeles 54, Calif.
300 W. Adams St., Chicago 6, Ill.

DOORS
THE BILCO COMPANY
New Haven, Conn.
Oakland: Geo. B. Schultz, 190 MacArthur Blvd.
Sacramento: Harry B. Ogle & Assoc., 1331 T St.
Fresno: Healey & Popovich, 1703 Fulton St.
Reseda: Daniel Dunner, 6200 Alonzo Ave.

Cold Storage Doors
BIRKENWALD
Portland: 310 N.W. 5th Ave.

Electric Doors
ROLY-DOOR SALES CO.
San Francisco, 5976 Mission St., PL 5-5089

Folding Doors
WALTER D. BATES & ASSOCIATES
San Francisco, 693 Mission St., GA 1-6971

Hardwood Doors
BELLWOOD CO. OF CALIF.
Orange, Calif., 533 W. Collins Ave.

Hollywood Doors
WEST COAST SCREEN CO.
Los Angeles: 1127 E. 63rd St., AD 1-1108
T. M. COBB CO.
Los Angeles & San Diego
W. P. FULLER CO.
Seattle, Tacoma, Portland
HOGAN LUMBER CO.
Oakland: 700 - 6th Ave.
HOUSTON SASH & DOOR
Houston, Texas
SOUTHWESTERN SASH & DOOR
Phoenix, Tucson, Arizona
El Paso, Texas
WESTERN PINE SUPPLY CO.
Emeryville: 5760 Shellmound St.
GEO. C. VAUGHAN & SONS
San Antonio & Houston, Texas

Screen Doors
WEST COAST SCREEN DOOR CO.

DRAFTING ROOM EQUIPMENT
GENERAL FIREPROOFING CO.
Oakland: 332-19th St., GL 2-4280
Los Angeles: 1200 South Hope St., RI 7-7501
San Francisco: 1025 Howard St., HE 1-7070

DRINKING FOUNTAINS
HAWS DRINKING FAUCET CO.
Berkeley: 1435 Fourth St., LA 5-3341

ELECTRICAL CONTRACTORS
COOPMAN ELECTRIC CO.
San Francisco: 85 - 14th St., MA 1-4438
ETS-HOKIN & GALVAN
San Francisco: 551 Mission St., EX 2-0432

ELECTRICAL CONTRACTORS (cont'd)
LEMOGE ELECTRIC CO.
San Francisco: 212 Clara St., DO 2-6010
LYNCH ELECTRIC CO.
San Francisco: 937 McAllister St., WI 5158
PACIFIC ELECTRIC & MECHANICAL CO.
San Francisco: Gough & Fell Sts., HE 1-5904

ELECTRIC HEATERS
WESIX ELECTRIC HEATER CO.
San Francisco: 390 First St., GA 1-2211

FIRE ESCAPES
MICHEL & PFEFFER IRON WORKS
South San Francisco: 212 Shaw Road, PLaza 5-8983

FIRE PROTECTION EQUIPMENT
FIRE PROTECTION PRODUCTS CO.
San Francisco: 1101-16th St., UN 1-2420
ETS-HOKIN & GALVAN
San Francisco: 551 Mission St., EX 2-0432
BARNARD ENGINEERING CO.
San Francisco: 35 Elmira St., JU 5-4642

FLOORS
Floor Tile
GLADDING McBEAN & CO.
San Francisco: Harrison at 9th St., UN 1-744
Los Angeles: 2901 Las Feliz Bldg., OL 2121
KRAFTILE CO.
Niles, Calif., Niles 3611

Resilient Floors
PETERSON-COBBY CO.
San Francisco: 218 Clara St., EX 2-8714
TURNER RESILIENT FLOORS CO.
San Francisco: 2280 Shafter Ave., AT 2-7720

FLOOR DRAINS
JOSAM PACIFIC COMPANY
San Francisco: 765 Folsom St., EX 2-3142

GAS VENTS
WM. WALLACE CO.
Belmont, Calif.

GENERAL CONTRACTORS
O. E. ANDERSON
San Jose: 1075 No. 10th St., CY 3-8844
BARRETT CONSTRUCTION CO.
San Francisco: 1800 Evans Ave., MI 7-9700
JOSEPH BETTANCOURT
South San Francisco: 125 So. Linden St., PL 5-9185
DINWIDDIE CONSTRUCTION CO.
San Francisco: Crocker Bldg., YU 6-2718
D. L. FAULL CONSTRUCTION CO.
Santa Rosa: 1236 Cleveland Ave.
HAAS & HAYNIE
San Francisco: 275 Pine St., DO 2-0678
HENDERSON CONSTRUCTION CO.
San Francisco: 33 Ritch St., GA 1-0856
JACKS & IRVINE
San Francisco: 620 Market St., YU 6-0511
G. P. W. JENSEN & SONS
San Francisco: 320 Market St., GA 1-2444
RALPH LARSEN & SON
San Francisco: 64 So. Park, YU 2-5682
LINDGREN & SWINERTON
San Francisco: 200 Bush St., GA 1-2980
MacDONALD, YOUNG & NELSON
San Francisco: 351 California St., YU 2-4700
MATTOCK CONSTRUCTION CO.
San Francisco: 220 Clara St., GA 1-5516
OLSEN CONSTRUCTION CO.
Santa Rosa: 125 Brookwood Ave., SR 2030
BEN ORTSKY
Cotati: Cypress Ave., Pet. 5-4383
PARKER, STEFFANS & PEARCE
San Mateo: 135 So. Park, EX 2-6639

RAPP, CHRISTENSEN & FOSTER
Santa Rosa: 705 Bennett Ave.
STOLTE, INC.
Oakland: 8451 San Leandro Ave., LO 2-4611
SWINERTON & WALBERG
San Francisco: 200 Bush St., GA 1-2980

FURNITURE—INSTITUTIONAL
GENERAL FIREPROOFING CO.
San Francisco: 1025 Howard St., HE 1-7070
Oakland: 332-19th St., GL 2-4280
Los Angeles: 1200 South Hope St., RI 7-7501

HEATING & VENTILATING
ATLAS HEATING & VENT. CO.
San Francisco: 557-4th St., DO 2-0377
E. C. BRAUN CO.
Berkeley: 2115 Fourth St., TH 5-2356
C. W. HALL
Santa Rosa: 1665 Sebastopol Rd., SR 6354
S. T. JOHNSON CO.
Oakland: 940 Arlington Ave., OL 2-6000
LOUIS V. KELLER
San Francisco: 289 Tehama St., JU 6-6252
L. J. KRUSE CO.
Oakland: 6247 College Ave., OL 2-8332
MALM METAL PRODUCTS
Santa Rosa: 724-2nd St., SR 454
JAS. A. NELSON CO.
San Francisco: 1375 Howard St., HE 1-0140
SCOTT COMPANY
Oakland: 1919 Market St., GL 1-1937
WESIX ELECTRIC HEATER CO.
San Francisco: 390 First St., GA 1-2211
Los Angeles: 530 W. 7th St., MI 8096

INSULATION WALL BOARD
PACIFIC CEMENT & AGGREGATES, INC.
San Francisco: 400 Alabama St., KL 2-1616

INTERCEPTING DEVICES
JOSAM PACIFIC CO.
San Francisco: 765 Folsom St., EX 2-3142

IRON—ORNAMENTAL
MICHEL & PFEFFER IRON WKS.
So. San Francisco: 212 Shaw Rd., PL 5-8983

LATHING & PLASTERING
ANGELO J. DANERI
San Francisco: 1433 Fairfax Ave., AT 8-1582
K-LATH CORP.
Alhambra: 909 So. Fremont St., Alhambra
A. E. KNOWLES CORP.
San Francisco: 3330 San Bruno Ave., JU 7-2091
G. H. & C. MARTINELLI
San Francisco: 174 Shotwell St., UN 3-6112
FREDERICK MEISWINKEL
San Francisco: 2155 Turk St., JO 7-7587
RHODES-JAMIESON LTD.
Oakland: 333-23rd Ave., KE 3-5225
PATRICK J. RUANE
San Francisco: 44 San Jose Ave., MI 7-6414

LIGHTING FIXTURES
SMOOT-HOLMAN COMPANY
Inglewood, Calif., OR 8-1217
San Francisco: 55 Mississippi St., MA 1-8474

LUMBER
CHRISTENSEN LUMBER CO.
San Francisco: Quint & Evans Ave., VA 4-5832
ART HOGAN LUMBER CO.
1701 Galvez Ave., ATwater 2-1157
MEAD CLARK LUMBER CO.
Santa Rosa: 3rd & Railroad
ROLANDO LUMBER CO.
San Francisco: 5th & Berry Sts., SU 1-6901
STERLING LUMBER CO.
Santa Rosa: 1129 College Ave., S. R. 82

MARBLE
JOS. MUSTO SONS-KEENAN CO.
San Francisco: 555 No. Point St., GR 4-6365
VERMONT MARBLE CO.
San Francisco: 6000-3rd St., VA 6-5024

MASONRY
BASALT ROCK CO.
Napa, Calif.
San Francisco: 260 Kearney St., GA 1-3758
WM. A. RAINEY & SON
San Francisco: 323 Clementina St., SU 1-0072
GEO. W. REED CO.
San Francisco: 1390 So. Van Ness Ave., AT 2-1226

METAL EXTERIOR WALLS
THE KAWNEER CO.
Berkeley: 930 Dwight Way, TH 5-8710

METAL FRAMING
UNISTRUT OF NORTHERN CALIFORNIA
Berkeley: 2547-9th St., TH 1-3031
Enterprise 1-2204

METAL GRATING
KLEMP METAL GRATING CORP.
Chicago, Ill.: 6601 So. Melvina St.

METAL LATH—EXPANDED
PACIFIC CEMENT & AGGREGATES, INC.
San Francisco: 400 Alabama St., KL 2-1616

METAL PARTITIONS
THE E. F. HAUSERMAN CO.
San Francisco: 485 Brannan St., YU 2-5477

METAL PRODUCTS
FORDERER CORNICE WORKS
San Francisco: 269 Potrero Ave., HE 1-4100

MILLWORK
CENTRAL MILL & CABINET CO.
San Francisco: 1595 Fairfax Ave., VA 4-7316
THE FINK & SCHINDLER CO.
San Francisco: 552 Brannan St., EX 2-1513
MULLEN MFG. CO.
San Francisco: 64 Rausch St., UN 1-5815
PACIFIC MFG. CO.
San Francisco: 16 Beale St., GA 1-7755
Santa Clara: 2610 The Alameda, S. C. 607
Los Angeles: 6820 McKinley Ave., TH 4156
SOUTH CITY LUMBER & SUPPLY CO.
So. San Francisco: Railroad & Spruce, PL 5-7085

OFFICE EQUIPMENT
GENERAL FIREPROOFING CO.
Los Angeles: 1200 South Hope St., RI 7-7501
San Francisco: 1025 Howard St., HE 1-7070
Oakland: 332-19th St., GL 2-4280

OIL BURNERS
S. T. JOHNSON CO.
Oakland: 940 Arlington Ave., GL 2-6000
San Francisco: 585 Potrero Ave., MA 1-2757
Philadelphia, Pa.: 401 North Broad St.

ORNAMENTAL IRON
MICHEL & PFEFFER IRON WORKS
So. San Francisco: 212 Shaw Rd., PL 5-8983

PAINTING
R. P. PAOLI & CO.
San Francisco: 2530 Lombard St., WE 1-1632
SINCLAIR PAINT CO.
San Francisco: 2112-15th St., HE 1-2196
D. ZELINSKY & SONS
San Francisco: 165 Groove St., MA 1-7400

PHOTOGRAPHS
Construction Progress
FRED ENGLISH
Belmont, Calif.: 1310 Old County Road, LY 1-0385

PLASTER
PACIFIC CEMENT & AGGREGATE INC.
San Francisco: 400 Alabama St., KL 2-1616

PLASTIC PRODUCTS
PLASTIC SALES & SERVICE
San Francisco: 409 Bryant St., DO 2-6433
WEST COAST INDUSTRIES
San Francisco: 3150-18th St., MA 1-5657

PLUMBING
BROADWAY PLUMBING CO.
San Francisco: 1790 Yosemite Ave., MI 8-4250
E. C. BRAUN CO.
Berkeley: 2175 Fourth St., TH 5-2356
C. W. HALL
Santa Rosa: 1665 Sebastopol Rd., SR 6354
HAWS DRINKING FAUCET CO.
Berkeley: 1435 Fourth St., LA 5-3341
JOSAM PACIFIC CO.
San Francisco: 765 Folsom St., EX 2-3143
LOUIS V. KELLER
San Francisco: 289 Tehama St., YU 6-6252
L. J. KRUSE CO.
Oakland: 6247 College Ave., OL 2-8332
JAS. A. NELSON CO.
San Francisco: 1375 Howard St., HE 1-0140
RODONI-BECKER CO., INC.
San Francisco: 455-10th St., MA 1-3662
SCOTT CO.
Oakland: 1919 Market St., GL 1-1937

POST PULLER
HOLLAND MFG. CO.
No. Sacramento: 1202 Dixieanne

PUMPING MACHINERY
SIMONDS MACHINERY CO.
San Francisco: 816 Folsom St, DO 2-6794

ROOFING
ANCHOR ROOFING CO.
San Francisco: 1671 Galvez Ave, VA 4-8140
ALTA ROOFING CO.
San Francisco: 1400 Egbert Ave, MI 7-2173
REGAL ROOFING CO.
San Francisco: 930 Innes Ave, VA 4-3261

ROOF SCUTTLES
THE BILCO CO.
New Haven, Conn.
Oakland: Geo. B. Schultz, 190 MacArthur Blvd.
Sacramento: Harry B. Ogle & Assoc., 1331 T St.
Fresno: Healey & Popovich, 1703 Fulton St.
Reseda: Daniel Dunner, 6200 Alonzo Ave.

ROOF TRUSSES
EASYBOW ENGINEERING & RESEARCH CO.
Oakland: 13th & Wood Sts., GL 2-0805

SAFES
THE HERMANN SAFE CO.
San Francisco: 1699 Market St., UN 1-6644

SEWER PIPE
GLADDING, McBEAN & CO.
San Francisco: 9th & Harrison, UN 1-7400
Los Angeles: 2901 Los Feliz Blvd., OL 2121

SHEET METAL
MICHEL & PFEFFER IRON WORKS
So. San Francisco: 212 Shaw Rd., PL 5-8983

SOUND EQUIPMENT
STROMBERG-CARLSON CO.
San Francisco: 1805 Rollins Rd., Burlingame, OX 7-3630
Los Angeles: 5414 York Blvd., CL 7-3939

SPRINKLERS
BARNARD ENGINEERING CO.
San Francisco: 35 Elmira St., JU 5-4642

STEEL—STRUCTURAL & REINFORCING
COLUMBIA-GENEVA DIV., U. S. STEEL CORP.
San Francisco: Russ Bldg., SU 1-2500
Los Angeles: 2087 E. Slauson, LA 1171
Portland, Ore.: 2345 N.W. Nicolai, BE 7261
Seattle, Wn.: 1331-3rd Ave. Bldg., MA 1972
Salt Lake City, Utah: Walker Bank Bldg., SL 3-6733
HERRICK IRON WORKS
Oakland 18th & Campbell, GL 1-1767
INDEPENDENT IRON WORKS, INC.
Oakland: 780 Pine St., TE 2-0160
JUDSON PACIFIC MURPHY CORP.
Emeryville: 4300 Eastshore Highway, OL 3-1717
REPUBLIC STEEL CORP.
San Francisco: 116 New Montgomery St., GA 1-0977
Los Angeles: Edison Bldg.
Seattle: White-Henry Stuart Bldg.
Salt Lake City: Walker Bank Bldg.
Denver: Continental Oil Bldg.
SOULE STEEL CO.
San Francisco: 1750 Army St., VA 4-4141

STEEL FORMS
STEELFORM CONTRACTING CO.
San Francisco: 666 Harrison St., DO 2-5582

SWIMMING POOLS
SIERRA MFG. CO.
Walnut Creek, Calif.: 1719 Mt. Diablo Blvd.

SWIMMING POOL FITTINGS
JOSAM PACIFIC CO.
San Francisco: 765 Folsom St., EX 2-3143

**TESTING LABORATORIES
(ENGINEERS & CHEMISTS**
ABBOT A. HANKS, INC.
San Francisco: 624 Sacramento St., GA 1-1697
ROBERT W. HUNT COMPANY
San Francisco: 500 Iowa, MI 7-0224
Los Angeles: 3050 E. Slauson, JE 9131
Chicago, New York, Pittsburgh
PITTSBURGH TESTING LABORATORY
San Francisco: 651 Howard St., EX 2-1747

TILE—CLAY & WALL
GLADDING McBEAN & CO.
San Francisco: 9th & Harrison Sts., UN 1-7400
Los Angeles: 2901 Los Feliz Blvd., OL 2121
Portland: 110 S.E. Main St., EA 6179
Seattle: 945 Elliott Ave. West, GA 0330
Spokane: 1102 No. Monroe St., BR 3259
KRAFTILE CO.
Niles, Calif.: Niles 3611
San Francisco: 50 Hawthorne St., DO 2-3780
Los Angeles: 406 So. Main St., MA 7241

TILE—TERRAZZO
NATIONAL TILE & TERAZZO CO.
San Francisco: 198 Mississippi St., UN 1-0273

TIMBER—TREATED
J. H. BAXTER CO.
San Francisco: 200 Bush St., YU 2-0200
Los Angeles: 3450 Wilshire Blvd., DU 8-9591

TIMBER TRUSSES
EASYBOW ENGINEERING & RESEARCH CO.
Oakland: 13th & Wood Sts., GL 2-0805

TRUCKING
PASSETTI TRUCKING CO.
San Francisco: 264 Clementina St., GA 1-5297

UNDERPINNING & SHORING
D. J. & T. SULLIVAN
San Francisco: 1942 Folsom St., MA 1-1545

WALL PAPER
WALLPAPERS, INC.
Oakland: 384 Grand Ave., GL 2-0451

WAREHOUSE AND STORAGE EQUIPMENT AND SHELVING
GENERAL FIREPROOFING CO.
Los Angeles: 1200 South Hope St., RI 7-7501
San Francisco: 1025 Howard St., HE 1-7070
Oakland: 332-19th St., GL 2-4280

WATERPROOFING MATERIALS
CONRAD SOVIG CO.
San Francisco: 875 Bryant St., HE 1-1345

WATERSTOPS (P.V.C.)
TECON PRODUCTS, LTD.
Vancouver, B.C.: 681 E. Hastings St.
Seattle: 304 So. Alaskan Way

WINDOW SHADES
SHADES, INC.
San Francisco: 80 Tehama St., DO 2-7092

CLASSIFIED ADVERTISING

RATE: 20c PER WORD . . . CASH WITH ORDER   MINIMUM $5.00

CONSTRUCTION INDUSTRY WAGE RATES

Table 1 has been prepared by the State of California, Department of Industrial Relations, Division of Labor Statistics and Research. The rates are the union hourly wage rates established by collective bargaining as of January 2, 1958, as reported by reliable sources.

TABLE 1—UNION HOURLY WAGE RATES, CONSTRUCTION INDUSTRY, CALIFORNIA

Following are the hourly rates of compensation established by collective bargaining, reported as of January 2, 1958 or later

CRAFT	San Francisco	Alameda	Contra Costa	Fresno	Sacramento	San Joaquin	Santa Clara	Solano	Los Angeles	San Bernardino	San Diego	Santa Barbara	Kern
ASBESTOS WORKER	$3.70	$3.70	$3.70	$3.70	$3.70	$3.70	$3.70	$3.70	$3.70	$3.70	$3.70	$3.70	$3.70
BOILERMAKER	3.675	3.675	3.675	3.675	3.675	3.675	3.675	3.675	3.675	3.675	3.675	3.675	3.675
BRICKLAYER	3.95	3.75	3.75	3.75	3.80	3.75	3.875	3.95	3.80	3.90	3.75		3.85
BRICKLAYER HODCARRIER	3.15	3.15	3.15	2.90	3.10	2.90	3.00	3.10	2.75	2.75	2.75		2.75
CARPENTER	3.175	3.175	3.225	3.225	3.225	3.225	3.225	3.225	3.225	3.225	3.225	3.225	3.225
CEMENT MASON	3.22	3.22	3.22	3.22	3.22	3.22	3.22	3.22	3.15	3.15	3.25	3.15	3.15
ELECTRICIAN	3.936A	3.936A	3.936A		3.94A	3.50	4.03A	3.666A	3.90A	3.92A	3.90	3.85A	3.70
GLAZIER	3.09	3.09	3.09	3.135	3.065	3.055	3.09	3.09	3.105	3.105	3.03	3.105	3.135
IRON WORKER ORNAMENTAL	3.625	3.625	3.625	3.625	3.625	3.625	3.625	3.625	3.625	3.625	3.625	3.625	3.625
REINFORCING	3.375	3.375	3.375	3.375	3.375	3.375	3.375	3.375	3.375	3.375	3.375	3.375	3.375
STRUCTURAL	3.625	3.625	3.625	3.625	3.625	3.625	3.625	3.625	3.625	3.625	3.625	3.625	3.625
LABORER, GENERAL OR CONSTRUCTION	2.505	2.505	2.505	2.505	2.505	2.505	2.505	2.505	2.50	2.50	2.48	2.50	2.50
LATHER	3.4375	3.84	3.84	3.45	3.60B	3.40C	3.60D	3.50E	3.9375		3.725	3.625F	
OPERATING ENGINEER Concrete mixer (up to 1 yard)	2.89	2.89	2.89	2.89	2.89	2.89	2.89	2.89					
Concrete mixer operator—Skip Type									2.96	2.96	2.96	2.96	2.96
Elevator Hoist Operator									3.19	3.19	3.19	3.19	3.19
Material Hoist (1 drum)	3.19	3.19	3.19	3.19	3.19	3.19	3.19	3.19					
Tractor Operator	3.33	3.33	3.33	3.33	3.33	3.33	3.33	3.33	3.47	3.47	3.47	3.47	3.47
PAINTER Brush	3.20	3.20	3.20	3.13	3.325	3.175	3.20	3.20	3.26G	3.25	3.19	3.13H	3.10
Spray	3.20	3.20	3.20	3.38	3.575	3.325	3.20	3.20	3.51G	3.50	3.74	3.38H	3.35
PILEDRIVERMAN	3.305	3.305	3.305	3.305	3.305	3.305	3.305	3.305	3.355	3.355		3.355	3.355
PLASTERER	3.69	3.545	3.545	3.35	3.60B	3.55C	3.58	3.50	3.9375	3.9375	3.725		
PLASTERER HODCARRIER	3.25	3.42	3.42	3.10	3.10	3.00C	3.20	3.15	3.6875	3.5625	3.475	3.50	3.6675
PLUMBER	3.47		3.935I	3.80J	3.70	3.80J	3.60	2.675	3.70	3.70	3.70	3.70	3.375
ROOFER	3.35	3.35	3.35	3.20	3.25	3.35	3.35	3.10K	3.20L	3.25	3.10	3.30	3.775
SHEET METAL WORKER	3.45	3.45	3.45	3.425	3.45	3.465	3.45	3.325	3.50	3.50	3.45	3.55	3.10
STEAMFITTER	3.67	3.96	3.96	3.80J	3.70	3.80J	3.60	3.675	3.70	3.70	3.70	3.70	3.775
TRUCK DRIVER— Dump Trucks under 4 yards	2.55	2.55	2.55	2.55	2.55	2.55	2.55	2.55	2.63	2.63	2.63	2.63	2.63
TILE SETTER	3.275	3.275	3.275	3.375	3.28	3.30	3.275	3.275	3.36	3.60	3.375	3.36	

A Includes 4% vacation allowance.
B Includes 5c hour for industry promotion and 5c hour for vacation fund.
C ½% withheld for industry promotion.
D 1½c withheld for industry promotion.
E Includes 5c hour for industry promotion and 5c hour for vacation fund. Hourly rate for part of county adjacent to Sacramento County is $3.60.
F Northern part of County: $3.75.

G Pomona Area: Brush $3.25; Spray $3.50.
H Southern half of County: Brush $3.28; Spray $3.28.
I Includes 30c hour for vacation pay.
J Includes 15c hour which local union may elect to use for vacation purposes.
K Includes 10c hour for vacation fund.
L Includes 10c hour savings fund wage.

ATTENTION: The above tabulation has been prepared by the State of California, Department of Industrial Relations, Division of Labor Statistics and Research, and represents data reported by building trades councils, union locals, contractor organizations, and other reliable sources. The above rates do not include any payments to funds for health and welfare, pensions, vacations, industry promotion, apprentice training, etc., except as shown in the footnotes.

CONSTRUCTION INDUSTRY WAGE RATES — TABLE 2

Employer Contributions to Health and Welfare, Pension, Vacation and Other Funds
California Union Contracts, Construction Industry

(Revised March, 1957)

CRAFT	San Francisco	Fresno	Sacramento	San Joaquin	Santa Clara	Los Angeles	San Bernardino	San Diego
ASBESTOS WORKER	.10 W .11 hr. V	.10 W .11 hr. V	.10 W .11 hr. V	.10 W .11 hr. V	.10 W .11 hr. V	.10 W	.10 W	.10 W
BRICKLAYER	.15 W .14 P .06 hr. V		.15 W .10 P		.15 W			
BRICKLAYER HODCARRIER	.10 W .10 P .10 V	.10 W	.10 W	.10 W	.10 W	.075 W	.075 W	.075 W
CARPENTER	.10 W .10 hr. V	.10 W	.10 W	.10 W	.10 W	.10 W	.10 W	.10 W
CEMENT MASON	.10 W	.10 W	.10 W	.10 W	.10 W	.10 W	.10 W	.10 W
ELECTRICAL WORKER	.10 W 1% P 4% V	.10 W 1% P 4% V	.075 W 1% P	.075 W 1% P 4% V	1% P	1% P	1% P	.10 W 1% P
GLAZIER	.075 W .085 V	.075 W 40 hr. V	.075 W .05 V	.075 W .05 V	.075 W .085 V	.075 W 40 hr. V	.075 W 40 hr. V	.075 W 10 hr. V
IRONWORKER: REINFORCING	.10 W	.10 W	.10 W	.10 W	.10 W	.10 W	.10 W	.10 W
STRUCTURAL	.10 W	.10 W	.10 W	.10 W	.10 W	.10 W	.10 W	.10 W
LABORER, GENERAL	.10 W	.10 W	.10 W	.10 W	.10 W	.075 W	.075 W	.075 W
LATHER	.60 day W .70 day V		.10 W	.10 W	.075 W .05 V	.90 day W	.70 day W	.10 W
OPERATING ENGINEER								
TRACTOR OPERATOR (MIN.)	.10 W	.10 W	.10 W	.10 W	.10 W	.10 W	.10 W	.10 W
POWER SHOVEL OP. (MIN.)	.10 W	.10 W	.10 W	.10 W	.10 W	.10 W	.10 W	.10 W
PAINTER, BRUSH	.095 W	.08 W	.075 W	.10 W	.095 W .07 V	.085 W	.08 W	.09 W
PLASTERER	.10 W .10 V	.10 W	.10 W	.10 W	.10 W .15 V	.10 W	.90 day W	.10 W
PLUMBER	.10 W .10 V	.15 W .10 P	.10 W .10 P .125 V	.10 W	.10 W .10 P .125 V	.10 W	.90 day W	.10 W
ROOFER	.10 W .10 V	.10 W	.10 W .10 V	.10 W	.075 W .10 V	.085 W	.10 W	.075 W
SHEET METAL WORKER	.075 W 4% V	.075 W 7 day V	.075 W .10 V	.075 W .12 V	.075 W 4% V	.085 W .10 V	.085 W .10 V	.085 W 5 day V
TILE SETTER	.075 W .09 V				.075 W .09 V	.025 W .06 V		

ATTENTION: The above tabulation has been prepared and compiled from the available data reported by building trades councils, union locals, contractor organizations and other reliable sources. The table was prepared from incomplete data; where no employer contributions are specified, it does not necessarily mean that none are required by the union contract.

The type of supplement is indicated by the following symbols: W—Health and Welfare; P—Pensions; V—Vacations; A—Apprentice training fund; Adm—Administration fund; JIB—Joint Industry Board; Prom—Promotion fund.

CONSTRUCTION CONTRACTS AWARDED AND MISCELLANEOUS PERSONNEL DATA

ARTS & CRAFTS BLDG., Fairgrounds, Yuba City, Sutter county. 13th District Agricultural Association, Yuba City, owner. 1-Story exhibit building to be used as arts and crafts building for county fair—$16,933. GENERAL CONTRACTOR: Vernon M. Hacker, 804 Colusa Ave., Yuba City.

RECREATION BLDG., Shoreview Park, San Mateo. City of San Mateo, owner. Construction to provide facilities for recreational building at city's park—$26,165. ARCHITECT: Alfred W. Johnson, AIA, 165 Jessie St., San Francisco.

CHAPEL & EDUCATIONAL, Church San Jose, Santa Clara county. Trinity Presbyterian Church, San Jose, owner. Work includes facilities for new Chapel, administration unit, and educational facilities—$107,619. ARCHITECT: Alfred W. Johnson, 165 Jessie St., San Francisco. GENERAL CONTRACTOR: Aiken Const. Co., 333 Phelan Ave., San Jose.

WAREHOUSE & DISTRIBUTION CENTER, South San Francisco, San Mateo county. Pellegrini Bros. Winery, San Francisco, owner. 1-Story combination building for offices, warehouse, and distribution center, 25,000 sq. ft. of area—$200,000. ARCHITECT & ENGINEER: Cline, Zerkle & Agee, 1810 6th St., Berkeley. GENERAL CONTRACTOR: A. S. Holmes & Son, Inc., 9300 G St., Oakland.

OPERATIONS & POWER BLDG., Sage Project, Reno. U. S. Army, Hamilton Air Force Base, Hamilton Field, Marin county, California, owner. Reinforced concrete construction, concrete roof slabs; facilities for operational building and power building and associated facilities—$492,519. GENERAL CONTRACTOR: Stolte Inc., 8451 San Leandro St., Oakland.

HIGH SCHOOL, Site Development, Walnut Creek, Contra Costa county. Acalanes Union High School District, Lafayette, owner. Work consists of site development for Tice High School to be built near Walnut Creek—$145,823. ARCHITECT: John Lyon Reid, 1019 Market St., San Francisco. GENERAL CONTRACTOR: Arvil O. Jones, 3420 San Pablo Dam Road, San Pablo.

LIBRARY, Concord, Contra Costa county. City of Concord, owner. "T" shaped new library building, main unit for storage and reading facilities, 1 wing for meeting rooms, 1 wing for Children's Department; concrete and wood frame construction—$200,000. ARCHITECT: Donald Powers Smith, 133 Kearny St., San Francisco. GENERAL CONTRACTOR: B. K. W. Const. Co., 1790 Mt. Diablo Blvd., Concord.

OFFICE BLDG., Fresno. Chester A. Bergfeld Enterprises, Inc., Fresno, owner. New modern office building — $124,464. AR-

CHITECT: Robert Stevens, 924 N. Van Ness Ave., Fresno. GENERAL CONTRACTOR: Harriss Const. Co., P. O. Box 109, Fresno.

MUNICIPAL IMPROVEMENTS, San Jose, Santa Clara county. City of San Jose, owner. Series of improvements to city's municipal airport to include 1) Aircraft parking apron, 2) Underground fire and water lines, 3) Electrical alterations to existing control tower building—$105,-805. GENERAL CONTRACTOR: Lew Jones Const. Co., 1535 So. 10th St., San Jose.

GLASS MFG. PLANT, San Leandro, Alameda county. Anchor Hocking Glass Corpn., Lancaster, Ohio., owner. Modern structural steel and concrete glass manufacturing plant center building. GENERAL CONTRACTOR: Indenco Inc., 2960 Merced St., San Leandro.

MEMORIAL BLDG., Additions and Alterations. Clovis, Fresno, county. Work consists of additions and alterations to existing memorial building — $38,635. ARCHITECT: Chester J. Lielan, 1461 N. Van Ness, Fresno. GENERAL CONTRACTOR: E. C. Stearns Const. Co., 137 E. Olive St., Fresno.

JR. COLLEGE ADD'N, Fresno, Fresno City Unified School District, owner. Construction of a shop building to present school plant facilities—$1,116,000. ARCHITECT: Walter Wagner & Partners, 1830 Van Ness, Fresno. GENERAL CONTRACTOR: Bob Long Const. Co., 2421 Hedges St., Fresno.

OFFICE BLDG., Sacramento. Sacramento Municipal Utility District, owner. Structural steel frame construction, precast panel and glass curtain walls—$4,297,000. ARCHITECT: Dreyfuss & Blackford, 2127 J St., Sacramento. GENERAL CONTRACTOR: Continental Const. & Lawrence Const. (joint venture), 3020 V St., Sacramento.

SERVICE CLUB, Ogden, Utah. U. S. Army Engineers, San Francisco, owner. Construction of a frame and reinforced concrete service club building at the Hill Air Force Base; 3,000 sq. ft. area, concrete block wall, cast-in-place gypsum roof, steel roof frame, paving — $258,700. ENGINEER: U. S. Corps of Engineers, San Francisco. GENERAL CONTRACTOR: Maurice B. McCullough Company, Salt Lake City.

OFFICE BLDG., San Jose, Santa Clara county. Draper Development Co., San

Francisco, owner. 1-Story, with provision for a 2nd story at a later date, grouted brick construction, glass, porcelain enamel curtain walls. ARCHITECT: Robert B. Liles, 340 Pine St., San Francisco. GENERAL CONTRACTOR: Leonard Semas Const., 2885 Homestead Road, Santa Clara.

SCHOOL ADD'N, Longbarn, Tuolumne county. Twain Harte-Longbarn Union School District, Twain Harte, owner. Addition to provide classrooms, kindergarten, and small kitchen — $54,152. ARCHITECT: John Lyon Reid & Partners, 1019 Market St., San Francisco. GENERAL CONTRACTOR: Covington & Wolverton, P. O. Box 573, Sonora.

MEDICAL CLINIC, Visalia, Tulare county. Visalia Clinic, Visalia, owner. Flagstone masonry, frame and stucco, interior plaster, concrete slab, metal sash, heating and ventilating, ceramic tile, electrical and related work to provide for physiotherapy, pharmacy, laboratory, X-ray, minor surgery and pediatrics. ARCHITECT: Robert C. Kaestner & Associates, 210 N. Encina, Visalia. GENERAL CONTRACTOR: Lauren Miner, W. Mineral King, Riverside.

COUNTY BOYS CAMP, near Visalia, Tulare county. County of Tulare, Visalia, owner. Work comprises construction of one new concrete block building with wood laminated roof, and remodel of other buildings — $84,300. GENERAL CONTRACTOR: Lewis C. Nelson & Sons, 2915 McCall St., Selma.

LIBRARY BLDG., Chico State College, Chico, Butte county. Division of Architecture, State of California, Sacramento, owner. Reinforced concrete foundations and piling, concrete reinforced brick masonry exterior walls, steel siding, roof decking — $600,000. ARCHITECT: Anson Boyd, California State Architect, Sacramento. GENERAL CONTRACTOR: Fred S. Macomber, 8818 Melrose Ave., Los Angeles.

MEDICAL OFFICE BLDG., Los Angeles. Causey & Rhodes, Glendale, owner. 4-Story brick medical office building, 44,000 sq. ft. of area, composition roofing, interior drywall, hardwood floors, metal sash, wood and glass doors, structural steel, pipe columns, asphalt concrete paving—$265,000. ARCHITECT: Henry N. Silvestri, 801 N. Cahuenga Blvd., Los Angeles.

OLYMPIC RINKS, Squaw Valley, Placer county. California Olympic Games Committee, San Francisco, owner. Project represents Phase 3 of the work in the Olympic area and skating rinks to be covered; 11,000 person seating capacity; 3 ice skating arenas and 1 speed-skating rink—$2,-411,000. ARCHITECT: Corlett & Spackman, AIA, and Kitchen & Hunt, AIA, 347 Clay St., San Francisco. GENERAL CONTRACTOR: Diversified Bldrs., P.O. Box 320 Montebello, Calif.

FELLOWSHIP HALL & CLASSROOM, Long Beach, Los Angeles county. Our Savior Lutheran Church, Long Beach, owner. Frame and stucco construction, composition and Spanish tile roofing, plaster, interior, acoustic tile ceiling, wood sash, concrete slab and wood parquet flooring, forced air heating, stainless steel kitchen equipment, metal toilet partitions, covered walks—$133,300. ARCHITECT:

Kenneth S. Wing, 30 Linden Ave., Long' Beach. GENERAL CONTRACTOR: Voge, Inc., 7601 Crenshaw Blvd., Los Angeles.

HONOR CAMP, Crystal Creek, Shasta county. California Dept. Public Works, Sacramento, owner. Work comprises construction of a group of buildings at the Crystal Creek Forestry Honor Camp including (1) wood frame type barracks, (2) wood frame mess hall, CDB office of wood frame, (3) CDF offices and shop and warehouse buildings, also sheet metal gas station — $183,000. ARCHITECT: Anson Boyd, California State Architect, Sacramento. GENERAL CONTRACTOR: Robert S. Bryant, 1242 Center St., Redding.

RECREATION FACILITIES, Strawberry Canyon, Berkeley, Alameda county. University of California, Berkeley, owner. Project comprises construction of recreational facilities in Strawberry Canyon as a part of the University of California campus—$344,000. GENERAL CONTRACTOR: Midstate Construction Co., 347 Clay Street, San Francisco.

ICE SKATING RINK, Downey, Los Angeles county. Mr. Smith, Downey, owner. 1-Story Switzer panel ice skating rink 50x-70 ft. in area, composition roof, tapered steel girders, steel casement cash, concrete slab floor, restrooms, plumbing and electrical work, black-top paving in parking areas. ENGINEER: Carter & Montgomery, Engineers, 2322A W. Beverly Blvd., Whittier; and D. & E. Drafting Service, 10604 E. Horley Ave., Downey. GENERAL CONTRACTOR: Marion Novosad, 10357 Mapledale Street, Bellflower.

SENIOR HIGH SCHOOL, Blythe, Riverside county. Palo Verde Unified School District, Blythe, owner. New high school of frame and stucco construction with total of 88,346 sq. ft. of area; includes all site improvements, classrooms, playground equipment and related work—$1,588,610. ARCHITECT: Harold Gimeno, 1400 N. Sycamore St., Santa Ana. GENERAL CONTRACTOR: L. P. Scherer, 208½ J Orange St., Redlands.

FELLOWSHIP HALL, Pasadena, Los Angeles county. Trinity Lutheran Church, Pasadena, owner. 2-Story fellowship hall, 5880 sq. ft. of area, composition roofing, frame and stucco construction, wood and metal sash, concrete slab, asphalt tile, unit heating. ARCHITECT: Edwin Westburg, 1199 E. Walnut St., Pasadena. GENERAL CONTRACTOR: Gloege & Shirar, 2110 E. Walnut St., Pasadena.

RACQUET CLUB FACILITIES, Sacramento. South Hills Racquet Club, Sacramento, owner. Work includes clubhouse with dressing rooms, shower and locker rooms, tennis courts, volley ball court, putting green, offstreet parking and an Olympic-size "L"-shaped swimming pool. ARCHITECT: Rickey & Brooks, 2015 J St., Sacramento. GENERAL CONTRACTOR: Charles F. Unger, 2112 Sutterville Rd., Sacramento.

OFFICE BLDG., Eagle Rock, Los Angeles county. Frances Roberts, Los Angeles, owner. Frame siding and stucco office building, 34x89 ft., composition roof, interior dry wall, acoustical tile ceilings, metal sash, asphalt tile and concrete slab floors, forced air heating, asphalt, concrete

paving and concrete block planter and retaining wall — $17,000. ARCHITECT: Geo. T. Kirkpatrick, 2171 Colorado Blvd., Los Angeles. GENERAL CONTRACTOR: Edwin Sylvis, 1125 Arbor Dell Rd., Los Angeles.

JONAS SALK, Elementary School, Carmichael, Sacramento county. Arden-Carmichael School District, Carmichael, owner. Light steel frame construction, grouted brick and precast slab, to provide facilities for administration unit, 15 classrooms, multi-purpose, also additional classrooms for mentally retarded children, kitchen and toilets—$664,105. ARCHITECT: Gordon Stafford, 1024½ J St., Sacramento. GENERAL CONTRACTOR: Lawrence Construction Co., 3020 V St., Sacramento.

INDUSTRIAL BLDG., Van Nuys, Los Angeles county. Harry Marks, Los Angeles, owner. Frame and stucco industrial building, 12,000 sq. ft. area, composition roof, steel sash, overhead doors, interior plaster, toilets, concrete slab, asphaltic-concrete paving — $54,000. ARCHITECT: Meyer and Alexander, Architects & Engineers, 11221 Burbank Blvd., North Hollywood.

RESTAURANT, Nut Tree reconstruction, Vacaville, Solano county. Nut Tree Restaurant, Vacaville, owner. Project includes program of long-term replacement of existing restaurant buildings and construction of a new outdoor restaurant and paved parking areas—$41,201. ARCHITECT: Dreyfuss & Blackford, 2127 J St., Sacramento. GENERAL CONTRACTOR: Syar & Harms, P.O. Box 1272 Vallejo.

BOTTLING PLANT, Emeryville, Alameda county. Pepsi Cola Bottling Co., Oakland, owner. The famed Oakland "Oaks" Pacific Coast baseball league park will be the site of a new concrete tilt-up, wood roof truss, bottling plant building, with related facilities to manufacture and service the Pepsi Cola Bottling Co. and the Belfast Beverages Co. CONSULTING ENGINEER, L. H. & B. L. Nishkian, 1045 Sansome St., San Francisco. GENERAL CONTRACTOR: Bishop · Mattei Construction Co., Pier 7, Embarcadero, San Francisco.

OFFICE BLDG., Sacramento. Jordan Jones, Sacramento, owner. 1-Story wood frame, concrete block office building and carports; built-up roofing, 25x80 ft.—$20,848. ARCHITECT: Herbert E. Goodpastor, 1012 J St., Sacramento. GENERAL CONTRACTOR: Edwin J. Mackey Construction, 720 Howe Ave., Sacramento.

SHOPPING CENTER, North Torrance, Los Angeles county. Dominguez Estate Co., Los Angeles, owner. Comprises Unit B of the North Torrance Shopping Center, 14,000 sq. ft. of floor area, concrete masonry, veneer, structural steel, metal doors and frames, mill work, sheet metal, composition roofing, plastering, glass store fronts, acoustical tile and terrazzo, resilient flooring, hardware, painting, plumbing, heating, ventilating, air conditioning, electric work. ENGINEERS: Quinton Engineers, Ltd., 812 W. 8th St., Los Angeles. GENERAL CONTRACTOR: Coordinated Construction, Inc., 12901 Crenshaw Blvd., Hawthorne.

ELEMENTARY SCHOOL, Blackford, Campbell, Santa Clara county. Campbell Union School District, Campbell, owner. Work consists of construction of 8 classrooms, shop building, home-making room —$206,486. ARCHITECT: Higgins & Root, 220 Meridian Road, San Jose. GENERAL CONTRACTOR: James Sakaguchi, 626 N. 1st St., San Jose.

TENNIS COURTS, High School, Covina, Los Angeles county. Covina High School District, Covina, owner. Work comprises construction of tennis courts at various city high schools—$16,689. ARCHITECT: Wright & Wright, 1125 W. 6th St., Los Angeles. GENERAL CONTRACTOR: E. C. Construction Co., 2213 N. Chico Ave., El Monte.

OFFICE BLDG., Van Nuys, Los Angeles county. Pancy Corpn., Van Nuys, owner. Cement block office building, 30x81 ft., mosaic tile, built-up roofing, aluminum sash, slab floor, open web steel joist, toilet facilities. ARCHITECT: Allison & Rible, 3670 Wilshire Blvd., Los Angeles. GENERAL CONTRACTOR: C. W. Driver, Inc., 2618 Temple St., Los Angeles.

TELEPHONE ACCOUNTING BLDG., Los Angeles. Pacific Tel. & Tel., Los Angeles, owner. 2-Story and basement. 81,000 sq. ft. floor space, reinforced concrete frame basement and first floor lightweight steel frame; second floor, masonry walls, built-up roofing, ceramic veneer work, metal sash, asphalt tile, air conditioning, acoustical and related trades—$1,250,000. ARCHITECT: Woodford & Bernard, 410 N. La Brea Ave., Los Angeles. GENERAL CONTRACTOR: Chotiner & Gumbiner, Inc., 5316 Venice Blvd., Los Angeles.

BURROUGHS HIGH SCHOOL, China Lake, Kern county. Kern County Union High School District, Bakersfield, owner. 1st Stage: 61,800 sq. ft. area, concrete block, composition roofing, concrete slab and asphalt tile floors, forced air heating and air floor heating, insulation, plastering, ceramic tile, aluminum sash, plywood partitions; complete facilities for administration unit, classrooms, shower and locker unit, library, study hall, toilet rooms—$1,126,600. ARCHITECT: Alford Thomas & Leyden Frost, 602 Habersfelde Bldg., Bakersfield. GENERAL CONTRACTOR: William A. Drennan, 1325 Castaic Avenue, Oildale.

MULTI-PURPOSE BLDG., Elementary School, Litchfield, Arizona. Maricopa County Board of Supervisors, owner. Construction of a multi-purpose school building—$119,850. ARCHITECT: Mel C. Ensign, 200 E. Bethany Home Rd., Phoenix. GENERAL CONTRACTOR: C. O. Johnson & Son, 1839 W. Buckeye Rd., Phoenix.

CHURCH, St. Ansgar, Salinas, Monterey county. Lutheran Church of Salinas, owner. Wood frame and stucco, 6 classrooms, kitchen, bell tower, toilets—$134,900. ARCHITECT: John H. Waterman & George Kuska, Associates, 1112 Pajaro St., Salinas. GENERAL CONTRACTOR: Ekelin & Small, P.O. Box 8, Salinas.

JAIL REMODEL, Sacramento. City of Sacramento, owner. Work consists of remodeling present jail facilities—$116,000. ARCHITECT: Harry J. Devine, 1012 J St., Sacramento. GENERAL CONTRACTOR: John F. Otto, 4332 24th St., Sacramento.

IN THE NEWS

ARCHITECT ALEXANDER ATTENDS AIA POLICY MEETING IN WASHINGTON

Architect Robert E. Alexander, former president of the Los Angeles City Planning Commission, flew to Washington, D.C., recently to attend the May meeting of the steering committee of The American Institute of Architects' community planning committee.

The purpose of the conference was to establish a plan of operation for Community Planning Committee action, and to report to the AIA Board of Directors.

AVCO AND PENN METAL OFFER BUILDING SYSTEM

A new architectural porcelain curtain wall system developed by the AK Division of Avco Mfg. Corp., is being marketed jointly with Penn Metal Co., according to a recent announcement by the two firms.

The system is engineered for office buildings, schools, stores, hospitals, clinics, industrial and commercial buildings and other one, two and three story buildings. Penn Metal will provide the structural framework and AK will supply modular porcelain-on-steel panels and accessories.

NATIONAL HOUSING CENTER APPOINTS RUFUS LISLE

Rufus Lisle has been appointed general manager of the National Housing Center, Washington, D. C., according to a recent announcement by Neal J. Hardy, director.

A graduate of Princeton University, Lisle has been with Frigidaire Division of General Motors for 16 years.

FRED KIRBY PROMOTED ASSISTANT SALES MGR. FOREST FIBER PRODUCTS

Fred Kirby, sales representative in the Pacific Northwest for the Forest Fiber Products Company, Forest Grove, Oregon, has been promoted to the post of Assistant Sales Manager in the jobber-dealer field, according to an announcement by F. M. Hughes, general manager.

Kirby was one of the original group of technical people who designed the Forest Fiber hardboard plant in Forest Grove, and at the time the plant was completed was appointed foreman supervising quality control of all products. He will continue to service the Oregon, Southern Washington, Utah and Idaho territories, plus serving in the field of assistance to regular dealer salesmen.

PROFESSOR LELAND VAUGHAN LANDSCAPE CONSULTANT FOR ALAMEDA SHORE DEVEOLPMENT

Professor Leland Vaughan, chairman of the University of California's Department of Landscape Architects, has been engaged as landscape consultant on Alameda's new South Shore Center and South Shore residential development, according to an announcement by Charles T. Travers, vice-president of the South Shore Center, Inc., Utah Construction Company subsidiary which is developing the project.

Prof. Vaughan will design and supervise the planting area in the new 65-acre regional shopping center and will develop a street and tree program plus a planting layout for pedestrian ways in residential areas of the project.

The new South Shore Center, expected to open in August of this year, will be the business hub of a new 400-acre community with more than 800 homes, a professional and administrative zone, more than 1500 luxury apartments plus a unique interior lagoon system and broad public beach on San Francisco Bay.

ANNOUNCING NEW JOSAM SEDIMENT INTERCEPTORS

A recently introduced improved type of sediment interceptor for use on pump suction for swimming pools, filters, water softeners, bleaching tanks and similar water supply systems; and waste lines from mechanical laundry equipment, has been announced by the Josam Manufacturing Company.

They are pressure tight units with a cylindrical body which can withstand a far greater suction pressure than square or rectangular designs. The protective leak-proof cover has a swing bolt locking arrangement, and the cover is easily removed for emptying the sediment basket. However, cover cannot be replaced unless sediment basket is in place, an exclusive feature. Available in sizes up to 10" connections, threaded or flange. Complete data from manufacturer Josam Mfg. Co., Michigan City, Indiana.

YALE OPENS FACTORY BRANCH IN SAN DIEGO

Yale and Towne Mfg., Co. has established a factory branch for the sale and service of industrial lift trucks in San Diego, under direction of James B. Cunningham, a veteran of more than 15 years experience in Yale truck sales and service and formerly Service Manager of the Yale Los Angeles branch.

Complete factory approved parts inventories will be maintained in the new San Diego facility.

JOHN S. BOLLES, AIA MOVES ARCHITECTURAL OFFICES

John S. Bolles, AIA, architect, recently announced the removal of his offices to new facilities at 14 Gold Street, San Francisco, adjacent to the north of the north-

west corner of Jackson and Sansome streets.

Bolles recently purchased and remodeled the 3-story building, and will occupy the second and third floors. Executive offices, conference rooms and a gallery for exhibit of his extensive collection of contemporary paintings and sculpture will occupy the second floor, while the third floor will be used for a drafting room.

A. C. HORN CO.
MOVES INTO
LARGER OFFICES

Stanford R. Horn, Pacific Coast manager of the A. C. Horn Company, manufacturers and distributors of materials for construction and maintenance, announces the firm's western division moved into larger quarters on April 1.

The new, modern, all concrete structure at 550 3rd Street, San Francisco, will house three times the previous space. Manufacturing and warehouse facilities will include three truck bays and railroad siding.

EARTH SCIENCES
BUILDING FOR
UC AT BERKELEY

The architectural firm of Warnecke & Warnecke, 111 New Montgomery Street, San Francisco, is preparing plans and specifications in co-ordination with Dudley Deane & Associates, Mechanical Engineers, 182 2nd Street, San Francisco, and Nishkian & Nishkian, Structural Engineers, 1045 Sansome Street, San Francisco, for the construction of a 6-story Earth Science building to be built on the University of California campus at Berkeley.

The new facilities will provide headquarters for the Department of Geography, Geology, Palentology and the University's Seismographic station. Present plans call for completion of the new building in the summer of 1960.

MOTEL FOR
DOWNTOWN
SAN FRANCISCO

Construction has started on a $2,000,000 Motor Hotel to be built on the southeast corner of Van Ness Avenue and Filbert Street in San Francisco.

Facilities will include 200 rooms, outdoor swimming pool; 57 suites will have own kitchen and bars; stalls for 160 automobiles in four adjacent garages operated by the motel management.

August Waegemann, Structural Engineer, 251 Post Street, San Francisco, is in charge of design and construction.

NEW CITY HALL
BEING BUILT
IN ALHAMBRA

Architect William Allen, 6112 Wilshire Blvd., Los Angeles, has been commissioned to draft plans and specifications for construction of a city hall on a newly acquired site in Alhambra for the City of Alhambra.

AIRPORT TERMINAL
BUILDING PLANNED
FOR ONTARIO

Associated Architects Jay D. Harnish and Eugene W. Fickes, Jr., 222 E. "B" St., Ontario, have completed plans and specifications for construction of a 2-story window wall and aluminum frame terminal building at the Ontario International Airport.

The new structure will contain 25,000 sq. ft. of area; two walls will be rigid steel frame and reinforced concrete, one end wall to be tilt-up concrete and the other end wall metal stud and plaster, composition roofing, restrooms, kitchen, bar, restaurant. Estimated cost $428,723.

ADDITION TO
GLENDALE COMMUNITY
HOSPITAL

Architect Frank Mosher, Bank of America, Glendale, is completing preliminary plans for construction of a 50-bed addition to the Glendale Community Hospital for the Hospital Board of Directors.

The 3-story and basement structure will be type 1, reinforced concrete, composition roofing, concrete slab, air conditioning, elevators and dumbwaiters, metal windows, sun control louvers on a portion of the addition, and also includes changes in the existing boiler plant.

NEW LAKE ROYAL
APARTMENT HOUSE
FOR OAKLAND

Gerson Bakar of Oakland has announced plans for construction of an 11-story "U" shaped apartment building facing Lake Merritt in downtown Oakland.

Architect George Meu, 693 Mission Street, San Francisco, has been commissioned to design the building which will provide 2 and 3-bedroom units; a swimming pool on the lobby floor; sun roof, two elevators; two levels will be devoted to automobile parking, and construction

will be of glass, steel and concrete.

Structural Engineers for the project, which will cost an estimated $2,000,000, are Fuller & Welisch of San Francisco.

**NEW HIGH SCHOOL
PLANNED FOR
COLFAX**

Architect Lawrence G. Thomson, 125 W. 3rd Street, Chico, has completed plans and specifications for construction of a new Colfax High School at an estimated cost of $700,000.

The new facilities will be of wood frame construction and will include administra-

tion unit, classrooms, multi-unit room, kitchen, cafeteria, shops, library, gymnasium, and toilets. Construction will be in various stages.

**SWIMMING POOL
AND BATH HOUSE
FOR MERCED**

Architect Lloyd J. Fletcher, 217 W. Main Street, Visalia, has completed plans and specifications for construction of a concrete block bath house and swimming pool for the Calvin Crest Conference Camp Grounds, Prsbytery of The San Joaquin at Merced.

The bath house will have a wood plank roof and wood beams, while the swimming pool will be of concrete block and plaster concrete slab construction.

**ARCHITECT
SELECTED
CHAPEL**

Architect Leonard S. Mosias, 1488 Howard Street, San Francisco, has been selected by the Division of Architecture, Department of Public Works, State of California, to design and prepare plans for construction of a new Chapel building at the California Veterans' Home in Yountville.

**AIR LINE
REMODELS
OFFICES**

MacDonald, Young and Nelson, Inc., general contractors, 8907 Railroad Avenue, Oakland, have started remodeling of the building at 350 Post Street, San Francisco, to provide modern facilities for North American headquarters for Qantas

Empire Airways, Ltd., who will occupy two floors of the building.

The building remodeling, 5200 sq. ft. on the first floor, and 2200 sq. ft. on the second floor, was designed by the San Francisco offices of Skidmore, Owings and Merrill, Architects.

**THREADLESS ALUMINUM
STUD CAP EXHIBITS
RETENTION STRENGTH**

A new threadless stud cap of aluminum alloy which features a positive interference lock for high retention strength is announced by the Huck Mfg. Co. of Detroit, Michigan. It is designed for use with special threadless steel studs and is available for either ⅛" or 3/16" nominal diameter. A variety of shank lengths is provided.

The studs with which the Huck caps are used are not threaded, but have annual grooves, and is installed by tapping it onto the stud with hammer. Optimum interference fit insures positive cap retention in assembly. Although designed specifically for installing insulation, the new device provides a low-cost, high-speed fastening method for other applications where use of a fastener of moderate strength is satisfactory. Full information from the manufacturer Huck Mfg. Co., 2480 Bellevue Ave., Detroit, Mich.

**NEW BANK UNDER
CONSTRUCTION
IN STOCKTON**

The architectural firm of Mayo & De Wolf, Exchange Building, Stockton, is completing plans and specifications for construction of a new bank building in the

City of Stockton for the Stockton Savings and Loan Bank.

The new building will be 96 x 160 ft. on a one-half block site and will be 1 or 2-story with full basement; drive-in and off street parking facilities. Work is scheduled to start as soon as site has been cleared.

NEW HIGH SCHOOL PLANS READIED FOR SALINAS

Architect Jerome Kasavan, 7 Winham Street, Salinas, has completed plans and specifications for construction of a new high school building to be built in Salinas for the Salinas Union High School District at an estimated cost of $2,000,000.

The new facilities will include an administration area, 41 teacher's stations, 5 shops, gymnasium, lunch room, kitchen, little theatre with a stage, locker rooms, and toilets. The academic buildings will be of Type 1 construction, while the shop buildings and gymnasium will be of Type 3 construction.

GOLF COURSE CLUBHOUSE AT SACRAMENTO

The architectural firm of Rickey & Brooks, 2015 J Street, Sacramento, has completed drawings for construction of a new clubhouse to be built at the William Land Park golf course in Sacramento for the City of Sacramento at an estimated cost of $30,000.

The new building will include a clubhouse, pro-shop, snack bar, two rest rooms and allied facilities. Construction will be of reinforced grouted masonry walls, wood frame, composition roofing, porcelain enamel, terrazzo tile, and aluminum store front materials.

WOODLAND HILLS ICE SKATING RINK PLANNED

Architect Carl Maston and Richard Banta of 922 N. La Cienega Blvd., Los Angeles, are preparing drawings for construction of a vaulted arch type ice skating rink in Woodland Hills.

The 90x200-ft. building to have laminated trusses, a snack bar, forced air heating, rest rooms, plumbing and electrical work. Also a paved auto parking area.

SHOPPING CENTER BEING BUILT IN HONOLULU

Ground breaking for the first stage of Kamehameha Shopping Center in Hono-

lulu, recently inaugurated construction of a 56,000 sq. ft. building which will provide complete facilities for 10 tenants with the principal being a supermarket of 33,-000 sq. ft. area.

Decorative accents of the building designed by Victor Gruen, Associates, 135 So. Doheny Drive, Beverly Hills, California, will be specially formed concrete columns for the high roof portion with imported glazed ceramic tile forming durable store front surfaces between the major glass areas.

Estimated cost of the project is $1,000,-000.

GRAEME K. MacDONALD IS ELECTED PRESIDENT OF SPANNAL OF THE PACIFIC

Graeme K. MacDonald, of MacDonald, Young & Nelson, General Contractors, has been elected president of the Spannal of the Pacific, Inc., and Charles E. Nelson, General Contractor, was named vice president; with Frederick C. Whitman, president of the St. Francis Investment Company, San Francisco, being named a member of the board of directors.

Spannal of the Pacific, Inc., has exclusive franchise rights for five western states, Alaska and Hawaii, for a newly developed building construction product which provides a new method of providing horizontal shoring for concrete floor slabs. Feature of the product is its ability for adjustment to meet any given need, plus the fact that it can be reused.

NEW YMCA BUILDING VAN NUYS

The firm of Larsen Associates, Architects and Engineers (H. L. Kahn, E. Farrell, Architects, and B. L. Larsen, Consulting Engineer), 6255 Van Nuys Blvd., Van Nuys, are completing drawings for construction of a steel frame, brick and concrete block Youth Center YMCA building in Van Nuys.

The building will be 60x110 ft., composition roof, steel beams, aluminum sash, fixed plate glass, store doors, concrete slab, interior plaster, resilient flooring; and will contain game room, offices, toilets, meeting rooms, kitchen and lobby. Project includes paving and landscaping.

LOS ANGELES ARCHITECT EXHIBITS

Victor Gruen Associates, Los Angeles architectural firm, will be represented at the Annual Convention of the Congress of the Union of Architects in Moscow, Russia, by a photographic display of the $7,000,000 Valley Fair Shopping Center in San Jose, California.

This shopping center exhibit is part of an overall presentation prepared by The American Institute of Architects to stress the new aspects of American life and will be on display in Moscow for several weeks this summer.

ROBERT F. DICK ELECTED TO BOARD OF PYLE-NATIONAL

Robert F. Dick, executive vice president of George Fry & Associates, Los Angeles and New York management consulting firm, has been elected to the board of directors of the Pyle-National Company, of Chicago, Ill., manufacturers of electrical

will be of glass, steel and concrete.

Structural Engineers for the project, which will cost an estimated $2,000,000, are Fuller & Welisch of San Francisco.

NEW HIGH SCHOOL
PLANNED FOR
COLFAX

Architect Lawrence G. Thomson, 125 W. 3rd Street, Chico, has completed plans and specifications for construction of a new Colfax High School at an estimated cost of $700,000.

The new facilities will be of wood frame construction and will include administra-

tion unit, classrooms, multi-ur room, kitchen, cafeteria, shops, library, ymnasi-um, and toilets. Construction wl be in various stages.

SWIMMING POOL
AND BATH HOUSE
FOR MERCED

Architect Lloyd J. Fletcher, .17 W. Main Street, Visalia, has comple d plans and specifications for construct n of a concrete block bath house and imming pool for the Calvin Crest C ference Camp Grounds, Prsbytery of he San Joaquin at Merced.

The bath house will have a u d plank roof and wood beams, while the imming pool will be of concrete block al plaster concrete slab construction.

ARCHITECT
SELECTED
CHAPEL

Architect Leonard S. Mosias, 138 How-ard Street, San Francisco, has be selected by the Division of Architectur Depart-ment of Public Works, State of lifornia, to design and prepare plans fo onstruc-tion of a new Chapel building the Cali-fornia Veterans' Home in You ville.

AIR LINE
REMODELS
OFFICES

MacDonald, Young and N n, Inc., general contractors, 8907 Rail ad Ave-nue, Oakland, have started ren eling of the building at 350 Post Street an Fran-cisco, to provide modern fa ities for North American headquarters r Qantas

Empire Airways, Ltd., who will two floors of the building.

The building remodeling, 520 on the first floor, and 2200 sq. second floor, was designed by Francisco offices of Skidmore, C Merrill, Architects.

THREADLESS ALUMINU
STUD CAP EXHIBITS
RETENTION STRENGT

A new threadless stud alloy which features a p lock for high retentie nounced by the Huck N Michigan. It is design cial threadless steel st for either 1/8" or 3/1 A variety of shank le

T
u
g

and air conditioning products, according to a recent announcement by William C. Croft, president.

An authority in the fields of sales, marketing and general management, Dick has been in the management consulting field for 15 years.

GYPSUM COMPANY PRODUCES SOUND COLOR FILM

The U.S. Gypsum Company has just produced, and has for distribution to architects, engineers, contractors and groups interested in the construction industry, a twenty-two minute, sound, color film on the functions of modern acoustical ceilings.

The film illustrates in detail sound absorption and isolation, structure, fire protection, beauty, comfort and economy features which are primary considerations in selecting acoustical materials for ceilings of new structures and remodeling projects. Prints are available for showing by request to the United States Gypsum Company, Dept. 136, 300 W. Adams St., Chicago, Ill.

UC EXTENSION DESIGN COURSE SANTA BARBARA

A two-week course in Optimum Design of Structures will be offered from June 30 to July 11 at the Santa Barbara campus of the University of California at Goleta, sponsored by the UCLA department of engineering, University Extension and the Rand Corporation.

The course will consist of three daily lectures and general discussion sessions. In addition, experts in the fields of modern painting, architecture and city planning will discuss the contributions of their respective specialties to structural design in a series of evening presentations.

The courses should be of special interest to structural engineers, particularly those responsible for preliminary and advanced design decisions, and to material specialists engaged in research and development on structural materials.

CONVALESCENT AND REST HOME

Architect Gates Burrows of 1606 Bush Street, Santa Ana, is completing plans and specifications for construction of a rest and convalescent home in Garden Grove for Dr. John F. Renshaw.

The 1-story building will be of frame and stucco construction, slab floor, asphalt shingle roof, plaster interior and a 36-bed unit hospital facilities including baths, kitchens and a black-top auto parking area.

THE CITY THAT DIDN'T EXIST A MONTH AGO

Every 30 days the U.S. adds as many new Americans as live in Norfolk, Va.—creating brand-new wants and needs which must be satisfied.

What does this mean to you? It means greater opportunities than ever before—in all fields. Home construction is expected to double by 1975. Power companies plan to increase output 250% in the next 20 years to provide the power for scores of new labor-saving devices. Clothing suppliers predict a one-third increase in 7 years.

With 11,000 new citizen-consumers born every day, there's a new wave of opportunity coming.

7 BIG REASONS FOR CONFIDENCE IN AMERICA'S FUTURE

1. **More people** . . . Four million babies yearly. U.S. population has *doubled* in last 50 years! And our prosperity curve has always followed our population curve.

2. **More jobs** . . . Though employment in some areas has fallen off, there are *15 million* more jobs than in 1939—and there will be *22 million more* in 1975 than today.

3. **More income** . . . Family income after taxes is at an all-time high of $5300—is expected to pass $7000 by 1975.

4. **More production** . . . U.S. production *doubles* every 20 years. We will require millions more people to make, sell and distribute our products.

5. **More savings** . . . Individual savings are at highest level ever—*$340 billion*—a record amount available for spending.

6. **More research** . . . *$10 billion* spent each year will pay off in more jobs, better living, whole new industries.

7. **More needs** . . . In the next few years we will need *$500 billion* worth of schools, highways, homes, durable equipment. Meeting these needs will create new opportunities for everyone.

Add them up and you have the makings of another big upswing. Wise planners, builders and buyers will act *now* to get ready for it.

FREE! Send for this new 24-page illustrated booklet, "Your Great Future in a Growing America." Every American should know these facts. Drop a card today to: ADVERTISING COUNCIL, Box 10, Midtown Station, New York 18, N. Y.

(This space contributed as a public service by this magazine.)

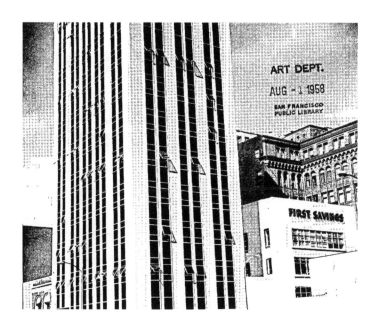

Vol. 214   No. 1

EDWIN H. WILDER
Editor

CONTRIBUTING EDITORS:

Education
SIDNEY W. LITTLE, Dean, College of Fine Arts and Department of Architecture, University of Arizona, Tucson, Arizona.

City Planning
CORWIN R. MOCINE, City Planning Engineer, Oakland, California

Urban Planning and Shopping Centers
FRANK EMERY COX, Sales Research & Business Development Analyst, Berkeley, California

Realty Development
ROY P. DRACHMAN, Subdivider and Realty Developer, Tucson, Arizona

School Planning
DR. J. D. McCONNEL, Stanford School Planning Dept., Palo Alto, California

Residential Planning
JEDD JONES, Architect, Boise, Idaho

General Architecture
ROBERT FIELD, Architect, Los Angeles, California

Engineering
JOHN A. BLUME, Consulting and Structural Engineer, San Francisco, California

Advertising
WILLIAM A. ULLNER, Manager
FRED JONES
Special Advertising

★

COVER PICTURE

FIRST SAVINGS BUILDING
Oakland, California

One of the newer remodeled commercial buildings of Oakland, designed by the late William B. Schirmer, Architect.

General Contractors were: Fentron Industries, Inc. (exterior curtain wall) and Gardner & Johnson (demolition and remodeling). The engineer was W. B. Clausen.

See page 16 for full details.

ARCHITECTS' REPORTS—
Published Daily
Archie MacCorkindale, Manager
Telephone DOuglas 2-8311

—*ARCHITECT & ENGINEER is indexed regularly by ENGINEERING INDEX, INC.; and ART INDEX*—

Contents for

JULY

ART DEPT.

AUG - 1 1958

SAN FRANCISCO
PUBLIC LIBRARY

THE OLDEST PROFESSIONAL MONTHLY BUSINESS MAGAZINE OF THE ELEVEN WESTERN STATES

ARCHITECT AND ENGINEER (Established 1905) is published on the 15th of the month by The Architect and Engineer, Inc., 68 Post St., San Francisco 4; Telephone EXbrook 2-7182. President, K. P. Kierulff; Vice-President and Manager, L. B. Penhorwood; Treasurer, E. N. Kierulff. — Los Angeles Office: Wentworth F. Green, 439 So. Western Ave., Telephone DUnkirk 7-8135 — Portland, Oregon, Office: R. V. Vaughn, 7117 Canyon Lane. — Entered as second class matter, November 2, 1905, at the Post Office in San Francisco, California, under the Act of March 3, 1879. Subscriptions United States and Pan America, $3.00 a year; $5.00 two years; foreign countries $5.00 a year; single copy, 50c.

. EDITORIAL NOTES .

NEW ENGINEERS

America's institutes of higher education with programs of less than four years' duration graduated some 11,742 students from engineering-related curricula during 1956.

These graduates were qualified for hard-to-fill technical positions in industry, where many of them might relieve professionally trained engineers for more creative, advanced assignments.

Total enrollment in engineering-related curricula in these schools at that time was 32,498 full time and 25,124 part-time students. Of these, 15,491 full time and 10,646 part-time students were enrolled for the first time during the year. These figures, covering 202 schools, of which 31 have at least one curricula accredited by Engineers Council for Professional Development, are the result of the first survey of "technical institute" enrollments ever made by the American Society for Engineering Education.

It is interesting to note that the total and first-time enrollment of full-time students is considerably larger than that of part-time students. The full-time students represent prospective additions to the labor force, whereas the majority of part-time students are already employed and do not represent new talent.

Subsequent reports can be expected to show developments and trends which can be used as a basis for meeting engineering manpower problems.

* * *

Lumber is the fifth largest employer among U. S. manufacturing industries. More than four out of five new houses are of wood frame construction.

* *

BUILDING INDUSTRY

Every plan advocated by economists and members of Congress to ease the "recession" has involved some phase of the construction industry and is an indication of the tremendous value of the industry, and its many ramifications, in our basic economy.

Here on the Pacific Coast the importance of the construction industry, light and heavy, is of considerable more value in any economic consideration than in most sectors of the nation. Industrial leaders have recognized the many advantages of product production in the West with the result that new industries, plants and facilities, are springing up in practically every community. This increased basic production has offered employment opportunities, with the result hundreds of thousands of families have moved to the West Coast.

Economy-wise, these new plants and facilities, and workers and families present an entirely new market to a multitude of products, in and out of the construction industry.

There is no question but that a tremendous opportunity awaits everyone who, in any way, serves the construction industry; the question is: "Will you see and take advantage of such an opportunity?"

* * *

Let businessmen supply leadership in marshalling public support and we'll soon have a military establishment capable of meeting any threat:—U.S. Chamber of Commerce.

* * *

WHO IS UNEMPLOYED — AND WHERE

To place unemployment in proper perspective, it is first necessary to separate facts from oratory. While it is not realistic to deny the individual tragedy which unemployment can cause, neither is it correct to assume that the unemployed are equally distributed among the 48 states. On the contrary, official figures disclose that eight states are bearing the preponderant share of total insured unemployment. Seven of these states, when visualized on a map, present a clearly discernible unemployment "belt" from Illinois eastward through Michigan, Ohio, Pennsylvania, New Jersey, New York and finally Massachusetts. California is the eighth of these states which together account for three out of every five of the nation's insured unemployed. In this context, comments concerning "nation-wide unemployment" lose much of their scare element.

Over one-third of presently unemployed workers come from factory jobs, about one-sixth from wholesale or retail trade, another sixth from construction, and the remainder principally from transportation, communication and public utilities.

Considering where the bulk of unemployment is, and the kinds of jobs involved, large-scale conservation programs offer little hope. The jobs which would gradually be opened would not be where most of the unemployment is concentrated. In addition, the nature of the work presents relatively few jobs in which the skills of the unemployed could be efficiently utilized.

* * *

It takes two-man years of labor to construct the average house.

* * *

HIGHER CONSTRUCTION COSTS

Substantial wage increases in construction workers' pay in many cities recently has raised June construction costs to an all record high, according to cost index reports.

. The index for June stands at the new high of 757.31 and is 5 per cent higher than the same period a year ago. Building costs are also at a new record level of 521.09, 3.4 per cent higher than a year ago.

Records show that most of the wage hikes are for skilled labor, the largest boost being in New York City where bricklayers received a 55-cent plus package deal over the next two years.

NEWS and COMMENT ON ART

CALIFORNIA PALACE OF THE LEGION OF HONOR

The California Palace of the Legion of Honor, Lincoln Park, San Francisco, under the direction of Thomas Carr Howe, Jr., has arranged a number of outstanding exhibitions and special events, designed to appeal to the many vacationists in the Bay Area.

Special Exhibitions: "The Fourth International Hallmark Art Award Exhibition"; "Paintings" by C. Frederick Hobbs; "Paintings" by N. C. Wyeth.

The ACHENBACH FOUNDATION for Graphic Arts is featuring "Artists at Work."

Special Events: Organ Recital each Saturday and Sunday at 3:00 P.M., featuring Mr. Richard Purvis and Mr. Ludwig Altman; Educational activities—six-weeks summer session of art classes for children and juniors will continue through July.

The Museum is open daily.

SAN FRANCISCO MUSEUM OF ART

The San Francisco Museum of Art, War Memorial Building, Civic Center, under the direction of Dr. Grace L. McCann Morley, is featuring the following special exhibits and events during July:

Exhibitions: The Art of Marquet; Contemporary Images, featuring the work of Margaret Peterson, Sonia Gechtoff and other painters from the San Francisco Bay Area; Bradley Walker Tomlin Memorial Exhibition, a retrospective exhibition of paintings by the late Bradley Walker Tomlin, organized jointly by the Whitney Museum and the Art Galleries of the University of California at Los Angeles. Contains paintings surveying the artist's work from about 1928 to the time of his death in 1953; Illustrations of Children's Books; Calligraphy by the Venerable Hodo Tobase; Six Japanese Painters, a Smithsonian Institution Traveling Exhibition; and the work of Alberto Burri.

Special Events: Lecture tours, based on current exhibitions, Sundays at 3 o'clock; Wednesday Art Programs, at 8:30; and recessed for the summer are Adventures in Drawing and Painting, Children's Saturday Morning Art Classes, and Studio Art for the Layman.

The Museum is open daily.

KATE NEAL KINLEY MEMORIAL FELLOWSHIP

The Board of Trustees of the University of Illinois has announced the twenty-seventh annual consideration of candidates for the Kate Neal Kinley Memorial Fellowship. Winner — David Ward-Steinman, composer of Alexandria, Louisiana.

This Fellowship was established in 1931 by the late President-Emeritus David Kinley in memory of his wife and in recognition of her influence in promoting the Fine Arts and similar interests upon the University of Illinois campus.

The Fellowship yields the sum of one thousand five hundred dollars to be used by the recipient toward defraying the expenses of advanced study of the Fine Arts in America or abroad.

Steinman has made many appearances as pianist and conductor, and has also performed bass and clarinet in various orchestras and symphonic bands. He plans to study musical composition in France.

OAKLAND ART MUSEUM

The Oakland Art Museum, 1000 Fallon Street, under the direction of Paul Mills, Curator, is presenting a number of special exhibitions during this month designed to fit into the summertime-vacation theme. Among them are:

Marsden Hartley Paintings. Hartley, pioneer modern American artist who died in 1943, is recognized for his rich, bold handling of American subjects, and this exhibition contains 20 paintings of the Southwest done between 1908 and 1920. They are from the Collection of Ione and Hudson Walker, courtesy of the University of Minnesota Gallery, and the Roswell Museum in New Mexico.

Paintings by Ray Boynton, for 25 years an art teacher at the University of California. They range from 1909 award winner in the museum collection to many from the decade preceding his death in 1951.

The Hayward Art Association's annual juried exhibition of paintings, for the most part realist in character, by members.

Ancient jewelry of the Near East, a collection of necklaces, earrings and other ornaments from archeological excavations in Egypt and other countries of the near East. Lent by the Susette Khayat Gallery of New York City.

Special Events: Include summer art classes for children and adults.

The William Keith Gallery, main Library Building, is currently exhibiting Keith Treasures from St. Mary's College and the Southwest Museum.

The Museum is open daily.

M. H. deYOUNG MEMORIAL MUSEUM

The M. H. deYoung Memorial Museum, Golden Gate Park, San Francisco, under the direction of

Walter Heil, is presenting a number of special exhibits and special events during the month of July, including:

EXHIBITIONS: "FRESH PAINT—1958", a selective survey of Western Painting compiled and arranged through the courtesy of the Committee for Art at Stanford University, Palo Alto; "WATERCOLORS" by Lois Langhorst; "SMALL GREEK BRONZES and RENAISSANCE MEDALS and PLAQUETTES", from the Collection of Sigmund Morgenroth of Santa Barbara.

SPECIAL EVENTS: Classes in Art Enjoyment, and Art Classes for the Children will be resumed during July.

The Museum is open Daily.

CALIFORNIA STATE FAIR ART SHOW ANNOUNCED

A grand total of $11,385 in prizes will be awarded this year to winners in the annual Art and Photogra-
(See page 30)

M. H. DE YOUNG MEMORIAL MUSEUM

Golden Gate Park   San Francisco

CLASSIC LANDSCAPE WITH FIGURES AT SUNSET

By CLAUDE GELLEE, called CLAUDE LORRAIN

French, 1600-1682

The Samuel H. Kress Collection

JULY, 1958

ONE OF NATION'S MOST MODERN HEAVY CLAY PRODUCTS PLANTS

NEW MICA PLANT
GLADDING McBEAN & COMPANY
GETS PROGRESS AWARD

SPOKANE, WASHINGTON

Located seventeen miles from Spokane, at Mica, Washington, the new two-million-dollar plant represents the most modern and highly automated heavy clay products plant in existance.

The new plant embraces nine rigid-frame steel buildings, covering an area of almost 200,000 square feet. These facilities include the most modern equipment for raw material preparation and the pressing, drying and firing of heavy clay products.

The clay preparation department includes facilities for two methods of batching. The stiff mud mixes are batched by blending the various clays together and placing them in apron feeders from which they are conveyed to the dry pan for grinding. After grinding, the batch is then ready for screening. For dry press mixes, each clay is ground and screened separately before being batched by weight.

Three Stiff Mud Lines

The plant contains three stiff mud lines. One line serves three kiln cars. Another line is equipped with
(See page 30)

PROGRESS AWARD: C. W. Planje, Gladding McBean & Co., president (left), receives Spokane Chamber of Commerce "Progress Award" from Joseph W. Kipper, Chamber president, while Governor Rosellini of Washington looks on.

MODERN
SERVICE
STATION

STANFORD
UNIVERSITY
CAMPUS

The new General Petroleum service station on the Stanford University campus at Palo Alto, California, is featured prominently in the film 'Industrial Parks, U.S.A." currently being shown at the Brussels, Belgium, Exposition.

Designed by Welton Becket, F.A.I.A. and Associates, San Francisco architects and engineers, the structure represents the successful attempt to combine beauty with normal utility of a service station. It is also designed to harmonize with the nearby Stanford Shopping Center.

Made of black tubular steel, red glazed brick, white porcelain enamel and plate glass, the station carries out the traditional colors of the operating oil company.

The main building—with office, salesroom, lubrication and wash areas, and restrooms—rests on a low rectangular grid of black tubular steel, which is also used for the vertical grid columns. The tubular col-

umns are arranged on a six foot module with plate glass filling most sections and the red glazed brick accenting the remainder. A white porcelain fascia forms a gleaming strip around the upper portion of the building.

A large free-standing metal canopy protects the pump stations which are also framed in black tubular steel to carry out further the motif of the main building.

Red glazed brick is appropriately used to form a separate enclosure beside the main building to screen vending machines, rubbish disposal and storage for service station accessories. Both structures cover a total of 1,500 square feet.

Landscaped areas have been set aside to aid the attractiveness of this unique station, and black top-rails and vertical posts have been used in the fencing behind and to the side of the station.

ASSISTANT STATE ARCHITECT
FOR CALIFORNIA RETIRES
AFTER THIRTY-SIX YEARS

P. T. Poage, for a third of a century Assistant State Architect of California, will retire on August 1st. During the 36 years he has worked in the Division

of Architecture of the California State Department of Public Works, Poage has seen the State building construction under his charge mount to a total of $1,000,000,000.

After his first four years in architectural designing positions, he became Assistant State Architect in charge of design and planning, a title he has retained since 1926.

P. T. POAGE
Retires

C. M. Gilliss, State Director of Public Works, in commenting on Poage's retirement said that "during his years supervising California's building program, he developed better and less expensive ways of building the State's different correctional and mental institutions, office facilities, colleges, and fairs, as well as lesser works."

Poage was also credited by Gilliss with "a big share in establishing the techniques California now uses in determining the scope of building projects, in programming space requirements, and in controlling costs of planning and building."

Projects which make up the billion dollar total Poage has supervised have ranged from building a bleacher for an athletic field to developing a $20,000,000 new plant for a State institution.

Poage was born in Bolivar, Missouri, January 28, 1896 and came to California in 1907. He received his Bachelor of Arts degree in architecture at the University of California at Berkeley in 1918.

(See page 32)

A small country "retreat" on a nearby hill had caught the attention of Mr. and Mrs. Bruce Johnstone. Mr. Johnstone was a member of a large law firm in

WILLIAM CLEMENT AMBROSE,
Architect

RESIDENCE

Mr. and Mrs.
BRUCE JOHNSTONE

INVERNESS, CALIFORNIA
(Marin County)

Chicago; Mrs. Johnstone was a member of a pioneer San Francisco family. For several years the Johnstones had spent the summers in Northern California and had decided that, upon retirement, they would live in Inverness.

When the Johnstones had selected the site of their California home, they got in touch with the architect of the Inverness place which they had admired and engaged him for the design and supervision of their new dwelling. They had particularly admired the merging of the house and the site of the "retreat" both

(See page 10)

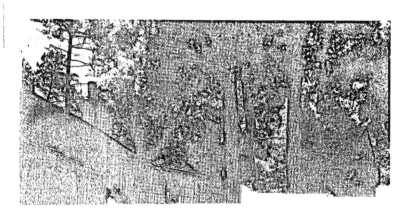

THE WORK OF
WM. CLEMENT AMBROSE

FELLOW, AMERICAN INSTITUTE OF ARCHITECTS

William Clement Ambrose, San Francisco architect, is a native Californian, being born in Tulare, California, on November 22, 1888, and until his retirement this year was a partner in the firm of Wm. Clement Ambrose, A.I.A. & Eldridge T. Spencer, F.A.I.A., San Francisco.

Award of Fellowship in The American Institute of Architects was given to Mr. Ambrose for his long record of "Service to the Institute." He was a member of the California State Board of Architectural Examiners from 1944 to 1952, and its pres-

WM. CLEMENT AMBROSE
Fellow, A.I.A.

ident in 1945 and 1949; past chairman of the Building Industry Conference Board; president of the Northern California Chapter A.I.A. in 1948 and chairman of the California Council of Architects A.I.A. Fees Committee in 1952-53.

W. Clement Ambrose received his B.S. from the University of California in 1910 and began his architectural career in the offices of Willis Polk, San Francisco architect, in 1911-13; the next two years were spent in study and travel in Europe and New York; from 1915 to 1927 Ambrose was with John Reid, Jr., Architect, San Francisco, taking time out to serve in the U.S. Army for two years during World War I.

Entering private practice of architecture in 1927, Ambrose opened offices in San Francisco, and in 1943 formed the partnership with Eldridge T. Spencer, Architect, maintaining such offices until his retirement from active practice of architecture this year.

(See next page)

KENNETH C.
HAMILTON
HOUSE

INVERNESS,
CALIFORNIA

WM. CLEMENT
AMBROSE,
Architect

... WM. CLEMENT AMBROSE, A.I.A.

(From preceding page)

Time was taken from practice to engage in many allied activities during the year: Lecturer in U.C. Extension, Instructor Summer Session, Architect for the Berkeley Board of Education, and in 1945 was given the Meritorious Civilian Service Award by the U. S. Navy.

Some of the work engaged in by the firm included buildings at Stanford University, University of California, San Francisco School Department, Yosemite Park, San Francisco Public Housing Authority.

JOHNSTONE RESIDENCE
(From page 8)

in relation to the contours of the property and the choice of materials of the construction, and desired the same qualities in their larger house. A winter of exchanges of ideas and sketches between Chicago and San Francisco resulted in final plans in the spring of 1932 and the construction of the house in that year.

An excellent contractor, A. F. Mattock, and an equally competent foreman in charge of the construction resulted in an accurate and skillful realization of the plans and specifications—and at 1932 prices. The house is of wood inside and out, with Douglas fir framing, hand split redwood shakes on the exterior and natural color redwood interior wall finish. The rock fireplaces and the exterior rock work are of material quarried in the Mt. Diablo district of Contra Costa County, California.

"ICELAND" Skating Rink, Berkeley, California ... Wm. Clement Ambrose, Architect

Wm. Clement Ambrose and Eldridge T. Spencer, Architects

YERBA BUENA PLAZA • Low Rent Housing

SAN FRANCISCO, CALIFORNIA

The Yerba Buena Plaza, Low Rent Housing Project, was completed in 1956. It consists of five concrete buildings which are twelve stories in height and one building of five stories. The six new buildings contain 608 dwelling units which have one to three bedrooms in each unit, which consists of living room-dining room-kitchenette combinations, and a bathroom for each dwelling unit. The project location is near the geographical center of the city and replaces old wooden "flat" buildings, many of which had degenerated to a slum condition.

WM. CLEMENT AMBROSE,

Fellow, American Institute

of Architects

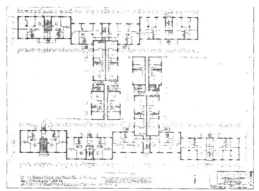

Typical Floor

ELDRIDGE T.
SPENCER
and
WILLIAM
CLEMENT
AMBROSE,
Architects

STERN HALL DORMITORY
STANFORD UNIVERSITY
PALO ALTO, CALIFORNIA

Stern Hall Dormitory, Stanford University, California is a composition of eight concrete buildings joined together around landscaped courts, and which provide living accommodations for men students, two in a room. There is a lavatory in each bedroom, and shower and toilet rooms on each floor of each unit.

Dining facilities and lounges are provided on the ground floor so arranged as to permit separation of units or joint meetings of adjacent units. The courts are landscaped and paved, and larger recreation areas have been provided adjacent to the dormitory.

12

WM. CLEMENT AMBROSE, Architect, Fellow, A.I.A.
(Wm. Clement Ambrose and Eldridge T. Spencer, Architects)

HUNT HALL

Plant Science Building

UNIVERSITY OF CALIFORNIA — DAVIS, CALIFORNIA

A two story and partial basement "V" shaped building of concrete construction containing laboratories for research and instruction in agronomy, plant pathology and related agricultural subjects. The building contains classrooms, lecture halls and experimental and demonstration laboratories for student instruction, and smaller laboratories where original research on agricultural problems, agricultural economics, chemistry of soils, etc. are studied and releases prepared for the information and guidance of the great farming and farm products industries of California. A lecture hall accessible from the exterior and distinct from the general circulation of the building is useful for farm conferences, lectures to larger groups, etc. at times when the main corridors are closed as well as for larger meetings of faculty and students.

WM. CLEMENT AMBROSE, Architect
Fellow, American Institute of Architects

JOHN McLAREN ELEMENTARY SCHOOL

SAN FRANCISCO, CALIFORNIA

The program for this school plant posed a difficult problem for the architect. Two sites were available—one in a hollow to the north of Sunnyvale Avenue, and the other on the side of the hill south of Sunny-vale Avenue. The low site also had some problems, but to build in a hole was not inspiring. Fortunately, the consultant for the school department, Nicholas Engelhardt, saw eye to eye with the architect, and the south side site was chosen, even though there was a difference in elevation of more than ninety feet from the lower to the upper corner of the property.

A system of terraces was decided upon for the various units of the school. This necessitated large cuts on the south and west sides of the property and engineered fill for practically all of the area to be covered by the buildings and play yards. But it did make possible an east exposure for the classrooms, shelter from the gale-like west winds for the classroom windows and a magnificent view over San Francisco Bay from the classrooms and play yards.

Cooperation between the school authorities, the school consultant and the architect has provided a clean-cut design, separate play areas for the children of different ages, an inspiring outlook from the school and colorful treatment of the classroom wall surfaces.

Wm. Clement Ambrose and Eldridge T. Spencer, Architects

STRUCTURAL ENGINEERS OF
SOUTHERN CALIFORNIA HEAR
CONCRETE REPORT

Members of the Structural Engineers Association were given a progress report on prestressed concrete at their dinner meeting held early this month in the Rodger Young Auditorium, Los Angeles. Edward K. Rice, partner of T. Y. Lin and Associates, gave a comprehensive report. Mr. Rice is a well-known authority in the field of prestressed concrete.

In the past year, prestressed concrete has taekn off its laboratory coat, put on working clothes and has gone to work. Fire rating tests, publication of recommended practice and advances in the economical use of prestressed concrete have made this structural system more available for common use.

High points in recent developments were presented by Mr. Rice. These developments have established basis for fire insurance ratings, codification, low-cost construction and improved structural behavior.

The first standard ASTM fire tests on prestressed concrete were held in April at the Fire Underwriters Laboratory in Chicago and were witnessed by Mr. Rice. The test results exceeded expectations. Two separate tests were made. The first consisted of a double-tee floor system on precast, pretensioned members with two-inch concrete cover on the steel tendons. Design live load was placed on the full scale specimen per ASTM standards and the furnace was ignited on the underside of the deck. After a two-hour exposure to heat no structural damage was noted.

Minor spalling of concrete cover along one edge of the beam stem occurred almost immediately after the furnace was ignited. The spalling apparently was caused by the use of green members that still contained a large amount of moisture. The moisture turned into steam and caused the concrete to spall. Test results were unaffected by this occurrence.

The second test consisted of a hollow-core slab deck eight inches thick that was precast and pretensioned. One and one-half inch concrete cover was provided over the steel tendons. At the end of a two-hour exposure the slab members were behaving well with no spalling and no increase in deflections. It was then decided to continue the test. At the end of four hours exposure the slab still successfully supported the design live load and passed the standard hose stream test. The stream test is conducted at the end of the fire exposure and consists of spraying water through a fire hose on the side exposed to the heat. The test was completed by loading the panels with two times the design live load 24 hours after the start of the test. Thus the standard four-hour fire test was passed very successfully. The complete results of the tests will be published soon.

A material that is to be readily accepted and widely used requires design and fabrication standards. This need has been satisfied by the recent publications by a joint ACI-ASCE committee of a report titled, "Tentative Recommendations for Prestressed Concrete."

Mr. Rice pointed out economies that have been effected to bring down the cost of prestressed concrete. Members that are made continuous over supports mean a saving in the weight of prestressing steel. Wider use of off-site precast elements that are adaptable to mass-production methods mean lower costs. Standardization of shapes and sizes by manufacturers can effect further savings. Several national committees are now working toward standardization of pre-stressed components.

Structural behavior of prestressed concrete has been improved by the present availability of consistent quality of materials. High strength concrete, 4000 to 5000 psi, can be delivered throughout the country. Casting yards can provide 3500 psi concrete at 16 hours with steam curing and a 7000 psi concrete at 28 days. Pre-stress wire is being produced with uniform quality. A national committee of manufacturers' representatives is preparing an ASTM specification for high-strength wire and rods.

Prestressing of floor and roof slabs is used to control deflections and provide watertight decks without the use of a waterproof membrane. Providing prestressed wires in lift slabs permits the slabs to be cast flat and remain flat after being lifted. Concrete parking decks are prestressed sufficiently to assure a leakproof surface.

Mr. Rice provided slides showing recent projects in prestressed concrete. Several long span bridges were shown, one of which was continuous for two spans and saved $1.00 per square foot of bridge deck over the cost of simple spans.

Precasting beds of manufacturers in Petaluma, San Diego, Sun Valley and Los Angeles were shown. Precast members for roof spans up to 120 feet are available. Mr. Rice noted that a 100-foot span can be roofed as economically as a 40-foot span.

A prestressed roof shell, cantilevering 90 feet, at a race track in Caracas, Venezuela, was shown. The shell is only 3 inches thick. Every downward force in the shell exerted by gravity is resisted by an upward force provided by prestressing. Henry Layne was the Structural Engineer on the project. T. Y. Lin and Associates were consultants.

SAN FRANCISCO ARCHITECTURAL CLUB

Marshall McDonnel was the principal speaker at a recent regular meeting.

Four Architectural Club members were among those recently passing the California State Board of Architectural Examiners and are now licensed to practice architecture in this state: Lyle Hood, Bob Lustig, Bob MacFarlane and Mel Rojko.

In exactly one hundred working days, the 10-story building on the hub corner of 17th and Broadway in downtown Oakland, has been completely transformed from the architectural style of 1914, when the building was originally erected, to modern functional design of simplified beauty and one of the city's growing skyline of "modern look" buildings.

The building, which was formerly known as the Western Professional Building, was purchased a year ago by the First Savings and Loan Association, which is located next door on 17th Street, and the firm's facilities are now expanded from this adjacent property to include the entire ground floor.

Renamed the First Savings Building, the facilities will represent the enlarged home office of the Savings institution headed by Stuart Davis, president.

According to Mr. Davis, head of the $65 million savings and loan institution with six offices in the Bay Area, it was determined to modernize the building with a new facade inasmuch as the location is almost the true center of Oakland's top rental area. Updating it to the design of today's architectural developments was decided, however, only after the building was thoroughly engineered and found to agree basically with present-day structural standards.

New architectural beauty has been captured with a skin of sand-color porcelain enamel over steel, complemented with aluminum metal trim around charcoal-tinted plate glass windows. This new look covers the entire building exterior of 10 stories. Flood lights will illuminate it at night.

The First Savings offices on the ground floor, which

GENERAL CONTRACTORS:

FENTRON INDUSTRIES, INC.
(Exterior Curtain Wall)

GARDNER & JOHNSON
(Demolition and Remodeling)

VIEW OF BUILDING

17th and Broadway in Oakland, prior to remodeling into a modern structure.

FIRST SAVINGS . . .

STUART DAVIS, President of First Savings & Loan Association, viewing new area.

extend through and include the former office, which is now entered from Broadway, is finished with marble-topped walnut counters, with coral, green and brown predominating the color atmosphere in the walls, tile flooring and carpeting. The acoustical ceiling is translucent plastic.

The outstanding feature of the first floor is the twelve - foot windows, separated only by marble columns, revealing the entire lobby and savings area to the street.

Westminster Carillons have been installed on the roof, which toll the hour during the day.

The new quarters has a translucent plastic ceiling which provides shadowless, ideal working light. Carpeting and large comfortable sofas in tweed mixture of brown, black and sand, repeat the colors of the black granite columns and walnut counters. Walls are painted a soft spruce green and the marquee, from the sidewalk to the inside, is a deeper tone of spruce.

The focal point of the room is the Federal Home Loan Bank and Federal Insurance Corporation insignia. This great double seal, eight by ten feet in oxidized metal was designed and executed by Don Clever of San Francisco.

In the back of the room, looking through two twelve-foot arches, one sees the original quarters done

INTERIOR—View from front entrance, showing decorative finishing and overhead lighting system and air conditioning.

MAIN OFFICE

Showing a portion
of the attractive
customer service
facilities area.

in complementary colors of soft coral and mahogany.

On the lower floors, besides ample lounge and dressing rooms for men and women employees, a large dining area has been created. Besides complete kitchen facilities, it is decorated like a French sidewalk cafe, with black and white floors, red and pink walls, striped canopy, and a street scene mural painted by George E. Dean. This room also has a full ceiling of translucent plastic.

This remodeling program has added 2600 square feet to the original office space, increasing facilities to expedite service to First Savings' thousands of savings and home loan customers.

Many skins and various treatments of the facade were studied before it was decided by the late William E. Schirmer, architect, that an exterior covering of light weight aluminum and steel would be the most practical to attach to the existing brick surface. The cost was estimated at $150,000 and the contract let to Architectural Porcelain Constructors.

Extensive tests proved that the brick walls could hold the facing by expansion anchors, and continued tests were made during the erection of the facade to substantiate these findings. The anchors actually tested to three times the load they would ultimately carry.

The curtain wall was kept four inches

FIRST SAVINGS . . .

EMPLOYEES' REST and LUNCH ROOM . . . carefree decor for atmosphere of relaxation and modern appearance.

from the existing brick wall to eliminate as much chip-ping of the ornamental trim as possible, and to allow space for the installation of supporting steel channels. Every precautionary measure was taken to prevent electrolysis between the steel and aluminum.

To insure waterproofing between panels, elastic thiocol was used to allow expansion and contraction due to temperature differential.

A definite repeat pattern in the existing windows of the original building, made it readily possible to pre-fabricate the projected windows, including spandrels of tempered colored glass. Long vertical mullions —sand-color porcelain enamel—extend from above the marquee to the parapet. Joining between these

mullions and the windows are continuous aluminum sections. Windows are charcoal tinted, glare-resistant glass.

On the interior, after the exterior was all completed, it was a simple matter to tie each existing window frame to the corresponding new window by removing the old window sash and encasing the opening with a hardwood panel and formica sill. In this way it was not necessary to remove the old frames, which would have caused the necessity of repainting each entire office. When designing the curtain wall, an aluminum channel was secured to the inside of the window wall to receive the hardwood panel.

The modernization program of the First Savings Building also calls for two new automatic elevators at a cost of $100,000 that will travel at the rate of 350 feet per minute. One of the three existing elevators will be retained for freight.

In addition to the new facing and modernization expenditures that have created one of the most desirable office addresses in Oakland, First Savings has exercised an expansion program which added 2600 square feet to its Oakland home office at a cost of $100,000. The entire ground floor of the new building is now occupied by First Savings in addition to the ground and mezzanine floors of the adjacent four-story building, also owned by First Savings and Loan Association.

Inasmuch as business was continued without interruption during the one hundred working days it took to complete the expansion portion of the program, no formal opening to the public was scheduled.

In the interest of Oakland's urban renewal program, the growth of Oakland and the development of downtown business properties, First Savings, according to Davis, is proud to be among those business enterprises to recognize the potential of this metropolitan center and to grow with it. "We feel a civic pride in our contribution," said Davis.

Over 20 years ago First Savings opened its Oakland office in the mid-

WITH
LIFETIME
PORCELAIN
ENAMEL

FIRST SAVINGS BUILDING, Oakland, California
Architect: William Edward Schirmer, A.I.A., (Deceased) Oakland
Structural Engineer: W. B. Clausen, Oakland
Porcelain Enamel Panels, Sign Letters at top of building:
  Manufacture and erection by APCO

FIRST SAVINGS . . .

dle of the block on 17th Street between Broadway and Franklin. Eight years later these quarters were out-grown which resulted in the purchase of the adjacent four-story building, using the ground floor for offices. Later a mezzanine floor was built for executive offices. The next move was to purchase the next adjacent building, which is the new present headquarters.

Other First Savings offices are located in Berkeley, Alameda, San Leandro, Walnut Creek and San Francisco.

ENTIRE SIXTH FLOOR is now occupied by Jeff Branscom, and designed for facilities of general insurance agency.

NOVEL CONSTRUCTION TECHNIQUES

By F. FRANK MAMMINI

Novel construction techniques were employed in erecting the new curtain wall system on the remodeled First Savings & Loan Association Building in Oakland, California. The 9-story aluminum curtain wall system was erected directly over the existing masonry facade of the building with no interior demolition taking place to disturb the business activity in the

FOYER

Designed to
create atmosphere
of homeyness—
carpeted floor,
frosted glass
office partitions,
and excellent overhead
lighting.

building. Total time for the remodeling of the facade was only 14 weeks.

The curtain wall, with its porcelain enamel covered vertical columns and panels of Spandrelite, was designed by the late architect William Edward Schirmer, A.I.A., of Oakland. Fentron Industries, Incorporated, of San Francisco and Seattle, manufactured and erected the curtain walls.

VIEW OF
SAN FRANCISCO SHOWROOM

LIGHTING
FIXTURE
DISPLAY

BENEFITS PUBLIC
AND INDUSTRY

Showroom styling strikes the keynote at the home office of Incandescent Supply Company in San Francisco, as well as the branches located in Redding, Sacramento, Oakland, San Jose, Fresno and Los Angeles, all of which boast sparkling lighting fixture showrooms.

Extensive redecorating and remodelling, and in the cases of Sacramento and San Jose moves to new quarters, have resulted in seven of the most modern showrooms in the country.

Established in 1913, Incandescent Supply Co. has long felt that proper surroundings are extremely important to the sale of lighting fixtures. Showrooms that compliment merchandise also compliment the customer and set a buying mood.

As stated by president Marvin H. Jankelson, "We at Incandescent feel proper lighting is a business carrying tremendous overtones of public importance. Though people are constantly becoming more aware of the right way to illuminate for various purposes there is still much to be done. We think

ABOVE: Marvin H. Jankelson.

AT LEFT: B. E. Buerkel, John F. Helms, M. H. Jankelson, Francis E. Showalter and Joseph Newland.

one of the best places to start is right at the business source of purchase. Display lighting fixtures well and they assume their rightful importance."

Modern Showrooms provide a framework for the active pursuit of merchandising and marketing. Service to the trade is more complete in surroundings designed to accentuate highly visual displays.

Incandescent Supply Co. stocks a complete line of electrical products in addition to lighting fixtures. The showrooms, however, have proved the key to better lighting fixture departments.

The growth of importance of good lighting is definitely on the rise. Display of lighting must keep abreast of the uses for which improved lighting is intended.

Incandescent Supply Co. has, through their showroom display facilities, taken the position that showing off lighting fixtures to best advantage keeps trust with manufacturers, dealers, the general public and the concepts of good business.

ARCHITECT RICHARD J. NEUTRA, FAIA, GIVEN INTERNATIONAL RECOGNITION

Richard J. Neutra, FAIA, architect and consultant of Los Angeles, has been awarded honorary membership in the Venice Academy of the College of the Academicians of Venice, an institute founded in 1750 and recently renewed.

Recognition was given to Architect Neutra for his "creative genius" in the field of architecture which has won international recognition.

In addition the city of Vienna honored Neutra with the "Prize for Architecture," an honor bestowed each year for outstanding artistic achievement in the realm of architecture, painting, sculpture, music and poetry.

Neutra was also recently nominated a director of planning and will serve as consultant to guide the planning and reconstruction of the Accademia di Belle Arti di Venzia, Collegio Degli Accademici, and as further recognition of his two-thirds of a century in the practice of architecture, his firm of Neutra and Alexander has been commissioned by the National Park Service in Washington, D.C., to design the Shrine of the Nation, the Lincoln Memorial Building, on the hallowed grounds of the Battlefield of Gettysburg, where the great, prophetic statesman pronounced his immortal address.

SAN DIEGO CHAPTER AIA

"School for Johnny" and "What Is a Home?" were the subjects of discussion at a recent meeting supplemented by the showing of motion pictures.

Herb Ringer, Chief City Building Inspector for the City of San Diego, also gave a brief talk of subjects related to his office and the practice of architecture.

New members: Ronald Keith Davis, Dale William Naegle and Robert Stephen Paul, corporate members.

J. MILTON HAGLER, *President*
Tay-Holbrook, Inc., Plumbing Supplies
Headquarters, San Francisco

AMERICAN INSTITUTE OF ARCHITECTS ANNUAL NATIONAL CONVENTION

Secretary of the Treasury Robert B. Anderson was the keynoter for the American Institute of Architects' annual convention in Cleveland, Ohio, July 7-11, according to an announcement by Leo Chatelain, AIA president.

Secretary Anderson's opening address was followed by the architectural keynote speech of Philadelphia architect Vincent G. Kling, and at the luncheon the same day, Harlan Hatcher, president of the University of Michigan, spoke on "The Western Reserve—Part of Our Heritage."

Specialists serving on panels discussed such practical matters as how to make better cost estimates, where to find construction money, developing today's building program, working with the homebuilder, urban planning, office organization, chapter affairs, and "Professional Status — Your Most Valuable Asset."

Because the architect's services are expanding and the demands upon him are greater and more diverse than ever before, the convention program was geared towards providing a deeper understanding of the economic forces of the nation that are influencing environmental patterns.

SANTA CLARA AND SANTA CRUZ COUNTIES CHAPTER AIA

William W. Wurster, Dean of the College of Architecture, University of California at Berkeley, was the principal speaker at the June 24th meeting held in the Stanford Room at Rickey's in Palo Alto, and it being the annual Draftsmen's Meeting, numerous comments of the speaker were directed to draftsmen.

It was announced that the July meeting would be a joint meeting with the Monterey Chapter and the Administrative Committee of the California Council, while the August meeting will be the annual meeting with the Engineers Society.

Recent new members include: Richard Norman Tipton and Frank Raphael Gonsalves, Junior Associates.

EAST BAY CHAPTER AIA

'What's A House?" the AIA motion picture film showing the evolution of the American residence from "carpenter classic" to residence of the future,

and presenting some of the problems of home building and the aid an architect can give; and the AIA film, "A School for Johnny," showing that the school building is a bargain today—a product of teamwork between educators and architects—were shown at the July meeting held in Pland's in Oakland. Preliminary remarks relative to the program were made by Frank Lockwood. Also shown was the Japan Consulate film, "The Japanese Carpenter."

Recent new members include: Henry Hill and John M. Evans, Members; and Albert Anthony Perata, Junior Associate.

ARCHITECT SPEAKER AT SOROPTOMIST MEETING

"The New Look in Architecture" was the subject of a talk given before the Soroptimist International of Oakland, June 23rd, by Leon Rimov, Architect and Area Planner, and member of the Berkeley architectural firm of Schmidts, Hardman & Wong.

The new look, according to Rimov, is the coordinated look of an entire area which comes about when the architect takes a broad perspective of the area into which a singe building will fit, rather than thinking of the building as a separate entity.

This new approach by an architect will result in a new look to cities and to parts of cities. Architects are more and more interpreting their responsibility as one toward the large area surrounding the individual building.

The Soroptimist Club is the oldest women's service club in Oakland, with Mrs. Ortha Wulfing serving as president currently.

PASADENA CHAPTER AIA

A Public Relations Workship was conducted by Irv Myers, nationally known public relations consultant and director of Architectural News Service, at the July meeting, with the meeting being in charge of William Rudolph, Chapter public relations chairman.

New members to the Chapter include: Edward James Reese, Corporate Member. Everett M. Simpson and Milton R. von Bargen, Associate Members.

SAN FRANCISCO ARCHITECTURAL CLUB

"Town Planning and Housing in Sweden" was the subject of an illustrated talk given at the July meeting by Lew Gelwicks, a new member of the Club who received his Master's Degree at the International Graduate School at the University of Stockholm, with his specialty being town planning.

CALIFORNIA COUNCIL AIA

Members of the Board of Directors decided at their June meeting to continue efforts at the 1959 session of the California State Legislature to obtain amendments to the Architectural Practice Act. Details of such changes will be worked out by the Architectural Practice Act Advisory Committee under Philip S. Buckingham, Fresno, chairman. In 1957, the Council amendments were passed by the State Assembly but killed by a State Senate committee.

PASADENA CHAPTER:
H. Douglas Byles, President; Edward D. Davies, Vice-President; Ward W. Deems, Secretary; Robert F. Gordon, Treasurer. Directors; Mal Gianni, Lee B. Kline, Keith B. Marston, Donald E. Neptune. Office of the Secy., 170 E. California St., Pasadena.

SAN DIEGO CHAPTER:
Raymond Lee Eggers, President; William F. Wilmurt, Vice-President; Lloyd P. A. Ruocco, Secretary; Delmar S. Mitchell, Treasurer. Directors: John C. Deardorf, Richard George Wheeler and Sam Bruce Richards. Office of the Secy., 3603 5th Ave., San Diego 3.

SAN JOAQUIN CHAPTER:
Robert C. Kaestner, President (Visalia); William G. Hyberg, Vice-President (Fresno); Lawrence B. Alexander, Secretary; Edwin S. Darden. Office of Secy., 128 E. 8th St., Hanford.

SANTA BARBARA CHAPTER:
Wallace W. Arendt, President (Santa Barbara); Darwin E. Fisher, Vice-President (Ventura); Walter Tibbetts, Secretary; Kenneth H. Hess, Treasurer. Office of Secy., 630 Para Grande Lane, Santa Barbara.

SOUTHERN CALIFORNIA CHAPTER:
George Vernon Russell, President; Maynard Lyndon, Vice-President; Ralph C. Crosby, Secretary; Thornton Abell, Treasurer. Office of Secy., 124 W. 4th St., Los Angeles.

SOUTHWEST WASHINGTON CHAPTER:
Robert Billsborough Price, President; Robert T. Olson, 1st Vice-President; Donald F. Burr, 2nd Vice-President; Percy G. Ball, Secretary; Alan C. Liddle, Treasurer; Charles T. Pearson and George Leonard Ekvall, Trustees. Office of Secy., 2715 Center St., Tacoma 2, Washington.

UTAH CHAPTER:
W. J. Monroe, Jr., President. 433 Atlas Bldg., Salt Lake City; M. E. Harris, Jr., Secretary, 703 Newhouse Bldg., Salt Lake City.

WASHINGTON STATE CHAPTER:
James J. Chiarelli (Seattle), President; Robert H. Dietz (Seattle), 1st Vice-President; Walter H. Rothe (Yakima), 2nd Vice-President; Talbot Wegg (Seattle), Secretary; Albert O. Bumgardner (Seattle), Treasurer. Directors: Arnold O. Gangnes, Harrison J. Overturf, Lloyd J. Lovegren, and John L. Wright. Miss Gwen Myer, Executive Secretary, 409 Central Bldg., Seattle 4.

SPOKANE CHAPTER:
Wm. C. James, President; Carl H. Johnson, Vice-President; Keith T. Boyington, Secretary; Ralph J. Bishop, Treasurer; Lawrence G. Evanoff, Carroll Martell, Kenneth W. Brooks, Directors. Office of the Secy., 615 Realty Bldg., Spokane.

HAWAII CHAPTER:
Robert M. Law, President; Harry W. Seckel, Vice-President; Richard Dennis, Secretary. Directors: Edwin Bauer, George J. Wimberly. Office of Secy., P. O. Box 3288, Honolulu, Hawaii.

CALIFORNIA COUNCIL, THE A.I.A.:
L. F. Richards, Santa Clara, President; Lee B. Kline, Los Angeles, Vice-President; Edward H. Fickett, Los Angeles, Secretary; Allen Y. Lew, Fresno, Treasurer. Miss Mary E. White, Office Secretary, 703 Market Street, San Francisco 3.

CALIFORNIA STATE BD. ARCHITECTURAL EXAMINERS:
Malcolm D. Reynolds, President (Oakland); Kenneth Wing, Secretary (Long Beach); Wendell R. Spackman (San Francisco); Paul Davis (Santa Ana), and Frank Cronin, Executive Secy., 1020 N St., Sacramento 14.

ALLIED ARCHITECTURAL ORGANIZATIONS

SAN FRANCISCO ARCHITECTURAL CLUB:
C. Van De Weghe, President; O. Hickenlooper, Vice-President; James O. Brummett, Secretary; J. W. Tasker, Treasurer. Directors: Morris Barnett, Art Swisher, Stan Howatt, Frank Barsoti, Frances Capone. Office of Secy., 507 Howard St., San Francisco 5.

PRODUCERS' COUNCIL—SOUTHERN CALIFORNIA CHAPTER:
Clay T. Snider, President. Minneapolis-Honeywell Regulator Co., L.A.; E. J. Lawson, Vice-President, Aluminum Company of America, L.A.; E. Phil Filsinger, Secretary, Gladding, McBean & Co., L.A.; William G. Aspy, Treasurer, H. H. Robertson Co., L.A.; Henry E. North, Jr., National Director, Arcadia Metal Products, L.A.; Office of the Secy., 2901 Los Feliz Blvd.

PRODUCERS' COUNCIL—NORTHERN CALIFORNIA CHAPTER:
John J. O'Connor, President, H. H. Robertson Co.; Stanley L. Basterash, Vice-President, Western Asbestos Co.; Howard W. DeWeese, Treasurer, Pomona Tile Mfg. Co.; Robert W. Harrington, Secretary, Clay Brick & Tile Assn. Office of Secy., 55 New Montgomery St., San Francisco 5.

PRODUCERS' COUNCIL—SAN DIEGO CHAPTER:
Eugene E. Bean, President, Fenestra Inc.; James J. Hayes, Vice-President, Westinghouse Electric Co.; E. R. Shelby, Secretary, The Celotex Corp. (El Cajon); Joseph C. Langley, Treasurer, Republic Steel Corp., Truscon Steel Div. (Lemon Grove). Office of Secy., 1832 Wedgemore Rd., El Cajon.

CONSTRUCTION SPECIFICATIONS INSTITUTE—LOS ANGELES:
R. R. Coghlan, Jr., President; George Lamb, Vice-President; E. Phil Filsinger, Secretary; Harry L. Miller, Treasurer; Directors; Harold Keller, Jack Whiteside, Walter Hagedohm, Raymond Whalley, Charles Field Wetherbee, Martin A. Hegsted, Advisory Member, D. Stewart Kerr. Office of Secy., 2901 Los Feliz Blvd., L.A.

CONSTRUCTION SPECIFICATIONS INSTITUTE— SAN FRANCISCO:
Henry P. Collins, President; Leonard M. Tivol, Vice-President; Leonard P. Grover, Treasurer; Marvin E. Hirchert, Secretary. Office of Secy., 585 Whitewood Drive, San Rafael.

WITH THE ENGINEERS

EAST BAY STRUCTURAL ENGINEERS SOCIETY

A. B. Sabin, Consulting Engineering of San Francisco, was a recent speaker at the Society's meeting discussing the subject "Point Four Program in Indonesia." Mr. Sabin emphasized his comments with the showing of numerous slides.

President Superak announced that R. Harrington, Manager of the Clay Brick and Tile Association, would address the Society's July meeting on the subject "Atomic Bomb versus Brick Masonry Construction."

Meetings are usually held at the Villa de la Paix resturant, 4th and Oak streets in Oakland.

ENGINEERING FOUNDATION GRANTS ADVANCE TWENTY-SIX PROJECTS

At a meeting held in New York recently, Engineering Foundation announced grants of $71,500 to advance research in the 1958-59 fiscal year.

These new allocations will further twenty-six projects that will also receive nearly $1,000,000 outside support from industry. The projects to which funds have been allocated represent all the important branches of the engineering profession. They are being carried out in university, government, and industrial laboratories all over the nation under sponsorship of the major engineering societies.

This year Engineering Foundation is making an initial grant to a program concerned with Documentation in Engineering, a joint project of four major engineering societies, the American Society for Metals, and Western Reserve University. The Council on Documentation Research was established at Western Reserve two years ago to promote wider use and better understanding of recorded scientific and technical information.

Formed in 1914, Engineering Foundation was a pioneer in recognizing the importance of research. Its current endowment fund is about $2,000,000. Though the income from this fund is very modest in comparison with present day research outlays, the Foundation has through the years initiated and kept alive many important research programs that were later able to obtain large scale financial backing from industry.

SOCIETY OF AMERICAN MILITARY ENGINEERS — San Francisco Post

Lt. Col. John A. Rankin, USA, Sixth US Army G-3 Section, was the principal speaker at the July meeting held in the Officer's Club, Presidio of San Francisco.

The speaker discussed "The Pentomic Army" and exhibited a motion picture showing the changes in organization and the technological advances that have been made in the Army since World War II.

The Society's Annual Golf Tournament will be held on the Ocean Course of the Olympic Club on July 25th, starting at 12:30 p.m. Entrance to the course is on Skyline Blvd, San Francisco.

AMERICAN SOCIETY OF CIVIL ENGINEERS

Papers on engineering aspects of water and wood, two items of considerable interest in the Northwest, will feature the program of the annual convention of the American Society of Civil Engineers, which was held in Portland, Oregon, June 23-27.

One of the highlights of the convention was a luncheon talk by Robert D. Holmes, Governor of Oregon. H. Loren Thompson was general chairman of the convention, and Norbert Leupold was chairman of the technical program committee.

USC ENGINEERING DEPARTMENT

More than 1000 Southland civil engineers, alumni and friends of the Civil Engineering Department of the University of Southern California, met in the Rodger Young Auditorium recently to launch a series of dinner meetings designed to stimulate interest in

and develop the SC civil engineering department.

Funds raised by the activity will provide a professorship in honor of David N. Wilson, head of the Civil Engineering Department. Prof. Wilson, a graduate of the University of Michigan, has been a member of the faculty at USC since 1929.

President of the group is Roy G. Johnston of Brandow and Johnston. Robert E. McClellan, Jr., of the California State Division of Architecture, is secretary, and Fred C. Walker of the P. J. Walker Co., is treasurer.

ANNUAL AWARDS ANNOUNCED BY ARCHITECTURAL GROUP

Two schools designed by San Francisco architect Mario J. Ciampi are among the five buildings selected by the jury to receive First Honor Awards in The American Institute of Architects' 1958 competition for outstanding architecture. They are the Sonoma Elementary School in Sonoma, and the Westmoor High School in Daly City.

Other awards went to Pereira & Luckman of Los Angeles for the Robinson's Palm Springs specialty shop and for the Beckman-Helipot Corporation Plant in Newport Beach; Thornton Ladd's own studio at Pasadena, and the Lakenan residence at Beverly Hills by Richard Dorman & Associates and Dan Morganelli Associate Architect of Beverly Hills.

The Honor Awards Program was established by the AIA in 1949 to encourage the appreciation of excellence in architecture and to afford recognition of exceptional merit in recently completed buildings. Eligible to submit work is any registered architect practicing professionally in the United States.

WOMEN'S AUXILIARY SEASC

A Fashion Show was staged by the Women's Auxiliary in Bullocks Wilshire store recently. The annual dinner dance was held July 19th at the Huntington.

CONSTRUCTION CONTRACTS UP

Heavy construction contract awards climbed again last month to score the fifth consecutive monthly increase, with the upsurge pushing recent contract volume to the largest record for any month since the all-time high of December, 1950.

Public works are primarily responsible for the gain.

CLIFFORD WAYNE MOLES IS AWARDED DMJM MENTORSHIP

Clifford Wayne Moles, third year architectural student at the University of Southern California, has been selected as recipient of the first annual Mentorship Award in a program established by the partners of the Los Angeles architectural-engineering firm of Daniel, Mann, Johnson & Mendenhall.

The DMJM Mentorship Award is available to a student of Architecture upon completion of the sophomore year and may continue for the undergraduate years. The student must be, and remain in, the top 10 per cent of his class. The student is selected by a committee of the faculty of the School of Architecture, the President of the Southern California Chapter of The American Institute of Architecture, and the partners of Daniel, Mann, Johnson and Mendenhall.

The program includes an interest-free loan of $900 per year to cover tuition and fees in the School of Architecture, this amount to be entirely cancelled upon successful completion of the year's training. The student will receive training in the offices of DMJM as a special employee, several hours per week during the school year and full time during vacations. He will receive prevailing wages for this effort.

GLADDING, McBEAN — MICA

(From page 6)

two re-presses which enable it to produce, in addition to the products made on the first line, stiff mud refractories, circle brick, rotary kiln block, refractory pavers and other shapes that need to be re-pressed. These two lines feed directly to the tunnel kiln on kiln cars. Another stiff mud line has been set up specifically for the manufacture of auger-extruded flue lining and drain tile. These products are burned in the tunnel kiln and in periodic kilns.

The stiff mud operation has been designed to provide maximum flexibility. It is possible to run the same mix and shape on the first two lines at the same time. Or one color can be run on one line with another color and shape running on the other line. Each line has a daily capacity of 60,000 eight-inch standard face brick, 40,000 Normans, or 40,000 re-pressed nine-inch straights. It is also possible to run both dry press and stiff mud through the dryer on the same car.

Holding Chamber Protects Brick

One very important unit in the new plant is a holding chamber with a capacity of 57 cars. Mica clays are difficult to work with because they have a high shrinkage and will not dry easily. In the past, drafts striking the green brick have caused cracking before the cars reached the dryer. Now these cars can be placed in the holding chamber to keep the green brick from drying too fast.

Two Latest Model Dry Presses

Dry-pressing needs can be easily filled with the two latest model dry presses, and is the means of making face brick, which units are finding a ready market in school partitions and like construction as both sides are smooth faced with no kiln marking.

Two Large Dryers

Drying facilities at Mica include two two-track dryers 134 feet long. The dryers are so constructed that air is injected underneath the car deck the full length of all tunnels and removed through roof slots in a false ceiling at the top of the load. This movement of air, under controlled temperature and humidity vertically throughout the ware, assures uniform drying.

Natural Gas Used to Fire Kiln

Another distinguishing feature of the plant is a 400-foot-long tunnel kiln which is fired by natural gas. No reburning of bricks is necessary because temperatures can be raised very rapidly in the kiln. The kiln is operated at three different cones, PCE 8 (2372° F), PCE 11 (2437° F) and PCE 14 (2458° F).

NEWS & COMMENT ON ART

(From page 5)

phy Shows at the California State Fair and Exposition to be held in Sacramento, August 27-September 7, according to Mrs. Florence M. Doe, director in charge.

Divisions in the big exhibition, which will be held in the Art Building on the Fairgrounds, will be oil paintings, water colors, sculpture, prints, metal work, ceramics, jewelry, hand-blocked textiles, hand-woven textiles, art movies, photography and student art. Student artists will compete for $2,625 in prizes. A $500 scholarship will be awarded to the student among all first-prize winners who, in the opinion of the judges, shows the greatest promise.

Photographers will take part in the 18th Annual North American International Photographic Exhibit, which will run concurrently with the Fair's Art Show.

Judges have been announced as follows: Oil Paintings—Duncan Gleason, Los Angeles; Leonard Edmondson, Pasadena; Edward A. Reep, Studio City; Glenn A. Wessels, Berkeley; Frank Scalise, Sacramento, and Lawrence Hosmer of Lodi.

Sculpture—Wayne Thiebaud and Ernest Van Harlingen, Sacramento; Robert W. Cremean, La Jolla; and Gurdon Woods, San Francisco.

Ceramics, Enameling, Metal Work, Jewelry and Textiles—Robert Dhaemers, Oakland; Doris Heineman, Sacramento; Evelyn M. Gulick, Spring Valley; Brooke Morris, Los Angeles; Antonio Prieto, Oakland; Edith Garland, San Francisco; Otto Natzler, Los Angeles, and Charles Eames, Santa Monica.

Student Art Work—Thiebaud, Van Harlingen, Woods and Cremean.

Photography Prints—Elmer Lew, Fresno; Eugene Kibbe, Fairfax, and Arthur M. Underwood, Rochester, New York. Photographic Color Slides—Robert W. L. Potts, San Francisco; Fred Bond, Los Angeles, and Mrs. Bertha Koch, Auburn.

ARCHITECT KERR NAMED TO BOARD SCHOOL COUNCIL

Architect D. Stewart Kerr, of the Los Angeles architectural firm of H. L. Gogerty Associates, 3123 W. 8th Street, has been elected a member of the governing board of the School Facilities Council, a national organization with headquarters in New York City.

Membership on the governing board, which comprises 36 members from the fields of architecture, education, industry, or other individuals with a direct responsibility for education, is for three years.

Purpose of the organization is to assist education through improvement of school building design, school sites, school facilities and school equipment.

TELEPHONE COMPANY PLANS NEW BUILDING FOR SAN FRANCISCO

Architect Aleck L. Wilson, 315 Montgomery Street, San Francisco, is working on plans and specifications for construction of a new telephone building to be built in San Francisco for the Pacific Tel. & Tel. Company at an estimated cost of $4,500,-000.

The new 7-story structure will contain 135,000 sq. ft. of area and will feature a glass and ceramic tile facade. Construction is scheduled to start this summer.

OAKLAND TO BUILD NEW HALL OF JUSTICE

The architectural firm of Confer & Willis, 366 40th Street, Oakland, has started working drawings for the construction of a $6,950,000 new Hall of Justice Building for the City of Oakland.

The new 10-story building will include a new police center including a jail and courts; electrically operated jail doors, criminology laboratory; employee cafeteria, exercise rooms, locker rooms, firing range, offices of district attorney and public defender, judges quarters, court officials facilities, and a violations bureau; approximate 255,000 sq. ft. area.

Building design will include a helicopter landing on roof and paved parking area.

STOCKTON SAVINGS AND LOAN TO BUILD BUILDING

The architectural firm of Mayo & DeWolf, Exchange Bldg., Stockton, is completing drawings for construction of a new bank building in Stockton for the Stockton Savings & Loan Bank.

The construction site covers a half-block 150x300 ft., with the building occupying 96x160 ft.; it will have a full basement, drive-in and off-street parking facilities. Work will start on site clearance at once.

NEW SAN DIEGO HEALTH ASS'N BUILDING

Ground breaking ceremonies for the 5-story San Diego Health Association building, at 328 Maple Street, San Diego; early this month, marked another milestone in the progress of the Association, according to George R. Stevenson, founder and president of the trustees of the association.

The San Diego Health Association, operating the medical clinic for the health association, is currently housed in the late Henry W. Putnam mansion, a noted land-

mark of San Diego.

The new building was designed by architect Charles G. Polacek, and contract for construction has been awarded to the Haas-Haynie-Frandsen, Inc., construction company of Beverly Hills.

TRINITY COUNTY CIVIL DEFENSE TRAINING CENTER

Architect Albert W. Kahl, 1120 7th Avenue, San Mateo, has completed plans for construction of a 1-story wood and frame building in Weaverville to serve as the Trinity County Civil Defense and Disaster Training Center.

The new building, with concrete basement to contain Civil Defense Communications Center, will cost an estimated $85,-000. The main building will contain an auditorium, executive offices, kitchen, facilities and defense training rooms.

TEACHERS TO BUILD BUILDING

Architect John H. Carter, 1401 21st Street, Sacramento, has completed plans and specifications and contract has been awarded for the construction of a wood frame and concrete block building in Sacramento for the Northern Section of the California Teachers Association.

Estimated cost of the project is $50,-882. Paul R. Christman, 2141 Madera Road, Sacramento, has been awarded the contract for construction.

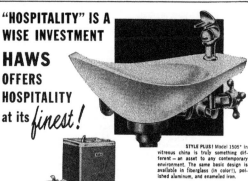

LESLIE R. ALT NAMED
FELLOW OF AMERICAN
CERAMIC SOCIETY

Leslie R. Alt of the Kraftile Company, Niles, California, was a made a Fellow of the American Ceramic Society at the 60th Annual Meeting of the Society recently held in Pittsburgh, Pennsylvania.

More than two thousand people from the widely diversified ceramic industries of the country attended the conference, one of the largest gatherings of ceramists in the world. Some 200 scientific papers were presented in nine divisions of the meetings.

LESLIE R. ALT
Fellow,
American Ceramic Society

Leslie R. Alt attended school in Woodbury county, Iowa, received his B.S. degree in ceramic engineering from Iowa State College; was with the Sioux City Brick and Tile Co. from 1924-1945, and is presently vice president in charge of production at the Kraftile Company plant in Niles. He is a member of the Tau Beta Pi, and has been active in the affairs of the Northern California Section of the Society, serving as chairman. He joined The American Ceramic Society in 1927 and is affiliated with the Structural Clay Products Division.

Fellows, one of the major honors conferred by the Society, are elected by a two-thirds vote of the Board of Trustees for achievement in their field and contributions to the ceramic arts and sciences.

ANNUAL AWARDS OF AMERICAN
MILITARY ENGINEERS MADE

Winners of the Society of American Military Engineers for military engineering achievement for 1957 have been announced with awards being presented at the 38th annual meeting of the society at the Mayflower Hotel in Washington, D.C.

Award winners include: Lt. Gen. Raymond A. Wheeler, U.S.A., retired, the George W. Goethals Medal; Donald A. Rice, U.S.C. & G.S., the Colbert Medal; Comdr. Richard A. Laughlin, CEC, U.S. Navy, the Morrell Medal; Brig. Gen. William F. Cassidy, CE, U.S.A., the Wheeler Medal; Col. Edward C. Gill, Installations, U.S. Air Force, the Newman Medal; Brig. Gen. John W. N. Schulz, U.S.A., retired, the Society Gold Medal; and Comdr. Charles J. Merdinger, CEC, U.S. Navy, the Toulmin Medal.

Rear Adm. Eugene J. Peltier, Chief of the Civil Engineers Corps and Bureau of Yards and Docks, U.S. Navy, was the honored guest speaker at the presentation ceremonies.

ARCHITECTURAL TRAIN

Two San Francisco architectural firms, John Lyon Reid & Partners, and John C. Warnecke, are represented in the exhibition train, "Schoolroom Progress U.S.A.," which started its country-wide tour last month in Grand Central Station, New York. Co-sponsored by the Henry Ford Museum and the Encyclopedia Americana, the exhibition is intended to stimulate viewers to think in terms of the new educational environment. Other California architects having an exhibit on the train are Smith, Powell & Morgridge, AIA, of Los Angeles.

ARCHITECT POAGE RETIRES
(From page 7)

After a short period in the Army, he did architectural work in Oakland, San Francisco and Hawaii before joining the State's Division of Architecture.

Poage was married to Marguerite Bennett in Berkeley in 1923. They have a daughter, Mrs. Ellen Doermer of Sacramento, and a son, Bennett Poage, who is associated with a Sacramento paving and grading firm.

After retirement, Poage plans to move his home from Sacramento to an oceanside area near Fort Bragg. He plans then to add geology and oceanography to his hobby interests, which now include old clocks, furniture, branding irons, early churches, books and people.

Poage's fellow employees honored him at a farewell dinner June 4 in the Empire Room of the Hotel Senator. He left his desk June 6 for nearly two months' terminal leave.

No successor to Poage has been named.

PHOTO CREDITS: Wm. Clement Ambrose, Architect, Page 10, 11-bottom, 12; Phil Fein, Page 11-top, 14; Rondal Partridge, Page 13; Fred English, Page 7-top; Hal Matson, Page 16, 17, 18-top, 20, 22; United Lighting & Ceiling Company, Page 18-bottom, 19, 23; Gladding, McBean & Company, Page 6.

HIGH SCHOOLS—Today and Tomorrow. By Charles W. Bursch and John Lyon Reid. Reinhold Publishing Co., 430 Park Ave., New York 22. Price $7.95. 127 pages, Illustrated.

Charles W. Bursch, a leader in the development of the modern California schoolhouse because of the years he headed the school plant service administration in the California State Department of Education, and John Lyon Reid, one of the best known architects of schools, collaborated to formulate a new solution to the problem that has been plaguing America since the end of the war: the development of a sound, workable high school program and the design of the building to house it. The educational and architectural theories presented here take full account of the individuals involved—teachers and students—and of the nature of the learnig activity.

INDUSTRIAL ELECTRONICS HANDBOOK. By R. Kretzmann. Philosophical Library, Inc., 15 E. 40th St., New York 16. Price $12.00. 298 pages, illustrated.

The first part of this book, 2nd enlarged edition, describes the principles and properties of the various classes of electronic tubes, together with typical applications and circuits.

In the second part a separate chapter is devoted to each of the main types of application, such as electronic relays, counting circuits, etc., containing a large number of practical examples, the operation of each being described in considerable detail with fully designed circuits.

The book is invaluable to technicians engaged in the supervision or mantenance of industrial equipment, to industrial engineers in the mechanical and electrical fields who desire to acquaint themselves with the possibilities of electronic control and the methods of application, and to students at technical colleges and universities.

INDUSTRIAL ELECTRONICS CIRCUITS. By R. Kretzmann. Philosophical Library, Inc., 15 E. 40th St., New York 16. Price $10.00, 194 pages, illustrated.

This book is a sequel to INDUSTRIAL ELECTRONICS HANDBOOK, and deals with the circuitry of industrial electronic apparatus and includes nearly 200 carefully chosen circuits. The functions of the various circuit elements are described, and comprehensive information is also supplied on the actual component values.

Instructive examples are given of photoelectric control devices, counting circuits for various purposes, stabilizing circuits and motor controls. Numerous photos are used to illustrate the design of the apparatus.

A valuable book for engineers and technicians directly concerned with the development and design of electronic apparatus, and to the student.

NEW CATALOGUES AVAILABLE

Architects, Engineers, Contractors, Planning Commission members—the catalogues, folders, new building products material, etc., described below may be obtained by directing your request to the name and address given in each item.

A tour of the Calaveras Cement Company plant. New 16-page brochure describes the cement manufacturing process in detail; 30 photographs and a flow chart accompany a simple explanatory text which in effect gives the reader a "tour" of the company's San Andreas plant in Calaveras county, California. Free to visitors at plant, also free upon request: DEPT-A&E, Calaveras Cement Company, 315 Montgomery St., San Francisco 4.

Self-sealing asphalt shingles. A new 8-page color brochure describes SEALCO Self-Sealing Asphalt Shingles; a new sealing agent developed by United States Gypsum research; when shingles are applied to a roof, and after short exposure to the sun's heat, the sealant spots fuse firmly with the backs of overlapping shingles to provide an over-all, sealed-down roof. Free copy write DEPT-A&E, United States Gypsum Company, Chicago, Ill.

Special hazard fire protection. New publication on "Special Hazard Fire Protection" presents this highly technical subject in an easily understandable manner; up-to-date and accurate thereby valuable to professional fire protection engineers,

architects and contractors. Write for copy, DEPT-A&E, Grinnell Co., Providence, R. I.

Belt conveyor systems. New brochure on latest design rope belt conveyor system; illustrated, great flexibility, lower cost, better load handling, increased belt life; spacing tables show proper placement of idlers support stands, and anchor points for various material weights and height limitations. Free copy write DEPT-A&E, Joy Mfg. Co., Henry W. Oliver Bldg., Pittsburgh, Pa.

Metal building. New brochure describes how pre-engineered metal buildings are being widely used, and are of increasing interest to commerce, industry and agriculture; mass production efficiency has brought cost of standard metal buildings down to the level where they can be economically used; use of specially designed facades gives architect and contractor ample opportunity to display talents. Write for free copy DEPT-A&E, Metal Building Mfgrs. Ass'n, 2130 Keith Bldg., Cleveland 15, Ohio.

Tables and stools. Colorful 24-page food and drink equipment Planning Catalog for architects, designers and contractors, shows very latest in stool and table design, color selection and installation ideas; many installation illustrations covering all types of use. Free copy write DEPT-A&E, Chicago Hardware Foundry Co., North Chicago, Ill.

Steel portable grandstands. New 8-page catalog designed for school administrators, architects and contractors; completely describes and illustrates the sectional and continuous styles of elevated and non-elevated grandstands; design details, specifications, a table of dimensions for various size units and a check list of accessories and variations for use in designing and installation. Free copy write DEPT-A&E, Wayne Iron Works, 147 N. Pembroke Ave., Wayne, Pa.

Highway bridges of steel. New 32-page, 2-color illustrated brochure designed as an aid in structural steel bridge design; divided into two sections: first discusses low alloy steels, erection, steel decking and complete design; second is devoted to examples of selected typical details showing solutions that have been used for some of the more troublesome problems encountered in steel bridge design; is of technical nature in presentation. Free copy write DEPT-A&E, American Institute of Steel Construction, 101 Park Ave., New York 17, N.Y.

Gas-fired winter air conditioners. Three-color data sheet describes and illustrates the newly developed Comet-572 series of factory wired and assembled gas-fired winter air conditioners; designed for fast, economical installation; descriptive material, charts giving engineering data and specifications. Free copy write DEPT-A&E, Thatcher Furnace Co., Garwood, N. J.

Specifications for metal lathing and furring. New 20-page booklet (AIA FILE No. 20-B-1) entitled "Specifications for Metal Lathing and Furring" includes technical data on specifications for solid and hollow partitions; wall furring; metal lath attached directly to wood supports; contact, furred, and suspended ceilings; beam and column protection for fireproofing; and reinforcing for exterior stucco; descriptive tables summarize various spans and spacings for supporting metal lath and plaster ceilings; page of fire resistant ratings. Free copy write DEPT-A&E, Metal Lath Mfgr's Ass'n, Engineers' Bldg., Cleveland, Ohio.

ARCHITECT AND ENGINEER

ESTIMATOR'S GUIDE

BUILDING AND CONSTRUCTION MATERIALS

PRICES GIVEN ARE FIGURING PRICES AND ARE MADE UP FROM AVERAGE QUOTATIONS FURNISHED BY LeROY CONSTRUCTION SERVICES. 4% SALES TAX ON ALL MATERIALS BUT NOT LABOR. ITEMS IN ITALIC INCLUDE LABOR AND SALES TAX.

BONDS—Performance or Performance plus Labor and Material Bond(s), $10 per $1000 on contract price. Labor and Material Bond(s) only, $5.00 per $1000 on contract price.

BRICKWORK & MASONRY

COMMON BRICKWORK, Reinforced:		
8" walls	SF	*2.95*
12" walls	SF	*4.15*
SELECT COMMON, Reinforced:		
8" walls	SF	*3.05*
12" walls	SF	*4.30*
CONCRETE BLOCK, Reinforced:		
6" walls	SF	*1.40*
8" walls	SF	*1.55*
12" walls	SF	*1.90*
BRICK VENEER:		
4" Select Common	SF	*1.65*
4" Roman	SF	*2.50*
4" Norman	SF	*2.40*
4" Aggrelite	SF	*2.40*

BRICKWORK & MASONRY

All Prices—F.O.B. Plant.

COMMON BRICK		
Common 2½ x 3¾ x 8¼	M	45.00
Select 2½ x 3¾ x 8¼	M	52.00
Clinker 2½ x 3¾ x 8¼	M	48.00
Jumbo 3½ x 3 x 11½	M	90.00
FACE BRICK		
Standard	M	59.80 - 83.20
Jumbo	M	114.40 - 130.00
Roman	M	88.40 - 109.20
Norman	M	101.40 - 124.80
Brik Blox (6")	M	202.80
(8")	M	239.20
Braile Veneer	M	26.00
BUILDING TILE		
8 x 5½ x 12 inches	M	165.78
6 x 5½ x 12 inches	M	128.96
HOLLOW TILE		
12 x 12 x 3 inches	M	163.12
12 x 12 x 4 inches	M	184.18
12 x 12 x 6 inches	M	244.71
MANTEL FIRE BRICK		
2½ x 9½ x 4½ inches	M	140.40
GLAZED STRUCTURAL UNITS		
2 x 6 x 12 Furring	SF	.90
4 x 6 x 12 Furring	SF	1.20
6 x 6 x 12 Furring	SF	1.50
4 x 6 x 12 Partition	SF	1.60
Add for color	SF	.20
CONCRETE BLOCKS		
4 x 8 x 16 inches	EA	.22
6 x 8 x 16 inches	EA	.265
8 x 8 x 16 inches	EA	.30
12 x 8 x 16 inches	EA	.435
Colored Add	EA	.02
AGGREGATE—Haydite or Basalite		
All sizes in bulk	CY	6.24

BUILDING PAPERS & FELTS

1 ply per 1000 ft. roll	3.95
2 ply per 1000 ft. roll	6.03
3 ply per 1000 ft. roll	8.22
Sisalkraft, reinf. 500 ft. roll	7.54
SHEATHING PAPERS:	
Asphalt sheathing, 15-lb. roll	2.50
30-lb. roll	3.50
Dampcourse, 216-ft. roll	3.05
FELT PAPERS:	
Deadening felt, ¾-lb. 50 ft. roll	4.10
1-lb. 50 ft. roll	4.78
Asphalt roofing, 15-lbs.	2.50
30-lbs.	3.50
ROOFING PAPERS:	
Standard Grade, Smooth Surface	
108-ft. roll, Light	2.35
Medium	2.75
Heavy	3.22
Extra Heavy	3.75

CHIMNEYS, PATENT

F.O.B. Warehouse

6"	LF	1.45
8"	LF	2.05
10"	LF	2.85
12"	LF	3.45

Rates for 10 - 50 Lin. Ft.

CONCRETE AGGREGATES

	Bunker Per Ton	Del'd Per Ton
Gravel, All Sizes	3.38	4.16
Top Sand	3.59	4.37
Concrete Mix	3.48	4.26
Crushed Rock		
¼" to ¾"	3.43	4.26
¾" to 1½"	3.43	4.26
Roofing Gravel	3.54	4.42
SAND		
Lapis (Nos. 2 & 4)	4.47	5.30
Olympia (Nos. 1 & 2)	3.75	4.32

CEMENT		
Common All Brands (Paper Sacks)		
Small Quantities	Per Sack	1.40
Large Quantities	Per Bbl.	4.00
Trinity White & Mendusa White	Per Sack	4.16
CONCRETE READY-MIX		
6 sack in 5 yd. loads	Per Yd.	15.40
CURING COMPOUND, Clear		
5 gal. drums	Per Gal.	1.46

CARPENTRY & MILLWORK

Hardware not included

FRAMING:		
Floors	BM	*.20 - .25*
Walls	BM	*.25 - .30*
Ceilings	BM	*.18 - .22*
Roofs	BM	*.22 - .27*
Furring & Blocking	BM	*.30 - .50*
SHEATHING:		
1 x 8 straight	BM	*.20 - .25*
1 x 8 diagonal	BM	*.23 - .28*
5/16" Plyscore	SF	*.16 - .20*
⅜" Plywood	SF	*.25 - .30*
SIDING:		
1 x 8 Bevel	BM	*.35 - .40*
1 x 4 V-Rustic	BM	*.40 - .45*
EXTERIOR TRIM:		
Fascia and Molds	BM	*.40 - .50*
Bolted Framing—Add 50%		
ENTRANCE DOORS & FRAMES:		
Singles		*60.00 & Up*
Doubles		*100.00 & Up*
INTERIOR DOORS & FRAMES:		
Singles		*35.00 & Up*
Pocket Sliding		*45.00 & Up*
Closet Sliding (Pr.)		*50.00 & Up*
WINDOWS:		
D/H Sash & Frames	SF	*1.75 & Up*
Casement Sash & Frames	SF	*1.90 & Up*
SHELVING:		
1 x 12 S4S	BM	*.30 - .50*
¾" Plywood	SF	*.40 - .60*
STAIRS:		
Oak steps D.F. Risers		
Under 36" wide	Riser	*12.00*
Under 60" wide	Riser	*17.00*
Newel posts and rail extra		
WOOD CASES & CABINETS:		
D.F. Wall Hung	LF	*13.00 - 18.00*
D.F. Counters	LF	*15.00 - 20.00*

DAMPPROOFING & WATERPROOFING

MEMBRANE:		
1 layer 50 lb. felt	SQ.	*9.00*
4 layers Dampcourse	SQ.	*13.00*
Hot coat walls	SQ.	*6.00*
Tricosal added to concrete	CY	*1.00*
Anti-Hydro added to concrete	CY	*1.50*

ELECTRIC WIRING

Per Outlet:		
Knob & Tube	EA	*9.00*
Armor	EA	*16.00*
Conduit	EA	*20.00*
110 V Circuit	EA	*25.00*
220 V Circuit	EA	*95.00*

ELEVATORS & ESCALATORS

Prices vary according to capacity, speed and type. Consult Elevator Companies.

Slow speed apartment house elevator including doors and trim, about $5000.00 per floor.

EXCAVATION

MACHINE WORK in common ground:		
Large Basements	CY	*.75 - 1.00*
Small Pits	CY	*1.25 - 1.75*
Trenches	CY	*1.50 - 2.25*
HAND WORK in common ground:		
Large pits and trenches	CY	*4.50 - 5.50*
Small pits and trimming	CY	*5.00 - 6.50*

Hard Clay & Shale 2 times above rates.
Rock and large boulders 4-6 times above rates.
Shoring, bracing and disposal of water not included.

FLOORS

⅛" Asp. tile, dark colors	SF	*.25 - .30*
⅛" Asp. tile, light colors	SF	*.30 - .35*
⅛" Rubber tile	SF	*.60 - .70*
.080 Vinyl Asbestos Tile	SF	*.40 - .45*
.080 Vinyl Tile	SF	*.85 - .95*
Lino, Standard Gauge	SY	*3.75 - 4.25*
Lino, Battleship	SY	*5.25 - 5.75*
4" Rubber Base, Black	LF	*.35 - .40*
Rubber Stair Nosing	LF	*1.00 - 1.75*

Above rates based on quantities of 1000 - 5000 SF per job.

HARDWOOD FLOORS

Select Oak, filled, sanded, stained and varnished:		
5/16" x 2¼" strip	SF	*.45 - .50*
5/16" Random Plank	SF	*.50 - .55*
25/32" x 2¼" T&G	SF	*.70 - .80*
Maple, 2nd Grade and Better, filled, sanded, stained and varnished:		
25/32" x 2¼" T&G	SF	*.80 - .95*
Wax Finish, add	SF	*.10*

HARDWOOD FLOORING

Oak 5/16" x 2" Strip—		
Clear	M	229.00
Select	M	218.00
#1 Common	M	203.00
Oak 5/16" Random Plank—		
Select & Btr.	M	286.00
#1 Common	M	244.00
Oak 25/32" x 2¼" T&G—		
Select	M	260.00
#1 Common	M	203.00
Maple 25/32" x 2¼" T&G—		
#1 Grade	M	317.00
#2 Grade	M	281.00
#3 Grade	M	208.00
Nails—1" Floor Brads	KEG	17.20

GLASS & GLAZING

S.S.B. Clear	SF	*.48*
D.S.B. Clear	SF	*.78*
Crystal	SF	*.92*
¼" Plate	SF	*2.17*
⅛" Obscure	SF	*.68*
⅛" Heat Absorbing	SF	*1.12*
¼" Tempered Plate	SF	*4.38*
½" Tempered Plate	SF	*7.84*
¼" Wire Plate, Clear	SF	*3.65*
¼" Wire Plate, Rough	SF	*1.08*

GLASS—CUT TO SIZE

F.O.B. Warehouse

S.S.B. Clear, Av. 6 SF	SF	.34
D.S.B. Clear, Av. 10 SF	SF	.56
Crystal, Av. 35 SF	SF	.66
¼" Polished Plate, Av. 100 SF	SF	1.55
⅛" Obscure, Av. 10 SF	SF	.49
⅛" Ribbed, Av. 10 SF	SF	.49
⅛" Rough, Av. 10 SF	SF	.49
¼" Wire Plate, Clear, Av. 40 SF	SF	2.61
¼" Wire Plate, Rough, Av. 40 SF	SF	.77
⅛" Heat Absorbing, Av. 10 SF	SF	.80
¼" Tempered Plate, Av. 50 SF	SF	3.13
½" Tempered Plate, Av. 50 SF	SF	5.60

Glazing—Approx. 40-50% of Glass
Glass Blocks—Check with Dealer

HEATING

FURNACES—Gas Fired—Av. Job:	
FLOOR FURNACE:	
25,000 BTU	*100.00 - 125.00*
35,000 BTU	*107.00 - 135.00*
45,000 BTU	*115.00 - 150.00*
AUTOMATIC CONTROL:	
Add	*25.00 - 35.00*

HEATING—Cont'd

DUAL WALL FURNACE:
23,000 BTU ....110.00 - 125.00
33,000 BTU ....125.00 - 145.00
50,000 BTU ....150.00 - 180.00
AUTOMATIC CONTROL:
Add .... 25.00 - 35.00
GRAVITY FURNACE:
75,000 BTU ....375.00 - 450.00
85,000 BTU ....425.00 - 525.00
95,000 BTU ....475.00 - 600.00
FORCED AIR FURNACE:
.... 75.00 - 125.00
AUTOMATIC CONTROL:
Add .... 15.00 - 25.00
HEAT REGISTERS:
Outlet .... 7.50 - 15.00

INSULATION & WALLBOARD
F.O.B. Warehouse
ROCKWOOL Insulation—
2" Semi-thick ....Per M SF 63.02
3½" Full Thick ....Per M SF 80.50
COTTON Insulation
1" Full Thick ....Per M SF 43.26
SOFTBOARDS—Wood Fiber—
½" thick ....Per M SF 88.00
1½" thick ....Per M SF 275.00
2" thick ....Per M SF 385.00
ALUMINUM Insulation—
80# Kraft paper with alum. foil
1 side only ....Per M SF 18.30
2 sides ....Per M SF 31.00
GYPSUM Wallboard—
⅜" thick ....Per M SF 49.50
½" thick ....Per M SF 54.50
⅝" thick ....Per M SF 83.00
¾" Gyplap ....Per M SF 85.00
HARDBOARDS—Wood Fiber—
⅛" thick, Sheathing ....Per M SF 78.75
¼" thick, Sheathing ....Per M SF 90.48
⁵⁄₁₆" thick, Sheathing ..Per M SF 109.20
⅛" thick, Tempered ....Per M SF 98.80
¼" thick, Tempered .....Per M SF 140.40
⁵⁄₁₆" thick, Tempered ..Per M SF 194.48
CEMENT ASBESTOS Board—
¼" C.A.B. Flat Sheets ..Per M SF 156.00
⅜" C.A.B. Flat Sheets ..Per M SF 218.40
½" C.A.B. Flat Sheets ..Per M SF 280.80

LATH & PLASTER
Diamond 3.40 copper bearing ....SY .50
Ribbed 3.40 copper bearing ....SY .55
⅜" rock lath ....SY .37
2" Standard Channel ....LF .085
1½" Standard Channel ....LF .065
¾" Standard Channel ....LF .045
3¾" steel studs ....LF .09
4" steel studs ....LF .105
Stud shoes ....EA .025
Hardwall, Browning ....Sack 1.46
Hardwall, Finish ....Sack 1.72
Stucco ....Sack 2.50

LATH & PLASTERWORK
CHANNEL FURRING:
Suspended Ceilings ....SY 2.20 - 2.50
Walls ....SY 2.30 - 2.60
METAL STUD PARTITIONS:
3¼" Studs ....SY 1.70 - 2.00
4" Studs ....SY 1.95 - 2.25
Over 10'0 high, add ....SY .20 - .30
3.40 METAL LATH AND PLASTER:
Ceilings ....SY 3.60 - 4.00
Walls ....SY 3.75 - 4.15
KEENE'S CEMENT FINISH:
Add ....SY .40 - .60
ROCK LATH & PLASTER:
Ceilings ....SY 2.50 - 2.80
Walls ....SY 2.60 - 2.90
WIRE MESH AND ⅞" STUCCO:
Walls ....SY 3.60 - 4.10
STUCCO ON CONCRETE:
Walls ....SY 2.30 - 2.80
METAL ACCESSORIES ....LF .20 - .50

LINOLEUM
Lino. Standard Gauge........................SY 2.65 - 2.85
Lino. Battleship ....SY 3.90 - 4.10
⅛" Asp. tile, Dark............................SF .10 - .11
⅛" Asp. tile, Light ....SF .14 - .16
⅛" Rubber Tile ....SF .40 - .44
.080 Vinyl Asb. tile..........................SF .18 - .19
.080 Vinyl tile ....SF .59 - .61
⅛" Vinyl tile ....SF .78 - .82
4" Base, Dark ....LF .15 - .16
4" Base, Light ....LF .24 - .26
Rubber Nosing ....LF .60 - 1.30
Lino Paste ....GAL .75 - .90
Above rates based on quantities of
1000-5000 SF per job.

LUMBER
DOUGLAS FIR: M.B.M.
#1 2x4—2x10 .... 88.00 - 92.00
#2 2x4—2x10 .... 85.00 - 90.00
#3 2x4—2x10 .... 68.00 - 74.00
#4 2x4—2x10 .... 64.00 - 72.00
Clear, Air Dried.................. 180.00 - 210.00
Clear, Kiln Dried................ 210.00 - 240.00

REDWOOD:
Foundation Grade .... 120.00 - 130.00
Construction Heart .... 110.00 - 120.00
A Grade .... 180.00 - 210.00
Clear Heart .... 190.00 - 220.00
D.F. PLYWOOD   M.S.F.
¼" AB .... 95.00 - 105.00
¼" AD .... 90.00 - 95.00
¼" Ext. Waterproof........... 115.00 - 125.00
⅜" AB .... 130.00 - 145.00
⅜" AD .... 115.00 - 125.00
½" CD .... 70.00 - 85.00
½" AB .... 170.00 - 185.00
½" AD .... 110.00 - 115.00
⅝" CD
⅝" AB .... 185.00 - 200.00
⅝" AD .... 165.00 - 180.00
¾" CD .... 115.00 - 125.00
¾" AB .... 210.00 - 230.00
¾" AD .... 195.00 - 210.00
¾" CD .... 125.00 - 140.00
⅝" Plyform .... 160.00 - 170.00
SHINGLES: Square
Cedar #1 .... 14.00 - 15.50
Cedar #2 .... 11.50 - 12.50
SHAKES:
CEDAR
½ to ¾" Butt.................... 17.50 - 18.50
¾ to 1¼" Butt.................. 18.50 - 19.50
REDWOOD
¾ to 1¼" Butt.................. 21.00 - 24.00

MILLWORK
All Prices F.O.B. Mill
D.F. CLEAR, AIR DRIED:
S4S ....MBM 220.00 - 250.00
D.F. CLEAR, KILN DRIED:
S4S ....MBM 225.00 - 275.00
DOOR FRAMES & TRIM:
Residential Entrance .... 17.00 & up
Interior Room Entrance...... 7.50 & up
DOORS:
1⅜" D.F. Slab, Hollow Core.... 8.00 & up
1⅜" D.F. Slab, Solid Core.... 19.00 & up
1⅜" Birch Slab, Hollow Core.. 10.00 & up
1⅜" Birch Slab, Solid Core... 22.00 & up
WINDOW FRAMES:
D/H Singles ....SF .80
Casement Singles ....SF .90
WOOD SASH:
D/H in pairs (1 lite) ....SF .45
Casement (1 lite) ....SP .50
WOOD CABINETS:
¾" D.F. Ply with ¼" ply backs
Wall Hung ....LF 10.00 - 15.00
Counter ....LF 12.00 - 17.00
BIRCH OR MAPLE—Add 25%

PAINTING
EXTERIOR:
Stucco Wash 1 ct. ....SY .30
Stucco Wash 2 cts. ....SY .35
Lead and Oil 2 cts. ....SY .80
Lead and Oil 3 cts. ....SY 1.30
INTERIOR:
Primer Sealer ....SY .40
Wall Paint, 1 ct. ....SY .30
Wall Paint, 2 cts. ....SY .55
Enamel, 1 ct. ....SY .60
Enamel, 2 cts. ....SY 1.10
Doors and Trim...................EA 10.00
Sash and Trim......................EA 12.00
Base and Molds....................LF .12
Old Work—Add 15-30%

PLUMBING
Lavatories ....EA 100.00 - 150.00
Toilets ....EA 200.00 - 300.00
Bath Tubs ....EA 300.00 - 330.00
Stall Shower ....EA 80.00 - 150.00
Sinks ....EA 125.00 - 175.00
Laundry Trays ....EA 80.00 - 130.00
Water Heaters ....EA 100.00 - 300.00
Prices based on average residential and commercial
work. Special fixtures and excessive piping not in-
cluded.

PAINT
All Prices F.O.B. Warehouse
Thinners—5-100 gals. ....GAL .45
Turpentine—5-100 gals. ....GAL 1.35
Linseed Oil, Raw................GAL 2.00
Linseed Oil, Boiled.............GAL 1.95
Primer-Sealer ....GAL 2.95
Enamel ....GAL 5.00
Enamel Undercoat ....GAL 3.25
White Lead in Oil ....LB .26
Red Lead in Oil ....LB .29
Litharge ....LB .24

ROOFING
STANDARD TAR & GRAVEL   Per Square
4 ply .... 14.00 - 18.00
5 ply .... 17.00 - 20.00
White Gravel Finish—Add.... 2.00 - 4.00
Asph. Compo. Shingles......... 16.00 - 20.00
Cedar Shingles .... 20.00 - 24.00
Cedar Shakes .... 26.00 - 30.00
Redwood Shakes .... 28.00 - 34.00
Clay Tiles .... 40.00 - 50.00

SEWER PIPE
VITRIFIED:
Standard 4 in......................LF .31
Standard 6 in......................LF .56
Standard 8 in......................LF .81
Standard 12 in......................LF 1.76
Standard 24 in......................LF 6.95
CLAY DRAIN PIPE:
Standard 6 in........................LF .34
Standard 8 in........................LF .59
Rate for 100 Lin. Ft. F.O.B. Warehouse

STEEL
REINFORCING BARS:
¼" rounds ....LB .122
⅜" rounds ....LB .111
½" rounds ....LB .108
⅝" rounds ....LB .104
¾" rounds ....LB .102
⅞" rounds ....LB .102
1" rounds ....LB .102
REINFORCING MESH (1050 SF Rolls)
6x6 x 10x10...........................SF .035
6x6 x 6x6...............................SF .067
16 GA. TYING WIRE............LB .130
Rates 100-1000 Lbs. F.O.B. Warehouse

STRUCTURAL STEEL
$325.00 and up per ton erected when out of mill.
$350.00 and up per ton erected when out of stock.

SHEET METAL
ROOF FLASHINGS:
18 ga. Galv. Steel.................SF .60 - 1.00
22 ga. Galv. Steel.................SF .50 - .90
26 ga. Galv. Steel.................SF .40 - .80
18 ga. Aluminum ....SF 1.00 - 1.50
22 ga. Aluminum ....SF .80 - 1.30
26 ga. Aluminum ....SF .60 - 1.10
24 oz. Copper ....SF 1.90 - 2.40
20 oz. Copper ....SF 1.50 - 2.00
16 oz. Copper ....SF 1.30 - 2.00
26 ga. Galv. Steel
4" o.g. gutter.......................LF .90 - 1.30
Mitres and Drops.................EA 2.00 - 4.00
22 ga. Galv. Louvres............SF 2.30 - 3.50
20 oz. Copper Louvres.........SF 3.00 - 4.50

TILE WORK
CERAMIC TILE, Stock colors:
Floors ....SF 1.95 - 2.45
Walls ....SF 2.05 - 2.55
Coved Base ....LF 1.05 - 1.45
QUARRY TILE:
6" x 6" x ½" Floors..............SF 1.60 - 2.00
6" x 6" x ¾" Floors..............SF 1.75 - 2.15
Treads and risers..................LF 3.00 - 4.30
Coved Base ....LF .90 - 1.30
Mosaic Tile — Rates vary with design and colors.
Each job should be priced from Manufacturer.

TERRAZZO & MARBLE
Terrazzo Floors ....SF 2.00 - 2.30
Cond. Terr. Floors...............SF 2.20 - 2.75
Precast treads and risers.......SF 3.50 - 4.30
Precast landing slabs.............SF 3.00 - 4.00

TILE
CERAMIC:
F.O.B. Warehouse
4¼" x 4¼" glazed................SF .69
4¼" x 4¼" hard glazed........SF .72
Random unglazed ....SF .73
6" x 2" cap...........................EA .17
6" coved base ....EA .22
¼" round bead......................LF .18
QUARRY:
6" x 6" x ½" Red..................SF .49
6" x 6" x ¾" Red..................SF .50
6" x 9" x ¾" Red..................SF .60
6" x 6" coved base................EA .21
White Cement Grout............Per 100 Lbs. 6.25

VENETIAN BLINDS
Residential ....SF .40 & Up
Commercial ....SF .45 & Up

WINDOWS
STEEL SASH:
Under 10 SF ....SP 2.50 & Up
Under 15 SF ....SP 2.00 & Up
Under 20 SF ....SP 1.50 & Up
Under 30 SF.........................SP 1.00 & Up
ALUMINUM SASH:
Under 10 SF ....SF 2.75 & Up
Under 15 SF ....SF 2.25 & Up
Under 20 SF ....SF 1.75 & Up
Under 30 SF.........................SF 1.25 & Up
Above rates are for standard sections and stock sizes
F.O.B. Warehouse

ESTIMATOR'S DIRECTORY
Building and Construction Materials

ACOUSTICAL ENGINEERS
L. D. REEDER CO.
San Francisco: 1255 Sansome St., DO 2-5050
Sacramento: 3026 V St., GL 7-3505

AIR CONDITIONING
E. C. BRAUN CO.
Berkeley: 2115 Fourth St., TH 5-2356
GILMORE AIR CONDITIONING SERVICE
San Francisco: 1617 Harrison St., UN 1-2000
KAEMPER & BARRETT
San Francisco: 233 Industrial St., JU 6-6200
LINFORD AIR & REFRIGERATION CO.
Oakland: 174-12th St., TW 3-6521
MALM METAL PRODUCTS
Santa Rosa: 724-2nd St., SR 454
JAMES A. NELSON CO.
San Francisco: 1375 Howard St., HE 1-0140

ALUMINUM BLDG. PRODUCTS
MICHEL & PFEFFER IRON WORKS (Wrought Iron)
So. San Francisco: 212 Shaw Road, PLaza 5-8983
REYNOLDS METALS CO.
San Francisco: 3201 Third St., MI 7-2990
SOULE STEEL CO.
San Francisco: 1750 Army St., VA 4-4141
UNIVERSAL WINDOW CO.
Berkeley: 950 Parker St., TH 1-1600

ARCHITECTURAL PORCELAIN ENAMEL
CALIFORNIA METAL ENAMELING CO.
Los Angeles: 6904 E. Slauson, RA 3-6351
San Francisco: Continental Bldg. Products Co.,
   178 Fremont St.
Portland: Portland Wire & Iron Works,
   4644 S.E. Seventeenth Ave,
Seattle: Foster-Bray Co., 2412 1st Ave. So.
Spokane: Bernhard Schafer, Inc., West 34, 2nd Ave.
Salt Lake City: S. A. Roberts & Co., 109 W. 2nd So.
Dallas: Offenhauser Co., 2201 Telephone Rd.
El Paso: Architectural Products Co.,
   506 E. Yandell Blvd.
Phoenix: Haskell-Thomas Co., 3808 No. Central
San Diego: Maloney Specialties, Inc., 823 W. Laurel St.
Boise: Intermountain Glass Co., 1417 Main St.

ARCHITECTURAL & AERIAL PHOTOGRAPHS
FRED ENGLISH
Belmont, Calif.: 1310 Old County Road, LY 1-0385

ARCHITECTURAL VENEER
Ceramic Veneer
GLADDING, McBEAN & CO.
San Francisco: Harrison at 9th St., UN 1-7400
Los Angeles: 2901 Los Feliz Blvd., OL 2121
Portland: 110 S.E. Main St., EA 6179
Seattle 99: 945 Elliott Ave., West. GA 0330
Spokane: 1102 N. Monroe St., BR 3259
KRAFTILE COMPANY
Niles, Calif., Niles 3611

Porcelain Veneer
PORCELAIN ENAMEL PUBLICITY BUREAU
Oakland 12: Room 601, Franklin Building
Pasadena 8: P. O. Box 186, East Pasadena Station
Granite Veneer
VERMONT MARBLE COMPANY
San Francisco 24: 6000 3rd St, VA 6-5024
Los Angeles: 3522 Council St., DU 2-6339
Marble Veneer
VERMONT MARBLE COMPANY
San Francisco 24: 6000 3rd St, VA 6-5024
Los Angeles: 3522 Council St., DU 2-6339

BANKS - FINANCING
CROCKER-ANGLO NATIONAL BANK
San Francisco: 13 Offices
BLINDS
PARAMOUNT VENETIAN BLIND CO.
San Francisco: 5929 Mission St., JU 5-2436
BRASS PRODUCTS
GREENBERG'S, M. SONS
San Francisco 7: 765 Folsom, EX 2-3143
Los Angeles 23: 1258 S. Boyle, AN 3-7108
Seattle 4:1016 First Ave. So., MA 5140
Phoenix: 3009 N. 19th Ave., Apt. 92, PH 2-7663
Portland 4: 510 Builders Exch. Bldg., AT 6443
BRICKWORK
Face Brick
GLADDING McBEAN & CO.
San Francisco: Harrison at 9th, UN 1-7400
KRAFTILE CO.
Niles, Calif., Niles 3611
UNITED MATERIALS & RICHMOND BRICK CO.
Point Richmond, BE 4-5032
BRONZE PRODUCTS
GREENBERG'S M. SONS
San Francisco: 765 Folsom St., EX 2-3143
MICHEL & PFEFFER IRON WORKS
So. San Francisco: 212 Shaw Road, PLaza 5-8983
C. E. TOLAND & SON
Oakland: 2635 Peralta St., GL 1-2580
BUILDING HARDWARE
E. M. HUNDLEY HARDWARE CO.
San Francisco: 662 Mission St., YU 2-3322
BUILDING PAPERS & FELTS
PACIFIC CEMENT & AGGREGATES INC.
San Francisco: 400 Alabama St., KL 2-1616
CABINETS & FIXTURES
CENTRAL MILL & CABINET CO.
San Francisco: 1595 Fairfax Ave., VA 4-7316
THE FINK & SCHINDLER CO.
San Francisco: 552 Brannan St., EX 2-1513
JONES KRAFT SHOP,
San Francisco: 1314 Ocean Avenue., JU 7-1545
MULLEN MFG. CO.
San Francisco: 64 Rausch St., UN 1-5815
PARAMOUNT BUILT IN FIXTURE CO.
Oakland: 962 Stanford Ave., OL 3-9911
ROYAL SHOWCASE CO.
San Francisco: 770 McAllister St., JO 7-0311
CEMENT
CALAVERAS CEMENT CO.
San Francisco: 315 Montgomery St.
DO 2-4224, Enterprise 1-7315
PACIFIC CEMENT & AGGREGATES INC.
San Francisco: 400 Alabama St., KL 2-1616
CONCRETE AGGREGATES
Ready Mixed Concrete
CENTRAL CONCRETE SUPPLY CO.
San Jose: 610 McKendrie St.
PACIFIC CEMENT & AGGREGATES INC.
San Francisco: 400 Alabama St., KL 2-1616
Sacramento: 16th and A Sts., GI 3-6586
San Jose: 790 Stockton Ave., CY 2-5620
Oakland: 2400 Peralta St., GL 1-0177
Stockton: 820 So. California St., ST 8-8643
READYMIX CONCRETE CO.
Santa Rosa: 50 W. Cottage Ave.
RHODES-JAMIESON LTD.
Oakland: 333-23rd Ave., KE 3-5225
SANTA ROSA BLDG. MATERIALS CO.
Santa Rosa: Roberts Ave.
CONCRETE ACCESSORIES
Screed Materials
C. & H. SPECIALTIES CO.
Berkeley: 909 Camelia St., LA 4-5358

CONCRETE BLOCKS
BASALT ROCK CO.
Napa, Calif.
CONCRETE COLORS—HARDENERS
CONRAD SOVIG CO.
875 Bryant St., HE 1-1345
CONSTRUCTION SERVICES
LE ROY CONSTRUCTION SERVICES
San Francisco, 143 Third St., SU 1-8914
DECKS—ROOF
UNITED STATES GYPSUM CO.
2322 W. 3rd St., Los Angeles 54, Calif.
300 W. Adams St., Chicago 6, Ill.
DOORS
THE BILCO COMPANY
New Haven, Conn.
Oakland: Geo. B. Schultz, 190 MacArthur Blvd.
Sacramento: Harry B. Ogle & Assoc., 1331 T St
Fresno: Healey & Popovich, 1703 Fulton St.
Reseda: Daniel Dunner, 6200 Alonzo Ave.
Cold Storage Doors
BIRKENWALD
Portland: 310 N.W. 5th Ave.
Electric Doors
ROLY-DOOR SALES CO.
San Francisco, 5976 Mission St., PL 5-5089
Folding Doors
WALTER D. BATES & ASSOCIATES
San Francisco, 693 Mission St., GA 1-6971
Hardwood Doors
BELLWOOD CO. OF CALIF.
Orange, Calif., 533 W. Collins Ave.
Hollywood Doors
WEST COAST SCREEN CO.
Los Angeles: 1127 E. 63rd St., AD 1-1108
T. M. COBB CO.
Los Angeles & San Diego
W. P. FULLER CO.
Seattle, Tacoma, Portland
HOGAN LUMBER CO.
Oakland: 700 - 6th Ave.
HOUSTON SASH & DOOR
Houston, Texas
SOUTHWESTERN SASH & DOOR
Phoenix, Tucson, Arizona
El Paso, Texas
WESTERN PINE SUPPLY CO.
Emeryville: 5760 Shellmound St.
GEO. C. VAUGHAN & SONS
San Antonio & Houston, Texas
Screen Doors
WEST COAST SCREEN DOOR CO.
DRAFTING ROOM EQUIPMENT
GENERAL FIREPROOFING CO.
Oakland: 332-19th St., GL 2-4280
Los Angeles: 1200 South Hope St., RI 7-7501
San Francisco: 1025 Howard St., HE 1-7070
DRINKING FOUNTAINS
HAWS DRINKING FAUCET CO.
Berkeley: 1435 Fourth St., LA 5-3341
ELECTRICAL CONTRACTORS
COOPMAN ELECTRIC CO.
San Francisco: B5 - 14th St., MA 1-4438
ETS-HOKIN & GALVAN
San Francisco: 551 Mission St., EX 2-0432

ELECTRICAL CONTRACTORS (cont'd)

LEMOGE ELECTRIC CO.
San Francisco: 212 Clara St., DO 2-6010
LYNCH ELECTRIC CO.
San Francisco: 937 McAllister St., WI 5158
PACIFIC ELECTRIC & MECHANICAL CO.
San Francisco: Gough & Fell Sts., HE 1-5904

ELECTRIC HEATERS

WESIX ELECTRIC HEATER CO.
San Francisco: 390 First St., GA 1-2211

FIRE ESCAPES

MICHEL & PFEFFER IRON WORKS
South San Francisco: 212 Shaw Road, PLaza 5-8983

FIRE PROTECTION EQUIPMENT

FIRE PROTECTION PRODUCTS CO.
San Francisco: 1101-16th St., UN 1-2420
ETS-HOKIN & GALVAN
San Francisco: 551 Mission St., EX 2-0432
BARNARD ENGINEERING CO.
San Francisco: 35 Elmira St., JU 5-4642

FLOORS

Floor Tile
GLADDING McBEAN & CO.
San Francisco: Harrison at 9th St., UN 1-744
Los Angeles: 2901 Las Feliz Bldg., OL 2121
KRAFTILE CO.
Niles, Calif., Niles 3611

Resilient Floors
PETERSON-COBBY CO.
San Francisco: 218 Clara St., EX 2-8714
TURNER RESILIENT FLOORS CO.
San Francisco: 2280 Shafter Ave., AT 2-7720

FLOOR DRAINS

JOSAM PACIFIC COMPANY
San Francisco: 765 Folsom St., EX 2-3142

GAS VENTS

WM. WALLACE CO.
Belmont, Calif.

GENERAL CONTRACTORS

O. E. ANDERSON
San Jose: 1075 No. 10th St., CY 3-8844
BARRETT CONSTRUCTION CO.
San Francisco: 1800 Evans Ave., MI 7-9700
JOSEPH BETTANCOURT
South San Francisco: 125 So. Linden St., PL 5-9185
DINWIDDIE CONSTRUCTION CO.
San Francisco: Crocker Bldg., YU 6-2718
D. L. FAULL CONSTRUCTION CO.
Santa Rosa: 1236 Cleveland Ave.
HAAS & HAYNIE
San Francisco: 275 Pine St., DO 2-0678
HENDERSON CONSTRUCTION CO.
San Francisco: 33 Ritch St., GA 1-0856
JACKS & IRVINE
San Francisco: 620 Market St., YU 6-0511
G. P. W. JENSEN & SONS
San Francisco: 320 Market St., GA 1-2444
RALPH LARSEN & SON
San Francisco: 64 So. Park, YU 2-5682
LINDGREN & SWINERTON
San Francisco: 200 Bush St., GA 1-2980
MacDONALD, YOUNG & NELSON
San Francisco: 351 California St., YU 2-4700
MATTOCK CONSTRUCTION CO.
San Francisco: 220 Clara St., GA 1-5516
OLSEN CONSTRUCTION CO.
Santa Rosa: 125 Brookwood Ave., SR 2030
BEN ORTSKY
Cotati: Cypress Ave., Pet. 5-4383
PARKER, STEFFANS & PEARCE
San Mateo: 135 So. Park, EX 2-6639
RAPP, CHRISTENSEN & FOSTER
Santa Rosa: 705 Bennett Ave.

STOLTE, INC.
Oakland: 8451 San Leandro Ave., LO 2-4611
SWINERTON & WALBERG   -
San Francisco: 200 Bush St., GA 1-2980

FURNITURE—INSTITUTIONAL

GENERAL FIREPROOFING CO.
San Francisco: 1025 Howard St., HE 1-7070
Oakland: 332-19th St., GL 2-4280
Los Angeles: 1200 South Hope St., RI 7-7501

HEATING & VENTILATING

ATLAS HEATING & VENT. CO.
San Francisco: 557-4th St., DO 2-0377
E. C. BRAUN CO.
Berkeley: 2115 Fourth St., TH 5-2356
C. W. HALL
Santa Rosa: 1665 Sebastopol Rd., SR 6354
S. T. JOHNSON CO.
Oakland: 940 Arlington Ave., OL 2-6000
LOUIS V. KELLER
San Francisco: 289 Tehama St., JU 6-6252
L. J. KRUSE CO.
Oakland: 6247 College Ave., OL 2-8332
MALM METAL PRODUCTS
Santa Rosa: 724-2nd St., SR 454
JAS. A. NELSON CO.
San Francisco: 1375 Howard St., HE 1-0140
SCOTT COMPANY
Oakland: 1919 Market St., GL 1-1937
WESIX ELECTRIC HEATER CO.
San Francisco: 390 First St., GA 1-2211
Los Angeles: 530 W. 7th St., MI 8096

INSULATION WALL BOARD

PACIFIC CEMENT & AGGREGATES, INC.
San Francisco: 400 Alabama St., KL 2-1616

INTERCEPTING DEVICES

JOSAM PACIFIC CO.
San Francisco: 765 Folsom St., EX 2-3142

IRON—ORNAMENTAL

MICHEL & PFEFFER IRON WKS.
So. San Francisco, 212 Shaw Rd., PL 5-8983

LATHING & PLASTERING

ANGELO J. DANERI
San Francisco: 1433 Fairfax Ave., AT 8-1582
K-LATH CORP.
Alhambra: 909 So. Fremont St., Alhambra
A. E. KNOWLES CORP.
San Francisco: 3330 San Bruno Ave., JU 7-2091
G. H. & C. MARTINELLI
San Francisco: 174 Shotwell St., UN 3-6112
FREDERICK MEISWINKEL
San Francisco: 2155 Turk St., JO 7-7587
RHODES-JAMIESON LTD.
Oakland: 333-23rd Ave., KE 3-5225
PATRICK J. RUANE
San Francisco: 44 San Jose Ave., MI 7-6414

LIGHTING FIXTURES

SMOOT-HOLMAN COMPANY
Inglewood, Calif., OR 8-1217
San Francisco: 55 Mississippi St., MA 1-8474

LIGHTING & CEILING SYSTEMS

UNITED LIGHTING AND FIXTURE CO.
Oakland: 3120 Chapman St., KE 3-8711

LUMBER

CHRISTENSEN LUMBER CO.
San Francisco: Quint & Evans Ave., VA 4-5832
ART HOGAN LUMBER CO.
1701 Galvez Ave., ATwater 2-1157
MEAD CLARK LUMBER CO.
Santa Rosa: 3rd & Railroad
ROLANDO LUMBER CO.
San Francisco: 5th & Berry Sts., SU 1-6901
STERLING LUMBER CO.
Santa Rosa: 1129 College Ave., S. R. 82

MARBLE

JOS. MUSTO SONS-KEENAN CO.
San Francisco: 555 No. Point St., GR 4-6365
VERMONT MARBLE CO.
San Francisco: 6000-3rd St., VA 6-5024

MASONRY

BASALT ROCK CO.
Napa, Calif.
San Francisco: 260 Kearney St., GA 1-3758
WM. A. RAINEY & SON
San Francisco: 323 Clementina St., SU 1-0072
GEO. W. REED CO.
San Francisco: 1390 So. Van Ness Ave., AT 2-1726

METAL EXTERIOR WALLS

THE KAWNEER CO.
Berkeley: 930 Dwight Way, TH 5-8710

METAL FRAMING

UNISTRUT OF NORTHERN CALIFORNIA
Berkeley: 2547-9th St., TH 1-3031
Enterprise 1-2204

METAL GRATING

KLEMP METAL GRATING CORP.
Chicago, Ill.: 6601 So. Melvina St.

METAL LATH—EXPANDED

PACIFIC CEMENT & AGGREGATES, INC.
San Francisco: 400 Alabama St., KL 2-1616

METAL PARTITIONS

THE E. F. HAUSERMAN CO.
San Francisco: 485 Brannan St., YU 2-5477

METAL PRODUCTS

FORDERER CORNICE WORKS
San Francisco: 269 Potrero Ave., HE 1-4100

MILLWORK

CENTRAL MILL & CABINET CO.
San Francisco: 1595 Fairfax Ave., VA 4-7316
THE FINK & SCHINDLER CO.
San Francisco: 552 Brannan St., EX 2-1513
MULLEN MFG. CO.
San Francisco: 64 Rausch St., UN 1-5815
PACIFIC MFG. CO.
San Francisco: 16 Beale St., GA 1-7755
Santa Clara: 2610 The Alameda, S. C. 607
Los Angeles: 6820 McKinley Ave., TH 4156
SOUTH CITY LUMBER & SUPPLY CO.
So. San Francisco: Railroad & Spruce, PL 5-7085

OFFICE EQUIPMENT

GENERAL FIREPROOFING CO.
Los Angeles: 1200 South Hope St., RI 7-7501
San Francisco: 1025 Howard St., HE 1-7070
Oakland: 332-19th St., GL 2-4280

OIL BURNERS

S. T. JOHNSON CO.
Oakland: 940 Arlington Ave., GL 2-6000
San Francisco: 585 Potrero Ave., MA 1-2757
Philadelphia, Pa.: 401 North Broad St.

ORNAMENTAL IRON

MICHEL & PFEFFER IRON WORKS
So. San Francisco: 212 Shaw Rd., PL 5-8983

PAINTING

R. P. PAOLI & CO.
San Francisco: 2530 Lombard St., WE 1-1632
SINCLAIR PAINT CO.
San Francisco: 2112-15th St., HE 1-2196
D. ZELINSKY & SONS
San Francisco: 165 Groove St., MA 1-7400

PHOTOGRAPHS

Construction Progress
FRED ENGLISH
Belmont, Calif.: 1310 Old County Road, LY 1-0385

PLASTER

PACIFIC CEMENT & AGGREGATE INC.
San Francisco: 400 Alabama St., KL 2-1616

PLASTIC PRODUCTS

PLASTIC SALES & SERVICE
San Francisco: 409 Bryant St., DO 2-6433
WEST COAST INDUSTRIES
San Francisco: 3150-18th St., MA 1-5657

38

PLUMBING
BROADWAY PLUMBING CO.
San Francisco: 1790 Yosemite Ave., MI 8-4250
E. C. BRAUN CO.
Berkeley: 2115 Fourth St., TH 5-2356
C. W. HALL
Santa Rosa: 1665 Sebastopol Rd., SR 6354
HAWS DRINKING FAUCET CO.
Berkeley: 1435 Fourth St., LA 5-3341
JOSAM PACIFIC CO.
San Francisco: 765 Folsom St., EX 2-3143
LOUIS V. KELLER
San Francisco: 289 Tehama St., YU 6-6252
L. J. KRUSE CO.
Oakland: 6247 College Ave., OL 2-8332
JAS. A. NELSON CO.
San Francisco: 1375 Howard St., HE 1-0140
RODONI-BECKER CO., INC.
San Francisco: 455-10th St., MA 1-3662
SCOTT CO.
Oakland: 1919 Market St., GL 1-1937

POST PULLER
HOLLAND MFG. CO.
No. Sacramento: 1202 Dixieanne

PUMPING MACHINERY
SIMONDS MACHINERY CO.
San Francisco: 816 Folsom St., DO 2-6794

ROOFING
ANCHOR ROOFING CO.
San Francisco: 1671 Galvez Ave., VA 4-8140
ALTA ROOFING CO.
San Francisco: 1400 Egbert Ave., MI 7-2173
REGAL ROOFING CO.
San Francisco: 930 Innes Ave., VA 4-3261

ROOF SCUTTLES
THE BILCO CO.
New Haven, Conn.
Oakland: Geo. B. Schultz, 190 MacArthur Blvd.
Sacramento: Harry B. Ogle & Assoc., 1331 T St.
Fresno: Healey & Popovich, 1703 Fulton St.
Reseda: Daniel Dunner, 6200 Alonzo Ave.

ROOF TRUSSES
EASYBOW ENGINEERING & RESEARCH CO.
Oakland: 13th & Wood Sts., GL 2-0805

SAFES
THE HERMANN SAFE CO.
San Francisco: 1699 Market St., UN 1-6644

SEWER PIPE
GLADDING, McBEAN & CO.
San Francisco: 9th & Harrison, UN 1-7400
Los Angeles: 2901 Los Feliz Blvd., OL 2121

SHEET METAL
MICHEL & PFEFFER IRON WORKS
So. San Francisco: 212 Shaw Rd., PL 5-8983

SOUND EQUIPMENT
STROMBERG-CARLSON CO.
San Francisco: 1805 Rollins Rd., Burlingame, OX 7-3630
Los Angeles: 5414 York Blvd., CL 7-3939

SPRINKLERS
BARNARD ENGINEERING CO.
San Francisco: 35 Elmira St., JU 5-4642

STEEL—STRUCTURAL & REINFORCING
COLUMBIA-GENEVA DIV., U. S. STEEL CORP.
San Francisco: Russ Bldg., SU 1-2500
Los Angeles: 2087 E. Slauson, LA 1171
Portland, Ore.: 2345 N.W. Nicolai, BE 7261
Seattle, Wn.: 1331-3rd Ave. Bldg., MA 1972
Salt Lake City, Utah: Walker Bank Bldg., SL 3-6733
HERRICK IRON WORKS
Oakland 18th & Campbell, GL 1-1767
INDEPENDENT IRON WORKS, INC.
Oakland: 780 Pine St., TE 2-0160
JUDSON PACIFIC MURPHY CORP.
Emeryville: 4300 Eastshore Highway, OL 3-1717
REPUBLIC STEEL CORP.
San Francisco: 116 New Montgomery St., GA 1-0977
Los Angeles: Edison Bldg.
Seattle: White-Henry Stuart Bldg.
Salt Lake City: Walker Bank Bldg.
Denver: Continental Oil Bldg.
SOULE STEEL CO.
San Francisco: 1750 Army St., VA 4-4141

STEEL FORMS
STEELFORM CONTRACTING CO.
San Francisco: 666 Harrison St, DO 2-5582

SWIMMING POOLS
SIERRA MFG. CO.
Walnut Creek, Calif.: 1719 Mt. Diablo Blvd.

SWIMMING POOL FITTINGS
JOSAM PACIFIC CO.
San Francisco: 765 Folsom St., EX 2-3143

**TESTING LABORATORIES
(ENGINEERS & CHEMISTS**
ABBOT A. HANKS, INC.
San Francisco: 624 Sacramento St., GA 1-1697
ROBERT W. HUNT COMPANY
San Francisco: 500 Iowa, MI 7-0224
Los Angeles: 3050 E. Slauson, JE 9131
Chicago, New York, Pittsburgh
PITTSBURGH TESTING LABORATORY
San Francisco: 651 Howard St., EX 2-1747

TILE—CLAY & WALL
GLADDING McBEAN & CO.
San Francisco: 9th & Harrison Sts., UN 1-7400
Los Angeles: 2901 Los Feliz Blvd., OL 2121
Portland: 110 S.E. Main St., EA 6179
Seattle: 945 Elliott Ave. West, GA 0330
Spokane: 1102 No. Monroe St., BR 3259
KRAFTILE CO.
Niles, Calif.: Niles 3611
San Francisco: 50 Hawthorne St., DO 2-3780
Los Angeles: 406 So. Main St., MA 7241

TILE—TERRAZZO
NATIONAL TILE & TERAZZO CO.
San Francisco: 198 Mississippi St., UN 1-0273

TIMBER—TREATED
J. H. BAXTER CO.
San Francisco: 200 Bush St., YU 2-0200
Los Angeles: 3450 Wilshire Blvd., DU 8-9591

TIMBER TRUSSES
EASYBOW ENGINEERING & RESEARCH CO.
Oakland: 13th & Wood Sts., GL 2-0805

TRUCKING
PASSETTI TRUCKING CO.
San Francisco: 264 Clementina St., GA 1-5297

UNDERPINNING & SHORING
D. J. & T. SULLIVAN
San Francisco: 1942 Folsom St., MA 1-1545

WALL PAPER
WALLPAPERS, INC.
Oakland: 384 Grand Ave., GL 2-0451

WAREHOUSE AND STORAGE EQUIPMENT AND SHELVING
GENERAL FIREPROOFING CO.
Los Angeles: 1200 South Hope St., RI 7-7501
San Francisco: 1025 Howard St., HE 1-7070
Oakland: 332-19th St., GL 2-4280

WATERPROOFING MATERIALS
CONRAD SOVIG CO.
San Francisco: 875 Bryant St., HE 1-1345

WATERSTOPS (P.V.C.)
TECON PRODUCTS, LTD.
Vancouver, B.C.: 681 E. Hastings St.
Seattle: 304 So. Alaskan Way

WINDOW SHADES
SHADES, INC.
San Francisco: 80 Tehama St., DO 2-7092

CONSTRUCTION INDUSTRY WAGE RATES

Table 1 has been prepared by the State of California, Department of Industrial Relations, Division of Labor Statistics and Research. The rates are the union hourly wage rates established by collective bargaining as of January 2, 1958, as reported by reliable sources.

TABLE 1—UNION HOURLY WAGE RATES, CONSTRUCTION INDUSTRY, CALIFORNIA

Following are the hourly rates of compensation established by collective bargaining, reported as of January 2, 1958 or later

CRAFT	San Francisco	Alameda	Contra Costa	Fresno	Sacramento	San Joaquin	Santa Clara	Solano	Los Angeles	San Bernardino	San Diego	Santa Barbara	Kern
ASBESTOS WORKER	$3.70	$3.70	$3.70	$3.70	$3.70	$3.70	$3.70	$3.70	$3.70	$3.70	$3.70	$3.70	$3.70
BOILERMAKER	3.675	3.675	3.675	3.675	3.675	3.675	3.675	3.675	3.675	3.675	3.675	3.675	3.675
BRICKLAYER	3.95	3.75	3.75	3.75	3.80	3.75	3.875	3.95	3.80	3.90	3.75		3.85
BRICKLAYER HODCARRIER	3.15	3.15	3.15	2.90	3.10	2.90	3.00	3.00	2.75	2.75	2.75		2.75
CARPENTER	3.175	3.175	3.225	3.225	3.225	3.225	3.225	3.225	3.225	3.225	3.225	3.225	3.225
CEMENT MASON	3.22	3.22	3.22	3.22	3.22	3.22	3.22	3.22	3.15	3.15	3.25	3.15	3.15
ELECTRICIAN	3.936ᴀ	3.936ᴀ	3.936ᴀ		3.94ᴀ	3.50	4.03ᴀ	3.666ᴀ	3.90ᴀ	3.90ᴀ	3.90	3.85ᴀ	3.70
GLAZIER	3.09	3.09	3.09	3.135	3.055	3.055	3.09	3.09	3.105	3.105	3.03	3.105	3.135
IRON WORKER ORNAMENTAL	3.625	3.625	3.625	3.625	3.625	3.625	3.625	3.625	3.625	3.625	3.625	3.625	3.625
REINFORCING	3.375	3.375	3.375	3.375	3.375	3.375	3.375	3.375	3.375	3.375	3.375	3.375	3.375
STRUCTURAL	3.625	3.625	3.625	3.625	3.625	3.625	3.625	3.625	3.625	3.625	3.625	3.625	3.625
LABORER, GENERAL OR CONSTRUCTION	2.505	2.505	2.505	2.505	2.505	2.505	2.505	2.505	2.50	2.50	2.48	2.50	2.50
LATHER	3.4375	3.84	3.84	3.45	3.60ʙ	3.40ᴄ	3.60ᴅ	3.50ᴇ	3.9375		3.725	3.625ꜰ	
OPERATING ENGINEER Concrete mixer (up to 1 yard)	2.89	2.89	2.89	2.89	2.89	2.89	2.89	2.89					
Concrete mixer operator—Skip Type									2.96	2.96	2.96	2.96	2.96
Elevator Hoist Operator									3.19	3.19	3.19	3.19	3.19
Material Hoist (1 drum)	3.19	3.19	3.19	3.19	3.19	3.19	3.19	3.19					
Tractor Operator	3.33	3.33	3.33	3.33	3.33	3.33	3.33	3.33	3.47	3.47	3.47	3.47	3.47
PAINTER Brush	3.20	3.20	3.20	3.13	3.325	3.175	3.20	3.20	3.26ᴳ	3.25	3.19	3.13ʜ	3.10
Spray	3.20	3.20	3.20	3.38	3.575	3.325	3.20	3.20	3.51ᴳ	3.50	3.74	3.38ʜ	3.35
PILEDRIVERMAN	3.305	3.305	3.305	3.305	3.305	3.305	3.305	3.305	3.355	3.355		3.355	3.355
PLASTERER	3.69	3.545	3.545	3.35	3.60ʙ	3.55ᴄ	3.58	3.50	3.9375	3.9375	3.725		
PLASTERER HODCARRIER	3.25	3.42	3.42	3.10	3.10	3.00ᴄ	3.20	3.15	3.6875	3.5625	3.475	3.50	3.6875
PLUMBER	3.67		3.935ɪ	3.80ᴊ	3.70	3.80ᴊ	3.60	3.675	3.70	3.70	3.70	3.70	3.375
ROOFER	3.35	3.35	3.35	3.20	3.25	3.35	3.35	3.10ᴋ	3.20ʟ	3.25	3.10	3.30	3.775
SHEET METAL WORKER	3.45	3.45	3.45	3.425	3.45	3.465	3.46	3.325	3.50	3.50	3.45	3.55	3.10
STEAMFITTER	3.67	3.96	3.96	3.80ᴊ	3.70	3.80ᴊ	3.60	3.675	3.70	3.70	3.70	3.70	3.775
TRUCK DRIVER— Dump Trucks under 4 yards	2.55	2.55	2.55	2.55	2.55	2.55	2.55	2.55	2.63	2.63	2.63	2.63	2.63
TILE SETTER	3.275	3.275	3.275	3.375	3.26	3.30	3.275	3.275	3.36	3.60	3.375	3.36	

ᴀ Includes 4% vacation allowance.
ʙ Includes 5c hour for Industry promotion and 5c hour for vacation fund.
ᴄ ½% withheld for industry promotion.
ᴅ 1½c withheld for industry promotion.
ᴇ Includes 5c hour for Industry promotion and 5c hour for vacation fund. Hourly rate for part of county adjacent to Sacramento County is $3.60.
ꜰ Northern part of County: $3.75.

ᴳ Pomona Area: Brush $3.25; Spray $3.50.
ʜ Southern half of County: Brush $3.28; Spray $3.28.
ɪ Includes 30c hour for vacation pay.
ᴊ Includes 15c hour which local union may elect to use for vacation purposes.
ᴋ Includes 10c hour for vacation fund.
ʟ Includes 10c hour savings fund wage.

ATTENTION: The above tabulation has been prepared by the State of California, Department of Industrial Relations, Division of Labor Statistics and Research, and represents data reported by building trades councils, union locals, contractor organizations, and other reliable sources. The above rates do not include any payments to funds for health and welfare, pensions, vacations, Industry promotion, apprentice training, etc., except as shown in the footnotes.

CONSTRUCTION INDUSTRY WAGE RATES — TABLE 2

Employer Contributions to Health and Welfare, Pension, Vacation and Other Funds
California Union Contracts, Construction Industry

(Revised March, 1957)

CRAFT	San Francisco	Fresno	Sacramento	San Joaquin	Santa Clara	Los Angeles	San Bernardino	San Diego
ASBESTOS WORKER	.10 W .11 hr. V	.10 W .11 hr. V	.10 W .11 hr. V	.10 W .11 hr. V	.10 W .11 hr. V	.10 W	.10 W	.10 W
BRICKLAYER	.15 W .14 P .05 hr. V		.15 W		.15 W			
			.10 P					
BRICKLAYER HODCARRIER	.10 W .10 P .10 V	.10 W	.10 W	.10 W	.10 W	.075 W	.075 W	.075 W
CARPENTER	.10 W .10 hr. V	.10 W	.10 W	.10 W	.10 W	.10 W	.10 W	.10 W
CEMENT MASON	.10 W	.10 W	.10 W	.10 W	.10 W	.10 W	.10 W	.10 W
ELECTRICAL WORKER	.10 W 1% P 4% V	.10 W 1% P 4% V	.075 W 1% P	.075 W 1% P 4% V	1% P	1% P	1% P	.10 W 1% P
GLAZIER	.075 W .085 V	.075 W 40 hr. V	.075 W .05 V	.075 W .05 V	.075 W .08S V	.075 W 40 hr. V	.075 W 40 hr. V	.075 W 10 hr. V
IRONWORKER: REINFORCING STRUCTURAL	.10 W .10 W	.10 W .10 W	.10 W .10 W	.10 W .10 W	.10 W .10 W	.10 W .10 W	.10 W .10 W	.10 W .10 W
LABORER, GENERAL	.10 W	.10 W	.10 W	.10 W	.10 W	.075 W	.075 W	.075 W
LATHER	.60 day W .70 day V		.10 W	.10 W	.075 W .05 V	.90 day W	.70 day W	.10 W
OPERATING ENGINEER TRACTOR OPERATOR (MIN.) POWER SHOVEL OP. (MIN.)	.10 W .10 W	.10 W .10 W	.10 W .10 W	.10 W .10 W	.10 W .10 W	.10 W .10 W	.10 W .10 W	.10 W .10 W
PAINTER, BRUSH	.095 W	.08 W	.075 W	.10 W	.095 W .07 V	.085 W	.08 W	.09 W
PLASTERER	.10 W .10 V	.10 W	.10 W	.10 W	.10 W .15 V	.10 W	.90 day W	.10 W
PLUMBER	.10 W .10 V	.15 W .10 P	.10 W .10 P .125 V	.10 W	.10 W .10 P .125 V	.10 W	.90 day W	.10 W
ROOFER	.10 W .10 V	.10 W	.10 W .10 V	.10 W	.075 W .10 V	.085 W	.10 W	.075 W
SHEET METAL WORKER	.075 W 4% V	.075 W 7 day V	.075 W .10 V	.075 W .12 V	.075 W 4% V	.085 W .10 V	.085 W .10 V	.085 W 5 day V
TILE SETTER	.075 W .09 V				.075 W .09 V	.025 W .06 V		

ATTENTION: The above tabulation has been prepared and compiled from the available data reported by building trades councils, union locals, contractor organizations and other reliable sources. The table was prepared from incomplete data; where no employer contributions are specified, it does not necessarily mean that none are required by the union contract.

The type of supplement is indicated by the following symbols: W—Health and Welfare; P—Pensions; V—Vacations; A—Apprentice training fund; Adm—Administration fund; JIB—Joint Industry Board; Prom—Promotion fund.

CONSTRUCTION CONTRACTS AWARDED AND MISCELLANEOUS PERSONNEL DATA

SCHOOL ADD'N, Luther Elementary, Live Oak, Sutter county. Live Oak School District, Live Oak, owner. 1-Story wood frame construction to provide facilities for 3 classrooms—$100,989. ARCHITECT: Lawrence G. Thomson, 125 W. 3rd St., Chico. GENERAL CONTRACTOR: Jay Dailey Construction Co., P.O. Box 148, Woodland.

SPEECH - ARTS, Little Theatre Bldg., Humboldt State College, Arcata, Humboldt county. Department of Public Works, State of California, Sacramento, owner. Work consists of a 2-story and basement building to provide facilities for Speech-Arts Little Theatre, also some site development, 66,000 sq. ft. of floor area—$1,298,000. ARCHITECT: Anson Boyd, California State Architect, Sacramento. GENERAL CONTRACTOR: B. & R.

Construction Co., 110 Market St., San Francisco.

MACHINE SHOP, South Gate, Los Angeles county. Wesier Lock Co., South Gate, owner. 1-Story concrete block machine shop building, 70x121 ft. in area, composition roofing, bowstring trusses, cyclone type dust collectors, concrete slab floor. STRUCTURAL ENGINEER: John E. Mackel, 306 S. Union Place, Los Angeles. GENERAL CONTRACTOR: Ecker Bros., 122 Gertrude Ct., Pasadena.

PHYSICAL SCIENCE BLDG., Arizona State College, Tempe, Arizona. Arizona State College, Tempe, owner. Construction of a new physical science building with all related facilities — $1,036,291. ARCHITECT: Kemper Goodwin, 115 E. 5th St., Tempe, Arizona. GENERAL

CONTRACTOR: Owens Redden Construction Co., 1616 W. Camelback Rd., Phoenix.

HIGH SCHOOL ADD'N, Ukiah, Mendocino county. Ukiah Union High School District, Ukiah, owner. Wood frame and stucco construction to provide facilities for classrooms, music room, science room—$575,887. ARCHITECT: C. A. Caulkins, Jr., Rosenberg Bldg., Santa Rosa. GENERAL CONTRACTORS: Reynolds Construction Co., 55 Mt. View Ave., Santa Rosa.

MEDICAL BLDG., REMODEL, Riverside. Drs. Miller, Mullen & Cline, Riverside, owners. Remodel work involves exterior metal screens, new plate glass and aluminum entry, new interior wall coverings, wood paneling, vinyl floor, new air conditioning system, relocation of interior partitions, electrical work, plumbing. ARCHITECT: Clinton Marr, 3646 9th St., Riverside. GENERAL CONTRACTOR: Eric Emtman, 3825 Vine, Riverside.

HIGH SCHOOL ADD'N, Paso Robles, San Luis Obispo county. Paso Robles Joint Union High School District, owner.

Work includes excavating, concrete work, masonry, structural steel, sheet metal, refrigeration, insulation, plastering, metal windows, metal toilet compartments, resilient floor covering, tile, plumbing, heating, ventilating and electrical work—$95,-479. ARCHITECT: Daniel Mann, Johnson & Mendenhall, 3325 Wilshire Blvd., Los Angeles. GENERAL CONTRACTOR: Maino Construction Co., P.O. Box 708, San Luis Obispo.

OFFICE BLDG., Los Angeles. Southern Counties Gas Co., Los Angeles, owner. 13-Story reinforced concrete construction, 152x52 ft. in area, composition roofing, concrete floor, painting, plastering, plumbing, electrical work, heating, ventilating, acoustical, wood and metal partitions, structural and miscellaneous metal, pipe railings, pneumatic system, air conditioning, metal sash — $2,268,950. ARCHITECT: Albert C. Martin & Associates, Architects and Engineers, 333 S. Beaudry Ave., Los Angeles. GENERAL CONTRACTORS: Lindgren & Swinerton, 1631 Beverly Blvd., Los Angeles.

SCHOOL, Alvin S. Hatch, Half Moon Bay, San Mateo county. Coastside Union School District, owner. 1-Story wood frame construction, stucco exterior to provide facilities for 3 classrooms, administration unit and toilets—$83,235. ARCHITECT: Peter Kump, 107 Curtis St., Menlo Park. GENERAL CONTRACTOR: Roth Construction Co., P.O. Box 827, Belmont.

AUTO SALES BLDG., Monterey. Roller Chevrolet Co., Monterey, owner. 1-Story structural steel, masonry and concrete slab floor; built-up roofing; work includes remodeling of present building—$38,200. ARCHITECT: Wallace Holm & Associates, 321 Webster St., Monterey. GENERAL CONTRACTOR: Harold C. Geyer, P.O. Box 1190, Monterey.

RECREATION BLDG., Beverly Hills, Los Angeles county. City of Beverly Hills, owner. Masonry construction "U"-shaped structure, containing assembly hall with meeting and craft buildings adjoining under one roof. 7400 sq. ft. area, composition roofing, concrete slab, interior plaster, heating, electric plumbing—$190,080. ARCHITECT: Allison & Rible, 3670 Wilshire Blvd., Los Angeles. GENERAL CONTRACTOR: Jim Medlin Construction Co., 10962 Pickford Way, Culver City.

SCHOOL ADD'N, Oak Manor, Fairfax, Marin county. Fairfax School District, Fairfax, owner. 1-Story wood frame, wood siding, tar and gravel roof, concrete slab and asphalt tile floors, plaster and wood paneling—$115,990. ARCHITECT: Eugene E. Crawford, 920 5th Ave., San Rafael. GENERAL CONTRACTOR: R.S. Miller, 5610 Jordan Ave., El Cerrito.

PUBLIC LIBRARY, Santa Ana, Orange county. City of Santa Ana, owner. New Public Library Building, 30,000 sq. ft. area, reinforced concrete construction—$729,349. ARCHITECT: Harold Gimeno, 1400 N. Sycamore St., Santa Ana. GENERAL CONTRACTOR: The Gallegos Corp., 2120 S. Main St., Santa Ana.

HIGH SCHOOL ADD'N, Sonoma Valley, Sonoma. Sonoma Valley Union High School District, owner. Work includes construction of a library, crafts room and 4-classroom addition to present high school building; concrete slab on

grade, wood frame and stucco, 9.000 sq. ft. in area — $110,188. ARCHITECT: John Lyon Reid & Partners, 1019 Market St., San Francisco. GENERAL CONTRACTOR: A. A. Douglas, 130 Franklin St., Napa.

TREAD RUBBER PLANT, Santa Ana, Orange county. Voit Rubber Corp., Santa Ana, owner. New tread rubber plant, 60,-000 sq. ft. area, excavating, drainage ditch, chain link fence, spur track, tilt-up concrete construction, concrete block masonry, structural steel, millwork, steel sash, metal doors and hollow metal frames, glass and glazing, sheet metal, built-up roofing, asphalt tile, ceramic tile, acoustical treatment, plumbing, air conditioning, suspended unit heaters, fire sprinklers. ENGINEER: Quinton Engineers, Ltd., 812 W. 8th St., Los Angeles. GENERAL CONTRACTOR: Oltmans Construction Co., 516 S. Monterey Pass Rd., Monterey Park.

ELEMENTARY SCHOOL ADD'N, Rancho Verde, Decoto, Alameda county. Decoto School District, owner. 1-story, 4-classroom addition to existing buildings, wood frame construction—$125,870. ARCHITECT: John Hudspeth, 339 15th St., Oakland. GENERAL CONTRACTOR: C. R. Lind, 447 Glencoe Dr., Centerville.

SCHOOL & CHAPEL, Santa Ana, Orange county. Roman Catholic Archbishop of Los Angeles, owner. Reinforced brick and frame school and chapel addition to the Mater Dei Church in Santa Ana; 5 classrooms and chapel, concrete slab flooring, asphalt tile, composition roofing, interior plaster, decorative glass. ARCHITECT: Barker and Ott, 4334 W. Pico Blvd., Los Angeles. GENERAL CONTRACTOR: Ogden Markel, 1814 Parton, Santa Ana.

RESIDENCE HALLS, Sacramento State College, Sacramento. State of California, owner. Work consists of construction of three 3-story Residence Halls on the Sacramento State College campus at Sacramento; reinforced brick masonry construction, also some site development—$1,282,000. ARCHITECT: Anson Boyd, California State Architect, Sacramento. GENERAL CONTRACTOR: Nomellini Const. Co., P.O. Box 1528, Stockton.

STORE & OFFICE, Sherman Oaks, Los Angeles county. Scotty Building Co., Sherman Oaks, owner. 2-story frame and stucco office and store building, with basement; glued laminated beams, rock roof, structural steel, concrete slab, plaster, acoustical tile, plumbing, electrical, plate glass, metal toilet partitions, asphalt paving. ARCHITECT: Martin Stern, Jr., 8325 Wilshire Blvd., Beverly Hills. GENERAL CONTRACTOR: Parthenon Const. Co., 14015 Ventura Blvd., Sherman Oaks.

ELEMENTARY SCHOOL ADD'N, Roosevelt, Redwood City, San Mateo county. Redwood City School District, owner. Work represents Unit No. 4, wood frame and concrete block construction—$253,-000. ARCHITECT: Janssen, Daseking & Keller, 1616 El Camino Real, Menlo Park. GENERAL CONTRACTOR: Stevenson-Pacific Co., 1135 Chestnut St., Redwood City.

ELEMENTARY SCHOOL, Nathaniel Hawthorne, Riverside. Riverside School District, owner. New elementary school

plant in Riverside—$298,000. GENERAL CONTRACTOR: Frank R. & Wm. E. Jones, 3649 Meyers, Arlington.

TRAILER COURT, 200 units, Bakersfield, Kern county. Development includes a recreational building, general store, swimming pool, recreation area, utility building, trailer sales area, board and batten construction, composition roofing, concrete slab floors, sliding glass doors, air conditioning, exterior lighting, asphalt paving; sewers, gas, water, electricity. ARCHITECT: Mikles & Boner, Architects and Engineers, 1224 Chester Ave., Bakersfield. GENERAL CONTRACTOR: E. V. Mikles & Associates, Bakersfield.

STORE BLDG., Woodland Hills, Los Angeles county. Martin L. Klein, Woodland Hills, owner. Brick veneer and stucco store building 76 x 50 ft., composition roofing, steel security sash, evaporative coolers, concrete slab, interior plaster, plate glass, toilets — $20,000. STRUCTURAL ENGINEER: W. D. Crouch, Jr., Santa Paula. GENERAL CONTRACTOR: Ainslee W. Buchingham, 19634 Ventura Blvd., Tarzana.

NEW HIGH SCHOOL, Kings Canyon, Fresno. Fresno Unified School District, owner. Project is located on a 20-acre site and will include construction of Administration unit, all-purpose unit with lunch facilities, library, wood shop, 15 classrooms, metal shop, art unit, storage room; wood frame construction combined with steel frame — $1,148,000. ARCHITECT: John P. Miller, 1910 Fresno St., Fresno. GENERAL CONTRACTOR: Harris Const. Co., P.O. Box 109, Fresno.

HOTEL & RESTAURANT, El Segundo, Los Angeles county. Allen E. Seigal Enterprises, Beverly Hills, owner. 5-story "Thunderbird" hotel, 100,000 sq. ft. of area, masonry, steel stud and plaster construction, composition roofing, terrazzo, asphalt tile, ceramic tile and carpeted floors, plaster walls and ceilings, plumbing, electrical, air conditioning, two elevators, aluminum sliding windows, private balconies, swimming pool, asphalt paving; also included is a 25,000 sq. ft. restaurant and cocktail lounge. ARCHITECT: Raymond Stockdale, 3260 Hillock, Los Angeles. GENERAL CONTRACTOR: Allen E. Siegal Enterprises.

JR. COLLEGE ADD'N, Hartnell College, Salinas, Monterey county. Hartnell Jr. College District, Salinas, owner. Work comprises the addition of a 1-story library building of Type II construction—$389,-000. ARCHITECT: Jerome Kasacan, 7 Winham St., Salinas. GENERAL CONTRACTOR: Ekelin & Small, P.O. Box 8, Salinas.

BOAT SALES & SERVICE BLDG., Sherman Oaks, Los Angeles county. Casa-De-Marina, Inc., Sherman Oaks, owner. New boat sales and service building, 48 x 72 x 80 ft., all metal construction, aluminum roof, metal siding, plate glass, overhead doors, electrical, plumbing, asphalt concrete paving—$26,000. ENGINEER: C. Read, Structural Engineer. GENERAL CONTRACTOR: Southwest Const. Co., 314 W. Redondo Beach Blvd., Gardenia.

VETERANS MEMORIAL, Petaluma, Sonoma county. Board of Supervisors County of Sonoma, owner. Concrete exterior walls, concrete floors, wood, composition roofing; facilities for auditorium,

banquet hall, 2 meeting rooms, kitchen, shower and locker rooms, toilet facilities—$394,490. ARCHITECT: J. Clarence Felciano, 4010 Montecito Ave., Santa Rosa. GENERAL CONTRACTOR: Wright & Oretsky, P.O. Box 2185, Santa Rosa.

STORE BLDG., Marysville, Sutter county. C. M. Morris, Marysville, owner. 1-story wood frame and masonry store building; 2,000 sq. ft. area. ARCHITECT: Robert S. Oliver, 916 F Street, Marysville. GENERAL CONTRACTOR: Paul D. Young, 586 Cassidy Ave., Yuba City.

RESTAURANT & COCKTAIL LOUNGE. Montebello, Los Angeles county. Harsol, Inc., Montebello, owner. 1-story frame. stucco and stone veneer restaurant and cocktail lounge; 75 x 65 ft. area, built-up composition roof, aluminum entrance, concrete slab floor with carpet and vinyl covering, interior plaster and wood paneling, air conditioning, restrooms, plumbing and electrical work, paved parking area. ARCHITECT: Raymond Dan Conwell and Associates, 919 S. Garfield Ave., Los Angeles. GENERAL CONTRACTOR: Howard Livingston, 428 W. Washington Blvd., Montebello.

FELLOWSHIP HALL & EDUCATIONAL BLDGS., Mountain View, Santa Clara county. 1st Presbyterian Church, Mt. View, owner. Work includes construction of a new Fellowship Hall and educational buildings—$356,980. ARCHITECT: Alfred W. Johnson, 165 Jessie St., San Francisco. GENERAL CONTRACTOR: Pacific Coast Builders, 1 So. Park, San Francisco.

VALLEY JUNIOR COLLEGE, Van Nuys, Los Angeles county. Los Angeles Board of Education, owner. Construction includes classroom buildings, laboratory building, administration building, library building — $2,414,000. ARCHITECT: Chambers & Hibbard, 124 W. 4th St., Los Angeles. GENERAL CONTRACTOR: Tom E. Norcross, 6053 Atlantic Ave., Long Beach.

HOSPITAL RENOVATION, Kern County Hospital, Bakersfield, Kern county. County of Kern, owner. Work includes rehabilitation of the present county hospital buildings; structural, gunite exterior walls, removal of some brick work, rehabilitation of electrical installations with new power supply, forced air heating, air conditioning—$175,990. GENERAL CONTRACTOR: Tobisch & Colombo, 1530 E. 19th, Bakersfield.

CHURCH, San Marino, Los Angeles county. First Church of Christ Scientist, San Marino, owner. Building will measure 110 x 83 ft. in area, reinforced brick construction, composition roofing, concrete floor, brick work, structural steel and miscellaneous metal, lath and plaster, tile and marble, steel windows, hollow metal doors and frames, glass, finish hardware, painting, plumbing, heating, air conditioning, electrical work, wood floor, resilient tile, acoustical tile, metal toilet partitions—$199,840. ARCHITECT: Smith, Powell & Morgridge, 208 W. 8th St., Los Angeles. GENERAL CONTRACTOR: Escherich Bros., 645 S. Avenue 21, Los Angeles.

WOMEN'S RESIDENCE HALL, Berkeley, Alameda county. Baptist Divinity School, Berkeley, owner. Represents Phase 2 of a $3,000,000 development program; 3 stories, structural steel, partial basement, wood frame construction—$130,900. ARCHITECT: Ratcliff & Ratcliff, 2286 Fulton St., Berkeley. GENERAL CONTRACTOR: A. B. Lahti, 21 Arlington Court, Berkeley.

BRANCH BANK, San Jose, Santa Clara county. Bank of America, San Francisco. owner. 1-story and mezzanine, concrete block construction — $144.940.. ARCHITECT: Continental Service Co., Flood Bldg., San Francisco. GENERAL CONTRACTOR: Aiken Const Co., 333 Phelan Ave., San Jose.

STORAGE & GARAGE, Placentia, Orange county. Orange county Board of Supervisors, Santa Ana, owner. New Civil Defense storage and garage building; 40 x 68 ft., frame and stucco construction, composition roofing, concrete slab, steel sash, overhead doors — $9,665. ARCHITECT: Willard Jordan. 771 W. 19th St., Costa Mesa. GENERAL CONTRACTOR: Vincent Joyce, 15421 S. Van Buren St., Westminster.

INDUSTRIAL ARTS BLDG., State College, San Jose, Santa Clara county. State of California, Sacramento, owner. 2-story Industrial Arts Building on the State College campus, concrete construction; 109,000 sq. ft. area; also vehicle shelter of 800 sq. ft. area; 2,500 sq. ft.—$1,107,633. ARCHITECT: Anson Boyd, California State Architect, Sacramento. GENERAL CONTRACTOR: O. E. Anderson, 1075 No. 10th St., San Jose.

OFFICE BUILDING REMODEL, Santa Barbara. Granada Building, Santa Barbara, owner. Remodeling interior and exterior of the lobby of the Granada Building in Santa Barbara; new terrazzo floors, granite exterior, mosaic tile walls, plaster ceilings, electric lighting, new elevator doors and frames, aluminum store fronts, tempered plate glass doors. ARCHITECT: Robert Kleigman, 8588 Melrose Ave., Los Angeles. GENERAL CONTRACTOR: J. W. Bailey Const. Co., 634 Santa Barbara St., Santa Barbara.

ADMINISTRATION & BUSINESS EDUCATION BLDG., Humboldt State College, Arcata, Humboldt county. State of California, Sacramento, owner. 2-story and basement building on Humboldt State College campus; reinforced concrete walls, exterior brick veneer, composition roofing, aluminum sash and entrances—$493,000. ARCHITECT: Anson Boyd, California State Architect, Sacramento. GENERAL CONTRACTOR: B & R Const. Co., 110 Market St., San Francisco.

GARAGE & APARTMENT, Long Beach, Los Angeles county. Bert Bond, Long Beach, owner. Garage · apartment building, 2576 sq. ft. area, frame and stucco construction, wood siding, composition and rock roofing, plaster and wood panel interior, plaster and open beam ceilings, thermal and sound insulation, aluminum louver sash, oak and linoleum flooring, gas wall heaters, ceramic tile stall showers, composition decking, wrought iron handrails. ENGINEER: Henry A. Ross, and Paul O. Neble, associate, 6169 Cherry Ave., Long Beach.

IN THE NEWS

LOS ANGELES ARCHITECTURAL FIRM ESTABLISHES A MENTORSHIP AWARD AT USC

The partners of Daniel, Mann, Johnson & Mendenhall, Los Angeles architectural and engineering firm, have established a Mentorship Award for students of Architecture at the University of Southern California, Los Angeles.

In making the announcement to the School of Architecture, S. Kenneth Johnson, spokesman for the firm and himself an alumnus of USC, stated: "The primary purpose of this award is to enable the student to obtain professinal guidance and

counseling, therefore in addition to the payment of his tuition and fees he will receive professional training in the DMJM home office in Los Angeles, as a special employee for eight hours of work per week during the school year and full-time during vacations.

The student will receive prevailing wages for his efforts and his assignments will be designed to enable him to have concentrated training in all phases of the profession.

The Award will be made to an architectural student at the end of his sophomore year and may be continued for the three remaining academic years. The student will be selected by a committee of representatives of the faculty of the School of Architecture, the President of the Southern California Chapter AIA, and partners of the DMJM firm. To be eligible, the student must be in, and remain in, the top 10% of his class.

SAN FRANCISCO ARCHITECT EXPANDS OFFICES

Rex Whitaker Allen, A.I.A. Architect and Hospital Planning Consultant, has announced the expansion of his offices in San Francisco at 693 Mission Street. The telephone number has also been changed to YUkon 2-0431.

I. C. CROUDACE NAMED PLANT MANAGER PORTLAND ROOFING

J. C. Croudace has been appointed plant manager of the Portland Roofing Plant of the "Pabco" Building Materials Division of Fiberboard Paper Products Corp., according to an announcement by R. R. Galloway, vice-president and general manager of the Building Materials Division.

He succeeds Walter Simon who has been promoted to the new position of purchasing agent, construction and equipment, at the company's headquarters in San Francisco.

The Portland Roofing Plant is located in Portland, Oregon.

FRED K. RAMLOW APPOINTED SALES MANAGER

Fred K. Ramlow has been named San Francisco district sales manager for Virginia Metal Products, Inc., according to Nicholas C. Gianakos, vice-president in charge of sales.

The territory served from the San Francisco district includes six western states: Arizona, California, Idaho, Nevada, Ore-

gon, and Washington. Offices of the firm are located at 1700 Madera Street in Berkeley, California.

Sales activities for the western states are under the direction of the firm's regional sales office in Orange, Virginia, and under the direction of Charles D. Hawkins.

PORTABLE OUTDOOR SHOWER ATTACHES TO WALL IN SECONDS

A new, portable outdoor shower for fun in the sun at home, farm, motel, cottage, beach, pool, or camp is now available, featuring a simple slotted bracket that attaches to any outside surface such as house, garage, cottage, barn, shed walls, post or tree.

The shower assembly slips into the slide-in, slide-out holding bracket in seconds and connects to the garden hose. It is just as quickly taken down and stored when not in use. The new Silver Rain Shower is made of rustproof anodized aluminum for long wear and stay-new appearance. The swivel shower head permits full wide spray in any direction. Available in red, green, blue, or silver, the unit is complete with shower assembly, adjustable swivel shower head, and fast acting attaching bracket. For full data write Forest Specialties Co., 13000 Athens Ave., Cleveland 7, Ohio.

TIMBER ENGINEERING COMPANY CHANGES CALIFORNIA NAME

The Timber Engineering Company of California, Inc., recently announced a change of corporate name and trademark. The new company name is "Timber Fasteners, Inc."

Coinciding with the firm name change is a new policy of production in which all products of the firm will be manufactured in the West.

The address of the firm remains the same in San Francisco and Los Angeles.

ARCHITECT GREGORY AIN RECEIVES SILVER MEDAL FROM STUDENTS USC

Architect Gregory Ain, Los Angeles, nationally honored for his residential and housing work, has been awarded the Silver Medal, annual award of the student chapter of Scarab, national architectural honorary fraternity, at the University of Southern California School of Architecture.

The award is given to the "person, firm, or organization contributing the most to the profession and to the community," and was given to architect Ain for "his

great contributions to contemporary architecture and the sincerity of his continuing efforts to bring young people in the field the benefits of his experience as an outstanding architect."

Ain has been a Visiting Critic in the Fourth Year design classes of the SC School of Architecture since 1949.

Presentation of the award was made by Art Silvers, president of Scarab, and fourth year SC architectural student.

EDWARD F. WANTLAND APPOINTED ARCHITECT FOR K-LATH CORP.

Edward F. Wantland, architect, has been appointed to the staff of the K-Lath Corporation of Alhambra, California, according to a recent announcement by Robert W. Davis, president of the firm who specialize in the field of galvanized, welded wire lath.

Wantland will consult with architects, engineers, contractors, and builders in the use of K-Lath. He was formerly with the architectural firm of Pereira & Luckman, and Gordon B. Kaufman, Bechtel, Parsons, Inc.

ASSOCIATION OF WOMEN IN ARCHITECTURE

The Association of Women in Architecture concluded its most successful national convention early this month in Los Angeles with the election of Architect Mary Jane Fournier of St. Louis, Missouri.

Other officers elected for the years 1958-1960 included Doris Danna, vice-president; Jane Godfrey, Secretary; Barbara Uthe, Treasurer; Betty Lou Custer, Administrative Advisor; Jane Stuessie, Public

Relations Chairman. Los Angeles members of the officers elected are May Steinmesch, Charter Chairman; Lorraine Rudoff, Expansion Chairman; and Rose Conner, Information Center Chairman.

The Association of Women in Architecture is the national organization of outstanding women in the field of architecture and allied arts such as interior design, landscape architecture, land planning, and engineering.

NEW CHEMICAL PLANT PLANNED FOR RICHMOND

The Stauffer Chemical Company, San Francisco, has announced plans for the construction of a new process development laboratory to be built in the City of Richmond at a cost of $100,000.

The new facilities will be ready for occupancy the latter part of September, according to present plans.

SURFACE MOUNTED STAINLESS STEEL SHOWER COMPONENT

A new surface mounted stainless steel shower component, factory tested and ready for installation, has been announced by the Logan Mfg. Co., of Glendale, California.

The new Logan Showergon, Arvin type, is available in multiples of one, two, three or four shower stations. Overlay connections, access panels and right angle corner units provide adequate stock fixture combinations to meet most shower room requirements. This design meets all of the many architectural advantages of concealed piping while retaining the accessibility nor-

mally found only in exposed piping installations. All interior portions are produced

from stainless steel, brass or copper, and all exposed brass fixtures are triple plated chrome finish and assembled with vandalproof stainless steel screws. Complete data from the Logan Mfg. Co., P.O. Box 111, Glendale, California.

KAISER ALUMINUM DISTRIBUTORS NAMED FOR NORTH CALIF.

U. S. Steel Supply, warehousing division of the U. S. Steel Corporation has been appointed a general line industrial distributor for Kaiser aluminum products in northern California, according to a recent announcement by the Oakland office of the Kaiser Aluminum & Chemical Sales, Inc.

JUDSON STUDIO EXECUTIVE ATTENDS STAINED GLASS MEET

J. William Rundstrom of Altadena, artist, vice-president and partner of the Jud-

son Studios in Southern California, attended the annual National Convention of the Stained Glass Association of America, recently held in Philadelphia, Pa.

He announced upon his return that the convention voted to hold the 1959 National Convention in Los Angeles, June 15-19.

EDGARDO CONTINI SPEAKER AT SANTA BARBARA

Edgardo Contini, partner in the architectural and planning firm of Victor Gruen Associates, was guest speaker early this month at the University of California Conference of Engineers held on the Santa Barbara campus at Goleta, discussing "The

SPECIFY CALAVERAS

TOP QUALITY CEMENTS FOR EVERY ARCHITECTURAL USE

CALAVERAS CEMENT COMPANY
315 MONTGOMERY ST., SAN FRANCISCO 4

Principles of Optimum Structural Design."

Other speakers included Howard Warshaw, assistant professor at Santa Barbara College, University of California; Milton Zolotow, advertising designer and art director; and Ira Bach, Commissioner of City Planning, Chicago, Ill.

HENRY DREYFUSS HONORED BY MUSEUM OF ART

Henry Dreyfuss, Pasadena industrial designer, has been honored by the Philadelphia Museum of Art for 28 years of design achievement in such fields as aviation, electronics, shipping, banking, railroads and petroleum.

Dreyfuss was cited for "the distinction he has brought to the youngest and most vigorous of the creative professions." He was interior designer of the 200-foot perisphere for the 1939 New York World's Fair, also received recognition for such familiar designs as telephones, round thermostats, plumbing fixtures and airplane passenger facilities.

An educator and author Dreyfuss is an instructor at UCLA and Cal Tech and has lectured at Harvard and MIT.

FORMICA OPENS NEW DISTRICT SALES OFFICES IN LA

The opening of a new Formica district sales office and creation of a new executive position in the Los Angeles district office, resulted in four sales personnel changes, according to F. C. Walter, general sales manager of the firm.

C. R. Bailey, who has been in charge of sales activities in the Columbus, Ohio, area,

has been named district manager; R. H. Cottle, in charge of the Jacksonville, Florida, office, has been appointed to the new position of assistant district manager of the Los Angeles office, under the direction of Glenn H. Taylor; and Ed Borchers, formerly sales representative in the New York office, has been named to the Jacksonville office, which also serves Tampa, Florida; and J. F. Clunell has been moved to the New York office.

REVOLUTIONARY NEW TYPE SPRING ROLLER CABINET CATCH

A revolutionary new type of Spring Roller Cabinet Catch that gives effortless closing and firmer holding because of an AJAX exclusive new hinged action pivot point roller, has just been announced.

Other design features of the new product includes double ridged strikes that cradle roller in front and back, eliminating necessity for accurate alignment, Quieter operation and a coiled spring that is locked in place and can not pop out. The frame is steel with a tough, krome-brite finish and the spring is finest steel piano wire. Available with a strike for lip door applications; under shelf or flush door applications; or with both strikes. Ajax Hardware Corp., 4355 Valley Blvd., Los Angeles, California.

JUNIOR COLLEGE FOR ALTA LOMA SAN BERNARDINO

Associated Architects Jay Dewey Harnish and Eugene Weldon Fickes, Jr., 222 E. "B" St., Ontario, are completing plans for construction of a business education building, social science building, library and language arts building at the new site of the Chaffey Junior College, Alta Loma, San Bernardino county.

Total floor area of the buildings will be 63,000 sq. ft. Steel frame with brick filler panels and tilt-up concrete end wall construction. Library will have a reinforced concrete basement and a mezzanine; metal roof decking, composition roofing, struc-

tural steel, rigid roof insulation, metal sash, interior exposed brick and plaster, accoustical tile ceilings, metal toilet partitions, ceramic tile and asphalt tile floors, metal door frames, slab and aluminum doors, winter and summer air conditioning.

NEW CITY
HALL FOR
HEALDSBURG

Architect J. Clarence Felciano, 4010 Montecito Avenue, Santa Rosa, is preparing plans for construction of a wood frame City Hall to be built in the city of Healdsburg.

KAPPA SIGMA
PLANS NEW
HOUSE

Architect George T. Kirkpatrick, 2171 Colorado Blvd., Los Angeles, has completed working drawings for construction of a new Fraternity House in Eagle Rock for the Kappa Sigma Fraternity.

The new building will contain 5000 sq. ft. of area and construction will include: composition roofing, frame and stucco, masonry chimney, wood siding, metal sash, plate glass, sliding glass doors, plywood and vinyl flooring, interior stucco, forced air heating, 1 fireplace, 2 baths with tile gang showers, and asphalt paving.

CENTRAL FIRE
STATION FOR
STOCKTON

The architectural firm of Mayo, DeWolf & Associates, Exchange Building, Stockton, is completing plans and specifications for construction of a new Central Fire Station in Stockton for the City of Stockton at a cost of $393,000.

The new facilities will be of reinforced concrete construction, also some grouted brick, structural steel frame, steel roof deck, and will contain 20,000 sq. ft. of floor area.

STORE BLDG.
AND NEW
APARTMENTS

Architect David Freedman, 231 N. Robertson Blvd., Beverly Hills, is preparing plans for construction of a frame, stucco and stone veneer building with four stores on the ground floor and 10 single apartments on the second floor.

The building will contain 14,760 sq. ft. of area; built-up roofing, concrete slab and vinyl tile flooring, plaster walls and ceilings, plumbing, electrical work, plate glass, aluminum store fronts, structural steel, metal windows, and asphalt paving.

FLEXIBLE METAL
WET HEAT
CONNECTORS

A complete line of flexible metal wet heat connectors in $\frac{1}{2}''$ and $\frac{3}{4}''$ ID has been introduced by Cobra Metal Hose, representing fourteen separate models in 30 combinations for hot water or steam heating systems.

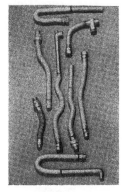

The new connector line was developed with the cooperation of independent contractors primarily for reducing the cost of installing wet heat systems and for speeding installations in industrial, residential and commercial buildings; eliminate many fittings, nipples and time consuming operations; completely flexible; eliminate noise; and Rafold constructed of high quality bronze metal tubing. Full information from Cobra Metal Hose, 5059 S. Kedzie Ave., Chicago, Ill.

WAREHOUSE AND
OFFICE BUILDING
LOS ANGELES

Edward F. Escalle, Engineer of 5140 Crenshaw Blvd., Los Angeles, is preparing plans and specifications for construction of a 2-story brick warehouse and office building to be built in Los Angeles.

The new building, 21x71 ft., will have a composition roof, interior dry wall work, insulation, acoustical tile ceiling, concrete slab floor, metal doors and stairs, wood and pipe railings, brick plaster and concrete canopy.

Estimated cost is $15,000.

BOWLING CENTER
BEING BUILT
IN BANNING

The firm of Johnson Engen & D'Agostino, Architects and Engineers, 4868 Oak Park Avenue, Encino, are preparing drawings for construction of a 16-lane bowling and recreation center in Banning.

The building will contain 18,000 sq. ft. of floor area and construction will be of reinforced brick, steel frame, tapered steel girders, concrete slab, insulation, acoustical tile, interior plaster, wood paneling, drywall, plate glass store doors, fixed glass,

metal toilet partitions, electric hand dryers, carpeting, air conditioning, automatic pin setters and underground ball returns; a coffee shop, cocktail lounge, locker rooms, complete nursery with play yard, and asphaltic concrete paving area for customer parking.

BAPTIST
CHURCH
FOR TAFT

Farrar, Hudson & Associates, Designers, 661 Highway 99, San Bernardino, have completed plans and specifications for construction of a new church in Taft for the First Baptist Church of Taft at an estimated cost of $250,000.

The new 1-story frame and stucco building will have a reinforced concrete basement and will provide complete facilities for a church and Sunday school.

REMODEL
KINGS COUNTY
HOSPITAL

Architect Lawrence B. Alexander, 128 E. 8th Street, Hanford, is preparing drawings for remodeling and construction of alterations to the Kings County Hospital in Hanford at an estimated cost of $115,000.

Four separate portions of the present building will be tied into one unit and construction will include anchoring roof trusses, steel trusses to be installed in the west wing to strengthen ceilings and floors. The exterior brick of the present building will be replaced with 4-inch reinforced concrete.

CORTE MADERA
VETERINARY
HOSPITAL

Architect Eugene E. Crawford, 920 5th Avenue, San Rafael, is completing plans for construction of a number of additions to the Corte Madera Pet Hospital in Corte Madera.

Work includes a new reception and waiting room, treatment room, new wards, an examination room, some demolition work and extensive remodeling of the existing buildings.

PENN METAL
ANNOUNCES
STAFF

Robert T. Mathis has been appointed western sales engineer for the structural sections division of Penn Metal Company, Inc., and will provide engineering assistance to the firm's Los Angeles, San Francisco, Seattle and Denver offices.

Index to Advertisers

HELP US KEEP THE
THINGS WORTH KEEPING

Speech is free for the asking, here in America. But it's not free for the *keeping!* Protecting our American heritages costs money—a great deal of money.

It takes money for strength to keep the peace. Money for science and education to help make peace lasting. And money saved by individuals.

Your Savings Bonds, as a direct investment in your country, make you a Partner in strengthening America's Peace Power—helping us keep the things worth keeping.

Good cash investment, too. Put 3 dollars into Series E Bonds—take out 4 in just 8 years, 11 months.

Safe. Both interest and principal guaranteed by the U.S. Government. Every Bond recorded, so if it's lost, stolen or destroyed it can be replaced, free.

Automatic saving. The Payroll Savings Plan is the *automatic* way to save for the big things in life. Look at the chart. See how easily you can get a nest egg!

HOW YOU CAN REACH YOUR SAVINGS GOAL WITH SERIES E BONDS *(in just 8 years, 11 months)*			
If you want about	$2,500	$5,000	$10,000
each week, save	$4.75	$9.50	$18.75

This shows only a few examples. You can save any sum, buying Bonds by Payroll Savings or where you bank. Start your program now!

HELP STRENGTHEN AMERICA'S PEACE POWER
BUY U. S. SAVINGS BONDS

Featuring The Work of Jacks & Irvine, General Contractors

THE HIBERNIA BANK   .   Downtown San Francisco Office

THE HIBERNIA BANK

1958

B-6965 SANITON: women's vitreous china, syphon jet wall-hung urinal.

B-6790 NOBLE: vitreous china wall-hung closet bowl.

B-4039-H PLANET: vitreous china fully-recessed combination drinking fountain and cuspidor.

B-3190-HS BYRON: 17" x 17" corner lavatory with 4" back, integral front.

THE SCULPTURED LOOK

Briggs puts more than 70 years of vitreous china experience into the creation of an all-new commercial fixture line!

Symmetry, simplicity, and continuity of design! These characteristics are evident throughout the line of Briggs new commercial fixtures. Designed by Harley Earl, Inc., these high-density vitreous china fixtures are a product of Briggs skill and the standards set by more than 70 years' continuous experience in the manufacture of vitreous china products. Available in Briggs colors or white. Specifications on request.

A COMPLETE LINE OF PLUMBING FIXTURES FOR RESIDENTIAL, COMMERCIAL, AND INDUSTRIAL USE

BRIGGS

B E A U T Y W A R E

LEADERSHIP FOR 53 YEARS
ON THE PACIFIC COAST

IN THE LIGHT CONSTRUCTION FIELD

SERVING ARCHITECTS...ENGINEERS...CONTRACTORS
...BUILDERS...AND GOVERNMENTAL AGENCIES
CONCERNED WITH PUBLIC WORKS

ARCHITECT & ENGINEER magazine serves the Building Industry
with information on new materials, new products, new equipment
and new methods. Its circulation covers builders and contractors,
architects and engineers, building supply dealers and governmental agencies concerned with public works.

ADVERTISE YOUR PRODUCT OR SERVICE IN
ARCHITECT & ENGINEER MAGAZINE

The Market Is Right—alive, rich, expanding. Because of new construction and expansion of existing plants, the Western market is
probably the most fertile in the nation.

The Medium Is Right—thorough coverage of key personnel . . .
the men who control the buying of your product. Deliver your
advertising message to them monthly by a messenger which has
been welcomed in Western building firms for over *53 years.*

ARCHITECT & ENGINEER MAGAZINE

Basic Coverage Through A Single Medium

68 POST STREET   SAN FRANCISCO, CALIFORNIA

Vol. 214   No. 2

EDWIN H. WILDER
Editor

CONTRIBUTING EDITORS:

Education
SIDNEY W. LITTLE, Dean,
College of Fine Arts and Department of Architecture, University
of Arizona, Tucson, Arizona.

City Planning
CORWIN R. MOCINE, City
Planning Engineer, Oakland,
California

*Urban Planning and
Shopping Centers*
FRANK EMERY COX, Sales
Research & Business Develop-
ment Analyst, Berkeley, Califor-
nia

Realty Development
ROY P. DRACHMAN, Sub-
divider and Realty Developer,
Tucson, Arizona

School Planning
DR. J. D. McCONNEL, Stan-
ford School Planning Dept.,
Palo Alto, California

Residential Planning
JEDD JONES, Architect,
Boise, Idaho

General Architecture
ROBERT FIELD, Architect,
Los Angeles, California

Engineering
JOHN A. BLUME, Consulting
and Structural Engineer, San
Francisco, California

Advertising
WILLIAM A. ULLNER,
Manager

FRED JONES
Special Advertising

★

COVER PICTURE

THE HIBERNIA
BANK

New Downtown San Francisco bank facility, designed by Hertzka & Knowles,
AIA Architects.

One of many modern structures of
which Jacks & Irvine have been the
General Contractor.

See page 10 for story of the Jacks
& Irvine Construction Company.

ARCHITECTS' REPORTS—
Published Daily
       Archie MacCorkindale, Manager
               Telephone DOuglas 2-8311

ARCHITECT & ENGINEER is indexed regularly by ENGINEERING INDEX, INC.; and ART INDEX

Contents for

AUGUST

THE OLDEST PROFESSIONAL MONTHLY BUSINESS MAGAZINE OF THE ELEVEN WESTERN STATES

ARCHITECT AND ENGINEER (Established 1905) is published on the 15th of the month by The Architect and
Engineer, Inc., 68 Post St., San Francisco 4; Telephone EXbrook 2-7182. President, K. P. Kierulff; Vice-
President and Manager, L. B. Penhorwood; Treasurer, E. N. Kierulff. — Los Angeles Office: Wentworth F.
Green, 439 So. Western Ave., Telephone DUnkirk 7-6135 — Entered as second class matter, November 2,
1905, at the Post Office in San Francisco, California, under the Act of March 3, 1879. Subscriptions: United
States and Pan America, $3.00 a year; $5.00 two years; foreign countries $5.00 a year; single copy 50c.

. EDITORIAL NOTES .

HOUSING SENIOR CITIZENS

Methods of expanding the volume of private housing for elderly persons was explored by leading builders of the nation, public interest groups, and governmental officials at an all-day conference at the National Housing Center in Washington, D.C., last month.

Sponsored by the National Housing Center and the National Association of Home Builders, the meeting on "Housing Our Senior Citizens" was the first national workshop set up to analyze intensively the practical problems and programs involved in constructing and financing such housing.

Consideration included the current market of housing for older people and its economic and social characteristics; available current programs; case studies of successful projects; construction features; unmet needs; and financing aids.

Housing for the elderly is one of the most important yet one of the most neglected market areas of our national living despite the fact that various types of Federal aids are available to elderly home buyers and builders of homes for them at the present time.

* * *

There are 2791 Registered architects in the State of California —11.6 percent of all architects registered to practice architecture in the United States—giving California 66 percent more architects than is the national average.

* * *

COMPULSORY SOCIAL SECURITY

The best way to understand the real justification of our compulsory Social Security program is to compare it with the purposes of compulsory education which has been generally accepted throughout the nation.

Thus, in the manner that compulsory education protects the body politic from bad judgments of illiteracy, the basic purpose of compulsory Social Security is to protect society from the political and economic consequences of leaving millions of elderly persons with no visible means of support.

If we had permitted a large part of today's electorate to remain unable to read and write, incapable of understanding the basic principles of sanitation, nutrition and public health, then our form of government in this Atomic Age would be doomed.

Similarly, if our worthy, growing, experience and resourceful older population were left completely adrift in today's economic tides, we could expect them to take a kind of concerted action that could easily lead to political, social and economic instability.

The basic purpose of Social Security is to provide a floor of protection against destitution in old age. It was never intended to meet all the economic needs of elderly persons, thus constant changing conditions require review of the situation and may bring pressure to

increase Social Security benefits, and social taxes. However, any attempt to stretch the Social Security program into a mechanism of total security will rob the individual of the necessity, the incentive, to build additional old age income protection through his own efforts.

* * *

It has been estimated that in the construction of a modern home about 3000 articles are used, helpful to all phases of our labor and business community.

* *

URBAN DEVELOPMENT

Problems created in your community by the changing patterns of modern life have some things in common and much that is different from the problems of other cities and towns. The best solutions, therefore, are those custom-made by the businessmen of each community rather than those following some general standard federal government formula.

The businessman and property owner is the logical one to provide the necessary leadership. They best know how blight and congestion drive away retail customers, discourage new business, increase transportation costs and lower employee morale. They also know the depressing effect of slum areas on property in adjoining neighborhoods.

True, local and State governments are being strained financially by the tremendous pressures for additional community facilities and public works, but local pride, initiative and hard work are the best answers to the problem, and not "federal aid" which costs the taxpayer many, many times the amount of funds which eventually trickle back in the form of "aid."

While municipal financing is a substantial problem for most communities, there is still much unused capacity for apportioning the costs of urban development among the people who most benefit from it.

* * *

NO GLOOM

Several Washington, D. C., sources now predict there will be between 1,200,000 and 1,300,000 new homes started throughout the nation this year, and with the population still on the move, about one out of every five persons one year old and over in the United States changed his place of residence between April, 1956 and April, 1957, prospects for continued residential building in the West look encouraging.

In Los Angeles alone, 630,000 residential units have been constructed since 1950, representing 30% of all housing in the city.

Improved financing, better housing, expanding industrial development in many areas, are all factors that contribute to a continuance of good business throughout the West.

STATE DIVISION OF ARCHITECTURE
READIES PLANS FOR CONSTRUCTION

SACRAMENTO, CALIFORNIA

Planning for the new, 1065-acre California State Fair and Exposition site north of the American River near Sacramento is proceeding rapidly, along with work toward the staging of this year's big exposition, August 27-September 7, on the present site.

The Fair is scheduled to open in its new home in 1961. State money for the project, including funds gained from the sale of the present 207-acre site and money from an approved revenue bond issue, total slightly more than $30,000,000. Participation by industry and commerce, however, is expected to push total investment in the exposition to more than $75,-000,000.

State Division of Architecture has primary responsibility for design and construction of the new facilities.

Anson Boyd, state architect, in a public meeting held for the purpose of programming and promoting the new Fair project, went on record to the effect that a project of this kind indicates that it would be logical to assume that Division of Architecture will employ, under contract, architects, engineers and artists outside of state service.

The Division already has completed an area plot plan which has been approved by the Fair directors, but no master plan or building designs have been drawn.

A preliminary development budget of $25,500,000 has been approved by the directors. The budget makes provision for a 17,000-person capacity race track grandstand to cost $2,550,000; a 100,000-square-foot counties building to cost $1,200,000; an administration and auditorium building of 80,000 square feet to cost $1,320,000, and a 60,000-square-foot youth dormitory to cost $2,240,000.

Preliminary plans call for the site to be developed in a series of stages. Much major work will be completed by opening day, 1961, but further development —for projects such as a stadium, air strip, yacht harbor, etc.—will continue during ensuing years.

Theodore Rosequist, former assistant manager of the Fair and now the new Fair planning coordinator, said that specific, modernistically-designed areas on

the site will be developed for special age groups and fairgoers with special interests.

These may include a Kiddies' Town, Teen Town, Gold Rush Town, etc. Possibilities of the establishment of a California Academy of Youth and Science are now being explored.

Among the suggestions for the academy are a planetarium, aquarium, museum of natural history, a space age museum, and a giant outdoor map of California through which fairgoers could walk on paths laid along the routes of principal highways.

In the meantime, the granddaddy of all western fairs is entering the 104th year in 1958, and the big show will be just as bright, brash and beautiful as it ever has been in the past.

The Fair has become the biggest and most successful annual show in California. It is aiming this year at a record attendance of 850,000 on its 207-acre Fairground, and in 1961 on the new 1065-acre American River site it is planning for visits by 1,250,000 Western fairgoers.

NEW FAIR PLAN: Theodore Rosequist (right) Planning Co-ordinator, outlines features of 1065 acre site on American River north of Sacramento, to Earl Lee Kelly, president of the Fair's Board of Directors.

NEWS and COMMENT ON ART

OAKLAND ART MUSEUM

The Oakland Art Museum, 1000 Fallon Street, under the direction of Paul Mills, Curator, is displaying the first showing of three new exhibitions this month. In the Museum's "Archives of California Art" gallery is a selection of paintings by Edwin Deakin, one of California's turn-of-the-century masters, and includes views of European churches and landmarks as well as historic scenes of California..

Featured also this month is a selection of recent work by Miriam Hoffman, distinguished California sculptress, including abstract figures and heads.

Members of the Alameda Art Association are holding their annual exhibition this month. The showing of paintings by this organization, primarily realistic in style, is a juried selection.

The exhibition of Chinese and Persian ceramics from the Reitz collection and the showing of ancient Near East jewelry, lent by the Susette Khayat Gallery, will continue through the month.

The Museum is open daily.

ARCHITECTURAL GALLERY

The architectural Gallery, Building Center, 7933 West Third Street, Los Angeles, is showing a SPECIAL EXHIBITION of the work of Richard Dorman AIA and Associates, architects, during August.

The Gallery features the work of a prominent Southern California architect each month. Public invited.

SAN FRANCISCO MUSEUM OF ART

The San Francisco Museum of Art, War Memorial Building, Civic Center, San Francisco, under the direction of Dr. Grace L. McCann Morley, announces a number of special summer exhibitions, including the following for August:

EXHIBITS: THE ART OF ALBERT MARQUET Exhibition will close early in the month; continuing Calligraphy, by the venerable Hodo Tobase; the Bradley Walker Tomlin Memorial Exhibition; and SIX JAPANESE PAINTERS, representing 31 recent works by six contemporary Japanese painters, organized by Dr. Chisaburch Yamada, in Tokyo, and assembled with the cooperation of the National Museum of Modern Art in Tokyo.

JUAN GRIS Exhibition from the Museum of Modern Art, Retrospective of the Cubist master.

The most complete retrospective of the work of the pioneer Cubist artist, Juan Gris (1887 - 1927) was assembled by the Museum of Modern Art for showing in New York and for three other United States cities.

It was one of the exhibitions on view at the time of the Museum of Modern Art fire in April, but miraculously was saved.

Private and public collections in Europe as well as in the United States were reviewed by James Thrall Soby, Director of the exhibition, who also wrote a monograph on the artist, in connection with the showing, in order to secure the finest examples of his work representative of his various periods. Over 70 works are included in the exhibition.

Picasso, Braque, Leger, and Juan Gris are generally considered the most important Cubist artists and Gris, somewhat younger than the others, has a distinctive place in the movement for his "refinement of calculation and a highly original color sense. . . ."

Gris has been seen here in San Francisco only in isolated examples and in the selection of twenty of his paintings included in the Spanish Masters exhibition shown at the San Francisco Museum of Art in 1948.

SPECIAL EVENTS: Lecture Tours on current exhibitions; Wednesday evening art discussions, 8:30 p.m.; Library and Rental Gallery.

The Museum is open daily.

CALIFORNIA PALACE OF THE LEGION OF HONOR

The California Palace of the Legion of Honor, Lincoln Park, San Francisco, under the direction of Thomas Carr Howe, Jr., is presenting the following special exhibitions and events during August.

EXHIBITS: PAINTINGS by N. C. Wyeth; SCULPTURES SEEN ANEW, a special group of photographs by Clarence John Laughlin; and COLLAGES by Don Reich.

The ACHENBACH FOUNDATION for GRAPHIC ARTS, is featuring "Artists At Work," and "Recent Works" by June Wayne.

SPECIAL EVENTS: Organ Program each Saturday and Sunday afternoon at 3 o'clock, by Richard Purvis and Ludwig Altman. The new series of art classes for children will be resumed in September.

The Museum is open daily—admission free.

M. H. deYOUNG MEMORIAL MUSEUM

The M. H. deYoung Memorial Museum, Golden Gate Park, San Francisco, under the direction of Walter Heil, announces a number of special exhibits have been arranged for this month, including the following:

EXHIBITIONS: "FRESH PAINT—1958," an exhibition of paintings from 11 western states and Ha-

waii, augmented by the works of 27 Bay Area painters. The exhibition was conceived and is sponsored by the friends of art at Stanford University and was shown at the Stanford Art Gallery in June as a survey of recent western painting selected by 21 Museum Directors and College Art Department heads.

By supplementing the original exhibition with representative works by additional Bay Area artists, its original scope and intent, to relate the important contribution of western art to American art as a whole, has been broadened to also highlight the Bay Area's contribution to the larger art picture.

SPECIAL EVENTS: Classes in Art Enjoyment, for adults and children, are available at no cost.

The Museum is open daily.

GRETA WILLIAMS GALLERY

The Greta Williams Gallery, 2059 Union Street, San Francisco, is featuring OILS and WATER-COLORS by Homer Turner, in a specially arranged exhibition during August.

The Gallery is open weekdays only, 12:00 noon to 6 p.m.

SAN FRANCISCO MUSEUM OF ART

WAR MEMORIAL BUILDING CIVIC CENTER

GUITAR AND FLOWERS

1912, oil, 44$\frac{1}{8}$ x 27$\frac{5}{8}$"

by

Juan Gris

(1887-1927)

This major artist of Cubism has his first comprehensive showing in the United States in this exhibition organized by New York's Museum of Modern Art. This important movement of about 1910 to 1920 was to influence strongly all the later developments in art of the 20th century, and to prepare the way for contemporary abstraction and the new approach of our time to painting and sculpture.

Collection of the Museum of Modern Art, New York, bequest of Anna Erickson Levene in memory of her husband. Dr. Phoebus Aaron Theodor Levene.

AUGUST, 1958

$4,500,000

CONVENTION CENTER

LAS VEGAS, NEVADA

Adrian Wilson & Associates, Architects and Engineers

The long-sought Las Vegas Convention Center, years in the dream stage, is now approximately 55% complete, according to the designers Adrian Wilson & Associates, Architects & Engineers. Completion date is scheduled for February 15, 1959, and the architects report that the project is now running ahead of the construction schedule.

The Convention Center is the result of efforts of the Clark County Fair & Recreation Board, and it is the first phase of a large civic program to develop Las Vegas as an important business community as well as a national resort attraction.

Cost of the current Convention Center is $4,500,-000. It is located on a 40-acre tract at Desert Inn Road and Paradise Valley Road, a site on the southern portion of the defunct race track in Las Vegas.

Architecturally, the Convention Center is a mush-room-shaped main building with a circular interior hall 240 feet in diameter. The large circular building is 440 feet across, including the outer concourse, where display facilities and exhibit areas are located.

Overall length of the building, including the exhibit wing, will be 1,000 feet, and total footage will be 275,285 square feet. The Center will have seating for 8,500 people in the assembly hall, and it will have seating for 7,500 people for such events as horse shows, ice shows, hockey, boxing, etc.

Among its facilities will be 20 meeting rooms, flexible in arrangement to take care of from 50 to 800 people each; two catering kitchens, serving from 50 to 3,000 people; two portable stages; completely air-conditioned; and advanced lighting systems will give the building unusual flexibility in use.

The building will contain the most modern installa-tions of electronics equipment for broadcasting, includ-ing closed circuit television, separate viewing screens, and intercommunicating devices.

Because of the requirement for advanced use of the building, particularly in conjunction with electronics and electrical effects, the architects employed nation-ally prominent consultants in those fields. Dr. Vern O. Knudsen, internationally famed sound technician, was the acoustical consultant; and J. S. Hamel, former New York theatrical illumination expert, was the special illumination effects consultant.

Structurally, a portion of the walls are of masonry curtain walls, with some veneers of textured Spanish tile. Steel metal decking is used throughout.

The impressive mushroom-like dome, which can be seen for miles on the flat desert, is formed by 16 steel trusses that are six feet deep. Surface of the dome will be of anodized aluminum, and special lighting effects will dramatize it at night.

The partitioned rooms and halls will employ fully automatic movable partitions of aluminum for soundproofing. Among the Center's many luxury features will be the finest upholstered theatre seating, using 22-inch wide seats instead of the normal 18 or 19-inch seats.

Main floor of the building has been designed with a concrete floor system to support heavy loads, for exhibits such as automobile, farm and mining equipment shows. A unique feature of the assembly hall is that the entire ceiling of the domed hall is suspended below the roof to: 1) lower the air conditioning operational cost by decreasing the volume of the hall, and providing additional insulation; 2) provide suitable profiles and materials to make the acoustics of the hall practically perfect; 3) provide space for a press booth and projection booth and other service facilities, television and special effects systems, etc.

Ceilings of the building are 25 feet high, with a unique grid paneling 2 x 4 feet; all conduit is run above the grid, and fluorescent lighting fixtures are suspended below. The grid panels can be easily lifted out to expose all utilities for easy service access.

The Las Vegas Convention Center has been described by the architects as a major advance by the city in its economic development. Las Vegas has over 10,000 hotel and motel rooms classed as "first class," which compares favorably with such large cities as Los Angeles and San Francisco.

Because of this large concentration of first-class hotel accommodations, and construction of one of America's most advanced convention meeting halls, the city of Las Vegas is expecting an increase of a new type of business income.

The convention center has been designed to accommodate meetings of almost any size now being held in America, including the comforts of complete air conditioning, the most modern of electronic installations for closed circuit television, special effects, and complete flexibility in use of floor area.

DOME

Huge mushroom shape of the Las Vegas, Nevada, Convention Center (nearly 55% completed) is dramatized by steel beams forming the roof of the auditorium, which can be seen for miles around desert city.

Feature of construction is 13-ton compression ring in top center, 16 steel roof trusses, each weighing nine tons. Finished surface will be of anodized aluminum.

35 YEARS OF

BUILDING

FEATURING THE WORK OF JACKS & IRVINE

General Contractors

by FRED JONES

A reader asked me: 'How come you never devoted an issue of Architect and Engineer to the work of Jacks & Irvine, general contractors, who have erected many fine buildings in San Francisco and the Bay Area? You have done a good job publicizing other well known contractors."

The query proved timely for both magazine and contractors as evidenced by this issue.

For nearly 40 years Jacks & Irvine have been build-ing—building San Francisco so to speak—first with beautiful homes, then apartment houses, commercial and industrial structures, schools and churches. Add Federal and State institutions, together with an ever mounting volume of major and minor alteration jobs, and it would seem no exaggeration to credit the firm with having done a fifty million dollar business over the years.

The Jacks & Irvine partnership began in 1921 with Henry Jacks and William K. Irvine equal owners. While active Mr. Jacks helped to form the San Fran-

INTERIOR VIEW . . . looking towards
Main Entrance to Bank.

cisco Builders Exchange and as an officer of the Associated General Contractors he contributed much of his time and energy. Upon Mr. Jacks' retirement in the mid-30's, Mr. Irvine continued to manage the business which later was expanded to its present personnel consisting of the senior Irvine, James W., George M., and William K. Irvine, Jr.

A summary of some of the more outstanding Jacks & Irvine projects:

During World War II, it built torpedo storage facilities for the Navy at Mare Island; a large machine shop at the Port of Oakland for the Army; several good size machine shops for the Bechtel Shipyard at Sausalito and remodeled office and storage facilities for the Army Engineers in San Francisco.

During this same period the firm engaged in a remodeling project of the former William Taylor Hotel in San Francisco for the U.S. Treasury Department. This half-million dollar job embraced the complete renovation of all 25 floors in the building and had to be completed in 75 days. Through day and night work this schedule was met.

During the post-war period some of its larger projects included the remodeling of the 7-story Ransohoff's Department Store, a ½-million job completed in 4 months; the Leon Russell residence for Architect Eric Mendolsohn in San Francisco (one of the most modern and unusual residences in this area); Corpus Christi Church, San Francisco, Mario Ciampi, architect; Spreckels-Russell Dairy Co. Ltd., San Francisco; remodeling of the Doe Library, University of Califor-

DETAILS of interior design of Bank.

JACKS & IRVINE . . .

nia, Berkeley campus; Heavy Ion Accelerator Building, University of California, Radiation Laboratory, Corlett & Spackman, architects; two automotive sales and service buildings in San Francisco. In 1956 the new St. Cecilia's Church in San Francisco was completed at a cost of $1,000,000 from plans by architect Martin Rist.

From 1946 to the present Jacks & Irvine built new offices for the Hibernia Bank in San Mateo, San Jose and San Francisco as well as renovating portions of the main office and four local branches. Value of work performed for this bank at present amounts to over $2,000,000. Two new branches for the Bank of California at Millbrae and Oakland were completed in the last two years, along with the remodeling of their Berkeley office. Other bank work included branches for the Anglo California National Bank.

In 1946 the firm was engaged to remodel the Paso Robles Inn after a serious fire had destroyed much of the building, and in 1951 it erected a new store building for J. C. Penney Company in Eureka.

Projects now under construction, or recently completed, include the new General Services Building for the University of California, Berkeley; St. Joseph's Hall on the campus of St. Mary's College High School; complete renovation of two buildings at 321 Bush Street in San Francisco, for the Associated Real Estate Corporation; the new International Longshoremen's and Warehousemen's Union Memorial Hall and Dispatch Building at Fisherman's Wharf, Henry Hill, Architect.

Completed last month were the new St. Bruno's Church in San Bruno, Wilton Smith, Architect, and the modernization of Di Maggio's Restaurant at Fisherman's Wharf, Hewitt Wells, Architect.

St. Bruno Church

In the new St. Bruno Church the architect has achieved a contemporary solution within the traditional form dictated by Catholic ritual. In the main entrance a covered atrium, designed to give protection during the rainy season and also to provide welcome

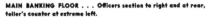

MAIN BANKING FLOOR . . . Officers section to right and at rear, teller's counter at extreme left.

Wilton Smith, Architect

shade during the hot summer, leads into a spacious Narthex. In the Nave exposed laminated arches frame the Sanctuary, which is finished in oak panelling, while the main altar is of marble with a Roman travertine reredos.

The large window in the north elevation has been designed for future stained glass as also have the tall aluminum windows in the Nave. Furnishing of the interior has been handled with dignity and restraint and the finished effect is one of repose and dignity.

**ST. BRUNO'S
CATHOLIC
CHURCH**

**San Bruno,
California**

**Exterior view (at top) shows
modernistic
trend in design.**

**At right is view of Nave
and Sanctuary.**

HOLIDAY LODGE

San Francisco,
California

At left is view of entrance to the
"Patio" area, also restaurant and
bar.

On the exterior the roof, with its large overhanging eaves, has been finished with shingle tiles. A striking feature of the main facade is the aluminum tower with its chevron ornament. In the layout of the site particular attention has been paid to the provision for lawns and planting areas and the parking lots have been connected to the entrances by concrete walks and steps.

GARDEN
COURT

Swimming Pool
and sun area.

TYPICAL ROOM INTERIOR
(at left)

INTERNATIONAL
LONGSHOREMEN'S
WAREHOUSE
UNION

San Francisco

Downtown Hibernia Bank

The Hibernia Bank at Sutter Street and Grant Avenue, San Francisco, is the first downtown expansion of the 99-year-old organization.

The newly opened branch office of the bank occupies the former Davis Schonwasser building, a 3-story and basement reinforced concrete structure which was completely renewed, except for the structural elements of the original building.

ILWU: Building begins to take form at North Point and Taylor Streets.

HENRY HILL, Architect

JOHN W. KRUSE, Associate Architect

ISADOR THOMPSON, Structural Engineer

ILWU MEMORIAL BUILDING . . .

BEGINNING TO TAKE FORM

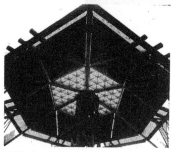

DETAIL view of the
roof construction.

Outline of Materials

Exterior

Curtain wall with gray tempered structural glass and clear glass. Aluminum and stainless steel trim.

Marble and granite—white Vermont marble with Dakota granite accents.

Interior

Main Floor—White Vermont marble, teak and vinyl wall coverings. Roman travertine floors, accents of darker Imperial travertine which is also used as an accent on walls adjacent to elevator.

Basement safe deposit areas have vinyl wall coverings

The building is air conditioned and equipped with the latest types of mechanical, electrical, and electronic devices for efficient banking and office operations. Safe deposit and coin vaults are of maximum security, class #10 construction in accordance with the standards of the "Manual of Burglary, Theft and Robbery Insurance Rates" issued by the National Bureau of Casualty Underwriters.

The exterior of the structure has been faced with a new light-weight curtain wall of aluminum, glass and marble. The main banking room has been finished in teak and marble, with wall coverings of vinyl fabric and floors of travertine.

17

JACKS & IRVINE . . .

and teak, with stainless steel trim. Floors are quarry tile.

Business offices on upper floors have acoustic ceilings throughout and the building is completely air conditioned.

After completion of structural work, including a new elevator penthouse, new reinforced concrete sidewalks on both streets, and construction of the concrete vault in the basement area, the owner required that all the interior and exterior finish work be completed by June 15, 1958. This meant that a rigid construction schedule had to be met as the contractor had only 4½ months to complete approximately $600,000 worth of work.

Through close cooperation of all sub-contractors and coordination of the overall schedule between the architect and general contractor the building was completed on schedule with a minimum of overtime involved. Only an all-out effort on the part of all contractors, suppliers and others made this posible. On-the-spot decisions were made when problems arose by the architects and general contractor in order that the schedule not be interrupted.

This building is an excellent example of what can be accomplished when close harmony exists between all firms involved in a project.

Holiday Lodge

Holiday Lodge, San Francisco's first garden hotel,

**THE BANK OF
CALIFORNIA**

Oakland Office

**Bank Building &
Equipment Corporation,
Architects.**

BANK OF CALIFORNIA
Millbrae Office
Robert B. Liles, Architect

designed by Hertzka & Knowles, architects, is a unique conception of a resort type hotel located close to the heart of downtown San Francisco, and is one of the major projects of the Jacks & Irvine organization.

The building is of concrete and wood frame con-

JACKS & IRVINE . . .

HEAVY ION ACCELERATOR BUILDING . . . University of California, Radiation Laboratory, Berkeley Campus, California.   **Corlett & Spackman, Architects.**

890 JACKSON MEDICAL-DENTAL BUILDING
San Francisco, California

Lun Chan & Associates, Architects.

Di MAGGIO'S RESTAURANT
Fisherman's Wharf,
San Francisco, California

Hewitt C. Wells, Architect.

...as permanent as masonry
...as beautiful as glass

APCO PORCELAIN ENAMEL PANELS

In San Francisco and throughout the world...
Architectural Porcelain Enamel provides
the key to permanent beauty. It complements
masonry and glass, providing arresting highlights of
deep-hued beauty. Pre-frabricated
window wall sections speed up the job,
for savings all around. When thinking
of the finest in modern construction,
think of Architectural Porcelain
Enamel...*by APCO!*

2320 SUTTER MEDICAL BUILDING
San Francisco, California
ARCHITECT:
Hertzka & Knowles, A.I.A., San Francisco
GENERAL CONTRACTOR:
Jacks and Irvine, San Francisco
Porcelain Enamel Panel
Manufacture and Erection: APCO

APCO ARCHITECTURAL PORCELAIN CONSTRUCTORS

2837 UNION STREET
OAKLAND 8, CALIFORNIA
TWINOAKS 3-9225

JACKS & IRVINE . . .

**MEDICAL CENTER
BUILDING**

**San Francisco,
California**

Wm. B. David & Associates, Designers.

struction. Concrete is used on the parking level. The remainder of the structure is wood frame with exterior walls finished in redwood and stone which latter treatment gives only a hint of what might be expected on the inside.

Guests are pleasantly surprised upon entering to view the beautifully landscaped interior court abundant with lush planting, paved terraces for sitting or sunning, a swimming pool and an atmosphere of an oasis in the heart of a busy city. Most unusual of all is that no automobiles are evident, as the garage is hidden from view.

The swimming pool, completely exposed, astounded San Franciscans when they heard about it because they felt it would not be used due to the cool climate. Located in the court as it is, however, it is completely shielded from winds and open to all the sunshine.

Not only is the water heated but the concrete deck around it has radiant heating installed. Consequently, the pool has become a favorite pastime with guests.

There are 64 rooms, a restaurant, bar, and banquet rooms. The restaurant wing faces the pool and court

LEON B. RUSSELL RESIDENCE
San Francisco, California

Eric Mendelsohn, Architect

JACKS & IRVINE . . .

and makes an interesting place to dine, either in day-time or at night.

The rooms are all finished in redwood and furnished in a contemporary style. They have separate dressing alcoves and fully tiled bathrooms. All rooms are completely soundproofed from street noises through the use of double glazed windows and insulated wall partitions. Ventilation is through an insulated louvred soundproof baffle.

All rooms have interesting views or outlooks into the court. On the first level above the garage, they have private patios, and this level is also completely landscaped.

Lawrence Halprin was the Landscape Architect and Knorr Interior Planning handled the furnishings.

Holiday's Mechanical Features

Keller & Gannon, mechanical engineers, describe

ARCHITECT AND ENGINEER

2320 SUTTER MEDICAL BUILDING

San Francisco, California

Hertzka & Knowles, Architects

the heating and ventilating of the Lodge as follows:

"The hotel rooms are heated by means of a forced hot water system with forced air units in each room. Temperature control is provided for each room by means of a manually operated speed control on each room unit.

"Domestic hot water is heated by means of indirect coils with heat provided by the gas fired space heating boilers. A circulating system for domestic hot water is provided for all areas.

"Circulating piping for heating system and domestic water piping is type L copper. All hot lines are insulated.

(See Page 32)

American Institute of Architects

John Noble Richards, President

Philip Will, Jr., 1st Vice-President
Henry L. Wright, 2nd Vice-President
Edmund R. Purves, Executive Secretary

Edward L. Wilson, Secretary
Raymond S. Kastendieck, Treasurer

National Headquarters—1735 New York Avenue, N.W., Washington, D. C.

REGIONAL DIRECTORS—Northwest District, Donald J. Stewart, Portland, Oregon; Western Mountain District, Frederick H. Porter, Sr., Cheyenne, Wyoming; California-Nevada-Hawaii District, Ulysses Floyd Rible, Los Angeles, California.

ARIZONA CHAPTERS:
CENTRAL ARIZONA: David Sholder, President; A. John Brenner, Vice-President; Jimmie R. Nunn, Secretary; Kemper Goodwin, Treasurer; James W. Elmore, Director; Ralph Haver, Director; Martin Ray Young, Jr., Director. Office of Secy., P.O. Box 904, Phoenix.
SOUTHERN ARIZONA: Santry Clay Fuller, President; Edward H. Nelson, Vice-President; David S. Swanson, Secretary; Robert J. Ambrose, Treasurer; D. Burr DuBois, Director; Eleazar D. Herreras, Director; Emerson C. Scholer, Director. Office of Secy., 2343 South Tucson Avenue, Tucson.

COAST VALLEYS CHAPTER:
William L. Higgins (San Jose), President; Paul J. Huston (Palo Alto), Vice-President; William H. Daseking (Menlo Park), Treasurer; Edward N. Chamberlain (San Jose), Secretary. Office of Secy., 390 Park Ave., San Jose.

CENTRAL VALLEY OF CALIFORNIA:
Joseph J. Jozens, President (Sacramento); Armsby Tod Hart, Vice-President (Sacramento); Albert M. Dreyfuss, Secretary (Sacramento); Whitson W. Cox, Treasurer. Office of Secy., 2127 "J" St., Sacramento.

COLORADO CHAPTER:
Casper F. Hegner, President; C. Gordon Sweet, Vice President; Norton Polivnick, Secretary; Richard Williams, Treasurer. Directors: James M. Hunter, Robert K. Fuller, Edward L. Bunts. Office of Secy., 1225 Bannock St., Denver, Colorado.

EAST BAY CHAPTER:
Hachiro Yuasa (Oakland), President; George T. Kern (Oakland), Vice-President; William M. Gillis (San Francisco), Secretary; J. A. Zerkle (Berkeley), Treasurer. Directors: H. B. Clausen, F. A. Lockwood, John Oyarzo, G. M. McCue, Marjorie Montgomery, Exec. Secy. Office of Secy., Mezzanine, Hotel Claremont, Berkeley 5.

IDAHO CHAPTER:
Anton E. Dropping, Boise, President; Charles W. Johnston, Payette, Vice-President; Glenn E. Cline, Boise, Sec.-Treas. Executive Committee: Chester L. Shawver and Nat J. Adams, Boise. Office of Secy., 624 Idaho Bldg., Boise.

MONTEREY BAY CHAPTER:
Robert Stanton, President (Carmel); Walter Burde, Vice-President; William L. Cranston, Secretary; George Kuska, Treasurer. Office of Secy., P.O. Box 1846, Carmel.

MONTANA CHAPTER:
William J. Hess, President (Great Falls); John E. Toohey, Vice-President (Billings); H. C. Cheever, Secy.-Treas. (Bozeman). Directors: Oscar J. Ballas, Wm. J. Hess, John E. Toohey. Office of Secy., Bozeman, Montana.

NEVADA CHAPTER:
RENO: William E. Cowell, President; Albert W. Alegre, Vice-President; Ralph A. Casazza, Secretary; John Crider, Treasurer. Directors Graham Erskine, George L. F. O'Brien, Laurence A. Gulling. Office of the Secy. 232 W. 1st St., Reno, Nevada.
WOMEN'S ARCHITECTURAL LEAGUE: (Reno) Mrs. Eileen Casazza, President; Mrs. Lucille Lackard, Vice-President; Mrs. Glades Cowell, Secretary; Mrs. Enid Hellman, Treasurer.
LAS VEGAS: Walter F. Zick, President; Aloyius McDonald, Vice-President; Edward B. Hendricks, Secy.-Treas. Directors: Walter F. Zick, Edward Hendricks, Charles E. Cox. Office of Secy., 106 S. Main St., Las Vegas.

NEVADA STATE BOARD OF ARCHITECTS:
L. A. Ferris, Chairman; Aloysius McDonald, Secy.-Treas. Members: Russell Mills (Reno), Edward S. Parsons (Reno), Richard R. Stadelman (Las Vegas). Office: 1420 S. 5th St., Las Vegas.

NORTHERN CALIFORNIA CHAPTER:
William Corlett, President; Donald Powers Smith, Vice-President; George T. Rockrise, Secretary; Richard S. Banwell, Treasurer. Directors: W. Clement Ambrose, John Kruse, Bernard J. Sabaroff, Corwin Booth. Exec. Secy., May B. Hipshman. Chapter Office, 47 Kearny St., San Francisco.

ORANGE COUNTY CHAPTER:
William T. Jordan, President (Costa Mesa); Donald M. Williamson, Vice-President (Laguna Beach); J. Herbert Brownell, Secretary; Rumont W. Hougan, Treasurer. Office of Secy., 1950 W. Coast Highway, Newport Beach.

OREGON CHAPTER:
John K. Dukehart, President; Keith R. Maguire, Vice-President; Robert Douglas, Secretary; Harry K. Stevens, Treasurer. Directors: Daniel McGoodwin, Earl P. Newberry, Everett B. Franks, Robert W. Fritsch, Donald W. Edmundson. Office of Secy., 2041 S.W. 58th Ave., Portland 1.

PASADENA CHAPTER AIA

Following dinner at Man Jen Low's in New Chinatown, Los Angeles, on August 6th, members were treated to a guided tour of the new Union Oil Center in Los Angeles, under supervision of Roland Logan Russell, program chairman.

Recent new members include: Harold F. Munselle and Joseph E. Kottra, Corporate Members; W. Giles McNeill, Associate Member.

SAN FRANCISCO ARCHITECTURAL CLUB

John McElheney, Assistant Manager of the Prudential Insurance Company spoke at the August meeting on the subject "The Impact of Insurance Upon Building and Architecture," and described the results of surveys currently being made by the firm's Los Angeles and San Francisco offices.

The Class Committee announces Fall Classes will be conducted in Engineering, Atelier, and Basic Drawing, which is a new class in architectural deliniation for young draftsmen.

On Saturday, August 23, members were treated to a tour of the Kraftile plant at Niles, California, where new equipment recently installed by Kraftile was put in demonstration for the visitors.

SOUTHERN CALIFORNIA CHAPTER AIA

Dean Stafford Warren of the University of California at Los Angeles Medical School, was a recent speaker at a Chapter meeting, taking as his subject "Professional Improvement." Dean Warren appraised the architect's status in society, drawing many comparable situations with the medical profession.

New members of the Chapter include: Dale Bragg, Zack Cook, Wayne Frederick, Robert Hernandez, Immanuel Lewin, Oscar Liff, Richard Pollock, John Scheidemen, E. Ray Schlick, Frank Schneider, Morris Stark, and John Williams, Corporate Members.

OREGON CHAPTER AIA

The next meeting of the Chapter is scheduled for September 16th in the Imperial Hotel.

Considerable discussion was recently given to problems and implications of the appeal to the State Supreme Court of the Glazier vs. State Board of Architect Examiner case. The appeal being based on the point of law that a Circuit Court Judge shall not usurp the duties of the Oregon State Board of Architectural Examiners by issuing a license to practice

architecture within the State of Oregon.

Glazier was recently issued a license by the Oregon State Board of Architect Examiner to practice architecture within the state, but such action did not nullify the pending court action.

EAST BAY CHAPTER AIA

The August meeting was devoted to the California Council AIA, with the following in attendance: Ulysses Floyd Rible of Los Angeles, Regional Director of the AIA; Don Canty of the California CouncilAIA; L. F. Richards, CCAIA President, and a member of the Coast Valleys Chapter; Lee B. Kline, of the Pasadena Chapter AIA, and vice-president of the CCAIA; Edward H. Fickett, Secretary, CCAIA, and member of the Southern California Chapter AIA; Allen Y. Lew, Treasurer, CCAIA, and member of the San Joaquin Valley Chapter AIA; Corwin Booth, Northern California Chapter AIA, and Member at Large; and the CCAIA Executive Director.

Recent new members include: Serifo J. Menegon, Corporate Member, and Elwood Hansen, formerly Junior Member, now a Corporate Member.

The work of five East Bay AIA firms is currently on view at the Junior Center of Art, Mosswood Park, Oakland. Exhibiting work is Schmidts, Hardman & Wong; Reynolds & Chamberlain; John C. Warnecke; David H. Horn, and Barbachano, Ivanitsky & Watanabe.

WASHINGTON STATE CHAPTER AIA

Harrison J. Overturf, partner in the architectural firm of Bain & Overturf, Seattle, has been elected president of the Washington State Chapter AIA, for the ensuing year, succeeding James J. Chiarelli.

Other officers elected to serve with him were: Lawrence G. Waldron, first vice-president; Thomas F. Hargis, Jr., second vice-president; Talbot Wegg, secretary, and David R. Anderson, treasurer. Retiring president Chiarelli and Hugo W. Osterman were elected to the Board of Directors.

The Chapter also elected the following delegates to the Northwest Regional Council and the 1959 annual convention of the AIA: Arnold G. Gangnes, William J. Bain, Robert H. Dietz, Robert L. Durham, Fred Bassetti, Albert O. Bumgardner, Victor Steinbrueck, Clare Moffitt, B. Marcus Priteca, and Edward J. Baar.

SANTA CLARA & SANTA CRUZ COUNTIES CHAPTER

The August meeting was a joint meeting with the Engineers Society, with the engineers in charge of the meeting.

NORTHWEST REGIONAL CONFERENCE AIA

The Northwest Regional Conference of the AIA will be held this year at Harrison Hot Springs, British Columbia, October 9-12.

PASADENA CHAPTER:
H. Douglas Byles, President; Edward D. Davies, Vice-President; Ward W. Deems, Secretary; Robert F. Gordon, Treasurer. Directors: Mal Gianni, Lee B. Kline, Keith B. Marston, Donald E. Neptune. Office of the Secy., 170 E. California St., Pasadena.

SAN DIEGO CHAPTER:
Raymond Lee Eggers, President; William P. Wilmurt, Vice-President; Lloyd P. A. Ruocco, Secretary; Delmar S. Mitchell, Treasurer. Directors: John C. Deardorf, Richard George Wheeler and Sam Bruce Richards. Office of the Secy., 3603 5th Ave., San Diego 3.

SAN JOAQUIN CHAPTER:
Robert C. Kaestner, President (Visalia); William G. Hyberg, Vice-President (Fresno); Lawrence B. Alexander, Secretary; Edwin S. Darden. Office of Secy., 128 E. 8th St., Hanford.

SANTA BARBARA CHAPTER:
Wallace W. Arendt, President (Santa Barbara); Darwin E. Fisher, Vice-President (Ventura); Walter Tibbetts, Secretary; Kenneth H. Hess, Treasurer. Office of Secy., 630 Para Grande Lane, Santa Barbara.

SOUTHERN CALIFORNIA CHAPTER:
George Vernon Russell, President; Maynard Lyndon, Vice-President; Ralph C. Crosby, Secretary; Thornton Abell, Treasurer. Office of Secy., 124 W. 4th St., Los Angeles.

SOUTHWEST WASHINGTON CHAPTER:
Robert Billsborough Price, President; Robert T. Olson, 1st Vice-President; Donald F. Burr, 2nd Vice-President; Percy G. Ball, Secretary; Alan C. Liddle, Treasurer; Charles T. Pearson and George Leonard Elkvall, Trustees. Office of Secy., 2715 Center St., Tacoma 2, Washington.

UTAH CHAPTER:
W. J. Monroe, Jr., President, 433 Atlas Bldg., Salt Lake City; M. E. Harris, Jr., Secretary, 703 Newhouse Bldg., Salt Lake City.

WASHINGTON STATE CHAPTER:
Harrison J. Overturf, President; Lawrence G. Waldron, 1st Vice-President; Thomas F. Hargis, Jr., 2nd Vice-President; Talbot Wegg, Secretary; David R. Anderson, Treasurer. Office of Secy., Miss Gwen Myer, Executive Secty., 409 Central Bldg., Seattle 4.

SPOKANE CHAPTER:
Wm. C. James, President; Carl H. Johnson, Vice-President; Keith T. Boyington, Secretary; Ralph J. Bishop, Treasurer; Lawrence G. Evanoff, Carroll Martell, Kenneth W. Brooks, Directors. Office of the Secy., 615 Realty Bldg., Spokane.

HAWAII CHAPTER:
Howard L. Cook, President; Douglas W. Freeth, Vice-President; Francis S. Haines, Secretary; Clifford F. Young, Treasurer. Directors, Richard N. Dennis, Frank Slavsky, William D. Merrill. Office of Secretary, 1410 Kapiolani Blvd., Honolulu 14.

CALIFORNIA COUNCIL, THE A.I.A.:
L. F. Richards, Santa Clara, President; Lee B. Kline, Los Angeles, Vice-President; Edward H. Fickett, Los Angeles, Secretary; Allen Y. Lew, Fresno, Treasurer. Miss Mary E. White, Office Secretary, 703 Market Street, San Francisco 3.

CALIFORNIA STATE BD. ARCHITECTURAL EXAMINERS:
Malcolm D. Reynolds, President (Oakland); Kenneth Wing, Secretary (Long Beach); Wendell R. Spackman (San Francisco); Paul Davis (Santa Ana), and Frank Cronin, Executive Secy., 1020 N St., Sacramento 14.

ALLIED ARCHITECTURAL ORGANIZATIONS

SAN FRANCISCO ARCHITECTURAL CLUB:
C. Van De Weghe, President; O. Hickenlooper, Vice-President; James O. Brummett, Secretary; J. W. Tasker, Treasurer. Directors: Morris Barnett, Art Swisher, Stan Hosmer, Frank Barsoti, Frances Capone. Office of Secy., 507 Howard St., San Francisco 5.

PRODUCERS' COUNCIL—SOUTHERN CALIFORNIA CHAPTER:
Clay T. Snider, President, Minneapolis-Honeywell Regulator Co., L.A.; E. J. Lawson, Vice-President, Aluminum Company of America, L.A.; E. Phil Filsinger, Secretary, Gladding, McBean & Co., L.A.; William G. Aspy, Treasurer, H. H. Robertson Co., L.A.; Henry E. North, Jr., National Director, Arcadia Metal Products, L.A.; Office of the Secy., 2901 Los Felis Blvd.

PRODUCERS' COUNCIL—NORTHERN CALIFORNIA CHAPTER:
R. W. Harrington, President, Clay Brick & Tile Ass'n.; P. C. Christensen, Vice-President, Truscon Steel Div., Republic Steel Corps.; Philip D. Mittell, Secretary, Otis Elevator Co.; William E. Black, III, Treas., Libby, Owens, Ford Glass Co.

PRODUCERS' COUNCIL—SAN DIEGO CHAPTER:
Eugene E. Bean, President, Fenestra Inc., James I. Hayes, Vice-President, Westinghouse Electric Co.; E. R. Shelby, Secretary, The Celotex Corp. (El Cajon); Joseph C. Langley, Treasurer, Republic Steel Corp., Truscon Steel Div. (Lemon Grove). Office of Secy., 1832 Wedgemore Rd., El Cajon.

CONSTRUCTION SPECIFICATIONS INSTITUTE—LOS ANGELES:
R. R. Coghlan, Jr., President; George Lamb, Vice-President; E. Phil Filsinger, Secretary; Harry L. Miller, Treasurer; Directors: Harold Keller, Jack Whiteside, Walter Hagedohm, Raymond Whalley, Charles Field Wetherbee, Martin A. Hegsted, Advisory Member, D. Stewart Kerr. Office of Secy., 2901 Los Felis Blvd., L.A.

CONSTRUCTION SPECIFICATIONS INSTITUTE—SAN FRANCISCO:
Henry P. Collins, President; Leonard M. Tivel, Vice-President; Leonard P. Grover, Treasurer; Marvin E. Hirchert, Secretary. Office of Secy., 585 Whitewood Drive, San Rafael.

WITH THE ENGINEERS

STRUCTURAL ENGINEERS ASSOCIATION OF CALIFORNIA

The Structural Engineers Association of California will hold their 27th Annual Convention, October 2, 3 and 4 at Ahwahnee Hotel in Yosemite, California.

Structural Engineers from California, Washington, Oregon and Arizona will convene for three days of busy sessions, according to Henry J. Degenkolb, president SEAOC, who announced the convention program.

The three-day program will feature technical topics including: "The Use of High Strength Tensile Reinforcing Bars"; "Composite Application of Pre-Stressed Concrete Units in Buildings"; "Engineering and Construction in Russia Today"; "Structural Aspects of Missile Towers" and a progress report on the State Earthquake Code. Technical Program Chairman Charles DeMaria will announce additional technical subjects at a later date.

Social activities for the ladies during the three-day conclave are under the chairmanship of Maribel Sandner. A tea and fashion show will be held during the early part of the convention during Thursday and Friday, October 2 and 3. There will also be ladies sports activities on Saturday.

Other convention social activities include a cocktail party, costume party and a dinner dance.

The business session of the Association will be held on Friday afternoon. In addition to the usual association business, members will hear a report on the present status of the Structural Engineers Registration Examination. The men delegates will take time off from their busy technical and business sessions for a golf tournament at the Wawona Course and tennis, ping pong and horse shoes.

STRUCTURAL ENGINEERS ASSOCIATION SOUTHERN CALIFORNIA

The Annual Field Day was observed this month at the Riviera Country Club, under the general chairmanship of Alex Laker, assisted by Charlie Nichols in charge of golf; Al Dambros, softball; and Don Hoover, show.

Recent new members include: Cy M. Beebe, William O. Miller, and Frederick A. Shaver, Affiliate Members. Hugo G. Conley, Robert E. Franklin, and Edwin C. Haggard, Members; and Ernest L. Constan, Junior Member.

STRUCTURAL ENGINEERS ASSOCIATION NORTHERN CALIFORNIA

The August meeting was arranged by the Junior Activities Committee, C. Vincent de Nevers, Chairman and Moderator, and included discussions by

Robert L. McNeill, Staff Engineer, Woodward, Clyde & Associates on "Tolerable Building Settlements"; William E. Edwards, District Engineer, Bethlehem Pacific Coast Steel Corpn., on "Economical Design of Structures from the Fabricator's Viewpoint"; and Kenneth E. Beebe and Sanford Tandowski, Pregnoff and Matheu on "Unusual Application of a Hyperbolic Parabolical Shell."

The well attended meeting was held in the San Francisco Engineers Club.

SAN FRANCISCO ENGINEERS SPEAKERS CLUB MEETINGS

The San Francisco Engineers Speakers Club will begin its 21st year of "Practice in Public Speaking" on September 9th. Meetings are held weekly at noon, and according to Carl Otto, President, Will Popert will again serve as Club Advisor.

AMERICAN SOCIETY OF CIVIL ENGINEERS SAN FRANCISCO SECTION

B. W. Booker, Assistant State Highway Engineer for the State of California, was the principal speaker at the August meeting in the Engineers Club, San Francisco, discussing the San Francisco Bay Area freeway system and existing and proposed bay crossings.

Booker served with the interstate Commerce Commission for a short time following his graduation from the University of California, and since has been with the State Division of Highways and for the past 16 years has been in charge of the State Highway District IV, with headquarters in San Francisco.

AMERICAN SOCIETY OF CIVIL ENGINEERS

Francis S. Friel of Philadelphia, Pennsylvania, has been named of President of the American Society of Civil Engineers for 1959 by the Board of Directors, at their recent meeting in Portland, Oregon.

Election will be by mail ballot of the 41,000-member

society and results announced at the October meeting of the organization in New York City.

NATIONAL SOCIETY OF PROFESSIONAL ENGINEERS

Annual Fall meeting will be held October 23-25 in the St. Francis Hotel, San Francisco, California.

"I Sure Love My Builder for Installing the New

ZONOLITE
GLASS FIBER INSULATION"

No wonder she's happy! Zonolite offers cucumber-coolness all summer. And saves her up to 40% in winter fuel while keeping her home warm and comfy.

Zonolite Glass Fiber is a light-weight blanket of superfine glass fibers that trap heat in billions of air pockets. And it's backed with a vapor barrier of reflective aluminum foil, providing moisture-vapor protection.

Easy to install! Won't rot, sag! Fireproof! Three thicknesses: Standard, Medium, Full-Thick.

Distributed by

Pacific Cement & Aggregates, Inc.

Contact the Nearest PCA Sales Office

| SAN FRANCISCO | OAKLAND | SAN JOSE |
| STOCKTON | SACRAMENTO | FRESNO |

CONSTRUCTION SPECIFICATIONS INSTITUTE OF SAN FRANCISCO

Andrew Stevens of H. J. Brunnier's office, who handled the waterproofing of the new Zellerbach building now being constructed at Sansome, Bush, and Market streets, San Francisco, served as moderator of a discussion at the August meeting relating to "specifications."

Discussions also included soil mechanics, and other phases of using modern materials and equipment in today's construction.

INTERNATIONAL STRUCTURAL ENGINEER CONFERENCE SCHEDULED AT CONVENTION

An international review of structural engineering developments will feature the national convention of the American Society of Civil Engineers in New York City, October 13-17.

The setting will provide a joint meeting of ASCE's Structural Division and the International Association for Bridge and Structural Engineering, at which the most recent advances in structural design, research in the behavior of structures and properties of materials, and construction techniques will be discussed in eight half-day sessions.

Thirteen European engineers, representing eight countries, and 14 American engineers will be on the program, among them: E. L. Durkee, Bethlehem Steel Company; Eivind Hognestad, Portland Cement Association; T. Y. Lin, University of California, Berkeley; and Alfred L. Parme of the Portland Cement Association.

SOCIETY OF AMERICAN MILITARY ENGINEERS—SAN FRANCISCO POST

Dr. Claude R. Schwob, U. S. Naval Radiological Defense Laboratory, San Francisco, was the speaker at the August meeting held in the Officer's Club, Presidio of San Francisco.

Dr. Schwob, in charge of a team of experts especially trained to cope with the after-effects of an accidental peacetime nuclear explosion, spoke on the subject "Nuclear Accidents." He discussed some of the types of accidents which have occurred to date, and the types which are anticipated in the future.

CALIFORNIA STRUCTURAL ENGINEERS EXAMINATION

The California State Board of Registration has announced an examination for Structural Engineer Authority will be given on November 28 and 29, 1958, with final date for filing for the examination on September 1.

CALIFORNIA STATE FAIR ART-CRAFT WINNERS

Winners in the competitive art classes of ceramics, jewelry, metal work, textiles and art movies at the California State Fair and Exposition, this year, as announced by Mrs. Florence M. Doe, Fair Director in charge of Art included fifty five winners from 559 entries.

Prizes consisted of purchase awards, non purchase awards and honorable mentions. Winners of purchase awards received cash prizes of $100 in ceramics; $100 in hand woven fabrics; $100 in hand blocked textiles; and $500 in art movies. Purchase award winners included: Ceramics—Ruth Rippon of Sacramento, Reese Bullen of Arcata, Harold J. Myers, Jr., of Bakersfield, Elena M. Netherby of Oakland, and Richard Steltzner of Piedmont. Hand-Blocked Textiles—Raul A. Coronel of Los Angeles, and Bernard Kester of Compton. Hand-Woven Textiles—Constance Tydeman Bevis, Marge Krejcik and Janet Van Evera, all of San Francisco.

ARCHITECTURAL GALLERY

The Architectural Gallery, located in the Building Center, 7933 West Third Street, Los Angeles, is featuring a SPECIAL EXHIBITION during this month of the work of A. Quincy Jones-Frederick E. Emmons, Architects and Site Planners, AIA, Los Angeles. Associated with the firm are Emil Becsky, Harry Saunders, and Kaz Nomura.

WALTER C. ORAM APPOINTED TO CEMENT STAFF

Walter C. Oram has been appointed Paving Engineer of the Rocky Mountain Regional Office of the Portland Cement Association, Denver, Colorado, according to an announcement by E. W. Thorson, Regional Manager.

Oram joined the Association in 1952 as special assignment engineer in the Highways and Municipal Bureau, and since March, 1955, has served as general field engineer at the Seattle, Washington, District Office.

He holds a Bachelor of Science degree in Civil Engineering from the University of Washington, and is a member of the American Society of Civil Engineers, National Reclamation Association and the Associated General Contractors of America. During World War II, Oram served in the U.S. Navy as an electronic technician's mate.

BOTANY BUILDING FOR U.C.L.A. NOW UNDER CONSTRUCTION

University of California at Los Angeles new Botany Building is "growing" out of one of the Southland's most beautiful botanical gardens, as the $1,080,000 glass-facaded building was designed by architect Paul R. Williams, AIA, to take advantage of the existing environment rather than change it, according to Lawrence H. Boyd, project Architect for the development.

The project is one of many buildings coming off drawing boards as part of U.C.L.A.'s multi-million dollar building program. The four-story structure will be located on the northwest corner of the sloping Botanical Garden, immediately south of the Plant Physiology Building on the campus.

The existing garden completely surrounds the building and many of the plants, which have been growing on the slope of the bank between the sidewalk and the north facade of the building, are being preserved.

MacIsaac and Menke Company of Los Angeles are the general contractors.

ARCHITECT NAMED FOR ROSSMOOR PROJECT

Chris Choate, Southern California, architect and R. G. Jones, have been appointed as project architects for Rossmoor, a 1200-acre community being developed near the Long Beach State College in Long Beach, according to Wm. Cheney, sales manager of the tract development.

The appointment places the architects in charge of design and all additional development of the $200,000,000 project, which already is occupied by 900 families. In addition to residential design, one of the first assignments the new architects will handle is the planning of an 1800 unit apartment house and a 100 unit motel.

CALIFORNIA HIGHWAY TO EXPERIMENT WITH ELECTRIC ROAD SIGN

The California Highway Commission recently approved an expenditure of $17,-000 for construction of experimental radio-controlled highway signs to keep motorists informed on up-to-the-minute changes in road conditions at the higher elevations of U. S. 40.

State Highway Engineer, G. T. McCoy, said the new signs will replace old style wooden signs at the customary winter con-

trol points, Colfax and Baxter. As road conditions change, the signs will be instantaneously changed by radio from the Highway Maintenance Station at Yuba Gap, which is nearer to the Donner Pass summit.

Each sign has three long, prism-shaped units, one above the other, which rotate on their long axes in accordance with electric impulses. By rotating the prism, various combinations descriptive of road conditions can be formed. "Chains required Ahead", "Road Clear Over Summit", "Road Closed Over Summit", and "Road Clear, Icy Ahead", are some of the combinations available.

Similar signs are currently in use on some eastern turnpikes.

LANDSCAPE ARCHITECTS HOLD NATIONAL MEET IN PHILADELPHIA

The National Conference of Instructors in Landscape Architecture was recently held at the University of Pennsylvania, Philadelphia, with Ian L. McHarg, head of the university's Department of Landscape Architecture chairman.

More than fifty teachers from all parts of the nation were in attendance and discussed the modern influence of religion, society and science on environment. Other topics discussed included air pollution in large cities and the degree to which the psychological environment endangers mental health influence landscape architectural planning.

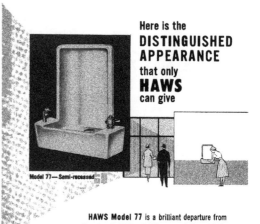

Model 77—Semi-recessed

Here is the
DISTINGUISHED
APPEARANCE
that only
HAWS
can give

WRITE FOR DETAILS
Ask for HAWS
complete
new catalog, too!

HAWS Model 77 is a brilliant departure from stereotyped drinking facilities...ready to match the imagination and dignity of your project, superbly styled, precision-engineered. Model 77 is a semi-recessed wall fountain—in durable vitreous china, available in striking colors, with automatic volume and pressure controls. And the same design is available in stainless steel (Model 73); or in remarkably tough, lightweight fiberglass (Model 69, in choice of colors at no extra cost).

For nearly 50 years, HAWS has provided finer drinking facilities to match forward-looking architectural design. Here's a design in vitreous china, stainless steel and fiberglass worthy of your attention.

DRINKING FAUCET COMPANY
1441 FOURTH STREET (Since 1909) BERKELEY 10, CALIFORNIA

George Vernon Russell, president of The Southern California Chapter, American Institute of Architects, and prominent Southern California Architect with

offices at 3275 Wilshire Boulevard, Los Angeles, has been advanced to Fellowship in The American Institute of Architects, national professional association of architects.

Born in San Bernardino, California, in 1905, Russell received his higher education at the California Institute of Technology, the University of Washington, and the Ecole des Beaux Arts Americaines en France, Fontainebleau. Following his education, Russell traveled extensively in Europe, South America, and America, before beginning his professional career as a draftsman with an architectural firm in New York City.

GEORGE VERNON RUSSELL
Fellow AIA

Russell entered the practice of architecture in Los Angeles in 1932, forming a partnership in 1935, from which his present firm of George Vernon Russell, Architect, developed.

Fellowship was awarded in the field of "Design."

F. H. PORTER ELECTED NEW REGIONAL DIRECTOR AIA

Frederick H. Porter, Sr., founder and first president of the Wyoming Chapter AIA, has been elected regional director of The American Institute of Architects to represent the Western Mountain District AIA.

Porter, a resident of Cheyenne, Wyoming, is a registered architect in Wyoming, Colorado, Nebraska,

and Utah, and has been practicing architecture since 1906. He is also secretary-treasurer of the Wyoming State Board of Architects.

OLIVER G. BOWEN, LOS ANGELES STRUCTURAL ENGINEER PASSES

Oliver G. Bowen, a leading structural engineer and a founding member of the Structural Engineer Association of Southern California and first president of the Structural Engineers Association of California, died June 3, 1958.

Mr. Bowen bridged the gap between the structural engineers who designed from basic fundamental analysis (as Mr. Bowen expressed it WL/8 engineers) and today's structural engineers whose designs incorporated highly complex theoretical analysis. Mr. Bowen not only bridged the gap but also became one of the most respected structural engineers in practice.

For years he was a member of the Advisory Board to the California State Division of Architecture. He was appointed chairman in 1958.

JACKS & IRVINE
(From Page 25)
"Electrical power is metered separately for the hotel and the restaurant areas. Wiring is in metallic conduit and provision for telephone and television is made for each hotel room. A fire alarm system of the non-coded supervised type is provided."

"Exhaust fans are provided for all hotel toilet rooms.

"Dining room, cocktail lounge, banquet rooms and kitchen are heated and ventilated by means of a forced air system with heating provided by means of a forced hot water system with heating coils in the air supply units. Ventilation consists of the use of 100 per cent outside air which is exhausted through broiler and

All the partners in the firm are active in both the office and field with the overall activity being directed by the senior partner, Wm. K. Irvine.

Whether the job be large or small the policy of this firm has been to give personal service and attention to all phases of the work right down to the smaller details. As a result the partners are more often to be found directing and coordinating work right at the site. Says James W. Irvine:

"We feel that this type of service and the quality of workmanship turned out has brought in future business as well as gaining for the company a reputation for work completed to the satisfaction of all and on time. This is the way we plan to keep it in the future."

PHOTO CREDITS: Moulin Studios, Cover and Page 11 (bottom), 13, 16, 17, 18, 19, 20, 21, 22, 23, 24; Rondal Partridge, Page 25; Hertzka & Knowles, Page 14, 25; Phil Fein, Page 15 (top); Pirkle Jones, Page 15 (bottom); George Knight, Page 14; Dickey and Harleen Studios, Page 10, 11 (top), 12; California State Fair, Page 5; Adrian Wilson & Associates, Page 8, 9.

BOOK REVIEWS
PAMPHLETS AND CATALOGUES

PROBLEMS OF DESIGN. By George Nelson. Whitney Publications, Inc., 18 E. 50th St., New York 22. 206 pages, $10.00

Here is a well illustrated volume of 26 of the best and most interesting articles written by the author over the past ten years, whose success and international reputation is firmly based on his achievements as an architect and a designer. The work of his office in architecture, furniture, product design and exhibition design is well known and widely publicized.

The book deals with architecture, design, town planning, education and the fine arts, with the depth and sincerity of discussions of the problems that interest the author, bringing the reader to a better understanding of the modern world and in particular, the parts of the modern world that are the special concern of the architect, the artist and the designer.

THE THEORY OF PROPORTION IN ARCHITECTURE. By P. H. Scholfield. Cambridge University Press, 32 E. 57th St., New York 22. 156 pages, Price $5.50.

A building cannot be good to look at if it is unplanned, with its parts totally unrelated to one another; but on the other hand, if the arrangement is too regular it becomes boring and dull. The object of architectural proportion is to strike the balance between these extremes, creating an interesting visible order by the repetition of similar shapes.

The author deals with the whole history of the theory of proportion, and in doing so develops his own positive theory, which reconciles the apparent contradictions of rival systems and serves as a key to historical understanding. Even when he is dealing with complex themes, the author's exposition can be followed by the uninitiated reader, while those interested in architecture and the visual arts will certainly want the book.

THE STRUCTURES OF EDUARDO TORROJA. An Autobiography of Engineering Accomplishment. F. W. Dodge Corp., 119 W. 40th St., New York 18. 198 pages, Price $8.50.

In this first published summation, the great Spanish architect-engineer describes and explains the major accomplishments of his career, and reveals with candor his unusual building philosophy. From his hundreds of works, the author has selected 30 of the most significant including bridges, churches, viaducts, stadia, water towers, factories, dams, and hangars. Many of them are in reinforced concrete, however, wood, brick and steel are used as well, all of them bearing the strong mark of Torroja's brilliant design, sound engineering, and delicate sense of beauty. Over 275 illustrations show the completed projects, models, details, and projects under construction.

AFRICAN SCULPTURE. By Ladislas Segy. Dover Publications, Inc., 920 Broadway, New York 10. Price $2.00

Some 50 years ago the world of art was elated with shock of discovery. It was suddenly recognized that within the so-called dark continent a great art tradition had been flourishing for centuries. And it was observed that this African art anticipated in practice many of the most modern theories of artistic creation and technique.

The author presents many illustrations of African art, religious and magic, of great interest, and the book is a welcome addition on the subject.

NEW CATALOGUES AVAILABLE

Architects, Engineers, Contractors, Planning Commission members—the catalogues, folders, new building products material, etc., described below may be obtained by directing your request to the name and address given in each item.

Photoswitch light control. New bulletin contains illustrated and descriptive data on Photoswitch Light Control, a new automatic on-off control for any lighting system whose operation should be keyed to outdoor light conditions; reduces cost of control and eliminates power waste in every case where illumination is essential as soon as sunlight drops below a predetermined level. Free copy write DEPT A&E, Electronics Corpn. of America, 1 Memorial Drive, Cambridge 42, Mass.

Structural steel tubing. New brochure describes structural steel tubing in sizes larger than ever before available; structural properties are shown for sections from 3x3 to 12x12

inches square and from 4x2 to 14x10 inches rectangular; data includes girth, wall thickness, weight per foot, cross section area, moment of inertia, section modules, and radius of gyration; also shows tolerances on squareness, straightness, parallelism, wall thickness, OD, flatness, corner radius, and length. Free copy write DEPT-A&E, Espro Tubing Division, Union Asbestos & Rubber Co., 2900 W. Vermont St., Blue Island, Ill.

Modern stone. New brochure entitled "The Modern Stone Age is Here" (AIA File No. 22-83) pictorially reviews the use of stone through the ages from the time of the cave man, the Egyptian, Grecian, Roman, Byzantine, Medieval, Renaissance periods, the present time and the future; depicts every type of quarried stone in natural colors; valuable to architect, builder, engineer, student, educator and home owner. Free copy write DEPT-A&E, Building Stone Institute, 420 Lexington Ave., New York 17, N.Y.

Air diffusers. New 20-page catalog gives full details on square and rectangular air diffusers; comprehensive engineering section makes the correct selection of diffusers for any application fast and easy; pattern chart, specifications. Free copy write DEPT-A&E, Titus Mfg. Corpn., Waterloo, Iowa.

Surgical lights. New architects handbook (AIA FILE No. 31-F-28) available on Surgical Lights; gives mounting specifications for major, minor, and specialty surgical lights; intended as a planning guide; contains illustrations of the principal types of surgical lights with short descriptions of each, specifications for maximum-minimum ceiling height, load weight in pounds, and the number and wattage of bulbs used with each light; rough-in drawings are included for typical structural and suspended ceiling construction. Free copy, write DEPT-A&E, Wilmot Castle Co., 1918 East Henrietta Road, Rochester, N. Y.

Drafting templates. New catalog, well illustrated, presents full line of Timely precisely made symbol, circle, ellipse, alphabet and other templates used by architects, builders and contractors, engineers, draftsmen, students and others; size, scale, description and uses, and prices are shown. Free copy write DEPT-A&E, Timely Drafting Template, Box 416, Basil, Ohio.

Sliding glass doors. New 36-page catalog (AIA FILE No. 16-E) contains illustrations, standards and options, and complete architectural specifications on all Arcadia aluminum or steel sliding glass doors, windows and window walls; complete descriptions and details are well illustrated with stock and custom types listed. Copy free, write DEPT-A&E, Arcadia Metal Products, 801 S. Acacia Ave., Fullerton, California.

Monolithic linings. Newly issued bulletin describes monolithic linings for full protection of stacks and breechings, utilizing Plicast castable refractories; covers structural and installation advantages of 1-piece construction as well as basic advantages of the products used; complete characteristics for five insulating grades; illustrations and typical installations. Free copy, write DEPT-A&E, Plibrico Company, 1800 Kingsbury St., Chicago 14, Ill.

Underfloor duct. New brochure (AIA FILE No. 31C62) features simplicity in distribution systems for electric power, telephone, and inter-com; section includes detailed dimensions, various types and sizes of junction boxes, ducts, all accessories, and service facilities. Free copy, write DEPT-A&E, Spang-Chalfant Division, The National Supply Co., Pittsburgh.

ESTIMATOR'S GUIDE

BUILDING AND CONSTRUCTION MATERIALS

PRICES GIVEN ARE FIGURING PRICES AND ARE MADE UP FROM AVERAGE QUOTATIONS FURNISHED BY LeROY CONSTRUCTION SERVICES. 4% SALES TAX ON ALL MATERIALS BUT NOT LABOR. ITEMS IN ITALIC INCLUDE LABOR AND SALES TAX.

BONDS—Performance or Performance plus Labor and Material Bond(s), $10 per $1000 on contract price. Labor and Material Bond(s) only, $5.00 per $1000 on contract price.

BRICKWORK & MASONRY

COMMON BRICKWORK, Reinforced:		
8" walls	SF	*2.95*
12" walls	SF	*4.15*
SELECT COMMON, Reinforced:		
8" walls	SF	*3.05*
12" walls	SF	*4.30*
CONCRETE BLOCK, Reinforced:		
6" walls	SF	*1.40*
8" walls	SF	*1.55*
12" walls	SF	*1.90*
BRICK VENEER:		
4" Select Common	SF	*1.65*
4" Roman	SF	*2.50*
4" Norman	SF	*2.40*
4" Aggrelite	SF	*2.40*

BRICKWORK & MASONRY

All Prices—F.O.B. Plant.

COMMON BRICK		
Common 2½ x 3¾ x 8¼	M	45.00
Select 2½ x 3¾ x 8¼	M	52.00
Clinker 2½ x 3¾ x 8¼	M	48.00
Jumbo 3½ x 3 x 11½	M	90.00
FACE BRICK		
Standard	M	59.80 - 83.20
Jumbo	M	114.40 - 130.00
Roman	M	88.40 - 109.20
Norman	M	101.40 - 124.80
Brik Blox (6")	M	202.80
(8")	M	239.20
Braile Veneer	M	26.00
BUILDING TILE		
8 x 5½ x 12 inches	M	165.78
6 x 5½ x 12 inches	M	128.96
HOLLOW TILE		
12 x 12 x 3 inches	M	163.12
12 x 12 x 4 inches	M	184.18
12 x 12 x 6 inches	M	244.71
MANTEL FIRE BRICK		
2½ x 9½ x 4½ inches	M	140.40
GLAZED STRUCTURAL UNITS		
2 x 6 x 12 Furring	SF	.90
4 x 6 x 12 Furring	SF	1.20
6 x 6 x 12 Furring	SF	1.50
4 x 6 x 12 Partition	SF	1.60
Add for color	SF	.20
CONCRETE BLOCKS		
4 x 8 x 16 inches	EA	.22
6 x 8 x 16 inches	EA	.265
8 x 8 x 16 inches	EA	.30
12 x 8 x 16 inches	EA	.435
Colored Add	EA	.02
AGGREGATE—Haydite or Basalite		
All sizes in bulk	CY	6.24

BUILDING PAPERS & FELTS

1 ply per 1000 ft. roll	3.95
2 ply per 1000 ft. roll	6.03
3 ply per 1000 ft. roll	8.22
Sisalkraft, reinf. 500 ft. roll	7.54
SHEATHING PAPERS:	
Asphalt sheathing, 15-lb. roll	2.40
30-lb. roll	3.37
Dampcourse, 216-ft. roll	3.05
FELT PAPERS:	
Deadening felt, ¾ lb., 50 ft. roll	3.94
Deadening felt, 1 lb., 50 ft. roll	4.60
Asphalt roofing, 15-lb.	2.50
30-lb.	3.50
ROOFING PAPERS:	
Standard Grade, Smooth Surface	
108 ft. roll, Light, 45 lb.	2.26
Medium 55 lb.	2.64
Heavy 65 lb.	3.10
Mineral Surfaced	3.60

CHIMNEYS, PATENT

F.O.B. Warehouse

6"	LF	1.45
8"	LF	2.05
10"	LF	2.85
12"	LF	3.45

Rates for 10 - 50 Lin. Ft.

CONCRETE AGGREGATES

	Bunker Per Ton	Del'd Per Ton
Gravel, All Sizes	3.25	4.00
Top Sand	3.45	4.20
Concrete Mix	3.35	4.20
Crushed Rock		
¼" to ¾"	3.30	4.20
¾" to 1½"	3.30	4.20
Roofing Gravel	3.46	4.15
SAND		
Lapis (Nos. 1 & 2)	4.30	5.10
Olympia (Nos. 1 & 2)	3.60	4.15

CEMENT		
Common, All brands (Paper sacks)		
Small quantities,	Per Sack	1.35
Large quantities,	Per bbl.	4.25
Trinity White & Mendusa White	Per Sack	4.00
CONCRETE MIX		
6 sacks in 5-yd. loads	Per yard	13.40
CURING COMPOUND, Clear		
5 gal drums	Per Gal.	1.46

CARPENTRY & MILLWORK

Hardware not included

FRAMING:		
Floors	BM	*.20 - .25*
Walls	BM	*.25 - .30*
Ceilings	BM	*.18 - .22*
Roofs	BM	*.22 - .27*
Furring & Blocking	BM	*.30 - .50*
SHEATHING:		
1 x 8 straight	BM	*.20 - .25*
1 x 8 diagonal	BM	*.23 - .28*
5/16" Plyscore	SF	*.16 - .20*
⅜" Plywood	SF	*.25 - .30*
SIDING:		
1 x 8 Bevel	BM	*.35 - .40*
1 x 4 V-Rustic	BM	*.40 - .45*
EXTERIOR TRIM:		
Fascia and Molds	BM	*.40 - .50*
Bolted Framing—Add 50%		
ENTRANCE DOORS & FRAMES:		
Singles		*60.00 & Up*
Doubles		*100.00 & Up*
INTERIOR DOORS & FRAMES:		
Singles		*35.00 & Up*
Pocket Sliding		*45.00 & Up*
Closet Sliding (Pr.)		*50.00 & Up*
WINDOWS:		
D/H Sash & Frames	SF	*1.75 & Up*
Casement Sash & Frames	SF	*1.90 & Up*
SHELVING:		
1 x 12 S4S	BM	*.30 - .50*
¾" Plywood	SF	*.40 - .60*
STAIRS:		
Oak steps D.F. Risers		
Under 36" wide	Riser	*12.00*
Under 60" wide	Riser	*17.00*
Newel posts and rail extra		
WOOD CASES & CABINETS:		
D.F. Wall Hung	LF	*13.00 - 18.00*
D.F. Counters	LF	*15.00 - 20.00*

DAMPPROOFING & WATERPROOFING

MEMBRANE:		
1 layer 50 lb. felt	SQ.	*9.00*
4 layers Dampcourse	SQ.	*13.00*
Hot coat walls	SQ.	*6.00*
Tricosal added to concrete	CY	*1.00*
Anti-Hydro added to concrete	CY	*1.50*

ELECTRIC WIRING

Per Outlet:

Knob & Tube	EA	*9.00*
Armor	EA	*16.00*
Conduit	EA	*20.00*
110 V Circuit	EA	*25.00*
220 V Circuit	EA	*95.00*

ELEVATORS & ESCALATORS

Prices vary according to capacity, speed and type. Consult Elevator Companies.

Slow speed apartment house elevator including doors and trim, about $5000.00 per floor.

EXCAVATION

MACHINE WORK in common ground:		
Large Basements	CY	*.75 - 1.00*
Small Pits	CY	*1.25 - 1.75*
Trenches	CY	*1.50 - 2.25*
HAND WORK in common ground:		
Large pits and trenches	CY	*4.50 - 5.50*
Small pits and trimming	CY	*5.00 - 6.50*

Hard Clay & Shale 2 times above rates.
Rock and large boulders 4-6 times above rates.
Shoring, bracing and disposal of water not included.

FLOORS

⅛" Asp. tile, dark colors	SF	*.25 - .30*
⅛" Asp. tile, light colors	SF	*.30 - .35*
⅛" Rubber tile	SF	*.60 - .70*
.080 Vinyl Asbestos Tile	SF	*.40 - .45*
.080 Vinyl Tile	SF	*.85 - .95*
Lino, Standard Gauge	SY	*3.75 - 4.25*
Lino, Battleship	SY	*5.25 - 5.75*
4" Rubber Base, Black	LF	*.35 - .40*
Rubber Stair Nosing	LF	*1.00 - 1.75*

Above rates based on quantities of 1000 - 5000 SF per job.

HARDWOOD FLOORS

Select Oak, filled, sanded, stained and varnished:		
5/16" x 2¼" strip	SF	*.45 - .50*
5/16" Random Plank	SF	*.50 - .55*
25/32" x 2¼" T&G	SF	*.70 - .80*
Maple, 2nd Grade and Better, filled, sanded, stained and varnished:		
25/32" x 2¼" T&G	SF	*.80 - .95*
Wax Finish, add	SF	*.10*

HARDWOOD FLOORING

Oak 5/16" x 2" Strip—		
Clear	M	229.00
Select	M	218.00
#1 Common	M	203.00
Oak 5/16" Random Plank—		
Select & Btr.	M	286.00
#1 Common	M	244.00
Oak 25/32" x 2¼" T&G—		
Select	M	260.00
#1 Common	M	203.00
Maple 25/32" x 2¼" T&G—		
#1 Grade	M	317.00
#2 Grade	M	281.00
#3 Grade	M	208.00
Nails—1" Floor Brads	KEG	17.20

GLASS & GLAZING

S.S.B. Clear	SF	*.48*
D.S.B. Clear	SF	*.78*
Crystal	SF	*.92*
¼" Plate	SF	*2.17*
⅛" Obscure	SF	*.68*
⅛" Heat Absorbing	SF	*1.12*
¼" Tempered Plate	SF	*4.38*
½" Tempered Plate	SF	*7.84*
¼" Wire Plate, Clear	SF	*3.65*
¼" Wire Plate, Rough	SF	*1.08*

GLASS—CUT TO SIZE

F.O.B. Warehouse

S.S.B. Clear, Av. 6 SF	SF	.34
D.S.B. Clear, Av. 10 SF	SF	.56
Crystal, Av. 35-SF	SF	.65
¼" Polished Plate, Av. 100 SF	SF	1.55
⅛" Obscure, Av. 10 SF	SF	.49
⅛" Ribbed, Av. 10 SF	SF	.49
⅛" Rough, Av. 10 SF	SF	.49
¼" Wire Plate, Clear, Av. 40 SF	SF	2.61
¼" Wire Plate, Rough, Av. 40 SF	SF	.77
⅛" Heat Absorbing, Av. 10 SF	SF	.80
¼" Tempered Plate, Av. 50 SF	SF	3.60
½" Tempered Plate, Av. 50 SF	SF	6.88
Glazing—Approx. 40-50% of Glass		
Glass Blocks—		
6"		.57
8"		.92
12"		2.39

HEATING

FURNACES—Gas Fired—Av. Job:	
FLOOR FURNACE:	
25,000 BTU	*100.00 - 125.00*
35,000 BTU	*107.00 - 135.00*
45,000 BTU	*115.00 - 150.00*
AUTOMATIC CONTROL:	
Add	*25.00 - 35.00*

HEATING—Cont'd

DUAL WALL FURNACE:
- 25,000 BTU .... 110.00 - 125.00
- 35,000 BTU .... 125.00 - 145.00
- 50,000 BTU .... 150.00 - 180.00

AUTOMATIC CONTROL:
- *Add* .... 25.00 - 35.00

GRAVITY FURNACE:
- 75,000 BTU .... 375.00 - 450.00
- 85,000 BTU .... 425.00 - 525.00
- 95,000 BTU .... 475.00 - 600.00

FORCED AIR FURNACE:
- *Add* .... 75.00 - 125.00

AUTOMATIC CONTROL:
- *Add* .... 15.00 - 25.00

HEAT REGISTERS:
- *Outlet* .... 7.50 - 15.00

INSULATION & WALLBOARD

F.O.B. Warehouse

ROCKWOOL Insulation—
- 2" Semi-thick .... Per M SF 60.60
- 3⅝" Full Thick .... Per M SF 77.40

COTTON Insulation
- 1" Full Thick .... Per M SF 43.26

SOFTBOARDS—Wood Fiber—
- ½" thick .... Per M SF 84.00
- 1½" thick .... Per M SF 275.00
- 2" thick .... Per M SF 385.00

ALUMINUM Insulation—
- 80# Kraft paper with alum. foil
- 1 side only .... Per M SF 18.30
- 2 sides .... Per M SF 31.00

GYPSUM Wallboard—
- ⅜" thick .... Per M SF 49.50
- ½" thick .... Per M SF 54.50
- ⅝" thick .... Per M SF 83.00
- ⅜" Gyplap .... Per M SF 85.00

HARDBOARDS—Wood Fiber—
- ⅛" thick, Sheathing .... Per M SF 84.00
- 3/16" thick, Sheathing .... Per M SF 90.48
- ¼" thick, Sheathing .... Per M SF 109.20
- ⅛" thick, Tempered .... Per M SF 108.00
- 3/16" thick, Tempered .... Per M SF 186.00
- ¼" thick, Tempered .... Per M SF 194.48

CEMENT Asbestos Board—
- ⅛" C.A.B. Flat Sheets .... Per M SF 151.20
- 3/16" C.A.B. Flat Sheets .... Per M SF 208.80
- ¼" C.A.B. Flat Sheets .... Per M SF 270.01

LATH & PLASTER

- Diamond 3.40 copper bearing .... SY .56
- Ribbed 3.40 copper bearing .... SY .62
- ⅜" rock lath .... SY .36
- 1½" Standard Channel .... LF .062
- ¾" Standard Channel .... LF .045
- 3¼" steel studs .... LF .092
- 4" steel studs .... LF .107
- Stud shoes .... EA .028
- Hardwall, Browning .... Sack 1.45
- Hardwall, Finish .... Sack 1.70
- Stucco .... Sack 2.50

LATH & PLASTERWORK

CHANNEL FURRING:
- *Suspended Ceilings* .... SY 2.20 - 2.50
- *Walls* .... SY 2.30 - 2.60

METAL STUD PARTITIONS:
- *3¼" Studs* .... SY 1.70 - 2.00
- *4" Studs* .... SY 1.95 - 2.25
- *Over 10'0 high, add* .... SY .20 - .30

3.40 METAL LATH AND PLASTER:
- *Ceilings* .... SY 3.60 - 4.00
- *Walls* .... SY 3.75 - 4.15

KEENE'S CEMENT FINISH:
- *Add* .... SY .40 - .60

ROCK LATH & PLASTER:
- *Ceilings* .... SY 2.50 - 2.80
- *Walls* .... SY 2.60 - 2.90

WIRE MESH AND ⅞" STUCCO:
- *Walls* .... SY 3.60 - 4.10

STUCCO ON CONCRETE:
- *Walls* .... SY 2.30 - 2.80

METAL ACCESSORIES .... LF .20 - .50

LINOLEUM

- Lino. Standard Gauge .... SY 2.65 - 2.85
- Lino. Battleship .... SY 2.95 - 3.11
- ⅛" Asp. tile, Dark .... SF .10 - .11
- ⅛" Asp. tile, Light .... SF .14 - .16
- ⅛" Rubber Tile .... SF .40 - .44
- .080 Vinyl tile .... SF .20 - .21
- .080 Vinyl Asb. tile .... SF .18 - .19
- ⅛" Vinyl tile .... SF .78 - .82
- 4" Base, Dark .... LF .15 - .16
- 4" Base, Light .... LF .24 - .26
- Rubber Nosing .... LF .60 - 1.30
- Lino Paste .... GAL .75 - .90

Above rates based on quantities of 1000-5000 SF per job.

LUMBER

DOUGLAS FIR: (M.B.M.)
- #1 2x4—2x10 .... 88.00 - 92.00
- #2 2x4—2x10 .... 85.00 - 90.00
- #3 2x4—2x10 .... 68.00 - 74.00
- #4 2x4—2x10 .... 64.00 - 72.00
- Clear, Air Dried .... 180.00 - 210.00
- Clear, Kiln Dried .... 210.00 - 240.00

REDWOOD:
- Foundation Grade .... 120.00 - 130.00
- Construction Heart .... 110.00 - 120.00
- A Grade .... 180.00 - 210.00
- Clear Heart .... 190.00 - 220.00

D.F. PLYWOOD (M.S.F.)
- ¼" AB .... 95.00 - 105.00
- ¼" AD .... 90.00 - 95.00
- ¼" Ext. Waterproof .... 115.00 - 125.00
- ⅜" AB .... 130.00 - 145.00
- ⅜" AD .... 115.00 - 125.00
- ⅜" CD .... 70.00 - 85.00
- ½" AB .... 170.00 - 185.00
- ½" AD .... 110.00 - 115.00
- ½" CD ....
- ⅝" AB .... 185.00 - 200.00
- ⅝" AD .... 165.00 - 180.00
- ⅝" CD .... 115.00 - 125.00
- ¾" AB .... 210.00 - 230.00
- ¾" AD .... 195.00 - 210.00
- ¾" CD .... 125.00 - 140.00
- ⅝" Plyform .... 160.00 - 170.00

SHINGLES: (Square)
- Cedar #1 .... 14.00 - 15.50
- Cedar #2 .... 11.50 - 12.50

SHAKES:
- CEDAR
  - ½ to ¾" Butt .... 17.50 - 18.50
  - ¾ to 1¼" Butt .... 18.50 - 19.50
- REDWOOD
  - ¾ to 1¼" Butt .... 21.00 - 24.00

MILLWORK

All Prices F.O.B. Mill

D.F. CLEAR, AIR DRIED:
- S4S .... MBM 220.00 - 250.00

D.F. CLEAR, KILN DRIED:
- S4S .... MBM 225.00 - 275.00

DOOR FRAMES & TRIM:
- Residential Entrance .... 17.00 & up
- Interior Room Entrance .... 7.50 & up

DOORS:
- 1⅜" D.F. Slab, Hollow Core .... 8.00 & up
- 1¾" D.F. Slab, Solid Core .... 19.00 & up
- 1⅜" Birch Slab, Hollow Core .... 10.00 & up
- 1¾" Birch Slab, Solid Core .... 22.00 & up

WINDOW FRAMES:
- D/H Singles .... SF .80
- Casement Singles .... SF .90

WOOD SASH:
- D/H in pairs (1 lite) .... SF .45
- Casement (1 lite) .... SF .50

WOOD CABINETS:
- ¾" D.F. Ply with ¼" ply backs
  - Wall Hung .... LF 10.00 - 15.00
  - Counter .... LF 12.00 - 17.00

BIRCH OR MAPLE—Add 25%

PAINT

All Prices F.O.B. Warehouse
- Thinners—5-100 gals. .... GAL. .57
- Turpentine—5-100 gals. .... GAL. 1.58
- Linseed Oil, Raw .... GAL. 2.51
- Linseed Oil, Boiled .... GAL. 2.57
- Primer-Sealer .... GAL. 3.10
- Enamel .... GAL. 5.45
- Enamel Undercoaters .... GAL. 5.45
- White Lead in Oil .... LB. .35
- Red Lead in Oil .... LB. .35
- Litharge .... LB. .30

PAINTING

EXTERIOR:
- *Stucco Wash 1 ct.* .... SY .30
- *Stucco Wash 2 cts.* .... SY .55
- *Lead and Oil 2 cts.* .... SY .90
- *Lead and Oil 3 cts.* .... SY 1.30

INTERIOR:
- *Primer Sealer* .... SY .40
- *Wall Paint, 1 ct.* .... SY .50
- *Wall Paint, 2 cts.* .... SY .95
- *Enamel, 1 ct.* .... SY .60
- *Enamel, 2 cts.* .... SY 1.10
- *Doors and Trim* .... EA 10.00
- *Sash and Trim* .... EA 12.00
- *Base and Molds* .... LF .12

Old Work—Add 15-30%

PLUMBING

- *Lavatories* .... EA 100.00 - 150.00
- *Toilets* .... EA 200.00 - 300.00
- *Bath Tubs* .... EA 250.00 - 350.00
- *Stall Shower* .... EA 80.00 - 150.00
- *Sinks* .... EA 125.00 - 175.00
- *Laundry Trays* .... EA 80.00 - 130.00
- *Water Heaters* .... EA 100.00 - 300.00

Prices based on average residential and commercial work. Special fixtures and excessive piping not included.

ROOFING

STANDARD TAR & GRAVEL (Per Square)
- *4 ply* .... 14.00 - 18.00
- *5 ply* .... 17.00 - 20.00
- *White Gravel Finish—Add* .... 2.00 - 4.00

- *Asph. Compo. Shingles* .... 16.00 - 20.00
- *Cedar Shingles* .... 20.00 - 24.00
- *Cedar Shakes* .... 26.00 - 30.00
- *Redwood Shakes* .... 28.00 - 34.00
- *Clay Tiles* .... 40.00 - 50.00

SEWER PIPE

VITRIFIED:
- Standard 4 in. .... LF .31
- Standard 6 in. .... LF .56
- Standard 8 in. .... LF .81
- Standard 12 in. .... LF 1.76
- Standard 24 in. .... LF 6.95

CLAY DRAIN PIPE:
- Standard 6 in. .... LF .34
- Standard 8 in. .... LF .59

Rate for 100 Lin. Ft. F.O.B. Warehouse

STEEL

REINFORCING BARS:
- ¼" rounds .... LB .122
- ⅜" rounds .... LB .111
- ½" rounds .... LB .107
- ⅝" rounds .... LB .104
- ¾" rounds .... LB .102
- ⅞" rounds .... LB .102
- 1" rounds .... LB .102

REINFORCING MESH (1050 SF Rolls)
- 6x6 x 10x10 .... SF .035
- 6x6 x 6x6 .... SF .067

16 GA. TYING WIRE .... LB .130

Rates 100-1000 Lbs. F.O.B. Warehouse

STRUCTURAL STEEL

$325.00 and up per ton erected when out of mill.
$350.00 and up per ton erected when out of stock.

SHEET METAL

ROOF FLASHINGS:
- *18 ga. Galv. Steel* .... SF .60 - 1.00
- *22 ga. Galv. Steel* .... SF .50 - .90
- *26 ga. Galv. Steel* .... SF .40 - .80
- *18 ga. Aluminum* .... SF 1.00 - 1.50
- *22 ga. Aluminum* .... SF .80 - 1.30
- *26 ga. Aluminum* .... SF .60 - 1.10
- *24 oz. Copper* .... SF 1.90 - 2.40
- *20 oz. Copper* .... SF 1.70 - 2.20
- *16 oz. Copper* .... SF 1.50 - 2.00
- *26 ga. Galv. Steel*
  - *4" o.g. gutter* .... LF .90 - 1.30
  - *Mitres and Drops* .... EA 2.00 - 4.00

- *22 ga. Galv. Louvres* .... SF 2.50 - 3.50
- *20 oz. Copper Louvres* .... SF 3.00 - 4.50

TILE WORK

CERAMIC TILE, Stock colors:
- *Floors* .... SF 1.95 - 2.45
- *Walls* .... SF 2.05 - 2.55
- *Coved Base* .... LF 1.05 - 1.45

QUARRY TILE:
- *6" x 6" x ½" Floors* .... SF 1.60 - 2.00
- *9" x 9" x ¾" Floors* .... SF 1.75 - 2.15
- *Treads and risers* .... LF 3.00 - 4.50
- *Coved Base* .... LF .90 - 1.30

Mosaic Tile — Rates vary with design and colors. Each job should be priced from Manufacturer.

TERRAZZO & MARBLE

- *Terrazzo Floors* .... SF 2.00 - 2.50
- *Cond. Terr. Floors* .... SF 2.20 - 2.75
- *Precast treads and risers* .... LF 3.50 - 4.50
- *Precast landing slabs* .... SF 3.00 - 4.00

TILE

CERAMIC:

F.O.B. Warehouse
- 4¼" x 4¼" glazed .... SF .69
- 4¼" x 4¼" hard glazed .... SF .72
- Random unglazed .... SF .73
- 6" x 2" cap .... EA .17
- 6" coved base .... EA .22
- ¼" round bead .... LF .18

QUARRY:
- 6 x 6 x ½" Red .... SF .49
- 6 x 6 x ¾" Red .... SF .52
- 9 x 9 x ¾" Red .... SF .60
- 6 x 6" coved base .... EA .21
- White Cement Grout .... Per 100 Lbs. 6.25

VENETIAN BLINDS

- Residential .... SF .40 & Up
- Commercial .... SF .45 & Up

WINDOWS

STEEL SASH:
- Under 10 SF .... SF 2.50 & Up
- Under 15 SF .... SF 2.00 & Up
- Under 20 SF .... SF 1.50 & Up
- Under 30 SF .... SF 1.00 & Up

ALUMINUM SASH:
- Under 10 SF .... SF 2.75 & Up
- Under 15 SF .... SF 2.25 & Up
- Under 20 SF .... SF 1.75 & Up
- Under 30 SF .... SF 1.25 & Up

Above rates are for standard sections and stock sizes F.O.B. Warehouse

CONSTRUCTION INDUSTRY WAGE RATES

Table 1 has been prepared by the State of California, Department of Industrial Relations, Division of Labor Statistics and Research. The rates are the union hourly wage rates established by collective bargaining as of January 2, 1958, as reported by reliable sources.

TABLE 1—UNION HOURLY WAGE RATES, CONSTRUCTION INDUSTRY, CALIFORNIA

Following are the hourly rates of compensation established by collective bargaining, reported as of January 2, 1958 or later

CRAFT	San Francisco	Alameda	Contra Costa	Fresno	Sacramento	San Joaquin	Santa Clara	Solano	Los Angeles	San Bernardino	San Diego	Santa Barbara	Kern
ASBESTOS WORKER	$3.70	$3.70	$3.70	$3.70	$3.70	$3.70	$3.70	$3.70	$3.70	$3.70	$3.70	$3.70	$3.70
BOILERMAKER	3.675	3.675	3.675	3.675	3.675	3.675	3.675	3.675	3.675	3.675	3.675	3.675	3.675
BRICKLAYER	3.95	3.75	3.75	3.75	3.80	3.75	3.875	3.95	3.80	3.90	3.75		3.85
BRICKLAYER HODCARRIER	3.15	3.15	3.15	2.90	3.10	2.90	3.00	3.10	2.75	2.75	2.75		2.75
CARPENTER	3.175	3.175	3.225	3.225	3.225	3.225	3.225	3.225	3.225	3.225	3.225	3.225	3.225
CEMENT MASON	3.22	3.22	3.22	3.22	3.22	3.22	3.22	3.22	3.15	3.15	3.25	3.15	3.15
ELECTRICIAN	3.936ᴀ	3.936ᴀ	3.936ᴀ		3.94ᴀ	3.50	4.03ᴀ	3.666ᴀ	3.90ᴀ	3.90ᴀ	3.90	3.85ᴀ	3.70
GLAZIER	3.09	3.09	3.09	3.135	3.055	3.055	3.09	3.09	3.105	3.105	3.03	3.105	3.135
IRON WORKER													
ORNAMENTAL	3.625	3.625	3.625	3.625	3.625	3.625	3.625	3.625	3.625	3.625	3.625	3.625	3.625
REINFORCING	3.375	3.375	3.375	3.375	3.375	3.375	3.375	3.375	3.375	3.375	3.375	3.375	3.375
STRUCTURAL	3.625	3.625	3.625	3.625	3.625	3.625	3.625	3.625	3.625	3.625	3.625	3.625	3.625
LABORER, GENERAL OR CONSTRUCTION	2.505	2.505	2.505	2.505	2.505	2.505	2.505	2.505	2.50	2.50	2.48	2.50	2.50
LATHER	3.4375	3.84	3.84	3.45	3.60ᴀ	3.40c	3.60ᴅ	3.50ᴇ	3.9375		3.725	3.625ꜰ	
OPERATING ENGINEER													
Concrete mixer (up to 1 yard)	2.89	2.89	2.89	2.89	2.89	2.89	2.89	2.89					
Concrete mixer operator—Skip Type									2.96	2.96	2.96	2.96	2.96
Elevator Hoist Operator									3.19	3.19	3.19	3.19	3.19
Material Hoist (1 drum)	3.19	3.19	3.19	3.19	3.19	3.19	3.19	3.19					
Tractor Operator	3.33	3.33	3.33	3.33	3.33	3.33	3.33	3.33	3.47	3.47	3.47	3.47	3.47
PAINTER													
Brush	3.20	3.20	3.20	3.13	3.325	3.175	3.20	3.20	3.26ɢ	3.25	3.19	3.13ʜ	3.10
Spray	3.20	3.20	3.20	3.38	3.575	3.325	3.20	3.20	3.51ɢ	3.50	3.74	3.38ʜ	3.35
PILEDRIVERMAN	3.305	3.305	3.305	3.305	3.305	3.305	3.305	3.305	3.355	3.355		3.355	3.355
PLASTERER	3.69	3.545	3.545	3.35	3.60ᴀ	3.55c	3.58	3.50	3.9375	3.9375	3.725		
PLASTERER HODCARRIER	3.25	3.42	3.42	3.10	3.10	3.00c	3.20	3.15	3.6875	3.5625	3.475	3.50	3.6875
PLUMBER	3.67		3.935ɪ	3.80ᴊ	3.70	3.80ᴊ	3.60	3.675	3.70	3.70	3.70	3.70	3.375
ROOFER	3.35	3.35	3.35	3.20	3.25	3.35	3.35	3.10ᴋ	3.20ʟ	3.25	3.10	3.30	3.775
SHEET METAL WORKER	3.45	3.45	3.45	3.425	3.45	3.465	3.45	3.325	3.50	3.50	3.45	3.55	3.10
STEAMFITTER	3.67	3.96	3.96	3.80ᴊ	3.70	3.80ᴊ	3.60	3.675	3.70	3.70	3.70	3.70	3.775
TRUCK DRIVER— Dump Trucks under 4 yards	2.55	2.55	2.55	2.53	2.55	2.55	2.55	2.55	2.63	2.63	2.63	2.63	2.63
TILE SETTER	3.275	3.275	3.275	3.375	3.26	3.30	3.275	3.275	3.36	3.60	3.375	3.36	

ᴀ Includes 4% vacation allowance.
ʙ Includes 5c hour for industry promotion and 5c hour for vacation fund.
c ½% withheld for industry promotion.
ᴅ 1½c withheld for industry promotion.
ᴇ Includes 5c hour for Industry promotion and 5c hour for vacation fund. Hourly rate for part of county adjacent to Sacramento County is $3.60.
ꜰ Northern part of County: $3.75.

ɢ Pomona Area: Brush $3.25; Spray $3.50.
ʜ Southern half of County: Brush $3.29; Spray $3.28.
ɪ Includes 30c hour for vacation pay.
ᴊ Includes 15c hour which local union may elect to use for vacation purposes.
ᴋ Includes 10c hour for vacation fund.
ʟ Includes 10c hour savings fund wage.

ATTENTION: The above tabulation has been prepared by the State of California, Department of Industrial Relations, Division of Labor Statistics and Research, and represents data reported by building trades councils, union locals, contractor organizations, and other reliable sources. The above rates do not include any payments to funds for health and welfare, pensions, vacations, industry promotion, apprentice training, etc., except as shown in the footnotes.

CONSTRUCTION INDUSTRY WAGE RATES — TABLE 2

Employer Contributions to Health and Welfare, Pension, Vacation and Other Funds
California Union Contracts, Construction Industry

(Revised March, 1957)

CRAFT	San Francisco	Fresno	Sacramento	San Joaquin	Santa Clara	Los Angeles	San Bernardino	San Diego
ASBESTOS WORKER	.10 W / .11 hr. V	.10 W / .11 hr. V	.10 W	.10 W / .11 hr. V	.10 W / .11 hr. V	.10 W	.10 W	.10 W
BRICKLAYER	.15 W / .14 P / .05 hr. V		.15 W / .10 P		.15 W			
BRICKLAYER HODCARRIER	.10 W / .10 P / .10 V	.10 W	.10 W	.10 W	.10 W	.075 W	.075 W	.075 W
CARPENTER	.10 W / .10 hr. V	.10 W	.10 W	.10 W	.10 W	.10 W	.10 W	.10 W
CEMENT MASON	.10 W	.10 W	.10 W	.10 W	.10 W	.10 W	.10 W	.10 W
ELECTRICAL WORKER	.10 W / 1% P / 4% V	.10 W / 1% P / 4% V	.075 W / 1% P	.075 W / 1% P / 4% V	1% P	1% P	1% P	.10 W / 1% P
GLAZIER	.075 W / .085 V	.075 W / 40 hr. V	.075 W / .05 V	.075 W / .05 V	.075 W / .085 V	.075 W / 40 hr. V	.075 W / 40 hr. V	.075 W / 10 hr. V
IRONWORKER; REINFORCING	.10 W	.10 W	.10 W	.10 W	.10 W	.10 W	.10 W	.10 W
STRUCTURAL	.10 W	.10 W	.10 W	.10 W	.10 W	.10 W	.10 W	.10 W
LABORER, GENERAL	.10 W	.10 W	.10 W	.10 W	.10 W	.075 W	.075 W	.075 W
LATHER	.60 day W / .70 day V		.10 W	.10 W	.075 W / .05 V	.90 day W	.70 day W	.10 W
OPERATING ENGINEER TRACTOR OPERATOR (MIN.)	.10 W	.10 W	.10 W	.10 W	.10 W	.10 W	.10 W	.10 W
POWER SHOVEL OP. (MIN.)	.10 W	.10 W	.10 W	.10 W	.10 W	.10 W	.10 W	.10 W
PAINTER, BRUSH	.095 W	.08 W	.075 W	.10 W	.095 W / .07 V	.085 W	.08 W	.09 W
PLASTERER	.10 W / .10 V	.10 W	.10 W	.10 W	.10 W / .15 V	.10 W	.90 day W	.10 W
PLUMBER	.10 W / .10 V	.15 W / .10 P	.10 W / .10 P / .125 V	.10 W	.10 W / .10 P / .125 V	.10 W	.90 day W	.10 W
ROOFER	.10 W / .10 V	.10 W	.10 W / .10 V	.10 W	.075 W / .10 V	.085 W	.10 W	.075 W
SHEET METAL WORKER	.075 W / 4% V	.075 W / 7 day V	.075 W / .10 V	.075 W / .12 V	.075 W / 4% V	.085 W / .10 V	.085 W / .10 V	.085 W / 5 day V
TILE SETTER	.075 W / .09 V				.075 W / .09 V			.025 W / .06 V

ATTENTION: The above tabulation has been prepared and compiled from the available data reported by building trades councils, union locals, contractor organizations and other reliable sources. The table was prepared from incomplete data; where no employer contributions are specified, it does not necessarily mean that none are required by the union contract.

The type of supplement is indicated by the following symbols: W—Health and Welfare; P—Pensions; V—Vacations; A—Apprentice training fund; Adm—Administration fund; JIB—Joint Industry Board; Prom—Promotion fund.

CLASSIFIED ADVERTISING

RATE: 20c PER WORD . . . CASH WITH ORDER   MINIMUM $5.00

ACOUSTICAL ENGINEERS
L. D. REEDER CO.
San Francisco: 1255 Sansome St., DO 2-5050
Sacramento: 3026 V St., GL 7-3505

AIR CONDITIONING
E. C. BRAUN CO.
Berkeley: 2115 Fourth St., TH 5-2356
GILMORE AIR CONDITIONING SERVICE
San Francisco: 1617 Harrison St., UN 1-2000
KAEMPER & BARRETT
San Francisco: 233 Industrial St., JU 6-6200
LINFORD AIR & REFRIGERATION CO.
Oakland: 174-12th St., TW 3-6521
MALM METAL PRODUCTS
Santa Rosa: 724-2nd St., SR 454
JAMES A. NELSON CO.
San Francisco: 1375 Howard St., HE 1-0140

ALUMINUM BLDG. PRODUCTS
MICHEL & PFEFFER IRON WORKS (Wrought Iron)
So. San Francisco: 212 Shaw Road, PLaza 5-8983
REYNOLDS METALS CO.
San Francisco: 3201 Third St., MI 7-2990
SOULE STEEL CO.
San Francisco: 1750 Army St., VA 4-4141
UNIVERSAL WINDOW CO.
Berkeley: 950 Parker St., TH 1-1600

ARCHITECTURAL PORCELAIN ENAMEL
CALIFORNIA METAL ENAMELING CO.
Los Angeles: 6904 E. Slauson, RA 3-6351
San Francisco: Continental Bldg. Products Co.,
178 Fremont St.
Portland: Portland Wire & Iron Works,
4644 S.E. Seventeenth Ave.
Seattle: Foster-Bray Co., 2412 1st Ave. So.
Spokane: Bernhard Schafer, Inc., West 34, 2nd Ave.
Salt Lake City: S. A. Roberts & Co., 109 W. 2nd So.
Dallas: Offenhauser Co., 2201 Telephone Rd.
El Paso: Architectural Products Co.,
506 E. Yandell Blvd.
Phoenix: Haskell-Thomas Co., 3808 No. Central
San Diego: Maloney Specialties, Inc., 823 W. Laurel St.
Boise: Intermountain Glass Co., 1417 Main St.

ARCHITECTURAL & AERIAL PHOTOGRAPHS
FRED ENGLISH
Belmont, Calif.: 1310 Old County Road, LY 1-0385

ARCHITECTURAL VENEER
Ceramic Veneer
GLADDING, McBEAN & CO.
San Francisco: Harrison at 9th St., UN 1-7400
Los Angeles: 2901 Los Feliz Blvd., OL 2121
Portland: 110 S.E. Main St., EA 6179
Seattle 99: 945 Elliott Ave., West, GA 0330
Spokane: 1102 N. Monroe St., BR 3259
KRAFTILE COMPANY
Niles, Calif., Niles 3611

Porcelain Veneer
PORCELAIN ENAMEL PUBLICITY BUREAU
Oakland 12: Room 601, Franklin Building
Pasadena 8: P. O. Box 186, East Pasadena Station
Granite Veneer
VERMONT MARBLE COMPANY
San Francisco 24: 6000 3rd St., VA 6-5024
Los Angeles: 3522 Council St., DU 2-6339
Marble Veneer
VERMONT MARBLE COMPANY
San Francisco 24: 6000 3rd St., VA 6-5024
Los Angeles: 3522 Council St., DU 2-6339

BANKS - FINANCING
CROCKER-ANGLO NATIONAL BANK
San Francisco: 13 Offices
BLINDS
PARAMOUNT VENETIAN BLIND CO.
San Francisco: 5929 Mission St., JU 5-2436
BRASS PRODUCTS
GREENBERG'S, M. SONS
San Francisco 7: 765 Folsom, EX 2-3143
Los Angeles 23: 1258 S. Boyle, AN 3-7108
Seattle 4:1016 First Ave. So., MA 5140
Phoenix: 3009 N. 19th Ave., Apt. 92, PH 2-7663
Portland 4: 510 Builders Exch. Bldg., AT 6443
BRICKWORK
Face Brick
GLADDING McBEAN & CO.
San Francisco: Harrison at 9th, UN 1-7400
KRAFTILE CO.
Niles, Calif., Niles 3611
UNITED MATERIALS & RICHMOND BRICK CO.
Point Richmond, BE 4-5032
BRONZE PRODUCTS
GREENBERG'S M. SONS
San Francisco: 765 Folsom St., EX 2-3143
MICHEL & PFEFFER IRON WORKS
So. San Francisco: 212 Shaw Road, PLaza 5-8983
C. E. TOLAND & SON
Oakland: 2635 Peralta St., GL 1-2580
BUILDING HARDWARE
E. M. HUNDLEY HARDWARE CO.
San Francisco: 662 Mission St., YU 2-3322
BUILDING PAPERS & FELTS
PACIFIC CEMENT & AGGREGATES INC.
San Francisco: 400 Alabama St., KL 2-1616
CABINETS & FIXTURES
CENTRAL MILL & CABINET CO.
San Francisco: 1595 Fairfax Ave., VA 4-7316
THE FINK & SCHINDLER CO.
San Francisco: 552 Brannan St., EX 2-1513
JONES KRAFT SHOP,
San Francisco: 1314 Ocean Avenue., JU 7-1545
MULLEN MFG. CO.
San Francisco: 64 Rausch St., UN 1-5815
PARAMOUNT BUILT IN FIXTURE CO.
Oakland: 962 Stanford Ave., OL 3-9911
ROYAL SHOWCASE CO.
San Francisco: 770 McAllister St., JO 7-0311
CEMENT
CALAVERAS CEMENT CO.
San Francisco: 315 Montgomery St.
DO 2-4224, Enterprise 1-2315
PACIFIC CEMENT & AGGREGATES INC.
San Francisco: 400 Alabama St., KL 2-1616
CONCRETE AGGREGATES
Ready Mixed Concrete
CENTRAL CONCRETE SUPPLY CO.
San Jose: 610 McKendrie St.
PACIFIC CEMENT & AGGREGATES INC.
San Francisco: 400 Alabama St., KL 2-1616
Sacramento: 16th and A Sts., GI 3-6586
San Jose: 790 Stockton Ave., CY 2-5620
Oakland: 2400 Peralta St., GL 1-0177
Stockton: 820 So. California St., ST 8-8643
READYMIX CONCRETE CO.
Santa Rosa: 50 W. Cottage Ave.
RHODES-JAMIESON LTD.
Oakland: 333-23rd Ave., KE 3-5225
SANTA ROSA BLDG. MATERIALS CO.
Santa Rosa: Roberts Ave.
CONCRETE ACCESSORIES
Screed Materials
C. & H. SPECIALTIES CO.
Berkeley: 909 Camelia St., LA 4-5358

CONCRETE BLOCKS
BASALT ROCK CO.
Napa, Calif.

CONCRETE COLORS—HARDENERS
CONRAD SOVIG CO.
875 Bryant St., HE 1-1345

CONSTRUCTION SERVICES
LE ROY CONSTRUCTION SERVICES
San Francisco, 143 Third St., SU 1-8914
DECKS—ROOF
UNITED STATES GYPSUM CO.
2322 W. 3rd St., Los Angeles 54, Calif.
300 W. Adams St., Chicago 6, Ill.
DOORS
THE BILCO COMPANY
New Haven, Conn.
Oakland: Geo. B. Schultz, 190 MacArthur Blvd.
Sacramento: Harry B. Ogle & Assoc., 1331 T St.
Fresno: Healey & Popovich, 1703 Fulton St.
Reseda: Daniel Dunner, 6200 Alonzo Ave.
Cold Storage Doors
BIRKENWALD
Portland: 310 N.W. 5th Ave.
Electric Doors
ROLY-DOOR SALES CO.
San Francisco, 5976 Mission St., PL 5-5089
Folding Doors
WALTER D. BATES & ASSOCIATES
San Francisco, 693 Mission St., GA 1-6971
Hardwood Doors
BELLWOOD CO. OF CALIF.
Orange, Calif., 533 W. Collins Ave.
Hollywood Doors
WEST COAST SCREEN CO.
Los Angeles: 1127 E. 63rd St., AD 1-1108
T. M. COBB CO.
Los Angeles & San Diego
W. P. FULLER CO.
Seattle, Tacoma, Portland
HOGAN LUMBER CO.
Oakland: 700 - 6th Ave.
HOUSTON SASH & DOOR
Houston, Texas
SOUTHWESTERN SASH & DOOR
Phoenix, Tucson, Arizona
El Paso, Texas
WESTERN PINE SUPPLY CO.
Emeryville: 5760 Shellmound St.
GEO. C. VAUGHAN & SONS
San Antonio & Houston, Texas
Screen Doors
WEST COAST SCREEN DOOR CO.
DRAFTING ROOM EQUIPMENT
GENERAL FIREPROOFING CO.
Oakland: 332-19th St., GL 2-4280
Los Angeles: 1200 South Hope St., RI 7-7501
San Francisco: 1025 Howard St., HE 1-7070
DRINKING FOUNTAINS
HAWS DRINKING FAUCET CO.
Berkeley: 1435 Fourth St., LA 5-3341
ELECTRICAL CONTRACTORS
COOPMAN ELECTRIC CO.
San Francisco: 85 - 14th St., MA 1-4438
ETS-HOKIN & GALVAN
San Francisco: 551 Mission St., EX 2-0432

ELECTRICAL CONTRACTORS (cont'd)

LEMOGE ELECTRIC CO.
San Francisco: 212 Clara St., DO 2-6010
LYNCH ELECTRIC CO.
San Francisco: 937 McAllister St., WI 5158
PACIFIC ELECTRIC & MECHANICAL CO.
San Francisco: Gough & Fell Sts., HE 1-5904

ELECTRIC HEATERS

WESIX ELECTRIC HEATER CO.
San Francisco: 390 First St., GA 1-2211

FIRE ESCAPES

MICHEL & PFEFFER IRON WORKS
South San Francisco: 212 Shaw Road, PLaza 5-8983

FIRE PROTECTION EQUIPMENT

FIRE PROTECTION PRODUCTS CO.
San Francisco: 1101-16th St, UN 1-2420
ETS-HOKIN & GALVAN
San Francisco: 551 Mission St, EX 2-0432
BARNARD ENGINEERING CO.
San Francisco: 35 Elmira St., JU 5-4642

FLOORS

Floor Tile

GLADDING McBEAN & CO.
San Francisco: Harrison at 9th St., UN 1-744
Los Angeles: 2901 Las Feliz Bldg., OL 2121
KRAFTILE CO.
Niles, Calif., Niles 3611

Resilient Floors

PETERSON-COBBY CO.
San Francisco: 218 Clara St., EX 2-8714
TURNER RESILIENT FLOORS CO.
San Francisco: 2280 Shafter Ave., AT 2-7720

FLOOR DRAINS

JOSAM PACIFIC COMPANY
San Francisco: 765 Folsom St., EX 2-3142

GAS VENTS

WM. WALLACE CO.
Belmont, Calif.

GENERAL CONTRACTORS

O. E. ANDERSON
San Jose: 1075 No. 10th St., CY 3-8844
BARRETT CONSTRUCTION CO.
San Francisco: 1800 Evans Ave., MI 7-9700
JOSEPH BETTENCOURT
South San Francisco: 125 So. Linden St., PL 5-9186
DINWIDDIE CONSTRUCTION CO.
San Francisco: Crocker Bldg., YU 6-2718
D. L. FAULL CONSTRUCTION CO.
Santa Rosa: 1236 Cleveland Ave.
HAAS & HAYNIE
San Francisco: 275 Pine St., DO 2-0678
HENDERSON CONSTRUCTION CO.
San Francisco: 33 Ritch St., GA 1-0856
JACKS & IRVINE
San Francisco: 620 Market St., YU 6-0511
G. P. W. JENSEN & SONS
San Francisco: 320 Market St., GA 1-2444
RALPH LARSEN & SON
San Francisco: 64 So. Park, YU 2-5682
LINDGREN & SWINERTON
San Francisco: 200 Bush St., GA 1-2980
MacDONALD, YOUNG & NELSON
San Francisco: 351 California St., YU 2-4700
MATTOCK CONSTRUCTION CO.
San Francisco: 220 Clara St., GA 1-5516
OLSEN CONSTRUCTION CO.
Santa Rosa: 125 Brookwood Ave., SR 2030
BEN ORTSKY
Cotati: Cypress Ave., Pet. 5-4383
PARKER, STEFFANS & PEARCE
San Mateo: 135 So. Park, EX 2-6639
RAPP, CHRISTENSEN & FOSTER
Santa Rosa: 705 Bennett Ave.

STOLTE, INC.
Oakland: 8451 San Leandro Ave., LO 2-4611
SWINERTON & WALBERG
San Francisco: 200 Bush St., GA 1-2980

FURNITURE—INSTITUTIONAL

GENERAL FIREPROOFING CO.
San Francisco: 1025 Howard St., HE 1-7070
Oakland: 332-19th St., GL 2-4280
Los Angeles: 1200 South Hope St., RI 7-7501

HEATING & VENTILATING

ATLAS HEATING & VENT. CO.
San Francisco: 557-4th St., DO 2-0377
E. C. BRAUN CO.
Berkeley: 2115 Fourth St., TH 5-2356
C. W. HALL
Santa Rosa: 1665 Sebastopol Rd., SR 6354
S. T. JOHNSON CO.
Oakland: 940 Arlington Ave., OL 2-6000
LOUIS V. KELLER
San Francisco: 289 Tehama St., JU 6-6252
L. J. KRUSE CO.
Oakland: 6247 College Ave., OL 2-8332
MALM METAL PRODUCTS
Santa Rosa: 724-2nd St., SR 454
JAS. A. NELSON CO.
San Francisco: 1375 Howard St., HE 1-0140
SCOTT COMPANY
Oakland: 1919 Market St., GL 1-1937
WESIX ELECTRIC HEATER CO.
San Francisco: 390 First St., GA 1-2211
Los Angeles: 530 W. 7th St., MI 8096

INSULATION WALL BOARD

PACIFIC CEMENT & AGGREGATES, INC.
San Francisco: 400 Alabama St., KL 2-1616

INTERCEPTING DEVICES

JOSAM PACIFIC CO.
San Francisco: 765 Folsom St., EX 2-3142

IRON—ORNAMENTAL

MICHEL & PFEFFER IRON WKS.
So. San Francisco, 212 Shaw Rd., PL 5-8983

LATHING & PLASTERING

ANGELO J. DANERI
San Francisco: 1433 Fairfax Ave., AT 8-1582
K-LATH CORP.
Alhambra: 909 So. Fremont St., Alhambra
A. E. KNOWLES CORP.
San Francisco: 3330 San Bruno Ave., JU 7-2091
G. H. & C. MARTINELLI
San Francisco: 174 Shotwell St., UN 3-6112
FREDERICK MEISWINKEL
San Francisco: 2155 Turk St., JO 7-7587
RHODES-JAMIESON LTD.
Oakland: 333-23rd Ave., KE 3-5225
PATRICK J. RUANE
San Francisco: 44 San Jose Ave., MI 7-6414

LIGHTING FIXTURES

SMOOT-HOLMAN COMPANY
Inglewood, Calif., OR 8-1217
San Francisco: 55 Mississippi St., MA 1-8474

LIGHTING & CEILING SYSTEMS

UNITED LIGHTING AND FIXTURE CO.
Oakland: 3120 Chapman St., KE 3-8711

LUMBER

CHRISTENSEN LUMBER CO.
San Francisco: Quint & Evans Ave., VA 4-5832
ART HOGAN LUMBER CO.
1701 Galvez Ave., ATwater 2-1157
MEAD CLARK LUMBER CO.
Santa Rosa: 3rd & Railroad
ROLANDO LUMBER CO.
San Francisco: 5th & Berry Sts., SU 1-6901
STERLING LUMBER CO.
Santa Rosa: 1129 College Ave., S. R. 82

MARBLE

JOS. MUSTO SONS-KEENAN CO.
San Francisco: 555 No. Point St., GR 4-6365
VERMONT MARBLE CO.
San Francisco: 6000-3rd St., VA 6-5024

MASONRY

BASALT ROCK CO.
Napa, Calif.
San Francisco: 260 Kearney St., GA 1-3758
WM. A. RAINEY & SON
San Francisco: 323 Clementina St SU.J-0072
GEO. W. REED CO.
San Francisco: 1390 So. Van Ness Ave, AT 2-1226

METAL EXTERIOR WALLS

THE KAWNEER CO.
Berkeley: 930 Dwight Way, TH 5-8710

METAL FRAMING

UNISTRUT OF NORTHERN CALIFORNIA
Berkeley: 2547-9th St., TH 1-3031
Enterprise 1-2204

METAL GRATING

KLEMP METAL GRATING CORP.
Chicago, Ill.: 6601 So. Melvina St.

METAL LATH—EXPANDED

PACIFIC CEMENT & AGGREGATES, INC.
San Francisco: 400 Alabama St., KL 2-1616

METAL PARTITIONS

THE E. F. HAUSERMAN CO.
San Francisco: 485 Brannan St., YU 2-5477

METAL PRODUCTS

FORDERER CORNICE WORKS
San Francisco: 269 Potrero Ave., HE 1-4100

MILLWORK

CENTRAL MILL & CABINET CO.
San Francisco: 1595 Fairfax Ave., VA 4-7316
THE FINK & SCHINDLER CO.
San Francisco: 552 Brannan St., EX 2-1513
MULLEN MFG. CO.
San Francisco: 64 Rausch St., UN 1-5815
PACIFIC MFG. CO.
San Francisco: 16 Beale St., GA 1-7755
Santa Clara: 2610 The Alameda, S. C. 607
Los Angeles: 6820 McKinley Ave., TH 4156
SOUTH CITY LUMBER & SUPPLY CO.
So. San Francisco: Railroad & Spruce, PL 5-7085

OFFICE EQUIPMENT

GENERAL FIREPROOFING CO.
Los Angeles: 1200 South Hope St., RI 7-7501
San Francisco: 1025 Howard St., HE 1-7070
Oakland: 332-19th St., GL 2-4280

OIL BURNERS

S. T. JOHNSON CO.
Oakland: 940 Arlington Ave., GL 2-6000
San Francisco: 585 Potrero Ave., MA 1-2757
Philadelphia, Pa.: 401 North Broad St.

ORNAMENTAL IRON

MICHEL & PFEFFER IRON WORKS
So. San Francisco: 212 Shaw Rd., PL 5-8983

PAINTING

R. P. PAOLI & CO.
San Francisco: 2530 Lombard St., WE 1-1632
SINCLAIR PAINT CO.
San Francisco: 2112-15th St., HE 1-2196
D. ZELINSKY & SONS
San Francisco: 165 Groove St., MA 1-7400

PHOTOGRAPHS

Construction Progress
FRED ENGLISH
Belmont, Calif.: 1310 Old County Road, LY 1-0385

PLASTER

PACIFIC CEMENT & AGGREGATE INC.
San Francisco: 400 Alabama St., KL 2-1616

PLASTIC PRODUCTS

PLASTIC SALES & SERVICE
San Francisco: 409 Bryant St., DO 2-6433
WEST COAST INDUSTRIES
San Francisco: 3150-18th St., MA 1-5657

PLUMBING
BROADWAY PLUMBING CO.
San Francisco: 1790 Yosemite Ave., MI 8-4250
E. C. BRAUN CO.
Berkeley: 2115 Fourth St., TH 5-2356
C. W. HALL
Santa Rosa: 1665 Sebastopol Rd., SR 6354
HAWS DRINKING FAUCET CO.
Berkeley: 1435 Fourth St., LA 5-3341
JOSAM PACIFIC CO.
San Francisco: 765 Folsom St., EX 2-3143
LOUIS V. KELLER
San Francisco: 289 Tehama St., YU 6-6252
L. J. KRUSE CO.
Oakland: 6247 College Ave., OL 2-8332
JAS. A. NELSON CO.
San Francisco: 1375 Howard St., HE 1-0140
RODONI-BECKER CO., INC.
San Francisco: 455-10th St., MA 1-3662
SCOTT CO.
Oakland: 1919 Market St., GL 1-1937

POST PULLER
HOLLAND MFG. CO.
No. Sacramento: 1202 Dixieanne

PUMPING MACHINERY
SIMONDS MACHINERY CO.
San Francisco: 816 Folsom St., DO 2-6794

ROOFING
ANCHOR ROOFING CO.
San Francisco: 1671 Galvez Ave., VA 4-8140
ALTA ROOFING CO.
San Francisco: 1400 Egbert Ave., MI 7-2173
REGAL ROOFING CO.
San Francisco: 930 Innes Ave., VA 4-3261

ROOF SCUTTLES
THE BILCO CO.
New Haven, Conn.
Oakland: Geo. B. Schultz, 190 MacArthur Blvd.
Sacramento: Harry B. Ogle & Assoc., 1331 T St.
Fresno: Healey & Rapovich, 1703 Fulton St.
Reseda: Daniel Dunner, 6200 Alonzo Ave.

ROOF TRUSSES
EASYBOW ENGINEERING & RESEARCH CO.
Oakland: 13th & Wood Sts., GL 2-0805

SAFES
THE HERMANN SAFE CO.
San Francisco: 1699 Market St., UN 1-6644

SEWER PIPE
GLADDING, McBEAN & CO.
San Francisco: 9th & Harrison, UN 1-7400
Los Angeles: 2901 Los Feliz Blvd., OL 2121

SHEET METAL
MICHEL & PFEFFER IRON WORKS
So. San Francisco: 212 Shaw Rd., PL 5-8983

SOUND EQUIPMENT
STROMBERG-CARLSON CO.
San Francisco: 1805 Rollins Rd., Burlingame, OX 7-3630
Los Angeles: 5414 York Blvd., CL 7-3939

SPRINKLERS
BARNARD ENGINEERING CO.
San Francisco: 35 Elmira St., JU 5-4642

STEEL—STRUCTURAL & REINFORCING
COLUMBIA-GENEVA DIV., U. S. STEEL CORP.
San Francisco: Russ Bldg., SU 1-2500
Los Angeles: 2087 E. Slauson, LA 1171
Portland, Ore.: 2345 N.W. Nicolai, BE 7261
Seattle, Wn.: 1331-3rd Ave. Bldg., MA 1972
Salt Lake City, Utah: Walker Bank Bldg., SL 3-6733
HERRICK IRON WORKS
Oakland 18th & Campbell, GL 1-1767
INDEPENDENT IRON WORKS, INC.
Oakland: 780 Pine St., TE 2-0160
JUDSON PACIFIC MURPHY CORP.
Emeryville: 4300 Eastshore Highway, OL 3-1717
REPUBLIC STEEL CORP.
San Francisco: 116 New Montgomery St., GA 1-0977
Los Angeles: Edison Bldg.
Seattle: White-Henry Stuart Bldg.
Salt Lake City: Walker Bank Bldg.
Denver: Continental Oil Bldg.
SOULE STEEL CO.
San Francisco: 1750 Army St., VA 4.4141

STEEL FORMS
STEELFORM CONTRACTING CO.
San Francisco: 666 Harrison St., DO 2-5582

SWIMMING POOLS
SIERRA MFG. CO.
Walnut Creek, Calif.: 1719 Mt. Diablo Blvd.

SWIMMING POOL FITTINGS
JOSAM PACIFIC CO.
San Francisco: 765 Folsom St, EX 2-3143

TESTING LABORATORIES
(ENGINEERS & CHEMISTS)
ABBOT A. HANKS, INC.
San Francisco: 624 Sacramento St, GA 1-1697
ROBERT W. HUNT COMPANY
San Francisco: 500 Iowa, MI 7-0224
Los Angeles: 3050 E. Slauson, JE 9131
Chicago, New York, Pittsburgh
PITTSBURGH TESTING LABORATORY
San Francisco: 651 Howard St., EX 2-1747

TILE—CLAY & WALL
GLADDING McBEAN & CO.
San Francisco: 9th & Harrison Sts., UN 1-7400
Los Angeles: 2901 Los Feliz Blvd., OL 2121
Portland: 110 S.E. Main St., EA 6179
Seattle: 945 Elliott Ave. West, GA 0330
Spokane: 1102 No. Monroe St., BR 3259
KRAFTILE CO.
Niles, Calif.: Niles 3611
San Francisco: 50 Hawthorne St., DO 2-3780
Los Angeles: 406 So. Main St., MA 7241

TILE—TERRAZZO
NATIONAL TILE & TERAZZO CO.
San Francisco: 198 Mississippi St., UN 1-0273

TIMBER—TREATED
J. H. BAXTER CO.
San Francisco: 200 Bush St., YU 2-0200
Los Angeles: 3450 Wilshire Blvd., DU 8-9591

TIMBER TRUSSES
EASYBOW ENGINEERING & RESEARCH CO.
Oakland: 13th & Wood Sts., GL 2-0805

TRUCKING
PASSETTI TRUCKING CO.
San Francisco: 264 Clementina St., GA 1-5297

UNDERPINNING & SHORING
D. J. & T. SULLIVAN
San Francisco: 1942 Folsom St., MA 1-1545

WALL PAPER
WALLPAPERS, INC.
Oakland: 384 Grand Ave., GL 2-0451

WAREHOUSE AND STORAGE EQUIPMENT AND SHELVING
GENERAL FIREPROOFING CO.
Los Angeles: 1200 South Hope St., RI 7-7501
San Francisco: 1025 Howard St., HE 1-7070
Oakland: 332-19th St., GL 2-4280

WATERPROOFING MATERIALS
CONRAD SOVIG CO.
San Francisco: 875 Bryant St., HE 1-1345

WATERSTOPS (P.V.C.)
TECON PRODUCTS, LTD.
Vancouver, B.C.: 681 E. Hastings St.
Seattle: 304 So. Alaskan Way

WINDOW SHADES
SHADES, INC.
San Francisco: 80 Tehama St., DO 2-7092

CONSTRUCTION CONTRACTS AWARDED AND MISCELLANEOUS PERSONNEL DATA

HOSPITAL ADD'N., Los Angeles. Board of Trustees of Monte Sano Hospital, Los Angeles, owner. Addition to present buildings; 42 x 52 ft., concrete work, composition roofing, interior plaster, slab and asphalt tile floors, glass doors, tile work, plastic counter tops, electrical, plumbing. ARCHITECTS: Sterner & Dunn, Architects and Associates, 2119 Griffith Park Blvd., Los Angeles. GENERAL CONTRACTOR: Vern Huck, 3021 Rowena Ave., Los Angeles.

SEWAGE TREATMENT PLANT, Benicia, Solano county, City of Benicia, owner. Work comprises construction of a 1,500,000 gal. sewage treatment plant including operations building, inlet works, sewage treatment facilities, pumping plant, pre-aerating and sedimentation tanks, sludge dredging beds—$487,850. ENGINEER: Brown & Caldwell, 66 Mint St., San Francisco. GENERAL CONTRACTOR: Fred J. Early, Jr. Co., 369 Pine St., San Francisco.

OFFICE BLDG., Santa Monica, Los Angeles county. E. H. Stoll, Los Angeles, owner. 2-story masonry office building—$40,000. ENGINEER: David Witherly, 8233 Beverly Blvd., Los Angeles. GENERAL CONTRACTOR: Robert L. Reeves Const. Co., 1620 Euclid, Santa Monica.

BANK BLDG., Stockton, San Joaquin county. First Western Bank & Trust Co., Stockton, owner. 2-story, 10,000 sq. ft. in area, 2 drive-in windows; main lobby panel in walnut with pre-cast Italian terrazzo tile flooring, Mexical glass and porcelain enamel exterior; main banking activities on ground floor, staff lounges and Trust Department on second floor. ARCHITECT: Clowdsley, Whipple & Johnson & Mortensen, 142 N. California St., Stockton. GENERAL CONTRACTOR: Beckett & Frederighi, 1441 Franklin St., Oakland.

SWIMMING POOL, University Club, Palo Alto. University Club, Palo Alto, owner. New swimming pool facilities—$54,490. ARCHITECT: Paul James Huston, 744 Cowper St., Palo Alto. GENERAL CONTRACTOR: R. L. Stanley Const. Co., 848 San Jude St., Palo Alto.

CHURCH, Richmond, Contra Costa county. 1st Church of Christ Scientist, Richmond, owner. Wood, structural steel, brick, built-up roofing, concrete slab floors—$81,336. ARCHITECT: Hunter & Benedict, 5758 Wilshire, Los Angeles. GENERAL CONTRACTOR: Carl Overa Const. Co., 520 16th St., Richmond.

FIRE HOUSE, Byron, Contra Costa county. County of Contra Costa, Martinez, owner. New fire house—$32,483. ARCHITECT: Dawson Dean, Jr., 510 W 3rd St.,

Antioch. GENERAL CONTRACTOR: Ace Builders, 1702 N. Parkside Dr., Pittsburg.

LAUNDRY ADD'N, South Gate, Los Angeles county. California Towel Supply Company, Los Angeles, owner.. Addition to laundry building 70 x 125 ft., metal roof, concrete slab floor, concrete ramp, metal exterior work and pipe railings—$40,000. ENGINEER: F. E. MacDonald, Jr., Civil Engineer. GENERAL CONTRACTOR: Butler Mfg. Co., 4014 Firestone Blvd., South Gate.

NEW SCHOOL, Lowell, San Diego. San Diego Unified School District, owner. Work comprises construction of the new James Russell Lowell Elementary School to be located in San Diego—$245,715. ARCHITECT: J. Thomas Erchul, 526 San Diego Trust & Savings Bldg., San Diego. GENERAL CONTRACTOR: Raymond A. Whitwer, 4470 Draburn Rd., San Diego.

OFFICE BLDG., San Francisco. Adjustment Bureau, owner. Concrete block construction, glued laminated beams, wood and structural steel frame—$122,822. ARCHITECT: J. Lloyd Conrich, 593 Market St., San Francisco. GENERAL CONTRACTOR: Ira W. Coburn Const. Co., 2440 Mariposa St., San Francisco.

BOOK STORE ADD'N, Student Body, State College, Long Beach, Los Angeles county. Long Beach State College, owner. 2-story office building, 5000 sq. ft. area, reinforced concrete construction, structural brick walls, composition and gravel roofing on concrete, plaster interior finish, metal movable partitions, acoustic tile ceilings, steel sash, terrazzo lobby and stairs, forced air heating — $110,716. ARCHITECT: Hugh Gibbs, 441 E. First St., Long Beach. GENERAL CONTRACTOR: O. L. Dahl Inc., P.O. Box 4056, 1825 Redondo Ave., Long Beach.

HIGH SCHOOL, Site Development, Daly City, San Mateo county. Jefferson Union High School District, Daly City, owner. Development of new Westmore school site — $166,620. ARCHITECT: Mario Ciampi; A. C. Martin, Associate Architect, 425 Bush St., San Francisco. GENERAL CONTRACTOR: Adam Arras & Son, 855 Treat Ave., San Francisco.

STORE BLDG., West Los Angeles. Brick store building to provide facilities for three stores; 4000 sq. ft. of area, composition roof, tapered steel girders, concrete slab, acoustic tile ceilings, plumbing, electrical, metal framed canopy, plate glass, asphalt paving. ARCHITECT: Robert Wielgman, 8588 Melrose Ave., Los Angeles. GENERAL CONTRACTOR: H. Kaplan Co., 5304 Venice Blvd., Los Angeles.

SHOPPING CENTER, Foothill Center, Roseville, Placer county. Foothill Center, Inc., Roseville, owner. 1-story reinforced concrete tilt-up construction, structural steel roof; 150 - 200 ft. ARCHITECT: Clarence C. Cuff, 1315 "Q" St., Sacramento. GENERAL CONTRACTOR: Erickson Const. Co., 1119 E. Bassettlaw Ave., North Sacramento.

SALVATION ARMY STORE, Van Nuys, Los Angeles county. The Salvation Army, Los Angeles, owner. 100 x 100 ft. concrete and masonry store building, structural steel, plastering, roofing, resilient floor covering, ceramic tile, insulation, acoustic tile, sheet metal, asphalt paving. ARCHITECT: Fisher & Wilder, 20 S. Ash St., Ventura. GENERAL CONTRACTOR: A. R. Willinger Co., 13417 Ventura Blvd., Sherman Oaks.

HEAD & GREENHOUSE, Berkeley, Alameda county. University of California, Berkeley, owner. Construction of a new Headhouse and two Greenhouses in Berkeley—$357,800. ARCHITECT: Donald S. Macky, 1444 Webster St., Oakland. STRUCTURAL ENGINEER: Frank E. McClure, 1444 Webster St., Oakland. MECHANICAL & ELECTRICAL ENGINEER: G. L. Gendler & Associates, 1044 University Ave., Berkeley.

OFFICE BLDG., Redlands, San Bernardino county. John G. Wilcoxson, Redlands, owner. 2-level, seven-unit steel frame and reinforced masonry office building; 4160 sq. ft. area, composition roofing, public access ramps, exit stairs at rear, metal stud and plaster interior partitions, vinyl asbestos floor covering, winter and summer air conditioning, mechanical ventilation, plate glass and aluminum store front, aluminum sash, toilet facilities, electrical work. ARCHITECT: Clare Henry Day, Suite 7, Investment Bldg., Redlands. GENERAL CONTRACTOR: Donald & McKee, 414 E. Central, Redlands.

ELEMENTARY SCHOOL ADD'N, San Miguel, Sunnyvale, Santa Clara county. Sunnyvale School District, owner. Masonry

block construction to provide facilities for 8 new classrooms — $130,528. ARCHITECT: Donald Powers Smith, 133 Kearny St., San Francisco. GENERAL CONTRACTOR: Oscar H. Liebert, 617 E. Arques St., Sunnyvale.

GOLF CLUBHOUSE, William Land Park, Sacramento. City of Sacramento, owner. New Clubhouse and facilities for Pro shop, snack bar, rest rooms, aluminum store front material, reinforced grouted masonry walls, wood frame, composition roofing, porcelain enamel, terrazzo tile floors — $34,497. ARCHITECT: Rickey & Brooks, 3015 "J" St., Sacramento. GENERAL CONTRACTOR: Paul Christman, 2141 Madera Rd., Sacramento.

CIVIC CENTER ANNEX, Monterey. City of Monterey, owner. Project includes a new Police and Fire Department building in the Civic Center; 1-story, with basement; jail of built-up concrete; wood frame, stucco, shake roof, reinforced concrete slab on grade—$367,000. ARCHITECT: Wallace Holm & Associates, 321 Webster St., Monterey. GENERAL CONTRACTOR: Joseph B. Fratessa Const. Co., P.O. Box 430, Monterey.

HIGH SCHOOL ADD'N, Wasco, Kern county. Wasco Union High School District, owner. Frame and stucco construction, rigid asbestos shingle roofing, ceramic tile, air conditioning, aluminum and steel sash; facilities for new administration building — $64,428. ARCHITECT: Stuhr & Hicks, 924 Truxton, Bakersfield. GENERAL CONTRACTOR: Elliott Const. Co., 1516 E. 19th St., Bakersfield.

RESIDENCE HALLS, University of California, Davis, Sacramento county. University of California at Davis, owner. Project to provide Residence Halls on the campus of the University of California at Davis — $785,500. GENERAL CONTRACTOR: Bishop-Mattei Const. Co., Pier 7, San Francisco.

HOME FOR AGED, Duarte, Los Angeles county. Royal Oaks Manor, Duarte, owner. Multi-story home for the aged, 200 occupant capacity, reinforced brick construction, non-combustible materials throughout, gypsum roof, slab, hydraulic elevators, aluminum sash, hot water heating, cooling, utility basement, interior plaster and acoustical work, kitchen and kitchen equipment, ceramic tile, electrical and plumbing. ARCHITECT: Orr, Strange & Inslee, 3142 Wilshire Blvd., Los Angeles. GENERAL CONTRACTOR: Peck and Roach, 816 W. 5th St., Los Angeles.

SEWAGE PLANT, Livermore, Alameda county. City of Livermore, owner. Construction of a new sewage treatment plant of the City of Livermore — $844,000. GENERAL CONTRACTOR: Hilp & Rhodes, 518 Harrison St., San Francisco.

SCHOOL WAREHOUSE, Carmichael, Sacramento county. Arden-Carmichael School District, owner. 50 x 200 ft., concrete tilt-up construction—$66,495. ARCHITECT: Dreyfuss & Blackford, 2127 "J" Street, Sacramento. GENERAL CONTRACTOR: Delta Const. Co., P.O. Box 457, Rio Vista.

CIVIC CENTER, L.A. Road Dept. Administration Center, Los Angeles. City of Los Angeles, owner. 2-story administration building, steel frame construction, concrete walls and slabs, and a Central Yard Office

Building: 163,000 sq. ft. area—$3,159,000. ARCHITECT: Walker, Kalionzes and Klingerman. Lunden & Associates, Associate Architects. GENERAL CONTRACTOR: Twaits-Wittenberg Co., Los Angeles.

CAFETERIA & WOMEN'S DORMITORY, Junior College, Coalinga, Fresno county. Coalinga Union High School Dist., Coalinga, owner. Construction of a new cafeteria building and dormitory—$485,513. ARCHITECT: Walter Wagner & Associates, 1830 Van Ness, Fresno. GENERAL CONTRACTOR: Remco Const. Co., P.O. Box 152, Avenal.

COUNTRY CLUB ADD'N, La Rinconada, Los Gatos, Santa Clara county. La Rinconada Country Club, Los Gatos, owner. 1-story wood frame construction to provide facilities for clubhouse, dining room, kitchen, storage space—$89,744. ARCHITECT: Kurt Gross, 390 Park Ave., San Jose. GENERAL CONTRACTOR: A. A. Rogers, 14900 La Rinconada Dr., Los Gatos.

ADM. & CLASSROOM BLDG., Bishop Garcia Diego High School, Santa Barbara. Roman Catholic Archbishop of Los Angeles, owner. Frame and stucco, composition roofing, concrete slab, glued laminated beams, toilet facilities, some grading and paving—$444,969. ARCHITECT: George Adams, 2439 Hyperion Ave., Los Angeles. GENERAL CONTRACTOR: J. W. Bailey Construction Co., 634 Santa Barbara St., Santa Barbara.

ALT. & ADD'N, Manteca High School, Manteca, San Joaquin county. Manteca Union High School District, owner. Work comprises alterations to existing buildings and construction of some additions to provide facilities for new classrooms, gymnasium; wood and frame construction—$194,350. ARCHITECT: Harry J. Devine, 1012 "J" St., Sacramento. GENERAL CONTRACTOR: Carvers Const. Co., P.O. Box 484, Stockton, California.

BANK BLDG., Pasadena, Los Angeles county. Security First National Bank of Los Angeles, owner. 1-story and mezzanine, frame and stucco and unglazed ceramic mosaic tile veneer; 8200 sq. ft. of area, composition asbestos roof, tapered steel girders, plate glass, concrete slab and terrazzo first floor, wood and resilient tile mezzanine, air conditioning, interior plaster and acoustical tile. ARCHITECT: Marion J. Varner & Associates, 524 S. Rosemead Blvd., Pasadena. GENERAL CONTRACTOR: Shepard & Morgan, 2302 Huntington Drive, San Marino.

CHURCH CLASSROOM, First Methodist Church, Salinas, Monterey county. First Methodist Church of Salinas, owner. Wood frame and concrete block construction, composition roofing—$54,303. ARCHITECT: Edwin Wadsworth, 130 Summer Hill Lane, Woodside. STRUCTURAL ENGINEER: Marvin A. Larson, 251 Kearny St., San Francisco. MECHANICAL ENGINEER: W. D. Davis, 1676 Eleanor Drive, San Mateo. GENERAL CONTRACTOR: Thomas H. Mill, 523 Central Ave., Salinas.

SCIENCE & CLASSROOM BLDG., Pacific College, Los Angeles. Pacific College, Los Angeles, owner. 2-story Science and Classroom Building, 5000 sq. ft. area, frame and stucco construction, metal sash, built-up roofing, slab and vinyl asbestos first floor, colored cement second floor,

acoustic tile, metal exterior doors, forced air heating, electrical—$56,984. ARCHITECT: Rowland Foreman, 425 Terrill Ave., Los Angeles. GENERAL CONTRACTOR: Vance Beaird, 5112 W. Washington Blvd., Los Angeles.

SCHOOL ADD'N, Santa Margarita, San Rafael, Marin county. Dixie School District, San Rafael, owner. Concrete slab on grade, wood frame and wood siding, aluminum windows; facilities for 2 kindergartens, storage and toilets — $52,990. ARCHITECT: John Lyon Reid & Partners, 1019 Market St., San Francisco. ELECTRICAL ENGINEER: Smith & Garthorne, 1122 Market St., San Francisco. MECHANICAL ENGINEER: K. T. Belotelkin & Associates, 1122 Market St., San Francisco. GENERAL CONTRACTOR: Lawrence Vantrease, 672 Olive St., Novato.

NEW HIGH SCHOOL, Del Mar High School, Campbell, Santa Clara county. Campbell Union High School District, owner. Complete new High School plant, frame and stucco construction, some structural steel and brick veneer—$2,162,726. ARCHITECT: Clark, Stromquist, Potter & Ehrlich, 3200 Hanover Street, Palo Alto. GENERAL CONTRACTOR: Howard J. White, Inc., 870 Charleston Rd., Palo Alto.

MORTUARY, East Los Angeles. Pierce Bros., East Los Angeles, owner. Frame and stucco concrete block mortuary building; 8000 sq. ft. area, composition roof, concrete slab, metal sash, air conditioning, vinyl flooring, toilets, interior plaster, wood trusses, steel beams, asphalt concrete paving. ARCHITECT: Clark & Montgomery, 18710 Sherman Way, Reseda. GENERAL CONTRACTOR: William J. Moran Co., 1011 S. Fremont, Alhambra.

ELEMENTARY SCHOOL ADD'N, Woods Elementary School, Richmond, Contra Costa county. Richmond School District, owner. Completion of multi-use building, and additions to administration building; rehabilitation of existing facilities, site work, appurtenant facilities; wood frame construction — $58,800. ARCHITECT: Barbachano, Ivanitsky & Watanabe, 11484 San Pablo Ave., El Cerrito. GENERAL CONTRACTOR: Jack Burns Const., 1612 Everett St., El Cerrito.

MEDICAL-DENTAL BLDG., Los Angeles. Dr. Franklin Gordon, owner. 5

medical suites, 1 dental suite, and pharmacy, 8000 sq. ft. area; frame and stucco construction, built-up roofing, concrete slab, terrazzo and asphalt tile floors, toilets, acoustical work, metal sash, air conditioning, garden court with concrete block walls, landscaping. ARCHITECT: David Hyun, 1025 N. Vermont Ave., Los Angeles. GENERAL CONTRACTOR: Bill Turpin, 10823 Sepulveda Blvd., San Fernando.

RECTORY & SCHOOL, St. Appollinaris Parish, Napa. Archdiocese of San Francisco, owner. Concrete block walls, wood roof, facilities for school and church; 2 buildings — $218,570. ARCHITECT: Beland & Ginaelli, 1221 Monterey St., Vallejo. GENERAL CONTRACTOR: Samson Const. Co., 856 98th Ave., Oakland.

IN THE NEWS

AIR CONDITIONING AND HEAT EXCLUSION COMBINED IN GLASS

"Safetee" Laminated "Screenlok" Glass, one of the newest heat exclusion and air conditioning construction materials, is manufactured by the Safetee Glass Company of Philadelphia, Pa., and represents a new assembly of glass, plastic and material containing small louvers tilted at a downward angle of 17 degrees from the horizontal to form a shatter resisting glass functioning as a sun shade screen which blocks the strongest, hottest rays of the sun.

Solar heat falling on glazed areas varies with many factors: geographical location of building, time of year, time of day, atmospheric conditions, and direction in which the window faces. Practical heat control results can be obtained by using several logical simplifications. Solar energy falls on the glass at an angle which changes constantly during the day, and heat reflected varies with the angle. In modern construction the size and number of windows do not depend primarily on the directions towards which they face. Use of this new product will represent savings in first cost and subsequent use.

The product is also used in air conditioned buildings to increase the efficiency of air cooling equipment, thereby reducing operating costs. Its modern, attractive, functional appearance gives a new look to old buildings as well as making an ideal original installation product in new construction. It may also be used for doors, partitions, and dividers at a minimum of maintenance. Complete specifications available from the manufacturer or West Coast distributors in major cities.

PRESTRESSED CONCRETE CHICAGO CONVENTION

The Annual Meeting and Convention of the Prestressed Concrete Institute will be held in the Edgewater Beach Hotel, Chicago, September 21-25, according to Philip E. Balcomb, Chairman General Arrangements Committee.

As a sequel to the highly successful World Conference on Prestressed Concrete held last year in San Francisco, plans have been made to hold an equally informative and educational meeting.

DR. ARTHUR BRAMLEY IS TECHNICAL SPECIALIST AT STROMBERG-CARLSON

Dr. Arthur Bramley has been named Technical Specialist at Stromberg-Carlson in San Diego, according to Harold P. Field, manager.

Prior to joining the Stromberg-Carlson staff, Bramley devoted his full time to research at Allen B. DuMont Laboratories where he served as Senior Research Engineer and Head of the Solid State Physics Section. In 1951-52, he was Program Director of Electronic Corporation of America where he worked on industrial applications of infra-red detectors.

Bramley is a graduate of the University of Oregon where he majored in Physics and Chemistry. He was awarded his Ph.D. in Physics from Princeton University in 1924.

NAMED ASSOCIATES IN LOS ANGELES ARCHITECTURAL FIRM

Architect James H. VanDyke has announced the appointment of five associate architects to his architectural and engineering firm.

The new associates include: Paul M. White, Ronald Hendrickson, Colvin B. Childs, Jr., Harry Foard, and Coleman Mullin.

Offices of the firm have recently been moved to new quarters at 3912 Oakwood Ave., Los Angeles.

IMPROVED SELF-TAPPING SCREW FOR THIN GAGE METALS IS ANNOUNCED

Parker-Kalon announces an improved Self-tapping screw especially developed for use with thin gage metal sheets, called "Hi-thred." It is threaded full to the head with the last thread actually terminating in an annular orifice in the head itself.

Because of the full thread under the head, considerably more resistance to stripping out is provided than is the case with conventional sheet metal screws whose last thread is not fully formed. Available in Type "A" and "Z" in production quantities in non-countersunk heads. Complete data from Parker-Kalon Division, Clifton, New Jersey.

CLAREMONT HOTEL BERKELEY BUILDS NEW ADDITION

Architect Angus McSweeney, 2960 Van Ness Avenue, San Francisco, is preparing drawings for construction of an 8-story addition to the Claremont Hotel in Berkeley.

The new addition will provide facilities for 85 new hotel apartments; a 4-story club building, Olympic-size swimming pool, radiant heated patio, outdoor skating rink, and will also provide for some additional office space.

SWIMMING POOL AND BATH HOUSE FOR VAN NUYS

The architectural and engineering firm of Larsen Associates, H. L. Kahn, Ed Farrell, Architects, and B. L. Larsen, Consulting Engineer, 6255 Van Nuys Blvd., Van Nuys, is preparing drawings for construction of a swimming pool and bathhouse at the Sepulveda Playground, Van Nuys, for the Los Angeles City Recreation and Park Commission.

The swimming pool is to be 60x120 ft.

and the bathhouse 30x170 ft., concrete block construction with composition roof, concrete slab and resilient flooring, projected aluminum sash, toilet facilities, showers and related electrical and plumbing work.

Michael Timke is the Electrical Engineer, and King and Benioff the Structural Engineers.

NOTED ARCHITECT ON LECTURE TOUR OF SOUTH AFRICA

Architect Richard J. Neutra of Los Angeles, recently delivered a series of lectures on "Architecture, Today and Tomorrow," at the University of Witwatersrand, Johannesburg, under sponsorship of the Student's Visiting Lectures Fund, administered by students who choose personalities to lecture on the fields in which they have won international recognition.

Neutra will fly home via Capetown, Accra, Rio, Caracas and Maracaibo.

STORE BUILDING AND APARTMENTS BEVERLY HILLS

Architect David Freedman, 221 N. Robertson Blvd., Beverly Hills, is preparing drawings for construction of a frame, stucco and stone veneer building in Los Angeles for the Lion Auto Parts.

The building will have four stores on the ground floor and ten apartments on the second floor; built-up roofing, concrete slab, asphalt tile, hardwood and rubber tile floors, plaster walls and ceilings, metal casement windows, office partitions, stall and tub showers, ceramic tile, aluminum framed glass doors, electric raceways, fluor-

escent lighting, steel beams and pipe columns, metal marquee, circulating hot water system, concrete sidewalks, asphalt paving; 15,000 sq.ft. of area.

LOW TEMPERATURE HEAT TRAP COIL DEFROSTAIR

The "Witt Defrostair" is a low temperature heat trap coil, requiring only a low cost single pole, double throw time clock for completely automatic defrosting.

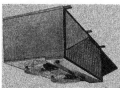

It is designed for freezing and storing frozen food, ice cream and many industrial applications. Installation cost is low, requiring no re-evaporation or special plumbing. Witt Defrostair is available in 17 models ranging in BTU capacities of from 1,880 to 38,000 at 10 degrees T.D. Full information from the manufacturer, A. H. Whitt Company, Inc., Los Angeles, California.

PLAN FIVE HUNDRED UNIT MOTEL FOR SAN LEANDRO

The Garden Hotels Company, Inc., of

Santa Rosa, have announced preliminary plans are being drawn by Lewis Smith of Santa Rosa, for construction of a new 500 unit Motel in San Leandro on a site at Castro Valley and East Shore Highway.

The first phase of construction, estimated cost of $6,000,000, will provide an initial construction of 160 units. Units will be 2-story in height set in developed 38-acre site which will include a large swimming pool, administration offices, medical center, and a neighborhood shopping center.

N. C. PRODUCERS COUNCIL ELECT BOB HARRINGTON PRESIDENT FOR 1958

R. W. Harrington, Executive Secretary of the Clay Brick & Tile Association, San Francisco, was elected 1958-59 president of the Northern California Chapter of the Producers' Council of America, at the organization's recent annual meeting.

Other officers named to serve with Harrington included: P. C. Christensen, Vice-President; Philip D. Mittell, Secretary; and William E. Black, III, Treasurer.

The Producers' Council is the national association of firms engaged in the manufacture, or distribution, of products identified with the construction industry of the nation.

NEW MEDICAL BUILDING FOR OAKLAND

Architect John Carl Warnecke, Financial Center Building, Oakland, is preparing plans and specifications for construction of a 2-story Medical Building in Oakland for Dave Sparber and Robert Hogan.

The new building will be of contempo-

rary design, glass wall surfaces, air conditioning. and will provide 20,000 sq. ft. of asphaltic paved parking area. Facilities will be provided for 15 suites of offices and a pharmacy.

Estimated cost is $600,000.

ARCHITECT SELECTED FOR SAN FRANCISCO AIRPORT BUILDINGS

The architectural firm of Welton Becket & Associates, 5657 Wilshire Blvd., Los Angeles and 153 Maiden Lane, San Francisco, has been selected by the Public Utilities Commission, City and County of San Francisco, to design a new passenger terminal, concourse, cargo terminal,

double-deck garage and appurtenant structures at the International Airport, San Francisco.

It is estimated cost of construction will be $10,000,000.

ARCHITECT OPENS NEW OFFICES IN LONG BEACH

Stanley Goldin AIA, Architect, has announced the opening of offices at 233 W. 7th Street in Long Beach, California, for the general practice of architecture.

Prior to opening the new offices, Goldin was associated with Warren Dedrick AIA, and James R. Friend, Architects Associated, with major responsibility for the design and execution of working drawings for the new $2,500,000 Long Beach Harbor Administration Building.

BLEACHERS AND ATHLETIC FACILITIES

The architectural firm of Allison & Roble, 3670 Wilshire Blvd., Los Angeles, is preparing working drawings for construction of bleachers and athletic department facilities at the Los Angeles City College.

Estimated cost of the project is $305,000.

MASONIC LODGE FOR NORTH HOLLYWOOD

The firm of Meyer & Alexander, Architects and Engineers, 11221 Burbank Blvd., North Hollywood, is preparing plans and specifications for construction of a frame and stucco Masonic Lodge building in

North Hollywood for the Home Lodge No. 721, A.&F.M.

The building will be 50 x 160 ft; composition roof, wood beams, concrete slab, aluminum store doors, toilet facilities, electrical, plumbing and paving. Estimated cost of work is $48,000.

NEW "JET AGE" ESCUTCHEON BY CHALLENGER

The Challenger Lock Company recently introduced a new escutcheon called "FLITE," which represents a real breakaway from conventional escutcheon design. Basic design elements are the free fluid lines which sweep upward in a manner that suggests jet-speed and unbroken flight.

It is designed for both upright and lefthand doors. Available in permanent luster sealed brass, bronze or aluminum finish. Measures 9" x 5⅜" and requires a 5" minimum backset lock. Complete details from Challenger Lock Co., 4865 Exposition Blvd., Los Angeles 16, California.

ARCHITECTS HAVE OPPORTUNITY OF FOREIGN STUDY

Young American architects and graduate students of architecture will have a chance to study in any of 43 foreign countries during 1959-60 under the International Education Exchange Program of the U. S. Department of State, according to a recent announcement by the Institute of International Education.

Recipients of awards under the Fulbright Act for study in Europe, Latin America, and the Asia-Pacific area will receive tuition, maintenance, and travel to and from the country of their choice. The Institute of International Education, New York, is

receiving applications for scholarships until November 1, 1958. Eligibility requires U. S. citizenship, a Bachelor's degree or its equivalent before departure, language ability sufficient to carry on the proposed study, and good health. A demonstrated capacity for independent study is also necessary, and preference is given to applicants under 35 years of age.

FLUOR CORPORATION ANNOUNCES PURCHASE OF SUMMERBELL

Summerbell Roof Structures, one of the oldest names in wood trusses and glued-laminated products in the construction industry, has recently been purchased by the Fluor Corporation, Ltd., according to an announcement by company officials.

Purchase of Summerbell is part of expansion plans by the Fluor company to expand Fluor products of their wood products division, and as part of their expanded program, a complete new glue-laminating and wood-fabricating plant is now under construction at Santa Rosa, California.

To better serve Northern California's greatly expanding construction industry, and in conjunction with the new Santa Rosa manufacturing and fabricating plant, new sales offices have been opened at 420 Market Street, San Francisco, with William B. Smith serving as northern division manager for Summerbell.

PORCELAIN ENAMEL INSTITUTE HOLDS ANNUAL MEETING

The Annual Meeting of the Porcelain Enamel Institute is scheduled to be held September 25-27 at the Greenbrier, White Sulphur Springs, West Virginia, with significant technical discussions on many phases of the industry, according to John Oliver, Managing Director of the Institute, whose national offices are maintained in Washington, D. C.

Among speakers scheduled to appear on the program is Paul J. Lovewell, Director of the Division of Economics Research at Stanford Research Institute, Menlo Park, California, a leading industrial economics expert of the nation.

ROGER D. McCOY JOINS CONSULTING ENGINEERING FIRM

Roger D. McCoy has joined the consulting engineering firm of Dudley Dean and Associates, San Francisco, as industrial engineer on automation.

McCoy is internationally known for his work in the mechanization of production,

packaging, material handling and warehousing. He was organizer and first president of the San Francisco and Peninsula chapters of the National Society of Professional Engineers and former chairman of the consulting engineers executive committee of the American Society of Mechanical Engineers.

NEW FLOOR DRAIN VALVE BUILT FOR DEPENDABILITY

An automatic floor drain valve that closes with a positive spring action whenever sewer water threatens to flood a basement, is being offered by HALLY MFG., INC., of Racine, Wisconsin, and is known as "Flood Check."

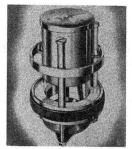

This new valve does not rely upon thue buoyancy of its float to seal off the drain. It is easily installed into any standard 4" drain by lifting up the floor drain cover, setting the unit in position, and tightening three screws. No special tools or recementing are necessary. All operating parts are protected from scum or debris deposited by water flowing through the drain, assuring year round protection against flooded basements. Needs no lubrication or electrical power, and is effective for use with septic tanks and cesspools. Complete details from manufacturer.

ENGINEERING FIRM ANNOUNCES A REORGANIZATION

Knock & Fowler, oldest consulting engineering firm of Dallas, Texas, has been reorganized as Koch & Fowler and Grafe, Inc., according to a recent announcement by Adam K. Grafe, new president of the company.

James D. Fowler, prominent Dallas engineer and Earl W. Sudderth have been named vice presidents of the firm.

Grafe, prior to entering the engineering field in 1955, was engaged in the oil business and had mining interests in Oklahoma. He is a licensed professional engineer in Texas, Colorado and Oklahoma.

The reorganized firm will institute an extended program of projects for the construction of water systems, sewer systems, highways and streets.

DENTAL OFFICE BUILDING FOR STUDIO CITY

Ridgeley & Wexler, Architects, 16610 Ventura Blvd., Encino, are preparing plans and specifications for construction of a 2-story, frame and stucco, masonry veneer,

dental office building in Studio City.

The new building will contain 2800 sq. ft. of area; composition roof, steel stairs, concrete slab floors, asphalt tile, terrazzo, interior plaster, plate glass, toilets and paving.

**MASTER PLAN FOR
CLAREMONT COLLEGE
IS APPROVED**

A master plan for the development of a $5,000,000 campus at the Southern California School of Theology in Claremont, has been accepted by the institution's Board of Trustees.

Prepared by the architectural firm of Pereira & Luckman, planning-architectural-engineering firm of Los Angeles and New York as supervising architects, and Criley and McDowell of Claremont as associate architects, the Plan will provide a completely modern spiritual and educational plant for instruction of graduate students at the school.

The first unit to be constructed will contain classrooms, offices and a library. Later units will consist of a worship center, including chapel and supporting elements; an academic center; additional classroom facilities and related areas; and administration building; a fellowship center with recreation, meeting and dining rooms and kitchen.

Some 200,000 sq.ft. of building area will be located on a 15-acre site. When completed, the campus will house the program serving approximately 300 full time graduate students, along with the faculty and administration to conduct a three-year course of study for training ministers.

**LIBRARY FOR
SANTA PAULA
HIGH SCHOOL**

The architectural firm of Wilson, Stroh & Wilson, Say Road, Santa Paula, have been commissioned by the Board of Education of the Santa Paula High School District, to prepare plans and specifications for the construction of additional library facilities at the Santa Paula High School.

**PLANS READIED
FOR ALL-STEEL
PUBLIC SCHOOL**

Roy Donley, Architect, 8810 Melrose Ave., Los Angeles, is completing plans for construction of an all-steel school in Lancaster School District, according to Ronald C. Henderson, superintendent.

Planned for an enrollment of 650 pupils from kindergarten through the sixth grade, the school will include 16-classrooms, two kindergartens, a multi-use and administrative building and connecting covered arcades.

It's actually easy to save—when you buy Series E Savings Bonds through the Payroll Savings Plan. Once you've signed up at your pay office, your saving is done *for you*. The Bonds you receive pay good interest—3% a year, compounded half-yearly when held to maturity. And the longer you hold them, the better your return. Even after maturity, they go on earning 10 years more. So hold on to your Bonds! . Join Payroll Savings today—or buy Bonds where you bank.

The bride wore goggles

On october 26, 1912, an ungainly biplane swooped into a Michigan pasture like an overfed duck and promptly nosed over on its back. Its contents proved to be a teen-age couple who got married as soon as they regained consciousness.

This was the world's first aerial elopement.

Art Smith, the groom, happened to have one of the country's few flying machines because he had built it, with his own hands, at age 15. And his parents had mortgaged their home to finance him. Their pride helped carry him through years of failure to soaring success as a famous early stunt flyer.

But he didn't remain a barnstormer long. In 1917 his pioneering skill was needed to train our World War I pilots. Then came America's first air-mail service. And again, Art helped break the way—though it eventually cost him his life.

As American as Tom Swift, Art Smith was the farseeing and confident son of a country that has always produced far more than her share of sure-footed visionaries. That's a good thing to know, especially if you've been putting some money into this country's Savings Bonds.

U. S. Savings Bonds aren't backed by gold or silver alone. They are backed by the character and abilities of 165 million Americans. That's why they're one of the world's greatest investments. Buy them regularly— and hold on to them!

Safe as America—U.S. Savings Bonds

St. Cecilia's Church, 17th Ave. and Vicente Street
San Francisco, California

Architect: MARTIN RIST
Structural Engineer: JAMES M. SMITH

●

JACKS & IRVINE

General Contractors

620 MARKET STREET, SAN FRANCISCO

YUKON 6-0511

Utah Construction Company's two great new industrial sites in South San Francisco—Lindenville Industrial Park (foreground) and South San Francisco Industrial Parks in background. Buildings already erected on the Lindenville site include Zellerbach Paper Company and Sterling Furniture Company.

FILL IN THIS SPACE

with your design for industrial development

Utah Construction Company has brought a new dimension to one of the West's most ideally located industrial centers, South San Francisco.

To light industry, it is offering 340 acres of prime sites in its new South San Francisco and Lindenville Industrial Parks — for sale or lease; with construction to suit, if desired.

To architects, engineers, contractors and brokers it is offering a complete package of highly skilled cooperation — both in the development of clients, and, if desired, in the technical planning and the financing of installations.

The land is there for you to use for tomorrow's most modern light industry and plants. Utah's half-century of experience in the construction and financing of major projects the world over is at your service.

Inquiries should be directed to:

Joseph K. Allen, Manager, South San Francisco Real Estate Division

UTAH CONSTRUCTION COMPANY

100 Bush Street, San Francisco 4 · YUkon 6-1700

Vol. 214   No. 3

EDWIN H. WILDER
Editor

CONTRIBUTING EDITORS:

Education
SIDNEY W. LITTLE, Dean,
College of Fine Arts and Department of Architecture, University
of Arizona, Tucson, Arizona.

City Planning
CORWIN R. MOCINE, City
Planning Engineer, Oakland,
California

*Urban Planning and
Shopping Centers*
FRANK EMERY COX, Sales
Research & Business Develop-
ment Analyst, Berkeley, Califor-
nia

Realty Development
ROY P. DRACHMAN, Sub-
divider and Realty Developer,
Tucson, Arizona

School Planning
DR. J. D. McCONNEL, Stan-
ford School Planning Dept.,
Palo Alto, California

Residential Planning
JEDD JONES, Architect,
Boise, Idaho

General Architecture
ROBERT FIELD, Architect,
Los Angeles, California

Engineering
JOHN A. BLUME, Consulting
and Structural Engineer, San
Francisco, California

Advertising
WILLIAM A. ULLNER,
Manager

FRED JONES
Special Advertising

★

COVER PICTURE

UTAH CONSTRUCTION
COMPANY'S INDUSTRIAL
DEVELOPMENT

South San Francisco, California

340-acre development project — Lindenville Industrial Park is outlined at
left; and South San Francisco Industrial Parks are shown at right center.
Further details on Page 3.

ARCHITECTS' REPORTS—
Published Daily
    Archie MacCorkindale, Manager
        Telephone DOuglas 2-8311

—ARCHITECT & ENGINEER *is indexed regularly by* ENGINEERING INDEX, INC.; *and* ART INDEX—

Contents for

SEPTEMBER

THE OLDEST PROFESSIONAL MONTHLY BUSINESS MAGAZINE OF THE ELEVEN WESTERN STATES

ARCHITECT AND ENGINEER (Established 1905) is published on the 15th of the month by The Architect and
Engineer, Inc., 68 Post St., San Francisco 4; Telephone EXbrook 2-7182, President, K. P. Kierulff; Vice-
President and Manager, L. B. Penhorwood; Treasurer, E. N. Kierulff. — Los Angeles Office: Wentworth F.
Green, 439 So. Western Ave., Telephone DUnkirk 7-8135 — Entered as second class matter, November 2,
1905, at the Post Office in San Francisco, California, under the Act of March 3, 1879. Subscriptions: United
States and Pan America, $3.00 a year; $5.00 two years; foreign countries $5.00 a year; single copy 50c.

. EDITORIAL NOTES .

DON'T KID YOURSELF

One of the reasons often offered in support of avoiding the normal appropriations process by funding programs through public debt transactions is that, unlike appropriationism these funds are to be paid back to the Treasury by the borrowing agency. As a consequence, the impression is sometimes created that this method of financing "doesn't really cost the taxpayer anything in the long run." To hold this view is to ignore two very significant features arising from past experiences in this area.

At a time not many months past, when the Treasury was borrowing money at an interest rate in excess of 3%, it was compelled by statute to lend money for such programs as rural electrification and college housing at rates well below this going rate. Unavoidably, the difference between the two rates had to come from the general taxpaying public.

Another example of the fallacy of the "doesn't cost anything" argument can be seen when the cancellation features of these transactions is considered. From time to time, when it has become apparent that the Treasury was not going to be able to collect in full on some of the notes it held, the Congress has authorized cancellation of this indebtedness of the borrowing agency. These cancellations have the same effect as an appropriation inasmuch as the money has to be paid out of the Treasury and there is no longer a requirement for payment.

As of June 30, 1957, Congress has authorized in excess of $16 billion of cancellations, which had been partly offset by cash recoveries from sales of surplus property and other means amounting to $2.6 billion.

Naturally, whatever difference remains between total cancellations and total cash recoveries must be borne by the taxpayer, despite any past assurances that such programs would pay their own way.

It's happened to each of us. We've wanted to stretch forth our hands in comfort, hope and help to others. We've wanted to do something and seemed unable somehow to find a way. Yet constantly we are approached by this organization or that service. We are asked to help as volunteers. We are asked to give and to give generously.

Although we may feel this cause is important or that service particularly necessary, we obviously cannot give to them all. This is the dilemma that confronts us . . . the perpetual frustration we face. And so some of us shrug our shoulders, mutter something about the total impossibility of it all and go about our business as usual.

Yet the problem is far from insoluble. A way has been found out of this distressing dilemma. Known as the United Way, it's the method by which one single appeal a year is made through United Fund and Community Chest campaigns for a whole family of health and welfare services. And that time of the year is now. From coast-to-coast, 2100 of these United Funds

and Community Chests are holding their all-out drives. Included in many of these drives are Red Cross . . . USO . . . funds to fight cancer, heart disease and other tragic illnesses; funds for the Boy and Girl Scouts, the Y's, Salvation Army and a multitude of other services, too.

Everybody benefits when everybody gives the United Way. Giving the United Way through United Funds and Community Chests saves time . . . saves campaign costs . . . helps more people and saves more lives than any other gift. It's the way to make sure our contributions really count.

STUART COMPANY PLANT at gateway to Industrial Development Park

A NEW DIMENSION
IN INDUSTRIAL DEVELOPEMENT

SOUTH SAN FRANCISCO, CALIFORNIA

UTAH CONSTRUCTION COMPANY, Developers

It seems like a far cry from a great dam on the Karnafuli River in East Pakistan or a mighty copper mine in Peru, to a trim, efficient beverage company plant in South San Francisco. And it is—yet it is all in a day's work for Utah Construction Company.

In the heavy construction field, Utah is known for its world-wide achievements. In half a century of steady and sturdy growth, it has dammed rivers on three continents, tunneled mountain ranges to reveal buried treasures of copper and iron products, pushed railroads across the plains and hills, lifted steel into the sky to make room for men to work in. It has taken fill from the bottom of a great Bay and created new land on which a growing community can stretch its cramped muscles.

Now Utah Construction has turned its experienced versatility to the development of convenient new sites for light industry. Moving into an area noted as one of the West's prime locations for heavy industrial development, the Company has brought a new dimension to South San Francisco—a $50,000,000 dimension, in fact.

That dimension encompasses not only the centrally located acreage that has been opened up in the heart of a thriving city; it includes a broad concept of co-operative effort with those who are going to fill those acres with productive industrial installations.

Utah Construction Company's 340 acres in South San Francisco—once part of the storied Miller ranch, and later owned by the historic South San Francisco Land and Development Company—are being made available for sale or lease. Utah itself offers any client a complete service—ownership, engineering, construction, but it also encourages the participation of architects, engineers, contractors and brokers on a coopera-

(See Page 11)

NEWS and COMMENT ON ART

OAKLAND ART MUSEUM

The Oakland Art Museum, 1000 Fallon Street, under the direction of Paul Mills, Curator, announces a number of new exhibitions at the Oakland Art Museum, including:

Contemporary Japanese Prints, an exhibition of woodblock prints by such masters as Saito, Munakata, and Azechi, as well as newer abstractionists not shown before in this country, opened at the Museum recently and will continue through Tuesday, September 23.

Art from Mexico, a selection of outstanding Mexican works of art organized by the National Museum Service of Mexico, will also be on view through September 23.

Opening on Saturday, September 6, an exhibition of paintings done in the last six years by Stanley William Hayter, noted modern printmaker, is being shown.

Contemporary Japanese ceramics, ancient Roman glass, and Egyptian objects, drawn from the Carl Rietz Collection and other museum collections, will be on display in the cases beginning Saturday, September 13.

Oakland Art Association members will show a juried exhibition of paintings September 27 through October 5, occupying the three galleries.

A new selection in the Art Rental Service includes nearly a hundred paintings in a great variety of styles, chosen by jury from the Jack London Square Art Festival.

The Gallery Shop has a new selection of crafts, including wooden ware by Bob Stocksdale, jewelry by Robert Dhaemers, and a selection of handweaving and ceramics.

William Keith paintings, some not previously shown and others just returned from Keith exhibitions elsewhere have been installed in the Keith Gallery, Northwest corner of the Oakland Public Library building. Open 10 till 4, Tuesday-Saturday, noon till 6, Sunday.

Museum Curator Paul Mills announces the autumn series of Wednesday night programs began September 10 with the showing of films on Japanese prints and S. W. Hayter. These films will be shown in connection with current exhibitions. Programs start at 8:30 p.m.

Entrance to the Museum is at the Southwest corner of the Municipal Auditorium, 10th and Fallon Streets. Open daily from 10 till 5.

CALIFORNIA PALACE OF THE LEGION OF HONOR

The California Palace of the Legion of Honor, Lincoln Park, San Francisco, under the direction of Thomas Carr Howe, Jr., has announced the following special exhibitions and events for this month:

EXHIBITS: A special exhibition of the artist members of the San Francisco Art Association; Collages by Don Reich. The Achenbach Foundation for Graphic Arts, will show recent works by June Wayne, and Prints by German Expressionists.

SPECIAL EVENTS: Featured will be Organ Program each Saturday and Sunday afternoon at 3 p.m.; Educational activities include a new Fall-Winter series of art classes for children and juniors, beginning September 27. Children, ages 6-11, will meet Saturday mornings from 10 to 11; and Juniors, age 12-17, will meet on Saturday afternoons 2 to 4.

The Museum is open daily.

SAN FRANCISCO MUSEUM OF ART

The San Francisco Museum of Art, War Memorial Building, Civic Center, under the direction of Dr. Grace L. McCann Morley, will feature the following special exhibitions and special events during September:

EXHIBITIONS: Juan Gris and Cubism; Three Bay Area Artists, featuring Claire Falkenstein, Sculpture; James Budd Dixon, Painting, and Walter Kuhlman, Painting. Miss Falkenstein, designer and teacher, has worked in Europe in recent years, showing her sculpture at the Stadler Gallery in Paris and Il Segno in Rome. James Budd Dixon has been prominent in the new movement in painting developed in the Bay Area, studied at the University of California, and has taught at the California School of Fine Arts, and has exhibited widely in Museums and Galleries of the Bay Area and at the Landeau Gallery in Los Angeles. Walter Kuhlman studied with Dixon at the California School of Fine Arts, and his work won him, in 1957, the $10,000 Graham Award.

Four Photographers, featuring Ruth Velissaratos, Bill Maund, William R. Hawkins and Clyde Smith, show work in photographic film to create abstract images resembling veils of cloth, shadows of leaves, and similar effects in nature. The other exhibits show use of the camera in searching for the structure underlying the pictorial image.

Latin American Works from The Museum's collection, honor the Pan-American Pacific Festival. Nature in Abstraction, an exhibit from the Whitney Museum of American Art; Ceramics by Bernard Leach; and the Autum Rental Gallery.

EVENTS: Tour of the Museum Sundays at 3 o'clock; Wednesday evening discussions on art at 8:30 p.m.; Adventures in Drawing and Painting, Friday

evenings at 7:30; Children's Saturday Morning Art Classes and Studio Art for the Laymen, recessed for the summer.

The Museum is open daily.

PAINTING BY ERNEST LUDWIG KIRSCHNER ACQUIRED BY SAN FRANCISCO MUSEUM

The San Francisco Museum of Art announces acquisition of a painting by the German Expressionist, Ernest Ludwig Kirschner (1888-1938), WINTER IN DAVOS, as a Memorial to Timothy L. Pflueger (1892-1946), Vice-President of the Museum from its reopening in the War Memorial in 1935 to his death, and art leader in the community as architect, President of the San Francisco Art Association, and chairman of the Art Building in the Golden Gate International Exposition of 1940.

Kirschner was among the leaders of modern movements in Germany during the first quarter of the century and, in his emotionally charged canvases, strong in color, powerfully drawn and boldly designed he contributed significantly to Expressionism which is being explored with great interest at present in this country. WINTER IN DAVOS painted in 1917 when he was at the height of his powers is a typical example of his landscape patterns, his expressionistic drawing of human and animal forms in movement, his strong and emotionally significant color. It strengthens the Museum's Collection in the direction of Northern painting and so adds a useful reference point as framework and introduction to its changing exhibitions. Currently it is being exhibited for the first time in the selection of art of the first thirty years of the century which serves as prelude to the Juan Gris and Cubism exhibitions.

NEW FALL ART CLASSES ANNOUNCED AT deYOUNG

New Fall Art Classes for adults and children will begin at the M. H. deYoung Memorial Museum on September 17.

Charles Lindstrom, director of education will conduct three new courses for adults. "Painting for Pleasure—Exercises in Perception" starting September 19 will be given Friday afternoons and will be repeated Saturday afternoons 2:00 to 3:30. This is a 12-week course in art appreciation through active practice designed for the absolute beginner. Required materials are drawing paper and colored chalks.

"Color Exercises—Part 3," a new course of weekly experiments in color organization will be given Wednesdays 10:30 a.m. to noon beginning September 17 and also Saturday mornings at the same time beginning September 20. Class members must equip themselves for painting in oil or casein.

Weekly "Seminars in the History of Art" will

resume Thursdays beginning September 18 from 10:30 a.m. to 11:30 a.m. Special subject for these illustrated lectures and discussions will be the art of Vincent Van Gogh during the next two months. The seminars will be conducted in a gallery of the museum newly equipped for this purpose.

Children's art classes conducted by Miriam Lindstrom will also resume in September. "Picture Making" for children 4 to 8 years old will be given Saturday mornings from 10:15 to 11:30 beginning September 20. "Art and Nature" for children 9 to 11 years old will be given Wednesdays 3:30 to 4:30 beginning September 17. "Art Club" for students 12 to 15 years old will meet Thursdays 3:30 to 4:30 beginning September 18.

All classes are free of charge.

DAVID GRAEME KEITH JOINS deYOUNG MUSEUM STAFF

David Graeme Keith has been appointed to the post of Curator of Decorative Arts at the M. H. de Young Memorial Museum, according to a recent announcement by Dr. Walter Heil, Museum director.

Born in Toronto, Canada in 1912, Keith studied history of art at the Western Reserve University in Cleveland where he obtained a Master's degree in Fine Arts in 1935. He later received additional training in art and museum administration at Harvard University and New York University.

For the past ten years he has served as assistant and later curator of Decorative Arts at the Rhode Island School for Design in Providence.

ART RENTAL PROGRAM WILL CONTINUE IN SAN FRANCISCO PUBLIC SCHOOLS

Following the success of its art rental program in the San Francisco City Schools, conducted over the past three years with the assistance of a $3,000 grant from the Rockefeller Foundation, the San Francisco Museum of Art has announced receipt of a new three-year grant from the Foundation for the continuation and expansion of the program, which will be conducted through the facilities of the Museum's Rental Gallery, sponsored by the Women's Board. Mrs. E. Morris Cox is Chairman of the School Rentals Committee of that Board.

The previous grant of The Rockefeller Foundation enabled the Committee to lend original works of art from the Rental Gallery to about one-half the elementary schools in the city. With the cooperation of the Art Department of the City Schools and the support provided by the Grant, the program for 1958-1961 will be expanded in the elementary schools and extended to cover selected secondary schools.

PLANT OF PACIFIC CEMENT & AGGREGATES ... Davenport, California

End Of Obsolete Era At
Pacific Cement & Aggregates Plant
DAVENPORT (near Santa Cruz), CALIFORNIA

Like the passing of the horse, then the steam engine, August marked the end of the oil-burning era for Pacific Cement & Aggregates plant at Davenport, California. The huge cement manufacturing plant is now being served by a recently completed 12-inch natural gas pipeline that runs from Santa Cruz to the plant.

Some 13 miles long, the line will bring eight million cubic feet of gas daily to the modern limestone burning kilns. Cost of the line is estimated at $750,000.

The new pipeline will carry enough natural gas in one day to supply heat for 2,000 homes for an entire month. PCA officials say the use of this large quantity of gas from the pipeline will have no adverse effect on home owners in the area. Should a gas shortage arise at any time, however, the company will revert to its fuel oil system of operation.

(See Page 25)

R. K. Humphries, President of Pacific Cement & Aggregates (L); Merle Whitesell, Mill Superintendent; Art Anderson, General Plant Superintendent, and Joe Vierra, Cement Union representative, turn on gas at recent plant ceremonies inaugurating the use of gas in manufacturing.

PRIVATE CONSTRUCTION
IN CALIFORNIA IN THE "SIXTIES"

By JOHN A. BLUME, President*

John A. Blume & Associates, Engineers

San Francisco

When Mr. Herrick first invited me to speak at this meeting on the subject "Private Construction in California in the Sixties" I thought it would be an interesting assignment. I am more than convinced of this now, not only from having the pleasure to address such a distinguished group from the California building industry but also because I found the subject to have even more interesting ramifications than I first suspected.

Although as part of my engineering work I often forecast the whims of nature such as windstorms, earthquakes, rainfall, ocean waves, etc., I am not a qualified expert in forecasting the whims of man. Forecasting and looking ahead, whether for natural phenomena or manmade situations, requires in the first place a fairly complete background on what has happened to date, proper analysis of cause-and-effect relationships, reasons for variations in the past, consideration of different situations that may develop in

JOHN A. BLUME
Engineer

the future, judgment, luck, a lot of nerve and a well-polished crystal ball. It also requires a temporary severance from any purely scientific attitudes the individual may have. I recall a former professor of mine who many years ago said with reference to some research work we were then undertaking that any damn fool could interpolate but a man would have to be completely out of his mind to extrapolate very far with any hope of being correct. So, let's go ahead with our extrapolation.

In these prophecies you have to at least try to think of everything which thought, combined with

these beautiful country club surroundings and the crystal ball, brings to mind a certain experience of a member of this group whose name I should not reveal.

Some Predictions of Others:

There are many predictions available in the present-day literature concerning the rosy economic future of the United States in general and California in particular. I would like to read a few of these.

Mr. Ralph Rotnem, financial analyst, was recently quoted as follows in the newspapers: "This recession is an economic coffee break preceding a tremendous upward move in the 1960s."

Frederick H. Mueller, Assistant Secretary of Commerce for Domestic Affairs, said in December, 1957, "I can't see anything but a tremendous up-surge three or four years from now."

Sylvia Porter, well-known author of a syndicated daily financial column carried in 218 newspapers in the United States and also a veteran of Wall Street, said recently in Life Magazine, 'In the '60s we will swing into the greatest business boom of modern times, a boom propelled by an exploding population's vast needs for everything from hairpins to houses, and by a dazzling variety of new products being created this minute in industry's research laboratories."

Robert P. Koenig, president, Cerro de Pasco Corporation, in his annual message to stockholders dated May 14, 1958, states: "Looking ahead to the longer term, particularly to the 1960s, there are persuasive reasons to believe the future for nonferrous metals is promising. The world population is growing, and family formations are expected to increase at a more rapid rate in the next decade—particularly here in the United States—than in recent years. This portends a considerable increase of activity in the construction industry and in the manufacture of durable goods."

There are, of course, many more such optimistic reports and all by highly qualified persons. However, as an engineer trained to gather all pertinent facts before coming to a conclusion, and with due allowances for the possibility that some of these reports may

*An address to the American Institute of Steel Construction and representatives of California's building industry—Oakland, California.

be influenced by a desire to generate more long-term optimism as a defense against the tendency to talk ourselves into a real recession, I decided to do some investigation and analysis on my own. Let us first kick this thing around a little bit and then see what it looks like.

The Present Situation

Before blasting off into outer space about our rosy future let us first consider where we are today. As most of you realize, private engineering construction, nationally and in the Far West, took an appreciable dive from 1956 to 1957. It was down 38% nationally and 47% in the Far West. This all happened at the same time that public engineering construction increased in California from $800,000,000 in 1956 to $1,050,000,000 in 1957. The year 1956 was a record year for California in private construction as was 1957 in public works. In good round numbers, the United States 1957 total physical construction (with correction for changes in dollar value) was about 2½ times the average annual construction of the late Roaring Twenties and about five times the average annual construction of the early Depression Thirties. I should define terms at this point: A "recession" is when your neighbor is out of work, and a "depression" is when you are out of work.

I have heard some people say that California today is over-built because it was in such a rush to make up for the slack construction years of World War II and the Korean conflict, and because it was in too much of a rush to build for its population increase. The inference was that things look pretty black for the private construction industry in the next several years. Let's toss this philosophy in the pot with the optimistic forecasts previously quoted and simmer them all in critical thought.

Some Factors that Affect Private Construction

(1) **Population:** In addition to the avoidance of hot, or shooting, wars, and disastrous social trends, private construction needs not only population but people with spending money and/or credit and people who desire to, or have to, buy at the offered price. Great population alone does not necessarily mean "work." I have seen great masses of people in the Middle East, India and in the Orient who had neither the spending money nor the desire to buy a single I-beam. So we have to look for more than population increase which we have had and which we know is continuing.

(2) **Type of Population:** A great deal has been written and much more will be written about the coming teen-age wave. A tremendous increase in the number of teen-age children is expected about 1960. This follows from the tremendous crop of post World War II babies, the reasons for which are beyond the scope of this talk. Roughly speaking, the number of

13-year-old people in the United States will increase to 4,000,000 in the 1960s as compared to a little over 2,000,000 in the late 1940s and early 1950s. California will have more than its share. There is no question that this is going to constitute a serious and important impact on American industry, particularly in the clothing business, the food industry, recreation, music, schools, etc. Every teen-ager will want a separate room, and a few years later before the 1960s are over he or she will want a family and a separate apartment or house. But before we completely take off on this ecstatic note, let's remember that somebody is going to have to pay for all this and the dentist bills besides. We have yet to solve the problem of where the teen-agers will get the money. Let's come back to that later.

(3) **Business Conditions:** The construction industry is a pretty good barometer for business in general. You can never accuse this industry of leading a dull, routine existence. It is apt to get chopped off at the boot straps when things are bad or even look bad, and it may have its work load increased many fold when the rush comes on to build ahead of the next guy when things look good or the financing money is drawing interest charges. Situations like this separate the men from the boys; a reasonable amount is healthy. The psychology and the thinking that affect the man with the spending money are very important. Whether negative thinking about new construction is produced by over-production, inventory troubles, lack of available capital at attractive interest rates, world situations, political or social situations, or many other conditions, the fact remains that if they won't spend, we can't build, and the construction industry feels the effect immediately.

(4) **Cost of Construction:** We must admit that the cost of construction has increased out of proportion to the rise in cost of most other products and utilities. In fact, it might be said that in some situations, regardless of the basic reasons, industry has temporarily priced itself out of work. Most manufacturers think of buildings as necessary evils for the simple reason that they don't sell buildings—they sell products. You can see why they would tend to resist any construction that might be postponed for a more favorable market condition. That is what a lot of them are doing right now. Only two things are needed—keep the costs down and convince them that they "auto build now" while the bargains are available.

(5) **Research and New Developments:** There is no question that we are in an age of intensified research, both basic and applied, and that this will have a great influence on the construction industry in the '60s. New products, new techniques, new businesses, all mean more construction, of course, but we must also look at the other side of the coin and realize that some managers are postponing construction of certain facilities because they might be outmoded by new developments. Also, those who move from one building or plant to another new one leave a vacancy which

is usually filled sooner or later by some new or smaller firm; not all new businesses build new buildings.

(6) **Standard of Living:** We hear a great deal about our standard of living—it is the most luxurious and costly in the world. Everybody will need television, two automobiles in the garage, radios in every room, and all the other items of recreation and luxury. This is fine and is undoubtedly a great stimulus to business, including ours. But I hate to come back to the inevitable fact that somebody has to pay for all of this. It would be ideal to spread this standard to other countries and have them buy the manufactured articles from us. The trouble with this is the only ones who are at all ready for this now or in the immediate future are selling things to us because they can make them and export them cheaper than we can under our present wage structures.

I do not want to imply that I am bearish or pessimistic about private construction now or in the 1960s. Actually I am not at all, but I do want to raise these questions in order that we keep our feet on the ground and consider all aspects of a highly complex problem. It is helpful to analyze ourselves at times. Let's divide the forecasting problem into two main categories: First, private demand in the 1960s, and second, private construction contracts in the 1960s.

Private Demand in the '60s

I have gone through a lot of statistical information and have also done some plotting, calculating and estimating of my own in order to answer the first question, "Assuming that people had money to spend, what volume of private engineering construction would they support in California during the 1960s?" A further assumption, of course, is that the cost of construction would be such that these people would be willing to finance what they wanted.

The first step was to estimate the amount of physical "hardware" per capita that is required on an average basis over a long period of time to keep the pressures of demand-and-supply in reasonable balance. In doing this I have attempted to allow for the temporary unbalances that were created by the depression of the 1930s, by World War II, and by the Korean conflict. I then applied adjustment factors to allow for the fact that modern technology, research and developments have and still are creating an increasingly greater per capita amount of physical goods than in prior years; for the fact that living standards and recreational time have changed; for the fact that we have this unprecedented teenage wave coming in the 1960s; and for other conditions.

There are various population forecasts for California. The figures finally selected are: 16,000,000 in 1960, 20,000,000 in 1965, and 23,000,000 in 1970. These, of course, could be in error, but if the population trend continues or increases they could be on the low side.

After applying all the correction factors year by year to the per capita demand for private construction I arrived at a total 10-year demand for private engineering type construction in California of at least $14,-000,000,000 and possibly more, up to $20,000,000,000. These figures are in 1957 dollars so the amount would have to be changed in the future in proportion to any variations in the building power of future dollars. If this were to average out evenly (and it won't), it would amount to $1.4 billion to $2.0 billion per year. It will undoubtedly vary considerably from the mean due to the many factors already discussed. For comparative purposes, the corresponding amount spent in this same phase of the industry in 1957 was 0.67 billion dollars and 1.20 billion dollars in 1956, the record high year. The 10-year period of 1948 to 1957 inclusive aggregated almost 6 billion actual dollars, or 7 billion equivalent 1957 dollars; thus 1957, in spite of its decline, had the same physical volume as the average annual amount of the past ten years. **My prediction is for the ten years of the sixties to have a cumulative demand in California of at least twice and possibly up to three times the physical engineering construction of the past ten years.** That is a lot of business to be added to the public works about which Mr. Gilliss will speak.

If in any year or period work is postponed, the potential backlog will increase and vice-versa. We thus will have peaks and valleys in our building industry as we have always had before. However, these can and will be leveled somewhat by the stabilizing effect of public works.

In addition to this new incoming demand, there will of course be an entering backlog demand, the amount of which will depend upon how much is done between now and 1960. At the present time the backlog pressure for California's private engineering construction is about 5 billion dollars. You would have to contract for about a billion dollars of work in 1958 and also in 1959 to enter 1960 with only the same $5 billion backlog.

Other Private Work

I have referred to the well-known ENR engineering construction category which includes mass housing, commercial building, industrial building, and other unclassified items of individual cost exceeding various minimum amounts. This is your principal source of private work; it consists mainly of commercial and industrial buildings. The remaining items which, with the above private engineering work, constitute the entire construction industry are new public works of all types, maintenance and repairs, and the "other" new construction items consisting mainly of housing. I realize that the AISC is, and properly so, interested in a greater participation in the small house field. Let us say that California small private housing demand will at least follow private engineering demand until the post World War II babies start reaching their

teens in 1960. Then the housing field could well exceed the gains of the heavier field.

Construction Contracts

In the preceding predictions I have used the term "demand," not actual construction. "Demand" is a pressure, a resource, a potential backlog of work. In order to convert the "demand" into contracts there will have to be sufficient money and credit, the price of the money and of the building will have to be what the buyer will pay, and the construction industry will have to have the capacity to do the work. If for one reason or another the cost gets too high, the work will be postponed until the pressure for contracts brings the price down and/or the postponement makes the buyer desperate. This is the good old rule of supply and demand—it could solve our problems if given the opportunity.

We, in the construction industry have a job to do of tremendous importance not only for our own business welfare, but for that of the State, the Nation, in fact, for the free world. I doubt it if a responsibility has ever been so important in peacetime. We have a chicken-and-egg situation; business needs construction, construction needs business; labor needs employment, the construction industry needs labor; the young people want to buy things (and we want them to) but they need money.

There is only one answer that I can see that would carry us through the surge of prosperity that potentially lies ahead. **The cost of materials, products and of construction has to be held in line with the buying capacity of the people.** If this is done, they will buy, they will have work and money, and California will break all of the construction records of the past. I'm no dreamer—I don't expect costs to decline on the long term, nor even much longer for the short term. There are bound to be further increases in the cost of everything sooner or later. However, costs have to be brought more into line with those of everything else. **Maladjustments in the ratio of wages to production have to be corrected for the long pull; whether this is done by labor, by industry, by the purchasing public or by combinations of these groups, is the key to unlocking the door to the "Sailing Sixties."** I think this can and will be done; in fact, some of the correcting is going on right now—look at your work volume.

To the many who have been raised in the climate of short working hours and long coffee breaks and who, in some cases, feel the world or the government owes them a nice living, I can only say that America is trying to enter a normal period of supply and demand, clean but tough competition, a world where results count. There is a lot of work and compensation ahead, you just have to be on the ball; if you get behind a few touchdowns, don't quit, just put all you have into the game. A forgotten truth is that "the man who is waiting for something to turn up might start with his shirtsleeves," or if you prefer, "The best place to find a helping hand is at the end of your arm."

Capacity for Work

Will the construction industry have the capacity to handle the work of the '60s? This is the least of our problems. The people and firms in California have the capacity for a great deal more work than they now have and this includes the design professions, suppliers, fabricators, the general contractors and the sub-contractors. In spite of any impressions to the contrary elsewhere in the country, we in California's private building industry could easily double our work load and not be strained. The low bids being submitted for construction and the many applications by architects and engineers for design assignments are indications of capacity. The reasons for this below capacity workload are many, including the temporary let-down in private construction, the influx of employees and firms from elsewhere in the country, and the fact that only a tiny fraction of our State public works program has been designed by private firms. We are strong in all respects to move into the "Sailing Sixties."

Fabricated Steel

The fabricated steel industry in California has a challenging future. Not only is the work load of private engineering construction going to build up to the point where physical construction will have to average in the '60s at least twice what it was in the last 10 years, but new trends in design and new knowledge and techniques from research are going to tend to increase steel's percentage of the construction dollar.

For example, the trends toward (1) exposing the framing of a building and treating it architecturally; (2) the greater use of glass and light-weight wall panels; (3) longer spans and unobstructed floor areas; (4) greater electrification of floor areas for modern business machines; (5) slender lines; (6) higher buildings; (7) improved light-weight fireproofing and relaxation of certain obsolete fireproofing requirements, etc., all tend toward the use of more structural steel in relation to the total building cost. These trends also involve relatively more structural engineering. But we in the design professions and you in the fabricating and erecting industry have to give the owner the most building for the least expenditure. Every problem and every material has to be considered on the basis of cost and value received for the particular application. Our clients are not only competing with other American firms but often with foreign firms as well. We are perhaps closer to the buying public than you fabricators are—they are **very** cost conscious! I predict they will be the same in the '60s.

Skyscrapers

Recent research work, in which we were happy to be involved, has shown that new modern skyscrapers

10

have entirely different structural characteristics than the traditional steel frame building with non-calculated concrete or masonry filler walls. The steel frame is on its own now, whereas before it could not function fully in lateral force resistance due to its envelopment by rigid walls. This means that many empirical or traditional design approaches have to be carefully reconsidered to avoid a building that will be so flexible as to cause human reactions to wind sway or to cause considerable architectural type damage in even moderately severe earthquakes. We have worked on several tall slender office buildings in recent years for which the steel design was at least in part controlled by sway considerations rather than unit stress. This again means a slightly greater participation by the steel industry in the total cost of modern skyscrapers, even though the building unit cost may be reduced or at least held firm in a rising labor market.

Earthquakes

This research also reveals that the ductility of steel, either by itself, or in supplementing other more brittle materials, has tremendous capacity to absorb energy from earthquake motion or blast if the designs are such as to allow motion without disturbing occupants under normal, non-emergency conditions. The increasing recognition of the true but complex nature of structural response to earthquakes, together with the need to not only build economically but to further reduce or eliminate the hazard of earthquake damage, is already creating new techniques which will affect the fabricating industry in California. Even today I believe the owners are obtaining more real building value per dollar under earthquake design than they would elsewhere without seismic considerations. The

little, if any, additional cost of modern earthquake resistant design should not deter any owner from building in California. But this is a job for structural engineers who know this problem—passing a building code is not enough.

Summary :

In summary, my analysis of the situation for private engineering construction in California, made with allowances for a great many factors, indicates that the total 10-year demand in the sixties will be at least $14,000,000,000, in 1957 value, and perhaps up to $20,000,000,000. This is two to three times the total physical volume of the last ten years ('48-'57 incl.). The annual amounts will vary from the average according to current conditions. The amount of fabricated steel for private consumption alone could well average 250,000 to 350,000 tons per year.

I have only one reservation besides hot war about this demand being turned into construction contracts and fabricated steel bookings. That would be if American industry and labor should fail to keep production costs in line with the buying ability of the people. Continued wage increases without increased production cannot do the job; such would price us out of the world market and also cause an ever-increasing flood of competitive foreign products.

I am confident that all concerned are beginning to sense these facts and that the sixties will be tremendous in volume, but also cost-conscious and competitive. We all have to give the owners a lot of building value for their money. The fabricated steel industry will have a big job to do as will the design professions and all the others in California's building industry. We are equal to it—let's get our shirt sleeves rolled up!

NEW DIMENSION IN INDUSTRIAL DEVELOPMENT
Utah Construction Company
(From Page 3)

tive partnership basis—and has thrown open to them its entire technical and sales facilities.

In a word, the Company—without charge—will go just as far as any one of those enterprisers wants it to in the development of a client agreement, financing the project (even to the extent of finding an owner if the client prefers to lease), planning and engineering, and so on. Or, once the land agreement has been reached, it will stay out of the development picture altogether . . . except, of course, for certain over-all regulations and restrictions that assure the highest quality of industrial development for the parks.

Both the 60-acre Lindenville Park and the 280-acre South San Francisco Industrial Parks have restrictive convenants that exclude unsightly operations or those that create obnoxious odors, dust, noise or smoke. Architectural landscaping and other standards important to the clients are high.

Contractors or architects planning a modern development for a prospective client will find Utah's industrial acreage has been engineered to provide unusually wide streets, storm and sanitary sewers, curbs and sidewalks, water, power and natural gas. The Parks are adjacent to U. S. Highway 101 (Bayshore Freeway) and are served by the Southern Pacific railway. One of the unusual features of the South San Francisco Industrial Parks is a section designated solely for half-acre sites served by rail transportation.

At the present time, Utah Construction Company is actively working with 150 prospective clients interested in relocating their plants in this area. These negotiations are being carried on in cooperation with brokers, architects, engineers, contractors and financial institutions.

Twenty companies already have purchased or arranged leases for sites in the two Parks: J. L. Stuart Company, McKesson & Robbins, Inc., California Metal Trades Association, Marshall-Newell Supply Company, Crane Packing Company, A. L. Young

(See Page 25)

**ENTRANCE
DETAIL**
Of this new Sacramento
Valley bank has a contem-
porary western look.

CROCKER-
ANGLO
NATIONAL
BANK

CARMICHAEL, CALIFORNIA

Barvetto & Thomas,
   Architects
United Construction Co.,
   General Contractors

Unusual building constructed to house its long established local office. Designed on low, wide-spreading
lines of modern ranch house. The contemporary style
is carried out by exposed pebble walls, redwood trim
and a hexagonal, tilt-up roof of crushed rock. "Wing"
at left, containing safe deposit department and vaults,
is repeated at rear of building to accommodate staff
facilities. Drive-in teller's window located at left side
of office, a night-and-holiday depository beside the
entrance, and a generous parking area at the rear. The
air conditioned interior features a wide, downward
curved panel of diffused lighting running the length
of the banking room, and is decorated in gray coral.
Structure occupies 6,700 square feet of area.

INTERIOR DESIGN

Modernistic teller's windows at left and executive work area at right, combine to provide convenient, pleasant customer relationships.

OVERHEAD LIGHTING, teller's and general banking areas are well lighted.

STEEL FRAME CONSTRUCTION

RESIDENCE

MR. & MRS HARRY C. NAIL

ATHERTON, CALIFORNIA

Architect: DAVID THORNE, Berkeley
Consulting Engineer: CARL REPLOGLE, Piedmont
Contractor: JOHN DAVENPORT

FLOOR
PLAN
DETAIL

LIVING ROOM

Floats over car port walls on two steel beams forming bottom chord of twin rigid steel frames. Wall serves double duty as inside living room wall and extends to enclose patio.

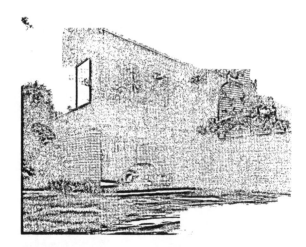

You can see right through the Harry C. Nail, Jr., house in Atherton, California.

Yet the owner has complete privacy in this unusual home designed by Architect David Thorne of Berkeley, California.

The house, containing 2,000 square feet of floor area, fronts on a clump of ancient oaks, the huge branches of which reach a height of 50 feet.

Eight-foot-high glass walls in the formal living room look out on this scene from a height 11 feet above

GLASS WALLS and clear glass clerestories permit viewer to look through house, yet occupant has complete privacy in every area.

STACKING
FIREPLACES

One fireplace on top of another in two level living room areas offers pleasing and unusual architectural effect.

All steel framework was left exposed, painted a dull black. Beam soaring across living room connects triangular steel frames for lateral strength and supports hearth slab.

LOWER VIEW: Shows oriental motif, interior colors of raw silk are toned to blend with furnishings, including rare Japanese screens. Sill is 11 feet off ground.

ground. Yet the level of the sill assures complete privacy. This same "openness with privacy" is expressed in smaller scale in every other living area. Where the architect used non-bearing panels of resawn redwood, he installed clear glass clerestories between panel wall and ceiling. The bedroom wing of the L-shaped house opens on a sun-swept patio and pool area, accessible through sliding glass doors connecting bedrooms and baths.

Interior walls separating the two bedrooms and two baths are also non-bearing and are either plaster wall or built-in cabinet walls. Clear glass clerestories are used over all interior as well as exterior walls, and at this level, one can actually see through the house.

Thorne designed this completely open interior plan to accommodate living facilities while lifting the formal living area over walls forming the carport to take full advantage of tree-top view. He did this with a series of rigid steel frames which he cleverly combined with concrete shear walls to give additional strength while allowing clear and uninterrupted span in the interior.

Thorne also avoided any dependence on a modular system, varying the distance between each of the rigid frames or bents. "I simply chose the space I was to cover, then framed it in," he says. "Because none of the walls run to the roof of the house, a steel frame was the only answer. This proved to be not only the simplest solution, but the most economical.

He set the two giant rigid steel frames 20-feet apart, forming the bents over the kitchen, family and living room areas, and varied the spacing for the smaller steel frames forming the bedroom wing.

The giant frames were composed of 10-inch-wide flange sections. The top chord supporting the pitched roof was 59-feet long, and the bottom horizontal chord 41-feet long.

The smaller frames for the wing of the house were composed of eight-inch-wide flange sections on four-by-four H columns. The architect also lessened the pitch of the roof over the wing to give proper balance to the structural whole. The carrier beams for the roof were tapered where they were carried out under the overhang.

The frames for the house were designed so that each

STAIRWAY connecting upper and lower living and dining areas is painted a lacquer red finish, maintaining Oriental motif.

could be shop fabricated down to the last detail into one unit.

Shipped to the job site, the entire steel framework was erected within two hours and the builder, John Davenport, had a steel skeleton framing the entire 2,000 square feet of house. The steel in place cost only $2,200. The consulting engineer was Carl Replogle of Piedmont.

Like most of Thorne's designs, the steel in the Nail house is left exposed to view and it fairly shouts its strength. One of his horizontal braces, an eight-inch steel wide flange section, soars across the family room, connecting the bottom chords of the two larger frames and forming a stairwell for the open tread stairs connecting the lower and upper living rooms. It also supports a reinforced concrete slab hearth for the fireplace in the upper level. The steel, the hearth, and the chimney form a monolithic structural unit, lending additional strength to the steel frame.

Thorne doesn't hesitate in making his structural materials serve a double purpose. "You can't afford to build for looks at today's prices," Thorne says. "You

have to combine architectural and structural use and make your materials do double duty."

Thorne's flair for this type of practical elegance is stamped into such imaginative uses as stacking one fireplace directly over another to utilize the same chimney. Because the chimney was tied in structurally, he could hang a black steel hood over the fireplace in the family room, and do the same thing for the formal living room immediately above it.

In designing the house and carport shear walls, Thorne extends them, and thus the wall serves not only a structural duty, but takes off from the house at the same level to enclose the patio.

There are no impediments in the ceiling of this house. The pitched roof over the kitchen, family and living room areas vaults out over the glass-walled living room, providing a four-foot overhang. Again using the same material to achieve two results, the designer used laminated two-by-sixes spanning the 20 feet over this area, and in the shallower bedroom wing laminated two-by-fours. Riding on the steel

(See Page 32)

MASTER BEDROOM looks out on patio and pool cabana, has ample access through sliding doors of glass. Glassed arcade through bathroom also has access to pool.

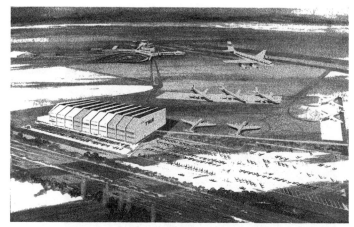

PREPARATION FOR A JET AGE

TWA HANGAR FACILITIES
SAN FRANCISCO INTERNATIONAL AIRPORT

Architect-Engineer: H. K. FERGUSON COMPANY

General Contractor: BARRETT CONSTRUCTION COMPANY

PORTION OF NEW HANGAR nearing completion.

CONSTRUCTION

All steel frame with structural system consisting of a single cantilever frame on 32'-0" centers.

Length of cantilever is 135'-0", which extends over the hangar portion of building.

Construction of Trans World Airlines new $2,000,-000 "jet age" hangar is well under way at the San Francisco International Airport, South San Francisco, on an appropriate 16½-acre site southwest of the main passenger terminal building.

Scheduled for completeion in December of this year, the hangar contains forty-three thousand square feet in area. It has a cantilevered roof 135 feet wide to eliminate columns and is the only such airline structure in this area at the present time. It will be 320 feet

long, 65 feet high, and 135 feet wide. A two-story office portion of the building is 320 feet long and 41 feet wide.

On completion, it will house two of TWA's "Jetstream" Constellations that will start service into and out of San Francisco this summer, or two of Boeing's new all-jet "707's" slated for delivery early in 1960. The work also provides for an outside ramp capable of mass parking of as many as ten of tomorrow's airliners.

In keeping with requirements of the City and County Art Commission, the building will incorporate a ribbed structural design to offset an otherwise box-like appearance. Its frame is being constructed of structural steel with exterior walls of pre-cast reinforced concrete and "Color-bestos" siding.

The front of the hangar facing the Bayshore Freeway will have three floors for use as offices, flight crew quarters, lunch and locker rooms. A 400-car parking lot will adjoin the building.

The hangar has been designed for easy expansion as TWA's jet fleet grows.

CUTAWAY VIEW: Timber-concrete girder bridge—girders support concrete deck.

NEW OREGON TIMBER - CONCRETE GIRDER BRIDGE

Boon To Cash - Short Road Budgets

By ARTHUR W. PRIAULX

A permanent, low-cost "do-it-yourself" timber-concrete girder bridge of surprising new design has just been developed by two Oregon counties in cooperation with the engineering staff of a timber structures manufacturer, which can stretch funds of cash-short county and state road budgets.

The economy of timber and durability of concrete are combined in this radical new design to give taxpayers the greatest value for their money.

In Josephine County, Oregon, County Roadmaster Buck Sharrah completed one of these girder bridges in one week with a five-man crew and without difficulty. No heavy power equipment was needed. The cost is far below conventionally designed bridges.

In addition to low cost, speed of erection is a factor, and since most of the work is done from

above, this design lends itself ideally for overpasses because they can be erected without interference with traffic below.

The timber-concrete girder bridge is delivered by the maker as a complete "package," including girders, girder bracing, wheel guards, hand rails and posts, all necessary hardware and formwork cut to size and ready for use. Accompanying each bridge "package" are complete working drawings, and to facilitate erection of the bridge, members are piece-marked to correspond to markings on the drawings.

"We were able to use our regular bridge crew," pointed out Roadmaster Sharrah, "and did not need expert bridge builders. We are happy with the way this first bridge went together. We feel the price is reasonable. After all, when you can erect a bridge

38 feet long and 23'-7" wide in a week with five men from your regular crews, you have the answer to a roadmaster's needs."

In the timber-concrete girder bridge, glulam timber girders and reinforced concrete deck are used together to bring out the best properties of each material. The large sizes of the glulam girders render them strongly resistant to destruction by fire. The concrete roadway is capable of generations of service. The new bridge is a long-time investment in public service, and will last beyond the time when inevitable highway relocation renders both road and bridge obsolete.

Construction is relatively simple. The design is intended for structures from 30 to 100 feet long, and it easily fits bridge widths up to six lanes by governing the number, spacing and section of glulam girders. From an economy standpoint, it should be pointed out that at a subsequent time, additional lanes can be added to accommodate increasing traffic load, by simply adding girders and pouring additional reinforced concrete deck.

Once abutments are in place, the bridge goes up rapidly. The engineered timber girders can be moved into place from either bank with power from a truck or tractor or by using a simple A-frame.

In construction of the bridge, shear developers and tension ties are installed in the glulam girders, formwork is placed, reinforcing steel is laid and the concrete deck is poured. In the composite beam action of the bridge, the timber girders take the tension and the concrete deck is the compression member.

The bridge is permanently rigid, and aside from the occasional maintenance of the handrails for appearance, no other upkeep is necessary. The heavy glulam girders are built of stress grades of durable Douglas fir lumber using exterior-type, waterproof glues which produce bonds as strong as the timber itself and as permanent.

One feature of the "package" bridge which appealed to Roadmaster Sharrah was the framework. This was supplied as part of the complete bridge package and was installed quickly and simply from the top, thus eliminating any need for shoring or scaffolding. Also, the formwork from the outer cantilevered deck areas was removed from the top and kept for use on other similar bridges.

THIRTY-EIGHT FOOT timber-concrete girder bridge over Murphy Creek near Grants Pass, Oregon.

Design loading is H20 S16.

Roadway width between wheels guards is 23'-7".

TIMBER-CONCRETE BRIDGE . . .

Ledgers and tongue-and-groove material which constitutes the formwork between the girders may be treated with preservative and left in place, generally for less than the cost of removal. However, if it is needed for re-use, it can be removed from beneath the deck, working from a planking laid across the bracing system, or from slings supported by the deck.

The timber-concrete girder bridge is a thoroughly engineered structure. The girders have been engineered to carry design loads with a wide safety factor for heavy impact and overloads. The concrete deck is permanently joined to the girders by engineered shear connections and tension ties which prevent movement of the deck in any direction. Other connections also are engineered to provide known factors of strength at all parts of the bridge. Shear plates are used for stressed wood-to-steel connections. All hardware used in the bridge receives a protective coat of galvanizing or other rust-preventive treatment.

This timber-concrete girder bridge is amazingly flexible. It can be designed for any loading, from farm access roads to main highways carrying huge transport trucks, logging trucks or heavy construction equipment.

Wheel guards most frequently are preservative-treated heavy timber used with treated timber scupper blocks. This system simplifies the finishing of the deck, since full-width screeds may be used. Concrete curbs may be substituted for the timber wheel guards if desired. Hand rails may be either wood or metal. When wood hand rails are furnished, they are usually untreated to permit application of paint.

Engineering design of the bridge conforms to the standards established by the American Association of State Highway Officials and the Bureau of Public Roads. It is approved for the Federal Aid program. Thermal-setting, waterproof glues conform to Military Specifications MIL-A-397B and manufacturing is in accordance with the "Timber Construction Standards" of the American Institute of Timber Construction, and of the "Standard Specifications for Structural Glued Laminated Douglas Fir Lumber" of the West Coast Lumbermen's Association.

Another similar bridge has been erected with very favorable results in Jackson County, Oregon, which immediately adjoins Josephine County on the south.

GIRDERS rest upon heavily galvanized steel pads. Diaphragm bracing is located at center of the bridge.

INDUSTRIAL DEVELOPMENT
(From Page 11)

Machinery Company, Zellerbach Paper Company, Pellegrini Bros. Winery, The Cleveland Cap Screw Company, Sullivan Pet Supply Co., A. E. Wilcox Co., Acme Towel Supply Company, Adam-Hill Company, Essex Wire Corporation, Mipro Metal Products Company, Sterling Furniture Company, Craig Corporation, Brennan-Hamilton Company, Par-T-Pak Beverages, Inc., Cadillac Plastics Company.

Among the noted Bay Area architects already contributing their designs to the Industrial landscape are:

John Boles, San Francisco (A. L. Young Machinery and Adam-Hill plants)

Frank Roller, San Francisco (Stuart Company)

Cline, Zerkle, Agee, Berkeley (Sterling Furniture, Pellegrini Brothers, Acme Towel)

J. Francis Ward, San Francisco (McKesson & Robbins, Crane Packing, Craig Corporation)

Wilsey and Ham, Millbrae (Cleveland Cap Screw)

Milton Leong, Oakland (Par-T-Pak)

Utah Construction Company's South San Francisco enterprise is under the direction of Joseph K. Allen, manager of the Company's South San Francisco Real Estate Division. H. L. Troutman is Director of Sales. Offices of the firm are at 100 Bush Street, San Francisco.

In Mr. Allen's words: "We aren't building any gigantic dams here in South San Francisco, although we did move a small mountain to create what might be called the 'north 80' of the South San Francisco Industrial Park. But in the opportunity we are offering to light industry for advantageous relocation, and to architects, engineers, brokers, and contractors for challenging and profitable expression of their talents, we feel that we are maintaining the standard expressed by Utah Construction Company's motto: 'The permanent public value of our work is the accurate measure of our success.' "

PACIFIC CEMENT
(From Page 6)

"It is our hope," said R. K. Humphries, president of PCA, "that we will not have to go back to fuel oil—even for a day. The convenience of natural gas and the saving in cost will ultimately offset the cash outlay made by the company for the line."

To commemorate the opening of the line, company officials met to honor the changeover. PG&E officials present were: L. J. Brundige, division manager; Eliott Ginocchio, division commercial manager, and Frank Thomas, district manager.

Literally hundreds of shiploads of heavy fuel oil have been brought in by the company since it started manufacturing "Santa Cruz Brand" portland cement over 50 years ago. With modern refining techniques developed by the oil companies, the move was necessary not only from an economic standpoint, but with the knowledge that fuel oil, too, would follow in the wake of the horse and the steam engine.

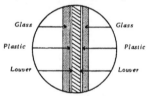

American Institute of Architects

John Noble Richards, President

Philip Will, Jr., 1st Vice-President
Henry L. Wright, 2nd Vice-President

Edward L. Wilson, Secretary
Raymond S. Kastendieck, Treasurer

Edmund R. Purves, Executive Secretary

National Headquarters—1735 New York Avenue, N.W., Washington, D. C.

REGIONAL DIRECTORS—Northwest District, Donald J. Stewart, Portland, Oregon; Western Mountain District, Frederick H. Porter, Sr., Cheyenne, Wyoming; California-Nevada-Hawaii District, Ulysses Floyd Rible, Los Angeles, California.

ARIZONA CHAPTERS:
CENTRAL ARIZONA: David Sholder, President; A. John Brenner, Vice-President; Jimmie R. Nunn, Secretary; Kemper Goodwin, Treasurer; James W. Elmore, Director; Ralph Haver, Director; Martin Ray Young, Jr., Director. Office of Secy., P.O. Box 904, Phoenix.

SOUTHERN ARIZONA: Santry Clay Fuller, President; Edward H. Nelson, Vice-President; David S. Swanson, Secretary; Robert J. Ambrose, Treasurer; D. Byrr DuBois, Director; Eleazar D. Herreras, Director; Emerson C. Scholer, Director. Office of Secy., 2343 South Tucson Avenue, Tucson.

COAST VALLEYS CHAPTER:
William L. Higgins (San Jose), President; Paul J. Huston (Palo Alto), Vice-President; William H. Daecking (Menlo Park), Treasurer; Edward N. Chamberlain (San Jose), Secretary. Office of Secy., 390 Park Ave., San Jose.

CENTRAL VALLEY OF CALIFORNIA:
Joseph J. Jozens, President (Sacramento); Armsby Tod Hart, Vice-President (Sacramento); Albert M. Dreyfuss, Secretary (Sacramento); Whitson W. Cox, Treasurer. Office of Secy., 2127 "J" St., Sacramento.

COLORADO CHAPTER:
Casper F. Hegner, President; C. Gordon Sweet, Vice President; Norton Polivnick, Secretary; Richard Williams, Treasurer; James M. Hunter, Robert K. Fuller, Edward L. Bunts. Office of Secy., 1225 Bannock St., Denver, Colorado.

EAST BAY CHAPTER:
Hachiro Yuasa (Oakland), President; George T. Kern (Oakland), Vice-President; William M. Gillis (San Francisco), Secretary; J. A. Zerkle (Berkeley), Treasurer. Directors: H. B. Clausen, F. A. Lockwood, John Oyarzo. G. M. McCue, Marjorie Montgomery, Exec. Secy. Office of Secy., Mezzanine, Hotel Claremont, Berkeley 5.

IDAHO CHAPTER:
Anton E. Dropping, Boise, President; Charles W. Johnston, Payette, Vice-President; Glenn E. Cline, Boise, Sec.-Treas. Executive Committee: Chester L. Shawver and Nat J. Adams, Boise. Office of Secy., 624 Idaho Bldg., Boise.

MONTEREY BAY CHAPTER:
Robert Stanton, President (Carmel); Walter Burde, Vice-President; William L. Cranston, Secretary; George Kuska, Treasurer. Office of Secy., P.O. Box 1846, Carmel.

MONTANA CHAPTER:
William J. Hess, President (Great Falls); John E. Toohey, Vice-President (Billings); H. C. Cheever, Secy.-Treas. (Bozeman). Directors: Oscar J. Ballas, Wm. J. Hess, John E. Toohey. Office of Sec., Bozeman, Montana.

NEVADA CHAPTER:
RENO: William E. Cowell, President; Albert W. Alegre, Vice-President; Ralph A. Casazza, Secretary; John Crider, Treasurer. Directors Graham Erskine, George L. F. O'Brien, Laurence A. Gulling. Office of the Secy. 232 W. 1st St., Reno, Nevada.
WOMEN'S ARCHITECTURAL LEAGUE: (Reno) Mrs. Eileen Casazza, President; Mrs. Lucille Lackard, Vice-President; Mrs. Glades Cowell, Secretary; Mrs. Enid Hellman, Treasurer.
LAS VEGAS: Walter F. Zick, President; Aloysius McDonald, Vice-President; Edward B. Hendricks, Secy.-Treas. Directors: Walter F. Zick, Edward Hendricks, Charles E. Cox. Office of Secy., 106 S. Main St., Las Vegas.

NEVADA STATE BOARD OF ARCHITECTS:
L. A. Ferris, Chairman; Aloysius McDonald, Secy.-Treas. Members: Russell Mills (Reno), Edward S. Parsons (Reno), Richard R. Stadelman (Las Vegas). Office: 1420 S. 5th St., Las Vegas.

NORTHERN CALIFORNIA CHAPTER:
William Corlett, President; Donald Powers Smith, Vice-President; George T. Rockrise, Secretary; Richard S. Banwell, Treasurer. Directors: W. Clement Ambrose, John Kruse, Bernard J. Sabaroff, Corwin Booth. Exec. Secy., May B. Hipshman. Chapter Office, 47 Kearny St., San Francisco.

ORANGE COUNTY CHAPTER:
William T. Jordan, President (Costa Mesa); Donald M. Williamson, Vice-President (Laguna Beach); J. Herbert Brownell, Secretary; Rumont W. Hougan, Treasurer. Office of Secy., 1950 W. Coast Highway, Newport Beach.

OREGON CHAPTER:
John K. Dukehart, President; Keith R. Maguire, Vice-President; Robert Douglas, Secretary; Harry K. Stevens, Treasurer. Directors: Daniel McGoodwin, Earl P. Newberry, Everett B. Franks, Robert W. Fritsch, Donald W. Edmundson. Office of Secy., 2041 S.W. 58th Ave., Portland 1.

SANTA CLARA AND SANTA CRUZ COUNTIES CHAPTER AIA

The September meeting was California State Legislature guest night with Senators and Assemblymen of the counties represented by the Chapter the honored guests including Senator and Mrs. Don Grunsky; Senator and Mrs. John F. Thompson; Assemblyman and Mrs. Bruce Allen; Assemblyman and Mrs. Clark Bradley; Assemblyman and Mrs. Carl Britschgi; Assemblyman and Mrs. Glenn Coolidge; and U. S. Congressman and Mrs. Charles Grubser.

Held at the Paul Masson Winery in Saratoga, the meeting was a barbecue and tour of the winery with Kurt Oper, wine master of the Paul Masson Winery, describing the methods of making wine and technique's of 'Wine Tasting.'

Recent new members include George Courtney and DeWitt J. Griffin, Corporate Members.

NORTHERN CALIFORNIA CHAPTER

"Metropolitan Growth and the Architect" was the subject of the September meeting held in the Canterbury Hotel, San Francisco, with William McCormick serving as program chairman and an eminent group of panelists taking part in the discussion.

The chapter again participated in the San Francisco Arts Festival, held this month at Fisherman's wharf, with construction of a "AIA pavilion" to house the exhibits comprising a photographic story of the process a client goes through from his first interview with the architect until he steps into his finished house, and a display of architectural panels showing work completed within the past two years.

Arrangements for the exhibits were in charge of George Quesada, chairman and James Leefe, John Wilkinson, Nick Primiani and Martin Rose.

NORTHWEST REGIONAL CONFERENCE AIA

"Making Today's Architecture A Richer Architecture" is the theme of the Seventh Annual Northwest Regional A.I.A. Conference to be held on October 9-12 at Harrison Hot Springs, British Columbia.

Among those scheduled to appear on the outstanding program is Louis Kahn.

SAN FRANCISCO ARCHITECTURAL CLUB

Three important meetings were held this month: The Annual Open Meeting on September 8th; The

26

Executive Meeting on the 17th, and the Fall Registration for Classes on September 11-15-16.

Helen Keller was the guest speaker at the Annual Open Meeting speaking on the subject "Errors and Omissions" and how to insure yourself against their consequences.

WASHINGTON STATE CHAPTER

Paul Thiry was the principal speaker at the September meeting, discussing the new Civic Center, and the Century 21 Exposition, events in which he was recently named primary architect in charge of design, planning and construction.

Recent new members include: William J. Bain, Jr., and W. Redmond Stout, Corporate Members. Norman G. Aehle, Donald L. Fraley, William H. Gardner, Donald A. Greve, George W. Heideman, Howard A. Kinney, Philip L. Jacobson, Edward J. LaBelle, Willis R. McClarty, David E. McDonald, Allen D. Moses, James R. Paul, Terry G. Quinn, Herbert L. Rodde, Dale M. Roff, Winifred L. Savery, Gary L. Shavey, Gerald F. Stark, and Quentin L. Sternberg, Associate Members.

SEATTLE ARCHITECTURAL GUILD

Auxiliary of the Washington State Chapter AIA, organized for the purpose of promoting unification and the advancement of the architectural profession, as well as friendship within the group, held their first Fall meeting on September 16th at the home of Mrs. Waldo Christenson.

The group, which also works to stimulate greater public interest in and understanding of architecture and the role of the architect in creating better environment, announced the November meeting would be devoted to the subject of "Gift Imports."

Offices of the Guild are: Mrs. Lon Wilson, president; Mrs. Arnold Gangnes, 1st vice-president; Mrs. George Wrede, 2nd vice-president; Mrs. John Wright, corresponding secretary; Mrs. Gene Zema, recording secretary, and Mrs. Austin VanDusen, treasurer.

CALIFORNIA COUNCIL ARCHITECTS

The 1958 Convention Advisory Committee has almost completed plans for the 12th annual CCAIA convention in Monterey, October 15-19. According to L. F. Richards, Council president, major plans are completed and only a few minor details remain.

While the fall meeting of the Board of Directors and a meeting of the California State Board of Architectural Examiners will meet on Tuesday, actual convention festivities will start on Wednesday with registration of delegates and guests at the Registration desk at the Monterey County Fair Grounds, where technical and business sessions of the convention are to be held.

Professional sessions will be held on Wednesday, Thursday, Friday and a Junior Associates' and Stu-
(See Page 30)

(See Page 30)

PASADENA CHAPTER:
H. Douglas Byles, President; Edward D. Davies, Vice-President; Ward W. Deems, Secretary; Robert F. Gordon, Treasurer. Directors: Mal Gianni, Lee B. Kline, Keith B. Marston, Donald E. Neptune. Office of the Secy., 170 E. California St., Pasadena.

SAN DIEGO CHAPTER:
Raymond Lee Eggers, President; William F. Wilmurt, Vice-President; Lloyd P. A. Ruocco, Secretary; Delmar S. Mitchell, Treasurer. Directors: John C. Deardorf, Richard George Wheeler and Sam Bruce Richards. Office of the Secy., 3603 5th Ave., San Diego 3.

SAN JOAQUIN CHAPTER:
Robert C. Kaestner, President (Visalia); William G. Hyberg, Vice-President (Fresno); Lawrence B. Alexander, Secretary; Edwin S. Darden. Office of Secy., 128 E. 8th St., Hanford.

SANTA BARBARA CHAPTER:
Wallace W. Arendt, President (Santa Barbara); Darwin E. Fisher, Vice-President (Ventura); Walter Tibbetts, Secretary; Kenneth H. Hess, Treasurer. Office of Secy., 630 Para Grande Lane, Santa Barbara.

SOUTHERN CALIFORNIA CHAPTER:
George Vernon Russell, President; Maynard Lyndon, Vice-President; Ralph C. Crosby, Secretary; Thornton Abell, Treasurer. Office of Secy., 124 W. 4th St., Los Angeles.

SOUTHWEST WASHINGTON CHAPTER:
Robert Billsborough Price, President; Robert T. Olson, 1st Vice-President; Donald F. Burr, 2nd Vice-President; Percy G. Ball, Secretary; Alan C. Liddle, Treasurer; Charles T. Pearson and George Leonard Elkvall, Trustees. Office of Secy., 2715 Center St., Tacoma 2, Washington.

UTAH CHAPTER:
W. J. Monroe, Jr., President, 433 Atlas Bldg., Salt Lake City; M. E. Harris, Jr., Secretary, 703 Newhouse Bldg., Salt Lake City.

WASHINGTON STATE CHAPTER:
Harrison J. Overturf, President; Lawrence G. Waldron, 1st Vice-President; Thomas F. Hargis, Jr., 2nd Vice-President; Talbot Wegg, Secretary; David R. Anderson, Treasurer. Office of Secy., Miss Gwen Myer, Executive Secty., 409 Central Bldg., Seattle 4.

SPOKANE CHAPTER:
Wm. C. James, President; Carl H. Johnson, Vice-President; Keith T. Boyington, Secretary; Ralph J. Bishop, Treasurer; Lawrence G. Evanoff, Carroll Martell, Kenneth W. Brooks, Directors. Office of the Secy., 615 Realty Bldg., Spokane.

HAWAII CHAPTER:
Howard L. Cook, President; Douglas W. Freeth, Vice-President; Francis S. Haines, Secretary; Clifford F. Young, Treasurer. Directors. Richard N. Dennis, Frank Slavsky, William D. Merrill. Office of Secretary, 1410 Kapiolani Blvd., Honolulu 14.

CALIFORNIA COUNCIL, THE A.I.A.:
L. F. Richards, Santa Clara, President; Lee B. Kline, Los Angeles, Vice-President; Edward H. Fickett, Los Angeles, Secretary; Allen Y. Lew, Fresno, Treasurer. Miss Mary E. White, Office Secretary, 703 Market Street, San Francisco 3.

CALIFORNIA STATE BD. ARCHITECTURAL EXAMINERS:
Malcolm D. Reynolds, President (Oakland); Kenneth Wing, Secretary (Long Beach); Wendell R. Spackman (San Francisco); Paul Davis (Santa Ana), and Frank Cronin, Executive Secy., 1020 N St., Sacramento 14.

ALLIED ARCHITECTURAL ORGANIZATIONS

SAN FRANCISCO ARCHITECTURAL CLUB:
C. Van De Weghe, President; O. Hickenlooper, Vice-President; James O. Brummett, Secretary; J. W. Tasker, Treasurer. Directors: Morris Barnett, Art Swisher, Stan Howatt, Frank Barsoti, Frances Capone. Office of Secy., 507 Howard St., San Francisco 5.

PRODUCERS' COUNCIL—SOUTHERN CALIFORNIA CHAPTER:
Clay T. Snider, President, Minneapolis-Honeywell Regulator Co., L.A.; E. J. Lawson, Vice-President, Aluminum Company of America, L.A.; E. Phil Filsinger, Secretary, Gladding, McBean & Co., L.A.; William G. Aspy, Treasurer, H. H. Robertson Co., L.A.; Henry E. North, Jr., National Director, Arcadia Metal Products, L.A.; Office of the Secy., 2901 Los Feliz Blvd.

PRODUCERS' COUNCIL—NORTHERN CALIFORNIA CHAPTER:
R. W. Harrington, President, Clay Brick & Tile Ass'n.; P. C. Christensen, Vice-President, Truscon Steel Div., Republic Steel Corpn.; Philip D. Mittell, Secretary, Otis Elevator Co.; William E. Black, III, Treas., Libby, Owens, Ford Glass Co.

PRODUCERS' COUNCIL—SAN DIEGO CHAPTER:
Eugene E. Bean, President, Fenestra Inc.; James I. Hayes, Vice-President, Westinghouse Electric Co.; E. R. Shelby, Secretary, The Celotex Corp. (El Cajon); Joseph C. Langley, Treasurer, Republic Steel Corp., Truscon Steel Div. (Lemon Grove). Office of Secy., 1832 Wedgemore Rd., El Cajon.

CONSTRUCTION SPECIFICATIONS INSTITUTE—LOS ANGELES:
R. R. Coghlan, Jr., President; George Lamb, Vice-President; E. Phil Filsinger, Secretary; Harry L. Miller, Treasurer; Directors: Harold Keller, Jack Whiteside, Walter Hagedohm, Raymond Whalley, Charles Field Wetherbee, Martin A. Hegsted, Advisory Member, D. Stewart Kerr. Office of Secy., 2901 Los Feliz Blvd., L.A.

CONSTRUCTION SPECIFICATIONS INSTITUTE—SAN FRANCISCO:
Henry P. Collins, President; Leonard M. Tivel, Vice-President; Leonard P. Grover, Treasurer; Marvin E. Hirchert, Secretary. Office of Secy., 585 Whitewood Drive, San Rafael.

STRUCTURAL ENGINEERS ASSOCIATION OF CALIFORNIA

An outstanding program of technical papers to be delivered by leading engineers of the nation has been announced for the 27th Annual Convention of the Structural Engineers Association of California, sched-uled to be held October 2-4, at Yosemite.

Convention registration of members and guests will start on Thursday morning, October 2nd, at the Ahwahnee Hotel, and the technical program will be-gin in the afternoon and continue through Friday and Saturday.

Included among speakers to appear at the meeting are: Prof. George Wastlund, Royal Institute of Tech-nology, Stockholm, Sweden, who will speak on the subject "The Use of High Strength Tensile Rein-forcing Bars"; Alfred A. Yee of the firm of Park and Yee, Consulting Engineers, Honolulu, who will speak on "Composite Application of Prestressed Concrete Units in Building Construction"; H. J. Andrews, Aluminum Company of America, "Structural Applica-tions of Aluminum"; Prof. T. Y. Lin, University of California, will speak on "Observations of Engineering and Construction Methods in Russia"; A. L. Collin, Kaiser Steel Corporation, "Structural Aspects of Mis-sile Towers and Other Ground Support Equipment."

Henry J. Stetina, American Institute of Steel Con-struction, will speak on "Fasteners for Structural Steel"; William T. Wheeler, Chairman, Seismology Committee of the SEOC, will discuss "A Progress Report on the State Earthquake Code"; and Prof. E. V. Laitone, University of California, "Missiles, Satellites and Out of This World."

Friday afternoon will be devoted to the annual business meeting, hearing of committee reports and a report on the Structural Engineer examination.

Entertainment and the ladies participation includes an amateur theatrical on Thursday evening, costume dance Friday night, and a cocktail party and dance on Saturday night, in addition to other ladies social ac-tivities. Included in the schedule of Convention ac-tivities is a men's golf tournament, on Wednesday morning, prior to the next day's convention registra-tion, and other events, such as tennis, horseshoes and ping pong, sightseeing and other activities.

STRUCTURAL ENGINEERS ASSOCIATION OF NORTHERN CALIFORNIA

Prof. T. Y. Lin, University of California at Berkeley, and Ben C. Gerwick, Jr., President of Prestressed Con-crete Institute and head of Ben C. Gerwick, Inc., San Francisco construction company, were the principal speakers at the September meeting held in the Clare-mont Hotel, Berkeley, as joint meeting with the East Bay Structural Engineers Society.

The subject of the meeting was "New Developments in European Prestressed Concrete Practice." Both Prof. Lin and Ben Gerwick recently returned from a six weeks tour of Europe, during which time they attended the 3rd International Conference on Prestressed Con-crete in Berlin, and later took part in a special tour through northern Europe.

Recent new members include: Robert D. Darragh, Oren L. Christensen, Donald S. Javete, Marko A. Jurjevich, Jack Kositsky, Burton A. Lewis, and Joseph P. Nicoletti, MEMBERS. Richard C. Calleti, Richard Lowell, Geoffrey T. Taylor, and C. William Tripp, AFFILIATE MEMBERS. Omer A. Kocaaslan, and Leland M. Davis, JUNIOR MEMBERS.

STRUCTURAL ENGINEERS ASSOCIATION OF SOUTHERN CALIFORNIA

"The Effects of Current Types of Construction on Fire Insurance Rates," was the subject of the Septem-ber meeting held in the Rodger Young Auditorium, Los Angeles, with Joseph T. Silveira, Pacific Fire Rating Bureau, the principal speaker.

Fire losses exceeded one billion dollars during the year of 1957 in the United States; with this figure as an introduction to his subject, Mr. Joseph Silveira noted that during the year 1952 the total U. S. fire losses were only about $800,000,000.

The two main reasons for the increase in fire losses

are inflation and an increasing fire experience. Silveira explained that the 2% annual inflation in our country is especially difficult for the insurance companies to absorb on their five year insurance contracts; there have been sufficient losses that the five-year contract is now a thing of the past.

The increasing fire loss experience, Silveira noted, emphasizes the fact that the fire insurance rating business is still an art. Many times buildings and fire-resistive assemblies have to be rated with little or no fire experience with the type of structure.

Because of the increasing fire losses most fire insurance companies have not been making any profits on their underwriting in the last few years. To overcome this difficulty, most of the rates have been raised a flat 8% just recently.

To find out the reasons for the great increase in fire loss experience in markets, the National Bureau of Fire Underwriters made a survey which disclosed many interesting facts. The two big items that have apparently led to the increase in market fires are the enclosed incinerators and the large area of the market which does not have fire division walls. The incinerator problem has been solved by removing it from the building proper. Since the store managers are not receptive to fire walls in their large display areas, automatic sprinklers have to be used to keep the rate low. Mr. Silveira noted that a small fire in a store can spread over a large area in a short time and also can produce sufficient smoke throughout the store that the firemen cannot readily locate the actual flames to put them out. In the event that the smoke throughout the building obscures the location of the fire, the firemen will chop holes through the roof to vent the room of the smoke. Mr. Silveira suggested that automatic fire vents in the roof would be a useful addition to the design of large markets.

Mr. Silveira stated that office building losses have been low, but that this could change if different types of occupancy would move into the ground floors and utilize more hazardous materials. He also expressed concern about the fact that fireproofing is tending to get lighter and lighter. He noted that adequate plaster fire protection is inexpensive, but that if an incorrect

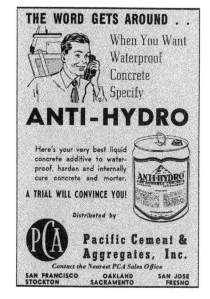

application is made the fire insurance rates for the building would be higher; in some cases this may lead to a 100% rate increase! Proper attention to accepted fire proofing assemblies is essential.

He also noted that every effort should be made in the design to help contain a fire to the story of origin. Air conditioning ducts, elevators, and stairs all need special care as they often have been responsible for the rapid spread of an office building fire.

Mr. Silveira concluded by saying that property owners will become more cognizant of their fire insurance design as their insurance costs mount. The cooperation of the architect and engineer with the insurance broker or agent in the early design stage can help to keep the insurance costs down.

SOCIETY OF AMERICAN MILITARY ENGINEERS—San Francisco

Rear Admiral Eugene J. Peltier, CEC, USN, Chief of Civil Engineers of the U. S. Navy, was the principal speaker at the September meeting held in the Presidio of San Francisco Officers' Club, taking as his subject "The Modern Navy's Influence on the Design of Facilities."

As head of the Navy's construction agency, the Bureau of Yards and Docks, Rear Admiral Peltier has the responsibility of designing, constructing, and maintaining all of the Navy's facilities ashore, and he discussed many of the new requirements of the work arising from the use of modern weapons systems.

SOCIETY OF AMERICAN ENGINEERS SAN FRANCISCO SECTION TO HOLD FALL BARBECUE

A fall barbecue for members and their families and guests will be held on Saturday, October 18th, in the Napa Valley at the Charles Krug Winery, St. Helena.

Program will include an hour's trip through the winery to see grapes being crushed and wine being made. Anyone wishing to attend should contact the San Francisco Post SAME, P. O. Box 9014, Presidio of San Francisco, for credentials and reservations.

AIA ACTIVITIES
(From Page 27)
dents' Seminar will close the convention on Saturday afternoon.

Among outstanding speakers scheduled to appear on various programs are: Philip Douglas Career, FAIA; Dr. Donald McKinnon, Charles Eames, Jo Sinel, Robert Billsbrough Price, David Countryman, Elmer Gunnette, Fred N. Severud, Victor Lundy, Walter Netsch, Paul Thiry, FAIA; Harry Weese, and appearing on the Junior Associate and Student Seminar are Neill Smith, Richard Hein, James Langenheim, members of the California State Board of Architectural Examiners.

Recreational attractions will be highlighted by the annual banquet on Friday night, cocktail party on Wednesday evening, steak barbecue and Hawaiian entertainment on Thursday afternoon, a fish barbecue, and the annual Producers' Council sports program on Saturday morning.

The Womens' Architectural League will take an important part in the five-day program and in addition to meetings devoted to their activities, will conduct an architectural tour of the Carmel Valley, stage a fashion show and participate in numerous convention activities.

EAST BAY CHAPTER

Newly licensed architects and non-members of the A.I.A. were guests at the September meeting held in The Trail's End, Oakland, with Loy Chamberlain speaking on the California Council of Architects and the annual convention scheduled for Monterey in October.

The Chapter has recently compiled and released for distribution to interested persons, a list of "member's work under construction," showing name of architect, type of work and location, and cost.

Recent new members include Morton A. Karp, Corporate Member.

ARCHITECTURAL SCHOOLS GET UNITED STATES STEEL FILM

The United States Steel Corporation is presenting prints of a film on the history of modern curtain wall construction to seventy-five schools of architecture throughout the country, and when the program is completed this fall the film will be in the libraries of all members of the Association of Collegiate Schools of Architecture.

The film, originally prepared as a half-hour educational television program, tells the story of the development of curtain wall construction from its inception in 1883, through the "Chicago school of architecture," to its culmination today in the modern skyscraper. The film was created as part of a promotion of modern architecture sponsored jointly last year in Chicago by the Chicago Chapter of The American Institute of Architects and the United States Steel Corporation.

PLASTIC ENGINEERS WILL HOLD MEETING IN SOUTHERN CALIF.

The Southern California Section of the Society of Plastic Engineers, Inc., will hold a Regional Technical Conference at the Ambassador Hotel in Los Angeles on November 13th, according to Edward J. Fitzpatrick, general Conference Chairman.

The theme of the meeting will be "Plastic Trends in Building Construction," and speakers will include Paul Hunter, Architect; R. Kenneth Gossett, national president of the S.P.I.; and panel discussions will feature New Materials, Walter H. Kadlec, moderator; Building Code, W. Demarest, moderator; Plastic Pipe, Martin Usab, moderator; and New Applications to Building Interiors, G. Huiseman, moderator.

WILLIAMS & PARUG FORM NEW ARCHITECTURAL FIRM IN BERKELEY

Robert C. Williams and Jane M. Parug, Architects, members of The American Institute of Architects, have announced their association for the preparation of Construction Specifications, under the name of Robert C. Williams and Associates, Specifications Consultants, with offices at 1091 Keith Ave., Berkeley 8, and 1628 Walnut St., Berkeley 9.

Spencer B. Lane of San Francisco, who has been engaged in civil engineering work and specifications writing for engineering firms and architects, will act as consultant to the firm.

MOUNTAIN VIEW PLANS NEW HOSPITAL

The architectural firm of Stone, Mulloy, Marraccini & Patterson, 536 Mission St., San Francisco, is preparing working drawings for construction of the El Camino Hospital in Mountain View for the Mt. View Hospital District.

Proposed is a four or five story building with facilities to serve 450 beds. Construction will be structural steel frame, reinforced concrete, and estimated cost is $7,000,000.

NEW YORK FIRM AND HAAS-HAYNIE IN JOINT VENTURE

Webb & Knapp Inc., of New York, has combined forces with Haas-Haynie General Contractors of San Francisco, in a joint venture representing one of San Francisco's urban redevelopment programs.

The project is the development of a 21-block area in the Western Addition Redevelopment Plan.

D. N. Stafford, western regional manager of Webb & Knapp, stated that Haas-Haynie would also participate in other urban renewal programs and business ventures on the Pacific Coast in which Webb & Knapp is interested.

H. LEE HIGLEY NAMED BUSINESS DIRECTOR OF ADRIAN WILSON ASSOCIATES

H. Lee Higley has been named Director of Business Development for the firm of Adrian Wilson & Associates, Architects and Engineers, Los Angeles, according to a recent announcement by Adrian Wilson.

Higley has been associated in the offices of Adrian Wilson & Associates since 1945 and became Chief Architect for the firm's Far Eastern offices in Nagoya, Japan, in 1953. He became Project Manager of the

Nagoya office in 1955, and in 1956 assisted in establishing the firm's offices in Manila. He has also assisted in master planning of major establishments on Formosa for the joint use of U.S. and Chinese Nationalists, including air fields and communications facilities.

Higley, a native of Glendale, California, studied architecture at the U.S.C. School of Architecture.

NEW FRATERNITY HOUSE FOR BERKELEY

Architect James Lucas, 61 Moraga Highway, Orinda, is preparing preliminary plans for construction of a new fraternity house in Berkeley for the Sigma Nu Fraternity.

The new building will be 5 stories, with basement, reinforced concrete construction, built-up roofing.

ARCHITECTURAL FIRM ANNOUNCES TWO NEW VICE PRESIDENTS

Otto H. Kilian and James H. Langenheim have been named vice-presidents of Pereira & Lukman, Los Angeles and New York, planning architectural and engineering firm.

Kilian, who has been with the firm since 1952, was formerly a project manager specializing in educational facilities, hotels, department stores and shopping centers.

Langenheim, now director of design, supervised and had active design and planning participation in projects for CBS and the Los Angeles International Airport.

SPECIFY HAWS FROM A COMPLETE LINEUP OF...

ELECTRIC WATER COOLERS!

Cafeteria Models

Hot & Cold Models

Bottle Types with & without Compartments

Pressure Bubblers with Compartments

Pressure Bubblers

You can specify water coolers for any specific requirement from the **complete** lineup of HAWS ELECTRIC WATER COOLERS! Pressure bubbler types, bottle-types, freezing compartment models, hot and colds, restaurant and cafeteria models of all sizes, remotes, wall inserts...they're ALL in the HAWS lineup with custom styling and advanced designs that guarantee client satisfaction.

Specify HAWS! Get Complete Water Cooler specification data from one dependable source... write today, for the new 1958 HAWS Catalog!

HAWS DRINKING FAUCET CO.
1441 FOURTH STREET (since 1909) BERKELEY 10, CALIFORNIA

William L. Pereira, Architect, with offices at 9220 Sunset Blvd., Los Angeles, has been advanced to Fellowship in The American Institute of Architects, by

the Jury of Fellows, for his outstanding contribution to the profession in the field of Design. He is a principal in the firm of Pereira and Luckman, and received AIA awards of merit for design of Robinsons' Beverly Department Store, Marineland of the Pacific, Columbia Broadcasting System's Television City, and the National Bureau of Standards Laboratory at

WILLIAM L. PEREIRA
Fellow A.I.A.

Boulder, Colorado. He is also a professor of architecture, design and planning at the University of Southern California graduate school.

Pereira was born in Chicago, April 25, 1909, and received his college education at the University of Illinois and his B.S. in 1930. Following a period of European travel, he began the practice of architecture in the offices of Holabird & Root in Chicago in 1930, and opened his own offices two years later. Moving to the West Coast, the present firm of Pereira and Luckman, Planners, Architects and Engineers, was organized in 1950 in Los Angeles.

He is a member of the American Society of Military Engineers; the Academy of Motion Picture Arts & Sciences; American Architects Foundation; and the Southern California Chapter of the A.I.A.

RESIDENCE
Mr. & Mrs. Hary C. Nail
(From Page 18)

frame these were left exposed and washed with a diluted paint in order to show the natural grain and color. Thorne also used two-by-eight laminated studs for the living-room floor over the carport. Not only did this system fulfill the structural need for strength over long spans, but proved attractive and provided the necessary insulation.

To avoid cramping the interior, Thorne designed a storage wall which he "hung" from the exterior by cantilevering his floor joists over the foundation in the bedroom wing of the house. The closet running the length of the wing is stuccoed on the exterior, giving it a more massive appearance to offset the dominance of the concrete shear walls and raised living room area. Since the closet faces on a hallway connecting the living areas, every compartment is completely accessible. The clerestory along the top between closet wall preserves the open feeling.

Thorne incorporated another wall to serve double duty as a patio wall as well as to close the house at the end of the bedroom wing. A "baby" bent of steel frames the clerestory over this wall which encloses the master bathroom and a glass-walled garden alcove with a handy entrance to the pool. Early morning swimmers don't have to track through the bedroom.

The interior colors of the house are toned to blend in with the furnishings. Mr. Nail, who is a connoisseur of oriental art, made liberal use of rare silk screen panels. Interior furnishings are a natural shade of raw silk. All steelwork is painted a dull black and the stairway connecting the upper and lower living rooms lends a splash of color in its bright red lacquer-ware finish. The kitchen is separated from the family dining room by a built-in cabinet of red birch with an overhead hooded light cove.

ARCHITECT SPEAKER AT
ARLINGTON WOMEN'S CLUB

Roland Kuechle, architect of Oakland and San Francisco, was a recent speaker at the regular meeting of the Home and Garden Section of the Arlington Woman's Club, Oakland, discussing the subject "What's A House?".

A colored film was shown in conjunction with the speaker's remarks.

Kuechle, AIA architect, is chief architect with the Rosener Engineering, Incorporated, San Francisco, and during his 17 years as a registered California architect, has designed many residences, as well as schools, store buildings, hospitals and other public buildings.

THE STORY OF ARCHAEOLOGY. By Agnes Allen. Philosophical Library, Inc., 15 E. 40th St., New York 16. Price $4.75, 245 pages, Illustrated by Jack Allen.

Archaeology is a subject that interests young and old at the present time.

It is the science by which we learn how men lived in the distant past through studying the relics they left behind them.

In this book the author has tried to tell something of the fascinating story of the enthusiastic, courageous, patient work of the early investigators and their successors, of the unexpected and astonishing things they found, of the dead and forgotten languages they learned to read and understand, of the myths and legends they unearthed. The exact work of the trained archaeologists of the present day is described and by such knowledge and experience the work has progressed.

REINFORCED CONCRETE IN ARCHITECTURE. By Aly Ahmed Raafat. Reinhold Publishing Corp., 430 Park Ave., New York 22. Price $15.00. 240 pages well illustrated with photos and drawings.

New structural forms, new plans, a new aesthetic—have all been brought into being by the use of reinforced concrete in architecture. This book is an available bridge between architectural knowledge and recently developed engineering principles, presented in simple, non-technical language. One of the greatest impacts upon architectural design today is being made in the field of thin shell construction. Surface-resistant forms, single curvature forms, double-curvature forms, prefabricated and prestressed units are all given added dimension by the illustrations. Architect and engineer alike find this book essential in his practice today and prophetic of the architecture of tomorrow.

COST CONTROL Through ELECTRONIC DATA PROCESSING. By Phil Carroll. Society for Advancement of Management, 74 5th Ave., New York 11. 32 pages, Price $1.50.

A publication of the Division of Management Research and Development, wherein the author details the practical groundrules of question asking (programming) and corrective managerial action in the use of EDP as a cost control instrument. He covers Systems and Procedures; Sales Forecasts; Production Scheduling and Control; Expense Budgeting; Direct and Indirect Costing; and the development of Decision-making ability in the managerial staff.

HOME BUILDERS MANUAL for LAND DEVELOPMENT, 2nd Revised Edition, 1958. National Association of Home Builders, 1625 "L" St., N. W., Washington 6, D. C. 264 pages, Price $5.00.

Everyone concerned with land planning, developers, municipal officials involved with the regulation of builder operations, land planners and technical schools, will find this Land Planning Manual an invaluable handbook. Well illustrated, the book is organized for ready reference, and among the many subjects covered are site considerations, utility systems, lot planning, shopping centers, proper methods of paving, and layout of streets and lots to take maximum advantage of natural terrain; special emphasis has been given to factors which result in cost saving through the use of proper materials and techniques.

NEW CATALOGUES AVAILABLE

Architects, Engineers, Contractors, Planning Commission members—the catalogues, folders, new building products material, etc., described below may be obtained by directing your request to the name and address given in each item.

"UNI-flo" air valve. New catalog fully describes new high velocity air valve, composed of gang operated, neoprene vane sections which provides simple, positive control of velocities and pressures and assures linear control of air volume; engineering data, dimensional, descriptive and application information. Write DEPT-A&E, Barber-Colman Co., Rockford, Ill.

"Family-proof" plywood paneling. Full color, 12-page booklet designed to help choose the right wall paneling for any room in the house; covers complete line of G-P factory finished and textured plywood paneling; shows five steps for

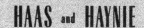

application; describes new "family-proof" finish, shows wood surfaces and paneled room settings, sizes available and average retail cost. Free copy write DEPT-A&E, Georgia-Pacific Corp., Equitable Bldg., Portland 4, Oregon.

Aluminum church windows. New catalog describes Twin-Beam aluminum church windows; completely illustrated to show how they guard against stained glass breakage, heat loss and outside noise; also diagrams four typical window designs; complete specifications, drawings of representative installations showing cross-sections of mounting and anchoring details. Free copy write DEPT-A&E, Industrial Engineering Works, 69 Bloomsbury St., Trenton 6, New Jersey.

Open floor grating. New 2-color, 16-page catalog on open floor grating and stair treads; features many product illustrations of rectangular grating with various wearing surfaces, Relgrit abrasive embedded non-skid grating, U-type grating, radial and numerous styles of treads; complete engineering details. Free copy write DEPT-A&E, Reliance Steel Products Co., P.O. Box 510, McKeesport, Pa.

Prime high strength, low alloy steel. A new 20-page booklet "KAISALOY" describes the development of three specialized grades of prime high strength, low alloy steel produced by the Kaiser Steel Corpn.; tells of wider range of uses for manufacturers and fabricators and details the mechanical characteristics of each grade, along with illustrations of actual applications. For free copies of booklet, write DEPT-A&E, Kaiser Steel Corpn., Engineering Sales Dept., P.O. Box 58, Oakland 12, Calif.

Low voltage switching systems. New 18-page, full colored brochure available to architects, contractors, engineers, electricians, and others interested in installing low voltage systems, features sections devoted to Designing a System, Architects Specifications, Planning the Installation, Installing a Touch-Plate System, Trouble Shooting and Installation, and Basic Components of a System; photographic illustrations; typical modern home floor plan with detailed layout. Free, write DEPT-A&E, Touch Plate Mfg. Corp., P.O. Box 1970, Long Beach, Calif.

Why and where to specify paint. New, color illustrated, brochure (AIA FILE No. 25-G) describes "Why and Where to Specify Latex Paint"; describes the development of latex paint, uses, minimum standards, performance characteristics— interior and exterior; types and glossary of terms; numerous color photographs of uses. Free copy, write DEPT-A&E, The Dow Chemical Co., Midland, Michigan.

Ceilings. New catalog (AIA FILE No. 31-F-231) entitled ". . . your future in sight"; describes and illustrates installations of Ceilglo, Ceilite, Ceilume, Ceilcell, and Ceilgrid; graphs, photographs, equipment data; of particular interest to architects, engineers, contractors. Free copy, write DEPT-A&E, United Lighting and Ceiling Co., 3120 Chapman Street, Oakland, California.

Hardboard lines. New 4-page pamphlet describes factory-finished, tempered, textured, utility, standard, perforated and smooth-both-sides boards; for builders and architects; includes complete specifications sheet listing exact size and thickness, strength, specific gravity and water absorption. Free copy, write DEPT-A&E, Georgia-Pacific Corp., Equitable Bldg., Portland 4, Oregon.

ESTIMATOR'S GUIDE

BUILDING AND CONSTRUCTION MATERIALS:

PRICES GIVEN ARE FIGURING PRICES AND ARE MADE UP FROM AVERAGE QUOTATIONS FURNISHED BY LeROY CONSTRUCTION SERVICES. 4% SALES TAX ON ALL MATERIALS BUT NOT LABOR. ITEMS IN ITALIC INCLUDE LABOR AND SALES TAX.

BONDS—Performance or Performance plus Labor and Material Bond(s), $10 per $1000 on contract price. Labor and Material Bond(s) only, $5.00 per $1000 on contract price.

BRICKWORK & MASONRY

COMMON BRICKWORK, Reinforced:
- *8" walls* ... SF *2.95*
- *12" walls* ... SF *4.15*

SELECT COMMON, Reinforced:
- *8" walls* ... SF *3.05*
- *12" walls* ... SF *4.30*

CONCRETE BLOCK, Reinforced:
- *6" walls* ... SF *1.40*
- *8" walls* ... SF *1.55*
- *12" walls* ... SF *1.90*

BRICK VENEER:
- *4" Select Common* ... SF *1.65*
- *4" Roman* ... SF *2.50*
- *4" Norman* ... SF *2.40*
- *4" Aggrelite* ... SF *2.40*

BRICKWORK & MASONRY

All Prices—F.O.B. Plant.

COMMON BRICK
- Common 2½ x 3¾ x 8¼ ... M 45.00
- Select 2½ x 3¾ x 8¼ ... M 52.00
- Clinker 2½ x 3¾ x 8¼ ... M 48.00
- Jumbo 3½ x 3 x 11½ ... M 90.00

FACE BRICK
- Standard ... M 59.80 - 83.20
- Jumbo ... M 114.40 - 130.00
- Roman ... M 88.40 - 109.20
- Norman ... M 101.40 - 124.80
- Brik Blox (6") ... M 202.80
- (8") ... M 239.20
- Braile Veneer ... M 26.00

BUILDING TILE
- 8 x 5½ x 12 inches ... M 165.78
- 6 x 5½ x 12 inches ... M 128.96

HOLLOW TILE
- 12 x 12 x 3 inches ... M 163.12
- 12 x 12 x 4 inches ... M 184.18
- 12 x 12 x 6 inches ... M 244.71

MANTEL FIRE BRICK
- 2½ x 9½ x 4½ inches ... M 140.40

GLAZED STRUCTURAL UNITS
- 2 x 6 x 12 Furring ... SF .90
- 4 x 6 x 12 Furring ... SF 1.20
- 6 x 6 x 12 Furring ... SF 1.50
- 4 x 6 x 12 Partition ... SF 1.60
- Add for color ... SF .20

CONCRETE BLOCKS
- 4 x 8 x 16 inches ... EA .22
- 6 x 8 x 16 inches ... EA .265
- 8 x 8 x 16 inches ... EA .30
- 12 x 8 x 16 inches ... EA .435
- Colored Add ... EA .02

AGGREGATE—Haydite or Basalite
- All sizes in bulk ... CY 6.24

BUILDING PAPERS & FELTS

- 1 ply per 1000 ft. roll ... .95
- 2 ply per 1000 ft. roll ... 03
- 3 ply per 1000 ft. roll ... 1.22
- Sisalkraft, reinf. 500 ft. roll ... 7.54

SHEATHING PAPERS:
- Asphalt sheathing, 15-lb. roll ... 2.40
- 30-lb. roll ... 3.37
- Dampcourse, 216-ft. roll ... 3.05

FELT PAPERS:
- Deadening felt, ¾ lb., 50 ft. roll ... 3.94
- Deadening felt, 1 lb., 50 ft. roll ... 4.60
- Asphalt roofing, 15-lb. ... 2.50
- 30-lb. ... 3.50

ROOFING PAPERS:
- Standard Grade, Smooth Surface
- 108 ft. roll, Light, 45 lb. ... 2.26
- Medium 55 lb. ... 2.64
- Heavy 65 lb. ... 3.10
- Mineral Surfaced ... 3.60

CHIMNEYS, PATENT

F.O.B. Warehouse
- 6" ... LF 1.45
- 8" ... LF 2.05
- 10" ... LF 2.85
- 12" ... LF 3.45

Rates for 10 - 50 Lin. Ft.

CONCRETE AGGREGATES

	Bunker Per Ton	Del'd Per Ton
Gravel, All Sizes	3.25	4.00
Top Sand	3.45	4.20
Concrete Mix	3.35	4.20
Crushed Rock		
¼" to ¾"	3.30	4.20
¾" to 1½"	3.30	4.20
Roofing Gravel	3.46	4.15
SAND		
Lapis (Nos. 1 & 2)	4.30	5.10
Olympia (Nos. 1 & 2)	3.60	4.15

CEMENT
- Common, All brands (Paper sacks)
- Small quantities, ... Per Sack 1.35
- Large quantities, ... Per bbl. 4.25
- Trinity White & Mendusa White ... Per Sack 4.00

CONCRETE MIX
- 6 sacks in 5-yd. loads ... Per yard 13.40

CURING COMPOUND, Clear
- 5 gal drums ... Per Gal. 1.46

CARPENTRY & MILLWORK

Hardware not included

FRAMING:
- *Floors* ... BM *.20 - .25*
- *Walls* ... BM *.25 - .30*
- *Ceilings* ... BM *.18 - .22*
- *Roofs* ... BM *.22 - .27*
- *Furring & Blocking* ... BM *.30 - .50*

SHEATHING:
- *1 x 8 straight* ... BM *.20 - .25*
- *1 x 8 diagonal* ... BM *.23 - .28*
- *5/16" Plyscore* ... SF *.16 - .20*
- *Plywood* ... SF *.25 - .30*

SIDING:
- *1 x 8 Bevel* ... BM *.35 - .40*
- *1 x 4 V-Rustic* ... BM *.40 - .45*

EXTERIOR TRIM:
- *Fascia and Molds* ... BM *.40 - .50*

Bolted Framing—Add 50%

ENTRANCE DOORS & FRAMES:
- *Singles* ... *60.00 & Up*
- *Doubles* ... *100.00 & Up*

INTERIOR DOORS & FRAMES:
- *Singles* ... *35.00 & Up*
- *Pocket Sliding* ... *45.00 & Up*
- *Closet Sliding (Pr.)* ... *50.00 & Up*

WINDOWS:
- *D/H Sash & Frames* ... SF *1.75 & Up*
- *Casement Sash & Frames* ... SF *1.90 & Up*

SHELVING:
- *1 x 12 S4S* ... BM *.30 - .50*
- *¾" Plywood* ... SF *.40 - .60*

STAIRS:
- *Oak steps D.F. Risers*
- *Under 36" wide* ... *Riser 12.00*
- *Under 60" wide* ... *Riser 17.00*
- *Newel posts and rail extra*

WOOD CASES & CABINETS:
- *D.F. Wall Hung* ... LF *13.00 - 18.00*
- *D.F. Counters* ... LF *15.00 - 20.00*

DAMPPROOFING & WATERPROOFING

MEMBRANE:
- *1 layer 50 lb. felt* ... *SQ. 9.00*
- *4 layers Dampcourse* ... *SQ. 13.00*
- *Hot coat walls* ... *SQ. 6.00*
- *Tricosal added to concrete* ... *CY 1.00*
- *Anti-Hydro added to concrete* ... *CY 1.50*

ELECTRIC WIRING

Per Outlet:
- *Knob & Tube* ... *EA 9.00*
- *Armor* ... *EA 16.00*
- *Conduit* ... *EA 20.00*
- *110 V Circuit* ... *EA 25.00*
- *220 V Circuit* ... *EA 95.00*

ELEVATORS & ESCALATORS

Prices vary according to capacity, speed and type. Consult Elevator Companies.

Slow speed apartment house elevator including doors and trim, about $5000.00 per floor.

EXCAVATION

MACHINE WORK in common ground:
- *Large Basements* ... CY *.75 - 1.00*
- *Small Pits* ... CY *1.25 - 1.75*
- *Trenches* ... CY *1.50 - 2.25*

HAND WORK in common ground:
- *Large pits and trenches* ... CY *4.50 - 5.50*
- *Small pits and trimming* ... CY *5.00 - 6.50*

Hard Clay & Shale 2 times above rates.
Rock and large boulders 4-6 times above rates.
Shoring, bracing and disposal of water not included.

FLOORS

- *⅛" Asp. tile, dark colors* ... SF *.25 - .30*
- *⅛" Asp. tile, light colors* ... SF *.30 - .35*
- *⅛" Rubber tile* ... SF *.60 - .70*
- *.080 Vinyl Asbestos Tile* ... SF *.40 - .45*
- *.080 Vinyl Tile* ... SF *.85 - .95*
- *Lino, Standard Gauge* ... SY *3.75 - 4.25*
- *Lino, Battleship* ... SY *5.25 - 5.75*
- *4" Rubber Base, Black* ... LF *.35 - .40*
- *Rubber Stair Nosing* ... LF *1.00 - 1.75*

Above rates based on quantities of 1000 - 5000 SF per job.

HARDWOOD FLOORS

Select Oak, filled, sanded, stained and varnished:
- *5/16" x 2¼" strip* ... SF *.45 - .50*
- *5/16" Random Plank* ... SF *.50 - .55*
- *25/32" x 2¼" T&G* ... SF *.70 - .80*

Maple, 2nd Grade and Better, filled, sanded, stained and varnished:
- *25/32" x 2¼" T&G* ... SF *.80 - .95*

Wax Finish, add ... SF *.10*

HARDWOOD FLOORING

Oak 5/16" x 2" Strip—
- Clear ... M 229.00
- Select ... M 218.00
- #1 Common ... M 203.00

Oak 5/16" Random Plank—
- Select & Btr. ... M 286.00
- #1 Common ... M 244.00

Oak 25/32" x 2¼" T&G—
- Select ... M 260.00
- #1 Common ... M 203.00

Maple 25/32" x 2¼" T&G—
- #1 Grade ... M 317.00
- #2 Grade ... M 281.00
- #3 Grade ... M 208.00

Nails—1" Floor Brads ... KEG 17.20

GLASS & GLAZING

- *S.S.B. Clear* ... SF *.48*
- *D.S.B. Clear* ... SF *.78*
- *Crystal* ... SF *.92*
- *¼" Plate* ... SF *2.17*
- *⅛" Obscure* ... SF *.68*
- *⅛" Heat Absorbing* ... SF *1.12*
- *¼" Tempered Plate* ... SF *4.38*
- *½" Tempered Plate* ... SF *7.84*
- *¼" Wire Plate, Clear* ... SF *3.65*
- *¼" Wire Plate, Rough* ... SF *1.08*

GLASS—CUT TO SIZE

F.O.B. Warehouse
- S.S.B. Clear, Av. 6 SF ... SF .34
- D.S.B. Clear, Av. 10 SF ... SF .56
- Crystal, Av. 35-SF ... SF .65
- ¼" Polished Plate, Av. 100 SF ... SF 1.55
- ⅛" Obscure, Av. 10 SF ... SF .49
- ⅛" Ribbed, Av. 10 SF ... SF .49
- ⅛" Rough, Av. 10 SF ... SF .49
- ¼" Wire Plate, Clear, Av. 40 SF ... SF 2.61
- ¼" Wire Plate, Rough, Av. 40 SF ... SF .77
- ⅛" Heat Absorbing, Av. 10 SF ... SF .80
- ¼" Tempered Plate, Av. 50 SF ... SF 3.60
- ½" Tempered Plate, Av. 50 SF ... SF 6.88
- Glazing—Approx. 40-50% of Glass
- Glass Blocks—
  - 6" ... .57
  - 8" ... .92
  - 12" ... 2.39

HEATING

FURNACES—Gas Fired—Av. Job:

FLOOR FURNACE:
- *25,000 BTU* ... *100.00 - 125.00*
- *35,000 BTU* ... *107.00 - 135.00*
- *45,000 BTU* ... *115.00 - 150.00*

AUTOMATIC CONTROL:
- *Add* ... *25.00 - 35.00*

HEATING—Cont'd

DUAL WALL FURNACE:
25,000 BTU .... 110.00 - 125.00
35,000 BTU .... 125.00 - 145.00
50,000 BTU .... 150.00 - 180.00
AUTOMATIC CONTROL:
Add .... 25.00 - 35.00
GRAVITY FURNACE:
75,000 BTU .... 375.00 - 450.00
85,000 BTU .... 425.00 - 525.00
95,000 BTU .... 475.00 - 600.00
FORCED AIR FURNACE:
Add .... 75.00 - 125.00
AUTOMATIC CONTROL:
Add .... 15.00 - 25.00
HEAT REGISTERS:
Outlet .... 7.50 - 15.00

INSULATION & WALLBOARD

F.O.B. Warehouse

ROCKWOOL Insulation—
2" Semi-thick .... Per M SF 60.60
3⅝" Full Thick .... Per M SF 77.40
COTTON Insulation
1" Full Thick .... Per M SF 43.26
SOFTBOARDS—Wood Fiber—
½" thick .... Per M SF 84.00
1½" thick .... Per M SF 275.00
2" thick .... Per M SF 385.00
ALUMINUM Insulation—
80# Kraft paper with alum. foil
1 side only .... Per M SF 18.30
2 sides .... Per M SF 31.00
GYPSUM Wallboard—
⅜" thick .... Per M SF 49.50
½" thick .... Per M SF 54.50
⅝" thick .... Per M SF 83.00
⅝" Gyplap .... Per M SF 85.00
HARDBOARDS—Wood Fiber—
⅛" thick, Sheathing .... Per M SF 84.00
3/16" thick, Sheathing .... Per M SF 90.48
¼" thick, Sheathing .... Per M SF 109.20
⅛" thick, Tempered .... Per M SF 108.00
3/16" thick, Tempered .... Per M SF 186.00
¼" thick, Tempered .... Per M SF 194.48
CEMENT Asbestos Board—
⅛" C.A.B. Flat Sheets .... Per M SF 151.20
3/16" C.A.B. Flat Sheets .... Per M SF 208.80
¼" C.A.B. Flat Sheets .... Per M SF 270.01

LATH & PLASTER

Diamond 3.40 copper bearing .... SY .56
Ribbed 3.40 copper bearing .... SY .62
⅜" rock lath .... SY .36
1½" Standard Channel .... LF .062
¾" Standard Channel .... LF .045
3¼" steel studs .... LF .092
4" steel studs .... LF .107
Stud shoes .... EA .028
Hardwall, Browning .... Sack 1.45
Hardwall, Finish .... Sack 1.70
Stucco .... Sack 2.50

LATH & PLASTERWORK

CHANNEL FURRING:
Suspended Ceilings .... SY 2.20 - 2.50
Walls .... SY 2.30 - 2.60
METAL STUD PARTITIONS:
3¼" Studs .... SY 1.70 - 2.00
4" Studs .... SY 1.95 - 2.25
Over 10'0 high, add .... SY .20 - .30
3.40 METAL LATH AND PLASTER:
Ceilings .... SY 3.60 - 4.00
Walls .... SY 3.75 - 4.15
KEENE'S CEMENT FINISH:
Add .... SY .40 - .60
ROCK LATH & PLASTER:
Ceilings .... SY 2.50 - 2.80
Walls .... SY 2.60 - 2.90
WIRE MESH AND ⅞" STUCCO:
Walls .... SY 3.60 - 4.10
STUCCO ON CONCRETE:
Walls .... SY 2.30 - 2.80
METAL ACCESSORIES .... LF .20 - .50

LINOLEUM

Lino. Standard Gauge .... SY 2.65 - 2.85
Lino. Battleship .... SY 2.95 - 3.11
⅛" Asp. tile, Dark .... SF .10 - .11
⅛" Asp. tile, Light .... SF .14 - .16
⅛" Rubber Tile .... SF .40 - .44
.080 Vinyl tile .... SF .20 - .21
.080 Vinyl Asb. tile .... SF .18 - .19
⅛" Vinyl tile .... SF .78 - .82
4" Base, Dark .... LF .15 - .16
4" Base, Light .... LF .24 - .26
Rubber Nosing .... LF .60 - 1.30
Lino Paste .... GAL .75 - .90
Above rates based on quantities of 1000-5000 SF per job.

LUMBER

DOUGLAS FIR: M.B.M.
#1 2x4—2x10 .... 88.00 - 92.00
#2 2x4—2x10 .... 85.00 - 90.00
#3 2x4—2x10 .... 68.00 - 74.00
#4 2x4—2x10 .... 64.00 - 72.00
Clear, Air Dried .... 180.00 - 210.00
Clear, Kiln Dried .... 210.00 - 240.00
REDWOOD:
Foundation Grade .... 120.00 - 130.00
Construction Heart .... 110.00 - 120.00
A Grade .... 180.00 - 210.00
Clear Heart .... 190.00 - 220.00
D.F. PLYWOOD M.S.F.
¼" AB .... 95.00 - 105.00
¼" AD .... 90.00 - 95.00
¼" Ext. Waterproof .... 115.00 - 125.00
⅜" AB .... 130.00 - 145.00
⅜" AD .... 115.00 - 125.00
⅜" CD .... 70.00 - 85.00
½" AB .... 170.00 - 185.00
½" AD .... 110.00 - 115.00
½" CD ....
⅝" AB .... 185.00 - 200.00
⅝" AD .... 165.00 - 180.00
⅝" CD .... 115.00 - 125.00
¾" AB .... 210.00 - 230.00
¾" AD .... 195.00 - 210.00
¾" CD .... 125.00 - 140.00
⅝" Plyform .... 160.00 - 170.00
SHINGLES: Square
Cedar #1 .... 14.00 - 15.50
Cedar #2 .... 11.50 - 12.50
SHAKES:
CEDAR
½ to ¾" Butt .... 17.50 - 18.50
¾ to 1¼" Butt .... 18.50 - 19.50
REDWOOD
¾ to 1¼" Butt .... 21.00 - 24.00

MILLWORK

All Prices F.O.B. Mill

D.F. CLEAR, AIR DRIED:
S4S .... MBM 220.00 - 250.00
D.F. CLEAR, KILN DRIED:
S4S .... MBM 225.00 - 275.00
DOOR FRAMES & TRIM:
Residential Entrance .... 17.00 & up
Interior Room Entrance .... 7.50 & up
DOORS:
1⅜" D.F. Slab, Hollow Core .... 8.00 & up
1¾" D.F. Slab, Solid Core .... 19.00 & up
1⅜" Birch Slab, Hollow Core .... 10.00 & up
1¾" Birch Slab, Solid Core .... 22.00 & up
WINDOW FRAMES:
D/H Singles .... SF .80
Casement Singles .... SF .90
WOOD SASH:
D/H in pairs (1 lite) .... SF .45
Casement (1 lite) .... SF .50
WOOD CABINETS:
¾" D.F. Ply with ¼" ply backs
Wall Hung .... LF 10.00 - 15.00
Counter .... LF 12.00 - 17.00
BIRCH OR MAPLE—Add 25%

PAINT

All Prices F.O.B. Warehouse

Thinners—5-100 gals. .... GAL. .57
Turpentine—5-100 gals. .... GAL. 1.58
Linseed Oil, Raw .... GAL. 2.51
Linseed Oil, Boiled .... GAL. 2.57
Primer-Sealer .... GAL. 3.10
Enamel .... GAL. 5.45
Enamel Undercoaters .... GAL. 5.45
White Lead in Oil .... LB. .35
Red Lead in Oil .... LB. .35
Litharge .... LB. .30

PAINTING

EXTERIOR:
Stucco Wash 1 ct. .... SY .30
Stucco Wash 2 cts. .... SY .55
Lead and Oil 2 cts. .... SY .90
Lead and Oil 3 cts. .... SY 1.30
INTERIOR:
Primer Sealer .... SY .40
Wall Paint, 1 ct. .... SY .50
Wall Paint, 2 cts. .... SY .95
Enamel, 1 ct. .... SY .60
Enamel, 2 cts. .... SY 1.10
Doors and Trim .... EA 10.00
Sash and Trim .... EA 12.00
Base and Molds .... LF .12
Old Work—Add 15-30%

PLUMBING

Lavatories .... EA 100.00 - 150.00
Toilets .... EA 200.00 - 300.00
Bath Tubs .... EA 250.00 - 350.00
Stall Shower .... EA 80.00 - 150.00
Sinks .... EA 125.00 - 175.00
Laundry Trays .... EA 80.00 - 130.00
Water Heaters .... EA 100.00 - 300.00
Prices based on average residential and commercial work. Special fixtures and excessive piping not included.

ROOFING

STANDARD TAR & GRAVEL Per Square
4 ply .... 14.00 - 18.00
5 ply .... 17.00 - 20.00
White Gravel Finish—Add .... 2.00 - 4.00
Asph. Compo. Shingles .... 16.00 - 20.00
Cedar Shingles .... 20.00 - 24.00
Cedar Shakes .... 26.00 - 30.00
Redwood Shakes .... 28.00 - 34.00
Clay Tiles .... 40.00 - 50.00

SEWER PIPE

VITRIFIED:
Standard 4 in. .... LF .31
Standard 6 in. .... LF .56
Standard 8 in. .... LF .81
Standard 12 in. .... LF 1.76
Standard 24 in. .... LF 6.95
CLAY DRAIN PIPE:
Standard 6 in. .... LF .34
Standard 8 in. .... LF .59
Rate for 100 Lin. Ft. F.O.B. Warehouse

STEEL

REINFORCING BARS:
¼" rounds .... LB .122
⅜" rounds .... LB .111
½" rounds .... LB .107
⅝" rounds .... LB .104
¾" rounds .... LB .102
⅞" rounds .... LB .102
1" rounds .... LB .102
REINFORCING MESH (1050 SF Rolls)
6x6 x 10x10 .... SF .035
6x6 x 6x6 .... SF .067
16 GA. TYING WIRE .... LB .130
Rates 100-1000 Lbs. F.O.B. Warehouse

STRUCTURAL STEEL

$325.00 and up per ton erected when out of mill.
$350.00 and up per ton erected when out of stock.

SHEET METAL

ROOF FLASHINGS:
18 ga. Galv. Steel .... SF .60 - 1.00
22 ga. Galv. Steel .... SF .50 - .90
26 ga. Galv. Steel .... SF .40 - .80
18 ga. Aluminum .... SF 1.00 - 1.50
22 ga. Aluminum .... SF .80 - 1.30
26 ga. Aluminum .... SF .60 - 1.10
24 oz. Copper .... SF 1.90 - 2.40
20 oz. Copper .... SF 1.70 - 2.20
16 oz. Copper .... SF 1.50 - 2.00
26 ga. Galv. Steel
4" o.g. gutter .... LF .90 - 1.30
Mitres and Drops .... EA 2.00 - 4.00
22 ga. Galv. Louvres .... SF 2.50 - 3.50
20 oz. Copper Louvres .... SF 3.00 - 4.50

TILE WORK

CERAMIC TILE, Stock colors:
Floors .... SF 1.95 - 2.45
Walls .... SF 2.05 - 2.55
Coved Base .... LF 1.05 - 1.45
QUARRY TILE:
6" x 6" x ½" Floors .... SF 1.60 - 2.00
9" x 9" x ¾" Floors .... SF 1.75 - 2.15
Treads and risers .... LF 3.00 - 4.50
Coved Base .... LF .90 - 1.30
Mosaic Tile — Rates vary with design and colors. Each job should be priced from Manufacturer.

TERRAZZO & MARBLE

Terrazzo Floors .... SF 2.00 - 2.50
Cond. Terr. Floors .... SF 2.20 - 2.75
Precast treads and risers .... LF 3.50 - 4.50
Precast landing slabs .... SF 3.00 - 4.00

TILE

CERAMIC:
F.O.B. Warehouse
4¼" x 4¼" glazed .... SF .69
4¼" x 4¼" hard glazed .... SF .72
Random unglazed .... SF .73
6" x 2" cap .... EA .17
6" coved base .... EA .22
¼" round bead .... LF .18
QUARRY:
6 x 6 x ½" Red .... SF .49
6 x 6 x ¾" Red .... SF .52
9 x 9 x ¾" Red .... SF .60
6 x 6" coved base .... EA .21
White Cement Grout .... Per 100 Lbs. 6.25

VENETIAN BLINDS

Residential .... SF .40 & Up
Commercial .... SF .45 & Up

WINDOWS

STEEL SASH:
Under 10 SF .... SF 2.50 & Up
Under 15 SF .... SF 2.00 & Up
Under 20 SF .... SF 1.50 & Up
Under 30 SF .... SF 1.00 & Up
ALUMINUM SASH:
Under 10 SF .... SF 2.75 & Up
Under 15 SF .... SF 2.25 & Up
Under 20 SF .... SF 1.75 & Up
Under 30 SF .... SF 1.25 & Up
Above rates are for standard sections and stock sizes F.O.B. Warehouse

CONSTRUCTION INDUSTRY WAGE RATES

Table 1 has been prepared by the State of California, Department of Industrial Relations, Division of Labor Statistics and Research. The rates are the union hourly wage rates established by collective bargaining as of January 2, 1958, as reported by reliable sources.

TABLE 1—UNION HOURLY WAGE RATES, CONSTRUCTION INDUSTRY, CALIFORNIA

Following are the hourly rates of compensation established by collective bargaining, reported as of January 2, 1958 or later

CRAFT	San Francisco	Alameda	Contra Costa	Fresno	Sacramento	San Joaquin	Santa Clara	Solano	Los Angeles	San Bernardino	San Diego	Santa Barbara	Kern
ASBESTOS WORKER	$3.70	$3.70	$3.70	$3.70	$3.70	$3.70	$3.70	$3.70	$3.70	$3.70	$3.70	$3.70	$3.70
BOILERMAKER	3.675	3.675	3.675	3.675	3.675	3.675	3.675	3.675	3.675	3.675	3.675	3.675	3.675
BRICKLAYER	3.95	3.75	3.75	3.75	3.80	3.75	3.875	3.95	3.80	3.90	3.75		3.85
BRICKLAYER HODCARRIER	3.15	3.15	3.15	2.90	3.10	2.90	3.00	3.10	2.75	2.75	2.75		2.75
CARPENTER	3.175	3.175	3.225	3.225	3.225	3.225	3.225	3.225	3.225	3.225	3.225	3.225	3.225
CEMENT MASON	3.22	3.22	3.22	3.22	3.22	3.22	3.22	3.22	3.15	3.15	3.25	3.15	3.15
ELECTRICIAN	3.936ᴀ	3.936ᴀ	3.936ᴀ		3.94ᴀ	3.50	4.03ᴀ	3.666ᴀ	3.90ᴀ	3.90ᴀ	3.90	3.85ᴀ	3.70
GLAZIER	3.09	3.09	3.09	3.135	3.055	3.055	3.09	3.09	3.105	3.105	3.03	3.106	3.135
IRON WORKER — ORNAMENTAL	3.625	3.625	3.625	3.625	3.625	3.625	3.625	3.625	3.625	3.625	3.625	3.625	3.625
REINFORCING	3.375	3.375	3.375	3.375	3.375	3.375	3.375	3.375	3.375	3.375	3.375	3.375	3.375
STRUCTURAL	3.625	3.625	3.625	3.625	3.625	3.625	3.625	3.625	3.625	3.625	3.625	3.625	3.625
LABORER, GENERAL OR CONSTRUCTION	2.505	2.505	2.505	2.505	2.505	2.505	2.505	2.505	2.50	2.50	2.48	2.50	2.50
LATHER	3.4375	3.84	3.84	3.45	3.60ɴ	3.40ᴄ	3.60ᴊ	3.50ᴇ	3.9375		3.725	3.625ꜰ	
OPERATING ENGINEER Concrete mixer (up to 1 yard)	2.89	2.89	2.89	2.89	2.89	2.89	2.89	2.89					
Concrete mixer operator—Skip Type									2.96	2.96	2.96	2.96	2.96
Elevator Hoist Operator									3.19	3.19	3.19	3.19	3.19
Material Hoist (1 drum)	3.19	3.19	3.19	3.19	3.19	3.19	3.19	3.19					
Tractor Operator	3.33	3.33	3.33	3.33	3.33	3.33	3.33	3.33	3.47	3.47	3.47	3.47	3.47
PAINTER Brush	3.20	3.20	3.20	3.13	3.325	3.175	3.20	3.20	3.26ɢ	3.25	3.19	3.13ʜ	3.10
Spray	3.20	3.20	3.20	3.38	3.575	3.325	3.20	3.20	3.51ɢ	3.50	3.74	3.38ʜ	3.35
PILEDRIVERMAN	3.305	3.305	3.305	3.305	3.305	3.305	3.305	3.305	3.355	3.355		3.355	3.355
PLASTERER	3.69	3.545	3.545	3.35	3.60ʙ	3.55ᴄ	3.58	3.50	3.9375	3.9375	3.725		
PLASTERER HODCARRIER	3.25	3.42	3.42	3.10	3.10	3.00ᴄ	3.20	3.15	3.6875	3.5625	3.475	3.50	3.6875
PLUMBER	3.67		3.935ɪ	3.80ᴊ	3.70	3.80ᴊ	3.60	3.675	3.70	3.70	3.70	3.70	3.375
ROOFER	3.35	3.35	3.35	3.20	3.25	3.35	3.35	3.10ᴋ	3.20ʟ	3.25	3.10	3.30	3.775
SHEET METAL WORKER	3.45	3.45	3.45	3.425	3.45	3.465	3.45	3.325	3.50	3.50	3.45	3.55	3.10
STEAMFITTER	3.67	3.96	3.96	3.80ᴊ	3.70	3.80ᴊ	3.60	3.675	3.70	3.70	3.70	3.70	3.775
TRUCK DRIVER — Dump Trucks under 4 yards	2.55	2.55	2.55	2.55	2.55	2.55	2.55	2.55	2.63	2.63	2.63	2.63	2.63
TILE SETTER	3.275	3.275	3.275	3.375	3.28	3.30	3.275	3.275	3.36	3.60	3.375	3.36	

ᴀ Includes 4% vacation allowance.
ʙ Includes 5c hour for industry promotion and 5c hour for vacation fund.
ᴄ ½% withheld for industry promotion.
ᴅ 1½c withheld for industry promotion.
ᴇ Includes 5c hour for industry promotion and 5c hour for vacation fund. Hourly rate for part of county adjacent to Sacramento County is $3.60.
ꜰ Northern part of County: $3.75.

ɢ Pomona Area: Brush $3.25; Spray $3.50.
ʜ Southern half of County: Brush $3.28; Spray $3.28.
ɪ Includes 30c hour for vacation pay.
ᴊ Includes 15c hour which local union may elect to use for vacation purposes.
ᴋ Includes 10c hour for vacation fund.
ʟ Includes 10c hour savings fund wage.

ATTENTION: The above tabulation has been prepared by the State of California, Department of Industrial Relations, Division of Labor Statistics and Research, and represents data reported by building trades councils, union locals, contractor organizations, and other reliable sources. The above rates do not include any payments to funds for health and welfare, pensions, vacations, industry promotion, apprentice training, etc., except as shown in the footnotes.

CONSTRUCTION INDUSTRY WAGE RATES — TABLE 2

Employer Contributions to Health and Welfare, Pension, Vacation and Other Funds
California Union Contracts, Construction Industry

(Revised March, 1957)

CRAFT	San Francisco	Fresno	Sacramento	San Joaquin	Santa Clara	Los Angeles	San Bernardino	San Diego
ASBESTOS WORKER	.10 W .11 hr. V	.10 W .11 hr. V	.10 W .11 hr. V	.10 W .11 hr. V	.10 W .11 hr. V	.10 W	.10 W	.10 W
BRICKLAYER	.15 W .14 P .05 hr. V		.15 W .10 P		.15 W			
BRICKLAYER HODCARRIER	.10 W .10 P .10 V	.10 W	.10 W	.10 W	.10 W	.075 W	.075 W	.075 W
CARPENTER	.10 W .10 hr. V	.10 W	.10 W	.10 W	.10 W	.10 W	.10 W	.10 W
CEMENT MASON	.10 W	.10 W	.10 W	.10 W	.10 W	.10 W	.10 W	.10 W .10 V
ELECTRICAL WORKER	.10 W 1% P 4% V	.10 W 1% P 4% V	.075 W 1% P	.075 W 1% P 4% V	1% P	1% P	1% P	1% P
GLAZIER	.075 W .085 V	.075 W 40 hr. V	.075 W .05 V	.075 W .05 V	.075 W .085 V	.075 W 40 hr. V	.075 W 40 hr. V	.075 W 80 hr. V
IRONWORKER: REINFORCING STRUCTURAL	.10 W .10 W	.10 W .10 W	.10 W .10 W	.10 W .10 W	.10 W .10 W	.10 W .10 W	.10 W .10 W	.10 W .10 W
LABORER, GENERAL	.10 W	.10 W	.10 W	.10 W	.10 W	.075 W	.075 W	.075 W
LATHER	.60 day W .70 day V		.10 W	.10 W	.075 W .05 V	.90 day W	.70 day V	.10 W
OPERATING ENGINEER TRACTOR OPERATOR (MIN.) POWER SHOVEL OP. (MIN.)	.10 W .10 W	.10 W .10 W	.10 W .10 W	.10 W .10 W	.10 W .10 W	.10 W .10 W	.10 W .10 W	.10 W .10 W
PAINTER, BRUSH	.095 W	.08 W	.075 W	.10 W	.095 W .07 V	.085 W	.08 W	.09 W
PLASTERER	.10 W .10 V	.10 W	.10 W	.10 W	.10 W .15 V	.10 W	.90 day W	.10 W
PLUMBER	.10 W .10 V	.15 W .10 P	.10 W .10 P .125 V	.10 W	.10 W .10 P .125 V	.10 W	.90 day W	.10 W
ROOFER	.10 W .10 V	.10 W	.10 W .10 V	.10 W	.075 W .10 V	.085 W	.10 W	.075 W
SHEET METAL WORKER	.075 W 4% V	.075 W 7 day V	.075 W .10 V	.075 W .12 V	.075 W 4% V	.085 W .10 V	.085 W .10 V	.085 W 5 day V
TILE SETTER	.075 W .09 V				.075 W .09 V	.025 W .06 V		

ATTENTION: The above tabulation has been prepared and compiled from the available data reported by building trades councils, union locals, contractor organizations and other reliable sources. The table was prepared from incomplete data; where no employer contributions are specified, it does not necessarily mean that none are required by the union contract.

The type of supplement is indicated by the following symbols: W—Health and Welfare; P—Pensions; V—Vacations; A—Apprentice training fund; Adm—Administration fund; JIB—Joint Industry Board; Prom—Promotion fund.

CLASSIFIED ADVERTISING

RATE: 20c PER WORD . . . CASH WITH ORDER   MINIMUM $5.00

QUICK REFERENCE
ESTIMATOR'S DIRECTORY
Building and Construction Materials

ACOUSTICAL ENGINEERS
L. D. REEDER CO.
San Francisco: 1255 Sansome St., DO 2-5050
Sacramento: 3026 V St., GL 7-3505

AIR CONDITIONING
E. C. BRAUN CO.
Berkeley: 2115 Fourth St., TH 5-2356
GILMORE AIR CONDITIONING SERVICE
San Francisco: 1617 Harrison St., UN 1-2000
KAEMPER & BARRETT
San Francisco: 233 Industrial St., JU 6-6200
LINFORD AIR & REFRIGERATION CO.
Oakland: 174-12th St., TW 3-6521
MALM METAL PRODUCTS
Santa Rosa: 724-2nd St., SR 454
JAMES A. NELSON CO.
San Francisco: 1375 Howard St., HE 1-0140

ALUMINUM BLDG. PRODUCTS
MICHEL & PFEFFER IRON WORKS (Wrought Iron)
So. San Francisco: 212 Shaw Road, PLaza 5-8983
REYNOLDS METALS CO.
San Francisco: 3201 Third St., MI 7-2990
SOULE STEEL CO.
San Francisco: 1750 Army St., VA 4-4141
UNIVERSAL WINDOW CO.
Berkeley: 950 Parker St., TH 1-1600

ARCHITECTURAL PORCELAIN ENAMEL
CALIFORNIA METAL ENAMELING CO.
Los Angeles: 6904 E. Slauson, RA 3-6351
San Francisco: Continental Bldg. Products Co.,
178 Fremont St.
Portland: Portland Wire & Iron Works,
4644 S.E. Seventeenth Ave.
Seattle: Foster-Bray Co., 2412 1st Ave. So.
Spokane: Bernhard Schafer, Inc., West 34, 2nd Ave.
Salt Lake City: S. A. Roberts & Co., 109 W. 2nd So.
Dallas: Offenhauser Co., 2201 Telephone Rd.
El Paso: Architectural Products Co.,
506 E. Yandell Blvd.
Phoenix: Haskell-Thomas Co., 3808 No. Central
San Diego: Maloney Specialties, Inc., 823 W. Laurel St.
Boise: Intermountain Glass Co., 1417 Main St.

ARCHITECTURAL & AERIAL PHOTOGRAPHS
FRED ENGLISH
Belmont, Calif.: 1310 Old County Road, LY 1-0385

ARCHITECTURAL VENEER
Ceramic Veneer
GLADDING, McBEAN & CO.
San Francisco: Harrison at 9th St., UN 1-7400
Los Angeles: 2901 Los Feliz Blvd., OL 2121
Portland: 110 S.E. Main St., EA 6199
Seattle 99: 945 Elliott Ave., West, GA 0330
Spokane: 1102 N. Monroe St., BR 3259
KRAFTILE COMPANY
Niles, Calif., Niles 3611

Porcelain Veneer
PORCELAIN ENAMEL PUBLICITY BUREAU
Oakland 12: Room 601, Franklin Building
Pasadena 8: P. O. Box 186, East Pasadena Station

Granite Veneer
VERMONT MARBLE COMPANY
San Francisco 24: 6000 3rd St., VA 6-5024
Los Angeles: 3522 Council St., DU 2-6339

Marble Veneer
VERMONT MARBLE COMPANY
San Francisco 24: 6000 3rd St., VA 6-5024
Los Angeles: 3522 Council St., DU 2-6339

BANKS - FINANCING
CROCKER-ANGLO NATIONAL BANK
San Francisco: 13 Offices

BLINDS
PARAMOUNT VENETIAN BLIND CO.
San Francisco: 5929 Mission St., JU 5-2436

BRASS PRODUCTS
GREENBERG'S, M. SONS
San Francisco 7: 765 Folsom, EX 2-3143
Los Angeles 23: 1258 S. Boyle, AN 3-7108
Seattle 4:1016 First Ave. So., MA 5140
Phoenix: 3009 N. 19th Ave., Apt. 92, PH 2-7663
Portland 4: 510 Builders Exch. Bldg., AT 6443

BRICKWORK
Face Brick
GLADDING McBEAN & CO.
San Francisco: Harrison at 9th, UN 1-7400
KRAFTILE CO.
Niles, Calif., Niles 3611
UNITED MATERIALS & RICHMOND BRICK CO.
Point Richmond, BE 4-5032

BRONZE PRODUCTS
GREENBERG'S M. SONS
San Francisco: 765 Folsom St., EX 2-3143
MICHEL & PFEFFER IRON WORKS
So. San Francisco: 212 Shaw Road, PLaza 5-8983
C. E. TOLAND & SON
Oakland: 2635 Peralta St., GL 1-2580

BUILDING HARDWARE
E. M. HUNDLEY HARDWARE CO.
San Francisco: 662 Mission St., YU 2-3322

BUILDING PAPERS & FELTS
PACIFIC CEMENT & AGGREGATES INC.
San Francisco: 400 Alabama St., KL 2-1616

CABINETS & FIXTURES
CENTRAL MILL & CABINET CO.
San Francisco: 1595 Fairfax Ave., VA 4-7316
THE FINK & SCHINDLER CO.
San Francisco: 552 Brannan St., EX 2-1513
JONES KRAFT SHOP,
San Francisco: 1314 Ocean Avenue., JU 7-1545
MULLEN MFG. CO.
San Francisco: 64 Rausch St., UN 1-5815
PARAMOUNT BUILT IN FIXTURE CO.
Oakland: 962 Stanford Ave., OL 3-9911
ROYAL SHOWCASE CO.
San Francisco: 770 McAllister St., JO 7-0311

CEMENT
CALAVERAS CEMENT CO.
San Francisco: 315 Montgomery St.
DO 2-4224, Enterprise 1-2315
PACIFIC CEMENT & AGGREGATES INC.
San Francisco: 400 Alabama St., KL 2-1616

CONCRETE AGGREGATES
Ready Mixed Concrete
CENTRAL CONCRETE SUPPLY CO.
San Jose: 610 McKendrie St.
PACIFIC CEMENT & AGGREGATES INC.
San Francisco: 400 Alabama St., KL 2-1616
Sacramento: 16th and A Sts., GI 3-6586
San Jose: 790 Stockton Ave., CY 2-5620
Oakland: 2400 Peralta St., GL 1-0177
Stockton: 820 So. California St., ST 8-8643
READYMIX CONCRETE CO.
Santa Rosa: 50 W. Cottage Ave.
RHODES-JAMIESON LTD.
Oakland: 333-23rd Ave., KE 3-5225
SANTA ROSA BLDG. MATERIALS CO.
Santa Rosa: Roberts Ave.

CONCRETE ACCESSORIES
Screed Materials
C. & H. SPECIALTIES CO.
Berkeley: 909 Camelia St., LA 4-5358

CONCRETE BLOCKS
BASALT ROCK CO.
Napa, Calif.

CONCRETE COLORS—HARDENERS
CONRAD SOVIG CO.
875 Bryant St., HE 1-1345

CONSTRUCTION SERVICES
LE ROY CONSTRUCTION SERVICES
San Francisco, 143 Third St., SU 1-8914

DECKS—ROOF
UNITED STATES GYPSUM CO.
2322 W. 3rd St., Los Angeles 54, Calif.
300 W. Adams St., Chicago 6, Ill.

DOORS
THE BILCO COMPANY
New Haven, Conn.
Oakland: Geo. B. Schultz, 190 MacArthur Blvd.
Sacramento: Harry B. Ogle & Assoc., 1331 T St.
Fresno: Healey & Popovich, 1703 Fulton St.
Reseda: Daniel Dunner, 6200 Alonzo Ave.

Cold Storage Doors
BIRKENWALD
Portland: 310 N.W. 5th Ave.

Electric Doors
ROLY-DOOR SALES CO.
San Francisco, 5976 Mission St., PL 5-5089

Folding Doors
WALTER D. BATES & ASSOCIATES
San Francisco, 693 Mission St., GA 1-6971

Hardwood Doors
BELLWOOD CO. OF CALIF.
Orange, Calif., 533 W. Collins Ave.

Hollywood Doors
WEST COAST SCREEN CO.
Los Angeles: 1127 E. 63rd St., AD 1-1108
T. M. COBB CO.
Los Angeles & San Diego
W. P. FULLER CO.
Seattle, Tacoma, Portland
HOGAN LUMBER CO.
Oakland: 700 - 6th Ave.
HOUSTON SASH & DOOR
Houston, Texas
SOUTHWESTERN SASH & DOOR
Phoenix, Tucson, Arizona
El Paso, Texas
WESTERN PINE SUPPLY CO.
Emeryville: 5760 Shellmound St.
GEO. C. VAUGHAN & SONS
San Antonio & Houston, Texas

Screen Doors
WEST COAST SCREEN DOOR CO.

DRAFTING ROOM EQUIPMENT
GENERAL FIREPROOFING CO.
Oakland: 332-19th St., GL 2-4280
Los Angeles: 1200 South Hope St., RI 7-7501
San Francisco: 1025 Howard St., HE 1-7070

DRINKING FOUNTAINS
HAWS DRINKING FAUCET CO.
Berkeley: 1435 Fourth St., LA 5-3341

ELECTRICAL CONTRACTORS
COOPMAN ELECTRIC CO.
San Francisco: 85 - 14th St., MA 1-4438
ETS-HOKIN & GALVAN
San Francisco: 551 Mission St., EX 2-0432

ELECTRICAL CONTRACTORS (cont'd)
LEMOGE ELECTRIC CO.
San Francisco: 212 Clara St., DO 2-6010
LYNCH ELECTRIC CO.
San Francisco: 937 McAllister St., WI 5158
PACIFIC ELECTRIC & MECHANICAL CO.
San Francisco: Gough & Fell Sts., HE 1-5904

ELECTRIC HEATERS
WESIX ELECTRIC HEATER CO.
San Francisco: 390 First St., GA 1-2211

FIRE ESCAPES
MICHEL & PFEFFER IRON WORKS
South San Francisco: 212 Shaw Road, PLaza 5-8983

FIRE PROTECTION EQUIPMENT
FIRE PROTECTION PRODUCTS CO.
San Francisco: 1101-16th St., UN 1-2420
ETS-HOKIN & GALVAN
San Francisco: 551 Mission St., EX 2-0432
BARNARD ENGINEERING CO.
San Francisco: 35 Elmira St., JU 5-4642

FLOORS
Floor Tile
GLADDING McBEAN & CO.
San Francisco: Harrison at 9th St., UN 1-744
Los Angeles: 2901 Las Feliz Bldg., OL 2121
KRAFTILE CO.
Niles, Calif., Niles 3611

Resilient Floors
PETERSON-COBBY CO.
San Francisco: 218 Clara St., EX 2-8714
TURNER RESILIENT FLOORS CO.
San Francisco: 2280 Shaffer Ave., AT 2-7720

FLOOR DRAINS
JOSAM PACIFIC COMPANY
San Francisco: 765 Folsom St., EX 2-3142

GAS VENTS
WM. WALLACE CO.
Belmont, Calif.

GENERAL CONTRACTORS
O. E. ANDERSON
San Jose: 1075 No. 10th St., CY 3-8844
BARRETT CONSTRUCTION CO.
San Francisco: 1800 Evans Ave., MI 7-9700
JOSEPH BETTANCOURT
South San Francisco: 125 So. Linden St., PL 5-9185
DINWIDDIE CONSTRUCTION CO.
San Francisco: Crocker Bldg., YU 6-2718
D. L. FAULL CONSTRUCTION CO.
Santa Rosa: 1236 Cleveland Ave.
HAAS & HAYNIE
San Francisco: 275 Pine St., DO 2-0678
HENDERSON CONSTRUCTION CO.
San Francisco: 33 Ritch St., GA 1-0856
JACKS & IRVINE
San Francisco: 620 Market St., YU 6-0511
G. P. W. JENSEN & SONS
San Francisco: 320 Market St., GA 1-2444
RALPH LARSEN & SON
San Francisco: 64 So. Park, YU 2-5682
LINDGREN & SWINERTON
San Francisco: 200 Bush St., GA 1-2980
MacDONALD, YOUNG & NELSON
San Francisco: 351 California St., YU 2-4700
MATTOCK CONSTRUCTION CO.
San Francisco: 220 Clara St., GA 1-5516
OLSEN CONSTRUCTION CO.
Santa Rosa: 125 Brookwood Ave., SR 2030
BEN ORTSKY
Cotati: Cypress Ave., Pet. 5-4383
PARKER, STEFFANS & PEARCE
San Mateo: 135 So. Park, EX 2-6639
RAPP, CHRISTENSEN & FOSTER
Santa Rosa: 705 Bennett Ave.

STOLTE, INC.
Oakland: 8451 San Leandro Ave., LO 2-4611
SWINERTON & WALBERG
San Francisco: 200 Bush St., GA 1-2980

FURNITURE—INSTITUTIONAL
GENERAL FIREPROOFING CO.
San Francisco: 1025 Howard St., HE 1-7070
Oakland: 332-19th St., GL 2-4280
Los Angeles: 1200 South Hope St., RI 7-7501

HEATING & VENTILATING
ATLAS HEATING & VENT. CO.
San Francisco: 557-4th St., DO 2-0377
E. C. BRAUN CO.
Berkeley: 2115 Fourth St., TH 5-2356
C. W. HALL
Santa Rosa: 1665 Sebastopol Rd., SR 6354
S. T. JOHNSON CO.
Oakland: 940 Arlington Ave., OL 2-6000
LOUIS V. KELLER
San Francisco: 289 Tehama St., JU 6-6252
L. J. KRUSE CO.
Oakland: 6247 College Ave., OL 2-8332
MALM METAL PRODUCTS
Santa Rosa: 724-2nd St., SR 454
JAS. A. NELSON CO.
San Francisco: 1375 Howard St., HE 1-0140
SCOTT COMPANY
Oakland: 1919 Market St., GL 1-1937
WESIX ELECTRIC HEATER CO.
San Francisco: 390 First St., GA 1-2211
Los Angeles: 530 W. 7th St., MI 8096

INSULATION WALL BOARD
PACIFIC CEMENT & AGGREGATES, INC.
San Francisco: 400 Alabama St., KL 2-1616

INTERCEPTING DEVICES
JOSAM PACIFIC CO.
San Francisco: 765 Folsom St., EX 2-3142

IRON—ORNAMENTAL
MICHEL & PFEFFER IRON WKS.
So. San Francisco: 212 Shaw Rd., PL 5-8983

LATHING & PLASTERING
ANGELO J. DANERI
San Francisco: 1433 Fairfax Ave., AT 8-1582
K-LATH CORP.
Alhambra: 909 So. Fremont St., Alhambra
A. E. KNOWLES CORP.
San Francisco: 3330 San Bruno Ave., JU 7-2091
G. H. & C. MARTINELLI
San Francisco: 174 Shotwell St., UN 3-6112
FREDERICK MEISWINKEL
San Francisco: 2155 Turk St., JO 7-7587
RHODES-JAMIESON LTD.
Oakland: 333-23rd Ave., KE 3-5225
PATRICK J. RUANE
San Francisco: 44 San Jose Ave., MI 7-6414

LIGHTING FIXTURES
SMOOT-HOLMAN COMPANY
Inglewood, Calif., OR 8-1217
San Francisco: 55 Mississippi St., MA 1-8474

LIGHTING & CEILING SYSTEMS
UNITED LIGHTING AND FIXTURE CO.
Oakland: 3120 Chapman St., KE 3-8711

LUMBER
CHRISTENSEN LUMBER CO.
San Francisco: Quint & Evans Ave., VA 4-5832
ART HOGAN LUMBER CO.
1701 Galvez Ave., ATwater 2-1157
MEAD CLARK LUMBER CO.
Santa Rosa: 3rd & Railroad
ROLANDO LUMBER CO.
San Francisco: 5th & Berry Sts., SU 1-6901
STERLING LUMBER CO.
Santa Rosa: 1129 College Ave., S. R. 82

MARBLE
JOS. MUSTO SONS-KEENAN CO.
San Francisco: 555 No. Point St., GR 4-6365
VERMONT MARBLE CO.
San Francisco: 6000-3rd St., VA 6-5024

MASONRY
BASALT ROCK CO.
Napa, Calif.
San Francisco: 260 Kearney St., GA 1-3758
WM. A. RAINEY & SON
San Francisco: 323 Clementina St., SU 1-0072
GEO. W. REED CO.
San Francisco: 1390 So. Van Ness Ave., AT 2-1226

METAL EXTERIOR WALLS
THE KAWNEER CO.
Berkeley: 930 Dwight Way, TH 5-8710

METAL FRAMING
UNISTRUT OF NORTHERN CALIFORNIA
Berkeley: 2547-9th St., TH 1-3031
Enterprise 1-2204

METAL GRATING
KLEMP METAL GRATING CORP.
Chicago, Ill.: 6601 So. Melvina St.

METAL LATH—EXPANDED
PACIFIC CEMENT & AGGREGATES, INC.
San Francisco: 400 Alabama St., KL 2-1616

METAL PARTITIONS
THE E. F. HAUSERMAN CO.
San Francisco: 485 Brannan St., YU 2-5477

METAL PRODUCTS
FORDERER CORNICE WORKS
San Francisco: 269 Potrero Ave., HE 1-4100

MILLWORK
CENTRAL MILL & CABINET CO.
San Francisco: 1595 Fairfax Ave., VA 4-7316
THE FINK & SCHINDLER CO.
San Francisco: 552 Brannan St., EX 2-1513
MULLEN MFG. CO.
San Francisco: 64 Rausch St., UN 1-5815
PACIFIC MFG. CO.
San Francisco: 16 Beale St., GA 1-7755
Santa Clara: 2610 The Alameda, S. C. 607
Los Angeles: 6820 McKinley Ave., TH 4156
SOUTH CITY LUMBER & SUPPLY CO.
So. San Francisco: Railroad & Spruce, PL 5-7085

OFFICE EQUIPMENT
GENERAL FIREPROOFING CO.
Los Angeles: 1200 South Hope St., RI 7-7501
San Francisco: 1025 Howard St., HE 1-7070
Oakland: 332-19th St., GL 2-4280

OIL BURNERS
S. T. JOHNSON CO.
Oakland: 940 Arlington Ave., GL 2-6000
San Francisco: 585 Potrero Ave., MA 1-2757
Philadelphia, Pa.: 401 North Broad St.

ORNAMENTAL IRON
MICHEL & PFEFFER IRON WORKS
So. San Francisco: 212 Shaw Rd., PL 5-8983

PAINTING
R. P. PAOLI & CO.
San Francisco: 2530 Lombard St., WE 1-1632
SINCLAIR PAINT CO.
San Francisco: 2112-15th St., HE 1-2196
D. ZELINSKY & SONS
San Francisco: 165 Groove St., MA 1-7400

PHOTOGRAPHS
Construction Progress
FRED ENGLISH
Belmont, Calif.: 1310 Old County Road, LY 1-0385

PLASTER
PACIFIC CEMENT & AGGREGATE INC.
San Francisco: 400 Alabama St., KL 2-1616

PLASTIC PRODUCTS
PLASTIC SALES & SERVICE
San Francisco: 409 Bryant St., DO 2-6433
WEST COAST INDUSTRIES
San Francisco: 3150-18th St., MA 1-5657

PLUMBING
BROADWAY PLUMBING CO.
San Francisco: 1790 Yosemite Ave., MI 8-4250
E. C. BRAUN CO.
Berkeley: 2115 Fourth St., TH 5-2356
C. W. HALL
Santa Rosa: 1665 Sebastopol Rd., SR 6354
HAWS DRINKING FAUCET CO.
Berkeley: 1435 Fourth St., LA 5-3341
JOSAM PACIFIC CO.
San Francisco: 765 Folsom St., EX 2-3143
LOUIS V. KELLER
San Francisco: 289 Tehama St., YU 6-6252
L. J. KRUSE CO.
Oakland: 6247 College Ave., OL 2-8332
JAS. A. NELSON CO.
San Francisco: 1375 Howard St., HE 1-0140
RODONI-BECKER CO., INC.
San Francisco: 455-10th St., MA 1-3662
SCOTT CO.
Oakland: 1919 Market St., GL 1-1937

POST PULLER
HOLLAND MFG. CO.
No. Sacramento: 1202 Dixieanne

PUMPING MACHINERY
SIMONDS MACHINERY CO.
San Francisco: 816 Folsom St., DO 2-6794

ROOFING
ANCHOR ROOFING CO.
San Francisco: 1671 Galvez Ave., VA 4-8140
ALTA ROOFING CO.
San Francisco: 1400 Egbert Ave., MI 7-2173
REGAL ROOFING CO.
San Francisco: 930 Innes Ave., VA 4-3261

ROOF SCUTTLES
THE BILCO CO.
New Haven, Conn.
Oakland: Geo. B. Schultz, 190 MacArthur Blvd.
Sacramento: Harry B. Ogle & Assoc., 1331 T St.
Fresno: Healey & Repovich, 1703 Fulton St.
Reseda: Daniel Dunner, 6200 Alonzo Ave.

ROOF TRUSSES
EASYBOW ENGINEERING & RESEARCH CO.
Oakland: 13th & Wood Sts., GL 2-0805

SAFES
THE HERMANN SAFE CO.
San Francisco: 1699 Market St., UN 1-6644

SEWER PIPE
GLADDING, McBEAN & CO.
San Francisco: 9th & Harrison, UN 1-7400
Los Angeles: 2901 Los Feliz Blvd., OL 2121

SHEET METAL
MICHEL & PFEFFER IRON WORKS
So. San Francisco: 212 Shaw Rd., PL 5-8983

SOUND EQUIPMENT
STROMBERG-CARLSON CO.
San Francisco: 1805 Rollins Rd., Burlingame, OX 7-3630
Los Angeles: 5414 York Blvd., CL 7-3939

SPRINKLERS
BARNARD ENGINEERING CO.
San Francisco: 35 Elmira St., JU 5-4642

STEEL—STRUCTURAL & REINFORCING
COLUMBIA-GENEVA DIV., U. S. STEEL CORP.
San Francisco: Russ Bldg., SU 1-2500
Los Angeles: 2087 E. Slauson, LA 1171
Portland, Ore.: 2345 N.W. Nicolai, BE 7261
Seattle, Wn.: 1331-3rd Ave. Bldg., MA 1972
Salt Lake City, Utah: Walker Bank Bldg., SL 3-6733
HERRICK IRON WORKS
Oakland 18th & Campbell, GL 1-1767
INDEPENDENT IRON WORKS, INC.
Oakland: 780 Pine St., TE 2-0160
JUDSON PACIFIC MURPHY CORP.
Emeryville: 4300 Eastshore Highway, OL 3-1717
REPUBLIC STEEL CORP.
San Francisco: 116 New Montgomery St., GA 1-0977
Los Angeles: Edison Bldg.
Seattle: White-Henry Stuart Bldg.
Salt Lake City: Walker Bank Bldg.
Denver: Continental Oil Bldg.
SOULE STEEL CO.
San Francisco: 1750 Army St., VA 4-4141

STEEL FORMS
STEELFORM CONTRACTING CO.
San Francisco: 666 Harrison St., DO 2-5582

SWIMMING POOLS
SIERRA MFG. CO.
Walnut Creek, Calif.: 1719 Mt. Diablo Blvd.

SWIMMING POOL FITTINGS
JOSAM PACIFIC CO.
San Francisco: 765 Folsom St., EX 2-3143

TESTING LABORATORIES
(ENGINEERS & CHEMISTS)
ABBOT A. HANKS, INC.
San Francisco: 624 Sacramento St., GA 1-1697
ROBERT W. HUNT COMPANY
San Francisco: 500 Iowa, MI 7-0224
Los Angeles: 3050 E. Slauson, JE 9131
Chicago, New York, Pittsburgh
PITTSBURGH TESTING LABORATORY
San Francisco: 651 Howard St., EX 2-1747

TILE—CLAY & WALL
GLADDING McBEAN & CO.
San Francisco: 9th & Harrison Sts., UN 1-7400
Los Angeles: 2901 Los Feliz Blvd., OL 2121
Portland: 110 S.E. Main St., EA 6179
Seattle: 945 Elliott Ave. West, 6A 0330
Spokane: 1102 No. Monroe St., BR 3259
KRAFTILE CO.
Niles, Calif.: Niles 3611.
San Francisco: 50 Hawthorne St., DO 2-3780
Los Angeles: 406 So. Main St., MA 7241

TILE—TERRAZZO
NATIONAL TILE & TERAZZO CO.
San Francisco: 198 Mississippi St., UN 1-0273

TIMBER—TREATED
J. H. BAXTER CO.
San Francisco: 200 Bush St., YU 2-0200
Los Angeles: 3450 Wilshire Blvd., DU 8-9591

TIMBER TRUSSES
EASYBOW ENGINEERING & RESEARCH CO.
Oakland: 13th & Wood Sts., GL 2-0805

TRUCKING
PASSETTI TRUCKING CO.
San Francisco: 264 Clementina St., GA 1-5297

UNDERPINNING & SHORING
D. J. & T. SULLIVAN
San Francisco: 1942 Folsom St., MA 1-1545

WALL PAPER
WALLPAPERS, INC.
Oakland: 384 Grand Ave., GL 2-0451

WAREHOUSE AND STORAGE EQUIPMENT AND SHELVING
GENERAL FIREPROOFING CO.
Los Angeles: 1200 South Hope St., RI 7-7501
San Francisco: 1025 Howard St., HE 1-7070
Oakland: 332-19th St., GL 2-4280

WATERPROOFING MATERIALS
CONRAD SOVIG CO.
San Francisco: 875 Bryant St., HE 1-1345

WATERSTOPS (P.V.C.)
TECON PRODUCTS, LTD.
Vancouver, B.C.: 681 E. Hastings St.
Seattle: 304 So. Alaskan Way

WINDOW SHADES
SHADES, INC.
San Francisco: 80 Tehama St., DO 2-7092

CONSTRUCTION CONTRACTS AWARDED AND MISCELLANEOUS PERSONNEL DATA

WAREHOUSE BLDG., San Leandro, Alameda county. Sears Roebuck & Co., Los Angeles, owner. Work consists of a new warehouse building at a cost of $1,202,000 and a Service Center Office at a cost of $72,000. ARCHITECT: A. E. Alexander, 918 Harrison St., San Francisco. GENERAL CONTRACTOR: Hilp & Rhodes, 918 Harrison St., San Francisco.

ELEMENTARY SCHOOL, Pico Street, Bakersfield. Bakersfield City School District, owner. Frame and stucco; 38,174 sq. ft. of area, rock roof, concrete and asphalt tile floors, radiant heating in Administration Building and Kindergarten; forced air heating in other portions; ceramic tile, interior plaster and plywood partitions, steel sash. fencing and paving—$491,900. ARCHITECT: Ernest L. McCoy, 2811

"H" St., Bakersfield. GENERAL CONTRACTOR: Fred S. Macomber, 2727 N. Cedar Ave., Fresno.

ELEMENTARY SCHOOL, Prairie, Shively, Humboldt county. Bluff Prairie School District, Shively, owner. Wood frame construction, 2 classrooms—$38,372. ARCHITECT: Gerald D. Matson, 537 "G" St., Eureka. GENERAL CONTRACTOR: Beacom Const. Co., P.O. Box 297, Fortuna.

CHURCH LIBRARY, Berkeley, Alameda county. Pacific Lutheran Theological Seminary, Berkeley, owner. 2-story masonry and structural steel, curtain wall construction—$145,000. ARCHITECT: Ratcliff & Ratcliff, 2286 Fulton St., Berkeley. GENERAL CONTRACTOR: Greuner Const. Co., 430 40th St., Oakland.

AUTO SALES BLDG. ADD'N, Arcadia, Los Angeles county. Charles Henderson, Arcadia, owner. 1-story steel frame and plate glass wall; 1645 sq. ft. of area, steel deck, composition roof, colored concrete slab floor, acoustical tile ceiling, aluminum entrance door, electrical work, painting, asphalt concrete paving—$16,238. ARCHITECT: Weimer & Fickes, 107 W. Huntington Dr., Arcadia. GENERAL CONTRACTOR: Hazen Albaugh, 225 Norumbega Dr., Monrovia.

OFFICE BLDG., Eureka, Humboldt county. Eureka Corp., Eureka, owner. 1-story; 13,000 sq. ft. in area, also 10,000 sq. ft. basement for auto parking. ARCHITECT: German Milono, 402 Jackson St., San Francisco. GENERAL CONTRACTOR: Crown Development Co., 1 Montgomery St., San Francisco.

HOSPITAL, Los Angeles. Southwest Foundation Hospital, Los Angeles, owner. 99-bed medical-surgical hospital; 54,452 sq. ft. of area, reinforced brick construction, composition roof, full basement, caissons, air conditioning, plumbing, electrical,

steel sash, X-ray facilities, elevators, remote controlled TV, piped oxygen, intercom system, asphalt paving. ARCHITECT: Nielsen & Moffatt, 4072 Crenshaw Blvd., Los Angeles. GENERAL CONTRACTOR: Parr Cont., Co., 5677 Selmaraine Dr., Culver City.

FIRE STATION, Enterprise, Shasta county. Enterprise Public Utility District, owner. Structural steel frame construction; facilities for equipment garage, living quarters and offices—$31,520. ENGINEER: Clair A. Hill & Associates, 1525 Court St., Redding. GENERAL CONTRACTOR: John Reiner, 1615 Walnut St., Redding.

STORE, Los Angeles. Jacob Felder, Los Angeles, owner. Brick building, 28 x 36 ft., composition roofing, interior plaster, acoustical tile ceiling, concrete slab and asphalt tile floors, security sash, structural steel, asphalt paving—$12,300. ARCHITECT: Cohn & Graham, 109 N. Larchmont Blvd., Los Angeles. GENERAL CONTRACTOR: B. C. G. Construction Co., 109 N. Larchmont Blvd., Los Angeles.

ELEMENTARY SCHOOL ADD'N, Burlingame, San Mateo county. Burlingame School District, owner. Wood frame construction, composition roofing; additional facilities for 4 classrooms—$113,-053. ARCHITECT: Hertzka & Knowles, 32 Fremont St., San Francisco. GENERAL CONTRACTOR: Stevenson-Pacific Co., 1135 Chestnut St., Redwood City.

CHURCH SCHOOL ADD'N, Covina, Los Angeles county. Roman Catholic Archbishop of Los Angeles, owner. Brick ma-

sonry classroom addition to Sacred Heart School; 5276 sq. ft. in area, composition roof, metal sash, slab and asphalt tile flooring, interior plaster, acoustical plaster, chalk and tack boards; facilities for 2 classrooms, kindergarten, Sisters faculty lounge and lay teachers faculty lounge. ARCHITECT: Verge & Clatworthy, 4342 Eagle Rock Blvd., Los Angeles. GENERAL CONTRACTOR: Clements and Hulst Co., 13220 Stanbridge Ave., Downey.

FACULTY OFFICE, State College, San Jose, Santa Clara county. State of Calif. Public Works Dept., Sacramento, owner. 2-story reinforced concrete building, designed for addition of 3rd and 4th floor at future time; to provide facilities for College faculty offices — $330,959. ARCHITECT: Anson Boyd, California State Architect, Sacramento. GENERAL CONTRACTOR: E. A. Hathaway & Co., 1098 So. 5th, San Jose.

WAREHOUSE ADD'N, Los Angeles. Stuart, Eckert, Willard Allers and David Chase, Los Angeles, owners. Work comprises 40 x 100 ft. addition to existing warehouse, composition roof, exterior brick, structural steel, security sash, metal rollup doors, pipe columns, asphalt concrete paving — $15,000. STRUCTURAL ENGINEER: John E. Mackel, 306 So. Union, Los Angeles. GENERAL CONTRACTOR: Morgan Lupher & Co., 453 S. Spring St., Los Angeles.

CHURCH, Corcoran, Kings county. First Presbyterian Church of Corcoran, owner. Work includes complete new Church structure — $198,484. ARCHITECT: Culver Heaton, 228 N. El Molino, Pasadena. GENERAL CONTRACTOR: Lewis C. Nelson & Sons, 2915 McCall St., Selma.

ELEMENTARY SCHOOL, Homer Jepson, Vacaville, Solano county. Vaca Valley Union High School District, Vacaville, owner. Wood frame, concrete tilt-up walls; facilities for administration building, homemaking, 6 classrooms, shop building, science, multi-purpose room, boys' and girls' shower and locker rooms, toilet facilities—$567,900. ARCHITECT: Beland & Gianelli & Hansen, 336 Merchant St., Vacaville. GENERAL CONTRACTOR: Carvers Const. Co., P. O. Box 484, Stockton.

GOLF CLUB HOUSE, Bermuda Dunes, Riverside county. Frame and plaster building; 5000 sq. ft. area, composition roof, concrete slab, plaster interior, stone work, air conditioning, plumbing, electrical work, aluminum windows, masonry and asphalt

paving. ARCHITECT: Chris Choate, 1334 Westwood Blvd., Los Angeles. GENERAL CONTRACTOR: Ernie Dunlevie, 40751 Adams St., Indio.

HANGAR ADD'N, and maintenance building, San Francisco International Airport. American Air Lines, San Francisco, owner. 4-bay addition to existing hangar facilities; structural steel frame, gypsum roof deck with steel sash, moving exit doors, heavy duty paving for planes, paved auto parking area, some exterior lighting, 3 concrete pads for aircraft parking, jet blast fence of precast concrete—$421,400. ARCHITECT: Warnecke & Warnecke, 111 New Montgomery St., San Francisco. GENERAL CONTRACTOR: Williams & Burrows, 500 Harbor Blvd., Belmont.

LABORATORY & OFFICE, Pacoima, Los Angeles county. Sundstrand Machine Tool Co., Pacoima, owner. Precast concrete, tilt-up general office and research and development laboratory building; 81 x 181 ft., gypsum roof decking, composition gravel roof, tapered steel girders, aluminum facia, concrete slab, asphalt tile, suspended ceiling, drywall, steel fire doors, acoustical tile ceilings, liquid oxygen storage tanks, metal toilet partitions, septic tanks, ceramic tile, air conditioning—$114,000. ENGINEER: Walter H. Preston, Consulting Engineer, 14542 Ventura Blvd., Sherman Oaks.

BARRACKS BLDG., Ranger Station, Bishop, Inyo county. U.S. Forest Service, San Francisco, owner. Construction of a 10-man barracks building at the Mammoth Ranger Station, Inyo National Forest — $24,547. GENERAL CONTRACTOR: George A. Jarvis, Bishop.

COMMERCIAL BLDG., Sacramento. Lamco Electric Co., Sacramento, owner. 1-story concrete block, wood truss roof—$64,444. ARCHITECT: Rickey & Brooks, 2015 "J" St., Sacramento. GENERAL CONTRACTOR: Holdener Const. Co., 2608 "R" St., Sacramento.

CHAPEL ADD'N., Berkeley, Alameda county. Berkeley Hills Chapel, Berkeley, owner. Wood and frame construction of an addition to the existing Chapel—$49,493. ARCHITECT: Nakahara & Nakahara, 2520 Shattuck Ave., Berkeley. GENERAL CONTRACTOR: William L. Wallace Const., 2735 Hilgard Ave., Berkeley.

ARMED FORCES HOUSING, Kirtland Air Force Base, Albuquerque, New Mexico. U. S. Air Force, owner. Work consists of the construction of a 490-unit armed forces housing project at the base — $8,000,000. ARCHITECT: Flatlow, Moore, Bryan & Farburn, 1840 Lomas Blvd., N. E. Albuquerque. GENERAL CONTRACTOR: Y & C Construction Co., 16 Republic Bldg., Oklahoma City, Okla.

SCHOOL, San Jose, Santa Clara county. Moreland School District, San Jose, owner. Precast concrete bents, concrete block and wood frame construction; to provide facilities for Administration offices, 14-classrooms, 2 kindergartens, toilet facilities—$380,412. ARCHITECT: Clark, Stromquist, Potter & Ehrlich, 3200 Hanover St., San Jose. GENERAL CONTRACTOR: Wayne F. Pendergraft, 21708 Alcazar Ave., Sunnyvale.

OFFICE BLDG., Redlands, San Bernardino county. Robert Van Roekel, Redlands, owner representative. 1-story, con-

crete block construction, composition roof, tapered steel girders, mosaic tile, acoustical tile, wood paneling, air conditioning, concrete slab, plate glass, resilient flooring, glass and aluminum store front work, asphalt paving — $23,667. ENGINEERS: Lockwood & Johnson, Engineers, 132 E. Foothill Blvd., Rialto. GENERAL CONTRACTOR: Swen Larsen, 722 Eureka, Redlands.

CONVALESCENT HOME, Walnut Creek, Contra Costa county. Concrete block construction, complete facilities for 24-bed convalescent home. ARCHITECT: Leonard Ford, 1644 N. Main St., Walnut Creek. GENERAL CONTRACTOR: F. C. Kirkman, 1290 Walden Road, Walnut Creek.

HIGH SCHOOL, Moro Bay, San Luis Obispo county. San Luis Obispo High School District, owner. Complete new high school facilities — $1,125,915. ARCHITECT: Falk & Booth, 16 Beale St., San Francisco. GENERAL CONTRACTOR: Barnhart Const. Co., 785 Walsh Ave., Santa Clara.

DEVELOPMENT, Leroy Heights San Pablo, Contra Costa county. Orinda Homes, Inc., San Pablo, owner. Initial contract for development work on the Leroy Heights project; 31-garden apartments, with swimming pools; 181 single family homes—$3,000,000. DESIGNER: Jimmy DeRade & Associates, 1520 Cypress St., Walnut Creek.

SCHOOL ADD'N., Van Nuys, Los Angeles, county. Roman Catholic Archbishop of Los Angeles, owner. Addition to the St. John De Salle School; 58 x 110 ft., composition roof, interior stucco and puttycoat plaster, exterior brick work, acoustical plaster, metal sash, metal partitions, mahogany wood slab doors, tile wainscoting—$125,000. ARCHITECT: Barker & Ott, 4334 W. Pico Blvd., Los Angeles. GENERAL CONTRACTOR: L. A. Lafavre and Sons, 1845 Clark St., Tarzana.

SCIENCE BLDG., Davis, Yolo county. University of California at Davis, owner. Administration building, Unit No. 1, Biological Sciences—$2,104,200. GENERAL CONTRACTOR: Stolte Inc., 8451 San Leandro St., Oakland.

CHURCH UNIT, South Pasadena, Los Angeles county. Calvary Prebyterian Church, South Pasadena, owner. Church educational unit and youth building. Composition roof, wood roof framing, concrete slab floor, interior plaster, asphalt tile, sliding doors, forced air heating, acoustical tile. ARCHITECT: Orr, Strange, & Islee, 3142 Wilshire Blvd., Los Angeles. GENERAL CONTRACTOR: Ted Tyler, 174 E. Belvue, Pasadena.

Y.M.C.A. ALTERATIONS, Redlands, San Bernardino county. Board of Directors, Redlands Young Men's Christian Association, owner. Construction of new additions and alterations to existing building — $21,154. ARCHITECT: C. Paul Ulmer, 1168 E. Highland Ave. San Bernardino. GENERAL CONTRACTOR: Swen Larsen, 722 Eureka, Redlands.

BOWLING ALLEY, Greenbrae, Marin county. Niels Schultz, Sr., Larkspur, owner. Contemporary design with all bowling alley facilities, including cocktail lounge, snack bar, nursery and play yard; 1-story wood and frame construction, wood truss, built-up roofing, aluminum sash,

stucco exterior; facilities for 24-lanes. ARCHITECT: Raad & Zahm, World Trade Center, San Francisco. GENERAL CONTRACTOR: Associated Const. Co., 127 Beacon St., South San Francisco.

COUNTRY CLUB ALTERATION, Victoria, San Bernardino county. Victoria Country Club, Riverside, owner. Work includes interior work in card room and locker room, plywood panel walls, new bar, stainless steel counter top, cabinet work, wood folding doors, acoustical tile, lighting, electrical, and concrete — $17,190. ARCHITECT: Herman O. Ruhnau, Mission Inn Rotunda, Riverside. GENERAL CONTRACTOR: C. V. Brown, 3514 9th St., Riverside.

PHYSICAL EDUCATION BLDGS., Polytechnic College, San Luis Obispo. State of California, Public Works Department, Los Angeles, owner. 2-story men's physical education gymnasium building; reinforced concrete and precast concrete wall and roof panel construction; structural steel framing, floor area approximately 70,250 sq. ft. Also outdoor physical educational facilities — $1,097,200. ARCHITECT: Anson Boyd, California State Architect, Sacramento. GENERAL CONTRACTOR: Maino Const. Co., 2238 S. Broad St., San Luis Obispo.

ALAMITOS SOUTH SCHOOL, Garden Grove, Los Angeles county. Board of Trustees, Alamitos School District, Garden Grove, owner. Facilities will provide complete educational plant—$477,800. ARCHITECT: Neutra & Alexander, 2379 Glendale Blvd., Los Angeles. GENERAL CONTRACTOR: Sherman Johnson, 10329 E. Weaver St., El Monte.

CHAPEL & EDUCATIONAL WING, McClellan Air Force Base, Sacramento county. U. S. Army Engineers, Corps of Engineers, Sacramento, owner. Project consists of a Chapel and educational wing; 164 x 114 ft., concrete masonry, structural steel and steel joists construction—$392,372. GENERAL CONTRACTOR: Campbell Const. Company, P. O. Box 390, Sacramento.

BOWLING ALLEY, Canoga Park, Los Angeles county. West Valley Bowl, Inc., Van Nuys, owner. Concrete panel bowling alley; 168 x 203 ft. in area, composition roof, tapered steel beams, concrete slab,

terrazzo, vinyl, carpet and parquet floors, suspended ceilings, plumbing, electrical, plate glass, air conditioning, acoustic tile, concrete block veneer, asphalt paving; facilities will include a club room, billiard room, nursery, locker room, restaurant and cocktail lounge. DESIGNER: Furukawa & Tamasaki Associates, Philip Furukawa, Architect, 15112½ S. Western Ave., Gardena.

OFFICE BLDG., Alhambra, Los Angeles county. Utica Mutual Insurance Co., Alhambra, owner. Reinforced brick and masonry office building, 5000 sq. ft. area, Type I Modified construction, metal sash, composition roofing, slab flooring, air conditioning, metal office partitions, plumbing and electrical — $151,170. ARCHITECT: Taylor and Conner, 285 S. Los Robles, Pasadena. GENERAL CONTRACTOR: Steed Brothers Const. Co., P. O. Box 350, Alhambra.

IN THE NEWS

AMERICAN CONCRETE INSTITUTE MEETING IN LOS ANGELES

Sam Hobbs, local chairman for the 1959 Convention of the American Concrete Institute to be held in Los Angeles, February 23-26, in the Statler-Hilton Hotel, has announced preliminary plans and committee appointments.

The general committee to correlate all local planning includes: John McNerney, Los Angeles District Engineer of the Portland Cement Association; Byron P. Weintz, Chief Engineer for Consolidated Rock Products; William F. Norton, Pacific Coast Regional Manager of Ceco Steel

Products Corp.; C. Taylor Test, Director, Technical Services, Riverside Cement Co.; Glenn C. Thomas, President, Thomas Concrete Accessory Company; and Lewis K. Osborn, associate, architectural firm of Kistner, Wright and Wright.

First two convention days will be devoted entirely to technical committee reports and the annual business sessions. Entertainment will be highlighted by a trip to Disneyland.

GEORGE BURR RETIRES FROM KRAFTILE COMPANY

George Burr, completing 32 years of service with the Kraftile Company, Niles, California, retired recently under the Kraftile Retirement Plan established in 1956 as the result of a previous plan which was put into effect by company management some ten years ago.

Burr is the fifth member of the firm's employees to benefit under the plan, and the occasion was marked by a bit of reminiscing by Burr and an exchange of presents, one to Burr from his fellow foreman and associates, and one from Burr to Chas. Kraft, president of the firm, in the form of a chromium plated open end wrench, which according to Burr "opened the first round kiln burner valve when natural gas was installed in the Kraftile manufacturing plant in 1929."

FIRST WESTERN BUILDS BANK IN VISALIA

Architect James P. Lockett, 121 E. Main St., Visalia, has completed plans for the construction of a new $150,000 bank building in Visalia for the First Western Bank & Trust Company of San Francisco.

The new facilities will include a 1-story building, with mezzanine, exterior walls of faced brick, suspended acoustical ceilings, terrazzo and rubber tile floors.

HAROLD P. FIELD NAMED MARKETING DIRECTOR BY STROMBERG-CARLSON

Appointment of Harold P. Field as Director of Marketing of the Eleectronics Division of Stromberg-Carlson, division of General Dynamics Corporation, has been announced by George A. Peck, Vice President and General Manager of the division in San Diego.

Field will continue as general manager of Stromberg-Carlson's plants in San Diego, a position he has held since 1956. A native of Rochester, he joined Stromberg-Carlson's Research Department in 1947 where

he worked on microwave communications. In 1949 he moved to the test equipment engineering section of the company's Television Division, and two years later became Assistant Manager of Production Engineering. In 1953 he was appointed Manager of Test Equipment Engineering, a position he held until his transfer to the San Diego position.

Field is a graduate of Phillips Exeter Academy and Harvard University where he received his Bachelor's degree in Physics in 1947.

TRUESDAIL LABORATORIES EXPAND FACILITIES TO TERMINAL ISLAND

Truesdail Laboratories has opened a new Terminal Island branch laboratory in Los Angeles, according to a recent announcement.

The new office is the only independent chemical and bacteriological laboratory in the Los Angeles-Long Beach Harbor area ready to serve the fish canneries and the fishing industry. Facilities for the bacteriological examination of water will also be maintained at Terminal Island.

ARCHITECT JOHN STORRS DESIGNS FOREST PRODUCT BUILDING IN PORTLAND

One of the world's most unusual and progressive structures will rise at Oregon Centennial Exposition and International Trade Fair next year as forest products industries pavilion.

The $250,000 building has been designed by Architect John Storrs of Portland, and James G. Pierson, also of Portland, and will cover 24,000 sq. ft. of area. It will remain as a permanent building following the Fair and will be used by 4-H groups of Oregon.

Announcement of the project was made by Roy Gould, president of the Diamond Lumber Company, Portland, chairman of a special forest industries centennial committee, and A. A. Lausmann, KOGAP Lumber Industries of Medford, chairman of the finance committee.

The huge building will consist of several sweeping hyperbolic paraboloids, each 50 feet square, supported by just six points. Unusual feature of the pavilion is that it is designed to be built completely of wooden 2 x 4's.

The Oregon centennial exposition and international trade fair will get underway June 10, 1959, and will run until September 17, 1959.

NEW OFFICE BUILDING FRESNO

Architect Leonard Malloy Abbott, 415 W. Center St., Visalia, has completed plans for construction of a 1-story, 140 x 40 ft. office building in Fresno for the Pittsburgh-Des Moines Steel Company.

The plans provide for addition of an additional story at a later date. Construction will be of concrete block walls, open web steel joists, concrete slab roof deck, pierced sun screen front and will include some 5,500 sq. ft. of area.

PLANS COMPLETE FOR NEW FEDERAL OFFICES IN SF

The architectural firms of Blanchard & Maher, 40 1st, San Francisco; Albert F. Roller, 1 Montgomery St., San Francisco; Stone, Mulloy, Marraccini & Patteson, 536 Mission St., San Francisco; and John Carl Warnecke, 111 New Montgomery St., San Francisco, as Associated Architects

have completed preliminary plans for the construction of a $45,000,000 new Federal Office Building in San Francisco for the General Services Administration.

Construction of the 20-story building is expected to be under way early in 1960.

SAN FRANCISCO ARCHITECTURAL CLUB CLASSES

Fall classes at the San Francisco Architectural Club, will include Structural Engineering, Fine Arts in Architecture and Atelier, plus the Architectural Seminar in the Spring of 1959.

The classes are designed for furthering Architectural knowledge. Complete information available from SFAC, 507 Howard St., San Francisco.

BUILDING DESIGN AND CONSTRUCTION COURSES OFFERED THIS FALL

Twenty-seven courses in Building Design and Construction will be offered in the Bay Area this fall by University of California Extension. Most of the classes meet in Berkeley and San Francisco; however, some are scheduled for San Leandro, Burlingame, Mountain View, Tracy, Castro Valley, Sunnyvale and Sacramento.

Course titles are Elementary Soil Mechanics; Theory of Thin Shells; Analysis of Indeterminate Structures; Mechanics of Materials; Structural Analysis; Reinforced Concrete Design; Structural Design in Timber; Structural Dynamics; Planning Today's House; Earthquake Resistant Design; Review of Civil Engineering; Building Design Development.

Estimating for Residential Construction; Construction Practices and Architectural Drawing; Review and Approval of Building Plans; Mechanics and Strength of Materials; Electrical and Mechanical Construction Inspection; School Building Inspection; Field Inspection of Building and Structures; Elementary Structural Analysis; Plastic Strength Design of Structural Steel; Structural Design; Applications of Structural Theory in Nuclear Engineering; Design of Reinforced Concrete; Structural Steel Detailing; Review of Structural Design for Architects; Inspection and Control of Concrete; and Prestressed Concrete.

TISHMAN REALTY TO BUILD LOS ANGELES SKYSCRAPER SOON

The Tishman Realty & Construction Co., Inc., will build a 22-story, multi-million dollar office building for general leasing in downtown Los Angeles, according to an announcement by Norman Tishman, president.

The air conditioned structure will contain 350,000 sq. ft. of area; high-speed electrically-controlled elevators, acoustical ceilings, flush fluorescent lighting, a large tenant garage. Work is scheduled to start in the Fall and completed in the Fall of 1959.

Site of the project is on Wilshire Blvd., between Flower and Lebanon Streets, just west of the General Petroleum Building.

DAN G. GILLHAM JOINS SAN FRANCISCO FIRM OF ENGINEERS

Dan G. Gillham has joined the consulting and engineering firm of Dudley Deane and Associates, San Francisco, as vice president and chief electrical engineer.

Formerly a Deane associate, Gillham has been most recently with International Engineering Company as senior engineer in charge of electrical work at Oxbow and Hell's Canyon dams in Idaho.

An Army Air Force major, Gillham was captured in Sicily and interned in Germany after participating in the African and Sicilian invasions. He is a Stanford University graduate.

ATOMIC ENERGY COMMISSION STUDY

The Atomic Energy Commission has awarded The Fluor Corporation, Ltd., Los Angeles, a modification to its current engineering contract to go forward on detailed engineering work for a waste calcination system to be built for the National Reactor Testing Station, near Arco, Idaho.

Essentially the system is a process to calcine and treat highly radioactive liquids that are produced in the recovery of fissionable materials from spent fuel elements in the chemical processing plant at the National Reactor Testing Station.

Presently the liquids are stored in cooled, stainless steel underground storage tanks. When the new system goes into operation, the radioactive liquids will be processed into a dry material and stored in underground stainless steel vaults.

KENNETH B. WOODS ELECTED PRESIDENT TESTING MATERIALS

Prof. Kenneth B. Woods, head of the School of Civil Engineering and director of the Joint Highway Research Project, Purdue University, was elected president of

the American Society for Testing Materials at the organization's recent 62nd annual meeting in Atlantic City, N.J.

A varied technical program filled with information useful to industry and commerce covered a wide range of important authentic data on materials featuring symposiums on Materials Research Frontiers, Radiation Effects on Materials, Bulk Sampling, and Particle Size Measurement highlighted the meetings.

A record attendance of 2988 made the meeting the largest in the Society's history. Other officers elected to serve for the ensuing year were: A. Allan Bates, vice-president of Research and Development, Portland Cement Association, was elected

vice-president for a two-year term; Frank L. LaQue, vice-president and manager, Development and Research Div., The International Nickel Co., vice-president for one year; directors included Lawrence A. O'Leary, head, Chemical Engineering and Research Dept., W. P. Fuller & Co., South San Francisco, California.

NEW CIVIC CENTER PLANNED FOR HAYWARD

Architect Mitchell Van Bourg, Hotel Claremont, Berkeley, is preparing preliminary drawings for construction of a new Civic Center to be built in the City of Hayward.

Included in the project is an administration building and multi-purpose auditorium. Estimated cost of the project is $3,800,000.

URBAN RENEWAL EXPERTS MEET IN SOUTH

Government and private experts on the social and economic problems of urban renewal met in a two-day conference in the Beverly-Wilshire Hotel, Beverly Hills, this month to discuss financing local programs, relocation, local code enforcement, and downtown renewal.

Speakers at the conference included Mayor Norris Poulson, Mayor of Los Angeles; Dr. Raymond B. Allen, Chancellor UCLA; M. Justin Herman, regional administrator of the Housing and Home Finance Agency; Joseph T. Bill, executive director of the Los Angeles Redevelopment

Agency; William Zeckendorf of New York; Harry N. Osgood of the Sears Roebuck & Company; and Dean Neil H. Jacoby of the UCLA Graduate School of Business Administration.

More than 200 participated in the conference discussions.

CHURCH ADDITION PLANNED

Floyd B. Comstock & Associates, Architects, 1620 Cypress Street, Walnut Creek, is preparing plans for construction of an addition to the First Congregational Church in Oroville.

The addition will be 2-stories in height and will provide facilities for an administration unit, offices, 13-classrooms, a kitchen, and a lecture hall.

STATION HOSPITAL FOR MARINE CORPS AIR STATION

The first permanent station hospital for the Marine Corps Air Station at El Toro, near Santa Ana, California, has been announced by Captain A. D. Hunter, CEC, USN, the District Public Works Officer and Officer in charge of construction of the Eleventh Naval District.

The structure will contain 42,000 sq. ft. of area, will serve as the clearing point for the Marine Corps Air Arm in the Pacific, and will cost an estimated $1,073,-812 to construct.

Working drawings and designs have been prepared by Welton Becket and Associates, Los Angeles architects and engineers, and construction contract has been awarded to Secrest and Fish, Inc., Whittier, California.

CALIFORNIA TEACHERS ASSOCIATION BUILDS NEW HEADQUARTERS

Construction of a new headquarters for the California Teachers Association in Burlingame will provide 60,000 sq. ft. of office space for the teachers and affiliated organizations, making it the educational center for California's professional groups.

Housed in the building in addition to the CTA will be the West Coast headquarters for the National Education Association and state offices of the California Association of Health, Physical Education and Recreation; California Association of School Administrators; California Junior College Association; California Scholarship Federation; California Secondary School Administrators Association; California School Supervisors Association, and

the California Business Education Association.

The building was designed by Welton Becket, F.A.I.A., and Associates, Los Angeles and San Francisco, architects and engineers. Robinson and Giddings, Structural Engineer, and Swinerton and Walberg, San Francisco, general contractors.

COOPERATIVE
APARTMENT
PROJECT

The first unit of "The Sandpiper," $9,900,000 luxury cooperative apartment project designed by architects Palmer and Krisel, A.I.A., Los Angeles, now under construction in Palm Desert, California, will be completed by September, according to present plans.

Each of the first units, consisting of 24 apartments, each selling for $18,000, have been sold to prospective residents.

When completed the project will cover an area of 72 acres, and the 550 apartments being planned will be in "clusters" of 24, with each cluster comprising eight triplex buildings, surrounding a swimming pool, sun terrace, and "ramuda." Included in the overall project are six tournament size tennis courts, twelve private putting greens and twelve children's play areas.

WIRTH ENGINEERING
COMPANY OPENS NEW
CULVER CITY OFFICE

The Wirth Engineering Company, Consulting Engineers, recently announced the opening of new offices at 9722 W. Washington Blvd., Culver City, California.

S. R. Wirth, Electrical Engineer, who heads the firm, is a graduate of Purdue University in electrical engineering, and a member of the National Society of Professional Engineers.

"PABCO" ENTERS THE
INDUSTRIAL INSULATIONS
CONTRACTING FIELD

"Pabco" Industrial Insulations Division of Fiberboard Paper Products Corp'n, San Francisco, has entered the industrial insulations contracting field throughout Southern California, according to an announcement by J. C. Voiles, general manager of the division.

"The new service is designed to serve the needs of both heavy industrial and commercial accounts," Voiles declared. For a number of years prior to 1948, Pabco participated in the contracting business throughout Southern California and Arizona, discontinuing the activity with the sale of business. The activity will now be resumed with commercial accounts being

serviced by Harry M. Voorhees, and the industrial accounts will be handled by R. E. Bounds.

Headquarters for the new Contract Department will be at 4231 E. Firestone Blvd., South Gate, California.

KENNETH S. TAYLOR
APPOINTED TO
ALL-BRITE STAFF

Kenneth S. Taylor has been appointed to the staff of All-Brite sales engineers, according to a recent announcement by Chas. D. Buchanan, vice-president of Fluorescent Fixtures of California, and will service the Northwest territory.

Taylor has long been identified with the lighting industry on the Pacific Coast.

MARKET GIVEN
SPECIAL CIVIC
RECOGNITION

Young's Market Company's new Metropolitan Distributing Center at 500 S. Central Avenue, Los Angeles, designed by Albert C. Martin & Associates, Architects, and built by Twaits-Wittenberg Co., constructors-engineers, has been given special Civic Recognition by the Los Angeles Beautiful Committee, according to an announcement by Arch L. Field, vice-president of the Los Angeles Board of Public Works and chairman of the Mayor's liaison committee with Los Angeles Beautiful.

The complex of buildings, located on the historic 10-acre Wolfskill Ranch site, consists of a large office and warehouse building, meat fabricating plant and garage. Extensive landscaping, decorative brick work, integration of parking areas, and clean design and careful engineering are emphasized.

OAKLAND PLANS
NEW HALL OF
JUSTICE BUILDING

Architects Confer & Willis, 366 40th St., Oakland, are completing working drawings for construction of a new Hall of Justice Building in Oakland for the City of Oakland.

The new facilities, estimated to cost $6,950,000, will comprise a new Police Department Center, Jail, and Courts to be flanked by a paved parking area. The basic design calls for a 10-story aluminum building; a 2-story jail building, and a 3-story courts building. Total area is 255,000 sq. ft.

M. M. PETTIS IS
APPOINTED REP
LITTLE BURNER

M. M. Pettis has been appointed Northern California factory representative for H. C. Little Burner Company, Inc., of San Rafael, California, according to a recent announcement by company officials.

Pettis was formerly connected with Thompson & Holmes as Sales Manager.

REGIONAL SHOPPING
CENTER IS PLANNED
FOR PHOENIX

Completion of plans for the first stage of the 120-acre Maryvale Shopping City in the 4000-acre Maryvale development project in suburban Phoenix, has been announced by the architectural firm of Victor Gruen Associates, Los Angeles.

The $18,500,000 project is being developed by John F. Long, Arizona's largest home builder, and will contain 120 stores with a total of 950,000 sq. ft. of store

space. Parking space will be provided for 9000 cars.

Complete plans of the area call for a community of more than 15,000 homes, schools, churches, community buildings, hospital and medical center, recreation park, golf course, and industrial and commercial areas.

GARDEN APARTMENT DEVELOPMENT FOR SACRAMENTO

Randolph Parks, 2449 Brentwood Drive, Sacramento, has started construction of a group of seven 2-story Garden Apartment buildings on a 7-acre site on Fair Oaks Boulevard in Sacramento county, estimated to cost $3,000,000.

All ground apartments will have private patios, electric kitchens, air conditioning, pear-shaped heated swimming pool, carports, and one of the proposed buildings will contain 8 offices.

ST. IGNATUS CHURCH AND RECTORY

Architect Harry Devine, 1012 J Street, Sacramento, has completed plans and specifications for construction of the St. Ignatus Church and Rectory on Arden Way, Sacramento, for the Archbishop of Sacramento.

The 1-story building will contain approximately 18,000 sq.ft. of area; construction will be tilt-up concrete, steel beams, grouted brick, concrete slab floors, gravel roofing.

LIBRARY BUILDING UCLA

Architects Jones and Emmons, 12248 Santa Monica Blvd., West Los Angeles, have been commissioned by the Board of Regents of the University of California, to prepare plans and specifications for construction of the North Campus Library on the University of California campus at Los Angeles.

ENLARGEMENT OF RENO HOSPITAL IS PLANNED

The Board of Directors of the Washoe Medical Center, Reno, Nevada, have announced plans for enlarging the facilities of the present Medical Center Hospital in Reno to a 350 bed capacity.

The Board proposes the issuance of a $1,000,000 bond issue to be voted upon sometime in the fall.

HELP US KEEP THE
THINGS WORTH KEEPING

One of the most precious American Heritages is the right to worship as you please. But protecting our American heritages costs money—because *peace costs money.*

It takes money for strength to keep the peace. Money for science and education to help make peace lasting. And money saved by individuals.

Your Savings Bonds, as a direct investment in your country, make you a Partner in strengthening America's Peace Power.

The chart below shows how the Bonds you buy will earn money for you. But the most important thing they earn is *peace.* They help us keep the things worth keeping.

Think it over. Are you buying as many Bonds as you *might?*

HOW YOU CAN REACH YOUR SAVINGS GOAL WITH SERIES E BONDS *(in just 8 years, 11 months)*			
If you want about	$2,500	$5,000	$10,000
each week, save	$4.75	$9.50	$18.75
This shows only a few examples. You can save any sum, buying Bonds by Payroll Savings or where you bank. Start your program now!			

HELP STRENGTHEN AMERICA'S PEACE POWER
BUY U. S. SAVINGS BONDS

MADE TO ORDER!

To fit your requirements for extra large roof openings

**Double Leaf
Roof Scuttles**

See our catalog
in Sweets Architectural
and Engineering Files
or write for
A.I.A. File No. 12P.

When a building function calls for bringing bulky equipment or materials in or out, Bilco Type D double leaf scuttles do the job best. An aid to your planning, too, by eliminating or reducing the number of extra wide doors required in rooms and corridors below.

Low and out of the sight line to complement your building design . . . easy to operate . . . economical . . . ruggedly built for long, troublefree service.

Bilco engineers will be happy to assist you in the design and fabrication of the proper scuttle to solve special or unusual roof access problems.

Advanced design, finest materials and careful attention to every detail by experienced craftsmen reflect in the quality of the finished product.

Effortless opening and closing of the huge covers is made possible by the right combination of tubular compression spring operators.

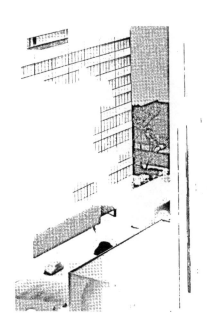

NEW
BEAUTYWARE
FITTINGS
...PERFECT COMPLEMENT
TO
BRIGGS
FIXTURES

Sleek, functional design with color impact

Briggs delivers the most advanced styling possible today in brass fittings! Contemporary lines in complete harmony with the modern look of Briggs Beautyware fixtures. Designed by Harley Earl, Inc., these bright chrome-plated brass fittings are available with interchangeable inserts to match Briggs compatible colors as well as white and chrome. Specify them for residential and commercial uses. Write now to Briggs for complete information.

BRIGGS MANUFACTURING COMPANY
WARREN, MICHIGAN

A T-8116. Combination bath-shower fitting, with automatic diverter valve in spout.

B T-8715-S. Shelf-back lavatory fitting, 5¾" centers, with aerator and pop-up drain.

BRIGGS
B E A U T Y W A R E

Versatile CERAMIC VENEER provides lasting beauty for Union Oil Center

UNION OIL CENTER

Pereira & Luckman, Architects; Del E. Webb Construction Co., General Contractor; A. H. Maxted, Inc., Masonry Contractor.

The new Union Oil Center in Los Angeles is distinguished by the effective use of light-grey adhesion type Ceramic Veneer.

Massive effect, beautiful fadeproof color and ease of maintenance were all obtained with modern, versatile CERAMIC VENEER.

Compatible with all materials, CV provides almost unlimited opportunity for originality, versatility and dramatic effect.

Ceramic Veneer

BY GLADDING, McBEAN & CO.

Since 1875

Detail shows how large scale appearance is accomplished by surrounding a group of pieces with a wide, slightly concave, contrasting color, accent joint. Smaller flush intermediate joints harmonize with the Ceramic Veneer color.

LIGHTSTEEL facilitated construction of suspended offices within hangar area.

Strength combined with light weight makes
LIGHTSTEEL the ideal choice for TWA hangar

LIGHTSTEEL was used for all interior partitions and ceilings in the office area.

TWA HANGAR LOT FACILITIES

Architect Engineer: H. K. Ferguson Co., San Francisco
General Contractor: Barrett Construction Company
LIGHTSTEEL furnished by: Tayler Products Corp., Millbrae, Calif.
LIGHTSTEEL erected by: Jack Dymond Lathing Corporation

Trans World Airlines' hangar lot facilities in San Francisco measure 320 ft. by 176 ft. Most of this is hangar space except for an elevated two-story area in the front of the building—containing offices, commissary, lavatories, etc. The structural system is a single cantilever frame on 32 foot centers.

Penmetal LIGHTSTEEL was specified for all interior partitions and ceilings in the two-story section, and for suspended offices in the hangar section. The LIGHTSTEEL provided a rigid, permanent construction, but because of its light weight afforded considerable savings in structural steel. And, of course, it also contributed to the fire integrity of the building.

In addition, LIGHTSTEEL helped to save on labor costs because it was easily fabricated, speedily positioned with minimum manpower and handling equipment.

For complete data on versatile LIGHTSTEEL, send for catalog SS-27.

TAYLER PRODUCTS CORPORATION
LIGHTSTEEL *distributor*
305 Adrian Road, Millbrae, California
OXford 7-4472

a name to remember   PM-192

ARCHITECT AND ENGINEER

EDWIN H. WILDER
Editor

CONTRIBUTING EDITORS:

Education
SIDNEY W. LITTLE, Dean,
College of Fine Arts and Department of Architecture, University
of Arizona, Tucson, Arizona.

City Planning
CORWIN R. MOCINE, City
Planning Engineer, Oakland,
California

*Urban Planning and
Shopping Centers*
FRANK EMERY COX, Sales
Research & Business Develop-
ment Analyst, Berkeley, Califor-
nia

Realty Development
ROY P. DRACHMAN, Sub-
divider and Realty Developer,
Tucson, Arizona

School Planning
DR. J. D. McCONNEL, Stan-
ford School Planning Dept.,
Palo Alto, California

Residential Planning
JEDD JONES, Architect,
Boise, Idaho

General Architecture
ROBERT FIELD, Architect,
Los Angeles, California

Engineering
JOHN A. BLUME, Consulting
and Structural Engineer, San
Francisco, California

Advertising
WILLIAM A. ULLNER,
Manager

FRED JONES
Special Advertising

★

COVER PICTURE

ALAMEDA COUNTY
HALL OF JUSTICE
Oakland, California
Confer & Willis,
Architects;
Donald W. Anderson,
Associate.

Artist's rendering of the new county
building as viewed from Seventh and
Broadway.

See page 22 for more details.

ARCHITECTS' REPORTS—
Published Daily
Archie MacCorkindale, Manager
Telephone DOuglas 2-8311

—*ARCHITECT & ENGINEER is indexed regularly by ENGINEERING INDEX, INC.; and ART INDEX*—

Contents for

OCTOBER

THE OLDEST PROFESSIONAL MONTHLY BUSINESS MAGAZINE OF THE ELEVEN WESTERN STATES

ARCHITECT AND ENGINEER (Established 1905) is published on the 15th of the month by The Architect and
Engineer, Inc., 68 Post St., San Francisco 4; Telephone EXbrook 2-7182. President, K. P. Kierulff; Vice-
President and Manager, L. B. Penhorwood; Treasurer, E. N. Kierulff. — Los Angeles Office: Wentworth F.
Green, 439 So. Western Ave., Telephone DUnkirk 7-8135 — Entered as second class matter, November 2,
1905, at the Post Office in San Francisco, California, under the Act of March 3, 1879. Subscriptions: United
States and Pan America, $3.00 a year; $5.00 two years; foreign countries $5.00 a year; single copy 50c.

. EDITORIAL NOTES .

SOMETHING TO THINK ABOUT

You are going to have an opportunity to "do something" about your representation in Congress this year, as the Fall elections will offer the choice of supporting, or rejecting, representation.

Measuring Congressional effectiveness, and determining whether a Congress has been a "good" one or not, depends on the individual point of view. One opinion is that a Congress which enacts a lot of new legislation is a "good" Congress. Another opinion is that a Congress which fails to enact much new legislation is a "do-nothing" Congress.

If we trace most of our economic ills to their sources we find that they are generally rooted deeply in bad legislation.

In any event, you as a voter have a chance every so often to make a decision as to your opinion of those who represent you in Congress. It's your responsibility to see that qualified men are elected.

* * ~

ECONOMIC CHANGES

Change is one of the striking characteristics of our national economic life. Individually, people attempting to "pursue the even tenor of their ways" are caught in an unceasing process of adjustment, readjustment and adaptation. Shifts are continuously taking place in the composition of output and the uses to which human, natural and capital resources are put.

These dynamic movements, though in part separate, are closely related to the growth of our productive capacities over time, and are essential to what we often term loosely "economic progress."

The process of growth and change is set in motion by the interplay of underlying economic forces as reflected in the markets for productive services and final products. Basically the forces of change are: 1) consumer demand; 2) technology; 3) changes in the supply of resources available and the improvement or deterioration of their quality; and 4) external economic relations.

In a competitive system of free markets these forces are constantly at work to modify both underlying cost and demand conditions of occupations and industries, to shift resources from one use to another and thereby enable society to obtain the optimum output of the right kinds of goods and services. The market does this automatically and without arbitrary coercion, by a system of positive and negative economic incentives—profit, loss, a flexible price structure, and wage differentials.

It is one of the great strengths of a free market competitive system that it does adapt automatically to changing conditions. The benefits of an economic system which is conducive and responsive to change accrue broadly to society as a whole. The increased output that results from transferring resources from less to more productive uses raises per capital real income. But, frequently, these changes produce pains and strains, especially in the short run.

However, because economic change is the common denominator of so many of our economic problems, our attitudes and policies relating to change merit most careful attention. In the final analysis, we can maintain our economic freedom only if we let the market do its essential work. It is tragic and ironic to contemplate the possibility that capitalism might become unworkable because of imperfections in the democratic process of our times.

*

BUILDING CODES

The realization of the gains from technological invention often requires changes in economic institutions and laws regulating economic activity. Our society must constantly wrestle with this facet of economic growth. One of the great problems is the multiplicity of local building codes, many of which are archaic and wasteful, and their effect on the costs of construction.

It has been estimated that the chaos and confusion created by hundreds of conflicting local building codes result in, on the average, an added cost of $1,000 per new house.

On the basis of one million new homes per year, this would add up to a billion dollars of legally enforced waste. If the costs of feather-bedding techniques and restrictions enforced in the construction industry were added to building code wastes, the unnecessary costs of home building, and the possibilities of savings, would appear staggering.

The answer, however, is quite simple. Today there are four widely recognized model construction codes specifying performance requirements rather than merely techniques and materials, as applied to residential construction. One of these model codes will fit any community wishing to take the step ahead.

* *

YOUR EFFORTS to trim costs and hold down prices are the best hope for a continued business recovery. Any over-all increase in business costs right now would be harmful to the nation's economy. Probably one of the best ways to improve economic conditions would be a realistic review of the tax situation, less government waste spending, and a reduction in give-away programs . . . just try it.

Greetings!

NEWS and
COMMENT ON ART

M. H. deYOUNG
MEMORIAL MUSEUM

The M. H. deYoung Memorial Museum, Golden Gate Park, San Francisco, under the direction of Walter Heil, is presenting a number of outstanding special exhibitions and events during this month, including:

EXHIBITS: Paintings and Drawings by Vincent Van Gogh, a major exhibition of 84 paintings and 71 drawings and watercolors by Vincent Van Gogh (1853-1890). This comprehensive exhibition contains many of the artist's most splendid and best known works, only a few of which have been shown in San Francisco. Many of the works are being shown in America for the first time.

SPECIAL EVENTS: Charles Lindstrom will discuss "The Art of Vincent Van Gogh" each Thursday morning at 10:30; Lecture tours of museum exhibitions; and special study classes in art for adults and children.

The Museum is open daily.

SAN FRANCISCO MUSEUM
OF ART

The San Francisco Museum of Art, War Memorial Building, Civic Center, under the direction of Dr. Grace L. McCann Morley, is featuring the following special exhibitions and events for October.

EXHIBITIONS: Autumn Rental Gallery, special exhibition; Sculpture by Leo Bigenwald and Woodcuts by Oskar Dalvit; exhibition of Swiss Graphic Designers; Nature in Abstraction, an exhibit from the Whitney Museum of American Art; Ceramics by Bernard Leach; and the work of Four Photographers—Ruth Velissaratos, William J. Maund, Jr., William R. Hawken, and Clyde B. Smith.

SPECIAL EVENTS: Wednesday Evening Series, programs presented each Wednesday evening at 8:30 comprising guest lecturers, outstanding film presentations, and social discussions; Discussions of art each Sunday afternoon at 3 o'clock; Saturday classes for children to help develop experience in visual forms, awareness of expressive opportunities in the visual arts, each Saturday 9:30 to 11 a.m. Study and discussion Classes in Art will be held for 8 sessions starting Tuesday, October 14th at 8:00 to 9:00 p.m.; and on Thursdays, 10:30 to 11:30 a.m., six sessions

will be held starting October 6th on the Theory of the Arts.

The Museum is open daily.

CALIFORNIA PALACE OF THE
LEGION OF HONOR

The California Palace of the Legion of Honor, Lincoln Park, San Francisco, under the direction of Thomas Carr Howe, Jr., has announced a special October showing of special exhibitions and events to include the following:

EXHIBITIONS: San Francisco Art Association—Artist Members Exhibition; Painting by Lada Hlavka; and The Metal Arts Guild Annual Exhibition.

The Achenbach Foundation for Graphic Arts will feature a special number of Prints by German expressionists.

Of special interest is the announcement that on October 15th a group of twenty-one paintings of the 19th and early 20th century French School, the gift of Mr. Andre J. Kahn of Paris, France, will be placed on exhibition. Included in the collection are works by Harpignies, Lebourg, Guillaumin, Besnard, Guerin and van Dongen.

SPECIAL EVENTS: Organ Program each Saturday and Sunday afternoon at 3 o'clock—Mr. Richard Purvis, and Mr. Ludwig Altman. Educational activities offer the Fall-Winter series of art classes for children and juniors, each Saturday morning 10 to 11, and Saturday afternoon 2 to 4 o'clock.

The Museum is open daily.

MAJOR ACQUISITION ANNOUNCED
BY M. H. deYOUNG MUSEUM

The M. H. deYoung Memorial Museum, San Francisco, announces a major acquisition, the latest gift of its great patron Roscoe F. Oakes. It is a marble bust of Cosimo d' Medici, 1st Grand Duke of Florence, by none other than Benvenuto Cellini, one of the most widely known men in the history of the arts.

Although its history can be traced back to the 18th century when it was acquired by an Englishman in Italy, and although it has been in America

for over thirty years, its traditional attribution to Cellini had not been verified, so that its recent identification as a work by Cellini clearly described in letters and other documents of his time, is in the nature of an actual discovery.

Various reasons may explain why the identification of the bust has been delayed for such a long time. Cellini himself has somehow been misjudged, both as a man and as an artist ever since his famous autobiography was first printed nearly two centuries after he had written it. The book, soon translated into other languages, became a world success, so that still today everyone knows the name Cellini and has read or somehow learned about his fabulous adventures.

The very "fabulousness" of his stories accounts for the lasting popularity of the book, but it also caused many a smiling doubt as to the veracity of the writer. The pronouncedly eccentric presentation of the life story with its colorful exaggerations quite logically led also to a certain distrust of the remarks Cellini made about his art. His praise of his own works and his scathing criticism of those of his fellow artists could easily be ascribed to vanity and envy.

Moreover, only a handful of Cellini's works have come down to us. As a goldsmith he shared the fate of other artisans famed in their days. Because of the preciousness of the material later generations whose taste had changed would break up their inherited jewelry and make use of gold and gems for other purposes. Hence, of all such works elaborately described by Cellini, only the gold salt cellar he had made for King Francis of France has survived. Incidently, this famous piece belonging to the Vienna Museum was in 1950 displayed in the deYoung Museum along with other Vienna art treasures then on tour in this country.

Until quite recently only five of his major sculptures were known. Among them was, of course, his monumental bronze statue of Perseus, standing most conspicuously in Florence and duly admired by every tourist.

Curiously enough, recent researches, undertaken almost simultaneously in the historical and the art fields, have largely vindicated Cellini. Documents, especially from French archives, have furnished evidence for the truth of some of the most unbelievable stories related by Cellini—for instance, about his soldierly exploits during the sack of Rome or about his being given the full use of a royal castle by the king of France. Altogether, these researchers have shown that Cellini, though occasionally in error as to dates and minor details, or carried away by his own emotions, never intentionally falsified the facts.

At the same time studies done by scholars, in particular by the German Friedrich Kriegbaum, have

thrown new light on Cellini as an artist. Kriegbaum in 1940 had made a discovery which startled the art world when he identified two marble statues which for centuries had been standing unnoticed amidst the shrubbery of the Boboli Garden in Florence as two major works by Cellini, amply described by the artist himself in his life story and clearly recorded in the inventory drawn up after his death. It was actually Kriegbaum's discovery of the lost marble statues of Apollo and Narcissus, and his study of them in relation to other works by Cellini and his fellow artists, which first led Kriegbaum himself and then others to a virtual rediscovery of Cellini the artist.

The result was that for the first time now in the twentieth century, he is really beginning to be recognized as what he believed himself to be, and actually was: the most important sculptor after Michelangelo in 16th century Italy, who through his successor, Giovanni Bologna, influenced sculpture throughout Europe.

Cellini's importance as a sculptor will be greatly enhanced through the discovery of the marble bust of Cosimo. Cellini himself wrote: "I always had a desire to do some great works in marble." But we know that his desire was constantly frustrated so that even the two marble figures re-discovered in 1940 had been done almost in secret and he had never been able to sell them. The emergence, therefore, of a new major marble work, well preserved in contrast to the statues of the Apollo and Narcissus, which have suffered from centuries of exposure, is of quite special importance.

There is little doubt that the bust will be regarded as the most important Italian High Renaissance sculpture existing in America and among the major works of this type in the world.

VAN GOGH PAINTINGS TO BE EXHIBITED AT THE deYOUNG MUSEUM

The largest and most comprehensive collection of Van Gogh paintings ever assembled on the West Coast will be exhibited at the deYoung Memorial Museum from October 7 through November 30th, according to an announcement by Dr. Walter Heil, museum director.

This all-Dutch Van Gogh exhibition, comprising 84 paintings and 71 drawing and water colors, is largely owned by Vincent W. Van Gogh, the artist's nephew, and usually hang in the Stedelijk Museum in Amsterdam. Other masterpieces of the exhibit come from the Kroller Muller collection, housed in the Rijksmuseum in Otterlo.

Many of the works shown have never been seen in America.

FIRST PHASE COMPLETED

SANTA MONICA STATE PARK
SANTA MONICA, CALIFORNIA

WELTON BECKET & ASSOCIATES, Architects and Engineers
ENCINO CONSTRUCTION CO., General Contractors
JACK EVANS & ASSOCIATES, Landscape Architects
RICHARD R. BRADSHAW, Structural Engineer

Development of the Santa Monica Beach State Park reached the end of its first phase and beginning of the second phase simultaneously this month.

Work was completed on the first beach facility and started on the second unit, according to Randall M. Dorton, Santa Monica City manager. The first beach facility, which will soon be open officially, is located between Ocean Park Boulevard and Grand Avenue. It contains dressing rooms, showers and toilets, a concession section, recreation area, picnic area, and parking for 2,000 cars. It covers an area of some 50,400 square feet, of which 18,764 square feet are devoted to the parking area.

Second phase of the $430,000 beach improvement program will be located about one-half mile north of this park area between Bicknell Street and Bay Place.

Welton Becket and Associates is preparing architectural plans for a two and one-half acre park which will be the largest in the total beach improvement program.

This second park will contain facilities similar to the first including shaded recreation areas and a children's playground area filled with sand, swings, and slides and enclosed by a chain link fence. Near the playground area a paved waiting area with wall seats for parents will permit supervision of the children at play. Another fenced, enclosed sand area, sort of a "junior Muscle Beach," will be complete with gym equipment, parallel bars, and bar bells for older children.

Grass-lawned picnic areas will contain seven barbecue hearths and wooden tables and benches for 125 picnickers. Three sunken concrete fire pits are also to

(See page 34)

UNIVERSITY OF ARIZONA

DEPARTMENT OF ARCHITECTURE

The University of Arizona, Tucson, has announced the establishment of a new Department of Architecture in the College of Fine Arts with a five-year curriculum, according to Sidney W. Little, AIA, Dean of the College.

The new five-year curriculum has been designed to prepare its graduates for the professional practice of architecture. The curriculum has as its basic aim the development of a student's awareness of the broadest expression of Architecture, and secondly, its means of achievement. The faculty is interested in developing and producing individuals with ideas and initiative as well as with Architectural ability.

The announced curriculum consists of two basic phases. The first, as a Pre-Professional phase, covers the Freshman and Sophomore years. During this period the student will be introduced to a fundamental vocabulary in Design, Architecture, Basic Science, and General Education. This period is intended to make the student aware of the fundamental problems of Architecture, and the position of the Architect in society.

The second, a Professional Phase, covers the last three years of the curriculum. The major emphasis during this period is on Architectural Design. It also has a complementary emphasis upon advanced courses in Theory of Structures, Technics, and History, all of which are conceived as a further resource to Design.

The Department of Architecture will offer instruction by stages beginning with this Fall. The curriculum has been designed to meet the requirements of professional accrediting by the National Architectural Accrediting Board and registration by the National Council of Architectural Registration Boards through the State of Arizona.

PAUL THIRY NAMED CHIEF ARCHITECT FOR SEATTLE CENTURY 21 EXPOSITION

Paul Thiry, F.A.I.A., of Seattle, has been named chief architect for the Century 21 Exposition, scheduled to be held in Seattle in 1961. Thiry was selected from a field of 35 architects considered for the assignment of converting Seattle's Civic Auditorium area into a 10-million-dollar Civic Center, serving as the setting for the International Exposition, and was the unanimous choice of the Seattle Civic Center Advisory Commission and the World Fair Commission.

PAUL THIRY
Fellow A.I.A.

Thiry, internationally known consultant and planning expert, is a master architectural planner for the Washington State Capitol Grounds, the University of Washington and Western Washington College of Education. He is a member of the National Capitol Committee of the National A.I.A., with Fellow Architects Stone, Saarinen, Shepley and Justament.

The first phase of Thiry's assignment will be to direct completion of site and building concepts, fol-

lowing which working drawings will be tendered for the construction program. Multi-level structures have been recommended for the 72-acre site, in a development featuring open courts, terraces and plazas, surrounded by or adjacent to exhibition buildings, providing up to 1,500,000 sq. ft. of exhibition space, or the equivalent of 35 to 40 large auditoriums. The state exposition facilities will remain for public use, including a permanent "home" for the Washington State International Trade Fair.

THE AMERICAN ENGINEERING ASSOCIATION

A call for unity in the engineering profession so that there will be a single "voice" to represent the more than half million engineers in the nation was made by Mason G. Lockwood, Past-President of The American Society of Civil Engineers, at the Society's annual meeting in Portland, Oregon, recently.

Lockwood proposed as an initial step that the name of the Engineers Joint Council, which now represents about fifty per cent of the engineering profession, be changed to "The American Engineering Association," so that it would be better able to attain popular recognition. Several other internal engineering organization suggestions were made which, if put into effect, would have a tendency to strengthen the engineering profession.

The engineering profession, like every other endeavor in today's highly specialized economy, can no longer exist on an individual basis, and if the profession is to survive the "atomic" era, unity must be attained.

VICTOR GRUEN, head of the firm of Victor Gruen Associates, Architects and Planners, Los Angeles, left the middle of last month for a six-week trip to Europe where he will visit Germany, France, Italy and Austria. In Vienna, he will address several professional groups on shopping centers and city planning.

BRICK HOUSE

DESIGNED BY STRUCTURAL CLAY PRODUCTS RESEARCH FOUNDATION

As a Result
of Nevada Atomic
Blast Testing

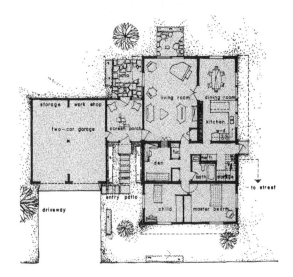

A new brick house design concept which offers protection against natural disasters has been announced by the Structural Clay Products Research Foundation, research arm of the nation's brick, structural tile and architectural terra cotta manufacturers.

The design concept was born out of research data obtained from the brick and tile industry's participation in the Federal Civil Defense Administration's Nevada atomic blast tests last year, Robert B. Taylor, SCPRF Director, explained. It was in these tests that a one-story reinforced brick structure successfully

(See page 36)

APARTMENT ... SAN DIEGO

HENRY H. HESTER, A.I.A. Architect

An outstanding example of modern San Diego architecture is the new four - story, million - dollar apartment house, topped by a penthouse, being erected at Sixth Avenue and Spruce Street in San Diego, which is called The Cecile Abbey.

The glass-front building, which will provide complete facilities for thirty large apartments, together with the penthouse, will face the city's famed Balboa Park, and will spread over a 210-foot frontage on Sixth Avenue and a 100-foot depth on Spruce Street.

Among the outstanding and unique features of the apartments are the large rooms, ample closet space for normal living, radiant heat with individual room controls, a basement garage with space for two cars if desired by the tenant, a spacious central patio in which is located a heated swimming pool and diving tower, a roof garden designed to provide relaxation area outdoors for tenants, and both passenger and service elevators.

Each of the apartments will be carpeted with wall-to-wall floor covering and each apartment will have a strictly modern kitchen with built-in appliances and plenty of cabinets. Each apartment will also be provided with an outdoor balcony which will

overlook the park.

Tenants who sign leases for occupancy before the new apartments are finished will have the added opportunity of choosing the interior colors they prefer, including the color of carpeting, as well as limited selections of cabinets and even arrangements of the partitions.

Every comfort and convenience of a luxury home has been incorporated in this project by the architect, Henry H. Hester, A.I.A.

CALIFORNIA COUNCIL ARCHITECTS

The California Council of Architects A.I.A., Convention Advisory Committee, headed by Loy Chamberlain of Oakland, has extended a special invitation to young people in architecture to attend the 13th Annual Convention, Oct. 15-19, in Monterey.

"We want to see more of the younger people in the profession at the convention — students, junior associates, architects just starting out on their own," Chamberlain said. "We feel they could get a tremendous amount out of it. The whole program this year has been planned with their interests in mind, as well as those of the established architects."

LADERA ELEMENTARY SCHOOL

MANHATTAN BEACH, CALIFORNIA

DANIEL, MANN, JOHNSON & MENDENHALL
Architects & Engineers

The Ladera Elementary School in Manhattan Beach, California, has been awarded an honorable mention citation in a national architectural design competition and in presenting the award to Phillip J. Daniel, A.I.A. partner, Daniel, Mann, Johnson & Mendenhall, the jury stated that it was highly impressed with the "fine architectural and engineering solution of a building on a difficult site."

The Ladera School was the only Southern California school selected for an award from 147 entries representing 31 states and Canada, and was planned, designed and engineered solely for the Manhattan Beach City School District.

The school has proven very popular not only with the students and parents, but also with the teachers because it "fits so well into the District's teaching program," and its beauty makes it a landmark for the city of Manhattan Beach and its compactness and cost make it a wonderful school building.

Phil Daniel, architect, said that he is "proud that another of our schools was singled out for an award. We are especially happy that it was the Ladera School as we feel it to have been a good architectural structure—functional in meeting the stringent requirements of the educational field and yet containing a strong element of architectural beauty."

This unique five-level Southern California school represents a dramatic solution to a difficult problem —the use of an "impossible" school site, a hill of shifting sand with a drop of 150 feet—the only site available to the district in the attendance area.

By designing a single building which follows the

sharp slope rather than a series of multiple units, the architects were able to achieve a remarkable economy of space. The initial development includes twelve classrooms, administrative offices, a health office and attendant facilities.

The plan provides for a series of terraced playgrounds, one for each classroom level, and allows the use of the roofdecks for outdoor teaching areas.

Structurally the building is an open framework with the cross walls serving not only as structural components but as earth - sand - retaining walls as well. Steel frame and wood joists have been employed for roof and floors, wood stud and plaster for walls.

Among the interesting design features is the continuous clerestory fenestration of low-light transmission glass, the extensive use of mahogany and the exterior covered ramp integrated into the structural plan of the building itself.

Construction was completed by the Bill Smith Construction Company, without change orders, in the same amount of time as that needed for a typical school plant on a level site, at a cost of $411,000. Currently under construction at the site are four additional classrooms, a double kindergarten, a multi-use building and extensive site development. Cost of this part of the project is $330,000.

WONDER PALACE

MULTIMILLION CONVENTION CENTER

DANIEL, MANN, JOHNSON, MENDENHALL, Architects and Engineers

ANAHEIM, CALIFORNIA

Located on a 37-acre site, minutes from the Santa Ana Freeway and adjacent to famed Disneyland, the project is geographically in the center of the vast Los Angeles metropolitan area. It calls for a plush 400-room skyscraper hotel, a spherical-shaped auditorium ball-sports arena to accommodate some 6,000 persons, an exhibit building covering 50,000 square feet and an outdoor exhibit area of 180,000 square feet.

Planned by Daniel, Mann, Johnson & Mendenhall, architects and engineers, Wonder Palace will represent the West's first completely integrated convention center. The project has been especially designed so that the business man can live next door

to the convention site and exhibit area, thereby saving valuable time in commuting between these elements.

According to Architect Arthur E. Mann, A.I.A. partner of DMJM, "The entire development has been so planned as to best satisfy the needs of the 78,000 populated area. In addition to serving as a convention center, it demonstrates a private enterprise solution to the off-season slump in local business. Wonder Palace will also provide an adult amusement center for the permanent residents of the Anaheim area by containing space for sports activities, spectacles and exhibits of interest to the community."

SOUTH SHORE CENTER · · · ALAMEDA, CALIFORNIA

ROBERT B. LILES, Architect and Engineer

Designed for Function and Beauty in One

Design of the 60 - acre shopping center at the South Shore, 400-created-acre development in Alameda, California, was conceived by the architectural and engineering firm of Robert B. Liles of San Francisco, with the civil engineering work involving streets and sanitary systems in the hands of Jones, Thenn & Associates of Alameda and Palo Alto, and the construction by the Utah Construction Company.

The attractive, colorful center, incorporating distinctive design and functional beauty, has been built around a colorful pedestrian mall.

Buildings are made of modern steel, aluminum and concrete, with the contemporary design of the facility to provide covered exterior circulation throughout for shopper convenience.

Total building area at the present time numbers 280,000 sq. ft. and is completely surrounded by 1,-250,000 square feet of parking area, sufficient to accommodate some 3,000 cars.

A distinctive feature of the exterior of the buildings is the use of exposed colored aggregates. Embedding of the stones was accomplished in conjunction with the use of 'tilt-up" construction. Casting of concrete panels was done flat, followed by the scattering of the colored rocks over the wet concrete. When dried, the panels were "tilted-up" and set in place, with the exposed colored aggregates highlighting the overall color scheme.

. "We have endeavored to develop an articulated group of buildings," Architect Liles stated, "rather than just a combination of individual stores. Every effort was made to maintain individuality for each business establishment, yet to coordinate each into the whole."

Because of the size of the center it was decided that the mall-type would prove most effective. Although the mall itself is over 1,000 feet long, the shopper is able to reach a maximum number of stores and businesses with minimum effort.

Throughout the center, color accents and decorative lighting have been used to add an atmosphere of gaiety. Every effort was made to "show off" each individual store to the best advantage of the tenant by developing, through the entrances and display windows, an invitation to enter.

CCAIA CONVENTION SPEAKERS

Four prominent American architects, an internationally known engineer, and a leading designer of contemporary furniture are among the thirteen speakers scheduled to appear on the 1958 CCAIA convention program, according to Loy Chamberlain, Oakland architect serving as Convention Advisory Committee Chairman.

Theme of the convention, in Monterey, is "Creativeness in Architecture," and will include consideration and discussions on such subjects as: "The Creative Mind," a panel discussion defining terms of convention theme and exploring characteristics of creativeness in man; "Materials as Creative Tools," "Structure in Creative Design," imaginative structural design and its relation to the whole of architecture; "Creativeness in Architecture: Analysis," and "Creativeness in Architecture: Synthesis."

THIRTEENTH ANNUAL CONVENTION

CALIFORNIA COUNCIL ARCHITECTS

MONTEREY, OCTOBER 14 - 18, 1958

Theme of the 1959 Annual Convention of the California Council of Architects AIA, scheduled for Monterey on October 15-19, has been designated as "Creativeness in Architecture" and unquestionably no better interpretation of the profession of architecture in modern economies and construction could have been chosen.

Several prominent American architects, an internationally known engineer, and a leading designer of contemporary furniture are among the many outstanding speakers who will appear in the technical sessions of the convention.

The CCAIA convention has gained in attendance each year until now it is difficult to find a non-metropolitan community with adequate facilities to handle the large attendance, and Monterey was selected as the convention city this year because of its historical background, adequate housing facilities plus the fact that the Monterey County Fair exhibit buildings were available for general meetings, round-table discussions, and panel conferences.

"The growing complexity of both our society and our buildings places heavy pressure on today's architects," Loy Chamberlain, prominent Oakland architect and Convention Advisory Committee Chairman, points out, "and these pressures sometimes make it difficult to practice architecture as an art, as well as a profession and a business.

"For this reason, we feel it is an appropriate time to re-emphasize the need of creativeness, to focus the profession's attention on creativeness as an essential quality of successful architecture, one that must be inherent in every phase of the architect's practice," Chamberlain said.

'Creativeness in Architecture" means the evolving of new forms from the materials at hand, and the development of inventive new solutions to building problems out of the architect's own thought and imagination, so the theme of this year's convention has been designated "Creativeness in Architecture."

Technical discussions will begin Wednesday afternoon with the first phase of the convention theme being devoted to "The Creative Mind," and will feature three prominent speakers: Dr. Donald McKinnon, psychologist and director of the Institute of Personality Assessment and Research, University of

California; Jo Sinel, industrial and graphic designer; and Charles Eames, well known for his designs for the Herman Miller Furniture Company.

Thursday morning will be devoted to the phase "Materials as Creative Tools," and three outstanding speakers, Robert B. Price, AIA, of Tacoma, Washington, president of the Southwest Washington Chapter AIA; David Countryman, one of the Douglas Fir Plywood Association research engineers, and Elmer Gunnette, District Engineer in Seattle for the American Institute of Steel Construction, will discuss the newest developments in plywood and steel, and the creative uses of these two basic materials.

"Structure in Creative Design" will highlight the Thursday afternoon technical sessions with Fred N. Severud, senior partner in the New York firm of Severud-Elstad-Krueger, Consulting Engineers, discussing phases of imaginative structural design and its relation to the whole of architecture.

Friday morning "Creativeness in Architecture: Analysis" will feature Victor Lundy, architect of Sarasota, Florida; Walter N. Netsch, Jr., architect and general partner in the firm of Skidmore, Owings and Merrill; and Paul Thiry, FAIA, Seattle, Washington, as speakers. Lundy, who received national recognition for his work, will analyze design of the Warm Mineral Springs Inn, winner of the AIA Award of Merit this year, and the Bee Ridge Presbyterian Church. Walter Netsch, Jr., will analyze the much discussed design of the Air Force Academy Chapel at Colorado Springs, Colorado; while Paul Thiry, long a leader in contemporary Northwest architecture will discuss several buildings at the University of Washington and Washington State College, the Church of Christ the King in Seattle and a number of residences.

"Creativeness in Architecture: Synthesis" will represent Friday afternoon discussions, and will consist of a summary address on the convention theme by Harry M. Weese, internationally noted architect of Chicago.

Well aware of contributing influences to the practice of architecture, the convention program committee has incorporated into the overall convention program a (See page 34)

A more complete detail of the convention program follows.

COMPLETE PROGRAM
CALIFORNIA COUNCIL ARCHITECTS, AIA

TUESDAY, OCTOBER 14

9:30 a.m. to 12 noon	Fall meeting, CCAIA Board of Directors—Mark Thomas Inn State Board of Architectural Examiners—Mark Thomas Inn
12 noon to 1:30 p.m.	Sunset magazine luncheon for CCAIA Board—Mark Thomas Inn
1:30 to 4 p.m.	Fall meeting, CCAIA Board of Directors—Mark Thomas Inn

WEDNESDAY, OCTOBER 15

9:30 a.m. to 12 noon	Registration—Fairgrounds Fall meeting, CCAIA Board of Directors—Fairgrounds State Board of Architectural Examiners—Mark Thomas Inn
12 noon to 1:30 p.m.	Regional luncheon—Hunt Club, Fairgrounds, Speaker: Philip Douglas Creer, FAIA
1 to 5 p.m.	Registration
1:30 to 6 p.m.	Exhibits open—Fairgrounds
2 to 4:30 p.m.	FIRST SESSION, PROFESSIONAL PROGRAM—Main hall, Fairgrounds. Panel discussion on "The Creative Mind." Participants: Dr. Donald McKinnon, Charles Eames, Jo Sinel
4:30 to 6 p.m.	Joint CCAIA-PC cocktail party—Fairgrounds exhibit area

THURSDAY, OCTOBER 16

9 a.m. to 12 noon	Registration State Board of Architectural Examiners—Mark Thomas Inn
9 a.m. to 3:30 p.m.	Exhibits open
9 to 10:30 a.m.	SECOND SESSION, PROFESSIONAL PROGRAM—"Materials as Creative Tools." Speakers: Robert Billsbrough Price, AIA, David Countryman, Elmer Gunnette
10 a.m. to 1 p.m.	WAL State Central Committee meeting—Mark Thomas Inn
10:30 to 11:30 a.m.	Coffee break—Fairgrounds exhibit area
11:30 a.m. to 1 p.m.	THIRD SESSION, PROFESSIONAL PROGRAM—"Structure in Creative Design." Speaker: Fred N. Severud
1 to 2:30 p.m.	Steak barbecue, Hawaiian entertainment—Fairgrounds
1 to 4 p.m.	Registration
2:45 p.m.	Door prize drawing—Fairgrounds exhibit area

The 1958 CONVENTION

MONTEREY, CALIFORNIA—OCTOBER 14-18, 1958

THURSDAY, OCTOBER 16 (continued)

3:15 p.m.	Architectural tours leave from Fairgrounds Chapter executive secretaries' meeting—Fairgrounds
6:30 p.m.	Dinner meeting, Regional Committee on Preservation of Historic Buildings—Mark Thomas Inn

FRIDAY, OCTOBER 17

9:30 a.m. to 5:30 p.m.	Exhibits open
9:30 a.m. to 12 noon	Registration State Board of Architectural Examiners—Mark Thomas Inn FOURTH SESSION, PROFESSIONAL PROGRAM—"Creativeness in Architecture: Analysis.' Speakers: Victor Lundy, AIA, Walter Netsch, AIA, Paul Thiry, AIA.
10 a.m. to 12 noon	WAL home tour—Carmel Valley
12 noon to 1:30 p.m.	Fish barbecue—Hunt Club, Fairgrounds WAL luncheon and fashion show—Los Laureles Lodge, Carmel Valley
1 to 5 p.m.	Registration
2:30 to 4 p.m.	FIFTH SESSION, PROFESSIONAL PROGRAM—"Creativeness in Architecture: Synthesis." Speaker: Harry Weese, AIA
4:30 p.m.	Door prize drawing—Fairgrounds exhibits area
7 p.m.	Cocktail hour—Fairgrounds
8 p.m.	Annual banquet—Fairgrounds
9:30 p.m.	Dancing—Naval Postgraduate School

SATURDAY, OCTOBER 18

All day	Producers' Council sports program San Simeon tour
9 a.m.	Buffet breakfast—Mark Thomas Inn
10:30 a.m.	JUNIOR ASSOCIATES' AND STUDENTS' SEMINAR—Mark Thomas Inn. Speakers: Neill Smith, Richard Hein, James Langenheim, members of State Board of Architectural Examiners
7:30 p.m.	PC Early California Fiesta—Casa Munras

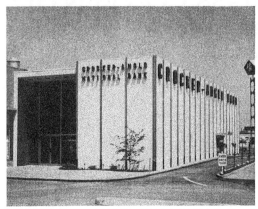

STEVENS CREEK
WINCHESTER
OFFICE

CROCKER-ANGLO BANK

SAN JOSE,
CALIFORNIA

HIGGINS & ROOT, Architects

The structure is notable for its simplicity of line and color. Exterior walls, of white with brown fleck, are accented by a gold-colored aluminum strip; they have black footings, and illuminated black sign letters are mounted directly on walls. The modern look of the interior features a high-ceilinged entrance area, lighting system combining luminous ceiling tubes and achitectural spotlights, and a color blend of beige, gold, brown and white. With a mezzanine for staff facilities, the building occupies a total of 5,100 square feet of floor area.

County Fair Grand-Stand

STOCKTON,
CALIFORNIA

Features cantilever roof supported by huge fabricated steel plate girders to give spectators an unobstructed view.

15 horseshoe shaped steel frames, standing 65 ft. high are set on 25 ft. centers to form 350 ft. long pavilion. Seating capacity 3,776.

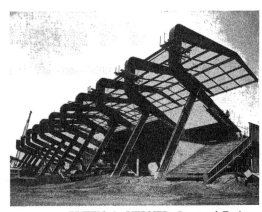

EDWIN A. VERNER, Structural Engineer

SCIENCE BUILDING - Occidental College
LOS ANGELES

PEREIRA & LUCKMAN,
Architects

The $1,350,000 three-story Norris Hall of Science building now under construction will contain the Mosher Science Auditorium and Lecture Halls and the Jorgensen Laboratories, providing Southern California with some of the nation's most advanced facilities for teaching research in chemistry and biology.

With a total of 44,000 square feet, the building has a contemporary design which relates to existing structures on the campus. Constructed of reinforced concrete, it will have a clay tile roof to match roof materials on other Occidental units.

Among design features is an entrance court with a canopy and garden on the first floor level which will lead into either the lecture hall or the science building itself. Pozzo Construction Company is the general contractor.

AIR VIEW of the recently completed Sea Arena, with original Marineland structures in the background. World's largest Oceanarium.

SEA ARENA - MARINELAND

PALOS VERDES, CALIFORNIA
PEREIRA & LUCKMAN, Architects

YOUNG'S MARKET

WAREHOUSE DISTRIBUTION CENTER
LOS ANGELES, CALIFORNIA

ALBERT C. MARTIN
and ASSOCIATES,
Architects and Engineers

The new plant is located in the heart of what was recently a major slum area and marks the rebirth of one of the city's most important central urban cores. It utilizes 400,000 sq. ft. of which 210,000 sq. ft. are under one roof.

A single-story warehouse of tilt-up concrete panel construction provides storage space, receiving and shipping facilities for wines and spirits and specialty groceries. Offices are in the same building with large areas of glass open to the exterior landscaping. A separate structure, with specially designed air conditioning to handle many different temperature requirements houses the meat storage and fabricating plant. A 5000-sq. ft. garage provides for the maintenance and repair of delivery trucks. Generous parking and extensive landscaping complete the site plan.

A.I.A. LEGISLATIVE PROGRAM

The California Council of Architects A.I.A., will follow the same general approach as heretofore employed in an effort to amend the Architectural Practice Act in the 1959 session of the California State Legislature as it did in 1957, the Board of Directors has announced.

Exact details of the bill which the Council will sponsor next year will be worked out by the Architectural Practice Act Advisory Committee under Philip S. Buckingham, the Board directed. In 1957, the Council amendments were passed by the State Assembly but killed by a Senate committee in the final days of the legislative session. Principal provisions were elimination of the "written notice" clause, establishment of a definition of architecture, and addition of exemptions paralleling those in the Engineers Act.

NEW WESTERN
HEADQUARTERS
BUILDING

TEXAS OIL COMPANY

LOS ANGELES, CALIFORNIA

WELTON BECKET &
ASSOCIATES
Architects & Engineers

The limit height building rising some 175 ft. from sidewalk, houses more than 700 employees; 217,000 sq. ft. of area; sheer areas of reinforced concrete cover ends of T-shaped bldg. while curtain wall system of aluminum framework, and porcelain enamel panels enclose remainder of structure.

CHANNEL 2
KTVU

JACK LONDON SQUARE

Oakland,
California

Designed by
Welton Becket &
Associates,
Architects &
Engineers

Washington Street Elevation

ALAMEDA COUNTY
HALL OF JUSTICE
A NEW TREND IN GOVERNMENTAL BUILDINGS

OAKLAND, CALIFORNIA

CONFER AND WILLIS,
Architects

DONALD W. ANDERSON,
Associate

By RAY WILLIS, A.I.A.

In the interest of economy and greater efficiency, a new trend in supplying buildings for city and county governments is developing. This concept involves the combining of the services of these two governmental bodies within the confines of one structure and under one roof. There are many advantages which accrue to such an arrangement. The biggest ones are efficiency and economy.

Such a venture is now in the process of building in the city of Oakland, California. It is a joint venture being carried out between the city of Oakland and the county of Alameda. Perhaps the best explanation

for what is going on can be found in the joint statement made by Mayor Clifford E. Rishell and Chairman, Board of Supervisors, Leland W. Sweeney, as
follows:

"The proposed Oakland Hall of Justice is the most
recent example of the new attitude toward cooperation existing between city and county officials. The
letters CCC, have again assumed special significance,
as they have become identified with City-County Cooperation.

"Until recent years, only lip-service was given to
efforts to cooperate on major projects of mutual concern. Now the people of Oakland are witnessing important cooperative enterprises in which Oakland's
role has been, in spirit as well as in name, that of an
All-American City. In addition to the joint planning
of a Hall of Justice which is to house agencies of
both the city and the county, some of the other principal areas of cooperation are: 1. The adoption of

the Mayor's formula for allocation of gas tax funds,
which resulted in the county providing the city with
$1,942,445 during a four-year period for improve-
ment of major streets and highways within the city;
2. Consolidation of city health services with those of
the county, which eliminated the double taxation of
Oakland citizens; 3. The arrangement whereby the
county provides custodial care for hundreds of Oakland prisoners at Santa Rita Rehabilitation Center at
less than one-half the cost of city jail care. This has
resulted in a savings of $770,000 to Oakland taxpayers
since January of 1956.

"The Mayor, City Council, and the Board of Supervisors are dedicated to furthering this cooperative
spirit to the end that the best possible service may be
rendered at the lowest possible cost.

"Having made reference to the proposed Oakland
Hall of Justice, the Mayor and Chairman of the Board
of Supervisors deem it appropriate to extend congratu-

Seventh Street Elevation

ALAMEDA COUNTY HALL OF JUSTICE . . .

lations to the architectural firm of Confer & Willis for the excellent plans for this structure."

These fundamentals were subscribed to by the councilmen of the city of Oakland, Lester M. Grant, John W. Holmdahl, Glenn E. Hoover, Fred Maggiora, Howard E. Rilea, Robert L. Osborne, Peter M. Tripp and Frank J. Youell; and the supervisors of Alameda County, Chairman Leland W. Sweeney, Chester E. Stanley, Francis Dunn, Kent D. Pursel and Emanuel P. Razeto. Cooperating in the program were City Manager Wayne E. Thompson, County Administrator Earl R. Strathman, City Architect John Papadakis; Director of Public Works Herbert G. Crowle, Chief, Engineering and Architectural Division, Karl F. Wieger; Auditor-Controller David V. Rosen, Chief of Police Wyman W. Vernon, and Presiding Judge Charles W. Fisher.

There are three basic and outstanding elements in the plan of the Oakland Hall of Justice which make for economy and efficiency. These three things are:

    a. Expandability

    b. Flexibility

    c. Utility.

This structure, which will house the city police department, city jail and the municipal court facilities for the Oakland-Piedmont Judicial District of the Alameda County courts system, is located on an entire block, bounded by Broadway, Washington, Sixth and Seventh Streets.

The concept of this structure is based on the realization that no building can be truly economical unless it has the three factors already mentioned. Perhaps it would be well to point out in somewhat more detail the three factors involved.

PLOT AND VICINITY PLAN Showing Proximity of Freeway and On & Off Ramps

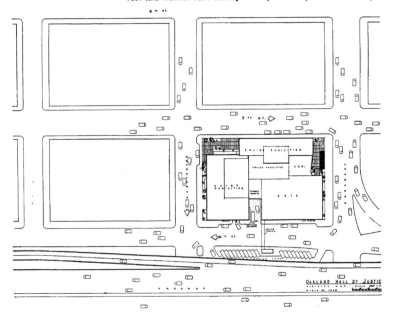

Expandability

The building is composed of three basic elements or "space containers" busing the following departments:

1. Police
2. Jail
3. Courts and related service areas.

This conception permits the expansion of the "space containers" vertically, and to some degree, horizontally, without interference or disruption of the functions of the others.

Flexibility

This element has been achieved by eliminating, to a great extent, interior bearing walls and columns, thus providing clear areas which, through the use of prefabricated metal movable partitions and a continuous underfloor electrical duct system, which provides for changing departmental needs in an efficient way.

Utility

The multi-story element, fronting on Seventh Street, is entered through a lobby which utilizes a "split-level"

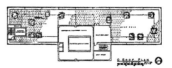

SEVENTH FLOOR PLAN . . . Top

EIGHTH FLOOR PLAN . . Center

ROOF PLAN . . . . Shown Third

Floor Plan at Street Level

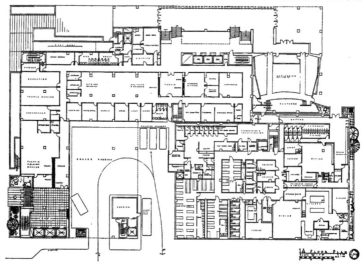

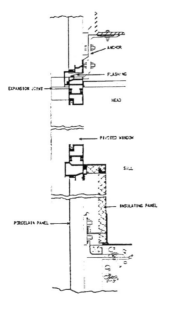

system, placing the main entry at a point midway between the two lower floors which contain the departments having the greatest public usage. Access is by way of a short flight of stairs, up or down. This system results in greater convenience to the public, reduces the elevators normally required to handle this great volume of public traffic and is one of the factors which reduces public circulation area to an abnormally low percentage of the total area constructed. This, together with complete air conditioning, intercommunication and pneumatic tube systems, acoustical treatment, high-level illumination and external sun control contributes to the high utilitarian characteristics of this building.

The major police activities include Patrol, Traffic, Inspectors, Records, Communication, Juvenile and Training Division, Criminalistics Laboratory and the Statistical Section. An auditorium for educational programs and large police "lineups" is on the ground level. Locker rooms, property and evidence storage,

FLOOR PLAN . . . Washington Street at left, Broadway at right.

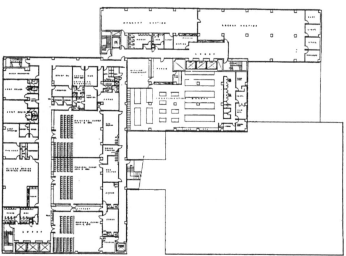

SECOND FLOOR PLAN

pistol range, building maintenance and mechanical equipment rooms are in the basement.

The Alameda County Courts section consists of six stories, and is in effect a separate and distinct building with its own lobby and elevator service. The ground floor is assigned to the traffic violations bureau which by necessity must be readily accessible to the public. In the next three floors are eight courts and their auxiliary departments. The entire fifth floor is allocated to the adult probation department, with the Prosecuting Attorney and domestic relations office occupying the top level.

The jail, designed as a holding facility for 400 persons, is a mechanically ventilated two-story windowless structure with a public entrance from Broadway and police and prisoner entry off of Sixth Street. The ground floor is devoted to the processing of prisoners, the administrative offices, dining facilities and holding areas. Dormitories and high security cells for both male and female prisoners are located on the second floor. The jail is connected directly to police "show-up" rooms and to the courts permitting the movement of prisoners to those areas without violation of security requirements.

Minimum maintenance has been the prime consideration in the selection of the materials to be used. The exterior of the building will be of glass, colored metal insulated panels and masonry veneer. The exterior walls are designed so that expansion and contraction

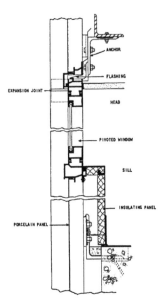

ANCHOR

FLASHING

EXPANSION JOINT

HEAD

PIVOTED WINDOW

SILL

INSULATING PANEL

PORCELAIN PANEL

VERTICAL SECTION at left: Is through wall showing vertically pivoted sash which is reversible for cleaning. Weathertightness is insured by the continuous flashing in the expansion joint at the window head and by designing each horizontal to allow for drainage. Anchors are designed for each adjustment to line, grade and centers and are welded in their final position. Insulating panel runs continuously behind wall diminishing heat loss through mullion.

system, placing the main entry at a point midway between the two lower floors which contain the departments having the greatest public usage. Access is by way of a short flight of stairs, up or down. This system results in greater convenience to the public, reduces the elevators normally required to handle this great volume of public traffic and is one of the factors which reduces public circulation area to an abnormally low percentage of the total area constructed. This, together with complete air conditioning, intercommunication and pneumatic tube systems, acoustical treatment, high-level illumination and external sun control contributes to the high utilitarian characteristics of this building.

The major police activities include Patrol, Traffic, Inspectors, Records, Communication, Juvenile and Training Division, Criminalistics Laboratory and the Statistical Section. An auditorium for educational programs and large police "lineups" is on the ground level. Locker rooms, property and evidence storage,

FLOOR PLAN . . . Washington Street at left, Broadway at right.

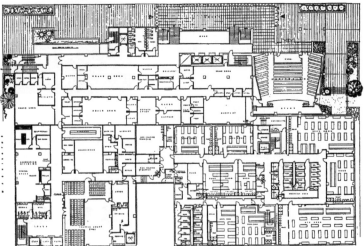

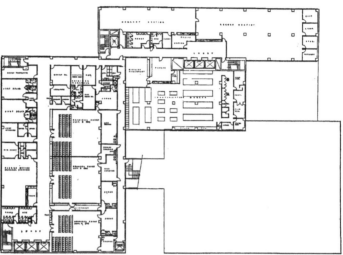

SECOND FLOOR PLAN

pistol range, building maintenance and mechanical equipment rooms are in the basement.

The Alameda County Courts section consists of six stories, and is in effect a separate and distinct building with its own lobby and elevator service. The ground floor is assigned to the traffic violations bureau which by necessity must be readily accessible to the public. In the next three floors are eight courts and their auxiliary departments. The entire fifth floor is allocated to the adult probation department, with the Prosecuting Attorney and domestic relations office occupying the top level.

The jail, designed as a holding facility for 400 persons, is a mechanically ventilated two-story windowless structure with a public entrance from Broadway and police and prisoner entry off of Sixth Street. The ground floor is devoted to the processing of prisoners, the administrative offices, dining facilities and holding areas. Dormitories and high security cells for both male and female prisoners are located on the second floor. The jail is connected directly to police "show-up" rooms and to the courts permitting the movement of prisoners to those areas without violation of security requirements.

Minimum maintenance has been the prime consideration in the selection of the materials to be used. The exterior of the building will be of glass, colored metal insulated panels and masonry veneer. The exterior walls are designed so that expansion and contraction

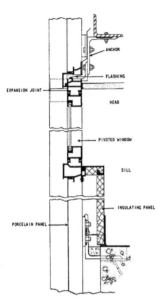

VERTICAL SECTION at left: is through wall showing vertically pivoted sash which is reversible for cleaning. Weathertightness is insured by the continuous flashing in the expansion joint at the window head and by designing each horizontal to allow for drainage. Anchors are designed for each adjustment to line, grade and centers and are welded in their final position. Insulating panel runs continuously behind wall diminishing heat loss through mullion.

system, placing the main entry at a point midway between the two lower floors which contain the departments having the greatest public usage. Access is by way of a short flight of stairs, up or down. This system results in greater convenience to the public, reduces the elevators normally required to handle this great volume of public traffic and is one of the factors which reduces public circulation area to an abnormally low percentage of the total area constructed. This, together with complete air conditioning, intercommunication and pneumatic tube systems, acoustical treatment, high-level illumination and external sun control contributes to the high utilitarian characteristics of this building.

The major police activities include Patrol, Traffic, Inspectors, Records, Communication, Juvenile and Training Division, Criminalistics Laboratory and the Statistical Section. An auditorium for educational programs and large police "lineups" is on the ground level. Locker rooms, property and evidence storage,

FLOOR PLAN . . . Washington Street at left, Broadway at right.

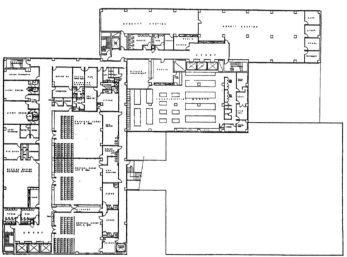

SECOND FLOOR PLAN

pistol range, building maintenance and mechanical equipment rooms are in the basement.

The Alameda County Courts section consists of six stories, and is in effect a separate and distinct building with its own lobby and elevator service. The ground floor is assigned to the traffic violations bureau which by necessity must be readily accessible to the public. In the next three floors are eight courts and their auxiliary departments. The entire fifth floor is allocated to the adult probation department, with the Prosecuting Attorney and domestic relations office occupying the top level.

The jail, designed as a holding facility for 400 persons, is a mechanically ventilated two-story windowless structure with a public entrance from Broadway and police and prisoner entry off of Sixth Street. The ground floor is devoted to the processing of prisoners, the administrative offices, dining facilities and holding areas. Dormitories and high security cells for both male and female prisoners are located on the second floor. The jail is connected directly to police "show-up" rooms and to the courts permitting the movement of prisoners to those areas without violation of security requirements.

Minimum maintenance has been the prime consideration in the selection of the materials to be used. The exterior of the building will be of glass, colored metal insulated panels and masonry veneer. The exterior walls are designed so that expansion and contraction

of the 'skin'" can take place without ripples occurring in the panels, or water leakage taking place where joints and various materials come together. Carefully designed and proven sealants are detailed and specified to assure a complete leak-proof job. The interior finishes vary from area to area but will consist mainly of terrazzo and vinyl tile for floors, metal movable partitions, permanent walls of metal lath and plaster and ceilings of acoustical plaster, acoustical tile, or of a luminous type.

Heating, ventilating and air-conditioning will be accomplished by a high velocity distribution system with zone control for each department. This, along with continuous fluorescent strips or luminous ceilings which will furnish a high level of illumination will provide comfort for the occupants and tend to increase the efficiency of the employees.

In summary, this building will provide comfortable, efficient, flexible space for housing the activities of the employees and will satisfy the demands of the future without penalizing the present. The foregoing all being accomplished within a container which can be maintained at minimum cost.

ARCHITECTS PARTICIPATE IN SCHOOL PLANNING LABORATORY

Stanford University has announced that a selection of addresses to be given at the Eighth Annual School Building Institute will be compiled and published

under the title, "New Dimensions in Planning Community Junior Colleges."

The unique role of the Community Junior College is presented by Edmund J. Gleazer, Jr., Executive Director of the American Association of Junior Colleges. Architects Mario Ciampi, Stanley Smith and James Fessenden share in discussions regarding development of administrative and student personnel facilities.

Germaine to the purpose of all discussions is the recognized need of cooperative planning of collegiate educational facilities. Included are a number of photographs, floor plans and other descriptive materials which portray successful experiences in the planning of Community Junior College facilities.

ENGINEERING FILM AVAILABLE FOR EDUCATIONAL GROUPS

"Building for Professional Growth," a 16mm film covering the activities of the National Society of Professional Engineers, has been released by the 46,000 member engineering group.

The 20-minute film will be "previewed" by the Board of Directors of the National Society at the organization's fall meeting in San Francisco, the latter part of this month.

Narrated by radio-TV network announcers, the film is centered around an explanation of the value and benefits of Society membership to the individual, and to the engineering profession as a whole. Included in the film are consideration of registration, legislative cooperation, income and salary surveys of engineers, public relations, and other professional activities.

MEDDLING BY PARISHIONERS MAY RUIN GOOD CHURCH DESIGN, ARCHITECTS REPORT

"The burning need in church architecture today is the recognition that good design does not evolve from compromise," Willis N. Mills, a partner of Serhoow, Mills & Smith, Stamford, Connecticut architectural firm, told the New England Regional Council of The American Institute of Architects last month.

Representing the Connecticut Chapter AIA on a panel on "Liturgical Requirements in Design," Mills

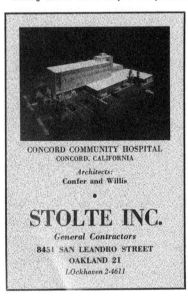

suggested each church planning a new building should have a small, representative group empowered to pass on the design of the new church as proposed by the architects.

"Too often, the design is subject to modifications by every group in the church," Mills said. "The result is mediocre design which pleases no one." He also made a plea for the wider use of contemporary design in modern churches, and defined contemporary architecture as design with basic simplicity, strength honesty, and repose.

JOINT SCHOOL CONFERENCE
TO BE HELD IN SAN DIEGO

A joint conference of architects and school administrators on the subject "The Three C's of School Planning — Communication, Cooperation, Coordination," will be held this month in the U.S. Grant Hotel, San Diego. Program for the conference, which opens the 1958 convention of the California Association of School Administrators, was announced recently by Drummond J. McCunn, co-chairman, Superintendent of the Contra Costa Junior College District, and Gordon Stafford, Architect, Sacramento.

Addressing the opening session will be Roy E. Simpson, California State Superintendent of Instruction; L. F. Richards, President of the California Council of Architects, Santa Clara, and James H. Corson, President of the California Association of School Administrators. Special sections of the conference will then consider such factors as "Educational Planning," "Architectural Services and Compensation," "Coordination of Agencies Involved in Planning," "Packaged Buildings, Pre-Fabrication, and Re-Use of Plans," and "Relation of Building and Grounds to Site Size."

A general session will also be held with William W. Caudill, Architect, of Caudill, Rowlett and Scott, as guest speaker.

CHANGE IN SCHOOL
CODE REJECTED

Title 21 Advisory Board of the California Council of Architects recently recommended against a change in the California School Code which would allow use of "L-1-R" plywood glue structurally on the exterior of California school buildings. The California State Division of Architecture subsequently announced that schools now under construction, or out to bid, on which such use of "L-1-R" had been approved would not be affected by the recommendation.

WYMAN BEAR, Portland, architect and prominent member of the Oregon Chapter The American Institute of Architects, has been appointed a member of the Oregon State Board of Architect Examiners to serve the unexpired term of architect Walter Gordon, recently resigned to accept the position of Dean of the School of Architecture and Allied Arts at the University of Oregon.

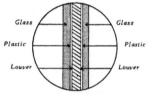

American Institute of Architects

John Noble Richards, President

Philip Will, Jr., 1st Vice-President   Edward L. Wilson, Secretary
Henry L. Wright, 2nd Vice-President   Raymond S. Kastendieck, Treasurer
Edmund R. Purves, Executive Secretary

National Headquarters—1735 New York Avenue, N.W., Washington, D. C.

REGIONAL DIRECTORS—**Northwest District**, Donald J. Stewart, Portland, Oregon; **Western Mountain District**, Frederick H. Porter, Sr., Cheyenne, Wyoming; **California-Nevada-Hawaii District**, Ulysses Floyd Rible, Los Angeles, California.

ARIZONA CHAPTERS:

CENTRAL ARIZONA: David Sholder, President; A. John Brenner, Vice-President; Jimmie R. Nunn, Secretary; Kemper Goodwin, Treasurer; James W. Elmore, Director; Ralph Haver, Director; Martin Ray Young, Jr., Director. Office of Secy., P.O. Box 904, Phoenix.

SOUTHERN ARIZONA: Santry Clay Fuller, President; Edward H. Nelson, Vice-President; David S. Swanson, Secretary; Robert J. Ambrose, Treasurer; D. Burr DuBois, Director; Eleazar D. Herreras, Director; Emerson C. Scholer, Director. Office of Secy., 2343 South Tucson Avenue, Tucson.

COAST VALLEYS CHAPTER:

William L. Higgins (San Jose), President; Paul J. Huston (Palo Alto), Vice-President; William H. Daseking (Menlo Park), Treasurer; Edward N. Chamberlain (San Jose), Secretary. Office of Secy., 390 Park Ave., San Jose.

CENTRAL VALLER OF CALIFORNIA:

Joseph J. Jozens, President (Sacramento); Armsby Tod Hart, Vice-President (Sacramento); Albert M. Dreyfuss, Secretary (Sacramento); Whitson W. Cox, Treasurer. Office of Secy., 2127 "J" St., Sacramento.

COLORADO CHAPTER:

Casper F. Hegner, President; C. Gordon Sweet, Vice President; Norton Polivnick, Secretary; Richard Williams, Treasurer. Directors: James M. Hunter, Robert K. Fuller, Edward L. Bunts. Office of Secy., 1225 Bannock St., Denver, Colorado.

EAST BAY CHAPTER:

Hachiro Yuasa (Oakland), President; George T. Kern (Oakland), Vice-President; William M. Gillis (San Francisco), Secretary; J. A. Zerkle (Berkeley), Treasurer. Directors: H. B. Clausen, F. A. Lockwood, John Oyarzo, G. M. McCue. Marjorie Montgomery, Exec. Secy. Office of Secy., Mezzanine, Hotel Claremont, Berkeley 5.

IDAHO CHAPTER:

Anton E. Dropping, Boise, President; Charles W. Johnston, Payette, Vice-President; Glenn E. Cline, Boise, Sec.-Treas. Executive Committee: Chester L. Shawver and Nat J. Adams, Boise. Office of Secy., 624 Idaho Bldg., Boise.

MONTEREY BAY CHAPTER:

Robert Stanton, President (Carmel); Walter Burde, Vice-President; William L. Cranston, Secretary; George Kuska, Treasurer. Office of Secy., P.O. Box 1846, Carmel.

MONTANA CHAPTER:

William J. Hess, President (Great Falls); John E. Toohey, Vice-President (Billings); H. C. Cheever, Secy.-Treas. (Bozeman). Directors: Oscar J. Ballas, Wm. J. Hess, John E. Toohey. Office of Sec., Bozeman, Montana.

NEVADA CHAPTER:

RENO: William E. Cowell, President; Albert W. Alegre, Vice-President; Ralph A. Casazza, Secretary; John Crider, Treasurer. Directors Graham Erskine, George L. F. O'Brien, Laurence A. Gulling. Office of the Secy. 232 W. 1st St., Reno, Nevada.

WOMEN'S ARCHITECTURAL LEAGUE: (Reno) Mrs. Eileen Casazza, President; Mrs. Lucille Lackard, Vice-President; Mrs. Glades Cowell, Secretary; Mrs. Enid Hellman, Treasurer.

LAS VEGAS: Walter F. Zick, President; Aloysius McDonald, Vice-President; Edward B. Hendricks, Secy.-Treas. Directors: Walter F. Zick, Edward Hendricks, Charles E. Cox. Office of Secy., 106 S. Main St., Las Vegas.

NEVADA STATE BOARD OF ARCHITECTS:

L. A. Ferris, Chairman; Aloysius McDonald, Secy.-Treas. Members: Russell Mills (Reno), Edward S. Parsons (Reno), Richard R. Stadelman (Las Vegas). Office: 1420 S. 5th St., Las Vegas.

NORTHERN CALIFORNIA CHAPTER:

William Corlett, President; Donald Powers Smith, Vice-President; George T. Rockrise, Secretary; Richard S. Banwell, Treasurer. Directors: W. Clement Ambrose, John Kruse, Bernard J. Sabaroff, Corwin Booth. Exec. Secy., May B. Hipshman. Chapter Office, 47 Kearny St., San Francisco.

ORANGE COUNTY CHAPTER:

William T. Jordan, President (Costa Mesa); Donald M. Williamson, Vice-President (Laguna Beach); J. Herbert Brownell, Secretary; Rumont W. Hougan, Treasurer. Office of Secy., 1910 W. Coast Highway, Newport Beach.

OREGON CHAPTER:

John K. Dukehart, President; Keith R. Maguire, Vice-President; Robert Douglas, Treasurer; Harry K. Stevens, Treasurer. Directors: Daniel McGoodwin, Earl P. Newberry, Everett B. Franks, Robert W. Prltsch, Donald W. Edmundson. Office of Secy., 2041 S.W. 58th Ave., Portland 1.

OREGON CHAPTER AIA

The first fall meeting of the Oregon Chapter, Inc., was held in the Imperial Hotel, Portland, the middle of last month with a special program devoted to a "Review of New Zoning Ordinances Proposal by Special Committee."

It was announced that there is a competition for the design of a bas-relief, sculpture or mosaic for the lobby of the new Logan Building in Seattle, Washington, with competition open to all artists, sculptors and architects in the Northwest. First prize is $4,500 plus cost of execution, 2nd through 5th a prize of $250 each and 6th through 10th a prize of $100 each.

Recent new members include: John W. Brooms, Wayne E. Huffstutter, Andrew B. Olson, and Charles E. Selig, Associate Members.

AMERICAN ARCHITECTURAL FOUNDATION AWARDS SCHOLARSHIP TO UNIVERSITY OF OKLAHOMA STUDENT STREUFERT

The first annual scholarship award for fifth year architectural students has been issued to a senior enrolled at the University of Oklahoma, according to Henry Davis, chairman of the public relations committee of the International Association of Blue Print and Allied Industries.

Norman Streufert, Milwaukee, Wisconsin, has been selected by the American Architectural Foundation, affiliated with The American Institute of Architects, through whom the Blue Print Association awards the scholarship, for the award which is designed to help promising students to complete their fifth year in an accredited architectural school.

PASADENA CHAPTER

Howard Alphson, Los Angeles attorney, was the principal speaker at the October meeting held in the Chef's Inn, Pasadena, taking as his subject "Is It Legal?"

Alphson pointed out that many phases of architecture require a knowledge and interpretation of the law, and endeavored to point out and clarify some of the more common issues.

Recent new members of the Chapter included H. Richard Adams, Associate.

NORTHWEST REGIONAL CONFERENCE

The Seventh Annual Northwest Regional Conference, sponsored by the Washington State Chapter AIA, and the Architectural Institute of British Columbia, at Harrison Hot Springs, B.C., this month, featured "Towards A Better Environment."

Guest speakers included Louis I. Kahn, FAIA, Philadelphia architect, planner, writer and Yale University design critic; John Noble Richards, FAIA, Toledo, Ohio, national President of the American Institute of Architects; Charles E. Pratt, MRAIC, Vancouver, B.C., architect; Gideon Kramer, Seattle industrial designer; and Melvin M. Rader, professor of philosophy, University of Washington.

HAWAII AIA CONFERENCE SET

The California Council of Architects AIA will sponsor a Pacific Rim Architectural Conference in October of 1959 in Hawaii, according to a decision of the Administrative Committee.

Site of the conference will be Henry J. Kaiser's new Hawaiian Village Hotel and will include the Annual CCAIA Convention, the California Regional Conference, and the Women's Architectural League Conference.

Architects from the entire Pacific area will be invited to attend.

SOUTHERN CALIFORNIA CHAPTER

The October meeting was devoted to the subject of "Redevelopment" with Joe Bill, Director of Redevelopment; and Milt Brievogel, Director of the Regional Planning Commission of the City and County of Los Angeles among the speakers.

The meeting was held October 7th in the Los Angeles Elks' Club with Robert E. Alexander serving as program chairman assisted by Charles O. Matcham, chairman of the Los Angeles Community Planning Committee.

CHARLES LUCKMAN OAKLAND SPEAKER

Charles Luckman, Architect, 9220 Sunset Blvd., Los Angeles, was the principal speaker at a meeting of Bay Area architects in Oakland early this month, at which government and industry leaders were in attendance.

Sponsored by the East Bay Chapter, The American Institute of Architects, the meeting was held in the Hotel Leamington to observe their 11th anniversary with Hachiro Yuasa, president, presiding.

SAN FRANCISCO ARCHITECTURAL CLUB

Engineering, Atelier and Art and Architecture classes have been resumed for the Fall season, and plans are being made for the Architectural Seminar to be held in the Spring, just prior to the examination of the California State Board of Architectural Examiners.

GORDON TRAPP, Portland, Oregon architect, has been appointed a member of the Multnomah County Planning Commission.

Structural Engineers Association of California
Henry J. Degenkolb, President (San Francisco); William T. Wheeler, Vice-President (Southern California); John M. Sardis, Sec.-Treas. (San Francisco). R. W. Binder, Henry J. Degenkolb, Charles D. DeMaria, Charles M. Herd, Harold L. Manley, Clarence E. Rinne, John M. Sardis, Arthur A. Sauer, William T. Wheeler, and David M. Wilson, Directors. Office of Secty., 64 Pine St., San Francisco.

Structural Engineers Association of Northern California
J. Albert Pacquette, President; Charles D. DeMaria, Vice-President; Arthur R. Weatherby, Secretary; Samuel H. Clark, Asst. Secy.; William K. Cloud, Treasurer. Henry J. Degenkolb, Harold S. Kellam, Marvin A. Larson, John M. Sardis and Richard J. Woodward, Charles D. DeMaria, J. Albert Pacquette, and Richard J. Woodward, Directors. Office of Secy., 417 Market St., San Francisco 5.

Structural Engineers Society of the East Bay
M. P. Superak, President; D. R. Judd, Vice-President; MacGregor Graham, Sec'y-Treas. Office of Sec'y, 1952 Wright Ave., Richmond.

Structural Engineers Association of Central California
A. L. Brinckman, President; Wendell F. Pond, Vice-President; Gordon M. Hart, Sec.-Treas.; Jack S. Barrish, Norman W. Beattie, Albert T. Brinckman, James J. Doody and Wendell F. Pond, Directors.

Structural Engineers Association of Southern California
Joseph Sheffet, President; Harold Omsted, Vice-President; Marvin J. Kudroff, Secy-Treas. Directors: Robert M. Wilder, Norman B. Green, Roy G. Johnston and William A. Jensen. Office of the Sec., 2808 Temple St., Los Angeles 26.

PLANS BEING PREPARED
FOR ENGINEERS' WEEK

Fifteen leading engineering figures throughout the nation representing a wide variety of fields of engineering, have agreed to act as sponsors for the 1959 National Engineers' Week, to be observed February 22-28.

Representing industry, education, private practice, government service, and the military the fifteen sponsors are:

Wernher von Braun, director, Development Opera-

tions Division, Army Ballistic Missile Agency; Allen B. DuMont, chairman of the board, Allen B. DuMont Laboratories, Inc.; T. Keith Glennan, president-on-leave, Case Institute of Technology, and administrator, National Aeronautics and Space Administration; Major General Emerson C. Itschner, chief of engineers, United States Army; Charles F. Kettering, General Motors Corporation; James R. Killian, Jr., special assistant to the President of the United States for science and technology; Clarence H. Linder, vice president, General Electric Company; Thomas E. Murray, consultant, Joint Committee on Atomic Energy; Granville M. Read, chief engineer, E. I. du Pont de Nemours and Company; Rear Admiral H. G. Rickover, chief of naval reactors, United States Atomic Energy Commission; Royal W. Sorensen, California Institute of Technology; Philip Sporn, president, American Gas and Electric Company; David B. Steinman, consulting engineer; Bertram D. Tallamy, Federal Highway Administrator; and Charles Allen Thomas, president, Monsanto Chemical Company.

MODERN MATHEMATICS FOR
THE ENGINEER SERIES

A lecture series in "Modern Mathematics for the Engineer" is being given in Berkeley and Menlo Park this fall by University of California Extension. It is also being given in Los Angeles and San Diego, and will consist of seventeen weekly lectures by experts in the field.

The purpose of the series is to help non-specialists deevlop an insight into certain aspects of modern mathematics. Those with training in engineering or science, high school and college teachers of mathematics and others wishing to remain informed concerning mahtematical development are invited to attend.

Among the lecturers will be David Blackwell, chairman of the Department of Statistics, University of California; William Feller, professor of mathematics, Princeton University; A. Erdelyi, professor of mathematics, California Institute of Technology; J. Barkley

Rosser, professor of mathematics, Cornell University; George B. Dantzig, research mathematician with the Rand Corporation, Santa Monica; S. Ulam, research advisor, Los Alamos Scientific Laboratory; S. Chandrasekhar, professor in the Departments of Physics and Astronomy, University of Chicago; Paul R. Garabediao, professor of mathematics, Stanford University; Samuel Karlin, professor of mathematics and statistics, Stanford University; and G. Polya, professor of mathematics, emeritus, Stanford University.

STRUCTURAL ENGINEERS HOLD CALIFORNIA CONVENTION

PLANNERS OF ENGINEERS CONVENTION: Responsible for this year's annual convention of the Structural Engineers Association of California, to be held this month at Yosemite National Park are: J. L. Stratta, seated (left to right); C. D. DeMaria; H. J. Degenkolb, President of the SEAOC; W. E. Dreusike, General Convention Chairman; A. M. Sperry; and standing B. B. Dunwoody, and D. B. Hicks. Other convention committee chairmen and members were not available at the time this photograph was taken.

FEMINEERS

The September meeting of the FEMINEERS, was held at the Women's Athletic Club, San Francisco, with Bill Wagner, Art Director of television station KRON the speaker. His subject was "Oodles of Doodles" and included many interesting and behind the scenes comment on TV station activities.

CONVENTION CALIFORNIA COUNCIL ARCHITECTS

(From page 15)

number of additional activities which include a Junior Associates' and Students' Seminar on Saturday morning led by three project designers from California architectural firms, followed by student discussions with State Board of Architectural Examiners. Scheduled to lead the general discussions are Richard Hein of Anshen & Allen, San Francisco; James Langenheim of Pereira and Luckman, Los Angeles; and Neil Smith of John Carl Warnecke, AIA, San Francisco.

Other convention events include a Regional Luncheon which will open the festivities at 12 noon on Wednesday with Philip Creer, FAIA, dean of the Texas University School of Architecture, as speaker. The Womens' Architectural League (WAL) will hold a business meeting on Thursday morning and a Carmel Valley field trip Friday morning, and luncheon and fashion show in Carmel Valley Friday noon.

The annual banquet will be held Friday night at the Fairgrounds' main dining hall with dancing following at the Naval Postgraduate School hosted by the Monterey Bay Chapter AIA.

The annual Producers' Council sports activities will be held Saturday and the famed Producers' Council Sports Dinner and entertainment is scheduled for Saturday evening.

A number of outstanding examples of Monterey Peninsula architecture, covering its development from early days to the present, are scheduled for Thursday afternoon, and an excursion to the newly acquired San Simeon California State Park will be held on Saturday.

ARCHITECT WALTER GORDON APPOINTED OREGON DEAN

Walter Gordon, Portland, architect prominent in architectural activities in the West, has been appointed Dean of the School of Architecture and Allied Arts at the University of Oregon.

Gordon has been serving as a member of the Oregon State Board of Architect Examiners, resigning from the Board to accept the University of Oregon position.

SANTA MONICA STATE PARK

(From page 8)

be located in the picnic area. Landscaping of the beach parks has been chosen for its colorfulness, shade quality, and suitability for oceanside climates. Bushes and trees will hide fences to give a more natural appearance to the areas.

A prominent feature of all the Santa Monica Beach Parks are the unique thin-shelled concrete vaults that cover the main building areas. Buildings are constructed of cement block while the grounds are surfaced in grass, asphalt, cement, and sand.

The second unit is due for construction this fall. Also included in the beach park development, which will be supervised by the Santa Monica Recreation Commission, is a new lifeguard headquarters located just south of the Santa Monica Municipal Pier. Plans for the lifeguard unit have been completed, according to Welton Becket architects, and are now out to bid with construction due to begin this year.

ALBERT SIGAL, AIA OPENS OFFICES IN PALO ALTO

Albert Sigal, Jr., AIA, a senior partner of Sigal, Johnson and Hawley, Architects, has formed his own firm for the practice of architecture and has opened offices in the Stanford Professional Center, 800 Welch Road, Palo Alto.

The new firm will offer personal service without specialization to the best needs of client and community in terms of planning, economy and design.

Sigal received his M.A. degree in Architecture at Stanford University in 1952.

FIBERBOARD PAPER APPOINTS J. B. FAGOT TO NEW POSITION

J. B. Fagot has been appointed Director of Management Development of the Fiberboard Paper Products Corporation, San Francisco, according to an announcement by W. K. Spence, vice president of personnel for the firm.

In his newly created position, Fagot will establish a program of management development methods and will institute management procedures for recruiting, placement, guidance, counseling, appraisal and promotion. The new management development program will give each employee a maximum opportunity for growth.

MARRIED STUDENTS FACILITIES EXPANDED AT STANFORD

Architects Wurster, Bernardi & Emmons of San Francisco, together with Supervising Architect Eldridge T. Spencer, San Francisco, have prepared preliminary plans for construction of a $3,000,-000 married students housing development at Stanford University.

The initial unit will comprise a group of 250 one and two story apartments of frame and wood construction to serve students during their educational period at Stanford.

ARCHITECT EISENSHTAT DESIGNS JEWISH COMMUNITY SERVICE BUILDING

Sidney Eisenshtat, AIA, Architect, has completed plans for construction of a new Jewish Community Service building and mortuary for Malinow and Silverman, to be constructed on the southwest corner of the 800 block on Venice Blvd. in Los Angeles.

The new building will contain 20,000 sq. ft. of area, and be of California contemporary architectural design. It will provide 33 rooms on two levels, a spacious chapel, slumber rooms, air conditioning, and traditional decorations. It will be ready for occupancy in February 1959.

DON DRIVER IS APPOINTED BY PAYNE COMPANY

Don Driver has been appointed sales engineering representative in Southern California for the Payne Company, according to the company's National sales manager Owen McComas.

Driver joined the firm in 1947 as a field service representative and has since gained additional technical background in the Sales Engineering Department and as a Service Manager. In his new assignment, Driver will devote his time to calling on customers in the Southern California areas, including Los Angeles, Ventura and Santa Barbara counties. He will maintain offices in La Puente.

ANNUAL CONVENTION OF HOME BUILDERS TO BE HELD IN CHICAGO

The fifteenth annual Convention and Exposition of the National Association of Home Builders will be held in Chicago, January 18-22, according to present plans. It will attract the largest attendance in recent years, according to Daniel B. Grady, chairman of the 1959 Convention Committee.

Three reasons are given to the predicted large attendance: 1) The current status of the building industry and a general recognition among builders and suppliers that if the indicated upturn in home building is to be fully capitalized upon, every advantage must be taken of improved techniques and materials; 2) An increase in the number of available exhibit spaces to a record of 809, and 3) An increase in the number of first class hotel accommodations in the downtown Chicago area, 1500 additional rooms are available this year.

Serving with Grady on the Convention Committee is Ben C. Deane of Van Nuys, California.

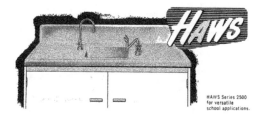

HAWS Series 2500 for versatile school applications.

ONE-PIECE INTEGRAL UNIT
deck-top, receptor and fountain in lightweight, tough fiberglass. Color, too, at no extra cost. Look – no rims, no cracks, no joints. It's all One Piece for ultimate ease of maintenance and sanitation.

Get the full story: write for detail sheets for Series 2500. A drinking fountain separate from main receptor is provided on Series 2700 "two receptor" units, to meet code requirements of certain localities.

DRINKING FAUCET CO.

1443 FOURTH STREET (Since 1909) BERKELEY 10, CALIFORNIA

CONVENTION CALIFORNIA COUNCIL ARCHITECTS

(From page 15)

number of additional activities which include a Junior Associates' and Students' Seminar on Saturday morning led by three project designers from California architectural firms, followed by student discussions with State Board of Architectural Examiners. Scheduled to lead the general discussions are Richard Hein of Anshen & Allen, San Francisco; James Langenheim of Pereira and Luckman, Los Angeles; and Neil Smith of John Carl Warnecke, AIA, San Francisco.

Other convention events include a Regional Luncheon which will open the festivities at 12 noon on Wednesday with Philip Creer, FAIA, dean of the Texas University School of Architecture, as speaker. The Womens' Architectural League (WAL) will hold a business meeting on Thursday morning and a Carmel Valley field trip Friday morning, and luncheon and fashion show in Carmel Valley Friday noon.

The annual banquet will be held Friday night at the Fairgrounds' main dining hall with dancing following at the Naval Postgraduate School hosted by the Monterey Bay Chapter AIA.

The annual Producers' Council sports activities will

be eld Saturday and the famed Producers' Co Sp ts Dinner and entertainment is scheduled Sa rday evening.

number of outstanding examples of Mon Pe nsula architecture, covering its development ea days to the present, are scheduled for Thur af noon, and an excursion to the newly acquired Si :on California State Park will be held on Satur

A CHITECT WALTER GORDON A OINTED OREGON DEAN

/alter Gordon, Portland, architect prominent ar itectural activities in the West, has been pc ited Dean of the School of Architecture and Al A s at the University of Oregon.

ordon has been serving as a member of the Ore St e Board of Architect Examiners, resigning fr th Board to accept the University of Oregon positi

S .NTA MONICA STATE PARK

(From page 8)

b located in the picnic area. Landscaping of r b ch parks has been chosen for its colorfulness, sh q lity, and suitability for oceanside climates. Busl a trees will hide fences to give a more natural ; p rance to the areas.

\ prominent feature of all the Santa Monica Bea P ks are the unique thin-shelled concrete vaults th c er the main building areas. Buildings are cc st cted of cement block while the grounds are s f. d in grass, asphalt, cement, and sand.

Che second unit is due for construction this fa A o included in the beach park development, whic w l be supervised by the Santa Monica Recreatic C mmission, is a new lifeguard headquarters locate m j't south of the Santa Monica Municipal Pier. Plai f the lifeguard unit have been completed, accordin t Welton Becket architects, and are now out to bi v h construction due to begin this year.

ONE-P

including Los Angeles, Ventura and Santa Barbara counties. He will maintain offices in La Puente.

ANNUAL CONVENTION OF HOME BUILDERS TO BE HELD IN CHICAGO

The fifteenth annual Convention and Exposition of the National Association of Home Builders will be held in Chicago, January 18-22, according to present plans. It will attract the largest attendance in recent years, according to Daniel B. Grady, chairman of the 1959 Convention Committee.

Three reasons are given to the predicted large attendance: 1) The current status of the building industry and a general recognition among builders and suppliers that if the indicated upturn in home building is to be fully capitalized upon, every advantage must be taken of improved techniques and materials; 2) An increase in the number of available exhibit spaces to a record of 809, and 3) An increase in the number of first class hotel accommodations in the downtown Chicago area, 1500 additional rooms are available this year.

Serving with Grady on the Convention Committee is Ben C. Deane of Van Nuys, California.

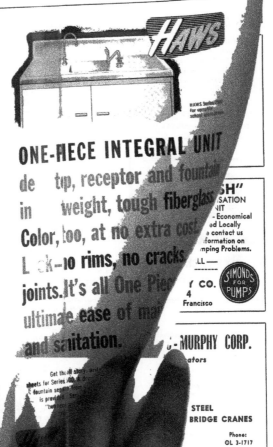

BRICK HOUSE DESIGN
(From page 10)

withstood the devastating force of nuclear blast.

Employing the principle of arching, clay industry research engineers designed a six-inch "SCR brick" residence in which the arching takes place vertically, by means of the roof being tied to the foundation by three-inch steel channels on 24-inch centers.

In addition to the walls of the one-story house being designed with the arching principle, the concept calls for a safety core of 10-inch reinforced brick masonry walls roofed with six and one-half inch reinforced

precast clay tile beams topped with a two and one-half inch concrete slab. The beams are of the same design which also successfully stood up during the FCDA blast tests.

The design of the house includes a three and one-quarter inch laminated plywood blast-resistant door with steel hinges which withstood atomic blast in the tests.

Besides protection against such natural disasters as hurricanes, tornadoes and earthquakes, this design concept affords good protection against loss of life in 90 per cent of the potential blast damage area of any size atomic or hydrogen weapon. Although not needed for natural disasters, a partial basement under the core area could be a safe refuge against severe atomic fallout.

A modern see-through fireplace between the living room and den which is decorative and useful would, in the event of disaster, serve an important role as a source of heat and a place for cooking.

Another advantage to the home owner in this core design concept for conventional housing is that it offers protection not only in the immediate disaster situation, but provides a place to live until the damaged conventional portion of the house is rebuilt.

SCPRF engineers estimate that, in new construction, this safety core could be incorporated in a conventional house design for about five per cent additional cost. The safety core plus the surrounding walls designed with the arching principle providing a complete disaster-resistant house could be built at an additional cost of less than 20 per cent.

In areas where natural disasters are a real danger, this design concept can give a family the protection it seeks at a cost not much above conventional construction.

ASSOCIATED GENERAL CONTRACTORS ISSUE ACCIDENT PREVENTION DATA

The Associated General Contractors of America have just published and released for general distribution two sectional reprints of its Manual of Accident Prevention in Construction. The sections are particularly designed for superintendents, foremen, and individual workers at the construction site.

The material presents much valuable information on such related subjects as Scaffolding, Ladders, Explosives and Power Actuated Tools, and is published in small booklet size convenient for coat pocket. Technological advances in the industry over the past few years are included.

*PHOTO CREDITS: Herrington-Olson Photography, Cover;
Vanguard Photo, page 8; Clay Products Research Foundation,
page 10; Daniel, Mann, Johnson & Mendenhall, page 12, 13;
Robert B. Liles, page 14; Steve Kirchner, page 18 top; Kaiser
Graphic Arts, page 18 bottom; Pereira & Luckman, page 19
top; Robert Donohue, page 19 bottom; Victor Haverman,
page 20; Julius Shulman, page 21 top; Joe De Narie, page 21
bottom; Willis & Confer, page 22, 23, 24, 25, 26, 27.*

BOOK REVIEWS
PAMPHLETS AND CATALOGUES

THEORY OF STRUCTURAL ANALYSIS AND DESIGN.
By James Michalos. The Ronald Press Company, 15 E.
26th St., New York 10, N. Y. 552 pages. Price $12.00.

Special features of this book include a thorough treatment
of arches, encompassing continuous arches, and arches having
stiff ties, with influence lines and tables for horizontal and
vertical leading; detailed illustrations of a number of procedures for determining the effects of secondary and participation stresses, with numerous charts; and it investigates by
numerical methods the stress intensification and buckling of
frameworks and arches.

This new, high level textbook integrates the theory, methods, and tools of structural analysis and related design concepts. Throughout, classical and modern numerical methods
are applied to obtain exact analyses. The book relates methods
of analysis to design procedures and mathematical treatment
to physical concepts and behavior. The author is Prof. and
Chm. Department of Civil Engineering, New York University.

COMPOSITE CONSTRUCTION IN STEEL AND CON-
CRETE—For Bridges and Buildings. By I. M. Viest, R.
S. Fountain & R. C. Singleton. McGraw-Hill Book Co.,
Inc., 330 W. 42nd St., New York 36, N. Y. 176 pages.
Price $7.50.

Here is an engineering manual on the design of steel beams
and concrete slabs for composite construction, showing the
advantages of the method and fully covering design procedures and practical applications. The well-rounded treatment
gives the basis of composite construction and its advantages,
devlops design equations and procedures, describes methods
of connecting slab to beams, and includes illustrative examples
of design procedure, and design charts and tables.

A rapid method for the composite design of beams is discussed in detail and illustrated by six complete examples.
Special problems are covered, such as the determination of
the length of cover plates, design of continuous beams, and
computation of deflections.

PHILOSOPHY OF STRUCTURES. By Eduardo Torroja.
University of California Press, Berkeley 4, Calif. 366
pages. Illustrated. Price $12.50.

The book is a comprehensive and systematic discussion of
the principles of advanced structural design by one of the
world's foremost architects and engineers. Writing of the
book was inspired by a visit of the author, at the suggestion
of J. J. Polivka, to Taliesin West. Torroja and Polivka then
set to work on the present English version. Milos Polivka,
assistant professor of engineering and architecture at the
University of California in Berkeley, assisted his father in a
close collaboration with Torroja, which insured a knowledge-
able presentation of the author's ideas for American readers.

SAMARIA—The Capital of the Kingdom of Israel. By Andre
Parrot. Philosophical Library, Inc., 15 E. 40th St., New
York 16. 142 pages, Price $2.75.

Translated from the French by S. H. Hooke, this is a fascinating account of the history of Samaria from the foundation
of the kingdom of Israel after the death of Solomon to the
Christian era. It is based on biblical sources and on the discoveries archaeologists have made in Samaria and the surrounding
district. Prof. Parrot tells of the fate of the city under the
Assyrians and Babylonians and in the Hellenistic and Roman
periods and examines the tradition that Samaria is the burial
place of John the Baptist.

NEW CATALOGUES AVAILABLE

*Architects, Engineers, Contractors, Planning Commission
members—the catalogues, folders, new building products
material, etc., described below may be obtained by directing
your request to the name and address given in each item.*

Longspan roof deck. New brochure (A.I.A. File No. 13-H)
describes in detail PIRIB Longspan Roof Deck for better
buildings; load tables, suggested framing, structural details,
specifications, and photographs of many installations. Free
copy write DEPT-A&E, Pacific Iron & Steel Corp., 11633 So.
Alameda St., Los Angeles 2, California.

"Discover ceramic tile." New consumer booklet designed
for ceramic tile contractors; explains in easy-to-read terms

various kinds of ceramic tile and their uses in the home—walls, floors, countertops and other surfaces. Free copy write DEPT·A&E, The Mosaic Tile Co., Zanesville, Ohio.

Air filters. New bulletin on Far-Air Roll-Kleen, an automatic renewable media air filter; described in simplest terms, contains detailed information about the component parts of the filter; describes operation controls, as well as engineering data and maintenance factors. Free copy write DEPT A&E, Farr Company, P. O. Box 45187, Airport Station, Los Angeles 45.

Arc and incandescent spotlights. Now available specification sheets and descriptive brochures on an entire line of arc and incandescent spotlights for schools, colleges, arenas, auditoriums, theatres, and stadiums, prepared for architectural use; foot candle readings and diameters for flood to small spot sizes at various lengths of throws. Free copies write DEPT A&E, The Strong Electric Corpn., 251 City Park Ave., Toledo 1, Ohio.

Indoor and outdoor switchgear. New 40-page bulletin provides detailed information on the operation, characteristics and application of GE's complete line of indoor and outdoor metal clad switchgear, rated 2.4 to 13.8 kilovolts with interrupting capacities of 75 to 1000 MVA; describes margins of versatility, system protection, safety, compactness, maintenance and ordering; includes equipment and application photos, dimensional drawings and lists basic and optional equipment; tables on indoor and outdoor units, and equipment diagrams. Free copy write DEPT A&E, General Electric Co., Schenectady 5, N. Y.

Foundation piles for permanent structures. New brochure just published by the Western Wood Preserving Operators Association, illustrates and describes in numerous details, many installations of pressure creosoted Douglas fir timber foundation; data includes number of pieces and length of piling, size, species of wood, treatment, and remarks. Free copy write DEPT A&E, Western Wood Preserving Operations Association, 1410 S. W. Morrison St., Portland 5, Oregon.

Moment distribution factors for beams of tapered I-section. New 40-page booklet by James M. Gere, Associate Professor of Civil Engineering at Stanford University, presents in graphical form the coefficients and factors which are necessary for the analysis of steel structures involving tapered beams by the moment distribution method; graphs give fixed-end moment coefficients, stiffness factors, and carry-over factors for beams of I-section or box section; the beams have a uniform taper along their length. Free copy write DEPT A&E, American Institute of Steel Construction, Inc., 101 Park Ave., New York 17, New York.

Laboratory supply catalog. Complete catalog, 1273 pages, complete revised and specially engineered to provide buyers of laboratory supplies and equipment with more effective descriptions, wide selection of laboratory items, faster finding aids and more efficient and convenient source for handling requisitions; 400 separate supplies and equipment sections with over 8,000 listings arranged in alphabetical order, completely cross-referenced; specifications. Copy write DEPT A&E, The Chemical Rubber Co., 2310 Superior Ave., Cleveland 14, Ohio.

ARCHITECT AND ENGINEER

ESTIMATOR'S GUIDE

BUILDING AND CONSTRUCTION MATERIALS

PRICES GIVEN ARE FIGURING PRICES AND ARE MADE UP FROM AVERAGE QUOTATIONS FURNISHED BY LeROY CONSTRUCTION SERVICES. 4% SALES TAX ON ALL MATERIALS BUT NOT LABOR. ITEMS IN ITALIC INCLUDE LABOR AND SALES TAX.

BONDS—Performance or Performance plus Labor and Material Bond(s), $10 per $1000 on contract price. Labor and Material Bond(s) only, $5.00 per $1000 on contract price.

BRICKWORK & MASONRY

COMMON BRICKWORK, Reinforced:		
8" walls	*SF*	*2.95*
12" walls	*SF*	*4.15*
SELECT COMMON, Reinforced:		
8" walls	*SF*	*3.05*
12" walls	*SF*	*4.30*
CONCRETE BLOCK, Reinforced:		
6" walls	*SF*	*1.40*
8" walls	*SF*	*1.55*
12" walls	*SF*	*1.90*
BRICK VENEER:		
4" Select Common	*SF*	*1.65*
4" Roman	*SF*	*2.50*
4" Norman	*SF*	*2.40*
4" Aggrelite	*SF*	*2.40*

BRICKWORK & MASONRY

All Prices—F.O.B. Plant.

COMMON BRICK		
Common 2½ x 3¾ x 8¼	M	45.00
Select 2½ x 3¾ x 8¼	M	52.00
Clinker 2½ x 3¾ x 8¼	M	48.00
Jumbo 3½ x 3 x 11½	M	90.00
FACE BRICK		
Standard	M	59.80 - 83.20
Jumbo	M	114.40 - 130.00
Roman	M	88.40 - 109.20
Norman	M	101.40 - 124.80
Brik Blox (6")	M	202.80
Brik Blox (8")	M	239.20
Braile Veneer	M	26.00
BUILDING TILE		
8 x 5½ x 12 inches	M	165.78
6 x 5½ x 12 inches	M	128.96
HOLLOW TILE		
12 x 12 x 3 inches	M	163.12
12 x 12 x 4 inches	M	184.18
12 x 12 x 6 inches	M	244.71
MANTEL FIRE BRICK		
2½ x 9½ x 4½ inches	M	140.40
GLAZED STRUCTURAL UNITS		
2 x 6 x 12 Furring	SF	.90
4 x 6 x 12 Furring	SF	1.20
6 x 6 x 12 Furring	SF	1.50
4 x 6 x 12 Partition	SF	1.60
Add for color	SF	.20
CONCRETE BLOCKS		
4 x 8 x 16 inches	EA	.22
6 x 8 x 16 inches	EA	.265
8 x 8 x 16 inches	EA	.30
12 x 8 x 16 inches	EA	.435
Colored Add	EA	.02
AGGREGATE—Haydite or Basalite		
All sizes in bulk	CY	6.24

BUILDING PAPERS & FELTS

1 ply per 1000 ft. roll	3.95
2 ply per 1000 ft. roll	6.03
3 ply per 1000 ft. roll	8.22
Sisalkraft, reinf. 500 ft. roll	7.54
SHEATHING PAPERS:	
Asphalt sheathing, 15-lb. roll	2.40
30-lb. roll	3.37
Dampcourse, 216-ft. roll	3.05
FELT PAPERS:	
Deadening felt, ¾ lb., 50 ft. roll	3.94
Deadening felt, 1 lb., 50 ft. roll	4.60
Asphalt roofing, 15-lb.	2.50
30-lb.	3.50
ROOFING PAPERS:	
Standard Grade, Smooth Surface	
108 ft. roll, Light, 45 lb.	2.26
Medium 55 lb.	2.64
Heavy 65 lb.	3.10
Mineral Surfaced	3.60

CHIMNEYS, PATENT

F.O.B. Warehouse

6"	LF	1.45
8"	LF	2.05
10"	LF	2.85
12"	LF	3.45

Rates for 10 - 50 Lin. Ft.

CONCRETE AGGREGATES

	Bunker Per Ton	Del'd Per Ton
Gravel, All Sizes	3.25	4.00
Top Sand	3.45	4.20
Concrete Mix	3.35	4.20
Crushed Rock		
¼" to ¾"	3.30	4.20
¾" to 1½"	3.30	4.20
Roofing Gravel	3.46	4.15
SAND		
Lapis (Nos. 1 & 2)	4.30	5.10
Olympia (Nos. 1 & 2)	3.60	4.15

CEMENT		
Common, All brands (Paper sacks)		
Small quantities,	Per Sack	1.35
Large quantities,	Per bbl.	4.25
Trinity White & Mendusa White	Per Sack	4.00
CONCRETE MIX		
6 sacks in 5-yd. loads	Per yard	13.40
CURING COMPOUND, Clear		
5 gal drums	Per Gal.	1.46

CARPENTRY & MILLWORK

Hardware not included

FRAMING:		
Floors	*BM*	*.20 - .25*
Walls	*BM*	*.25 - .30*
Ceilings	*BM*	*.18 - .22*
Roofs	*BM*	*.22 - .27*
Furring & Blocking	*BM*	*.30 - .50*
SHEATHING:		
1 x 8 straight	*BM*	*.20 - .25*
1 x 8 diagonal	*BM*	*.23 - .28*
5/16" Plyscore	*SF*	*.16 - .20*
⅜" Plywood	*SF*	*.25 - .30*
SIDING:		
1 x 8 Bevel	*BM*	*.35 - .40*
1 x 4 V-Rustic	*BM*	*.40 - .45*
EXTERIOR TRIM:		
Fascia and Molds	*BM*	*.40 - .50*
Bolted Framing—Add 50%		
ENTRANCE DOORS & FRAMES:		
Singles		*60.00 & Up*
Doubles		*100.00 & Up*
INTERIOR DOORS & FRAMES:		
Singles		*35.00 & Up*
Pocket Sliding		*45.00 & Up*
Closet Sliding (Pr.)		*50.00 & Up*
WINDOWS:		
D/H Sash & Frames	*SF*	*1.75 & Up*
Casement Sash & Frames	*SF*	*1.90 & Up*
SHELVING:		
1 x 12 S4S	*BM*	*.30 - .50*
¾" Plywood	*SF*	*.40 - .60*
STAIRS:		
Oak steps D.F. Risers		
Under 36" wide	*Riser*	*12.00*
Under 60" wide	*Riser*	*17.00*
Newel posts and rail extra		
WOOD CASES & CABINETS:		
D.F. Wall Hung	*LF*	*13.00 - 18.00*
D.F. Counters	*LF*	*15.00 - 20.00*

DAMPPROOFING & WATERPROOFING

MEMBRANE:		
1 layer 50 lb. felt	*SQ.*	*9.00*
4 layers Dampcourse	*SQ.*	*13.00*
Hot coat walls	*SQ.*	*6.00*
Tricosal added to concrete	*CY*	*1.00*
Anti-Hydro added to concrete	*CY*	*1.50*

ELECTRIC WIRING

Per Outlet:		
Knob & Tube	*EA*	*9.00*
Armor	*EA*	*16.00*
Conduit	*EA*	*20.00*
110 V Circuit	*EA*	*25.00*
220 V Circuit	*EA*	*95.00*

ELEVATORS & ESCALATORS

Prices vary according to capacity, speed and type. Consult Elevator Companies.

Slow speed apartment house elevator including doors and trim, about $5000.00 per floor.

EXCAVATION

MACHINE WORK in common ground:		
Large Basements	*CY*	*.75 - 1.00*
Small Pits	*CY*	*1.25 - 1.75*
Trenches	*CY*	*1.50 - 2.25*
HAND WORK in common ground:		
Large pits and trenches	*CY*	*4.50 - 5.50*
Small pits and trimming	*CY*	*5.00 - 6.50*

Hard Clay & Shale 2 times above rates.
Rock and large boulders 4-6 times above rates.
Shoring, bracing and disposal of water not included.

FLOORS

⅛" Asp. tile, dark colors	*SF*	*.25 - .30*
⅛" Asp. tile, light colors	*SF*	*.30 - .35*
⅛" Rubber tile	*SF*	*.60 - .70*
.080 Vinyl Asbestos Tile	*SF*	*.40 - .45*
.080 Vinyl Tile	*SF*	*.85 - .95*
Lino, Standard Gauge	*SY*	*3.75 - 4.25*
Lino, Battleship	*SY*	*5.25 - 5.75*
4" Rubber Base, Black	*LF*	*.35 - .40*
Rubber Stair Nosing	*LF*	*1.00 - 1.75*

Above rates based on quantities of 1000 - 5000 SF per job.

HARDWOOD FLOORS

Select Oak, filled, sanded, stained and varnished:		
5/16" x 2¼" strip	*SF*	*.45 - .50*
5/16" Random Plank	*SF*	*.50 - .55*
25/32" x 2¼" T&G	*SF*	*.70 - .80*
Maple, 2nd Grade and Better, filled, sanded, stained and varnished:		
25/32" x 2¼" T&G	*SF*	*.80 - .95*
Wax Finish, add	*SF*	*.10*

HARDWOOD FLOORING

Oak 5/16" x 2" Strip—		
Clear	M	229.00
Select	M	218.00
#1 Common	M	203.00
Oak 5/16" Random Plank—		
Select & Btr.	M	286.00
#1 Common	M	244.00
Oak 25/32" x 2¼" T&G—		
Select	M	260.00
#1 Common	M	203.00
Maple 25/32" x 2¼" T&G—		
#1 Grade	M	317.00
#2 Grade	M	281.00
#3 Grade	M	208.00
Nails—1" Floor Brads	KEG	17.20

GLASS & GLAZING

S.S.B. Clear	*SF*	*.48*
D.S.B. Clear	*SF*	*.78*
Crystal	*SF*	*.92*
¼" Plate	*SF*	*2.17*
⅛" Obscure	*SF*	*.68*
⅛" Heat Absorbing	*SF*	*1.12*
¼" Tempered Plate	*SF*	*4.38*
½" Tempered Plate	*SF*	*7.84*
¼" Wire Plate, Clear	*SF*	*3.65*
¼" Wire Plate, Rough	*SF*	*1.08*

GLASS—CUT TO SIZE

F.O.B. Warehouse

S.S.B. Clear, Av. 6 SF	SF	.34
D.S.B. Clear, Av. 10 SF	SF	.56
Crystal, Av. 35-SF	SF	.65
¼" Polished Plate, Av. 100 SF	SF	1.55
⅛" Obscure, Av. 10 SF	SF	.49
⅛" Ribbed, Av. 10 SF	SF	.49
⅛" Rough, Av. 10 SF	SF	.49
¼" Wire Plate, Clear, Av. 40 SF	SF	2.61
¼" Wire Plate, Rough, Av. 40 SF	SF	.77
⅛" Heat Absorbing, Av. 10 SF	SF	.80
¼" Tempered Plate, Av. 50 SF	SF	3.60
½" Tempered Plate, Av. 50 SF	SF	6.88
Glazing—Approx. 40-50% of Glass		
Glass Blocks—		
6"		.57
8"		.92
12"		2.39

HEATING

FURNACES—Gas Fired—Av. Job:	
FLOOR FURNACE:	
25,000 BTU	*100.00 - 125.00*
35,000 BTU	*107.00 - 135.00*
45,000 BTU	*115.00 - 150.00*
AUTOMATIC CONTROL:	
Add	*25.00 - 35.00*

HEATING—Cont'd

DUAL WALL FURNACE:		
25,000 BTU		*110.00 - 125.00*
35,000 BTU		*125.00 - 145.00*
50,000 BTU		*150.00 - 180.00*
AUTOMATIC CONTROL:		
Add		*25.00 - 35.00*
GRAVITY FURNACE:		
75,000 BTU		*375.00 - 450.00*
85,000 BTU		*425.00 - 525.00*
95,000 BTU		*475.00 - 600.00*
FORCED AIR FURNACE:		
Add		*75.00 - 125.00*
AUTOMATIC CONTROL:		
Add		*15.00 - 25.00*
HEAT REGISTERS:		
Outlet		*7.50 - 15.00*

INSULATION & WALLBOARD

F.O.B. Warehouse

ROCKWOOL Insulation—		
2" Semi-thick	Per M SF	60.60
3⅝" Full Thick	Per M SF	77.40
COTTON Insulation		
1" Full Thick	Per M SF	43.26
SOFTBOARDS—Wood Fiber—		
½" thick	Per M SF	84.00
1½" thick	Per M SF	275.00
2" thick	Per M SF	385.00
ALUMINUM Insulation—		
80# Kraft paper with alum. foil		
1 side only	Per M SF	18.30
2 sides	Per M SF	31.00
GYPSUM Wallboard—		
⅜" thick	Per M SF	49.50
½" thick	Per M SF	54.50
⅝" thick	Per M SF	83.00
⅝" Gyplap	Per M SF	85.00
HARDBOARDS—Wood Fiber—		
⅛" thick, Sheathing	Per M SF	84.00
3/16" thick, Sheathing	Per M SF	90.48
¼" thick, Sheathing	Per M SF	109.20
⅛" thick, Tempered	Per M SF	108.00
3/16" thick, Tempered	Per M SF	186.00
¼" thick, Tempered	Per M SF	194.48
CEMENT Asbestos Board—		
⅛" C.A.B. Flat Sheets	Per M SF	151.20
3/16" C.A.B. Flat Sheets	Per M SF	208.80
¼" C.A.B. Flat Sheets	Per M SF	270.01

LATH & PLASTER

Diamond 3.40 copper bearing	SY	.56
Ribbed 3.40 copper bearing	SY	.62
⅜" rock lath	SY	.36
1½" Standard Channel	LF	.062
¾" Standard Channel	LF	.045
3¼" steel studs	LF	.092
4" steel studs	LF	.107
Stud shoes	EA	.028
Hardwall, Browning	Sack	1.45
Hardwall, Finish	Sack	1.70
Stucco	Sack	2.50

LATH & PLASTERWORK

CHANNEL FURRING:		
Suspended Ceilings	*SY*	*2.20 - 2.50*
Walls	*SY*	*2.30 - 2.60*
METAL STUD PARTITIONS:		
3¼" Studs	*SY*	*1.70 - 2.00*
4" Studs	*SY*	*1.95 - 2.25*
Over 10'0 high, add	*SY*	*.20 - .30*
3.40 METAL LATH AND PLASTER:		
Ceilings	*SY*	*3.60 - 4.00*
Walls	*SY*	*3.75 - 4.15*
KEENE'S CEMENT FINISH:		
Add	*SY*	*.40 - .60*
ROCK LATH & PLASTER:		
Ceilings	*SY*	*2.50 - 2.80*
Walls	*SY*	*2.60 - 2.90*
WIRE MESH AND ⅞" STUCCO:		
Walls	*SY*	*3.60 - 4.10*
STUCCO ON CONCRETE:		
Walls	*SY*	*2.30 - 2.80*
METAL ACCESSORIES	*LF*	*.20 - .50*

LINOLEUM

Lino. Standard Gauge	SY	2.65 - 2.85
Lino. Battleship	SY	2.95 - 3.11
⅛" Asp. tile, Dark	SF	.10 - .11
⅛" Asp. tile, Light	SF	.14 - .16
⅛" Rubber Tile	SF	.40 - .44
.080 Vinyl tile	SF	.20 - .21
.080 Vinyl Asb. tile	SF	.18 - .19
⅛" Vinyl tile	SF	.78 - .82
4" Base, Dark	LF	.15 - .16
4" Base, Light	LF	.24 - .26
Rubber Nosing	LF	.60 - 1.30
Lino Paste	GAL	.75 - .90

Above rates based on quantities of 1000-5000 SF per job.

LUMBER

DOUGLAS FIR:	M.B.M.
#1 2x4—2x10	88.00 - 92.00
#2 2x4—2x10	85.00 - 90.00
#3 2x4—2x10	68.00 - 74.00
#4 2x4—2x10	64.00 - 72.00
Clear, Air Dried	180.00 - 210.00
Clear, Kiln Dried	210.00 - 240.00
REDWOOD:	
Foundation Grade	120.00 - 130.00
Construction Heart	110.00 - 120.00
A Grade	180.00 - 210.00
Clear Heart	190.00 - 220.00
D.F. PLYWOOD	M.S.F.
¼" AB	95.00 - 105.00
¼" AD	90.00 - 95.00
¼" Ext. Waterproof	115.00 - 125.00
⅜" AB	130.00 - 145.00
⅜" AD	115.00 - 125.00
⅜" CD	70.00 - 85.00
½" AB	170.00 - 185.00
½" AD	110.00 - 115.00
½" CD	.... - ....
⅝" AB	185.00 - 200.00
⅝" AD	165.00 - 180.00
⅝" CD	115.00 - 125.00
¾" AB	210.00 - 230.00
¾" AD	195.00 - 210.00
¾" CD	125.00 - 140.00
⅝" Plyform	160.00 - 170.00
SHINGLES:	Square
Cedar #1	14.00 - 15.50
Cedar #2	11.50 - 12.50
SHAKES:	
CEDAR	
½ to ¾" Butt	17.50 - 18.50
¾ to 1¼" Butt	18.50 - 19.50
REDWOOD	
¾ to 1¼" Butt	21.00 - 24.00

MILLWORK

All Prices F.O.B. Mill

D.F. CLEAR, AIR DRIED:		
S4S	MBM	220.00 - 250.00
D.F. CLEAR, KILN DRIED:		
S4S	MBM	225.00 - 275.00
DOOR FRAMES & TRIM:		
Residential Entrance		17.00 & up
Interior Room Entrance		7.50 & up
DOORS:		
1⅜" D.F. Slab, Hollow Core		8.00 & up
1¾" D.F. Slab, Solid Core		19.00 & up
1⅜" Birch Slab, Hollow Core		10.00 & up
1¾" Birch Slab, Solid Core		22.00 & up
WINDOW FRAMES:		
D/H Singles	SF	.80
Casement Singles	SF	.90
WOOD SASH:		
D/H in pairs (1 lite)	SF	.45
Casement (1 lite)	SF	.50
WOOD CABINETS:		
¾" D.F. Ply with ¼" ply backs		
Wall Hung	LF	10.00 - 15.00
Counter	LF	12.00 - 17.00
BIRCH OR MAPLE—Add 25%		

PAINT

All Prices F.O.B. Warehouse

Thinners—5-100 gals.	GAL.	.57
Turpentine—5-100 gals.	GAL.	1.58
Linseed Oil, Raw	GAL.	2.51
Linseed Oil, Boiled	GAL.	2.57
Primer-Sealer	GAL.	3.10
Enamel	GAL.	5.45
Enamel Undercoaters	GAL.	5.45
White Lead in Oil	LB.	.35
Red Lead in Oil	LB.	.35
Litharge	LB.	.30

PAINTING

EXTERIOR:		
Stucco Wash 1 ct.	*SY*	*.30*
Stucco Wash 2 cts.	*SY*	*.55*
Lead and Oil 2 cts.	*SY*	*.90*
Lead and Oil 3 cts.	*SY*	*1.30*
INTERIOR:		
Primer Sealer	*SY*	*.40*
Wall Paint, 1 ct.	*SY*	*.50*
Wall Paint, 2 cts.	*SY*	*.95*
Enamel, 1 ct.	*SY*	*.60*
Enamel, 2 cts.	*SY*	*1.10*
Doors and Trim	*EA*	*10.00*
Sash and Trim	*EA*	*12.00*
Base and Molds	*LF*	*.12*

Old Work—Add 15-30%

PLUMBING

Lavatories	*EA*	*100.00 - 150.00*
Toilets	*EA*	*200.00 - 300.00*
Bath Tubs	*EA*	*250.00 - 350.00*
Stall Shower	*EA*	*80.00 - 150.00*
Sinks	*EA*	*125.00 - 175.00*
Laundry Trays	*EA*	*80.00 - 130.00*
Water Heaters	*EA*	*100.00 - 300.00*

Prices based on average residential and commercial work. Special fixtures and excessive piping not included.

ROOFING

STANDARD TAR & GRAVEL	Per Square
4 ply	*14.00 - 18.00*
5 ply	*17.00 - 20.00*
White Gravel Finish—Add	*2.00 - 4.00*
Asph. Compo. Shingles	*16.00 - 20.00*
Cedar Shingles	*20.00 - 24.00*
Cedar Shakes	*26.00 - 30.00*
Redwood Shakes	*28.00 - 34.00*
Clay Tiles	*40.00 - 50.00*

SEWER PIPE

VITRIFIED:		
Standard 4 in.	LF	.31
Standard 6 in.	LF	.56
Standard 8 in.	LF	.81
Standard 12 in.	LF	1.76
Standard 24 in.	LF	6.95
CLAY DRAIN PIPE:		
Standard 6 in.	LF	.34
Standard 8 in.	LF	.59

Rate for 100 Lin. Ft. F.O.B. Warehouse

STEEL

REINFORCING BARS:		
¼" rounds	LB	.122
⅜" rounds	LB	.111
½" rounds	LB	.107
⅝" rounds	LB	.104
¾" rounds	LB	.102
⅞" rounds	LB	.102
1" rounds	LB	.102
REINFORCING MESH (1050 SF Rolls)		
6x6 x 10x10	SF	.035
6x6 x 6x6	SF	.067
16 GA. TYING WIRE	LB	.130

Rates 100-1000 Lbs. F.O.B. Warehouse

STRUCTURAL STEEL

$325.00 and up per ton erected when out of mill.
$350.00 and up per ton erected when out of stock.

SHEET METAL

ROOF FLASHINGS:		
18 ga. Galv. Steel	*SF*	*.60 - 1.00*
22 ga. Galv. Steel	*SF*	*.50 - .90*
26 ga. Galv. Steel	*SF*	*.40 - .80*
18 ga. Aluminum	*SF*	*1.00 - 1.50*
22 ga. Aluminum	*SF*	*.80 - 1.30*
26 ga. Aluminum	*SF*	*.60 - 1.10*
24 oz. Copper	*SF*	*1.90 - 2.40*
20 oz. Copper	*SF*	*1.70 - 2.20*
16 oz. Copper	*SF*	*1.50 - 2.00*
26 ga. Galv. Steel		
4" o.g. gutter	*LF*	*.90 - 1.30*
Mitres and Drops	*EA*	*2.00 - 4.00*
22 ga. Galv. Louvres	*SF*	*2.50 - 3.50*
20 oz. Copper Louvres	*SF*	*3.00 - 4.50*

TILE WORK

CERAMIC TILE, Stock colors:		
Floors	*SF*	*1.95 - 2.45*
Walls	*SF*	*2.05 - 2.55*
Coved Base	*LF*	*1.05 - 1.45*
QUARRY TILE:		
6" x 6" x ½" Floors	*SF*	*1.60 - 2.00*
9" x 9" x ¾" Floors	*SF*	*1.75 - 2.15*
Treads and risers	*LF*	*3.00 - 4.50*
Coved Base	*LF*	*.90 - 1.30*

Mosaic Tile — Rates vary with design and colors. Each job should be priced from Manufacturer.

TERRAZZO & MARBLE

Terrazzo Floors	*SF*	*2.00 - 2.50*
Cond. Terr. Floors	*SF*	*2.20 - 2.75*
Precast treads and risers	*LF*	*3.50 - 4.50*
Precast landing slabs	*SF*	*3.00 - 4.00*

TILE

CERAMIC:

F.O.B. Warehouse

4¼" x 4¼" glazed	SF	.69
4¼" x 4¼" hard glazed	SF	.72
Random unglazed	SF	.73
6" x 2" cap	EA	.17
6" coved base	EA	.22
¼" round bead	LF	.18
QUARRY:		
6 x 6 x ½" Red	SF	.49
6 x 6 x ¾" Red	SF	.52
9 x 9 x ¾" Red	SF	.60
6 x 6" coved base	EA	.21
White Cement Grout	Per 100 Lbs.	6.25

VENETIAN BLINDS

Residential	SF	.40 & Up
Commercial	SF	.45 & Up

WINDOWS

STEEL SASH:		
Under 10 SF	SF	2.50 & Up
Under 15 SF	SF	2.00 & Up
Under 20 SF	SF	1.50 & Up
Under 30 SF	SF	1.00 & Up
ALUMINUM SASH:		
Under 10 SF	SF	2.75 & Up
Under 15 SF	SF	2.25 & Up
Under 20 SF	SF	1.75 & Up
Under 30 SF	SF	1.25 & Up

Above rates are for standard sections and stock sizes F.O.B. Warehouse

CONSTRUCTION INDUSTRY WAGE RATES

Table 1 has been prepared by the State of California, Department of Industrial Relations, Division of Labor Statistics and Research. The rates are the union hourly wage rates established by collective bargaining as of January 2, 1958, as reported by reliable sources.

TABLE 1—UNION HOURLY WAGE RATES, CONSTRUCTION INDUSTRY, CALIFORNIA

Following are the hourly rates of compensation established by collective bargaining, reported as of January 2, 1958 or later

CRAFT	San Francisco	Alameda	Contra Costa	Fresno	Sacramento	San Joaquin	Santa Clara	Solano	Los Angeles	San Bernardino	San Diego	Santa Barbara	Kern
BESTOS WORKER	$3.70	$3.70	$3.70	$3.70	$3.70	$3.70	$3.70	$3.70	$3.70	$3.70	$3.70	$3.70	$3.70
ILERMAKER	3.675	3.675	3.675	3.675	3.675	3.675	3.675	3.675	3.675	3.675	3.675	3.675	3.675
ICKLAYER	3.95	3.75	2.75	3.75	3.80	3.75	3.875	3.95	3.80	3.90	3.75		3.85
RICKLAYER HODCARRIER	3.15	3.15	3.15	2.90	3.10	2.90	3.00	3.10	2.75	2.75	2.75		2.75
ARPENTER	3.175	3.175	3.225	3.225	3.225	3.225	3.225	3.225	3.225	3.225	3.225	3.225	3.225
EMENT MASON	3.22	3.22	3.22	3.22	3.22	3.22	3.22	3.22	3.15	3.15	3.25	3.15	3.15
LECTRICIAN	3.936A	3.936A	3.936A		3.94A	3.50	4.03A	3.666A	3.90A	3.90A	3.90	3.85A	3.70
LAZIER	3.09	3.09	3.09	3.135	3.055	3.055	3.09	3.09	3.105	3.105	3.03	3.105	3.135
RON WORKER													
ORNAMENTAL	3.625	3.625	3.625	3.625	3.625	3.625	3.625	3.625	3.625	3.625	3.625	3.625	3.625
REINFORCING	3.375	3.375	3.375	3.375	3.375	3.375	3.375	3.375	3.375	3.375	3.375	3.375	3.375
STRUCTURAL	3.625	3.625	3.625	3.625	3.625	3.625	3.625	3.625	3.625	3.625	3.625	3.625	3.625
BORER, GENERAL OR CONSTRUCTION	2.505	2.505	2.505	2.505	2.505	2.505	2.505	2.505	2.50	2.50	2.48	2.50	2.50
LATHER	3.4375	3.84	3.84	3.45	3.60B	3.40C	3.40D	3.50E	3.9375		3.725	3.625F	
OPERATING ENGINEER													
Concrete mixer (up to 1 yard)	2.89	2.89	2.89	2.89	2.89	2.89	2.89	2.89					
Concrete mixer operator—Skip Type									2.96	2.96	2.96	2.96	2.96
Elevator Hoist Operator									3.19	3.19	3.19	3.19	3.19
Material Hoist (1 drum)	3.19	3.19	3.19	3.19	3.19	3.19	3.19	3.19					
Tractor Operator	3.33	3.33	3.33	3.33	3.33	3.33	3.33	3.33	3.47	3.47	3.47	3.47	3.47
PAINTER													
Brush	3.20	3.20	3.20	3.13	3.325	3.175	3.20	3.20	3.26a	3.25	3.19	3.13H	3.10
Spray	3.20	3.20	3.20	3.38	3.575	3.325	3.20	3.20	3.51a	3.50	3.74	3.38H	3.35
PILEDRIVERMAN	3.305	3.305	3.305	3.305	3.305	3.305	3.305	3.305	3.355	3.355		3.355	3.355
PLASTERER	3.69	3.545	3.545	3.35	3.60B	3.55C	3.58	3.50	3.9375	3.9375	3.725		
PLASTERER HODCARRIER	3.25	3.42	3.42	3.10	3.10	3.00C	3.20	3.15	3.6875	3.5625	3.475	3.50	3.6875
PLUMBER	3.67		3.935i	3.80J	3.70	3.80J	3.60	3.675	3.70	3.70	3.70	3.70	3.375
ROOFER	3.35	3.35	3.35	3.20	3.25	3.35	3.35	3.10K	3.20L	3.25	3.10	3.30	3.775
SHEET METAL WORKER	3.45	3.45	3.45	3.425	3.45	3.465	3.45	3.325	3.50	3.50	3.45	3.55	3.10
STEAMFITTER	3.67	3.96	3.96	3.80J	3.70	3.80J	3.60	3.675	3.70	3.70	3.70	3.70	3.775
TRUCK DRIVER— Dump Trucks under 4 yards	2.55	2.55	2.55	2.55	2.55	2.55	2.55	2.55	2.63	2.63	2.63	2.63	2.63
TILE SETTER	3.275	3.275	3.275	3.375	3.28	3.30	3.275	3.275	3.34	3.40	3.375	3.36	

A Includes 4% vacation allowance.
B Includes 5c hour for industry promotion and 5c hour for vacation fund.
C 1½% withheld for industry promotion.
D 1½c withheld for industry promotion.
E Includes 5c hour for industry promotion and 5c hour for vacation fund. Hourly rate for part of county adjacent to Sacramento County is $3.60.
F Northern part of County: $3.75.

a Pomona Area: Brush $3.25; Spray $3.50.
H Southern half of County: Brush $3.20; Spray $3.28.
i Includes 30c hour for vacation pay.
J Includes 15c hour which local union may elect to use for vacation purposes.
K Includes 10c hour for vacation fund.
L Includes 10c hour savings fund wage.

ATTENTION: The above tabulation has been prepared by the State of California, Department of Industrial Relations, Division of Labor Statistics and Research, and represents data reported by building trades councils, union locals, contractor organizations, and other reliable sources. The above rates do not include any payments to funds for health and welfare, pensions, vacations, industry promotion, apprentice training, etc., except as shown in the footnotes.

CONSTRUCTION INDUSTRY WAGE RATES — TABLE 2

Employer Contributions to Health and Welfare, Pension, Vacation and Other Funds
California Union Contracts, Construction Industry

(Revised March, 1957)

CRAFT	San Francisco	Fresno	Sacramento	San Joaquin	Santa Clara	Los Angeles	San Bernardino	San Diego
ASBESTOS WORKER	.10 W .11 hr. V	.10 W .11 hr. V	.10 W .11 hr. V	.10 W .11 hr. V	.10 W .11 hr. V	.10 W	.10 W	.10 W
BRICKLAYER	.15 W .14 P .05 hr. V		.15 W .10 P		.15 W			
BRICKLAYER HODCARRIER	.10 W .10 P .10 V	.10 W	.10 W	.10 W	.10 W	.075 W	.075 W	.075 W
CARPENTER	.10 W .10 hr. V	.10 W	.10 W	.10 W	.10 W	.10 W	.10 W	.10 W
CEMENT MASON	.10 W	.10 W	.10 W	.10 W	.10 W	.10 W	.10 W	.10 W .10 V
ELECTRICAL WORKER	.10 W 1% P 4% V	.10 W 1% P 4% V	.075 W 1% P	.075 W 1% P 4% V	1% P	1% P	1% P	1% P
GLAZIER	.075 W .085 V	.075 W 40 hr. V	.075 W .05 V	.075 W .05 V	.075 W .085 V	.075 W 40 hr. V	.075 W 40 hr. V	.075 W 10 hr. V
IRONWORKER: REINFORCING STRUCTURAL	.10 W .10 W	.10 W .10 W	.10 W .10 W	.10 W .10 W	.10 W .10 W	.10 W .10 W	.10 W .10 W	.10 W .10 W
LABORER, GENERAL	.10 W	.10 W	.10 W	.10 W	.10 W	.075 W	.075 W	.075 W
LATHER	.60 day W .70 day V		.10 W	.10 W	.075 W .05 V	.90 day W	.70 day W	.10 W
OPERATING ENGINEER TRACTOR OPERATOR (MIN.) POWER SHOVEL OP. (MIN.)	.10 W .10 W	.10 W .10 W	.10 W .10 W	.10 W .10 W	.10 W .10 W	.10 W .10 W	.10 W .10 W	.10 W .10 W
PAINTER, BRUSH	.095 W	.08 W	.075 W	.10 W	.095 W .07 V	.085 W	.08 W	.09 W
PLASTERER	.10 W .10 V	.10 W	.10 W	.10 W	.10 W .15 V	.10 W	.90 day W	.10 W
PLUMBER	.10 W .10 V	.15 W .10 P	.10 W .10 P .125 V	.10 W	.10 W .10 P .125 V	.10 W	.90 day W	.10 W
ROOFER	.10 W .10 V	.10 W	.10 W .10 V	.10 W	.075 W .10 V	.085 W	.10 W	.075 W
SHEET METAL WORKER	.075 W 4% V	.075 W 7 day V	.075 W .10 V	.075 W .12 V	.075 W 4% V	.095 W .10 V	.085 W .10 V	.085 W 6 day V
TILE SETTER	.075 W .09 V				.075 W .09 V	.025 W .06 V		

ATTENTION: The above tabulation has been prepared and compiled from the available data reported by building trades councils, union locals, contractor organizations and other reliable sources. The table was prepared from incomplete data; where no employer contributions are specified, it does not necessarily mean that none are required by the union contract.

The type of supplement is indicated by the following symbols: W—Health and Welfare; P—Pensions; V—Vacations; A—Apprentice training fund; Adm—Administration fund; JIB—Joint Industry Board; Prom—Promotion fund.

QUICK REFERENCE
ESTIMATOR'S DIRECTORY
Building and Construction Materials

ACOUSTICAL ENGINEERS
L. D. REEDER CO.
San Francisco: 1255 Sansome St., DO 2-5050
Sacramento: 3026 V St., GL 7-3505

AIR CONDITIONING
E. C. BRAUN CO.
Berkeley: 2115 Fourth St., TH 5-2356
GILMORE AIR CONDITIONING SERVICE
San Francisco: 1617 Harrison St., UN 1-2000
KAEMPER & BARRETT
San Francisco: 233 Industrial St., JU 6-6200
LINFORD AIR & REFRIGERATION CO.
Oakland: 174-12th St., TW 3-6521
MALM METAL PRODUCTS
Santa Rosa: 724-2nd St., SR 454
JAMES A. NELSON CO.
San Francisco: 1375 Howard St., HE 1-0140

ALUMINUM BLDG. PRODUCTS
MICHEL & PFEFFER IRON WORKS (Wrought Iron)
So. San Francisco: 212 Shaw Road, PLaza 5-8983
REYNOLDS METALS CO.
San Francisco: 3201 Third St., MI 7-2990
SOULE STEEL CO.
San Francisco: 1750 Army St., VA 4-4141
UNIVERSAL WINDOW CO.
Berkeley: 950 Parker St., TH 1-1600

ARCHITECTURAL PORCELAIN ENAMEL
CALIFORNIA METAL ENAMELING CO.
Los Angeles: 6904 E. Slauson, RA 3-6351
San Francisco: Continental Bldg. Products Co.,
178 Fremont St.
Portland: Portland Wire & Iron Works,
4644 S.E. Seventeenth Ave.
Seattle: Foster-Bray Co., 2412 1st Ave. So.
Spokane: Bernhard Schafer, Inc., West 34, 2nd Ave.
Salt Lake City: S. A. Roberts & Co., 109 W. 2nd So.
Dallas: Offenhauser Co., 2201 Telephone Rd.
El Paso: Architectural Products Co.,
506 E. Yandell Blvd.
Phoenix: Haskell-Thomas Co., 3808 No. Central
San Diego: Maloney Specialties, Inc., 823 W. Laurel St.
Boise: Intermountain Glass Co., 1417 Main St.

ARCHITECTURAL & AERIAL PHOTOGRAPHS
FRED ENGLISH
Belmont, Calif.: 1310 Old County Road, LY 1-0385

ARCHITECTURAL VENEER
Ceramic Veneer
GLADDING, McBEAN & CO.
San Francisco: Harrison at 9th St., UN 1-7400
Los Angeles: 2901 Los Feliz Blvd., OL 2121
Portland: 110 S.E. Main St., EA 6179
Seattle 99: 945 Elliott Ave., West, GA 0330
Spokane: 1102 N. Monroe St., BR 3259
KRAFTILE COMPANY
Niles, Calif., Niles 3611

Porcelain Veneer
PORCELAIN ENAMEL PUBLICITY BUREAU
Oakland 12: Room 601, Franklin Building
Pasadena 8: P. O. Box 186, East Pasadena Station

Granite Veneer
VERMONT MARBLE COMPANY
San Francisco 24: 6000 3rd St., VA 6-5024
Los Angeles: 3522 Council St., DU 2-6339

Marble Veneer
VERMONT MARBLE COMPANY
San Francisco 24: 6000 3rd St., VA 6-5024
Los Angeles: 3522 Council St., DU 2-6339

BANKS - FINANCING
CROCKER-ANGLO NATIONAL BANK
San Francisco: 13 Offices

BLINDS
PARAMOUNT VENETIAN BLIND CO.
San Francisco: 5929 Mission St., JU 5-2436

BRASS PRODUCTS
GREENBERG'S, M. SONS
San Francisco 7: 765 Folsom, EX 2-3143
Los Angeles 23: 1258 S. Boyle, AN 3-7108
Seattle 4:1016 First Ave. So., MA 5140
Phoenix: 3009 N. 19th Ave., Apt. 92, PH 2-7663
Portland 4: 510 Builders Exch. Bldg., AT 6443

BRICKWORK
Face Brick
GLADDING McBEAN & CO.
San Francisco: Harrison at 9th, UN 1-7400
KRAFTILE CO.
Niles, Calif., Niles 3611
UNITED MATERIALS & RICHMOND BRICK CO.
Point Richmond, BE 4-5032

BRONZE PRODUCTS
GREENBERG'S M. SONS
San Francisco: 765 Folsom St., EX 2-3143
MICHEL & PFEFFER IRON WORKS
So. San Francisco: 212 Shaw Road, PLaza 5-8983
C. E. TOLAND & SON
Oakland: 2635 Peralta St., GL 1-2580

BUILDING HARDWARE
E. M. HUNDLEY HARDWARE CO.
San Francisco: 662 Mission St., YU 2-3322

BUILDING PAPERS & FELTS
PACIFIC CEMENT & AGGREGATES INC.
San Francisco: 400 Alabama St., KL 2-1616

CABINETS & FIXTURES
CENTRAL MILL & CABINET CO.
San Francisco: 1595 Fairfax Ave., VA 4-7316
THE FINK & SCHINDLER CO.
San Francisco: 552 Brannan St., EX 2-1513
JONES KRAFT SHOP
San Francisco: 1314 Ocean Avenue., JU 7-1545
MULLEN MFG. CO.
San Francisco: 64 Rausch St., UN 1-5815
PARAMOUNT BUILT IN FIXTURE CO.
Oakland: 962 Stanford Ave., OL 3-9911
ROYAL SHOWCASE CO.
San Francisco: 770 McAllister St., JO 7-0311

CEMENT
CALAVERAS CEMENT CO.
San Francisco: 315 Montgomery St.
DO 2-4224, Enterprise 1-2315
PACIFIC CEMENT & AGGREGATES INC.
San Francisco: 400 Alabama St., KL 2-1616

CONCRETE AGGREGATES
Ready Mixed Concrete
CENTRAL CONCRETE SUPPLY CO.
San Jose: 610 McKendrie St.
PACIFIC CEMENT & AGGREGATES INC.
San Francisco: 400 Alabama St., KL 2-1616
Sacramento: 16th and A Sts., GI 3-6586
San Jose: 790 Stockton Ave., CY 2-5620
Oakland: 2400 Peralta St., GL 1-0177
Stockton: 820 So. California St., ST 8-8643
READYMIX CONCRETE CO.
Santa Rosa: 50 W. Cottage Ave.
RHODES-JAMIESON LTD.
Oakland: 333-23rd Ave., KE 3-5225
SANTA ROSA BLDG. MATERIALS CO.
Santa Rosa: Roberts Ave.

CONCRETE ACCESSORIES
Screed Materials
C. & H. SPECIALTIES CO.
Berkeley: 909 Camelia St., LA 4-5358

CONCRETE BLOCKS
BASALT ROCK CO.
Napa, Calif.

CONCRETE COLORS—HARDENERS
CONRAD SOVIG CO.
875 Bryant St., HE 1-1345

CONSTRUCTION SERVICES
LE ROY CONSTRUCTION SERVICES
San Francisco, 143 Third St., SU 1-8914

DECKS—ROOF
UNITED STATES GYPSUM CO.
2322 W. 3rd St., Los Angeles 54, Calif.
300 W. Adams St., Chicago 6, Ill.

DOORS
THE BILCO COMPANY
New Haven, Conn.
Oakland: Geo. B. Schultz, 190 MacArthur Blvd.
Sacramento: Harry B. Ogle & Assoc., 1331 T St.
Fresno: Healey & Popovich, 1703 Fulton St.
Reseda: Daniel Dunner, 6200 Alonzo Ave.

Cold Storage Doors
BIRKENWALD
Portland: 310 N.W. 5th Ave.

Electric Doors
ROLY-DOOR SALES CO.
San Francisco, 5976 Mission St., PL 5-5089

Folding Doors
WALTER D. BATES & ASSOCIATES
San Francisco, 693 Mission St., GA 1-6971

Hardwood Doors
BELLWOOD CO. OF CALIF.
Orange, Calif., 533 W. Collins Ave.

Hollywood Doors
WEST COAST SCREEN CO.
Los Angeles: 1127 E. 63rd St., AD 1-1108
T. M. COBB CO.
Los Angeles & San Diego
W. P. FULLER CO.
Seattle, Tacoma, Portland
HOGAN LUMBER CO.
Oakland: 700 - 6th Ave.
HOUSTON SASH & DOOR
Houston, Texas
SOUTHWESTERN SASH & DOOR
Phoenix, Tucson, Arizona
El Paso, Texas
WESTERN PINE SUPPLY CO.
Emeryville: 5760 Shellmound St.
GEO. C. VAUGHAN & SONS
San Antonio & Houston, Texas

Screen Doors
WEST COAST SCREEN DOOR CO.

DRAFTING ROOM EQUIPMENT
GENERAL FIREPROOFING CO.
Oakland: 332-19th St., GL 2-4280
Los Angeles: 1200 South Hope St., RI 7-7501
San Francisco: 1025 Howard St., HE 1-7070

DRINKING FOUNTAINS
HAWS DRINKING FAUCET CO.
Berkeley: 1435 Fourth St., LA 5-3341

ELECTRICAL CONTRACTORS
COOPMAN ELECTRIC CO.
San Francisco: 85 - 14th St., MA 1-4438
ETS-HOKIN & GALVAN
San Francisco: 551 Mission St., EX 2-0432

43

ELECTRICAL CONTRACTORS (cont'd)

LEMOGE ELECTRIC CO.
San Francisco: 212 Clara St., DO 2-6010
LYNCH ELECTRIC CO.
San Francisco: 937 McAllister St., WI 5158
PACIFIC ELECTRIC & MECHANICAL CO.
San Francisco: Gough & Fell Sts., HE 1-5904

ELECTRIC HEATERS

WESIX ELECTRIC HEATER CO.
San Francisco: 390 First St., GA 1-2211

FIRE ESCAPES

MICHEL & PFEFFER IRON WORKS
South San Francisco: 212 Shaw Road, PLaza 5-8983

FIRE PROTECTION EQUIPMENT

FIRE PROTECTION PRODUCTS CO.
San Francisco: 1101-16th St., UN 1-2420
ETS-HOKIN & GALVAN
San Francisco: 551 Mission St., EX 2-0432
BARNARD ENGINEERING CO.
San Francisco: 35 Elmira St., JU 5-4642

FLOORS

Floor Tile
GLADDING McBEAN & CO.
San Francisco: Harrison at 9th St., UN 1-744
Los Angeles: 2901 Las Feliz Bldg., OL 2121
KRAFTILE CO.
Niles, Calif., Niles 3611

Resilient Floors
PETERSON-COBBY CO.
San Francisco: 218 Clara St., EX 2-8714
TURNER RESILIENT FLOORS CO.
San Francisco: 2280 Shafter Ave., AT 2-7720

FLOOR DRAINS
JOSAM PACIFIC COMPANY
San Francisco: 765 Folsom St., EX 2-3142

GAS VENTS
WM. WALLACE CO.
Belmont, Calif.

GENERAL CONTRACTORS

O. E. ANDERSON
San Jose: 1075 No. 10th St., CY 3-8844
BARRETT CONSTRUCTION CO.
San Francisco: 1800 Evans Ave., MI 7-9700
JOSEPH BETTANCOURT
South San Francisco: 125 So. Linden St., PL 5-9185
DINWIDDIE CONSTRUCTION CO.
San Francisco: Crocker Bldg., YU 6-2718
D. L. FAULL CONSTRUCTION CO.
Santa Rosa: 1236 Cleveland Ave.
HAAS & HAYNIE
San Francisco: 275 Pine St., DO 2-0678
HENDERSON CONSTRUCTION CO.
San Francisco: 33 Ritch St., GA 1-0856
JACKS & IRVINE
San Francisco: 620 Market St., YU 6-0511
G. P. W. JENSEN & SONS
San Francisco: 320 Market St., GA 1-2444
RALPH LARSEN & SON
San Francisco: 64 So. Park, YU 2-5682
LINDGREN & SWINERTON
San Francisco: 200 Bush St., GA 1-2980
MacDONALD, YOUNG & NELSON
San Francisco: 351 California St., YU 2-4700
MATTOCK CONSTRUCTION CO.
San Francisco: 220 Clara St., GA 1-5516
OLSEN CONSTRUCTION CO.
Santa Rosa: 125 Brookwood Ave., SR 2030
BEN ORTSKY
Cotati: Cypress Ave., Pet. 5-4383
PARKER, STEFFANS & PEARCE
San Mateo: 135 So. Park, EX 2-6639
RAPP, CHRISTENSEN & FOSTER
Santa Rosa: 705 Bennett Ave.

STOLTE, INC.
Oakland: 8451 San Leandro Ave., LO 2-4611
SWINERTON & WALBERG
San Francisco: 200 Bush St., GA 1-2980

FURNITURE—INSTITUTIONAL
GENERAL FIREPROOFING CO.
San Francisco: 1025 Howard St., HE 1-7070
Oakland: 332-19th St., GL 2-4280
Los Angeles: 1200 South Hope St., RI 7-7501

HEATING & VENTILATING
ATLAS HEATING & VENT. CO.
San Francisco: 557-4th St., DO 2-0377
E. C. BRAUN CO.
Berkeley: 2115 Fourth St., TH 5-2356
C. W. HALL
Santa Rosa: 1665 Sebastopol Rd., SR 6354
S. T. JOHNSON CO.
Oakland: 940 Arlington Ave., OL 2-6000
LOUIS V. KELLER
San Francisco: 289 Tehama St., JU 6-6252
L. J. KRUSE CO.
Oakland: 6247 College Ave., OL 2-8332
MALM METAL PRODUCTS
Santa Rosa: 724-2nd St., SR 454
JAS. A. NELSON CO.
San Francisco: 1375 Howard St., HE 1-0140
SCOTT COMPANY
Oakland: 1919 Market St., GL 1-1937
WESIX ELECTRIC HEATER CO.
San Francisco: 390 First St., GA 1-2211
Los Angeles: 530 W. 7th St., MI 8096

INSULATION WALL BOARD
PACIFIC CEMENT & AGGREGATES, INC.
San Francisco: 400 Alabama St., KL 2-1616

INTERCEPTING DEVICES
JOSAM PACIFIC CO.
San Francisco: 765 Folsom St., EX 2-3142

IRON—ORNAMENTAL
MICHEL & PFEFFER IRON WKS.
So. San Francisco: 212 Shaw Road, PL 5-8983

LATHING & PLASTERING
ANGELO J. DANERI
San Francisco: 1433 Fairfax Ave., AT 8-1582
K-LATH CORP.
Alhambra: 909 So. Fremont St., Alhambra
A. E. KNOWLES CORP.
San Francisco: 3330 San Bruno Ave., JU 7-2091
G. H. & C. MARTINELLI
San Francisco: 174 Shotwell St., UN 3-6112
FREDERICK MEISWINKEL
San Francisco: 2155 Turk St., JO 7-7587
RHODES-JAMIESON LTD.
Oakland: 333-23rd Ave., KE 3-5225
PATRICK J. RUANE
San Francisco: 44 San Jose Ave., MI 7-6414

LIGHTING FIXTURES
SMOOT-HOLMAN COMPANY
Inglewood, Calif., OR 8-1217
San Francisco: 55 Mississippi St., MA 1-8474

LIGHTING & CEILING SYSTEMS
UNITED LIGHTING AND FIXTURE CO.
Oakland: 3120 Chapman St., KE 3-8711

LUMBER
CHRISTENSEN LUMBER CO.
San Francisco: Quint & Evans Ave., VA 4-5832
ART HOGAN LUMBER CO.
1701 Galvez Ave., ATwater 2-1157
MEAD CLARK LUMBER CO.
Santa Rosa: 3rd & Railroad
ROLANDO LUMBER CO.
San Francisco: 5th & Berry Sts., SU 1-6901
STERLING LUMBER CO.
Santa Rosa: 1129 College Ave., S. R. 82

MARBLE
JOS. MUSTO SONS-KEENAN CO.
San Francisco: 555 No. Point St., GR 4-6365
VERMONT MARBLE CO.
San Francisco: 6000-3rd St., VA 6-5024

MASONRY
BASALT ROCK CO.
Napa, Calif.
San Francisco: 260 Kearney St., GA 1-3758
WM. A. RAINEY & SON
San Francisco: 323 Clementina St., SU 1-0072
GEO. W. REED CO.
San Francisco: 1390 So. Van Ness Ave., AT 2-1226

METAL EXTERIOR WALLS
THE KAWNEER CO.
Berkeley: 930 Dwight Way, TH 5-8710

METAL FRAMING
UNISTRUT OF NORTHERN CALIFORNIA
Berkeley: 2547-9th St., TH 1-3031
Enterprise 1-2204

METAL GRATING
KLEMP METAL GRATING CORP.
Chicago, Ill.: 6601 So. Melvina St.

METAL LATH—EXPANDED
PACIFIC CEMENT & AGGREGATES, INC.
San Francisco: 400 Alabama St., KL 2-1616

METAL PARTITIONS
THE E. F. HAUSERMAN CO.
San Francisco: 485 Brannan St., YU 2-5477

METAL PRODUCTS
FORDERER CORNICE WORKS
San Francisco: 269 Potrero Ave., HE 1-4100

MILLWORK
CENTRAL MILL & CABINET CO.
San Francisco: 1595 Fairfax Ave., VA 4-7316
THE FINK & SCHINDLER CO.
San Francisco: 552 Brannan St., EX 2-1513
MULLEN MFG. CO.
San Francisco: 64 Rausch St., UN 1-5815
PACIFIC MFG. CO.
San Francisco: 16 Beale St., GA 1-7755
Santa Clara: 2610 The Alameda, S. C. 607
Los Angeles: 6820 McKinley Ave., TH 4156
SOUTH CITY LUMBER & SUPPLY CO.
So. San Francisco: Railroad & Spruce, PL 5-7085

OFFICE EQUIPMENT
GENERAL FIREPROOFING CO.
Los Angeles: 1200 South Hope St., RI 7-7501
San Francisco: 1025 Howard St., HE 1-7070
Oakland: 332-19th St., GL 2-4280

OIL BURNERS
S. T. JOHNSON CO.
Oakland: 940 Arlington Ave., GL 2-6000
San Francisco: 585 Potrero Ave., MA 1-2757
Philadelphia, Pa.: 401 North Broad St.

ORNAMENTAL IRON
MICHEL & PFEFFER IRON WORKS
So. San Francisco: 212 Shaw Rd., PL 5-8983

PAINTING
R. P. PAOLI & CO.
San Francisco: 2530 Lombard St., WE 1-1632
SINCLAIR PAINT CO.
San Francisco: 2112-15th St., HE 1-2196
D. ZELINSKY & SONS
San Francisco: 165 Groove St., MA 1-7400

PHOTOGRAPHS
Construction Progress
FRED ENGLISH
Belmont, Calif.: 1310 Old County Road, LY 1-0385

PLASTER
PACIFIC CEMENT & AGGREGATE INC.
San Francisco: 400 Alabama St., KL 2-1616

PLASTIC PRODUCTS
PLASTIC SALES & SERVICE
San Francisco: 409 Bryant St., DO 2-6433
WEST COAST INDUSTRIES
San Francisco: 3150-18th St., MA 1-5657

CONSTRUCTION CONTRACTS AWARDED AND MISCELLANEOUS PERSONNEL DATA

PLAYGROUND AND FIELD HOUSE, San Francisco. City and County of San Francisco, owner. Hayes Valley Playground facilities construction—$108,739. ARCHITECT: Chas. W. Griffiths, City Architect, San Francisco City Hall. GENERAL CONTRACTOR: De Narde & Ganske, 1950 Oakdale Ave., San Francisco.

MEDICAL OFFICE, Redwood City, San Mateo county. Kaiser Foundation Hospital, San Francisco, owner. Wood frame construction of a medical office building. ARCHITECT: Clarence Mayhew, 251 Post St., San Francisco. GENERAL CONTRACTOR: Vance M. Brown & Sons, 351 Pepper Ave., Palo Alto.

MARKET BLDG., La Habra, Orange county. Sansimena Corp., La Habra, owner. Reinforced brick and masonry market building; 30,000 sq. ft. area with 10,400 sq. ft. of mezzanine, composition roof, metal sash, aluminum store front also plate glass, slab, terrazzo and asphalt tile floors, pipe columns, structural steel, tapered steel beams, air conditioning, asphalt paving, loading ramps. ARCHITECT: Robert H. Ainsworth, 1199 E. Walnut St., Pasadena. GENERAL CONTRACTOR: Ernest W. Hahn, Inc., 219 S. Hawthorne Blvd., Hawthorne.

HIGH SCHOOL, Moro Bay, San Luis Obispo County. San Luis Obispo School District, owner. 1-story, wood frame construction, concrete slab floors, concrete block walls, facilities for administration room, 7 classrooms, arts and crafts, music, home making, shop, physical education, teachers room, dining room, student dining, toilet rooms, and some site work—$1,215,915. ARCHITECT: Falk & Booth,

16 Beale St., San Francisco: GENERAL CONTRACTOR: Barnhart Const. Co., 785 Walsh Ave., Santa Clara.

FIRE STATION, Pasadena, Los Angeles county. City of Pasadena, owner. Linda Vista Fire Station, all facilities—$58,080. ARCHITECT: Frick and Frick, 30 N. Altadena Dr., Pasadena. GENERAL CONTRACTOR: Samuelson Bros., 341 Ocean View Blvd., Glendale.

HOSPITAL ADDN., Chico, Butte county. Emloe Hospital, Chico, owner. Wood frame construction, plaster interior, stucco exterior; facilities for 20 additional bed wing including multi-purpose room, nursery, shower room, toilet facilities—$106,470. ARCHITECT: Thomas F. Dunlap, 304 Broadway, Chico. CONSULTING ARCHITECTS: Stone, Mulloy, Marraccini & Paterson, 536 Mission St., San Francisco. GENERAL CONTRACTOR: Fred S. Macomber, 2727 N. Cedar Ave., Fresno.

PARISH HOUSE ALTERATION, Pasadena, Los Angeles county. All Saints Episcopal Church, Pasadena, owner. Alter-

ations to kitchen and classrooms in the Parish House. ARCHITECT: Bennett and Bennett, 109 So. Los Robles, Pasadena. GENERAL CONTRACTOR: Glen E. Hummer Const. Co., 3242 E. Colorado Blvd., Pasadena.

SCHOOL ADDN., Bowers School, Santa Clara. Jefferson Union High School District, Santa Clara, owner. Facilities to include multi-purpose room, kitchen, service facilities, utilities, some site development—$109,240. ARCHITECT: Clyde D. Goudie, 307 Phelan Ave., San Jose. GENERAL CONTRACTOR: Leonard Semas Const. Co., 2885 Homestead Rd., Santa Clara.

OFFICE BLDG., Hayward, Alameda county. Star Leader Company, Hayward, owner. 1-story concrete block construction, steel joists, gypsum roof—$43,735. ARCHITECT: George McCue, 2007 Hopkins Street, Berkeley. ASSOCIATE ARCHITECT: Huntington & Brelsford, Denver, Colorado. GENERAL CONTRACTOR: Hugo Muller, Jr., 6089 Claremont Ave., Oakland.

WAREHOUSE, Pacoima, Los Angeles county. Keene W. Thomas, Canoga Park, owner. Frame and stucco warehouse; 72 x 150 ft., composition roof, tapered steel girders, concrete slab, pipe columns, sliding doors, toilets, interior plaster, wall furnaces in office—$36,690. ENGINEER: G. R. Campbell, Consulting Engineer, 4155 Bellaire, Studio City.

CHURCH, Larkspur, Marin county. Redwood Presbyterian Church, Larkspur,

owner. New building to include complete church facilities—$106,875. ARCHITECT: Donald Powers Smith, 133 Kearny St., San Francisco. GENERAL CONTRACTOR: Ray I. Johnson Const. Co., P. O. Box 98, Kentfield.

ANIMAL HOUSE, Stanford University Campus, Santa Clara county. Stanford University, Board of Trustees, Palo Alto, owner. Wood frame and concrete block construction—$38,300. ARCHITECT: Spencer & Lee, 251 Kearny St., San Francisco. GENERAL CONTRACTOR: Brickman Const. Co., 1702 Miramonte Ave., Mountain View.

ARMED FORCES HOUSING, Travis Air Force Base, Solano county. U. S. Air Force Base Procurement Office, Travis Air Force Base, owner. Work comprises construction of 48 units of housing for armed service personnel—$782,713. GENERAL CONTRACTOR: Gresham Const. Co., P. O. Box 300, Santa Clara.

DRIVE - IN REALTY OFFICE, Richmond, Contra Costa county. West Contra Costa Board of Realtors, owner. 2-Story concrete block construction; 25x51 ft., wood exterior, 150 foot street frontage; 2nd floor entire conference room to seat 20 persons; ground floor consists of general offices and two-story lobby; drive-in facilities and parking area for 16 vehicles—$33,000. GENERAL CONTRACTOR: Edward Eoff Co., 1430 Nevin Ave., Richmond.

LOW RENT HOUSING, Outler, Tulare county. Tulare County Housing Authority, Visalia, owner. Project consists of complete construction, with all facilities, of 24 low rent housing units—$237,800. ARCHITECT: James P. Lockett, 121 E. Main St., Visalia. GENERAL CONTRACTOR: Guy I. Munson Co., 275 W. Tulare St., Dinuba.

LUXURY APARTMENT, Sacramento. Morris & Lillian Tamres, Sacramento, owner. 3-Story building, 229x173 ft., to contain 42 complete apartment units; one and two bedrooms, heated, swimming pool; individual foyer and terraces; self-service elevator, parking area for 40 vehicles—$500,000. DESIGNER: Jules F. Reither, 3415 Fulton Ave., Sacramento. GENERAL CONTRACTOR: Stoddard Const. Co., 5308 Valhalla Dr., Carmichael.

JUNIOR HIGH SCHOOL, Frick-Oakland, Alameda county. Oakland Unified School District, Oakland, owner. Rein-

forced concrete, slab floors, wood frame and wood siding, stucco exterior walls; to provide complete facilities for administration unit, 16 classrooms, dining room, kitchen, multiple-use buildings, 3 music rooms, portable shop buildings, storage facilities, gymnasium, boys' and girls' shower and locker rooms, toilet facilities—$1,604,500. ARCHITECT: Anderson & Simonds, 2800 Park Blvd., Oakland. GENERAL CONTRACTOR: John E. Branagh, 42 La Salle Ave., Piedmont.

MEDICAL BLDG., Richmond, Contra Costa county, Richmond Medical Center, Richmond, owner. 1-Story, frame and stucco addition to an existing medical building, 1,500 sq. ft. area, plate glass, concrete slab floor, composition roof, heating, ventilating, plumbing, electrical work. ARCHITECT: William L. Duquette, 330 S. Rosemead Blvd., Pasadena. GENERAL CONTRACTOR: Carl Overaa Const. Co., 520-16th St., Richmond.

BANK, Ione, Amador county. Bank of America, San Francisco, owner. Complete new banking building and facilities—$48,998. DESIGNER: Continental Service Company, San Francisco. GENERAL CONTRACTOR: Jay Bailey Const. Co., P. O. Box 148, Woodland.

MAUSOLEUM, Oakland, Alameda county, Mt. View Cemetery Association, Oakland, owner. Project comprises construction of a new mausoleum—$475,000. ARCHITECT: Kitchen & Hunt, 40-1st Street, San Francisco. GENERAL CONTRACTOR: Dinwiddie Const. Co., Crocker Bldg., San Francisco.

FIRE STATION, Mountain View, Santa Clara county. City of Mt. View, owner. Modern, contemporary design new fire station will house two pieces of equipment and dormitory facilities for six firemen—$33,995. ARCHITECT: Joel E. Bowman, 748 Arroyo Road, Los Altos. GENERAL CONTRACTOR: John J. Mauro, 889 Middle Rincon Road, Santa Rosa.

CAFETORIUM, Montvue School, Pomona, Los Angeles county. Pomona School District, owner. Construction of a multi-purpose cafetorium and all facilities—$112,936. ARCHITECT: Don L. Yinger, 565 E. Holt Ave., Pomona. GENERAL CONTRACTOR: Herman Rempel, 537 N. 6th Ave., Upland.

STUDENT HEALTH SERVICE BLDG., State Polytechnic College, San Luis Obispo. State of California, Div. of Architecture, Sacramento, owner. 1-Story building with total floor area of 13,200 sq. ft.; facilities for 30-bed hospital unit and all appurtenances—$238,000. ARCHITECT: Anson Boyd, California State Architect, Sacramento. GENERAL CONTRACTOR: Harris Construction Company, P. O. Box 109, Fresno.

ELEMENTARY SCHOOL, Pollock Pines, El Dorado county. Pollock Pines School District, owner. Wood frame, aluminum walls, brick and stucco exterior, concrete slab floors; facilities for administration unit, 3 classrooms, multi - use rooms, and toilets—$122,000. ARCHITECT: Cox & Liske, Whitson W. Cox, Architect, 926 "J" St., Sacramento. GENERAL CONTRACTOR: Bingham Const. Co., 6329 Eastern Ave., Sacramento.

JUNIOR HIGH ADD'N, Yucaipa Junior High, Redlands, San Bernardino county. Redlands High School District, owner. 1-

Story, frame and stucco storage room, and a 1-story, frame and stucco addition to the library—$26,275. ARCHITECT: Ulmer & Rack, 9½ E. State St., Redlands. GENERAL CONTRACTOR: E. E. Hunt, P. O. Box 781, Beaumont.

POLICE GARAGE, Civic Center, San Jose, Santa Clara county. City of San Jose, owner. Project includes construction of a new police garage building in the civic center with all usual facilities—$416,-800. GENERAL CONTRACTOR: Carl N. Swenson Co., 1095 Stockton Ave., San Jose.

FACTORY ADD'N, North Hollywood, Los Angeles county. Fred Johnsman, Los Angeles, owner. Concrete block factory building; 44x50 ft., composition roof, skylights, metal sash, concrete slab, tapered steel girders, overhead doors, unit air conditioning, toilets. ARCHITECT: Jay Cowan, 141 S. Barrington Ave., Los Angeles.

BLEACHERS & LIBRARY ADD'N, Sierra Joint Union High School, Fresno. Sierra Joint Union High School District, Fresno, owner. Work comprises construction of new bleachers at the athletic field and an addition to the present library building—$325,577. ARCHITECT: Alastair Simpson, 64 N. Fulton, Fresno. GENERAL CONTRACTOR: Lewis C. Nelson & Sons, 2915 McCall St., Selma.

CHURCH ADD'N, Burlingame, San Mateo county. First Methodist Church, Burlingame, owner. Wood frame construction of an addition to the second-story of existing church building, and alterations; facilities for classrooms and miscellaneous uses. ARCHITECT: Edwin Wadsworth, 2720 El Camino Real, Redwood City. GENERAL CONTRACTOR: Charles J. Pedersen Co., 311-7th Avenue, San Mateo.

FIRE STATION, South Gate, Los Angeles county. City of South Gate, owner, 1-Story concrete block building to be known as Fire Station No. 3; 4000 sq. ft. of area, dormitory, hose tower, concrete paving, personal exercise area, painting, plumbing, electrical work—$57,758. ARCHITECT: Wallner, Bostock & Wallis, Architect and Engineers, 3260 E. Florence Ave., Huntington Park. GENERAL CONTRACTOR: John H. Parrish, 7919 Wilcox Ave., Bell.

HIGH SCHOOL ADD'N, Union High School, Alturas, Modoc county. Modoc Union High School District, Alturas, owner. Wood frame construction to provide complete shop building facilities—$76,694. ARCHITECT: Howard R. Perrin, 1120 Main St., Klamath Falls, Oregon. GENERAL CONTRACTOR: Gibbons & Zick, P. O. Box 631, Alturas.

JR. HIGH SCHOOL, Arlington; Riverside, Riverside county. Riverside High School District, owner. Completely new Junior High School in Riverside to be known as the Arlington Junior High School—$789,381. ARCHITECT: Herman O. Ruhnau, Mission Inn Rotunda, Riverside. GENERAL CONTRACTOR: Taylor & Clark, 10691 Magnolia Ave., Arlington.

MARRIED STUDENTS, Housing Development, Stanford University, Santa Clara county. Stanford University, Palo Alto, owner. Initial unit of construction to provide housing for married students to con-

sist of 250 one and 2-story apartments; also a 2-story structure of wood frame construction—$2,164,000. ARCHITECT: Wurster, Bernardi & Emmons, 202 Green St., San Francisco. SUPERVISING ARCHITECT: Eldridge T. Spencer, 251 Kearny St., San Francisco. GENERAL CONTRACTOR: Williams & Burrows, Inc., 500 Harbor Blvd., Belmont.

LABORATORY EXTENSION, Palo Alto, Santa Clara county. Stanford University, owner. Reinforced concrete office and laboratory extension of high energy laboratory, some wood frame—$255,900. ARCHITECT: Spencer & Lee, 251 Kearny St., San Francisco. GENERAL CONTRACTOR: Dickman Const. Co., 1702 Miramonte Ave., Mt. View.

MEDICAL BLDG., Saratoga, Santa Clara county. George Oldham, Saratoga, owner. Wood frame construction medical building with all needed facilities—$38,410. ARCHITECT: Knox & Lincoln, 2181 Moorpark Ave., San Jose. GENERAL CONTRACTOR: Fred W. Winniger, 1244 Laurie Ave., San Jose.

HIGH SCHOOL ADD'N, Carmel, Monterey county. Carmel Unified School District, owner. Wood frame and stone, adobe veneer construction of a shop building at the Carmel High School—$55,500. ARCHITECT: Elstone & Cranston, 6th and Junipero, Carmel. GENERAL CONTRACTOR: Harold C. Geyer, P. O. Box 1190, Monterey.

SEWER-DRAINAGE, Yountville, State of California, Sacramento, owner. Work comprises furnishing and installing sewage equipment and piping, manholes, cleanouts, pumps, heating equipment, sand trap, storm drains, concrete catch basins, gutters, retaining wall, plant mix surfacing and site clearance at the California State Veterans Home in Yountville—$31,450. ARCHITECT: Anson Boyd, State Architect, Sacramento. GENERAL CONTRACTOR: E. R. Koller Const., 1907 Merchant St., Crockett.

NEVADA STATE MUSEUM ADD'N, Carson City, Nevada. State of Nevada, Planning Board, Carson City, owner. Work comprises construction of an addition to the existing Nevada State Museum building in Carson City — $190,-581. ARCHITECT: De Longchamps &

O'Brien, 160 No. Arlington Ave., Reno. GENERAL CONTRACTOR: Savini Const. Co., Caron City, Nevada.

MAXIMUM SECURITY CELL BLOCK, State Prison, Carson City, Nevada. State of Nevada, owner. Construction of a new maximum security cell block at the Nevada State Prison near Carson City, Nevada—$259,917. ARCHITECT: Edward S. Parsons, 210 W. 2nd St., Carson City, Nevada. GENERAL CONTRACTOR: McKenzie Const. Co., P. O. Box 137, Reno, Nevada.

OFFICE BLDG., San Jose, Santa Clara county. Eggco Products, San Jose, owner. Construction of a new office building—$40,816. ARCHITECT: Binder & Curtis, 35 W. San Carlos St., San Jose. GENERAL CONTRACTOR: Elmo Pardini, 1741 Hamilton Ave., San Jose.

IN THE NEWS

NEW TECHNIQUES IN INDUSTRIAL ENGINEERING OFFERED IN COURSE

New techniques and development in industrial engineering and management will be presented by top experts in a 10-day course at the University of California, Los Angeles, from January 26-February 5, 1959.

Requirements of the Engineering and Management course will be a flexible mind and interest in higher job possibilities, rather than a formal educational background. Participants will attend four classes daily, selected from 24 highly diversified subjects, including work measurement, work simplification, automation, leadership laboratory, industrial human relations, statistics, and data processing.

CLEVELAND CAP SCREW COMPANY TO BUILD PLANT

The Cleveland Cap Screw Company, a subsidiary of the Standard Pressed Steel Corp. of Jenkintown, Pa., have acquired a site in the new 80-acre upland tract in the Utah Construction Company's South San Francisco Industrial Park, and will build a combination office and warehouse facility costing an estimated $200,000 and containing 24,000 sq. ft. of floor space.

Cleveland selected the site as ideally suited for unusually heavy floor load requirements because of its solid rock foundation.

SAFEWAY BUILDS NEW SUNNYVALE STORE

Safeway Stores, Inc., is building a new supermarket in Sunnyvale, California, containing 16,000 sq. ft. of interior space, and provision for 116 automobiles in adjacent parking facilities.

The design and construction of the structure will be similar to the Safeway pattern, with concrete floor, tilt-up walls and laminated glued wood beams.

The San Francisco-Oakland construction firm of MacDonald, Young & Nelson, Inc., are the general contractors, and according to Graeme K. MacDonald, firm president, work is scheduled for completion in January.

NEW ELKS CLUB BUILDING FOR REDDING

The architectural firm of Smart & Clabaugh, 1001 Yuba St., Redding, is preparing preliminary plans for construction of a new building to house activities of the B.P.O. Elks in Redding.

REPRESENTATIVES APPOINTED BY FARR COMPANY

The Farr Company, national manufacturing engineers of commercial and industrial air filtration equipment, has appointed five new representatives to handle its product line, according to a recent announcement by Gordon F. Thruelsen, general sales manager of the firm.

The new representatives and their general territories are: Air Filter & Service, Sacramento—Northern California and Nevada; R. H. Sparks, Des Moines—Iowa, Nebraska and Rock Island county, Illinois; R. N. Toucey, Pittsburgh—Pennsylvania; Air Filter & Sales Service, Kansas City—Kansas and Western Missouri; and Industrial Supply Co., Syracuse—New York.

NEW SERIES FIBER GLASS ARCHITECTURAL SPEAKER BAFFLES ANNOUNCED

An entirely new series of Fiber Glass Architectural Speaker Baffles has been announced by Fourjay Industries, Dayton 39, Ohio, including Round and Square Faceplates, complete Bass Reflex Units, and a complete line of accessories for installation in new or existing construction.

Highlight is the new "Spiral-Jector" Baffle, available in two types for eight-inch speakers. This provides an entirely new concept in diffusion type baffles by the use of non-resonant materials for best sound quality. This material has the impact strength of steel, the lightness of aluminum and the beauty of wood. Sound is dispersed by the special fiber glass diffusion plate to give an overall feeling of presence, so that sound seems to fill the entire area in which the speakers are located. Two tone finish, full data from manufacturer.

ARCHITECTURAL FIRM TO EXPAND NEW YORK OFFICES

Welton Becket & Associates, Los Angeles architects and engineers, have announced immediate plans for extension of their offices in New York City, according to a recent announcement by Welton Becket, head of the firm.

A five-story and basement building at 116 East 55th Street, New York, has been purchased and will be completely remodeled to offer facilities of the architectural and engineering organization in New York City.

COUNTY SCHOOL OFFICE BLDG. FOR HANFORD

The architectural firm of Alexander & Dorman, 128 E. 8th St., Hanford, has completed plans for construction of a reinforced brick, wood frame and glu-laminated beam county school office building in Hanford for the County of Kings.

STROMBERG-CARLSON APPOINTS ALEXANDER ASST. GEN. MANAGER

William G. Alexander, Chief Engineer of Stromberg-Carlson's San Diego plant since joining the organization in January 1957, has been appointed Assistant General manager of the firm's San Diego operations, according to an announcement

by Harold P. Field, general manager.

Alexander is a member of the Institute of Radio Engineers, American Ordnance Association and the Harbor Optimists' Club of San Diego.

GEORGE J. TAYLOR ELECTED PRESIDENT ILLUMINATING ENGINEERING SOCIETY

George J. Taylor, vice president of eastern operations for Day-Brite Lighting, Inc., has been elected president of the Illuminating Engineering Society for the ensuing year, succeeding Kirk M. Reid, senior illuminating engineer of the General Electric Company, Cleveland.

Taylor has been active in the Society for many years, serving successfully as regional vice-president Northeastern region, treasurer and general secretary, and vice-president. He is currently chairman of the President's advisory board and a member of the Executive Council Committee.

PASSENGER-CARGO TERMINAL FOR SAN PEDRO

The architectural firm of Kistner, Wright & Wright, with Edward H. Fickett and S. G. Barnes & Associates, has been commissioned by the Los Angeles Board of Harbor Commissioners to design a new multi-million dollar passenger-cargo terminal, according to Lloyd A. Menveg, Board President.

The terminal, to be located at Boschke Slough on the Main Channel, will include a two-story passenger-cargo structure 1000 feet long and 200 feet wide, clear span,

with the passenger facilities on the upper floor; and a second building, 630 feet long and 200 feet wide, clear span, to be used entirely for cargo.

Cargo capacity for the two sheds will be about 35,000 tons, and other features will include 2400 linear feet of wharf, dockside rail and truck facilities, latex tanks and refrigerated cargo space. Work is to be completed in four years.

HI-LO DOCKBOARD HELPS CUT LOADING TIME IN HALF

A modern, new, 1200 Series HI-LO Dockboard, manufactured by the Kelley Company and specially designed for existing dock installations, was the answer to the Blatz Brewing Company's problem of loading trucks that were 2" to 14" above dock level.

A revolutionary counterbalance system makes it possible to install these permanent

semi-automatic 12,000 lb capacity units without any pit construction or dock alteration. Loading time has been cut over 60 per cent in this one instance. The 8' long by 6' wide boards allow smooth, easy and fast movement of loading equipment even with fragile 7 case high pallet loads. Manufactured by HI-LO Automatic Dockboards, Kelley Company, Inc., 2129 West Mill Road, Milwaukee 9, Wisconsin.

ORRIN E. BURWELL PROMOTED BY THE PAYNE COMPANY

Orrin E. "Bud" Burwell has been promoted to managing director of the Product Application and Engineering Department of the Payne Company at La Puente. He has been serving as Southern California Sales Representative.

He has previously served the firm in capacities of sales engineer, field sales engineer, customer relations manager, and more recently sales representative.

A graduate of the University of Wyoming with B.S. in mechanical engineering, he specialized in heating and air conditioning studies during his undergraduate years.

LOS ANGELES HARBOR GENERAL HOSPITAL WORK STARTS

Plans and specifications have been completed and work started on a new General Heating and Refrigeration Plant and Library Building for the Los Angeles County Harbor General Hospital at Torrance.

The hospital plant will be divided into two sections. One section will house the laundry facilities; 2-stories high with base-

ment and elevator penthouse. The second
section will house the heating and refrigeration facilities; 1-story with provision for
future expansion. Added to the structure
will be a cooling tower, power center, and
distribution tunnels to carry a network of
pipe lines.

M. A. Nishkian & Co., Consulting Engineers of Long Beach, prepared the .plans
and specifications.

**ARCHITECT
SELECTED
AT CHICO**

Lawrence G. Thomson, 125 W. 3rd St.,
Chico, has been commissioned by the
Chico Fire District, to design and plan

construction of a new firehouse in Chico.

The District has allocated an item of
$60,000 in their budget to provide for the
necessary construction.

**HOUSING CONFERENCE
IN HAWAII BACKED
BY HOME BUILDERS**

The Home Builders Association of Hawaii is again presenting a Mid-Pacific
Housing Conference in Honolulu on November 3, 4, 5 and 6, according to an
announcement by "Buck" Gregory, executive director of the Association.

More than 1000 builders and members
of the allied industries are expected to
attend the informative business sessions
and partake of the "island's" hospitality.

**SAFEWAY STORES
BUYS SITE FOR
SACRAMENTO STORE**

Safeway Stores, Inc., San Francisco, recently acquired a site for a new Safeway
Store building in Sacramento, at an estimated cost of $105,000.

A new store of 16,500 sq. ft. will be
erected on the 55,000 sq. ft. site; provision will be made for ample parking. Estimated cost of the building is $376,000.

**BYRON C. BLOOMFIELD
NAMED EXECUTIVE
DIRECTOR**

Byron C. Bloomfield, formerly secretary
for professional development with The
American Institute of Architects, has been
appointed Executive Director of the recently formed Modular Building Standards
Association, according to an announce-

ment by Cyrus E. Silling, MBSA president,
Charleston, W. Va.

Bloomfield is a civil and architectural
engineering graduate of Iowa State College, and holds an advanced degree in
building engineering and construction
from Massachusetts Intitute of Technology. He engaged in active practice and
taught architecture at the University of
Colorado prior to joining the AIA.

The MBSA was formed in 1957 under
the joint sponsorship of the American
Institute of Architects, Associated General Contractors of America, National Association of Home Builders, and the Producers' Council, Inc.

**NEW LINE EXHAUST
VENTILATION FANS
BY GENERAL BLOWER**

A new line of low cost package-ventilat-
ing units has been announced by General
Blower Co., designed to exhaust air from
small enclosed rooms, commercial dryers,
restaurant steam tables, hoods and vats
where gases and odors need removing, cor-
rosive gases, and generator cooling.

The new units, "FAN-PAC," are avail-
able either direct drive, or belt driven.
Direct drive exhausters deliver up to 2290
CFM, and belt-driven models up to 1800
CFM. Standard finish is weather resistant,
light acid resistant zinc chromatic primer.
Complete details from General Blower
Co., Morton Grove, Ill.

**BAY AREA RAPID
TRANSIT DISTRICT
SEEKS ENGINEER**

Directors of the San Francisco Bay Area
Rapid Transit District recently created the
position of "chief engineer" on the district's staff and established a salary range
of from $20,000 to $30,000.

General Manager John M. Peirce is
seeking applicants to fill the newly created
position. The successful applicant will
have full charge of engineering activities
for the district involving a "rapid transit
system" serving the five "core" counties
of the San Francisco Bay Area.

**HOUSING ADMINISTRATION
APPROVES USE OF
STRUCTURAL STEEL**

The Public Housing Administration in
Washington, D. C., issued a circular to
Regional Directors on July 29, 1958, ad-
vising them on the economies of high-
rise structural systems, and encouraged

Contra Costa Junior College District of Concord.

Estimated cost of the work is $1,000,000.

**HOSPITAL
ADDITION
AT FORTUNA**

Architect Gerald D. Matson, 537 "G" St., Eureka, is preparing plans for construction of a new ward-wing to the Redwood Memorial Hospital in Fortuna.

**REMOVABLE BACK-UP
FLANGE SIMPLIFIES
INSTALLATION**

A new two-piece removable back-up flange that slips over the pipe after stub ends are welded in place eliminates the necessity of handling the combined weight of pipe and flanges during fabrication, installation and maintenance of Van Stone piping systems.

Made of steel, or stainless segments welded into single units, the end leaves of the two halves are interlocked, and when bolted in place, make a positive connection that is stronger yet lighter than is possible with cast iron or forged steel flanges. It is built to A.S.A. specifications for Van Stone flanges at 150 lbs. service and is available in two-inch through thirty-inch tube and pipe sizes. Complete information from Farwell Metal Fabricating, 81 W. Fairfield, St. Paul 7, Minn.

**ARCHITECT STUDENTS
PUBLISH BOOK ON
SCHOOL WORK**

A new annual publication, edited by architectural students to illustrate architectural work in over 50 schools of architecture in the United States, has been published by The American Institute of Architects.

The 1957-58 "Annual" consists of 102 pages of illustrations and photographs showing student designs for all types of buildings, structures and art considered representative of the work of students at various college levels. Each architectural school is represented with selections of work made by the students.

**UNIQUE DESIGN
SCHOOL COMPLETED
IN SAN FERNANDO**

The new $500,000 Osceola Street Elementary School constructed in the Sylmar area of the San Fernando Valley has been completed, according to officials of the Burch Construction Company, general contractors.

Designed by the architectural firm of Victor Gruen Associates, 135 So. Doheny Drive, Beverly Hills, the new educational plant is located on a 10-acre site and provides facilities for 500 students. Included are 10 classrooms, 2 kindergarten class-

rooms, assembly-cafeteria building, library and textbook unit, administrative offices and a gardening unit. Provision has been made for expansion to a total of 20 classrooms for peak enrollment.

A unique feature is the back-to-back arrangement of the classrooms with provision for outdoor study areas adjacent to each classroom.

APPOINTED EXCLUSIVE REFRIGERATION AGENT

The Authorized Supply Corpn., of Los Angeles, who for more than 18 years has sold Drayer-Hanson's refrigeration products on a non-exclusive basis, was recently appointed exclusive sales agent for the manufacturer's commercial refrigeration products in the Los Angeles area and the State of Arizona.

The appointment was announced by C. W. Pollock, manager, Air Conditioning & Refrigeration, Drayer-Hanson, and Rober E. Shaw, vice president and general manager of Authorized Supply.

SWIMMING CENTER PLANNED FOR SANTA ROSA

Architect L. F. Richards, 1033 Jackson Street, Santa Clara, is completing plans and specifications for construction of a Swimming Center for the City of Santa Rosa.

The project will comprise a swimming pool, bathhouse, bleachers for spectators at water sports, a snack bar, and all sanitary facilities.

NEW VETERAN HOSPITAL FOR MARTINEZ

Col. R. Edgar, Assistant Administrator of Construction for the Veterans Administration, Washington, D. C., has announced the purchase of a site near Martinez, California, where the Veterans Administration proposes to construct a new 500 bed Veteran's Hospital.

The acquired site is on Arnold Road near Muir Road. Estimated cost of the project, which will not be started until July 1960, is $10,000,000.

PROPOSED NEW SHOPPING CENTER FOR SAN DIEGO

Architect Richard George Wheeler & Associates, 3276 Rosencrans, San Diego, has completed the preparation of plans and specifications for construction of a shopping center to be located at the northwest corner of 54th and University St., San Diego.

First unit to be constructed is a "Buy 'N' Save" Market, with the remainder of the center to be retail stores, miscellaneous shops and offices.

LARGE HOTEL PROJECT FOR SAN FRANCISCO

Engineer August E. Waegemann, 251 Post Street, San Francisco, is preparing preliminary plans for construction of a $20,000,000 new hotel building at the corner of California and Jones Streets, San Francisco, for owner Joseph Massaglia, Jr.

The proposed luxury hotel will be 31 stories in height, with a roof-top restaurant and cocktail lounge, convention rooms, garage space for several hundred automobiles, and other dining and entertainment facilities and features.

"Don't worry,
I'm not going to sing"

THE OLD LADY had lost her voice. That rich, vibrant contralto which had rung through opera's golden age was long gone. And she made no bones about it.

Standing at the network microphones, she'd loudly promise her audience: "Don't worry, I'm not going to sing."

Yet, every Christmas Eve, she did sing. And millions of homes hushed to listen. For *Stille Nacht, Heilige Nacht* does not demand a big voice. Rather, a big heart.

And Ernestine Schumann-Heink had always had that. From the beginning, when she threw away her budding career for love, only to wind up deserted with her four children. Through World War I, when she sang to sell Liberty Bonds while she had sons fighting—on both sides. Right up to the end of her turbulent life, she stayed warm, generous and brave.

Naturally, her adopted country loved her. Because Americans admire heart, and as the little stories in every daily paper show, they have plenty of it. That's one of the vital reasons why America is strong and why her Savings Bonds are a tremendous guarantee of security.

The heart and strength of 165 million Americans stand behind these Bonds.

There could be no better guarantee. So, for yourself, and for your country, invest in U.S. Savings Bonds regularly. And hold on to them.

It's actually easy to save—when you buy Series E Savings Bonds through the Payroll Savings Plan. Once you've signed up at your pay office, your saving is done *for you*. The Bonds you receive pay good interest—3% a year, compounded half-yearly when held to maturity. And the longer you hold them, the better your return. Even after maturity, they go on earning 10 years more. So hold on to your Bonds! Join Payroll Savings today—or buy Bonds where you bank.

Safe as America—U.S. Savings Bonds

MODERN DESIGN
USES
WEST COAST
LUMBER

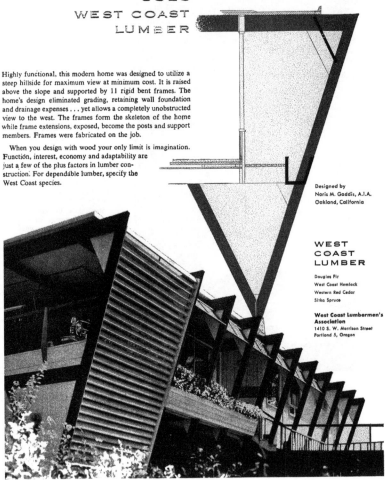

Highly functional, this modern home was designed to utilize a steep hillside for maximum view at minimum cost. It is raised above the slope and supported by 11 rigid bent frames. The home's design eliminated grading, retaining wall foundation and drainage expenses . . . yet allows a completely unobstructed view to the west. The frames form the skeleton of the home while frame extensions, exposed, become the posts and support members. Frames were fabricated on the job.

When you design with wood your only limit is imagination. Function, interest, economy and adaptability are just a few of the plus factors in lumber construction. For dependable lumber, specify the West Coast species.

Designed by
Noris M. Gaddis, A.I.A.
Oakland, California

**WEST
COAST
LUMBER**

Douglas Fir
West Coast Hemlock
Western Red Cedar
Sitka Spruce

**West Coast Lumbermen's
Association**
1410 S. W. Morrison Street
Portland 5, Oregon

MODERN DESIGN
USES
WEST COAST
LUMBER

Highly functional, this modern home was designed to utilize a steep hillside for maximum view at minimum cost. It is raised above the slope and supported by 11 rigid bent frames. The home's design eliminated grading, retaining wall foundation and drainage expenses . . . yet allows a completely unobstructed view to the west. The frames form the skeleton of the home while frame extensions, exposed, become the posts and support members. Frames were fabricated on the job.

When you design with wood your only limit is imagination. Function, interest, economy and adaptability are just a few of the plus factors in lumber construction. For dependable lumber, specify the West Coast species.

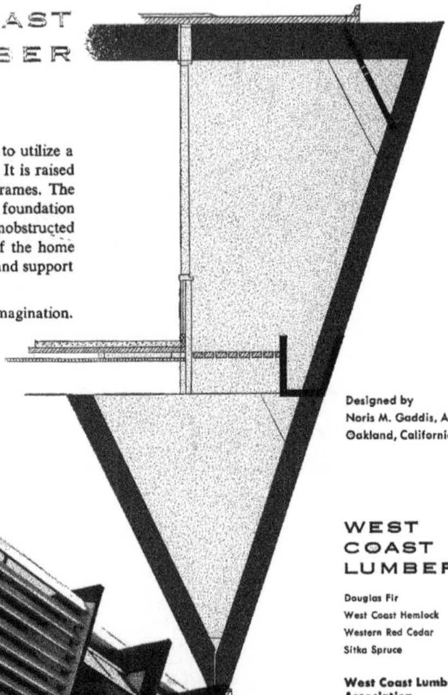

Designed by
Naris M. Gaddis, A.I.A.
Oakland, California

WEST
COAST
LUMBER

Douglas Fir
West Coast Hemlock
Western Red Cedar
Sitka Spruce

West Coast Lumbermen's Association
1410 S. W. Morrison Street
Portland 3, Oregon

Vol. 215   No. 2

EDWIN H. WILDER
Editor

CONTRIBUTING EDITORS:

Education
  SIDNEY W. LITTLE, Dean, College of Fine Arts and Department of Architecture, University of Arizona, Tucson, Arizona.

City Planning
  CORWIN R. MOCINE, City Planning Engineer, Oakland, California

Urban Planning and Shopping Centers
  FRANK EMERY COX, Sales Research & Business Development Analyst, Berkeley, California

Realty Development
  ROY P. DRACHMAN, Subdivider and Realty Developer, Tucson, Arizona

School Planning
  DR. J. D. McCONNEL, Stanford School Planning Dept., Palo Alto, California

Residential Planning
  JEDD JONES, Architect, Boise, Idaho

General Architecture
  ROBERT FIELD, Architect, Los Angeles, California

Engineering
  JOHN A. BLUME, Consulting and Structural Engineer, San Francisco, California

Advertising
  WILLIAM A. ULLNER, Manager

  FRED JONES
  Special Advertising

★

COVER PICTURE

1960 OLYMPIC
WINTER GAMES
ARENA
Squaw Valley,
California

Architectural drawing of the Olympic Arena, showing exterior view of the South side of the building—outdoor and indoor exhibition and competition.
See page 16 for complete story and pictures.

ARCHITECTS' REPORTS—
Published Daily
  Archie MacCorkindale, Manager
  Telephone DOuglas 2-8311

—ARCHITECT & ENGINEER *is indexed regularly by* ENGINEERING INDEX, INC.; *and* ART INDEX—

Contents for

NOVEMBER

THE OLDEST PROFESSIONAL MONTHLY BUSINESS MAGAZINE OF THE ELEVEN WESTERN STATES

ARCHITECT AND ENGINEER (Established 1905) is published on the 15th of the month by The Architect and Engineer, Inc., 68 Post St., San Francisco 4; Telephone EXbrook 2-7182. President, K. P. Kierulff; Vice-President and Manager, L. B. Penhorwood; Treasurer, E. N. Kierulff. — Los Angeles Office: Wentworth F. Green, 439 So. Western Ave., Telephone DUnkirk 7-8135 — Entered as second class matter, November 2, 1905, at the Post Office in San Francisco, California, under the Act of March 3, 1879. Subscriptions: United States and Pan America, $3.00 a year; $5.00 two years; foreign countries $5.00 a year; single copy 50c.

. EDITORIAL NOTES .

RESEARCH IS AVAILABLE TO YOU

Never in the history of civilization has research played such a crucial role in forward planning, gaining understanding, or running a business. Never were research facilities as relatively cheap as they are today.

Frequently, it has been thought that research is only for the large firm; the little fellow can't carry it on, and must do without. However, this is not true anymore.

Recently, the National Science Foundation published the Directory of Independent Commercial Laboratories Performing Research and Development — 1957, which compiles the names, addresses, and identifies the type of research of more than 565 independent commercial laboratories performing research and development in the natural sciences.

Earlier, the National Academy of Sciences-National Research Council's "Industrial Research Laboratories of the United States," listed 4,834 laboratories of all kinds classified according to their sponsorship, such as manufacturing companies, trade associations, non profit organizations, or independent commercial laboratories.

Here, for a small fee, competitively determined, a small business or any business can get research of all kinds done, cheaply, effectively, and competently.

* * *

BANKRUPTCY BY CHOICE

With the controversial elections of this month out of the way let's take a look and see what is ahead of those elected to represent the "people" in Washington during the next session of Congress and the Congresses to come.

Taxes imposed against the "people" supply the funds to meet federal budget spending, and the federal budget determines the amount to be taxed against the people, but, unlike the unsolved question of which came first the chicken or the egg, a look at the financial position of the nation's government indicates that the spending of taxpayers' money comes first and then comes the application of taxation to try and catch up with the spending.

It has been customary, though not accurate, for supporters of increased federal spending to lay the chief blame at the door of the "cold war." It has even been said that the size of this country's budget is dictated by Moscow. A close look at the actual figures, however, tells a somewhat different story. In the period since the Korean conflict, expenditures for programs related to national security, although near the war-time peak, have remained relatively constant. During this same period, expenditures for non-defense

programs have increased from $22.5 billion in 1955 to an estimated $32.4 billion for 1959.

This represents an increase in non-defense programs of almost 50 per cent.

The present estimate of a $12.2 billion 1959 deficit marks the twenty-fourth year in the thirty years since 1929 that the government will have spent more than it took in. On a cumulative basis over the same period, we have had budget deficits totaling $280 billion. On the other side of the ledger, the total of the six years' surpluses add up to but $16.6 billion.

The cold statistics become more meaningful when it is realized that during the period from 1929 to date, the purchasing power of the dollar has been reduced by about 40 per cent. While deficit spending is not the sole culprit in the inflation picture, it is, except in time of war, or other national emergency, the factor most susceptible to remedy.

The predecessors of those currently elected to serve us in Congress, have slowly but surely been taking us down the road to bankruptcy, let's see how many campaign promises of economy our new representatives will keep.

- ‒ -

THE ADVERTISING COUNCIL

As a private, non-partisan, non-profit organization acting as a channel of mass communication, the Advertising Council brings citizen interest and action to bear on many of our nation's most serious current problems. It does this through the medium of advertising, .with contributed support from all phases of business.

American business and advertising are the sole support of the Council. Advertisers and advertising media, large and small, contribute free space and time to Council projects which are prepared without charge by advertising agencies under the direction of volunteer coordinators, usually company advertising and public relations executives.

A Board of Directors representing industry, advertising agencies and media supervises the Council's operation and plans its policies. All campaigns except those in which the public interest has been clearly established by an Act of Congress, must be approved by a three-fourths vote of the Public Policy Committee. This Committee, which acts to ensure that all Council projects are genuinely in the public interest, is made up of twenty distinguished citizens from widely varied fields.

ARCHITECT & ENGINEER magazine is a part of this American Business Program and contributes monthly towards its success.

Ten
Million
Dollar
Research
Laboratory

GENERAL ATOMIC FACILITIES

NEAR COMPLETION

SAN DIEGO, CALIFORNIA

Pereira & Luckman,
Architects-Engineers

Final construction stages are being reached on the $10 million atomic research laboratory for the General Atomic Division of General Dynamics Corp. at Torrey Pines Mesa near San Diego.

According to Dr. Frederic de Hoffman, vice president of General Dynamics and division general manager of General Atomic, the entire General Atomic staff is now located at the new facilities which are named the John Jay Hopkins Laboratory for Pure and Applied Science.

Master planned by Pereira & Luckman, planning architectural-engineering firm of Los Angeles and New York, the basic facilities consist of an administration-engineering building, an experimental building, two laboratory buildings and a technical information services building.

The design provided rectilinear and circular forms for the various units to take advantage of the natural configuration of the site and to establish intimate but carefully spaced building locations.

General objective of the design was to achieve a campus-like appearance while satisfying functional considerations.

The buildings are constructed of a custom designed tapered bent of structural steel plate and girder frame. Roofs and upper portions of the side walls and canopies are steel corrugated decking. Walls below the decking are integral colored, textured concrete block and steel window wall.

A construction feature is the exposure of the structural frame as architectural elements to achieve sun control support and a striking appearance by use of simple repetitive detail, as well as to lower construction costs and speed the completion schedule.

Haas-Haynie-Frandsen, Inc., of Los Angeles was general contractor on the project.

NEWS and COMMENT ON ART

SAN FRANCISCO MUSEUM OF ART

The San Francisco Museum of Art, War Memorial Building, Civic Center, under the direction of Dr. Grace G. L. McCann Morley, is showing the following special exhibitions and events for this month:

Exhibitions: Swiss Graphic Designers; Sculpture by Leo Bigenwald and Woodcuts by Oskar Dalvit; Thirty-Third Annual Exhibition of The San Francisco Women Artists; A Reappraisal—Masterworks from the Museum's permanent collection; and Paintings by Ruth Armer, Ralph Du Casse, and Carl Morris.

Special Events: Members' Social Hour each Wednesday evening at 8:30; Lectures, and Tours.

The Museum is open daily.

M. H. deYOUNG MEMORIAL MUSEUM

The M. H. deYoung Memorial Museum, Golden Gate Park, San Francisco, under the direction of Walter Heil, announces the following schedule of special exhibits and special events for November:

Exhibits: A major exhibition of 84 paintings, and 71 watercolors and drawings by VINCENT VAN GOGH (1853-1890) opened to the public October 7 and will continue through November. This comprehensive exhibition contains many of the artist's most splendid and best-known works, only a few of which have previously been seen in San Francisco. Many of the works are being shown in America for the first time. Selections were made by the deYoung Museum's director, Walter Heil, principally from the famous collection belonging to Vincent W. van Gogh, the artist's nephew, and are lent through the Vincent van Gogh Foundation. Other important works are lent by the Stedelijk Museum in Amsterdam and the Rijksmuseum Kroeller-Mueller in Otterlo. Admission: General, 50 cents; Children, 25 cents; Members of The deYoung Museum Society, free upon presentation of card.

The Museum is open daily.

CALIFORNIA PALACE OF THE LEGION OF HONOR

The California Palace of the Legion of Honor, Lincoln Park, San Francisco, under the direction of Thomas Carr Howe, Jr., has arranged the following special exhibitions and events for public showing during this month:

Exhibitions: Masterpieces of Korean Art, an exhibition consisting of the major national art treasures of Korea, being shown in San Francisco following its showing at the National Gallery of Art, Washington,

the Metropolitan Museum of Art, New York, the Museum of Fine Arts, Boston, and other leading museums of the country.

The Andre J. Kahn Gift—the inaugural showing of a distinguished group of paintings which has come to the Museum from Paris as the gift of Mr. Andre J. Kahn; Paintings by Madeleine Reichert, Watercolors by Jerome Land, and the Metal Arts Guild Annual Exhibition.

The Achenbach Foundation for Graphic Arts is showing the annual Bay Area Printmakers Exhibition.

Special Events: Organ Program each Saturday and Sunday at 3 p.m. Educational activities include the Fall-Winter series of art classes for children and juniors on Saturdays.

The Museum is open daily.

OAKLAND ART MUSEUM

The Oakland Art Museum, 1000 Fallon Street, under the direction of Paul Mills, Curator, is presenting the Fourth National Exhibition of the Bay Area Printmakers' Society — distinguished printmakers as well as outstanding young artists from throughout the country are included in the selection made by juror Ernst Gunter Troche, Director of the Achenbach Foundation.

Other exhibitions to be shown during the month include the California Sculptors' Annual—held concurrently with the print exhibition, it is the museum's annual sculpture competition with David Silvka of New York, visiting sculptor at the University of California, the juror. The work of Mauricio Lasansky, Wally Hedrick and Claire Falkenstein, selected by last year's jurors as outstanding artists, will be shown. The Craftsmen's Festival, showing this month, is a juried exhibition of weaving, ceramics and jewelry by members of the Loom and Shuttle Guild, the Metal Arts Guild and the Mills College Ceramic Guild.

"A World of Art for Christmas," a special holiday exhibition during November, and the East Bay Artists' Association Annual Exhibition will be shown November 29 to December 7th.

Special events are scheduled for each Wednesday evening at 8:30.

The Museum is open daily.

UCLA ART GALLERIES

The works of architect Richard Neutra, shown in 200 photographs, will highlight three art exhibits to be displayed simultaneously by the University of California at Los Angeles Art Galleries this month, and extending through January 11th.

Other exhibits are the Ruth McC. Maitland Memo-

rial Exhibition, showing works of Picasso, Braque, Miro, Matisse, Chirico, Kandinsky, Rembrandt, Durer, and Cranach; and an exhibit of the engravings of the late Middle Ages artist Pieter Brueghel the Elder.

Neutra, a pioneer modern architect, was born in Austria, coming to this country in 1923. He settled in southern California two years later and has made the southland his home ever since. An architect "who designs to meet the needs of people," Neutra's structures and influence are to be found in Europe, Asia and South America.

Professor Frederick S. Wight, director of the UCLA Art Galleries, described Neutra as a humanist 'whose work is based on a philosophy which sees human beings and their needs as the architect's most important data.

"Accordingly," he said, "the major part of his work is in the field of domestic building. But he has also been deeply concerned with building for education and health, and he is famous as a pioneer designer of modern schools."

Among Neutra's graceful yet functionally-modern school buildings is the latest addition (now under con-
(See Page 32)

M. H. DE YOUNG MEMORIAL MUSEUM

Golden Gate Park   San Francisco

Self Portrait

VINCENT VAN GOGH

Paris, 1887

One of the 84 paintings and 71 watercolors and drawings by Vincent van Gogh (1853-1890) principally from the famous collection belonging to Vincent W. van Gogh, a nephew, and lent to the Museum by the Vincent van Gogh Foundation.

WE ENGINEERED AN IDEA

By CARL OTTO*
Civil Engineer

It is an honor for me to represent the San Francisco Engineers' Speakers Club and the engineering profession at this meeting of your organization. It occurs to me that this opportunity has a parable I once heard. I have here a quarter. If I should give this quarter to one of you, and you, in turn, should give me a quarter, neither one of us would be any better off. On the other hand, if you give me an idea, and I offer you my idea, we are both enriched. This exchange will bring enjoyment and satisfaction to those who participated and will cause the idea to grow and prosper and benefit more and more people in an ever-widening circle. I have received many ideas, as well as a delicious lunch, in the conversations and discussions of this gathering. Now I shall try to explain an idea which is related to this year's celebration of Engineers' Week.

CARL OTTO
Engineer

Not too far from here is a mountainous tree-covered island, where the people cannot have the normal forms of transportation we all take for granted. Where the slope is so steep that roads and streets are built by digging one edge into the hill and supporting the other on a log which has been pushed into the ground like a toothpick into a martini olive. Where the terrain is so rough that it is impractical to build an airport. Where there are no railroads. Where it will cost you an average of 75c or $1 to have each small common carton of goods brought in by steamship or seaplane.

Gentlemen, I visited this place last summer, and, believe it or not, the experiences associated with that visit are exhilarating to me even when I think about them today. In response to your request to learn something about the work done by professional engineers I thought you might like to hear about the job which has been done for the people who live on this island. I chose this topic because I think it shows that engineering is interesting work, is sometimes a little different from the normally accepted concept, and is extremely satisfying to those who engage in it.

The place I visited is Ketchikan, Alaska. As you probably know, Alaska is a large peninsula jutting out from the North American continent towards Siberia. However, there is a smaller but important part of Alaska which comes down the coast towards the United States. This long, narrow strip of mountainous, coastal land with its many beautiful islands is known as Southeastern Alaska. Ketchikan is the southernmost city of any importance in Southeastern Alaska, and is only about 700 miles north of Seattle. That is approximately the same distance as from San Francisco to Portland. The city of Ketchikan has a beautiful setting. The mountains rise quickly from the smooth protected waters which meander like blue ribbons among the green islands and coastal lands. The City is perched, almost precariously, between the mountain and the water. But Ketchikan has a problem.

Ketchikan has no railroad, no highway transportation connected to Canada or the U. S., no direct connection with land-based airplanes, and is almost entirely dependent for its needs on water transportation. Because their transportation was limited only to water transportation, there was no competition from other forms of transportation to keep the rates low. The people had a feeling that the rates were too high but they had no real basis for saying it was too high. Because of this feeling they thought that the answer to the high rates might be solved by building new port facilities. But to do this they had to get concrete facts, they had to know how much freight was entering and leaving the city, they had to know what kinds of freight it was, what it would cost for this freight movement, and what freight might develop in the future. They had to receive an impartial opinion whether or not it was feasible to institute a different method of cargo handling and transportation than the one that exists now. They had to know what it would cost to get any new system into operation and whether or not the revenues from any such system would pay for its construction and operation. In short they wanted to know if the project was feasible. In order to

*NOTE: This address was prepared by Carl Otto, Civil Engineer with the Ralph Tudor Engineering Company, San Francisco, and delivered before the San Francisco Chinatown Lions Club, in conjunction with national observation of ENGINEERS' WEEK, receiving first award recognition as being the most outstanding paper prepared in San Francisco to acquaint the public with the engineering profession.

obtain the answers to these questions the City of Ketchikan asked our firm to make a feasibility study for new port facilities.

Before going on with the Ketchikan project, it might be a good idea to relate this feasibility study to the whole field of engineering so we know where we are. Engineering is like a lot of other things, you don't know how much is involved until you get into it. In any construction project, there are several fields of engineering involved. There is an initial study to determine whether or not the project can be financed. Then there is the actual design of the project, where it is decided what materials are to be used, concrete, steel, or timber, and then getting these decisions down on paper in the form of drawings, designs, figures. Then there's the actual construction. Here the engineer estimates costs, schedules the work, interprets the drawings and makes sure the project is built the way the designer intended. The first phase I mentioned, the feasibility study, probably is the least known field of engineering. The phase that we call supervision of construction is fairly well-known because people are always attracted by a construction project . . . sidewalk superintendents. They actually see the concrete being poured and the steel being erected and take for granted that someone must be there to see that it is being built the way it was supposed to be. Also, the very fact that the building is going up or the dam being built, is evidence that someone must have designed it, and so they are at least aware of the second phase of the engineering, the design field. But many times the question—"Why is it here, rather than some place else?" or "Why is it even being built at all?" is not asked. And yet this is the basic question which must be answered before any action can be started on the project, before any design can be accomplished, any construction can start, before any real work is done. The Ketchikan project was limited to the first phase—the feasibility study.

One of our first jobs was to do some research and find out what published reports were available from government agencies and private industry. These gave us some figures on the amount of cargo that went into and came out of Ketchikan, and also a general idea of the published rates, and in some instances, the actual costs of transportation. But this data was not adequate, so a survey team was sent into Kethcikan to get information directly from the merchants and industries located in the area. The people were very cooperative and opened their books for our inspection. This gave us a good insight on the kinds and amounts of cargo, and what it cost them to import or export that cargo. Of course, the interviews made by us with representatives of industry and transportation were very revealing too. These people gave us a lot of information which is not available from the normal sources of written publications. In fact this is probably one of the best reasons for having an impartial organization

come in to perform a certain job. It has been a real source of satisfaction to me to find out that people are more than willing to divulge nearly all the information needed to let us arrive at a sound conclusion. I believe that in situations like this the people are more willing to talk to an outside impartial third party, than to any member in their own community.

While our survey people were in Ketchikan they inspected and made an inventory of all the existing port facilities. There were lots of piers and wharves. But most of them accommodated small activities designed for one specialized function and were built many years ago. They could not accommodate cargo and ships in the modern method of today. For instance the transit shed, a building in which materials are held while awaiting further movement, was built only a few feet from the face of the wharf, which made it very handy in the days when one used hand trucks to haul materials, but it left no room to maneuver with mechanical equipment such as fork trucks and tow tractors which are used at modern terminals today.

Our survey and research work revealed that nearly all of the incoming cargo was of the general type items that are used for ordinary everyday living, such as groceries, furniture, appliances, etc. About two thirds of this was brought in by one steamship company, and most of the rest by a locally formed cooperative, which chartered small coastal vessels to bring the cargo in. Basically there are only two exports. One is fish and the other is timber. The fishing industry is very important and provides the livelihood either directly or indirectly for over half the people in the city. But it is also very seasonal, starting in May or June and is over by the end of September. The movement of canned fish follows this same pattern, and there is no activity during the other months of the year. Nearly all of the canned fish is transported by one steamship company from the cannery docks to the warehouses of the Seattle area. The fishing industry is also very volatile with catches in some years being very good, and in others extremely poor. There has been a definite decreasing trend in the catch for the past eight years. The timber industry provides a year around activity and probably has the best potential for resource development in Southeastern Alaska. There are two species of timber, hemlock and spruce. The spruce industry has been going on for many years, furnishing the lumber requirements for much of Alaska, and high-quality items such as flooring and stock for pianos. The hemlock is being used in a new industry for Alaska in making pulp, and there are indications that this pulp industry will increase as the demands for paper products develop. Nearly all the timber products are shipped by barge under contracts made with private companies by the timber firm. The shipping pattern of these products is disorganized and sporadic. It means that

one outfit is coming up loaded and going back empty, and another is coming up empty and going back loaded. It was our feeling that this is one of the major causes of the high cost of transportation.

We also felt that there was one other area where savings could be made in the cost of transportation. We found out that it cost on the average of 31 dollars a ton to haul cargo from Seattle to Ketchikan. Of this 31 dollars over five dollars represented the cost of handling the cargo in Ketchikan, and nearly three dollars was spent in handling the cargo in Seattle. We felt that this eight dollars which was required only for taking the material from the transit shed and putting it in the hold of the ship and then taking it out of the hold of this ship and into the transit shed was excessive, and could be reduced by changing the method of cargo handling.

Before going on to the recommended methods of improving cargo shipping and handling and reducing costs, I want to mention that by this time in our study we had also studied the situation to try and determine what the future cargo would be. It is not an easy thing to try and predict what is going to happen in the future, but we had to get some idea on whether or not the type of probable cargo would change or whether the amounts would change. We obtained some idea of the potential of resource development from the published information of government agencies. We obtained a good idea of the policies which would determine how these resources would be developed by talking to the agency representatives and reviewing the laws pertaining to those resources. We also contacted private industry to get their feeling on the market potential for the resources and their plans for its development.

We had to have some yardstick for determining the probable growth of commerce and trade in the area. This was obtained by looking at certain key factors such as population growth use of electrical power. From these investigations we concluded that there would be no startling increase in the types or amounts of cargo but that a reasonable rate of growth could be expected for the next 20 or 25 years.

At this point in the survey we knew what the problem of the community was in regard to transportation. Now we had the problem of determining how to fulfill the transportation needs in a manner which was more economical than the way in which it was being done at the present time.

There is not much probabilty that a revolutionary new idea will come out of study. Whatever schemes may be thought of have probably already been considered by someone in the transportation business. So an important part of this phase is to determine why these ideas have not been incorporated into the transportation system.

Basically, we had two problems. One was to consolidate the cargo and the other was to improve the

cargo handling between the shipping and shore. It was obvious that the transportation companies could not consolidate the cargo because each company was trying to get all he could. And in this respect we were very fortunate in having the city of Ketchikan as a client because it would seem that an agency such as a city is the logical one to initiate the cooperative steps necessary to get the cargo consolidated.

As to the second problem, improvements in cargo handling between the ships and shore could not be done in an isolated operation. We had to keep in mind the overall operation in getting the cargo from Seattle to Ketchikan. The water route connecting the two points of Seattle and Ketchikan is very well protected from the weather and the ocean. It is popularly known as the scenic Inside Passage. It looks more like a river or canal than part of the ocean. And in all the rivers and canals throughout the United States nearly all the river traffic consists of tugs and barges. Tugs and barges carried some of the cargo to Alaska already, and the proportion which they were carrying was increasing each year. This in itself would indicate that they are an economical method of transportation. Certainly it is easier to load and unload cargo from barges than in the holds of existing ships. Another evident trend in the shipping industry is the increasing use of larger units of cargo. Instead of handling 1, 2, or half a dozen sacks of sugar, they now put many of them into a big box, or strap them together on a large flat board and handle these larger units in terms of 2, 3, 5, and 10 tons, with the aid of fork lift trucks, tow tractors, and wharves, and buildings which have lots of space inside for maneuvering. One of the main reasons this system had not been more widely instituted is that it required a considerable outlay of money to buy these containers or pallets. And there is, as yet, no universal system of exchange for these items. The transportation companies were therefore reluctant to take the steps necessary for providing this kind of service. Accordingly, we are recommending that the City of Ketchikan buy the necessary containers to get the system started. Admittedly, this is a little unusual, but sometimes unusual things need to be done for the sake of progress.

From this point on, the feasibility study was relatively easier. We made field reconnaissance of the shoreline surrounding Ketchikan to determine several locations which could be recommended for a new port facility which could handle container-type cargo. We made preliminary designs for the main elements of the facility, such as the transit shed and pier, which by the way can accommodate a car ferry when such a system of transportation is started in Southeastern Alaska. We made up estimates of cost for construction which, of course, required a little research since the costs and methods are different from those in, say, the Bay Area. And the final step in the feasibility study is to determine how all this is going to be paid

for. Certainly, it does no good to dream up all this grandiose changeover only to find that there is no way to finance it, so a general idea of benefits and costs must be kept in mind all through the study, but in the final step you actually get down to figures, and interest rates, and bonds, and security and all those other financial terms—which is another business in itself. We found that for Ketchikan, by instituting the recommended consolidation of cargo and guaranteeing a minimum tonage of freight to a single carrier who would use container system of cargo handling, freight costs could be reduced substantially, and considerable benefits would accrue to the community.

This was the idea we presented to the City of Ketchikan. Yesterday, I was enjoying the satisfying experience of participating in the formulation of this idea. Today, I am enjoying the happy experience of relating this idea to all of you—who have been very receptive. Tomorrow? Well, perhaps tomorrow, this idea will grow and prove beneficial not only to the people of Ketchikan, but also in one form or another to each of you.

NORTHERN CALIFORNIA CHAPTER

Associated General Contractors
40th ANNUAL CONVENTION
San Francisco, California

The 40th Annual Convention of the Northern California Chapter, Associated General Contractors of America, will be held next month, December 5-6, at the Sheraton-Palace Hotel in San Francisco.

President Milt Simpson points out "This year's convention marks the fourth decade since the formation of our organization," and business sessions and other activities have been geared to a fitting observance of this anniversary.

Several prominent industry representatives from outside California are scheduled to appear on the business sessions Friday noon and afternoon, among them National AGC President Fred W. Heldenfels, Jr., Corpus Christi, Texas; Chairman of the National Association's Highway Division Max C. Harrison, Pittsburgh, Pennsylvania; National Advisory Board Member M. Clare Miller, McPherson, Kansas; and National Executive Committeeman W. Ray Rogers, Portland, Oregon.

The Fifth Annual Associates' Party will also be held on Friday evening in the Garden Court, Rose Room and Concert Room, with John M. Connolly serving as Committee Chairman of the event.

Highlights of an entertainment program will be a "Fashion Show" with Mrs. John M. Connolly, serving as chairman. This is the second year such an event has been scheduled and will be staged at the Hotel Mark Hopkins' Peacock Court. Named to assist Mrs. Connolly are Mrs. M. L. Simpson, wife of the Chapter President, Honorary Chairman; Mrs. William H. Baldwin, Mrs. Frank W. Callahan, Mrs. Nelson Hyde Chick, Mrs. Gardiner Johnson, Mrs. Mel J. London, and Mrs. J. P. Silvestri.

Chairman of the convention and committee members are:

Convention Committee Chairman Nelson Hyde Chick, Underground Construction Company, Oakland, and his committee members are William H. Baldwin, Baldwin Contracting Company, Inc., Marysville; John M. Connolly, John M. Connolly Co., San Francisco; Eugene G. Finn, North Bay Construction Co., Santa Rosa; Robert Gwinn, A. Teichert & Son, Inc., Sacramento; Mel J. London, Calaveras Cement Company, San Francisco; Ben Nehrbass, Jr., Harms Bros., Sacramento; Albert A. Shansky, S & Q Con-

CHAPTER OFFICERS: Treasurer L. D. Weirick, Rothchild, Raffin & Weirick, San Francisco; President Milt Simpson, Ball & Simpson, Berkeley; and Vice-President, John Dephia of Patterson. (l to r.)

Oakland; Frank Castellucci, Peterson Tractor Co., San Leandro; Charles J. Fox, Rods, Inc., Berkeley; G. V. Garner, The Texas Company, San Francisco; Albert P. Hahn, Edward R. Bacon Company, San Francisco; Mel J. London; Paul N. McCarron, Associated Employers, Inc., San Francisco; G. E. McGavran, Daily Pacific Builder, San Francisco; and Felix H. Siri.

struction Company, South San Francisco; Felix H. Siri, Piombo Construction Company, San Carlos; and L. D. Weirick, Rothschild, Raffin & Weirick, San Francisco

Chairman of the Associates' Party Committee is John M. Connolly, and his committee members are John F. Blakemore, Blakemore Equipment Company,

The Annual Banquet, which will be the closing event of the two-day convention, will be held on Saturday evening, December 6th, in the Garden Court of the Sheraton-Palace Hotel.

COURTLAND P. PAUL ELECTED PRESIDENT OF CALIFORNIA LANDSCAPE ARCHITECTS

Courtland P. Paul, Pasadena landscape architect, is the new president of the California Council of Landscape Architects, elected at its fourth annual convention at El Mirador Hotel in Palm Springs, October 16 through 19.

Paul succeeds C. Mason Whitney of Berkeley as president. Other new officers are: Theodore Osmundson, Jr., San Francisco, vice-president; and Lynn M. F. Harriss, Oakland, executive secretary.

COURTLAND P. PAUL
Landscape Architect

The landscape architects took action to urge that California's new 12,500-mile freeway program be so planned as to preserve the natural beauty of the State and provide a scenic showcase for visitors. They resolved to support the new California Roadside Council "Beautiful Highways" program which includes the landscaping of freeways, control of billboards on the new interstate highway system in California, and a state wide anti-litter campaign.

First annual honor awards of C.C.L.A. for outstanding service to the profession were given to Ralph

D. Cornell of Los Angeles, Dr. John W. Gregg and Professor Emeritus Harry W. Shepherd, both of Berkeley.

Public relations for landscape architects was the principal theme of the meeting, with stress being placed by speakers on creating a better understanding of the work and value of the profession in making California a more beautiful place in which to live.

Dr. Robert Fenton Craig of the University of Southern California made the principal address at the kick-off luncheon on Friday, emphasizing the need for close cooperation between landscape architects, architects, engineers, landscape and irrigation contractors, and other in allied fields to insure that the public receives the finest in professional skills in future landscaping development.

Craig warned against a tendency in some public agencies for "empire builders" to bypass the services of landscape architects and contractors and conduct their own landscaping programs on a "green thumb" basis, resulting in poor planning and waste of public funds.

Raymond E. Page, Sr., of Beverly Hills, member of the California State Board of Landscape Architects, cautioned the group that their legal responsibilities required written contracts with clients and close study of local and State building codes.

Gordon Whitnall, planning consultant and landscape architect; Robert Hamill, southwest editor of Sunset Magazine; Phillip J. Daniel, Los Angeles archi-

tect; and Andre Anastasion, Los Angeles public relations counsellor, were among the other speakers. All stressed the need for landscape architects to widen public understanding and acceptance of their profession.

The next convention is to be held in Yosemite on October 15 through 17 of next year.

SPOKESMAN FOR CLAY PRODUCTS INDUSTRY SEES GOOD TIMES

In the face of powerful competitors on the construction scene today, the masonry industry has every reason to view the future with enthusiasm, Douglas Whitlock, Chairman of the Board of the Structural Clay Products Institute, reported to the 20th biennial convention of the Bricklayers, Masons & Plasterers International Union, meeting in Atlantic City, New Jersey, recently. "I am not only optimistic — I am truthfully inspired by the prospects for our future prosperity," he declared.

Whitlock indicated that the underlying reasons for his optimism for the future are to be found in the unique masonry industry cooperation between the materials manufacturers, the mason contractors and the Bricklayers' Union. "No other segment of the construction industry can show a greater degree of teamwork for a common goal than ours," he said.

Reporting on the residential market, he cited the rise in the number of brick houses in the post-war years. In 1949, 25 per cent of the houses being built were brick. By 1957, 40 per cent of the houses being built were brick, he reported. Today, 70 per cent of brick shipments go into the residential market.

Whitlock credited this increase to several factors. One is the stepped-up promotional programs by brick and structural tile manufacturers through their organization, the Structural Clay Products Institute. Another is the progressive efforts of the Bricklayers' Union to train apprentices and to encourage bricklayers to become qualified mason contractors. He said that the establishment of mason contractor associations on the local level through the Mason Contractors Association of America has also contributed to the residential market increase.

Turning to the non-residential market, Whitlock admitted that the masonry industry has lost ground to its competitors. While this loss of market is a matter of concern to all segments of the masonry industry, there are many elements which make him optimistic, he said. The focal point for these hopeful elements is the organization three years ago of the Allied Masonry Council, a working alliance of masonry building material producers, bricklayers and mason contractors. Through the work of the Allied

Masonry Council, of which Whitlock is Chairman, large educational and promotional programs are being conducted to tell the American public the positive story of masonry's economy, durability and beauty. He said that the continuing efforts of AMC will ultimately result in masonry regaining its lost ground in non-residential construction.

Another cause for optimism in the masonry industry is the extensive research activities of the brick and tile industry through its research arm, the Structural Clay Products Research Foundation, Whitlock said. He cited successful research projects in the field of lightweight clay products, brick packaging, atomic blast resistance, prefabricated brick panels as examples of the forward-looking program which will help insure the future of the masonry industry.

Added to these masonry industry activities is the fact that a growing American population will create greater future markets in an expanding economy. Whitlock underscored this idea by telling the bricklayer delegates that during their convention, the 175 millionth American will be born.

ENGINEERING EDUCATORS TO STUDY RUSSIAN ENGINEERING SYSTEMS

Dr. Frederick C. Lindvall, Chairman of the Division of Engineering, California Institute of Technology, will serve as chairman of a group of eight American engineering educators who will serve as an Exchange Mission on Engineering to study engineering schools in Russia.

The American group hope to see engineering classrooms and laboratories and meet teachers and students throughout Russia, including Siberia, and to bring back curricula, syllabi, textbooks, and other material pertaining to Russian engineering education not now in the United States. The proposed itinerary includes institutions in Moscow, Kharkov, Novosibirsk, Tomsk, Stalinsk, and Frunze.

In return, a group of Russian engineering educators is expected to tour schools in this country.

LOS ANGELES ARCHITECTURAL FIRM BECOMES WORLD'S LARGEST

According to the results of a survey just published, the architectural firm of Daniel, Mann, Johnson & Mendenhall, Los Angeles, will become the nation's largest Architectural-Engineering firm in 1959. The firm held third place in 1957, having completed projects with a construction value in excess of $150 million.

The firm was founded in 1946 in Santa Maria, California, and has grown from a three-man office to a world-wide, 480-man organization, designing and planning projects in all corners of the globe.

MARRIED STUDENTS

HOUSING PROJECT

UNIVERSITY OF MONTANA

Missoula, Montana

ARCHITECTS: WITWER & PRICE, Architects and Engineers

STRUCTURAL ENGINEER:
Jack M. Lyerla
Spokane, Washington

GENERAL CONTRACTOR:
C. B. Lauch Construction Co.
Boise, Idaho

MECHANICAL ENGINEER:
W. M. Walterskirchen
Missoula, Montana

MECHANICAL CONTRACTOR:
Fullerton's Plumbing and Heating Co.
Hamilton, Montana

ELECTRICAL ENGINEER:
James F. Parr
Hamilton, Montana

ELECTRICAL CONTRACTOR:
The Electrical Shop
Missoula, Montana

Two three-story apartment houses, each containing sixty apartments, varying from four-bedroom units to bachelor units, with a total area of 123,130 square feet. Three-story precast concrete bents, colored concrete and vinyl-asbestos floors, wood stud partitions with gypsum wallboard finish, concrete ceilings, exterior walls of precast tilt-up sandwich panels composed of insulated cement-asbestos board and pumice concrete, brick cavity walls with pumice block back-up, aluminum window sash with half-inch insulating glass, steel exterior doors and frames, built-up roof on pumice concrete fill, sound insulating partitions between apartments, enameled steel kitchen cabinets with formica tops, electric ranges and kitchen exhaust fans, hot water baseboard heat with thermostatic control for each apartment, 3300 volt primary service with a transformer vault in each building and secondary distribution to breaker panels in each apartment by aluminum bus duct.

GENERAL VIEW of new residence hall project, showing site area in relation to city's residential district—wide overhang roofs and protected outside passageways are seen on the two completed buildings.

UNIVERSITY RESIDENCE HALLS . . .

PROJECT COSTS:

General Contract..$ 947,765.00
Mechanical Contract... 175,852.00
Electrical Contract.. 111,761.00

$1,235,378.00

COST BREAKDOWN: (Architect's fees not included)

General Contract..$ 7.70 per square foot
Mechanical Contract... 1.43 per square foot
Electrical Contract.. .91 per square foot

$10.04 per square foot

Cost Per Apartment—$10,300 exclusive of architect's fees.

Construction started: April, 1956.

Construction completed: July, 1957.

**WORKMEN are shown erecting pre-cast concrete frames in
construction of the new University dormitories.**

144 three-story concrete bents at 10'-0" O.C. spanning 24'-8" with 4'-0" cantilevers. Each bent required 6.5 cubic yards of concrete and weighed approximately 14 tons. Bents were cast in piles six high using a bond breaking agent between pours and were sprayed with a liquid concrete compound. Bents were designed on the basis of 3750 p.s.i. Concrete at 28 days and test cylinders taken exceeded this value in all cases.

Bents were erected with a 35-ton capacity truck crane, and after some experimenting they were handled without difficulty. Bents were erected from 7-10 days after casting or when test cylinders showed that concrete reached a strength of 2500 p.s.i. A total of 144 bents were required for the job, and after the technique of erecting them was mastered, the contractor was able to erect them at the rate of one per hour.

The roof slab and suspended floor slab were cast in place on plywood lined forms supported by the precast bents. Concrete struts between bents were poured integrally with the slabs and were threaded into the same inserts in the bents that were used for lifting the bents.

Bents were fastened to footing piers by means of a steel baseplate anchored to bents and bolted to the piers, with the first floor slab, being poured on grade, covering the connection.

After a careful study of several framing systems, this system of framing was chosen for several reasons.

It was found that the primary considerations of economy and appearance could best be met by using a precast system. The use of metal forms provided a smooth surface on the bents, so that very little hand rubbing was required. Also all 144 bents were cast using only six sets of steel forms. Other economies were affected because of the speed of erection and the elimination of shoring for the floor slab forms. The architect's estimates were substantiated by the bid results, which showed a savings of approximately $86,000 over cast-in-place construction.

Tilt-Up Wall Panels

Tilt-up wall panels below the windows were constructed of 1-9/16 insulated cement-asbestos board with 2½" of pumice on the exterior face. This was accomplished by laying the sheets of insulated cement-

(See Page 30)

Forming Tilt-up
wall panels

1960 OLYMPIC WINTER SPORTS ARENA . . . North View

PICTURE PREVIEW

1960 OLYMPIC WINTER GAMES

SQUAW VALLEY, CALIFORNIA

By JACK GEYER

ARCHITECTS: Left to right, Robert S. Kitchen, Frank B. Hunt, Wendell R. Spackman, and William Corlett.

CORLETT & SPACKMAN, and
KITCHEN & HUNT, A.I.A. Architects

H. J. BRUNNIER, and
JOHN M. SARIS, Structural Engineers

PUNNETT, PAREZ & HUTCHINSON, Consulting Engineers

OFFICE of CLYDE C. KENNEDY, Sanitary Engineers

VANDAMENT & DARMSTED, Mechanical and Electrical
Engineers

ECKBO, ROYSTON & WILLIAMS, Landscape Architects

ANNE KNORR, Delineator

For the first time since 1932 the entwined rings of the Olympic Flag will wave over United States soil in 1960. Squaw Valley, California, a remote but beautiful wilderness, will host the VIII Olympic Winter Games from February 18 through February 28, 1960.

The last time the International Olympic Committee honored the United States for an Olympic event was 26 years ago when the Winter Games were staged at Lake Placid, New York and the Summer Games were held at Los Angeles.

Although it is a tremendous undertaking for a wilderness area like Squaw Valley to stage an event like the Olympic Games, there is every assurance that they will reach the high standards of past competitions. The joint effort of the federal government, the state governments of California and Nevada, and various civic groups have made this possible.

Construction at Squaw Valley is proceeding at a rapid pace. Four dormitories that will house 1200

EDITOR'S NOTE: The entire Squaw Valley 1960 Olympic Winter Games project is being designed by a joint venture consisting of architects and engineers listed on the opposite page.

men and women from 30 nations are nearing completion in the Olympic Village. Work is well under way on an Athletes' Center and a Reception Center.

Foundations are being poured for the 11,000-seat Ice Arena, biggest single project of Squaw Valley construction, and contractors are ahead of schedule on the Press and Administration Buildings.

On Alpine and Cross-Country ski courses, work crews under Ski Events Director Willy Schaeffler, and Technical Advisors Wendal Broomhall, Allison Merrill and Birger Torrissen have cleared brush and trees and are laying communications cable.

Workmen for Diversified Builders, Inc. of Paramount, California—the major contractor on Squaw Valley projects—are constructing the Ski Jumps and Skating Rinks.

Meanwhile, the State Division of Highways is proceeding around-the-clock with the widening of California sections of U. S. 40, the main transcontinental road leading to the region, and State Highway 89, the road linking U. S. 40 and Squaw Valley.

MAIN FACILITIES AREA

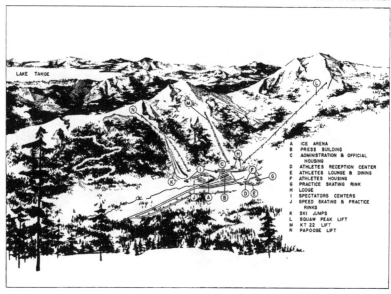

A   ICE ARENA
B   PRESS BUILDING
C   ADMINISTRATION & OFFICIAL
    HOUSING
D   ATHLETES RECEPTION CENTER
E   ATHLETES LOUNGE & DINING
F   ATHLETES HOUSING
G   PRACTICE SKATING RINK
H   LODGE
I   SPECTATORS CENTERS
J   SPEED SKATING & PRACTICE
    RINKS
K   SKI JUMPS
L   SQUAW PEAK LIFT
M   KT 22 LIFT
N   PAPOOSE LIFT

After the Games, the California Commission, a State agency, will turn over the permit lands and all of the facilities to the State Park Commission. The Arena, Rinks, Village, Ski Lifts and Runs will then be operated as a part of the State Park System.

The Organizing Committee anticipates that as many as 35,000 spectators will witness **each** of the 11 days of competition at the Olympic Winter Games.

The flow and parking of automobiles in this snow-covered area could become a major problem. In order to meet it, the Organizing Committee conducted a snow-compaction experiment during the winter of 1957. At that time the United States Navy utilized knowledge and techniques gained in Arctic explorations to ascertain the feasibility of parking buses, automobiles and other vehicles on large areas of packed snow. An experimental area, known affection-

ately to the Navy as "the pad," was made available for public parking and successfully carried an estimated 200 vehicular tons at one time.

If the experiment continues to prove workable, the Organizing Committee hopes to make available a snow-compacted surface to park 12,000 automobiles An alternate parking system will be planned for emergencies.

Description of Ice Arena

The enclosed ice arena, in which will be held the opening and closing ceremonies for the Games, figure skating, and ice hockey events, is designed for permanent use after the Games as a year-round ice skating and hockey rink which can quickly and easily be converted to house conventions, shows and similar events.

The 300-foot clear span roof shelter of the arena rises at a 4 in 12 pitch to a height at the ridge of 90

ARCHITECTURAL DRAWING OF THE MAIN FACILITIES AREA

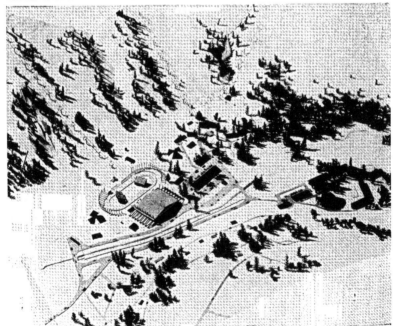

feet above the skating rink. Enclosed on three sides, the fourth side is completely open to the warming sun from the south, offering a view of the speed skating rink, Olympic torch and the ski jumps beyond, and places in silhouette a large Olympic symbol suspended from the roof.

The 85' x 190' ice hockey and figure skating rink is flanked on the three enclosed sides by permanent seating, augmented by movable temporary bleachers on the open side. The temporary seats are located parallel to the rink for skating events; perpendicular and in line with the permanent seating at the ends of the rink for the opening and closing Olympic ceremonies. Approximately 8,000 seats are provided under the roof augmented with 3,000 seats located at the open end. The bleachers have been designed and will be installed by an independent iron works in Oakland.

The ridge of the roof being located perpendicular to the long axis of the rink permits the maximum rise and number of choice seats parallel to the rink and facing the open vista of the valley, as well as providing for press, radio and television facilities with an unobstructed view over the entire arena.

Access to the main seating section is through dormitories at the mezzanine level eliminating the need for cross aisles with subsequent loss of seats and obstruction of sight lines. Bleacher seats can be reached from above or below.

Separate facilities are provided for the figure skaters and the hockey players under the main seating section at the first floor level which is also the level of the ice. Speed skaters have facilities on the left flank of the arena and adjacent to the speed skating rink.

The main access to the arena is through the lobby which extends the full length of the north elevation.

SPECTATORS' CENTER: One of two such structures which will support the Olympic Ice Arena, speed skating rink, ski-jumps, and Alpine ski courses. The identical wood framed structures utilize laminated wood beams for major spans. Three ridges open glazed wall surfaces to views from the main floor and mezzanine. A free standing fireplace center serves the main floor which also contains food serving facilities, restrooms, lounge and eating areas.

PRESS BUILDING: Takes form as workmen prepare to pour concrete wall.

Panels in the lobby and on the exterior of the north elevation will display the decorative crests and seals of the participating nations. Colors of golden yellow, deep spruce green, Indian red and black will decorate the interior and exterior of the building, in contrast with the white of the snow. The deeply corrugated surface of the steel roof deck will be sprayed with grey green plastic. The steel columns supporting the roof will be Indian red, the main roof beams spruce green. An Indian motif will recall the past history of Squaw Valley.

Structural Features

The main structural feature of the ice arena is the 300-ft. clear span of the roof which must be capable of supporting heavy snow loads.

ARCHITECTURAL DRAWING OF THE "SPECTATORS' CENTER"—Exterior view.

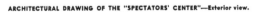

ICE ARENA

Workers pour concrete for foundation of the Ice Arena —men's and women's slalom, men's and women's giant slalom and women's downhill ski races will be held on the mountains in the background.

BELOW: Artists drawing of the completed Ice Arena.

The roof structure consists of a cellular steel deck spaning 11'-4", rolled steel beam purlins spanning 32'-0", and the main supporting frames at 32'-0" centers, spanning 300 ft.

The main suporting frames consist of tapered columns built up from steel plates, tapered steel box

CONSTRUCTION
Carpenters build floors and walls for a dormitory in "athletes' village"—four of such dormitories will accommodate 300 competitors.

BELOW: View of progress work on a dormitory. Twelve hundred athletes will be housed in this secluded and scenic corner of Squaw Valley.

ADMINISTRATION BUILDING

Crane swings a wooden beam into place as construction moves rapidly ahead on the Administration Building.

In right background are ridges of the mountain KT-22, where women's downhill, women's giant slalom and men's giant slalom ski races will be run.

girders, and inclined cable tension members. Each half of the main frame acts independently in somewhat the manner of a guy derrick, with the roof girder functioning as the boom, the column as the mast, and the inclined cables as the guys.

Cable anchorages are provided by piers of concrete supported on piles designed for tension, with the roof

girders extended resisting the horizontal thrust.

Several persistent problems arose in relation to design of the ice arena.

(1) In the Sierra Nevada Mountains, snow accumulates to great depths and roofs must be designed to carry such loads or a means of snow removal developed.

**ATHLETE'S
CENTER**

Located in the Olympic Village
is adjacent to the dormitory
buildings, one of which may be
seen in the background.

(2) Temperatures are very erratic and are often moderate or relatively warm even with heavy snow conditions.

(3) Condensation occurs in enclosed ice arenas resulting in dripping from roof mem-

bers on the occupants and on the skating surface.

(4) Events may take place in very cold weather with the occupants suffering considerable discomfort unless some heat is provided.

Consideration was given to heating this entire building and/or the roof, using reverse cycle refrigeration as a heat source. The refrigerating plant has a capacity of approximately 600 tons which will provide the largest expanse of artificially frozen ice ever refrigerated. Generally about 15,000 BTUs of heat per ton must be dissipated or wasted in a normal refrigeration system. 600 tons would produce 9,000,000 BTUs and this is much more heat than required. A complete analysis indicated that such a system can be used economically to melt the snow, reduce condensa-

**Completed
DORMITORY BUILDING**

This is one of four such dormitories to be built in "Athletes' Village."

Portion of building seen at extreme right in the picture is the "Athletes' Center."

tion, and partially heat the entire building.

Economical methods were sought to distribute the heated air. The roof deck of formed cellular steel is used to carry heated air for melting the snow and preventing condensation. Ducts between the roof purlins and above the bleachers are used to carry the main air. This will partly warm the seats and permit such ducts to be inconspicuous.

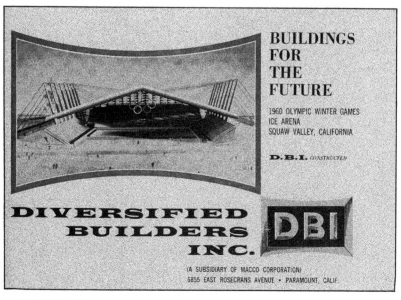

American Institute of Architects

John Noble Richards, President

Philip Will, Jr., 1st Vice-President
Henry L. Wright, 2nd Vice-President
Edmund R. Purves, Executive Secretary

Edward L. Wilson, Secretary
Raymond S. Kastendieck, Treasurer

National Headquarters—1735 New York Avenue, N.W., Washington, D. C.

REGIONAL DIRECTORS—Northwest District, Donald J. Stewart, Portland, Oregon; Western Mountain District, Frederick H. Porter, Sr., Cheyenne, Wyoming; California-Nevada-Hawaii District, Ulysses Floyd Rible, Los Angeles, California.

ARIZONA CHAPTERS:
CENTRAL ARIZONA: David Sholder, President; A. John Brenner, Vice-President; Jimmie R. Nunn, Secretary; Kemper Goodwin, Treasurer; James W. Elmore, Director; Ralph Haver, Director; Martin Ray Young, Jr., Director. Office of Secy., P.O. Box 904, Phoenix.

SOUTHERN ARIZONA: Santry Clay Fuller, President; Edward H. Nelson, Vice-President; David S. Swanson, Secretary; Robert J. Ambrose, Treasurer; D. Burr DuBois, Director; Eleazar D. Herreras, Director; Emerson C. Scholer, Director. Office of Secy., 2343 South Tucson Avenue, Tucson.

COAST VALLEYS CHAPTER:
William L. Higgins (San Jose), President; Paul J. Huston (Palo Alto), Vice-President; William H. Daseking (Menlo Park), Treasurer; Edward N. Chamberlain (San Jose), Secretary. Office of Secy., 390 Park Ave., San Jose.

CENTRAL VALLEY OF CALIFORNIA:
Joseph J. Jozens, President (Sacramento); Armsby Tod Hart, Vice-President (Sacramento); Albert M. Dreyfuss, Secretary (Sacramento); Whitson W. Cox, Treasurer. Office of Secy., 2127 "J" St., Sacramento.

COLORADO CHAPTER:
Casper F. Hegner, President; C. Gordon Sweet, Vice President; Norton Polivnick, Secretary; Richard Williams, Treasurer. Directors: James M. Hunter, Robert K. Fuller, Edward L. Bunts. Office of Secy., 1225 Bannock St., Denver, Colorado.

EAST BAY CHAPTER:
Hachiro Yuasa (Oakland), President; George T. Kern (Oakland), Vice-President; William M. Gillis (San Francisco), Secretary; J. A. Zerkle (Berkeley), Treasurer. Directors: H. B. Clausen, F. A. Lockwood, John Ovarto. G. M. McCue, Marjorie Montgomery, Exec. Secy. Office of Secy., Mezzanine, Hotel Claremont, Berkeley 5.

IDAHO CHAPTER:
Anton E. Dropping, Boise, President; Charles W. Johnston, Payette, Vice-President; Glenn E. Cline, Boise, Sec.-Treas. Executive Committee: Chester L. Shawver and Nat J. Adams, Boise. Office of Secy., 624 Idaho Bldg., Boise.

MONTEREY BAY CHAPTER:
Robert Stanton, President (Carmel); Walter Burde, Vice-President; William L. Cranston, Secretary; George Kuska, Treasurer. Office of Secy., P.O. Box 1846, Carmel.

MONTANA CHAPTER:
William J. Hess, President (Great Falls); John E. Toohey, Vice-President (Billings); H. C. Cheever. Secy.-Treas. (Bozeman). Directors: Oscar J. Ballas, Wm. J. Hess, John E. Toohey. Office of Sec., Bozeman, Montana.

NEVADA CHAPTER:
RENO: William E. Cowell, President; Albert W. Alegre, Vice-President; Ralph A. Casazza, Secretary; John Crider, Treasurer. Directors Graham Erskine, George L. F. O'Brien, Laurence A. Gulling. Office of the Secy. 232 W. 1st St., Reno, Nevada.
WOMEN'S ARCHITECTURAL LEAGUE: (Reno) Mrs. Eileen Casazza, President; Mrs. Lucille Lackard, Vice-President; Mrs. Gladea Cowell, Secretary; Mrs. Enid Hellman, Treasurer.
LAS VEGAS: Walter F. Zick, President; Aloysius McDonald, Vice-President; Edward B. Hendricks, Secy.-Treas. Directors: Walter F. Zick, Edward Hendricks, Charles E. Cox. Office of Secy., 106 S. Main St., Las Vegas.

NEVADA STATE BOARD OF ARCHITECTS:
Russell Mills, Chairman (Reno); Aloysius McDonald, Sec-Treas. Members: L. A. Ferris, Elmo C. Bruner, Edward S. Parsons. Office, 1420 S. 5th St., Las Vegas.

NORTHERN CALIFORNIA CHAPTER:
William Corlett, President; Donald Powers Smith, Vice-President; George T. Rockrise, Secretary; Richard S. Banwell, Treasurer. Directors: W. Clement Ambrose, John Kruse, Bernard J. Sabaroff, Corwin Booth. Exec. Secy., May B. Hipahman. Chapter Office, 47 Kearny St., San Francisco.

ORANGE COUNTY CHAPTER:
William T. Jordan, President (Costa Mesa); Donald M. Williamson, Vice-President (Laguna Beach); J. Herbert Brownell, Secretary; Rumont W. Hougan, Treasurer. Office of Secy., 1950 W. Coast Highway, Newport Beach.

OREGON CHAPTER:
John K. Dukehart, President; Keith R. Maguire, Vice-President; Robert Douglas, Secretary; Harry K. Stevens, Treasurer. Directors: Daniel McGoodwin, Earl P. Newberry, Everett B. Franks, Robert W. Fritsch, Donald W. Edmundson. Office of Secy., 2041 S.W. 58th Ave., Portland 1.

WASHINGTON STATE CHAPTER AIA

"Slides of Brussels" by Bob Durham featured this month's meeting in the Engineers' Club, Seattle. Durham has just returned from the Brussels Fair, and brought back a number of interesting observations in color slides.

Members were also treated to a discussion on "King County Planning Procedures and Problems" at a special meeting this month when Gordon Whitnall nationally recognized authority on planning, spoke on his observations while serving as a consultant to the King County Planning Commission.

Recent new members to the Chapter include Benjamin C. Stanford, Associate, and Wilbur P. Rosval, Junior Associate.

NORTHERN CALIFORNIA CHAPTER AIA

With the "official" announcement that San Francisco has been picked as the site city for the 1960 Annual Convention of The American Institute of Architects, the Chapter Executive Committee has appointed an interim 4-man Steering Committee, composed of William S. Allen, Henry Schubart, John Lyon Reid and George T. Rockrise to do the preliminary work of preparing for the national conference. The Steering Committee has been empowered to appoint Chapter members as the need arises.

ARCHITECT MARIO GAIDANO HONORED:

Mario Gaidano, AIA, San Francisco architect, has won the National Interiors Award program conducted by Institutions magazine of Chicago, Ill., for the fifth consecutive year. This year's award was for his design of Alioto's Mediterranean Room, a restaurant at Fisherman's Wharf in San Francisco.

OREGON CHAPTER

Glenn Stanton, Chapter member architect, presented an interesting group of color slides on the near East, Suez, Jordan, Lebanon, etc., at the October meeting in the Imperial Hotel, Portland.

Reports on the Northwest Regional Conference showed John Toohey elected as nominee for Regional Director, and Earl Newberry was elected to the Regional Judiciary Committee.

Recent new members include: Clive F. Kienle, Associate; Stanley F. Adam, J. Warren Carkin, Seaton

B. Griswold, David A. Pugh and John W. Reese Corporate Members.

SANTA CLARA & SANTA CRUZ COUNTIES

The October meeting held at Rickey's Palo Alto Restaurant, was devoted to a program showing slides supplied by members. Each participant was given 5 minutes to describe his slides and subjects.

Among recent new members to the Chapter is Arnold Flunkinger, Junior Associate.

WAL-SOUTHERN CALIFORNIA

The Southern California Chapter of the Women's Architectural League held their social meeting this month at the Women's City Club of Pasadena, with Dr. and Mrs. Robert Burt guest speakers on the subject "Intimate View of Japan," which included the showing of numerous slides.

Announcement was made that the Chapter would hold their Second Annual Architects' Home Tour in the Spring of 1959.

EAST BAY CHAPTER AIA

Richard Haag, landscape architect of Richard Haag Associates, San Francisco, was the principal speaker at this month's meeting discussing "Japanese Architecture and Japanese Landscape Architecture," showing also a number of slides taken by the speaker during a two-year stay in Japan where he was a Fulbright Scholar.

Recent new members include: Theodore R. Moist, Corporate, and Ralph K. Zimmerman, Junior Associate.

SAN FRANCISCO ARCHITECTURAL CLUB

"Plastics in Modern Architecture" was the subject of a talk at the November meeting by John Finke, Chief Chemist at Montanto Chemical Company's Santa Clara plant. Also shown was a motion picture film of Pacific Gas & Electric's participation in the new atomic reactor power plant at Livermore, Calif.

Ladies' Night was observed November 13th, and the annual "Jinx" is scheduled for the 21st.

SOUTHERN CALIFORNIA CHAPTER AIA

Announcement was made that the Craftsmanship Awards will be the subject of the December 12th meeting, Robert E. Alexander, program chairman.

The fifth annual craftsmanship program was instituted by S. Kenneth Johnson, and this year has as its chairman Edward A. Killingsworth, who heads the Chapter Awards and Scholarship committee. Purpose of the meeting is to identify and honor those persons and firms that have made a contribution to craftsmanship to the construction industry within the past three years.

Awards will be given in three classifications including decorative arts, basic and finish subtrades of all categories and special achievements in other allied architectural fields.

The meeting will be held in the Los Angeles Elks Club, 6th and Parkview.

PASADENA CHAPTER:
H. Douglas Byles, President; Edward D. Davies, Vice-President; Ward W. Deems, Secretary; Robert F. Gordon, Treasurer. Directors: Mal Gianni, Lee B. Kline, Keith B. Marston, Donald E. Neptune. Office of the Secy., 170 E. California St., Pasadena.

SAN DIEGO CHAPTER:
Raymond Lee Eggers, President; William F. Wilmurt, Vice-President; Lloyd P. A. Ruocco, Secretary; Delmar S. Mitchell, Treasurer. Directors: John C. Deardorf, Richard George Wheeler and Sam Bruce Richards. Office of the Secy., 3603 5th Ave., San Diego 3

SAN JOAQUIN CHAPTER:
Robert C. Kaestner, President (Visalia); William G. Hyberg, Vice-President (Fresno); Lawrence B. Alexander, Secretary; Edwin S. Darden. Office of Secy., 128 E. 8th St., Hanford.

SANTA BARBARA CHAPTER:
Wallace W. Arendt, President (Santa Barbara); Darwin E. Fisher, Vice-President (Ventura); Walter Tibbetts, Secretary; Kenneth H. Hess, Treasurer. Office of Secy., 630 Para Grande Lane, Santa Barbara.

SOUTHERN CALIFORNIA CHAPTER:
George Vernon Russell, President; Maynard Lyndon, Vice-President; Ralph C. Crosby, Secretary; Thornton Abell, Treasurer. Office of Secy., 124 W. 4th St., Los Angeles.

SOUTHWEST WASHINGTON CHAPTER:
Robert Billsborough Price, President; Robert T. Olson, 1st Vice-President; Donald F. Burr, 2nd Vice-President; Percy G. Ball, Secretary; Alan C. Liddle, Treasurer; Charles T. Pearson and George Leonard Elkvall, Trustees. Office of Secy., 2715 Center St., Tacoma 2, Washington.

UTAH CHAPTER:
W. J. Monroe, Jr., President. 433 Atlas Bldg., Salt Lake City; M. E. Harris, Jr., Secretary, 703 Newhouse Bldg., Salt Lake City.

WASHINGTON STATE CHAPTER:
Harrison J. Overturf, President; Lawrence G. Waldron, 1st Vice-President; Thomas F. Hargis, Jr., 2nd Vice-President; Talbot Wegg, Secretary; David R. Anderson, Treasurer. Office of Secy., Miss Gwen Myer, Executive Secty., 409 Central Bldg., Seattle 4.

SPOKANE CHAPTER:
Wm. C. James, President; Carl H. Johnson, Vice-President; Keith T. Boyington, Secretary; Ralph J. Bishop, Treasurer; Lawrence G. Evanoff, Carroll Martell, Kenneth W. Brooks, Directors. Office of the Secy., 615 Realty Bldg., Spokane.

HAWAII CHAPTER:
Howard L. Cook, President; Douglas W. Freeth, Vice-President; Francis S. Haines, Secretary; Clifford F. Young, Treasurer. Directors, Richard N. Dennis, Frank Slavsky, William D. Merrill. Office of Secretary, 1410 Kapiolani Blvd., Honolulu 14.

CALIFORNIA COUNCIL, THE A.I.A.:
L. F. Richards, Santa Clara, President; Lee B. Kline, Los Angeles, Vice-President; Edward H. Fickett, Los Angeles, Secretary; Allen Y. Lew, Fresno, Treasurer. Miss Mary E. White, Office Secretary, 703 Market Street, San Francisco 3.

CALIFORNIA STATE BD. ARCHITECTURAL EXAMINERS:
Malcolm D. Reynolds, President (Oakland); Kenneth Wing, Secretary (Long Beach); Wendell R. Spackman (San Francisco); Paul Davis (Santa Ana), and Frank Cronin, Executive Secy., 1020 N St., Sacramento 14.

ALLIED ARCHITECTURAL ORGANIZATIONS

SAN FRANCISCO ARCHITECTURAL CLUB:
C. Van De Weghe, President; O. Hickenlooper, Vice-President; James O. Brummett, Secretary; J. W. Tasker, Treasurer. Directors: Morris Barnett, Art Swisher, Stan Howatt, Frank Barsotti, Frances Capone. Office of Secy., 507 Howard St., San Francisco 5.

PRODUCERS' COUNCIL—SOUTHERN CALIFORNIA CHAPTER:
Clay T. Snider, President, Minneapolis-Honeywell Regulator Co., L.A.; E. J. Lawton, Vice-President, Aluminum Company of America, L.A.; E. Phil Filsinger, Secretary, Gladding, McBean & Co., L.A.; William G. Aspy, Treasurer, H. H. Robertson Co., L.A.; Henry E. North, Jr., National Director, Arcadia Metal Products, L.A.; Office of the Secy., 2901 Los Feliz Blvd.

PRODUCERS' COUNCIL—NORTHERN CALIFORNIA CHAPTER:
R. W. Harrington, President, Clay Brick & Tile Ass'n.; P. C. Christensen, Vice-President, Truscon Steel Div., Republic Steel Corp.; Philip D. Mittell, Secretary, Otis Elevator Co.; William E. Black, III, Treasurer, Libby, Owens, Ford Glass Co.

PRODUCERS' COUNCIL—SAN DIEGO CHAPTER:
Eugene E. Bean, President, Fenestra Inc., James I. Hayes, Vice-President, Westinghouse Electric Co.; E. R. Shelby, Secretary, The Celotex Corp. (El Cajon); Joseph C. Langley, Treasurer, Republic Steel Corp., Truscon Steel Div. (Lemon Grove). Office of Secy., 1832 Wedgemore Rd., El Cajon.

CONSTRUCTION SPECIFICATIONS INSTITUTE—LOS ANGELES:
George Lamb, President; Herman Boisclair, Vice-President; Jack Whiteside, Secretary; Frank Rasche, Treasurer. DIRECTORS: Walter Hagedohm, Raymond Whalley, Martin A. Hegsted. Chas. F. Wetherbee, Arthur T. Raitt and E. Phil Filsinger. Advisory Member: R. R. Coghlan, Jr. Office of Secy., Box 26114, Edendale Sta., Los Angeles 22.

CONSTRUCTION SPECIFICATIONS INSTITUTE
San Francisco Area Chapter:
Leonard M. Tivol, President; Emery Theo. Hirschman, Vice-President; Roual D. Shelly, Treas.; William LaGette, Secty. Directors: Frank L. Barsotti, Herman R. Jobst, Walter M. Krohn, Charles S. Pope, Erland Siran. Office of Secty., Kaiser Aluminum & Sales Co., 360 22nd St., Oakland 12.

ENGINEERS WEEK SET
FOR FEBRUARY NEXT

National Engineers' Week, sponsored by the National Society of Professional Engineers, has been set
for February 22-28, 1959, the week of George Washington's birthday, in commemoration of the fact that
our first President was, himself, a notable engineer.
Along with his great accomplishments as a soldier
and statesman, Washington was one of the first
engineer-builders who laid the foundation for modern America. He was a trained land surveyor, a builder
of roads and fortifications, and a life long believer in
technical progress.

Engineers' Week will be proclaimed nationally by
President Eisenhower, and locally by State governors
and city officials.

The theme for the 1959 observance is "Engineering
—for the Age of Space," and was selected to emphasize the role played by engineering the translating
scientific theory regarding the exploration of space
into everyday realities.

SEAOC DELEGATE APPOINTED: William A.
Jensen and Joseph Sheffet have been appointed delegates to the Structural Engineers Association of California for the year 1959-1960, to represent the Structural Engineers Association of Southern California.

STRUCTURAL ENGINEERS ASSOCIATION
OF CALIFORNIA CONVENTION

Reports of the 27th Annual Structural Engineers
Association of California convention in Yosemite
Valley, early in October, indicated a record attend-
ance at the three day technical conference.

Presided over by President Henry Degenkolb, and
under direction of General Chairman Bill Dreusikè, the
convention was an outstanding success with the technical sessions well attended and highly educational.
As stimulating was the business session which included
considerable discussion of the proposed lateral force
code submitted by the Seismology Committee, and a

discussion on the efforts of the Civil Engineers Act
on licensed and unlicensed persons with attention
given to specific cases.

While the men were busy with technical meetings
and discussions, the ladies were enjoying the perfect
fall weather and entertainment program arranged by
Maribel Sander and her committee.

FEMINEERS OF
SAN FRANCISCO

The Femineers held their annual Scholarship Benefit
Ball on November 15th at the Fairmont Hotel, San
Francisco, with dining and dancing to the music of
Ray Hackett's orchestra.

All proceeds derived from the event go into the
Scholarship Fund for the use of a worthy student
in engineering in college.

STRUCTURAL ENGINEERS ASSOCIATION
SOUTHERN CALIFORNIA

"Geological Hazards in the Los Angeles Hillside
Areas," was the subject of discussions led by Bruce
Lockwood, geologist of Schroeter & Lockwood, and
Milford Bliss, grading engineer, Department of Build-
ing Safety, City of Los Angeles.

As available real estate in the Los Angeles basin is
used up, more attention is focused on hillside areas
previously considered unsuitable for construction.
Many of these hillside areas are hazardous from the
standpoint of landsliding, failure of fills, erosion, and
mudflow. These factors were discussed from the standpoint of geology, and numerous failures of the past
were described and their causes given.

Results of the recent election show officers and
directors elected to serve the SEASC for next year
included: Harold Omstead, President; Jack Sparling,
1st Vice President; Roy Johnston, 2nd Vice President;
C. M. Biddison, Treasurer; and Carl Nelson, Irvan
Mendenhall, William Ropp, Charles Peterson, Robert
Wilder, and Norman Green, Directors.

Recent new members include: William F. Lever,

Kenneth L. Perry and Armand Saltman, Associate; Eugene A. Meier and Gordon T. Farrell, Members. Glen E. Bratzler, Lawrence O. Mackel, and Elbert J. Porteous, Jr., Junior; and Wayne B. Quinlan, Affiliate.

BRUNNIER GIVEN AWARD

Henry J. Brunnier, San Francisco structural engineer, was awarded the Structural Engineers Association of California's highest honor, Honorary Membership, at the Association's recent annual convention in Yosemite.

This is the fourth Honorary Membership awarded in the Association's almost 30-year history.

STRUCTURAL ENGINEERS ASSOCIATION OF NORTHERN CALIFORNIA

"The Digital Computor as a Tool in Structural Analysis" was the subject of discussion at the November meeting held in the Engineers Club, San Francisco, with Charles F. Scheffey, Associate Professor, University of California and Research Consultant on applications of digital computors to engineering problems, and Ray W. Clough, Assistant and Associate Professor, University of California and also a Research Consultant, the principal speakers. The program was an introduction to the terminology and procedures of computor use, and included a survey of programming devices and structural analysis methods which have been used to facilitate practical analysis.

Recent new members include: John E. Brown, William A. Eck, and James R. Spirz, Members. Robert H. Singer, and Tait Smith, Affiliates.

CALIFORNIA CIVIL ENGINEERS AND LAND SURVEYORS SET MEETING

Directors of the California Council of Civil Engineers and Land Surveyors have announced the annual professional conference of the organization will be held in Los Angeles on January 23-24, 1959, with headquarters in the Statler-Hilton Hotel.

A major feature of the convention program will be a report on the most extensive study ever undertaken in this country on the status of surveying and mapping. Consideration will also be given to California's highway program and the encroachment of government upon the private practice of the civil engineering and land surveying professions.

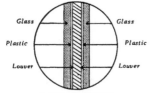
UNIVERSITY OF MONTANA
HOUSING PROJECT

(From Page 15)

asbestos board on the floor, and edge forming them with wood forms. Then a layer of number 6 ga. 6" x 6" wire mesh was attached by steel drive nails. The pumice aggregate concrete was then poured into the forms, screeded off and given a light broom finish. The panel was then scored vertically at the third points with a jointing tool to provide an inconspicuous place for shrinkage of the concrete to take place. Panels were cured with a sprayed-on curing compound.

After curing and stripping of forms, panels were tilted into position by hand. (Three or four men could handle a 4 x 9-foot panel without difficulty.) Panels were fastened at the columns by means of a specially devised anchorage and grouted in with cement grout.

Use of these panels provided a durable exterior and interior surface. The use of a 9" cavity wall of brick and pumice block was considered in the preliminary planing; however a study of the panel system showed that a better wall would be achieved, both from the standpoint of thermal insulation and of economy. A check of actual job costs showed a savings of $1.00 per square foot for a total savings of $23,000 on the project.

CALAVERAS CEMENT COMPANY
FORMS SUBSIDIARY FIRM

Formation of the Calco Supply Company as a wholly owned subsidiary of Calaveras Cement Company has been announced. The new firm will function as sales representative for major manufacturers of machinery and equipment in the industrial field, and will concentrate activities in northern and central California.

Calco officers include E. M. Barker, president; B. B. Woodward, Jr., vice president; Joseph Tedesco, treasurer; and Emmett J. Norris, Jr., secretary. James Whiter will serve as manager of sales. Headquarters of the firm will be in San Francisco.

FIRE RESISTANT COATINGS
AND TREATMENTS DISCUSSED

Fire resistant coatings and treatments were discussed at a panel meeting of the San Francisco Area Chapter, Construction Specifications Institute held in the Leopold Cafe, San Francisco, this month.

State Fire Marshal Joseph R. Yockers headed the

(See Page 32)

ROBERT A. WILLIAMSON PROMOTED CHIEF STRUCTURAL ENGINEER

Robert A. Williamson has been promoted to chief structural engineer and Harold Soliday to chief electrical engineer of Holmes & Narver, Inc., engineers and constructors of Los Angeles, according to a recent announcement by David L. Narver, Jr., engineering vice president of the firm.

Both positions are new and follow a recent company reorganization which placed operations on a division basis.

NEW HIGH SCHOOL PLANNED FOR MT. VIEW

Architect Ernest J. Kump, 450 Ramona Ave., Palo Alto, is preparing drawings for construction of a new High School in Mt. View for the Mt. View Union High School District, with the first phase of construction estimated to cost $1,895,000, and to provide complete educational facilities for 1,500 students.

Bonds for the project amounting to $2,000,000 were voted in February of this year and a 51-acre site acquired. Completion of the work is scheduled for September 1960.

UNITARIAN SOCIETY TO BUILD CHURCH IN SACRAMENTO

Architect John H. Carter, 1401-21st St., Sacramento, is preparing drawings for the construction of a thin shell concrete church building in Sacramento for the First Unitarian Society of Sacramento.

The first phase of construction will provide a social hall and two Sunday school departments. Construction will include steel arches, a flat roof and preliminary construction costs will be about $125,000. The complete church plant will cost an estimated $450,000.

NATIONAL CIVIC DEVELOPMENT MEMBERS NAMED BY CHAMBER

Nels G. Severin of the Severin Construction Company, San Diego; Calvin K. Snyder, Manager, Denver Chamber of Commerce, and Quigg Newton, President of the University of Colorado, Boulder, have been named members of the Construction and Civic Development Committee of the Chamber of Commerce of the United States. Fred I. Rowe, partner and general manager of W. L. Johnson Construction Company and Associates, Columbus, Ohio, has been named Chairman.

The Construction and Civic Development Committee studies major problems affecting the construction industry and urban development, and presents the business viewpoint on national legislative issues to Congressional Committees and government.

DANIEL S. DEFENBACHER BECOMES MEMBER OF THE VICTOR GRUEN FIRM

Daniel S. Defenbacher, a former president of the California College of Arts and Crafts in Oakland, has been appointed to the firm of Victor Gruen Associates, and will be principally involved with research and development on projects in Northern California.

Defenbacher is nationally known in architectural, industrial design and art

museum fields. He is a graduate in architecture of the Carnegie Institute of Technology in Pittsburgh, and has served as Assistant National Director of the Federal Art Project; established and developed the Walker Art Center in Minneapolis, Minn.; designer and director of a new modern community center for the arts in Fort Worth, Texas; and president of the Oakland college.

WESTERN PINE ASSOCIATION SUGGESTS NAMES

The Western Pine Association proposed its industry adopt grade names in place of present number grades in effect on most of its lumber products, such suggestion being made at the group's 1958 Semi-Annual meeting recently held in Portland. About

250 representatives from mills scattered throughout the 12-state Western Pine region attended the three-day sessions.

In recommending the change to name grades, the association's Board of Directors referred the proposal to a referendum vote of the group's 400 member mills. As proposed, all but shop grades would change from numbers to names. Final action will be taken at the Association's meeting in San Francisco in March, 1959.

PLANNING NEW HOSPITAL WING AT ATWATER

Architect Warren C. T. Wong, 2644 Pacific Ave., Stockton, is preparing plans for construction of a 15-bed addition to the Bloss Memorial Hospital in Atwater.

FIRE RESISTANT COATINGS

panel made up of Thomas R. Edwards of "Albi Flame Retarding Coatings" and Mrs. Gabrielle M. Hearst of the Flameort Chemical Company. A short moving picture showing a test of such coatings was shown. The panel moderator was Frank L. Barsotti from the office of the architectural firm of Skidmore, Owings and Merrill.

Many architects and structural engineers took advantage of the opportunity to learn more about the rulings of the State Fire Marshal.

CLYDE E. LEE AWARDED AMERICAN BITUMULS FELLOWSHIP AGAIN

Clyde E. Lee, University of California highway research student, Berkeley, and a resident of Richmond, California, has been awarded five scholarships within the past three years, with the most recent fellowship being granted him by the American Bitumuls and Asphalt Company of San Francisco.

In making the award, C. W. Turner, president of the sponsoring company stated that Lee's work "was perfectly aligned with the aims and purposes for which the fellowship was established, in that it represents a valuable contribution to the paving industry."

Last summer, at the University of California, Lee acted as Laboratory Instructor in Bituminous Research, a course especially designed for college instructors.

ARCHITECTURE'S LARGEST FIRMS DO BIG BUSINESS

Nearly one-tenth of all the new construction in the nation last year was accounted for by just 100 architectural and architectural-engineering firms. The 100 biggest firms were responsible for $4.4 billion of new construction in 1957, or 9.1 per cent of the total of $48.5 billion that was spent on new building of all kinds. Yet these firms represented only 1 per cent of the estimated 9,800 architectural offices in the country.

Forty-eight firms, or nearly half of those listed in the survey are located in five cities: New York, twenty; Los Angeles, nine; Chicago, eight; Detroit, six, and

FORDERER CORNICE WORKS

Manufacturers of

Hollow Metal Products • Interior Metal Trim
Elevator Fronts and Cabs
Metal Plaster Accessories • Sanitary Metal Base
Flat and Roll Metal Screens
Metal Cabinets • Commercial Refrigerators

269 POTRERO AVE.

SAN FRANCISCO, CALIF.   HEMLOCK 1-4100

Philadelphia, five. Of the nine firms listed in Los Angeles, Daniel, Mann, Johnson & Mendenhall rate third in the nation for total volume of construction; Welton Becket & Associates are eighth in the national rating; and J. E. Stanton & William F. Stockwell, Adrian Wilson & Associates, and Arthur Froehlich and Associates rate among the nations top twenty-five firms.

Of the total $4.4 billion of construction represented by the 100 firms, about one-fifth is industrial building, one-fifth is office building, and another fifth educational building. Hospital and institutional construction represents about thirteen per cent of the total, while a varied assortment of other building makes up a remaining 29 per cent.

About 52 of the 100 firms expect to do a greater amount of work during this year, thirteen foresee no change, and the rest feel their volume will decrease.

NEAL BUTLER, Associate in the Architectural and Planning firm of Victor Gruen Associates, Los Angeles, was guest speaker at a recent meeting of the Apartment and Rental Owners Association in San Diego.

LONG BEACH ARCHITECTS ASSOCIATION recently presented a special exhibition of architectural work in the Los Angeles Architectural Gallery in the Building Center, 7933 West 3rd Street.

NEWS & COMMENT ON ART
(From Page 5)

struction) to UCLA's teacher-training facility, the University Elementary School. Codesigner of this structure is architect Robert Alexander.

As a result of Neutra's interest in education, he was employed by the United States government to take on the problem of schools and health centers in Puerto Rico, and educational and government buildings in Guam.

The Ruth McC. Maitland Memorial Exhibition will be shown in its totality for the first time. It is described by Professor Wight as a "memorial to the daring, judgment, and taste of a sensitive and discerning collector—the late Mrs. McC. Maitland."

The third exhibit is composed of the engravings of Pieter Brueghel the Elder who worked in the Low Countries toward the close of the Middle Ages.

Breaking the artistic traditions of his time, the artist, according to Professor Wight, "brought art down to earth to give a democratic account of the life around him in all its pain, vitality, and rich humor." The engravings, lent by Mr. and Mrs. Jake Zeitlin, are shown by the Grunwald Graphic Arts Foundation.

Free to the public, the exhibits may be seen weekdays from 12:30 to 5 p.m., and on Sundays from 1:30 to 4 p.m. The galleries, located in the Dickson Art Center at UCLA, are closed on Saturdays.

BABYLON and the Old Testament. By Andre Parrot. Philosophical Library, Inc., 15 E. 40th St., New York 16. 166 pages. Price $2.75.

Translated from the French by Beatrice Hooke. Nothing remains of Babylon except ruins. But from these ruins archaeologists have been able to trace the sites of many of the important buildings in this great city. The author opens with the story of Babylonian archaeology, describing the palaces and temples, the citadels and walls which were found there. The second section gives an account of the history and civilization of this mighty empire as revealed by what the Old Testament tells us about the relations between Babylon and the Jewish peolpe.

DICTIONARY OF EUROPEAN ART. By Emerich Schaffran. Philosophical Library, Inc. 15 E. 40th St., New York 16, N. Y. 283 pages. Price $4.75.

Here is an indispensable handbook for all who wish to study, or merely add to the enjoyment of, the artistic landmarks of Western culture. In it is found the significant figures, terms, movements and masterpieces in the fine arts, from Classical antiquity to twentieth-century Europe. In addition to clarifying those basic concepts which add incalculably to the appreciation of an artwork, this book contains the biographies and major works of the supreme masters, as well as a host of lesser known artists who kept the creative tradition alive through its less fertile periods. A comprehensive introduction traces the evolution of art forms, and the rise and fall of art styles from Greek Classiciscm to modern Expressionism, Cubism and Surrealism.

THE GOLDEN NUMBER—And the Scientific Aesthetics of Architecture. By M. Borissavlievitch. Philosophical Library, Inc., 15 E. 40th St., New York 16, N. Y. 91 pages. Price $4.75

An essay on the Golden Section, and aesthetic geometry in architectural composition. The author discusses the difference between aesthetics and mathematics and makes comments on mathematical methods of investigations in aesthetic phenomena. He then pursues scientific aesthetics in architecture and the Golden Number, examines compositions based upon the Golden Number, and tenders laws for architectural harmony and composition including the Law of Tympanum. His strong support of aesthetics in architectural composition, and his opposition to the purely mathematical approach to the subject, together with his proposed laws for aesthetics in architecture, will arouse discussion.

THE MODERNS and Their World. Sir John Rothenstein. Philosophical Library, Inc., 15 E. 40th St., New York 16. 96 pages. Illustrated in color. Price $12.00.

This book is a gallery from the whole world of the painters of our time. Based on Ezra Pound's dictum that the way to understand pictures it to look at pictures, it contains 96 plates (48 in color), and has a long introduction by Sir John Rothenstein of the Tate Gallery, London, England. About fifty artists are represented, some by several pictures.

NEW CATALOGUES AVAILABLE

Architects, Engineers, Contractors, Planning Commission members—the catalogues, folders, new building products material, etc., described below may be obtained by directing your request to the name and address given in each item.

Overhead door opener. New, illustrated bulletin describes features of electric operator for commercial and industrial overhead doors; specifications in detail; new features including safety switch; standard control is from a 3-button, open, close, stop, switch; momentary contact opens or closes the door or reverses it at any point in the stroke. Free copy write DEPT A&E, Barber-Colman Co., Rockford, Ill.

Hornflex thiokol sealant. Unusual compression and expansion coefficients of 50 and 100 per cent in a temperature range of 0° F. to 250° F. are among the outstanding features of the Hornflex Thiokol LP-32 Sealant described in a new 8-page brochure; details application, physical properties and many functions served by the sealant including curtain wall construction, preparation of watertight joints and solving prob-

lems where extreme expansion and contraction are encountered. Free copy write DEPT-A&E, A. C. Horn Companies, Sun Chemical Corp., 750 3rd Ave., New York 17, N. Y.

Shaft mounted speed reducers. New 24-page book describes completely new line of shaft-mounted speed reducers; contains engineering and selection information on single drive in six sizes with nominal ratios of 5-1 and capacities up to 50-horsepower; and double reduction drives in 7 sizes, with nominal ratios of 15-1 and up to 40-horsepower; can be mounted at angular as well as horizontal positions; positive lubrication. Free copy write DEPT A&E, Link-Belt Co., Prudential Plaza, Chicago 1, Ill.

Metal framing system. Newly revised 2-color brochure features applications of Unistrut all-purpose, metal framing system; fully illustrated, shows typical electrical and mechanical applications; sketches of typical fittings and descriptions of channel units and specifications; easy installation, complete adjustability and reusability. Free copy write DEPT-A&E, Unistrut Products Co., 933 W. Washington Blvd., Chicago 7, Ill.

Light steel framing. New booklet (AIA File No. 13G) describes and fully illustrates some ideas for light occupancy structures with light steel framing; several architectural examples shown. Free copy write DEPT-A&E, Bethlehem Pacific Coast Steel Corp., San Francisco, California.

Panels for translucent ceilings. New brochure (AIA File No. 39-B) describes modern high level, low brightness shadow-free illumination with "lumicel" and "acousti-lux" panels; numerous illustrations of installations; specifications, materials. Free copy write DEPT-A&E, F. K. Pinney, Inc., San Francisco, or Sacramento, California.

Dust collectors. New 12-page, 2-color details the Joy Microdyne Dust Collector; wet inertial type, installed as part of the duct, and 1/10 the size of collectors with comparable performance; collection efficiencies are 95% of all dust 5 microns in size, 80% of dusts in the 1 micron range; illustrated, performance curves, complete specifications, cut-away drawings of inner construction, as well as description of a related filter for reclamation or removal of the collected sturry. Free copy write DEPT-A&E, Joy Mfg. Co., Oliver Bldg., Pittsburgh 22, Pa.

"How to be more comfortable and live for less." New illustrated 24-page booklet, in color, explains to home owners the values of thick insulation for comfort and economy; eliminates drafts, reduces radiation of heat both inward and outward, summer and winter; scientifically tested data. Available to builders, architects, engineers, contractors free, write DEPT-A&E, National Mineral Wool Ass'n, 2906 Americas Bldg., Rockefeller Center, New York 20, N. Y.

"Sound absorption coefficients of architectural acoustical materials." New 1959 edition published by Acoustical Materials Association to provide architects, builders and acoustical contractors, engineers and consultants with comprehensive technical data on various acoustical materials produced by the association's member firms; includes noise reduction coefficients and recommended specifications; materials are listed by manufacturers with individual trade names; section on installation recommendations. Copy free write DEPT-A&E, Acoustical Materials Association, 335 E. 45th St., New York 17, N. Y.

ARCHITECT AND ENGINEER

ESTIMATOR'S GUIDE

BUILDING AND CONSTRUCTION MATERIALS

PRICES GIVEN ARE FIGURING PRICES AND ARE MADE UP FROM AVERAGE QUOTATIONS FURNISHED BY LeROY CONSTRUCTION SERVICES. 4% SALES TAX ON ALL MATERIALS BUT NOT LABOR. ITEMS IN ITALIC INCLUDE LABOR AND SALES TAX.

BONDS—Performance or Performance plus Labor and Material Bond(s), $10 per $1000 on contract price. Labor and Material Bond(s) only, $5.00 per $1000 on contract price.

BRICKWORK & MASONRY

COMMON BRICKWORK, Reinforced:		
8" walls	*SF*	*2.95*
12" walls	*SF*	*4.15*
SELECT COMMON, Reinforced:		
8" walls	*SF*	*3.05*
12" walls	*SF*	*4.30*
CONCRETE BLOCK, Reinforced:		
6" walls	*SF*	*1.40*
8" walls	*SF*	*1.55*
12" walls	*SF*	*1.90*
BRICK VENEER:		
4" Select Common	*SF*	*1.65*
4" Roman	*SF*	*2.50*
4" Norman	*SF*	*2.40*
4" Aggrelite	*SF*	*2.40*

BRICKWORK & MASONRY

All Prices—F.O.B. Plant.

COMMON BRICK		
Common 2½ x 3¾ x 8¼	M	45.00
Select 2½ x 3¾ x 8¼	M	52.00
Clinker 2½ x 3¾ x 8¼	M	48.00
Jumbo 3½ x 3 x 11½	M	90.00
FACE BRICK		
Standard	M	59.80 - 83.20
Jumbo	M	114.40 - 130.00
Roman	M	88.40 - 109.20
Norman	M	101.40 - 124.80
Brik Blox (6")	M	202.80
(8")	M	239.20
Braile Veneer	M	26.00
BUILDING TILE		
8 x 5½ x 12 inches	M	165.78
6 x 5½ x 12 inches	M	128.96
HOLLOW TILE		
12 x 12 x 3 inches	M	163.12
12 x 12 x 4 inches	M	184.18
12 x 12 x 6 inches	M	244.71
MANTEL FIRE BRICK		
2½ x 9½ x 4½ inches	M	140.40
GLAZED STRUCTURAL UNITS		
2 x 6 x 12 Furring	SF	.90
4 x 6 x 12 Furring	SF	1.20
6 x 6 x 12 Furring	SF	1.50
4 x 6 x 12 Partition	SF	1.60
Add for color	SF	.20
CONCRETE BLOCKS		
4 x 8 x 16 inches	EA	.22
6 x 8 x 16 inches	EA	.265
8 x 8 x 16 inches	EA	.30
12 x 8 x 16 inches	EA	.435
Colored Add	EA	.02
AGGREGATE—Haydite or Basalite		
All sizes in bulk	CY	6.24

BUILDING PAPERS & FELTS

1 ply per 1000 ft. roll	3.95
2 ply per 1000 ft. roll	6.03
3 ply per 1000 ft. roll	8.22
Sisalkraft, reinf. 500 ft. roll	7.54
SHEATHING PAPERS:	
Asphalt sheathing, 15-lb. roll	2.40
30-lb. roll	3.37
Dampcourse, 216-ft. roll	3.05
FELT PAPERS:	
Deadening felt, ¾ lb., 50 ft. roll	3.94
Deadening felt, 1 lb., 50 ft. roll	4.60
Asphalt roofing, 15-lb.	2.50
30-lb.	3.50
ROOFING PAPERS:	
Standard Grade, Smooth Surface	
108 ft. roll, Light, 45 lb.	2.26
Medium 55 lb.	2.64
Heavy 65 lb.	3.10
Mineral Surfaced	3.60

CHIMNEYS, PATENT

F.O.B. Warehouse

6"	LF	1.45
8"	LF	2.05
10"	LF	2.85
12"	LF	3.45

Rates for 10 - 50 Lin. Ft.

CONCRETE AGGREGATES

	Bunker Per Ton	Del'd Per Ton
Gravel, All Sizes	3.25	4.00
Top Sand	3.45	4.20
Concrete Mix	3.35	4.20
Crushed Rock		
¼" to ¾"	3.30	4.20
¾" to 1½"	3.30	4.20
Roofing Gravel	3.46	4.15
SAND		
Lapis (Nos. 1 & 2)	4.30	5.10
Olympia (Nos. 1 & 2)	3.60	4.15

CEMENT		
Common, All brands (Paper sacks)		
Small quantities,	Per Sack	1.35
Large quantities,	Per bbl.	4.25
Trinity White & Meudusa White	Per Sack	4.00
CONCRETE MIX		
6 sacks in 5-yd. loads	Per yard	13.40
CURING COMPOUND, Clear		
5 gal drums	Per Gal.	1.46

CARPENTRY & MILLWORK

Hardware not included

FRAMING:		
Floors	*BM*	*.20 - .25*
Walls	*BM*	*.25 - .30*
Ceilings	*BM*	*.18 - .22*
Roofs	*BM*	*.22 - .27*
Furring & Blocking	*BM*	*.30 - .50*
SHEATHING:		
1 x 8 straight	*BM*	*.20 - .25*
1 x 8 diagonal	*BM*	*.23 - .28*
5/16" Plyscore	*SF*	*.16 - .20*
⅜" Plywood	*SF*	*.25 - .30*
SIDING:		
1 x 8 Bevel	*BM*	*.35 - .40*
1 x 4 V-Rustic	*BM*	*.40 - .45*
EXTERIOR TRIM:		
Fascia and Molds	*BM*	*.40 - .50*
Bolted Framing—Add 50%		
ENTRANCE DOORS & FRAMES:		
Singles		*60.00 & Up*
Doubles		*100.00 & Up*
INTERIOR DOORS & FRAMES:		
Singles		*35.00 & Up*
Pocket Sliding		*45.00 & Up*
Closet Sliding (Pr.)		*50.00 & Up*
WINDOWS:		
D/H Sash & Frames	*SF*	*1.75 & Up*
Casement Sash & Frames	*SF*	*1.90 & Up*
SHELVING:		
1 x 12 S4S	*BM*	*.30 - .50*
¾" Plywood	*SF*	*.40 - .60*
STAIRS:		
Oak steps D.F. Risers		
Under 36" wide	*Riser*	*12.00*
Under 60" wide	*Riser*	*17.00*
Newel posts and rail extra		
WOOD CASES & CABINETS:		
D.F. Wall Hung	*LF*	*13.00 - 18.00*
D.F. Counters	*LF*	*15.00 - 20.00*

DAMPPROOFING & WATERPROOFING

MEMBRANE:		
1 layer 50 lb. felt	*SQ.*	*9.00*
4 layers Dampcourse	*SQ.*	*13.00*
Hot coat walls	*SQ.*	*6.00*
Tricosal added to concrete	*CY*	*1.00*
Anti-Hydro added to concrete	*CY*	*1.50*

ELECTRIC WIRING

Per Outlet:		
Knob & Tube	*EA*	*9.00*
Armor	*EA*	*16.00*
Conduit	*EA*	*20.00*
110 V Circuit	*EA*	*25.00*
220 V Circuit	*EA*	*95.00*

ELEVATORS & ESCALATORS

Prices vary according to capacity, speed and type. Consult Elevator Companies.

Slow speed apartment house elevator including doors and trim, about $5000.00 per floor.

EXCAVATION

MACHINE WORK in common ground:		
Large Basements	*CY*	*.75 - 1.00*
Small Pits	*CY*	*1.25 - 1.75*
Trenches	*CY*	*1.50 - 2.25*
HAND WORK in common ground:		
Large pits and trenches	*CY*	*4.50 - 5.50*
Small pits and trimming	*CY*	*5.00 - 6.50*

Hard Clay & Shale 2 times above rates.
Rock and large boulders 4-6 times above rates.
Shoring, bracing and disposal of water not included.

FLOORS

⅛" Asp. tile, dark colors	*SF*	*.25 - .30*
⅛" Asp. tile, light colors	*SF*	*.30 - .35*
⅛" Rubber tile	*SF*	*.60 - .70*
.080 Vinyl Asbestos Tile	*SF*	*.40 - .45*
.080 Vinyl Tile	*SF*	*.85 - .95*
Lino, Standard Gauge	*SY*	*3.75 - 4.25*
Lino, Battleship	*SY*	*5.25 - 5.75*
4" Rubber Base, Black	*LF*	*.35 - .40*
Rubber Stair Nosing	*LF*	*1.00 - 1.75*

Above rates based on quantities of 1000 - 5000 SF per job.

HARDWOOD FLOORS

Select Oak, filled, sanded, stained and varnished:		
5/16" x 2¼" strip	*SF*	*.45 - .50*
5/16" Random Plank	*SF*	*.50 - .55*
25/32" x 2¼" T&G	*SF*	*.70 - .80*
Maple, 2nd Grade and Better, filled, sanded, stained and varnished:		
25/32" x 2¼" T&G	*SF*	*.80 - .95*
Wax Finish, add	*SF*	*.10*

HARDWOOD FLOORING

Oak 5/16" x 2" Strip—		
Clear	M	229.00
Select	M	218.00
#1 Common	M	203.00
Oak 5/16" Random Plank—		
Select & Btr.	M	286.00
#1 Common	M	244.00
Oak 25/32" x 2¼" T&G—		
Select	M	260.00
#1 Common	M	203.00
Maple 25/32" x 2¼" T&G—		
#1 Grade	M	317.00
#2 Grade	M	281.00
#3 Grade	M	208.00
Nails—1" Floor Brads	KEG	17.20

GLASS & GLAZING

S.S.B. Clear	*SF*	*.48*
D.S.B. Clear	*SF*	*.78*
Crystal	*SF*	*.92*
¼" Plate	*SF*	*2.17*
⅛" Obscure	*SF*	*.68*
⅛" Heat Absorbing	*SF*	*1.12*
¼" Tempered Plate	*SF*	*4.38*
½" Tempered Plate	*SF*	*7.84*
¼" Wire Plate, Clear	*SF*	*3.65*
¼" Wire Plate, Rough	*SF*	*1.08*

GLASS—CUT TO SIZE

F.O.B. Warehouse

S.S.B. Clear, Av. 6 SF	SF	.34
D.S.B. Clear, Av. 10 SF	SF	.56
Crystal, Av. 35-SF	SF	.65
¼" Polished Plate, Av. 100 SF	SF	1.55
⅛" Obscure, Av. 10 SF	SF	.49
⅛" Ribbed, Av. 10 SF	SF	.49
⅛" Rough, Av. 10 SF	SF	.49
¼" Wire Plate, Clear, Av. 40 SF	SF	2.61
¼" Wire Plate, Rough, Av. 40 SF	SF	.77
⅛" Heat Absorbing, Av. 10 SF	SF	.80
¼" Tempered Plate, Av. 50 SF	SF	3.60
½" Tempered Plate, Av. 50 SF	SF	6.88
Glazing—Approx. 40-50% of Glass		
Glass Blocks—		
6"		.57
8"		.92
12"		2.39

HEATING

FURNACES—Gas Fired—Av. Job:	
FLOOR FURNACE:	
25,000 BTU	*100.00 - 125.00*
35,000 BTU	*107.00 - 135.00*
45,000 BTU	*115.00 - 150.00*
AUTOMATIC CONTROL:	
Add	*25.00 - 35.00*

HEATING—Cont'd

DUAL WALL FURNACE:
25,000 BTU ... *110.00 - 125.00*
35,000 BTU ... *125.00 - 145.00*
50,000 BTU ... *150.00 - 180.00*
AUTOMATIC CONTROL:
Add ... *25.00 - 35.00*
GRAVITY FURNACE:
75,000 BTU ... *375.00 - 450.00*
85,000 BTU ... *425.00 - 525.00*
95,000 BTU ... *475.00 - 600.00*
FORCED AIR FURNACE:
Add ... *75.00 - 125.00*
AUTOMATIC CONTROL:
Add ... *15.00 - 25.00*
HEAT REGISTERS:
Outlet ... *7.50 - 15.00*

INSULATION & WALLBOARD

F.O.B. Warehouse

ROCKWOOL Insulation—
2" Semi-thick ... Per M SF 60.60
3⅝" Full Thick ... Per M SF 77.40
COTTON Insulation
1" Full Thick ... Per M SF 43.26
SOFTBOARDS—Wood Fiber—
½" thick ... Per M SF 84.00
1½" thick ... Per M SF 275.00
2" thick ... Per M SF 385.00
ALUMINUM Insulation—
80# Kraft paper with alum. foil
1 side only ... Per M SF 18.30
2 sides ... Per M SF 31.00
GYPSUM Wallboard—
⅜" thick ... Per M SF 49.50
½" thick ... Per M SF 54.50
⅝" thick ... Per M SF 83.00
⅜" Gyplap ... Per M SF 85.00
HARDBOARDS—Wood Fiber—
⅛" thick, Sheathing ... Per M SF 84.00
3/16" thick, Sheathing ... Per M SF 90.48
¼" thick, Sheathing ... Per M SF 109.20
⅛" thick, Tempered ... Per M SF 108.00
3/16" thick, Tempered ... Per M SF 186.00
¼" thick, Tempered ... Per M SF 194.48
CEMENT Asbestos Board—
⅛" C.A.B. Flat Sheets ... Per M SF 151.20
3/16" C.A.B. Flat Sheets ... Per M SF 208.80
¼" C.A.B. Flat Sheets ... Per M SF 270.01

LATH & PLASTER

Diamond 3.40 copper bearing ... SY .56
Ribbed 3.40 copper bearing ... SY .62
⅜" rock lath ... SY .36
1½" Standard Channel ... LF .062
¾" Standard Channel ... LF .045
3¼" steel studs ... LF .092
4" steel studs ... LF .107
Stud shoes ... EA .028
Hardwall, Browning ... Sack 1.45
Hardwall, Finish ... Sack 1.70
Stucco ... Sack 2.50

LATH & PLASTERWORK

CHANNEL FURRING:
Suspended Ceilings ... *SY 2.20 - 2.50*
Walls ... *SY 2.30 - 2.60*
METAL STUD PARTITIONS:
3¼" Studs ... *SY 1.70 - 2.00*
4" Studs ... *SY 1.95 - 2.25*
Over 10'0 high, add ... *SY .20 - .30*
3.40 METAL LATH AND PLASTER:
Ceilings ... *SY 3.60 - 4.00*
Walls ... *SY 3.75 - 4.15*
KEENE'S CEMENT FINISH:
Add ... *SY .40 - .60*
ROCK LATH & PLASTER:
Ceilings ... *SY 2.50 - 2.80*
Walls ... *SY 2.60 - 2.90*
WIRE MESH AND ⅞" STUCCO:
Walls ... *SY 3.60 - 4.10*
STUCCO ON CONCRETE:
Walls ... *SY 2.30 - 2.80*
METAL ACCESSORIES ... *LF .20 - .50*

LINOLEUM

Lino. Standard Gauge ... SY 2.65 - 2.85
Lino. Battleship ... SY 2.95 - 3.11
⅛" Asp. tile, Dark ... SF .10 - .11
⅛" Asp. tile, Light ... SF .14 - .16
⅛" Rubber Tile ... SF .40 - .44
.080 Vinyl tile ... SF .20 - .21
.080 Vinyl Asb. tile ... SF .18 - .19
⅛" Vinyl tile ... SF .78 - .82
4" Base, Dark ... LF .15 - .16
4" Base, Light ... LF .24 - .26
Rubber Nosing ... LF .60 - 1.30
Lino Paste ... GAL .75 - .90
Above rates based on quantities of 1000-5000 SF per job.

LUMBER

DOUGLAS FIR: M.B.M.
#1 2x4—2x10 ... 88.00 - 92.00
#2 2x4—2x10 ... 85.00 - 90.00
#3 2x4—2x10 ... 68.00 - 74.00
#4 2x4—2x10 ... 64.00 - 72.00
Clear, Air Dried ... 180.00 - 210.00
Clear, Kiln Dried ... 210.00 - 240.00

REDWOOD:
Foundation Grade ... 120.00 - 130.00
Construction Heart ... 110.00 - 120.00
A Grade ... 180.00 - 210.00
Clear Heart ... 190.00 - 220.00
D.F. PLYWOOD M.S.F.
¼" AB ... 95.00 - 105.00
¼" AD ... 90.00 - 95.00
¼" Ext. Waterproof ... 115.00 - 125.00
⅜" AB ... 130.00 - 145.00
⅜" AD ... 115.00 - 125.00
⅜" CD ... 70.00 - 85.00
½" AB ... 170.00 - 185.00
½" AD ... 110.00 - 115.00
½" CD ... .
⅝" AB ... 185.00 - 200.00
⅝" AD ... 165.00 - 180.00
⅝" CD ... 115.00 - 125.00
¾" AB ... 210.00 - 230.00
¾" AD ... 195.00 - 210.00
¾" CD ... 125.00 - 140.00
⅝" Plyform ... 160.00 - 170.00
SHINGLES: Square
Cedar #1 ... 14.00 - 15.50
Cedar #2 ... 11.50 - 12.50
SHAKES:
CEDAR
½ to ¾" Butt ... 17.50 - 18.50
¾ to 1¼" Butt ... 18.50 - 19.50
REDWOOD
¾ to 1¼" Butt ... 21.00 - 24.00

MILLWORK

All Prices F.O.B. Mill

D.F. CLEAR, AIR DRIED:
S4S ... MBM 220.00 - 250.00
D.F. CLEAR, KILN DRIED:
S4S ... MBM 225.00 - 275.00
DOOR FRAMES & TRIM:
Residential Entrance ... 17.00 & up
Interior Room Entrance ... 7.50 & up
DOORS:
1⅜" D.F. Slab, Hollow Core ... 8.00 & up
1¾" D.F. Slab, Solid Core ... 19.00 & up
1⅜" Birch Slab, Hollow Core ... 10.00 & up
1¾" Birch Slab, Solid Core ... 22.00 & up
WINDOW FRAMES:
D/H Singles ... SF .80
Casement Singles ... SF .90
WOOD SASH:
D/H in pairs (1 lite) ... SF .45
Casement (1 lite) ... SF .50
WOOD CABINETS:
¾" D.F. Ply with ¼" ply backs
Wall Hung ... LF 10.00 - 15.00
Counter ... LF 12.00 - 17.00
BIRCH OR MAPLE—Add 25%

PAINT

All Prices F.O.B. Warehouse

Thinners—5-100 gals. ... GAL. .57
Turpentine—5-100 gals. ... GAL. 1.58
Linseed Oil, Raw ... GAL. 2.51
Linseed Oil, Boiled ... GAL. 2.57
Primer-Sealer ... GAL. 3.10
Enamel ... GAL. 5.45
Enamel Undercoaters ... GAL. 5.45
White Lead in Oil ... LB. .35
Red Lead in Oil ... LB. .35
Litharge ... LB. .30

PAINTING

EXTERIOR:
Stucco Wash 1 ct. ... *SY .30*
Stucco Wash 2 cts. ... *SY .55*
Lead and Oil 2 cts. ... *SY .90*
Lead and Oil 3 cts. ... *SY 1.30*
INTERIOR:
Primer Sealer ... *SY .40*
Wall Paint, 1 ct. ... *SY .50*
Wall Paint, 2 cts. ... *SY .95*
Enamel, 1 ct. ... *SY .60*
Enamel, 2 cts. ... *SY 1.10*
Doors and Trim ... *EA 10.00*
Sash and Trim ... *EA 12.00*
Base and Molds ... *LF .12*
Old Work—Add 15-30%

PLUMBING

Lavatories ... *EA 100.00 - 150.00*
Toilets ... *EA 200.00 - 300.00*
Bath Tubs ... *EA 250.00 - 350.00*
Stall Shower ... *EA 80.00 - 150.00*
Sinks ... *EA 125.00 - 175.00*
Laundry Trays ... *EA 80.00 - 130.00*
Water Heaters ... *EA 100.00 - 300.00*
Prices based on average residential and commercial work. Special fixtures and excessive piping not included.

ROOFING

STANDARD TAR & GRAVEL Per Square
4 ply ... *14.00 - 18.00*
5 ply ... *17.00 - 20.00*
White Gravel Finish—Add ... *2.00 - 4.00*
Asph. Compo. Shingles ... *16.00 - 20.00*
Cedar Shingles ... *20.00 - 24.00*
Cedar Shakes ... *26.00 - 30.00*
Redwood Shakes ... *28.00 - 34.00*
Clay Tiles ... *40.00 - 50.00*

SEWER PIPE

VITRIFIED:
Standard 4 in. ... LF .31
Standard 6 in. ... LF .56
Standard 8 in. ... LF .81
Standard 12 in. ... LF 1.76
Standard 24 in. ... LF 6.95
CLAY DRAIN PIPE:
Standard 6 in. ... LF .34
Standard 8 in. ... LF .59
Rate for 100 Lin. Ft. F.O.B. Warehouse

STEEL

REINFORCING BARS:
¼" rounds ... LB .122
⅜" rounds ... LB .111
½" rounds ... LB .107
⅝" rounds ... LB .104
¾" rounds ... LB .102
⅞" rounds ... LB .102
1" rounds ... LB .102
REINFORCING MESH (1050 SF Rolls)
6x6 x 10x10 ... SF .035
6x6 x 6x6 ... SF .067
16 GA. TYING WIRE ... LB .130
Rates 100-1000 Lbs. F.O.B. Warehouse

STRUCTURAL STEEL

$325.00 and up per ton erected when out of mill.
$350.00 and up per ton erected when out of stock.

SHEET METAL

ROOF FLASHINGS:
18 ga. Galv. Steel ... *SF .60 - 1.00*
22 ga. Galv. Steel ... *SF .50 - .90*
26 ga. Galv. Steel ... *SF .40 - .80*
18 ga. Aluminum ... *SF 1.00 - 1.50*
22 ga. Aluminum ... *SF .80 - 1.30*
26 ga. Aluminum ... *SF .60 - 1.10*
24 oz. Copper ... *SF 1.90 - 2.40*
20 oz. Copper ... *SF 1.70 - 2.20*
16 oz. Copper ... *SF 1.50 - 2.00*
26 ga. Galv. Steel
4" o.g. gutter ... *LF .90 - 1.30*
Mitres and Drops ... *EA 2.00 - 4.00*
22 ga. Galv. Louvres ... *SF 2.50 - 3.50*
20 oz. Copper Louvres ... *SF 3.00 - 4.50*

TILE WORK

CERAMIC TILE, Stock colors:
Floors ... *SF 1.95 - 2.45*
Walls ... *SF 2.05 - 2.55*
Coved Base ... *LF 1.05 - 1.45*
QUARRY TILE:
6" x 6" x ½" Floors ... *SF 1.60 - 2.00*
9" x 9" x ¾" Floors ... *SF 1.75 - 2.15*
Treads and risers ... *LF 3.00 - 4.50*
Coved Base ... *LF .90 - 1.30*
Mosaic Tile — Rates vary with design and colors. Each job should be priced from Manufacturer.

TERRAZZO & MARBLE

Terrazzo Floors ... *SF 2.00 - 2.50*
Cond. Terr. Floors ... *SF 2.20 - 2.75*
Precast treads and risers ... *LF 3.50 - 4.50*
Precast landing slabs ... *SF 3.00 - 4.00*

TILE

CERAMIC:
F.O.B. Warehouse
4¼" x 4¼" glazed ... SF .69
4¼" x 4¼" hard glazed ... SF .72
Random unglazed ... SF .73
6" x 2" cap ... EA .17
6" coved base ... EA .22
¼" round bead ... LF .18
QUARRY:
6 x 6 x ½" Red ... SF .49
6 x 6 x ¾" Red ... SF .52
9 x 9 x ¾" Red ... SF .60
6 x 6" coved base ... EA .21
White Cement Grout ... Per 100 Lbs. 6.25

VENETIAN BLINDS

Residential ... SF .40 & Up
Commercial ... SF .45 & Up

WINDOWS

STEEL SASH:
Under 10 SF ... SF 2.50 & Up
Under 15 SF ... SF 2.00 & Up
Under 20 SF ... SF 1.50 & Up
Under 30 SF ... SF 1.00 & Up
ALUMINUM SASH:
Under 10 SF ... SF 2.75 & Up
Under 15 SF ... SF 2.25 & Up
Under 20 SF ... SF 1.75 & Up
Under 30 SF ... SF 1.25 & Up
Above rates are for standard sections and stock sizes F.O.B. Warehouse

CONSTRUCTION INDUSTRY WAGE RATES

Table 1 has been prepared by the State of California, Department of Industrial Relations, Division of Labor Statistics and Research. The rates are the union hourly wage rates established by collective bargaining as of January 2, 1958, as reported by reliable sources.

TABLE 1—UNION HOURLY WAGE RATES, CONSTRUCTION INDUSTRY, CALIFORNIA

Following are the hourly rates of compensation established by collective bargaining, reported as of January 2, 1958 or later

CRAFT	San Francisco	Alameda	Contra Costa	Fresno	Sacramento	San Joaquin	Santa Clara	Solano	Los Angeles	San Bernardino	San Diego	Santa Barbara	Kern
ASBESTOS WORKER	$3.70	$3.70	$3.70	$3.70	$3.70	$3.70	$3.70	$3.70	$3.70	$3.70	$3.70	$3.70	$3.70
BOILERMAKER	3.675	3.675	3.675	3.675	3.675	3.675	3.675	3.675	3.675	3.675	3.675	3.675	3.675
BRICKLAYER	3.95	3.75	3.75	3.75	3.80	3.75	3.875	3.95	3.80	3.90	3.75		3.85
BRICKLAYER HODCARRIER	3.15	3.15	3.15	3.10	2.90	3.00	3.10	2.75	2.75	2.75		2.75	
CARPENTER	3.175	3.175	3.225	3.225	3.225	3.225	3.225	3.225	3.225	3.225	3.225	3.225	3.225
CEMENT MASON	3.22	3.22	3.22	3.22	3.22	3.22	3.22	3.22	3.15	3.15	3.25	3.15	3.15
ELECTRICIAN	3.936A	3.936A	3.936A		3.94A	3.50	4.03A	3.666A	3.90A	3.90A	3.90	3.85A	3.70
GLAZIER	3.09	3.09	3.09	3.135	3.055	3.055	3.09	3.09	3.105	3.105	3.03	3.105	3.135
IRON WORKER													
ORNAMENTAL	3.625	3.625	3.625	3.625	3.625	3.625	3.625	3.625	3.625	3.625	3.625	3.625	3.625
REINFORCING	3.375	3.375	3.375	3.375	3.375	3.375	3.375	3.375	3.375	3.375	3.375	3.375	3.375
STRUCTURAL	3.625	3.625	3.625	3.625	3.625	3.625	3.625	3.625	3.625	3.625	3.625	3.625	3.625
LABORER, GENERAL OR CONSTRUCTION	2.505	2.505	2.505	2.505	2.505	2.506	2.505	2.505	2.50	2.50	2.48	2.50	2.50
LATHER	3.4375	3.84	3.84	3.45	3.60B	3.40G	3.60D	3.50E	3.9375		3.725	3.625F	
OPERATING ENGINEER													
Concrete mixer (up to 1 yard)	2.89	2.89	2.89	2.89	2.89	2.89	2.89	2.89					
Concrete mixer operator—Skip Type									2.96	2.96	2.96	2.96	2.96
Elevator Hoist Operator									3.19	3.19	3.19	3.19	3.19
Material Hoist (1 drum)	3.19	3.19	3.19	3.19	3.19	3.19	3.19	3.19					
Tractor Operator	3.33	3.33	3.33	3.33	3.33	3.33	3.33	3.33	3.47	3.47	3.47	3.47	3.47
PAINTER													
Brush	3.20	3.20	3.20	3.13	3.325	3.175	3.20	3.20	3.26a	3.25	3.19	3.13H	3.10
Spray	3.20	3.20	3.20	3.38	3.575	3.325	3.20	3.20	3.51a	3.50	3.74	3.38H	3.35
PILEDRIVERMAN	3.305	3.305	3.305	3.305	3.305	3.305	3.305	3.305	3.355	3.355		3.355	3.355
PLASTERER	3.69	3.545	3.545	3.35	3.60a	3.55c	3.58	3.50	3.9375	3.9375	3.725		
PLASTERER HODCARRIER	3.25	3.42	3.42	3.10	3.10	3.00c	3.20	3.15	3.6875	3.5625	3.475	3.50	3.6875
PLUMBER	3.67		3.935i	3.80J	3.70	3.80J	3.60	3.675	3.70	3.70	3.70	3.70	3.375
ROOFER	3.35	3.35	3.35	3.20	3.25	3.35	3.35	3.10K	3.20L	3.25	3.10	3.30	3.775
SHEET METAL WORKER	3.45	3.45	3.45	3.425	3.45	3.465	3.45	3.325	3.50	3.50	3.45	3.55	3.10
STEAMFITTER	3.67	3.96	3.96	3.80J	3.70	3.80J	3.60	3.675	3.70	3.70	3.70	3.70	3.775
TRUCK DRIVER—													
Dump Trucks under 4 yards	2.55	2.55	2.55	2.55	2.55	2.55	2.55	2.55	2.63	2.63	2.63	2.63	2.63
TILE SETTER	3.275	3.275	3.275	3.375	3.28	3.30	3.275	3.275	3.36	3.60	3.375	3.36	

A Includes 4% vacation allowance.
B Includes 5c hour for industry promotion and 5c hour for vacation fund.
c ½% withheld for industry promotion.
D 1½c withheld for industry promotion.
E Includes 5c hour for industry promotion and 5c hour for vacation fund. Hourly rate for part of county adjacent to Sacramento County is $3.60.
F Northern part of County: $3.75.

G Pomona Area: Brush $3.25; Spray $3.50.
H Southern half of County: Brush $3.28; Spray $3.28.
I Includes 30c hour for vacation pay.
J Includes 15c hour which local union may elect to use for vacation purposes.
K Includes 10c hour for vacation fund.
L Includes 10c hour savings fund wage.

ATTENTION: The above tabulation has been prepared by the State of California, Department of Industrial Relations, Division of Labor Statistics and Research, and represents data reported by building trades councils, union locals, contractor organizations, and other reliable sources. The above rates do not include any payments to funds for health and welfare, pensions, vacations, industry promotion, apprentice training, etc., except as shown in the footnotes.

CONSTRUCTION INDUSTRY WAGE RATES — TABLE 2

Employer Contributions to Health and Welfare, Pension, Vacation and Other Funds
California Union Contracts, Construction Industry

(Revised March, 1957)

CRAFT	San Francisco	Fresno	Sacramento	San Joaquin	Santa Clara	Los Angeles	San Bernardino	San Diego
ASBESTOS WORKER	.10 W .11 hr. V	.10 W .11 hr. V	.10 W .11 hr. V	.10 W .11 hr. V	.10 W .11 hr. V	.10 W	.10 W	.10 W
BRICKLAYER	.15 W .14 P .05 hr. V		.15 W .10 P		.15 W			
BRICKLAYER HODCARRIER	.10 W .10 P .10 V	.10 W	.10 W	.10 W	.10 W	.075 W	.075 W	.075 W
CARPENTER	.10 W .10 hr. V	.10 W	.10 W	.10 W	.10 W	.10 W	.10 W	.10 W
CEMENT MASON	.10 W	.10 W	.10 W	.10 W	.10 W	.10 W	.10 W	.10 W
ELECTRICAL WORKER	.10 W 1% P 4% V	.10 W 1% P 4% V	.075 W 1% P	.075 W 1% P 4% V	1% P	1% P	1% P	.10 W 1% P
GLAZIER	.075 W .085 V	.075 W 40 hr. V	.075 W .05 V	.075 W .05 V	.075 W .085 V	.075 W 40 hr. V	.075 W 40 hr. V	.075 W 40 hr. V
IRONWORKER: REINFORCING STRUCTURAL	.10 W .10 W	.10 W .10 W	.10 W .10 W	.10 W .10 W	.10 W .10 W	.10 W .10 W	.10 W .10 W	.10 W .10 W
LABORER, GENERAL	.10 W	.10 W	.10 W	.10 W	.10 W	.075 W	.075 W	.075 W
LATHER	.60 day W .70 day V		.10 W	.10 W	.075 W .05 V	.90 day W	.70 day V	.10 W
OPERATING ENGINEER TRACTOR OPERATOR (MIN.) POWER SHOVEL OP. (MIN.)	.10 W .10 W	.10 W .10 W	.10 W .10 W	.10 W .10 W	.10 W .10 W	10 W .10 W	.10 W .10 W	.10 W .10 W
PAINTER, BRUSH	.095 W	.08 W	.075 W	.10 W	.095 W .07 V	085 W	.08 W	.09 W
PLASTERER	.10 W .10 V	.10 W	.10 W	.10 W	.10 W .15 V	.10 W	.90 day W	.10 W
PLUMBER	.10 W .10 V	.15 W .10 P	.10 W .10 P .125 V	.10 W	.10 W .10 P .125 V	.10 W	.90 day W	.10 W
ROOFER	.10 W .10 V	.10 W	.10 W .10 V	.10 W	.075 W .10 V	.085 W	.10 W	.075 W
SHEET METAL WORKER	.075 W 4% V	.075 W 7 day V	.075 W .10 V	.075 W .12 V	.075 W 4% V	.085 W .10 V	.085 W .10 V	.085 W 5 day V
TILE SETTER	.075 W .09 V				.075 W .09 V	.025 W .06 V		

ATTENTION: The above tabulation has been prepared and compiled from the available data reported by building trades councils, union locals, contracto organizations and other reliable sources. The table was prepared from incomplete data; where no employer contributions are specified, it does not necessaril mean that none are required by the union contract.

The type of supplement is indicated by the following symbols: W—Health and Welfare; P—Pensions; V—Vacations; A—Apprentice training fund; Adm—Admini stration fund; JIB—Joint Industry Board; Prom—Promotion fund.

QUICK REFERENCE
ESTIMATOR'S DIRECTORY
Building and Construction Materials

ACOUSTICAL ENGINEERS
L. D. REEDER CO.
San Francisco: 1255 Sansome St., DO 2-5050
Sacramento: 3026 V St., GL 7-3505

AIR CONDITIONING
E. C. BRAUN CO.
Berkeley: 2115 Fourth St., TH 5-2356
GILMORE AIR CONDITIONING SERVICE
San Francisco: 1617 Harrison St., UN 1-2000
KAEMPER & BARRETT
San Francisco: 233 Industrial St., JU 6-6200
LINFORD AIR & REFRIGERATION CO.
Oakland: 174-12th St., TW 3-6521
JAMES A. NELSON CO.
San Francisco: 1375 Howard St., HE 1-0140

ALUMINUM BLDG. PRODUCTS
MICHEL & PFEFFER IRON WORKS (Wrought Iron)
So. San Francisco: 212 Shaw Road, PLaza 5-8983
REYNOLDS METALS CO.
San Francisco: 3201 Third St., MI 7-2990
UNIVERSAL WINDOW CO.
Berkeley: 950 Parker St., TH 1-1600

ARCHITECTURAL PORCELAIN ENAMEL
CALIFORNIA METAL ENAMELING CO.
Los Angeles: 6904 E. Slauson, RA 3-6351
San Francisco: Continental Bldg. Products Co.,
178 Fremont St.
Portland: Portland Wire & Iron Works,
4644 S.E. Seventeenth Ave.
Seattle: Foster-Bray Co., 2412 1st Ave. So.
Spokane: Bernhard Schafer, Inc., West 34, 2nd Ave.
Salt Lake City: S. A. Roberts & Co., 109 W. 2nd So.
Dallas: Offenhauser Co., 2201 Telephone Rd.
El Paso: Architectural Products Co.,
506 E. Yandell Blvd.
Phoenix: Haskell-Thomas Co., 3808 No. Central
San Diego: Maloney Specialties, Inc., 823 W. Laurel St.
Boise: Intermountain Glass Co., 1417 Main St.

ARCHITECTURAL & AERIAL PHOTOGRAPHS
FRED ENGLISH
Belmont, Calif.: 1310 Old County Road, LY 1-0385

ARCHITECTURAL VENEER
Ceramic Veneer
GLADDING, McBEAN & CO.
San Francisco: Harrison at 9th St., UN 1-7400
Los Angeles: 2901 Los Feliz Blvd., OL 2121
Portland: 110 S.E. Main St., EA 6179
Seattle 99: 945 Elliott Ave., West, GA 0330
Spokane: 1102 N. Monroe St., BR 3259
KRAFTILE COMPANY
Niles, Calif., Niles 3611

Porcelain Veneer
PORCELAIN ENAMEL PUBLICITY BUREAU
Oakland 12: Room 601, Franklin Building
Pasadena 8: P. O. Box 186, East Pasadena Station

Granite Veneer
VERMONT MARBLE COMPANY
San Francisco 24: 6000 3rd St., VA 6-5024
Los Angeles: 3522 Council St., DU 2-6339

Marble Veneer
VERMONT MARBLE COMPANY
San Francisco 24: 6000 3rd St., VA 6-5024
Los Angeles: 3522 Council St., DU 2-6339

BANKS - FINANCING
CROCKER-ANGLO NATIONAL BANK
San Francisco: 13 Offices

BLINDS
PARAMOUNT VENETIAN BLIND CO.
San Francisco: 5929 Mission St., JU 5-2436

BRASS PRODUCTS
GREENBERG'S, M. SONS
San Francisco 7: 765 Folsom, EX 2-3143
Los Angeles 23: 1258 S. Boyle, AN 3-7108
Seattle 4:1016 First Ave. So., MA 5140
Phoenix 3009 N. 19th Ave., Apt. 92, PH 2-7663
Portland 4: 510 Builders Exch. Bldg., AT 6443

BRICKWORK
Face Brick
GLADDING McBEAN & CO.
San Francisco: Harrison at 9th, UN 1-7400
KRAFTILE CO.
Niles, Calif., Niles 3611
UNITED MATERIALS & RICHMOND BRICK CO.
Point Richmond, BE 4-5032

BRONZE PRODUCTS
GREENBERG'S M. SONS
San Francisco: 765 Folsom St., EX 2-3143
MICHEL & PFEFFER IRON WORKS
So. San Francisco: 212 Shaw Road, PLaza 5-8983
C. E. TOLAND & SON
Oakland: 2635 Peralta St., GL 1-2580

BUILDING HARDWARE
E. M. HUNDLEY HARDWARE CO.
San Francisco: 662 Mission St., YU 2-3322

BUILDING PAPERS & FELTS
PACIFIC CEMENT & AGGREGATES INC.
San Francisco: 400 Alabama St., KL 2-1616

CABINETS & FIXTURES
CENTRAL MILL & CABINET CO.
San Francisco: 1595 Fairfax Ave., VA 4-7316
THE FINK & SCHINDLER CO.
San Francisco: 552 Brannan St., EX 2-1513
MULLEN MFG. CO.
San Francisco: 64 Rausch St., UN 1-5815
PARAMOUNT BUILT IN FIXTURE CO.
Oakland: 962 Stanford Ave., OL 3-9911
ROYAL SHOWCASE CO.
San Francisco: 770 McAllister St., JO 7-0311

CEMENT
CALAVERAS CEMENT CO.
San Francisco: 315 Montgomery St.
DO 2-4224, Enterprise 1-2315
PACIFIC CEMENT & AGGREGATES INC.
San Francisco: 400 Alabama St., KL 2-1616

CONCRETE AGGREGATES
Ready Mixed Concrete
PACIFIC CEMENT & AGGREGATES INC.
San Francisco: 400 Alabama St., KL 2-1616
Sacramento: 16th and A Sts., GI 3-6586
San Jose: 790 Stockton Ave., CY 2-5620
Oakland: 2400 Peralta St., GL 1-0177
Stockton: 820 So. California St., ST 8-8643
RHODES-JAMIESON LTD.
Oakland: 333-23rd Ave., KE 3-5225

CONCRETE ACCESSORIES
Screed Materials
C. & H. SPECIALTIES CO.
Berkeley: 909 Camelia St., LA 4-5358

CONCRETE BLOCKS
BASALT ROCK CO.
Napa, Calif.

CONCRETE COLORS—HARDENERS
CONRAD SOVIG CO.
875 Bryant St., HE 1-1345

CONSTRUCTION SERVICES
LE ROY CONSTRUCTION SERVICES
San Francisco, 143 Third St., SU 1-8914

DECKS—ROOF
UNITED STATES GYPSUM CO.
2322 W. 3rd St., Los Angeles 54, Calif.
300 W. Adams St., Chicago 6, Ill.

DOORS
THE BILCO COMPANY
New Haven, Conn.
Oakland: Geo. B. Schultz, 190 MacArthur Blvd.
Sacramento: Harry B. Ogle & Assoc., 1331 T St.
Fresno: Healey & Popovich, 1703 Fulton St.
Reseda: Daniel Dunner, 6200 Alonzo Ave.

Electric Doors
ROLY-DOOR SALES CO.
San Francisco, 5976 Mission St., PL 5-5089

Folding Doors
WALTER D. BATES & ASSOCIATES
San Francisco, 693 Mission St., GA 1-6971

Hardwood Doors
BELLWOOD CO. OF CALIF.
Orange, Calif., 533 W. Collins Ave.

Hollywood Doors
WEST COAST SCREEN CO.
Los Angeles: 1127 E. 63rd St., AD 1-1108
T. M. COBB CO.
Los Angeles & San Diego
HOGAN LUMBER CO.
Oakland: 700 - 6th Ave.
HOUSTON SASH & DOOR
Houston, Texas
SOUTHWESTERN SASH & DOOR
Phoenix, Tucson, Arizona
El Paso, Texas
WESTERN PINE SUPPLY CO.
Emeryville: 5760 Shellmound St.
GEO. C. VAUGHAN & SONS
San Antonio & Houston, Texas

DRAFTING ROOM EQUIPMENT
GENERAL FIREPROOFING CO.
Oakland: 332-19th St., GL 2-4280
Los Angeles: 1200 South Hope St., RI 7-7501
San Francisco: 1025 Howard St., HE 1-7070

DRINKING FOUNTAINS
HAWS DRINKING FAUCET CO.
Berkeley: 1435 Fourth St., LA 5-3341

ELECTRICAL CONTRACTORS
COOPMAN ELECTRIC CO.
San Francisco: 85 - 14th St., MA 1-4438

ELECTRICAL CONTRACTORS (cont'd)

LEMOGE ELECTRIC CO.
San Francisco: 212 Clara St., DO 2-6010

LYNCH ELECTRIC CO.
San Francisco: 937 McAllister St., WI 5158

PACIFIC ELECTRIC & MECHANICAL CO.
San Francisco: Gough & Fell Sts., HE 1-5904

ELECTRIC HEATERS

WESIX ELECTRIC HEATER CO.
San Francisco: 390 First St., GA 1-2211

FIRE ESCAPES

MICHEL & PFEFFER IRON WORKS
South San Francisco: 212 Shaw Road, PLaza 5-8983

FIRE PROTECTION EQUIPMENT

FIRE PROTECTION PRODUCTS CO.
San Francisco: 1101-16th St., UN 1-2420

BARNARD ENGINEERING CO.
San Francisco: 35 Elmira St., JU 5-4642

FLOORS

Floor Tile

GLADDING McBEAN & CO.
San Francisco: Harrison at 9th St., UN 1-744
Los Angeles: 2901 Las Feliz Bldg., OL 2121

KRAFTILE CO.
Niles, Calif., Niles 3611

Resilient Floors

PETERSON-COBBY CO.
San Francisco: 218 Clara St., EX 2-8714

TURNER RESILIENT FLOORS CO.
San Francisco: 2280 Shafter Ave., AT 2-7720

FLOOR DRAINS

JOSAM PACIFIC COMPANY
San Francisco: 765 Folsom St., EX 2-3142

GAS VENTS

WM. WALLACE CO.
Belmont, Calif.

GENERAL CONTRACTORS

BARRETT CONSTRUCTION CO.
San Francisco: 1800 Evans Ave., MI 7-9700

JOSEPH BETTANCOURT
South San Francisco: 125 So. Linden St., PL 5-9185

DINWIDDIE CONSTRUCTION CO.
San Francisco: Crocker Bldg., YU 6-2718

D. L. FAULL CONSTRUCTION CO.
Santa Rosa: 1236 Cleveland Ave.

HAAS & HAYNIE
San Francisco: 275 Pine St., DO 2-0678

HENDERSON CONSTRUCTION CO.
San Francisco: 33 Ritch St., GA 1-0856

JACKS & IRVINE
San Francisco: 620 Market St., YU 6-0511

RALPH LARSEN & SON
San Francisco: 64 So. Park, YU 2-5682

LINDGREN & SWINERTON
San Francisco: 200 Bush St., GA 1-2980

MacDONALD, YOUNG & NELSON
Oakland: 8907 Railroad Ave.

MATTOCK CONSTRUCTION CO.
San Francisco: 220 Clara St., GA 1-5516

RAPP, CHRISTENSEN & FOSTER
Santa Rosa: 705 Bennett Ave.

STOLTE, INC.
Oakland: 8451 San Leandro Ave., LO 2-4611

SWINERTON & WALBERG
San Francisco: 200 Bush St., GA 1-2980

FURNITURE—INSTITUTIONAL –

GENERAL FIREPROOFING CO.
San Francisco: 1025 Howard St., HE 1-7070
Oakland: 332-19th St., GL 2-4280
Los Angeles: 1200 South Hope St., RI 7-7501

HEATING & VENTILATING

ATLAS HEATING & VENT. CO.
San Francisco: 557-4th St., DO 2-0377

E. C. BRAUN CO.
Berkeley: 2115 Fourth St., TH 5-2356

S. T. JOHNSON CO.
Oakland: 940 Arlington Ave., OL 2-6000

LOUIS V. KELLER
San Francisco: 289 Tehama St., JU 6-6252

L. J. KRUSE CO.
Oakland: 6247 College Ave., OL 2-8332

JAS. A. NELSON CO.
San Francisco: 1375 Howard St., HE 1-0140

SCOTT COMPANY
Oakland: 1919 Market St., GL 1-1937

WESIX ELECTRIC HEATER CO.
San Francisco: 390 First St., GA 1-2211
Los Angeles: 530 W. 7th St., MI 8096

INSULATION WALL BOARD

PACIFIC CEMENT & AGGREGATES, INC.
San Francisco: 400 Alabama St., KL 2-1616

INTERCEPTING DEVICES

JOSAM PACIFIC CO.
San Francisco: 765 Folsom St., EX 2-3142

IRON—ORNAMENTAL

MICHEL & PFEFFER IRON WKS.
So. San Francisco, 212 Shaw Rd., PL 5-8983

LATHING & PLASTERING

ANGELO J. DANERI
San Francisco: 1433 Fairfax Ave., AT 8-1582

K-LATH CORP.
Alhambra: 909 So. Fremont St., Alhambra

A. E. KNOWLES CORP.
San Francisco: 3330 San Bruno Ave., JU 7-2091

G. H. & C. MARTINELLI
San Francisco: 174 Shotwell St., UN 3-6112

PATRICK J. RUANE
San Francisco: 44 San Jose Ave., MI 7-6414

LIGHTING FIXTURES

SMOOT-HOLMAN COMPANY
Inglewood, Calif., OR 8-1217
San Francisco: 55 Mississippi St., MA 1-8474

LIGHTING & CEILING SYSTEMS

UNITED LIGHTING AND FIXTURE CO.
Oakland: 3120 Chapman St., KE 3-8711

LUMBER

CHRISTENSEN LUMBER CO.
San Francisco: Quint & Evans Ave., VA 4-5832

ART HOGAN LUMBER CO.
San Francisco: 1701 Galvez Ave., ATwater 2-1157

ROLANDO LUMBER CO.
San Francisco: 5th & Berry Sts., SU 1-6901

WEST COAST LUMBERMEN'S ASS'N
Portland 5, Oregon

MARBLE

JOS. MUSTO SONS-KEENAN CO.
San Francisco: 555 No. Point St., GR 4-6365

VERMONT MARBLE CO.
San Francisco: 6000-3rd St., VA 6-5024

MASONRY

BASALT ROCK CO.
Napa, Calif.
San Francisco: 260 Kearney St., GA 1-3758

WM. A. RAINEY & SON
San Francisco: 323 Clementina St., SU 1-0072

GEO. W. REED CO.
San Francisco: 1390 So. Van Ness Ave., AT 2-1226

METAL EXTERIOR WALLS

THE KAWNEER CO.
Berkeley: 930 Dwight Way, TH 5-8710

METAL FRAMING

UNISTRUT OF NORTHERN CALIFORNIA
Berkeley: 2547-9th St., TH 1-3031
Enterprise 1-220

METAL GRATING

KLEMP METAL GRATING CORP.
Chicago, Ill.: 6601 So. Melvina St.

METAL LATH—EXPANDED

PACIFIC CEMENT & AGGREGATES, INC.
San Francisco: 400 Alabama St., KL 2-1616

METAL PARTITIONS

THE E. F. HAUSERMAN CO.
San Francisco: 485 Brannan St., YU 2-5477

METAL PRODUCTS

FORDERER CORNICE WORKS
San Francisco: 269 Potrero Ave., HE 1-4100

MILLWORK

CENTRAL MILL & CABINET CO.
San Francisco: 1595 Fairfax Ave., VA 4-7316

THE FINK & SCHINDLER CO.
San Francisco: 552 Brannan St., EX 2-1513

MULLEN MFG. CO.
San Francisco: 64 Rausch St., UN 1-5815

PACIFIC MFG. CO.
San Francisco: 16 Beale St., GA 1-7755
Santa Clara: 2610 The Alameda, S. C. 607
Los Angeles: 6820 McKinley Ave., TH 4156

SOUTH CITY LUMBER & SUPPLY CO.
So. San Francisco: Railroad & Spruce, PL 5-7075

OFFICE EQUIPMENT

GENERAL FIREPROOFING CO.
Los Angeles: 1200 South Hope St., RI 7-7501
San Francisco: 1025 Howard St., HE 1-7070
Oakland: 332-19th St., GL 2-4280

OIL BURNERS

S. T. JOHNSON CO.
Oakland: 940 Arlington Ave., GL 2-6000
San Francisco: 585 Potrero Ave., MA 1-2757
Philadelphia, Pa.: 401 North Broad St.

ORNAMENTAL IRON

MICHEL & PFEFFER IRON WORKS
So. San Francisco: 212 Shaw Rd., PL 5-8983

PAINTING

R. P. PAOLI & CO.
San Francisco: 2530 Lombard St., WE 1-1632

SINCLAIR PAINT CO.
San Francisco: 2112-15th St., HE 1-2196

D. ZELINSKY & SONS
San Francisco: 165 Groove St., MA 1-7400

PHOTOGRAPHS

Construction Progress

FRED ENGLISH
Belmont, Calif.: 1310 Old County Road, LY 1-0385

PLASTER

PACIFIC CEMENT & AGGREGATE INC.
San Francisco: 400 Alabama St., KL 2-1616

PLASTIC PRODUCTS

PLASTIC SALES & SERVICE
San Francisco: 409 Bryant St., DO 2-6435

WEST COAST INDUSTRIES
San Francisco: 3150-18th St., MA 1-5657

PLUMBING
BRIGGS MFG. CO.
Warren, Michigan
BROADWAY PLUMBING CO.
San Francisco: 1790 Yosemite Ave., MI 8-4250
E. C. BRAUN CO.
Berkeley: 2115 Fourth St., TH 5-2356
HAWS DRINKING FAUCET CO.
Berkeley: 1435 Fourth St., LA 5-3341
JOSAM PACIFIC CO.
San Francisco: 765 Folsom St., EX 2-3143
LOUIS V. KELLER
San Francisco: 289 Tehama St., YU 6-6252
JAS. A. NELSON CO.
San Francisco: 1375 Howard St., HE 1-0140
RODONI-BECKER CO., INC.
San Francisco: 455-10th St., MA 1-3662
SCOTT CO.
Oakland: 1919 Market St., GL 1-1937

POST PULLER
HOLLAND MFG. CO.
No. Sacramento: 1202 Dixieanne

PUMPING MACHINERY
SIMONDS MACHINERY CO.
San Francisco: 816 Folsom St., DO 2-6794

ROOFING
ANCHOR ROOFING CO.
San Francisco: 1671 Galvez Ave., VA 4-8140
ALTA ROOFING CO.
San Francisco: 1400 Egbert Ave., MI 7-2173
REGAL ROOFING CO.
San Francisco: 930 Innes Ave., VA 4-3261

ROOF SCUTTLES
THE BILCO CO.
New Haven, Conn.
Oakland: Geo. B. Schultz, 190 MacArthur Blvd.
Sacramento: Harry B. Ogle & Assoc., 1331 T St.
Fresno: Healey & Popovich, 1703 Fulton St.
Reseda: Daniel Dunner, 6200 Alonzo Ave.

ROOF TRUSSES
EASYBOW ENGINEERING & RESEARCH CO.
Oakland: 13th & Wood Sts., GL 2-0805
SUMMERBELL ROOF STRUCTURES
San Francisco: 420 Market St., EX 7-2796

SAFES
THE HERMANN SAFE CO.
San Francisco: 1699 Market St., UN 1-6644

SEWER PIPE
GLADDING, McBEAN & CO.
San Francisco: 9th & Harrison, UN 1-7400
Los Angeles: 2901 Los Feliz Blvd., OL 2121

SHEET METAL
MICHEL & PFEFFER IRON WORKS
So. San Francisco: 212 Shaw Rd., PL 5-8983

SOUND EQUIPMENT
STROMBERG-CARLSON CO.
San Francisco: 1805 Rollins Rd., Burlingame, OX 7-3630
Los Angeles: 5414 York Blvd., CL 7-2939

SPRINKLERS
BARNARD ENGINEERING CO.
San Francisco: 35 Elmira St., JU 5-4642

STEEL—STRUCTURAL & REINFORCING
COLUMBIA-GENEVA DIV., U. S. STEEL CORP.
San Francisco: Russ Bldg., SU 1-2500
Los Angeles: 2087 E. Slauson, LA 1171
Portland, Ore.: 2345 N.W. Nicolai, BE 7261
Seattle, Wn.: 1331-3rd Ave. Bldg., MA 1972
Salt Lake City, Utah: Walker Bank Bldg., SL 3-6733
HERRICK IRON WORKS
Hayward: Box 3007, LU 1-4451
INDEPENDENT IRON WORKS, INC.
Oakland: 780 Pine St., TE 2-0160
JUDSON PACIFIC MURPHY CORP.
Emeryville: 4300 Eastshore Highway, OL 3-1717
REPUBLIC STEEL CORP.
San Francisco: 116 New Montgomery St., GA 1-0977
Los Angeles: Edison Bldg.
Seattle: White-Henry Stuart Bldg.
Salt Lake City: Walker Bank Bldg.
Denver: Continental Oil Bldg.

STEEL FORMS
STEELFORM CONTRACTING CO.
San Francisco: 666 Harrison St., DO 2-5582

SWIMMING POOLS
SIERRA MFG. CO.
Walnut Creek, Calif.: 1719 Mt. Diablo Blvd.

SWIMMING POOL FITTINGS
JOSAM PACIFIC CO.
San Francisco: 765 Folsom St., EX 2-3143

TESTING LABORATORIES
(ENGINEERS & CHEMISTS
ABBOT A. HANKS, INC.
San Francisco: 624 Sacramento St., GA 1-1697
ROBERT W. HUNT COMPANY
San Francisco: 500 Iowa, MI 7-0224
Los Angeles: 3050 E. Slauson, JE 9131
Chicago, New York, Pittsburgh
PITTSBURGH TESTING LABORATORY
San Francisco: 651 Howard St., EX 2-1747

TILE—CLAY & WALL
GLADDING McBEAN & CO.
San Francisco: 9th & Harrison Sts., UN 1-7400
Los Angeles: 2901 Los Feliz Blvd., OL 2121
Portland: 110 S.E. Main St., EA 6179
Seattle: 945 Elliott Ave. West, GA 0330
Spokane: 1102 No. Monroe St., BR 3259
KRAFTILE CO.
Niles, Calif.: Niles 3611
San Francisco: 50 Hawthorne St., DO 2-3780
Los Angeles: 406 So. Main St., MA 7241

TILE—TERRAZZO
NATIONAL TILE & TERRAZZO CO.
San Francisco: 198 Mississippi St., UN 1-0273

TIMBER—TREATED
J. H. BAXTER CO.
San Francisco: 200 Bush St., YU 2-0200
Los Angeles: 3450 Wilshire Blvd., DU 8-9591

TIMBER TRUSSES
EASYBOW ENGINEERING & RESEARCH CO.
Oakland: 13th & Wood Sts., GL 2-0805

TRUCKING
PASSETTI TRUCKING CO.
San Francisco: 264 Clementina St., GA 1-5297

UNDERPINNING & SHORING
D. J. & T. SULLIVAN
San Francisco: 1942 Folsom St., MA 1-1545

WALL PAPER
WALLPAPERS, INC.
Oakland: 384 Grand Ave., GL 2-0451

WAREHOUSE AND STORAGE EQUIPMENT AND SHELVING
GENERAL FIREPROOFING CO.
Los Angeles: 1200 South Hope St., RI 7-7501
San Francisco: 1025 Howard St., HE 1-7070
Oakland: 332-19th St., GL 2-4280

WATERPROOFING MATERIALS
CONRAD SOVIG CO.
San Francisco: 875 Bryant St., HE 1-1345

WATERSTOPS (P.V.C.)
TECON PRODUCTS, LTD.
Vancouver, B.C.: 681 E. Hastings St.
Seattle: 2 Hanford St.

WINDOW SHADES
SHADES, INC.
San Francisco: 80 Tehama St., DO 2-7092

CONSTRUCTION CONTRACTS AWARDED AND MISCELLANEOUS PERSONNEL DATA

BANK BLDG., Visalia, Tulare county. First Western Bank & Trust Co., San Francisco, owner. 1-Story, mezzanine, exterior walls of faced brick, suspended acoustical ceilings, terrazzo and rubber tile floors—$146,000. ARCHITECT: James P. Lockett, 121 E. Main St., Visalia. GENERAL· CONTRACTOR: Harris Const. Co., P. O. Box 109, Fresno.

APARTMENT, Reno, Nevada. Co-operative Developers, Reno, owner. 4-Story and penthouse new apartment house building with 22 units; structural steel frame and concrete construction, brick walls—$840,000. ARCHITECT: Lockard & Casazza, R. A. Casazza, architect, 232 West 1st St., Reno.

HIGH SCHOOL ADD'N, Folsom, Sacramento county. Folsom Unified School District, owner. Construction of additions to the Mills Jr. High School to include administration unit, 9 classrooms, 2 science rooms, teacher's room, storage and heater rooms, toilet facilities and some site improvement—$298,295. ARCHITECT: Koblik & Fisher, 2203-13th St., Sacramento. GENERAL CONTRACTOR: Arthur Odman, P. O. Box 147, Fair Oaks.

ELEMENTARY SCHOOL ADD'N, Georgetown, El Dorado county. Georgetown School District, owner. Wood frame construction to provide facilities for a new administration unit, classrooms—$125,335. ARCHITECT: Grant D. Caywood, 1435 Alhambra Blvd., Sacramento. GENERAL CONTRACTOR: James P. Morton, 33 Clay St., Placerville.

CHURCH ADD'N, San Jose, Santa Clara county. Foothill Community Presbyterian Church, San Jose, owner. Work includes erection and completion of an administrative unit at the present church—$35,644. ARCHITECT: John H. Waterman & George Kuska, Associate Architects, 1112 Pajaro St., Salinas. GENERAL CONTRACTOR: Oscar Meyer Const., 1681 Dry Creek Road, San Jose.

CALIFORNIA STATE OFFICE BLDG., Oakland, Alameda county. State of California, Sacramento, owner. 8-Story office building with 1-story building with basement and roof structure; 200,000 sq. ft. area, Type 1 construction — $1,388,900. ARCHITECT: Anson Boyd, State Architect, Sacramento. GENERAL CONTRACTOR: Stolte Inc., 8451 San Leandro St., Oakland.

PROFESSIONAL BLDG., Ontario, San Bernardino county. J. Ross Gange, Ontario, owner. 1-story and basement, concrete block and stone professional building; wood beams, composition roof, pipe columns, extensive plate glass, winter and summer air conditioning, resilient tile floors, covered colored concrete walks,

toilet facilities; black-top parking area. ARCHITECT: Pierre Woodman, 191-F, N. Euclid Ave., Upland. GENERAL CONTRACTOR: Carl Harvey, Box 386, Ontario.

APARTMENT PROJECT, Sausalito, Marin county. F. Bruce Bernhard, Mill Valley, owner. Work comprises construction of 21 1-bedroom suites; 4 2-bedroom suites and 3 studio apartments; wood and frame—$191,222. DESIGNER: Jane A. Duncombe, 4 El Paseo, Mill Valley. GENERAL CONTRACTOR: William H. McDevitt Const., 1934 4th St., San Rafael.

MARKET BLDG., El Monte, Los Angeles county. Food Giant Markets, El Monte, owner. 1-Story reinforced brick market building; 36,000 sq. ft. of area, composition roof, concrete floor, stone veneer, sprinkler system, painting, plastering, plumbing, electrical, heating, ventilating, air conditioning, sheet metal, structural and miscellaneous metal. ARCHITECT: Stiles and Robert Clements, Architects and Engineers, 210 W. 7th St., Los Angeles. GENERAL CONTRACTORS: B. L. Metcalf Co., 1460 N. Glassell Ave., Orange.

SHOPPING CENTER, Montecito, (East San Rafael), Marin county. Montecito Properties, Inc., San Rafael, owner. Work includes two buildings to house 14 shops; 15,000 sq. ft area in each; one 2-story structure with 8 shops on 1st floor and office space on second floor; contemporary design; poured concrete walls; paved parking area for 400 cars—$400,000. DESIGNER: William B. David & Associates, 938 Market St., San Francisco. GENERAL CONTRACTOR: William H. McDevitt Co., 1934 4th St., San Rafael.

MOTOR TRUCK BRANCH, Van Nuys, Los Angeles county. International Harvester Co., Chicago, Ill., owner. Concrete block construction, plate glass, composition slab flooring, interior plaster, composition roof, plumbing, heating and ventilating. ENGINEER: David T. Whitherly, 7233 W. Beverly Blvd., Los Angeles. GENERAL CONTRACTOR: Pomeroy and Lawson, 901 El Centro, South Pasadena.

OFFICE BLDG., Carson City, Nevada. Nevada Industrial Commission, Carson City, owner. Work includes construction of a modern office building in Carson City for the Nevada State Industrial Commission—$657,717. ARCHITECT: De Long-

champs & O'Brien, 160 N. Arlington St., Reno, Nevada. GENERAL CONTRACTOR: Halvorsen Const. Co., 630 Judge Bldg., Salt Lake City, Utah.

JUNIOR HIGH SCHOOL, Mable E. O'Farrell, San Diego. San Diego Unified School District, San Diego, owner. Work comprises construction of a new Junior High School building to be known as the Mabel E. O'Farrell Junior High School Building in San Diego—$1,788,138. ARCHITECT: Frank Hope, 1447 6th St., San Diego. GENERAL CONTRACTOR: James Stewart Co., 411 No. Central Ave., Phoenix, Arizona.

CHURCH EDUCATIONAL FACILITIES, Palo Alto, Santa Clara county. Covenant Presbyterian Church, Palo Alto, owner. Project comprises construction of complete church educational facilities—$69,015. ARCHITECT: Alfred W. Johnson & William Sargent, Associates, 165 Jessie St., San Francisco. GENERAL CONTRACTOR: Cortleyou & Cole Construction, 546 Oxford St., Palo Alto.

DRUG STORE REMODEL, Sherman Oaks, Los Angeles county. Sheinborg-Horwitz & Lee, Sherman Oaks, owner. Remodel of present building includes revising floor plan, interior partitions, terrazzo floors, suspended ceiling—$20,000. ARCHITECT: S. Charles Lee, 258 Beverly Dr., Beverly Hills. GENERAL CONTRACTOR: Baingo Bros., 8929 Exposition Blvd., Los Angeles.

FORESTRY HONOR CAMP, Chamberlain Creek, Mendocino county. State of California, Public Works Department, Sacramento, owner. Division of Forestry Chamberlain Creek Honor Camp consists of a group of buildings; barracks, mess hall, two offices, warehouse and shop, and gas and oil station. ARCHITECT: Anson Boyd, California State Architect, Sacramento. GENERAL CONTRACTOR: Rapp Const. Co., P.O. Box 551, Santa ROSA.

MOTEL, Oceanside, San Diego county. Miramar Restaurant, Oceanside, owner. Thirty-two unit motel, 2-story frame-stucco and concrete construction; parking facilities; remodel existing building, demolition and repair work; earthwork, painting and decorating, plumbing, resilient floors, roof, sheet metal, structural steel and swimming pool — $182,282. ARCHITECTS: Mitchell & Dean, 521 "B" St.,

San Diego. GENERAL CONTRACTOR: Albert E. Betraun, 104 S. Barnes, Oceanside.

PROCESSING PLANT, Burlingame, San Mateo county. American Can Company, San Francisco, owner. 1-Story, 11,000 sq. ft. data processing plant building located on a 2.65 acre site with facilities to handle payroll, inventory control and sales statistics—$200,000. GENERAL CONTRACTOR: Neils P. Larsen, 1881 Rollins Road, Burlingame.

CHURCH BLDG., Anaheim, Orange county. Mount Calvary Lutheran Church of Anaheim, owner. Frame and stucco, stone veneer Chapel; 2820 sq. ft. of area, gravel roof, aluminum sash, slab floors, oak and vinyl asbestos flooring, interior plaster, acoustical plaster, toilet facilities, metal partitions, accordion doors, ornamental concrete grill wall, laminated wood cross, steel beams and suspended ceiling. ARCHITECT: Orr, Strange and Inslee, 3142 Wilshire Blvd., Los Angeles. GENERAL CONTRACTOR: Voge Inc., 7601 Crenshaw Blvd., Los Angeles.

PLANT ADDN., Millbrae, San Mateo county. Rundel Electric Co., Millbrae, owner. Concrete tilt-up construction of an addition to existing manufacturing plant building, 75 x 110 ft. of area—$100,000. STRUCTURAL ENGINEERS: Robinson & Giddings, Structural Engineers, 80 Stonestown, San Francisco. GENERAL CONTRACTOR: Bayshore Const. Co., 360 22nd St., Oakland.

CHURCH BLDG., Burbank, Los Angeles county. MacArthur Memorial Church, Burbank, owner. New Church Building in Burbank, 11,200 sq. ft. of area, frame and stucco construction; composition roof, interior plaster, concrete slab floor, asphalt tile, acoustic plaster, heating and ventilating. ARCHITECT: Joe B. Jordan, 213 S. 3rd St., Burbank.

JUNIOR COLLEGE ADDN., San Jose, Santa Clara county. San Jose Unified School District, owner. Wood and frame addition to administration unit and library for vocational sciences and arts—$422,265. ARCHITECT: Higgins & Root, 220 Meridian Road, San Jose. GENERAL CONTRACTOR: Nielsen & Nielsen, 1071 Westwood Dr., San Jose.

CLINIC, North Napa. Kaiser Foundation Health Plan, 368 42nd St., Oakland, owner. Work includes offices for 6 doctors, several out-patient treatment rooms, Pharmacy, X-ray room, laboratory, business offices—$150,000. ARCHITECT: Clarence W. Mayhew, 251 Post St., San Francisco. GENERAL CONTRACTOR: Samuel R. Geddes, 942 Main St., Napa.

ELEMENTARY SCHOOL SITE, Larkspur, Marin county. Larkspur School District, owner. Project comprises grading and preparation for later construction, 10 acre site—$180,000. ARCHITECT: John Lyon Reid & Partners, 1019 Market St., San Francisco. GENERAL CONTRACTOR: Charles L. Harney, 575 Berry St., San Francisco.

MULTI-PURPOSE BLDGS., Santa Clara. Santa Clara School District, owner. Work includes construction of multi - purpose buildings at the Hamann, Scott Lane, Westwood and Washington schools; wood frame, some structural steel construction—$280,889. ARCHITECT: L. F. Richards,

)33 Jackson St., Santa Clara. GENERAL
ONTRACTOR: Floyd B. Day Const.,
)5 Dell Ave., Campbell.

AVINGS & LOAN ASSN., Santa
[aria, Santa Barbara county. Santa Maria
avings & Loan Association, owner. 2-
tory reinforced brick savings and loan
·sociation building; 98 x 55 ft., composi-
on roof, concrete slab, vinyl, terrazzo,
arpet and cork floors, luminous ceiling,
late glass, vault, machine room, structural
ad reinforcing steel, insulation, ornamen-
l metal and air conditioning. ARCHI-
ECT: Clifford B. Holser, 156 Montgom-
y St., San Francisco. GENERAL
ONTRACTOR: Doane Bldg. Co., 212
. Russell St., Santa Maria.

OWLING ALLEY, Los Angeles, Anjola
orp., Los Angeles, owner. Reinforced
oncrete bowling alley; 124 x 160 ft.,
omposition roof, aluminum storefront,
oncrete slab and terrazzo flooring, interior
laster, acoustical tile, wood paneling, air
onditioning, electric, plumbing, mosaic
ile and ceramic tile work; facilities for
offee shop, cocktail lounge, nursery, pin-
etting machines for twenty-four lanes.
ARCHITECT: William Rudolph, 622 S.
Lake St., Pasadena. GENERAL CON-
TRACTOR: Roger Creed, 3630 Sun-
swept Drive, Studio City.

WAREHOUSE, Los Angeles. Sam Stone,
Los Angeles, owner. Concrete warehouse
building; 71 x 142 ft., composition roof,
interior drywall and exposed concrete
work, concrete slab, wood sectional, overhead doors, tile wainscoting, brick planter,
structural steel and canopy, $35,287. EN-
GINEER: Paul Toien, Consulting Engineer, 8217 Beverly Blvd., Los Angeles.
GENERAL CONTRACTOR: Excel Construction Co., 8600 Venice Blvd., Los
Angeles.

CITY HALL, Stanton, Orange County.
Stanton City Council, owners. Concrete
block, built-up roofing, concrete slab, as-
phalt slab, asphalt tile, acoustical plaster—
$60,800. ARCHITECT: Wiseman, Regan
& Tebault, Architects and Engineers, 2027
N. Main St., Santa Ana. GENERAL
CONTRACTOR: Larry & Jack Builders,
Inc., 13131 Brookhurst St., Garden Grove.

BANK BLDG., Redlands, San Bernardino
county. Bank of America, Los Angeles,
owner. New bank building, 118 x 65 ft.;
composition roof, concrete floor, iron and
steel ornamental metal, lath and plaster,
drywall finish, ceramic tile, aluminum
doors and frames, metal toilet partitions—
$221,600. ARCHITECT: Kistner, Wright
& Wright, 1125 W. 6th St., Los Angeles.
GENERAL CONTRACTOR: E. F. Gladding Co., 9178 Olive St., Fontana.

BOY SCOUT CAMP, Green Valley Lake,
San Bernardino. North Orange County
Council Boy Scouts, owner. Cabin 900 sq.
ft. in area, and a 20 x 20 ft. garage, storage
building, 960 sq. ft. area, and craft bldg.,
2080 sq. ft. area; asphalt shingle roof, cedar
siding, aluminum casement and commercial steel windows, interior plywood and
gypsum board, concrete slab floor—$24,-
500. ARCHITECT: Everett L. Childs,
1424 N. Spadra, Fullerton. GENERAL
CONTRACTOR: Newdigate Const· Co.,
2400 N. Highlands, San Bernardino.

BANK-OFFICE BLDG., Sacramento.
Bank of America, San Francisco, owner.
Reinforced concrete and steel main bank

and office building—$2,250,000. DESIGN:
Continental Service Co., 260 5th St., San
Francisco. GENERAL CONTRACTOR:
Campbell-Erickson Const., 1119 E. Bassett-
law Ave., North Sacramento.

METHODIST CHURCH, Redlands, San
Bernardino county. Free Methodist Church
of Redlands, owner. Complete new church,
1-story frame, stucco and stone and a 300
seat chapel; 5 classrooms, auditorium,
minister and church offices, storage areas:
13,000 sq. ft. of area, wood frame roof,
toilets, black-top paving. ARCHITECT:
C. Paul Ulmer, 1168 E. Highland Ave.,
San Bernardino. GENERAL CONTRAC-
TOR: Individual Contracts by owner.

PRESBYTERIAN CHURCH, Riverside,
First United Presbyterian Church, Riverside, owner. First phase of construction
will include Sanctuary and fellowship education building involving a total floor area
of 6800 sq. ft.; concrete block, wood
frame, laminated arches, composition roof,
cathedral glass, aluminum casement sash,
slab and asphalt tile floors with some carpeting, acoustical treatment, forced air
heating and mechanical ventilation, natural wood interior, toilets, metal toilet
partitions, ceramic tile, folding partitions
in education building, stone fireplace and
barbecue, black-top off-street parking for
70 cars. ARCHITECT: Wm. Lee Gates,
6533 Brockton Ave., Riverside. GENER-
AL CONTRACTOR: Russell Walling,
4728 Sedgewick, Riverside.

SANCTUARY, San Bernardino. Grace
Brethren Church, San Bernardino, owner.
1-Story and full basement, concrete block
sanctuary; 4000 sq. ft. area, built-up gravel
roof, laminated trusses, stained glass, slab
and wood floors with wall-to-wall carpeting,
asphalt tile in basement, interior exposed
block, acoustical plaster, choir loft, incandescent lighting, winter and summer air
conditioning, built-in pews, baptistry and
appurtenant facilities, raised platform with
pulpit, church spire, stone work, kitchen
facilities, folding partitions, toilet facilities,
black-top parking area. ARCHITECT:
Jimmie N. Cartee, 248 E. Highland Ave.,
San Bernardino. GENERAL CONTRAC-
TOR: Gordon Stokes, 1275 E. Pacific,
San Bernardino.

NEW HIGH SCHOOL, Saratoga, Santa
Clara county. Los Gatos Union High
School District, Saratoga, owner. 1-Story,

70,000 sq. ft. area, concrete block High
School building providing facilities for
administration unit, 21 classrooms, library,
toilets — $1,246,000. ARCHITECT, Hig-
gins & Root, 220 Meridian Road, San
Jose. GENERAL CONTRACTOR; Samuel E. Barth, 1801 McDaniel Ave., San
Jose.

OFFICE & MFG. PLANT, Van Nuys,
Los Angeles county. W. C. Dillion Co.,
Van Nuys, owner. Brick veneer, office and
manufacturing building addition; 8000 sq.
ft. of area, composition roofing, tapered
steel beams, evaporative coolers, concrete
slab, asphalt tile, interior plaster, alumi-
num overhead doors, toilets—$40,000.
ENGINEER: F. J. Baudino, Consulting
Engineer, 10638 Magnolia Blvd., North
Hollywood. GENERAL CONTRACTOR:
Gordon T. Davidson, 7310 Varna Ave.,
North Hollywood.

IN THE NEWS

ARCHITECTS REPORTS
ISSUE 127,000TH REPORT
IN CONTINUOUS SERVICE

Architects Reports, 68 Post Street, San Francisco, confidential advance construction report information, recently issued its 127,000th report to subscribers in the construction and allied industries.

Publication of the 127,00th report represents a continuous service for more than 25 years, or an average of 5,080 individual reports per year. The service comprises individual, confidential, reports on such phases of the construction industry as: selection of site and architect or engineer; announcement of preparation of prelimi-

nary drawings and plans; building permits; advertising for bids; awarding of contracts; selection of contractors and sub-contractors, and other miscellaneous data pertinent to the light construction industry.

DELANO PLANS
HIGH SCHOOL
ADDITIONS

Architects Stuhr & Hicks of 924 Truxton Ave., Bakersfield, are preparing plans for construction of a number of additions to the Delano High School for the Delano High School District.

The project comprises construction of a new music and shop building, gymnasium to seat 1,800 persons; a girls' gymnasium, science building, homemaking, administration unit and conversion of existing cafeteria into an arts and crafts building. Also installation of a public address system, gas, sewer, steam and water lines, sprinkler system and site improvements. Estimated cost of the work is $1,750,000.

GLEN G. GALLAGHER
NAMED OFFICER OF
INSTRUMENT SOCIETY

Glen G. Gallagher, principal instrument engineer for Fluor Corp., Los Angeles, has been elected vice president of the Standards and Practices Department of the Instrument Society of America at the 13th Annual Instrument Automation Conference and Exhibit, held in Philadelphia, Pa.

Gallagher is recognized as one of the leading engineers and trainers of engineers in the country. In his particular field of petroleum process instrumentation, he has distinguished himself as an author and speaker.

DIVINITY SCHOOL
EXPANSION NEARS
COMPLETION

Construction of an Academic building at the Church Divinity School of the Pacific in Berkeley is practically completed in the drawing board stage according to the San Francisco offices of Architects Skidmore, Owings & Merrill.

The first phase of improvements at the school will cost an estimated $650,000 with total cost in excess of $3,000,000.

The present construction will be of reinforced concrete.

SYRACUSE UNIVERSITY
APPOINTS WEST COAST
ARCHITECT CRITIC

George T. Rickrise, San Francisco architect, has been named "visiting critic"

of Syracuse University, Syracuse, New York, according to a recent announcement by D. Kenneth Sargent, Dean of the School of Architecture.

A graduate of the Syracuse University School of Architecture, Rockrise has been associated with the firm of Edward D. Stone and has been a member of the staff of the United Nations Headquarters Planning Commission. He has also served on the faculty of the College of Architecture, University of California, and as visiting professor in architecture at the National University, Caracas, Venezuela.

NEW VINYL WALL
COVERING IS
ANNOUNCED

To fulfill architects and decorators need for a plain, wear-resistant, easy-to-clean wall finish this new vinyl wall covering called STIP-L-TEX has been created.

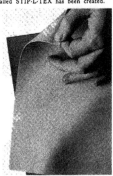

It is ideal for general offices where nicks, scratches and marks start appearing the day the office is occupied; also excellent for corridors, dividing partitions and many other places where a designer would not think of using vinyl ordinarily. Exciting shades—grays, charcoals, and sharp accent colors; has beautiful, fine flat mat finish without sheen or shine; completely washable, fadeproof, crackproof and peelproof; may be hung on wood, metal, glass or plaster. Full information available, L. E. Carpenter & Co., Inc., Empire State Bldg., New York 1.

EXTENSIVE FOOD
DISTRIBUTION
CENTER PLANNED

The Board of Port Commissioners of the Port of Oakland, recently announced plans for construction of a food distribution center near the Oakland Municipal Airport at an estimated cost of $20,000,000.

The proposed plant will serve all of northern California and is adjacent to water, rail bus and air transportation.

ARCHITECT NAMED
AS "RED FEATHER"
COORDINATOR

Architect Winston Cordes, associate in the firm of Albert C. Martin & Associates, architects and engineers, Los Angeles, has been appointed Chairman of the Construction Industry Division of the Community

Chest for the Los Angeles area, according to Rudolph Ostengaard, vice president of the California Bank, general chairman of the Commerce and Industry group for the 1958 Red Feather campaign.

Cordes will be assisted by William E. Kappler of North American Aviation.

RECREATION CENTER PLANNED FOR THE CITY OF SAN RAFAEL

Ferd J. Masberg, partner in the firm of Masberg & McKillip of Portland, Oregon, has announced plans for the construction of a large recreation center in San Rafael, the estimated cost being $2,500,000.

Facilities will be on a 3-acre site at Vivian and Belvedere streets, San Rafael, and will include a 90,000 sq. ft., 1 story building, 40 bowling alleys, Olympic size swimming pool and diving tower, billiard room, restaurant, cocktail lounge, dancing floor, and children's nursery.

AMERICAN CONCRETE INSTITUTE MEETS IN LOS ANGELES

The American Concrete Institute will hold their 1959 annual convention in Los Angeles, February 23-26, according to Sam Hobbs of Los Angeles, local chairman of the convention.

The general committee appointed to handle and correlate all local planning includes John McNerney, Los Angeles District Engineer of the Portland Cement Association; Byron P. Weintz, chief engineer, Consolidated Rock Products; William F. Norton, Pacific Coast regional manager, Ceco Steel Products Corp.; C. Taylor Teet, director technical services, Riverside Ce-

ment Co.; Glenn C. Thomas, president Thomas Concrete Accessory Co.; and Lewis K. Osborn, associate, architectural firm of Kistner, Wright & Wright.

NEW MODEL RECESSED INCANDESCENT LIGHT ELEMENT INTRODUCED

A single frame only ⅜" thin, and the largest lens area available for a 12" sq. opening are a few of the many features of UNI-FRAME, a new recessed incandescent lighting element introduced by Day-Brite Lighting, Inc.

Two models feature the same sculptured styling and identical mechanical dimensions, differ only in wattage rating: Frame 200 handles 100, 150 and 200 watt lamps, while frame 300 takes 300 watt medium base lamps. The Pyrex lens, 11¾ in. sq., features "Bifocal" prism design to boost light in the extremities of the distribution pattern. Frames are available in flat white enamel, anodized aluminum in brass or

natural aluminum. Rigid seamless box requires no plaster frame and can be installed in poured concrete box. Complete data from Day-Brite Lighting, Inc., 6260 N. Broadway, St. Louis 15, Mo.

LOUIS O. BRITT NAMED GENERAL MANAGER OF ENGINEERING FIRM

Louis O. Britt, vice-president of the consulting engineering firm of Dudley Deane and Associates, has been promoted to general manager, and Donald R. Lundy has joined the firm as chief mechanical engineer.

Dudley Deane and Associates is currently at work on the Federal Office Building, Civic Center, San Francisco; the Kaiser Center, Oakland; Lockheed Missiles Division research and development facility at Sunnyvale; the San Francisco International Airport expansion; and the new Bethlehem Pacific Coast Steel Corporation office building in San Francisco.

NEW JUNIOR HIGH SCHOOL TO BE BUILT IN ORANGE

Architects Smith, Powell & Morgridge, 208 W. 8th St., Los Angeles, are preparing plans for construction of a frame, stucco and concrete block junior high school building in Orange, for the Orange School District.

The project will include 8 classrooms, 2 music, 2 science, and 2 homemaking rooms, mechanical drawing, art, 2 shops, multi-purpose building, administration units, showers and lockers. The plant will contain some 56,700 sq. ft. of floor space. Work will include composition roof, con-

crete and wood floor, asphalt tile floor covering, ceramic tile, metal sash, heating, ventilating, painting, plastering, plumbing, electrical work, structural steel, and laminated wood beams.

DRYWALL CONTRACTORS ASSOCIATION ELECTS NEW OFFICERS

The annual election of the Drywall Contractors Association of Southern California recently in Los Angeles, resulted in the election of Reuben L. Casey of Garden Grove as president.

Other officers named to serve during the ensuing year were: Edwin H. Busch, Jr.,

of La Canada, vice-president; L. M. Lawson, North Hollywood, secretary; and Wayne W. Vaughan of West Los Angeles, treasurer.

MACHINE SHOP DEVELOPMENT AT SIGNAL HILL

Architect Francis O. Merchant, 4605 E. Anaheim St., Long Beach, has completed drawings for construction of two machine shop buildings containing offices, manufacturing and lavatory facilities in Signal Hill for Ted Matson.

Construction will be frame and stucco, tapered steel girders, composition and gravel roof, plaster interior, commercial alumnium projected sash and aluminum louver sash, concrete slab floor, mechanical roof ventilation, fluorescent lighting, metal overhead doors and wood sliding doors, and an asphaltic concrete paved driveway.

JAMES W. CAWDREY SEATTLE CONTRACTOR 1959 AGC PRESIDENT

James W. Cawdrey of Cawdrey & Vemo, Seattle contractors, has been nominated for president and former Federal Highway Administrator John A. Volpe, Malden, Massachusetts, for vice-president of The Associated General Contractors of America.

The election will be conducted by mail ballots in December, and the president and vice-president for 1959 will be installed at the 40th annual convention of the AGC at Miami Beach, Florida, in January.

Cawdrey has been active in local and national AGC affairs for many years, being president of the Seattle Chapter in

1949, and serving as chairman of the Building Contractor's Division of the national group in 1955. He has also served as a national director for three terms, a member of the Executive Committee as well as Finance, Labor, Membership, Contract Forms and Specifications and The American Institute of Architects AGC Joint Cooperative Committee.

YALE ANNOUNCES NEW LINE OF RESIDENTIALS

A major addition to Yale & Towne's broad range of key-in-the-knob type locksets is this new line of residential locksets, developed to reduce installation time and cost for residential builders and at the same time to provide them with a choice of design in moderately priced locksets unprecedented in the lock and hardware industry.

Incorporates many new labor-saving features, simplifies installation with only three preassembled units and no knob screw is required to fasten the knob to the spindle. An important safety feature is the panic-proof locking button which is automatically released when the knob is turned. Known as the 5280 series, complete data is available from the manufacturer, Yale & Towne Mfg. Co., Chrysler Bldg., New York 17, N. Y.

GLADDING McBEAN RETIRES JAMES COLE IN SEATTLE

James S. Cole, for more than 50 years associated with Gladding, McBean & Company, and sales manager for the company's building products in the Pacific Northwest area, retired on October 1st, according to an announcement by C. E. Goudge, vice president and general manager of the

Pacific Northwest Division of Gladding, McBean & Company, Seattle.

Cole began his career with Gladding, McBean & Company at the Lincoln, Calif., plant in 1908, following graduation from Syracuse University as a Civil Engineer. From 1912 to 1929 he served in various sales capacities in the company's San Francisco office, being named sales manager of all products for the Central Division in 1928.

In 1929 Gladding, McBean & Co. purchased the American Fire Brick Company in Spokane and Cole was transferred to become manager of the Spokane office. From 1932 to 1936 he served as manager of the Portland office, and since 1936 has served as sales manager, Building Products, Pacific Northwest area, with headquarters in Seattle.

Active in civic affairs he has served as a member of the Construction and Civic Development Committee, Seattle Chamber of Commerce, and is a past president of the Washington State Chapter, Producers' Council, Inc.

NEW SEVENTH DAY ADVENTIST ACADEMY FOR HEALDSBURG

The design department of the Pacific Union College, St. Helena, is preparing plans for construction of a new Seventh Day Adventist Academy, representing a boys' dormitory, near Healdsburg.

The first stage of constructing the new academy will include an administration unit with classrooms and offices, boys' and girls' dormitory buildings, home economics and science building, dining room and kitchen, boiler and shop buildings, manual training, gymnasium. All buildings will be of concrete block construction. Estimated cost on the first unit is $2,000,000.

IRWIN M. JOHNSON ARCHITECT MOVES TO NEW OFFICES

Architect Irwin M. Johnson has announced the removal of his offices to 503 49th Street, Oakland, according to a recent announcement.

The new office location is in the Bank of America building at 49th and Telegraph.

RESTAURANT AND WAREHOUSE BLDG., WEST LOS ANGELES

Consulting Engineer H. L. Standefer, 4344 Laurel Canyon Blvd., Studio City, is preparing plans for construction of a frame and stucco restaurant and a brick warehouse building on Santa Monica Boulevard, which will be 41x89 ft. and 90x100 feet.

Construction will be composition roofing, tapered steel girders, concrete slab floors, plate glass, terrazzo, toilets, ceramic tile work and air conditioning.

PRESSURE FILTER FOR LARGER SWIMMING POOLS

A new intermediate size Diatomite pressure filter designed for swimming pools requiring a filtration rate of 4000 to 7000 gallons per hour, or multiples, is known as the "Suburban."

The unit is of ROMAR down-flow design and is built in two models with average capacities of 4200 and 7200 gallons per hour, and filtering surfaces of 35 and 60 sq.ft. The larger model needs only 9 sq.ft. of base space and 5 ft. 6 in. headroom. Either model can be mounted in banks of two or more units for higher, more flexible filtering requirements where increased capacities are needed. Part of complete swimming pool equipment, write Romar Filter Corp., Milwaukee 12, Wis.

PLASTERERS AWARD FOUR SCHOLARSHIPS IN SOUTHERN CALIFORNIA

The Southern California Plastering Institute has announced the four recipients of the Institute's first scholarship grants to the College of Architecture of the University of Southern California.

The four third- and fourth-year architectural students are Howard Abos, Thomas W. Benton, William W. Preston and William S. Walsh.

Members of the architectural selection committee were H. Douglas Byles, William T. Jordan, George Vernon Russell and Dean Arthur B. Gallion of the University of Southern California.

AIR REDUCTION OF PACIFIC PROMOTES TWO STAFF MEMBERS

L. J. Fife, district sales manager at the Emeryville sales office of Air Reduction Pacific Company, has just been appointed executive staff assistant at Airco Pacific's executive offices in San Francisco, and G. G. Drake succeeds Fife as district sales manager at Emeryville.

RECREATIONAL FACILITIES IN SARATOGA

Architect William May, 1565 The Alameda, San Jose, has completed preliminary plans for construction of new recreational facilities at the Brookside Club in Saratoga.

comprising a swimming pool, tennis courts, bath house and showers.

Construction is scheduled for the Spring of 1959.

WALLACE R. HARPER NAMED BY AMERICAN INSTITUTE OF STEEL CONSTRUCTION

Wallace R. Harper has been named assistant executive vice-president of the American Institute of Steel Construction, according to a recent announcement by N. P. Hayes, president.

A former vice-president of Pittsburgh Plate Glass Company, Harper assumed his duties with the Institute on October 1st. Since January, 1957, Harper has been a sales consultant to the Hanley Company, a national manufacturer of structural clay products.

STATEMENT REQUIRED BY THE ACT OF AUGUST 24, 1912, AS AMENDED BY THE ACTS OF MARCH 3, 1933, AND JULY 2, 1946 (Title 39, United States Code, Section 233) SHOWING THE OWNERSHIP, MANAGEMENT, AND CIRCULATION OF

Architect and Engineer, published monthly at San Francisco, Calif., for October 1, 1958.

1. The names and addresses of the publisher, editor, managing editor, and business managers are:

Publisher, The Architect and Engineer, Inc., 68 Post St., San Francisco, Calif.

Editor, Edwin H. Wilder, 68 Post St., San Francisco, Calif.

Managing Editor, None.

Business Manager, L. B. Penhorwood, 68 Post St., San Francisco, Calif.

2. The owner is: (If owned by a corporation, its name and address must be stated and also immediately thereunder the names and addresses of stockholders owning or holding 1 percent or more of total amount of stock. If not owned by a corporation, the names and addresses of the individual owners must be given. If owned by a partnership or other unincorporated firm, its name and address, as well as that of each individual member, must be given.)

The Architect and Engineer, Inc., 68 Post St., San Francisco, Calif.

Kate P. Kierulff, 68 Post St., San Francisco, Calif.

E. N. Kierulff, 68 Post St., San Francisco, Calif.

L. B. Penhorwood, 68 Post St., San Francisco, Calif.

F. W. Jones, 1154 McKinley Ave., Oakland, Calif.

E. J. Cardinal, 942 Howard St., San Francisco, Calif.

3. The known bondholders, mortgagees, and other security holders owning or holding 1 percent or more of total amount of bonds, mortgages, or other securities are: (If there are none, so state.)

None.

4. Paragraphs 2 and 3 include, in cases where the stockholder or security holder appears upon the books of the company as trustee or in any other fiduciary relation, the name of the person or corporation for whom such trustee is acting; also the statements in the two paragraphs show the affiant's full knowledge and belief as to the circumstances and conditions under which stockholders and security holders who do not appear upon the books of the company as trustees, hold stock and securities in a capacity other than that of a bona fide owner.

5. The average number of copies of each issue of this publication sold or distributed, through the mails or otherwise, to paid subscribers during the 12 months preceding the date shown above was: (This information is required from daily, weekly, semiweekly, and triweekly newspapers only.)

L. B. Penhorwood, Business Mgr.

Sworn to and subscribed before me this 5th day of September, 1958.

(SEAL)   IRENE CRESPI

Notary Public in and for the City and County of San Francisco, State of California.

(My commission expires Jan. 3, 1959.)

A painter prompted a new look

When one of our maintenance department painters was redecorating the treasurer's office, he asked about U.S. Savings Bonds. "If I could buy these Bonds on installments," he said, "and you could take my payments out before I got my paycheck, I'd hardly miss it."

Our treasurer explained that the Payroll Savings Plan does exactly that and gave the painter an application card. But the matter didn't end there, for our painter had given *us* something, too: an idea that helped to put real color into our plan.

He made us realize that if he was unfamiliar with this plan, many others must be in exactly the same position.

Our State Savings Bond Director helped us pass the word. Under his direction, we set up a company-wide campaign that gave the whole Payroll Savings story to every person in the Company. Within a few days we had the best employee participation we've had since the mid-forties.

People are quick to take advantage of this sound, automatic way to save money. Today there are more payroll savers than ever before in peacetime. Look up your State Director in the phone book or write: Savings Bonds Division, U.S. Treasury Department, Washington, D.C.

ALIVE TODAY!

Arch Lightbody is one
of 800,000 Americans cured of cancer
because they went to their doctors in time.
They learned that many cancers
are curable if detected early
and treated promptly.
That's why an annual health checkup
is your best cancer insurance.

AMERICAN
CANCER
SOCIETY

No. 3

ER

EDITORS:

ITTLE, Dean,
Arts and Depart-
ture, University
son, Arizona.

MOCINE, City
ineer, Oakland,

md

tY COX, Sales
siness Develop-
Berkeley, Califor-

ent

.CHMAN, Sub-
ealty Developer,
a

:CONNEL, Stan-
Planning Dept.,
lifornia

ing
Architect,

ture
.D, Architect,
California

JME, Consulting
Engineer, San
ifornia

ULLNER,

sing

PICTURE

AL

on, Freeth, Haines
cts, it is a tasteful
ve stone and wood.
western Churches

REPORTS—

ARCHITECT & ENGINEER is indexed regularly by ENGINEERING INDEX, INC.; and ART INDEX

Contents for DECEMBER

THE OLDEST PROFESSIONAL MONTHLY BUSINESS MAGAZINE OF THE ELEVEN WESTERN STA

ARCHITECT AND ENGINEER (Established 1905) is published on the 15th of the month by The Architect Engineer, Inc., 68 Post St., San Francisco 4; Telephone EXbrook 2-7182. President, K. P. Kierulff; President and Manager, L. B. Penhorwood; Treasurer, E. N. Kierulff. — Los Angeles Office: Wentwor

Merry Christmas

and a

Happy New

Year

NEWS and COMMENT ON ART

SAN FRANCISCO MUSEUM OF ART

The San Francisco Museum of Art, War Memorial Building, Civic Center, under the direction of Dr. Grace L. McCann Morley, has announced the following schedule of special exhibitions and events for the holiday season:

EXHIBITS: The Twenty-Second Annual Drawing and Print Exhibition of the San Francisco Art Association; A Reappraisal—Masterworks from the Museum's Permanent Collection; Paintings by Ruth Armer, Ralph du Casse, and Carl Morris; The Christmas Exhibitions—featuring Christmas trees, Holiday Boutique, and Art for the Christmas Giving; The Art of Animation—A Retrospective Exhibition by Walt Disney.

EVENTS: Annual Christmas Party. Classes in Art will be resumed after the holidays.

The Museum will be open daily EXCEPT Christmas Day when it will be closed.

M. H. deYOUNG MEMORIAL MUSEUM

The M. H. deYoung Memorial Museum, Golden Gate Park, San Francisco, under the direction of Walter Heil, is featuring the following special exhibitions for the month of December:

EXHIBITIONS: Into The Child World, an exhibition of Art Works by San Francisco Public and Private School Children, from pre-school age to 12; Color Woodcuts, by Ande Hiroshige, 1797-1858, lent for exhibition by Mr. and Mrs. Edwin Grabhorn; Persian and Indian Miniatures—from the Collection of K. Demirdjian and lent by A. Demirdjian.

SPECIAL EVENTS: Classes in Art Enjoyment for adults and children; Exercises in Oil Painting; Seminars in the History of Art, and for the children, Picture Making, Art and Nature, and the Art Club.

The Museum is open daily.

CALIFORNIA PALACE OF THE LEGION OF HONOR

The California Palace of the Legion of Honor, Lincoln Park, San Francisco, under the direction of Thomas Carr Howe, Jr., announces the following exhibitions and special activities for December:

SPECIAL EXHIBITIONS: Masterpieces of Korean Art—This exhibition, consisting of the major national art treasures of Korea—comes to San Francisco following its showing at the National Gallery of Art, Washington, the Metropolitan Museum of Art, New York, the Museum of Fine Arts, Boston, and other leading museums of the country. Paintings by Madeleine Reichart; Watercolors by Jerome Land; Ivory Carv-

ings by Japanese Masters; Stoneware by Frank Hamilton; Recent Paintings by Harry Krell; and Sketchbook Drawings by Lee D. Stillwell, Jr.

The Achenbach Foundation for Graphic Arts, features gifts and acquisitions of the years 1957 and 1958.

EVENTS: Organ Program each Saturday and Sunday at 3 o'clock, p.m., featuring Richard Purvis and Ludwig Altman. Educational activities include the Fall-Winter series of Art classes for children and juniors.

The Museum is open daily.

OAKLAND ART MUSEUM

The Oakland Art Museum, 1000 Fallon Street, under the direction of Paul Mills, Curator, is featuring a number of special holiday exhibitions including:

EXHIBITS: Background for Brussels—Hans Namuth photographs and Fred Martin, guest of honor; A new Eye on Oakland—Bruce Brown photographs, and Ancient Palestinian Pottery; Toys of Yesteryears; and the Origin of Santa Claus.

SPECIAL EVENTS include Museum exhibit lectures and motion picture films.

The Museum is open daily.

ARCHITECTURAL GALLERY

The Architectural Gallery, 7933 West Third Street (Building Center) Los Angeles, is featuring a Special Exhibition of the work of Richard J. Neutra, F.A.I.A., and the architectural firm of Neutra & Alexander, F.A.I.A., during December.

COMPREHENSIVE ART EXHIBITION FOR CHILDREN AT deYOUNG

A juried exhibition of nearly 800 pieces of children's art planned especially to coincide with the Christmas season will be displayed at the M. H. deYoung Memorial Museum through January 5. "Into the Child's World" includes paintings, drawings, and three dimensional objects submitted by school children up to and including 12 years of age. Now a unique and nationally acclaimed educational event, the exhibition is the 7th to be presented since its inception in 1949.

Purpose of the comprehensive exhibition according to Archie Wedemeyer, Director of Art Education for the San Francisco Unified School District, and Chairman of the exhibition's Steering Committee, is to recognize children's art as a personal, creative expression and to aid parents and adults in the appreciation and understanding of children's art. Only the limitation of space restricted the acceptance of entries.

"Into the Child's World" is jointly sponsored by the San Francisco Unified School District and the Board of Education, the San Francisco News, and the Junior Committee of The deYoung Museum Society.

Today's

Design

Dominates

Western Church Architecture

By ARTHUR W. PRIAULX

The world, a century hence, may well refer to the mid-Twentieth Century as the period of great religious resurgence in the United States.

Also, it may well be that architects of that day will point to this very same period as having originated the Western church form. There is unfolding today a Western style in church design which is as contemporary as today's approach to religion by most faiths.

This religious resurgence and renaissance in church design are closely bound together, for the vast increase in church membership and attendance is, in

ST. DANIEL the PHOPHET Church, Ouray, Colorado, parish church built of native rock, contrasting wood and laminated arches.

LUTHERAN CHURCH of the Good Shepherd, Olympia, Washington, designed by Johnson and Austin, Architects.

A low budget church with interesting design solution. Post-and-beam design helps reduce cost.

fact, the real reason for the development of the new form. The resulting and amazing increase in church building has come at a time when modern, progressive architects are searching for that intangible quality which marks a religious building and are unwilling in this search to be bound by the rigidity of the past.

There are today no really accepted standards for church design such as those which, in past centuries, have guided, but more particularly bound or limited, the architect. Our mid-Twentieth Century architect lets his imagination range freely across the idea spectrum, from the highly romantic to the stiff and unrelenting. Some modern churches come close to touching the bizarre, as each architect strives to interpret and to achieve the lofty purpose of the church building. However, most contemporary churches are exciting and interesting, beautiful and functional, modern and restrained; and the great majority of the new churches show good taste and judgment on the part of the architect and illustrate his dedication to the purpose.

If the Western church has an identifying symbol, it is the capture of space in simple dignity and strong character. The subtle influence of the past is apparent everywhere, but there is the feeling, as one studies and enjoys these new churches, that the modern theme is dominant, self-assertive and powerful, although bow-

GOOD SHEPHERD LUTHERAN CHURCH

Tacoma, Washington

Designed by K. Walter Johnson and John V. Watson, Architects.

Church connects with parsonage, view shows two story canopy entry and clerestory.

WESTERN CHURCH ARCHITECTURE . . .

CROWN LUTHERAN CHURCH
Seattle, Washington

Designed by Oliver W. Olson, Architect.

ing ever so slightly to symbolic memories of the past.
An excellent definition of the Western church comes from Robert L. Durham, outstanding Seattle architect whose churches have long been a dominant part of the northwest landscape, who has just returned from an eight-day trip by air through Germany, Holland, Switzerland, and a week at the Brussels World's Fair.

"I have seen some fabulous new churches," Durham observed. "All of them were contemporary without any dependence on traditional detail, even when they were built in the very shadow of a historical structure. The thought occurred to me, while looking at them, that they are quite un-Western in character. Perhaps this is partially because of their lack of wood materials.

A large percentage of them depend upon reinforced concrete for their main structural concept. One or two to them have a wood plank roof resting on pre-cast reinforced beams, but, in the main, they are constructed of hard masonry materials."

Then Architect Durham made a most significant observation: "The one thing which is most common between our Pacific Coast buildings and those in Europe is the fact that neither one of them is 'warmed-over Georgian' or 'pseudo-Gothic'. By and large, the work being done on the Pacific Coast is completely of today's design."

Architect Durham frequently mentions wood as one of the typifying trademarks of the Western church, and other architects agree that much of the freedom

One of the most distinctive churches of the northwest is the exterior shown above.

Unusual glass panel wall beside chancel, and post and beam interior design, is seen at left.

FIRST LUTHERAN CHURCH

Kennewick, Washington

Designed by Durham, Anderson and Freed. Unusual view of nave with lovely wood arches contrasted with stone.

Two more views of church are shown below.

they enjoy today in church design unquestionably comes from the great flexibility of the glued laminated wood arch and its almost limitless variations in form.

With each passing year, Western churches become more interesting, more varied and more a tribute to the limitless imagination of the architect. Some of the finest ideas coming from the Western architect's drafting board involve the church form.

The First Lutheran Church of Kennewick, Washington, design by Durham, Anderson and Freed, see page 7, is an outstanding example of the Western church. Imaginative use of the giant glu-lam arches has created a nave with cathedral dignity, but which, the architects point out, is in no way Gothic. Here the low side aisles contrast with the high roof, and the texture of the stone forms another contrast with the wood. Small pieces of glass one inch thick have been set in the chancel wall to form a cross, and a plastic skylite is carried around the back of the last arch. The shape of the side walls has been so arranged as to cut off a view of the windows as you face towards the altar, but designed to open up the full view of the windows as you face the side. This church features the first exposed organ in the Northwest. Every new church in Europe seen by Robert L. Durham on his recent trip has an exposed organ.

Unusual is the five-sided fellowship hall, a part of the Kennewick First Lutheran Church. Five large

glu-lam beams are supported by a tension ring at the eave line to make up the dramatic roof of the structure.

When the First Presbyterian Church of Yakima found its 2,000 members crowding all its facilities, it commissioned Durham, Anderson and Freed to design the Westminster Presbyterian Church as a branch. (See page 12 top.) The $300,000 church had no congregation and was located in a 70-acre peach orchard. Now, a year later, it is full to capacity twice on Sunday. This church fits the classic 1000-300-300-300 formula which this firm has developed, that is, the potential 1000 members and 300 seats in the sanctuary, 300 people for dinner in the social hall, and 300 chil-

CENTRAL UNION CHURCH
Windward, Hawaii

Designed by Potter and Potter, Architects. Main church walls can be opened to include adjacent lanais during warm weather.

protruding bricks in the design form an interesting pattern when the light from the clerestory windows is cast across its face. The thick wall also serves to keep out street noises. Notice that a Celtic cross was chosen; this is being extensively used by the Presbyterian church. The structure for the 540-member congregation cost only $140,000.

Durham, Anderson and Freed demonstrate the flexibility of wood design in the Bothell Methodist Church near Seattle. (See page 10 bottom.) The congregation was moving to a wooded site near a new high school a mile away. The long range plans call for a sanctuary to seat 400 to 500 people. However, due to limited funds, only the heart of the master plan has been constructed which includes half the social hall, the narthex, a chapel to seat 160, and one half the future education and administration wing. This much was built for $130,000. The laminated beams of the roof are held from spreading by tie rods which express the structure, but are not noticeable. The sidewalls of the chapel are made with 2x8 pieces on an angle with glass fitted between. There is a row of clear glass at the top and bottom of the splayed wood screen. The end of the room is plate glass looking out into a small northwest garden. This is an excellent example of the ease with which properly designed wood structures can ultimately be enlarged and radically expanded without material loss in the original building and with minimum inconvenience to the occupants.

dren for one session in Sunday school. The exterior of the building is finished in brick and rough-sawn cedar. The spire is made of wood laminated sections with thick glass inserts held in with welded angle irons. Interesting is the brick wall in the narthex where 4x8 inch openings have been fitted with brilliantly colored inch-thick glass.

The Woodland Park Presbyterian Church of Seattle, another Durham, Anderson and Freed design (see page 10 top) shows still another form of the modern church. Here the architects used the parabolic shaped arch to achieve lofty, sweeping lines in the nave. Light is brought in through clerestory windows above the side aisles. A 12-inch-thick brick wall back of the chancel introduces a great deal of texture, and the

ST. ALBANS EPISCOPAL CHURCH
Tillamook, Oregon

**Designed by William G. Holford, Architect. A
small parish church with big church facilities.**

Three prominent architectural firms of Honolulu
have made genuine contributions to the development
of church designs in the western theme to suit the
particular and specific problems of their climate and
the island traditions.

A remarkably beautiful building is the Waiokeola
Congregational Church designed by Lemmon, Freeth,
Haines and Jones (see cover) which uses native stone
in combination with wood in a dramatic and impressive manner. The problem was to design a church to
accommodate 250 people plus a 30-seat choir and
six classrooms in a Sunday school building all for
$85,000. It was decided to use a church design which
would seat the choir off slightly to one side and, for
that reason, the "transept" plan was developed. The
transept opposite the choir is to be used for the church
offices over which a small overflow balcony is placed.

The original design, advises Paul D. Jones, was
based upon a framing system utilizing precast concrete
frames. Previous experience had shown this material
to be the cheapest. As might easily be imagined, Mr.

Jones points out, the cross vaulting at the intersection
of the transept and nave resulted in rather complicated
detailing of the precast concrete work. For that reason,
an alternative bid was invited for the substitution of

**CALVARY BAPTIST CHURCH of Tacoma, Washington. Designed by Silas E. Nelson, Archi-
tect, combines traditional styling with modern design of sidewalls and effective use of
dark stained arches.**

WESTERN CHURCH ARCHITECTURE . . .

WOODLAND PARK PRESBYTERIAN CHURCH
Seattle, Washington

Designed by Durham, Anderson and Freed, Architects, with exciting, upsweeping arches creating a frame for chancel wall.

material involved and was erected a great deal more easily and quickly. The contractor, S. Miyoski, had the foundations ready and waiting when the timbers were delivered and with a single crane was able to erect all the framing in a single day and a half.

Architect Jones points out that the framing system is based on 15-foot bay spacing which is easily spanned with 4x5 double tongue-and-groove cedar sheathing. The use of side aisles in the nave accentuates the rise of the arches and the entire design has been most satisfactory from all standpoints, he states, evoking many favorable comments. Best of all, he continues, it has proven to us that glu-lam framing has many advantages that are not always reflected in first cost. However, in this case, he adds, first cost was the determining factor, but it proved that the solution to a complicated framing problem can be more economically solved with glu-lam than with our normal, comparable framing methods.

glu-lam wood arches in lieu of the precast concrete. The alternate bid proved to be considerably less expensive, Mr. Jones states, as it resulted in a much more refined cross vaulting due to the reduction in the mass of the

An open type of architectural design was employed by Architects Potter and Potter in the design of the lovely Central Union Church, Windward, set in a beautiful site with 700 feet frontage on Kaneohe Bay Drive, Windward, Oahu, commanding an inspiring view of Kailua Bay. (See page 8.)

BOTHELL METHODIST CHURCH

Bothell, Washington

Designed by Durham, Anderson and Freed, Architects.

Emphasizes effectiveness of simplicity in medium budget church.

KALIHI UNION CHURCH
of Hawaii

Designed by Law and Wilson,
Architects.

Achieves a grace and dignity
with an economical spanning and
inclusion of space.

The church building proper is 56 by 119 feet with a 28 by 75 foot administrative wing placed at right angles to form a rear side courtyard. This courtyard is surrounded with open lanais connected to the main church, thus providing circulation between units. The seating capacity of the nave is 400, with an additional 200 on side lanais for especially crowded occasions. The Sunday school accommodates 200 and has lanais capable of seating 100 more. Suited to the Hawaiian climate, sides of the church and administrative wing open on to open, but roofed, lanais. The openings of these sides are practically 100%, only supporting posts being solid. In favorable weather, which Architect Mark Potter, designer of the church, assures us is practically all the time, these openings give excellent

ventilation and a wonderful view of the bay. The ends of the church are of native lava stone and brick providing a solidity of design and sound barrier from the highway. Glu-lam arches were used, Mr. Potter advises, as the best means of obtaining clean ecclesiastical architectural character desired at a minimum of cost.

When architects Law and Wilson designed the gracious Kalihi Union Church (see above and below) they set as their paramount objective a church with the maximum spiritual character consistent with minimum funds available. In achieving this objective, the design reflects the use of laminated timber arches which span the space most economically and yet evidence grace and dignity, the use of native lava stone masonry to

EXTERIOR VIEW:

Showing an interesting use of
the outrigger symbol for the
covered walkway.

WESTERN CHURCH ARCHITECTURE . . .

achieve serenity and humility as a background for the service, and the development of garden spaces on either side of the sanctuary to serve as a peaceful outlook and a barrier from external noises.

Certain features were incorporated by Law and Wilson to achieve this over-all feeling and character. The effect of the tracery in the rear of the chancel facing the morning sun, broken into small panes of light by using hand-blown golden glass from the windows of the old church, gives a rich color to the natural materials and finishes. The dossal has been formed of vertical redwood members to achieve the feeling of height at the communion table and has incorporated a simple wood cross symbolic of the true experience of the liturgy. The use of Japanese shoji

doors permits complete openness of the chancel in suitable weather. The structure was carefully fitted into the site with wide, covered walkways for rainy weather.

One of the strikingly dramatic churches of the Seattle area is the Crown Lutheran Church designed by Architect Oliver W. Olson, of Seattle. (See page 6.) The rugged and vaulted lines of the post and beam frame of the structure give the church the appearance of great solidity. The nave was designed to accommodate 350 worshipers, with a choir loft for 60 people. To the right of the nave is God's Garden, a delightful, formal garden brought from the outside to the inside through plate glass windows.

A social hall of proportionate size serves as overflow

WESTPARK CHURCH
Yakima, Washington

Designed by Champ Sanford, Architect, is an excellent example of possibilities for beauty and utility in the economy church; provides spacious, pleasant church quarters.

from the nave. Between the two principal areas, a large and spacious narthex is provided for social visiting. Adjacent to the social hall is a fireside room for youth and committee activities. The church was designed to utilize every square foot of space the city ordinances would allow, and, at the same time, avoid a crowded feeling. There has been an extensive use of brick and lumber in this structure which has been designed with a one-hour fire rating. A most dramatic lighting effect over the chancel is created by a large glass wall of varicolored glass panels at the right of the chancel. Here is an excellent example of the values which church organizations receive today in their buildings, for this fine church cost only $11.83 per square foot.

St. Albans Episcopal congregation of Tillamook, Oregon (see page 9 top) had only a small parish hall for a growing enrollment, so employed Architect William G. Holford of Nehalem, Oregon, to design a cottage type of church. The result is a charming structure which has grace and dignity and a western friendliness in its well planned facilities. Built for only $48,000, the nave seats 168 worshipers and Sunday school rooms added will accommodate 120 pupils. Although this had to be an economical church, Rev. Charles B. Traill reports that it is a solidly built, very attractive building which has become a community center and influenced new members to come in,

doubling the membership. Glu-lam arches form an attractive structural shape for the nave, and exposed wood decking and exterior cedar siding relate it with the surrounding wooded countryside.

In the St. Mary's Episcopal Church of Lakewood, Washington (see page 12 bottom) Architect Robert Billsbrough Price of Tacoma has created one of the distinguished and dramatic church structures of the northwest region. The roof is the center of attention from which the rest of the building stems. Wood glu-lam beams form the roof and extend through the side walls to anchor into concrete buttresses. A roof overhang follows these beams, giving extra emphasis

COOS BAY METHODIST CHURCH . . . Designed by James L. Paine, Salem

ST. MATHEW'S EPISCOPAL CHURCH
Parkrose, Oregon

Designed by Don Byers, Architect. An unusual use
of glass-end wall to delineate curve of arch
forms. Parabolic arches give lofty impression
and side windows give two-level effect.

to the dominant roof. The gable end facing the street is all glass, with vertical slats diffusing the light, and is one of the dramatic features of this extraordinary church.

Diffused light is one of the interesting developments of this church and Architect Price has used three components for diffusion: vertical wood slats, colored plastic panels, and glass jalousies. The slats, set in

frames, open out like doors. Cedar siding was used because of its affinity for the wooded surroundings.

When money-short members of the Westpark Church, Yakima, Washington (see page 13 top) employed Architect Champ Sanford to design their new church, they had one thing in common with most congregations: they, too, were short of money. They needed some 13,000 square feet of floor space, but couldn't spend over $125,000. Architect Sanford soon came to the conclusion that the only way he could get this much space for the money available was to design an attractive roof and close it in with inexpensive materials. He chose glu-laminated fir beams for his roof structural form and shalex block for the budget walls. The interior laminated arches set the design more or less for the entrance way and the open bell tower. The entryways of many churches, Architect Sanford comments, are dark and rather uninviting. The design problem here was to give protection while allowing plenty of light penetration. Indirect light was allowed to penetrate into the chancel area.

The design encompasses the use of a planter box which extends the entire width of the chancel and is eight feet high at the back wall, thus keeping the

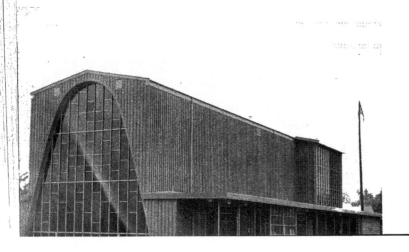

OAK GROVE METHODIST CHURCH
Oak Grove, Oregon

Designed by Stuart Mockford, Architect, combines an interesting use of native stone and wood for textural effect both inside and outside the church. Deck is nailed laminated, rough-sawn two-by-threes, which form the finished ceiling. Night-lighted copper spire contrasts with texture of stone and wood.

plants out of the way of movement in the chancel. The burning red glass cross was used as final emphasis to designate the spirit and program of the church. Rather slim tapered arches were used, and Architect Sanford designed them in this size so they would not dominate the auditorium, and he recessed them into the ceiling system just enough to prevent domination, yet to permit them to add the beauty of curved wood forms to the room.

Architect Silas E. Nelsen of Tacoma designed the Calvary Baptist Church (see page 9 bottom) of that city so as to preserve some of the traditional characteristics of early churches in keeping with the wishes of the building committee which also set economy as

ALL SAINTS EPISCOPAL CHURCH
Portland, Oregon

Designed by Stuart Mockford, Architect. Is fine example of an economy budget church which has all the charm and grace of a more costly structure. Roof system of glu-lam arches and purlins with exposed decking forms a light and cheerful interior.

one of the limitations. Architect Nelsen found that by using wood as the main structural component, he could have a colorful building with natural warmth of texture. Glu-laminated arches and beams with exposed purlins and decking form the design pattern for the roof system in both the church auditorium and the Sunday school and Fellowship wings. The church cost $11 per square foot, and much of this saving was due to the flexibility of design of the roof systems offered by the liberal use of glue laminated beams in the wing rooms and arches in the nave.

Two other rather distinctive churches in Washing-

ton came from the drafting boards of the K. Walter Johnson and John V. Austin architectural firm of Lakewood, Tacoma.

The Good Shepherd Lutheran Church of Tacoma (see page 5 bottom) presents a most unusual view, since the roof of the building extends to the ground level. The church takes the shape of the near parabolic arches which form the giant ribs of the structure and which are sheathed with wood decking left exposed inside and covered outside with heavy shakes. The arches are set in heavy buttresses of concrete. The gable end of the building is sided in cedar. A two-story canopied entrance in the center of the long wall enters the lower Sunday school and provides a clerestory system for the church nave on the second level. An interesting feature of this church is the inclusion of a four-bedroom parsonage in the rear portion of the building, but it in no way interferes with

FIRST BAPTIST CHURCH
Bloomington, Indiana

Designed by Sovik, Mathre and Associates, Architects, uses Indiana limestone and heavy timber to create a church with a contemporary theme.

Canopies relate interior and exterior most effectively.

Heavy timber beams give a rugged dignity and strength to the nave.

the unusual and distinctive roof line of the main church building.

Another of the many Lutheran churches designed by Johnson and Austin is the Lutheran Church of the Good Shepherd in Olympia, see page 5 top. This takes a completely different form from its near namesake in Tacoma. The brick-walled structure has clean, functional lines. The main structure gets its shape from flat beam and post frames, and much of the charm of the building comes from a pleasing blending

of the textures of the brick and cedar of the exterior and the brick and exposed wood of the interior.

One of the most interesting churches in the Oregon country is the Coos Bay Methodist Church, designed by James L. Paine of Salem, (see page 13 bottom). Here is a structure ideally adapted to its wooded site and designed to take full advantage of all possible natural light in an area where skies are frequently cloudy and somber. In order to properly accomplish this, a

(See Page 28)

FIRST
BAPTIST
CHURCH

Bloomington,
Indiana

VAN NESS AVENUE ENTRANCE . . . and driveway ramp to roof parking area.

PACIFIC NORTHERN SALES DIVISION

EASTMAN KODAK BUILDING

San Francisco, California

ARCHITECTS: KITCHEN & HUNT, A.I.A.
STRUCTURAL ENGINEER: H. J. BRUNNIER
MECHANICAL & ELECTRICAL ENGINEERS: VANDAMENT & DARMSTED
INTERIORS: MAURICE SANDS
GENERAL CONTRACTOR: LOUIS C. DUNN, INC.

ROOF PARKING

Cafeteria, Assembly Hall are on right, roof gardens and general offices are beyond.

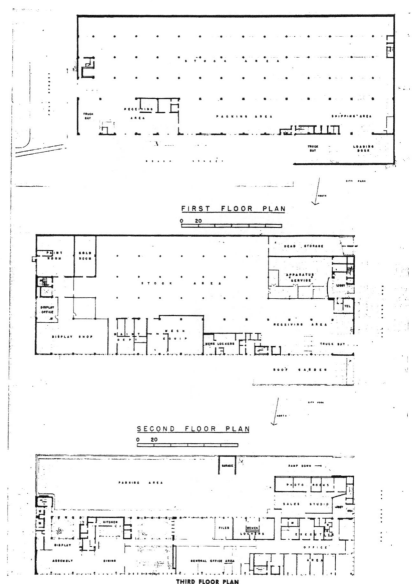

FIRST FLOOR PLAN

0 20

SECOND FLOOR PLAN

0 20

THIRD FLOOR PLAN

**GLAZED PASSAGE WAY from cafeteria to general
offices through the attractive roof garden.**

Of the several major commercial buildings to be erected in San Francisco and the Bay Area this year, the Eastman Kodak Company's new home on Van Ness avenue in San Francisco stands out as a good example of today's trend in office building design. It may be categorized as a structure unique for its many features such as its warehouse, display studios and executive offices, a beautiful exterior, landscaped roof garden and patios, cafeteria, assembly hall and parking facilities on the roof.

The building is situated on a sloping site near the south shore of San Francisco Bay, adjoining the Aquatic Park and opposite the Maritime Museum.

The half city block site is bounded by Van Ness avenue, Beach and Polk streets with a maximum land elevation differential of thirty-two feet permitting vehicular access to all three floors of the building. First floor warehouse receiving is by rail and truck from Beach street and at second floor level by truck from Van Ness avenue. By creating a ramp from Van Ness avenue off-street parking for automobiles of office and technical personnel is provided on the second floor roof with direct covered access to the adjacent third floor offices and demonstration rooms.

Most offices have a north exposure and a superb view across the bay with its colorful ships. The landscaped roof garden and patios designed by the architects adjoin the offices, cafeteria and assembly hall, and allow for future office expansion.

Complete studio and demonstration dark and light rooms are especially designed for display and use of company products. The assembly hall adjacent to cafeteria will also provide space for display and product projection for training personnel and dealer-customer meetings.

COVERED WALKWAY to Third Floor Entrance.

All warehouse receiving docks on both first and second floors are recessed within the building to accommodate large trucks and trailers thus leaving the street free for public traffic. The shipping dock at the end of Beach street is similarly planned except that the one-story roof will support a landscaped roof garden and lawn to blend the exterior appearance with adjacent city park and bocci ball courts.

For the flexibility of handling stock between the two warehouse floors when seasonal occasions demand, in addition to two large elevators, space is provided for a future vertical conveyor that will automatically transfer pallets of stock from floor to floor including the loading and unloading at the floors.

Structure Details

First and second floors are of reinforced concrete, flat slab of 350 lbs. per square foot live load.

The third floor is of light steel frame, with steel roof deck and a plaster fireproofing. The building's exterior is buff colored Norman brick veneer laid shinerwise from grade to third floor window sill. The third floor metal curtain wall is gold anodized aluminum with black anodized aluminum trim and parapet railing.

All sash is black anodized aluminum.

The third floor has large vertically pivoting sash

provided for ease of washing windows, as all offices are air conditioned.

Aluminum sun control louvers operated by solar time clock mechanism is integrated with illuminated plastic trademark sign on the west facade only, facing Van Ness avenue.

Interior Finish

Concrete walls and ceilings in the warehouse and similar areas are painted.

The office partitions are metal lath and plaster with

movable partitions in the general office areas. The general offices, executive offices and adjacent interior corridors, have luminous ceilings, while the other office areas have vinyl tile floors, with terrazzo in entrance and lobbies and toilet rooms.

Reflecting the tradition of the nautical site of the building, drift oak and teakwood finishes are used in the executive offices, conference room and part of the

ASSEMBLY HALL—Display gallery and adjacent roof garden next to roof parking.

Detail—Covered Walkway to Third Floor Entrance, Eastman Kodak Building
Kitchen & Hunt, Architects

Building faced with

RICHMOND BUFF COLORED NORMAN BRICK
(First Quality Hard Burned Brick)
"There is a Material Difference"

RICHMOND BRICK CO., LTD.
Since 1908
PORT RICHMOND • BEacon 4-5032

PHOTO APPARATUS Repair Department on second floor, adjacent to the Van Ness avenue lobby.

**SALES REPRESENTATIVE
OFFICES**

Demonstration photo studio is adjacent to photographic laboratory at the left of the studio.

assembly hall and cafeteria.

Mechanical

All offices are air conditioned. The first and second warehouse floors have automatic sprinkling systems; a refrigerated 50 degree cold room is provided for storage of special type film.

All offices have complete electrification in floor with major electrical distribution at 440 volts.

American Institute of Architects

John Noble Richards, President

Philip Will, Jr., 1st Vice-President   Edward L. Wilson, Secretary
Henry L. Wright, 2nd Vice-President   Raymond S. Kastendieck, Treasurer
Edmund R. Purves, Executive Secretary

National Headquarters—1735 New York Avenue, N.W., Washington, D. C.

REGIONAL DIRECTORS—Northwest District, Donald J. Stewart, Portland, Oregon; **Western Mountain District**, Frederick H. Porter, Sr., Cheyenne, Wyoming; California-Nevada-Hawaii District, Ulysses Floyd Rible, Los Angeles, California.

ARIZONA CHAPTERS:

CENTRAL ARIZONA: David Sholder, President; A. John Brenner, Vice-President; Jimmie R. Nunn, Secretary; Kemper Goodwin, Treasurer; James W. Elmore, Director; Ralph Haver, Director; Martin Ray Young, Jr., Director. Office of Secy., P.O. Box 904, Phoenix.

SOUTHERN ARIZONA: Santry Clay Fuller, President; Edward H. Nelson, Vice-President; David S. Swanson, Secretary; Robert J. Ambrose, Treasurer; D. Burr DuBois, Director; Eleazar D. Herreras, Director; Emerson C. Scholer, Director. Office of Secy., 2343 South Tucson Avenue, Tucson.

COAST VALLEYS CHAPTER:

William L. Higgins (San Jose), President; Paul J. Huston (Palo Alto), Vice-President; William H. Daseking (Menlo Park), Treasurer; Edward N. Chamberlain (San Jose), Secretary. Office of Secy., 390 Park Ave., San Jose.

CENTRAL VALLEY OF CALIFORNIA:

Joseph J. Jozens, President (Sacramento); Armsby Tod Hart, Vice-President (Sacramento); Albert M. Dreyfuss, Secretary (Sacramento); Whitson W. Cox, Treasurer. Office of Secy., 2127 "J" St., Sacramento.

COLORADO CHAPTER:

Casper F. Hegner, President; C. Gordon Sweet, Vice President; Norton Polivnick, Secretary; Richard Williams, Treasurer; James M. Hunter, Robert K. Fuller, Edward L. Bunts. Office of Secy., 1225 Bannock St., Denver, Colorado.

EAST BAY CHAPTER:

Hachiro Yuasa (Oakland), President; George T. Kern (Oakland), Vice-President; William M. Gillis (San Francisco), Secretary; J. A. Zerkle (Berkeley), Treasurer. Directors: H. B. Clausen, F. A. Lockwood, John Oyarzo, G. M. McCue, Marjorie Montgomery, Exec. Secy. Office of Secy., Mezzanine, Hotel Claremont, Berkeley 5.

IDAHO CHAPTER:

Anton E. Dropping, Boise, President; Charles W. Johnston, Payette, Vice-President; Glenn E. Cline, Boise, Sec.-Treas. Directors: Chester L. Shawver and Nat J. Adams, Boise. Office of Secy., 624 Idaho Bldg., Boise.

MONTEREY BAY CHAPTER:

Robert Stanton, President (Carmel); Walter Burde, Vice-President; William L. Cranston, Secretary; George Kuska, Treasurer. Office of Secy., P.O. Box 1846, Carmel.

MONTANA CHAPTER:

William J. Hess, President (Great Falls); John E. Toohey, Vice-President (Billings); H. C. Cheever, Secy.-Treas. (Bozeman). Directors: Oscar J. Ballas, Wm. J. Hess, John E. Toohey. Office of Sec., Bozeman, Montana.

NEVADA CHAPTER:

RENO: William E. Cowell, President; Albert W. Alegre, Vice-President; Ralph A. Casazza, Secretary; John Crider, Treasurer. Directors Graham Erskine, George L. F. O'Brien, Laurence A. Gulling. Office of the Secy. 232 W. 1st St., Reno, Nevada.

WOMEN'S ARCHITECTURAL LEAGUE: (Reno) Mrs. Eileen Casazza, President; Mrs. Lucille Lackard, Vice-President; Mrs. Gladys Cowell, Secretary; Mrs. Enid Hellman, Treasurer.

LAS VEGAS: Walter F. Zick, President; Aloysius McDonald, Vice-President; Edward B. Hendricks, Secy.-Treas. Directors: Walter F. Zick, Edward Hendricks, Charles E. Cox. Office of Secy., 106 S. Main St., Las Vegas.

NEVADA STATE BOARD OF ARCHITECTS:

Russell Mills, Chairman (Reno); Aloysius McDonald, Sec-Treas. Members: L. A. Ferris, Elmo C. Bruner, Edward S. Parsons. Office, 1420 S. 5th St., Los Vegas.

NORTHERN CALIFORNIA CHAPTER:

William Corlett, President; Donald Powers Smith, Vice-President; George T. Rockrise, Secretary; Richard S. Banwell, Treasurer. Directors: W. Clement Ambrose, John Kruse, Bernard J. Sabaroff, Corwin Booth. Exec. Secy., May B. Hipshman. Chapter Office, 47 Kearny St., San Francisco.

ORANGE COUNTY CHAPTER:

William T. Jordan, President (Costa Mesa); Donald M. Williamson, Vice-President (Laguna Beach); J. Herbert Brownell, Secretary; Rumont W. Hougan, Treasurer. Office of Secy., 1950 W. Coast Highway, Newport Beach.

OREGON CHAPTER:

John K. Dukehart, President; Keith R. Maguire, Vice-President; Robert Douglas, Secretary; Harry K. Stevens, Treasurer. Directors: Daniel McGoodwin, Earl P. Newberry, Everett B. Franks, Robert W. Fritsch, Donald W. Edmundson. Office of Secy., 2041 S.W. 58th Ave., Portland 1.

PASADENA CHAPTER

Roger Hayward, architect and artist, was the principal speaker at the December meeting held in the Rancho Hillcrest, Pasadena, taking as his subject "Color and You". The meeting also represented the annual joint meeting with the Pasadena Architectural Club.

Recent new additions to the Chapter roster include George T. Kirkpatrick, Corporate Member and Allan M. Chipp, Associate Member.

CALIFORNIA COUNCIL AIA

During December offices of the Council will be moved into new quarters at 916 Kearny Street, San Francisco.

The Council has gone on record as being opposed to a proposed change in Title 17 of the State Administrative Code relating to review of hospital plans for adherence to fire codes. The change would require that architects designing hospitals south of the Tehachapi Mountains who propose to personally bring their drawings to the State Fire Marshal and Bureau of Hospitals go to the Sacramento office of the fire marshal unless the projects are related to the Hill-Burton subsidy. It was proposed that architects designing hospitals south of the Tehachapis be directed to Los Angeles, rather than Sacramento.

Announcement has been made that reservations are now being accepted for the Pacific Rim Architectural Conference to be held in Honolulu next October.

EAST BAY CHAPTER

The California Redwood Association hosted the Chapter at the December meeting in Art's Buffet, Oakland, with the showing of two motion picture films — "The New Architecture" and "Space for Learning," both films having been produced by the Association.

Also featuring the program was a discussion of architecture led by John Banister, Executive Director of the Builders Exchange of Oakland.

SOUTHERN CALIFORNIA CHAPTER

Dr. Norman Topping, President of the University of Southern California, was the principal speaker at the December meeting held in the Elks Club, Los Angeles. Dr. Topping has just returned to California from the University of Pennsylvania where he has been vice-president for Medical Affairs for six years.

He was formerly Assistant Surgeon General of the U. S. Public Health Service at Bethesda Maryland Branch of the USTHS, and served on the Interdepartmental Committee for Scientific Research and Development, on an appointment by the President of the United States.

Dr. Topping spoke on the subject "Architecture and the University."

SANTA CLARA & SANTA CRUZ COUNTIES

William Andrew Goss, Edward G. Lee, Richard Wallace Lee and William May, architect members and associates were honored at the December meeting held in Saratoga. Other matters taken under consideration were the introduction of new officers, budget, and other Chapter matters.

The annual Chapter-WAL Christmas party was observed on the 16th at Bill and Ginny Higgins in Saratoga.

AMERICAN INSTITUTE OF ARCHITECTS ANNOUNCE AWARD

The American Institute of Architects have announced a new set of regulations for the annual $25,000 R. S. Reynolds Memorial Award for Significant use of aluminum in architecture.

The new rules increase the emphasis on the creative and architectural value of the structure selected to receive the Reynolds Award, which is conferred annually on an architect who has designed a significant work of architecture, in the creation of which aluminum has been an important contributing factor.

Under the new regulations, an architect may be nominated for the Reynolds Award by anyone, including himself or his firm, according to Edmund R. Purves, Executive Director of the AIA, Washington, D. C.

In addition to the $25,000 honorary payment, the recipient also receives an appropriate sculptured piece specially created by a prominent contemporary artist.

Nominations for the 1959 Reynolds Award will be accepted until February 2, 1959. Programs giving details of the Award will be sent by the AIA to each one of the 12,560 members of the Institute as well as to foreign architectural societies. Nomination forms are included with the programs.

The Award, with the honoratium and the sculptured piece, will be formally presented at the annual convention of the AIA in the summer of 1959.

SAN FRANCISCO ARCHITECTURAL CLUB

The Annual Christmas Party and meeting were observed in the Club's quarters early in December, with arrangements for the meeting being in charge of President Van De Wegbe and Orv Hickenlooper.

ARCHITECTS TO TOUR KAWNEER PLANT

The Kawneer Company will conduct a tour of architects through its new headquarters at 600 Parr Boulevard on January 8, 1959. Arrangements are in charge of Arthur Iwata.

AMERICAN SOCIETY OF CIVIL
ENGINEERS—San Francisco

The December meeting, held in the Engineers' Club, San Francisco, was devoted to the presentation of Life Member certificates on behalf of the National Society to seventeen members of the San Francisco Section, including:

Charles R. Blood, Albert E. Challenger, Howard F. Cozzens, Clinton De Well, Charles T. Dickerman, John M. Evans, Edmund C. Flynn, Russell G. Hackett, Harry L. Hess, Theodore S. Hersey, Bruce Jameyson,

Morgan M. Lewis, Albert G. Mett, John H. Peaslee, Ernest A. Rolison, Paul A. Swafford, and George E. Troxell.

It was announced that the Daniel W. Mead Prize for the best 2000 word paper by a Junior Member on Engineering Ethics would be presented at the 1959 Annual Convention of the ASCE.

FEMINEERS

"Christmas in the Islands" was the theme of the annual Christmas Party held in the Lakeside Olympic Club on December 17th. The Hawaiian motif ap-peared in tapa clothes, fish nets, sea shells, leis, surf-boards, ukeleles and mumus, with Santa Kris Kioni arriving on a surfboard to distribute gifts from Hawaii.

Mrs. John August Blume served as chairman of the event, assisted by Mesdames Mark Falk, Tom Wosser, William W. Brewer, Howard A. Schirmer and F. R. Preece.

SAN FRANCISCO ENGINEERS
SPEAKERS CLUB

Members of the San Francisco Engineers' Speakers Club are preparing for the 1959 Bay Area Engineers' Week observation which will be held in conjunction with National Engineers' Week, February 22-28, 1959.

The theme for this event has been selected as "Engineering for the Age of Space," according to John Sardis, Chairman of the 1959 Engineers' Week for the Bay Area.

Members of the Speakers' Club appear before Serv-ice Clubs, church organizations, fraternal groups and educational groups to discuss engineering during the nationally observed Engineers' Week.

STRUCTURAL ENGINEERS ASSOCIATION
OF SOUTHERN CALIFORNIA

"Management In The Space Age" was the subject of a speech given by W. L. Rogers, Vice-President, Aerojet General Corporation, Azusa Operations, at the December meeting of the Association held in the Rodger Young Memorial Auditorium in Los Angeles.

The activities at Aerojet cover a broad range of

ARCHITECT AND ENGINEER

engineering specialties, both rocket and non-rocket, as well as hundreds of other distinct projects. Underlying all the engineering effort is the unremitting battle with weight. Minimum weight has always been important in airborne applications and is even more important in space applications.

Rogers believes that Management today has two main areas: that of getting business and that of controlling performance of the job once you have it in the house.

Recent new members include: Edwin M. Bennett, Donald K. Diemer, Robert A. Eldridge, Harvey H. Hicks, Jr., James W. Pereira, and William C. Trude, Jr., Associate Members. Bertrand W. Greynald, John P. Jamison and Chris H. Kortner, Members. James C. Hamilton, Allied Member and Nels A. Roselund, Student Member.

STRUCTURAL ENGINEERS ASSOCIATION OF NORTHERN CALIFORNIA

The December meeting, held in the Engineers' Club, San Francisco, was devoted to a consideration of Association matters including By-Laws.

Recent new members include Frederick B. Bunting, and John E. McCarthy, Members. Fred A. Nicholson, Affiliate Member.

NAMED TO STUDY ENGINEERING SCHOOL IN INDIA

Emeritus Professor Royal W. Sorensen, Department of Electrical Engineering, California Institute of Technology, is one of six experts in engineering teaching named by the American Society for Engineering Education to study plans for a new engineering school at Kanpur, India, under a contract with the U. S. International Cooperative Administration.

The group will visit existing Universities and Colleges and Industrial plants in Roorke, Chandigrah, Delhi, Calcutta, Kharagpur, Tatanagar, Poona, Bombay, Bangalore and Madras. Their task, undertaken at the request of the India Ministry of Scientific Research and Cultural Affairs, is to evaluate tentative plans for a new institute of technology at Kanpur, and to make "comprehensive recommendations" for its size, physical plant, laboratory and workshop facilities, organization, curricula, teaching and examinations, library and personnel.

WESTERN CHURCH
ARCHITECTURE

(From Page 17)

plastic glazed skylight was introduced which brings the natural southern light into the entire sanctuary and chancel areas of the church. This skylight is glazed with multi-colored plastic sheets and is louvered for light control. Architect Paine said he was extremely happy with this installation and has received many compliments on this feature of the building.

In this church, as in each of the other eighteen designed by this firm in the Northwest, glued laminated structural members establish the basic chancel structural design. We have found, said Architect Paine, that glued laminated arches and purlins allow us unlimited freedom in our design and eliminate many of the problems.

Another innovation in connection with this church is its unique steeple, which is also glazed with multi-colored panels. This steeple glazing provides a flood of multi-colored radiance at the altar during daylight periods of worship. Fluorescent and incandescent lighting accomplishes the same purpose at night. Exterior of the building is covered with rough-sawn cedar and the roof with hand-split shakes. The interior features native paneling within the chancel area and within the chapel, as well as in several other areas of the building.

Two features of this church deserve special mention, the reredos directly behind the altar and the pierced wood screen separating the chapel and the sanctuary. The screen is constructed of a series of 1x3, 1x6 and 2x6 clear fir arranged in such a manner that light filters through the screen into the sanctuary area. This construction gives privacy for the chapel and is extremely decorative in its over-all effect. These features add a great deal of character to the church.

Saint Mathews Episcopal Church of Parkrose, Oregon, a suburb of Portland, was designed by Architect Don Byers (see page 16) and combines many of the modern features so familiar to the Western church theme, manages to retain enough of the traditional to result in a most pleasing and satisfying church design. Giant parabolic arches form a continuing curved roof system and the large wood members are set firmly in concrete to form the framework for both the roof and the curtain walls. A feature of this distinctive structure is a full wall of glass panels which fit the parabolic shape of the arches. A solid brick wall forms fine texture for the chancel background.

The church is wood framed with plywood sheathing used for bracing. Interior surface of the arch is covered with plywood skin with one-by-four fir boards nailed to this surface spaced one inch apart to give a board-and-batten effect. The exterior of the church features two types of wood finishes: 1x10 cedar lap siding installed horizontally on the low Sunday school wing, and vertical 1x6 fir boards with 2x6 battens. This gives a fine shadow line and the vertical installation

adds height to the structure. This is a most impressive church imparting much charm and dignity.

In the lovely, modern Oak Grove Methodist Church, Stuart B. Mockford, architect from nearby Oregon City (see page 17) has combined native stone and native wood to create a remarkably attractive and beautiful church structure at comparatively low cost. Construction is of solid 8-inch-thick volcanic Tuffa which comes from Sublimity, Oregon, quarries. The rough stone both inside and out, says Architect Mockford, gives an air of stability to the structure. The roof structure and the west end of the building comprising the narthex, youth chapel, and basement is frame. Laminated fir arches support a laminated rough-sawn 2x3-inch roof deck which forms the finished ceiling. Painted off-white, the ceiling catches the indirect lighting and diffuses it all over the church in a very effective manner. A copper clad spire reaches 75 feet into the air and terminates Central Avenue most satisfactorily. It is dramatically lighted at night.

Another church designed by Architect Stuart Mockford is the All Saints Episcopal Church of Woodstock, Portland, (see page 18) which presented the designer with some difficult problems. The church was to be an addition to an already existing frame parish hall, together with the old, original church which has been retained for a Sunday school. Due to the limited (200 by 200 foot) lot and the fact that off-street parking was required by the city, the architect had a time providing the desired 13,800 square feet of floor space and, also, fitting this building within his $185,000 budget.

The new church is completely separated from the older buildings by a fire wall, and the exterior walls are masonry, cavity wall construction with fine Roman brick on the interior and common brick on the exterior. The roof structure is glued laminated fir arches with 2x6 tongue-and-groove, V-joint hemlock laid over purlins to form the ceiling of the church. Perhaps the most novel feature is the long ridge skylight of plexiglass which supplements the north windows to do a fine job of lighting at all times. Another feature is the Chapel of Our Savior, which is so placed at the end of the nave that, by opening a set of large folding doors, it is possible to throw the chapel space into the church and accommodate about 80 additional worshipers. The copper clad spire rising 75 feet has already become a familiar landmark and is especially effective with lighting at night.

The First Baptist Church of Bloomington, Indiana, designed by Architects Sovik, Mathre and Associates, (see page 19), is a modern church with some exciting new design ideas. A combination of Indiana limestone and heavy timber construction was settled on by the architects as the ideal solution. The roof structure throughout depends upon laminated beams and timber deck of two-, three- and four-inch thicknesses, and the architects detailed the building in such a way that

(See Page 30)

NEW FINE ART
BUILDING FOR
UNIVERSITY

Architects Neutra & Alexander, 2379 Glendale Blvd., Los Angeles, are completing plans for construction of a Fine Arts Building at the University of Nevada, Reno.

The new facilities will be 2-story, with basement; 45,000 sq.ft. of area; two wings separated by a Theater, the two wings will provide for music and the silent arts; the theater will have a 300 person capacity; theater classrooms, stage, shop, dressing rooms, related units will be constructed of reinforced concrete with exposed brick walls, metal curtain wall around the art wing.

FRANK J. ANDERSON
PROMOTED DISTRICT
MANAGER AT SEATTLE

Frank J. Anderson has been promoted from outside salesman to district manager of the Seattle, Washington, offices of the Chase Brass & Copper Company, according to a recent announcement by Walter E. Evans, general sales manager of the firm. Evans also announced the retirement of Melvin A. Pugh as district manager there, after 36 years of service with Chase.

Anderson started work at Chase as a mill employee in Waterbury in 1943 and was a section foreman in the Tube Mill when in 1945 he joined the sales force as an inside salesman in their Los Angeles office. Two years later he was promoted to outside salesman at Seattle.

GLOBE HOIST
ACQUIRES PACIFIC
CURTAINWALL

Controlling interest in Pacific Curtainwall, Inc., of Long Beach, California, has been acquired by Globe Hoist Company, manufacturers of automotive hoists and industrial materials handling equipment, firm.

Douglas B. McFarland general manager of Pacific Curtainwall, Inc., will remain with the company continuing its overall management.

HOWARD A. LIBBEY
ELECTED PRESIDENT
REDWOOD ASSOCIATION

Howard A. Libbey, president and general manager of the Arcata Redwood Company, Arcata, California, was elected president of the California Redwood Association at their recent annual meeting. Re-elected were Philip T. Farnsworth, executive vice-president, and Selwyn J. Sharp, secretary-treasurer. Willard E. Pratt was elected to the new post of assistant secretary-treasurer.

In addition to his connections with the Arcata Redwood Company, Libbey is general manager of Hill-Davis Co., Ltd., operators of timberlands.

KAISER GYPSUM COMPANY
APPOINTS ROCKWELL
SALES ENGINEER

Deane W. Rockwell has been appointed technical sales engineer for Kaiser Gypsum Company, according to Colin L. Campbell, sales manager of the company.

He will be responsible for development of new products and systems, sales training programs, field sales of structural gypsum and technical liaison with building code groups, architects and industry associations.

Rockwell was previously architectural

sales representative for Kaiser Gypsum in Southern California, and his new headquarters will be in Oakland.

ROBERT B. McQUARRIE
APPOINTED NORTHWEST
FIELD ENGINEER

Robert B. McQuarrie of Seattle has been assigned Northwest Coast field service engineer for A. M. Byers Company, acocrding to a recent announcement by A. D. Sheere, Byers Pacific Coast Division sales manager.

He was formerly associated with Albers Mining Company of Seattle; Bechtel Corp. of San Francisco and Los Angeles; and the Reynolds Metals Company of Seattle. His offices will be located in Seattle.

BUILDING PERMIT IS
GRANTED FOR BIG
OAKLAND APARTMENTS

The City of Oakland has granted a building permit to Gerson Bakar, Oakland, for the construction of a $1,500,000 apartment house at the corner of 19th Street and Jackson.

The new building will be 12 stories in height and will contain 56 two- and three-bedroom units—286 rooms. It will be "U" shaped and face Lake Merritt; lobby with pool, two levels for parking cars, sun room, glass and steel and reinforced concrete construction.

George Meu, 693 Mission St., San Francisco, is the architect. Fuller & Welisch, San Francisco, Structural Engineers.

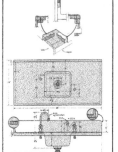

WESTERN CHURCH
ARCHITECTURE

(From Page 28)

the structural qualities of the framing is excellent everywhere.

The cost was about $14.25 a square foot which includes partial air conditioning. The timber is painted in some situations, but, for the most part, has been finished with a dark stain for contrast. The pole and bottom siding is somewhat heavier than the material usually used so that the scale of the building is maintained.

The architect's interest in building canopies over the entrances developed from an attempt to relate interior and exterior spaces and to control some of the exterior space by the partial enclosure the canopies provide and by projecting the canopies out into space to suggest the idea of welcome. The detailing of the ventilation involved a good many space details. As a result, they did not make use of standard windows to any degree.

This is a church with dignity and with maximum utility which uses simplicity as a virtue.

Father Joseph Halloran, of the St. Daniel the Prophet Catholic Church of Ouray, Colorado, (see page 6) deep in the Rockies, when it came time to build a new church, designed the beautiful and distinctive new building for his parish. Here is a church which is a part of the mountains, built of native stone and wood. Texture of these two fine natural materials has been used most efficiently to form the decorative theme for the church. Wood is the predominant material, in evidence everywhere. Upsweeping glued laminated arches form the frame for purlins of fir over which decking has been placed so that decking covering each section is at an angle different from that of adjoining section. This creates an unusually attractive ceiling design. The church steeple is of stone and stands nearly free of the frame structure of the church.

Church design, Western style, continues to ferment. There is no set pattern, even though most architects who have achieved some recognition in church design admit they have welcomed the chance at freedom.

Certainly, there is an unwillingness to depart completely from the traditional, and most architects save some semblance of the old form in one way or another, although in many of the modern, sleek lined, ecclesiastical structures, one must search for a sign that it is a house of worship, at least from an exterior view.

There seems to be little doubt that church design today offers the architect one of his great opportunities for individual expression, for imaginative creation, for satisfying invention, and for freedom to explore new fields. There are limitations, to be sure, but a study of some of the outstanding churches designed and built in these western states during the past year is a rewarding adventure into modern architecture at its best.

Given a set problem, the average architect will take the same basic materials, generally timber and wood, glass and stone, but there the similarity ends. It is absolutely amazing what ten different architects or twenty, or thirty, can make a set of glued laminated arches or beams do. As a matter of fact, it is interesting to see how many different variations of a few basic forms these talented designers can develop.

Each year we are impressed with the churches built in the twelve months just passed. Each year we think we have seen everything, but when another year rolls around and we start our interesting search for the new in churches, we know that here is a field in which man will never be static, never be satisfied, always be reaching and searching for a new way to express his faith. Faith is boundless, and so, apparently, are church designs. For that we are pleased.

CANDLESTICK POINT STADIUM FOR
SAN FRANCISCO GIANTS STARTS

MacDonald, Young & Nelson, Inc., San Francisco Bay Area general contractors have received from Charles L. Harney, Inc., the award for managing the general construction of the Giants' Baseball Stadium at Candlestick Point in San Francisco. Announcement of the award was made by Graeme K. MacDonald, president, and Dallas Young, vice president of MacDonald, Young & Nelson, and Charles L. Harney.

The new baseball stadium will lack nothing in the facilities it will provide both for fans and players. It will seat some 40,000 fans, with a projected future expansion area for 49,000 more. The parking area will have space for 8500 cars.

John S. Boles, San Francisco, is architect for the project.

BUILDINGS FOR RESEARCH. F. W. Dodge Corp., 119 W. 40th St., New York 18. 224 pages. Illustrated. Price $9.50.

A new book by the editors of Architectural Record, presenting surveys of 44 outstanding research facilities with covering commentary and photographs, plus additional longer text sections by men prominent in the field of research building design. Erected by industry, government agencies, universities, and branches of the armed forces, these research projects serve such diverse fields as communications, nuclear energy, textiles, chemistry, medicine, foods and petroleum products. There can be no standard model for a research laboratory; each design is dictated by the operation it houses and each has incorporated the ultimate in flexibility to allow for inexpensive, rapid change-over as new discoveries blast old conceptions.

The book should be of extreme interest to architects, engineers, designers, research directors and all persons charged with planning and devloping research facilities.

THE WEATHER CONDITIONED HOUSE. By Groff Conklin. Reinhold Publishing Corp., 430 Park Ave., New York 22. 237 pages. Illustrated. Price $14.75.

First intensive analysis of the task of making houses fit their total environment. Thoroughly delineated and simplified, the book is directed specifically to residential architects, builders, and contractors; architectural and engineering students; and intelligent laymen.

The Weather Conditioned House presents a comprehensive study of the problems of: general environment, climate, cold weather condensation, hot climate design, heating and cooling equipment, acoustical problems, and materials deterioration.

PARKING. By Geoffrey Baker and Bruno Funaro. Reinhold Publishing Corp., 430 Park Avenue, New York 22, N. Y. Illustrated, 202 pages. Price $9.50.

This book is the first to answer such questions as "Why Is There a Parking Problem", "Where Should the Cars Be Put," "How Much Space Is Really Needed," and "Who's To Pay for It." Here are photographs and plans of parking lots, ramp garages, parking decks, underground garages, and elevator garages. Examples are drawn from large cities and small towns, and range from suburban shopping centers, to downtown stores, from hotels to drive-in banks, from office buildings to fringe parking lots connected to bus to downtown. Special attention is directed to plans for redevelopment of existing cities and there are suggestions for zoning requirements and freight dock areas. There is a special ten page section of easy-to-use diagrams and tables, showing parking patterns and stall sizes for most advantageous use of a given site under various parking conditions. An essential handbook for engineers, architects, town planners, city officials, and planning commission members.

NEW CATALOGUES AVAILABLE

Architects, Engineers, Contractors, Planning Commission members—the catalogues, folders, new building products material, etc., described below may be obtained by directing your request to the name and address given in each item.

Color line—New concept in partitions. New 28-page catalog (A.I.A. File No. 35-H-6) by Unistrut Products Company; shows installations of movable partitions and new ideas in space dividing for office, factories, warehouses and stores with fast, simple assembly saving time and money; typical sections, design, layout, and specifications. Free copy, write DEPT-A&E, Unistrut, 2547 9th St., Berkeley, Calif.

Stagelighting handbook. New 28-page manual for architects, engineers and drama directors to guide them in planning and designing modern stagelighting installations for theater, hotel, school and church. Prepared under the direction of Ariel R. Davis, stagelighting authority; divided into two sections and features many specially prepared illustrations. Free copy, write DEPT-A&E, Ariel Davis Mfg., Co., 3687 South State Street, Salt Lake City 15, Utah.

Integrated ceiling lighting. New brochure (A.I.A. File No. 31-F-231) describes integrated ceiling lighting systems using

recessed lamps; diagrams, charts, specifications. Free copy, write DEPT-A&E, United Lighting and Ceiling Co., 3120 Chapman St., Oakland, California.

- **Pressure treated wood.** New brochure is an architects guide to pressure treated wood, protected from insects, decay and fire; explains conditions that lead to attack and gives corrective measures; photographs, drawings, recommendations. Free copy, write DEPT-A&E, Western Wood Preserving Operators Association, 1410 S. W. Morrison St., Portland 5, Oregon.

Boiler feed systems. New brochure is a quick summary and selection guide to Schaub engineered condensation drainage and automatic boiler feed systems for industrial and heating requirements; numerous drawings, photographs, specifications, installation examples. Free copy, write DEPT-A&E, Fred H. Schaub Engineering Co., 2110 S. Marshall Blvd., Chicago 23, Ill.

Light steel framing. New Booklet presenting some ideas for light-occupancy structures (A.I.A. File No. 13G); features illustrations and descriptive material on residences, service stations, supermarkets, religious structures and apartments. Free copy, write DEPT-A&E, Bethlehem Pacific Coast Steel Corp., San Francisco.

Centrifugal refrigeration. New bulletin features two-stage centrifugal refrigeration compressors; 28 pages, describes features, specifications for evaporator and condenser, instruments, safety controls, capacity control, purge systems, drives and auxiliary equipment; explains and illustrates the complete refrigeration cycle of operation. Free copy write DEPT-A&E, Worthington Corp., Harrison, N. J.

"101 Home ideas." Newly published 24-page, color, book features all 10 of the Western Pine Region species of wood in actual use; displays most popular paneling patterns, both in contour profile drawings and in photos. Free copy write DEPT-A&E, Western Pine Association, Yean Bldg., Portland, Oregon.

"Year round concreting." An 8-page pamphlet summarizes the new American Concrete Institute's standard recommendation (AIA File No. 3-B2) for cold weather concreting; tells how calcium chloride and other developments aid in placing durable, quality concrete in cold weather; includes section on accelerators, preparation before concreting, winter concreting objectives, and production required; charts, guide specifications. Available, write DEPT-A&E, Calcium Chloride Institute, 909 Ring Bldg., Washington 6, D. C.

Sump pumps. Newly revised bulletin (A.I.A. File No. 29-C-1) emphasizes 12 points of superior construction of heavy duty pumps made by Deming; outlines various guide bearing assemblies available; factual data includes ordering data, installation, horsepower, dimensions, optional control equipment, and two pages devoted to smaller residential cellar drainers; diagrams, cut-away drawings and price list. Free copy write DEPT-A&E, Deming Company, Salem, Ohio.

Poured-in-place gypsum roof decks. New 8-page booklet describes nine important advantages of this type roof construction; complete application notes including design data, weight and thermal properties and working drawings for a typical gypsum roof deck construction. Free copy write DEPT-A&E, The Celotex Corp., 120 S. LaSalle St., Chicago 3, Ill.

ARCHITECT AND ENGINEER

ESTIMATOR'S GUIDE

BUILDING AND CONSTRUCTION MATERIALS

PRICES GIVEN ARE FIGURING PRICES AND ARE MADE UP FROM AVERAGE QUOTATIONS FURNISHED BY LeROY CONSTRUCTION SERVICES. 4% SALES TAX ON ALL MATERIALS BUT NOT LABOR. ITEMS IN ITALIC INCLUDE LABOR AND SALES TAX.

BONDS—Performance or Performance plus Labor and Material Bond(s), $10 per $1000 on contract price. Labor and Material Bond(s) only, $5.00 per $1000 on contract price.

BRICKWORK & MASONRY

COMMON BRICKWORK, Reinforced:
- *8" walls* ... *SF 2.95*
- *12" walls* ... *SF 4.15*

SELECT COMMON, Reinforced:
- *8" walls* ... *SF 3.05*
- *12" walls* ... *SF 4.30*

CONCRETE BLOCK, Reinforced:
- *6" walls* ... *SF 1.40*
- *8" walls* ... *SF 1.55*
- *12" walls* ... *SF 1.90*

BRICK VENEER:
- *4" Select Common* ... *SF 1.65*
- *4" Roman* ... *SF 2.50*
- *4" Norman* ... *SF 2.40*
- *4" Aggrelite* ... *SF 2.40*

BRICKWORK & MASONRY

All Prices—F.O.B. Plant.

COMMON BRICK
- Common 2½ x 3¾ x 8¼ ... M 45.00
- Select 2½ x 3¾ x 8¼ ... M 52.00
- Clinker 2½ x ¾ x 8¼ ... M 48.00
- Jumbo 3½ x 3¾ x 11½ ... M 90.00

FACE BRICK
- Standard ... M 59.80 - 83.20
- Jumbo ... M 114.40 - 130.00
- Roman ... M 88.40 - 109.20
- Norman ... M 101.40 - 124.80
- Brik Blox (6") ... M 202.80
- (8") ... M 239.20
- Braile Veneer ... M 26.00

BUILDING TILE
- 8 x 5½ x 12 inches ... M 165.78
- 6 x 5½ x 12 inches ... M 128.96

HOLLOW TILE
- 12 x 12 x 3 inches ... M 163.12
- 12 x 12 x 4 inches ... M 184.18
- 12 x 12 x 6 inches ... M 244.71

MANTEL FIRE BRICK
- 2½ x 9½ x 4½ inches ... M 140.40

GLAZED STRUCTURAL UNITS
- 2 x 6 x 12 Furring ... SF .90
- 4 x 6 x 12 Furring ... SF 1.20
- 6 x 6 x 12 Furring ... SF 1.50
- 4 x 6 x 12 Partition ... SF 1.60
- Add for color ... SF .20

CONCRETE BLOCKS
- 4 x 8 x 16 inches ... EA .22
- 6 x 8 x 16 inches ... EA .265
- 8 x 8 x 16 inches ... EA .30
- 12 x 8 x 16 inches ... EA .435
- Colored Add ... EA .02

AGGREGATE—Haydite or Basalite
- All sizes in bulk ... CY 6.24

BUILDING PAPERS & FELTS

- 1 ply per 1000 ft. roll ... 3.95
- 2 ply per 1000 ft. roll ... 6.03
- 3 ply per 1000 ft. roll ... 8.22
- Sisalkraft, reinf. 500 ft. roll ... 7.54

SHEATHING PAPERS:
- Asphalt sheathing, 15-lb. roll ... 2.40
- 30-lb. roll ... 3.37
- Dampcourse, 216-ft. roll ... 3.05

FELT PAPERS:
- Deadening felt, ¾ lb., 50 ft. roll ... 3.94
- Deadening felt, 1 lb., 50 ft. roll ... 4.60
- Asphalt roofing, 15-lb. ... 2.50
- 30-lb. ... 3.50

ROOFING PAPERS:

Standard Grade, Smooth Surface
- 108 ft. roll, Light, 45 lb. ... 2.26
- Medium 55 lb. ... 2.64
- Heavy 65 lb. ... 3.10
- Mineral Surfaced ... 3.60

CHIMNEYS, PATENT

F.O.B. Warehouse
- 6" ... LF 1.45
- 8" ... LF 2.05
- 10" ... LF 2.85
- 12" ... LF 3.45

Rates for 10 - 50 Lin. Ft.

CONCRETE AGGREGATES

	Bunker Per Ton	Del'd Per Ton
Gravel, All Sizes	3.25	4.00
Top Sand	3.45	4.20
Concrete Mix	3.35	4.20
Crushed Rock		
¼" to ¾"	3.30	4.20
¾" to 1½"	3.30	4.20
Roofing Gravel	3.46	4.15
SAND		
Lapis (Nos. 1 & 2)	4.30	5.10
Olympia (Nos. 1 & 2)	3.60	4.15

CEMENT

Common, All brands (Paper sacks)
- Small quantities, ... Per Sack 1.35
- Large quantities, ... Per bbl. 4.25
- Trinity White & Mendusa White ... Per Sack 4.00

CONCRETE MIX
- 6 sacks in 5-yd. loads ... Per yard 13.40

CURING COMPOUND, Clear
- 5 gal drums ... Per Gal. 1.46

CARPENTRY & MILLWORK

Hardware not included

FRAMING:
- *Floors* ... *BM .20 - .25*
- *Walls* ... *BM .25 - .30*
- *Ceilings* ... *BM .18 - .22*
- *Roofs* ... *BM .22 - .27*
- *Furring & Blocking* ... *BM .30 - .50*

SHEATHING:
- *1 x 8 straight* ... *BM .20 - .25*
- *1 x 8 diagonal* ... *BM .23 - .28*
- *5/16" Plyscore* ... *SF .16 - .20*
- *⅜" Plywood* ... *SF .25 - .30*

SIDING:
- *1 x 8 Bevel* ... *BM .35 - .40*
- *1 x 4 V-Rustic* ... *BM .40 - .45*

EXTERIOR TRIM:
- *Fascia and Molds* ... *BM .40 - .50*

Bolted Framing—Add 50%

ENTRANCE DOORS & FRAMES:
- *Singles* ... *60.00 & Up*
- *Doubles* ... *100.00 & Up*

INTERIOR DOORS & FRAMES:
- *Singles* ... *35.00 & Up*
- *Pocket Sliding* ... *45.00 & Up*
- *Closet Sliding (Pr.)* ... *50.00 & Up*

WINDOWS:
- *D/H Sash & Frames* ... *SF 1.75 & Up*
- *Casement Sash & Frames* ... *SF 1.90 & Up*

SHELVING:
- *1 x 12 S4S* ... *BM .30 - .50*
- *¾" Plywood* ... *SF .40 - .60*

STAIRS:

Oak steps D.F. Risers
- *Under 36" wide* ... *Riser 12.00*
- *Under 60" wide* ... *Riser 17.00*

Newel posts and rail extra

WOOD CASES & CABINETS:
- *D.F. Wall Hung* ... *LF 13.00 - 18.00*
- *D.F. Counters* ... *LF 15.00 - 20.00*

DAMPPROOFING & WATERPROOFING

MEMBRANE:
- *1 layer 50 lb. felt* ... *SQ. 9.00*
- *4 layers Dampcourse* ... *SQ. 13.00*
- *Hot coat walls* ... *SQ. 6.00*
- *Tricosal added to concrete* ... *CY 1.00*
- *Anti-Hydro added to concrete* ... *CY 1.50*

ELECTRIC WIRING

Per Outlet:
- *Knob & Tube* ... *EA 9.00*
- *Armor* ... *EA 16.00*
- *Conduit* ... *EA 20.00*
- *110 V Circuit* ... *EA 25.00*
- *220 V Circuit* ... *EA 95.00*

ELEVATORS & ESCALATORS

Prices vary according to capacity, speed and type. Consult Elevator Companies.

Slow speed apartment house elevator including doors and trim, about $5000.00 per floor.

EXCAVATION

MACHINE WORK in common ground:
- *Large Basements* ... *CY .75 - 1.00*
- *Small Pits* ... *CY 1.25 - 1.75*
- *Trenches* ... *CY 1.50 - 2.25*

HAND WORK in common ground:
- *Large pits and trenches* ... *CY 4.50 - 5.50*
- *Small pits and trimming* ... *CY 5.00 - 6.50*

Hard Clay & Shale 2 times above rates.
Rock and large boulders 4-6 times above rates.
Shoring, bracing and disposal of water not included.

FLOORS

- *⅛" Asp. tile, dark colors* ... *SF .25 - .30*
- *⅛" Asp. tile, light colors* ... *SF .30 - .35*
- *⅛" Rubber tile* ... *SF .60 - .70*
- *.080 Vinyl Asbestos Tile* ... *SF .40 - .45*
- *.080 Vinyl Tile* ... *SF .85 - .95*
- *Lino, Standard Gauge* ... *SY 3.75 - 4.25*
- *Lino, Battleship* ... *SY 5.25 - 5.75*
- *4" Rubber Base, Black* ... *LF .35 - .40*
- *Rubber Stair Nosing* ... *LF 1.00 - 1.75*

Above rates based on quantities of 1000 - 5000 SF per job.

HARDWOOD FLOORS

Select Oak, filled, sanded, stained and varnished:
- *5/16" x 2¼" strip* ... *SF .45 - .50*
- *5/16" Random Plank* ... *SF .50 - .55*
- *25/32" x 2¼" T&G* ... *SF .70 - .80*

Maple, 2nd Grade and Better, filled, sanded, stained and varnished:
- *25/32" x 2¼" T&G* ... *SF .80 - .95*

Wax Finish, add ... *SF .10*

HARDWOOD FLOORING

Oak 5/16" x 2" Strip—
- Clear ... M 229.00
- Select ... M 218.00
- #1 Common ... M 203.00

Oak 5/16" Random Plank—
- Select & Btr. ... M 286.00
- #1 Common ... M 244.00

Oak 25/32" x 2¼" T&G—
- Select ... M 260.00
- #1 Common ... M 203.00

Maple 25/32" x 2¼" T&G—
- #1 Grade ... M 317.00
- #2 Grade ... M 281.00
- #3 Grade ... M 208.00

Nails—1" Floor Brads ... KEG 17.20

GLASS & GLAZING

- *S.S.B. Clear* ... *SF .48*
- *D.S.B. Clear* ... *SF .78*
- *Crystal* ... *SF .92*
- *¼" Plate* ... *SF 2.17*
- *⅛" Obscure* ... *SF .68*
- *⅛" Heat Absorbing* ... *SF 1.12*
- *¼" Tempered Plate* ... *SF 4.38*
- *½" Tempered Plate* ... *SF 7.84*
- *¼" Wire Plate, Clear* ... *SF 3.65*
- *¼" Wire Plate, Rough* ... *SF 1.08*

GLASS—CUT TO SIZE

F.O.B. Warehouse
- S.S.B. Clear, Av. 6 SF ... SF .34
- D.S.B. Clear, Av. 10 SF ... SF .56
- Crystal, Av. 35-SF ... SF .65
- ¼" Polished Plate, Av. 100 SF ... SF 1.55
- ⅛" Obscure, Av. 10 SF ... SF .49
- ⅛" Ribbed, Av. 10 SF ... SF .49
- ⅛" Rough, Av. 10 SF ... SF .49
- ¼" Wire Plate, Clear, Av. 40 SF ... SF 2.61
- ¼" Wire Plate, Rough, Av. 40 SF ... SF .77
- ⅛" Heat Absorbing, Av. 10 SF ... SF .80
- ¼" Tempered Plate, Av. 50 SF ... SF 3.60
- ½" Tempered Plate, Av. 50 SF ... SF 6.88

Glazing—Approx. 40-50% of Glass

Glass Blocks—
- 6" ... .57
- 8" ... .92
- 12" ... 2.39

HEATING

FURNACES—Gas Fired—Av. Job:

FLOOR FURNACE:
- *25,000 BTU* ... *100.00 - 125.00*
- *35,000 BTU* ... *107.00 - 135.00*
- *45,000 BTU* ... *115.00 - 130.00*

AUTOMATIC CONTROL:
- *Add* ... *25.00 - 35.00*

HEATING—Cont'd

DUAL WALL FURNACE:		
25,000 BTU		*110.00 - 125.00*
35,000 BTU		*125.00 - 145.00*
50,000 BTU		*150.00 - 180.00*
AUTOMATIC CONTROL:		
Add		*25.00 - 35.00*
GRAVITY FURNACE:		
75,000 BTU		*375.00 - 450.00*
85,000 BTU		*425.00 - 525.00*
95,000 BTU		*475.00 - 600.00*
FORCED AIR FURNACE:		
Add		*75.00 - 125.00*
AUTOMATIC CONTROL:		
Add		*15.00 - 25.00*
HEAT REGISTERS:		
Outlet		*7.50 - 15.00*

INSULATION & WALLBOARD

F.O.B. Warehouse

ROCKWOOL Insulation—		
2" Semi-thick	Per M SF	60.60
3⅝" Full Thick	Per M SF	77.40
COTTON Insulation		
1" Full Thick	Per M SF	43.26
SOFTBOARDS—Wood Fiber—		
½" thick	Per M SF	84.00
1½" thick	Per M SF	275.00
2" thick	Per M SF	385.00
ALUMINUM Insulation—		
80# Kraft paper with alum. foil		
1 side only	Per M SF	18.30
2 sides	Per M SF	31.00
GYPSUM Wallboard—		
⅜" thick	Per M SF	49.50
½" thick	Per M SF	54.50
⅝" thick	Per M SF	83.00
⅜" Gyplap	Per M SF	85.00
HARDBOARDS—Wood Fiber—		
⅛" thick, Sheathing	Per M SF	84.00
3/16" thick, Sheathing	Per M SF	90.48
¼" thick, Sheathing	Per M SF	109.20
⅛" thick, Tempered	Per M SF	108.00
3/16" thick, Tempered	Per M SF	186.00
¼" thick, Tempered	Per M SF	194.48
CEMENT Asbestos Board—		
⅛" C.A.B. Flat Sheets	Per M SF	151.20
3/16" C.A.B. Flat Sheets	Per M SF	208.80
¼" C.A.B. Flat Sheets	Per M SF	270.01

LATH & PLASTER

Diamond 3.40 copper bearing	SY	.56
Ribbed 3.40 copper bearing	SY	.62
⅜" rock lath	SY	.36
1½" Standard Channel	LF	.062
¾" Standard Channel	LF	.045
3¼" steel studs	LF	.092
4" steel studs	LF	.107
Stud shoes	EA	.028
Hardwall, Browning	Sack	1.45
Hardwall, Finish	Sack	1.70
Stucco	Sack	2.50

LATH & PLASTERWORK

CHANNEL FURRING:		
Suspended Ceilings	*SY*	*2.20 - 2.50*
Walls	*SY*	*2.30 - 2.60*
METAL STUD PARTITIONS:		
3¼" Studs	*SY*	*1.70 - 2.00*
4" Studs	*SY*	*1.95 - 2.25*
Over 10'0 high, add	*SY*	*.20 - .30*
3.40 METAL LATH AND PLASTER:		
Ceilings	*SY*	*3.60 - 4.00*
Walls	*SY*	*3.75 - 4.15*
KEENE'S CEMENT FINISH:		
Add	*SY*	*.40 - .60*
ROCK LATH & PLASTER:		
Ceilings	*SY*	*2.50 - 2.80*
Walls	*SY*	*2.60 - 2.90*
WIRE MESH AND ⅞" STUCCO:		
Walls	*SY*	*3.60 - 4.10*
STUCCO ON CONCRETE:		
Walls	*SY*	*2.30 - 2.80*
METAL ACCESSORIES	*LF*	*.20 - .50*

LINOLEUM

Lino. Standard Gauge	SY	2.65 - 2.85
Lino. Battleship	SY	2.95 - 3.11
⅛" Asp. tile, Dark	SF	.10 - .11
⅛" Asp. tile, Light	SF	.14 - .16
⅛" Rubber Tile	SF	.40 - .44
.080 Vinyl tile	SF	.20 - .21
.080 Vinyl Asb. tile	SF	.18 - .19
⅛" Vinyl tile	SF	.78 - .82
4" Base, Dark	LF	.15 - .16
4" Base, Light	LF	.24 - .26
Rubber Nosing	LF	.60 - 1.30
Lino Paste	GAL	.75 - .90

Above rates based on quantities of 1000-5000 SF per job.

LUMBER

DOUGLAS FIR:	M.B.M.
#1 2x4—2x10	88.00 - 92.00
#2 2x4—2x10	85.00 - 90.00
#3 2x4—2x10	68.00 - 74.00
#4 2x4—2x10	64.00 - 72.00
Clear, Air Dried	180.00 - 210.00
Clear, Kiln Dried	210.00 - 240.00
REDWOOD:	
Foundation Grade	120.00 - 130.00
Construction Heart	110.00 - 120.00
A Grade	180.00 - 210.00
Clear Heart	190.00 - 220.00
D.F. PLYWOOD	M.S.F.
¼" AB	95.00 - 105.00
¼" AD	90.00 - 95.00
¼" Ext. Waterproof	115.00 - 125.00
⅜" AB	130.00 - 145.00
⅜" AD	115.00 - 125.00
⅜" CD	70.00 - 85.00
½" AB	170.00 - 185.00
½" AD	110.00 - 115.00
½" CD	....
⅝" AB	185.00 - 200.00
⅝" AD	165.00 - 180.00
⅝" CD	115.00 - 125.00
¾" AB	210.00 - 230.00
¾" AD	195.00 - 210.00
¾" CD	125.00 - 140.00
⅝" Plyform	160.00 - 170.00
SHINGLES:	Square
Cedar #1	14.00 - 15.50
Cedar #2	11.50 - 12.50
SHAKES:	
CEDAR	
½ to ¾" Butt	17.50 - 18.50
¾ to 1¼" Butt	18.50 - 19.50
REDWOOD	
¾ to 1¼" Butt	21.00 - 24.00

MILLWORK

All Prices F.O.B. Mill

D.F. CLEAR, AIR DRIED:		
S4S	MBM	220.00 - 250.00
D.F. CLEAR, KILN DRIED:		
S4S	MBM	225.00 - 275.00
DOOR FRAMES & TRIM:		
Residential Entrance		17.00 & up
Interior Room Entrance		7.50 & up
DOORS:		
1⅜" D.F. Slab, Hollow Core		8.00 & up
1¾" D.F. Slab, Solid Core		19.00 & up
1⅜" Birch Slab, Hollow Core		10.00 & up
1¾" Birch Slab, Solid Core		22.00 & up
WINDOW FRAMES:		
D/H Singles	SF	.80
Casement Singles	SF	.90
WOOD SASH:		
D/H in pairs (1 lite)	SF	.45
Casement (1 lite)	SF	.50
WOOD CABINETS:		
¾" D.F. Ply with ¼" ply backs		
Wall Hung	LF	10.00 - 15.00
Counter	LF	12.00 - 17.00

BIRCH OR MAPLE—Add 25%

PAINT

All Prices F.O.B. Warehouse

Thinners—5-100 gals.	GAL.	.57
Turpentine—5-100 gals.	GAL.	1.58
Linseed Oil, Raw	GAL.	2.51
Linseed Oil, Boiled	GAL.	2.57
Primer-Sealer	GAL.	3.10
Enamel	GAL.	5.45
Enamel Undercoaters	GAL.	5.45
White Lead in Oil	LB.	.35
Red Lead in Oil	LB.	.35
Litharge	LB.	.30

PAINTING

EXTERIOR:		
Stucco Wash 1 ct.	*SY*	*.30*
Stucco Wash 2 cts	*SY*	*.55*
Lead and Oil 2 cts	*SY*	*.90*
Lead and Oil 3 cts	*SY*	*1.30*
INTERIOR:		
Primer Sealer	*SY*	*.40*
Wall Paint, 1 ct.	*SY*	*.50*
Wall Paint, 2 cts	*SY*	*.95*
Enamel, 1 ct.	*SY*	*.60*
Enamel, 2 cts	*SY*	*1.10*
Doors and Trim	*EA*	*10.00*
Sash and Trim	*EA*	*12.00*
Base and Molds	*LF*	*.12*

Old Work—Add 15-30%

PLUMBING

Lavatories	*EA*	*100.00 - 150.00*
Toilets	*EA*	*200.00 - 300.00*
Bath Tubs	*EA*	*250.00 - 350.00*
Stall Shower	*EA*	*80.00 - 150.00*
Sinks	*EA*	*125.00 - 175.00*
Laundry Trays	*EA*	*80.00 - 130.00*
Water Heaters	*EA*	*100.00 - 300.00*

Prices based on average residential and commercial work. Special fixtures and excessive piping not included.

ROOFING

STANDARD TAR & GRAVEL	Per Square
4 ply	*14.00 - 18.00*
5 ply	*17.00 - 20.00*
White Gravel Finish—Add	*2.00 - 4.00*
Asph. Compo. Shingles	*16.00 - 20.00*
Cedar Shingles	*20.00 - 24.00*
Cedar Shakes	*26.00 - 30.00*
Redwood Shakes	*28.00 - 34.00*
Clay Tiles	*40.00 - 50.00*

SEWER PIPE

VITRIFIED:		
Standard 4 in.	LF	.31
Standard 6 in.	LF	.56
Standard 8 in.	LF	.81
Standard 12 in.	LF	1.76
Standard 24 in.	LF	6.95
CLAY DRAIN PIPE:		
Standard 6 in.	LF	.34
Standard 8 in.	LF	.59

Rate for 100 Lin. Ft. F.O.B. Warehouse

STEEL

REINFORCING BARS:		
¼" rounds	LB	.122
⅜" rounds	LB	.111
½" rounds	LB	.107
⅝" rounds	LB	.104
¾" rounds	LB	.102
⅞" rounds	LB	.102
1" rounds	LB	.102
REINFORCING MESH (1050 SF Rolls)		
6x6 x 10x10	SF	.035
6x6 x 6x6	SF	.067
16 GA. TYING WIRE	LB	.130

Rates 100-1000 Lbs. F.O.B. Warehouse

STRUCTURAL STEEL

$325.00 and up per ton erected when out of mill.
$350.00 and up per ton erected when out of stock.

SHEET METAL

ROOF FLASHINGS:		
18 ga. Galv. Steel	*SF*	*.60 - 1.00*
22 ga. Galv. Steel	*SF*	*.50 - .90*
26 ga. Galv. Steel	*SF*	*.40 - .80*
18 ga. Aluminum	*SF*	*1.00 - 1.50*
22 ga. Aluminum	*SF*	*.80 - 1.30*
26 ga. Aluminum	*SF*	*.60 - 1.10*
24 oz. Copper	*SF*	*1.90 - 2.40*
20 oz. Copper	*SF*	*1.70 - 2.20*
16 oz. Copper	*SF*	*1.50 - 2.00*
26 ga. Galv. Steel		
4" o.g. gutter	*LF*	*.90 - 1.30*
Mitres and Drops	*EA*	*2.00 - 4.00*
22 ga. Galv. Louvres	*SF*	*2.50 - 3.50*
20 oz. Copper Louvres	*SF*	*3.00 - 4.50*

TILE WORK

CERAMIC TILE, Stock colors:		
Floors	*SF*	*1.95 - 2.45*
Walls	*SF*	*2.05 - 2.55*
Coved Base	*LF*	*1.05 - 1.45*
QUARRY TILE:		
6" x 6" x ½" Floors	*SF*	*1.60 - 2.00*
9" x 9" x ¾" Floors	*SF*	*1.75 - 2.15*
Treads and risers	*LF*	*3.00 - 4.50*
Coved Base	*LF*	*.90 - 1.30*

Mosaic Tile — Rates vary with design and colors. Each job should be priced from Manufacturer.

TERRAZZO & MARBLE

Terrazzo Floors	*SF*	*2.00 - 2.50*
Cond. Terr. Floors	*SF*	*2.20 - 2.75*
Precast treads and risers	*LF*	*3.50 - 4.50*
Precast landing slabs	*SF*	*3.00 - 4.00*

TILE

CERAMIC:

F.O.B. Warehouse

4¼" x 4¼" glazed	SF	.69
4¼" x 4¼" hard glazed	SF	.72
Random unglazed	SF	.73
6" x 2" cap	EA	.17
6" coved base	EA	.22
¼" round bead	LF	.18
QUARRY:		
6 x 6 x ½" Red	SF	.49
6 x 6 x ¾" Red	SF	.52
9 x 9 x ¾" Red	SF	.60
6 x 6" coved base	EA	.21
White Cement Grout	Per 100 Lbs.	6.25

VENETIAN BLINDS

Residential	SF	.40 & Up
Commercial	SF	.45 & Up

WINDOWS

STEEL SASH:		
Under 10 SF	SF	2.50 & Up
Under 15 SF	SF	2.00 & Up
Under 20 SF	SF	1.50 & Up
Under 30 SF	SF	1.00 & Up
ALUMINUM SASH:		
Under 10 SF	SF	2.75 & Up
Under 15 SF	SF	2.25 & Up
Under 20 SF	SF	1.75 & Up
Under 30 SF	SF	1.25 & Up

Above rates are for standard sections and stock sizes F.O.B. Warehouse

CONSTRUCTION INDUSTRY WAGE RATES

Table 1 has been prepared by the State of California, Department of Industrial Relations, Division of Labor Statistics and Research. The rates are the union hourly wage rates established by collective bargaining as of January 2, 1958, as reported by reliable sources.

TABLE 1—UNION HOURLY WAGE RATES, CONSTRUCTION INDUSTRY, CALIFORNIA

Following are the hourly rates of compensation established by collective bargaining, reported as of January 2, 1958 or later

CRAFT	San Francisco	Alameda	Contra Costa	Fresno	Sacramento	San Joaquin	Santa Clara	Solano	Los Angeles	San Bernardino	San Diego	Santa Barbara	Kern
ASBESTOS WORKER	$3.70	$3.70	$3.70	$3.70	$3.70	$3.70	$3.70	$3.70	$3.70	$3.70	$3.70	$3.70	$3.70
BOILERMAKER	3.675	3.675	3.675	3.675	3.675	3.675	3.675	3.675	3.675	3.675	3.675	3.675	3.675
BRICKLAYER	3.95	3.75	3.75	3.75	3.80	3.75	3.875	3.95	3.80	3.90	3.75		3.85
BRICKLAYER HODCARRIER	3.15	3.15	3.15	2.90	3.10	2.90	3.00	3.10	2.75	2.75	2.75		2.75
CARPENTER	3.175	3.175	3.225	3.225	3.225	3.225	3.225	3.225	3.225	3.225	3.225	3.225	3.225
CEMENT MASON	3.22	3.22	3.22	3.22	3.22	3.22	3.22	3.22	3.15	3.15	3.25	3.15	3.15
ELECTRICIAN	3.936A	3.936A	3.936A		3.94A	3.50	4.03A	3.666A	3.90A	3.90A	3.90	3.85A	3.70
GLAZIER	3.09	3.09	3.09	3.135	3.055	3.055	3.09	3.09	3.105	3.105	3.03	3.105	3.135
IRON WORKER													
ORNAMENTAL	3.625	3.625	3.625	3.625	3.625	3.625	3.625	3.625	3.625	3.625	3.625	3.625	3.625
REINFORCING	3.375	3.375	3.375	3.375	3.375	3.375	3.375	3.375	3.375	3.375	3.375	3.375	3.375
STRUCTURAL	3.625	3.625	3.625	3.625	3.625	3.625	3.625	3.625	3.625	3.625	3.625	3.625	3.625
LABORER, GENERAL OR CONSTRUCTION	2.505	2.505	2.505	2.505	2.505	2.505	2.505	2.505	2.50	2.50	2.48	2.50	2.50
LATHER	3.4375	3.84	3.84	3.45	3.60B	3.40c	3.60D	3.50E	3.9375		3.725	3.625F	
OPERATING ENGINEER													
Concrete mixer (up to 1 yard)	2.89	2.89	2.89	2.89	2.89	2.89	2.89	2.89					
Concrete mixer operator—Skip Type									2.96	2.96	2.96	2.96	2.96
Elevator Hoist Operator									3.19	3.19	3.19	3.19	3.19
Material Hoist (1 drum)	3.19	3.19	3.19	3.19	3.19	3.19	3.19	3.19					
Tractor Operator	3.33	3.33	3.33	3.33	3.33	3.33	3.33	3.33	3.47	3.47	3.47	3.47	3.47
PAINTER													
Brush	3.20	3.20	3.20	3.13	3.325	3.175	3.20	3.20	3.26G	3.25	3.19	3.13H	3.10
Spray	3.20	3.20	3.20	3.38	3.575	3.325	3.20	3.20	3.51G	3.50	3.74	3.38H	3.35
PILEDRIVERMAN	3.305	3.305	3.305	3.305	3.305	3.305	3.305	3.305	3.355	3.355		3.355	3.355
PLASTERER	3.69	3.645	3.645	3.35	3.60B	3.56	3.50	3.9375	3.9375	3.725			
PLASTERER HODCARRIER	3.25	3.42	3.42	3.10	3.10	3.00c	3.20	3.15	3.6875	3.5625	3.475	3.50	3.6875
PLUMBER	3.67		3.935I	3.80J	3.70	3.80J	3.60	3.675	3.70	3.70	3.70	3.70	3.375
ROOFER	3.35	3.35	3.35	3.20	3.25	3.35	3.35	3.10K	3.20L	3.25	3.10	3.30	3.775
SHEET METAL WORKER	3.45	2.45	3.45	3.425	3.45	3.465	3.45	3.325	3.50	3.50	3.45	3.55	3.10
STEAMFITTER	3.67	3.96	3.96	3.80J	3.70	3.80J	3.60	3.675	3.70	3.70	3.70	3.70	3.775
TRUCK DRIVER— Dump Trucks under 4 yards	2.55	2.55	2.55	2.55	2.55	2.55	2.55	2.55	2.63	2.63	2.63	2.63	2.63
TILE SETTER	3.275	3.275	3.275	3.375	3.28	3.30	3.275	3.275	3.36	3.60	3.375	3.36	

A Includes 4% vacation allowance.
B Includes 5c hour for industry promotion and 5c hour for vacation fund.
C ½% withheld for industry promotion.
D 1½c withheld for industry promotion.
E Includes 5c hour for industry promotion and 5c hour for vacation fund.
F Northern part of County: $3.75.
G Pomona Area: Brush $3.25; Spray $3.50.
H Southern half of County: Brush $3.28; Spray $3.28.
I Includes 30c hour for vacation pay.
J Includes 15c hour which local union may elect to use for vacation purposes.
K Includes 10c hour for vacation fund.
L Includes 10c hour savings fund wage.

Hourly rate for part of county adjacent to Sacramento County is $3.60.

ATTENTION: The above tabulation has been prepared by the State of California, Department of Industrial Relations, Division of Labor Statistics and Research, and represents data reported by building trades councils, union locals, contractor organizations, and other reliable sources. The above rates do not include any payments to funds for health and welfare, pensions, vacations, industry promotion, apprentice training, etc., except as shown in the footnotes.

CONSTRUCTION INDUSTRY WAGE RATES — TABLE 2

Employer Contributions to Health and Welfare, Pension, Vacation and Other Funds
California Union Contracts, Construction Industry

(Revised March, 1957)

CRAFT	San Francisco	Fresno	Sacramento	San Joaquin	Santa Clara	Los Angeles	San Bernardino	San Diego
ASBESTOS WORKER	.10 W .11 hr. V	.10 W .11 hr. V	.10 W .11 hr. V	.10 W .11 hr. V	.10 W .11 hr. V	.10 W	.10 W	.10 W
BRICKLAYER	.15 W .14 P .05 hr. V		.15 W .10 P		.15 W			
BRICKLAYER HODCARRIER	.10 W .10 P .10 V	.10 W	.10 W	.10 W	.10 W	.075 W	.075 W	.075 W
CARPENTER	.10 W .10 hr. V	.10 W	.10 W	.10 W	.10 W	.10 W	.10 W	.10 W
CEMENT MASON	.10 W	.10 W	.10 W	.10 W	.10 W	.10 W	.10 W	.10 W
ELECTRICAL WORKER	.10 W 1% P 4% V	.10 W 1% P 4% V	.075 W 1% P	.075 W 1% P 4% V	1% P	1% P	1% P	.10 W 1% P
GLAZIER	.075 W .085 V	.075 W 40 hr. V	.075 W .05 V	.075 W .05 V	.075 W .085 V	.075 W 40 hr. V	.075 W 40 hr. V	.075 W 10 hr. V
IRONWORKER: REINFORCING	.10 W	.10 W	.10 W	.10 W	.10 W	.10 W	.10 W	.10 W
STRUCTURAL	.10 W	.10 W	.10 W	.10 W	.10 W	.10 W	.10 W	.10 W
LABORER, GENERAL	.10 W	.10 W	.10 W	.10 W	.10 W	.075 W	.075 W	.075 W
LATHER	.60 day W .70 day V		.10 W	.10 W	.075 W .05 V	.90 day W	.70 day W	.10 W
OPERATING ENGINEER TRACTOR OPERATOR (MIN.) POWER SHOVEL OP. (MIN.)	.10 W .10 W	.10 W .10 W	.10 W .10 W	.10 W .10 W	.10 W .10 W	.10 W .10 W	.10 W .10 W	.10 W .10 W
PAINTER, BRUSH	.095 W	.08 W	.075 W	.10 W	.095 W .07 V	.085 W	.08 W	.09 W
PLASTERER	.10 W .10 V	.10 W	.10 W	.10 W	.10 W .15 V	.10 W	.90 day W	.10 W
PLUMBER	.10 W .10 V	.15 W .10 P	.10 W .10 P .125 V	.10 W	.10 W .10 P .125 V	.10 W	.90 day W	.10 W
ROOFER	.10 W .10 V	.10 W	.10 W .10 V	.10 W	.075 W .10 V	.085 W	.10 W	.075 W
SHEET METAL WORKER	.075 W 4% V	.075 W 7 day V	.075 W .10 V	.075 W .12 V	.075 W 4% V	.085 W .10 V	.085 W .10 V	.085 W 5 day V
TILE SETTER	.075 W .09 V				.075 W .09 V	.025 W .06 V		

ATTENTION: The above tabulation has been prepared and compiled from the available data reported by building trades councils, union locals, contractor organizations and other reliable sources. The table was prepared from incomplete data; where no employer contributions are specified, it does not necessarily mean that none are required by the union contract.

The type of supplement is indicated by the following symbols: W—Health and Welfare; P—Pensions; V—Vacations; A—Apprentice training fund; Adm—Administration fund; JIB—Joint Industry Board; Prom—Promotion fund.

ESTIMATOR'S DIRECTORY
Building and Construction Materials

ACOUSTICAL ENGINEERS
L. D. REEDER CO.
San Francisco: 1255 Sansome St., DO 2-5050
Sacramento: 3026 V St., GL 7-3505

AIR CONDITIONING
E. C. BRAUN CO.
Berkeley: 2115 Fourth St., TH 5-2356
GILMORE AIR CONDITIONING SERVICE
San Francisco: 1617 Harrison St., UN 1-2000
KAEMPER & BARRETT
San Francisco: 233 Industrial St., JU 6-6200
LINFORD AIR & REFRIGERATION CO.
Oakland: 174-12th St., TW 3-6521
JAMES A. NELSON CO.
San Francisco: 1375 Howard St., HE 1-0140

ALUMINUM BLDG. PRODUCTS
MICHEL & PFEFFER IRON WORKS (Wrought Iron)
So. San Francisco: 212 Shaw Road, PLaza 5-8983
REYNOLDS METALS CO.
San Francisco: 3201 Third St., MI 7-2990
UNIVERSAL WINDOW CO.
Berkeley: 950 Parker St., TH 1-1600

ARCHITECTURAL PORCELAIN ENAMEL
CALIFORNIA METAL ENAMELING CO.
Los Angeles: 6904 E. Slauson, RA 3-6351
San Francisco: Continental Bldg. Products Co.,
178 Fremont St.
Portland: Portland Wire & Iron Works,
4644 S.E. Seventeenth Ave.
Seattle: Foster-Bray Co., 2412 1st Ave. So.
Spokane: Bernhard Schafer, Inc., West 34, 2nd Ave.
Salt Lake City: S. A. Roberts & Co., 109 W. 2nd So.
Dallas: Offenhauser Co., 2201 Telephone Rd.
El Paso: Architectural Products Co.,
506 E. Yandell Blvd.
Phoenix: Haskell-Thomas Co., 3808 No. Central
San Diego: Maloney Specialties, Inc., 823 W. Laurel St.
Boise: Intermountain Glass Co., 1417 Main St.

ARCHITECTURAL & AERIAL PHOTOGRAPHS
FRED ENGLISH
Belmont, Calif.: 1310 Old County Road, LY 1-0385

ARCHITECTURAL VENEER
Ceramic Veneer
GLADDING, McBEAN & CO.
San Francisco: Harrison at 9th St., UN 1-7400
Los Angeles: 2901 Los Feliz Blvd., OL 2121
Portland: 110 S.E. Main St., EA 6179
Seattle 99: 945 Elliott Ave., West, GA 0330
Spokane: 1102 N. Monroe St., BR 3259
KRAFTILE COMPANY
Niles, Calif., Niles 3611

Porcelain Veneer
PORCELAIN ENAMEL PUBLICITY BUREAU
Oakland 12: Room 601, Franklin Building
Pasadena 8: P. O. Box 186, East Pasadena Station

Granite Veneer
VERMONT MARBLE COMPANY
San Francisco 24: 6000 3rd St., VA 6-5024
Los Angeles: 3522 Council St., DU 2-6339

Marble Veneer
VERMONT MARBLE COMPANY
San Francisco 24: 6000 3rd St., VA 6-5024
Los Angeles: 3522 Council St., DU 2-6339

BANKS - FINANCING
CROCKER-ANGLO NATIONAL BANK
San Francisco: 13 Offices

BLINDS
PARAMOUNT VENETIAN BLIND CO.
San Francisco: 5929 Mission St., JU 5-2436

BRASS PRODUCTS
GREENBERG'S, M. SONS
San Francisco 7: 765 Folsom, EX 2-3143
Los Angeles 23: 1258 S. Boyle, AN 3-7108
Seattle 4:1016 First Ave. So., MA 5140
Phoenix: 3009 N. 19th Ave., Apt. 92, PH 2-7663
Portland 4: 510 Builders Exch. Bldg., AT 6443

BRICKWORK
Face Brick
GLADDING McBEAN & CO.
San Francisco: Harrison at 9th, UN 1-7400
KRAFTILE CO.
Niles, Calif., Niles 3611
UNITED MATERIALS & RICHMOND BRICK CO.
Point Richmond, BE 4-5032

BRONZE PRODUCTS
GREENBERG'S M. SONS
San Francisco: 765 Folsom St., EX 2-3143
MICHEL & PFEFFER IRON WORKS
So. San Francisco: 212 Shaw Road, PLaza 5-8983
C. E. TOLAND & SON
Oakland: 2635 Peralta St., GL 1-2580

BUILDING HARDWARE
E. M. HUNDLEY HARDWARE CO.
San Francisco: 662 Mission St., YU 2-3322

BUILDING PAPERS & FELTS
PACIFIC CEMENT & AGGREGATES INC.
San Francisco: 400 Alabama St., KL 2-1616

CABINETS & FIXTURES
CENTRAL MILL & CABINET CO.
San Francisco: 1595 Fairfax Ave., VA 4-7316
THE FINK & SCHINDLER CO.
San Francisco: 552 Brannan St., EX 2-1513
MULLEN MFG. CO.
San Francisco: 64 Rausch St., UN 1-5815
PARAMOUNT BUILT IN FIXTURE CO.
Oakland: 962 Stanford Ave., OL 3-9911
ROYAL SHOWCASE CO.
San Francisco: 770 McAllister St., JO 7-0311

CEMENT
CALAVERAS CEMENT CO.
San Francisco: 315 Montgomery St.
DO 2-4224, Enterprise 1-2315
PACIFIC CEMENT & AGGREGATES INC.
San Francisco: 400 Alabama St., KL 2-1616

CONCRETE AGGREGATES
Ready Mixed Concrete
PACIFIC CEMENT & AGGREGATES INC.
San Francisco: 400 Alabama St., KL 2-1616
Sacramento: 16th and A Sts., GI 3-6586
San Jose: 790 Stockton Ave., CY 2-5620
Oakland: 2400 Peralta St., GL 1-0177
Stockton: 820 So. California St., ST 8-8643
RHODES-JAMIESON LTD.
Oakland: 333-23rd Ave., KE 3-5225

CONCRETE ACCESSORIES
Screed Materials
C. & H. SPECIALTIES CO.
Berkeley: 909 Camelia St., LA 4-5358

CONCRETE BLOCKS
BASALT ROCK CO.
Napa, Calif.

CONCRETE COLORS—HARDENERS
CONRAD SOVIG CO.
875 Bryant St., HE 1-1345

CONSTRUCTION SERVICES
LE ROY CONSTRUCTION SERVICES
San Francisco, 143 Third St., SU 1-8914

DECKS—ROOF
UNITED STATES GYPSUM CO.
2322 W. 3rd St., Los Angeles 54, Calif.
300 W. Adams St., Chicago 6, Ill.

DOORS
THE BILCO COMPANY
New Haven, Conn.
Oakland: Geo. B. Schultz, 190 MacArthur Blvd.
Sacramento: Harry B. Ogle & Assoc., 1331 T St.
Fresno: Healey & Popovich, 1703 Fulton St.
Reseda: Daniel Dunner, 6200 Alonzo Ave.

Electric Doors
ROLY-DOOR SALES CO.
San Francisco, 5976 Mission St., PL 5-5089

Folding Doors
WALTER D. BATES & ASSOCIATES
San Francisco, 693 Mission St., GA 1-6971

Hardwood Doors
BELLWOOD CO. OF CALIF.
Orange, Calif., 533 W. Collins Ave.

Hollywood Doors
WEST COAST SCREEN CO.
Los Angeles: 1127 E. 63rd St., AD 1-1108
T. M. COBB CO.
Los Angeles & San Diego
HOGAN LUMBER CO.
Oakland: 700 - 6th Ave.
HOUSTON SASH & DOOR
Houston, Texas
SOUTHWESTERN SASH & DOOR
Phoenix, Tucson, Arizona
El Paso, Texas
WESTERN PINE SUPPLY CO.
Emeryville: 5760 Shellmound St.
GEO. C. VAUGHAN & SONS
San Antonio & Houston, Texas

DRAFTING ROOM EQUIPMENT
GENERAL FIREPROOFING CO.
Oakland: 332-19th St., GL 2-4280
Los Angeles: 1200 South Hope St., RI 7-7501
San Francisco: 1025 Howard St., HE 1-7070

DRINKING FOUNTAINS
HAWS DRINKING FAUCET CO.
Berkeley: 1435 Fourth St., LA 5-3341

ELECTRICAL CONTRACTORS
COOPMAN ELECTRIC CO.
San Francisco: 85 - 14th St., MA 1-4438

ELECTRICAL CONTRACTORS (cont'd)

LEMOGE ELECTRIC CO.
San Francisco: 212 Clara St., DO 2-6010

LYNCH ELECTRIC CO.
San Francisco: 937 McAllister St., WI 5158

PACIFIC ELECTRIC & MECHANICAL CO.
San Francisco: Gough & Fell Sts., HE 1-5904

ELECTRIC HEATERS

WESIX ELECTRIC HEATER CO.
San Francisco: 390 First St., GA 1-2211

FIRE ESCAPES

MICHEL & PFEFFER IRON WORKS
South San Francisco: 212 Shaw Road, PLaza 5-8983

FIRE PROTECTION EQUIPMENT

FIRE PROTECTION PRODUCTS CO.
San Francisco: 1101-16th St., UN 1-2420

BARNARD ENGINEERING CO.
San Francisco: 35 Elmira St., JU 5-4642

FLOORS

Floor Tile

GLADDING McBEAN & CO.
San Francisco: Harrison at 9th St., UN 1-744
Los Angeles: 2901 Las Feliz Bldg., OL 2121

KRAFTILE CO.
Niles, Calif., Niles 3611

Resilient Floors

PETERSON-COBBY CO.
San Francisco: 218 Clara St., EX 2-8714

TURNER RESILIENT FLOORS CO.
San Francisco: 2280 Shafter Ave., AT 2-7720

FLOOR DRAINS

JOSAM PACIFIC COMPANY
San Francisco: 765 Folsom St., EX 2-3142

GAS VENTS

WM. WALLACE CO.
Belmont, Calif.

GENERAL CONTRACTORS

BARRETT CONSTRUCTION CO.
San Francisco: 1800 Evans Ave., MI 7-9700

JOSEPH BETTANCOURT
South San Francisco: 125 So. Linden St., PL 5-9185

DINWIDDIE CONSTRUCTION CO.
San Francisco: Crocker Bldg., YU 6-2718

D. L. FAULL CONSTRUCTION CO.
Santa Rosa: 1236 Cleveland Ave.

HAAS & HAYNIE
San Francisco: 275 Pine St., DO 2-0678

HENDERSON CONSTRUCTION CO.
San Francisco: 33 Ritch St., GA 1-0856

JACKS & IRVINE
San Francisco: 620 Market St., YU 6-0511

RALPH LARSEN & SON
San Francisco: 64 So. Park, YU 2-5682

LINDGREN & SWINERTON
San Francisco: 200 Bush St., GA 1-2980

MacDONALD, YOUNG & NELSON
Oakland: 8907 Railroad Ave.

MATTOCK CONSTRUCTION CO.
San Francisco: 220 Clara St., GA 1-5516

RAPP, CHRISTENSEN & FOSTER
Santa Rosa: 705 Bennett Ave.

STOLTE, INC.
Oakland: 8451 San Leandro Ave., LO 2-4611

SWINERTON & WALBERG
San Francisco: 200 Bush St., GA 1-2980

FURNITURE—INSTITUTIONAL

GENERAL FIREPROOFING CO.
San Francisco: 1025 Howard St., HE 1-7070
Oakland: 332-19th St., GL 2-4280
Los Angeles: 1200 South Hope St., RI 7-7501

HEATING & VENTILATING

ATLAS HEATING & VENT. CO.
San Francisco: 557-4th St., DO 2-0377

E. C. BRAUN CO.
Berkeley: 2115 Fourth St., TH 5-2356

S. T. JOHNSON CO.
Oakland: 940 Arlington Ave., OL 2-6000

LOUIS V. KELLER
San Francisco: 289 Tehama St., JU 6-6252

L. J. KRUSE CO.
Oakland: 6247 College Ave., OL 2-8332

JAS. A. NELSON CO.
San Francisco: 1375 Howard St., HE 1-0140

SCOTT COMPANY
Oakland: 1919 Market St., GL 1-1937

WESIX ELECTRIC HEATER CO.
San Francisco: 390 First St., GA 1-2211
Los Angeles: 530 W. 7th St., MI 8096

INSULATION WALL BOARD

PACIFIC CEMENT & AGGREGATES, INC.
San Francisco: 400 Alabama St., KL 2-1616

INTERCEPTING DEVICES

JOSAM PACIFIC CO.
San Francisco: 765 Folsom St., EX 2-3142

IRON—ORNAMENTAL

MICHEL & PFEFFER IRON WKS.
So. San Francisco, 212 Shaw Rd., PL 5-8983

LATHING & PLASTERING

ANGELO J. DANERI
San Francisco: 1433 Fairfax Ave., AT 8-1582

K-LATH CORP.
Alhambra: 909 So. Fremont St., Alhambra

A. E. KNOWLES CORP.
San Francisco: 3330 San Bruno Ave., JU 7-2091

G. H. & C. MARTINELLI
San Francisco: 174 Shotwell St., UN 3-6112

PATRICK J. RUANE
San Francisco: 44 San Jose Ave., MI 7-6414

LIGHTING FIXTURES

SMOOT-HOLMAN COMPANY
Inglewood, Calif., OR 8-1217
San Francisco: 55 Mississippi St., MA 1-8474

LIGHTING & CEILING SYSTEMS

UNITED LIGHTING AND FIXTURE CO.
Oakland: 3120 Chapman St., KE 3-8711

LUMBER

CHRISTENSEN LUMBER CO.
San Francisco: Quint & Evans Ave., VA 4-5832

ART HOGAN LUMBER CO.
San Francisco: 1701 Galvez Ave., ATwater 2-1157

ROLANDO LUMBER CO.
San Francisco: 5th & Berry Sts., SU 1-6901

WEST COAST LUMBERMEN'S ASS'N
Portland 5, Oregon

MARBLE

JOS. MUSTO SONS-KEENAN CO.
San Francisco: 555 No. Point St., GR 4-6365

VERMONT MARBLE CO.
San Francisco: 6000-3rd St., VA 6-5024

MASONRY

BASALT ROCK CO.
Napa, Calif.
San Francisco: 260 Kearney St., GA 1-3758

WM. A. RAINEY & SON
San Francisco: 323 Clementina St., SU 1-0072

GEO. W. REED CO.
San Francisco: 1390 So. Van Ness Ave., AT 2-1226

METAL EXTERIOR WALLS

THE KAWNEER CO.
Berkeley: 930 Dwight Way, TH 5-8710

METAL FRAMING

UNISTRUT OF NORTHERN CALIFORNIA
Berkeley: 2547-9th St., TH 1-3031
Enterprise 1-2204

METAL GRATING

KLEMP METAL GRATING CORP.
Chicago, Ill.: 6601 So. Melvina St.

METAL LATH—EXPANDED

PACIFIC CEMENT & AGGREGATES, INC.
San Francisco: 400 Alabama St., KL 2-1616

METAL PARTITIONS

THE E. F. HAUSERMAN CO.
San Francisco: 485 Brannan St., YU 2-5477

METAL PRODUCTS

FORDERER CORNICE WORKS
San Francisco: 269 Potrero Ave., HE 1-4100

MILLWORK

CENTRAL MILL & CABINET CO.
San Francisco: 1595 Fairfax Ave., VA 4-7316

THE FINK & SCHINDLER CO.
San Francisco: 552 Brannan St., EX 2-1513

MULLEN MFG. CO.
San Francisco: 64 Rausch St., UN 1-5815

PACIFIC MFG. CO.
San Francisco: 16 Beale St., GA 1-7755
Santa Clara: 2610 The Alameda, S. C. 607
Los Angeles: 6820 McKinley Ave., TH 4156

SOUTH CITY LUMBER & SUPPLY CO.
So. San Francisco: Railroad & Spruce, PL 5-70P5

OFFICE EQUIPMENT

GENERAL FIREPROOFING CO.
Los Angeles: 1200 South Hope St., RI 7-7501
San Francisco: 1025 Howard St., HE 1-7070
Oakland: 332-19th St., GL 2-4280

OIL BURNERS

S. T. JOHNSON CO.
Oakland: 940 Arlington Ave., GL 2-6000
San Francisco: 585 Potrero Ave., MA 1-2757
Philadelphia, Pa.: 401 North Broad St.

ORNAMENTAL IRON

MICHEL & PFEFFER IRON WORKS
So. San Francisco: 212 Shaw Rd., PL 5-8983

PAINTING

R. P. PAOLI & CO.
San Francisco: 2530 Lombard St., WE 1-1632

SINCLAIR PAINT CO.
San Francisco: 2112-15th St., HE 1-2196

D. ZELINSKY & SONS
San Francisco: 165 Groove St., MA 1-7400

PHOTOGRAPHS

Construction Progress
FRED ENGLISH
Belmont, Calif.: 1310 Old County Road, LY 1-0385

PLASTER

PACIFIC CEMENT & AGGREGATE INC.
San Francisco: 400 Alabama St., KL 2-1616

PLASTIC PRODUCTS

PLASTIC SALES & SERVICE
San Francisco: 409 Bryant St., DO 2-6433

WEST COAST INDUSTRIES
San Francisco: 3150-18th St., MA 1-5657

San Francisco: 930 Innes Ave., VA 4-3261

ROOF SCUTTLES
THE BILCO CO.
New Haven, Conn.
Oakland: Geo. B. Schultz, 190 MacArthur Blvd.
Sacramento: Harry B. Ogle & Assoc., 1331 T St.
Fresno: Healey & Ropovich, 1703 Fulton St.
Reseda: Daniel Dunner, 6200 Alonzo Ave.

ROOF TRUSSES
EASYBOW ENGINEERING & RESEARCH CO.
Oakland: 13th & Wood Sts., GL 2-0805
SUMMERBELL ROOF STRUCTURES
San Francisco: 420 Market St., EX 7-2796

SAFES
THE HERMANN SAFE CO.
San Francisco: 1699 Market St., UN 1-6644

SEWER PIPE
GLADDING, McBEAN & CO.
San Francisco: 9th & Harrison, UN 1-7400
Los Angeles: 2901 Los Feliz Blvd., OL 2121

STEEL FORMS
STEELFORM CONTRACTING CO.
San Francisco: 666 Harrison St., DO 2-5582

SWIMMING POOLS
SIERRA MFG. CO.
Walnut Creek, Calif.: 1719 Mt. Diablo Blvd.

SWIMMING POOL FITTINGS
JOSAM PACIFIC CO.
San Francisco: 765 Folsom St., EX 2-3143

TESTING LABORATORIES
(ENGINEERS & CHEMISTS
ABBOT A. HANKS, INC.
San Francisco: 624 Sacramento St., GA 1-1697
ROBERT W. HUNT COMPANY
San Francisco: 500 Iowa, MI 7-0224
Los Angeles: 3050 E. Slauson, JE 9131
Chicago, New York, Pittsburgh
PITTSBURGH TESTING LABORATORY
San Francisco: 651 Howard St., EX 2-1747

WALL PAPER
WALLPAPERS, INC.
Oakland: 384 Grand Ave., GL 2-0451

WAREHOUSE AND STORAGE EQUIPMENT AND SHELVING
GENERAL FIREPROOFING CO.
Los Angeles: 1200 South Hope St., RI 7-7501
San Francisco: 1025 Howard St., HE 1-7070
Oakland: 332-19th St., GL 2-4280

WATERPROOFING MATERIALS
CONRAD SOVIG CO.
San Francisco: 875 Bryant St., HE 1-1345

WATERSTOPS (P.V.C.)
TECON PRODUCTS, LTD.
Vancouver, B.C.: 681 E. Hastings St.
Seattle: 2 Hanford St.

WINDOW SHADES
SHADES, INC.
San Francisco: 80 Tehama St., DO 2-7092

CONSTRUCTION CONTRACTS AWARDED AND MISCELLANEOUS PERSONNEL DATA

2 DORMITORIES, Chapman College, Orange county. Chapman College, Orange, owner. Work consists of construction of boys' and girls' dormitories at the Chapman College; two-stories to accommodate 133 persons each; concrete and masonry construction with 55,000 sq. ft. of area—$738,493. ARCHITECT: Rule & Conkle, Architects and Engineers, 2835 Gilroy St., Los Angeles. GENERAL CONTRACTOR: Harwick & Son, Inc., 2254 Cahuenga Blvd., Hollywood.

VARIETY STORE, Monterey Park, Los Angeles county. Crawford's Modern Village Stores. Inc., El Monte, owner. 1-story and partial second floor variety store; includes excavating, concrete work, masonry, reinforcing steel, structural steel, lathing and plastering, roofing, insulation, sheet metal, glass and glazing, metal doors and frames, metal toilet partitions, automatic door operators, terrazzo, ceramic tile, ventilating and air conditioning, automatic fire sprinklers, and asphaltic paving in parking area. ENGINEER: Richard N. Jasper, Civil Engineer, 1610 Beverly Blvd., Los Angeles. GENERAL CONTRACTOR: Conant & Liberman, 5951 Venice Blvd., Los Angeles.

MARYMOUNT COLLEGE, Palos Verdes, Los Angeles county. Order of Sacred Heart of Mary, Palos Verdes, owner. Work includes site preparation, grading and excavating at the new Marymount College; construction will include 12 separate buildings consisting of administration, library, classrooms, theater, dining rooms, residence halls, convent, fine arts building and social halls; accommodations for 300 students. ARCHITECT: Montgomery & Mullay, 1109 N. Vermont Ave., Los Angeles. GENERAL CONTRACTOR: J. A. McNeil, 3115 W. Mission Road, Alhambra.

SHOP BLDG., Arcadia, Los Angeles county. William Jeffries, Arcadia, owner. 1-Story concrete block shop building; 1780 sq. ft. in area, composition and gravel roofing, plate glass windows, overhead doors, concrete slab floors, exposed block interior walls, exposed rafters, asphalt paving in yard. ENGINEER: Clyde Carpenter & Associates, Consulting Engineers, 614 S. Peck Rd., Monrovia. GENERAL CONTRACTOR: Worrell Construction Co., 1425 S. Myrtle Ave., Monrovia.

AUTO SALES & SERVICE, Fontana, San Bernardino county. Frank Mosher, Fontana, owner. 2-Story concrete block and frame and stucco auto sales and service building; 9000 sq. ft. of area, plate glass, composition roof, glued laminated beams, structural steel, toilet facilities, vinyl floors, interior plaster, slab doors, acoustical tile,

39

fluorescent lighting, automatic turntable, pneumatic tube, winter and summer air conditioning, black-top yard paving, concrete curbs and sidewalks — $88,000. ARCHITECT: Jay Wheaton, 333 No. Riverside Ave., Rialto. GENERAL CONTRACTOR: L. J. Construction Co., P.O. Box 606, Bloomington.

WAREHOUSE & OFFICE, Glendale, Los Angeles county. Havaskamp, Yates & Richardson, Glendale, owner. Reinforced brick warehouse and offices building, 49 x 153 ft., composition roof, tapered steel girders, plywood sheting, concrete slab floors, overhead doors, office partitions, asphalt paving — $60,000. GENERAL CONTRACTOR: Don Hatfield, 633 N. Brand Blvd., Glendale.

HIGH SCHOOL ADDN., Montebello, Los Angeles county. Montebello Unified School District, owner. 2-Story light steel frame and concrete 20-classroom addition to the Montebello High School—$355,000. ARCHITECT: Kistner, Wright & Wright, 1125 W. 6th St., Los Angeles. GENERAL CONTRACTOR: A. J. Marek, 450 La Merced Ave., Montebello.

PARISH HALL, Oakland, Alameda county. St. Paschal Parish, Oakland, owner. Concrete block construction of a new parish hall in Oakland, glu-laminated beams, tar and gravel roof—$108,417. ARCHITECT: Albert Hunter, Jr., and Shig Iyama, Architects and Associates, 656 31st St., Oakland. GENERAL CONTRACTOR: Samson Const. Co., 856 98th AVE., Oakland.

HALL OF JUSTICE, San Francisco. City and County of San Francisco, owner. Seven story hall of justice building, marble facing; adjacent 1-story building with roof deck parking; 637,000 sq. ft. of area—$13,508,800. ARCHITECT: Weihe, Frick & Kruse, 414 Mason St., San Francisco, and San Francisco City Architect, Charles W. Griffiths, City Hall, San Francisco. STRUCTURAL ENGINEER: Hall, Pregnoff & Matheu, 251 Kearny St., San Francisco. MECHANICAL & ELECTRICAL ENGINEERS: G. M. Simonson, 517 Howard St., San Francisco. GENERAL CONTRACTOR: M. & K. Corp., 519 California St., San Francisco.

WAREHOUSE ADDN., Los Angeles. Arrowhead Brass, Los Angeles, owner. Work comprises an addition to present warehouse building, 50 x 86 ft. in area, metal roof, exterior brick work, concrete slab floor, structural steel and security sash—$13,000. ENGINEER: H. M. Hansen, Structural Engineer, 5549 N. Rosemead Blvd., Temple City.

ELEMENTARY SCHOOL, Lancaster, Los Angeles county. Mariposa Elementary School, Lancaster, owner. New School plant, all steel construction; 6-classrooms, 2 kindergartens, administration buildings, multi-purpose building, steel roof deck, aluminum sash, concrete slab and vinyl asbestos tile flooring, suspended acoustical ceilings, forced air heating, outdoor dining area, asphaltic concrete, covered walks, site work turfing and sprinklers—$578,000. ARCHITECT: Roy Donley, 8320 Melrose

Ave., Los Angeles. GENERAL CONTRACTOR: Calcor Corp., 3383 E. Gage, Huntington Park.

COUNTY OFFICE BLDG., Stockton, San Joaquin county. County of San Joaquin, Stockton, owner. 1-Story building, 2,000 sq. ft. of area, light steel frame and concrete construction—$61,642. ARCHITECT: Clowdsley & Whipple, 142 No. Calif. St., Stockton. GENERAL CONTRACTOR: E. L. French, 1731 Oxford Way, Stockton.

SCHOOL ADMINISTRATION BLDG., Hanford, Kings county. Kings County School District, Hanford, owner. Reinforced brick, glu-laminated beams—$109,400. ARCHITECT: Lawrence B. Alexander, 128 E. 8th St., Hanford GENERAL CONTRACTOR: R. G. Fisher Const. Co., P.O. Box 4081, Fresno.

CHURCH EDUCATIONAL BLDG., Bakersfield, Kern county. First Baptist Church, Bakersfield, owner. 1-Story concrete frame, concrete, wood and rock roofing, concrete and asphalt tile floors, forced air heating, block curtain walls, acoustical tile, evaporative cooler system—$81,995. ARCHITECT: Whitney Biggar, 3601 Stockdale Highway, Bakersfield. GENERAL CONTRACTOR: Joe B. King Const. Co., 2909 Barnett St., Bakersfield.

ELECTRONICS LABORATORY, Palo Alto, Santa Clara county. Philco Co., Redwood City, owner. Construction includes two wings to present building, 2,000 sq. ft. area, tilt-up concrete slab construction, 100 x 120 ft. office area—$400,000. DESIGNER: Simpson & Stratta, 325 5th St., San Francisco. GENERAL CONTRACTOR: Johnson & Mape Const. Co., 540 Santa Cruz Ave., Menlo Park.

OFFICE BLDG., Van Nuys, Los Angeles county. A. G. Hoiby, Encino, owner. Work comprises alterations to present office building interior; interior partitions, plaster, acoustical tile, asphalt tile, flooring, electrical work—$20,000. ARCHITECT: Welton Becket and Associates, 5657 Wilshire Blvd., Los Angeles.

CARMEL HIGH SCHOOL, Carmel, Monterey county. Carmel Unified School District, Carmel, owner. Work comprises an addition to the Administration Bldg.—$44,000. ARCHITECT: Elston & Cranston, 6th & Junipero, Carmel. GENERAL CONTRACTOR: Joseph B. Fratessa, P.O. Box 430, Monterey.

WAREHOUSE & OFFICE, Los Angeles. James Wood, Los Angeles, owner. Precast concrete, dock high, warehouse and office building; 14,000 sq. ft. area, tapered steel beams, excavation and earth fill, ornamental concrete block, plumbing, electrical, metal sash, spur track, truck doors, asphalt paving. ENGINEER: David T. Witherly, Engineer, 7233 Beverly Blvd., Los Angeles. GENERAL CONTRACTOR: Carpenter & Smallwood, 3838 W. Santa Barbara Ave., Los Angeles.

MFG. PLANT, South San Francisco, San Mateo county. Dux, Inc., San Francisco, owner. 1-Story plant and office building, 46,000 sq. ft. in area. Additional office and plant space to be constructed later. Office of wood frame construction; plant of tilt-

of area, tapered steel girders, plumbing, electrical, aluminum loading doors, demolition of present buildings on site, panelized roof, fire sprinkler system. ENGINEER: Novikoff Engineers, 3858 W. Santa Barbara Ave., Los Angeles. GENERAL CONTRACTOR: Carpenter & Smallwood, 3838 W. Santa Barbara Ave., Los Angeles.

BANK BLDG., Stockton, San Joaquin county. Bank of Stockton, Stockton, owner. Work comprises two structures 1 and 2 stories high, type 1 construction, full basement with drive-in teller's window, off street parking facilities — $824,000. ARCHITECT: Mayo, De Wolf & Associates, Exchange Bldg., Stockton. GENERAL CONTRACTOR: Shepherd & Green, P.O. Box 1078, Stockton.

COMMERCIAL BLDG., Los Angeles. Zeigler & Fagin, Los Angeles, owner. Brick commercial building, composition roofing, tapered steel girders, concrete slab floors, metal windows, plumbing, electrical decorative concrete block walls, plate glass and asphaltic paving. ENGINEER: David T. Witherly, Engineer, 7233 Beverly Blvd., Los Angeles. GENERAL CONTRACTOR: Carpenter & Smallwood, 3838 W. Santa Barbara Ave., Los Angeles.

ELEMENTARY SCHOOL, Orangevale, Sacramento county. Orangevale School District, Orangevale, owner. New elementary school building, 1-story, wood with structural steel frame: to provide facilities for 7 classrooms, administration room, toilets—$250,000. ARCHITECT: Barovetto & Thomas, 718 Alhambra Blvd., Sacramento. GENERAL CONTRACTOR: Robert E. Hart, 3808 Walnut, Carmichael.

WAREHOUSE & OFFICE, Los Angeles. James Wood and Richard Newton, Los Angeles, owners. Pre-cast concrete warehouse and office building, 33,000 sq. ft. in area, composition roofing, tapered steel girders, dock-high floor, plumbing, electrical, glass and glazing. ENGINEER: David T. Wetherly, Engineer, 7233 Beverly Blvd., Los Angeles. GENERAL CONTRACTOR: Carpenter & Smallwood, 3838 W. Santa Barbara Ave., Los Angeles.

CHURCH ADDN., Castro Valley, Alameda county. Methodist Church of Castro Valley, owner. Concrete block construction of a new Fellowship Hall—$86,000. ARCHITECT: Gerald M. McCue & Associates, 2007 Hopkins St., Berkeley. GENERAL CONTRACTOR: C. A. Gossett & Sons, 10084 Madison Ave., Castro Valley.

MARKET, El Monte, Los Angeles county. Safeway Stores, El Monte, owner. Concrete tilt-up and glass market building: 21,000 sq. ft., of area, composition roofing, concrete slab floors, plumbing, electrical, air conditioning, asphalt paving. ARCHITECT: Chapman & McCorkell, Thomas W. McCorkell, Architect, 9304

OFFICE BLDG., Bakersfield, Kern county. Kern County Title Company, Bakersfield, owner. 1-story, 7,200 sq. ft. in area, wood frame, stucco, brick, composition roofing, concrete floors, air conditioning, asphaltic concrete paving, metal lath, wood sash, wood roof trusses — $76,985. ARCHITECT: C. Barton Alford, 15161 California Ave., Bakersfield. GENERAL CONTRACTOR: Reil & Terry, 1120 Greenwood Drive, Bakersfield.

PARK FACILITIES, Pomona. City of Pomona, owner. Work comprises construction of new facilities at Kellogg Park — $30,500. ARCHITECT: Everett L. Tozier, 556 N. Park Ave., Pomona. GENERAL CONTRACTOR: Lee C. Hess, Box 1168, Pomona.

FIRE STATION, Richmond, Contra Costa county. City of Richmond, owner. Steel frame construction, concrete block, built-up roofing, concrete slab floors — $108,200. ARCHITECT: Donald Hardison & Associates, 160 Broadway, Richmond. GENERAL CONTRACTOR: Marvin E. Collins, 635 San Diego St., El Cerrito.

OFFICE BLDG., Los Angeles. Shoppers Market, Los Angeles, owner. 2-story office building, masonry and frame construction, built-up roofing, slab, wood and asphalt tile floors, metal sash, acoustical work, air conditioning, ceramic tile, plastering, plumbing, sheet metal work, asphalt concrete paving, electrical, structural steel—$100,000. ARCHITECT: Leach & Cleveland, Ron Cleveland, Architect, 434 S. Robertson Blvd., Los Angeles. GENERAL CONTRACTOR: Edward M. Pozzo, 1052 W. 6th St., Los Angeles.

CHAPEL BLDG., Yountville, Napa county. State of California, Sacramento, owner. 1-story new chapel building at the California Veterans Home, 7,600 sq. ft. of area, concrete and concrete block con-

Bldg., Salt Lake City, Utah.

WAREHOUSE & OFFICE, Los Angeles. Willy P. Daetwyler, Los Angeles, owner. New warehouse and office building, 110,000 sq. ft. in area, tilt-up concrete construction, structural steel, built-up roofing, slab floors, metal sash, metal doors, electrical, plumbing, asphalt tile floors, paving.

IN THE NEWS

JOHN A. NELSON
CONTRACTORS
IN NEW OFFICE
John A. Nelson, Inc., General Contractors, have recently moved into new general offices at 1734 Mission Street, San Francisco.
The firm was formerly located at 430 West Portal, San Francisco.

NEW ASSOCIATES
APPOINTED TO
FIRM
The appointment of four new associates, Borice Boris, Olive Emslie, John Gilchrist and John Kerr to the architectural

firm of Victor Gruen Associates, has been announced.
Boris is in charge of the electrical engineering department with nineteen years experience; is a graduate of the California Institute of Technology and attended the University of California at Berkeley.
Olive Emslie is a designer in the New York office and is a graduate of Cornell University.
John Gilchrist is color consultant and head of the Graphics Department, and a graduate of the Institute of Design of the Illinois Institute of Technology.
Kerr is chief mechanical engineer and a graduate of the University of Arizona. He attended Cornell University and the University of Southern California and is also a registered professional engineer and a member of the American Society of Mechanical Engineers.

EXCHANGE BANK
BUILDS BRANCH
AT SANTA ROSA
The Exchange Bank of Santa Rosa, Sonoma county, has announced plans to build an $80,000 branch bank building in the City of Santa Rosa.
The single-story concrete block building, composition roof, and completely air conditioned, will contain some 3,500 sq. ft. of area.
Plans are being prepared by architects Steel & Van Dyke, 3960 Montgomery St., Santa Rosa.

KENDALL R. PECK
APPOINTED GENERAL
SALES MANAGER
Kendall R. Peck has been appointed general sales manager for the Montebello fabricating division plant of Kaiser Steel company, according to a recent announcement by Jack J. Carlson, vice president and general manager.
A native of Oakland, California, Peck is a graduate of Stanford University; is member of the Structural Engineers Association of Southern California and is prior to joining Kaiser Steel's sales department in 1954, was associated with Leonard Bosch, contractors of San Francisco.

NEW CITY HALL
PLANNED FOR
ALHAMBRA
Architect William Allen, 6112 Wilshire Blvd., Los Angeles, is preparing drawings for construction of a new 2-story, type 1, City Hall for the Alhambra City Commissioners; 42,520 sq.ft. of area; construction will include composition roofing, metal

sash, concrete slab floor, electric, plumbing, ornamental concrete block, two elevators and council chamber with a seating capacity of 124, Civil Defense office and maintenance rooms.

NEW 150 AMPERE
FUSIBLE SERVICE
EQUIPMENT
Wadsworth's new 150 Ampere main lugs only device is 3 pole, solid neutral directly attached to cabinet, 120-240 volt a.c. has recently been announced.

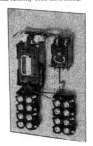

Has one 100 ampere Main Light Renu-Fuse unit and one 60 Ampere Range, or other use, Renu-Fuse unit, which are wired to the line terminals. The line slugs on the lighting unit are double lugs. In addition there are 16 plug fuse circuits and sub-feed Terminals, which are controled by the 100 Ampere main light Renu-Fuse unit. Construction is either surface or flush mounting with dead front, and finished in durable baked blue-gray enamel. Complete data from The Wadsworth Electric Mfg. Co., Inc., Covington, Ky.

NEW HIGH SCHOOL
BEING PLANNED
FOR SAN CARLOS
Architect Delp W. Johnson, 166 Geary Street, San Francisco, is preparing preliminary drawings for construction of a new High School at San Carlos for the Sequoia Union High School District of Redwood City.
The facilities will be a completely new High School building. Estimated cost is $2,500,000.

EDGARDO CONTINI
NAMED ASSOCIATE
PLANNER MEMBER
Edgardo Contini, engineer-planner and partner in the Architectural firm of Victor Gruen Associates, Los Angeles, has been appointed an Associate Member of The American Institute of Planners.
As chief engineer for the Gruen firm, Contini is in charge of the Los Angeles County Parking Garage project, the $13,000,000 Wilshire Terrace Apartments in Beverly Hills, and the $10,000,000 downtown Los Angeles office building for Tishman Realty and Construction Company.

SITE PURCHASED
FOR SAN ANSELMO
SUPER MARKET
Architect Jacob Van Der Ploeg, 2378 39th Ave., San Francisco, is preparing drawings for construction of a new super-

market to be built on a site recently acquired in San Anselmo by R. A. Conyer of San Pablo, California.

To cost $750,000, the building will be of tilt-up concrete construction, 10-ft., cantilevered canopy and acoustical ceilings. Work is scheduled to begin immediately following demolition of buildings on the site.

SIEGLER CORP. NAMES TWO NEW OFFICERS

Dan W. Burns and Robert T. Campion have been elected vice presidents of the Siegler Corporation of Los Angeles, by action of the Board of Directors, according to an announcement by John G. Brooks, firm president.

Campion, who joined the electronics firm in 1957 as secretary of the corporation, will continue to hold that position along with his new duties. Earlier in the year, Burns was named president of The Hufford Corp., a Siegler subsidiary located in El Secundo, California.

TWAITS-WITTENBERG COMPANY LOS ANGELES CONSTRUCTORS PUBLISH BOOK OF WORKS

The Twaits-Wittenberg Co., Los Angeles, constructors and engineers, has just released a book which documents its construction accomplishments during the past 40-years, its services, and construction approach.

The book describes various operations, including job management and such extended services as joint-ventures, site selection, and financing. Among some of the projects depicted are The Pershing Square Garage, Santa Fe Dam, Ramo-Wooldridge

Research and Development Center, and the Methodist Hospital of Southern California at Arcadia.

REVOLUTIONARY NEW CEILING HEATER

New ceiling mounted electric bathroom heater has just been announced by Thermador Electrical Mfg. Co., of Los Angeles, California.

Among important and desirable features is its flush-to-ceiling mounting. No rough-in box required since it is U.L. approved for surface mounting to a standard 3" or 4" junction box (with or without a plaster ring). Neoprene gasket on rim conforms to any irregularities of ceiling surface and allows snug clean fit.

Completely erosion proof with stainless steel rim and aluminum grille and reflector; instant radiant heat is provided from nickel chrome heating coil supported by ceramic bushings and mounted below polished aluminum reflector. Air is circulated by a 4-blade 6½" fan. Complete data from

Thermador Electrical Mfg. Co., 5119 District Blvd., Los Angeles 22.

JR. HIGH SCHOOL IS PLANNED FOR BORON

Architect Ernest L. McCoy, 2811 "H" St., Bakersfield, is preparing plans and specifications for construction of a 7th and 8th grade junior high school in Boron, Kern county, for the Muroc Unified School District at Edwards.

The 1-story, 13,980-sq. ft. in area building will be of concrete block construction, concrete and asphalt tile flooring, metal lath, ornamental iron, plaster, reinforced steel, sheet metal, steel sash, steel roof trusses, tile work, and asphaltic concrete paving. Estimated cost is $270,000.

NEW MORTUARY IS PLANNED FOR UPLAND

Architect Pierre Woodman, 191 "F" N. Euclid Ave., Upland, is completing plans for construction of a 1-story frame, stucco and stone mortuary building to be known as "The Stone Mortuary" in Upland.

Construction will include mortuary facilities and will represent 9,000 sq.ft. of area; glued laminated arches, rock and composition roofing, plate glass and aluminum store front, two air conditioning units, and patio gardens.

STROMBERG-CARLSON APPOINTS WETHERILL CHIEF ENGINEER

Clarence A. Wetherill has been appointed Chief Engineer of Stromberg-Carlson at San Diego, according to an announce-

ment by Harold P. Field, General Manager.

Wetherill has been Assistant Chief Engineer of Stromberg-Carlson, San Diego, since joining the organization in August 1957, and prior to that was Assistant Chief Electronics Engineer and head of the Electronic Development Group for Convair at San Diego.

DORMITORY BUILDING PLANNED FOR VILLA CABRINI ACADEMY

Architects Baker and Ott, 4334 W. Pico, Los Angeles, have completed plans for construction of a dormitory building at

the Villa Cabrini Academy, Burbank, for the Missionary Sisters of the Sacred Heart.

The building will contain 5200 sq. ft. of area, will be of reinforced brick construction, composition roofing, metal sash, asphalt tile flooring, interior plaster, forced air heating, plumbing, electrical, ornamental iron railings, insulation and shelving. Estimated cost is $75,000.

HUGH D. BARNES APPOINTED BY PORTLAND CEMENT ASSOCIATION

Hugh D. Barnes has been appointed to the position of Supervisor of Field Promotion for the Portland Cement Association, according to an announcement by G. Donald Kennedy, Association President.

Barnes has been serving as Manager of the Western Regional Offices in Los Angeles since 1956, and his new duties will take him to Chicago, where he will direct and have complete authority and responsibility for all operations of the Association's 32 district and 6 regional offices. John M. McNerney, District Engineer for the Association's Los Angeles office will succeed Barnes as Western Regional Manager.

HIGH SCHOOL ADDITION FOR LOMPOC PLANNED

Architect Pierre Claeyssens, 11941 Wilshire Blvd., Los Angeles is preparing plans for construction of a 1 and 2-story, concrete block addition to the Lompoc High School.

The work will include shop building, science building, library, and 3 classrooms.

Construction will be a composition roof, concrete and wood floor, painting, plastering, plumbing, electrical work, heating, ventilating, acoustical, ceramic tile, structural metal and sheet metal. The estimated cost of the project is $600,000.

NEW ALL PURPOSE LIGHTING FIXTURE IS NOW AVAILABLE

Complete versatility, unrivaled beauty, outstanding efficiency and unbelievable economy are featured in this new island lighting fixture known as the Golden-T.

It combines the finest idea in styling and design with newest decor for accenting its beauty! gives high light output over a wide area, as well as concentrated light pattern on the island itself; available at surprisingly low initial cost and has low operating and maintenance costs. Accommodates all popular types of fluorescent lamps. Complete data and specifications from the manufacturer, Guardian Light Company, Oak Park, Ill.

FRANK D. ROBERTS APPOINTED TO POSITION

Frank D. Roberts of Seattle, Washington, has been appointed to the Technical Services Department of the Western Red Cedar Lumber Association, Arthur I. Ellsworth. secretary-manager announced recently.

Roberts, a consulting engineer, will engage in field service work for Western Cedar directed primarily to architects and builders, with the objective of the service to aid in developing accurate specifications and proper building methods for best sidewall performance.

VOTERS APPROVE BONDS FOR SCHOOL

Voters of the Placerville School District, El Dorado county, recently approved the issuance of $140,000 in school bonds for the purpose of constructing a new school building in the City of Placerville.

A State Aid Grant in an amount of $750,000 was also obtained for the project. Architect Raymond R. Franceschini, Sacramento, has been commissioned by the school district to draw plans and specifications for the new building.

CONCRETE AND AGGREGATE PRODUCERS ORGANIZE NEW ASSOCIATION

The formation of a national joint cooperative committee by the National Sand and Gravel Association, the National Ready-Mix Concrete Association, and the Associated General Contractors of America, has been completed and will be known as the Concrete and Aggregate Producers-

Associated General Contractors Joint Co-operative Committee.

The joint committee was especially needed because of important problems arising from the vast expansion of highway construction under the long-range federal-aid program and the steady increase in the dollar volume of construction activity in general. Objectives will be to provide a medium for the discussion of problems affecting members of the three associations and the formulation of recommendations concerning them for the consideration of the parent organizations.

Among those selected to serve the new activity were: Robert Mitchell, Consolidated Rock Products Co., Los Angeles; John W. Murphy, Union Sand & Gravel Co., Spokane, Washington; R. W. McKinney, Nacognaches, Texas; B. B. Armstrong, Armstrong & Armstrong, Roswell, New Mexico; and D. J. Mooney, Cahill-Mooney Const. Co., Butte, Montana.

COLLEGE CHURCH BUILDING FOR LOMA LINDA

The architectural firm of Farrar, Hudson & Associates, 661 Highway 99, San Bernardino, has completed plans for construction of a 2-story reinforced concrete, reinforced masonry and frame and stucco church building at the campus of the College of Medical Evangelists at Loma Linda.

The new building will contain 44,000 sq.ft. of area and will comprise a chapel, sanctuary, classrooms, business offices and storage rooms.

PRESTRESSED CONCRETE INSTITUTE ELECTS NEW OFFICERS

At the annual Prestressed Concrete Institute meetings, among the new officers and directors elected to serve the Institute for the ensuing year were Prof. T. Y. Lin, University of California at Berkeley; Ben C. Gerwick, Ben C. Gerwick Company Inc., San Francisco.

It was announced at the meeting that the Prestressed Concrete Manufacturers Association of California, Inc., Robert H. Singer, President, has been admitted as an "Affiliate" of the Institute.

ARCHITECT SELECTED FOR SANITORIUM

Architect Warren C. T. Wong, 2644 Pacific Ave., Stockton, has been commissioned by the Bret Harte Central Committee of Stockton, to draft plans and specifications for construction of a new ward addition to the Sanitorium at Murphys,

near Stockton, in San Joaquin county.

The addition will comprise 8 rooms and accommodations for 28 beds. Estimated cost of the work is $33,000.

PLANNING COMMISSION APPROVES PLANS FOR SAN LEANDRO MOTEL

The San Leandro Planning Commission has approved plans for construction of a 350-unit Motor Motel to be built in San Leandro by the Garden Hotels, Inc., of Santa Rosa, at an estimated cost of $12,000,000.

First phase of construction will include 200 units, plus a department store, bowling center, swimming pool, service station, restaurant and tavern, and meeting rooms.

Plans are being prepared by Lewis Smith, 1645 4th St., Santa Rosa.

FIFTEENTH ANNUAL HOME BUILDERS CONVENTION

The Fifteenth Annual Convention & Exposition of the National Association of Home Builders, will be held January 18-22, 1959, in Chicago.

From a modest beginning 15 years ago, the convention has grown impressively to international proportions with approximately 30,000 expected to be in attendance this time.

AMERICAN INSTITUTE OF PLANNERS WILL MEET IN SAN DIEGO

Members of the California State Chapter of the American Institute of Planners will convene in San Diego, California, February 6-8, 1959, for their annual state meeting, with Woody Marshall of Los Altos City Planning serving as program committee chairman. The hosting local chapter, under the direction of Harry C. Haelsing, Director of the San Diego City Planning, is preparing a program of events which will include general sessions, workshops, field trips, and a special program of entertainment for the ladies.

ELEMENTARY SCHOOL PLANNED FOR PLACENTIA

Architects Pleger, Blurock, Hougan & Ellerbroek, 2515 Coast Highway, Corona del Mar, are preparing drawings for construction of a new administration building and three buildings containing four classrooms each at the Kramer Elementary School for the Placentia Unified School District.

The new structures will contain 14,250 sq.ft. in area, and construction will be of wood frame, glued laminated beams, stucco, composition roofing, and plaster interior. Outdoor gymnasium facilities include four basketball courts, two handball courts, and asphaltic paving.

JAMES R. PROBERT APPOINTED COLORADO SALES REPRESENTATIVE

James R. Probert has been appointed "Insulite" territory representative with headquarters at Colorado Springs, Colo., for the Insulite Division of Minnesota and according to an

Grand counties in Utah, and San Juan county of New Mexico. He will work with lumber and building material dealers handling the complete Insulite line of structural insulation board products.

A native of Colorado, Probert will make his home in Denver until the end of the year.

LUMINOUS CEILINGS BECOMING MORE POPULAR

Construction trends in industrial offices and commercial building are emphasizing more and more the importance of interior lighting. Development of new materials and wider use of conventional facilities is offering the architect, engineer, contractor and builder many opportunities to meet lighting problems with specific equipment.

Luminous ceilings, with many types and variations, are being considered in most instances where a specific lighting problem or effect is desired, and one of the most complete brochures illustrating and evaluating luminous ceilings has recently been issued by, and may be obtained by writing, Luminous Ceilings, Inc., 2500 W. North Avenue, Chicago 47, Ill.

LARGE APARTMENT PROJECT PLANNED FOR SAN FRANCISCO

Architect Angus McSweeney, 2960 Van Ness Ave., San Francisco, is preparing plans for construction of a 22-story apartment building in the Lake Merced area near old Fort Funston.

The project has been approved by the San Francisco Planning Commission and construction is scheduled to start in the Spring, with completion in about a year and a half.

The facilities will provide housing for approximately 1700 persons and will cost an estimated $10,000,000.

NEW CHURCH AND RECTORY PLANNED FOR SACRAMENTO

Architect Harry J. Devine, 1012 "J" St., Sacramento, has completed plans for construction of a 1-story, 18,000 sq. ft. Church and Rectory building in Sacramento for The Roman Catholic Archbishop of Sacramento.

The new facilities will be of built-up concrete construction, 6 structural steel beams, grouted brick, concrete slab floors, gravel roofing, and will provide seating for 1000 persons.

MONTEREY PENINSULA COLLEGE ADDITION BEING READIED

The architectural firm of Wallace Holm & Associates, 321 Webster St., Monterey, is preparing plans for construction of a library building addition to The Monterey Peninsula College at Monterey.

The new building will be part 1- and part 2-story construction and will contain approximately 18,000 sq. ft. of area. Estimated cost is $300,000.

ARCHITECT & ENGINEER

INDEX OF ARTICLES AND ILLUSTRATIONS

VOLUMES 212-215 — 1958

HELP US KEEP THE
THINGS WORTH KEEPING

All is calm, all is bright. In America we are free to worship as we please, where we please. And we worship in peace.

But like so many precious things, peace doesn't come easy. Peace costs money.

Money for strength to keep the peace. Money for science and education to help make peace lasting. And money saved by individuals.

Your Savings Bonds, as a direct investment in your country, make you a Partner in strengthening America's Peace Power.

The chart below shows how the Bonds you buy will earn money for you. But the most important thing they earn is *peace*. They help us keep the things worth keeping.

Think it over. Are you buying as many Bonds as you *might?*

HOW YOU CAN REACH YOUR SAVINGS GOAL WITH SERIES E BONDS (in just 8 years, 11 months)		
If you want about	$2,500	$5,000	$10,000
each week, save	$4.75	$9.50	$18.75

This shows only a few examples. You can save any sum, buying Bonds by Payroll Savings or where you bank. Start your program now!

HELP STRENGTHEN AMERICA'S PEACE POWER
BUY U. S. SAVINGS BONDS

Lightning Source UK Ltd.
Milton Keynes UK
UKHW012305140219
337323UK00011B/411/P